to the moon via the beach

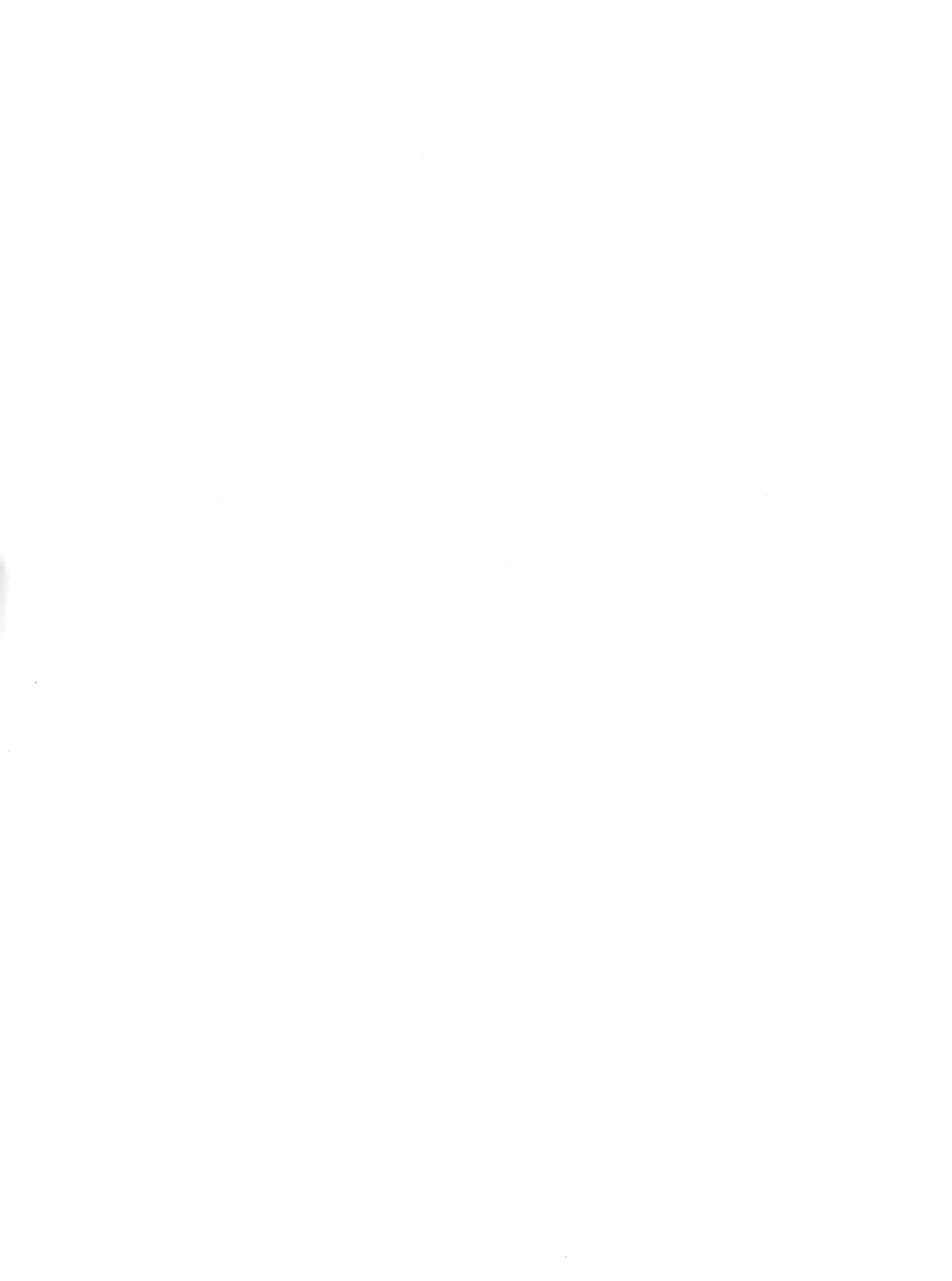

Foreword

Since 2010, the LUMA Foundation in Arles has produced a number of multifaceted artistic projects to explore the possibilities of its new arts campus in the Parc des Ateliers d'Arles, designed by the Foundation in conjunction with the artists Liam Gillick and Philippe Parreno, the curators Tom Eccles, Hans Ulrich Obrist, and Beatrix Ruf, the architects Frank Gehry and Annabelle Selldorf, and the land-scape designer Bas Smets.

Alongside exhibitions focusing on image-making such as How Soon is Now? and Neue Welt,[1] both held as part of the Arles' Rencontres Internationales de la Photographie festival, and The Human Snapshot conference organized jointly with Bard College,[2] To the Moon via the Beach, held in the Arles Amphi-theater in 2012, was a bold, radical new departure in the Foundation's dedication to cultural experimentation.

At the invitation of the LUMA Foundation, Tom Eccles, Liam Gillick, Hans Ulrich Obrist, Philippe Parreno, and Beatrix Ruf selected 20 artists representing different generations from around the world to come and work together in the Roman amphitheater, a site of considerable historical significance as a venue for popular culture, often used for bullfights and other traditional events. On this occasion, it played host to a constantly evolving exhibition whose title evoked at once an expedition, a quest, and an experiment. To the Moon via the Beach represented possibilities coming together, expanding space and time, and enabling unforeseen encounters to take place.

Our aim was to give locals and tourists alike the experience of rubbing shoulders with artists and trying out a new kind of interaction with art, while discovering that exhibitions can take unexpected forms.

I asked the two artists from the core group of the LUMA Foundation in Arles, Liam Gillick and Philippe Parreno, who first came up with the idea, to shape the exhibition. The way they presented the project was very simple: "Announcement that work has commenced will be made by three short blasts on an air horn —drawing people to the Amphitheater. This is an exhibition about work, production, and change—ideas in constant motion. A moonscape will be created around which artists will develop new ideas. Everything will be visible—no difference between production, presentation, and exchange."

I see this exhibition as one of the foundational acts of our center for creating, producing, and exhibiting art and ideas in Arles. It has given shape and life to the community of artists that we set out to build in a place that will become a tool for thinking, imagining, formulating, and producing striking art and ideas for the 21st century.

This founding principle is likewise materialized in the sand used to create the Arena's shifting artistic landscape, which will become a catalyst for new art when it is re-cycled on the building site to help underpin the foundations for the building designed by Frank Gehry within the Parc des Ateliers.

—Maja Hoffmann, May 2014

1 How Soon is Now? was a group exhibition curated in 2010 by Tom Eccles, Liam Gillick, Hans Ulrich Obrist, Philippe Parreno, and Beatrix Ruf with the aim of unveiling a new aspect of photography. Neue Welt was a solo exhibition of work by Wolfgang Tillmans curated by Beatrix Ruf in 2013 at the Kunsthalle Zürich and in Arles.

2 The conference explored the issue of the universality of images and human rights based on the emblematic exhibition The Family of Man, presented at MoMA in New York in 1953. The research based on the conference is one example of the future post-doctoral program on offer at the LUMA art campus in Arles.

Program

Le narrateur ou la narratrice parle calmement en anglais et en français, dans les deux langues, mais pas forcément dans cet ordre. Il ou elle essaye d'être le plus précis possible. Cette manière d'insister et d'être clair donne une direction de jeu précise à l'acteur.

A narrator speaks calmly and evenly:

To the Moon via the Beach, c'est le titre. Vers la lune en passant par la plage, c'est le titre de l'exposition présentée par la Fondation LUMA, presented by the LUMA Foundation.

C'est une exposition qui dure quatre jours.

An exhibition that develops over four days.

La piste des arènes est un lieu de travail.

The surface of the arena is a place of work.

Du sable y a été amené. Il est toujours en mouvement. Le paysage de plage se transforme peu à peu en surface lunaire.

In constant transformation from a beach to a lunar landscape.

L'équipe qui se charge de produire cela a été réunie autour du sculpteur de sable Wilfred Stijger.

The sand sculpture is carried out by Wilfred Stijger and his team.

Des artistes ont été invités à venir travailler aussi.

Several artists are working here too.

Ils ont tous produit des œuvres nouvelles ou énoncé de nouvelles idées.

They are producing new works and distributing some ideas.

Here is Uri Aran. He is making a film, the film is untitled. It's a text-based film, it's a film about two friends played by Dan Aran and Harry Ackland.

Il y a Uri Aran qui fait un film qui s'intitule *Sans titre*. C'est un film basé sur le texte et le langage, joué et parlé par Dan Aran et Harry Ackland.

Here is Daniel Buren. *Like Flags on the Moon*. Flags are deployed around the arena.

Il y a Daniel Buren qui propose un projet consistant en une série de petits drapeaux disposés aléatoirement sur la piste et autour d'elle. Le titre est : *Like Flags on the Moon*, travail in situ.

Here is Elvire Bonduelle distributing some Individual Lunar Modules made from space blankets.

Et voici Elvire Bonduelle qui distribue ses Modules lunaires individuels : des parapluies taillés dans des couvertures de survie pour une expérience esthétique confortable.

Here are Fischli & Weiss presenting Kling Klong, a sound sculpture. Two stones carrying remixed sound of wind chimes and communication machines.

Il y a Fischli & Weiss qui montrent une nouvelle sculpture sonore. Deux pierres qui diffusent des sons remixés de carillon éolien et de machines communicantes.

Here is Jef Geys, Les noms propres et Kempens Informatieblad: the top 100 art world names plus local people whose name starts with "G" are inserted in the list.

Et il y a Jef Geys qui vend deux journaux intitulés Kempens Informatieblad et cette action déclenche une réaction en chaîne.

Here are Dominique Gonzalez-Foerster, Tristan Bera, and Ari Benjamin Meyers presenting The 4th Act of Peer Gynt, After Edvard Grieg and Henrik Ibsen on Friday 6th of July at 10 pm. Music deployed for one night only.

Il y a Dominique Gonzalez-Foerster, Tristan Bera et Ari Benjamin Meyers qui présentent vendredi 6 juillet à dix heures du soir Le quatrième acte de la pièce de théâtre Peer Gynt écrit par Edvard Grieg sur une musique de Henrik Ibsen. De la musique et de la lumière sont mises en scène un soir seulement.

Here is Douglas Gordon.

Il y a Douglas Gordon.

Here is Pierre Huyghe with Colony Collapse. Marlon Middek (the performer) and Danny Jöckel (the beekeeper).

Il y a Pierre Huyghe. Une colonie d'abeilles se constitue sur le visage de Marlon Middek. L'œuvre est intitulée Colony Collapse.

Here is Klara Lidén's Moonwalk, on Saturday 7th of July at 9 pm.

Il y a aussi Klara Lidén qui dancera le 7 juillet un Moonwalk à 21 heures autour de la piste.

Here is Benoît Maire and his idea-measuring sculpture.

Voici Benoît Maire et sa sculpture sonore mesurante.

Here is Oscar Murillo, Work Just Happens with Joel Muggleton, Valentina Atamirano, Christian Camacho Reynoso, and Erica Bartrum. Coconut water is distributed.

Voilà Oscar Murillo, Work Just Happens avec Joel Muggleton, Valentina Atamirano, Christian Camacho Reynoso et Erica Bartrum. De l'eau de noix de coco est distribué.

Here is Lili Reynaud-Dewar: Why should our bodies end at the skin or include at best other beings encapsulated by skin? on Friday 6th of July, 10:30 am, 5 pm, and 8 pm. Featuring Zaza Tralala, Tatiana Defraine, Hendrik Hegray, Erik Minkinnen, Thomas Royer, and Jean-Baptiste Couronne.

Il y a Lili Reynaud-Dewar: Pourquoi nos corps devraient-ils

s'arrêter à la frontière de la peau ou ne comprendre, au mieux, que d'autres êtres encapsulés dans cette peau ?, sera montrée vendredi 6 juillet à 10h30, 17h et 20h. Avec Zaza Tralala, Tatiana Defraine, Hendrik Hegray, Erik Minkinnen, Thomas Royer et Jean-Baptiste Couronne.

Here is Anri Sala: Where the Moon Notes Equal the Beach Bridges, featuring Andre Vida on saxophone and Hilary Jeffery on trombone. Bridges made from songs about the moon and the beach.

Il y a Anri Sala qui présente une nouvelle œuvre musicale intitulée Where the Moon Notes Equal the Beach Bridges avec comme interprètes Andre Vida au saxophone et Hilary Jeffery au trombone. Ils jouent des ponts musicaux.

Here is Pilvi Takala, The Take Home Experience, providing candid images of those who visit.

Il y a Pilvi Takala. Elle présente The Take Home Experience. Une impression étrange que vous ressentirez certainement en sortant de ces arènes.

Here is Rirkrit Tiravanija, The Big Big Bang, featuring Sami Moor. In a spacesuit playing the harmonica.

Il y a Rirkrit Tiravanija et son œuvre intitulée The Big Big Bang dans laquelle se produit Sami Moor. Un cosmonaute joue de l'harmonica.

Here is Tris Vonna-Michell, Capitol Complex, a sound work produced with Martin Ehrencrona at Kobra Studio, Stockholm. Featuring Orestes Grediaga. It is located in the tunnels.

Il y a Tris Vonna-Michell et Capitol Complex, un travail sonore produit avec Martin Ehrencrona au Studio Kobra de Stockholm avec Orestes Grediaga. Cette bande-son est diffusée dans le tunnel.

Here is Lawrence Weiner, & THEN UNTENDED AS… A structure for use.

Il y a Lawrence Weiner, & THEN UNTENDED AS… Une structure abandonnée.

Artists

Announcement that work has commenced will be made by three short blasts on an air horn—drawing people to the Amphitheater. This is an exhibition about work, production, and change—ideas in constant motion. A moonscape will be created around which artists will develop new ideas. Everything will be visible —no difference between production, presentation, and exchange.

—Liam Gillick and Philippe Parreno, 2012

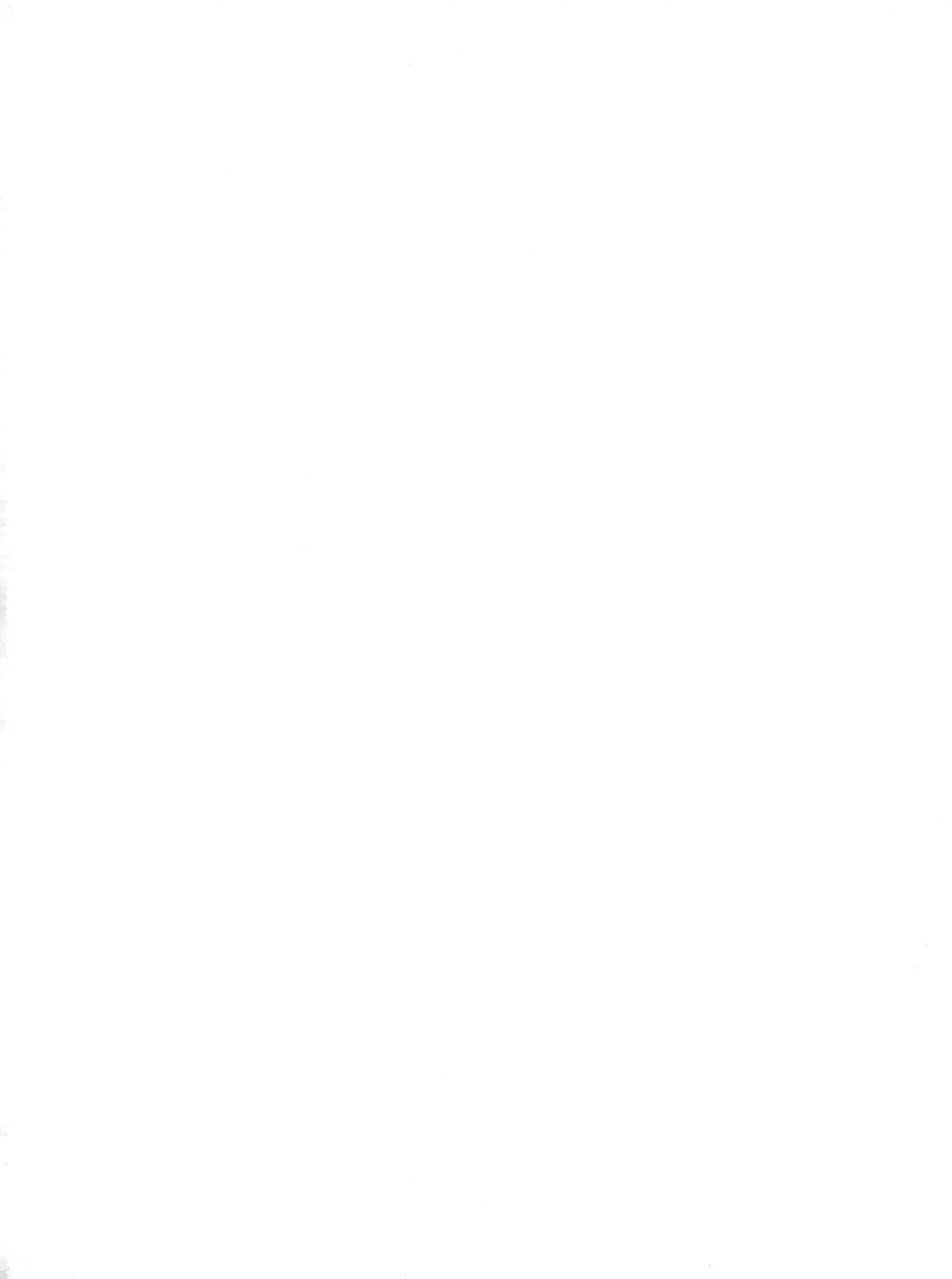

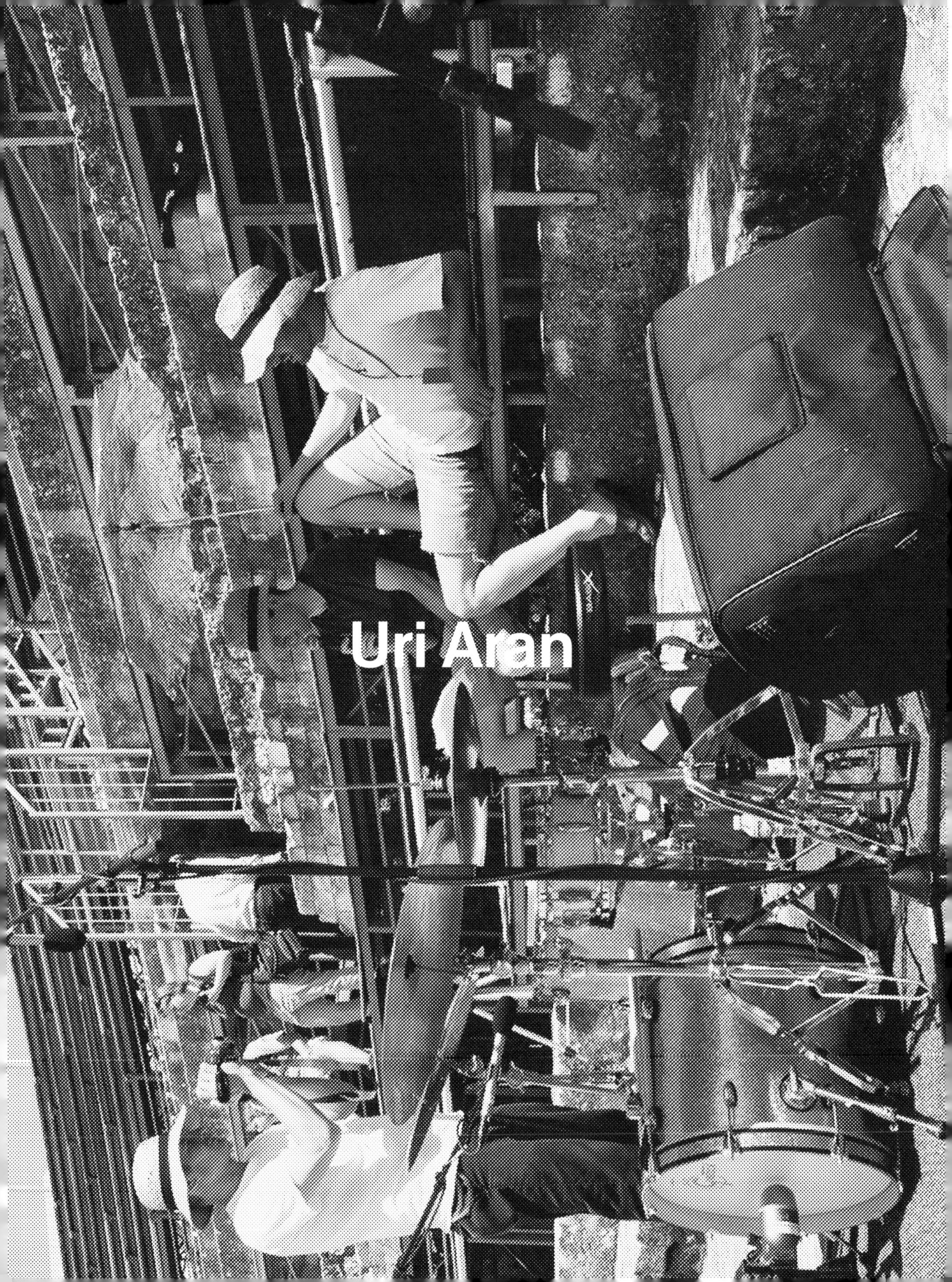
Uri Aran

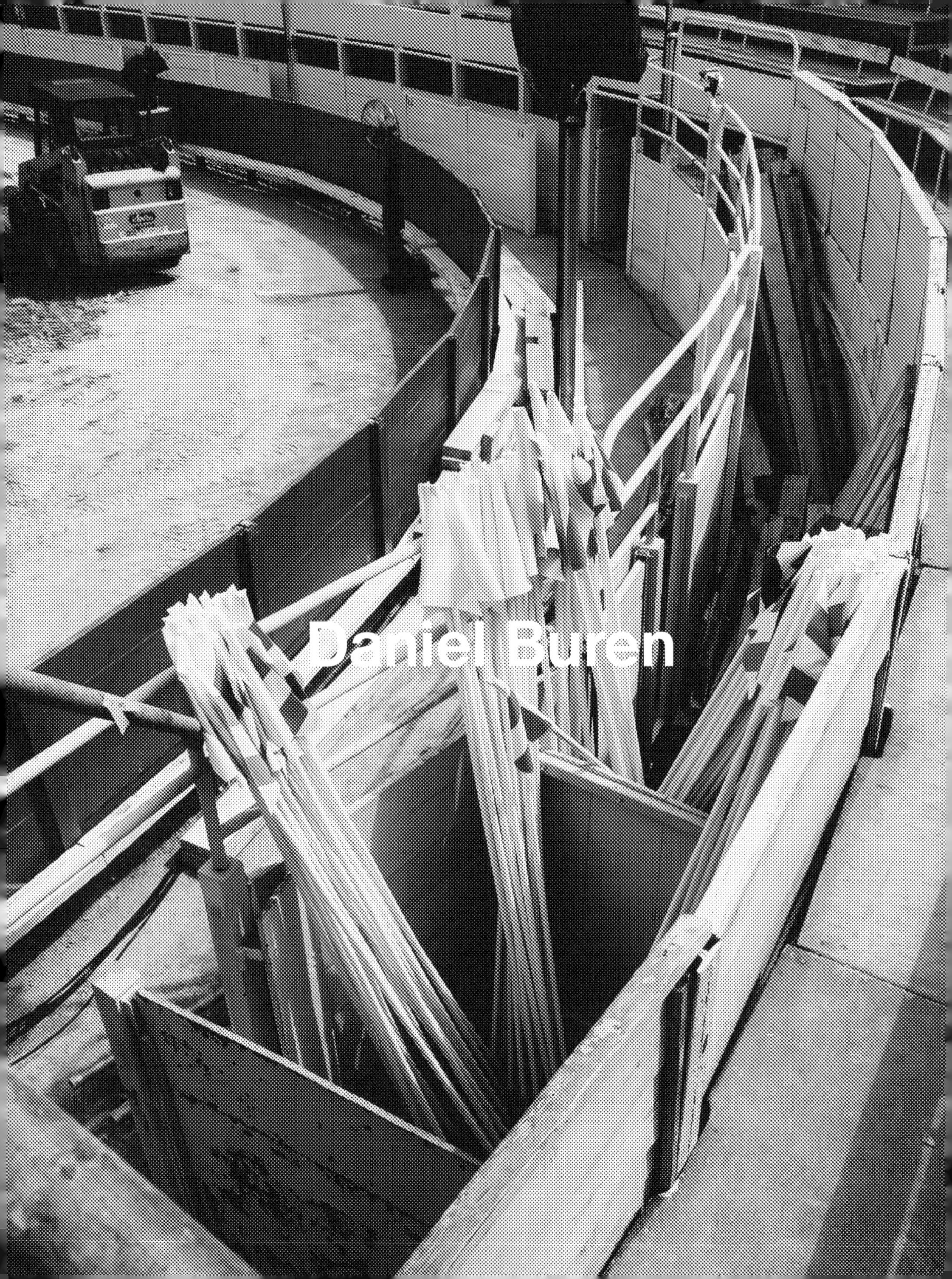
Daniel Buren

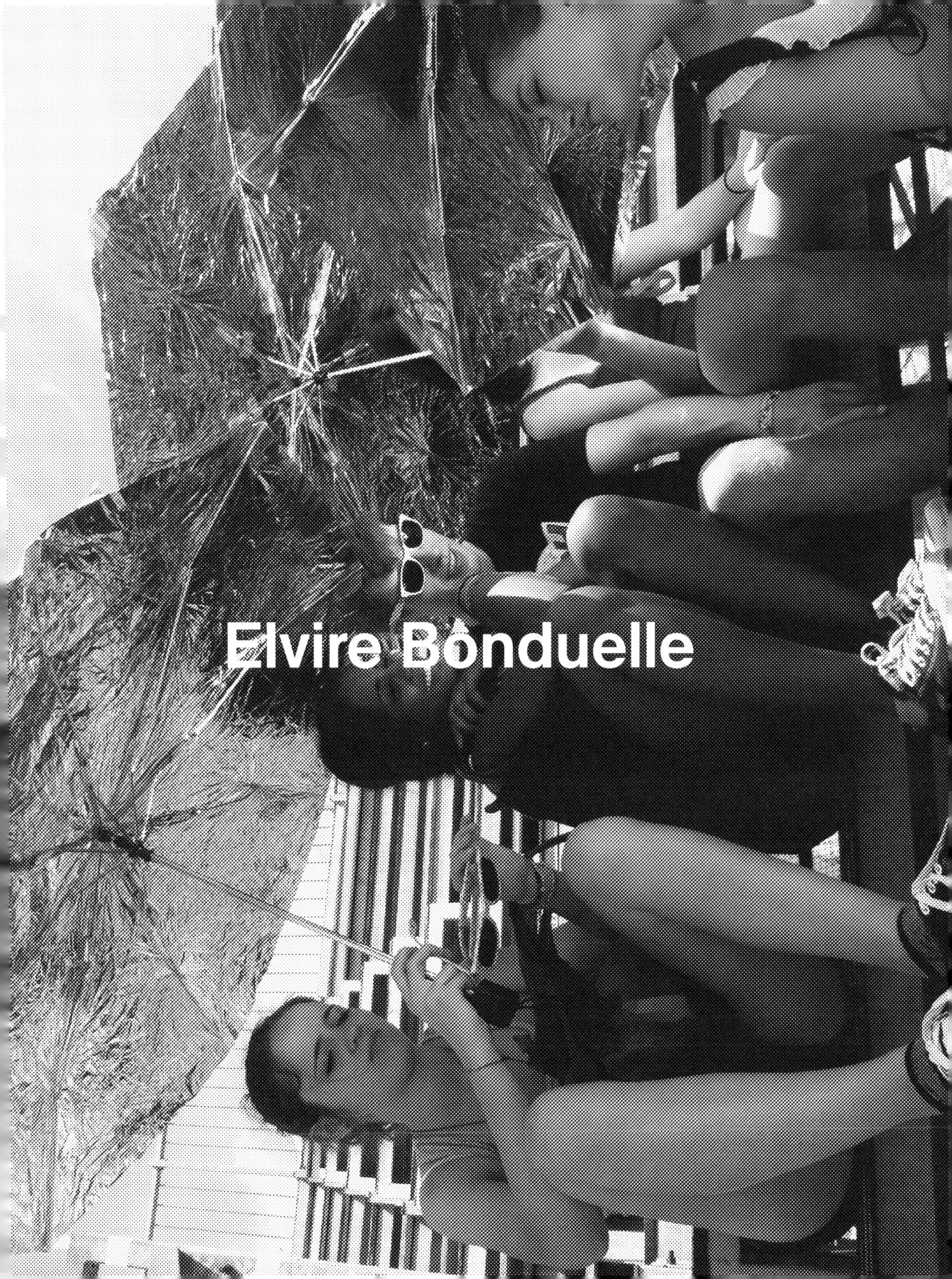

Elvire Bonduelle

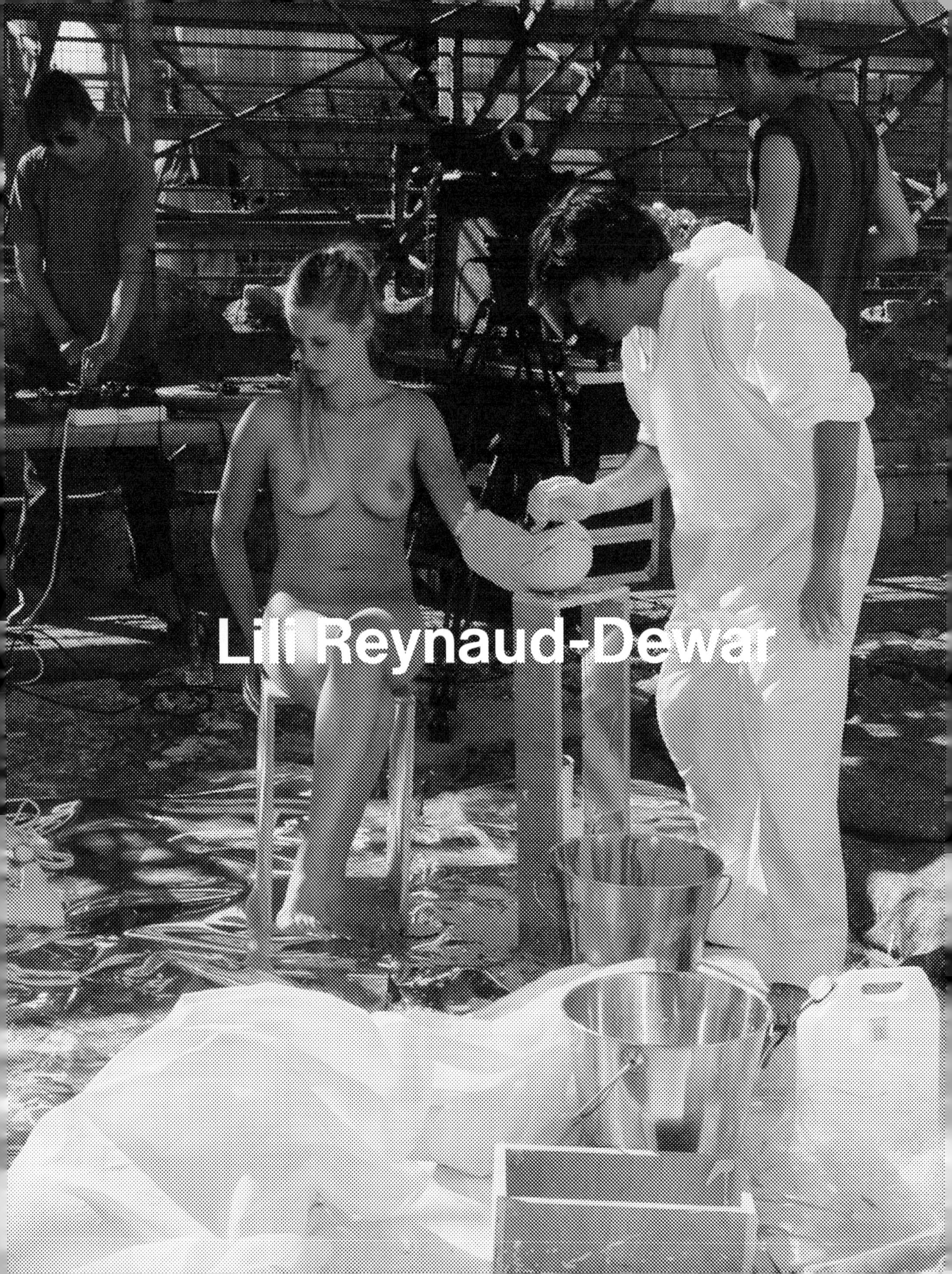
Lili Reynaud-Dewar

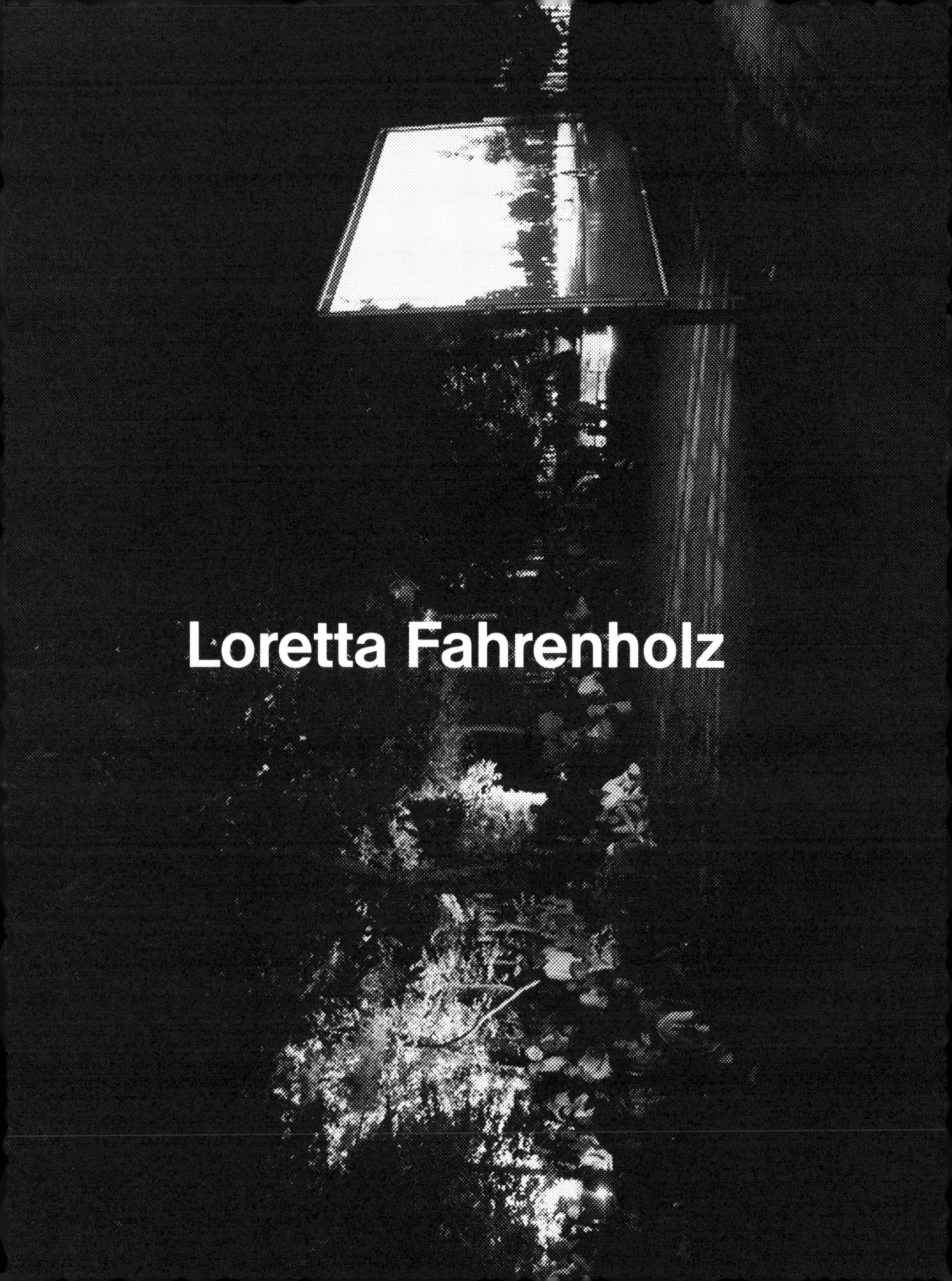

Loretta Fahrenholz

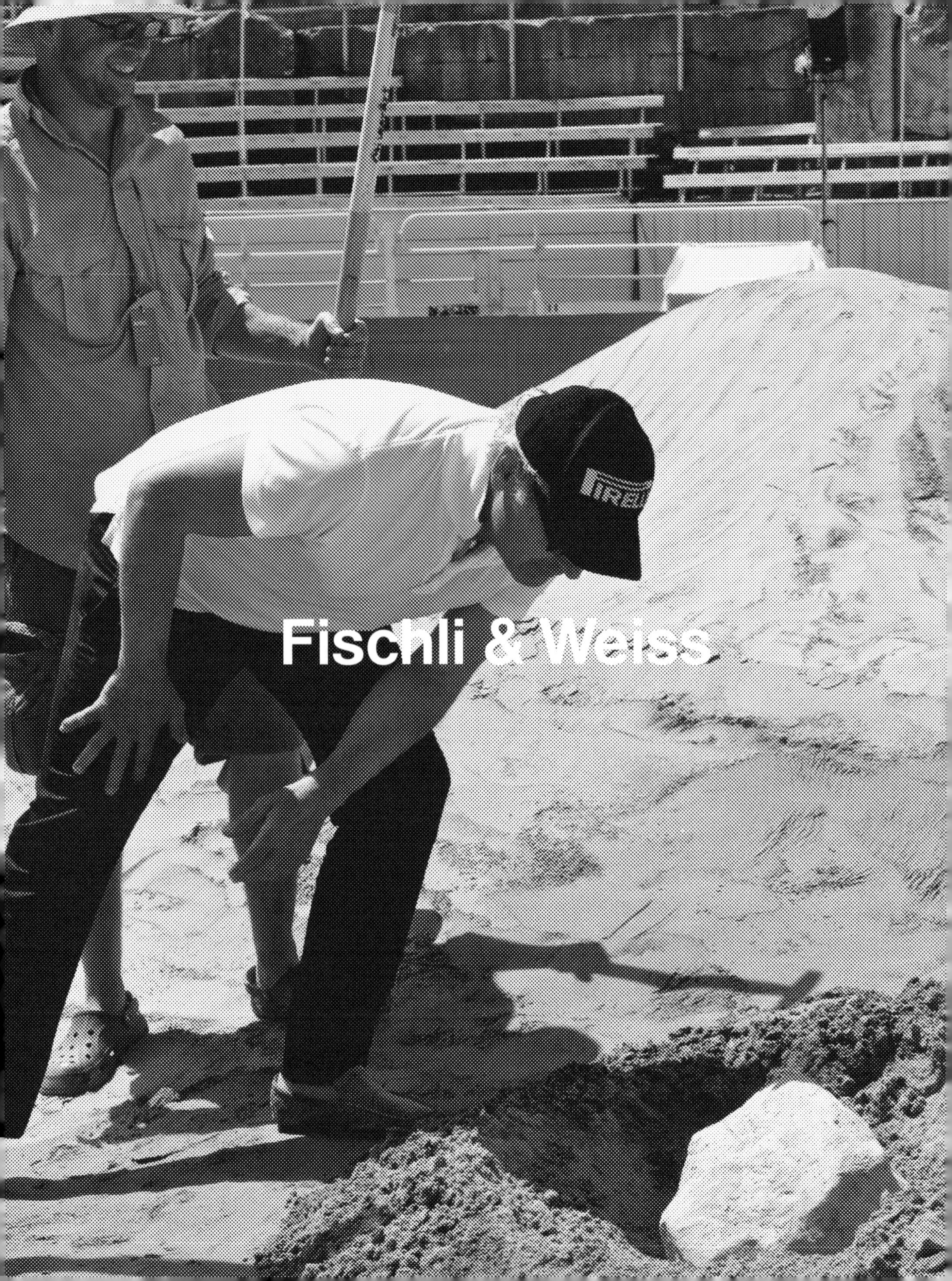
Fischli & Weiss

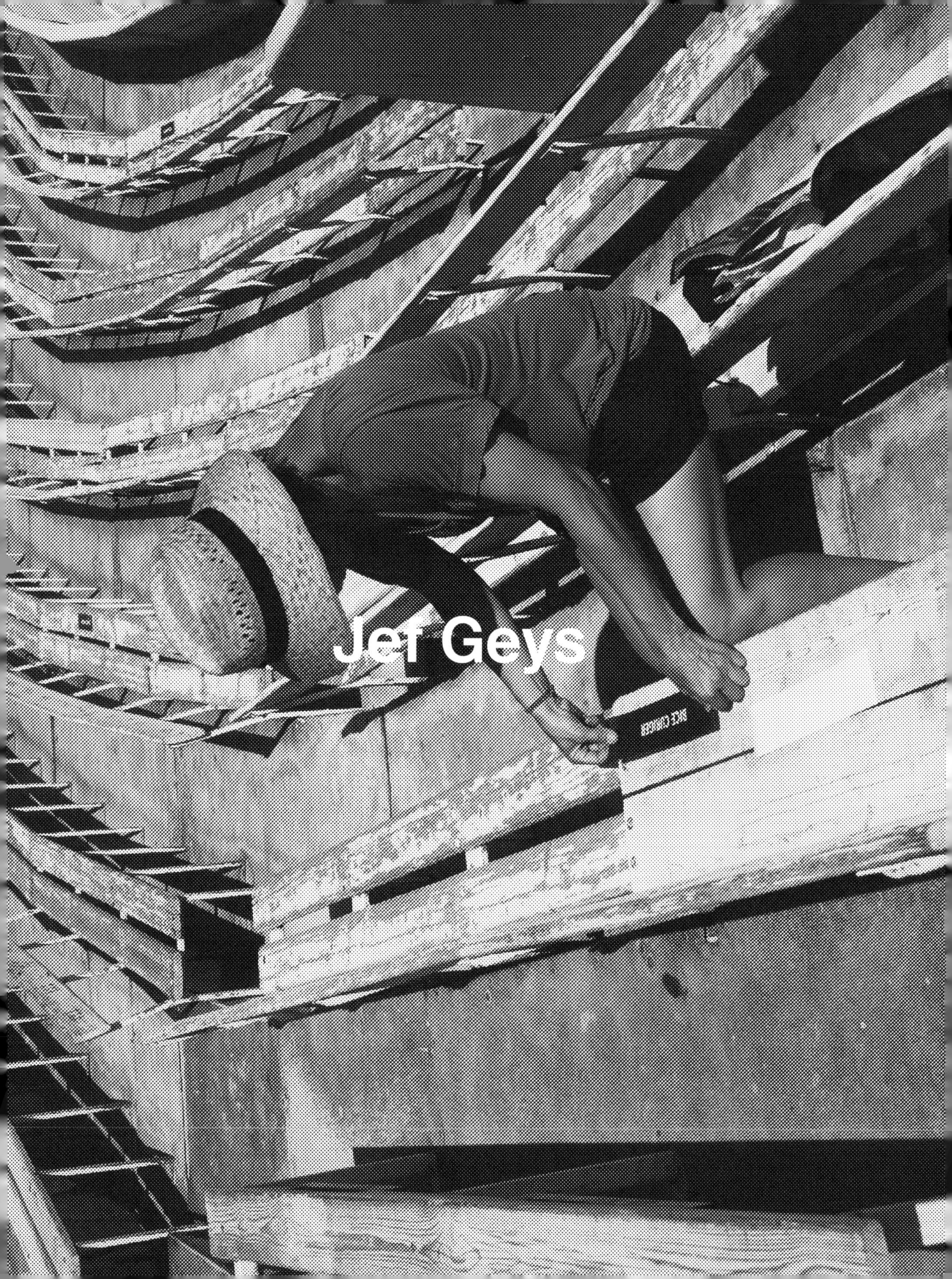
Jef Geys

Dominique Gonzalez-Foerster/ Ari Benjamin Meyers/ Tristan Bera

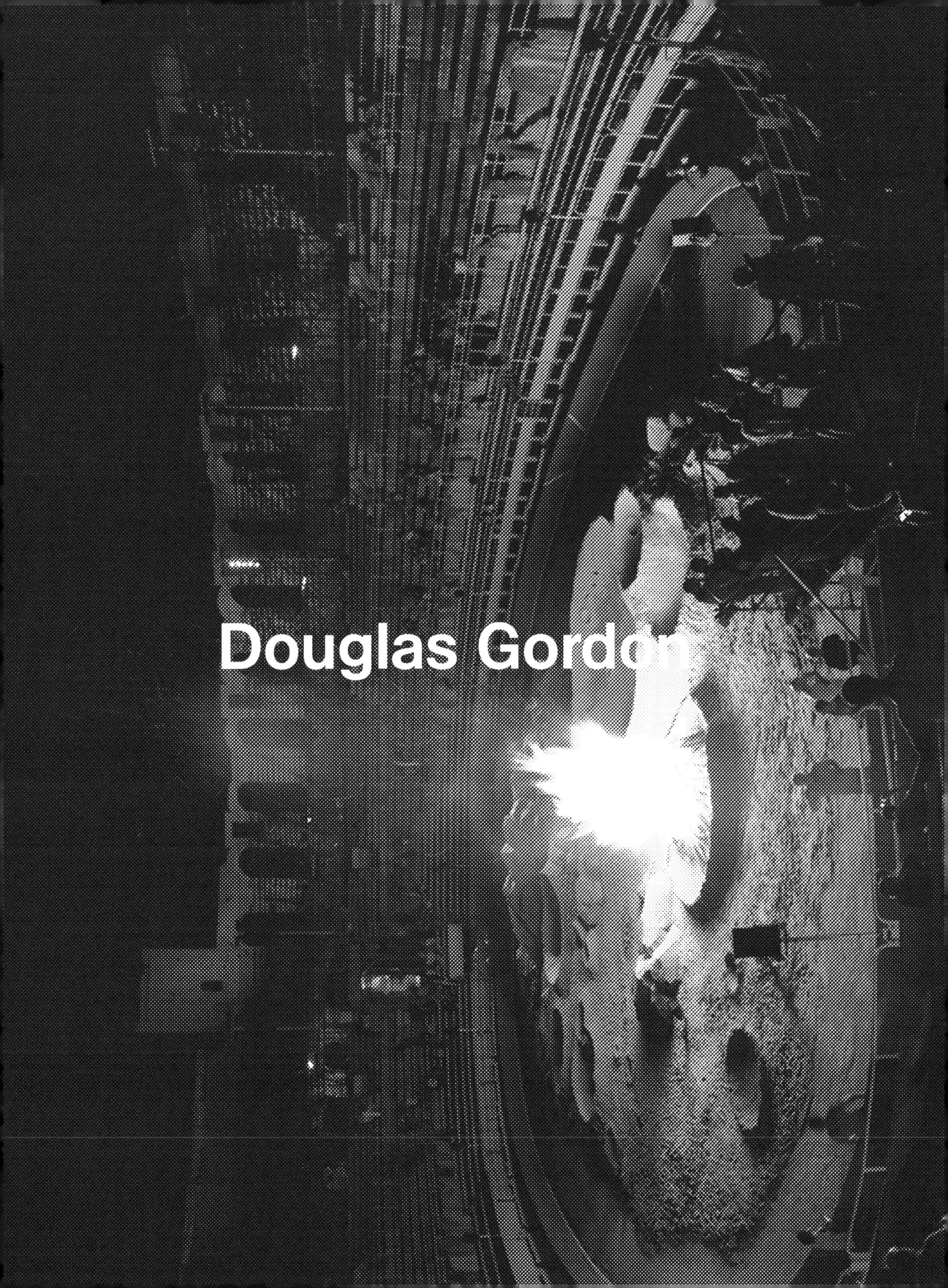

Douglas Gordon

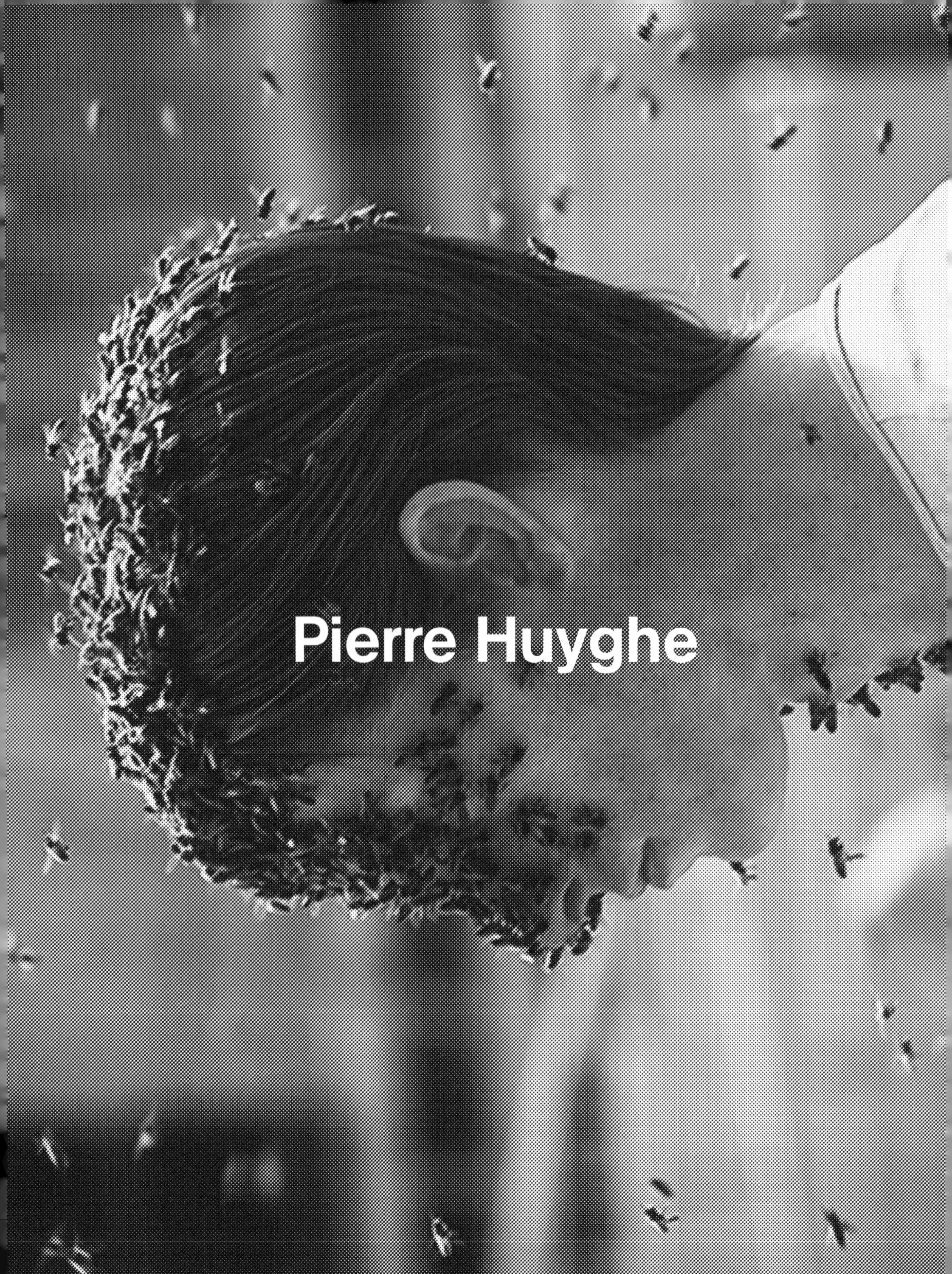
Pierre Huyghe

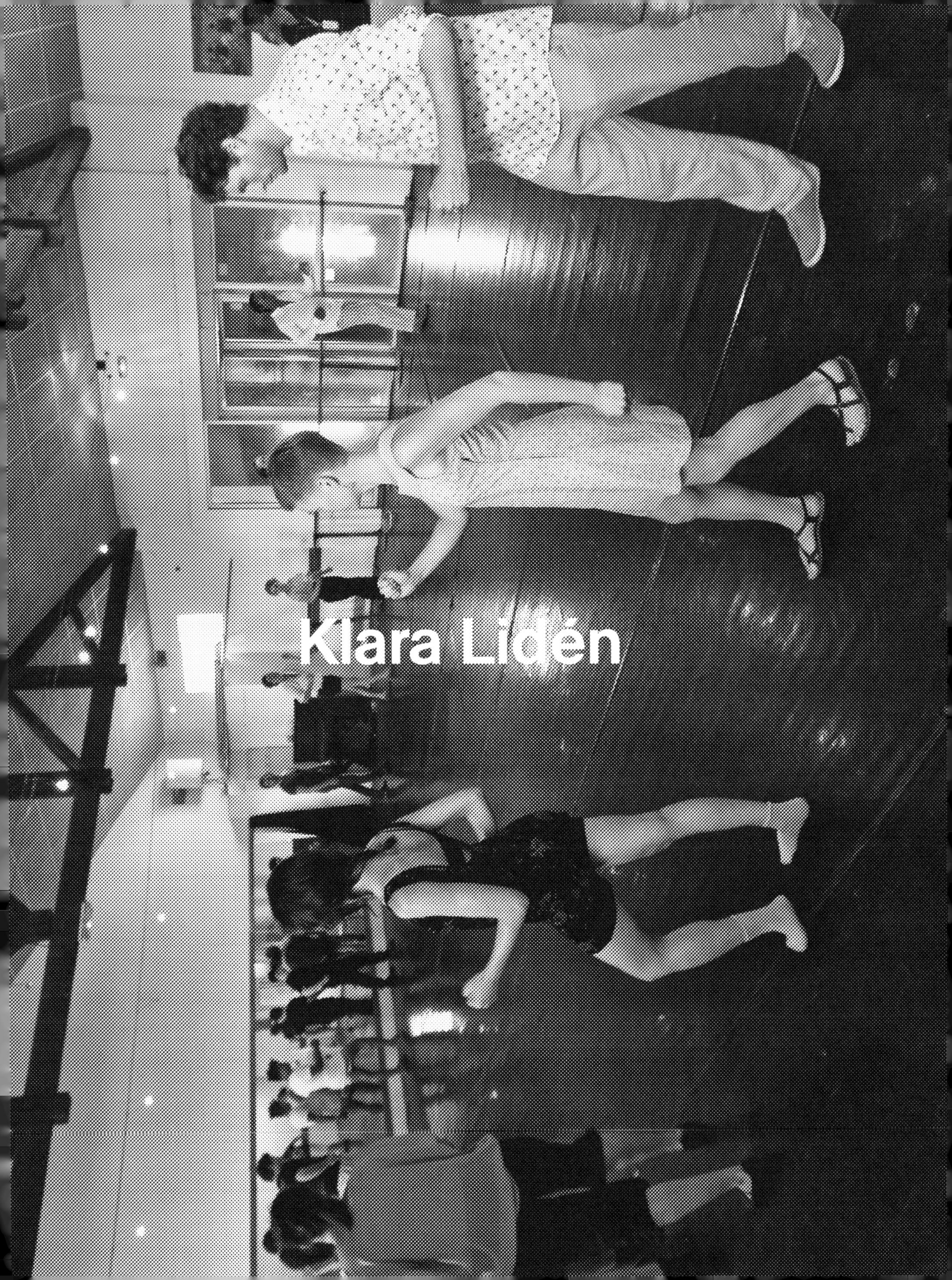

Klara Lidén

Renata Lucas

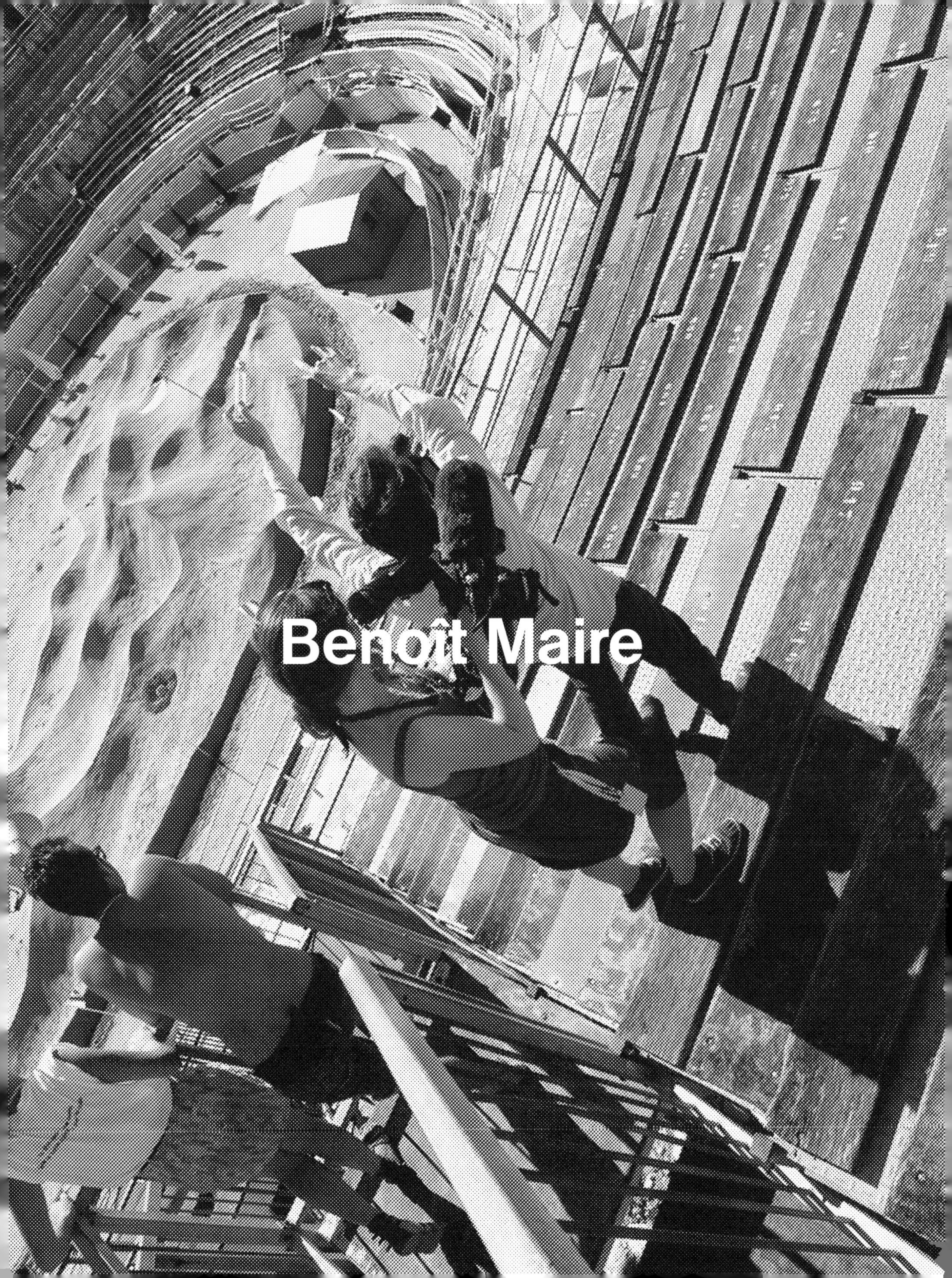

Benoît Maire

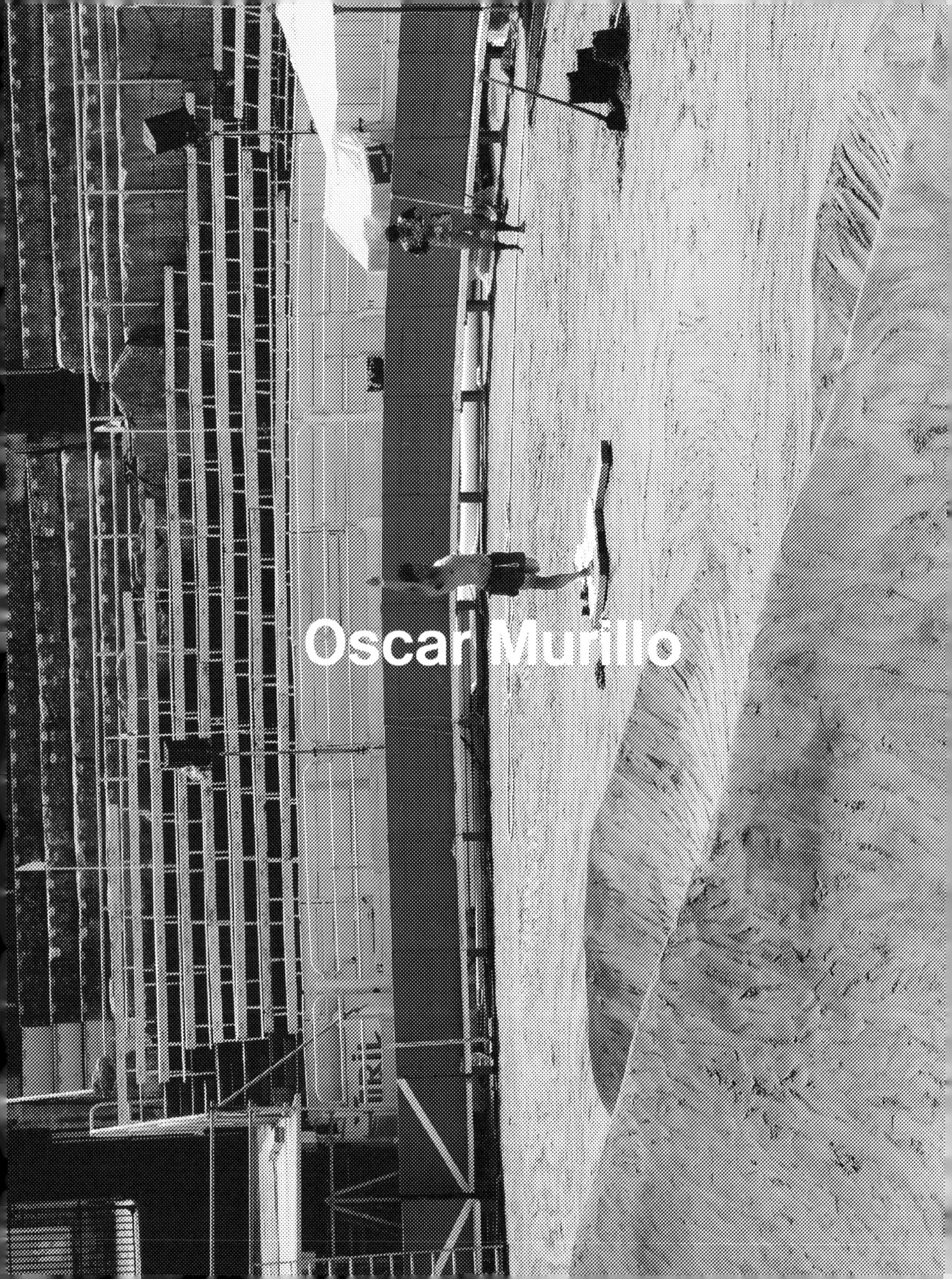
Oscar Murillo

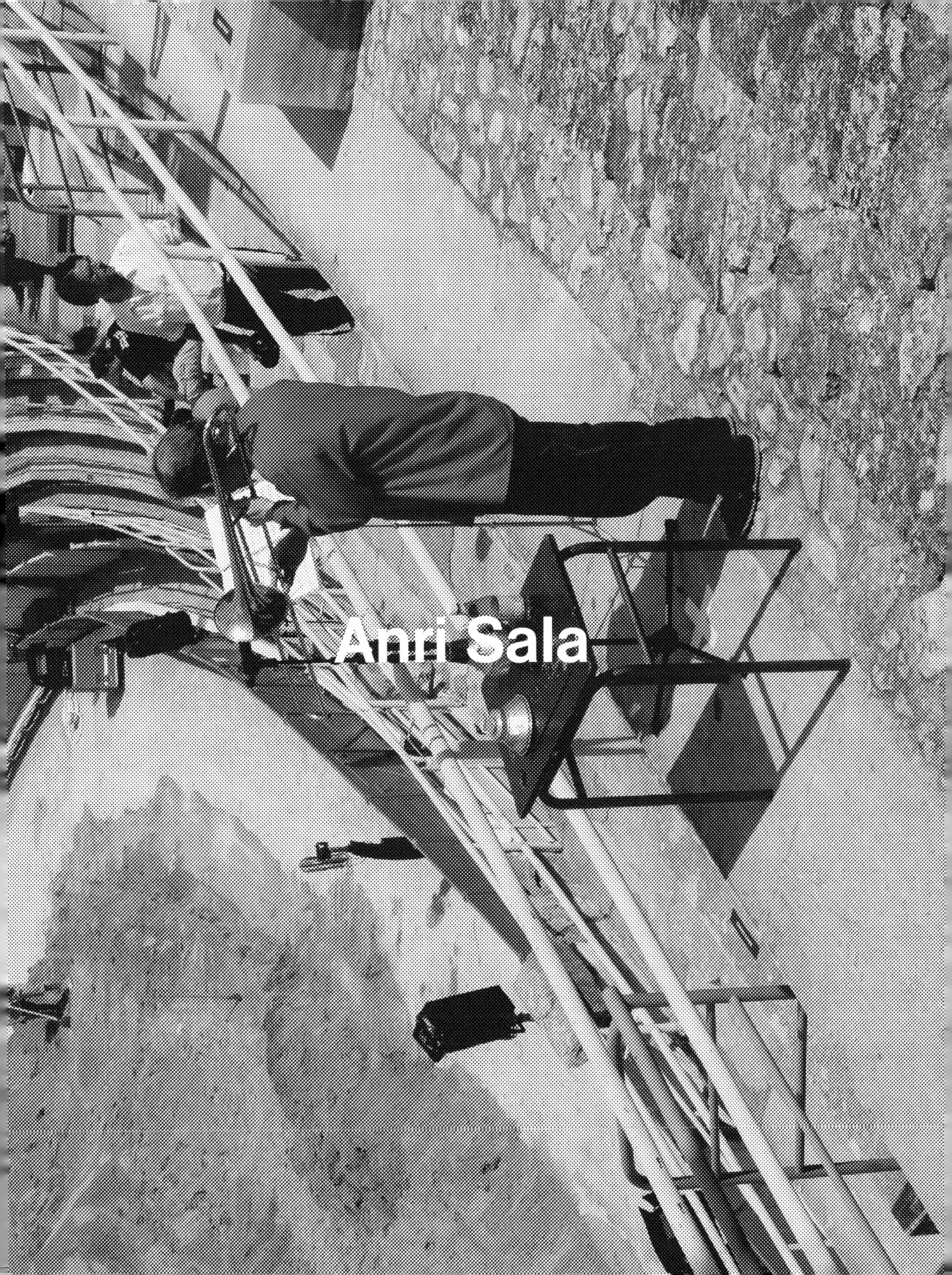
Anri Sala

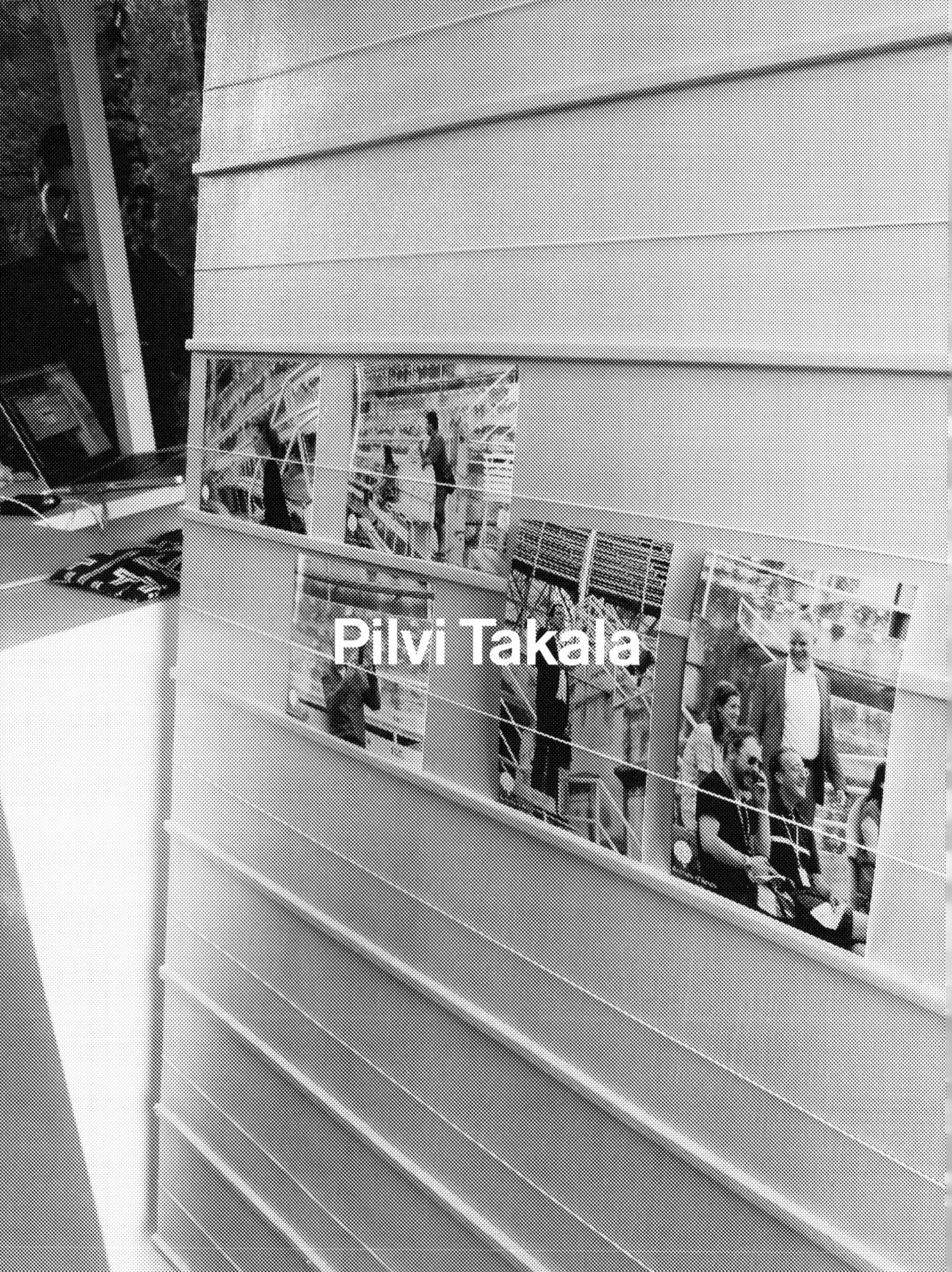

Pilvi Takala

Rirkrit Tiravanija

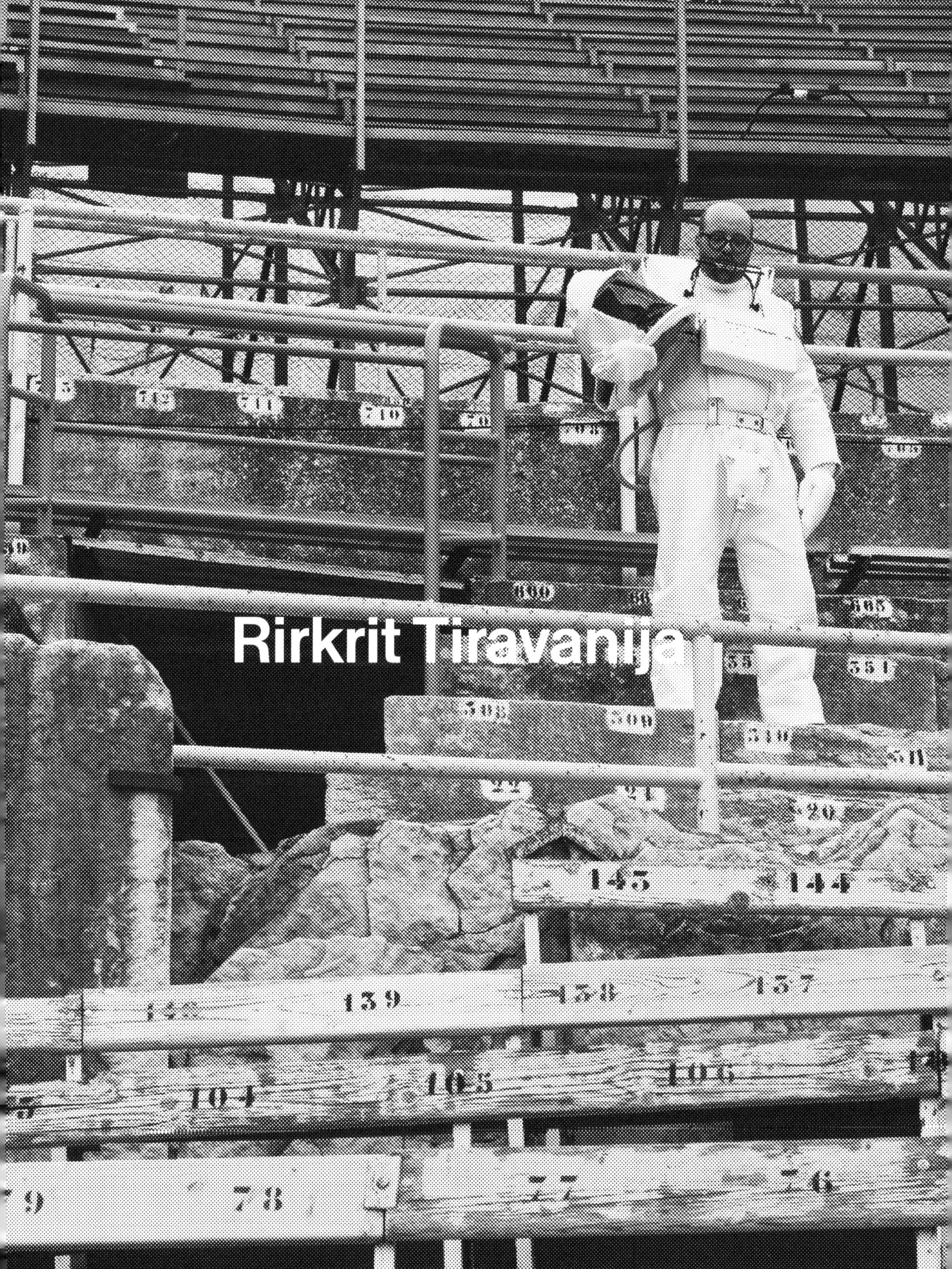

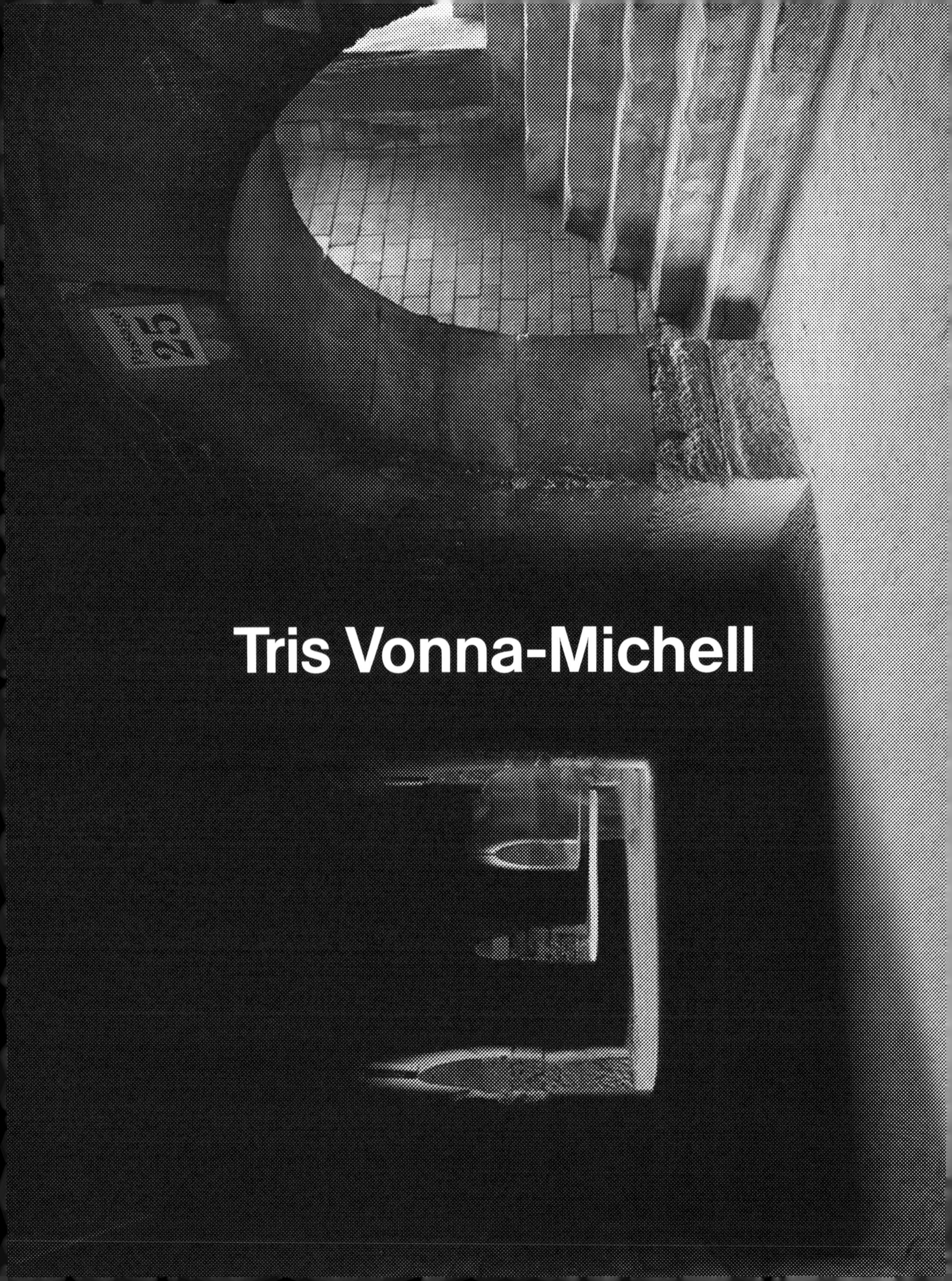

Tris Vonna-Michell

Lawrence Weiner

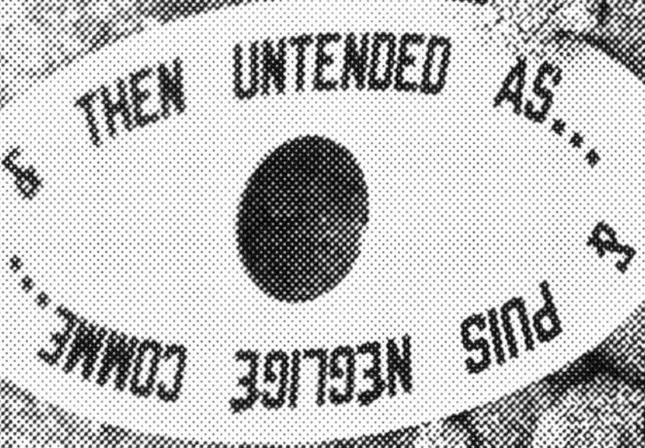

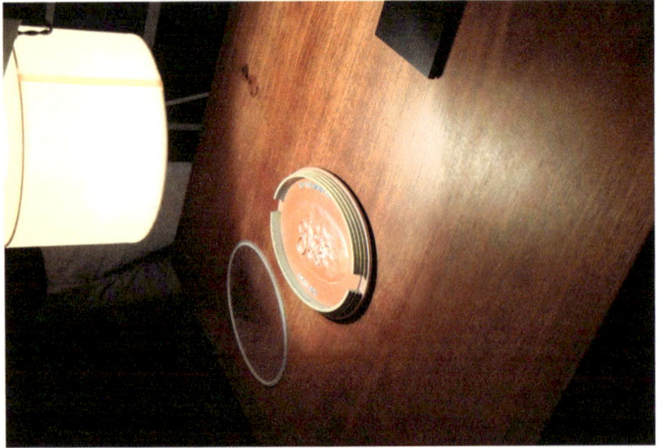

7/1/12—5:14:40 PM

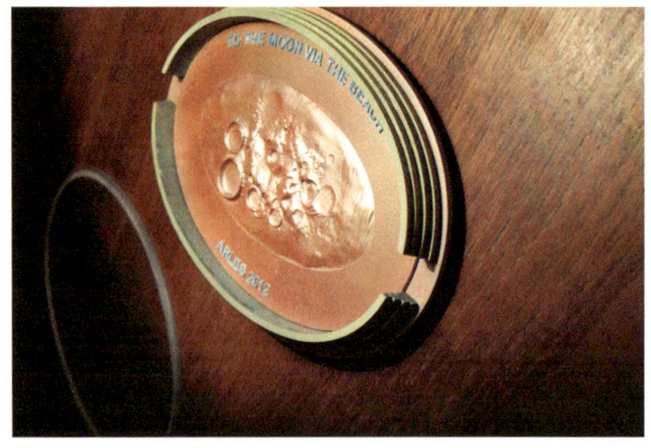

7/1/12—5:14:43 PM

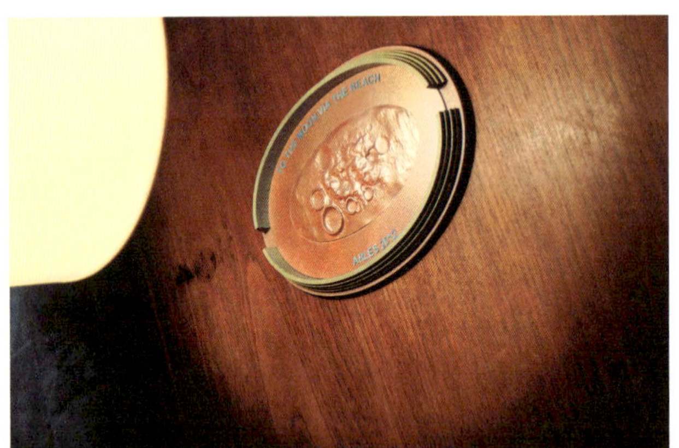

7/1/12—5:14:53 PM

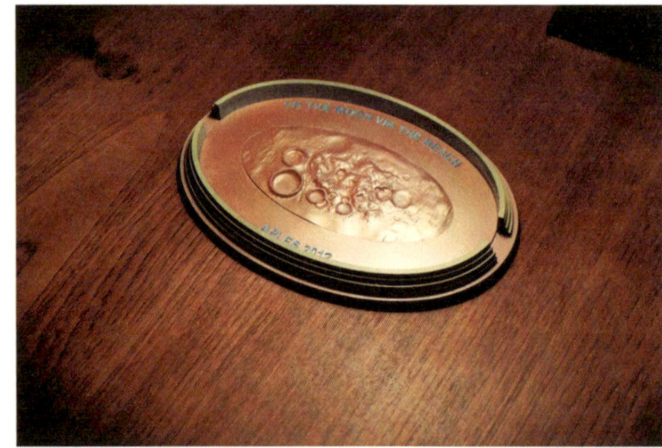

7/1/12—5:15:07 PM

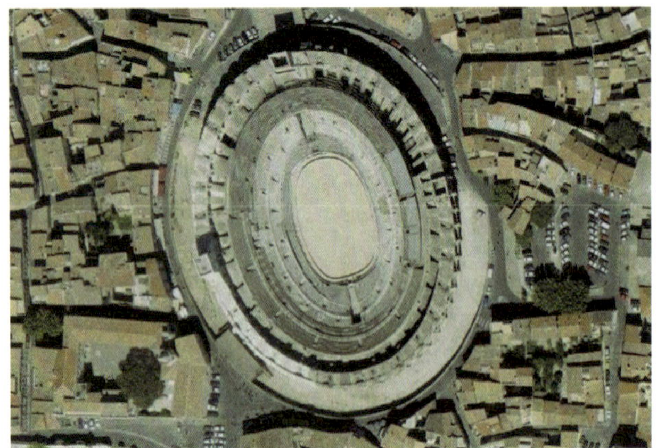

7/2/12—9:48:16 AM

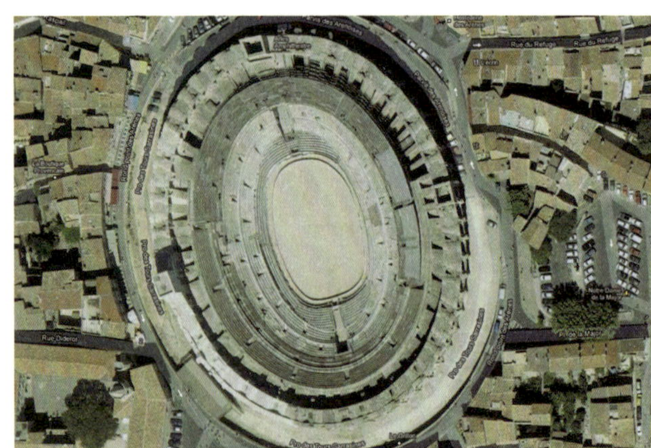

7/2/12—10:55:29 AM

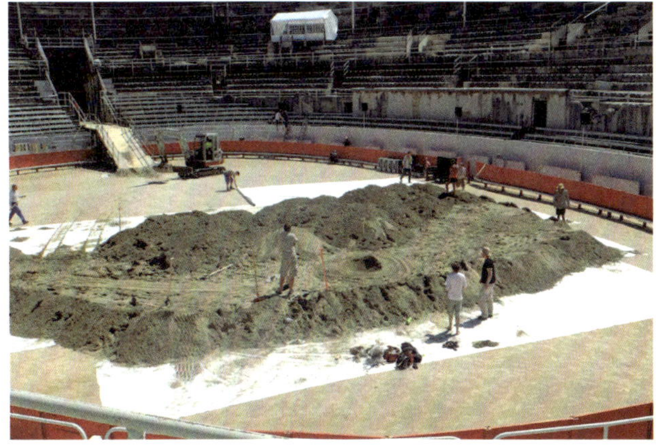
7/3/12—6:04:33 PM

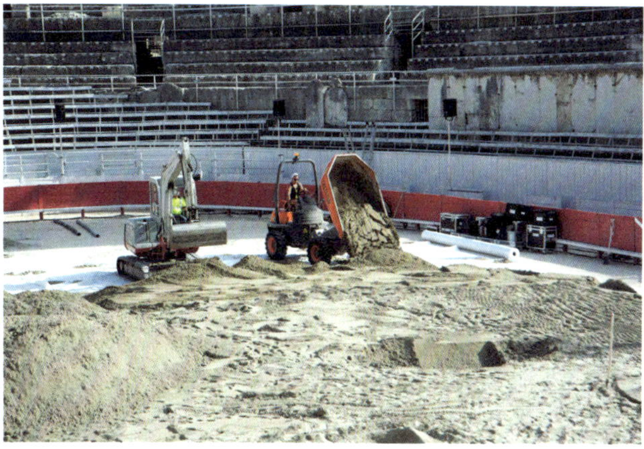
7/3/12—6:04:41 PM

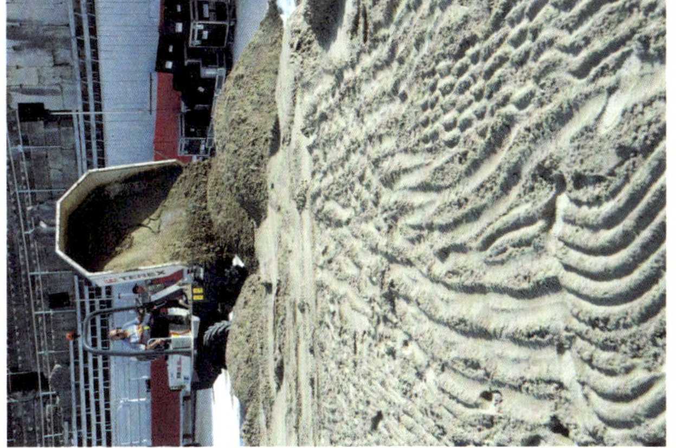
7/3/12—6:14:58 PM

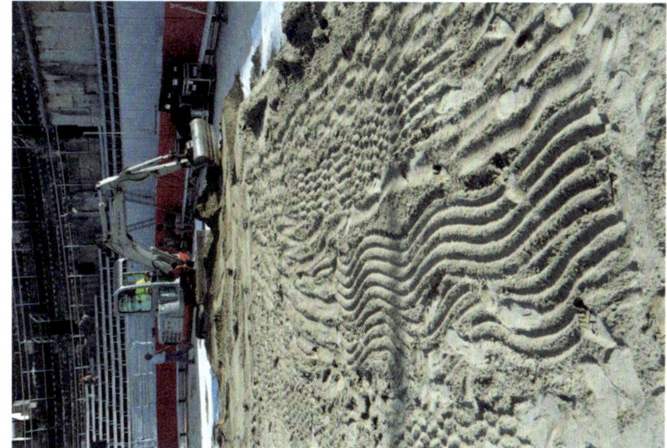
7/3/12—6:17:06 PM

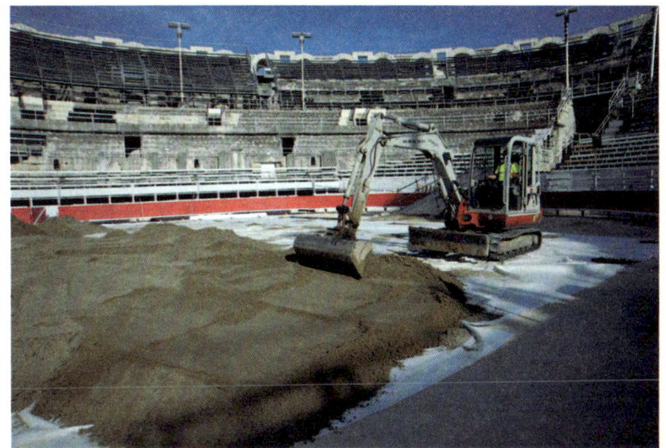
7/3/12—6:17:30 PM

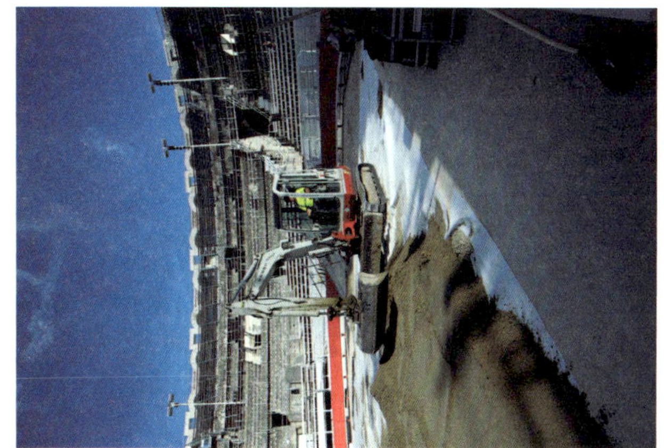
7/3/12—6:17:33 PM

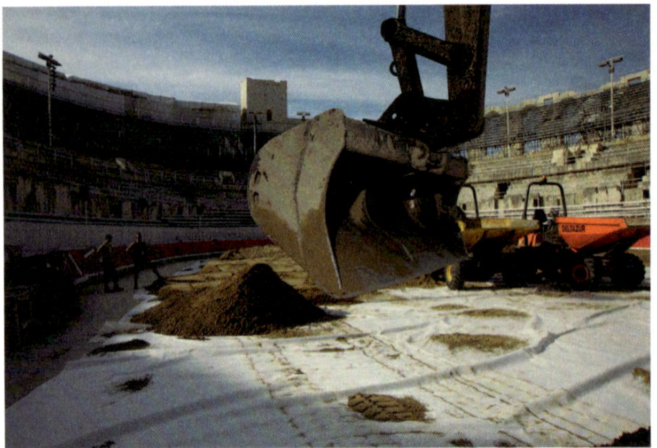

7/3/12—6:20:52 PM

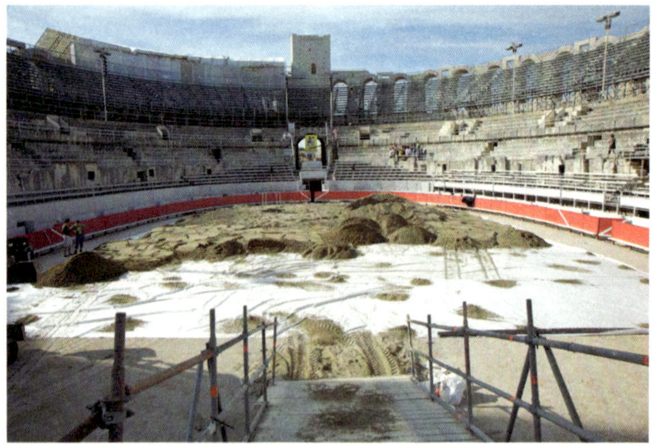

7/3/12—6:22:16 PM

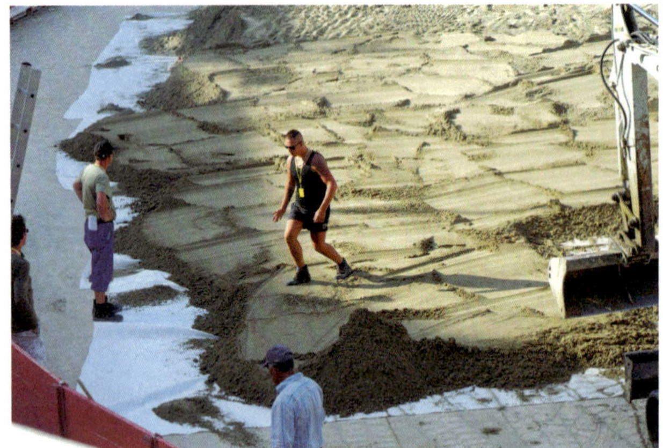

7/3/12—6:32:53 PM

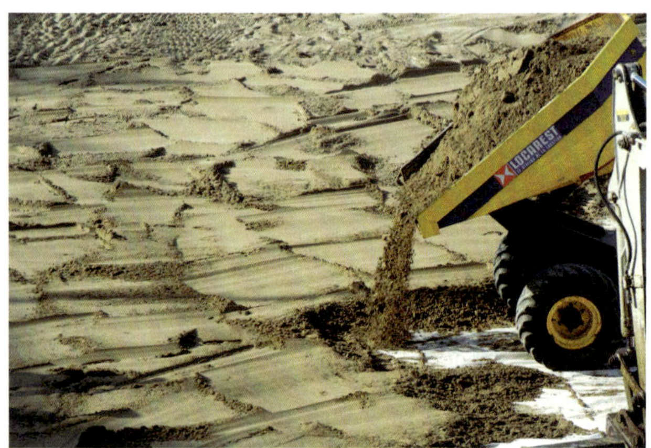

7/3/12—6:33:19 PM

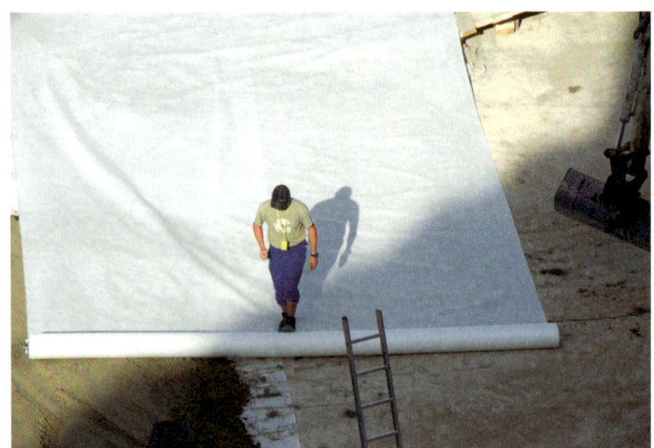

7/3/12—6:36:07 PM

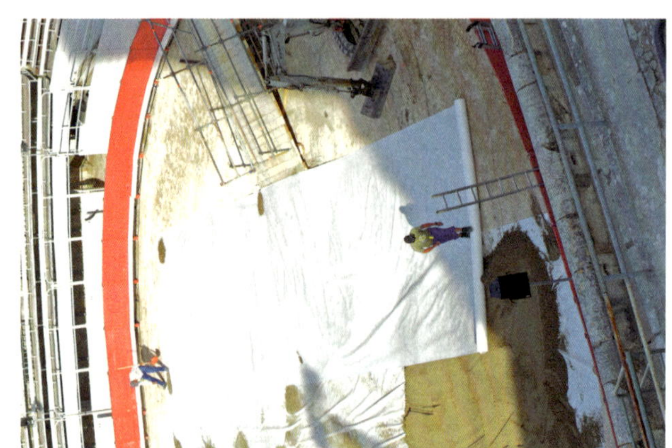

7/3/12—6:36:09 PM

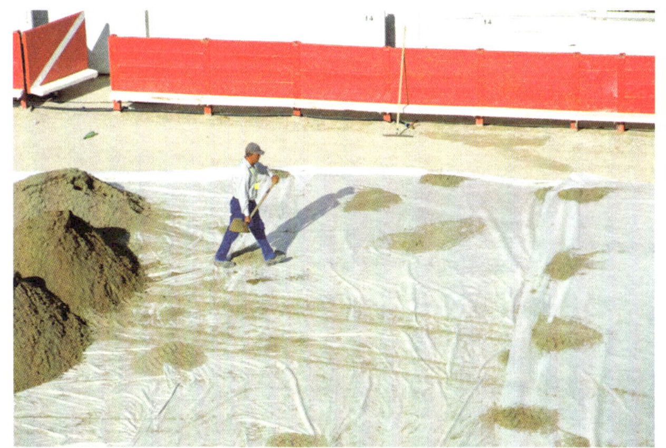

7/3/12—6:36:22 PM

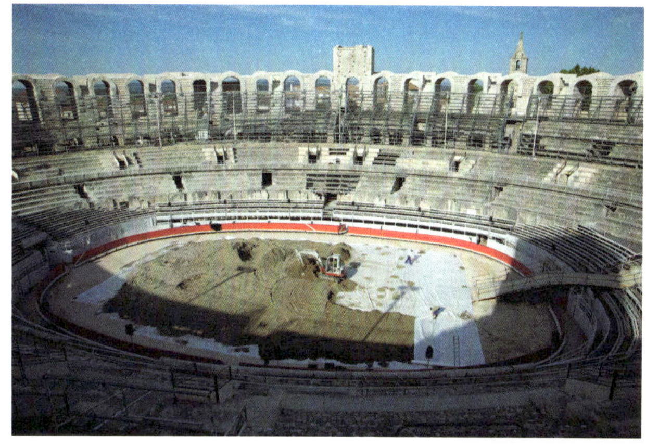

7/3/12—6:37:13 PM

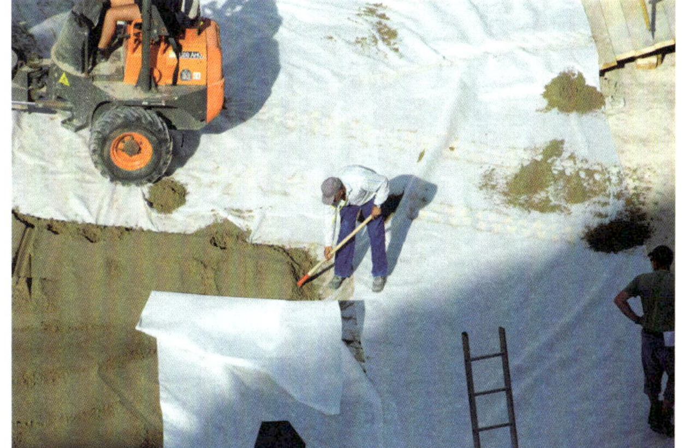

7/3/12—6:38:16 PM

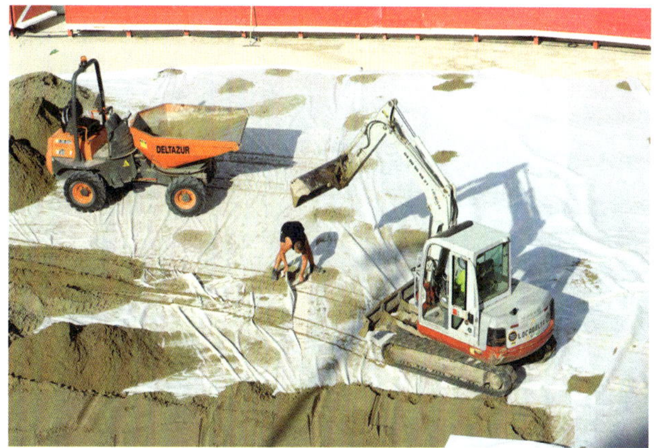

7/3/12—6:38:44 PM

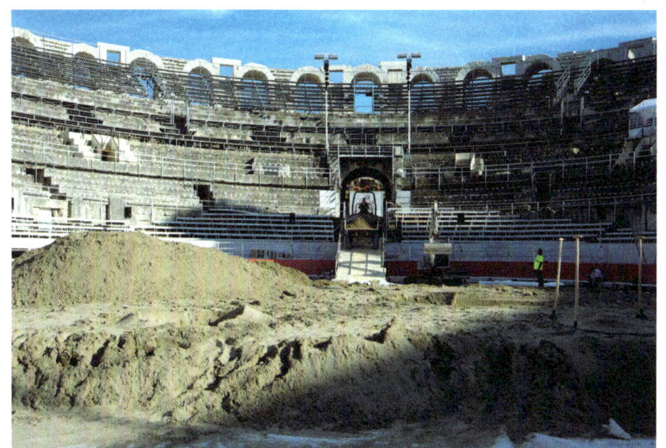

7/3/12—6:47:51 PM

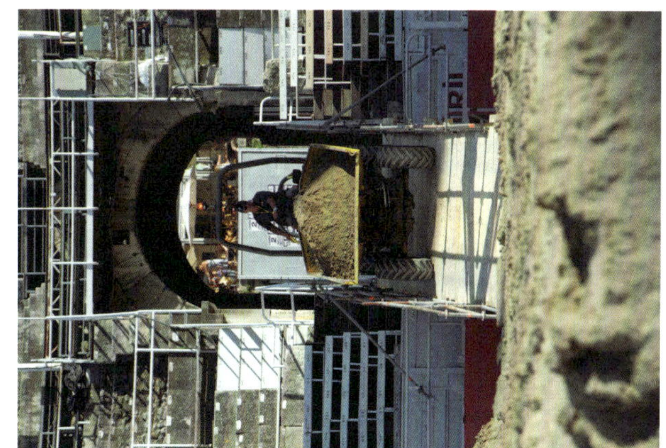

7/3/12—6:48:21 PM

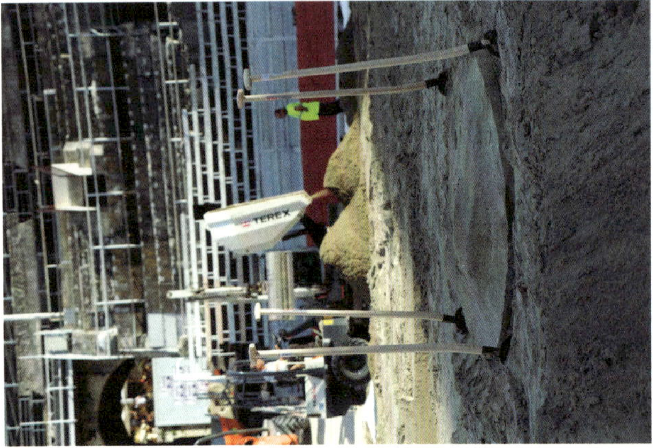

7/3/12—6:49:19 PM

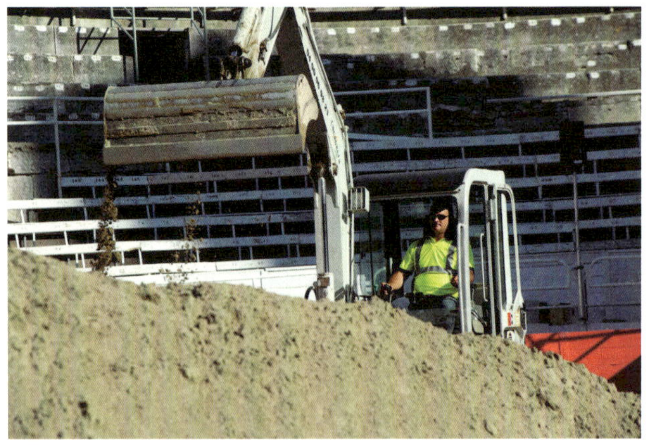

7/3/12—6:54:33 PM

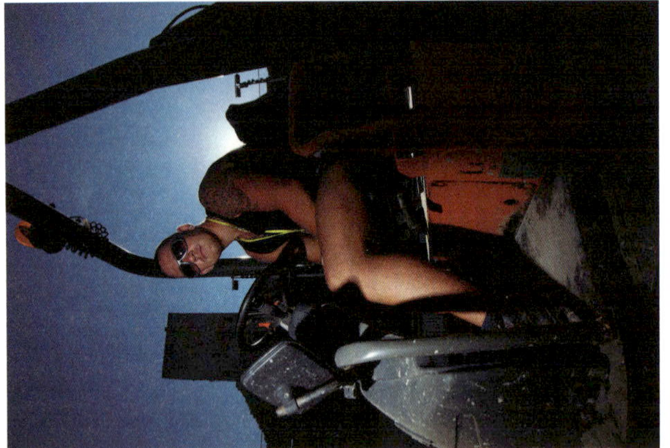

7/3/12—7:00:39 PM

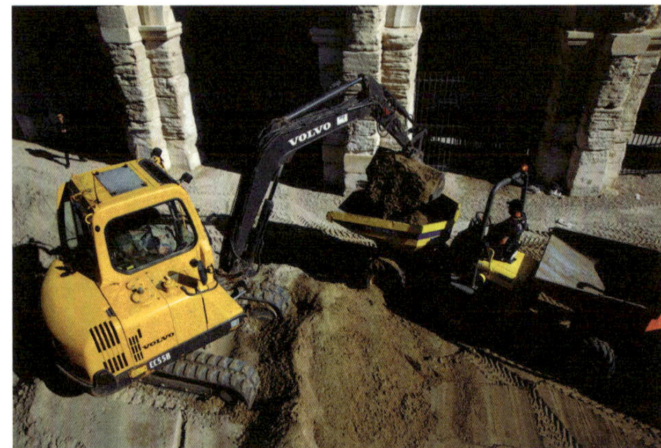

7/4/12—9:11:05 AM

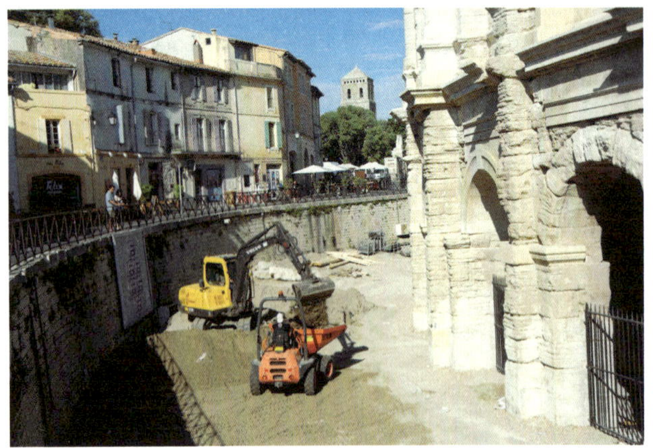

7/4/12—9:12:36 AM

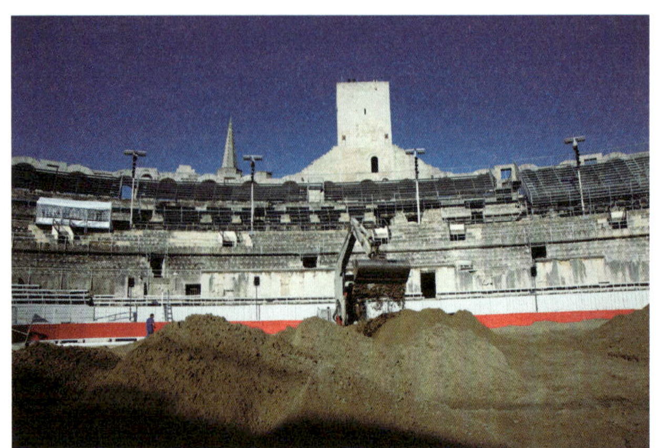

7/4/12—9:15:58 AM

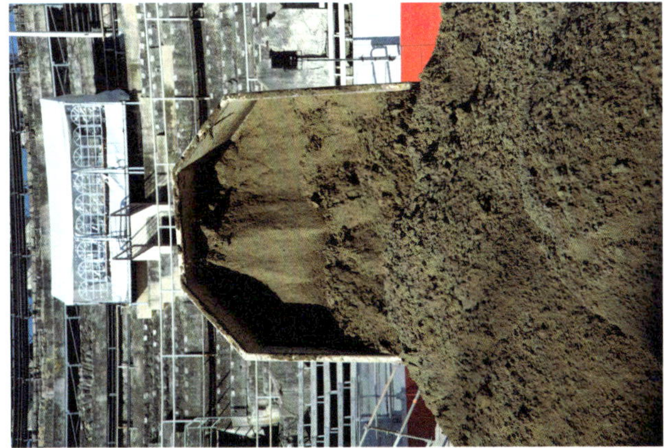

7/4/12—9:16:21 AM

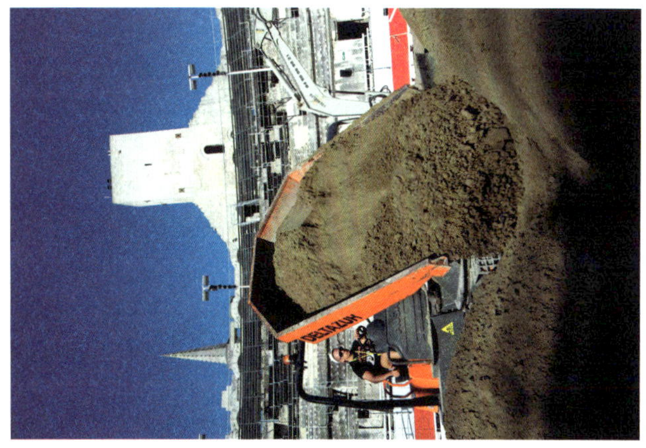

7/4/12—9:20:25 AM

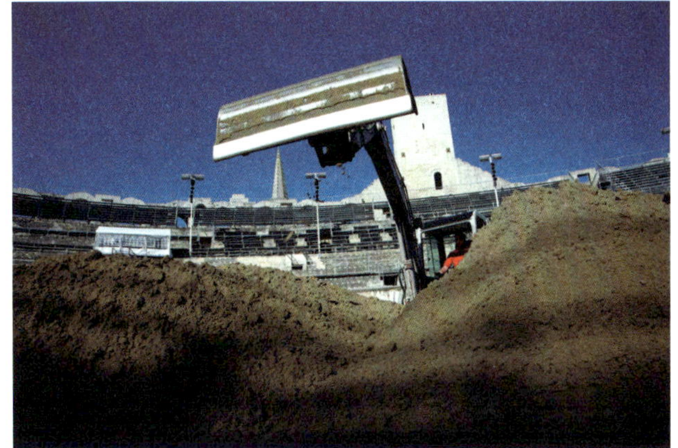

7/4/12—9:21:00 AM

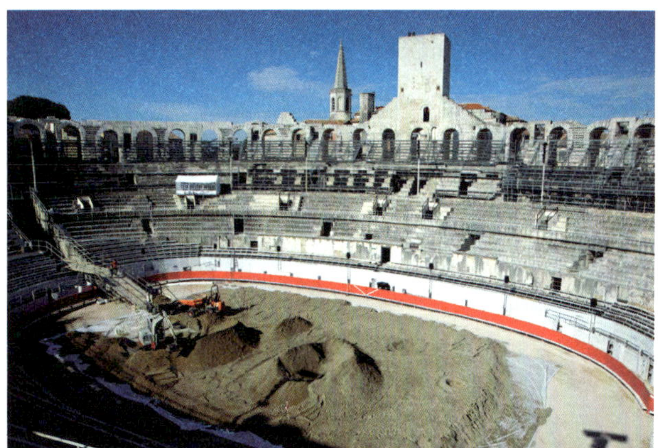

7/4/12—9:25:58 AM

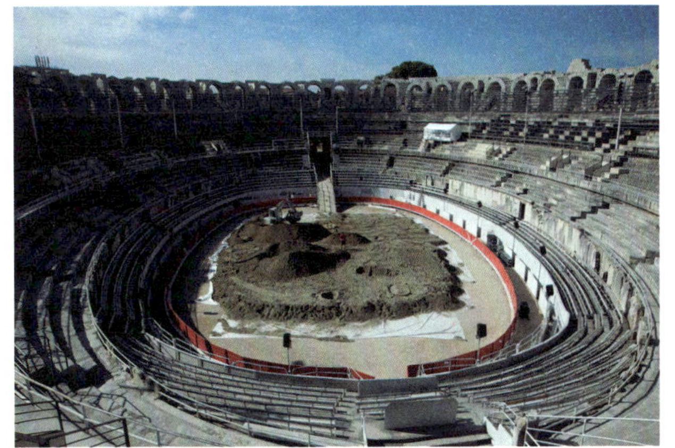

7/4/12—9:34:53 AM

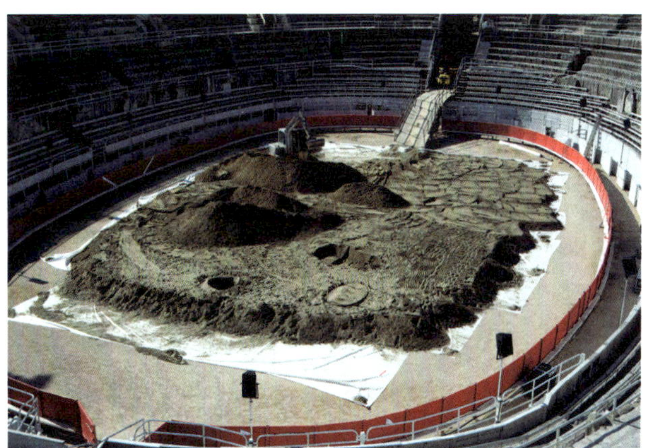

7/4/12—9:39:18 AM

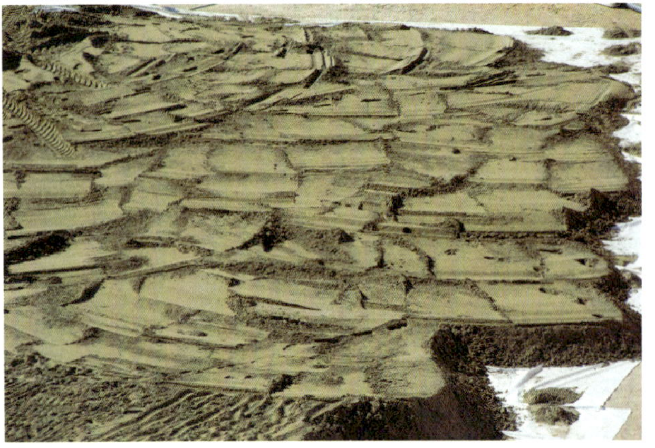

7/4/12—9:40:07 AM

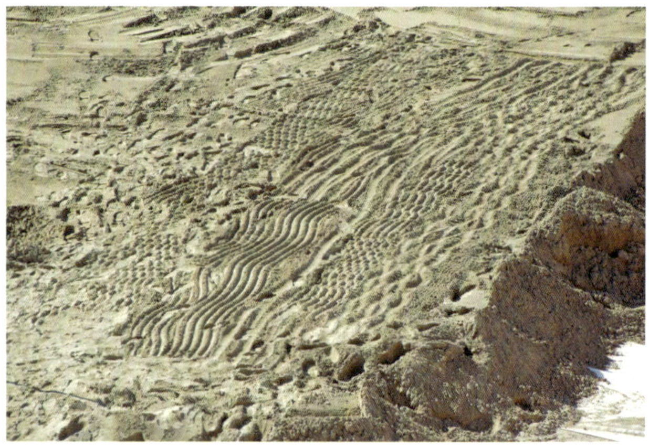

7/4/12—9:40:09 AM

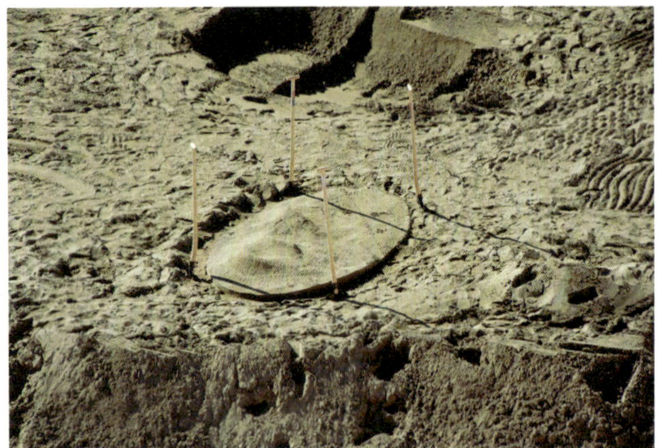

7/4/12—9:40:10 AM

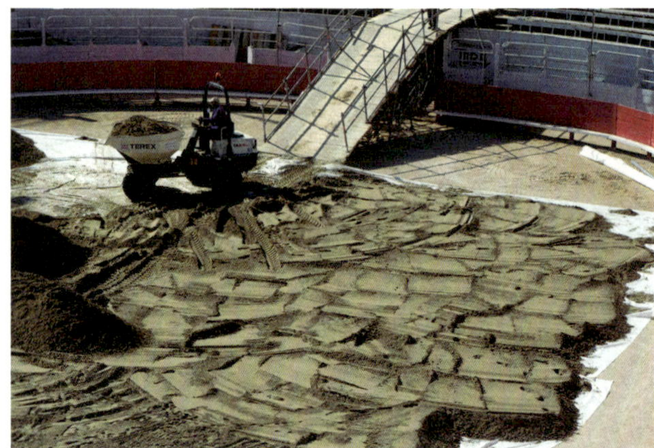

7/4/12—9:40:29 AM

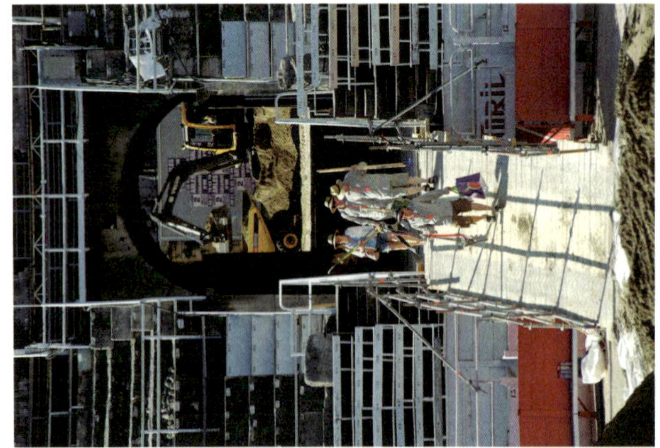

7/4/12—9:42:50 AM

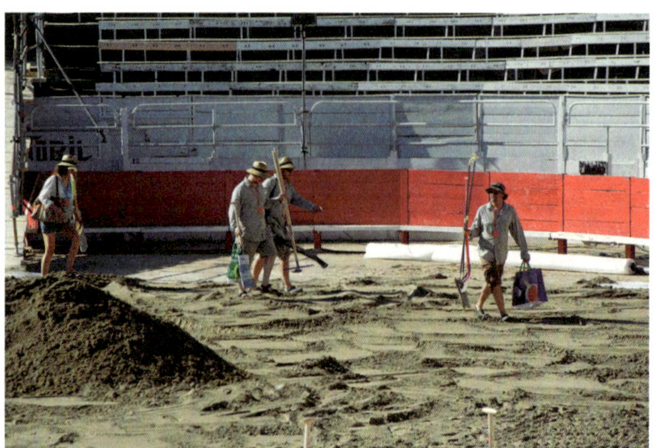

7/4/12—9:43:02 AM

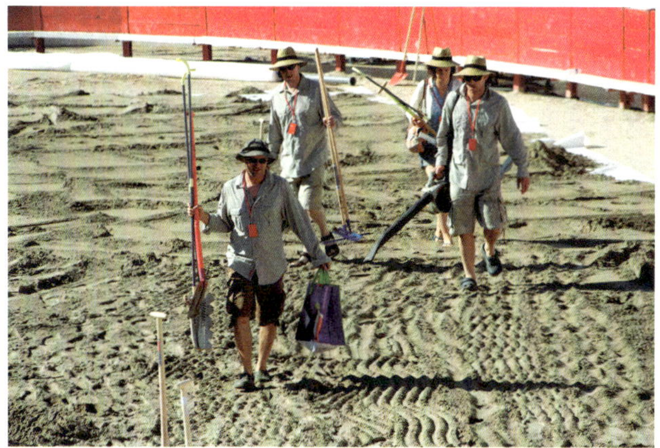

7/4/12—9:43:22 AM

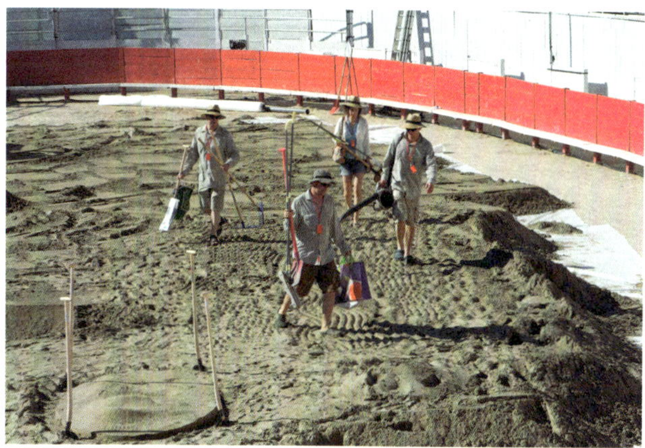

7/4/12—9:43:24 AM

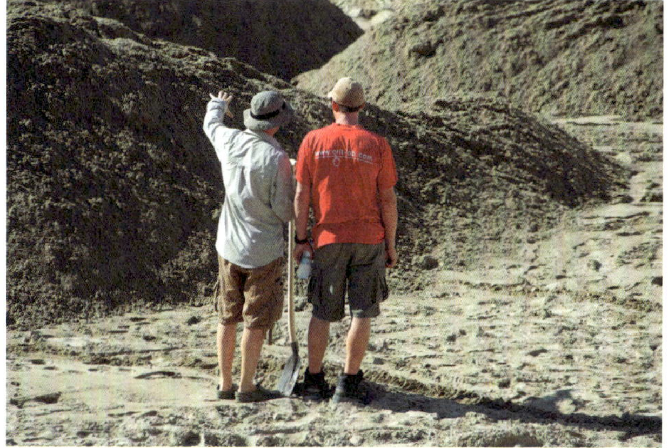

7/4/12—9:46:19 AM

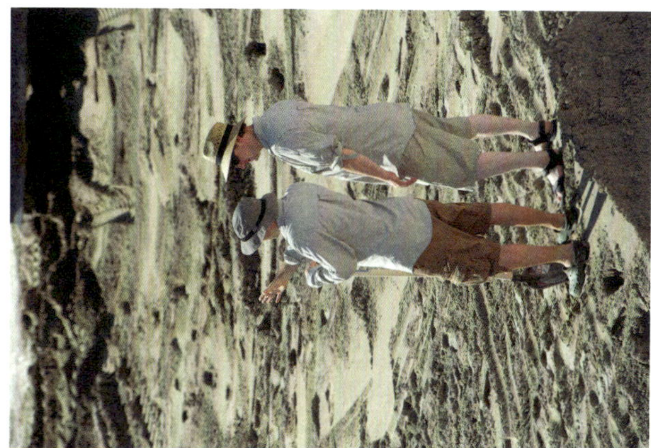

7/4/12—9:48:35 AM

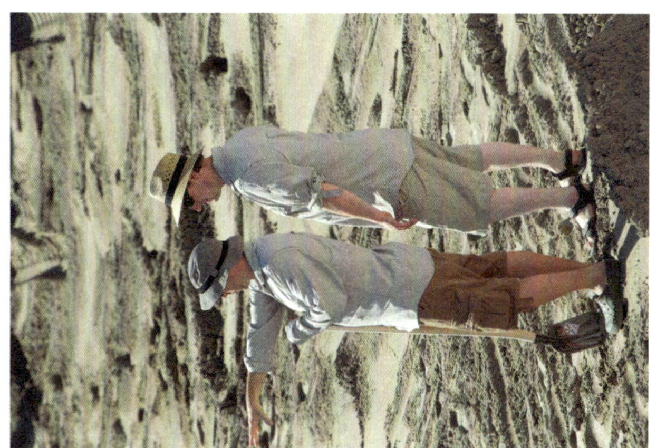

7/4/12—9:48:36 AM

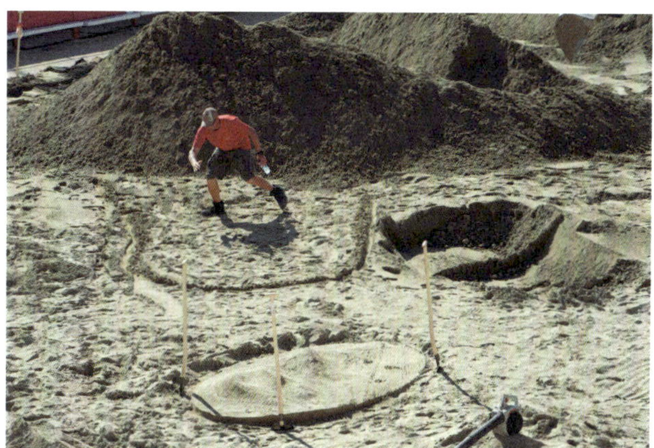

7/4/12—9:49:25 AM

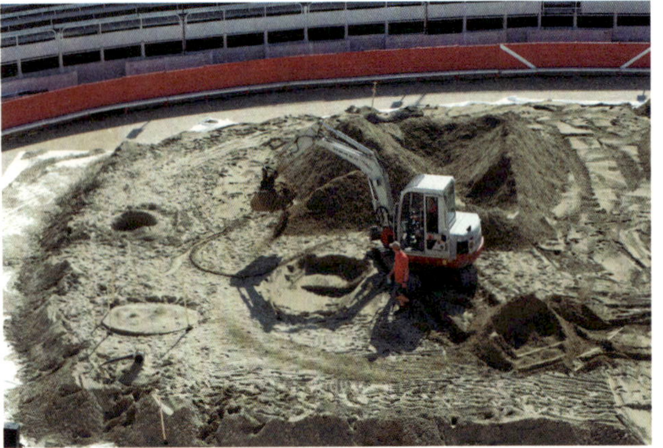
7/4/12—9:52:54 AM

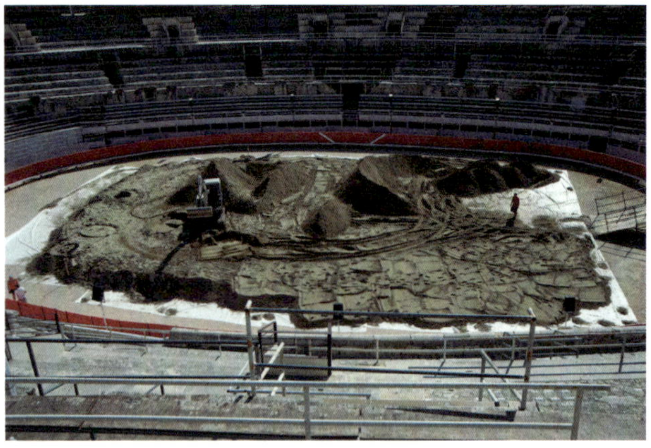
7/4/12—9:53:56 AM

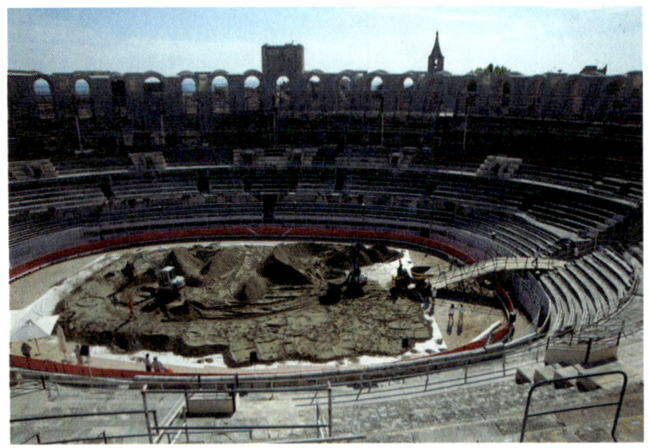
7/4/12—9:57:49 AM

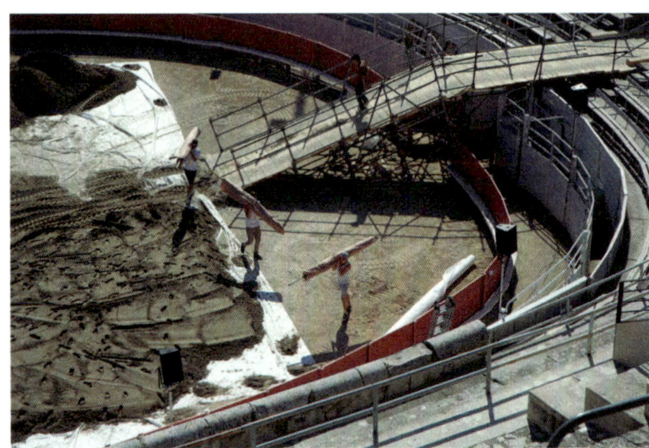
7/4/12—9:58:53 AM

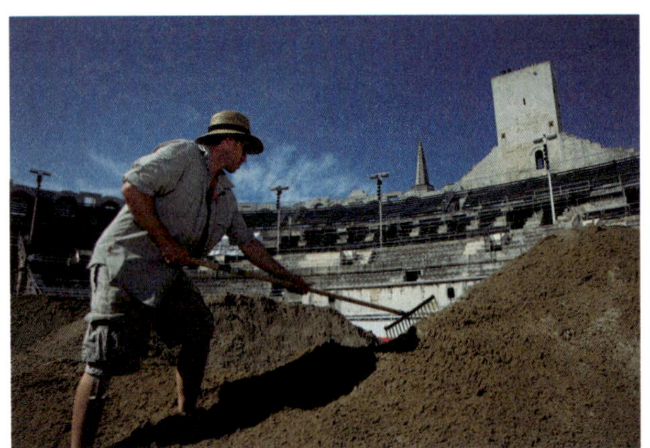
7/4/12—10:38:37 AM

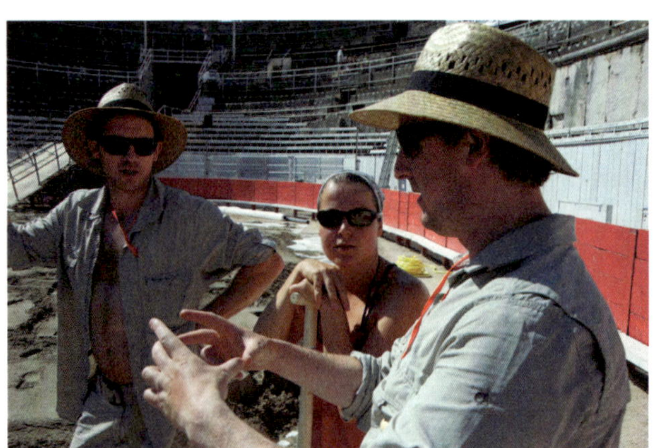
7/4/12—10:41:19 AM

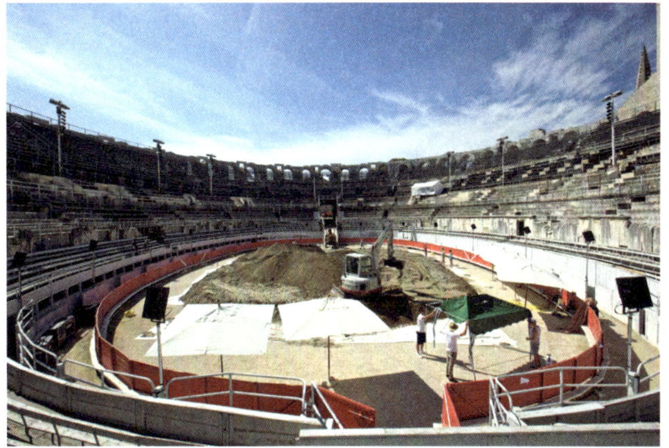

7/4/12—10:45:45 AM

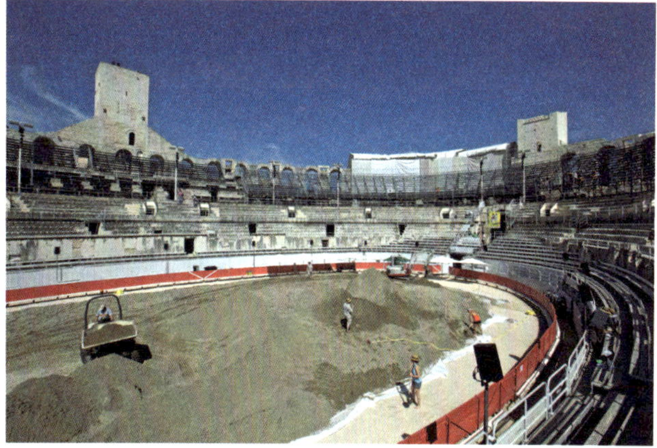

7/4/12—10:56:56 AM

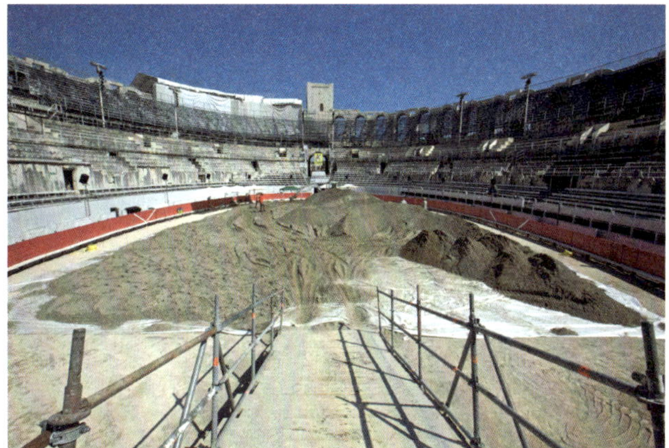

7/4/12—10:58:20 AM

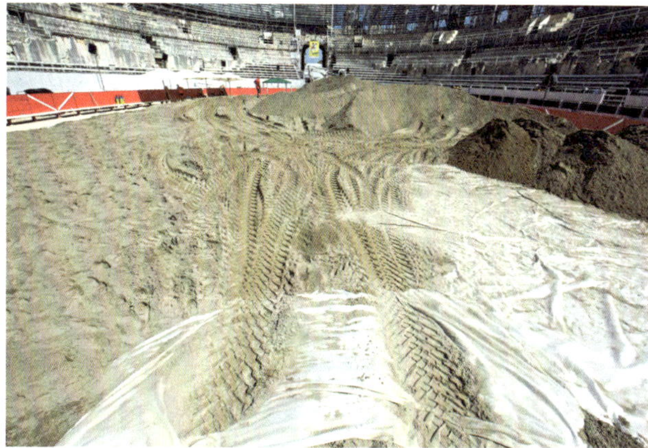

7/4/12—10:58:33 AM

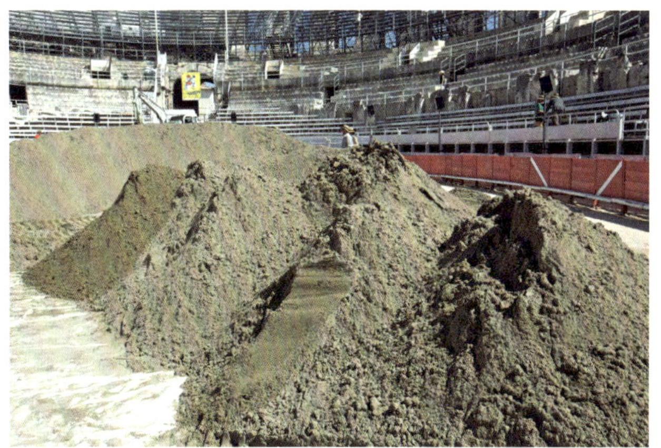

7/4/12—10:58:50 AM

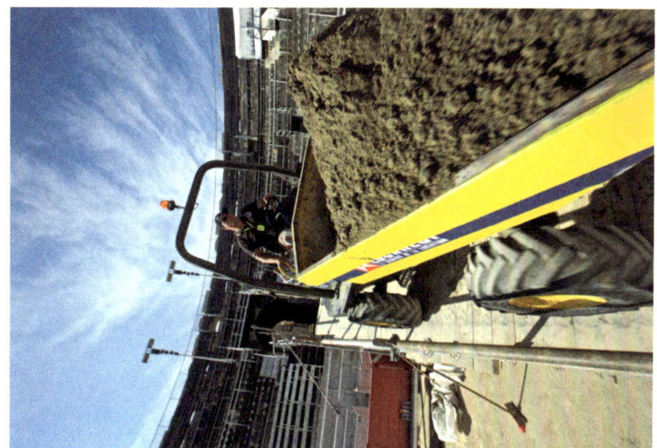

7/4/12—10:59:29 AM

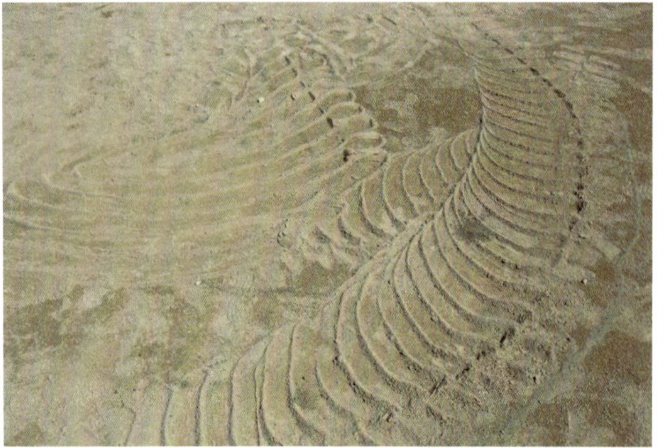
7/4/12—11:00:12 AM

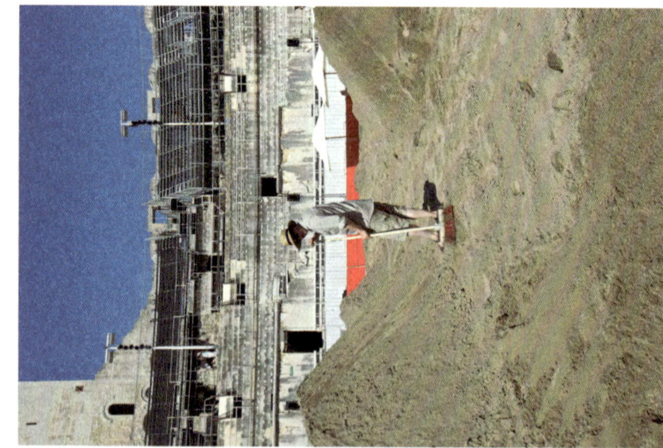
7/4/12—11:00:38 AM

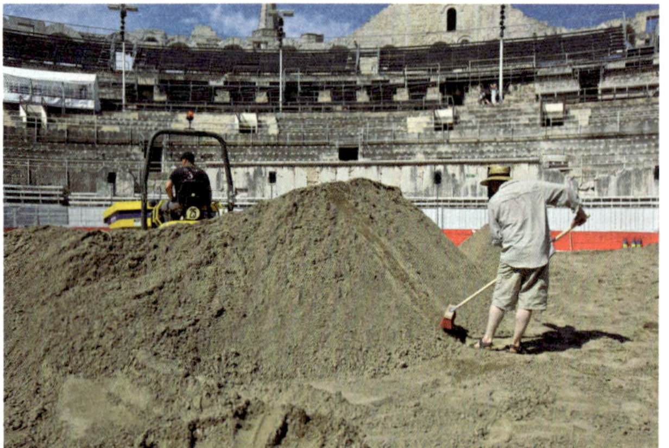
7/4/12—11:00:43 AM

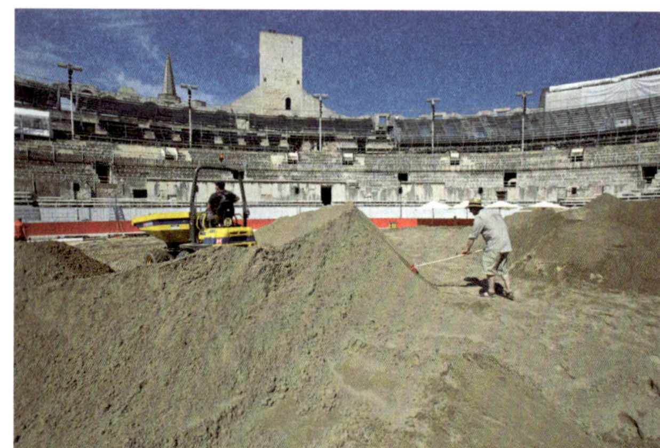
7/4/12—11:00:51 AM

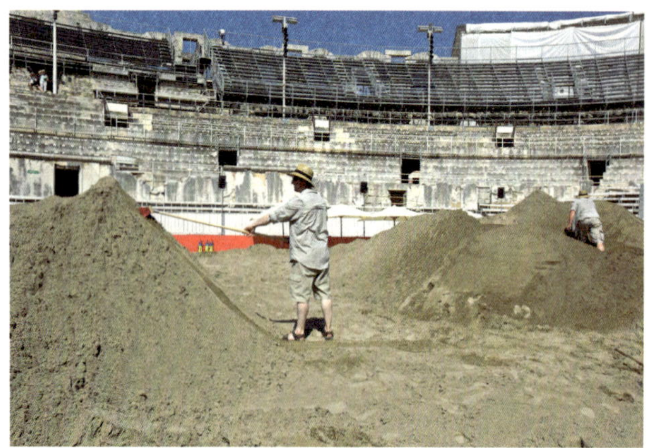
7/4/12—11:01:07 AM

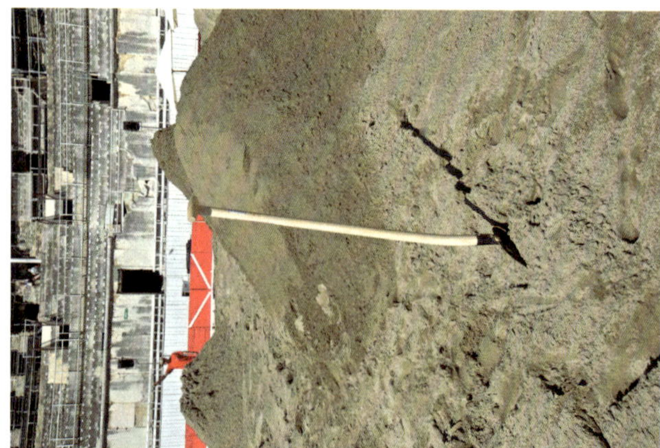
7/4/12—11:01:17 AM

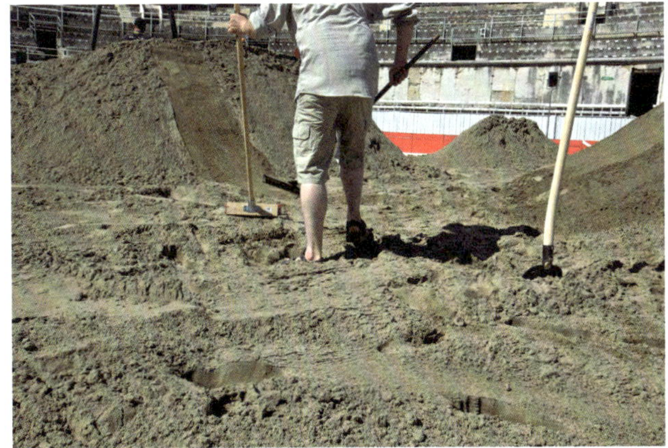

7/4/12—11:01:32 AM

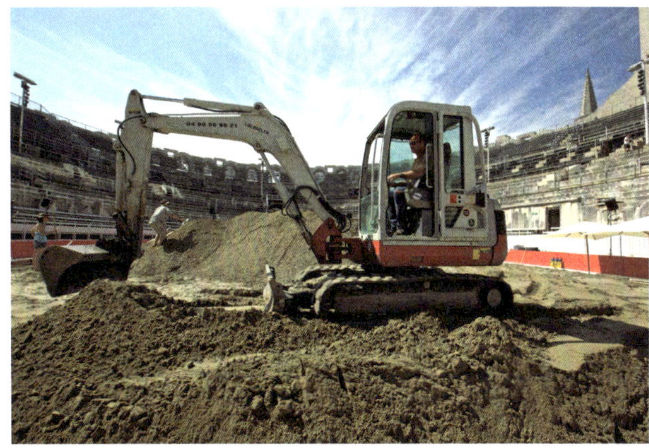

7/4/12—11:02:11 AM

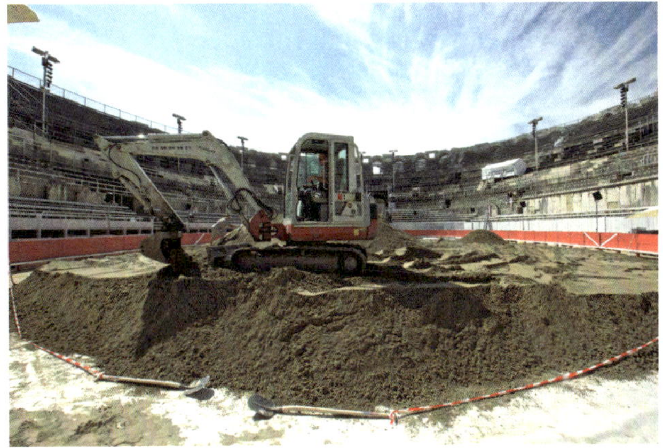

7/4/12—11:02:37 AM

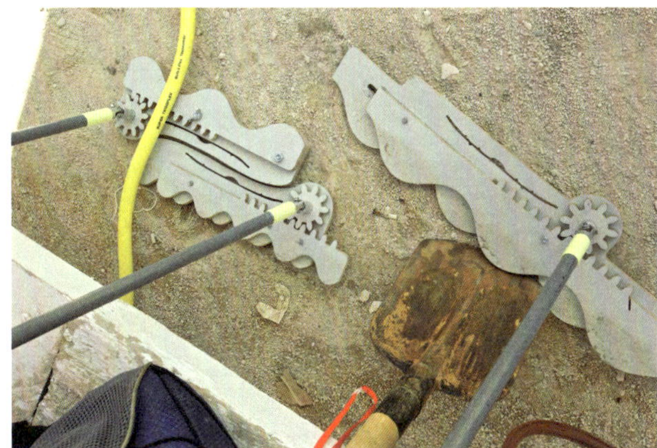

7/4/12—11:03:18 AM

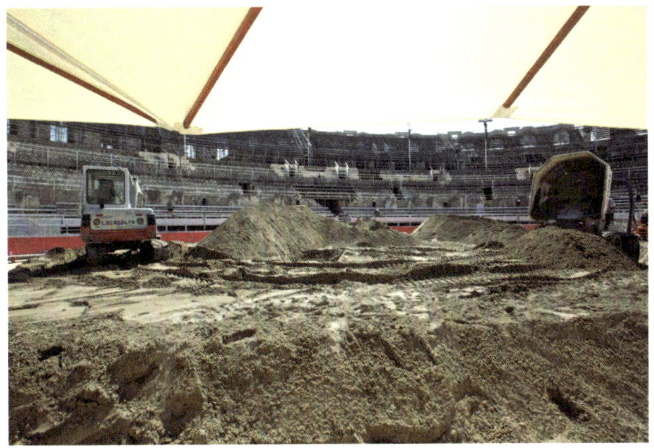

7/4/12—11:03:32 AM

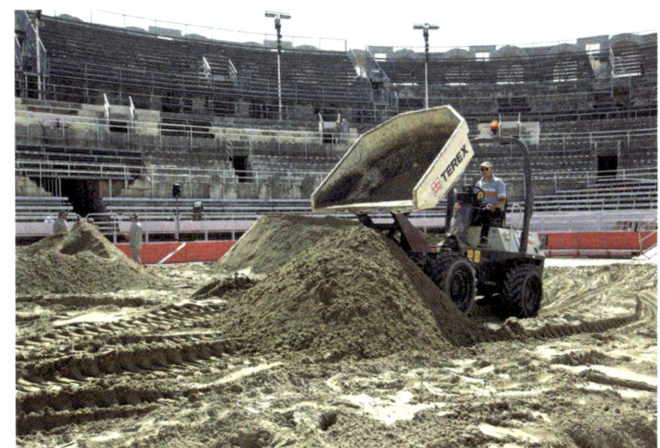

7/4/12—11:03:42 AM

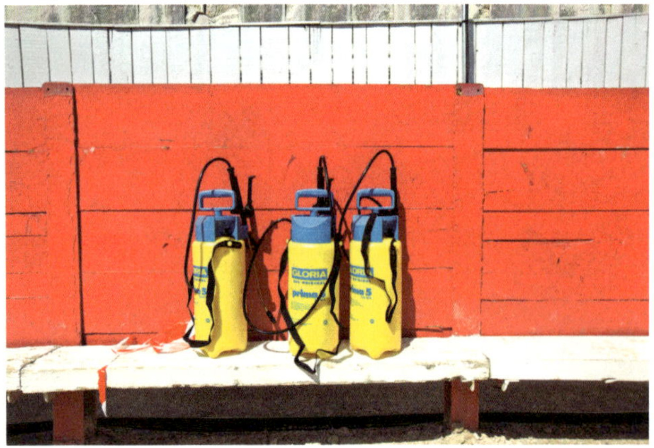

7/4/12—11:04:02 AM

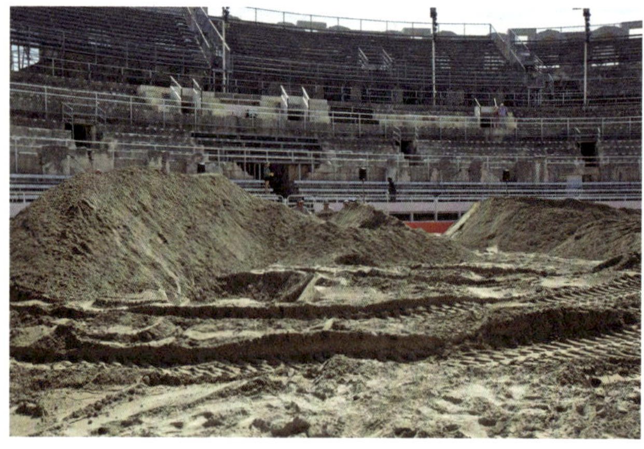
7/4/12—11:05:11 AM

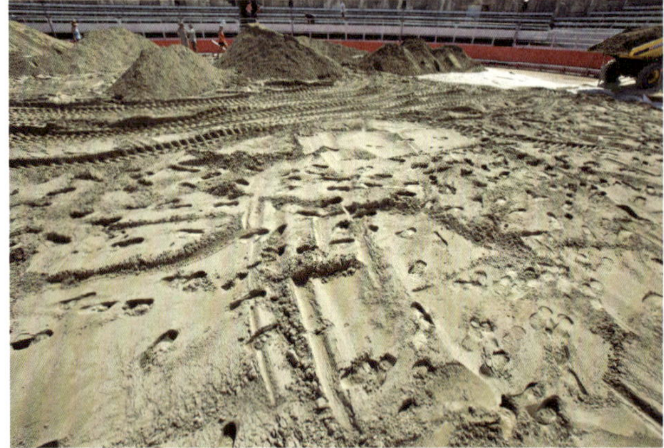
7/4/12—11:05:29 AM

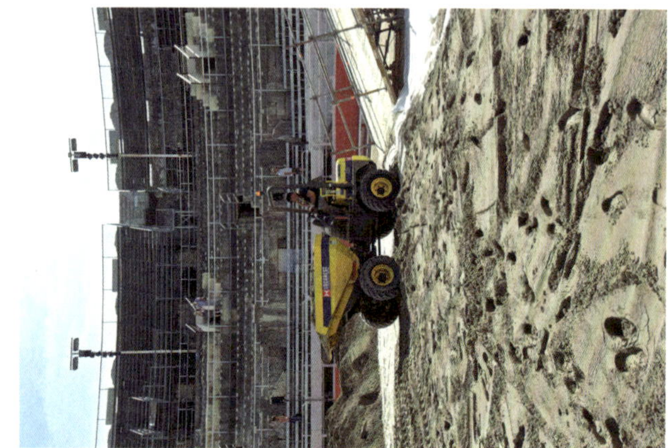
7/4/12—11:05:41 AM

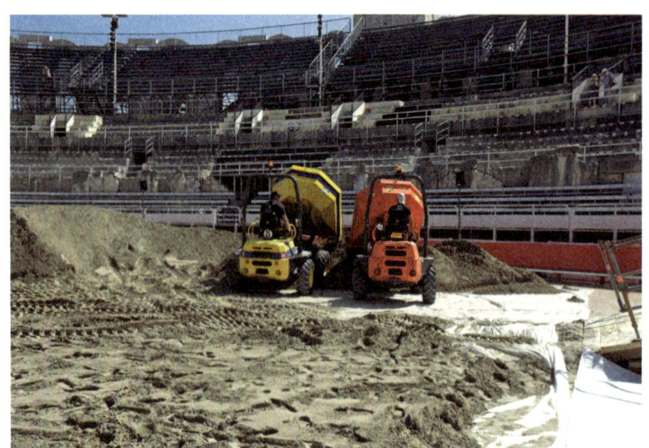
7/4/12—11:05:59 AM

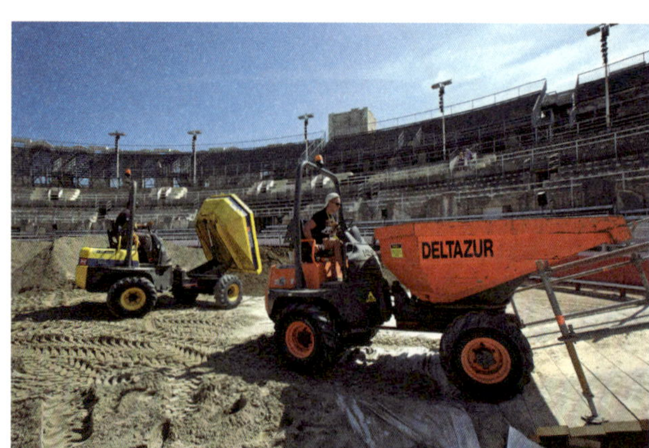

7/4/12—11:06:15 AM

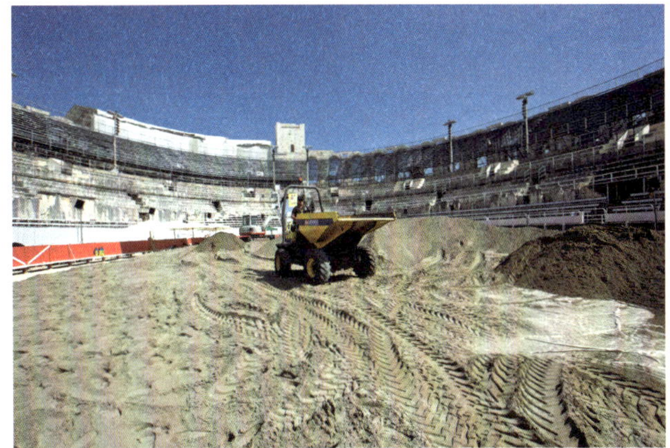

7/4/12—11:06:27 AM

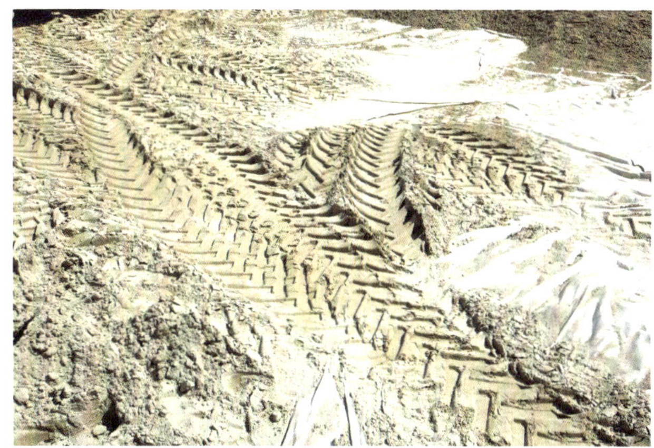

7/4/12—11:06:37 AM

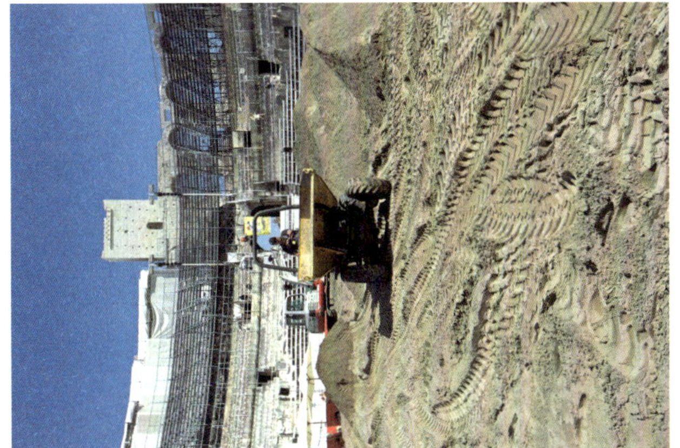

7/4/12—11:06:51 AM

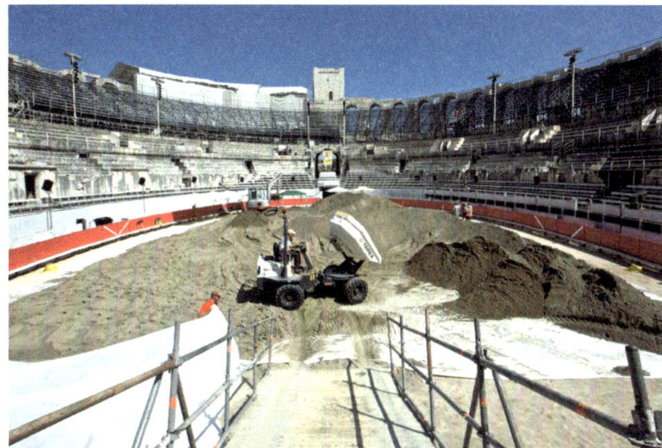

7/4/12—11:07:56 AM

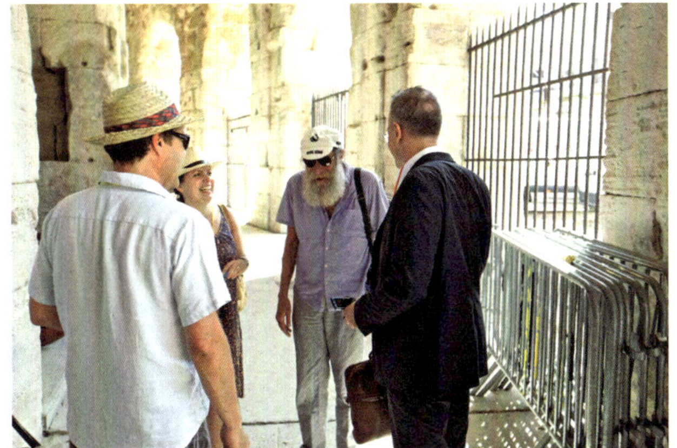

7/4/12—11:09:31 AM

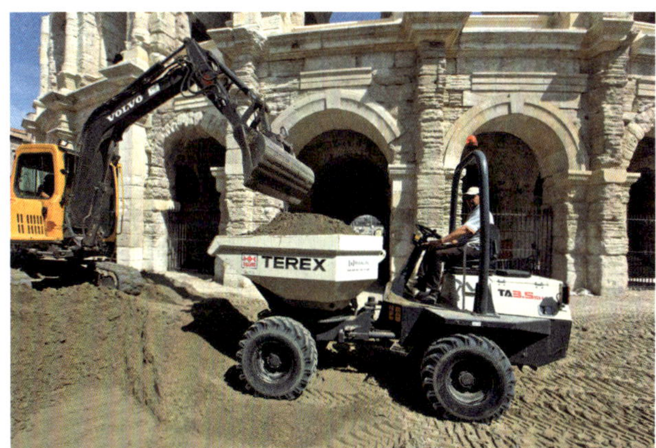

7/4/12—11:11:51 AM

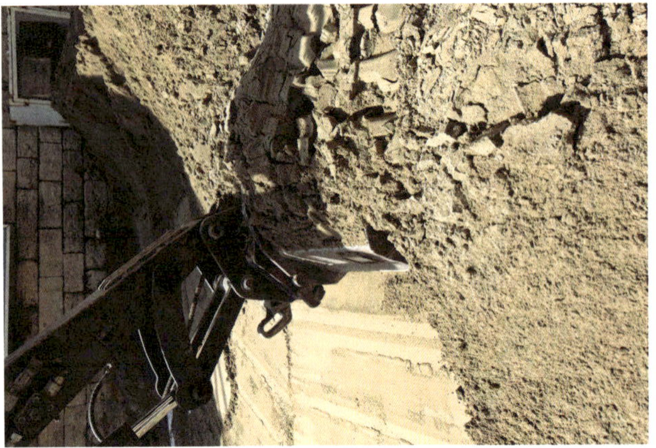

7/4/12—11:12:21 AM

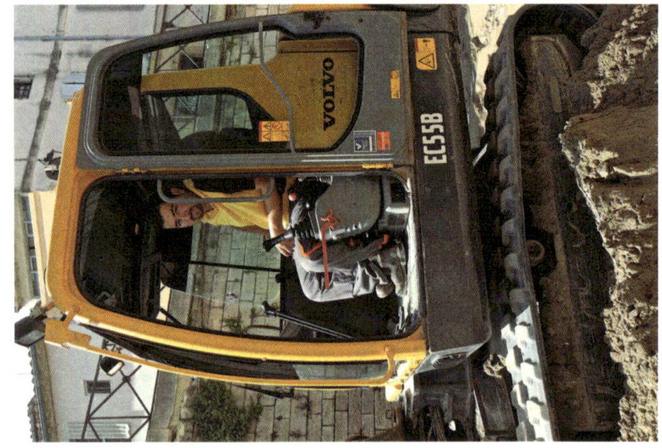

7/4/12—11:13:11 AM

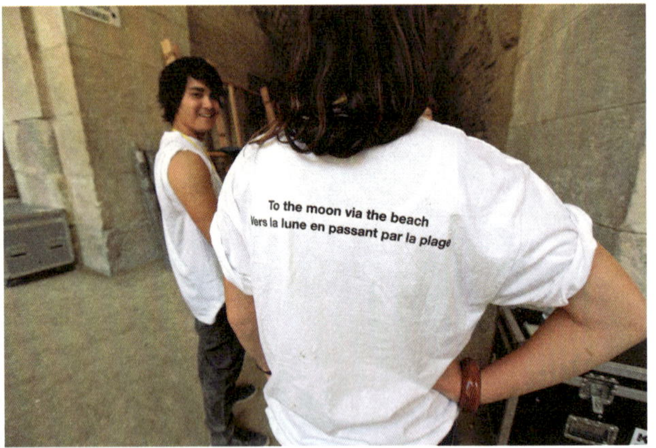

7/4/12—11:13:52 AM

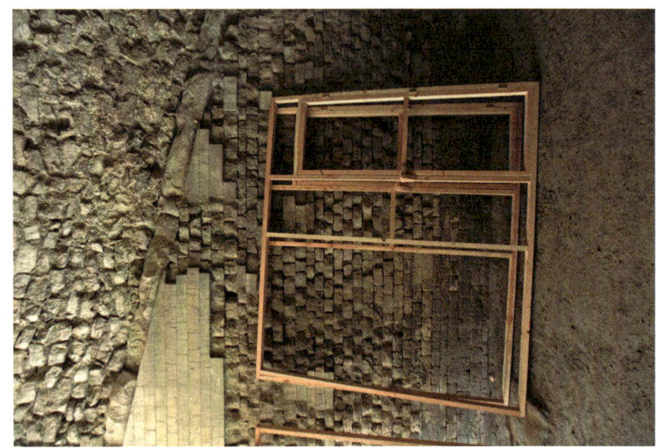

7/4/12—11:14:32 AM

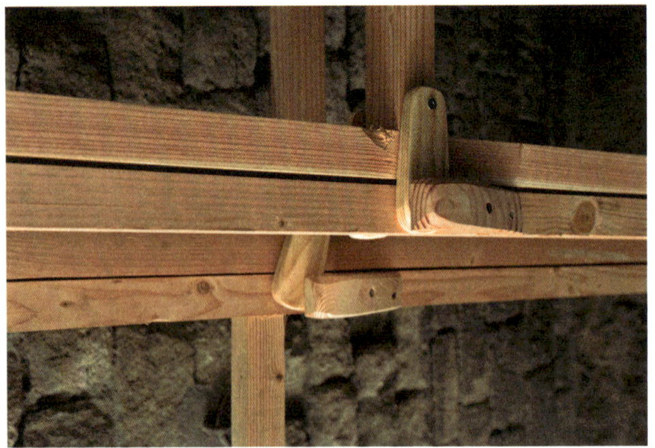

7/4/12—11:15:01 AM

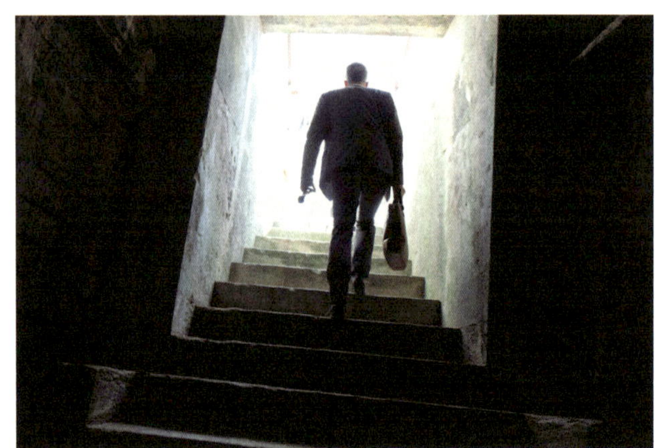

7/4/12—11:15:41 AM

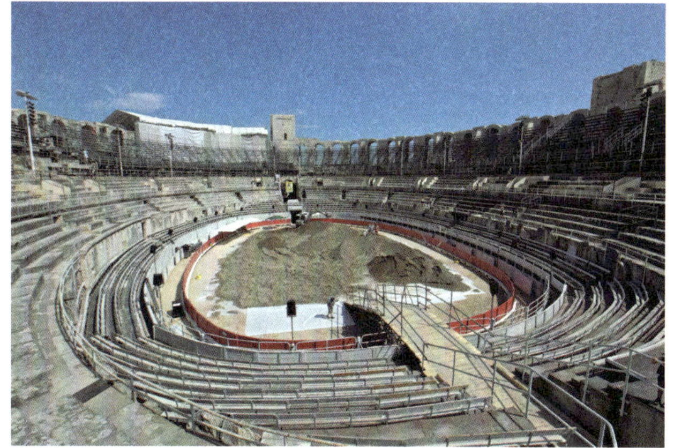
7/4/12—11:16:18 AM

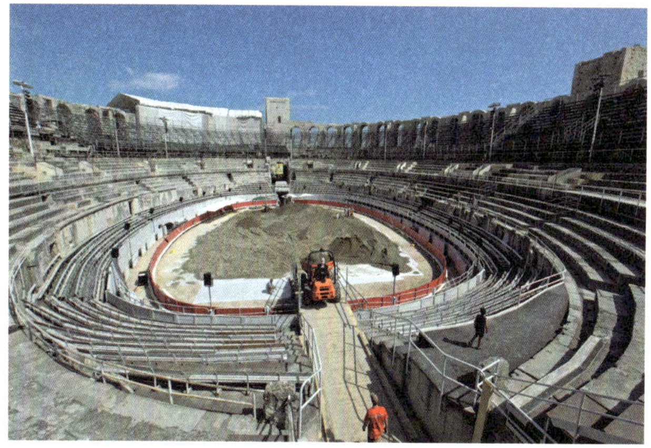
7/4/12—11:16:31 AM

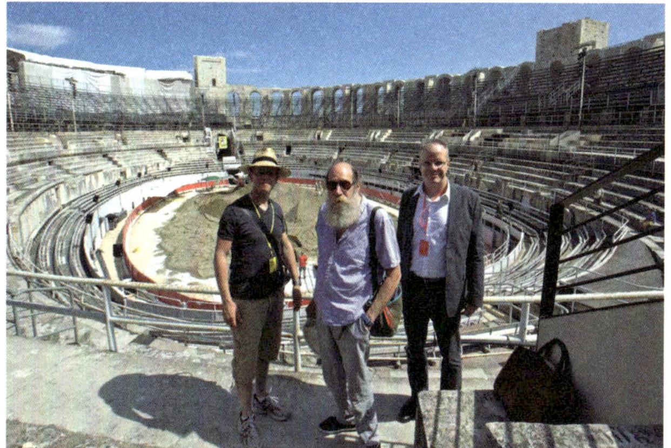
7/4/12—11:20:03 AM

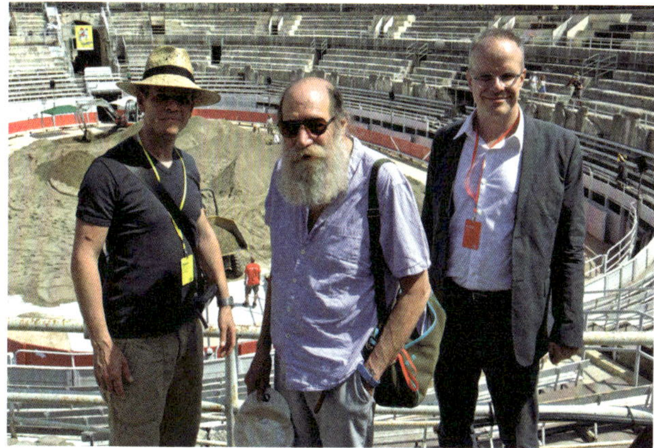
7/4/12—11:20:08 AM

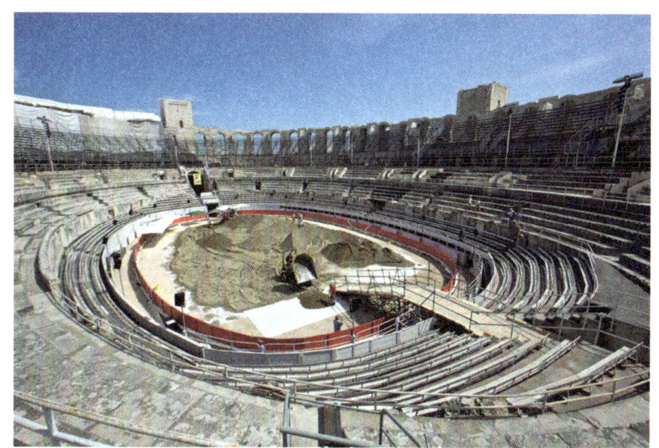
7/4/12—11:20:26 AM

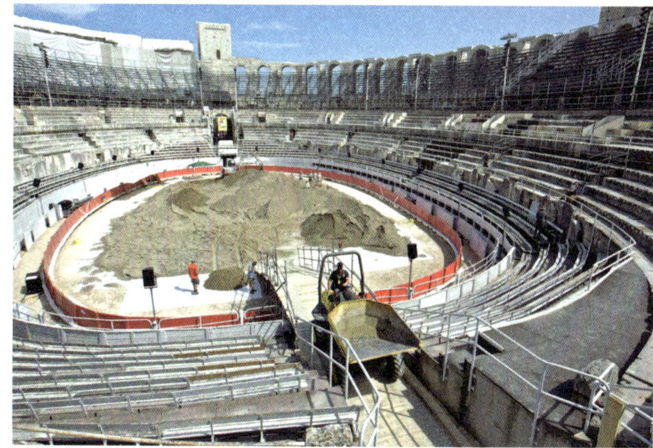
7/4/12—11:21:00 AM

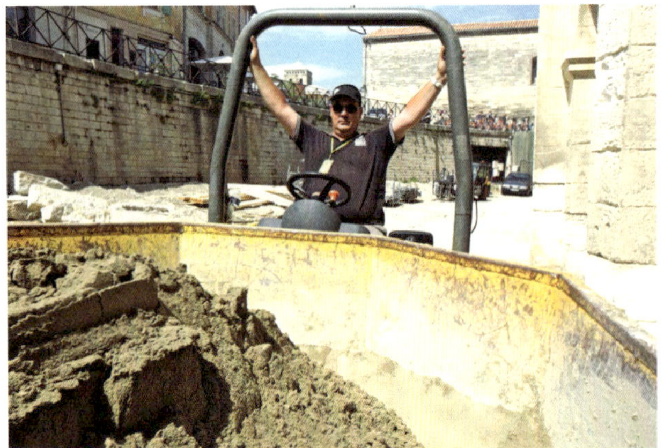

7/4/12—11:23:17 AM

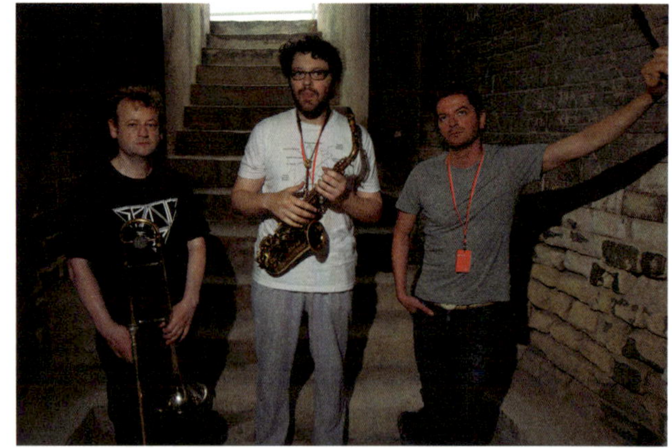

7/4/12—11:51:21 AM

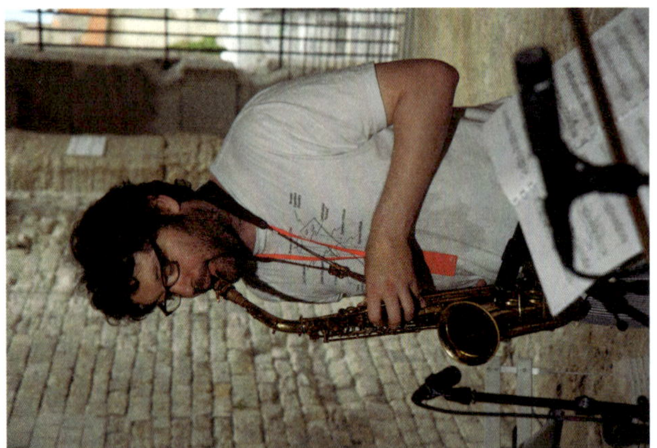

7/4/12—11:52:43 AM

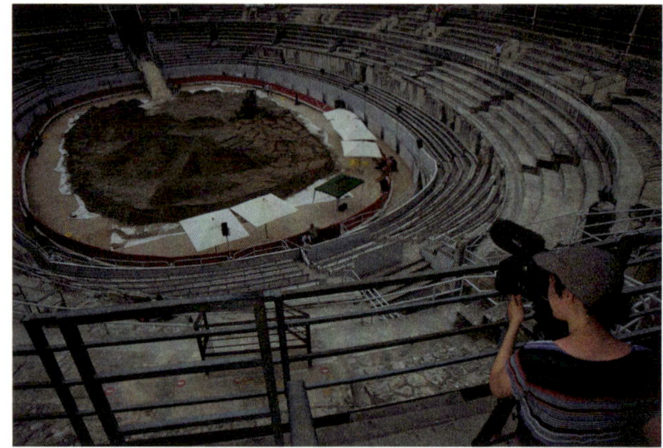

7/4/12—11:58:06 AM

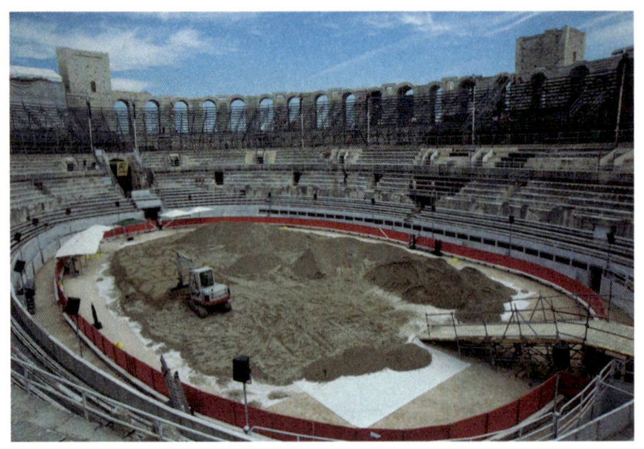

7/4/12—12:00:47 PM

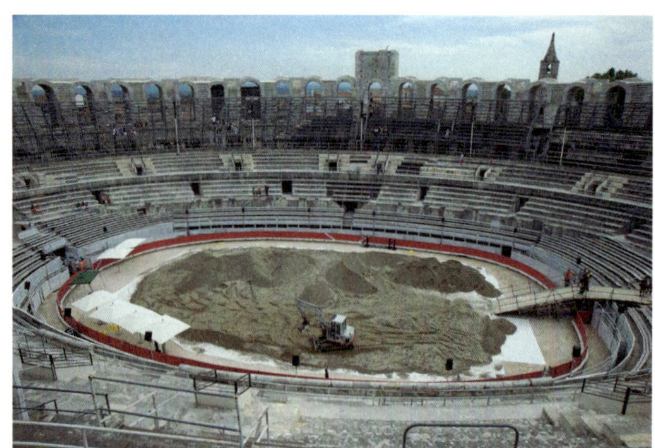

7/4/12—12:04:21 PM

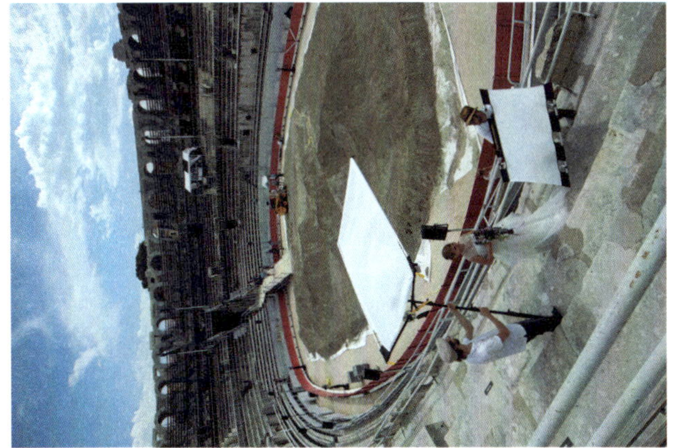

7/4/12—3:48:33 PM

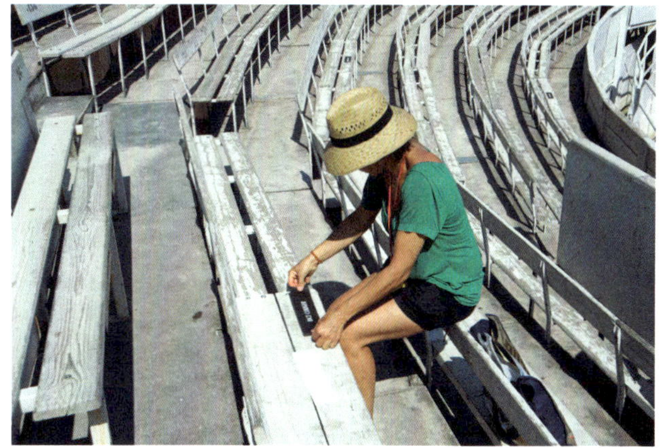

7/4/12—4:49:02 PM

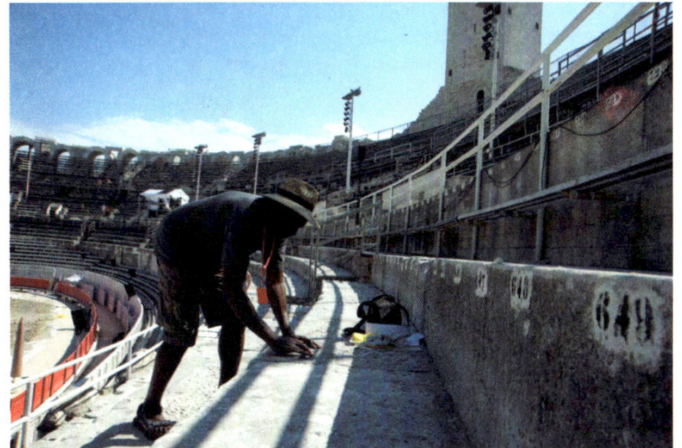

7/4/12—4:50:21 PM

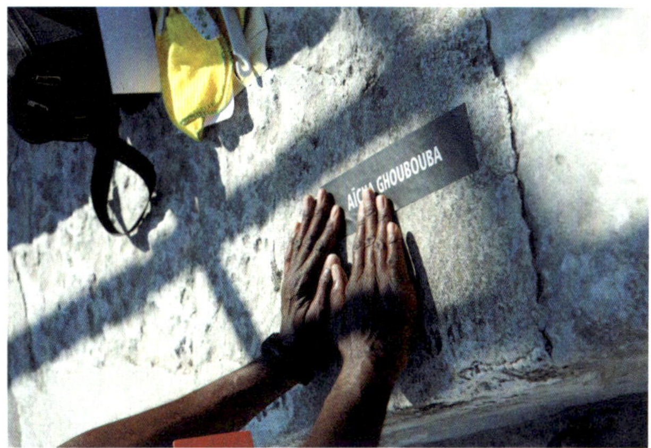

7/4/12—4:50:25 PM

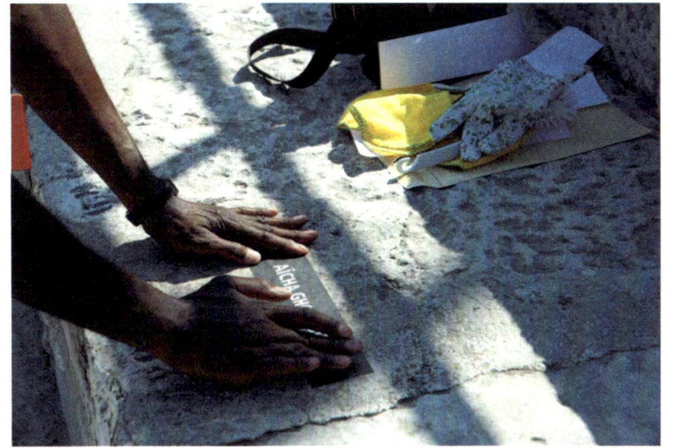

7/4/12—4:50:29 PM

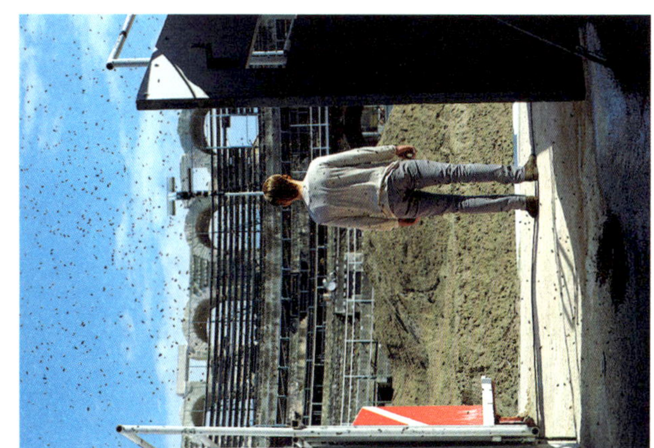

7/4/12—5:00:42 PM

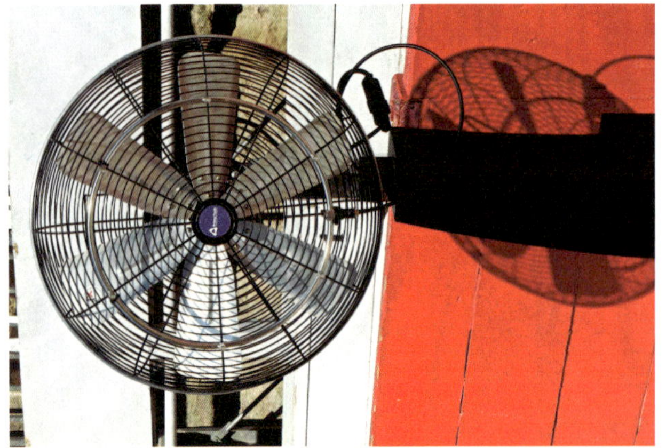

7/4/12—5:03:21 PM

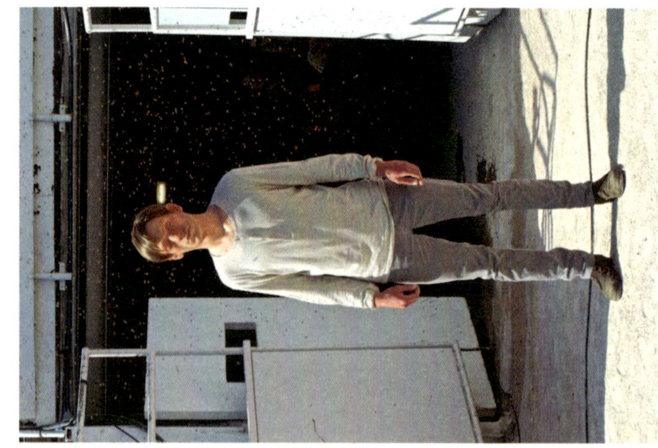

7/4/12—5:04:42 PM

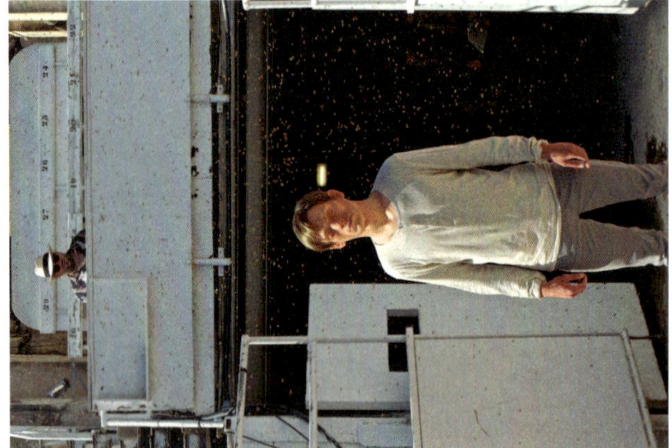

7/4/12—5:04:44 PM

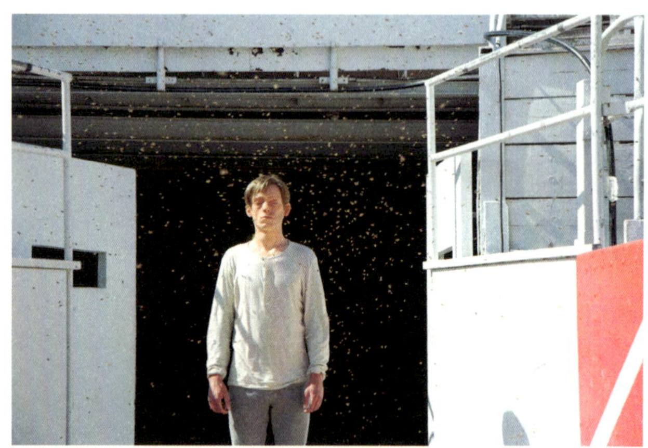

7/4/12—5:04:51 PM

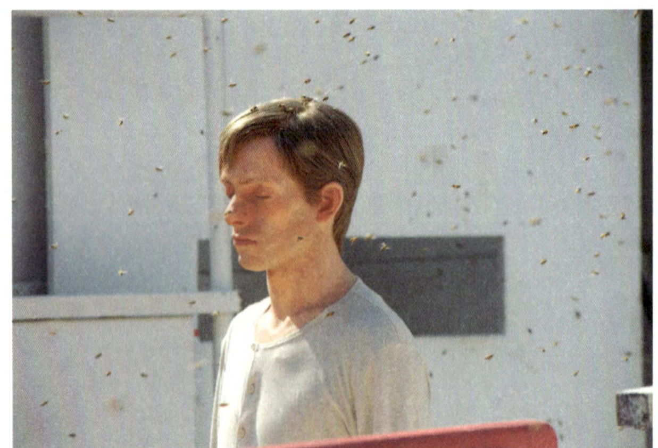

7/4/12—5:05:47 PM

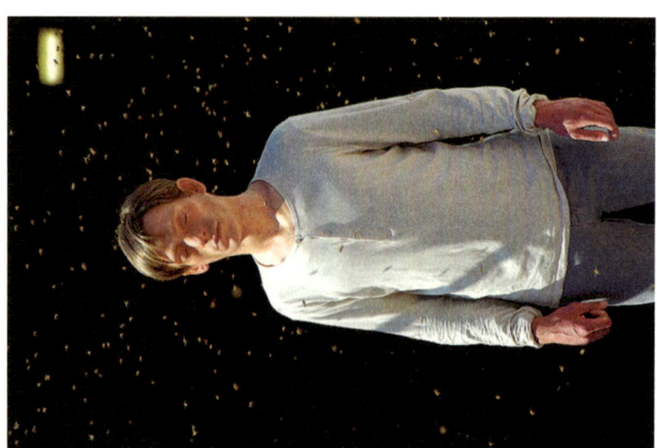

7/4/12—5:05:49 PM

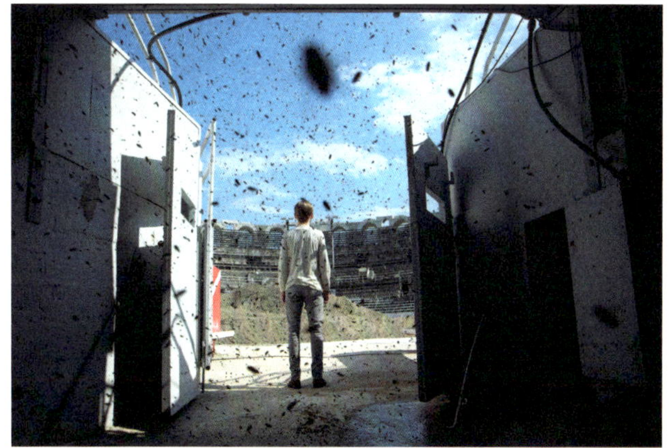

7/4/12—5:08:43 PM

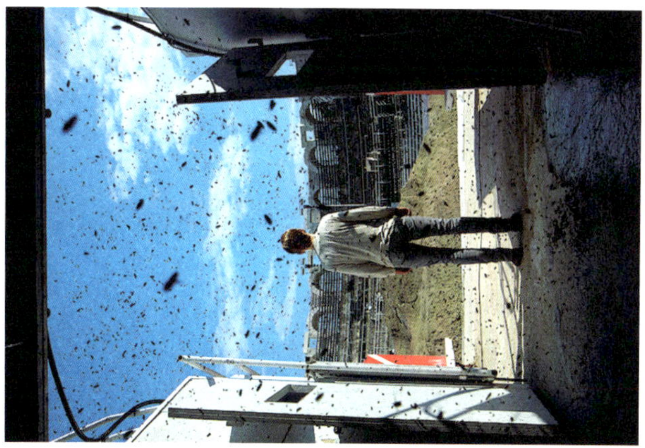

7/4/12—5:08:49 PM

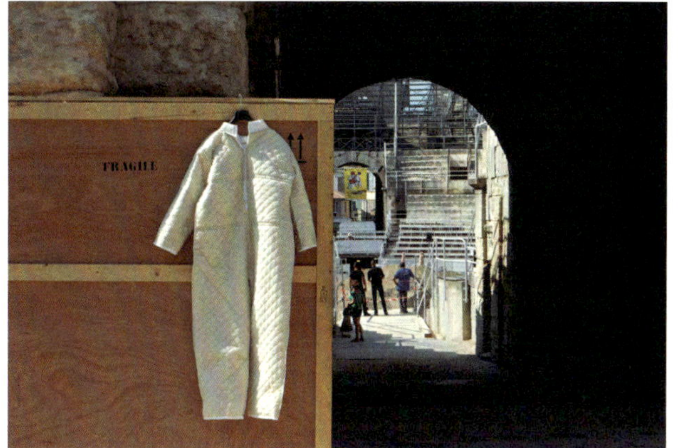

7/4/12—5:09:30 PM

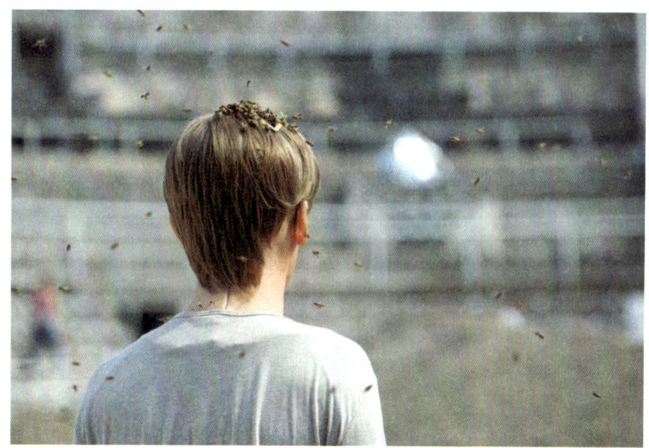

7/4/12—5:14:09 PM

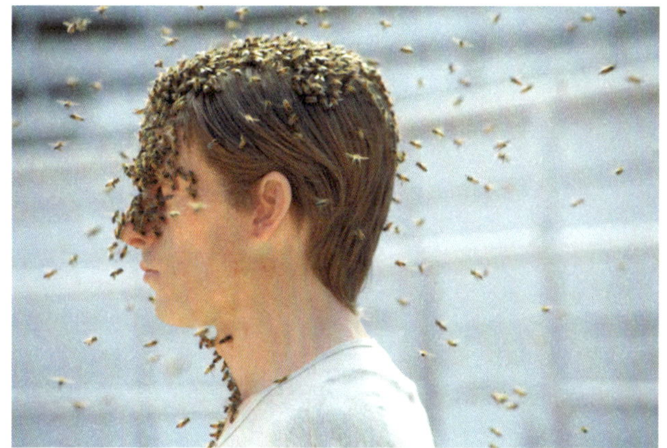

7/4/12—5:18:42 PM

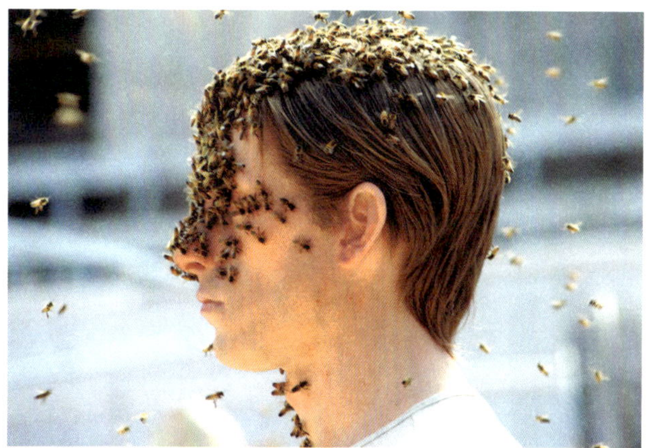

7/4/12—5:18:58 PM

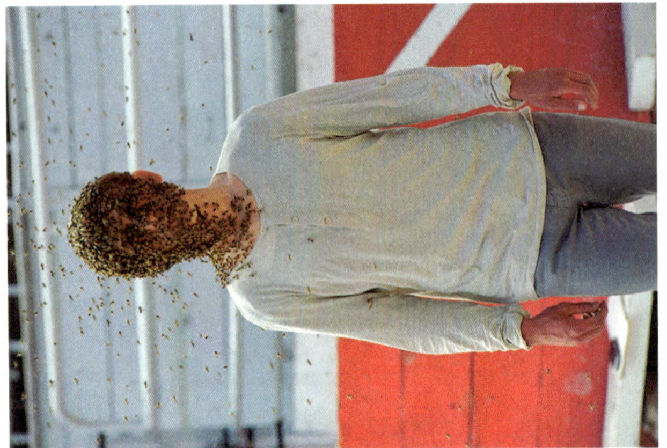

7/4/12—5:19:18 PM

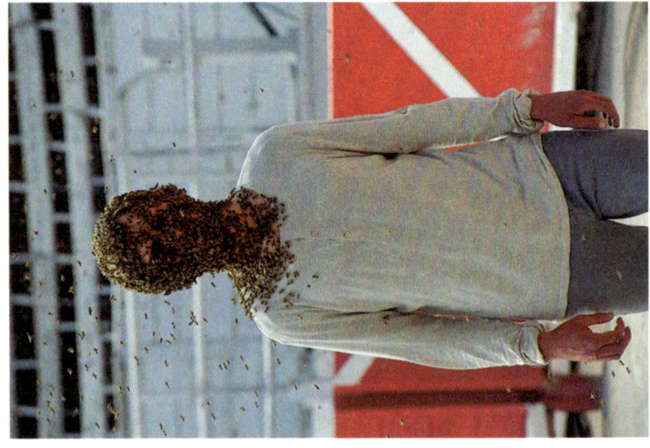

7/4/12—5:19:54 PM

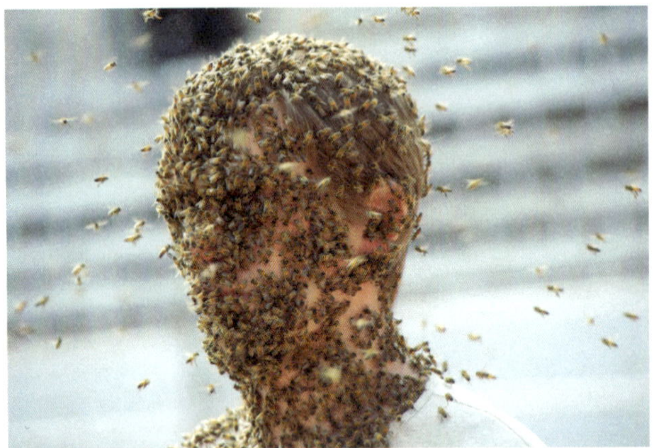

7/4/12—5:20:15 PM

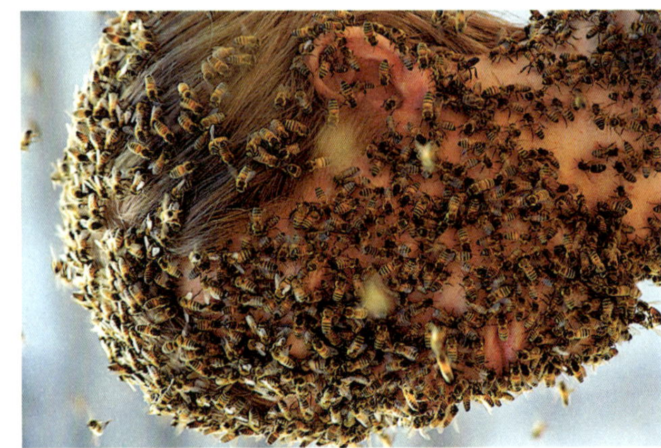

7/4/12—5:20:18 PM

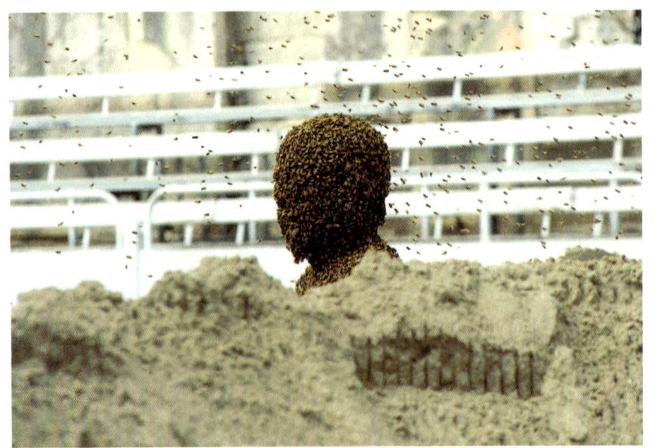

7/4/12—5:27:11 PM

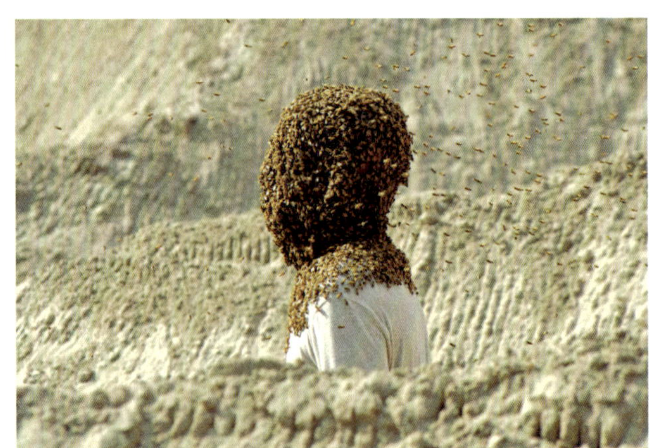

7/4/12—5:29:31 PM

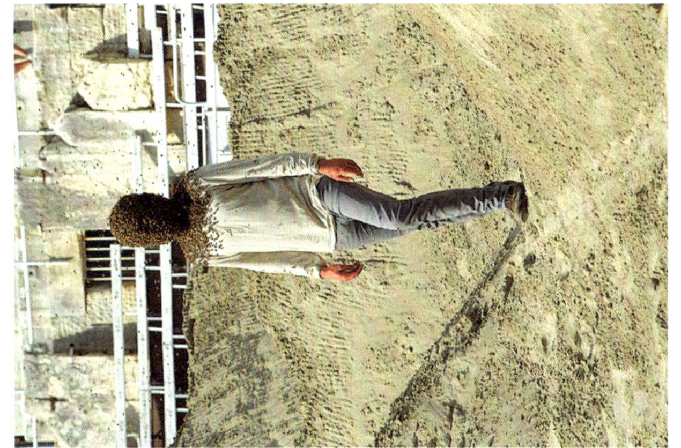

7/4/12—5:29:46 PM

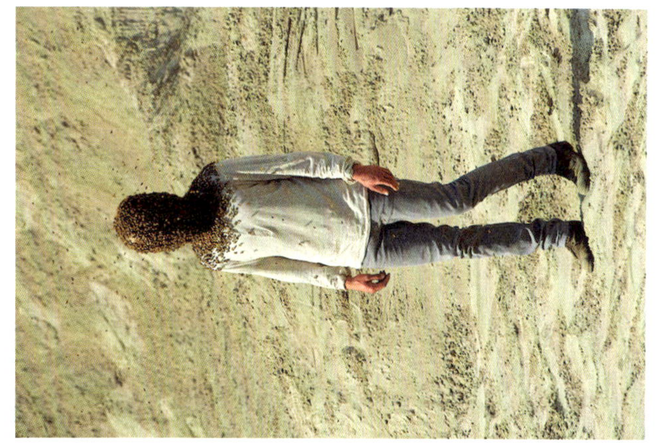

7/4/12—5:30:21 PM

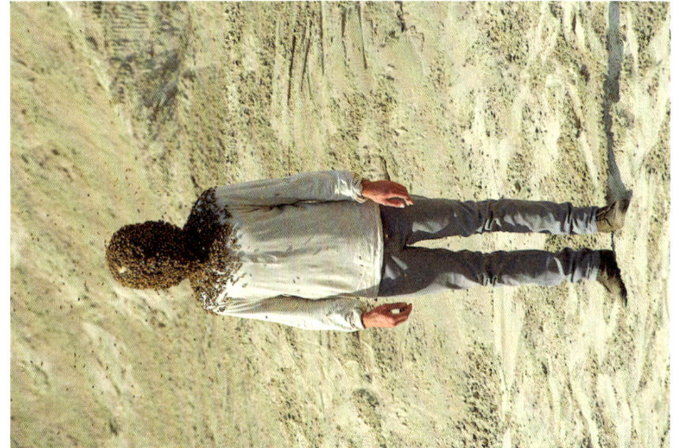

7/4/12—5:30:25 PM

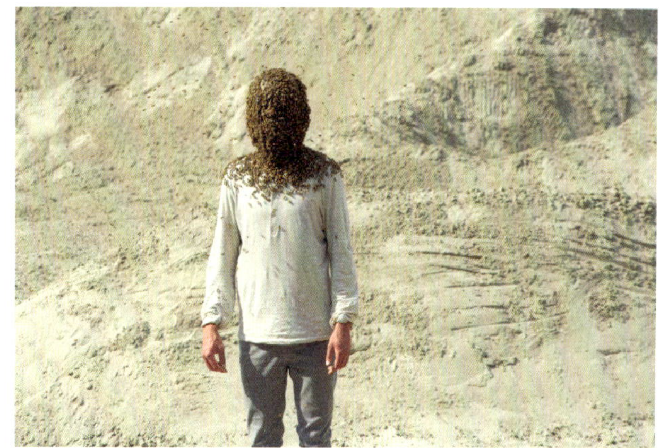

7/4/12—5:30:28 PM

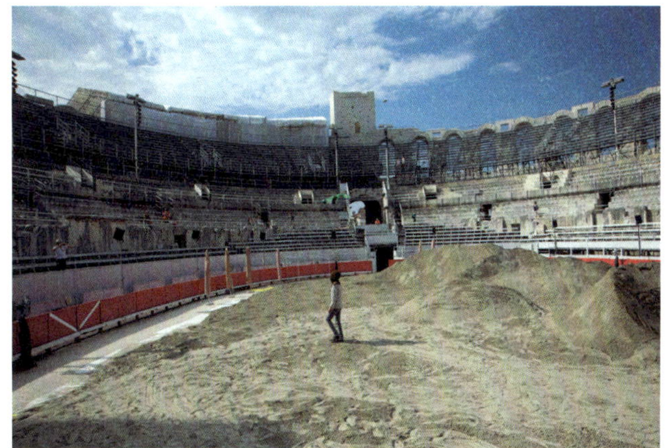

7/4/12—5:30:44 PM

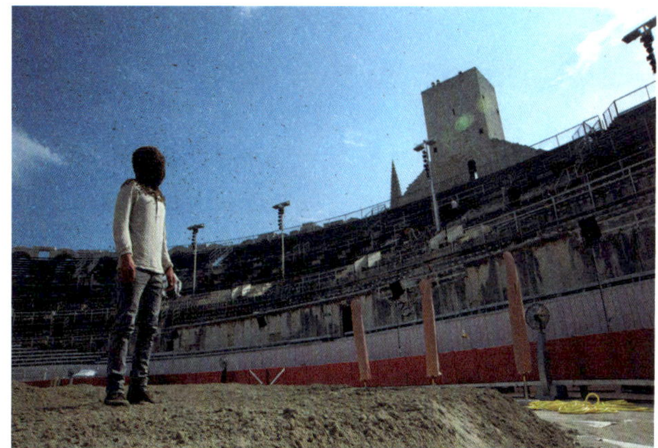

7/4/12—5:32:30 PM

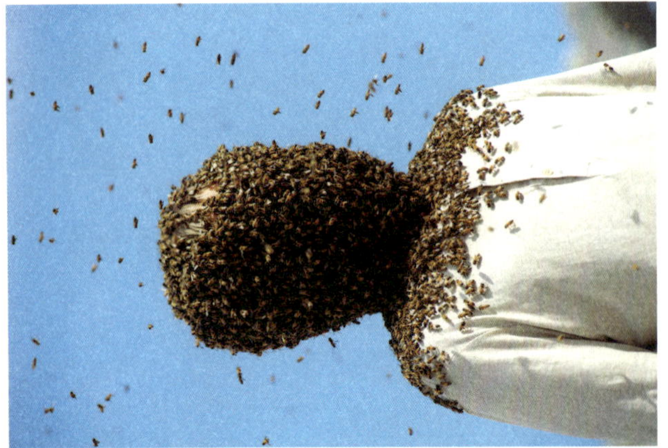
7/4/12—5:33:04 PM

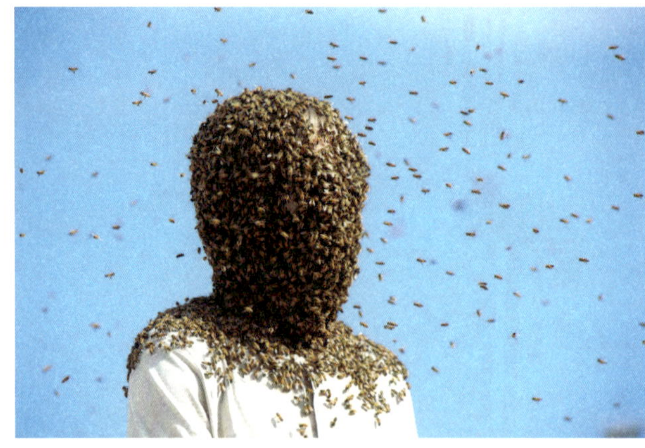
7/4/12—5:33:09 PM

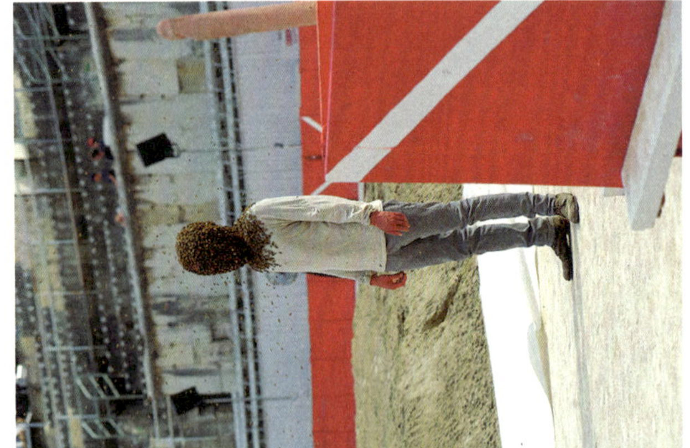
7/4/12—5:33:50 PM

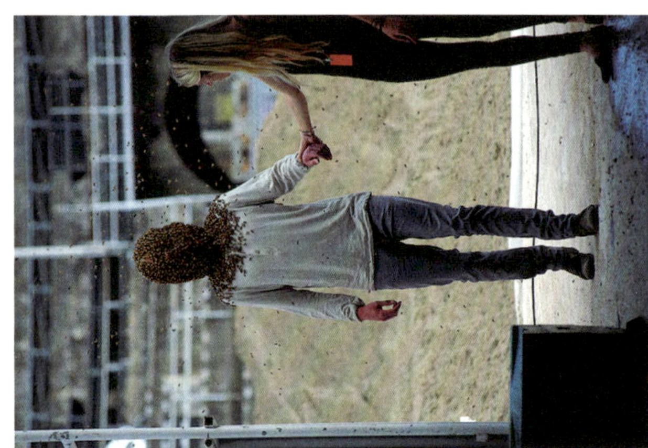
7/4/12—5:34:16 PM

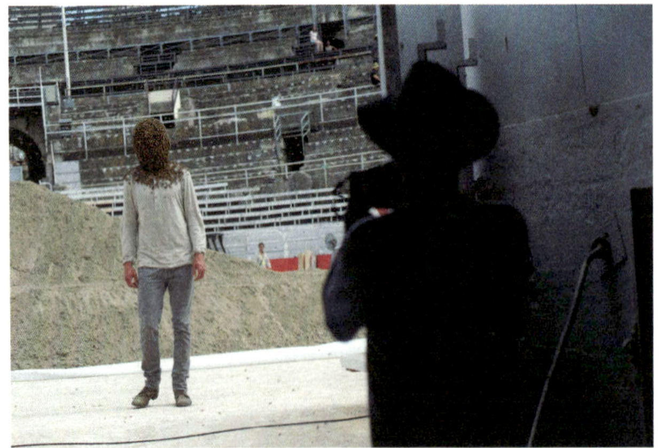
7/4/12—5:34:19 PM

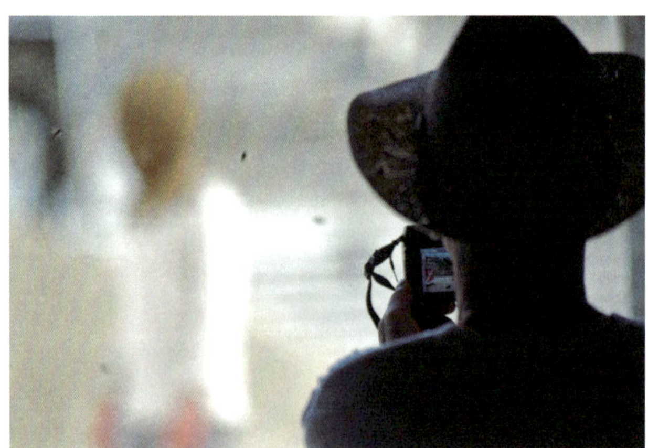
7/4/12—5:35:00 PM

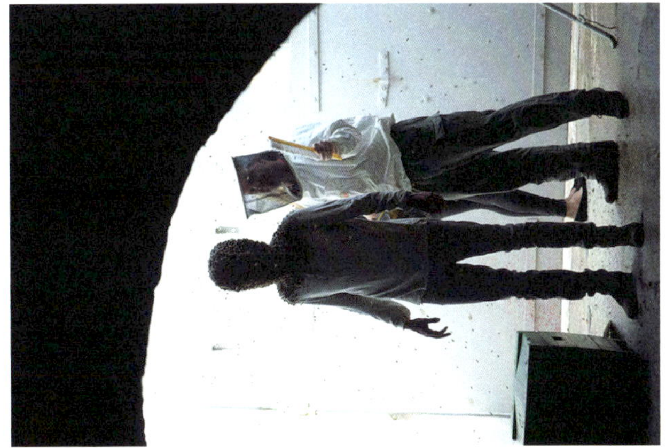

7/4/12—5:35:54 PM

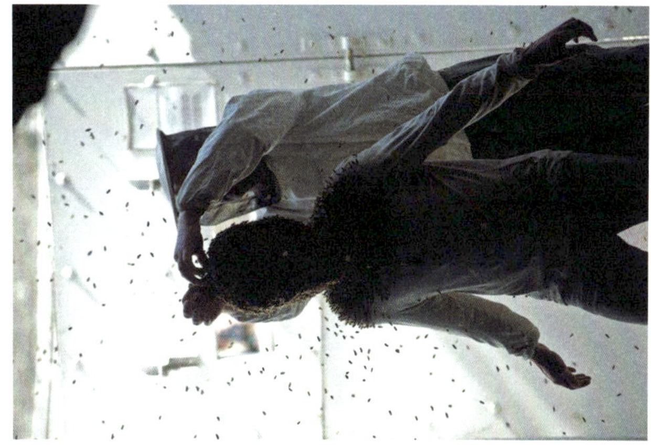

7/4/12—5:36:36 PM

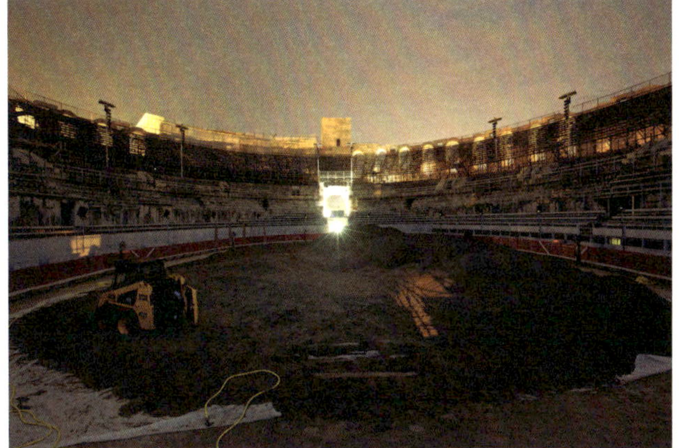

7/5/12—12:49:20 AM

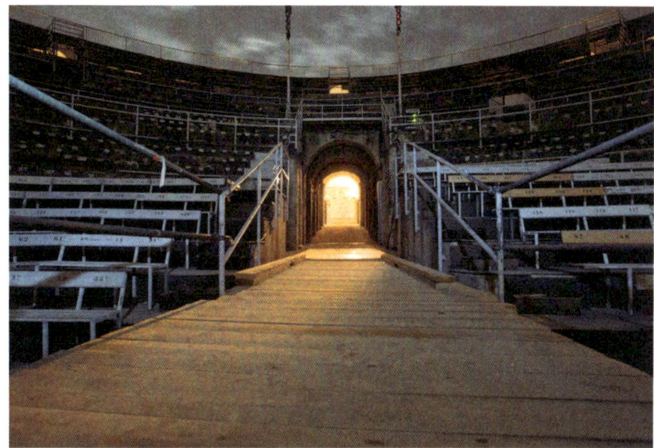

7/5/12—12:50:19 AM

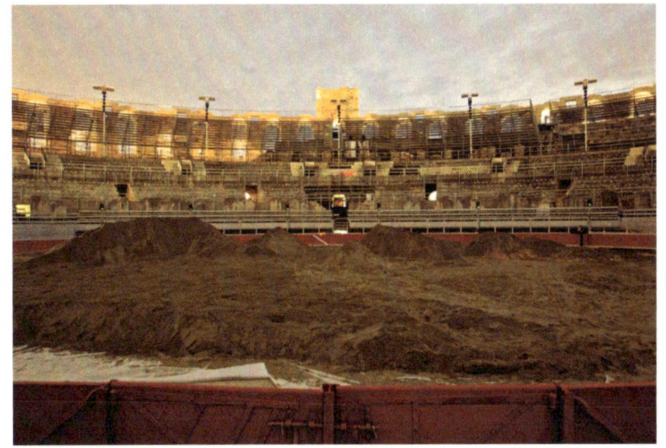

7/5/12—12:52:38 AM

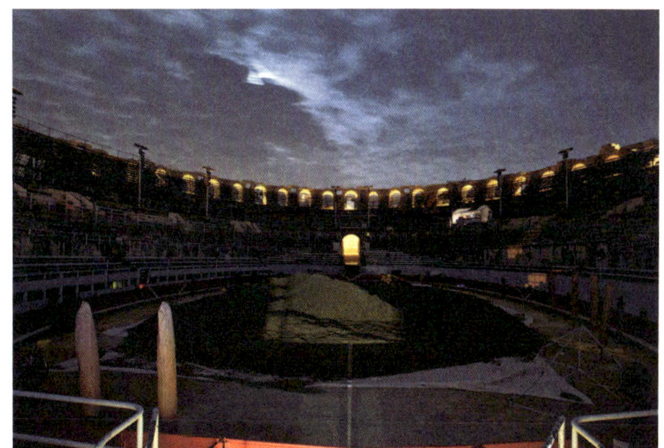

7/5/12—12:57:44 AM

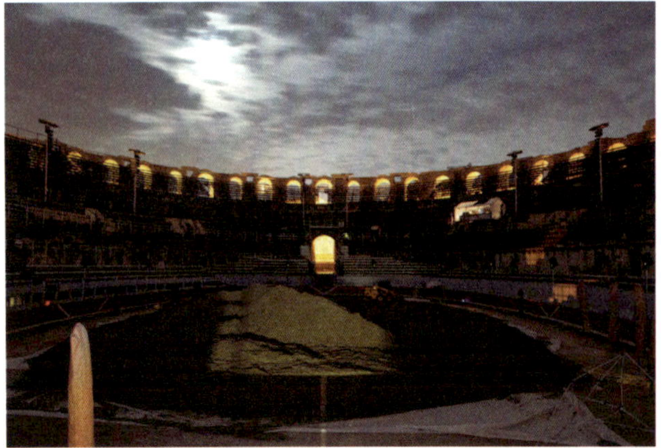

7/5/12—1:02:03 AM

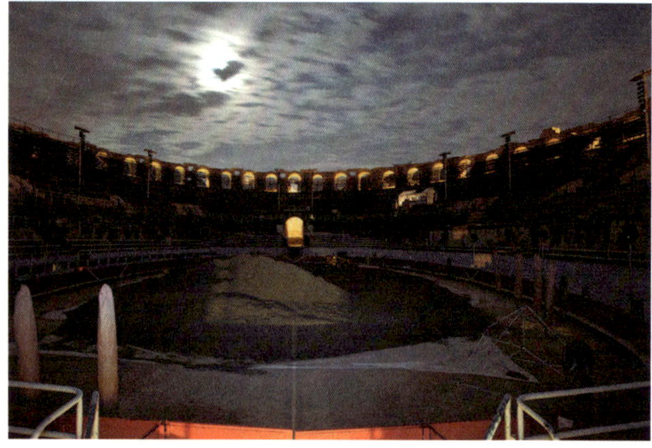

7/5/12—1:12:21 AM

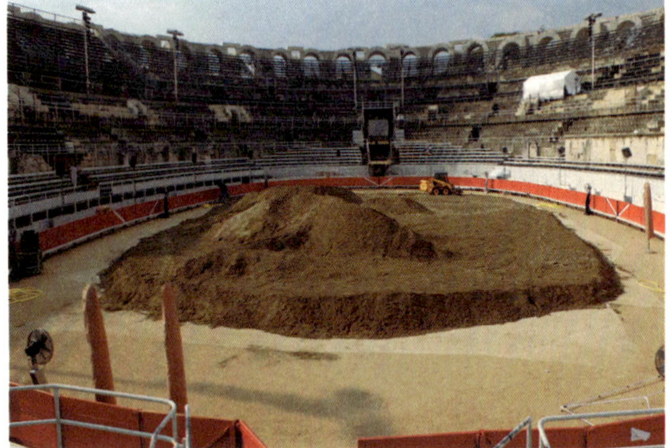

7/5/12—9:15:08 AM

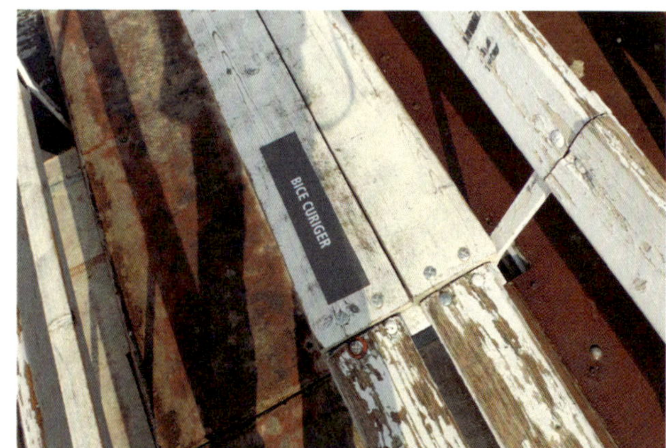

7/5/12—9:15:13 AM

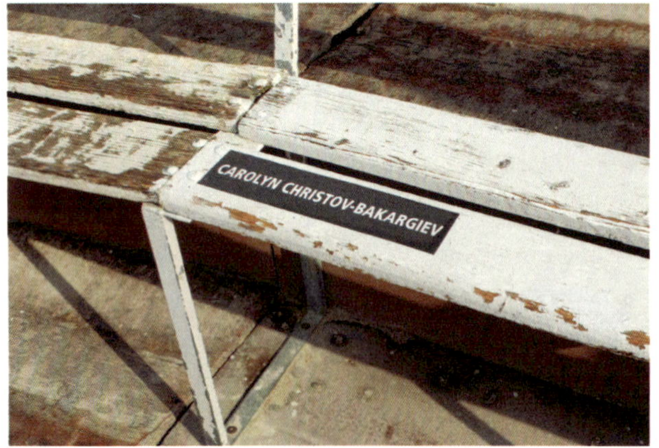

7/5/12—9:15:26 AM

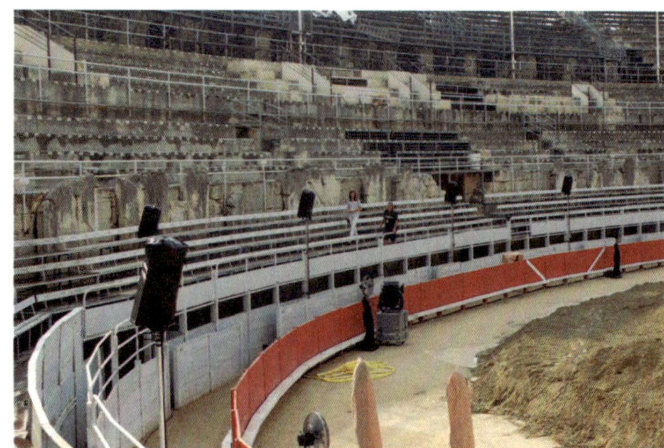

7/5/12—9:15:41 AM

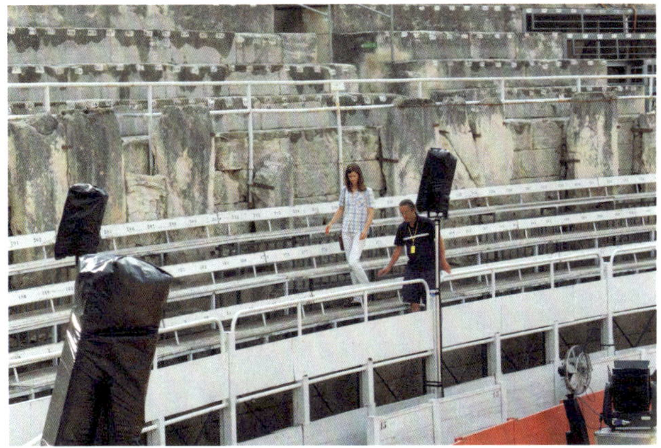
7/5/12—9:15:47 AM

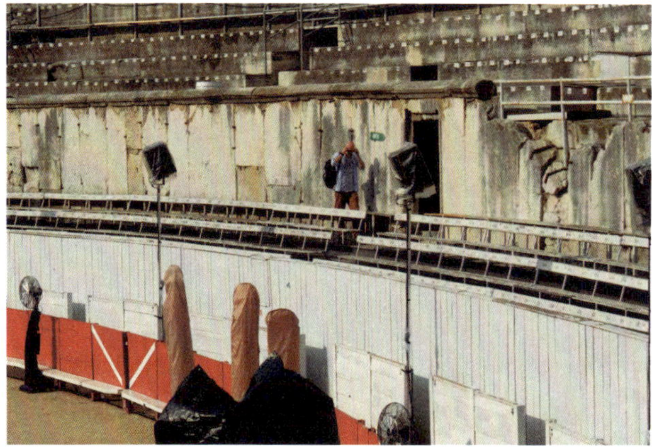
7/5/12—9:15:53 AM

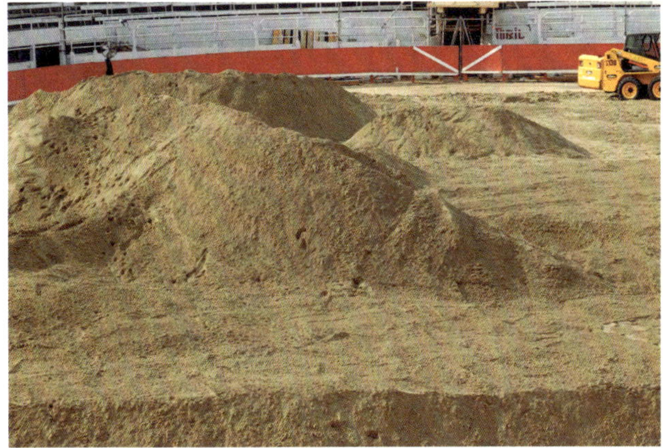
7/5/12—9:15:56 AM

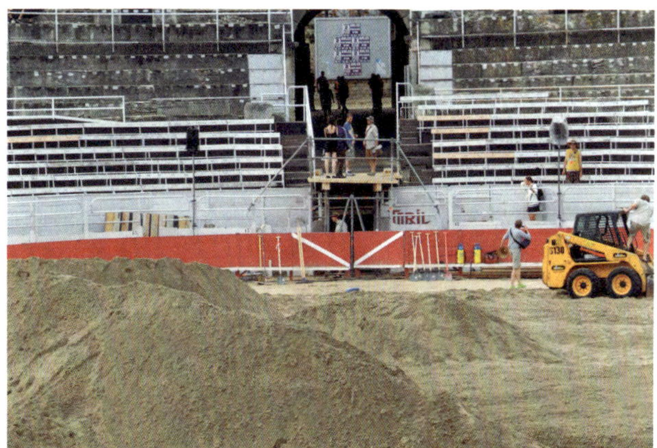
7/5/12—9:21:53 AM

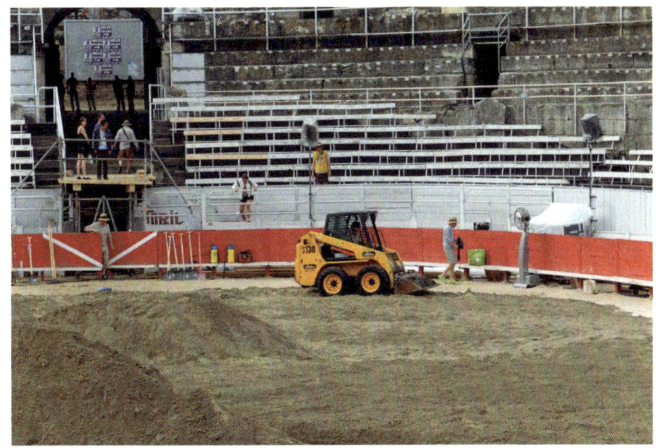
7/5/12—9:21:59 AM

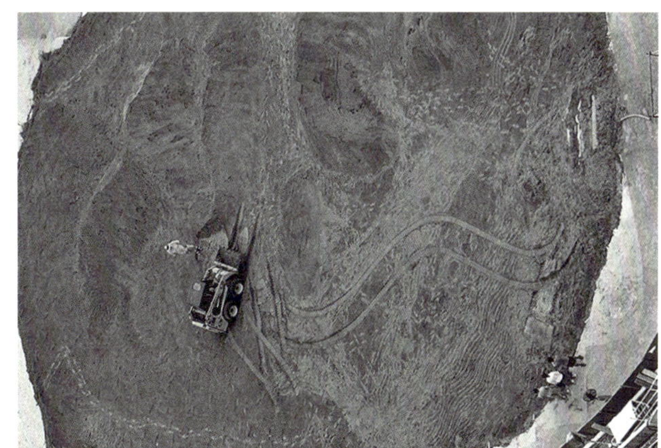
7/5/12—9:25:33 AM

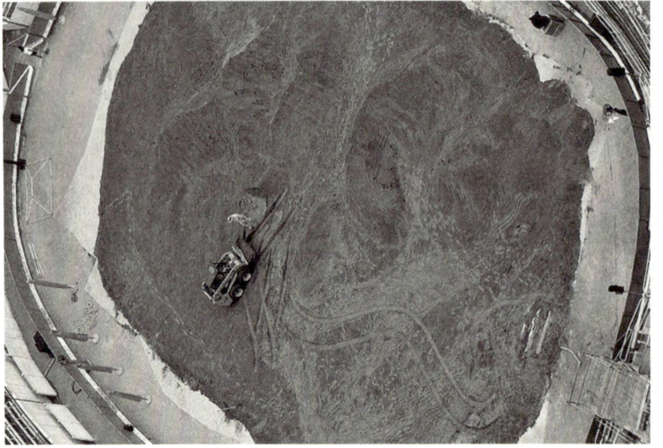
7/5/12—9:25:38 AM

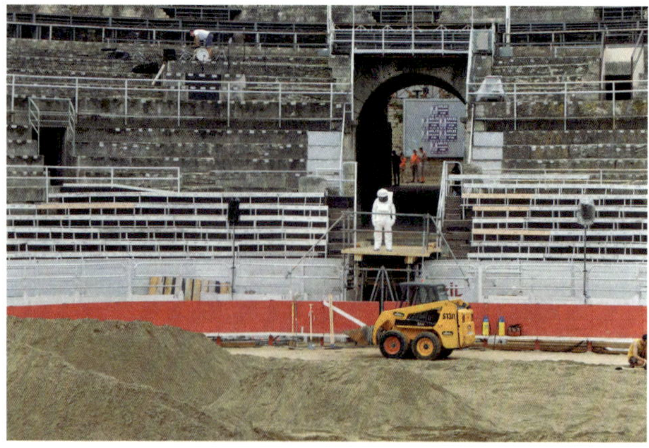
7/5/12—9:28:06 AM

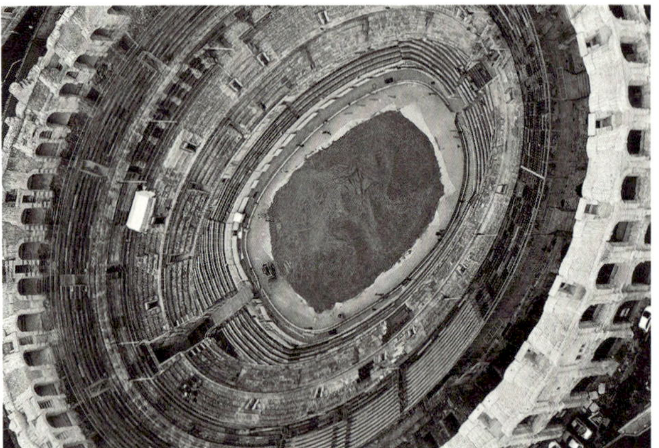
7/5/12—9:28:33 AM

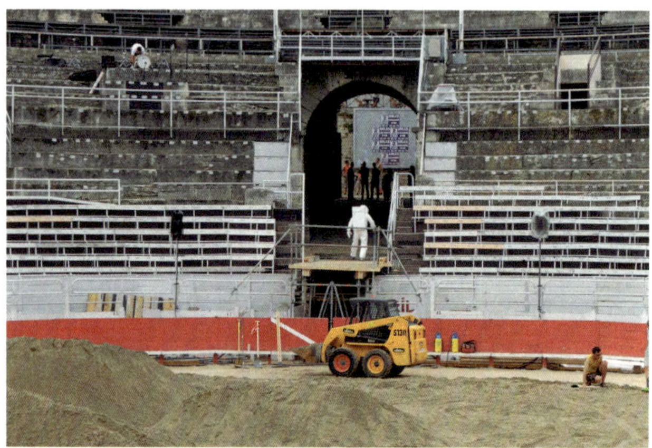
7/5/12—9:28:41 AM

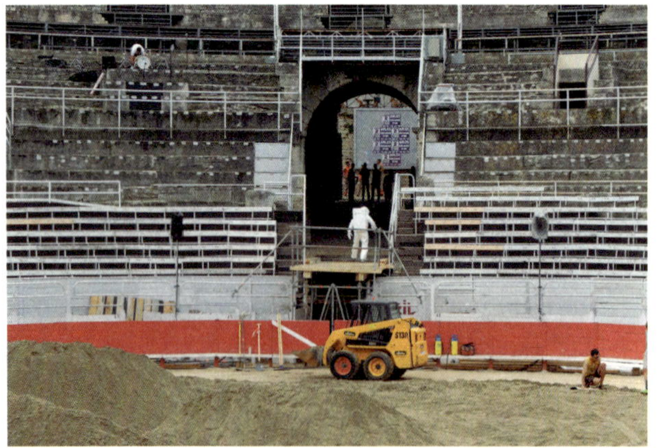
7/5/12—9:28:46 AM

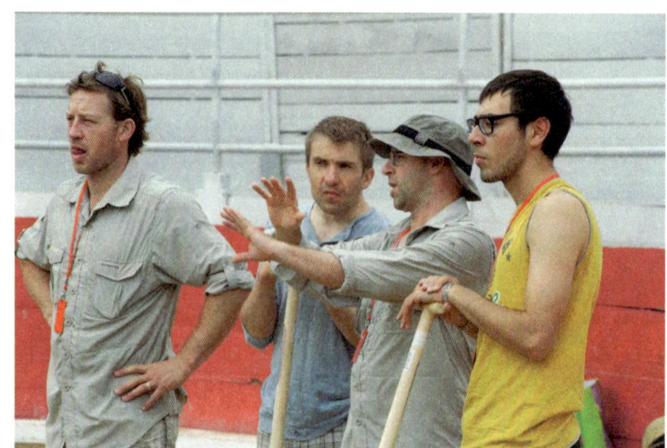
7/5/12—9:30:30 AM

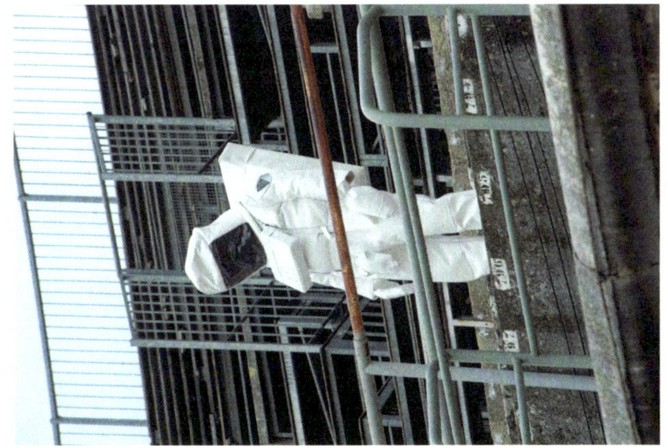

7/5/12—9:31:57 AM

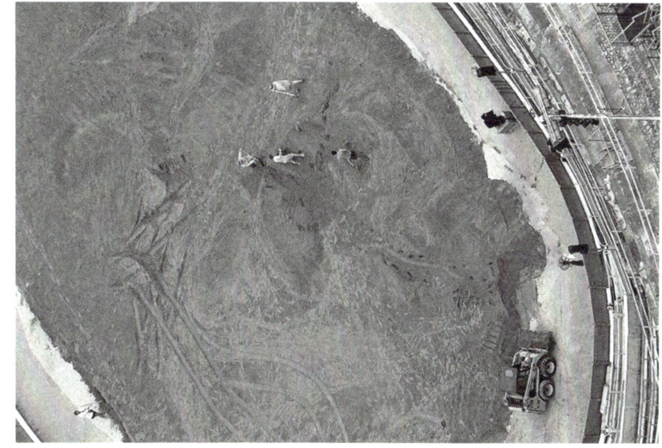

7/5/12—9:34:01 AM

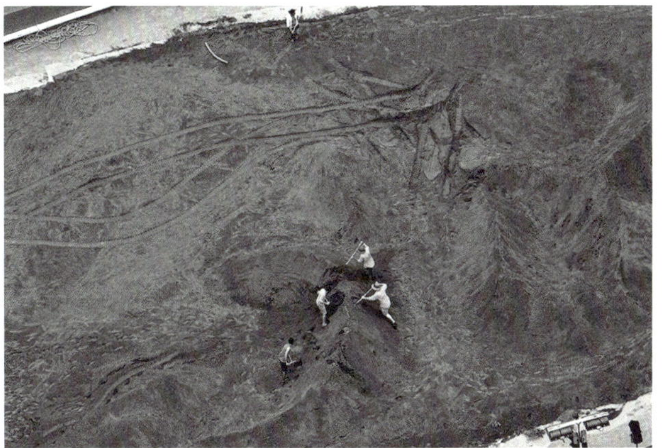

7/5/12—9:34:06 AM

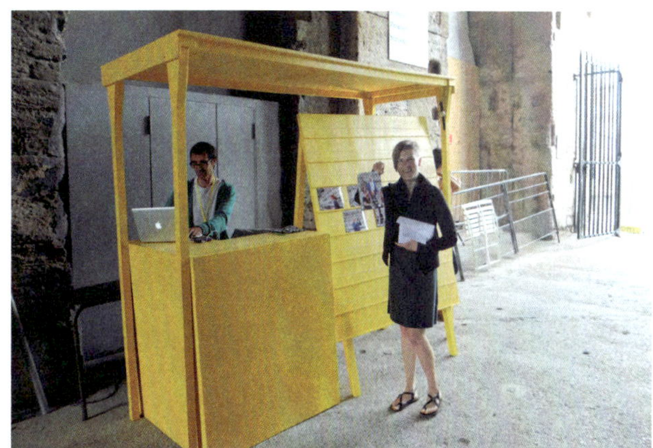

7/5/12—9:34:45 AM

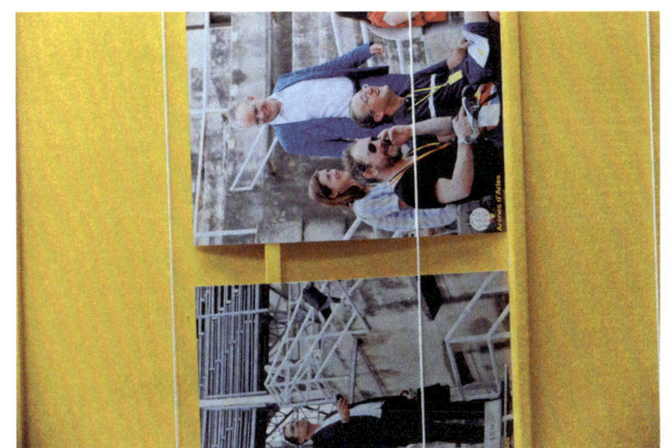

7/5/12—9:35:04 AM

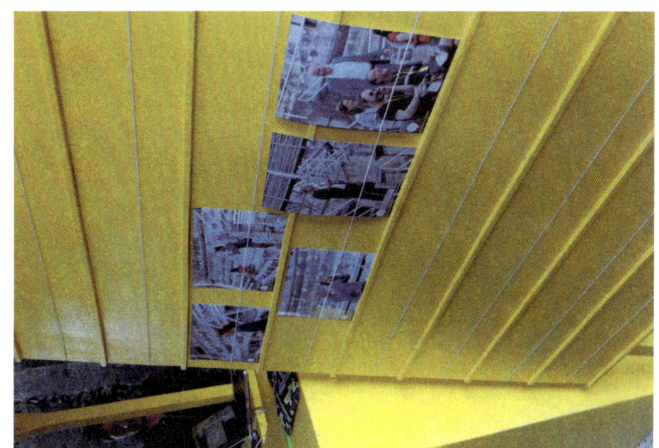

7/5/12—9:35:14 AM

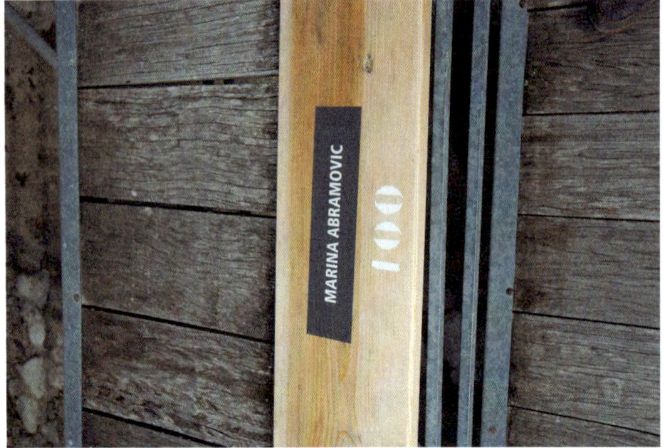

7/5/12—9:42:34 AM

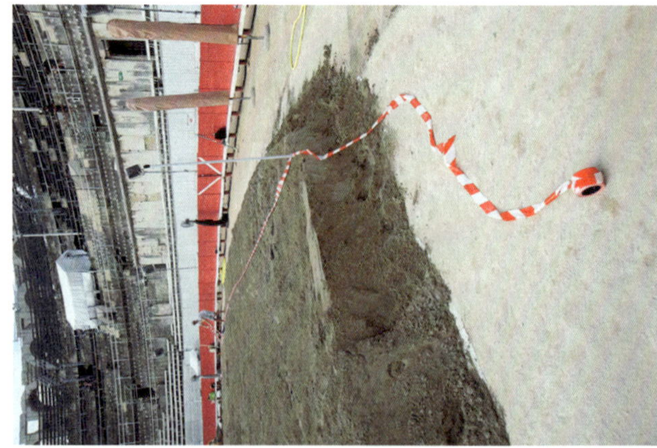

7/5/12—9:51:37 AM

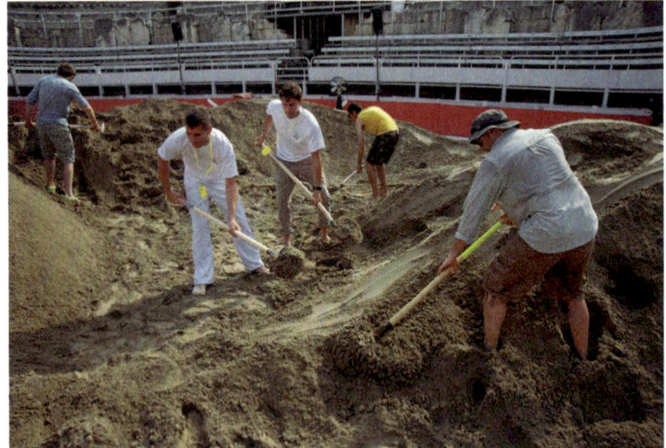

7/5/12—9:52:51 AM

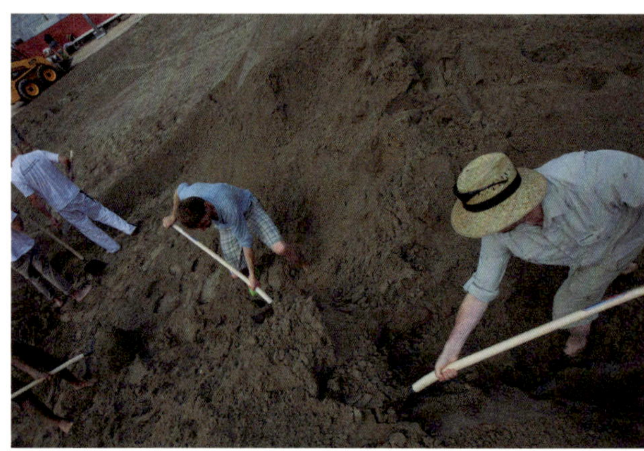

7/5/12—9:54:09 AM

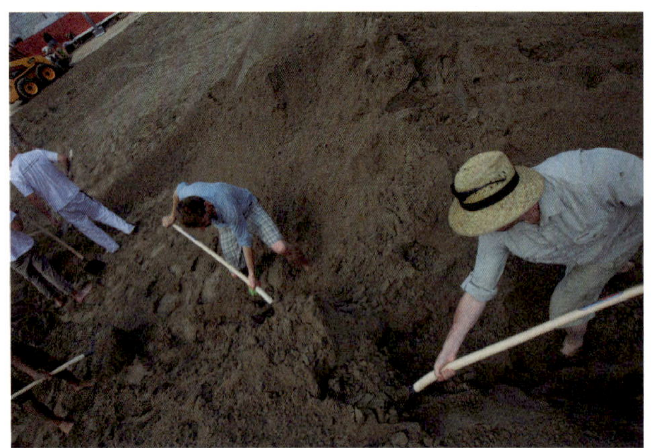

7/5/12—9:54:11 AM

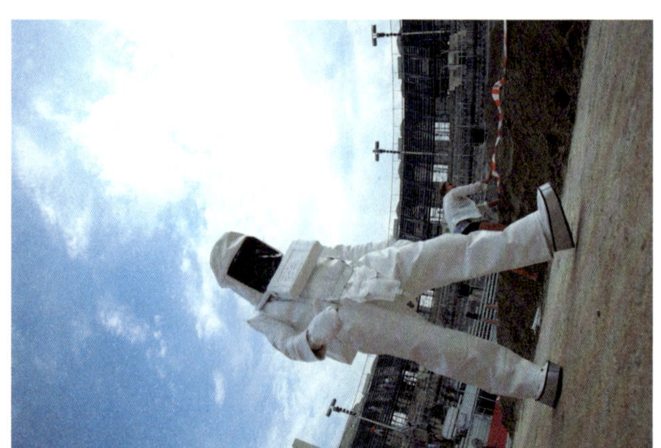

7/5/12—9:55:59 AM

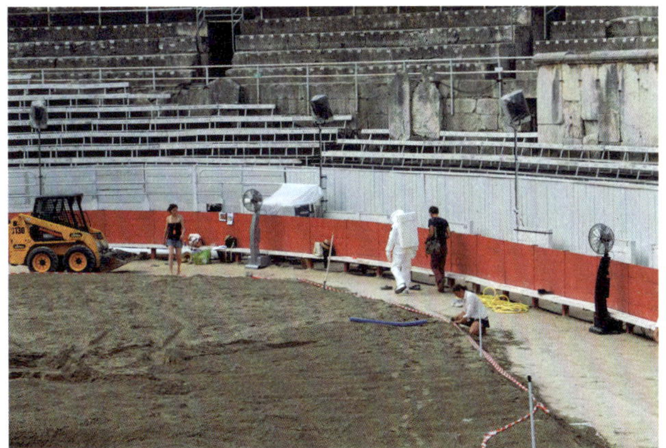

7/5/12—9:56:05 AM

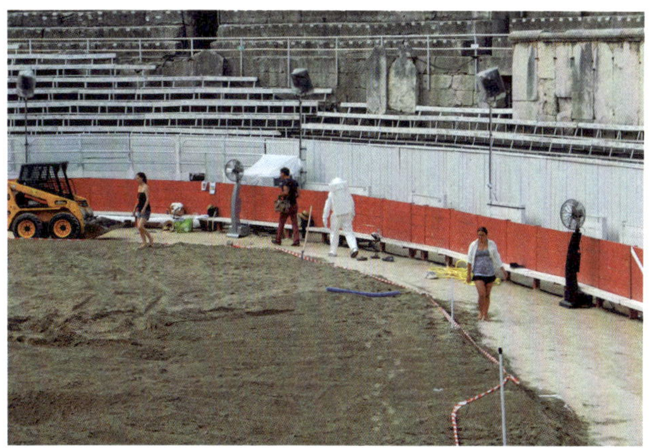

7/5/12—9:56:08 AM

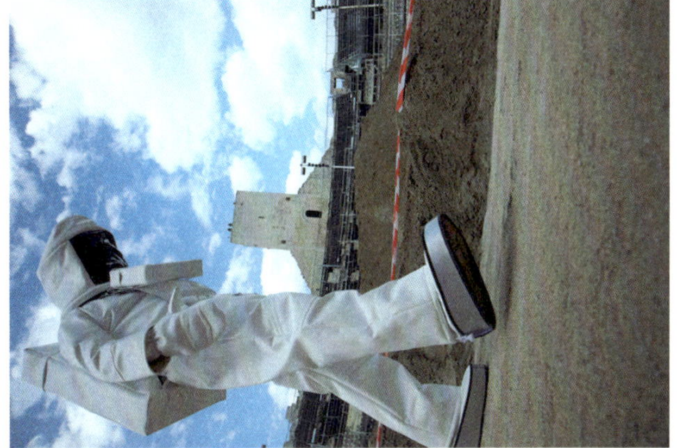

7/5/12—9:59:10 AM

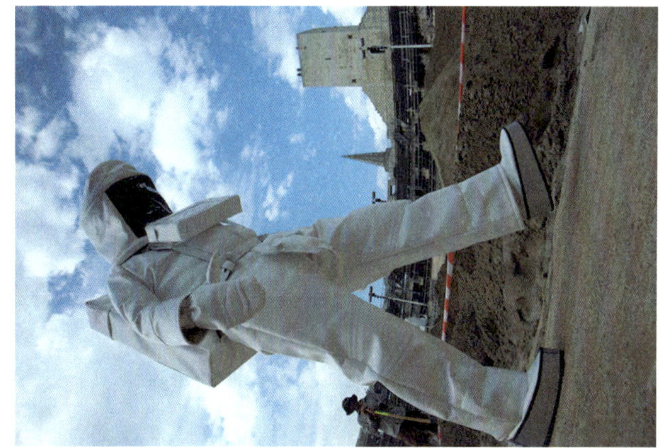

7/5/12—9:59:59 AM

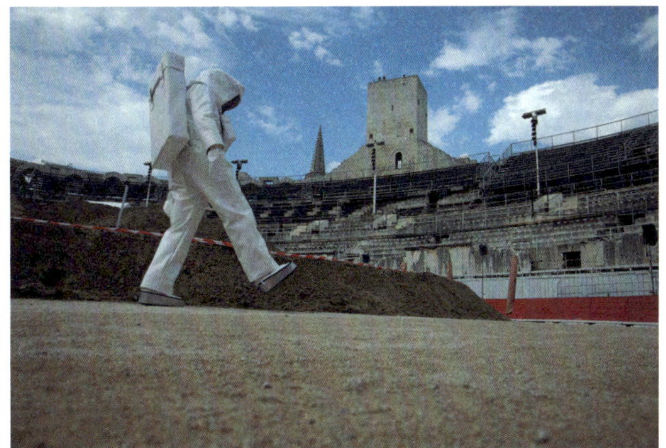

7/5/12—10:00:01 AM

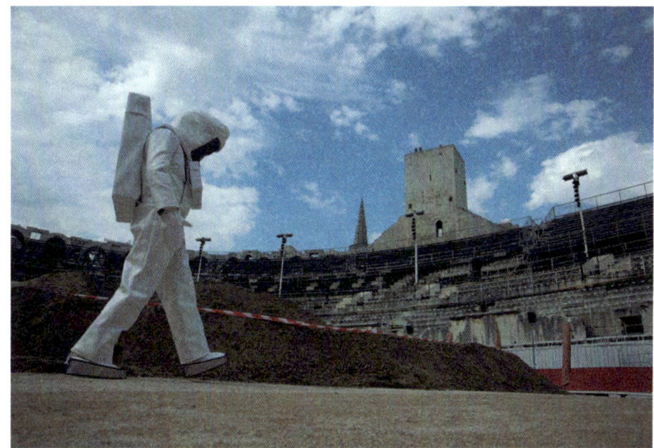

7/5/12—10:00:02 AM

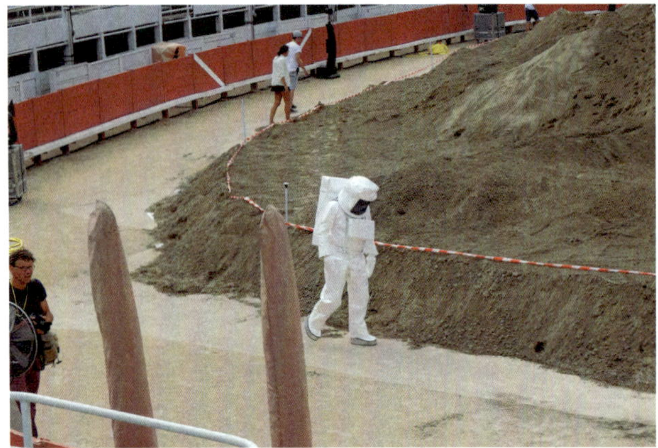
7/5/12—10:00:04 AM

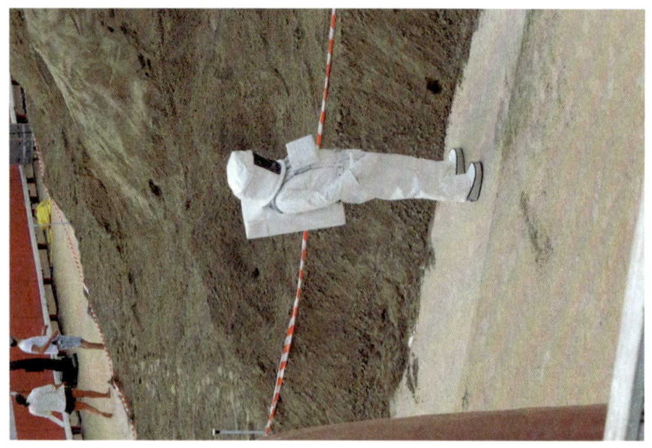
7/5/12—10:00:09 AM

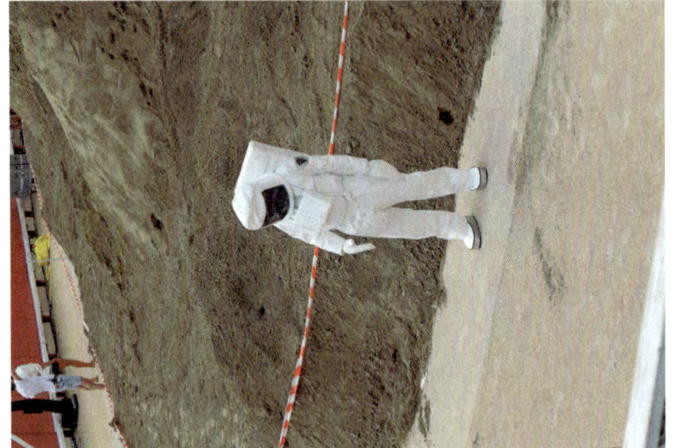
7/5/12—10:00:10 AM

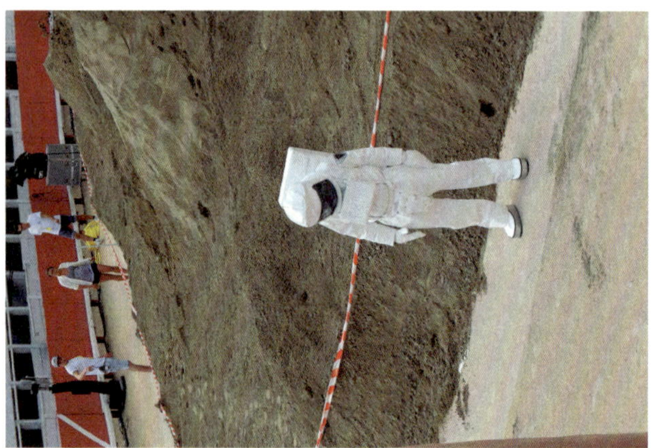
7/5/12—10:00:13 AM

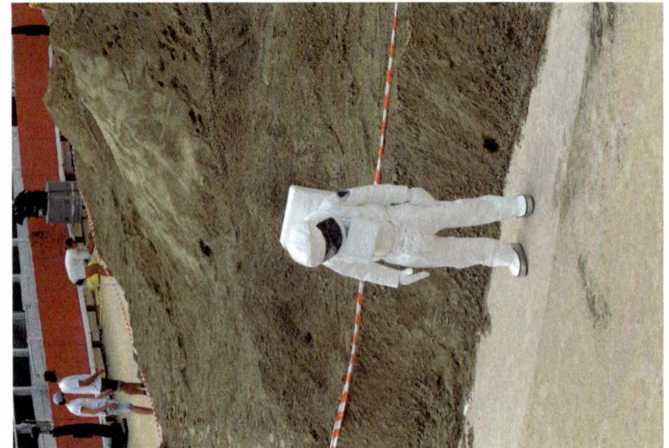
7/5/12—10:00:20 AM

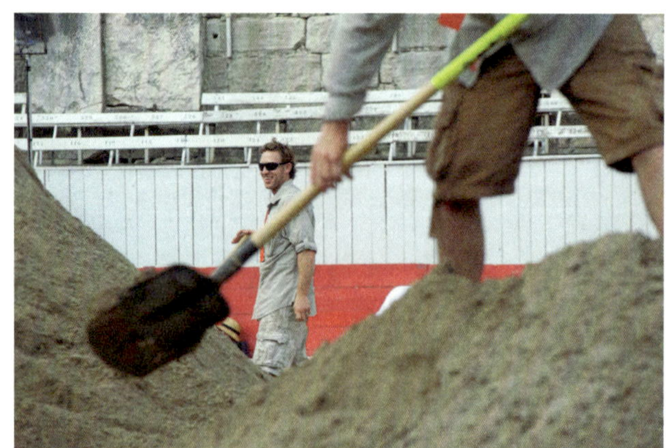
7/5/12—10:03:50 AM

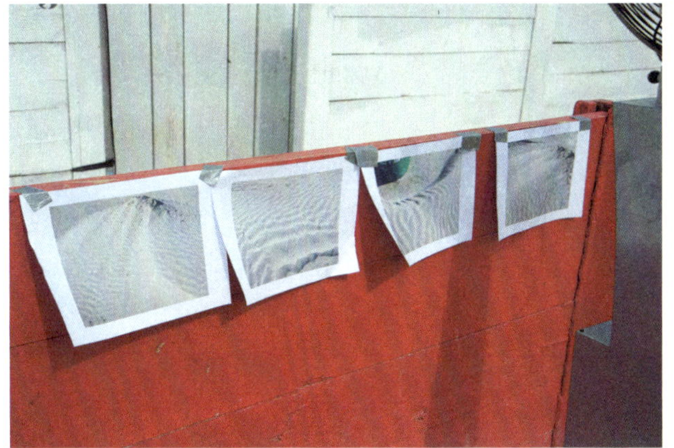

7/5/12—10:05:31 AM

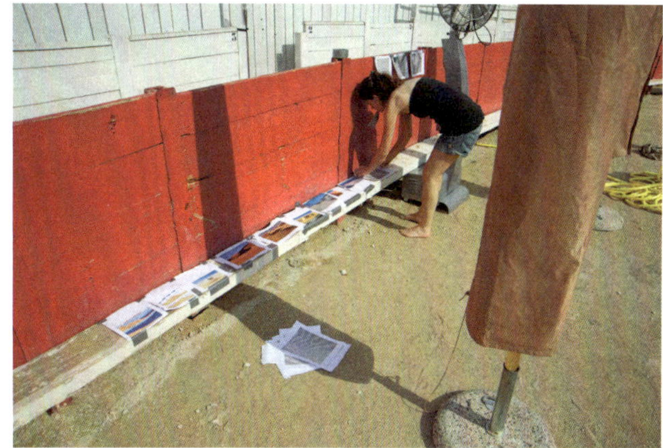

7/5/12—10:05:42 AM

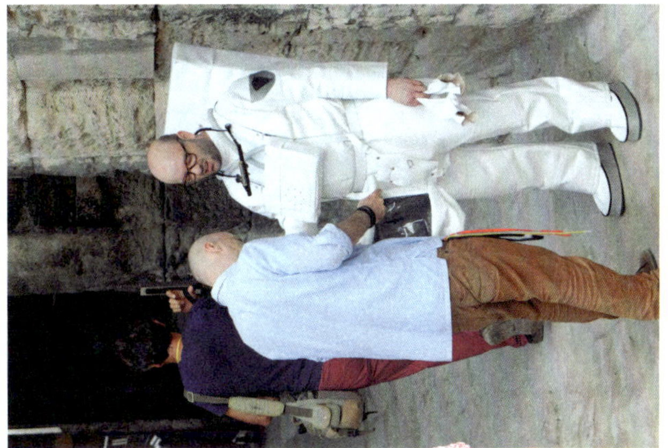

7/5/12—10:07:35 AM

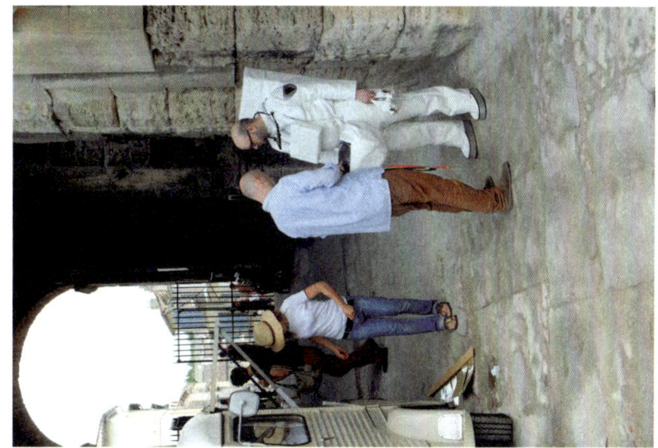

7/5/12—10:07:39 AM

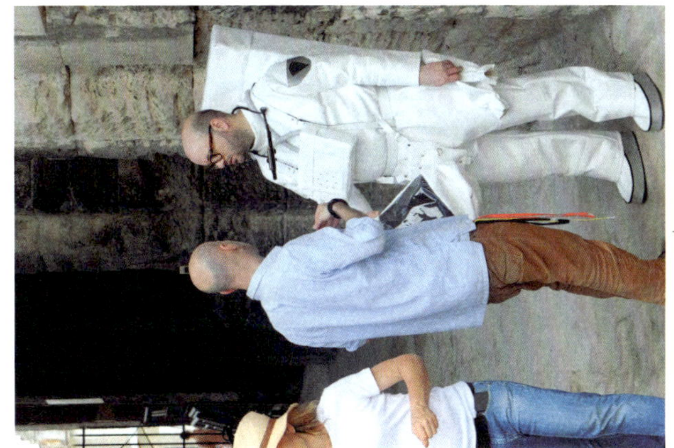

7/5/12—10:07:45 AM

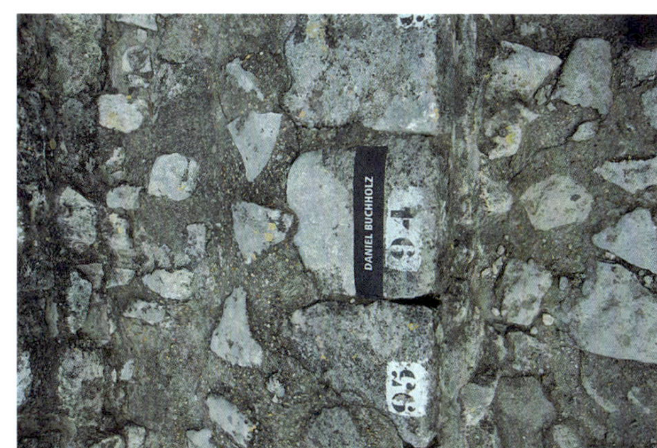

7/5/12—10:10:58 AM

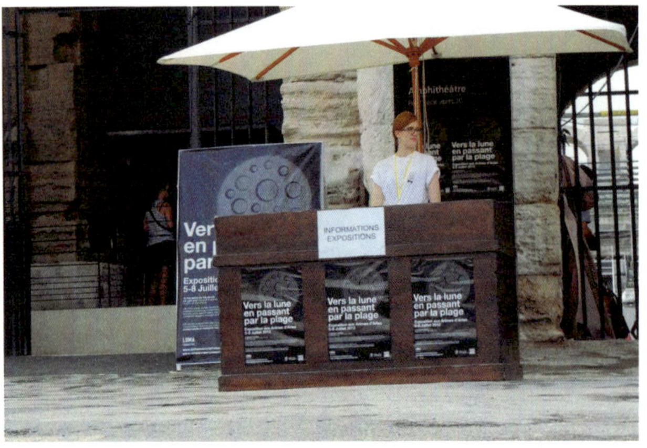

7/5/12—10:27:37 AM

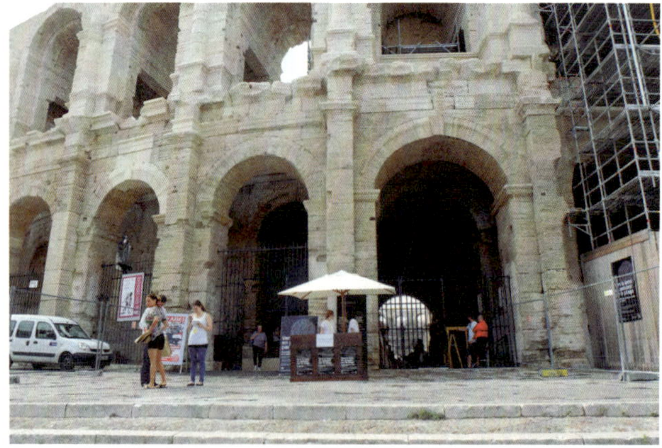

7/5/12—10:27:42 AM

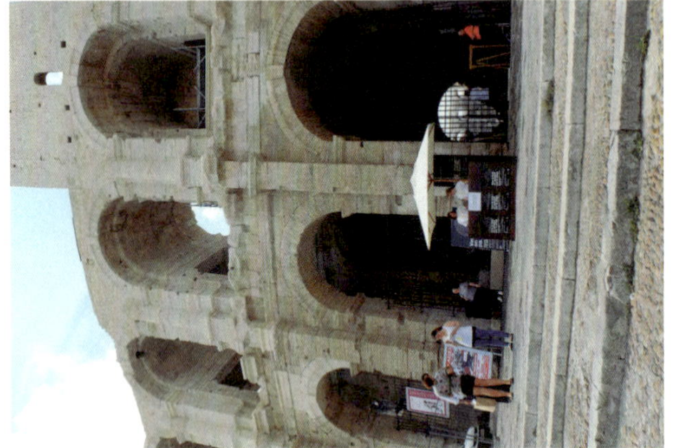

7/5/12—10:27:46 AM

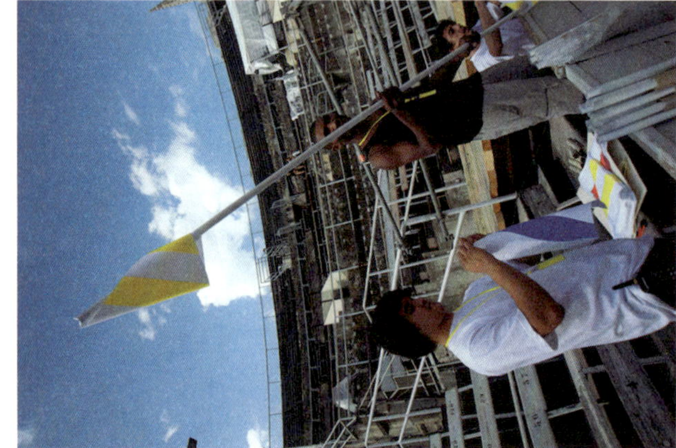

7/5/12—10:29:59 AM

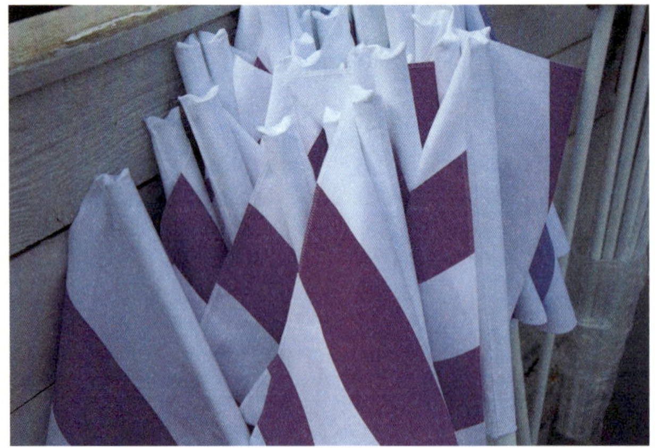

7/5/12—10:30:08 AM

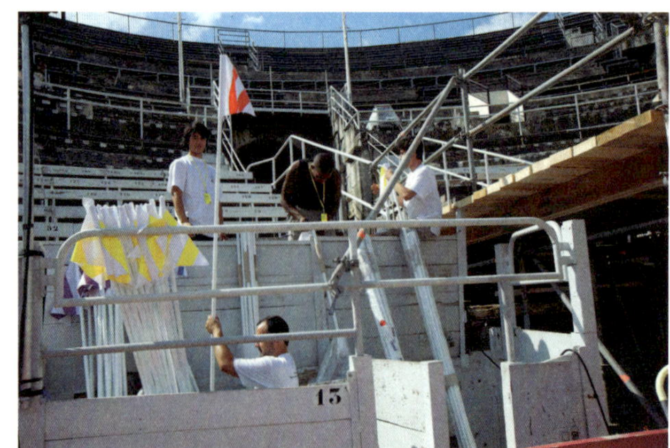

7/5/12—10:33:54 AM

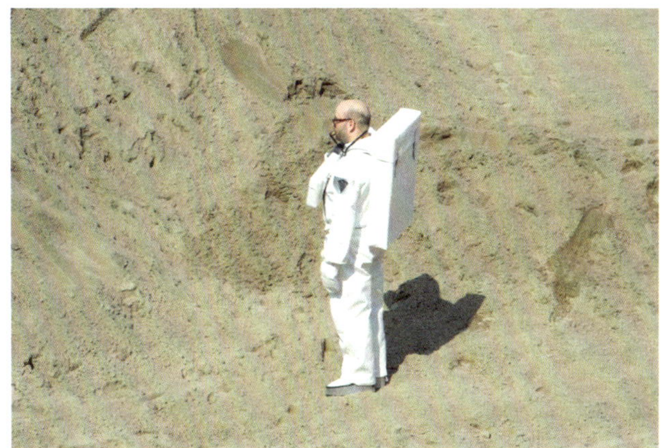

7/5/12—10:39:28 AM

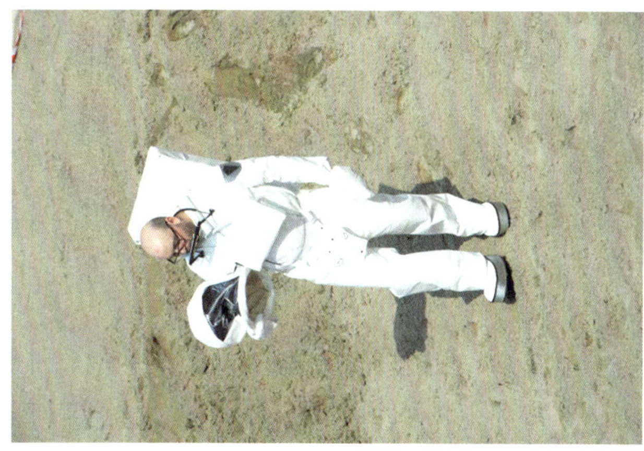

7/5/12—10:39:41 AM

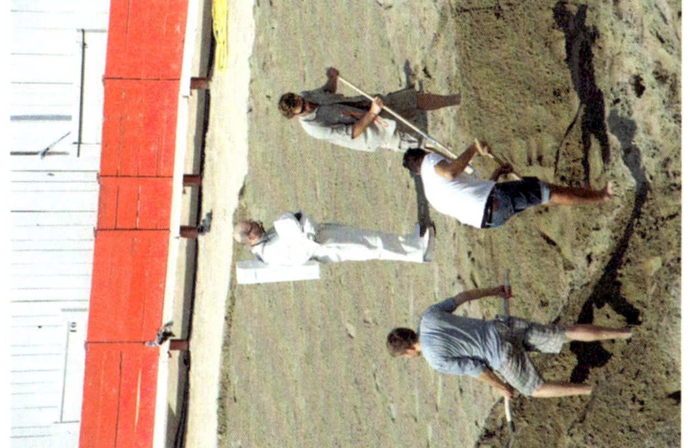

7/5/12—10:41:52 AM

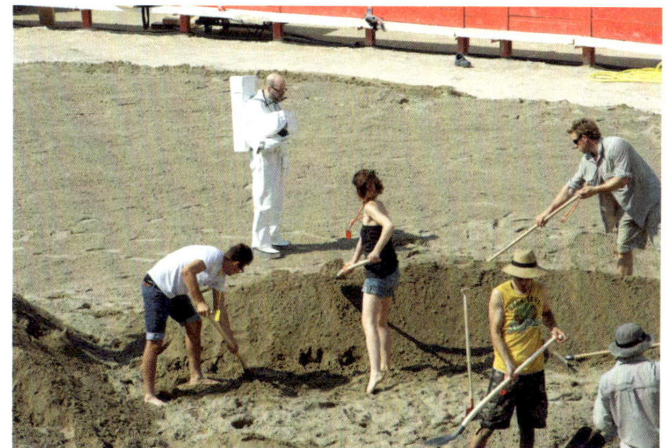

7/5/12—10:42:15 AM

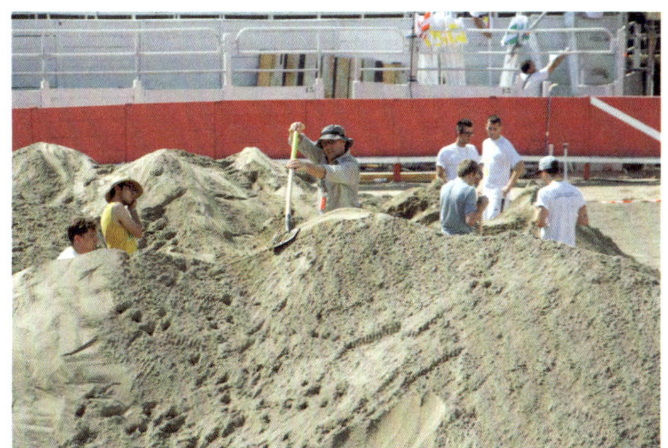

7/5/12—10:44:57 AM

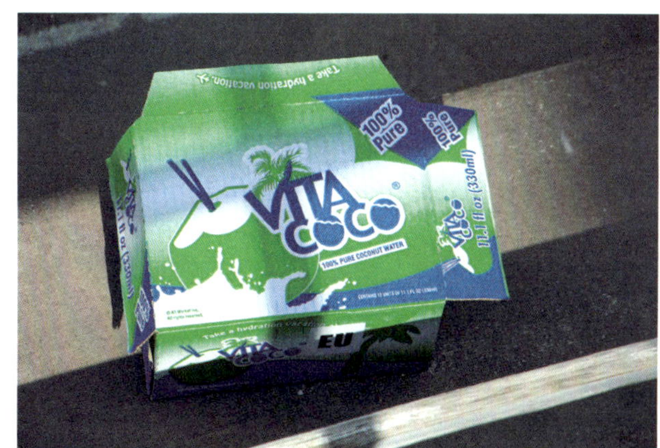

7/5/12—11:06:27 AM

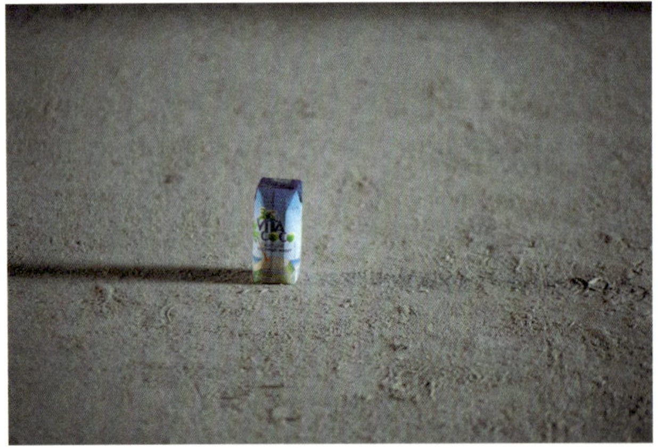

7/5/12—11:07:35 AM

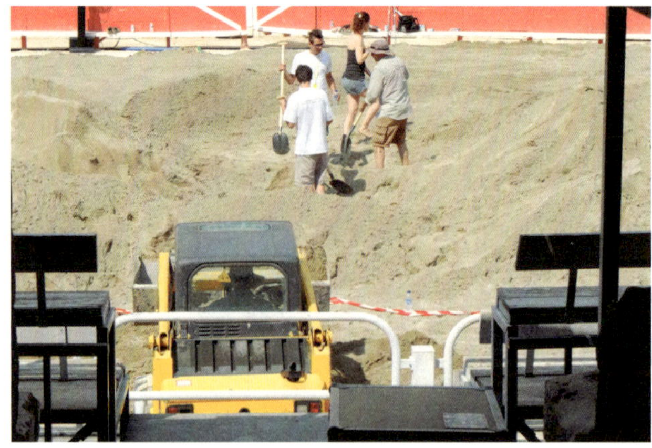

7/5/12—11:07:59 AM

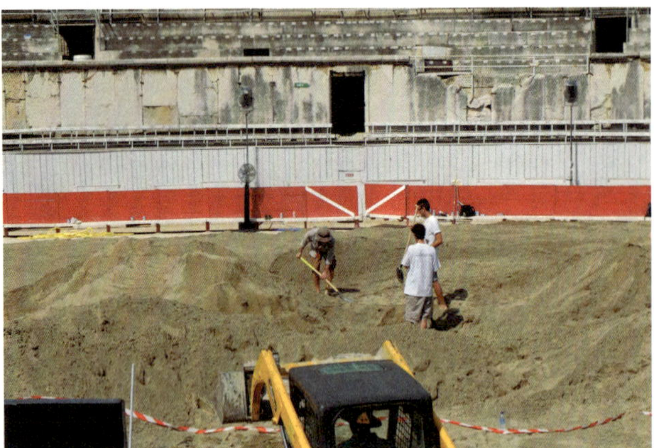

7/5/12—11:08:13 AM

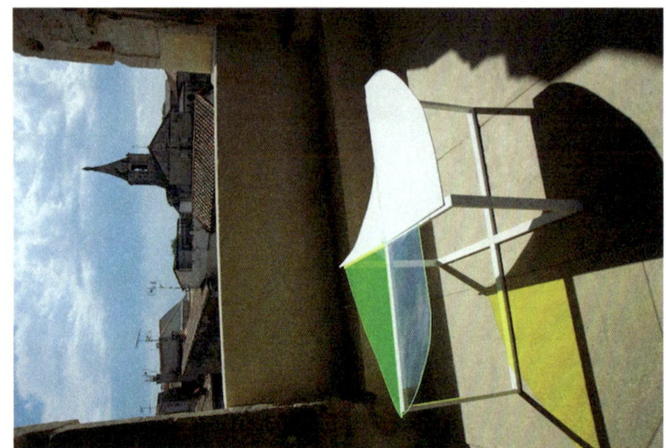

7/5/12—11:11:33 AM

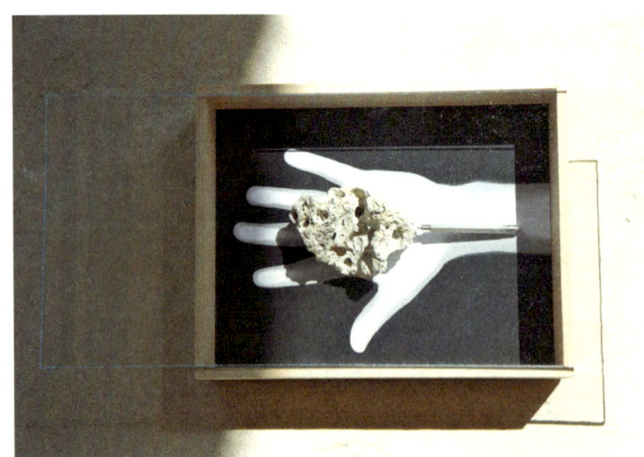

7/5/12—11:12:19 AM

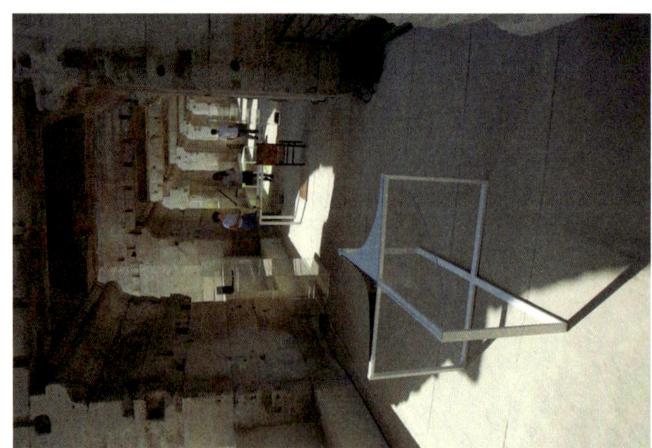

7/5/12—11:12:25 AM

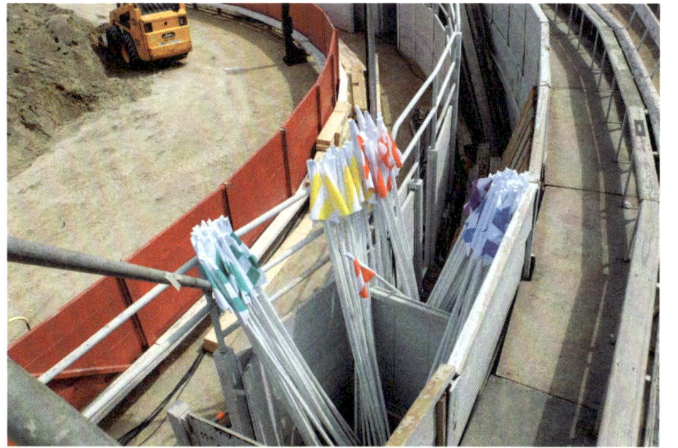
7/5/12—11:22:29 AM

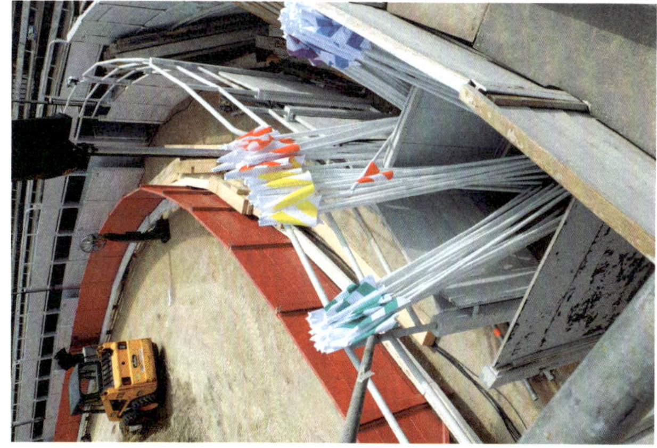
7/5/12—11:22:32 AM

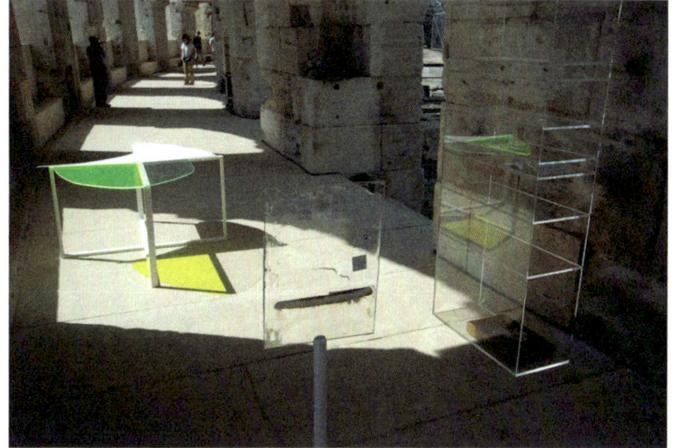
7/5/12—11:23:05 AM

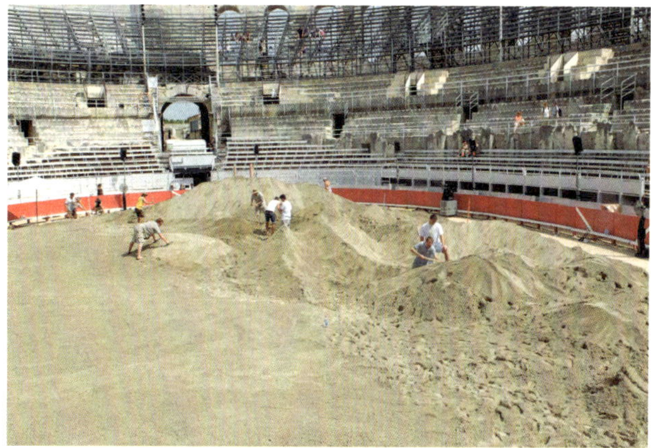
7/5/12—11:23:16 AM

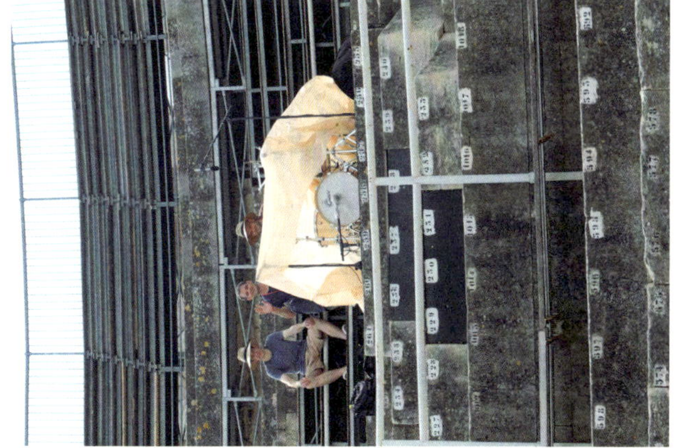
7/5/12—11:23:54 AM

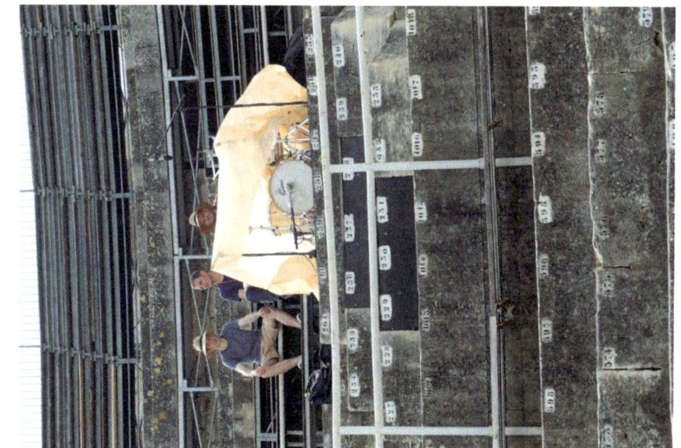
7/5/12—11:24:01 AM

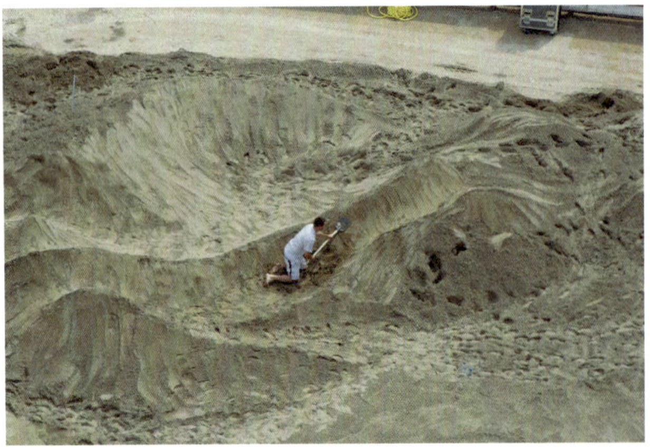

7/5/12—11:28:00 AM

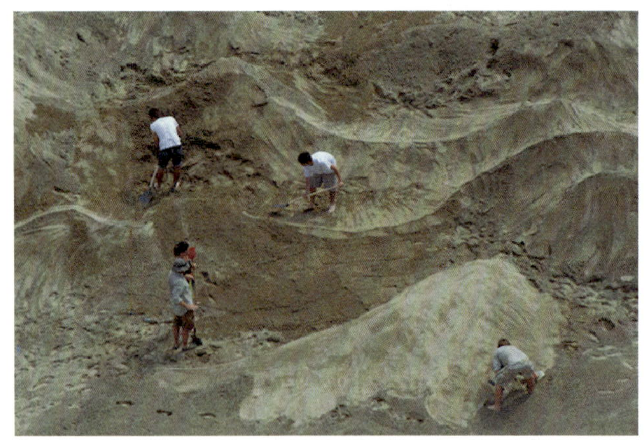

7/5/12—11:28:01 AM

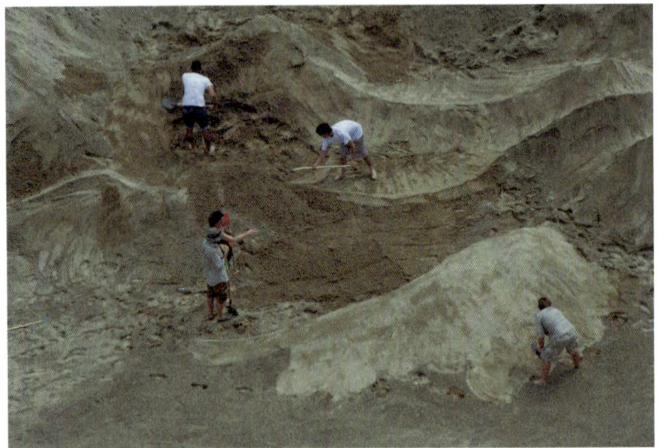

7/5/12—11:28:04 AM

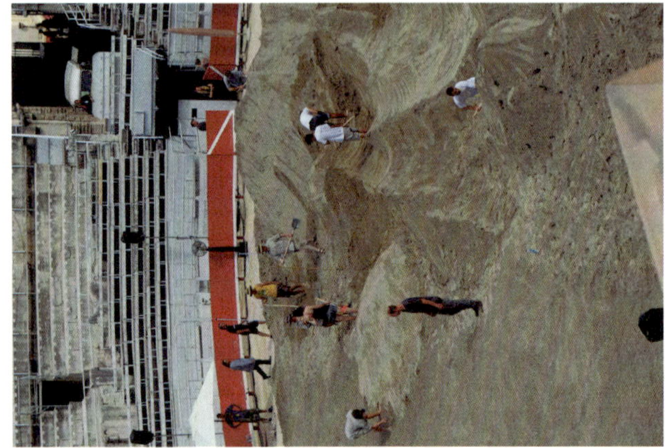

7/5/12—11:28:33 AM

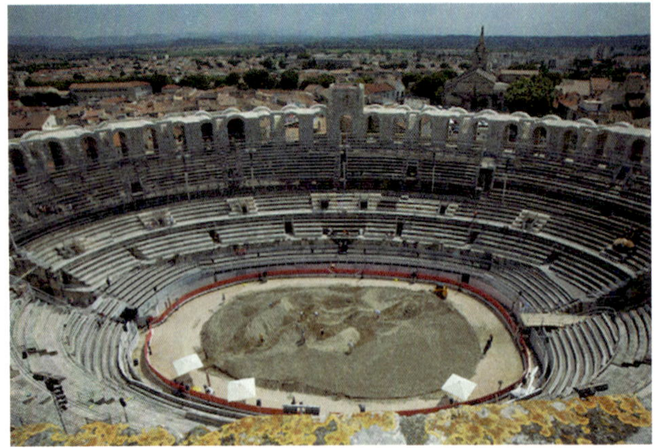

7/5/12—11:30:32 AM

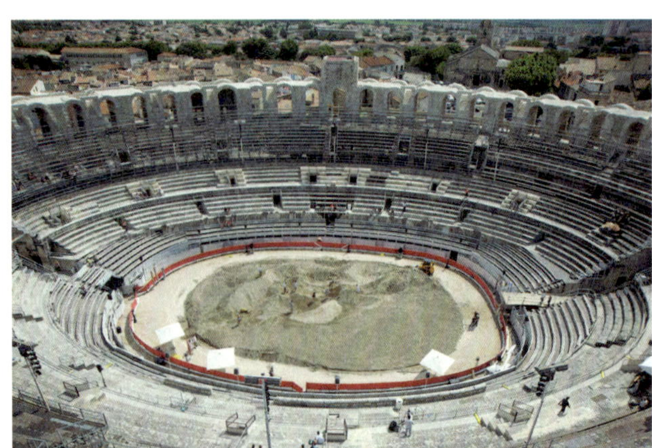

7/5/12—11:32:08 AM

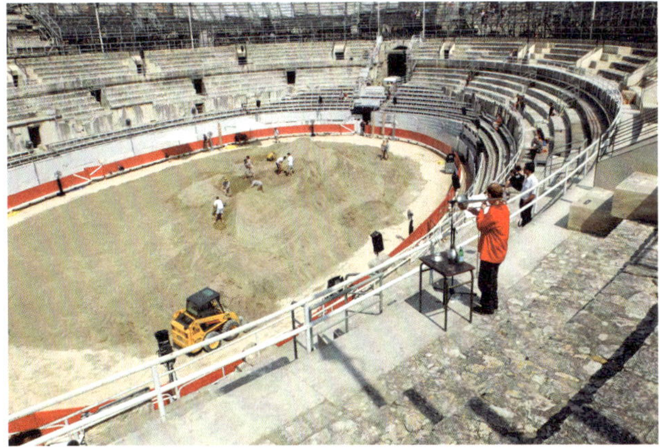

7/5/12—11:32:36 AM

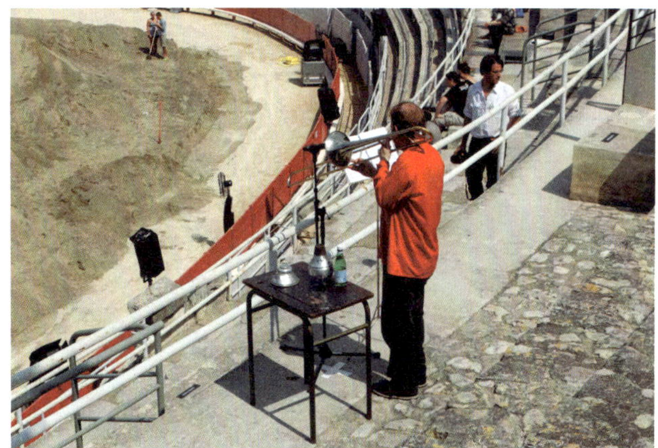

7/5/12—11:32:41 AM

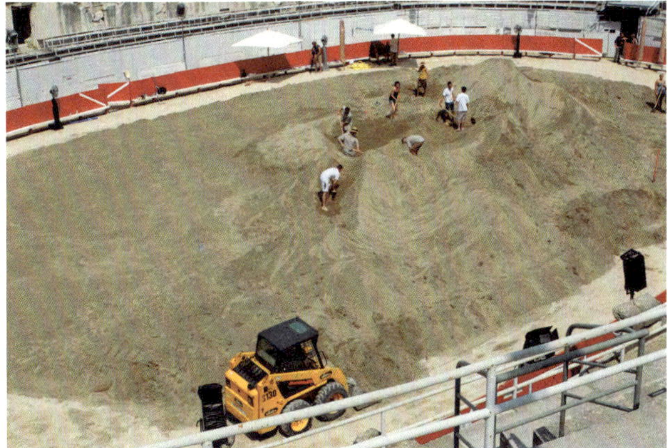

7/5/12—11:32:48 AM

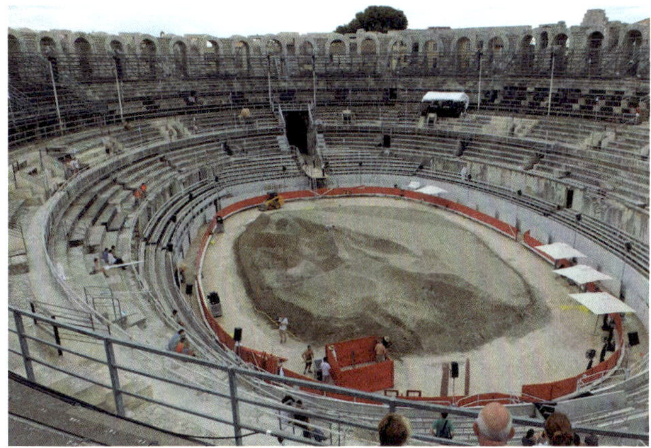

7/5/12—11:45:06 AM

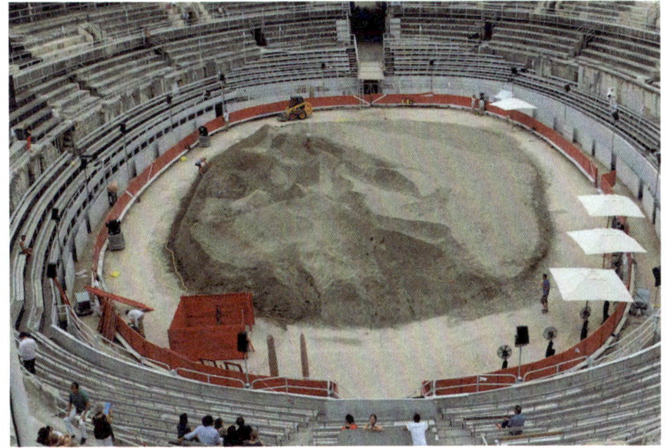

7/5/12—11:47:18 AM

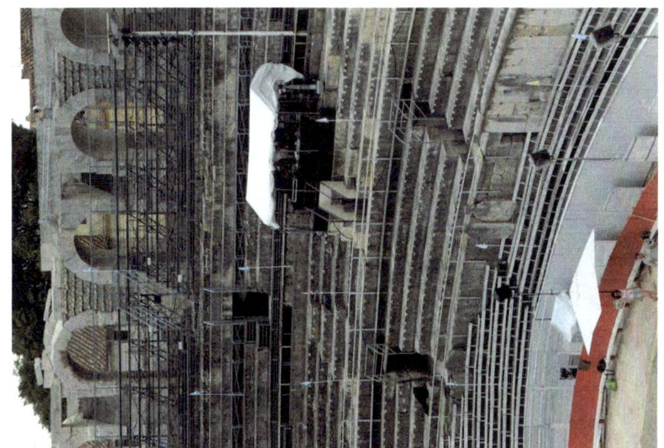

7/5/12—11:47:32 AM

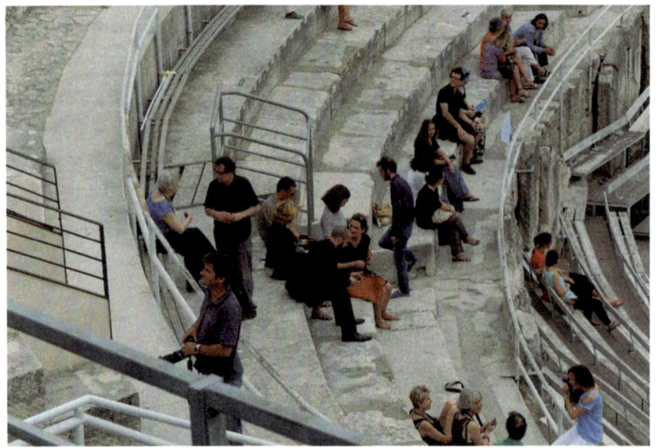
7/5/12—11:54:56 AM

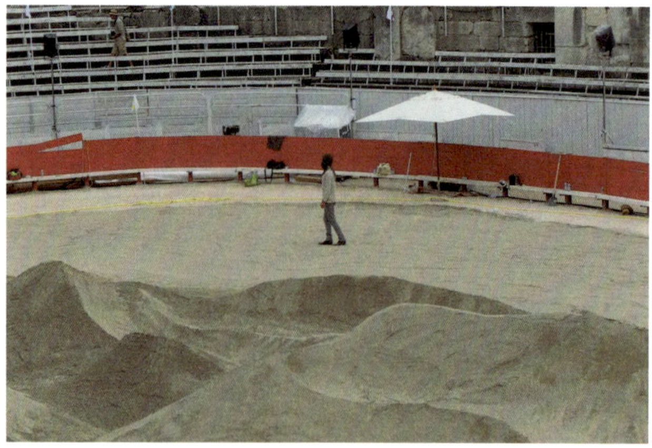
7/5/12—12:13:29 PM

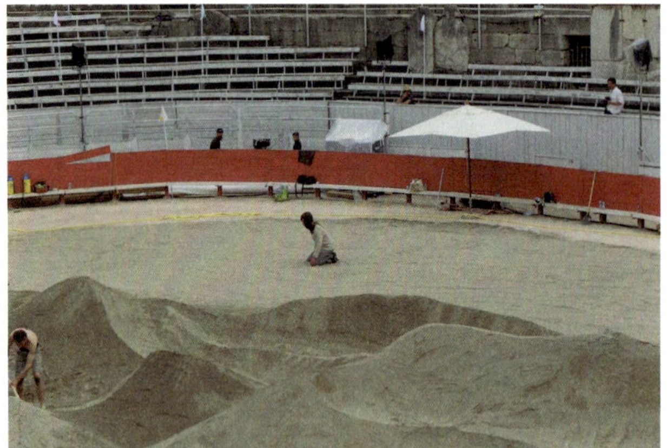
7/5/12—12:14:44 PM

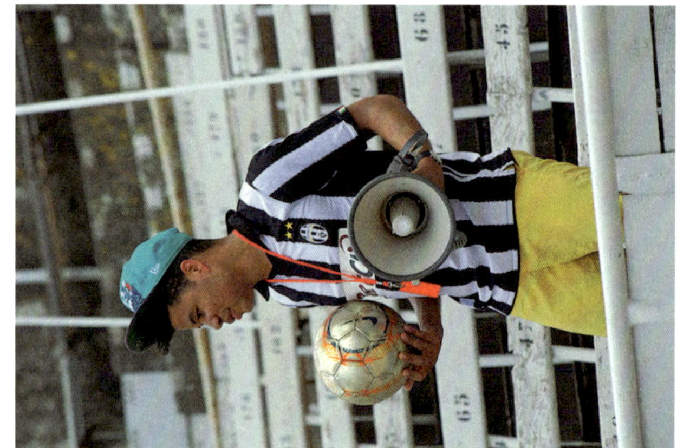
7/5/12—3:57:21 PM

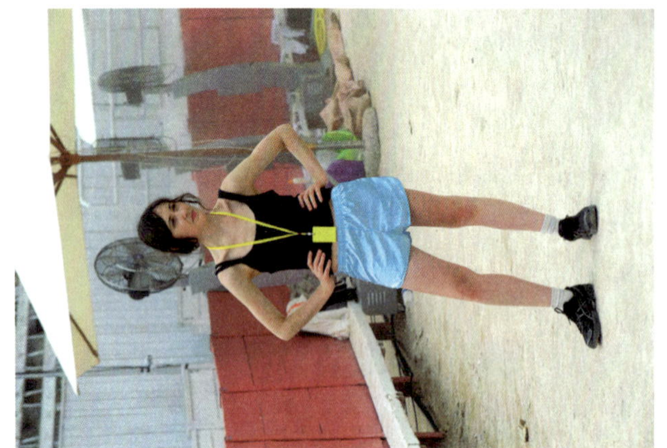
7/5/12—4:00:20 PM

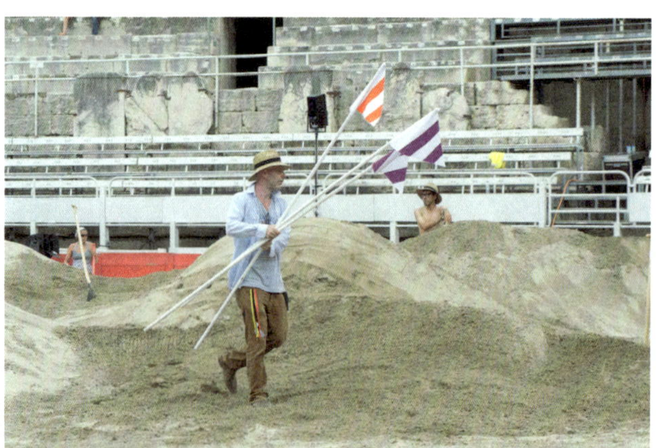
7/5/12—4:00:55 PM

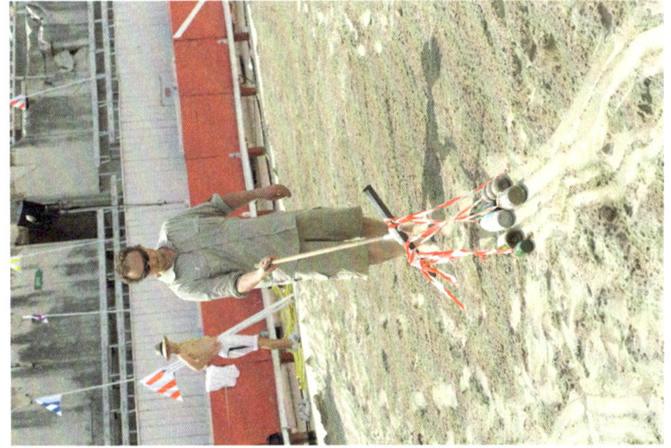

7/5/12—4:03:51 PM

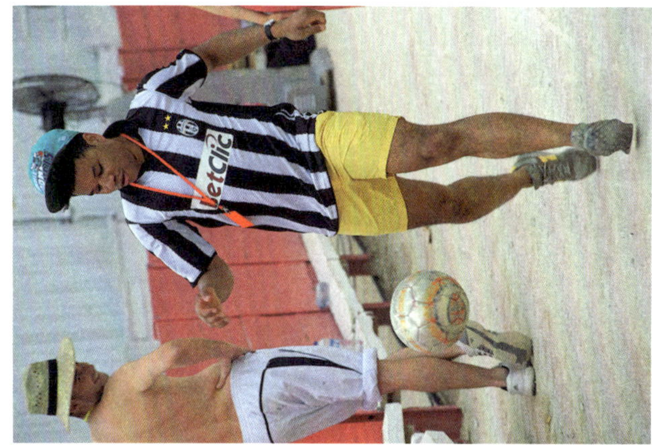

7/5/12—4:04:26 PM

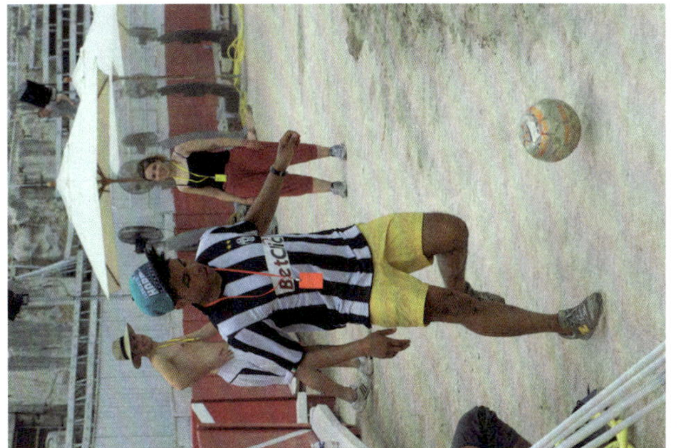

7/5/12—4:04:27 PM

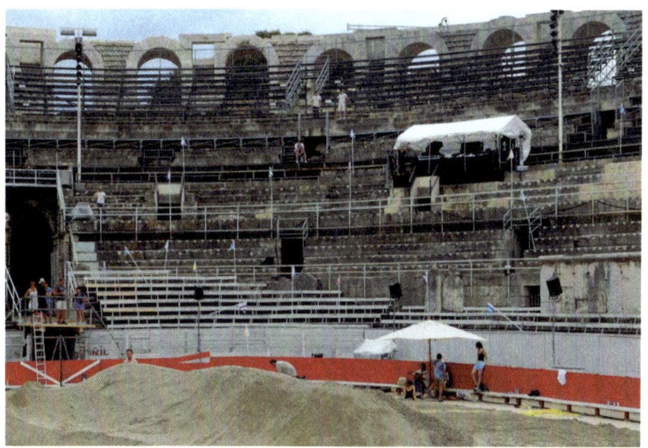

7/5/12—4:27:06 PM

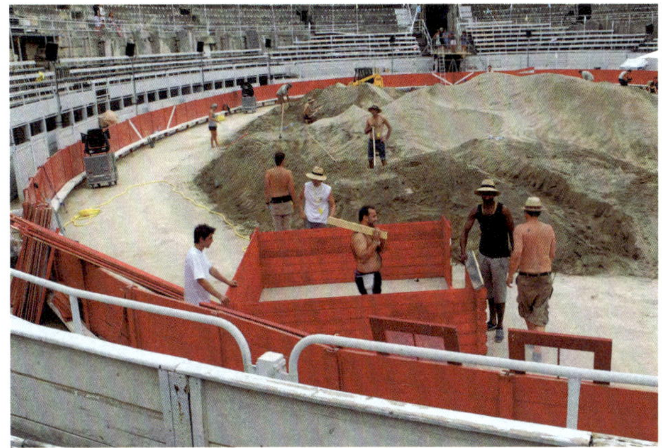

7/5/12—4:27:08 PM

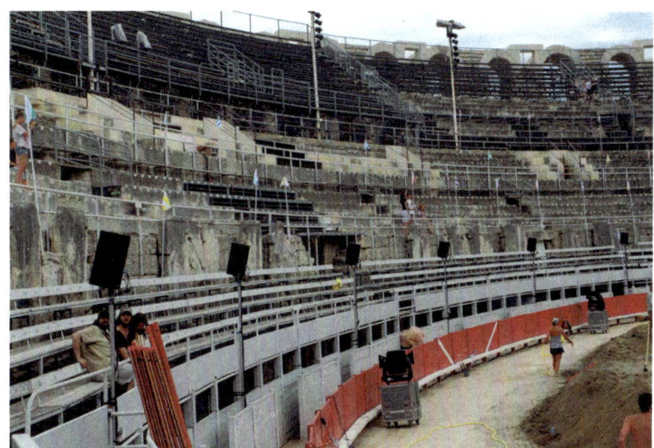

7/5/12—4:27:13 PM

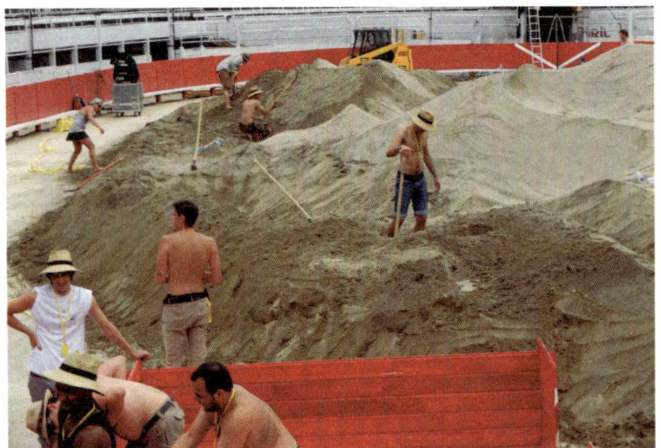

7/5/12—4:27:23 PM

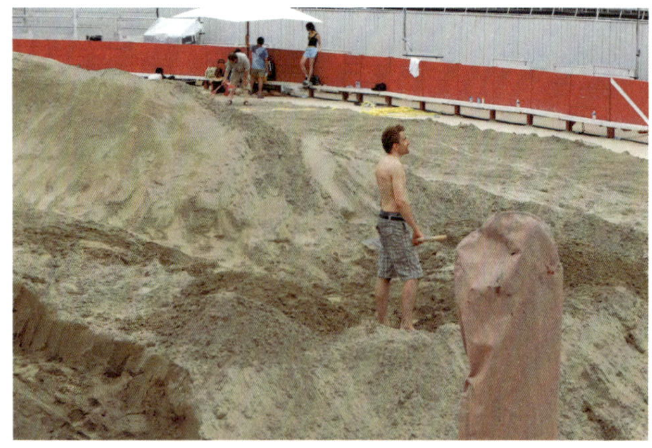

7/5/12—4:27:27 PM

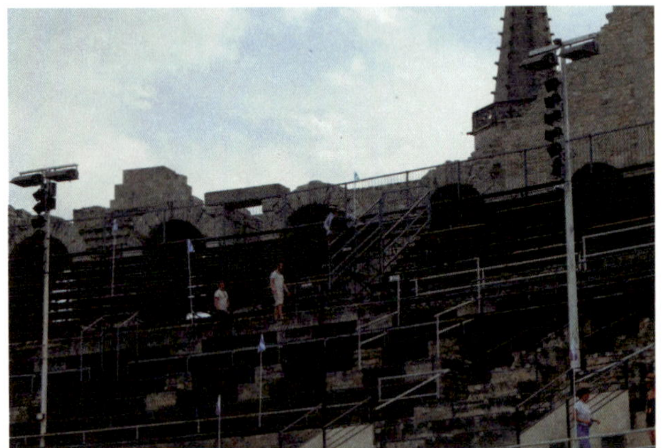

7/5/12—4:28:51 PM

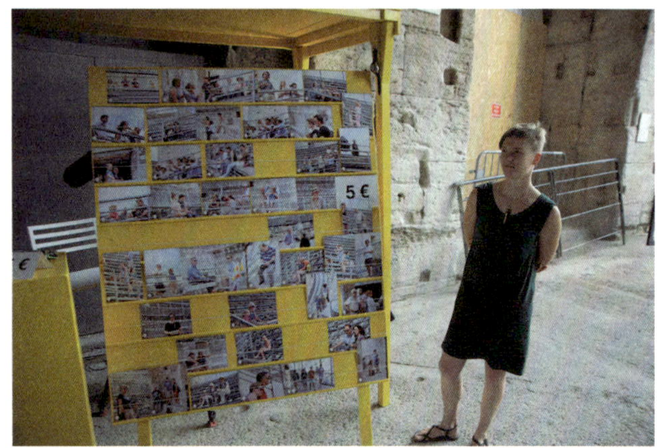

7/5/12—4:30:40 PM

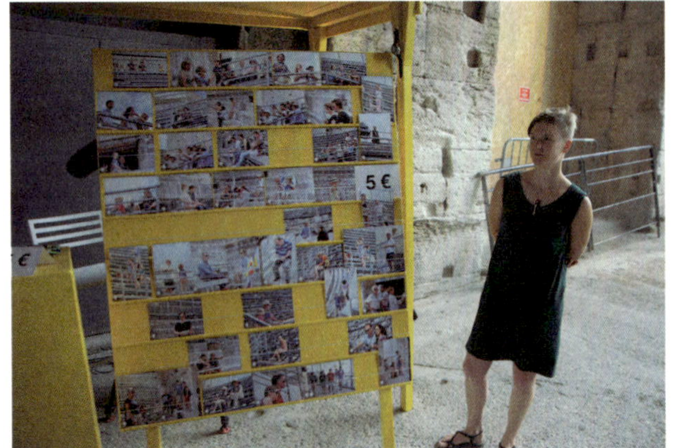

7/5/12—4:30:42 PM

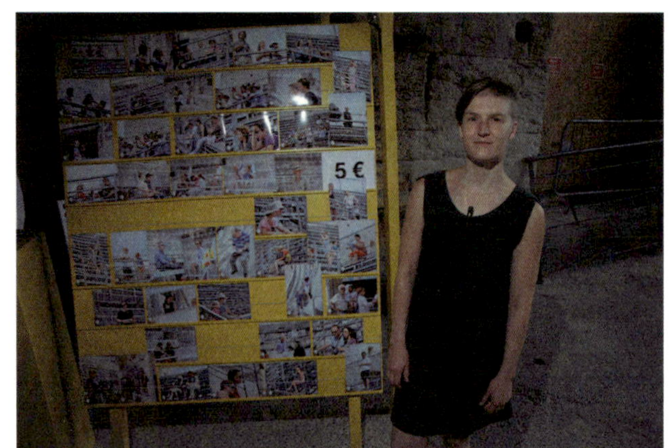

7/5/12—4:32:56 PM

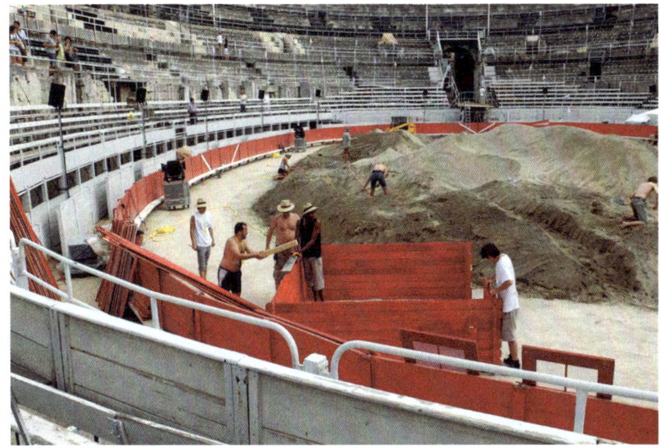

7/5/12—4:34:27 PM

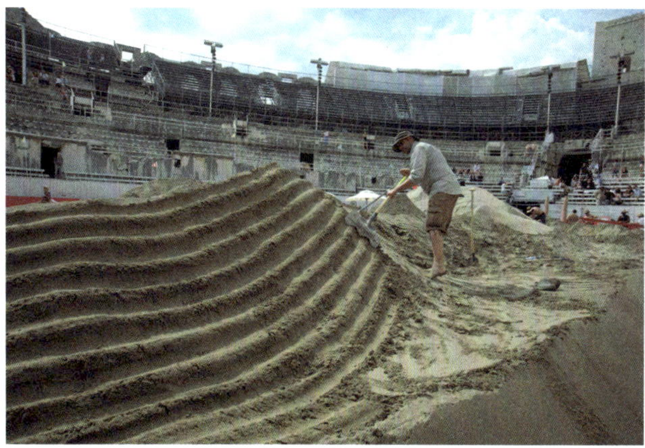

7/5/12—4:36:31 PM

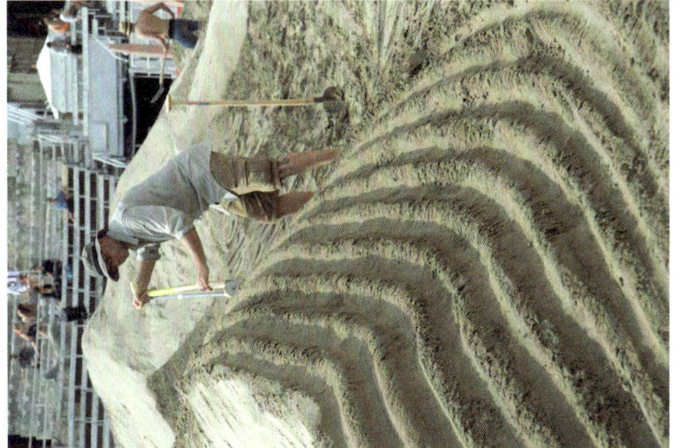

7/5/12—4:36:45 PM

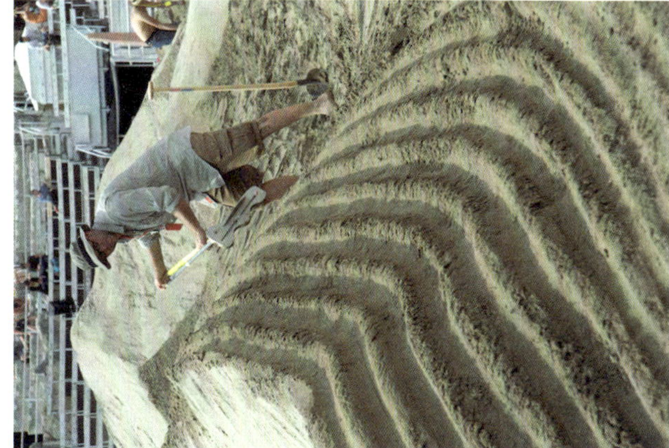

7/5/12—4:36:52 PM

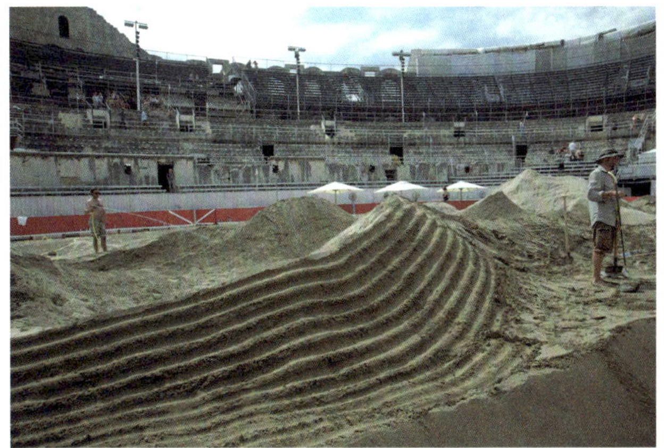

7/5/12—4:38:35 PM

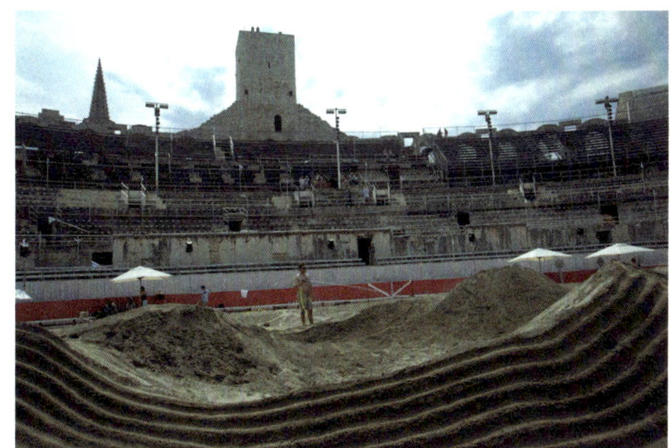

7/5/12—4:38:37 PM

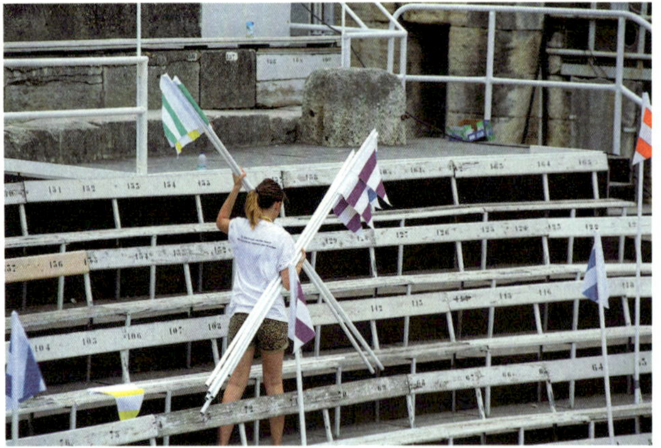
7/5/12—4:57:26 PM

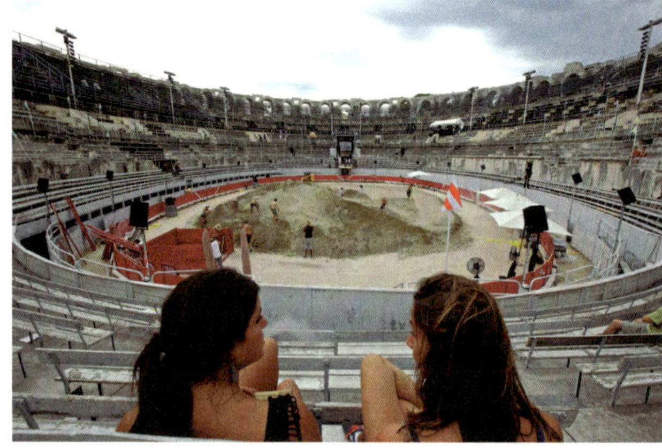
7/5/12—5:05:00 PM

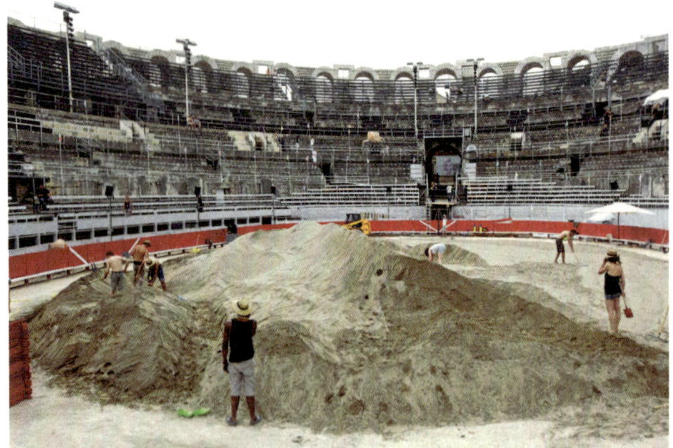
7/5/12—5:05:30 PM

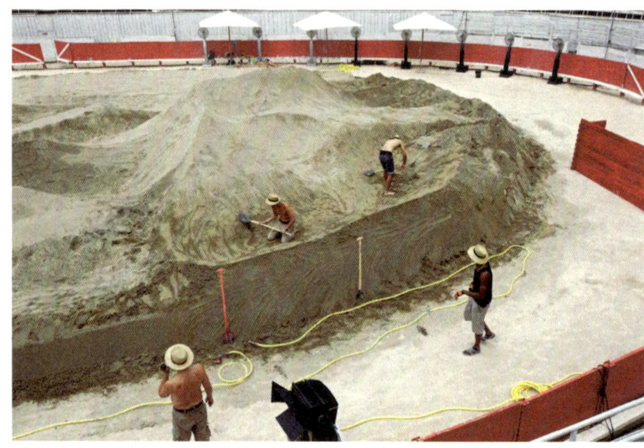
7/5/12—5:09:41 PM

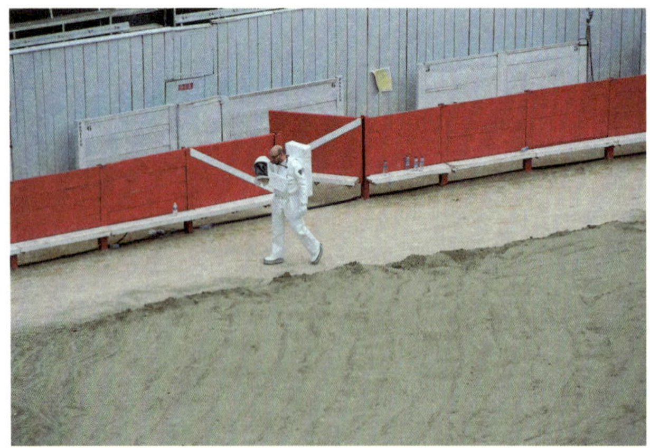
7/5/12—5:11:17 PM

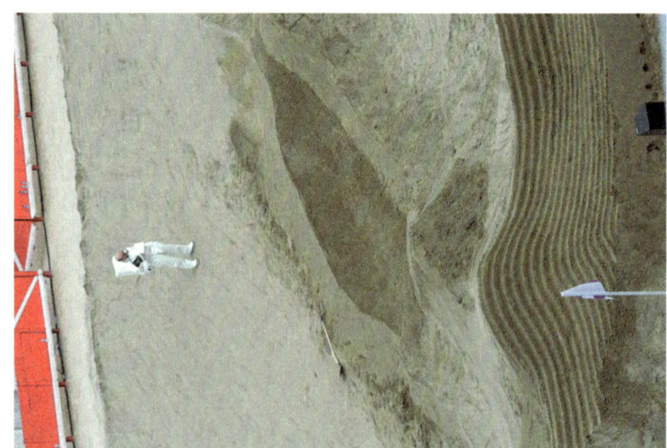
7/5/12—5:11:41 PM

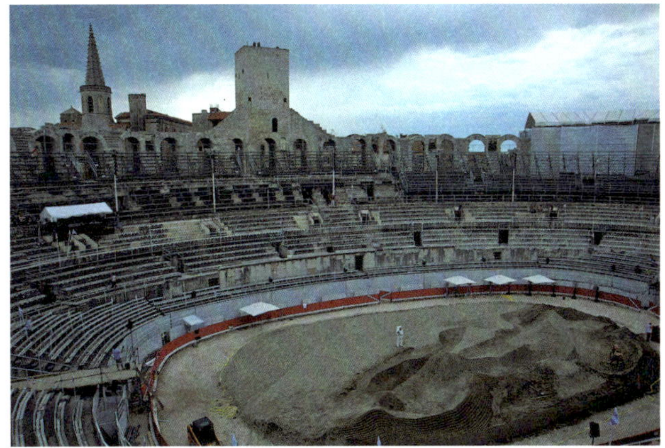

7/5/12—5:12:29 PM

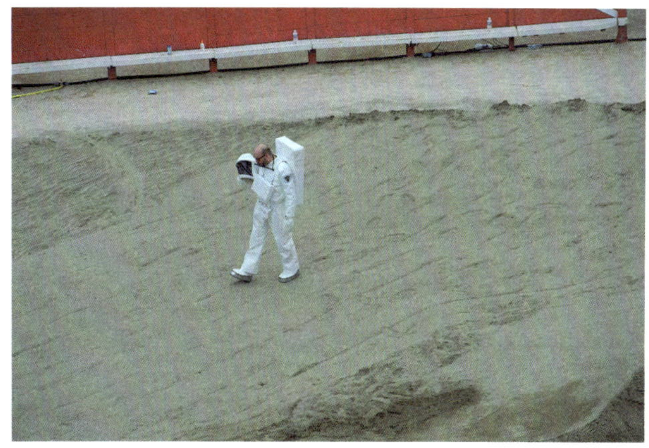

7/5/12—5:12:32 PM

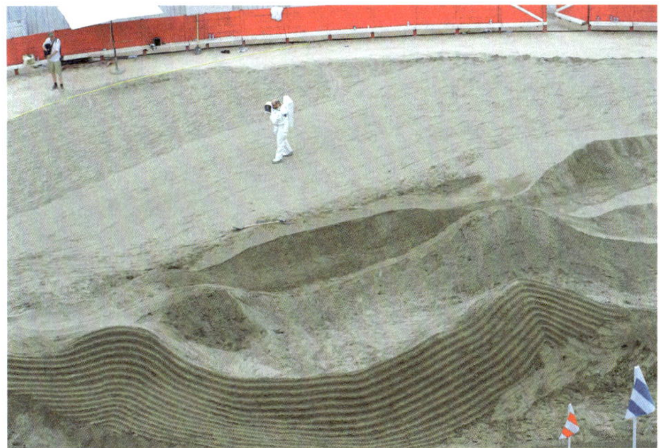

7/5/12—5:16:50 PM

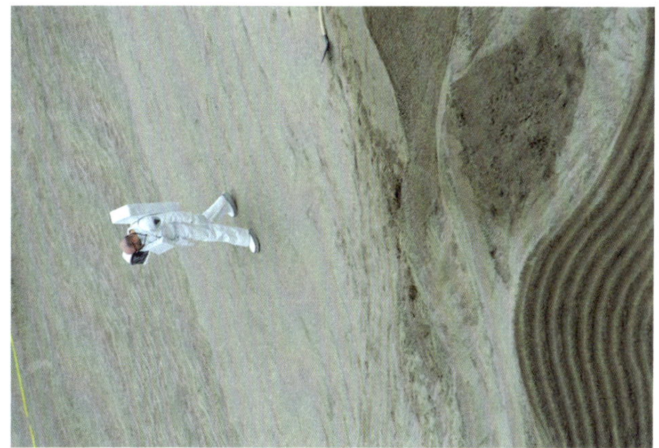

7/5/12—5:16:59 PM

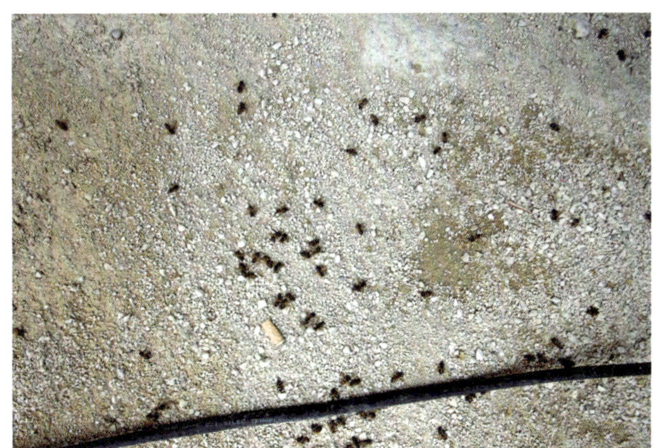

7/5/12—5:17:22 PM

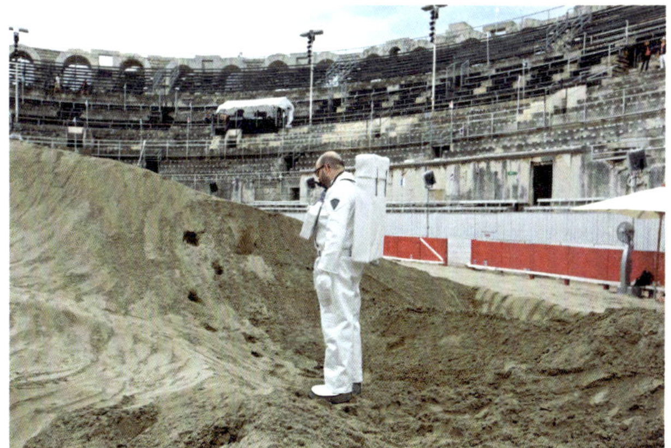

7/5/12—5:17:40 PM

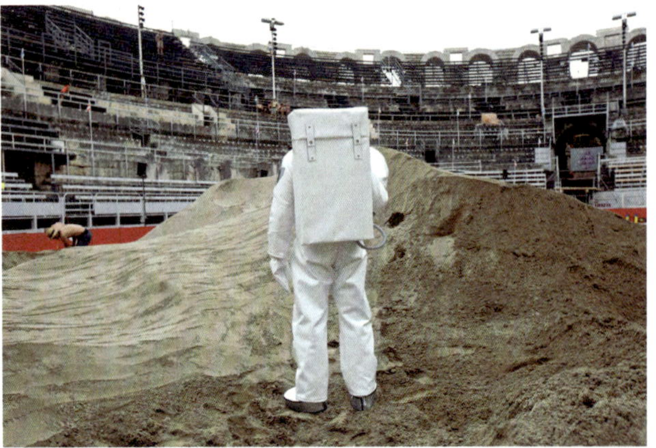

7/5/12—5:17:47 PM

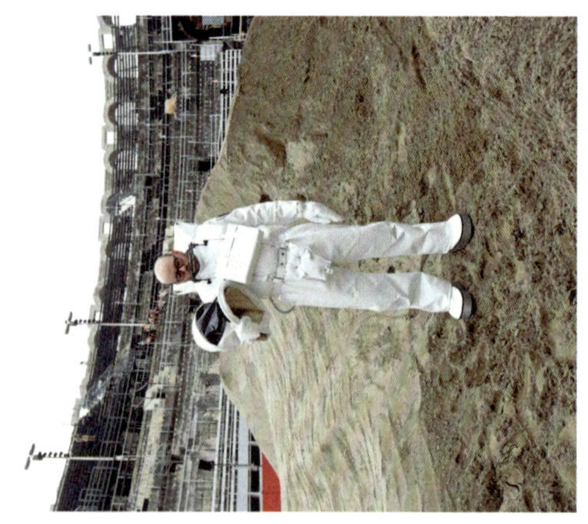

7/5/12—5:17:55 PM

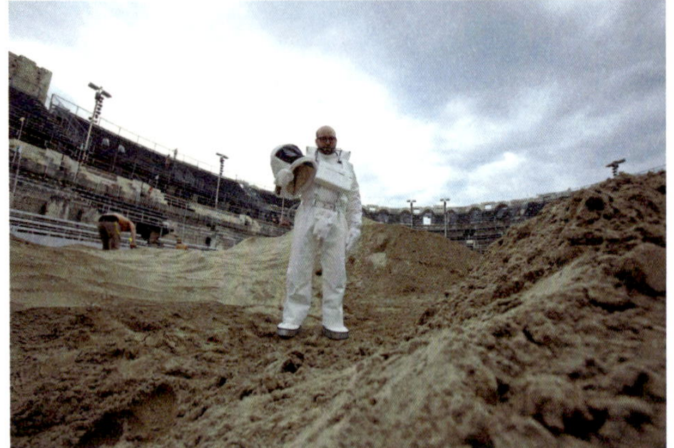

7/5/12—5:18:11 PM

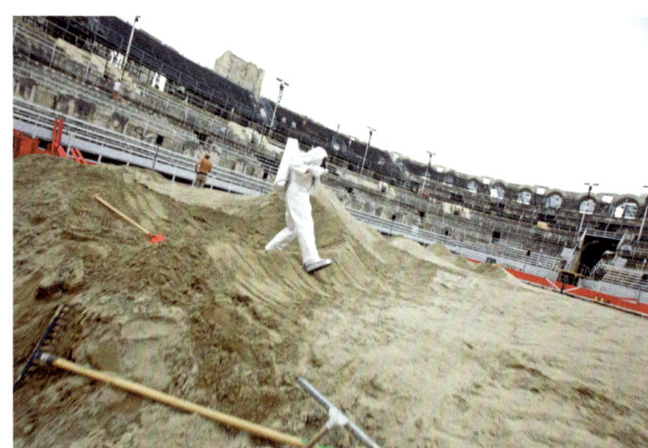

7/5/12—5:18:30 PM

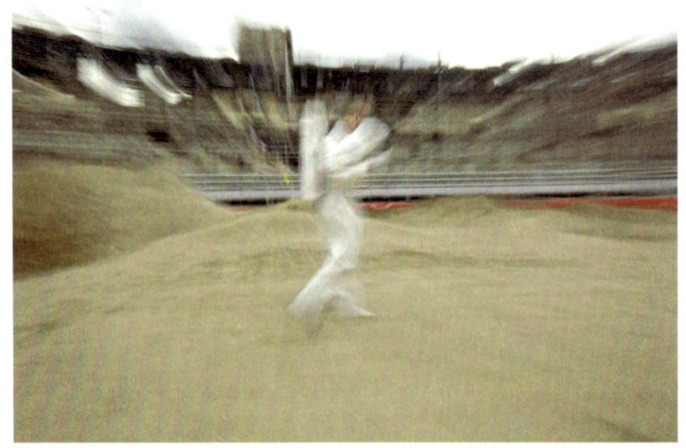

7/5/12—5:18:49 PM

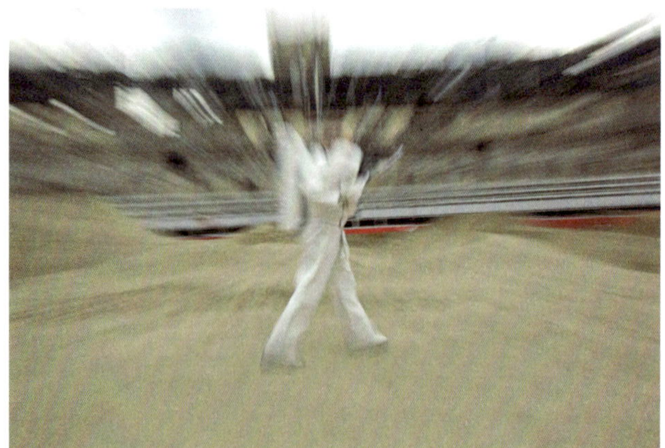

7/5/12—5:18:54 PM

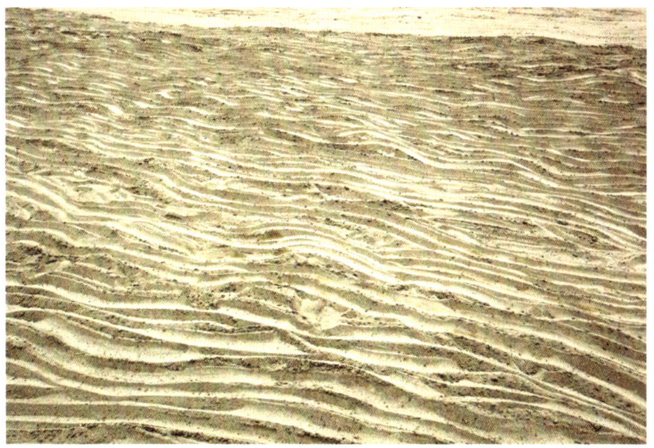
7/5/12—5:21:08 PM

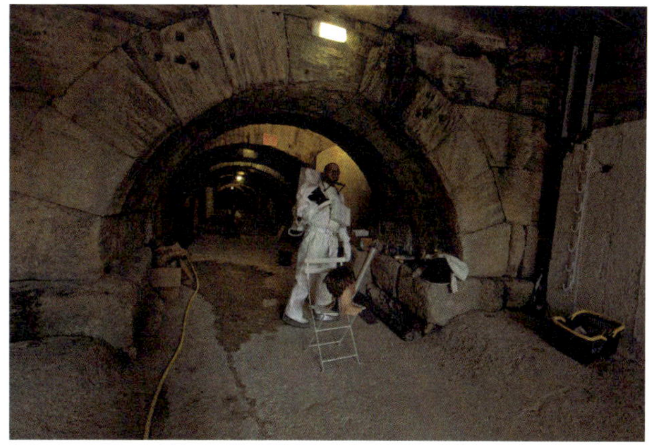
7/5/12—5:22:21 PM

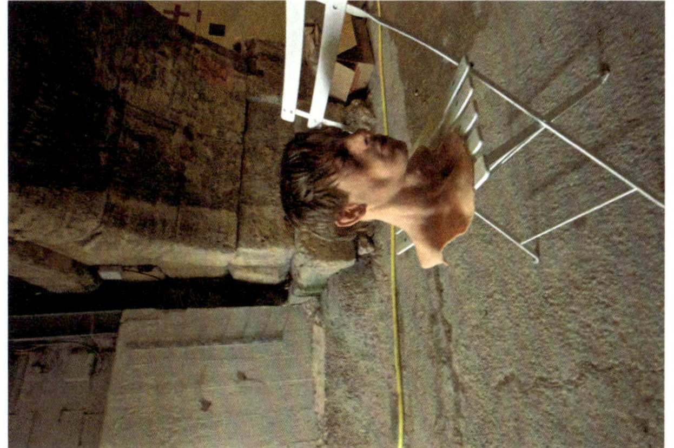
7/5/12—5:22:32 PM

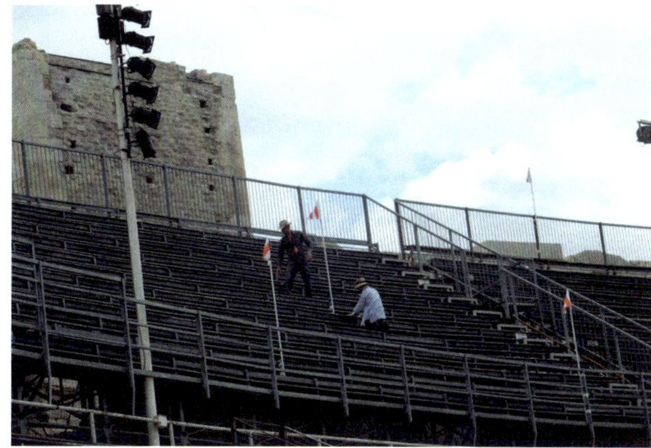
7/5/12—5:32:50 PM

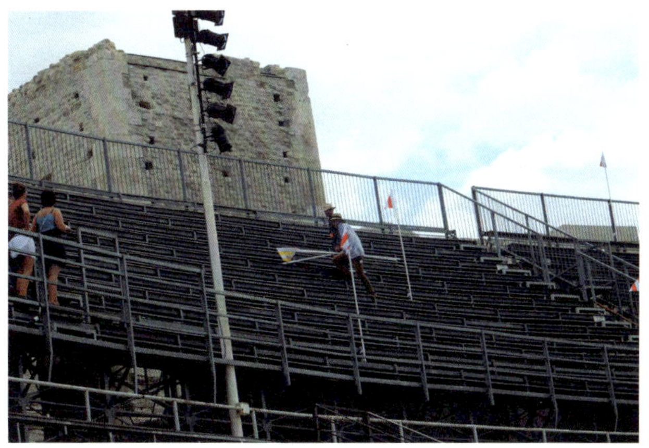
7/5/12—5:32:56 PM

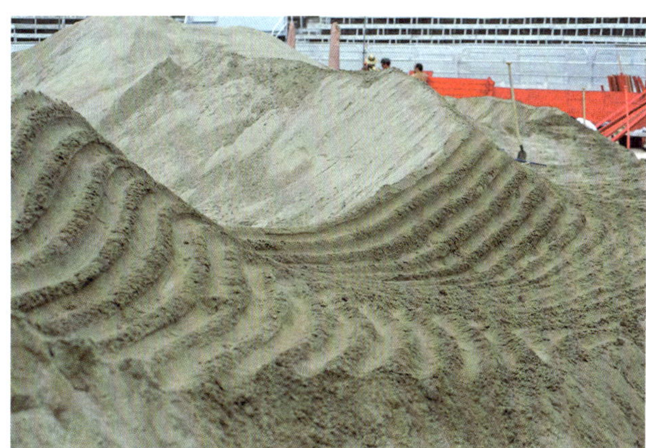
7/5/12—5:33:01 PM

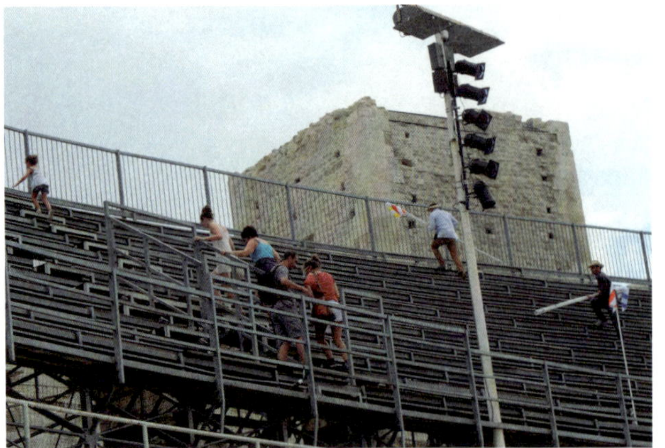
7/5/12—5:33:04 PM

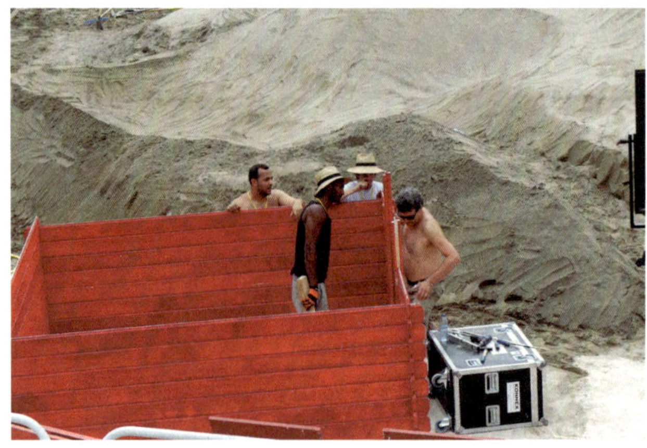
7/5/12—5:33:24 PM

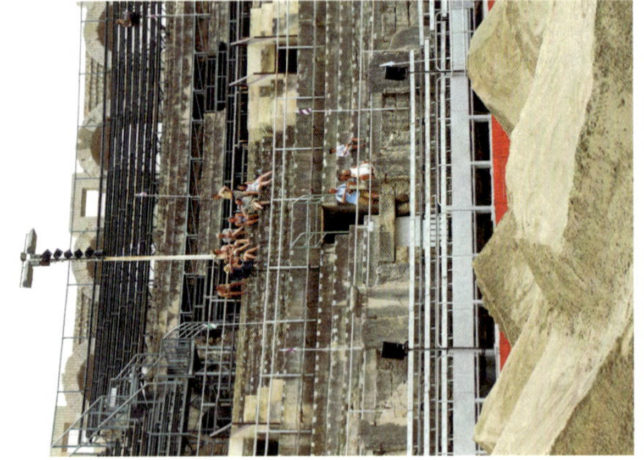
7/5/12—5:33:51 PM

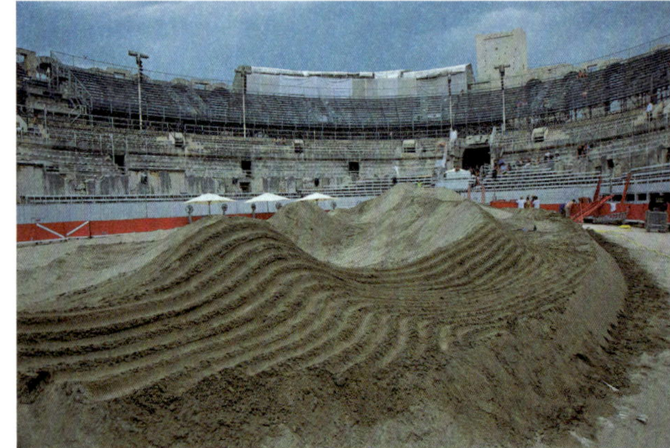
7/5/12—5:34:52 PM

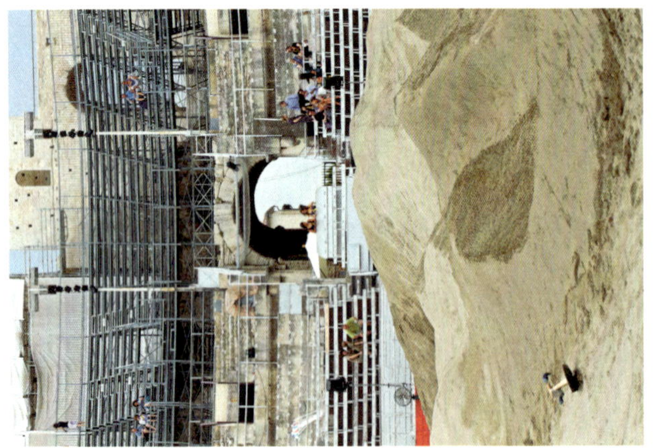
7/5/12—5:34:57 PM

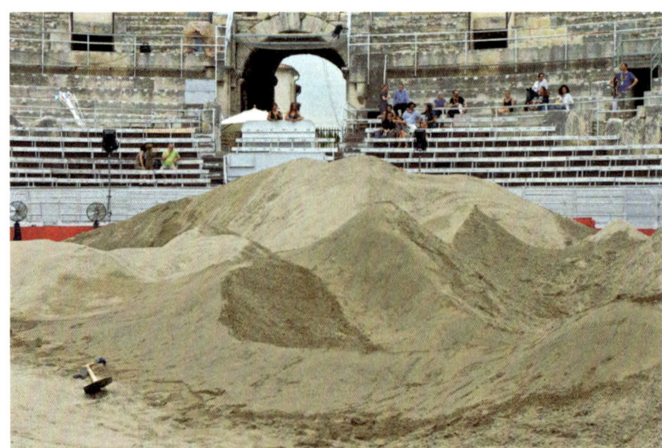
7/5/12—5:35:28 PM

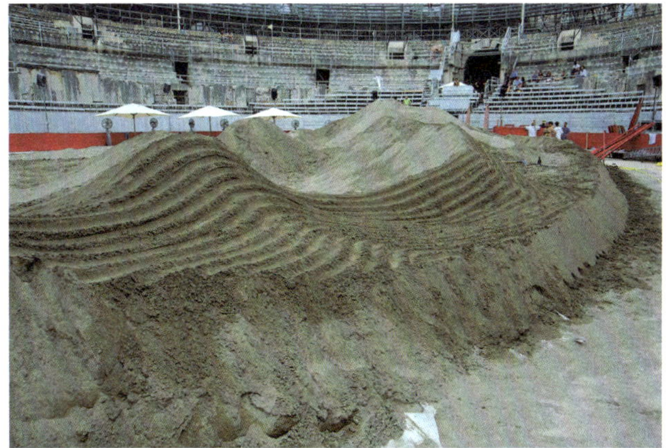

7/5/12—5:35:41 PM

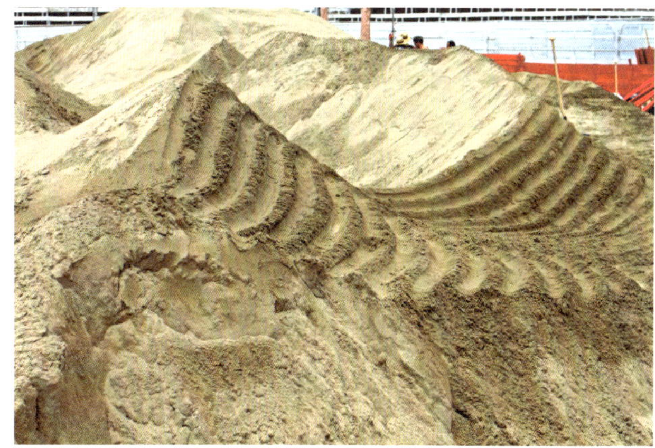

7/5/12—5:35:42 PM

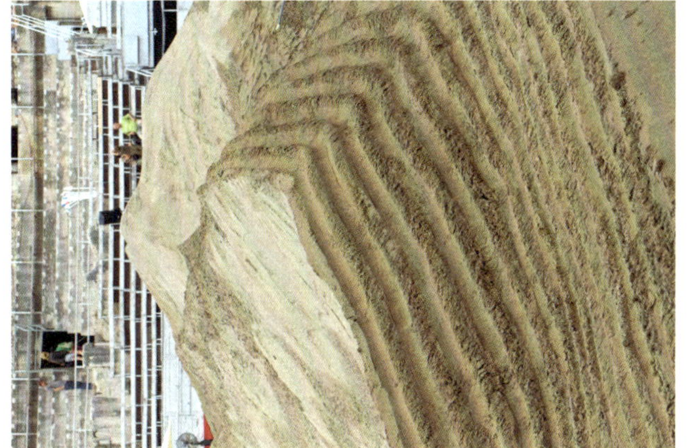

7/5/12—5:36:46 PM

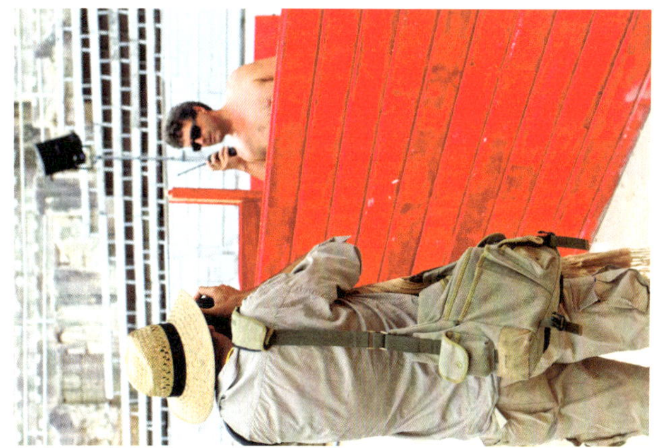

7/5/12—5:40:35 PM

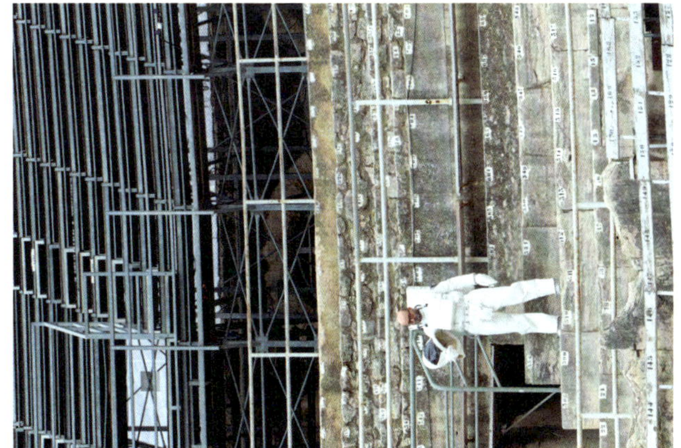

7/5/12—5:41:02 PM

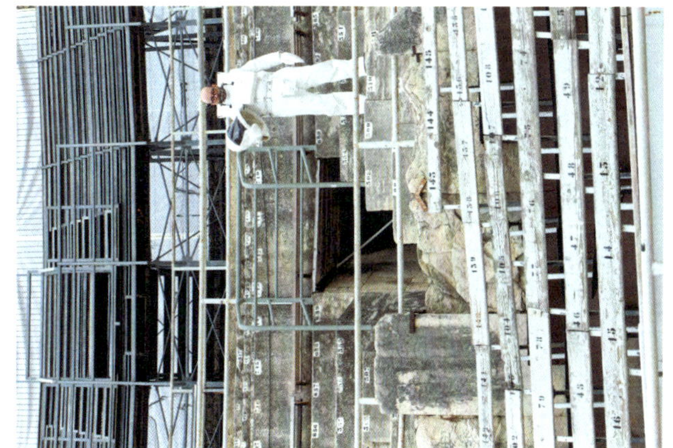

7/5/12—5:41:20 PM

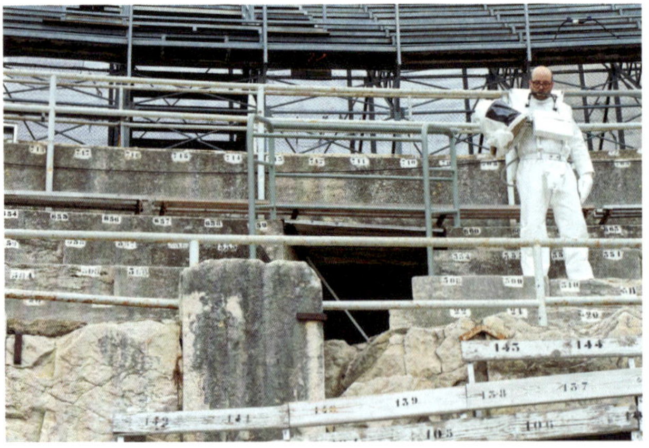

7/5/12—5:41:50 PM

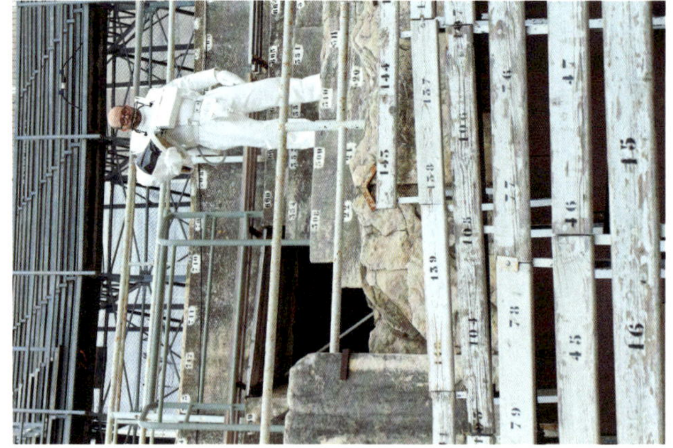

7/5/12—5:42:37 PM

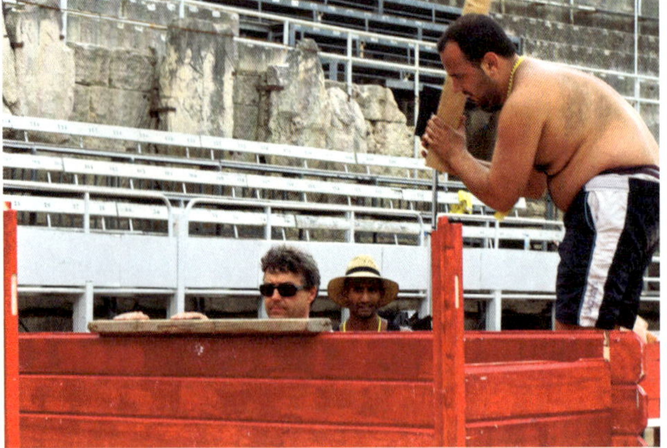

7/5/12—5:43:09 PM

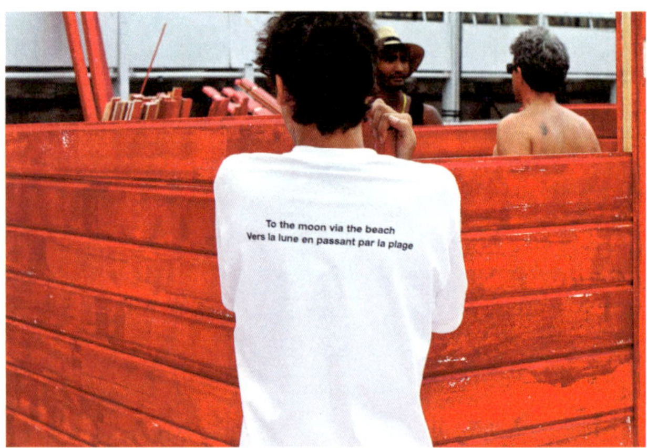

7/5/12—5:43:26 PM

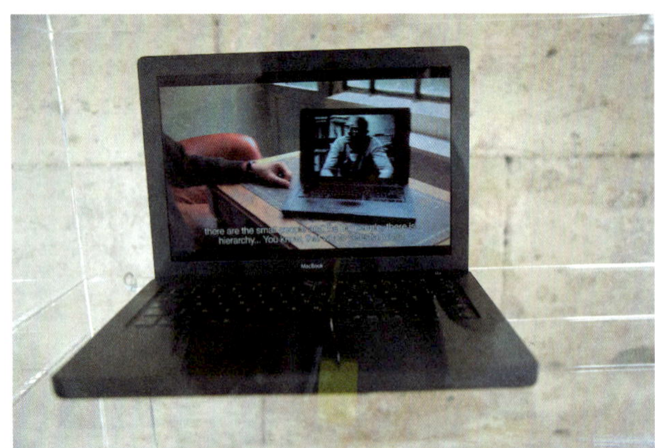

7/5/12—5:43:53 PM

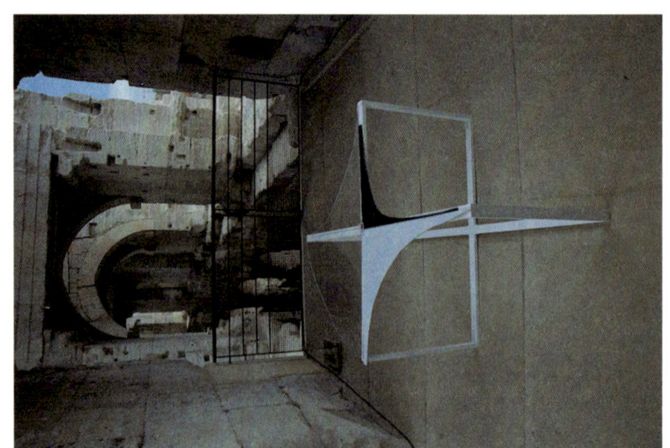

7/5/12—5:43:54 PM

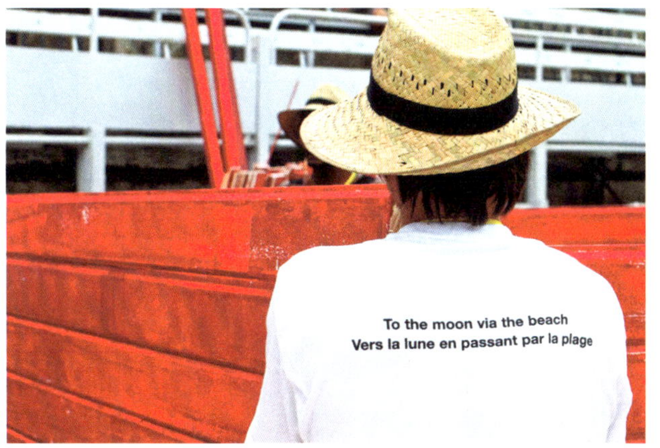

7/5/12—5:43:55 PM

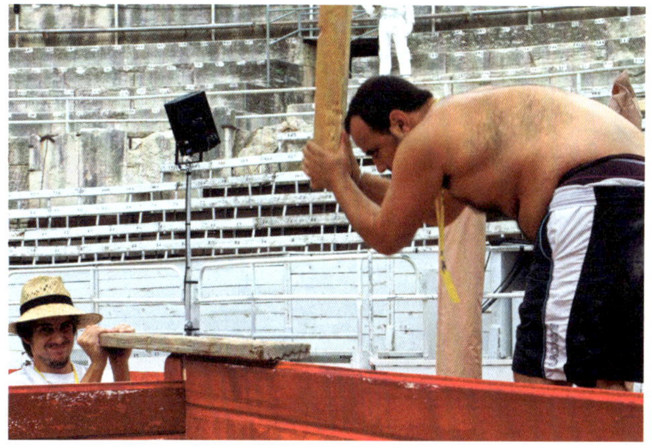

7/5/12—5:44:27 PM

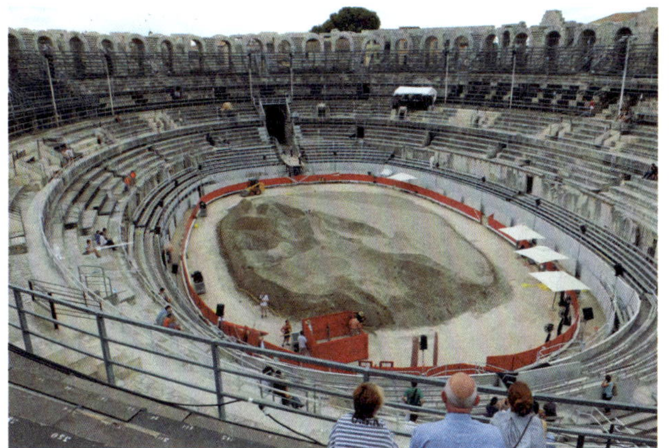

7/5/12—5:45:06 PM

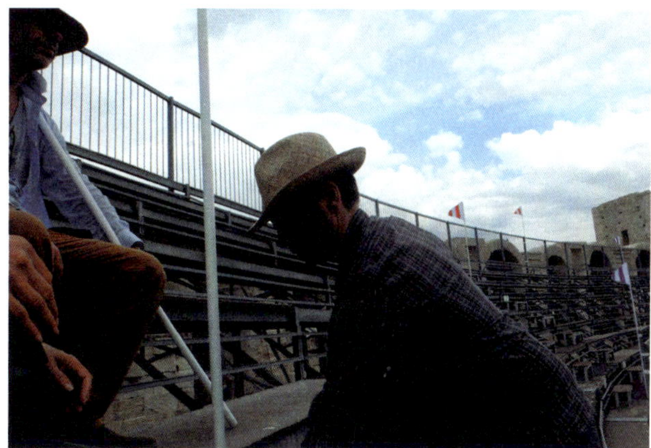

7/5/12—5:45:10 PM

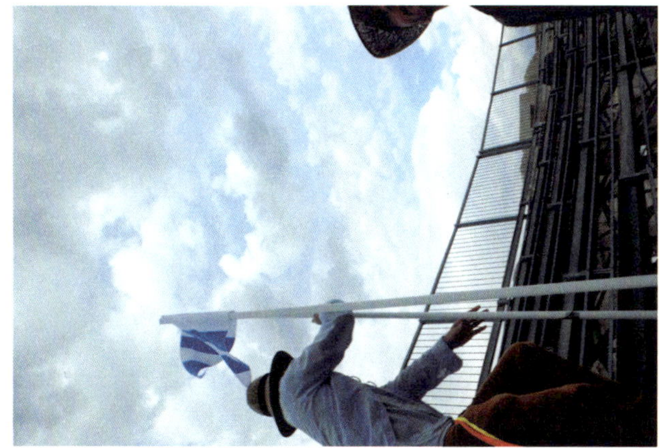

7/5/12—5:45:14 PM

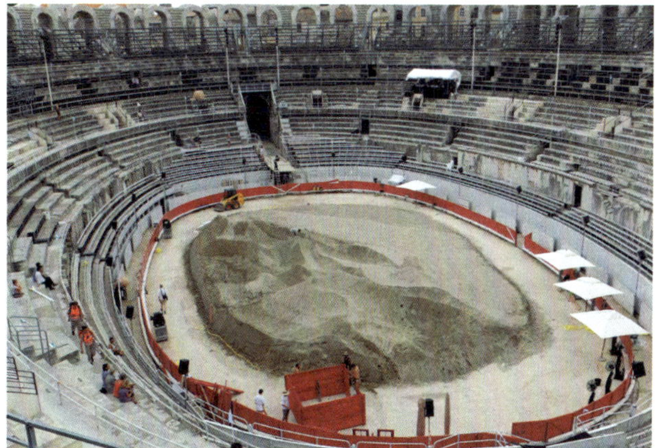

7/5/12—5:45:38 PM

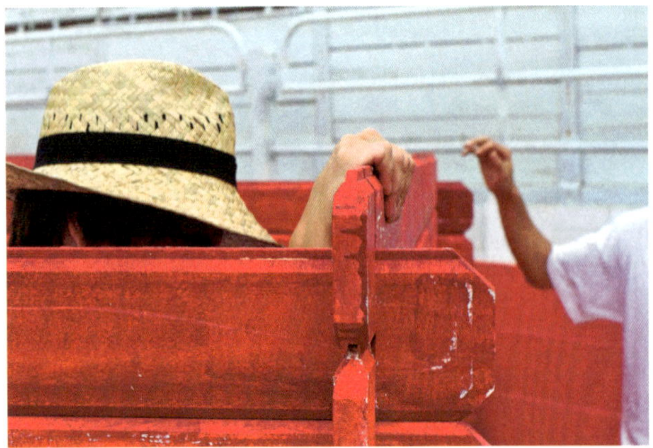

7/5/12—5:45:44 PM

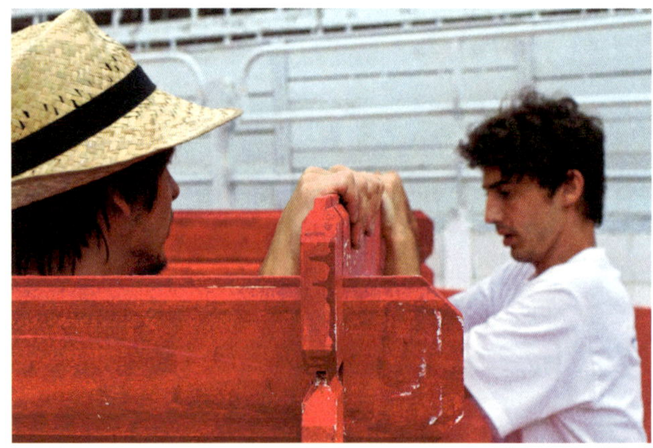

7/5/12—5:45:46 PM

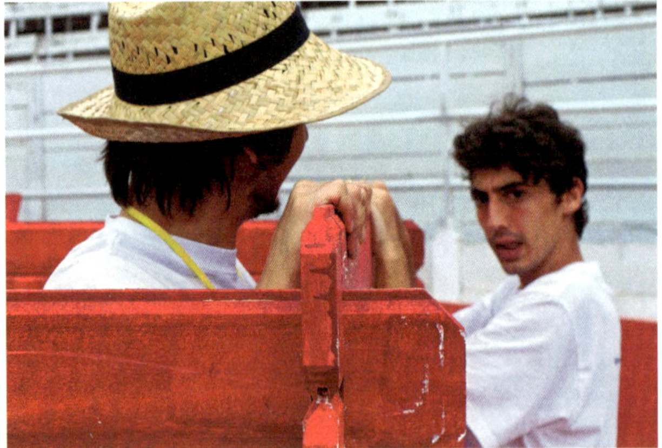

7/5/12—5:45:47 PM

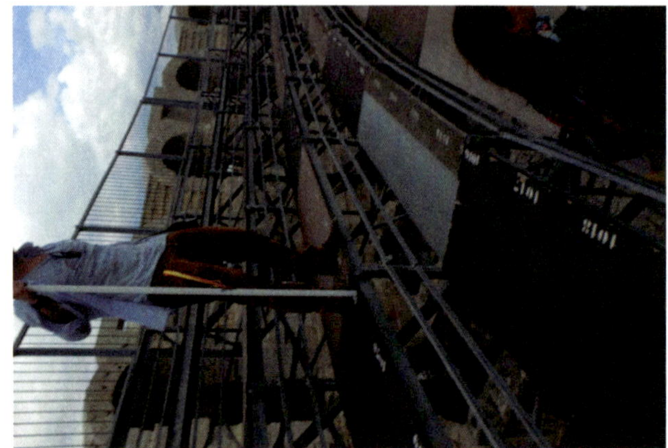

7/5/12—5:45:55 PM

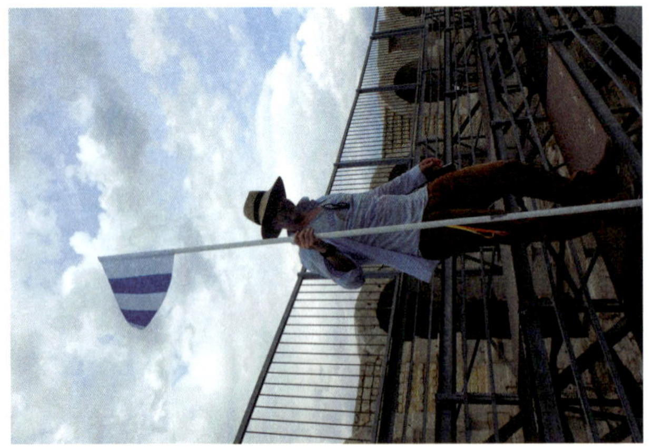

7/5/12—5:45:59 PM

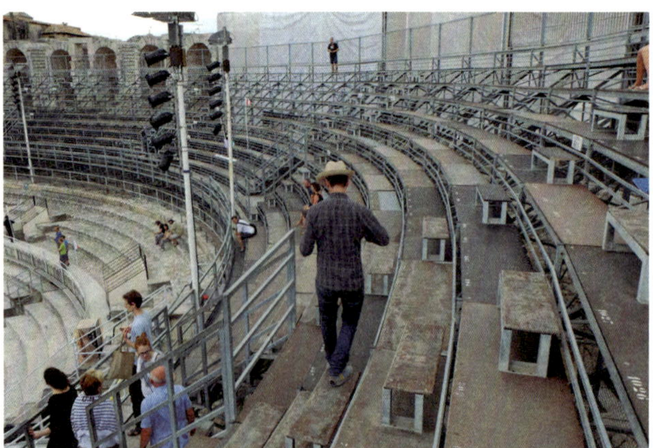

7/5/12—5:46:06 PM

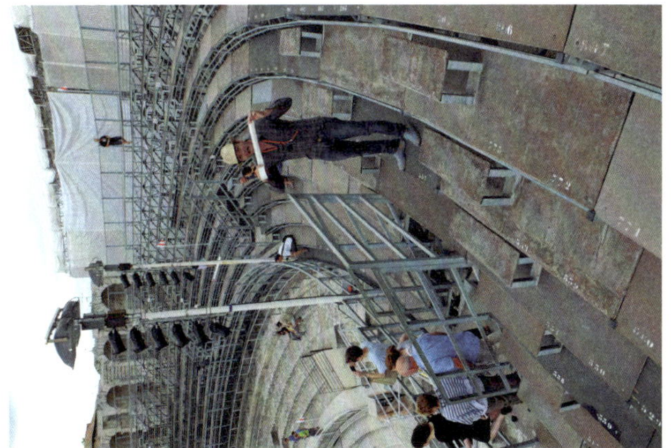
7/5/12—5:46:10 PM

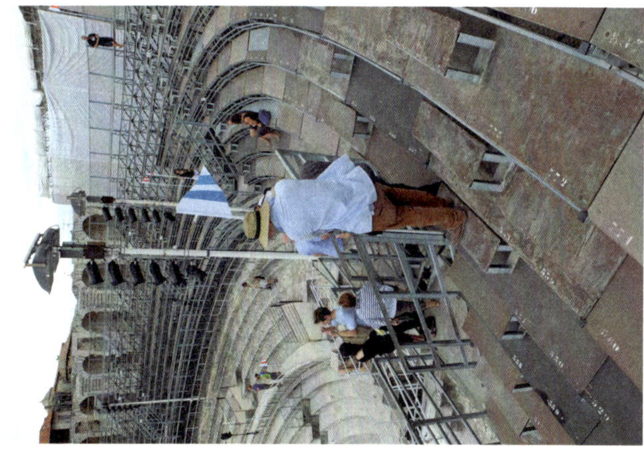
7/5/12—5:46:24 PM

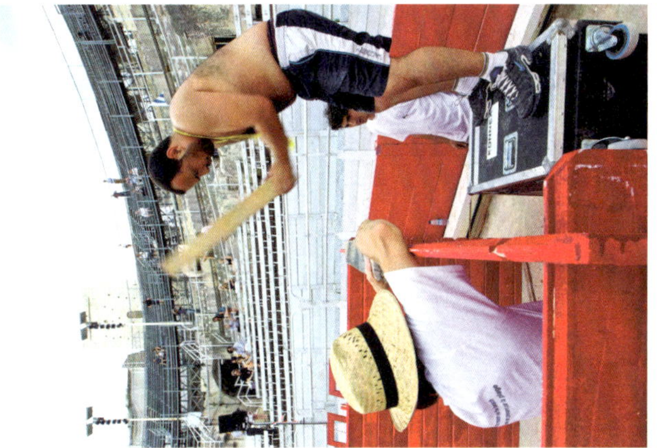
7/5/12—5:46:31 PM

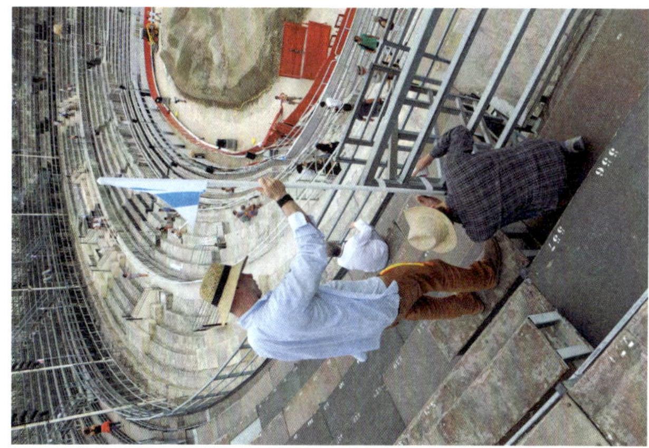
7/5/12—5:46:36 PM

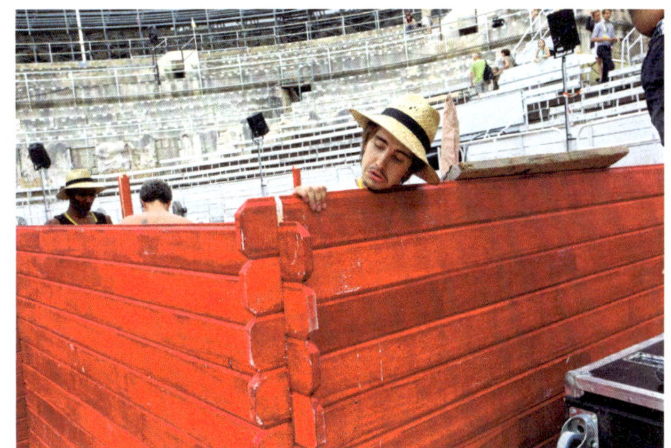
7/5/12—5:46:39 PM

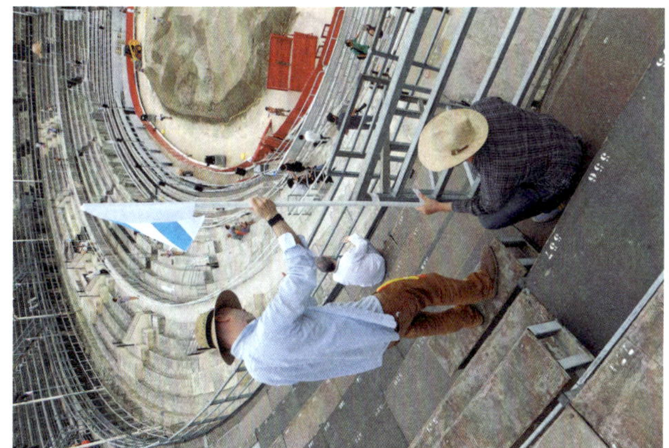
7/5/12—5:46:40 PM

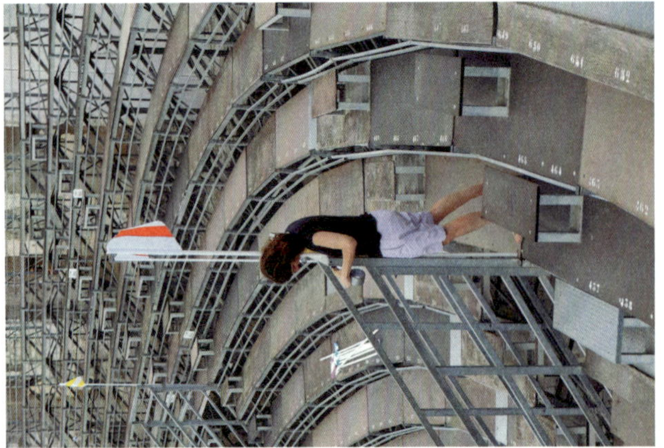
7/5/12—5:46:59 PM

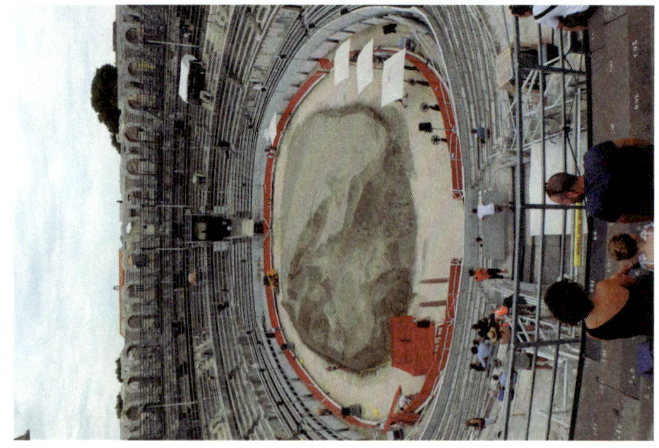
7/5/12—5:47:09 PM

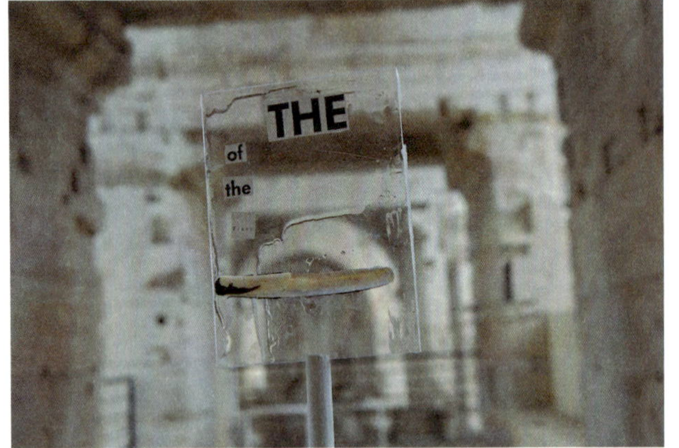

7/5/12—5:47:11 PM

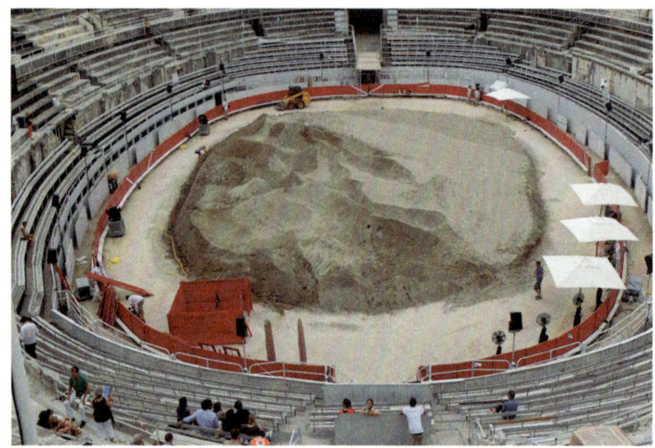
7/5/12—5:47:18 PM

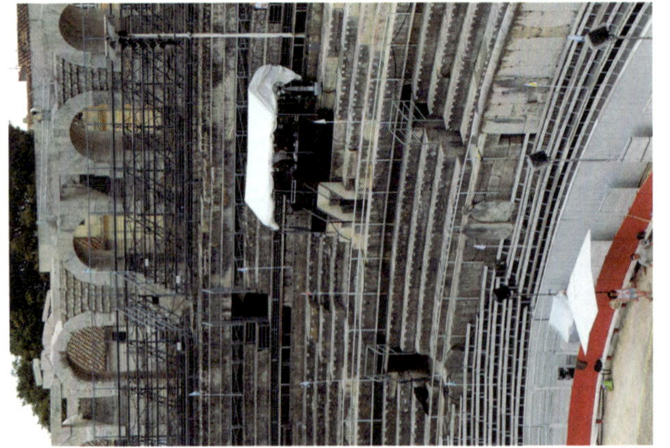
7/5/12—5:47:32 PM

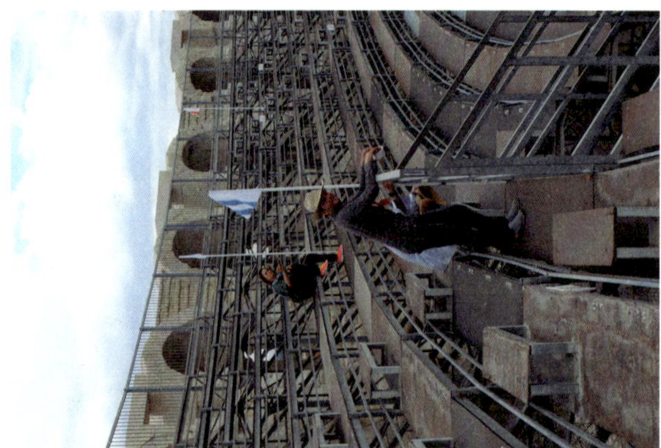
7/5/12—5:47:46 PM

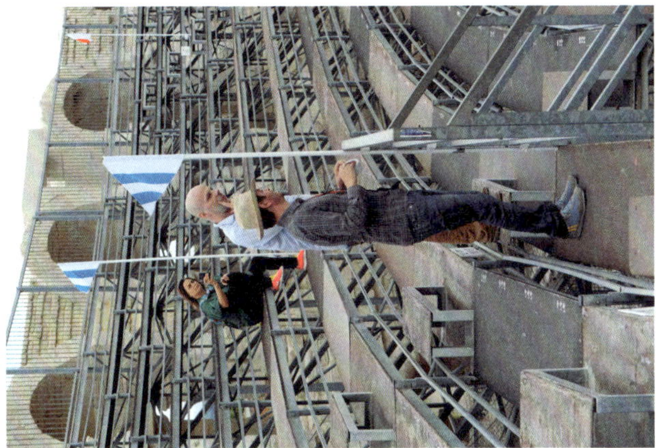
7/5/12—5:47:49 PM

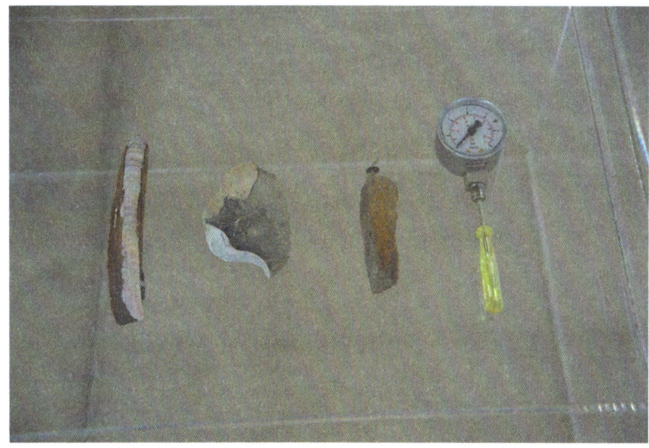
7/5/12—5:47:56 PM

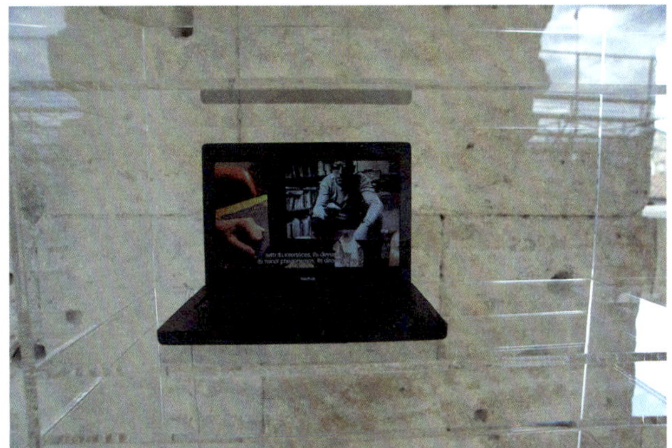
7/5/12—5:48:12 PM

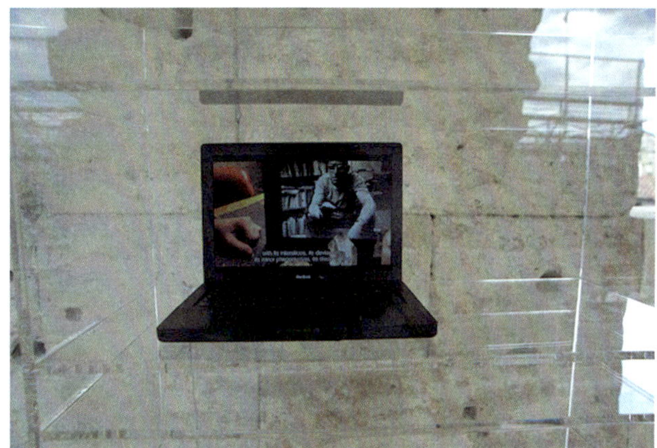
7/5/12—5:48:13 PM

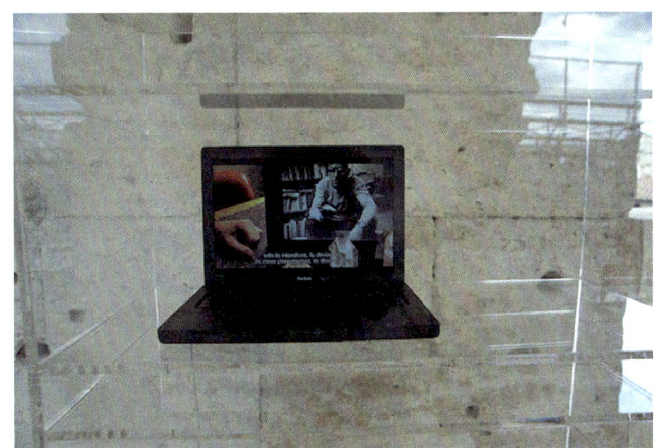
7/5/12—5:48:14 PM

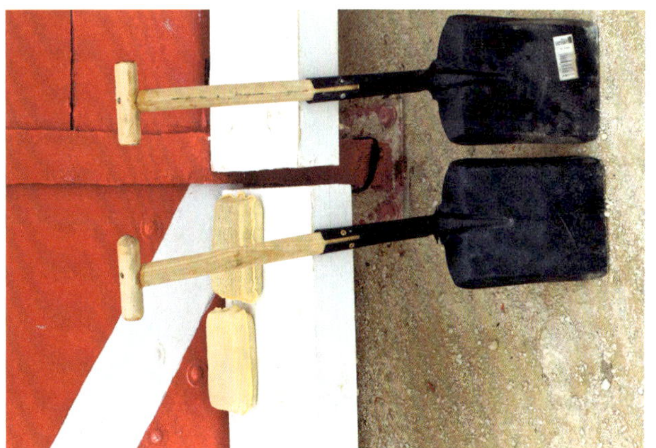
7/5/12—5:48:46 PM

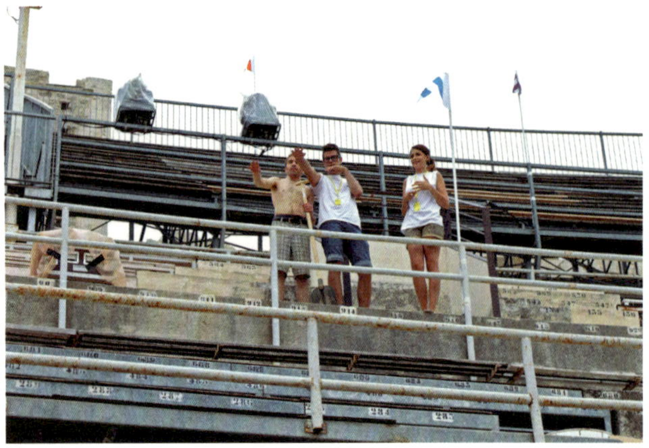

7/5/12—5:48:57 PM

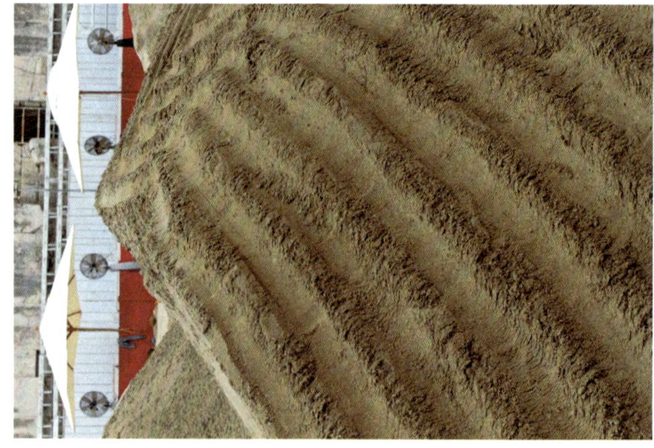

7/5/12—5:49:51 PM

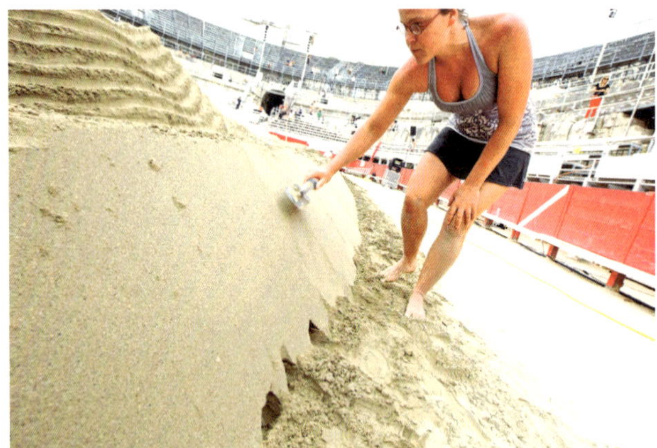

7/5/12—5:50:51 PM

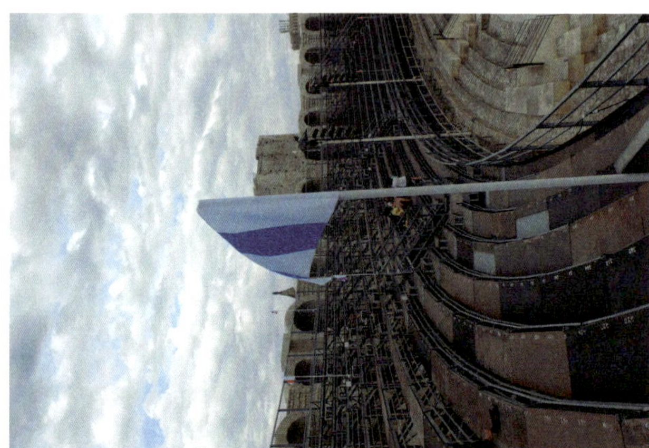

7/5/12—5:51:45 PM

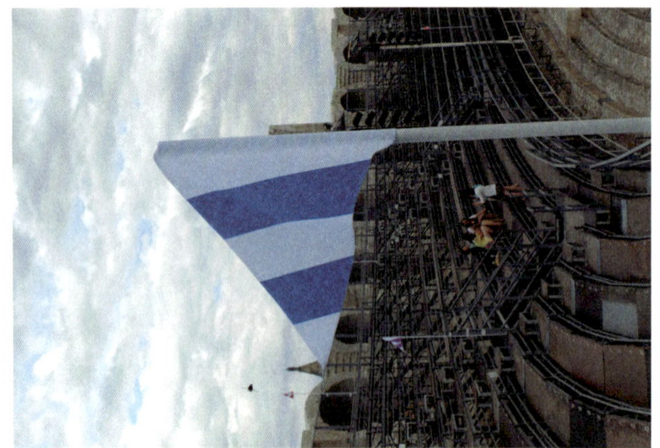

7/5/12—5:51:50 PM

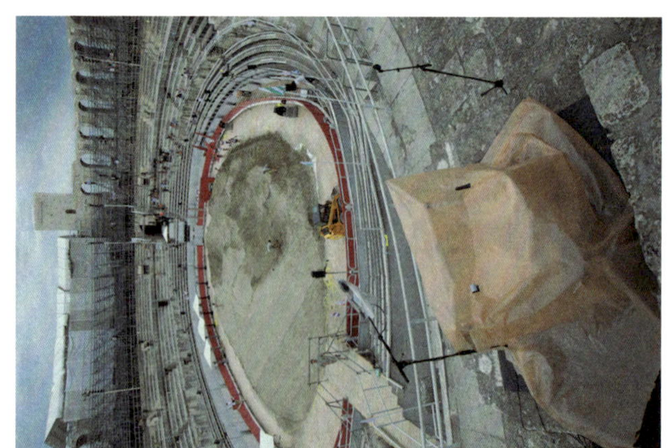

7/5/12—5:52:35 PM

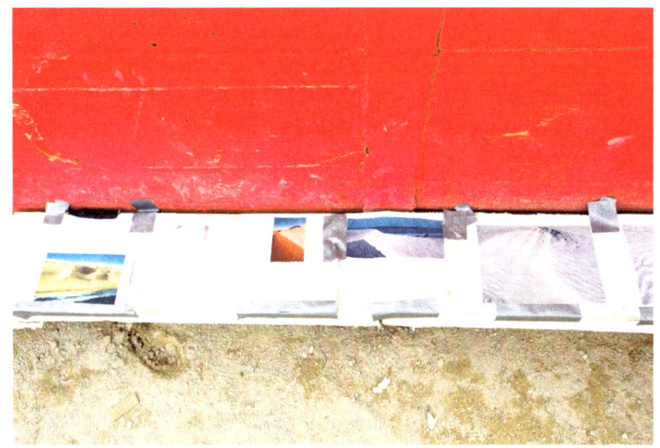

7/5/12—5:53:53 PM

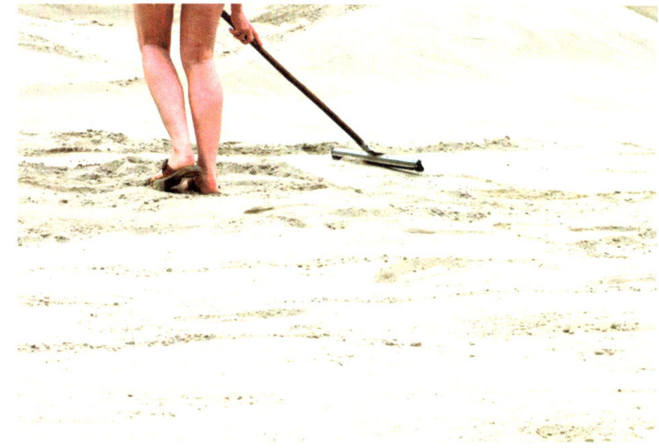

7/5/12—5:54:34 PM

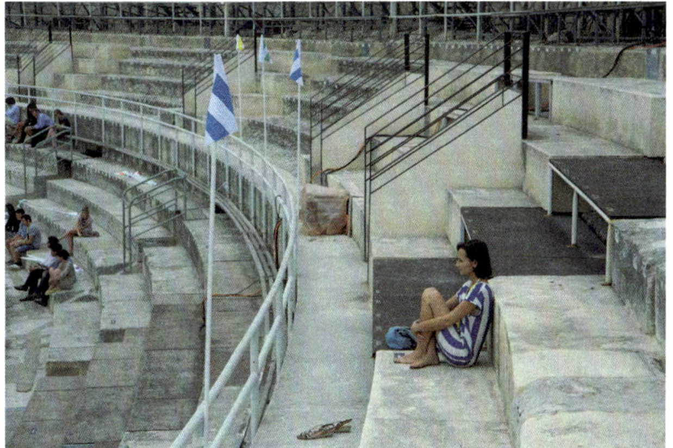

7/5/12—5:54:57 PM

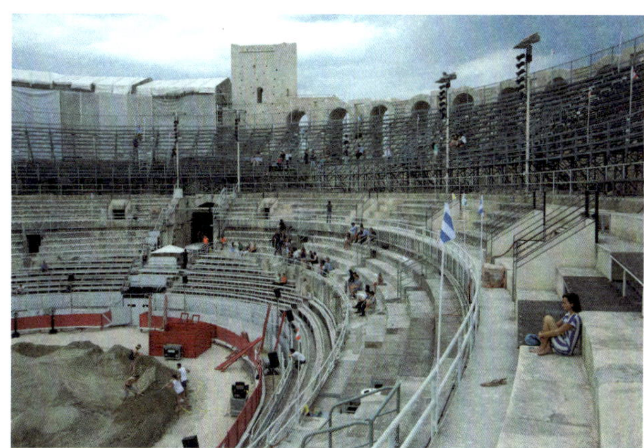

7/5/12—5:55:00 PM

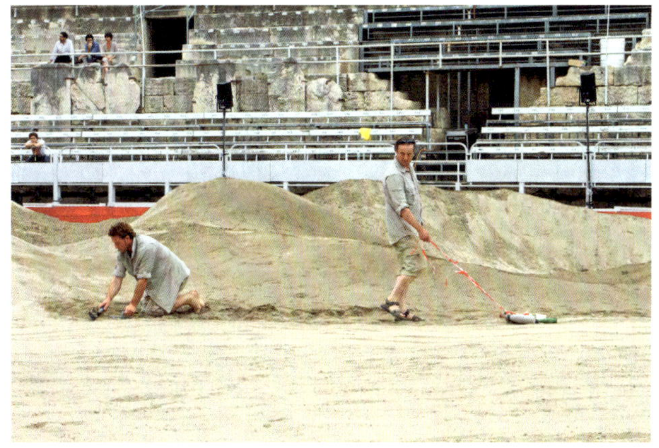

7/5/12—5:58:29 PM

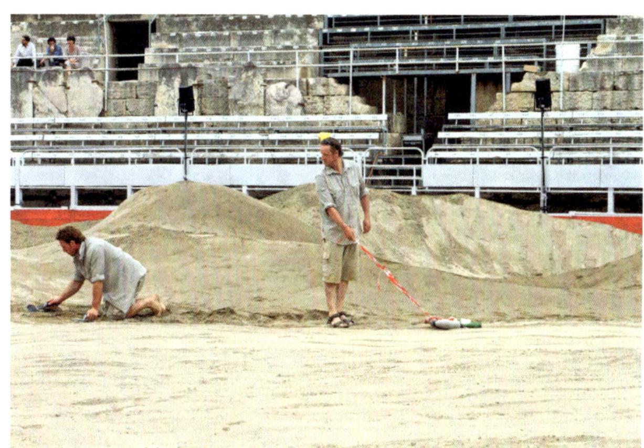

7/5/12—5:58:30 PM

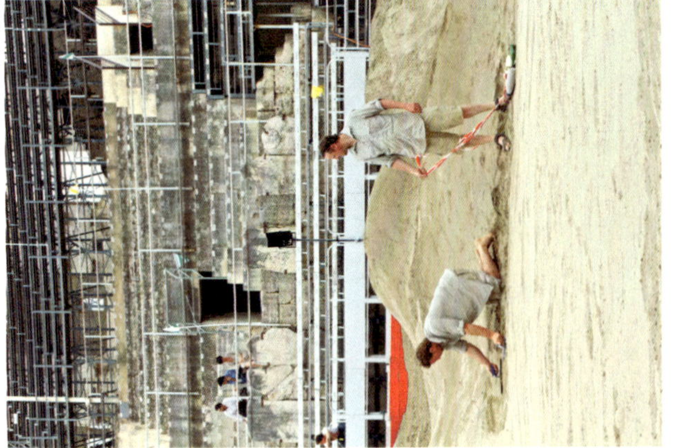
7/5/12—5:58:36 PM

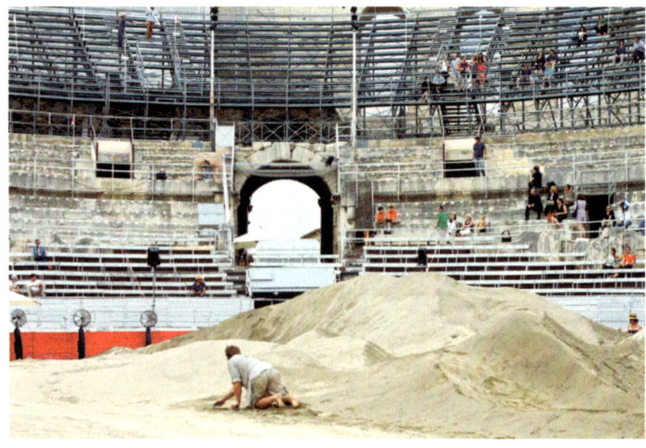
7/5/12—5:59:29 PM

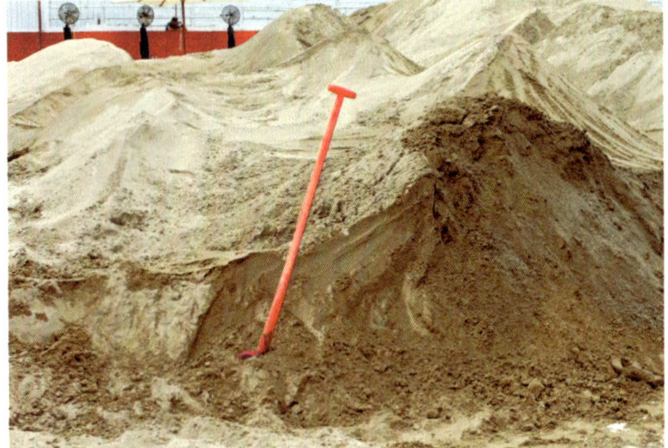
7/5/12—6:00:06 PM

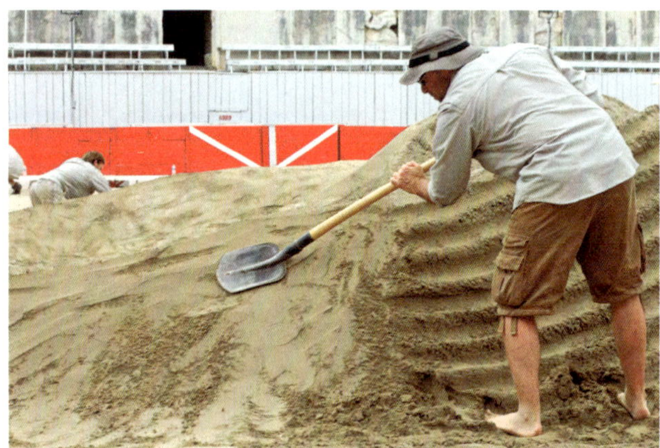
7/5/12—6:00:43 PM

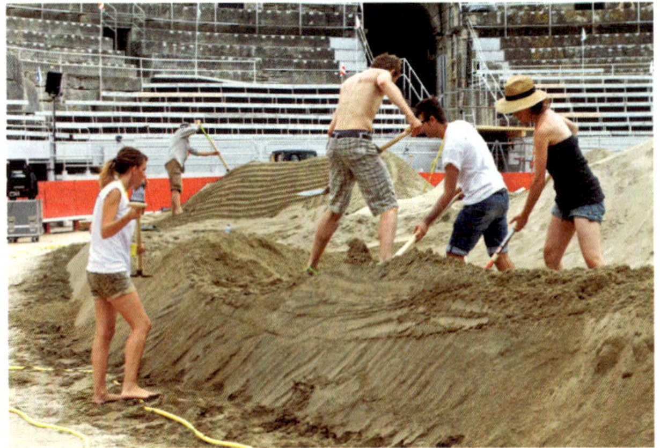
7/5/12—6:01:44 PM

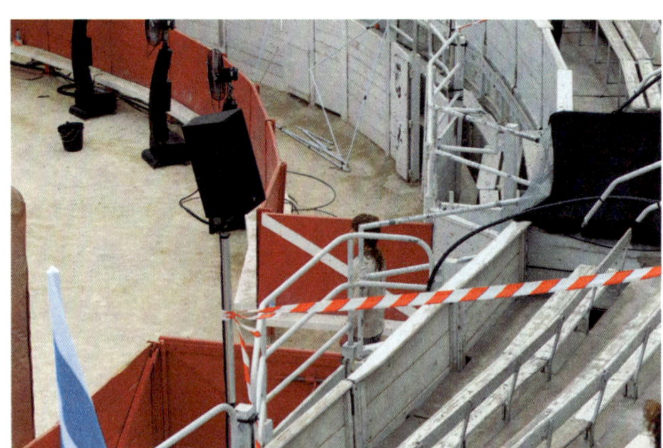
7/5/12—6:01:45 PM

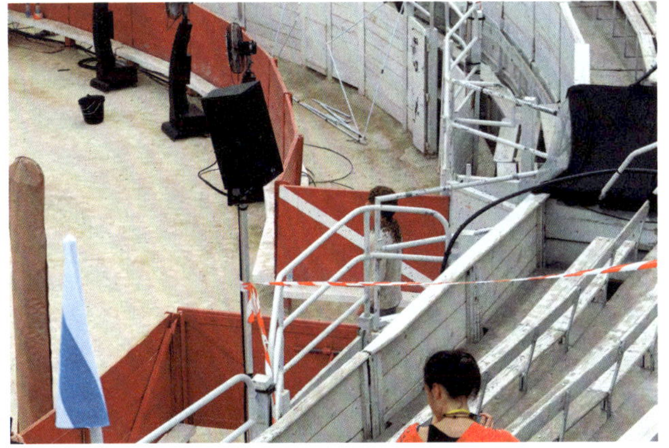
7/5/12—6:02:12 PM

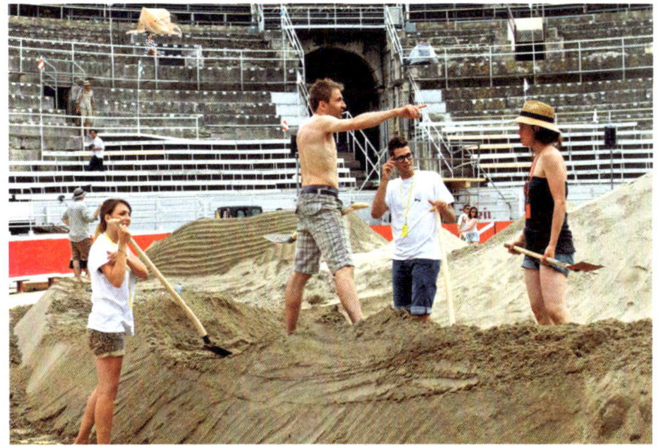
7/5/12—6:02:31 PM

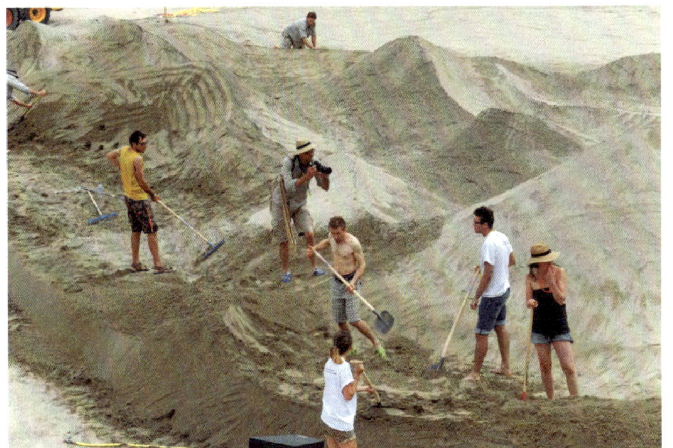
7/5/12—6:03:33 PM

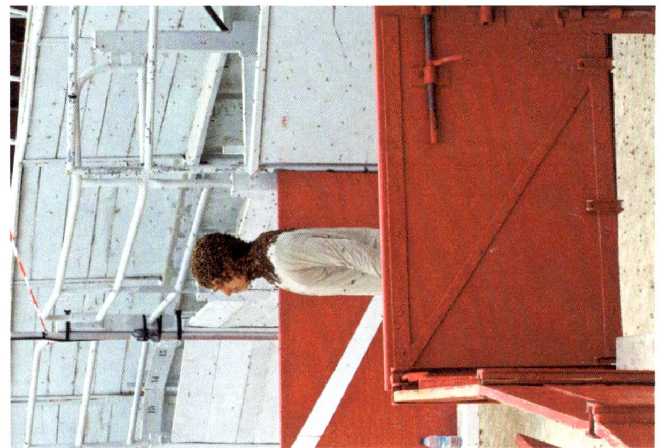
7/5/12—6:06:17 PM

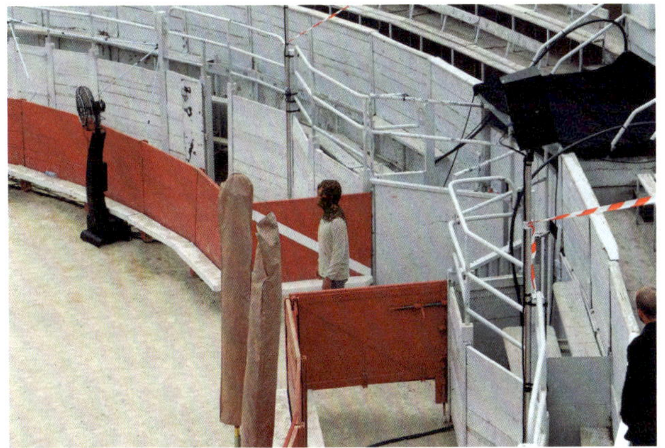
7/5/12—6:06:33 PM

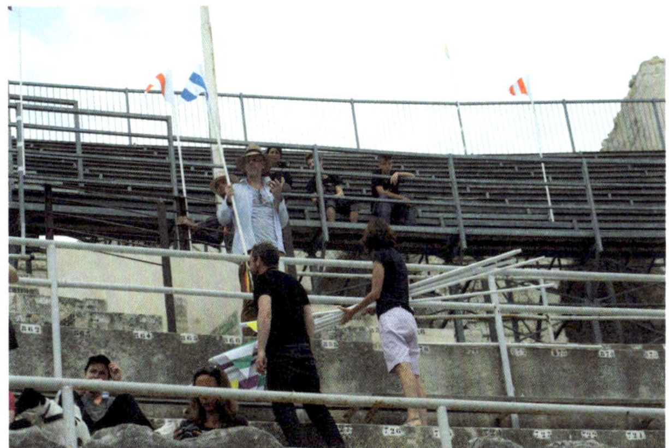
7/5/12—6:06:34 PM

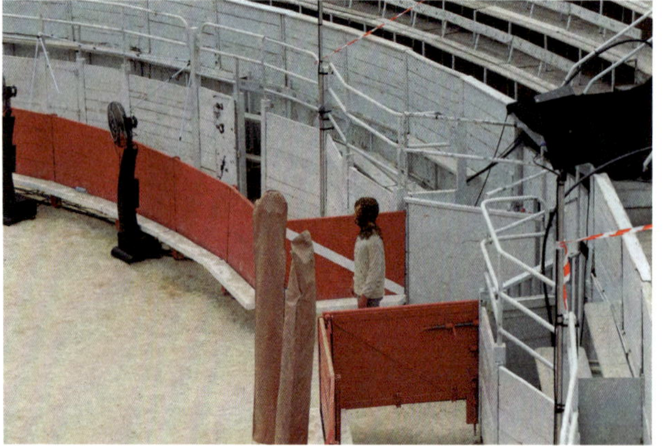
7/5/12—6:06:37 PM

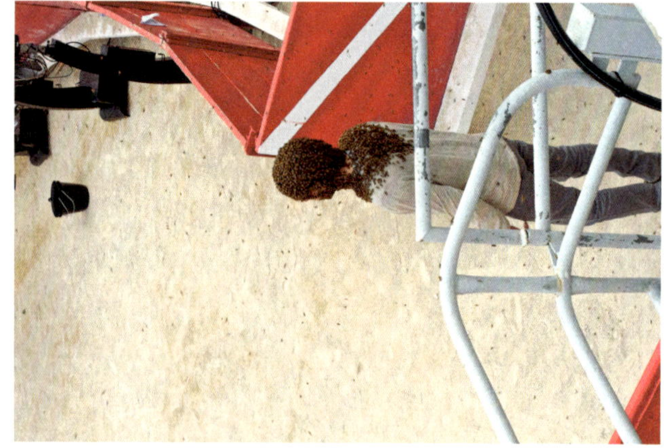
7/5/12—6:06:39 PM

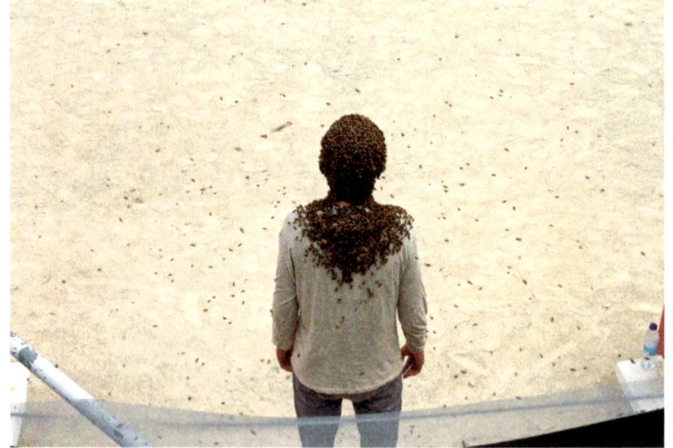
7/5/12—6:07:01 PM

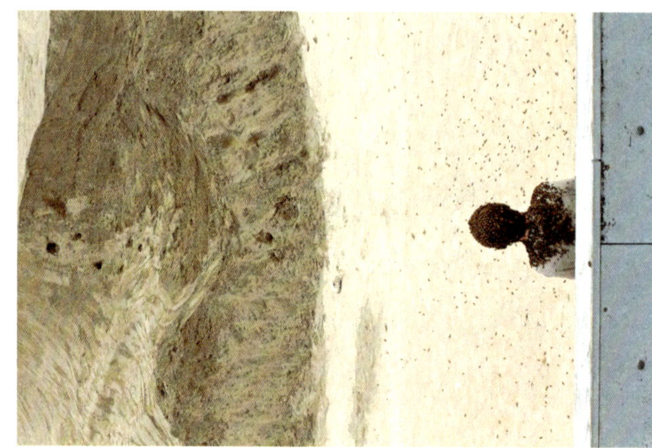
7/5/12—6:08:01 PM

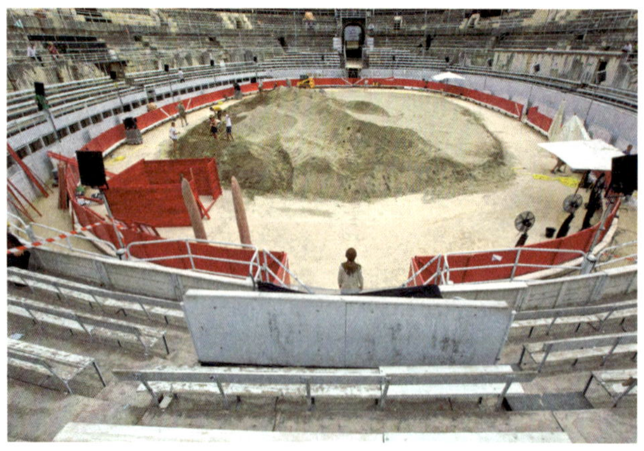
7/5/12—6:08:24 PM

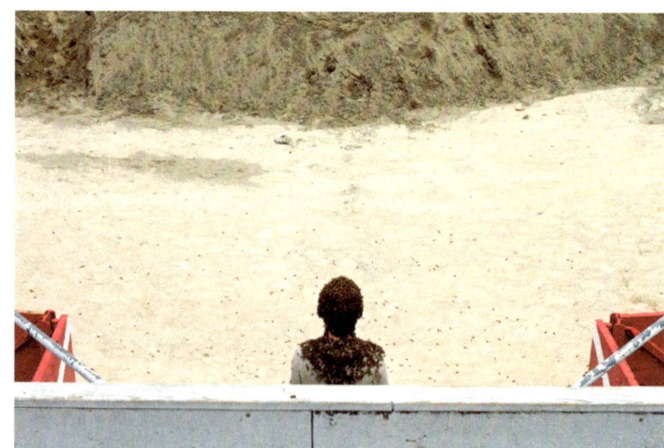
7/5/12—6:08:47 PM

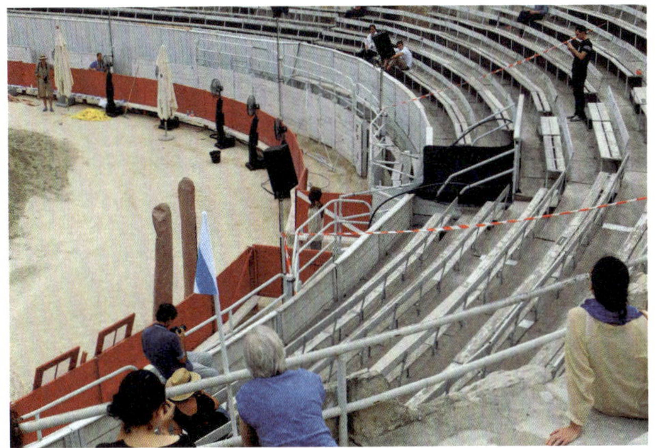
7/5/12—6:09:00 PM

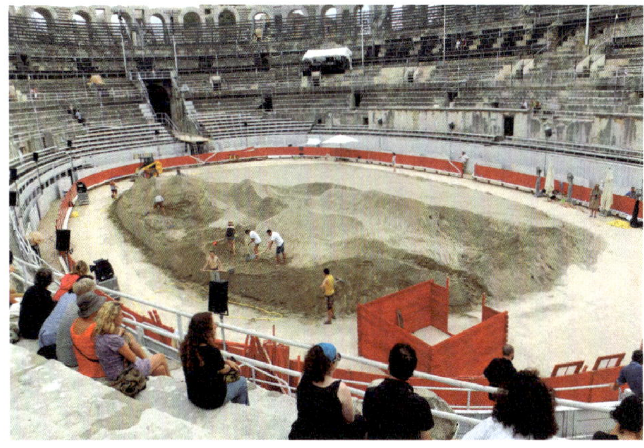
7/5/12—6:09:05 PM

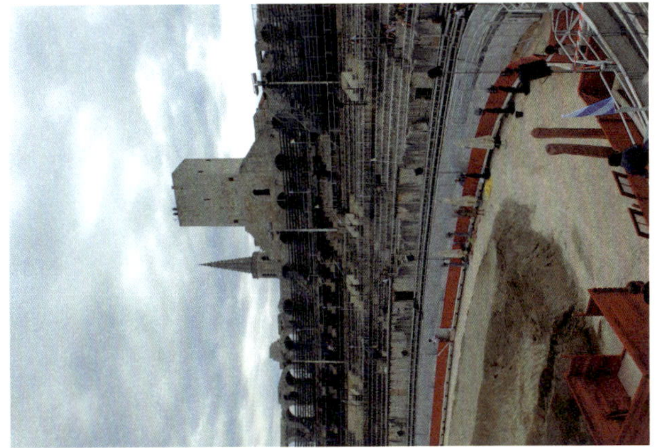
7/5/12—6:09:11 PM

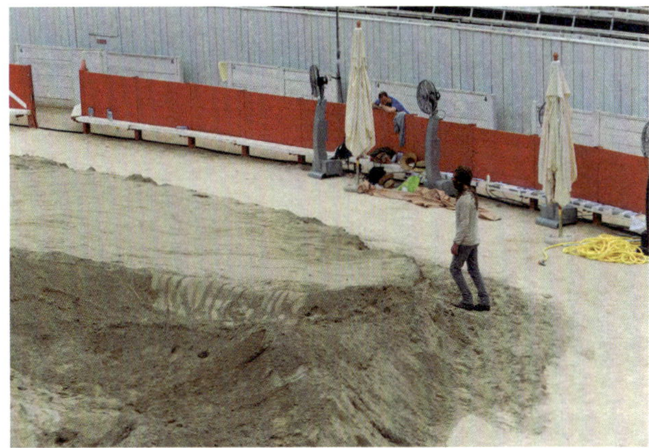
7/5/12—6:11:24 PM

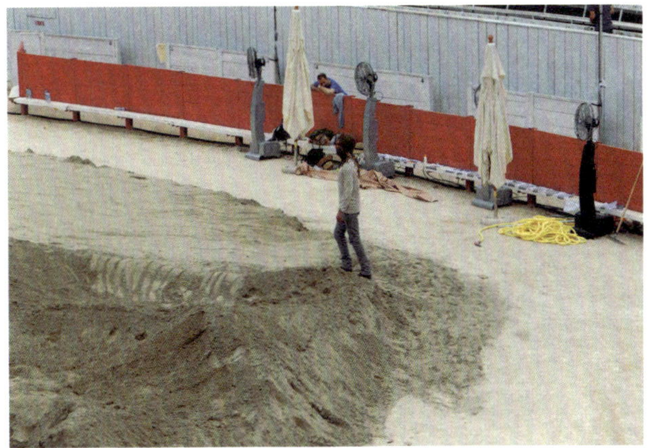
7/5/12—6:11:28 PM

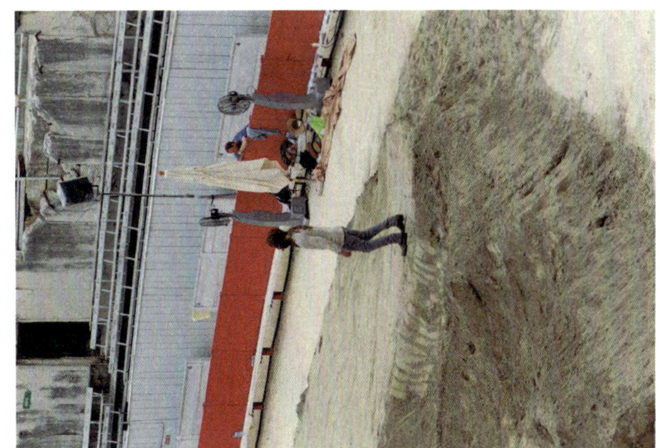
7/5/12—6:11:36 PM

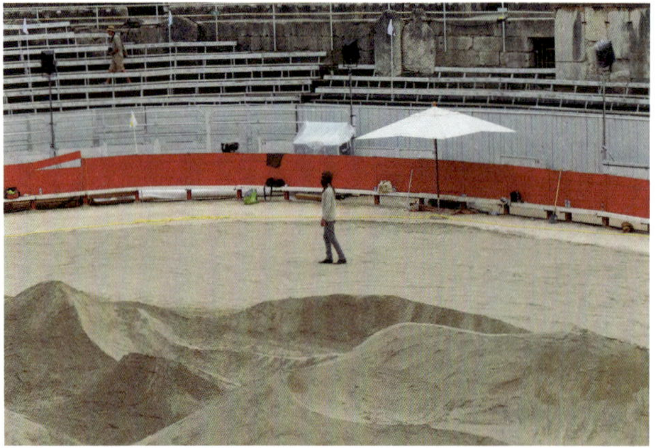

7/5/12—6:13:29 PM

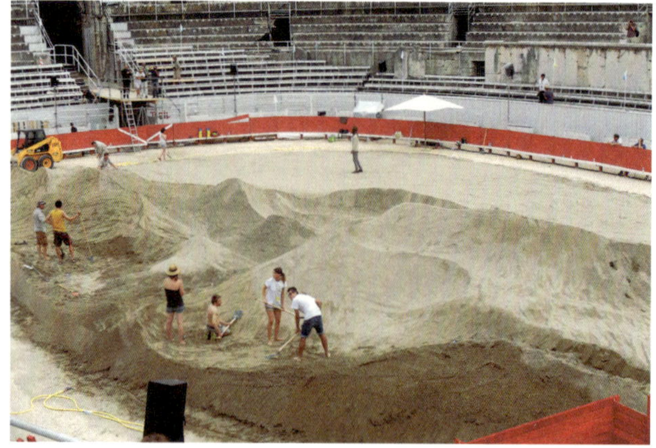

7/5/12—6:13:34 PM

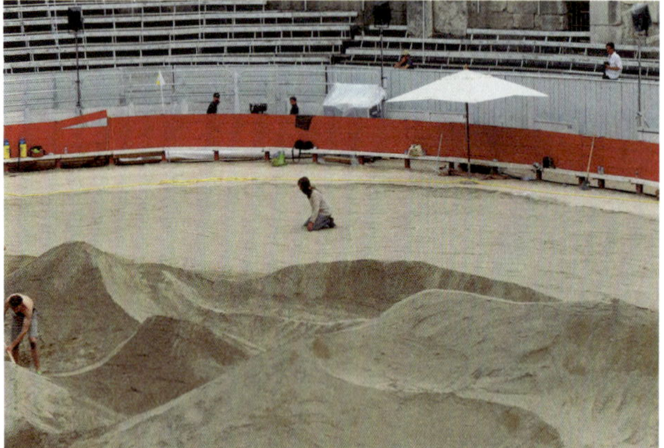

7/5/12—6:14:44 PM

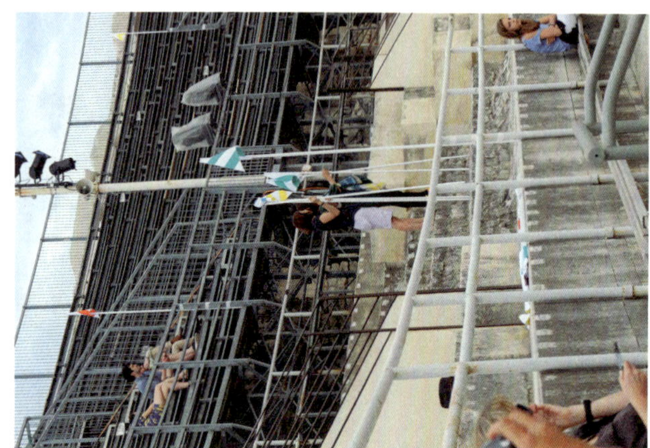

7/5/12—6:15:29 PM

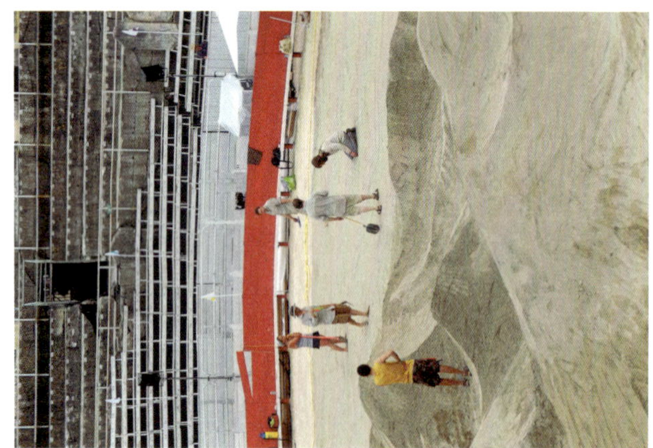

7/5/12—6:15:35 PM

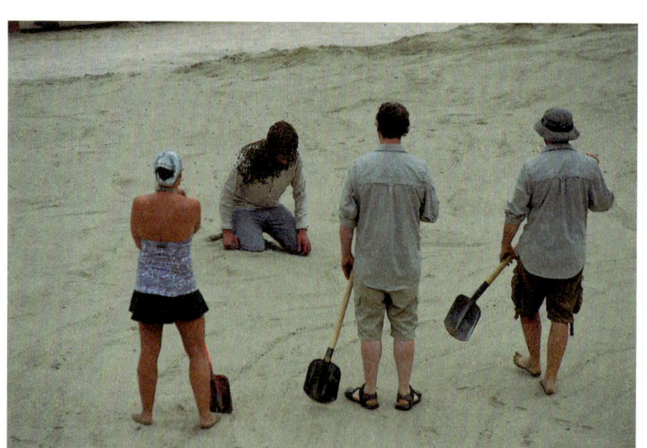

7/5/12—6:15:37 PM

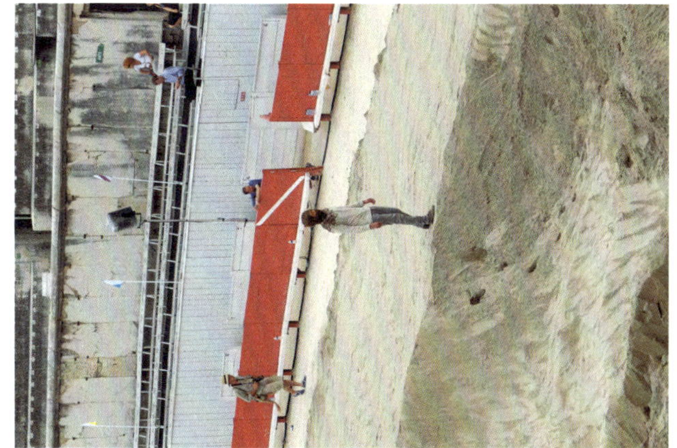

7/5/12—6:18:28 PM

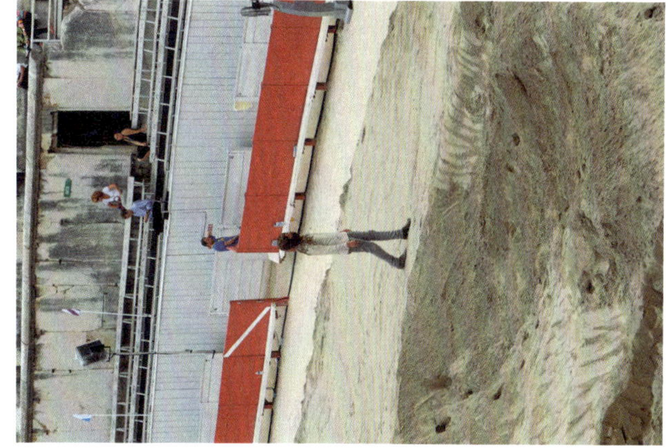

7/5/12—6:18:37 PM

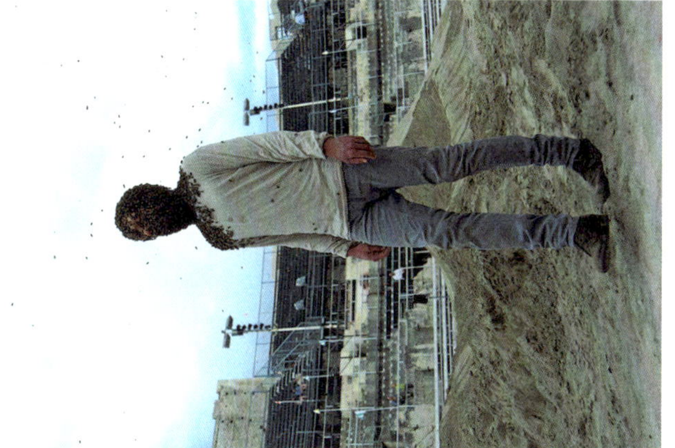

7/5/12—6:19:24 PM

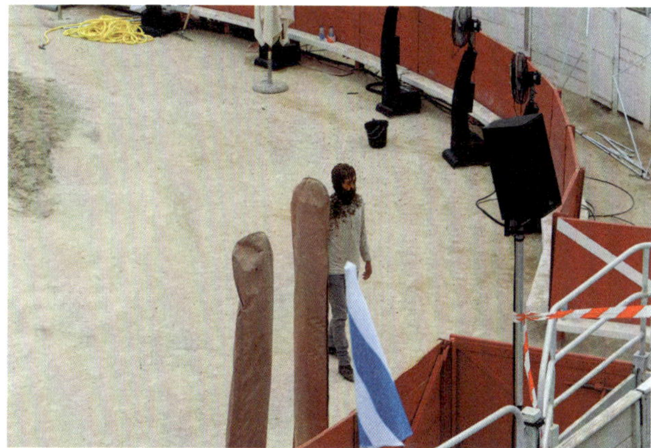

7/5/12—6:19:32 PM

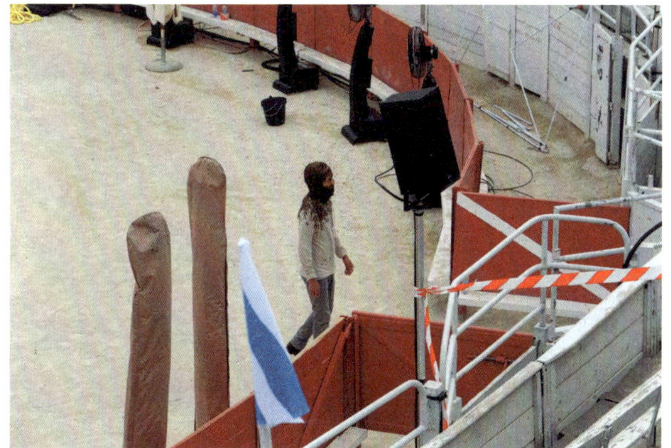

7/5/12—6:19:35 PM

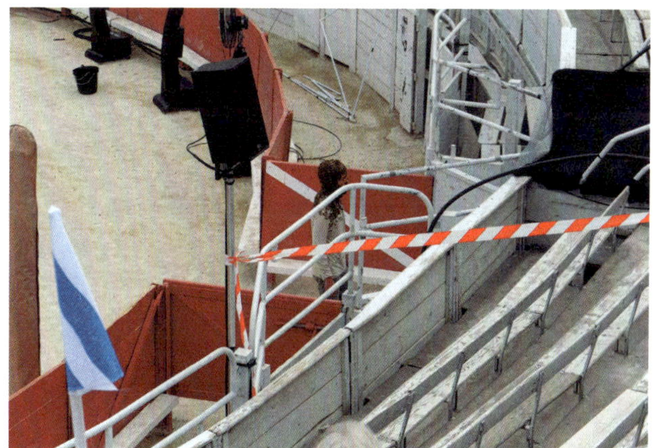

7/5/12—6:19:41 PM

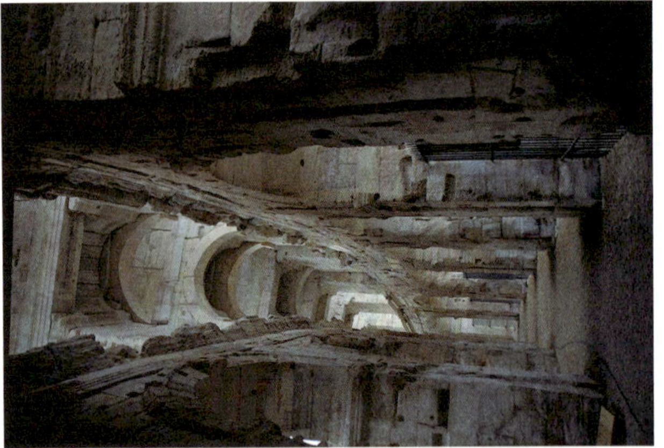

7/5/12—6:28:54 PM

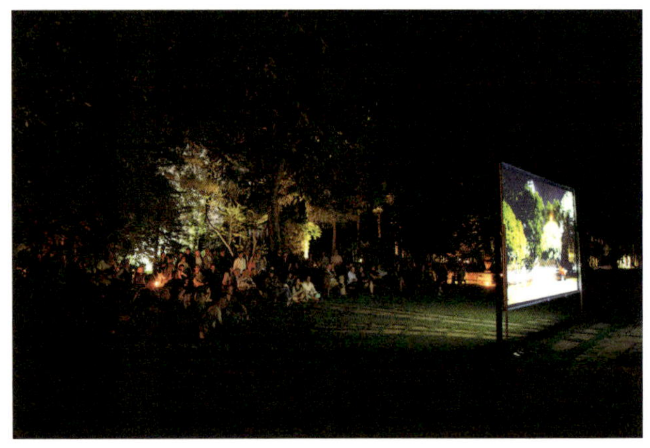

7/5/12—10:30:27 PM

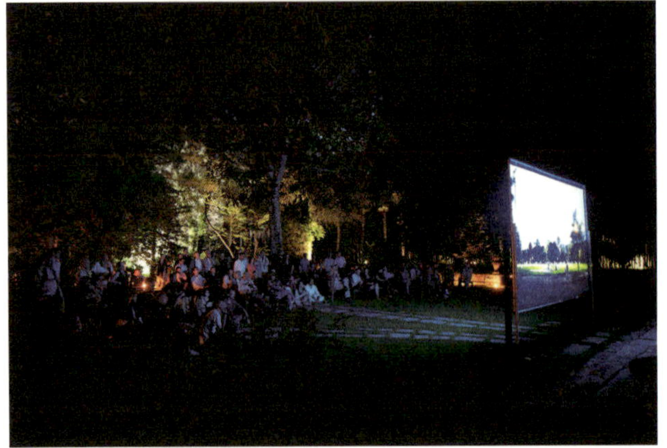

7/5/12—10:30:51 PM

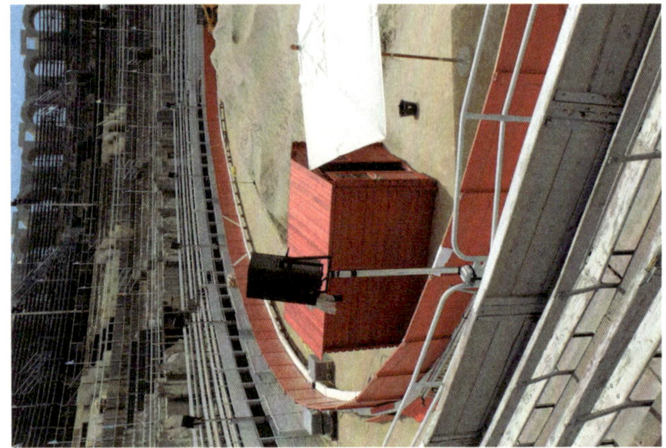

7/6/12—7:06:34 AM

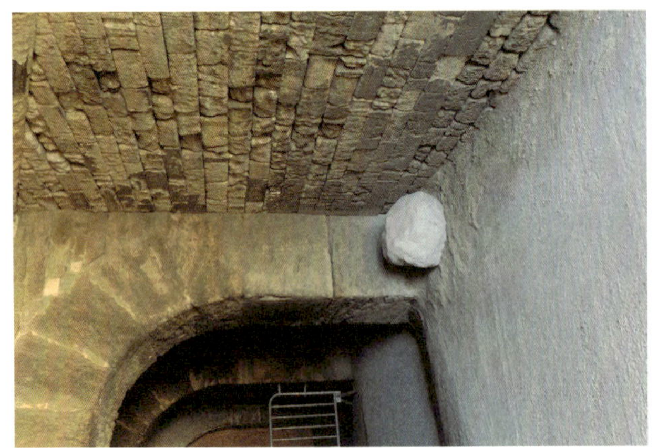

7/6/12—7:07:45 AM

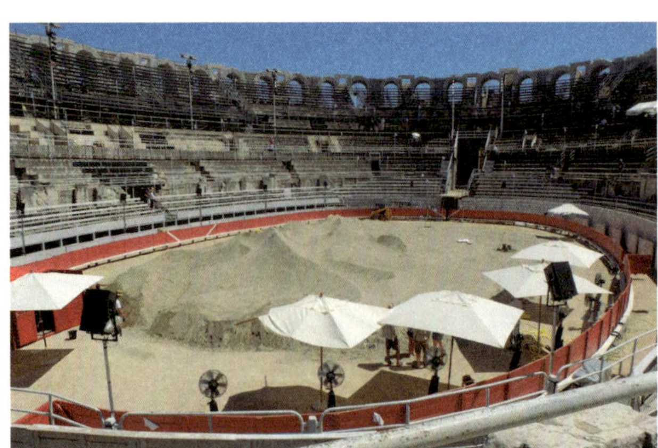

7/6/12—7:08:46 AM

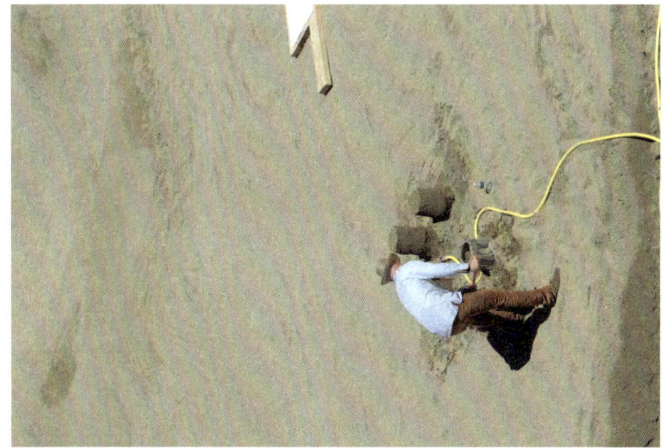

7/6/12—7:10:59 AM

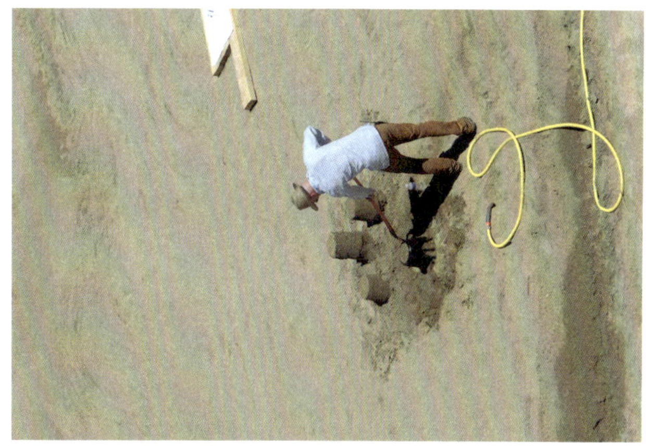

7/6/12—7:11:45 AM

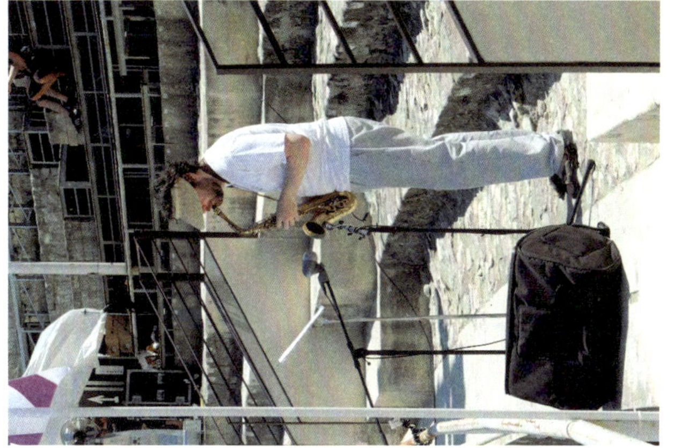

7/6/12—7:12:07 AM

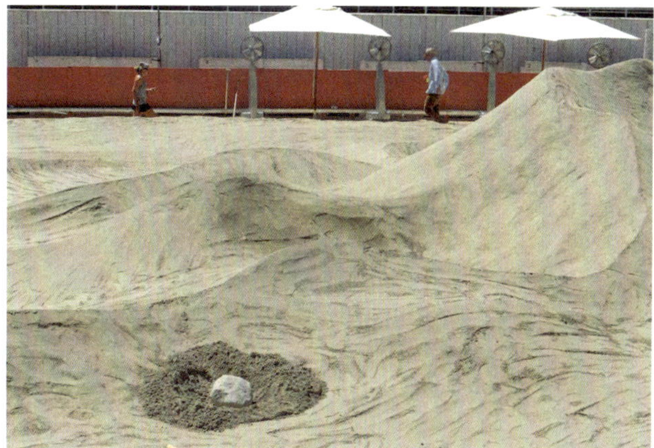

7/6/12—7:17:44 AM

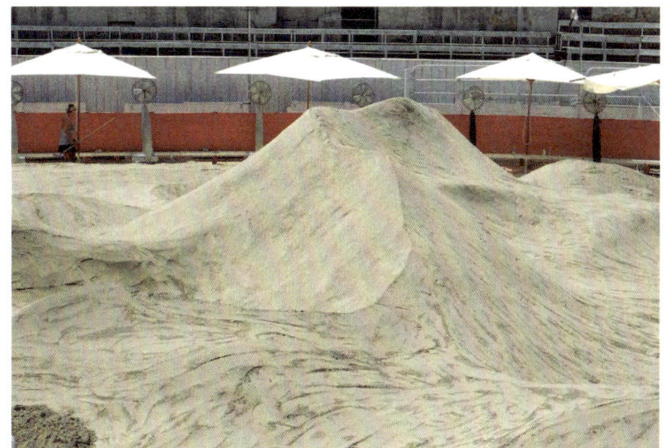

7/6/12—7:17:47 AM

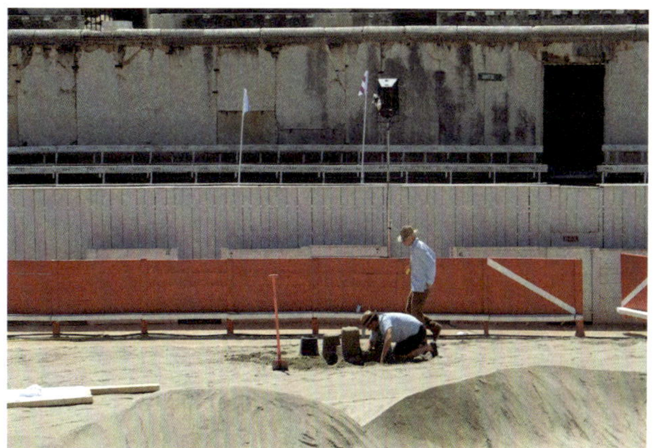

7/6/12—7:17:54 AM

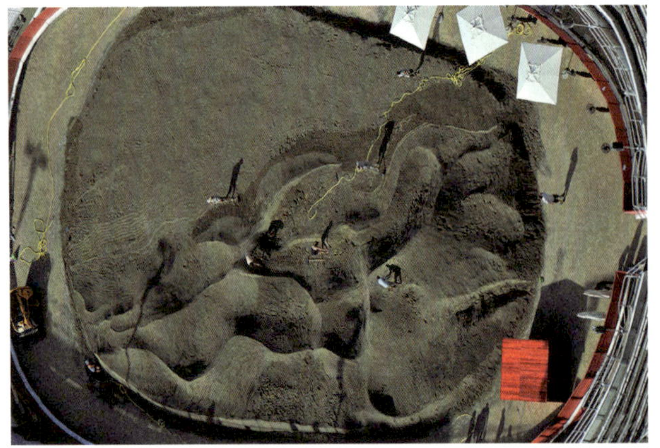

7/6/12—7:25:24 AM

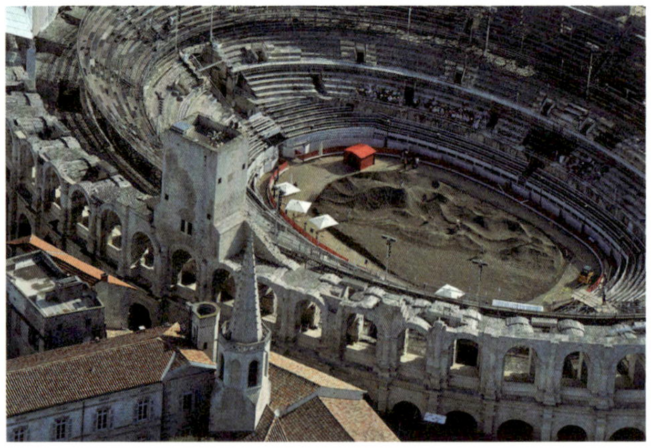

7/6/12—7:25:46 AM

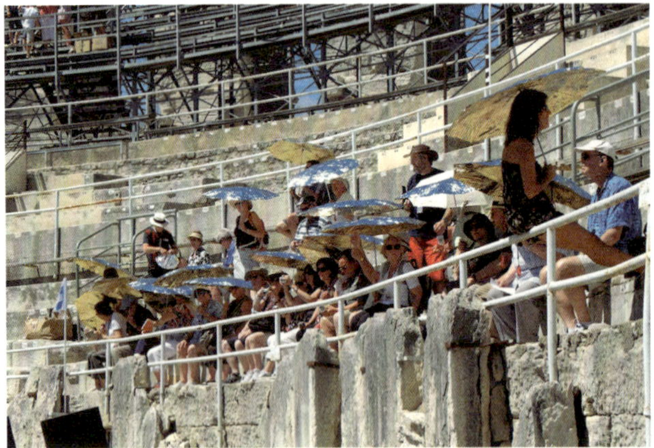

7/6/12—7:27:31 AM

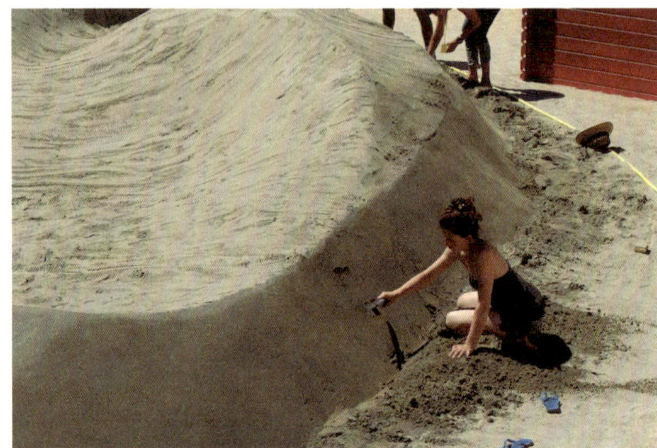

7/6/12—7:27:39 AM

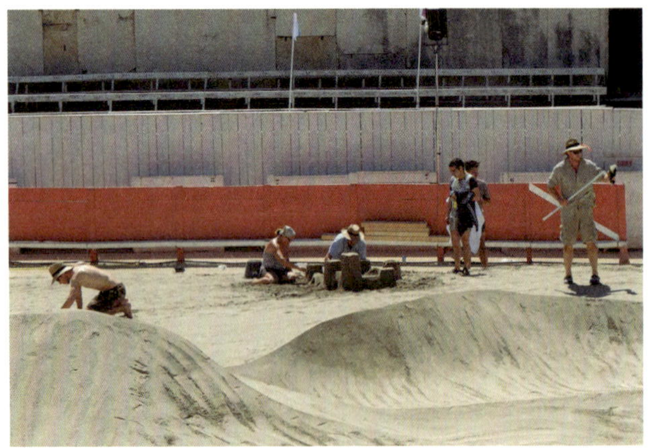

7/6/12—7:27:41 AM

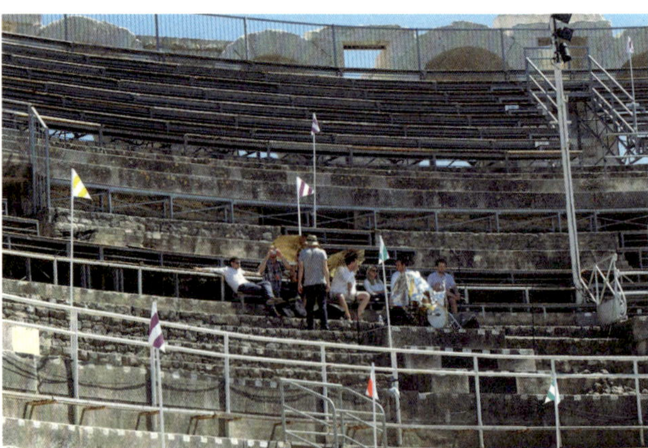

7/6/12—7:28:29 AM

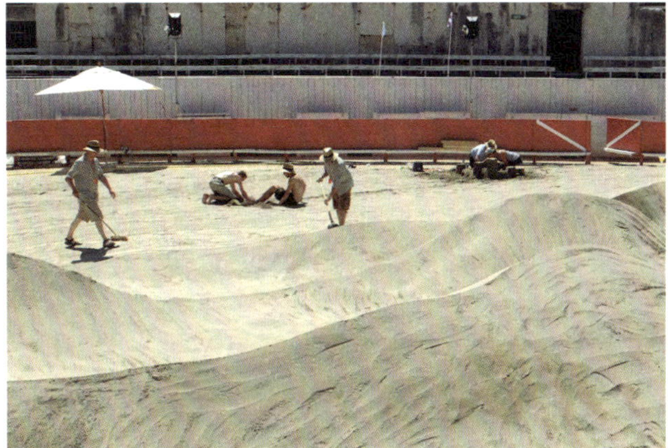

7/6/12—7:28:42 AM

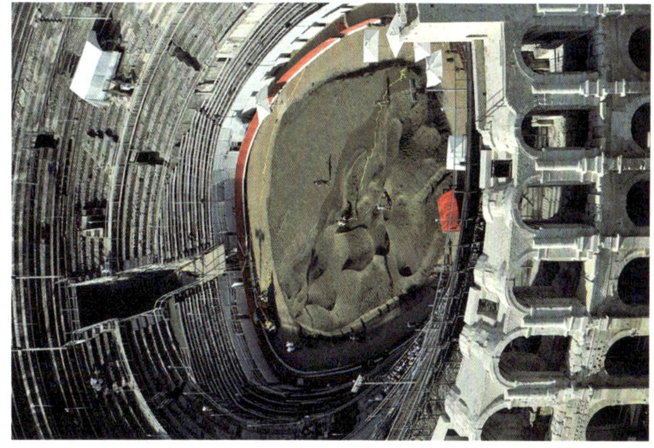

7/6/12—7:29:01 AM

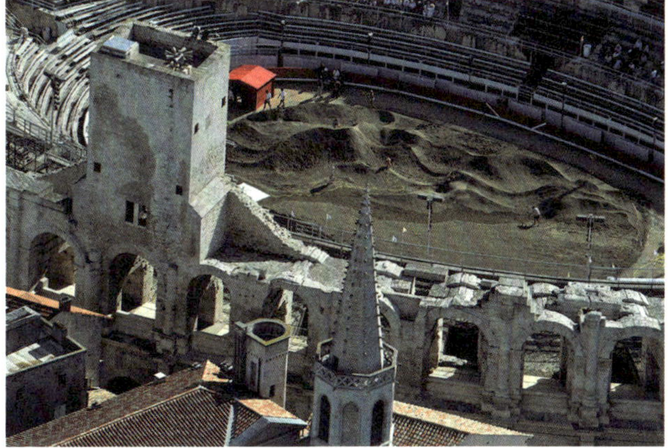

6/7/12—7:29:32 AM

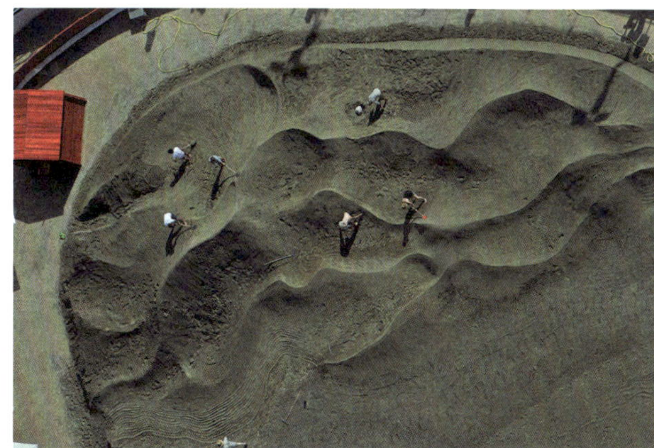

7/6/12—7:34:40 AM

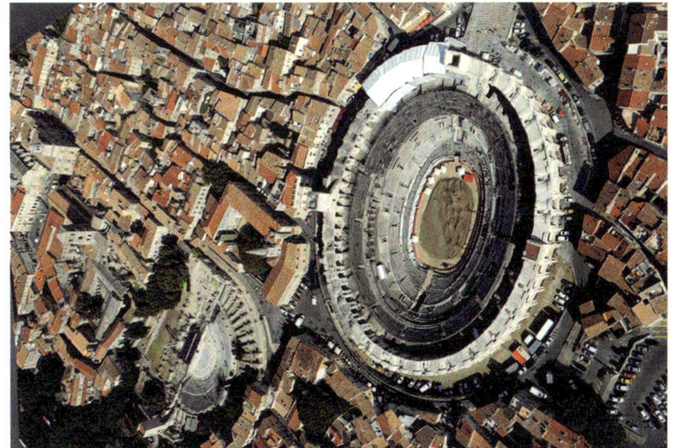

7/6/12—7:35:32 AM

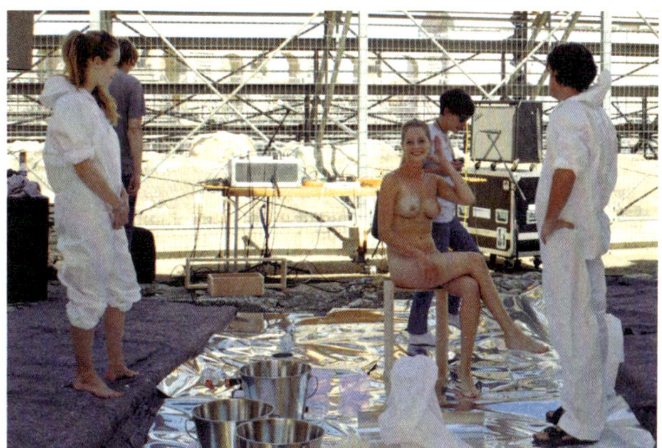

7/6/12—7:37:13 AM

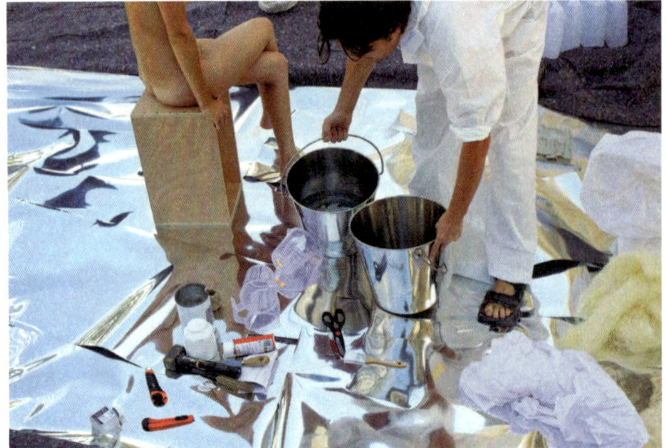

7/6/12—7:39:14 AM

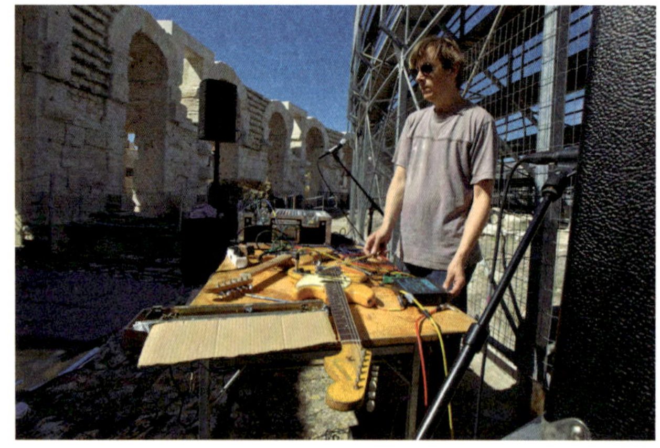

7/6/12—7:41:00 AM

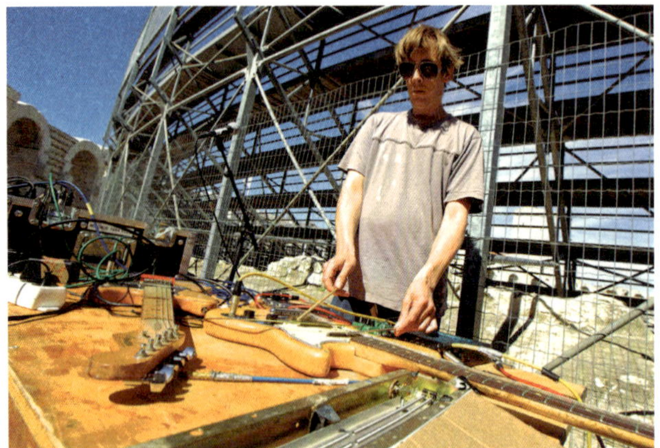

7/6/12—7:41:13 AM

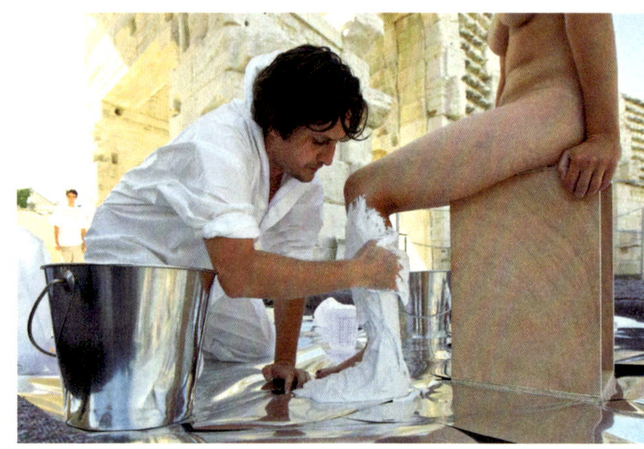

7/6/12—7:41:36 AM

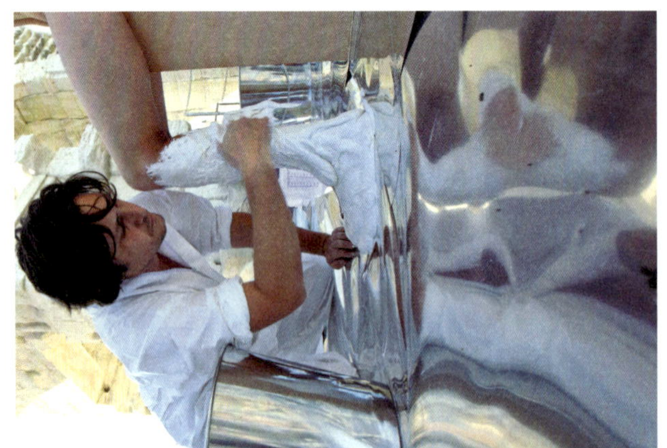

7/6/12—7:41:46 AM

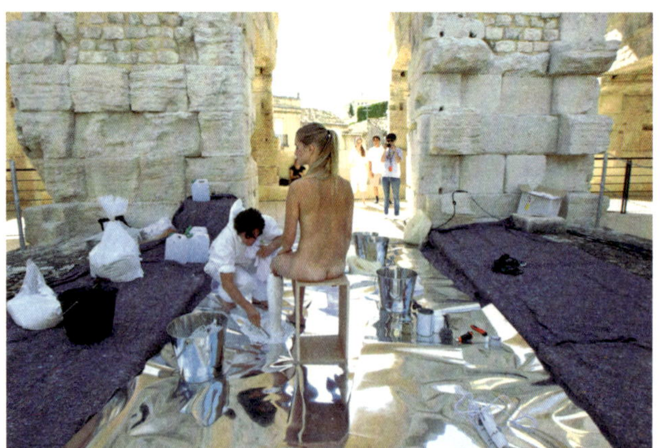

7/6/12—7:46:24 AM

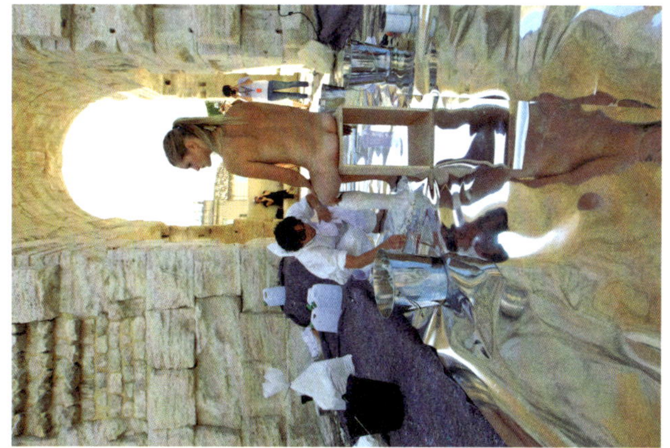
7/6/12—7:46:30 AM

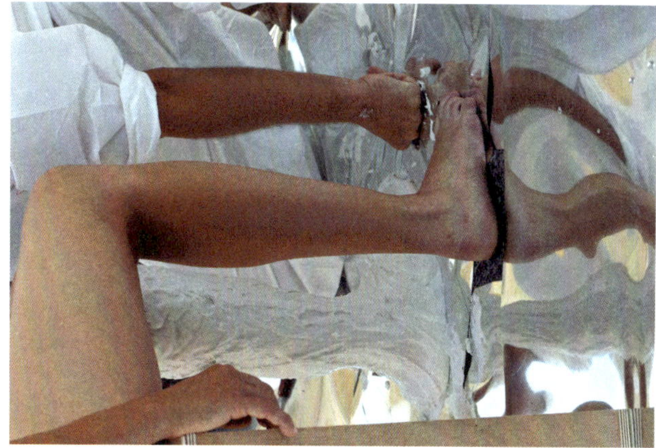
7/6/12—7:46:58 AM

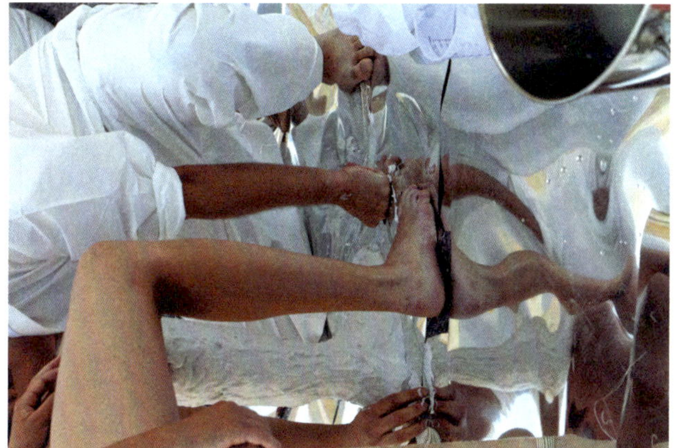
7/6/12—7:47:01 AM

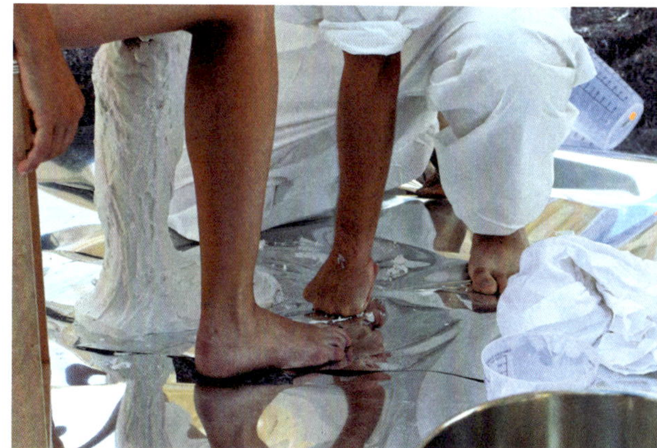
7/6/12—7:47:06 AM

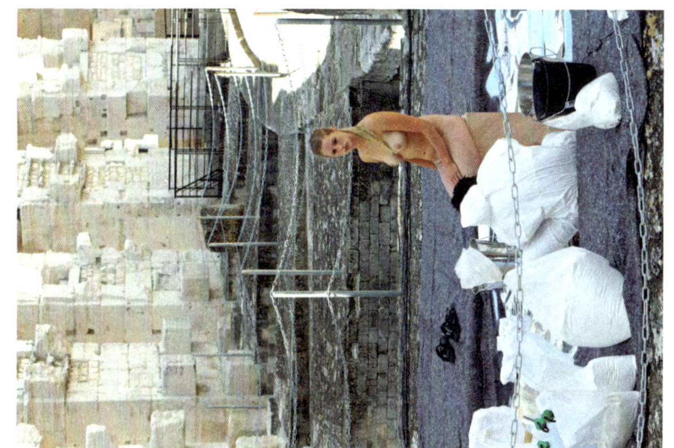
7/6/12—7:49:49 AM

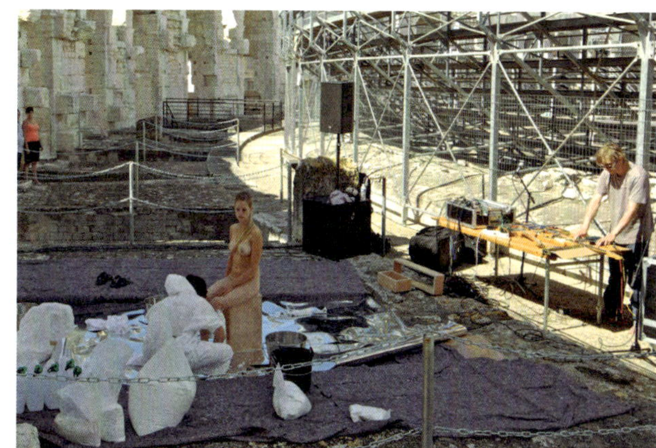
7/6/12—7:50:15 AM

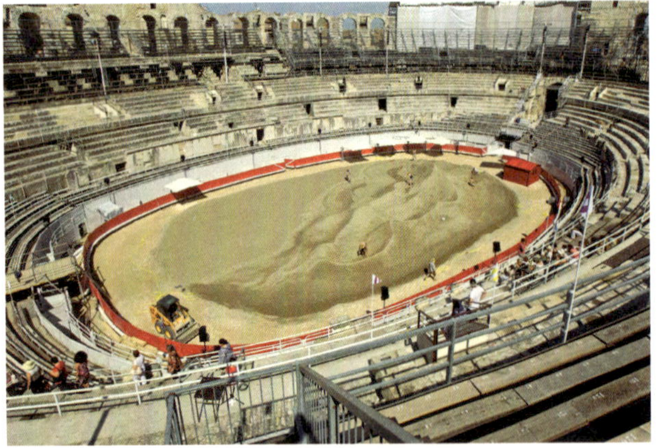

7/6/12—7:54:16 AM

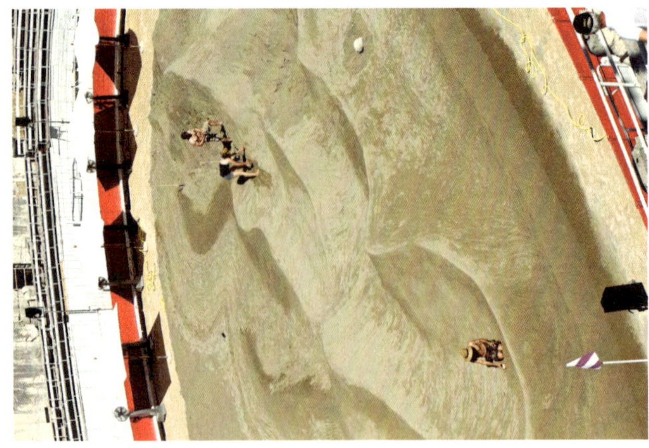

7/6/12—7:54:28 AM

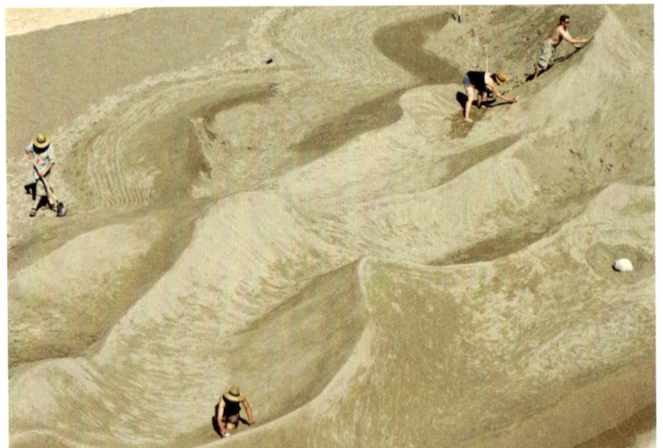

7/6/12—7:54:32 AM

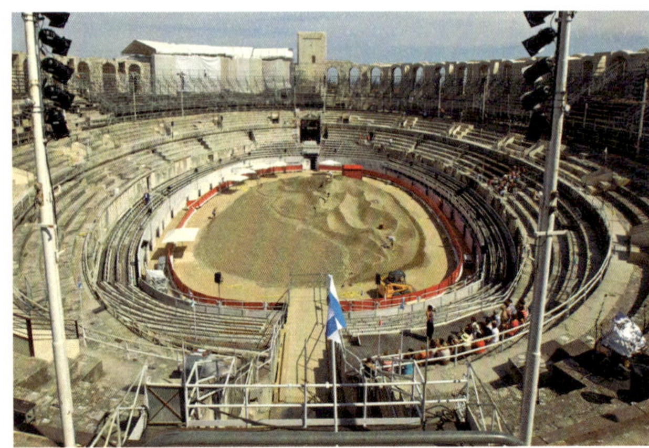

7/6/12—7:57:56 AM

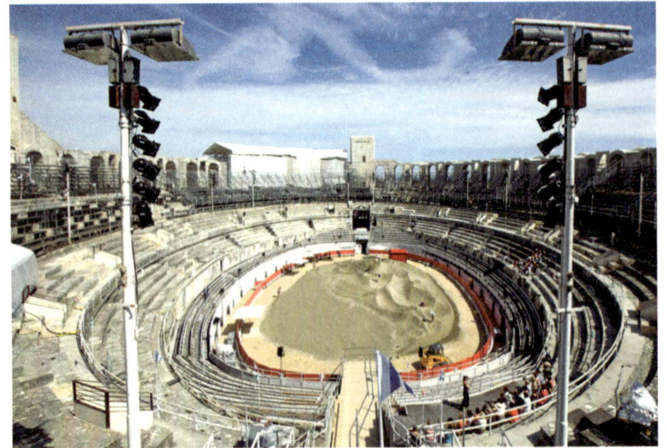

7/6/12—7:58:03 AM

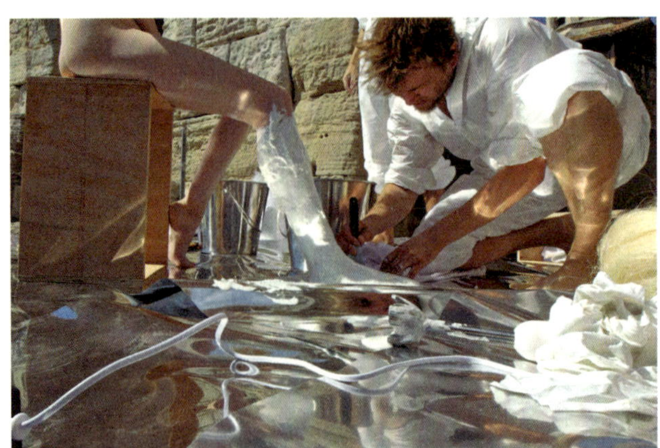

7/6/12—8:00:50 AM

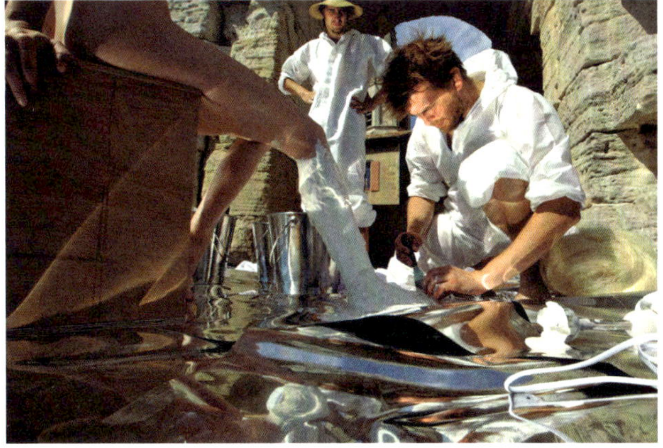

7/6/12—8:01:07 AM

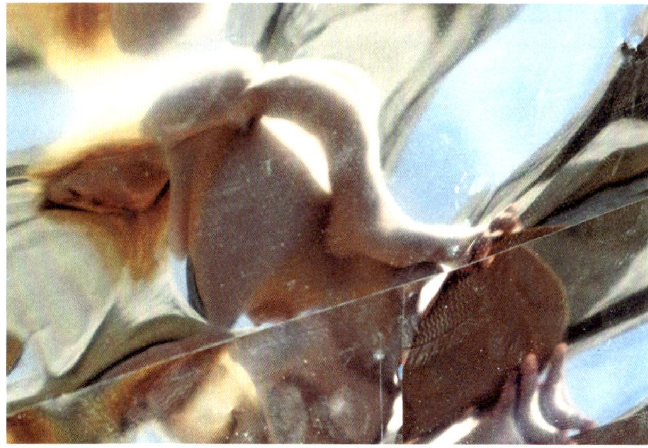

7/6/12—8:01:11 AM

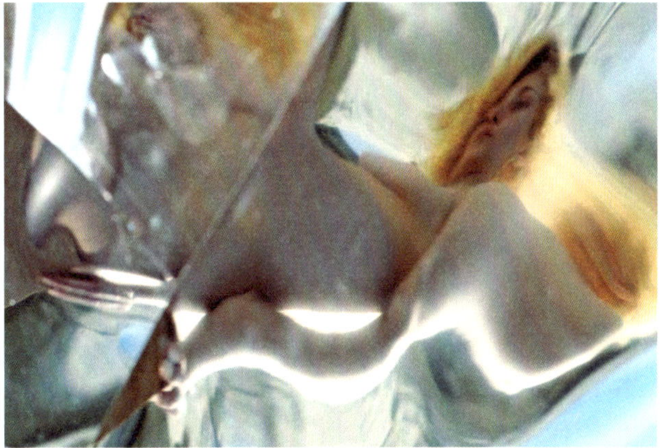

7/6/12—8:01:26 AM

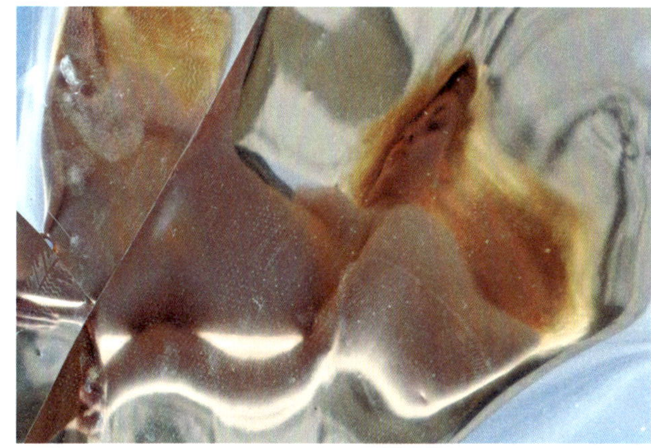

7/6/12—8:01:27 AM

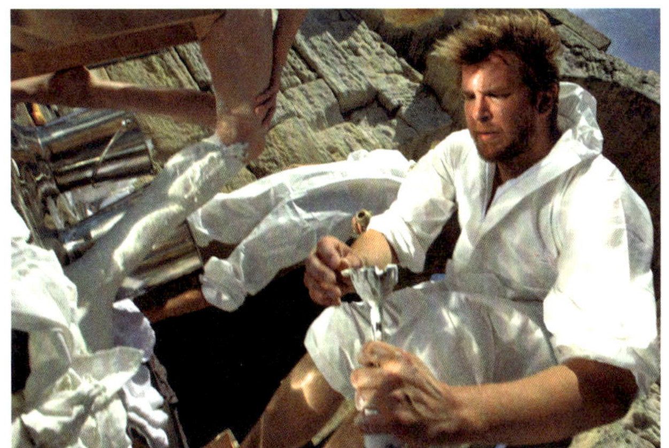

7/6/12—8:02:08 AM

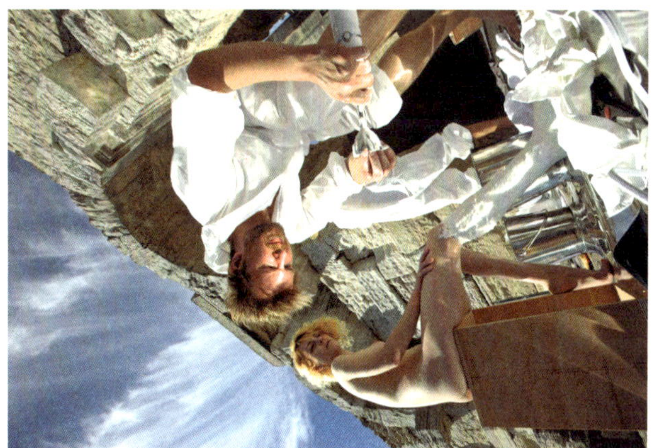

7/6/12—8:02:08 AM

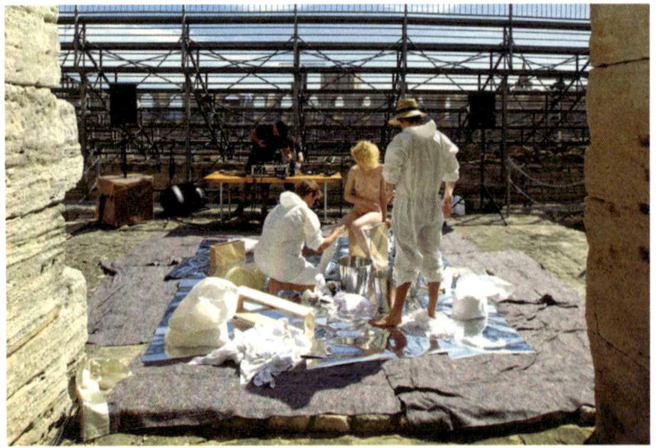

7/6/12—8:03:14 AM

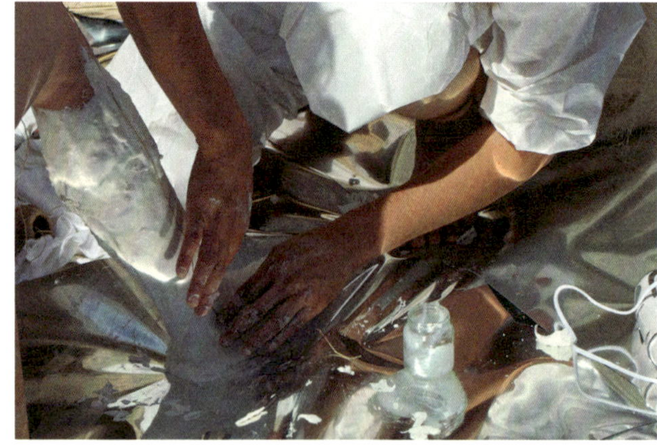

7/6/12—8:03:58 AM

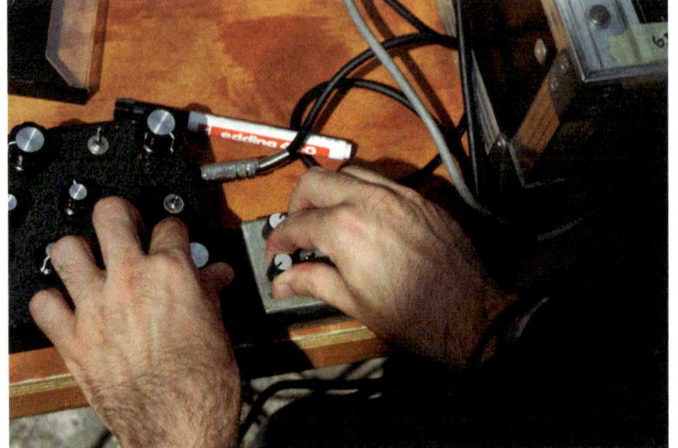

7/6/12—8:04:16 AM

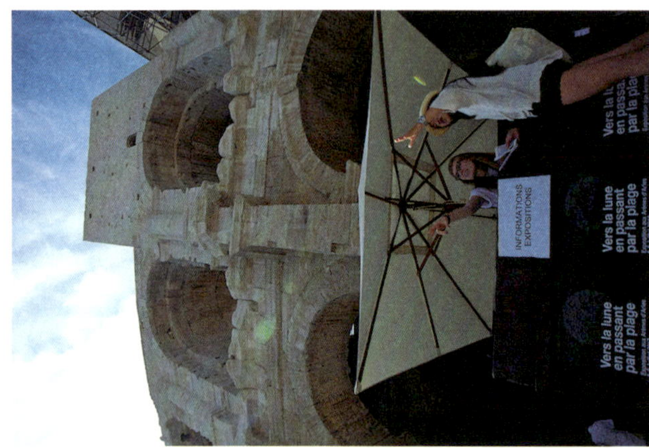

7/6/12—8:06:35 AM

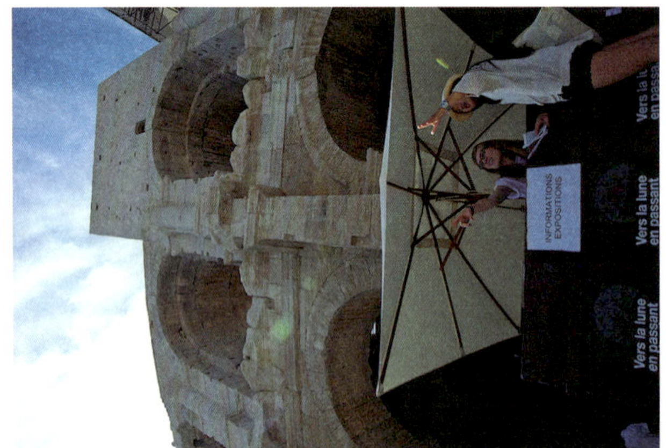

7/6/12—8:06:36 AM

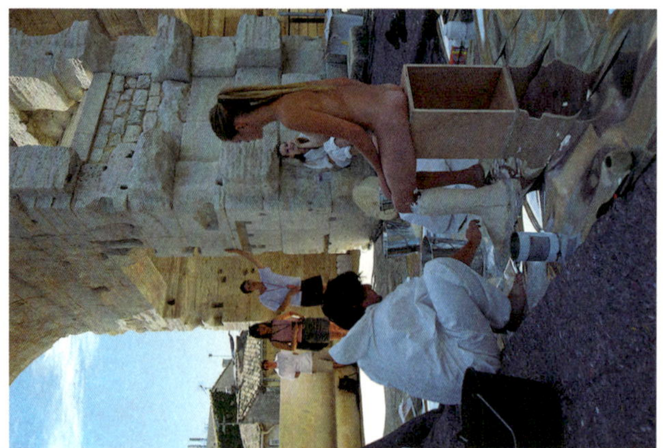

7/6/12—8:16:36 AM

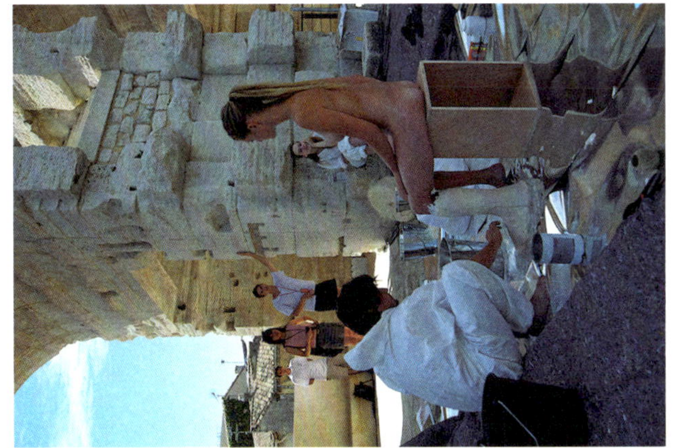
7/6/12—8:16:37 AM

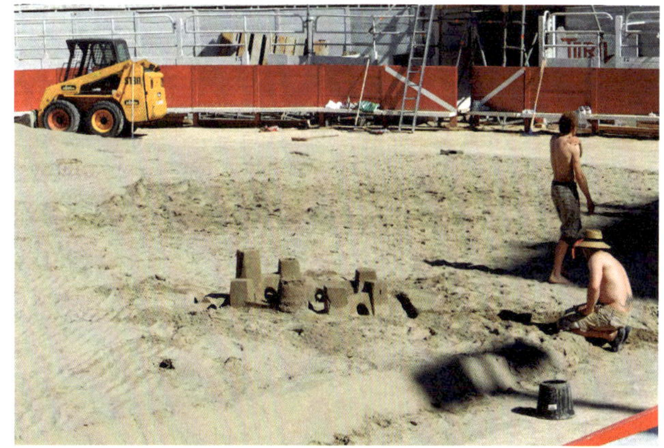
7/6/12—8:17:13 AM

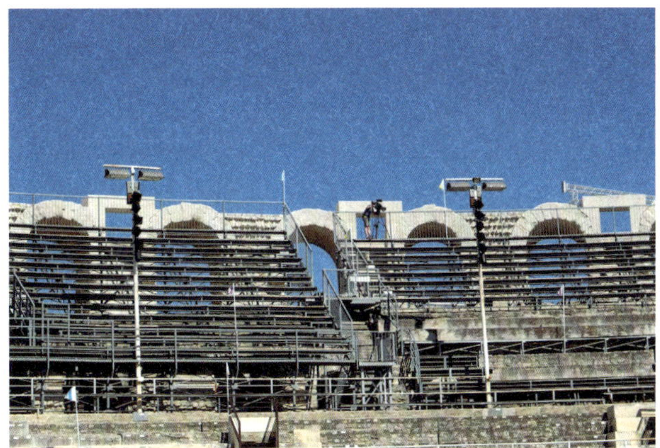
7/6/12—8:17:36 AM

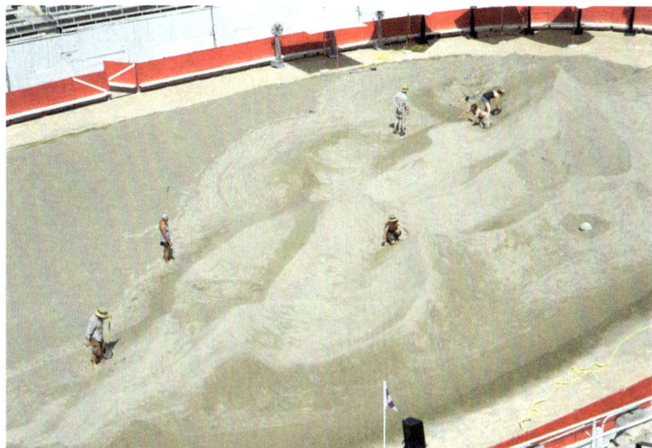
7/6/12—8:18:05 AM

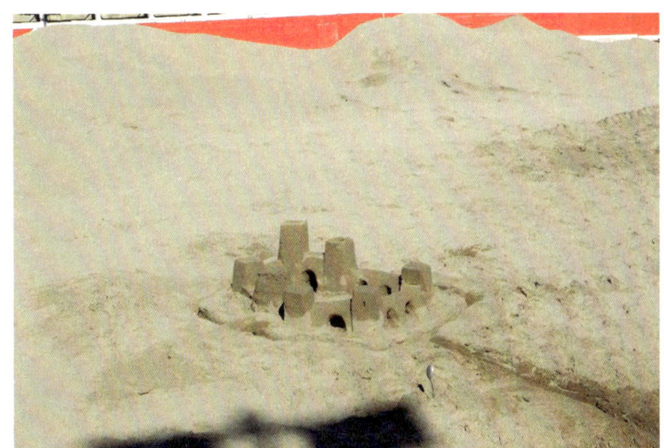
7/6/12—8:18:47 AM

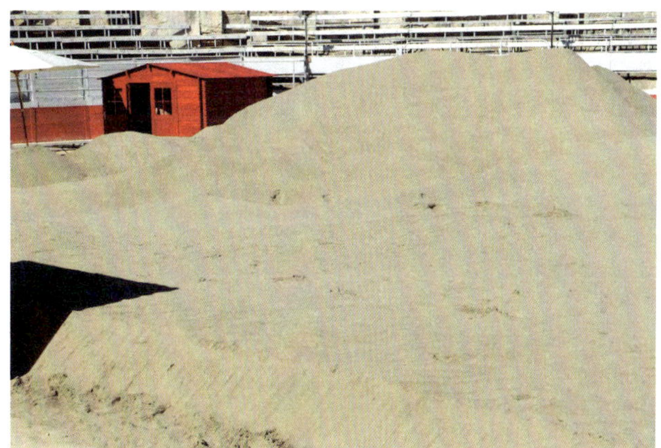
7/6/12—8:18:54 AM

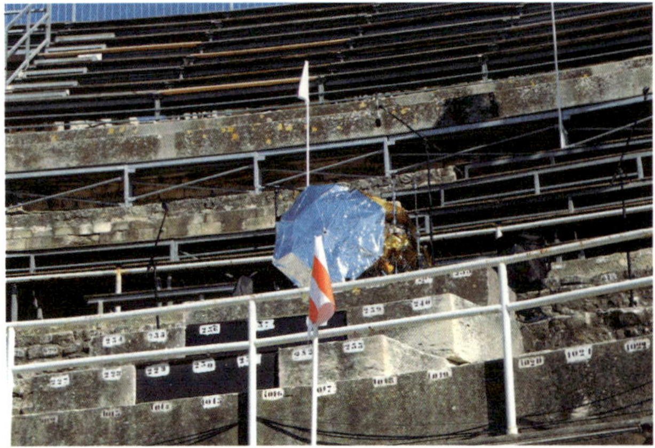

7/6/12—8:19:48 AM

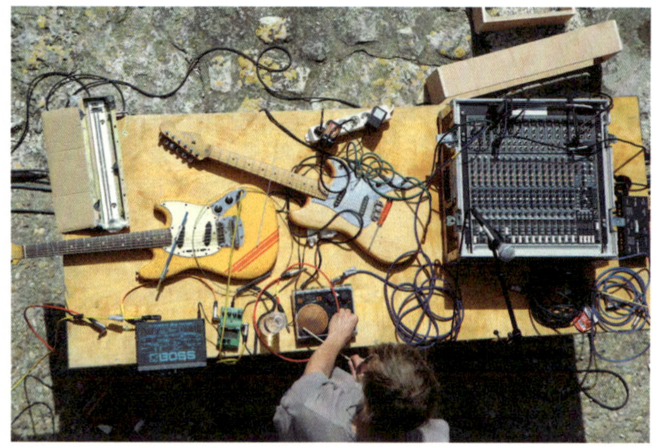

7/6/12—8:21:53 AM

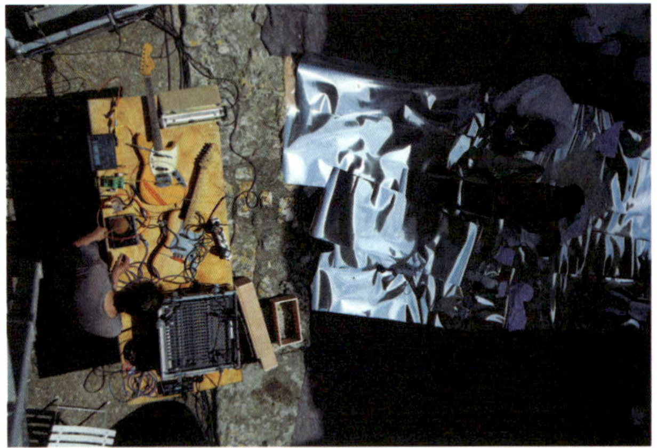

7/6/12—8:21:57 AM

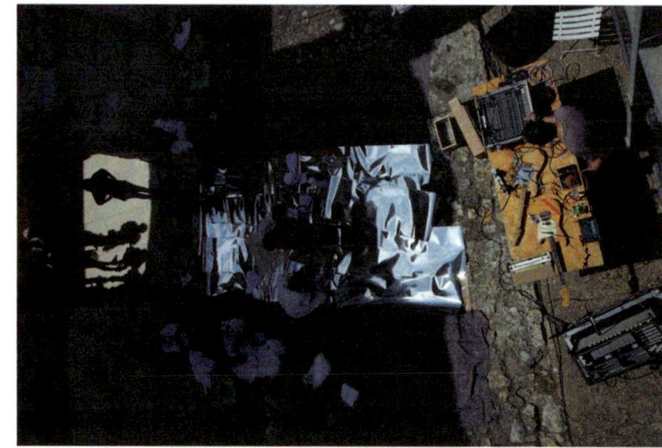

7/6/12—8:22:02 AM

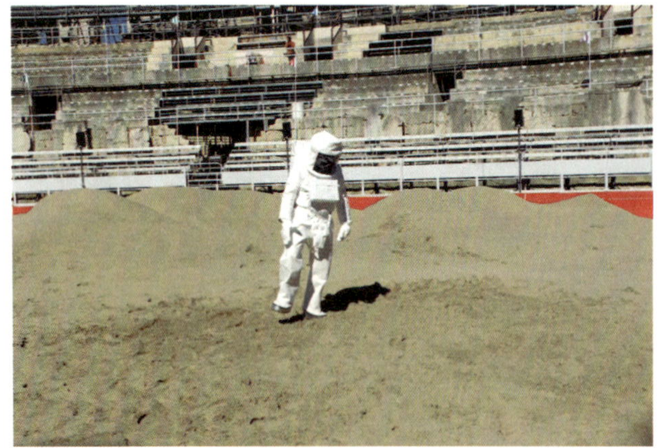

7/6/12—8:22:18 PM

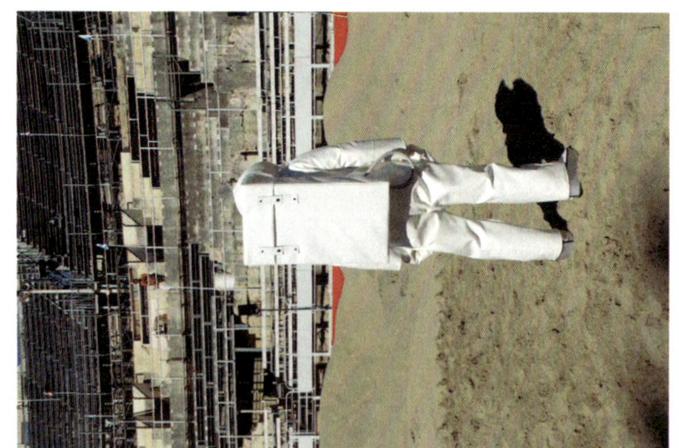

7/6/12—8:22:21 AM

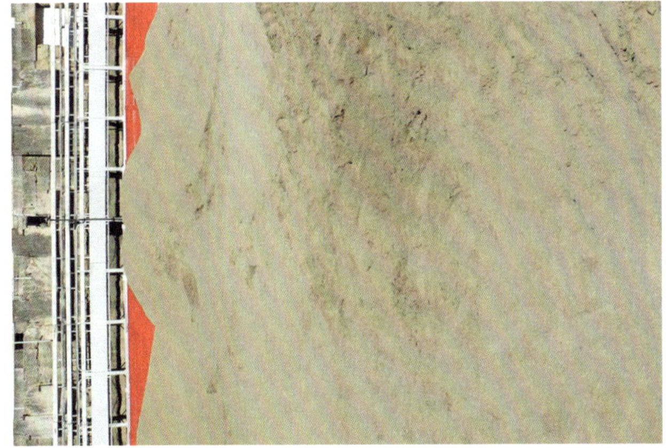
7/6/12—8:22:40 AM

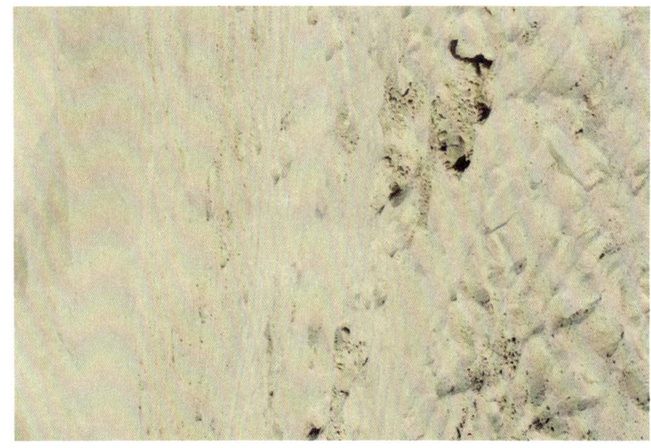
7/6/12—8:22:49 AM

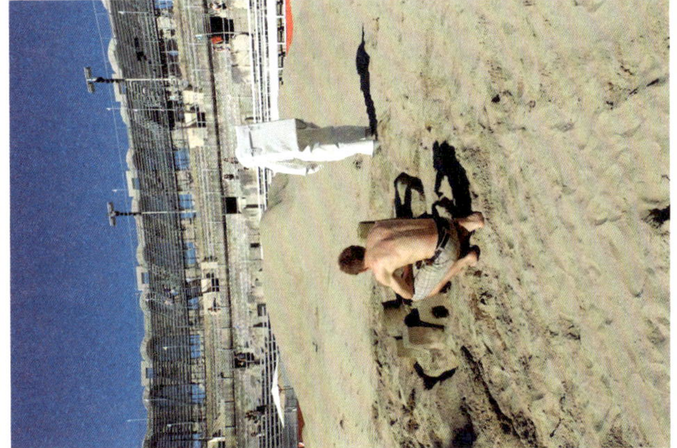
7/6/12—8:24:24 AM

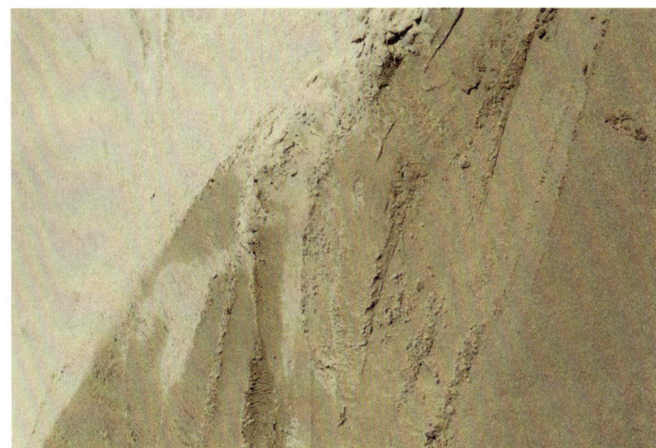
7/6/12—8:26:31 AM

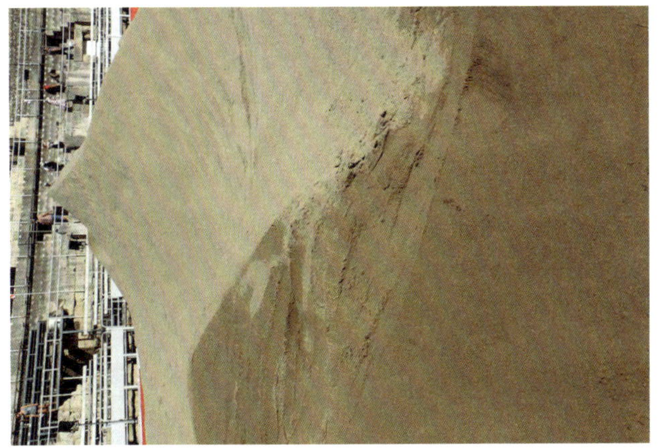
7/6/12—8:26:33 AM

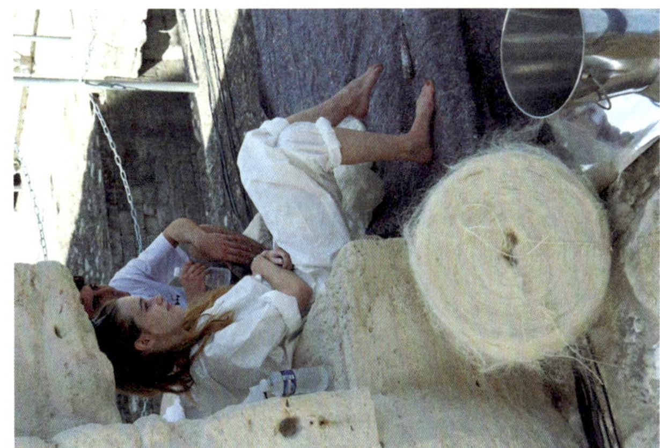
7/6/12—8:30:10 AM

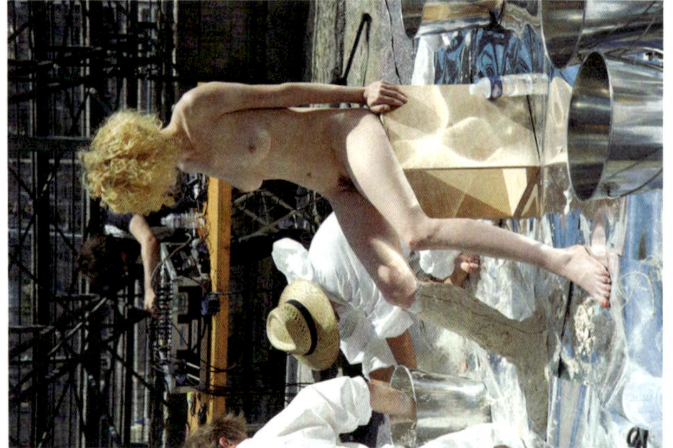
7/6/12—8:32:02 AM

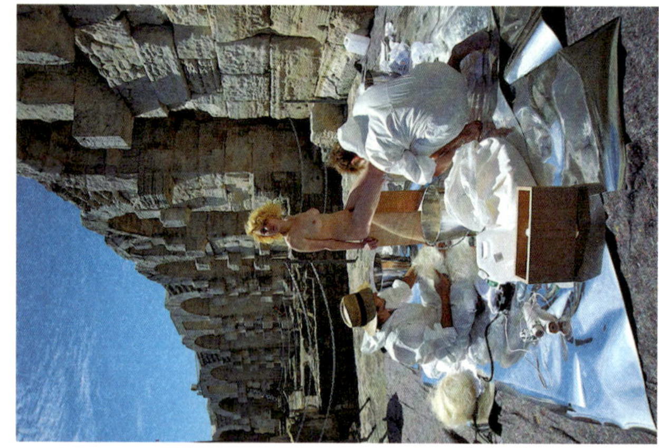
7/6/12—8:33:00 AM

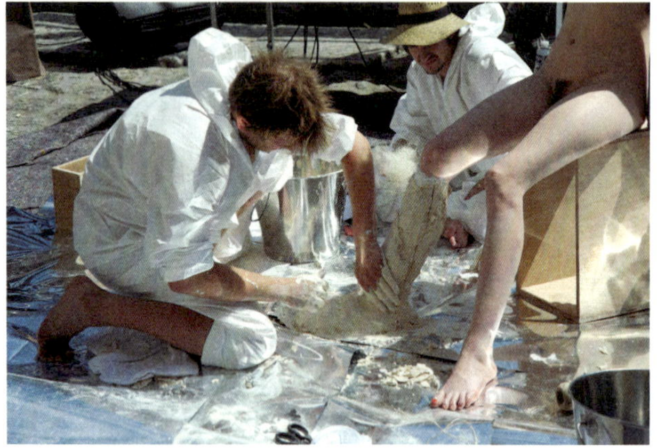
7/6/12—8:34:26 AM

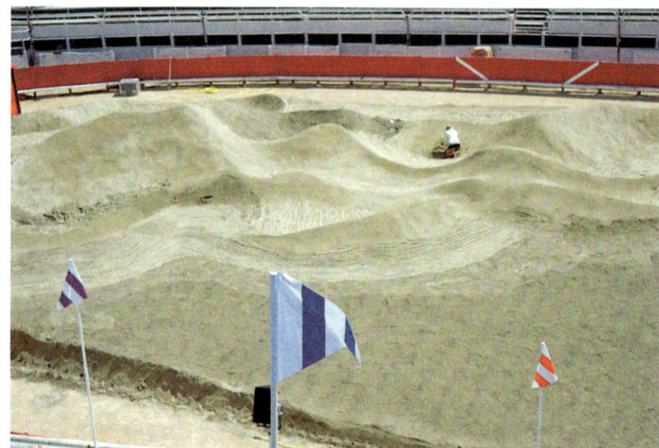
7/6/12—8:35:43 AM

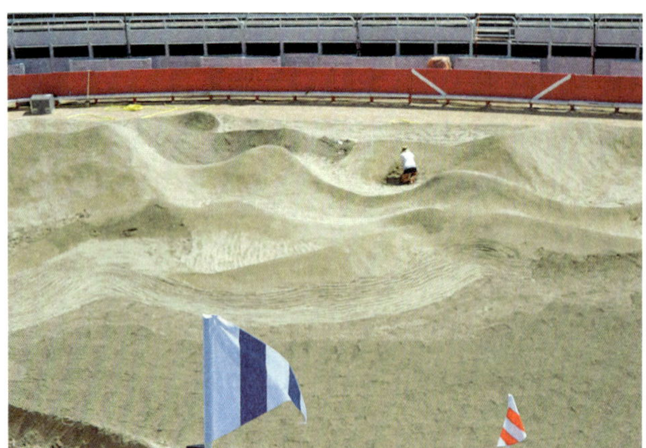
7/6/12—8:35:44 AM

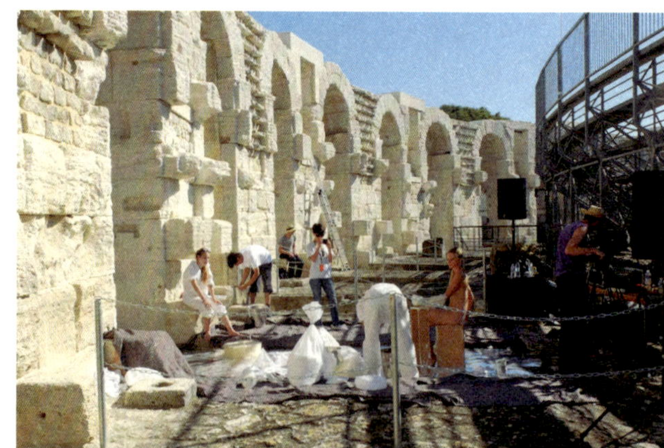
7/6/12—8:35:57 AM

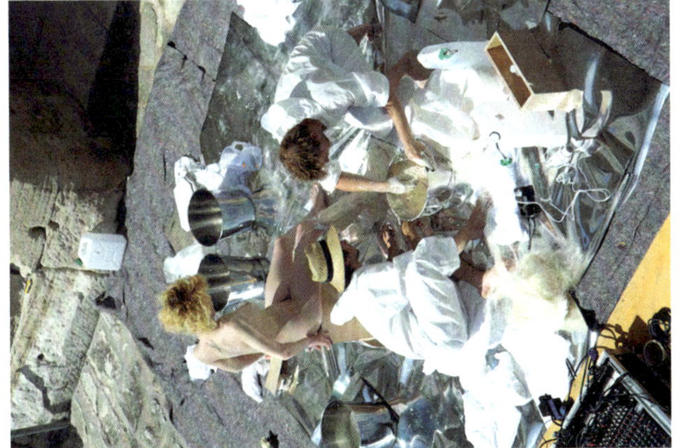
7/6/12—8:36:40 AM

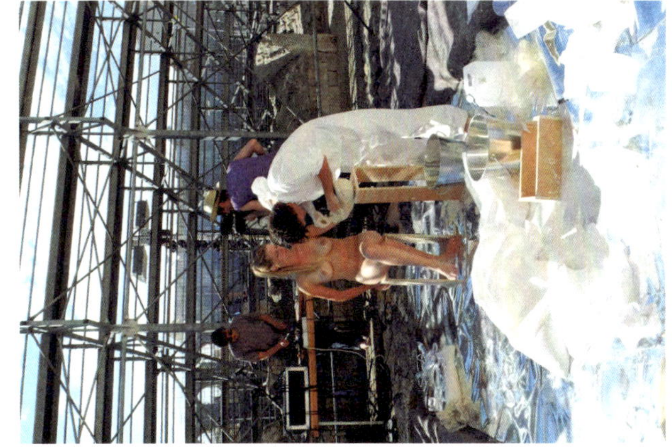
7/6/12—8:36:49 AM

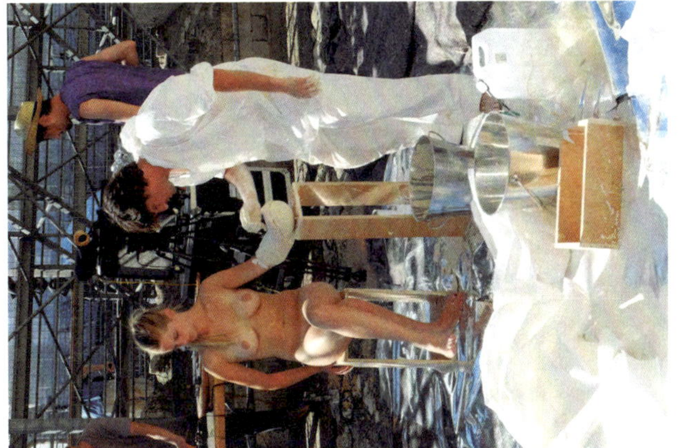
7/6/12—8:37:11 AM

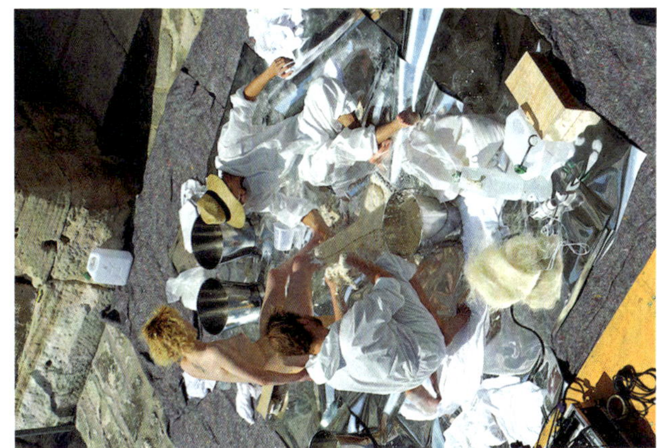
7/6/12—8:37:59 AM

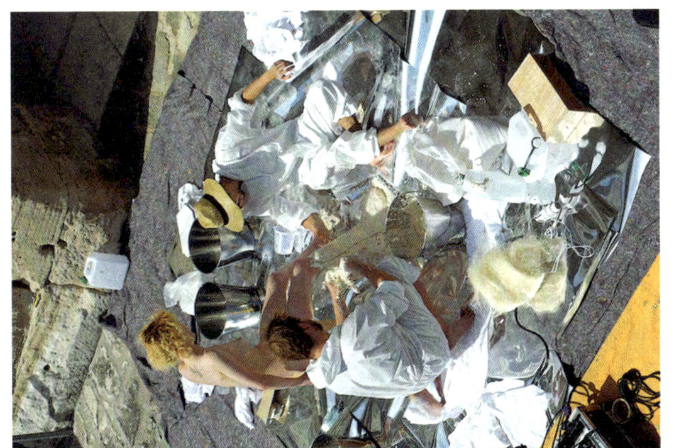
7/6/12—8:40:08 AM

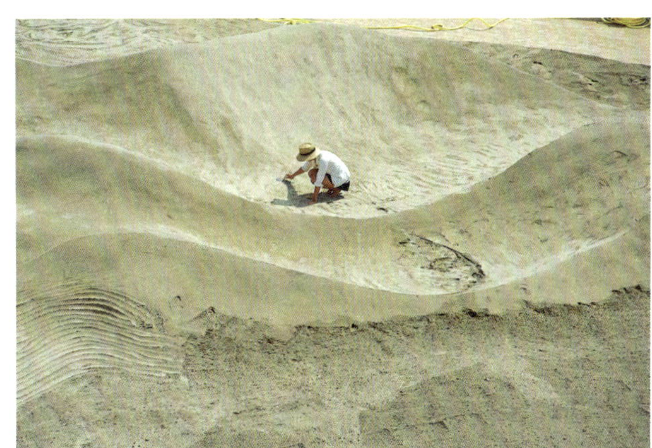
7/6/12—8:40:50 AM

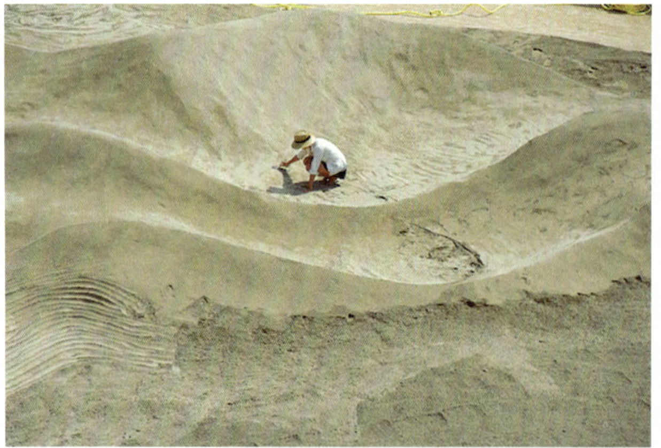
7/6/12—8:40:51 AM

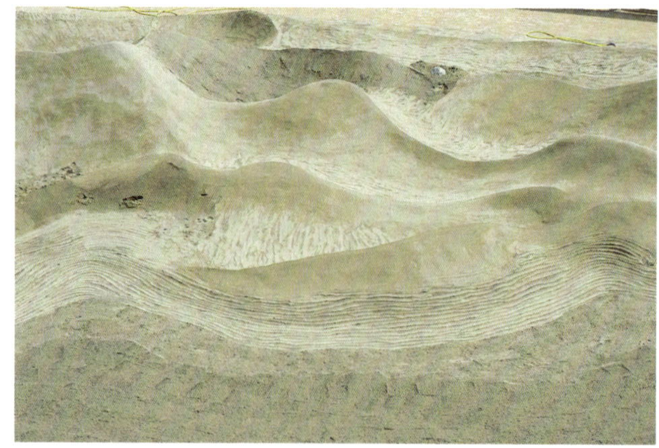
7/6/12—8:40:52 AM

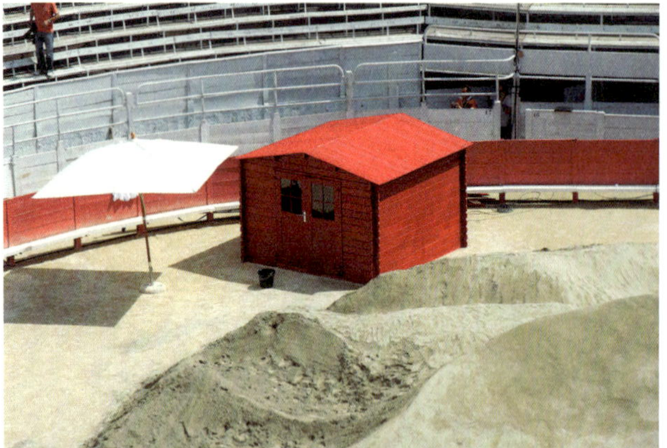
7/6/12—8:40:59 AM

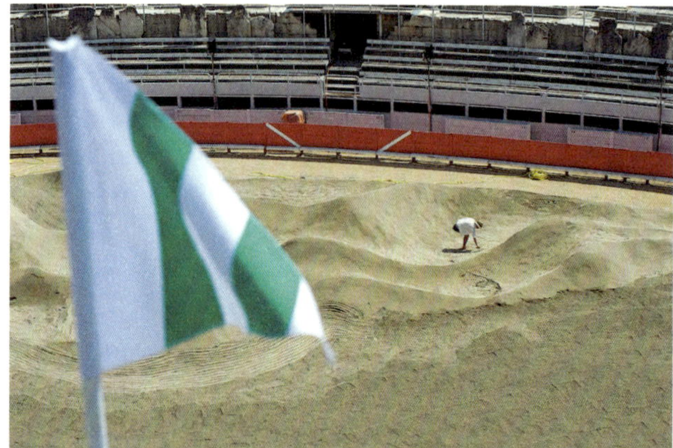
7/6/12—8:42:07 AM

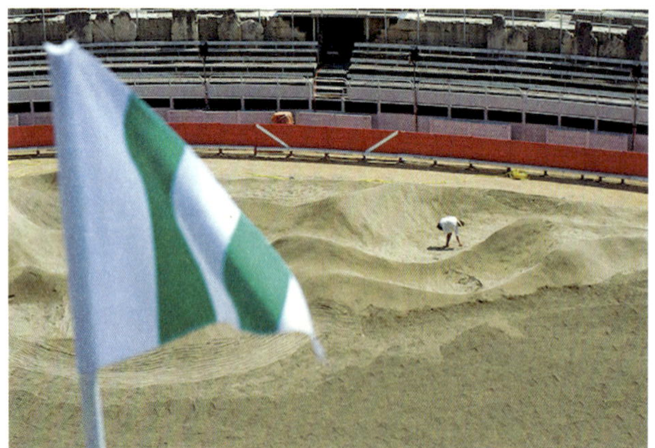
7/6/12—8:42:08 AM

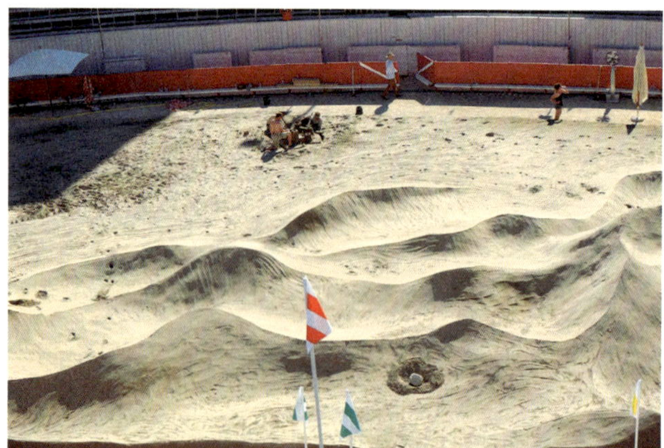
7/6/12—8:43:14 AM

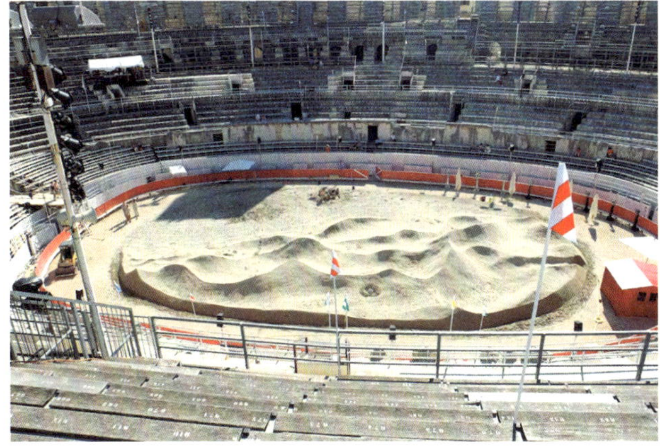

7/6/12—8:43:20 AM

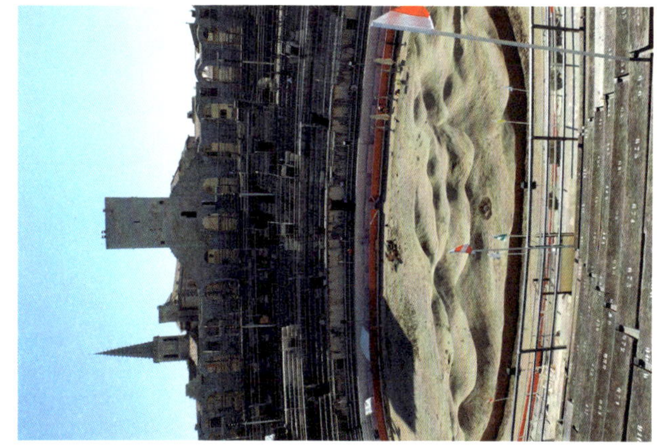

7/6/12—8:43:28 AM

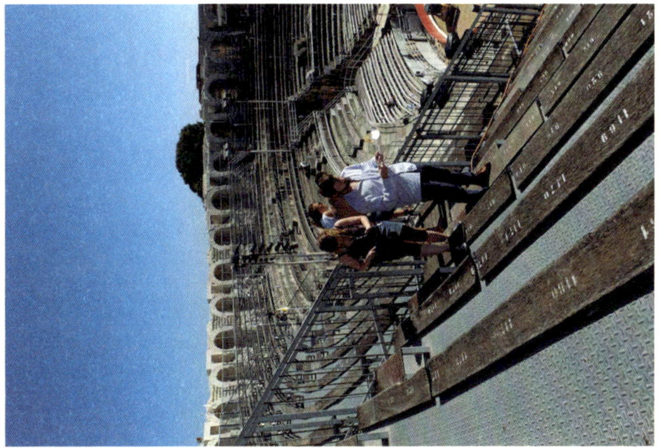

7/6/12—8:43:39 AM

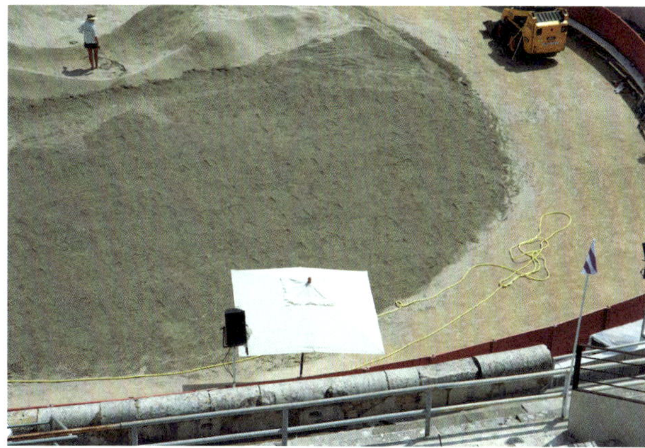

7/6/12—8:44:15 AM

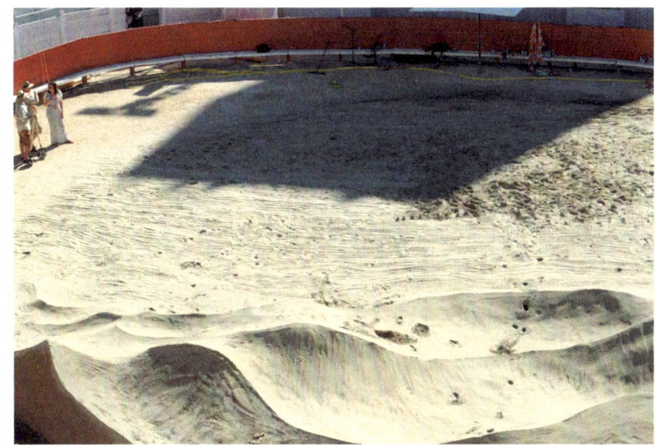

7/6/12—8:44:29 AM

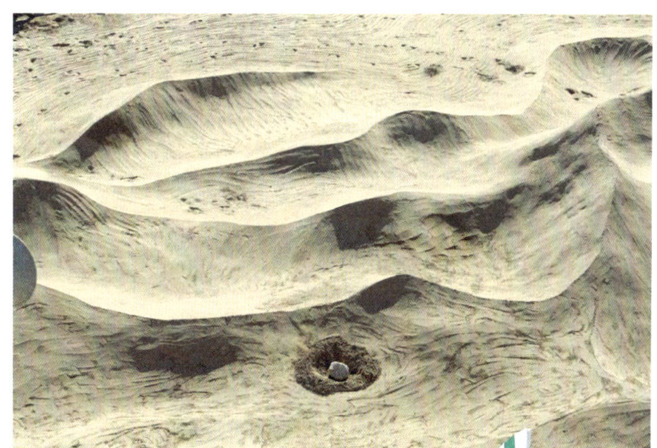

7/6/12—8:44:49 AM

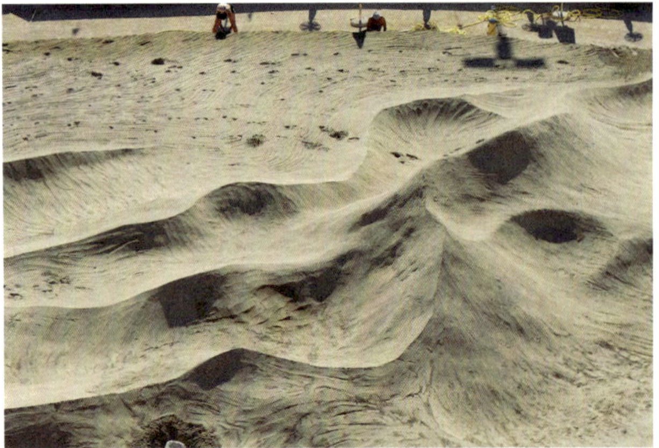

7/6/12—8:44:57 AM

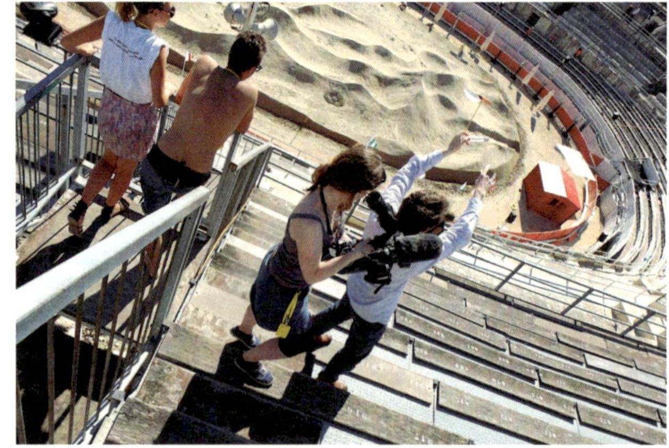

7/6/12—8:45:05 AM

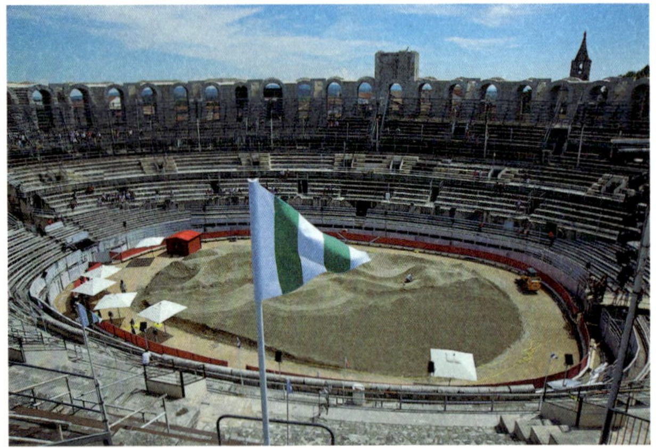

7/6/12—8:45:10 AM

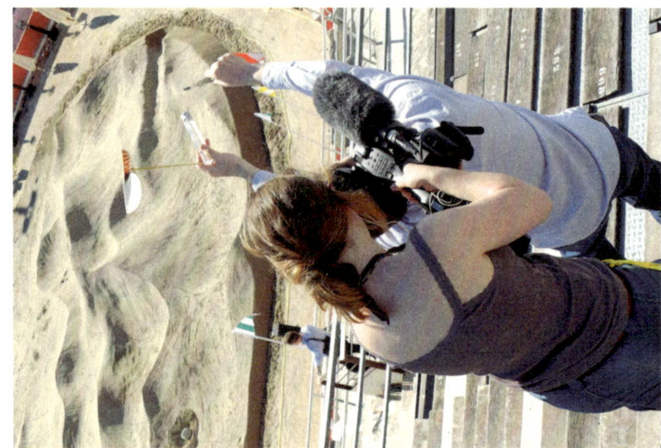

7/6/12—8:45:15 AM

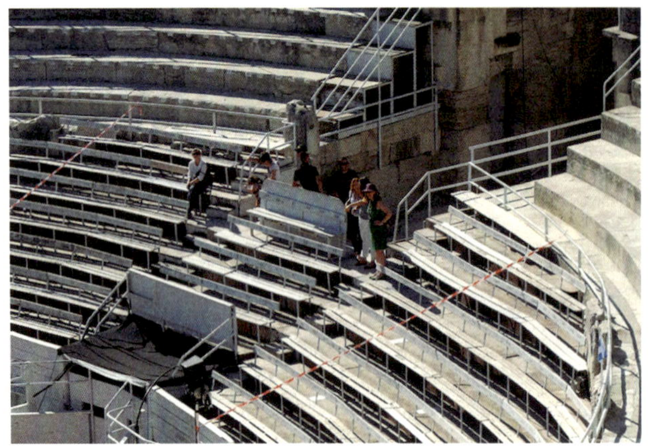

7/6/12—8:45:34 AM

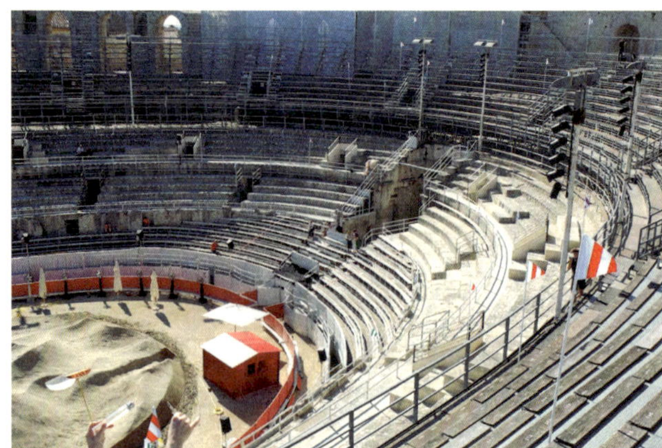

7/6/12—8:45:38 AM

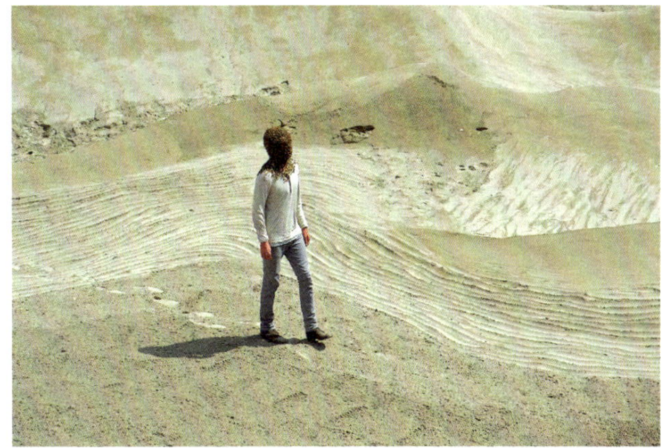

7/6/12—8:46:52 AM

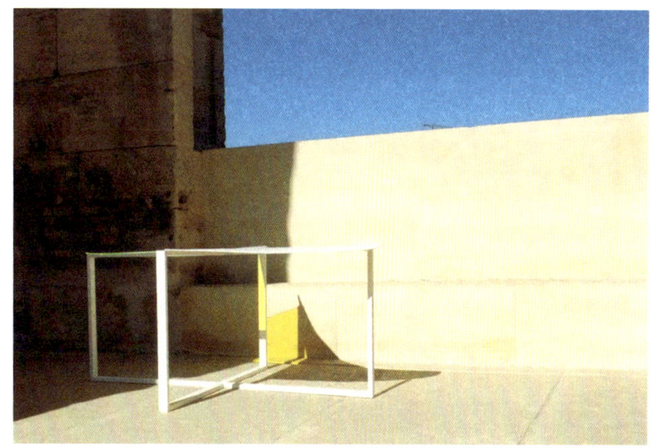

7/6/12—8:46:53 AM

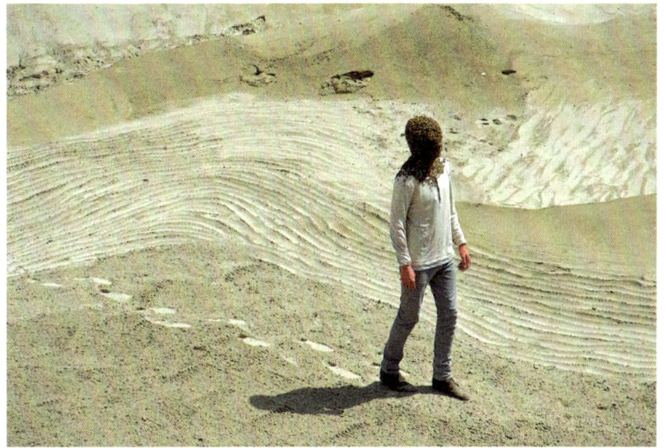

7/6/12—8:47:00 AM

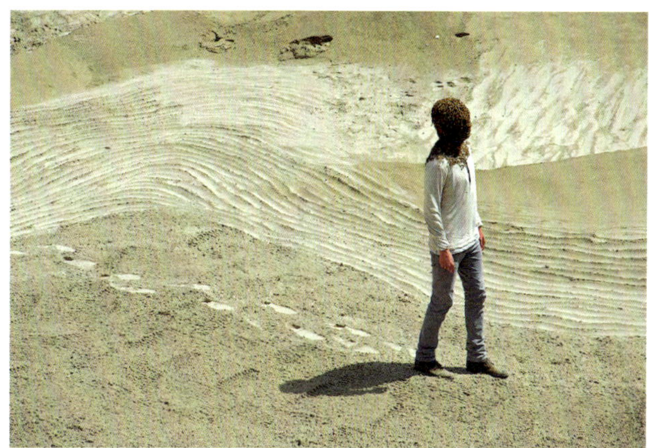

7/6/12—8:47:03 AM

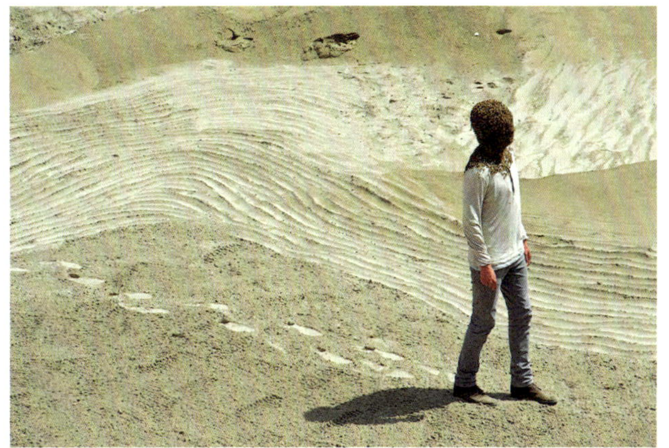

7/6/12—8:47:04 AM

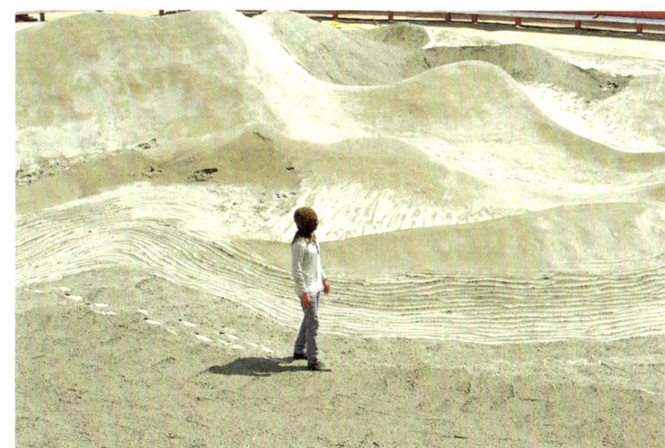

7/6/12—8:47:05 AM

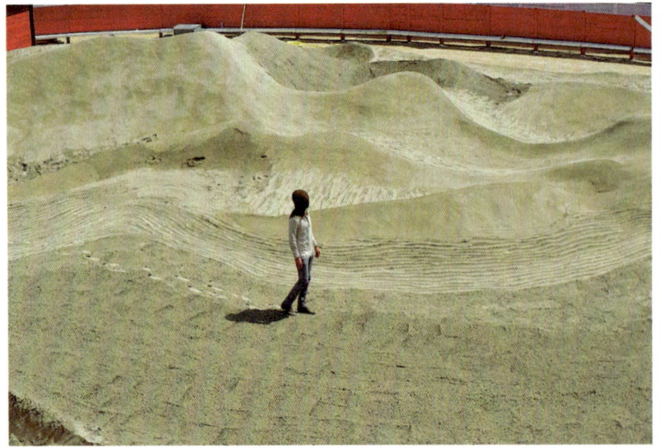
7/6/12—8:47:07 AM

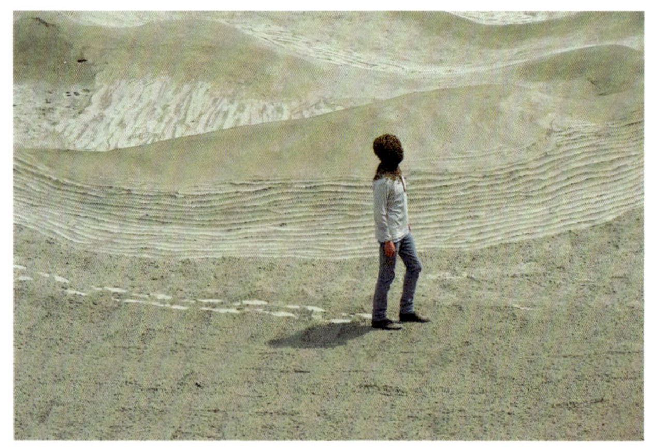
7/6/12—8:47:22 AM

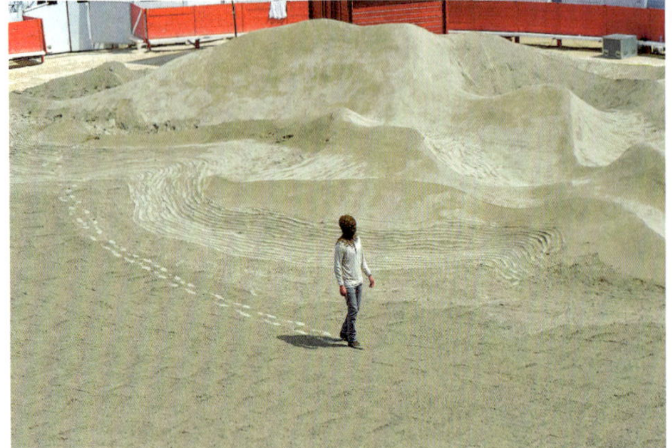
7/6/12—8:47:42 AM

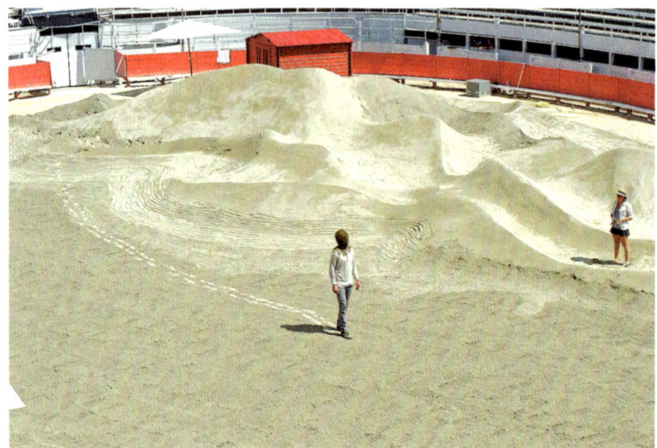
7/6/12—8:47:58 AM

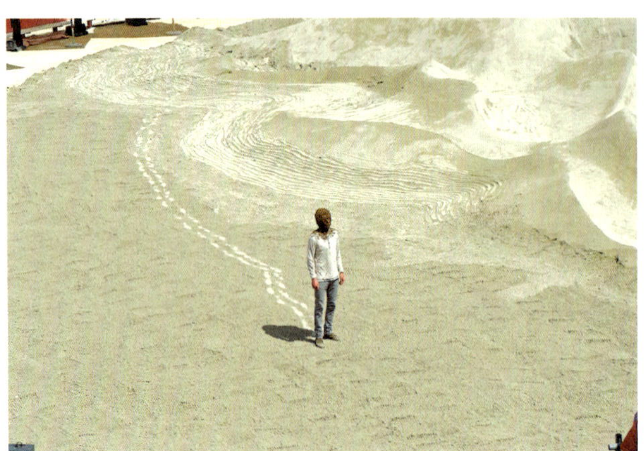
7/6/12—8:48:26 AM

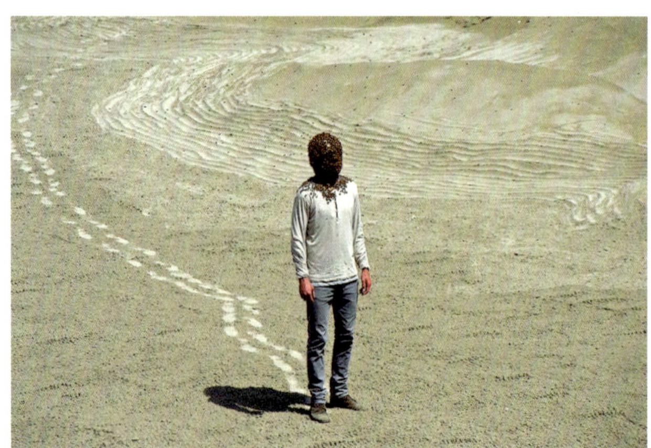
7/6/12—8:49:23 AM

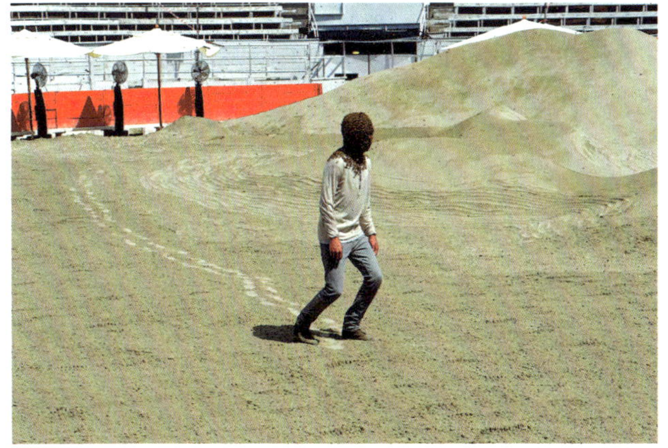
7/6/12—8:50:01 AM

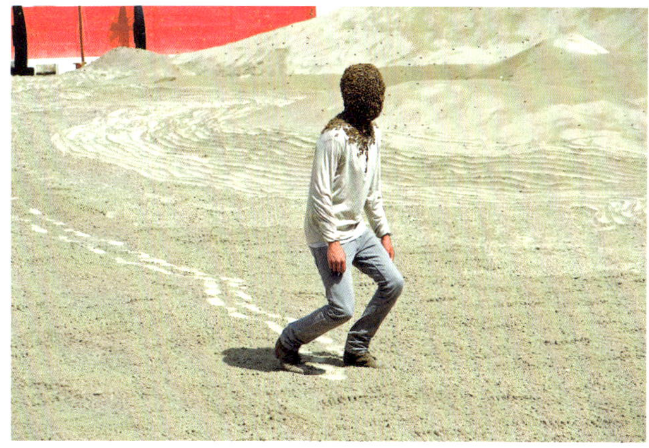
7/6/12—8:50:02 AM

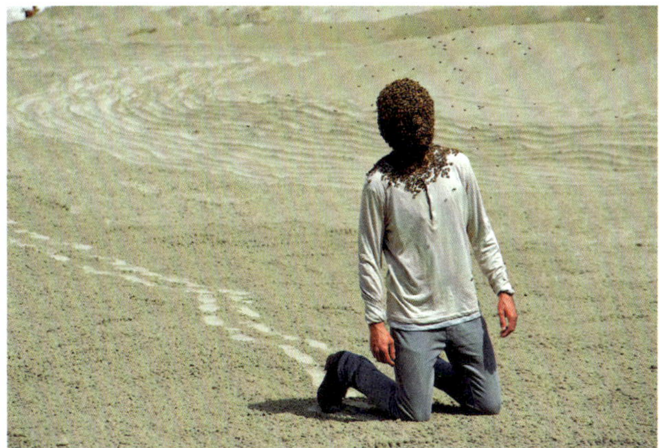
7/6/12—8:50:06 AM

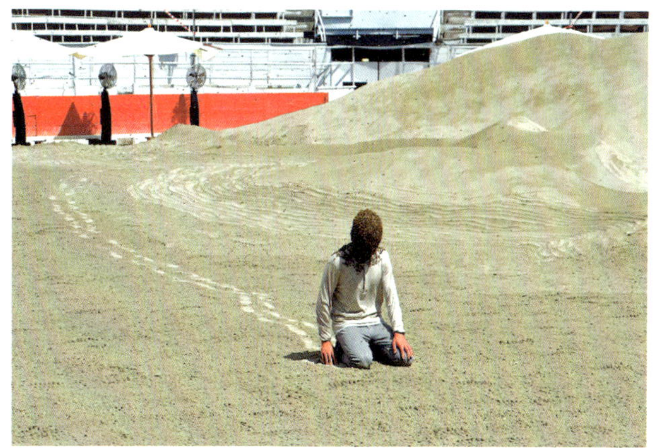
7/6/12—8:50:46 AM

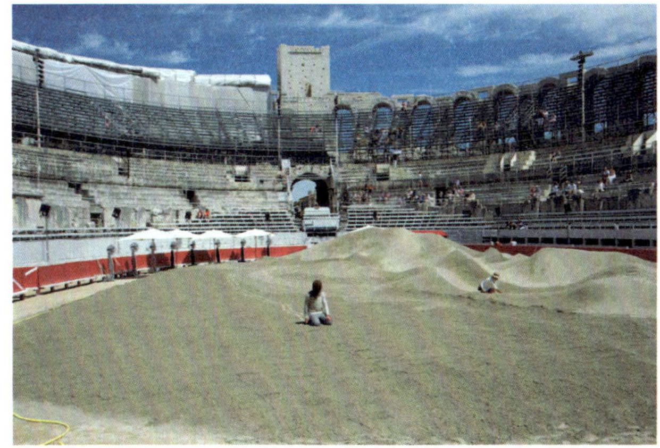
7/6/12—8:51:23 AM

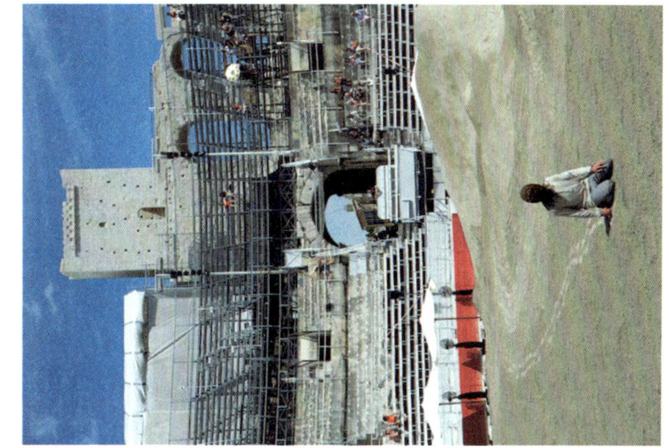
7/6/12—8:51:37 AM

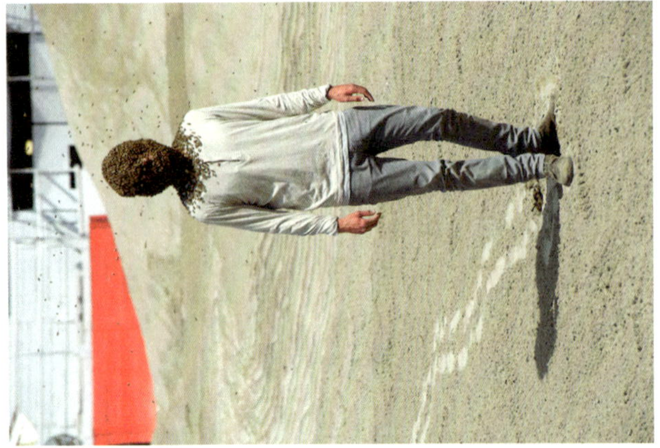
7/6/12—8:52:09 AM

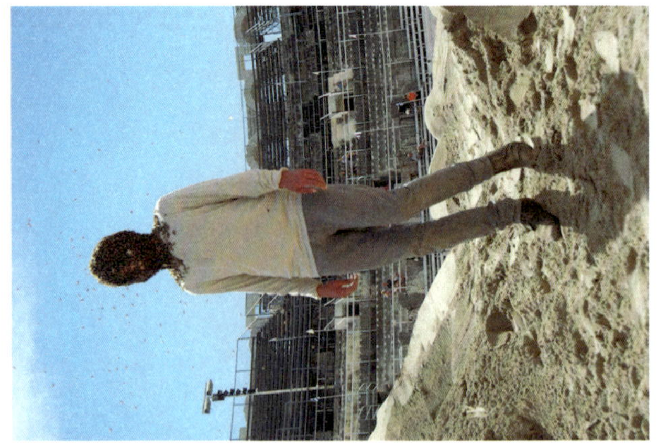
7/6/12—8:54:13 AM

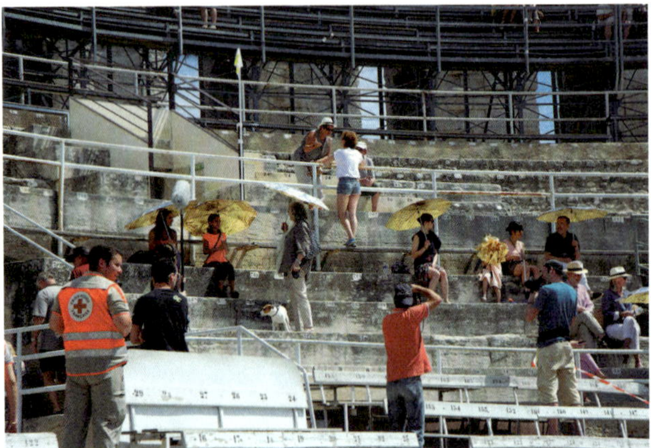
7/6/12—8:55:59 AM

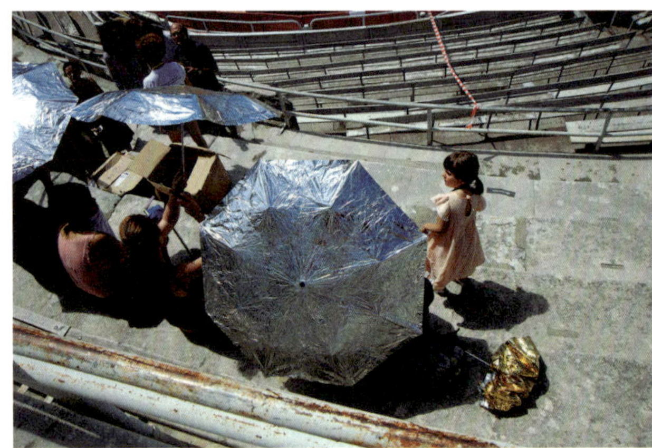
7/6/12—9:1:54 AM

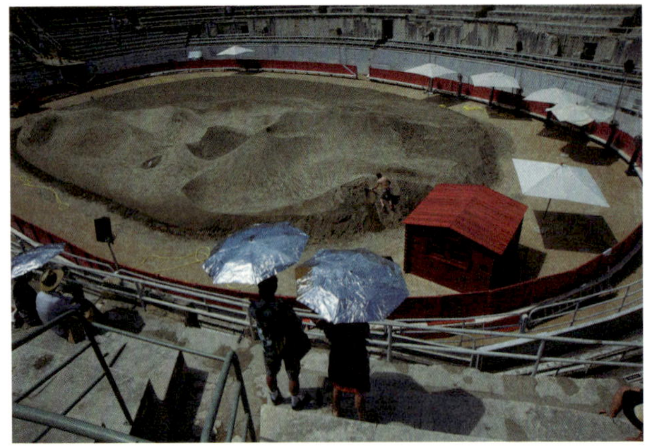
7/6/12—9:02:51 AM

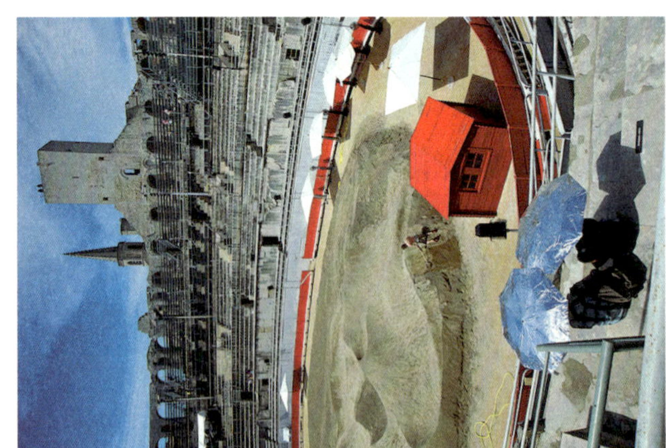
7/6/12—9:03:41 AM

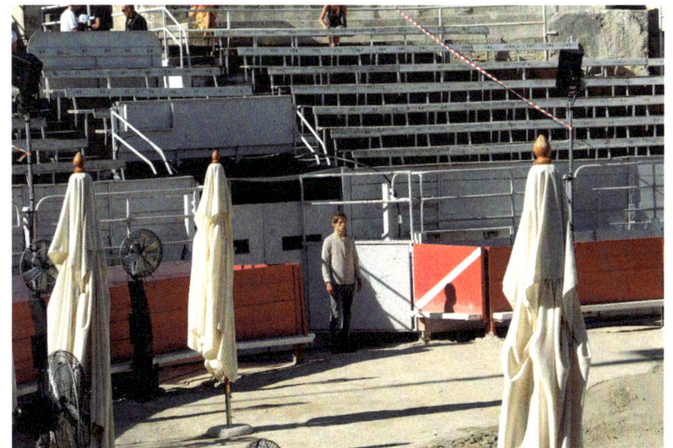

7/6/12—9:04:17 AM

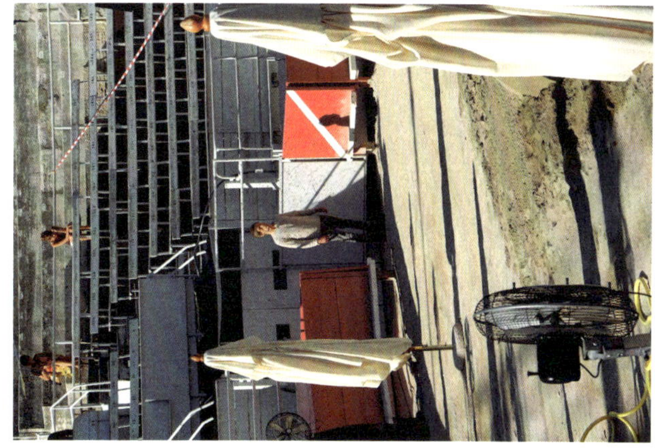

7/6/12—9:04:29 AM

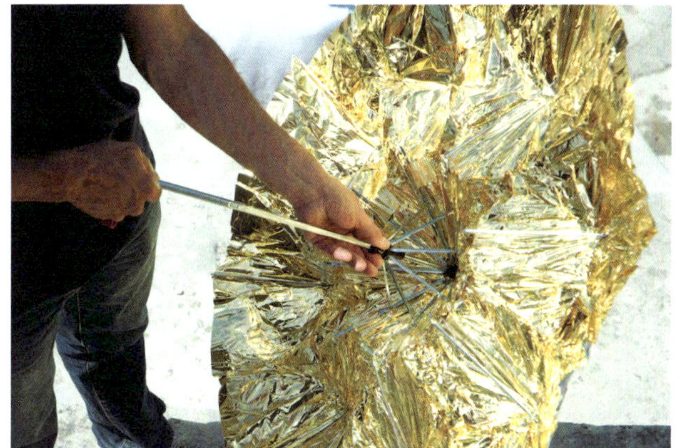

7/6/12—9:08:15 AM

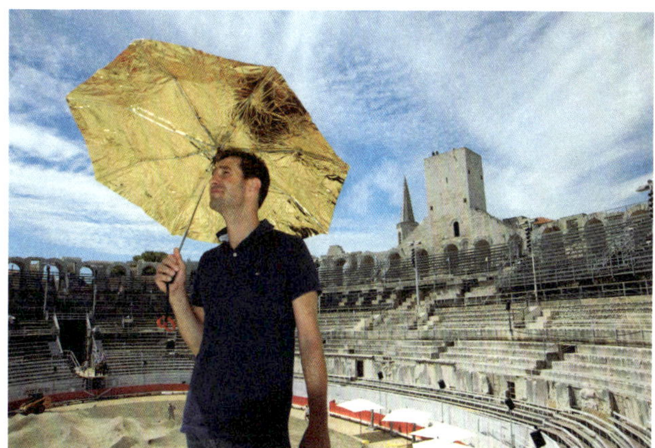

7/6/12—9:09:24 AM

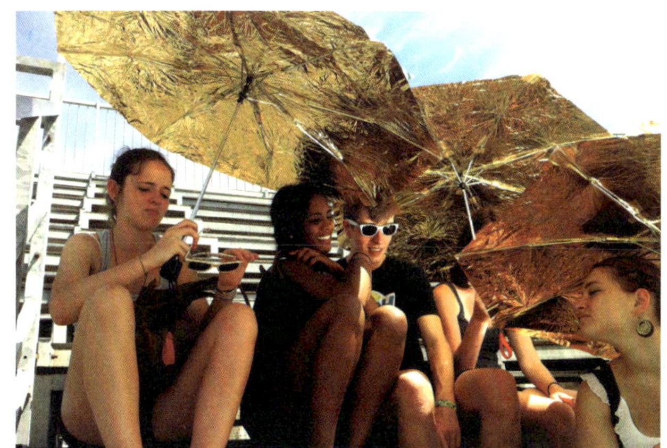

7/6/12—9:11:57 AM

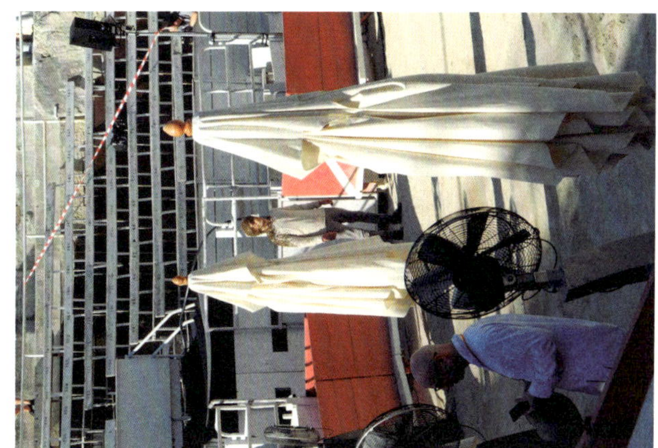

7/6/12—9:13:13 AM

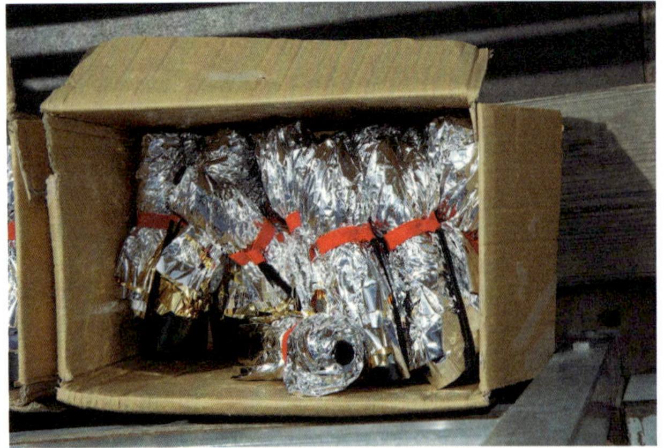

7/6/12—9:13:46 AM

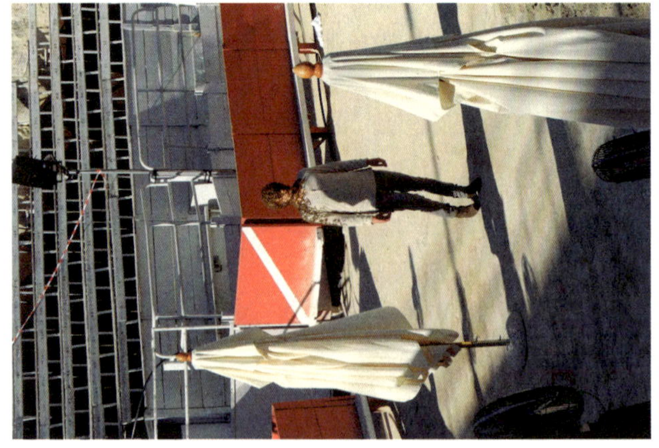

7/6/12—9:16:23 AM

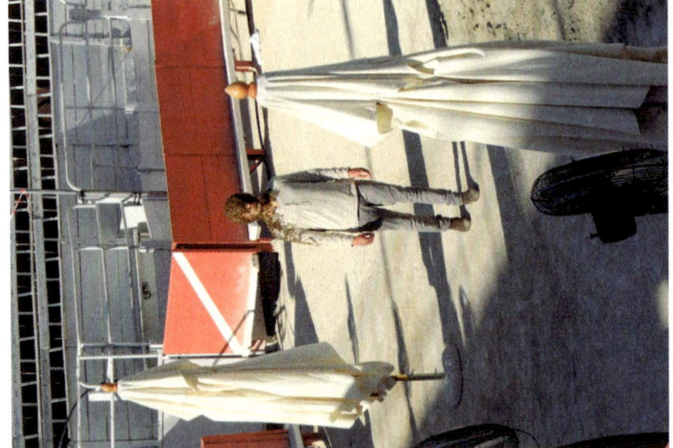

7/6/12—9:16:30 AM

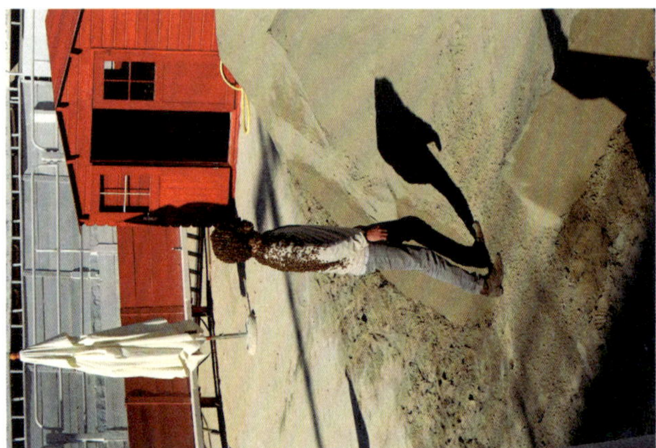

7/6/12—9:16:47 AM

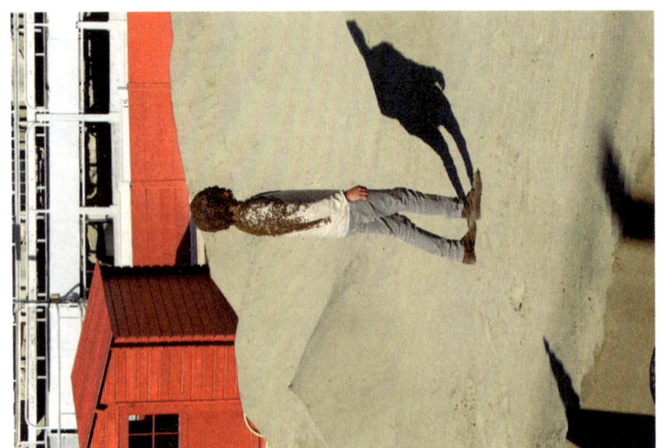

7/6/12—9:17:01 AM

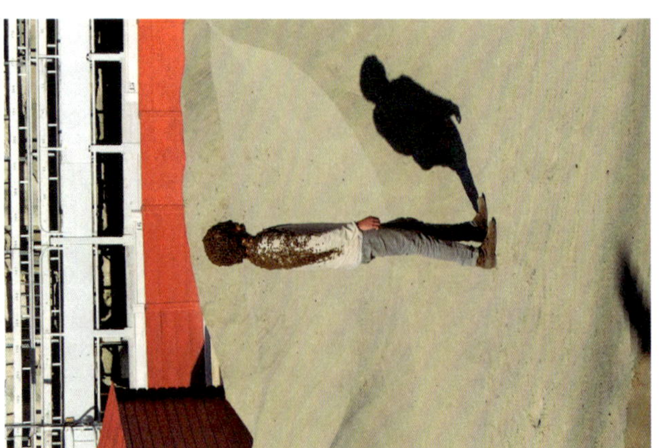

7/6/12—9:17:05 AM

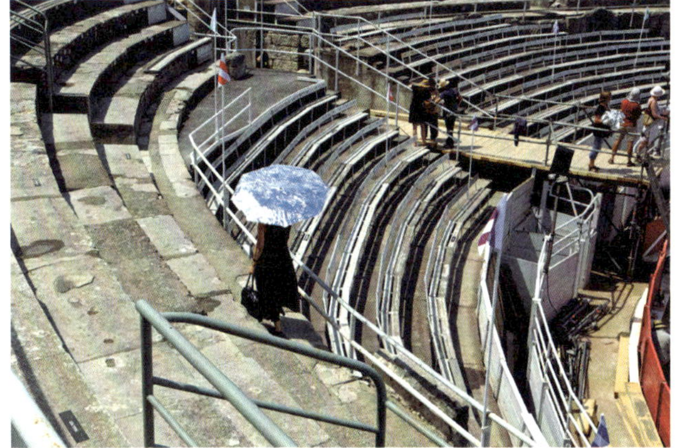
7/6/12—9:29:59 AM

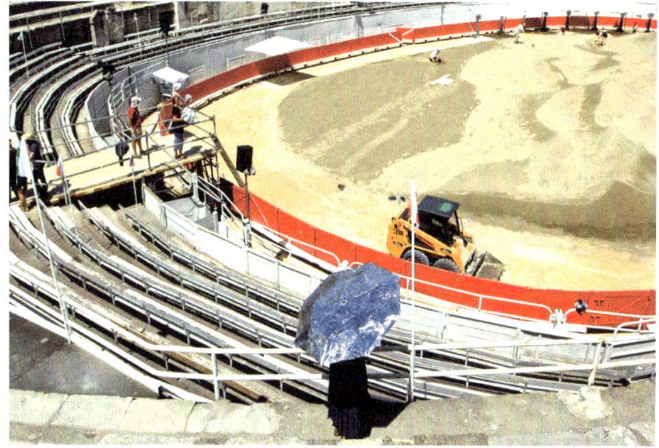
7/6/12—9:30:15 AM

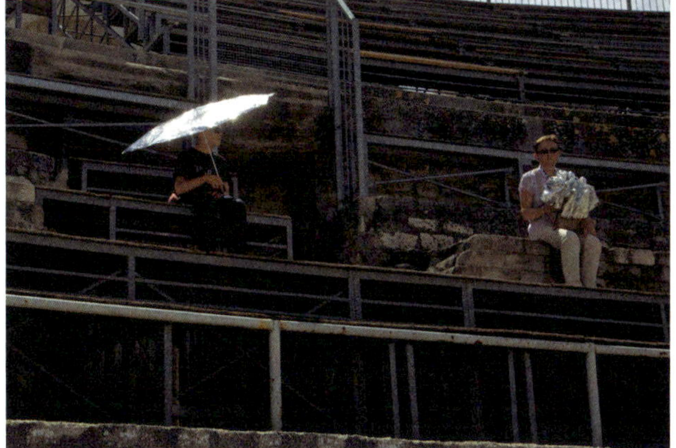
7/6/12—9:30:30 AM

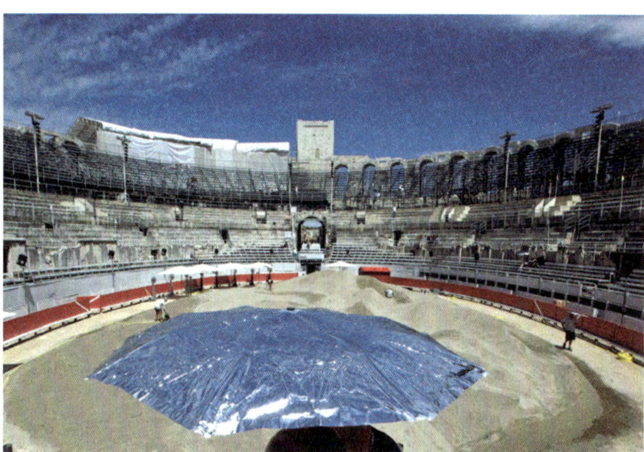
7/6/12—9:32:59 AM

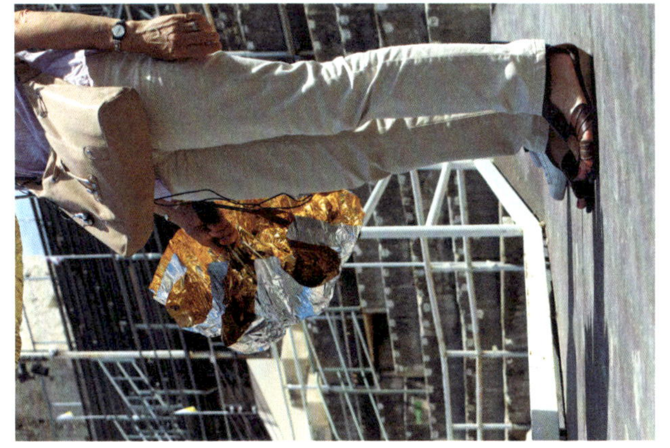
7/6/12—9:34:36 AM

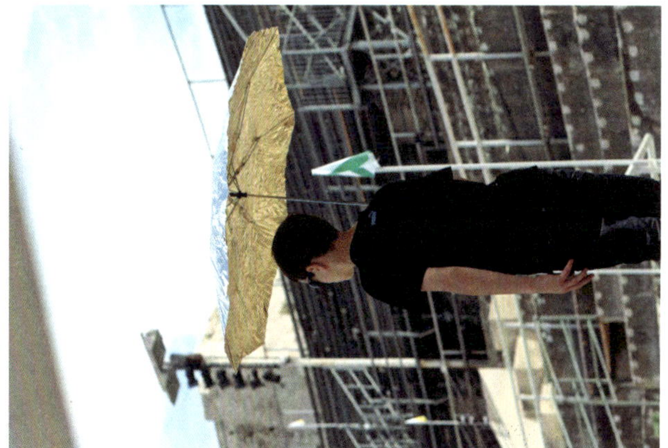
7/6/12—9:34:44 AM

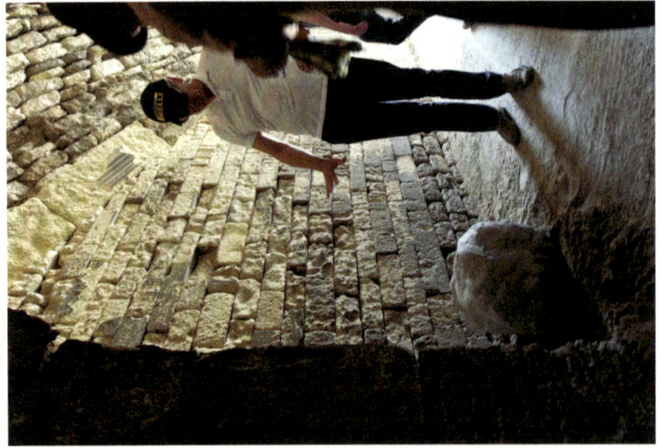
7/6/12—9:37:28 AM

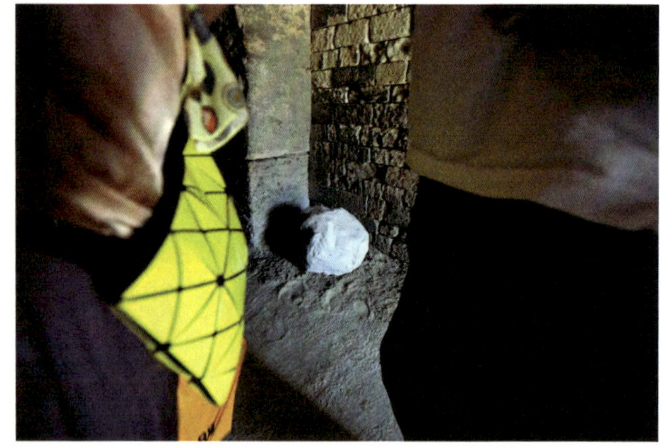
7/6/12—9:38:45 AM

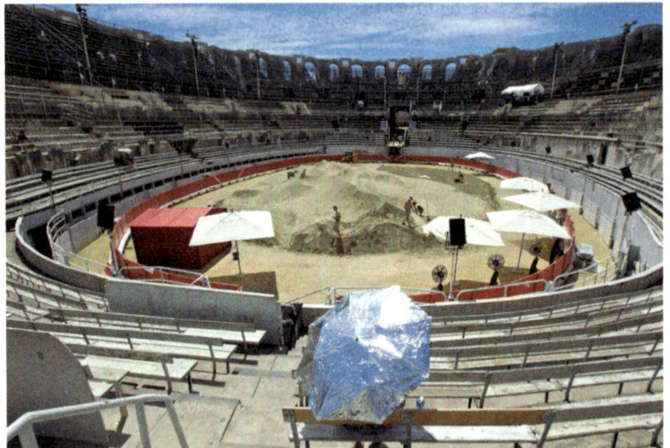
7/6/12—9:42:20 AM

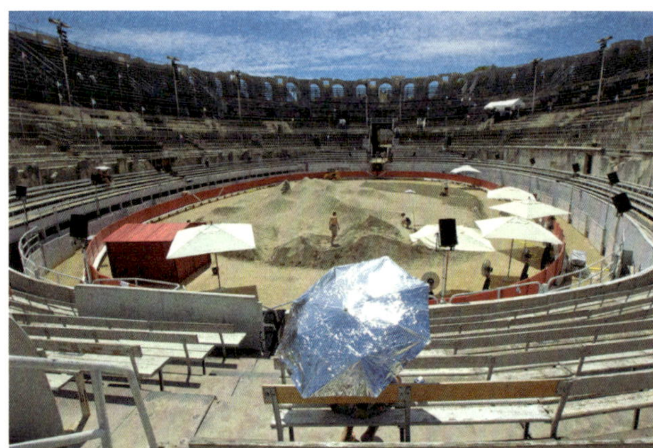
7/6/12—9:42:31 AM

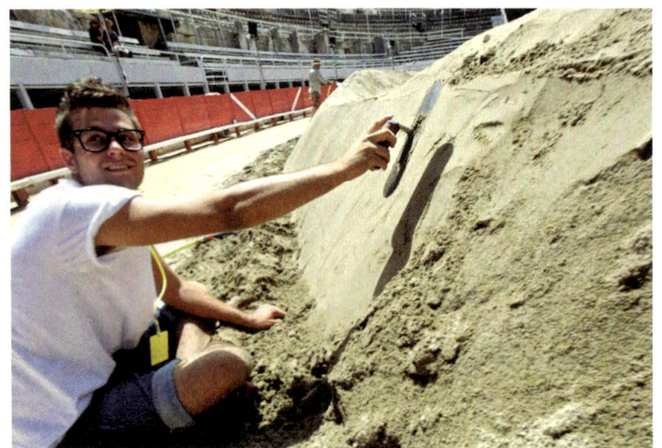
7/6/12—9:43:52 AM

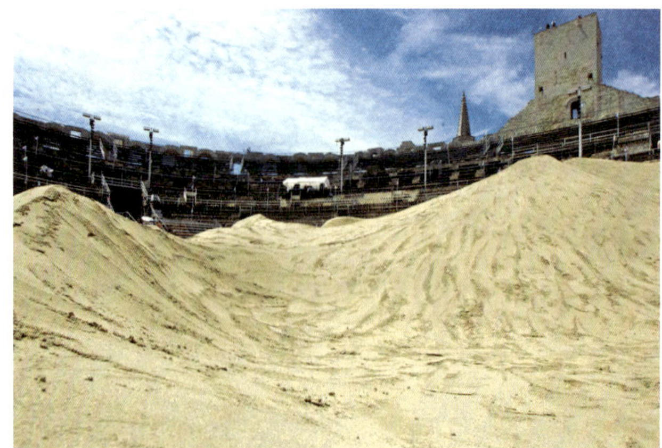
7/6/12—9:48:18 AM

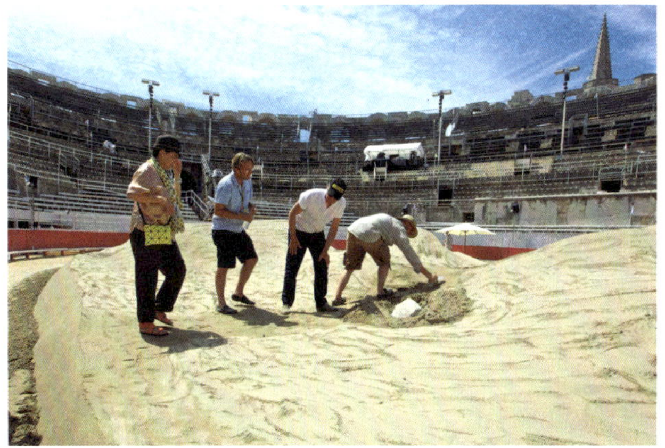

7/6/12—9:49:49 AM

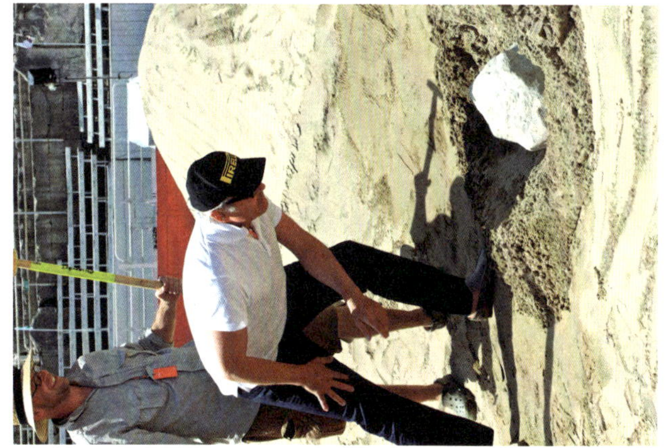

7/6/12—9:50:09 AM

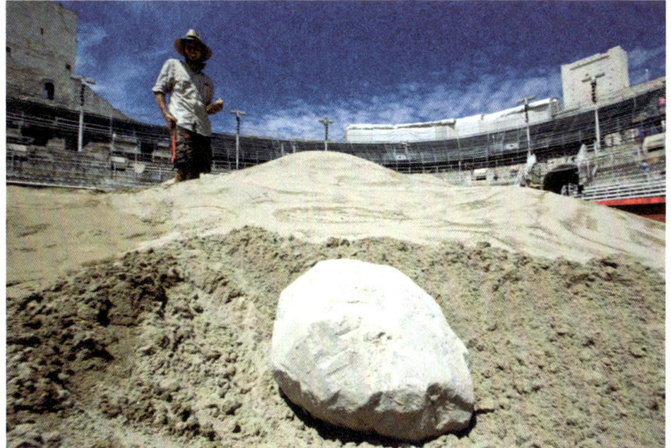

7/6/12—9:51:26 AM

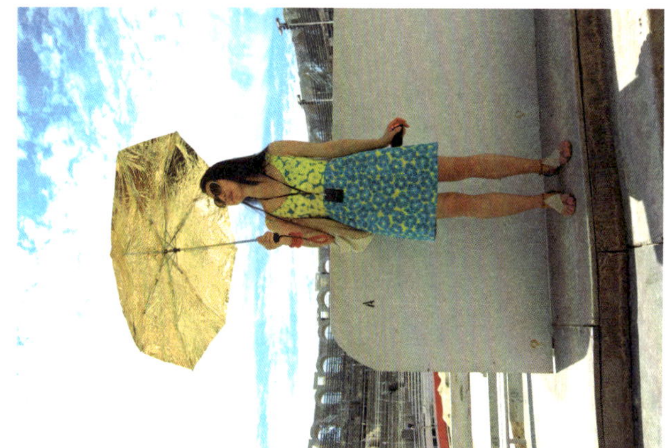

7/6/12—9:54:20 AM

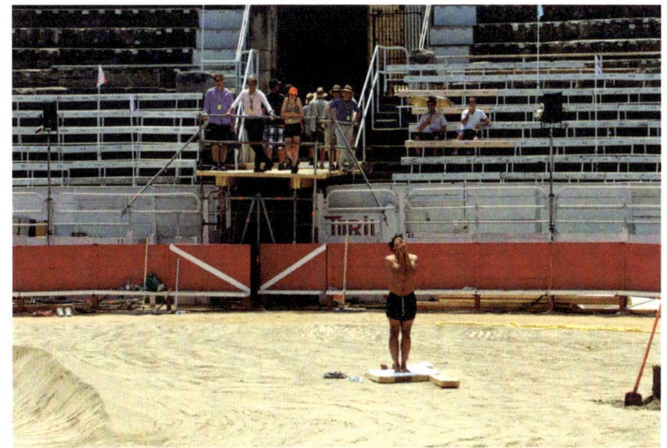

7/6/12—10:05:09 AM

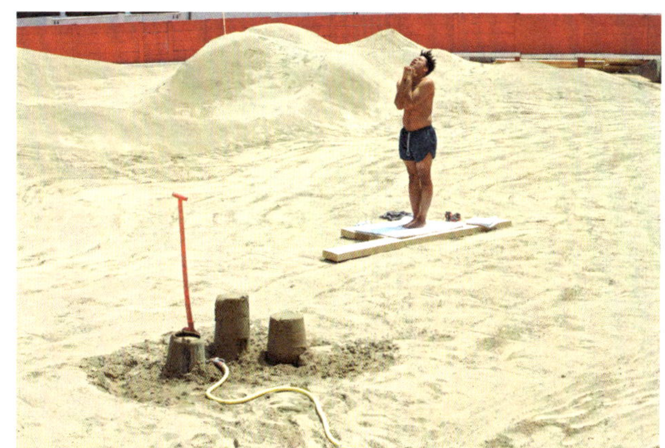

7/6/12—10:05:40 AM

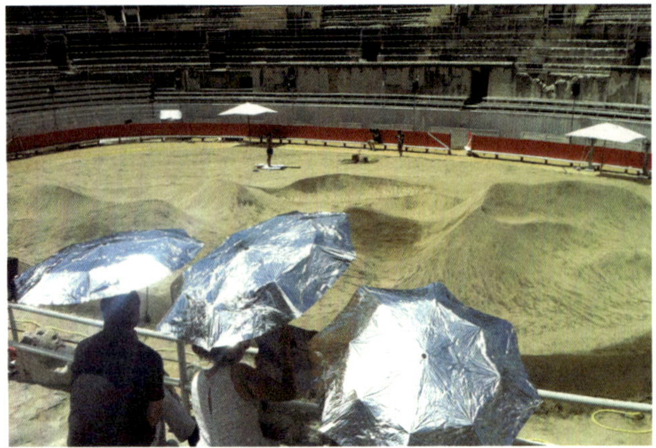

7/6/12—10:06:18 AM

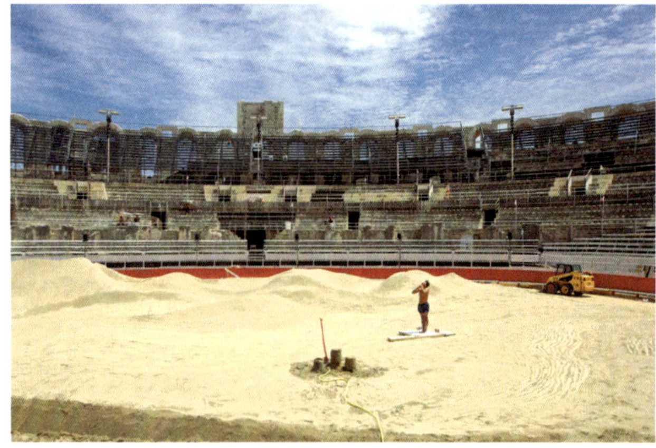

7/6/12—10:06:40 AM

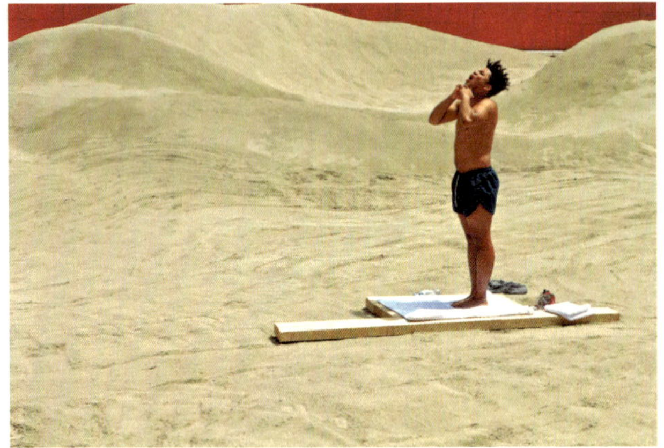

7/6/12—10:06:50 AM

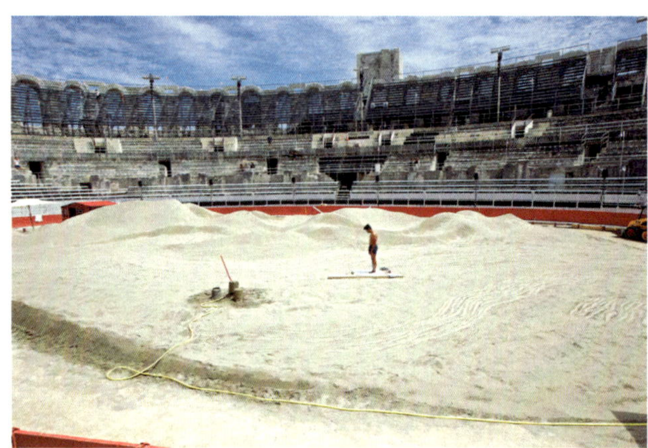

7/6/12—1:07:07 PM

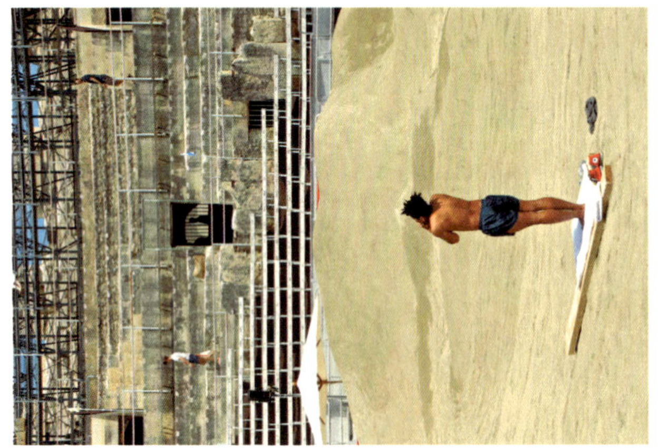

7/6/12—1:07:28 PM

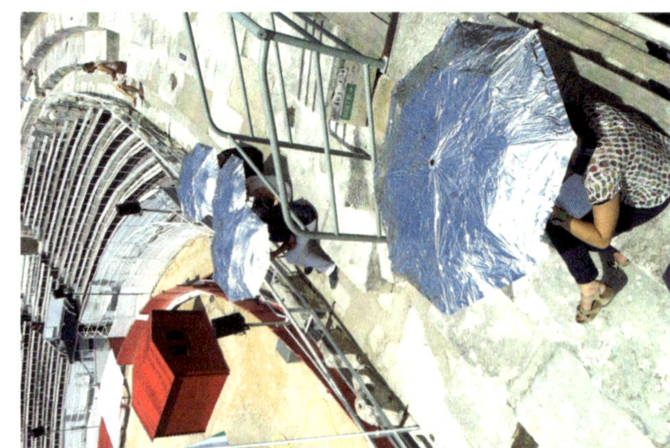

7/6/12—1:07:45 PM

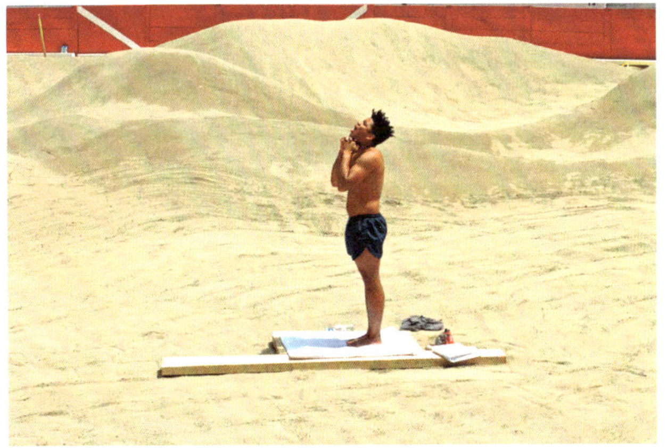

7/6/12—1:08:38 PM

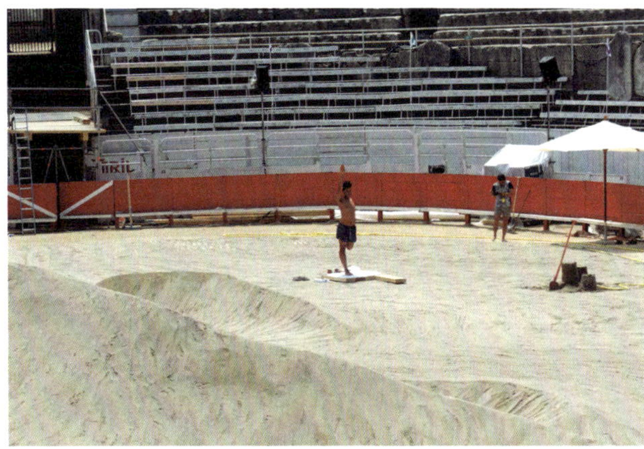

7/6/12—1:31:16 PM

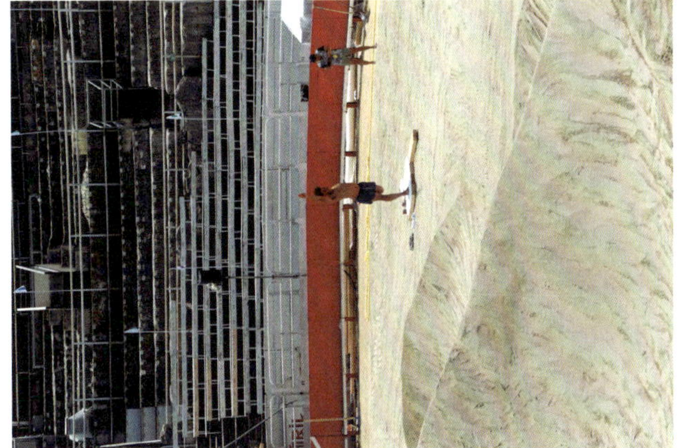

7/6/12—1:31:21 PM

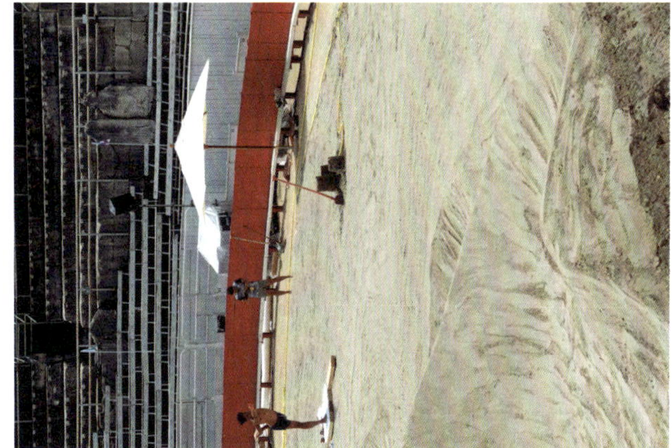

7/6/12—1:31:26 PM

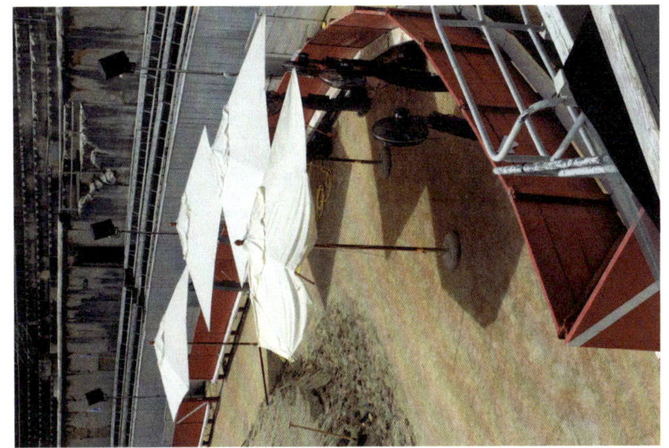

7/6/12—1:31:30 PM

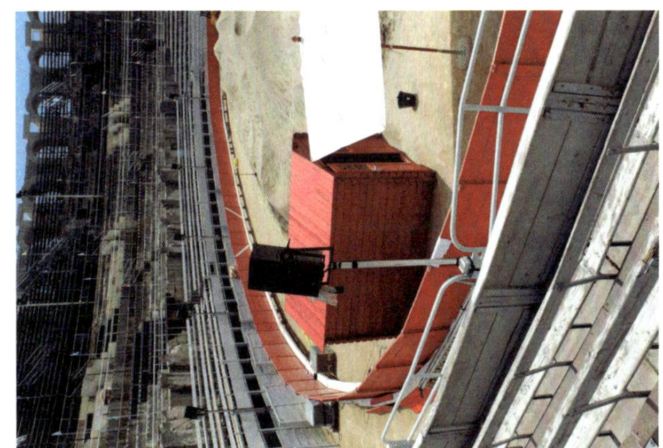

7/6/12—1:31:34 PM

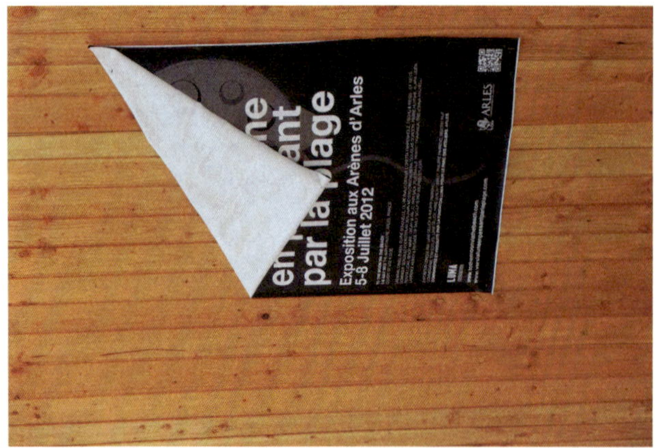

7/6/12—1:35:53 PM

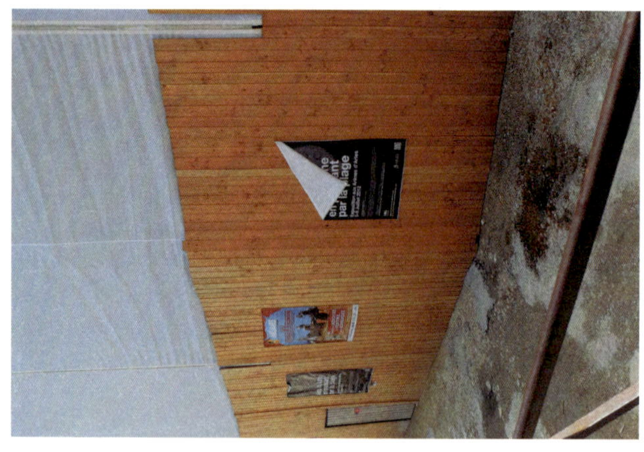

7/6/12—1:35:57 PM

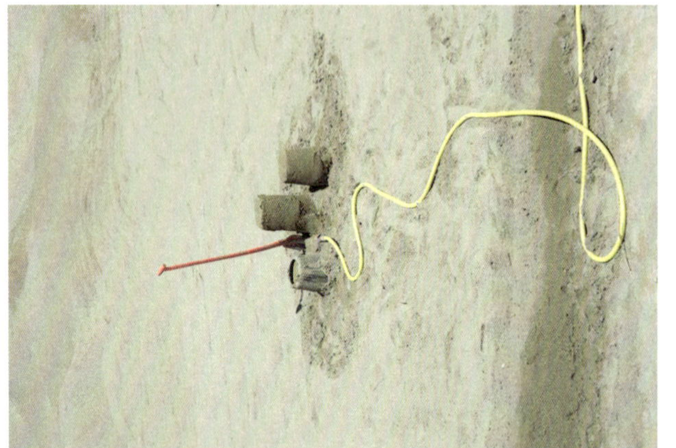

7/6/12—2:56:39 PM

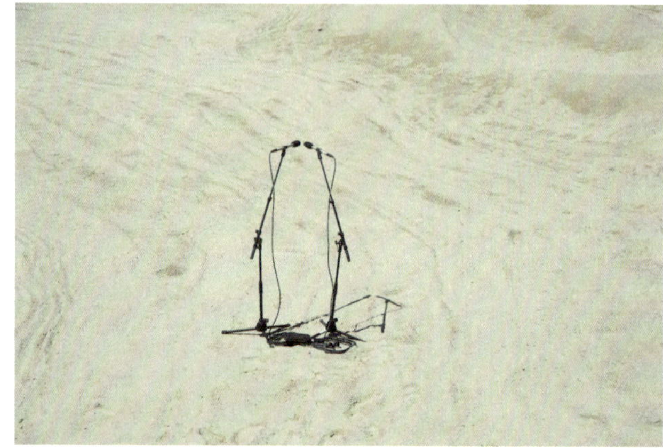

7/6/12—2:57:59 PM

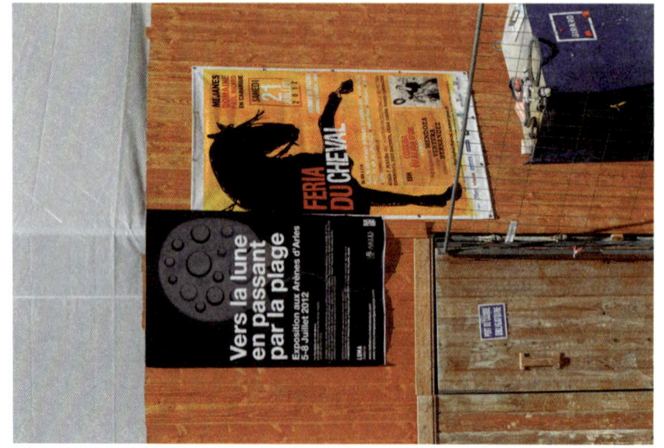

7/6/12—2:58:18 PM

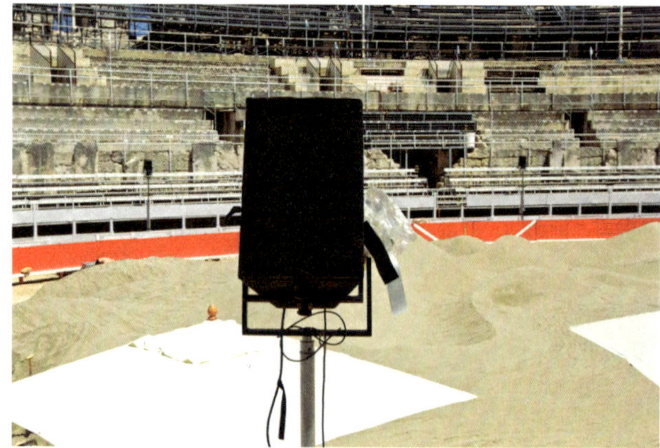

7/6/12—2:59:40 PM

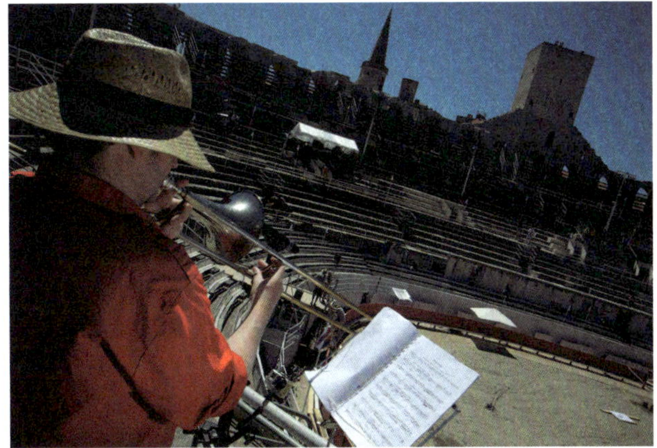

7/6/12—3:00:16 PM

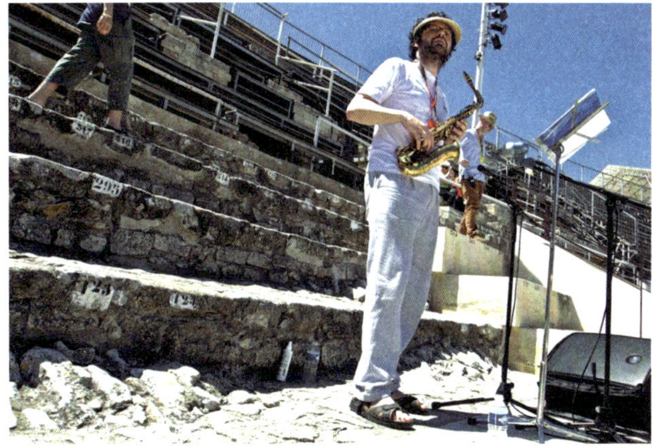

7/6/12—3:00:30 PM

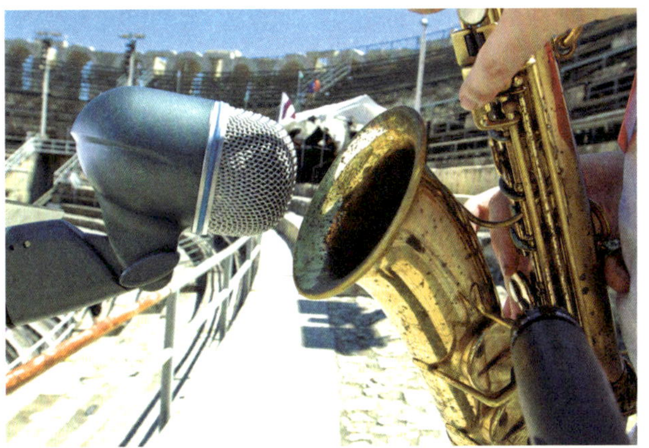

7/6/12—3:02:21 PM

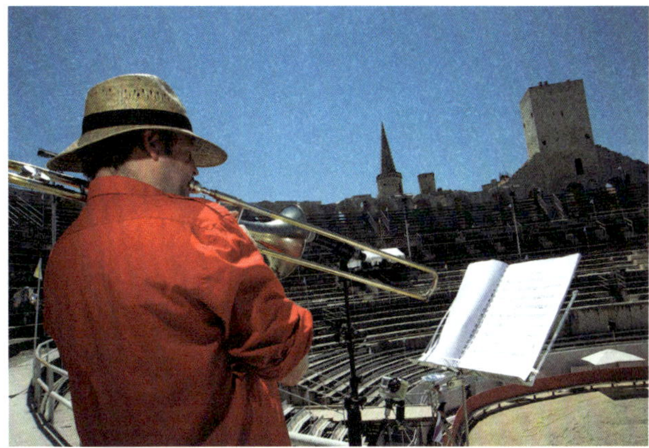

7/6/12—3:03:27 PM

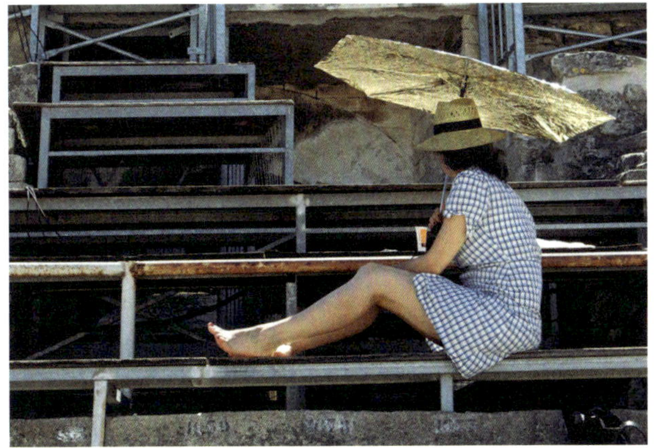

7/6/12—3:03:40 PM

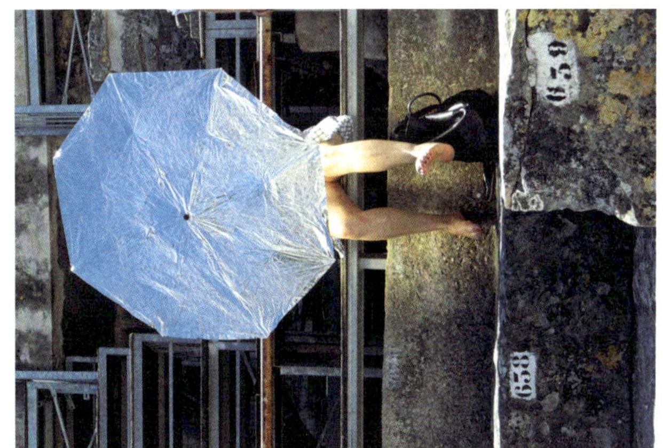

7/6/12—3:03:59 PM

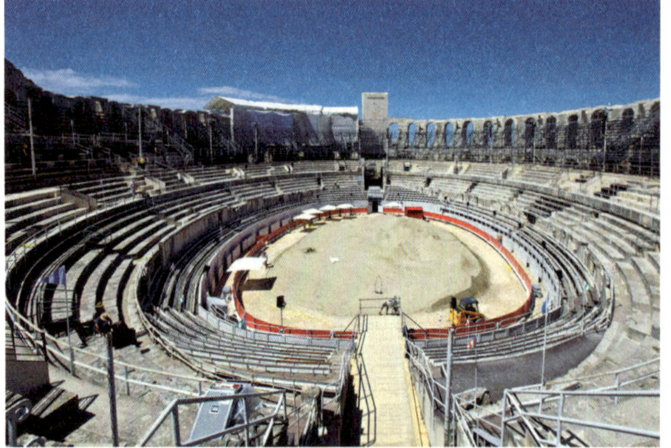

7/6/12—3:04:40 PM

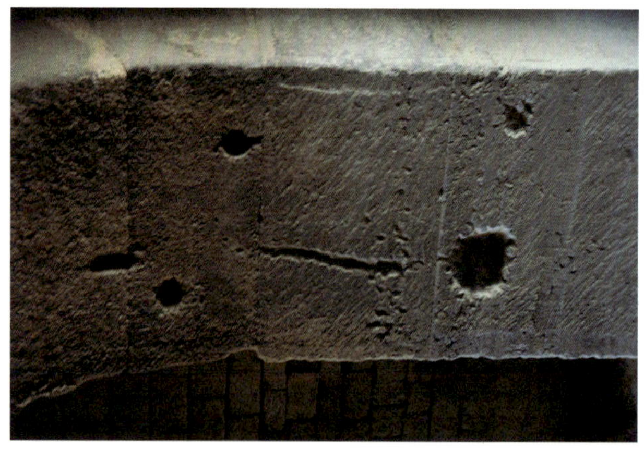

7/6/12—3:06:05 PM

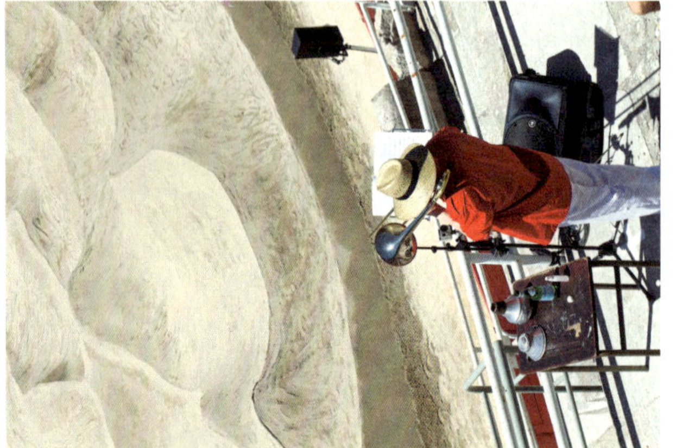

7/6/12—3:06:09 PM

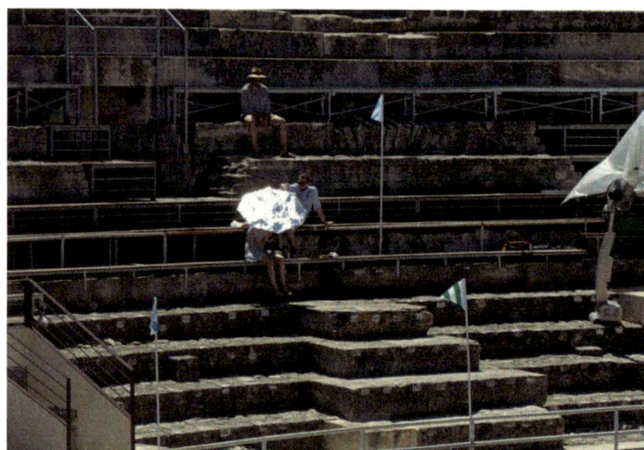

7/6/12—3:07:11 PM

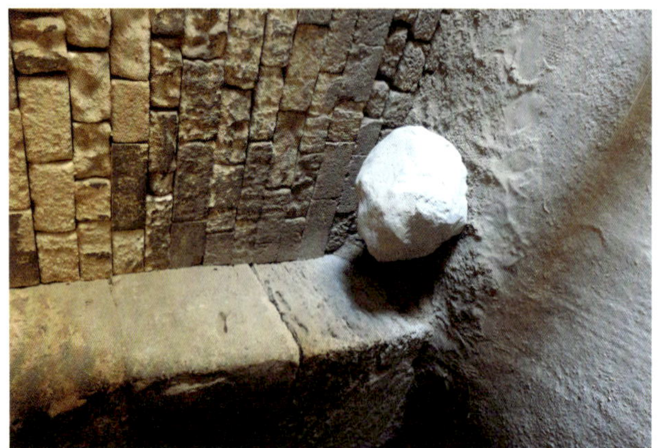

7/6/12—3:07:31 PM

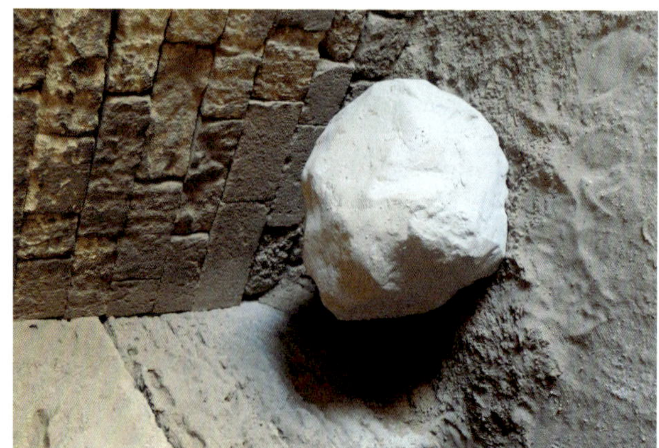

7/6/12—3:07:36 PM

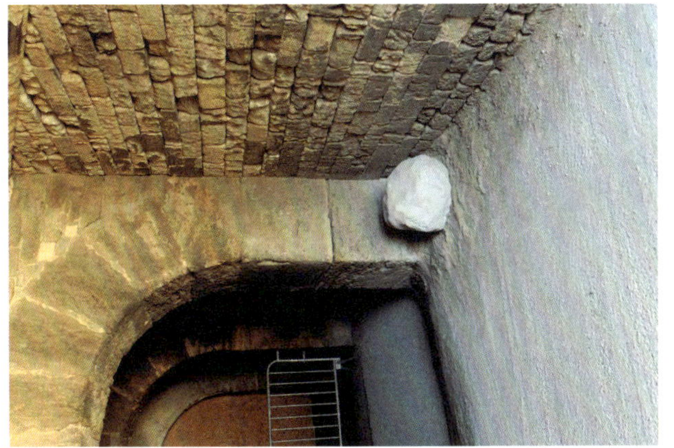
7/6/12—3:07:45 PM

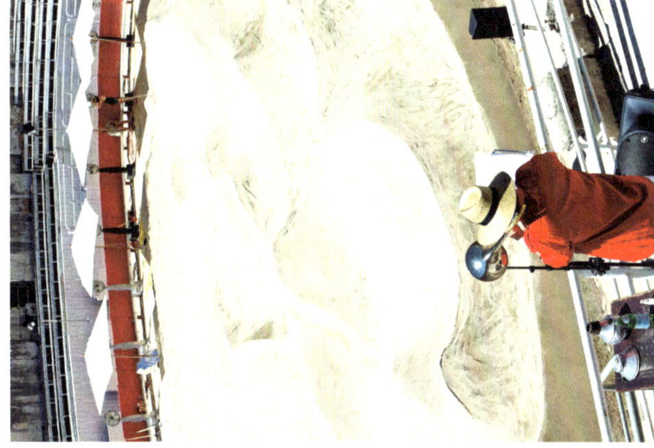
7/6/12—3:08:15 PM

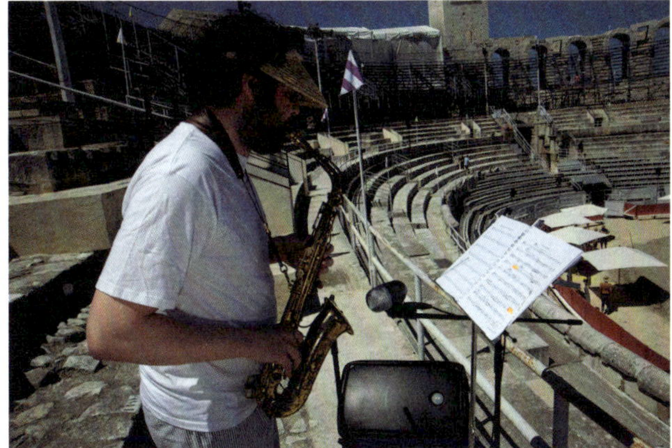
7/6/12—3:08:19 PM

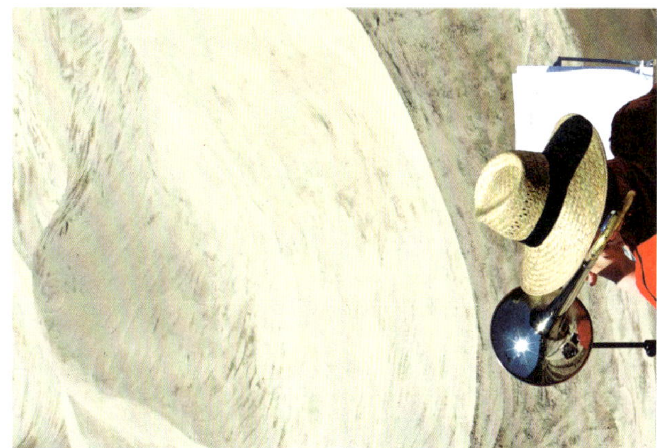
7/6/12—3:08:28 PM

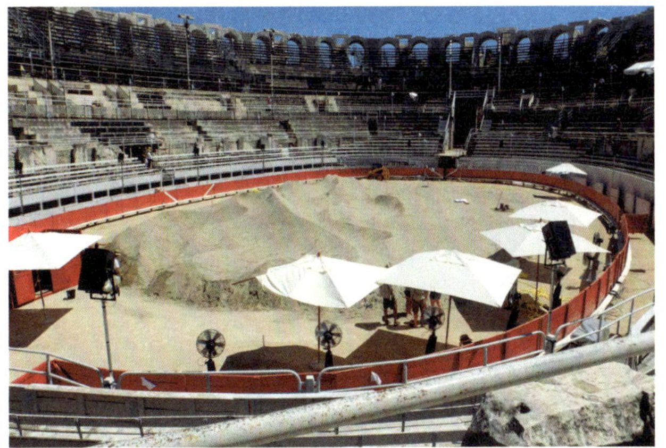
7/6/12—3:08:46 PM

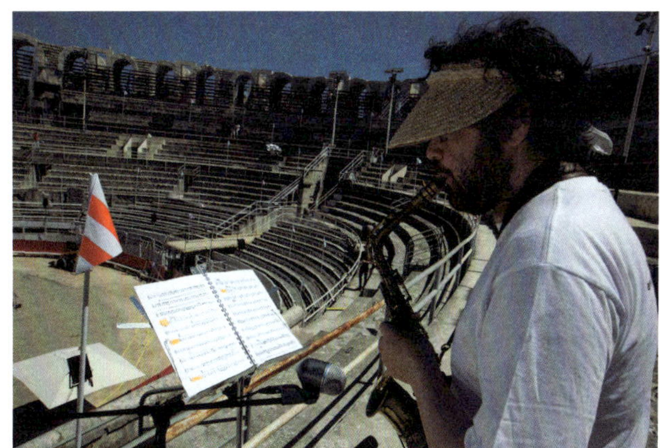
7/6/12—3:08:57 PM

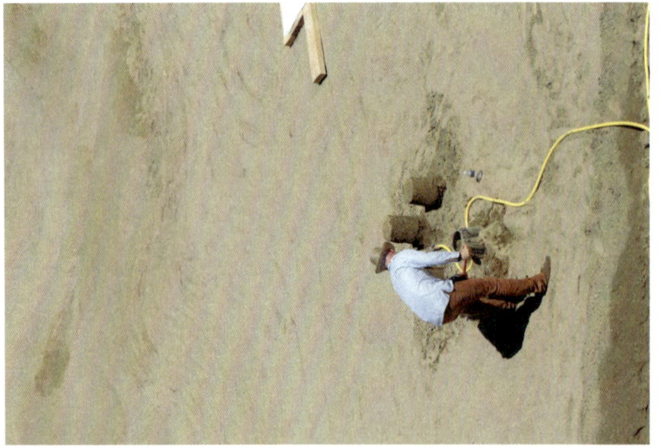

7/6/12—3:10:59 PM

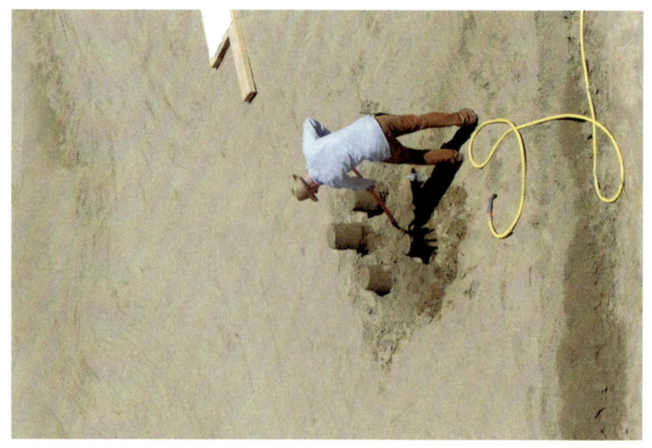

7/6/12—3:11:45 PM

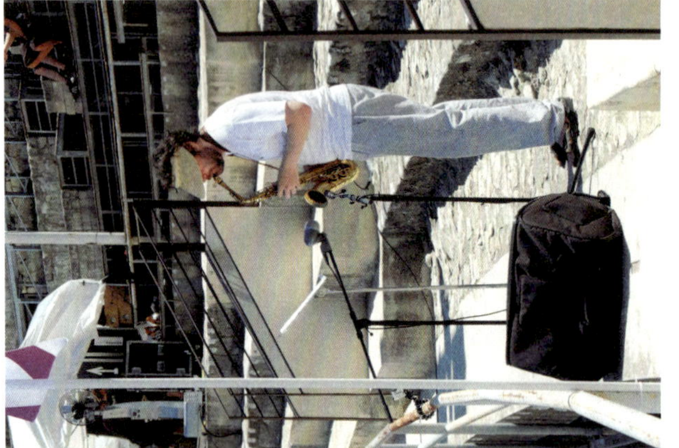

7/6/12—3:12:07 PM

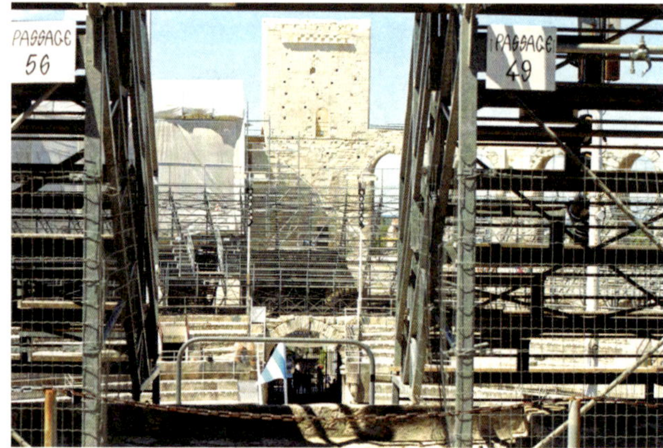

7/6/12—3:14:35 PM

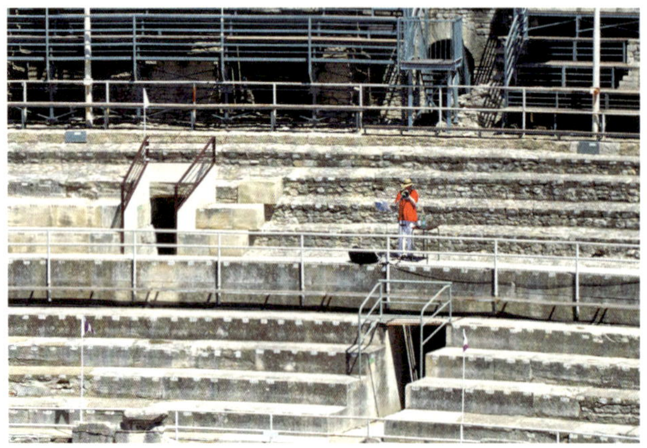

7/6/12—3:16:34 PM

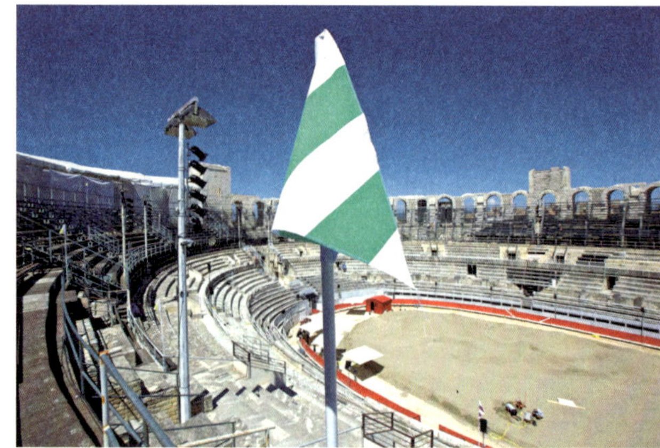

7/6/12—3:17:26 PM

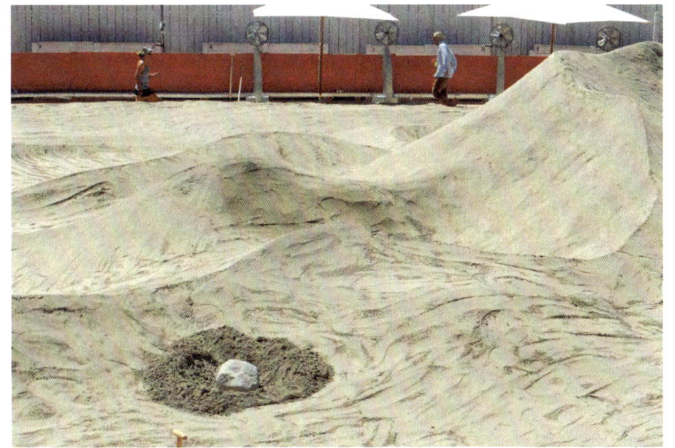

7/6/12—3:17:44 PM

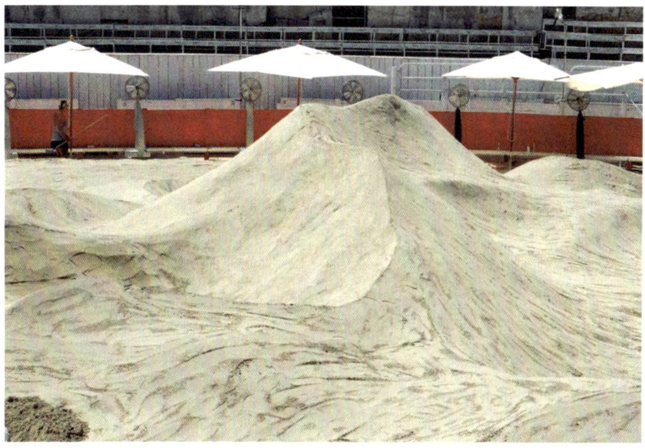

7/6/12—3:17:47 PM

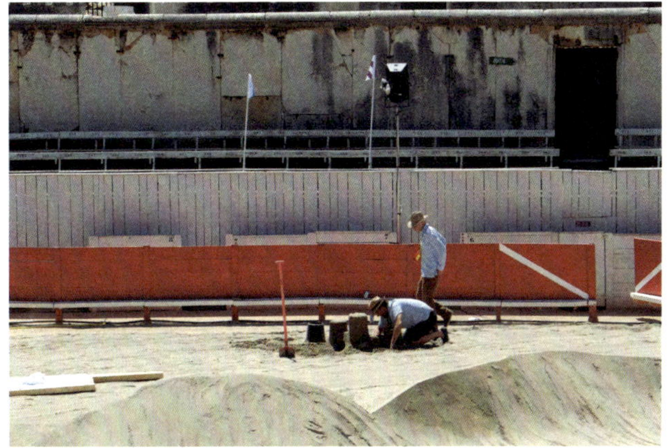

7/6/12—3:17:54 PM

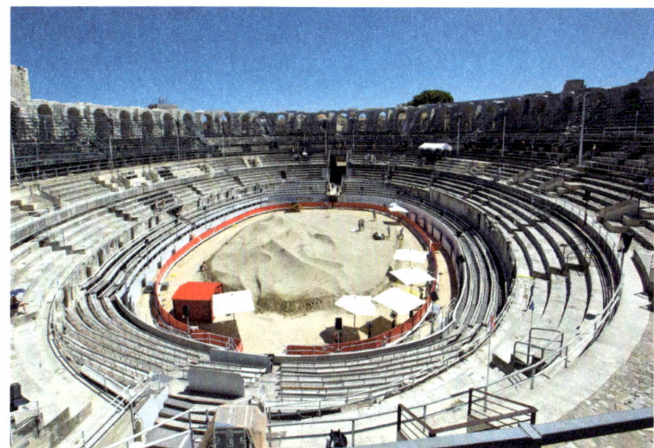

7/6/12—3:20:17 PM

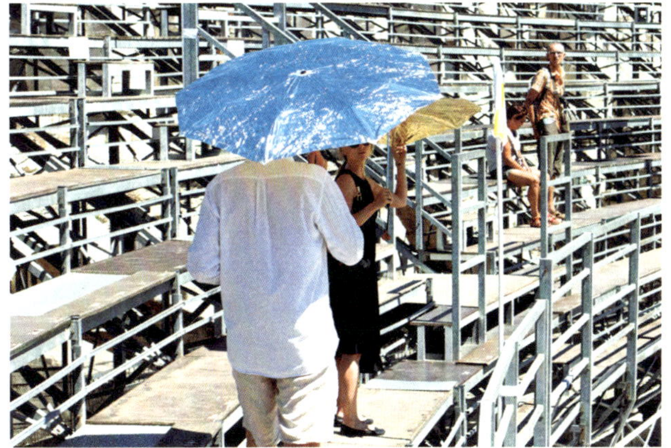

7/6/12—3:22:40 PM

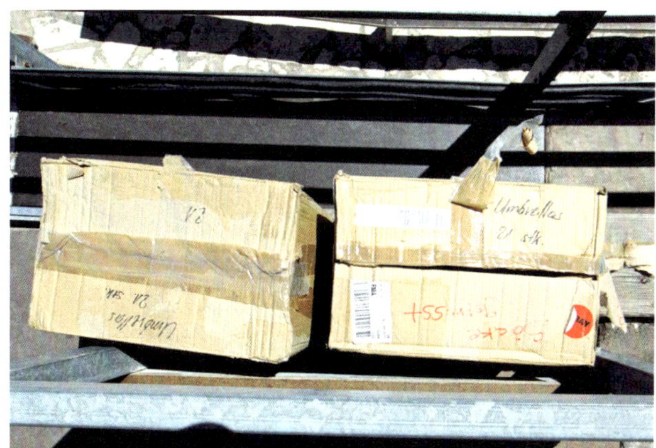

7/6/12—3:22:58 PM

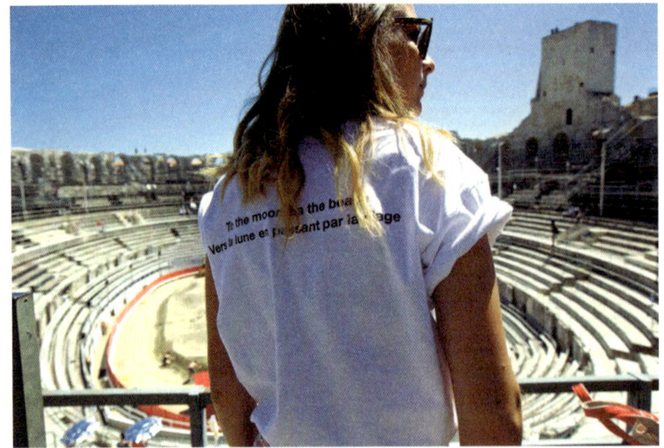

7/6/12—3:24:03 PM

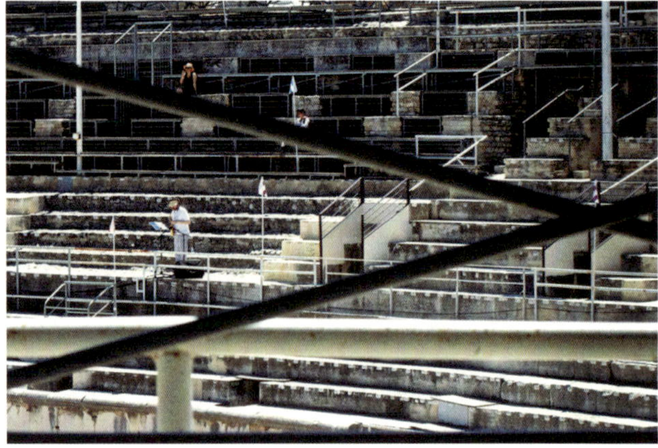

7/6/12—3:26:08 PM

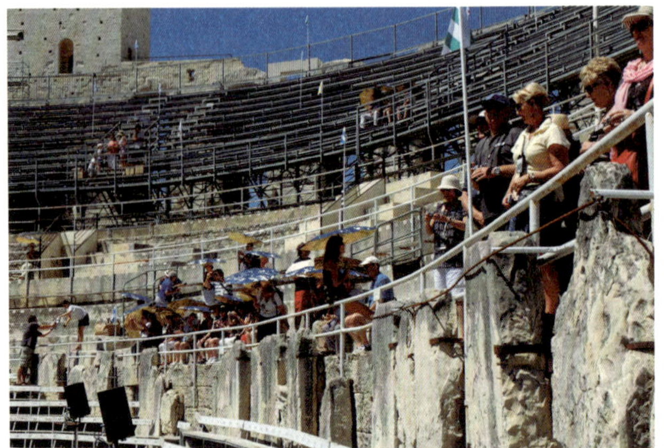

7/6/12—3:27:20 PM

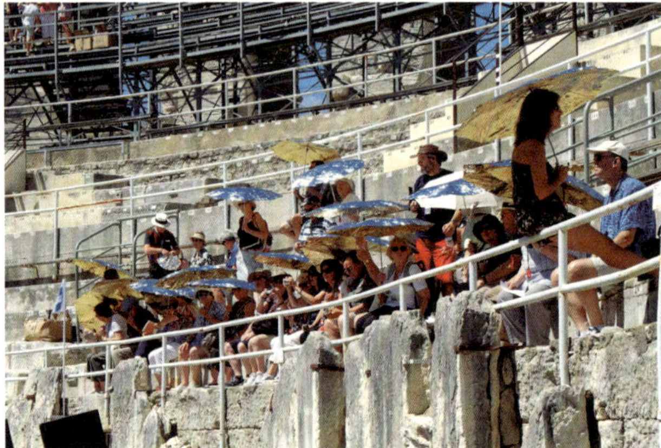

7/6/12—3:27:31 PM

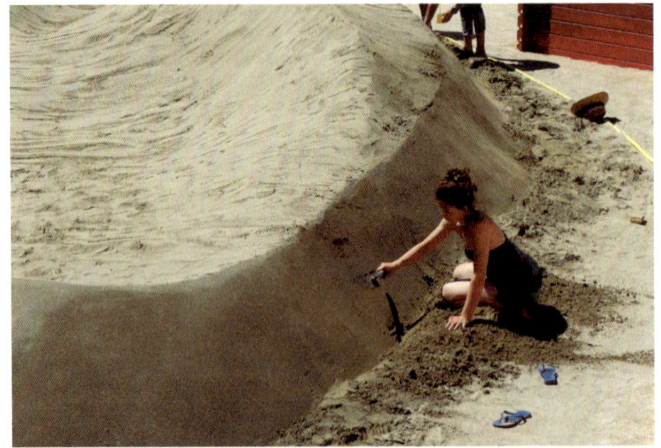

7/6/12—3:27:39 PM

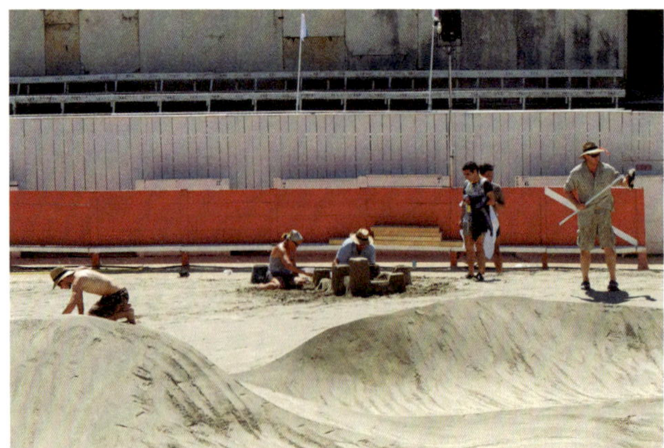

7/6/12—3:27:41 PM

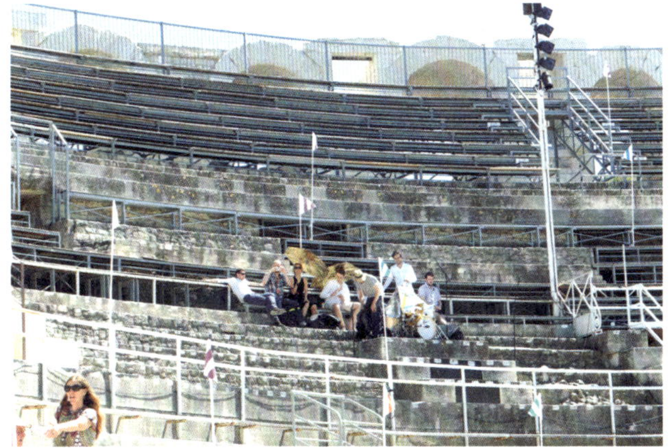
7/6/12—3:28:12 PM

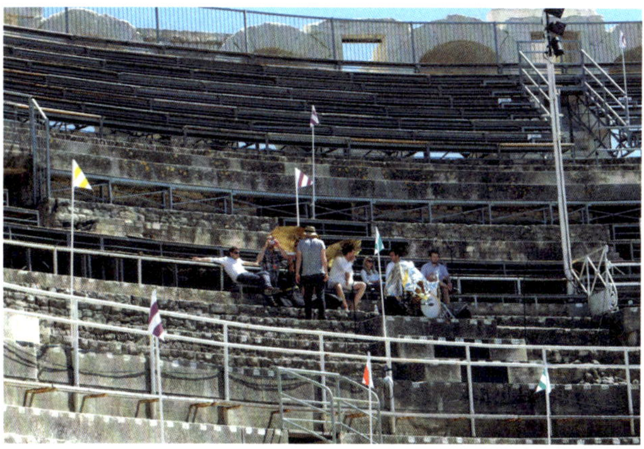
7/6/12—3:28:29 PM

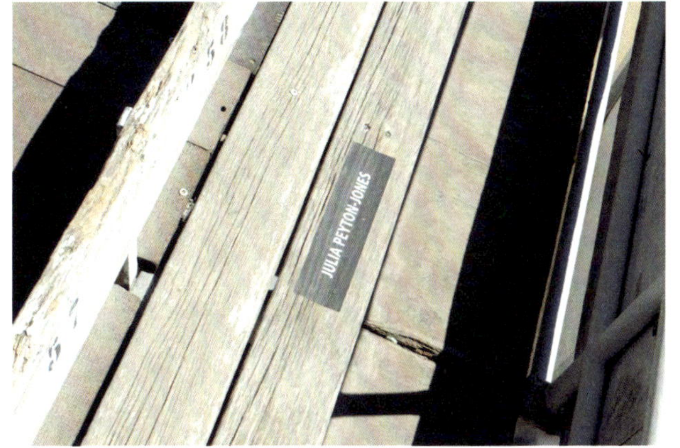

7/6/12—3:28:36 PM

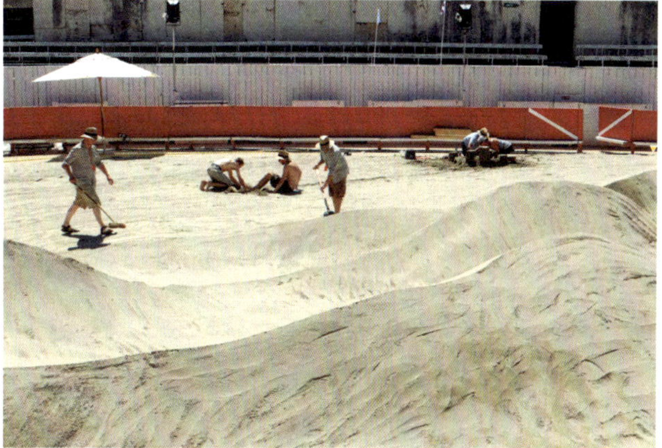
7/6/12—3:28:42 PM

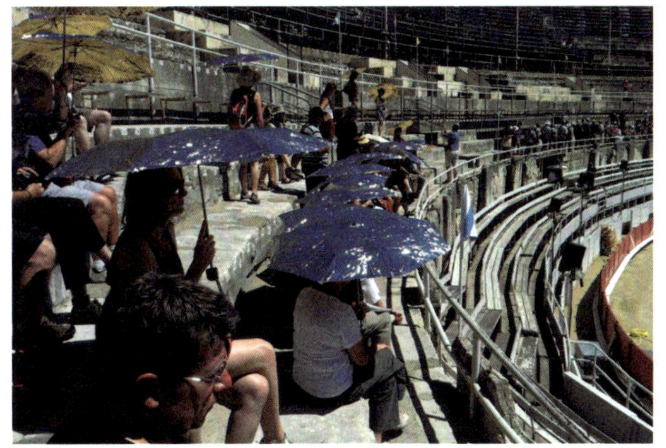
7/6/12—3:29:09 PM

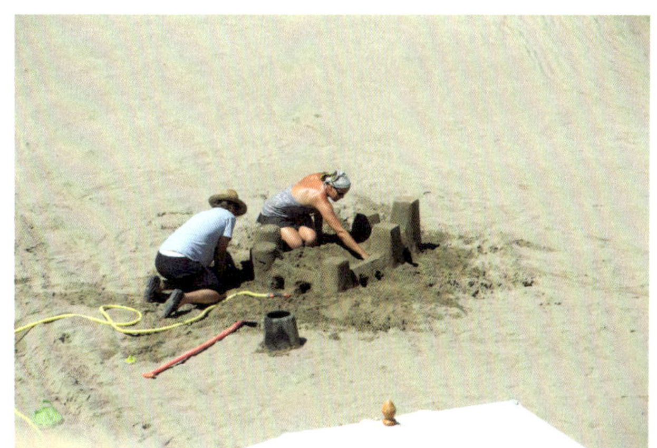
7/6/12—3:29:20 PM

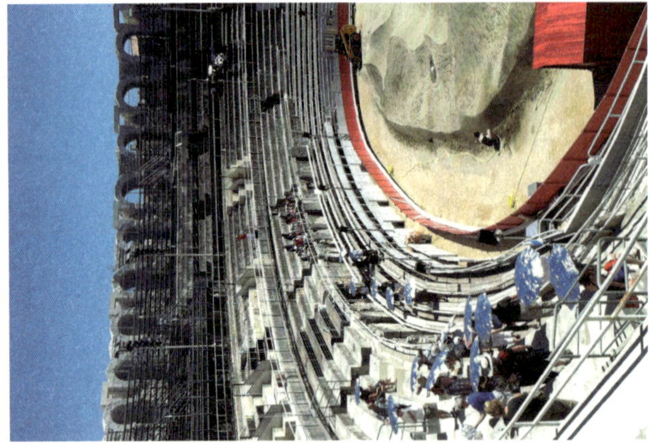
7/6/12—3:30:51 PM

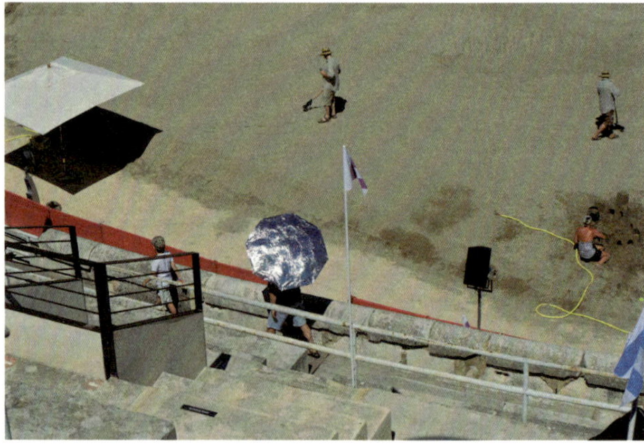
7/6/12—3:40:14 PM

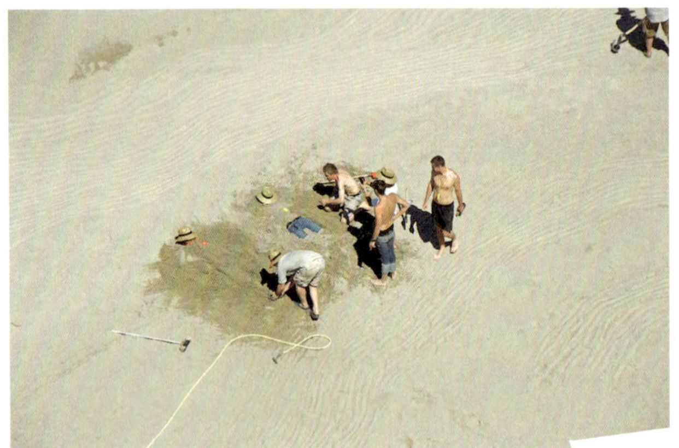
7/6/12—3:52:54 PM

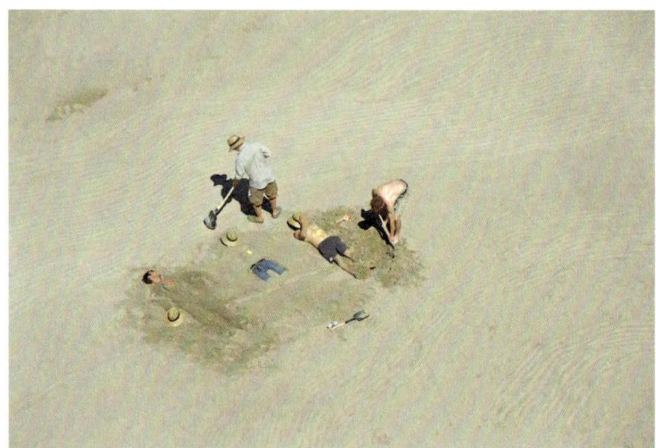
7/6/12—4:00:34 PM

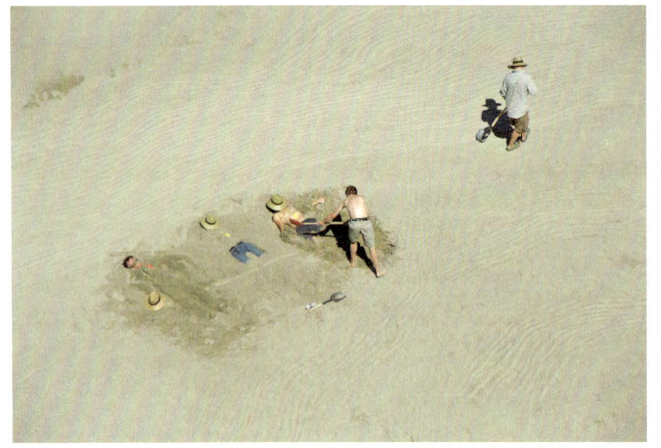
7/6/12—4:01:08 PM

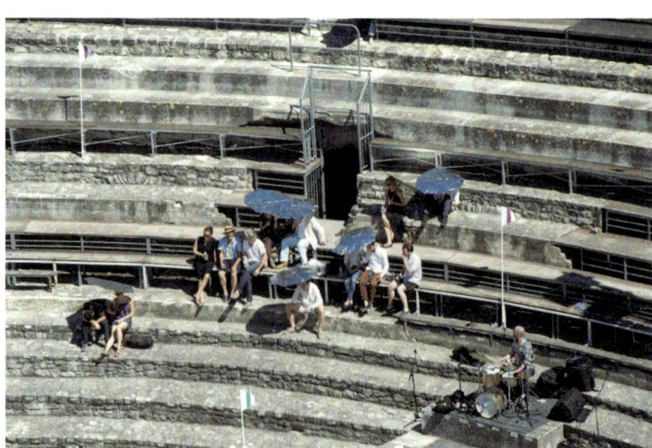
7/6/12—4:02:35 PM

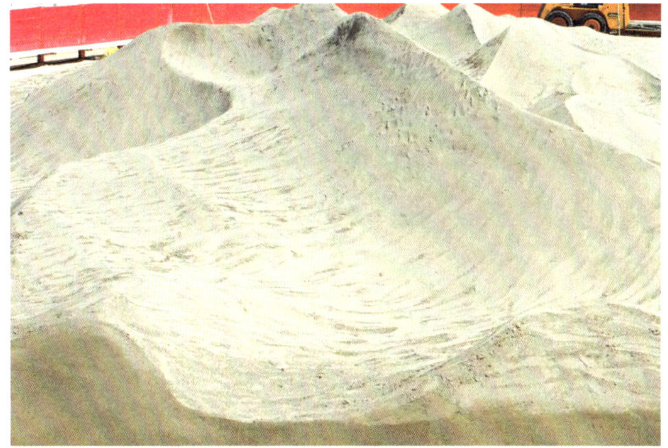

7/6/12—4:04:01 PM

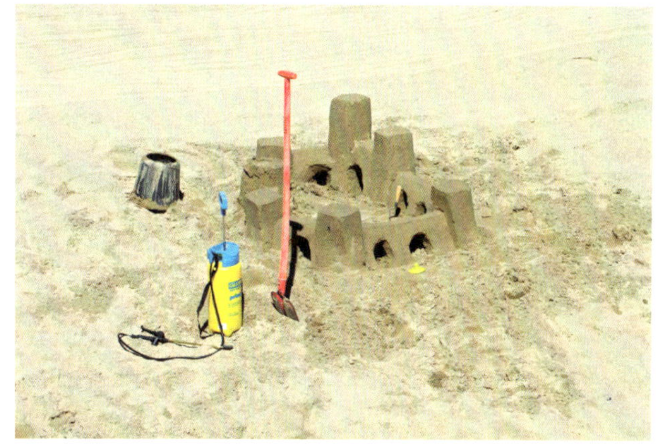

7/6/12—4:05:08 PM

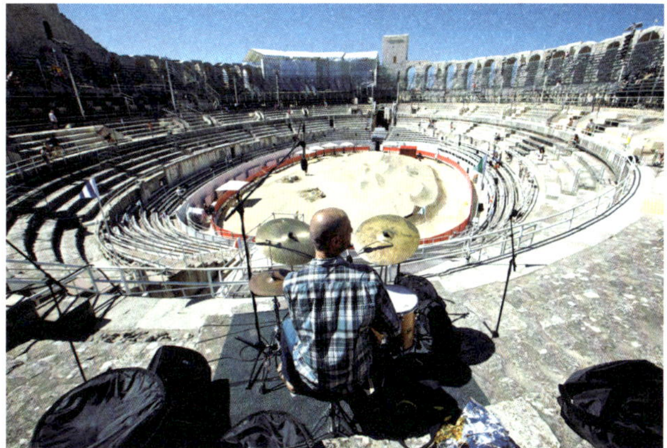

7/6/12—4:08:59 PM

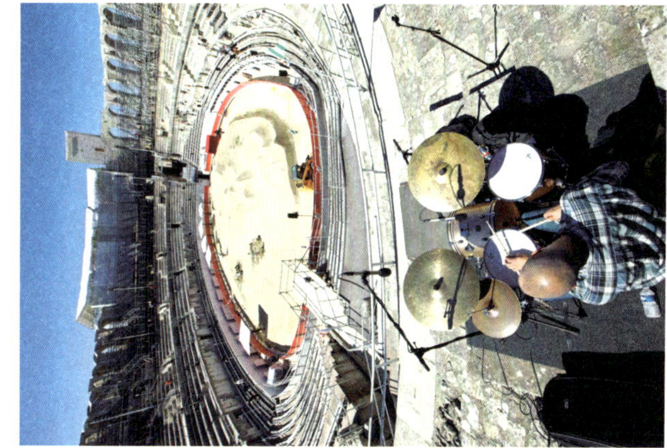

7/6/12—4:09:20 PM

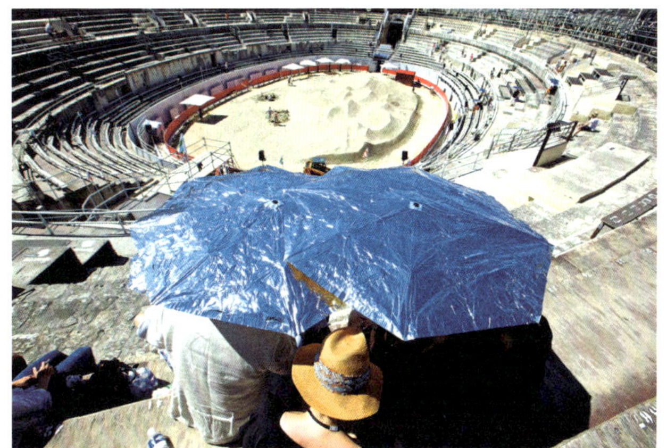

7/6/12—4:09:39 PM

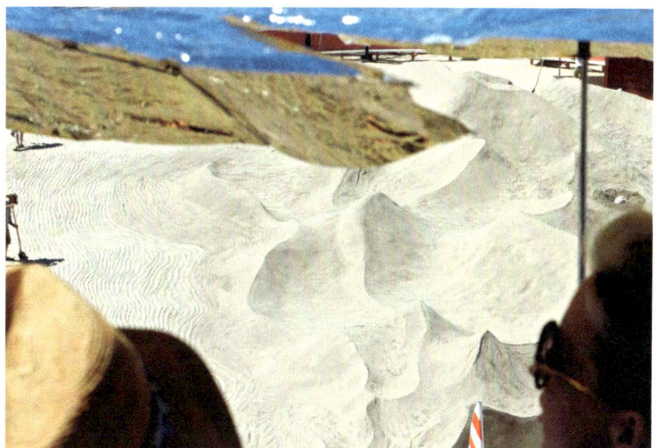

7/6/12—4:10:41 PM

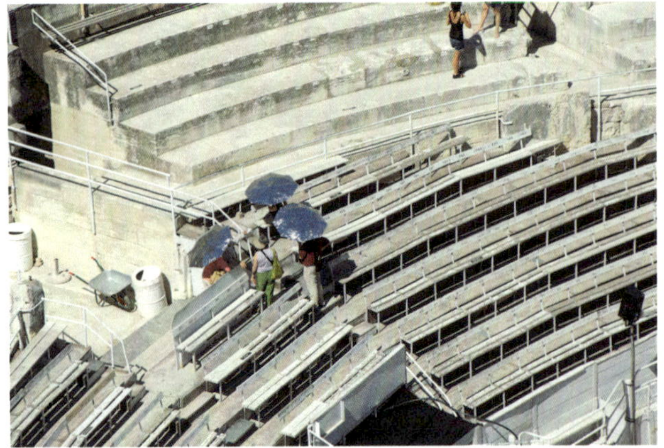
7/6/12—4:20:30 PM

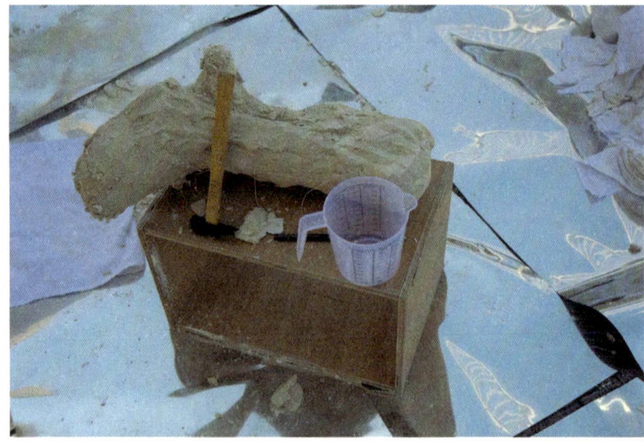
7/6/12—4:29:59 PM

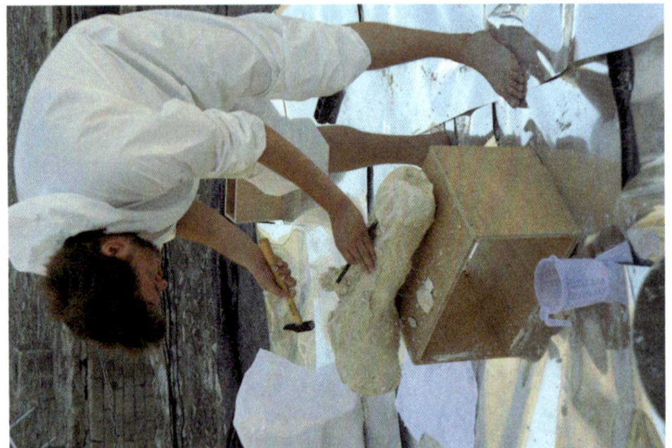
7/6/12—4:30:49 PM

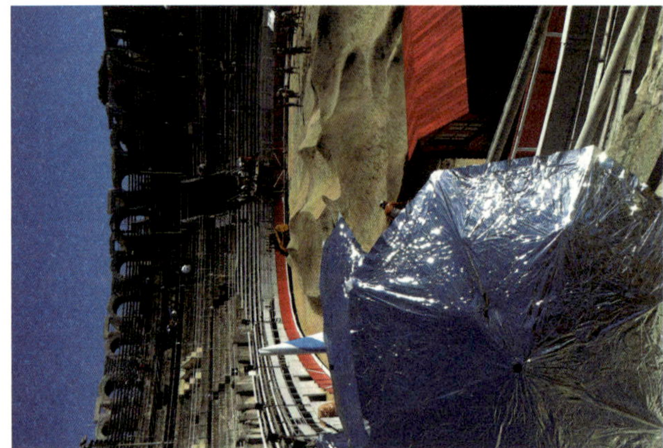
7/6/12—4:31:01 PM

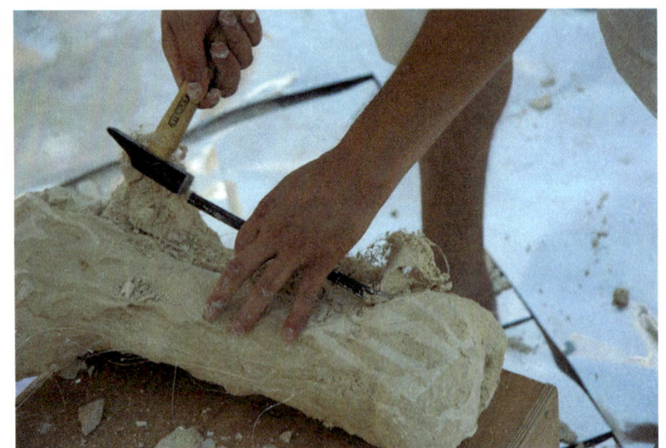
7/6/12—4:31:09 PM

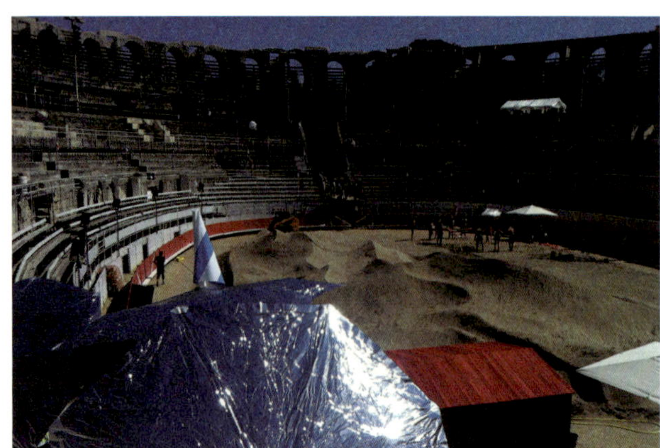
7/6/12—4:31:13 PM

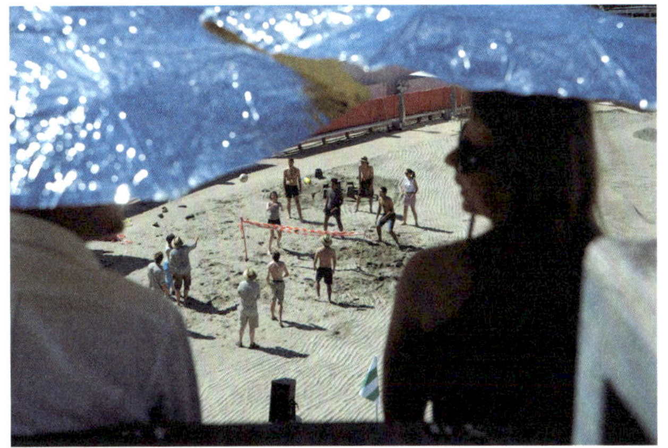

7/6/12—4:33:17 PM

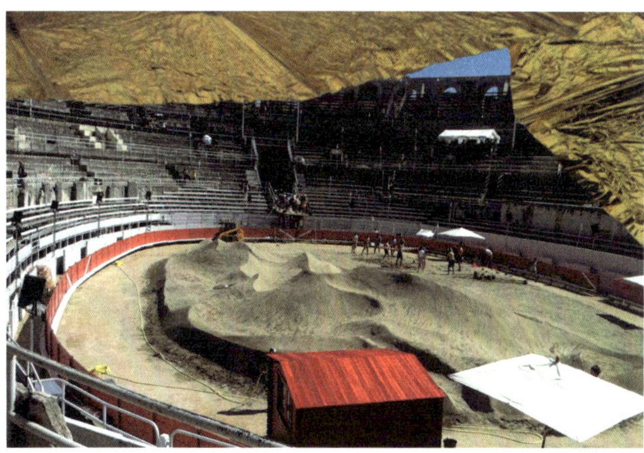

7/6/12—4:33:23 PM

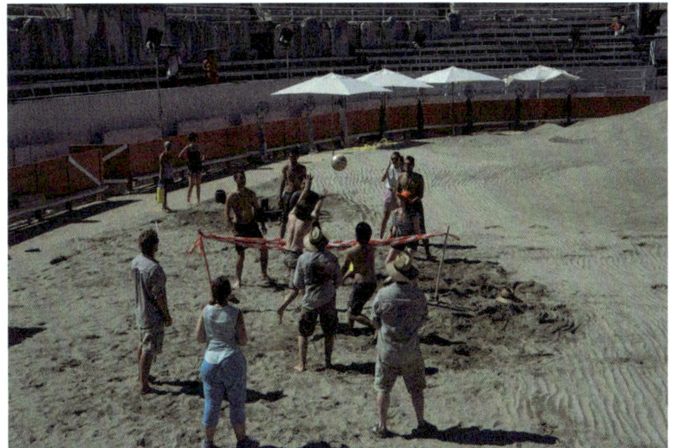

7/6/12—4:37:08 PM

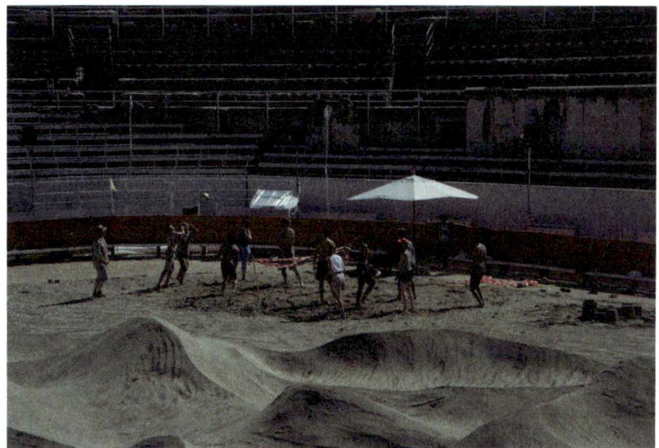

7/6/12—4:44:28 PM

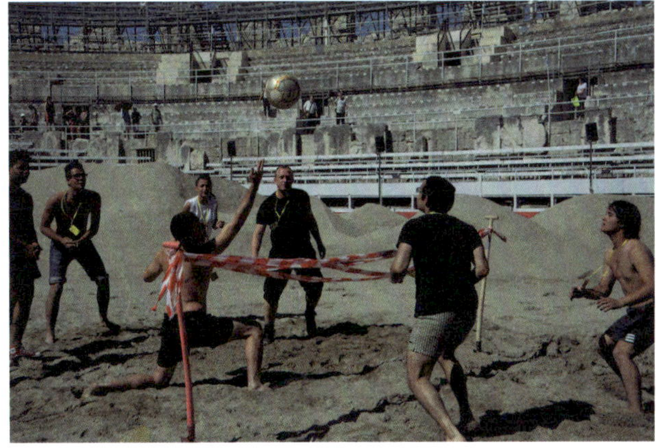

7/6/12—4:49:04 PM

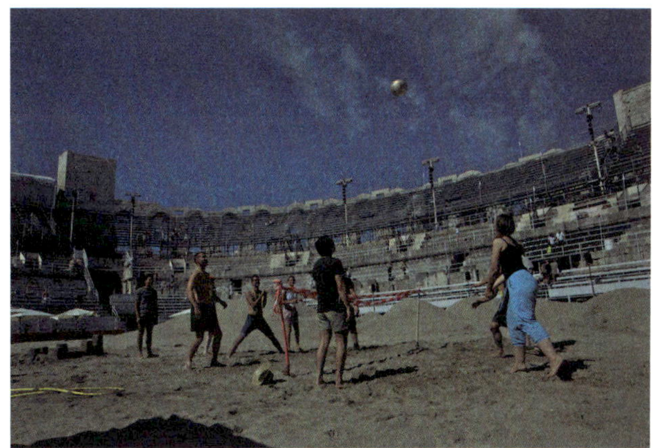

7/6/12—4:49:45 PM

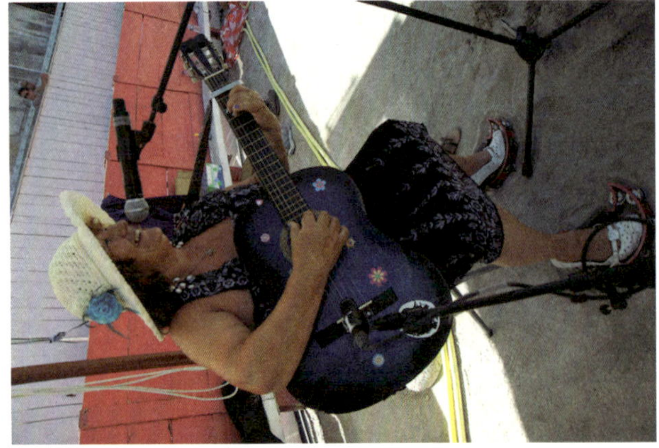
7/6/12—4:52:10 PM

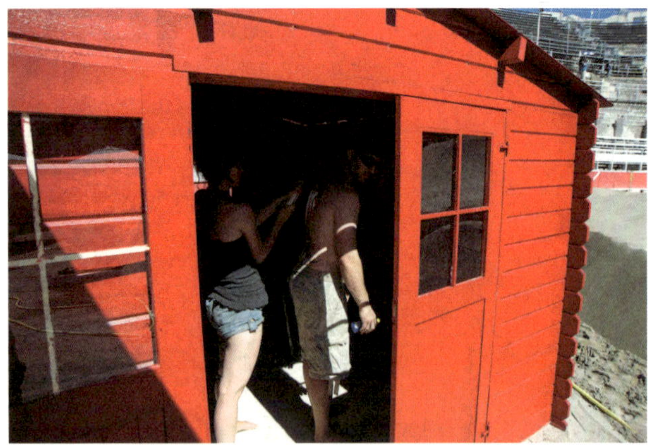
7/6/12—4:53:52 PM

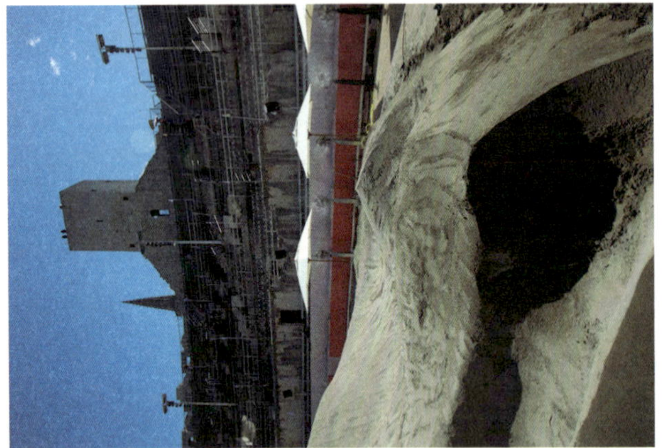
7/6/12—4:54:10 PM

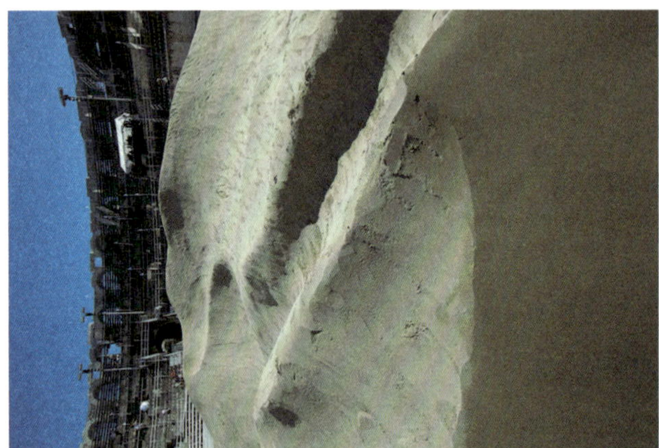
7/6/12—4:54:12 PM

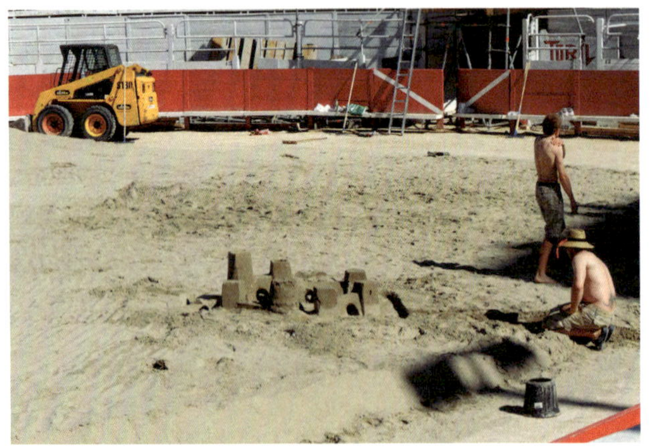
7/6/12—5:17:13 PM

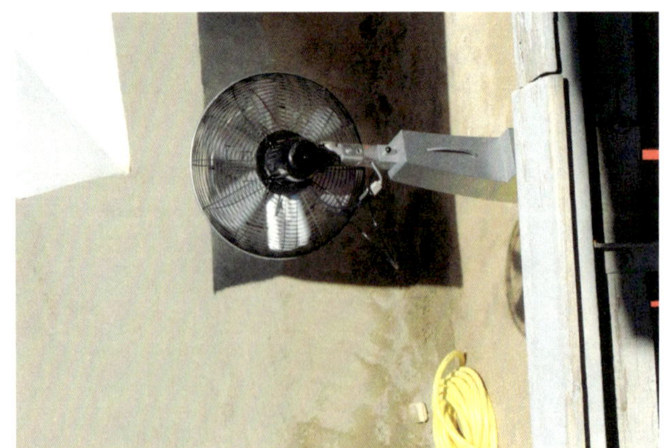
7/6/12—5:17:19 PM

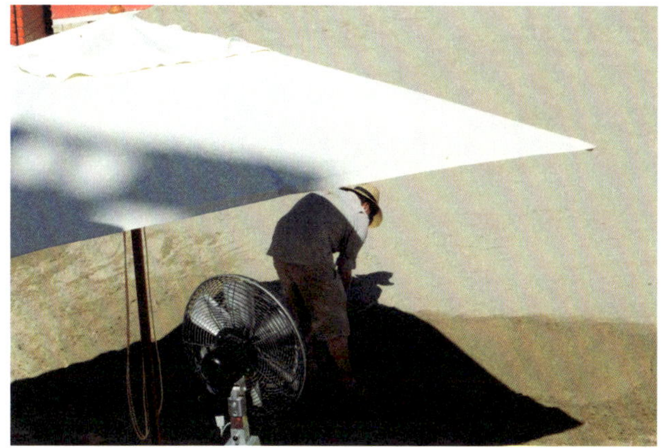

7/6/12—5:17:25 PM

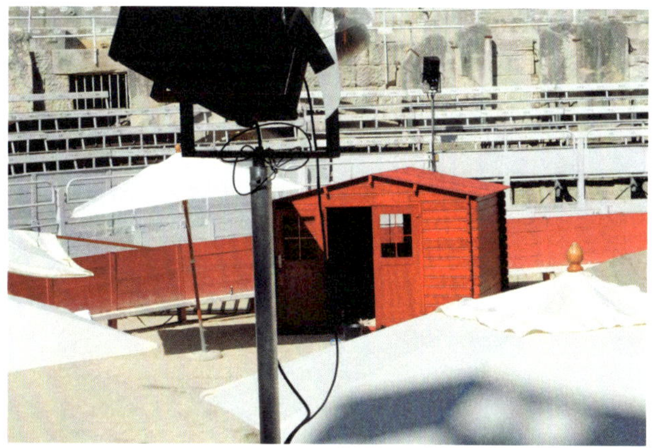

7/6/12—5:17:29 PM

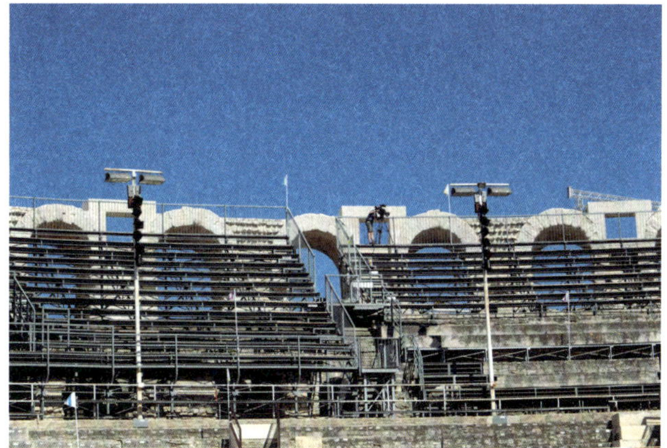

7/6/12—5:17:36 PM

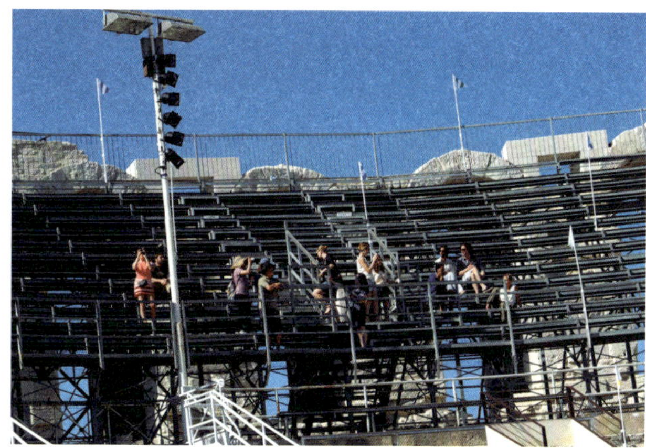

7/6/12—5:17:48 PM

7/6/12—5:18:44 PM

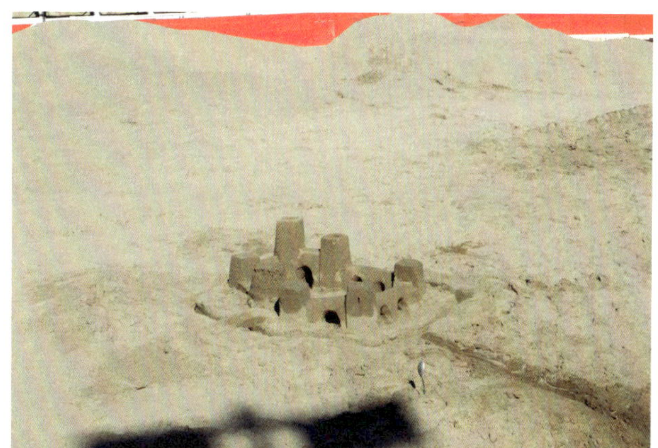

7/6/12—5:18:47 PM

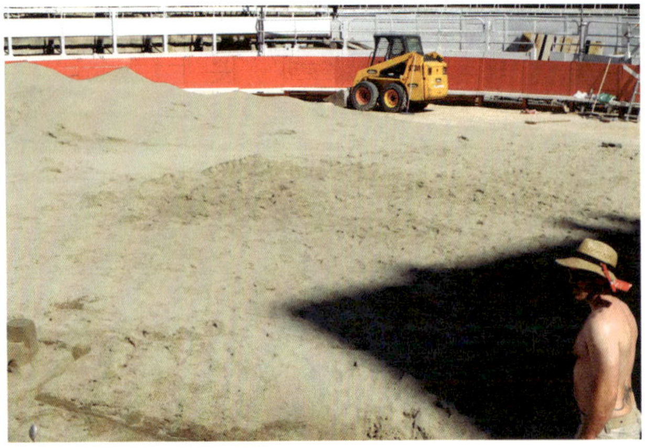
7/6/12—5:18:50 PM

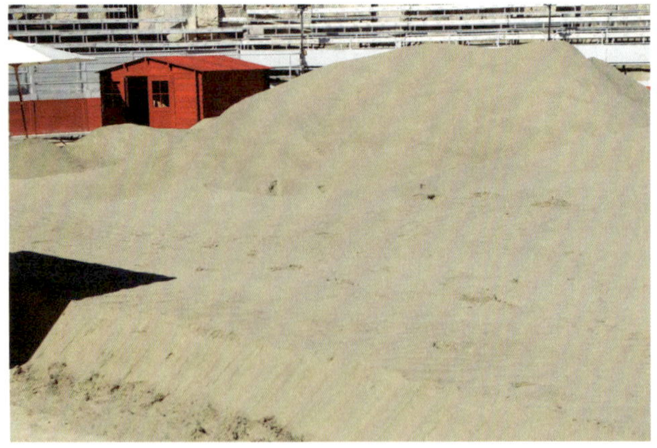
7/6/12—5:18:54 PM

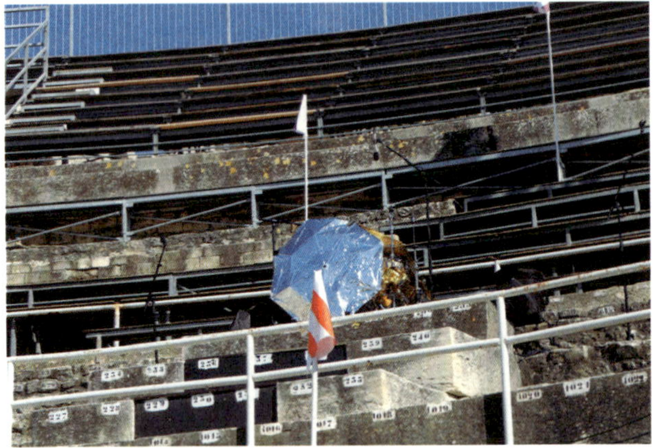
7/6/12—5:19:48 PM

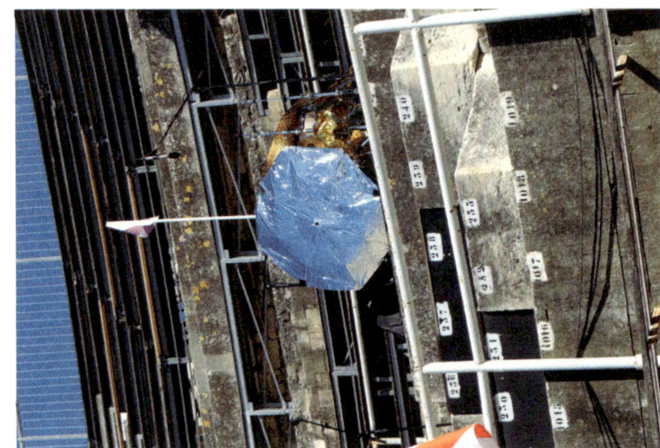
7/6/12—5:20:05 PM

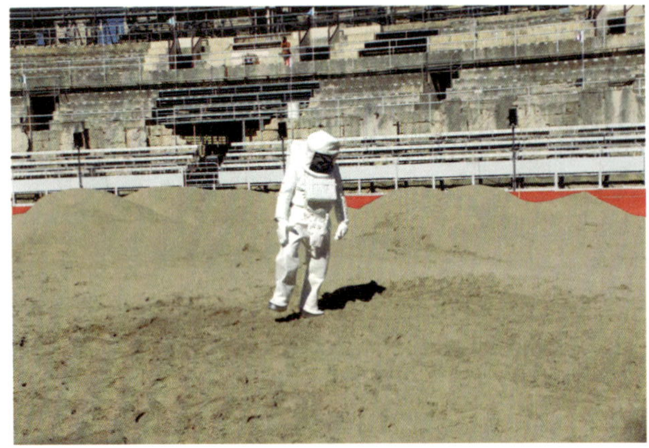
7/6/12—5:22:04 PM

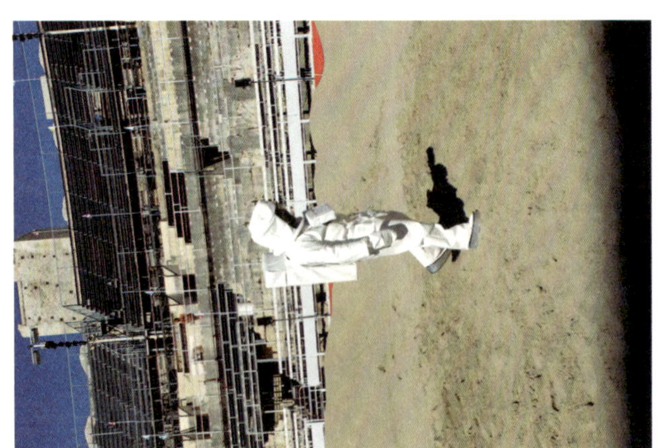
7/6/12—5:22:07 PM

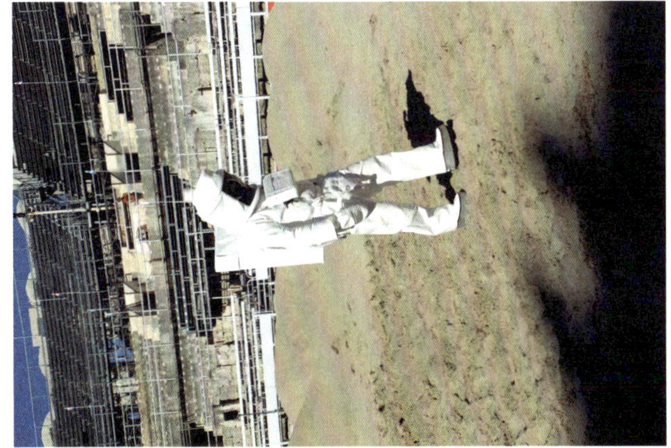

7/6/12—5:22:13 PM

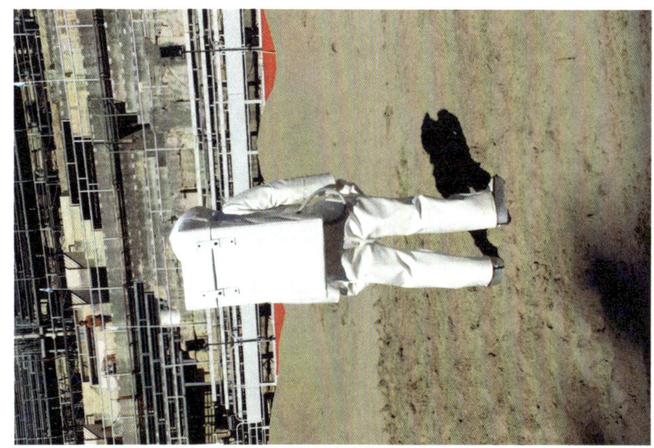

7/6/12—5:22:17 PM

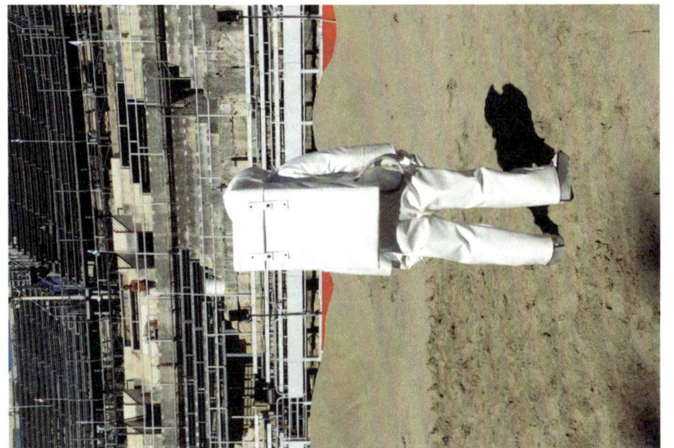

7/6/12—5:22:21 PM

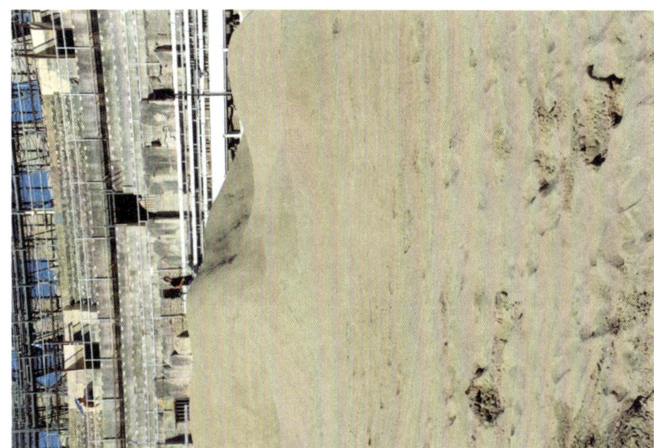

7/6/12—5:22:32 PM

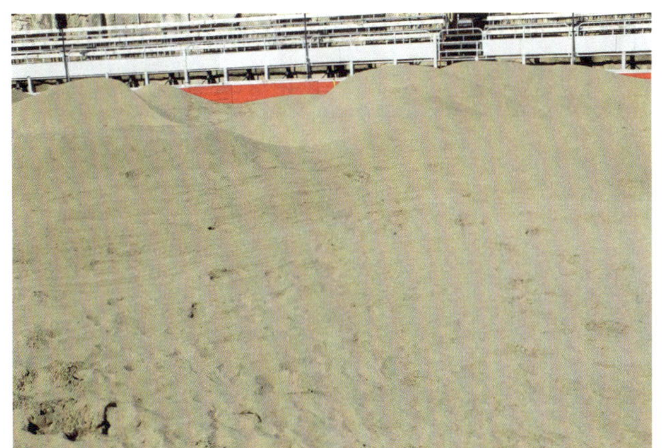

7/6/12—5:22:36 PM

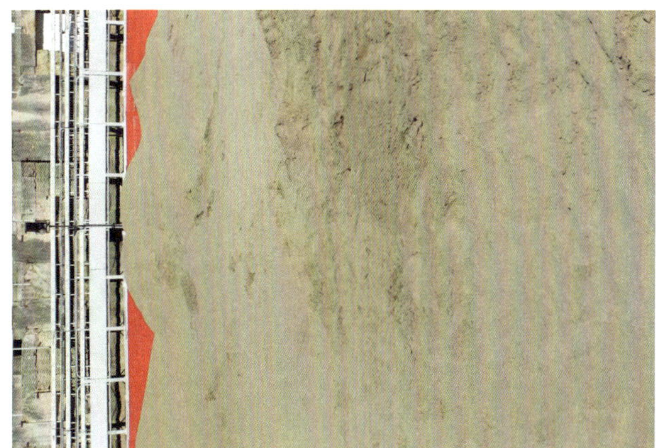

7/6/12—5:22:40 PM

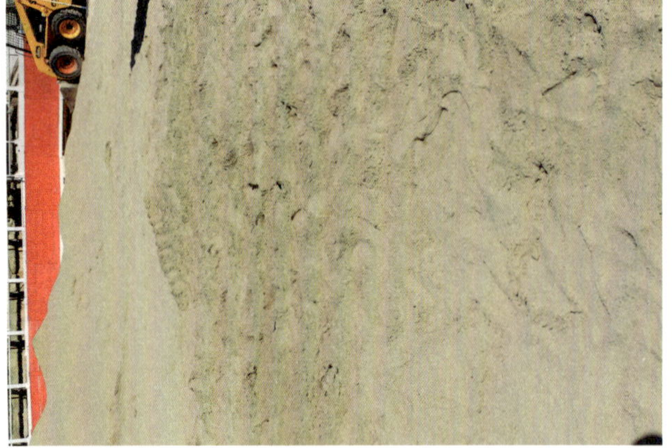
7/6/12—5:22:42 PM

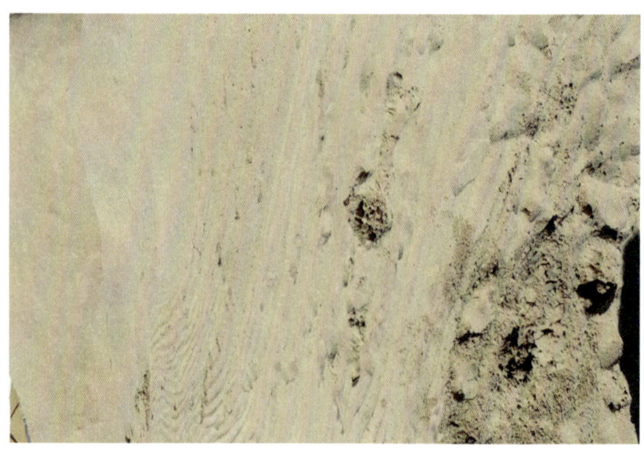
7/6/12—5:22:47 PM

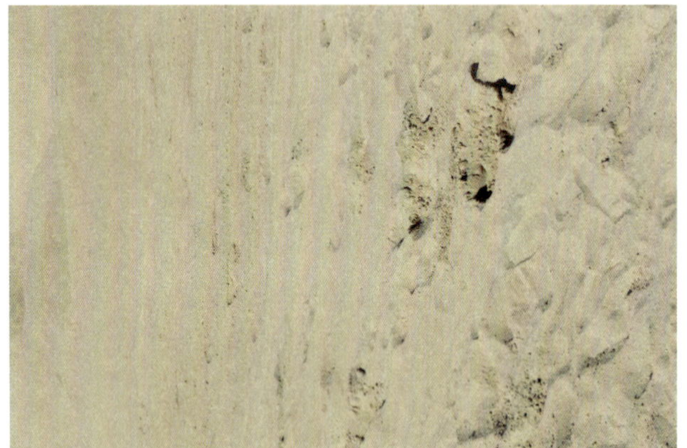
7/6/12—5:22:49 PM

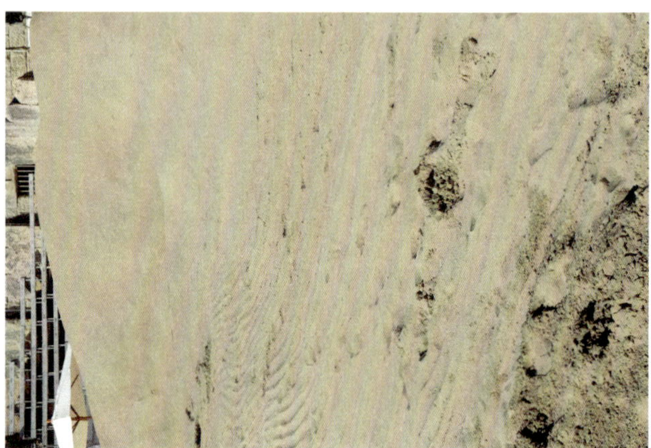
7/6/12—5:22:53 PM

7/6/12—5:22:55 PM

7/6/12—5:23:23 PM

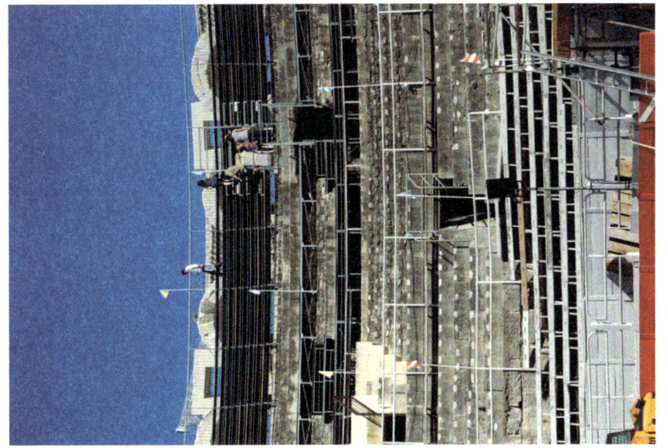

7/6/12—5:23:35 PM

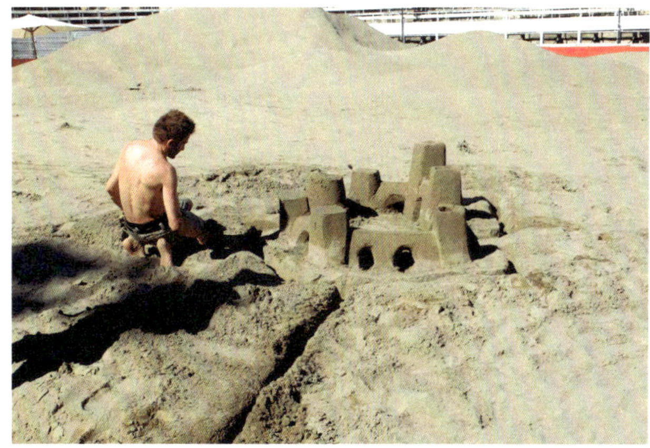

7/6/12—5:23:51 PM

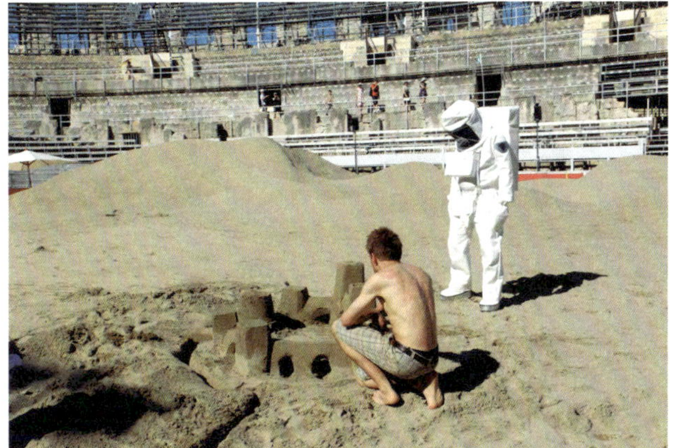

7/6/12—5:24:04 PM

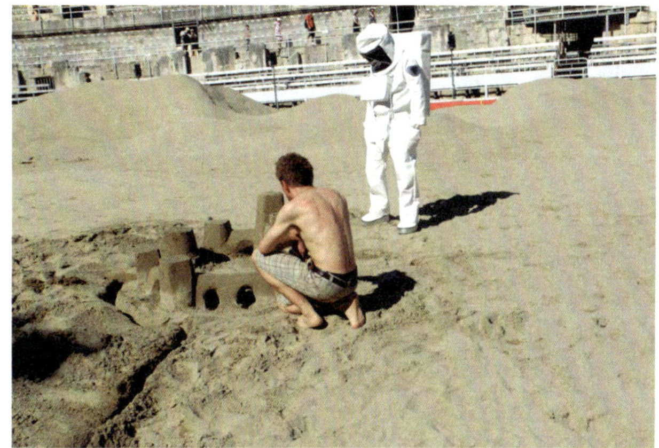

7/6/12—5:24:07 PM

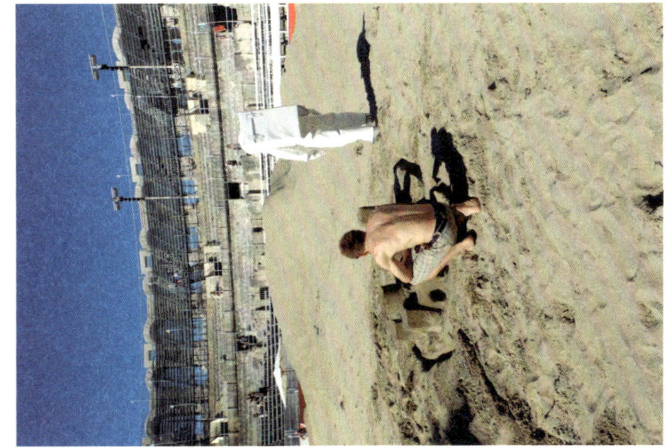

7/6/12—5:24:24 PM

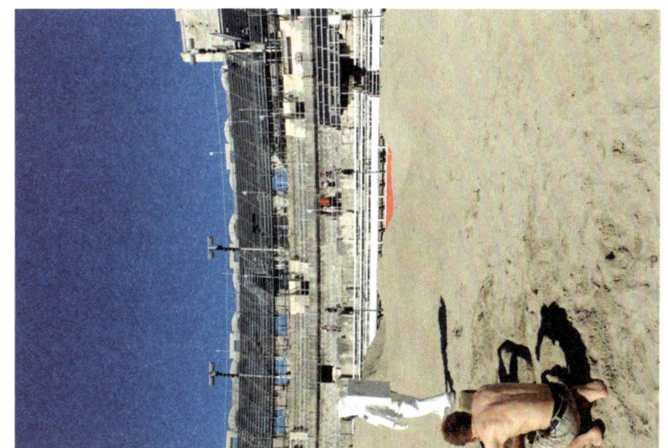

7/6/12—5:24:29 PM

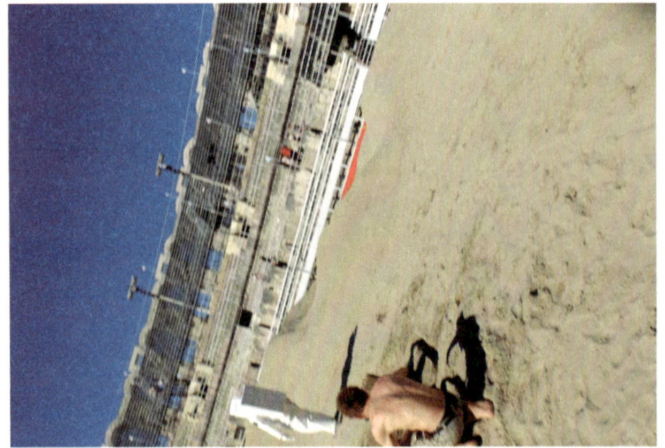
7/6/12—5:24:31 PM

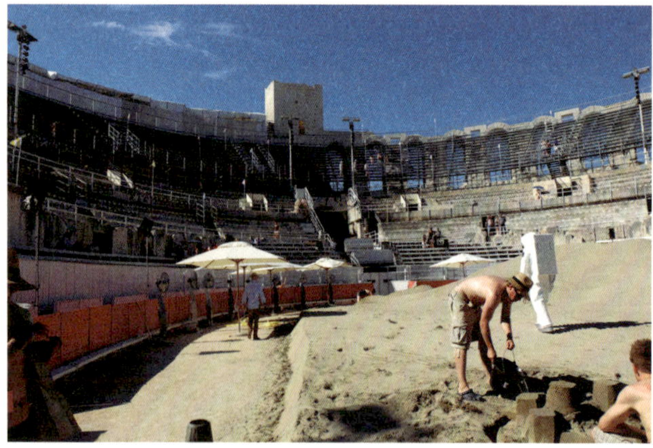
7/6/12—5:24:34 PM

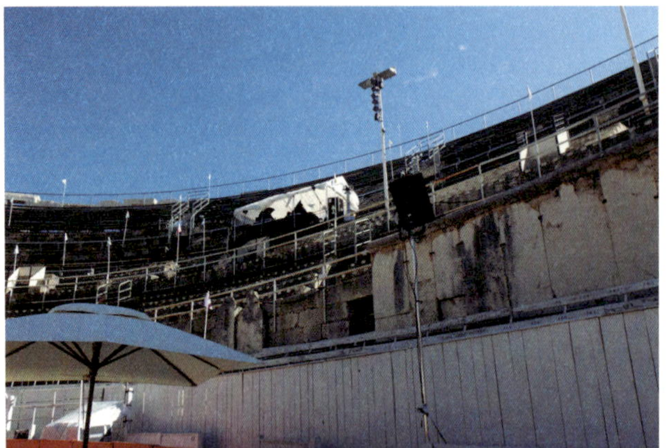
7/6/12—5:24:39 PM

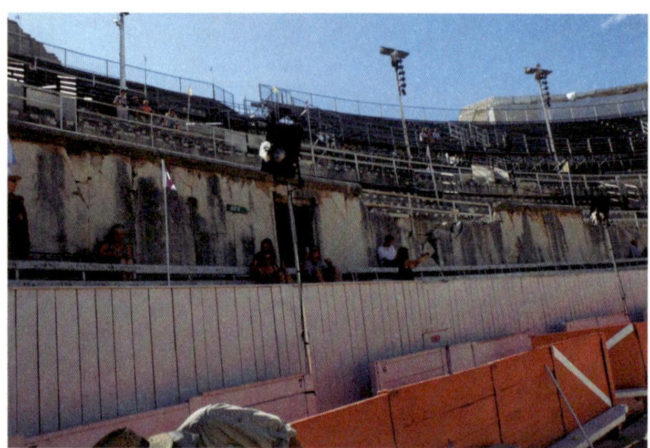
7/6/12—5:24:44 PM

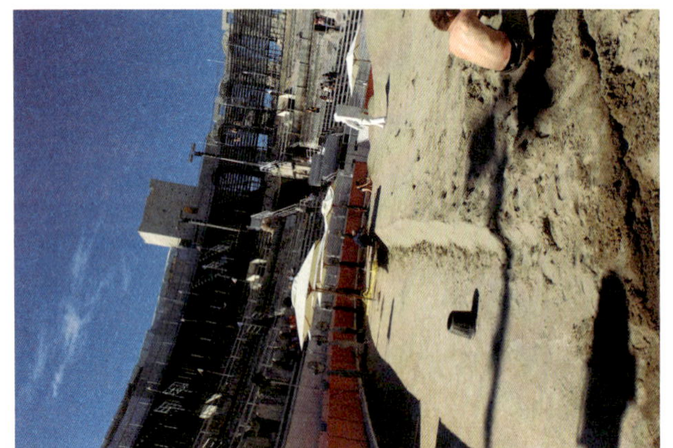
7/6/12—5:24:54 PM

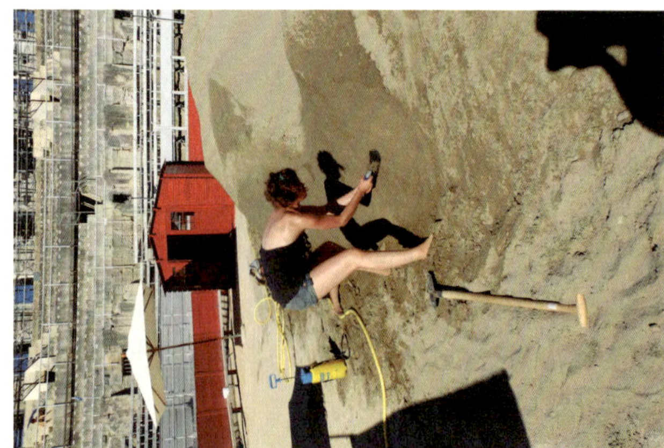
7/6/12—5:26:02 PM

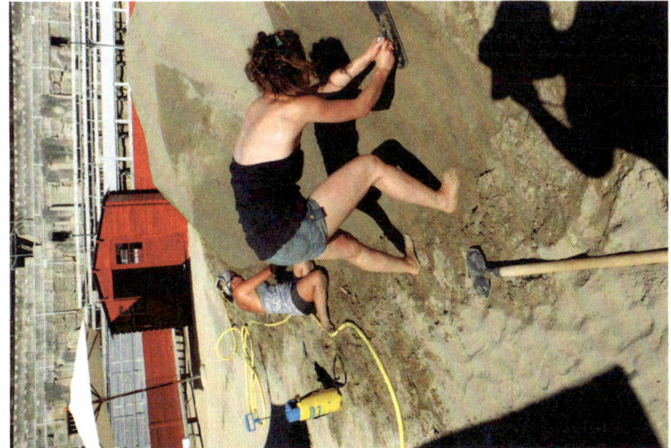

7/6/12—5:26:08 PM

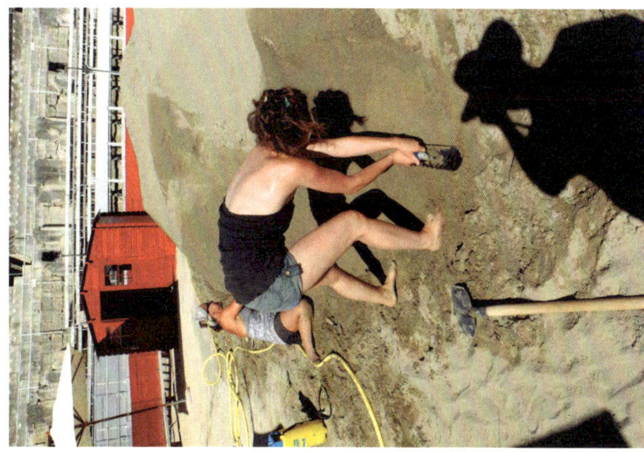

7/6/12—5:26:12 PM

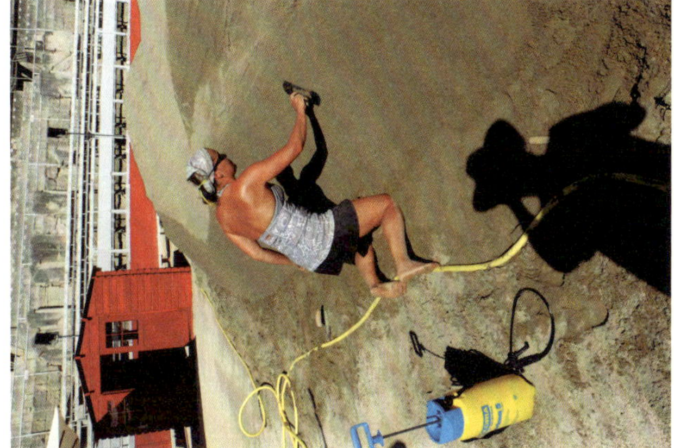

7/6/12—5:26:18 PM

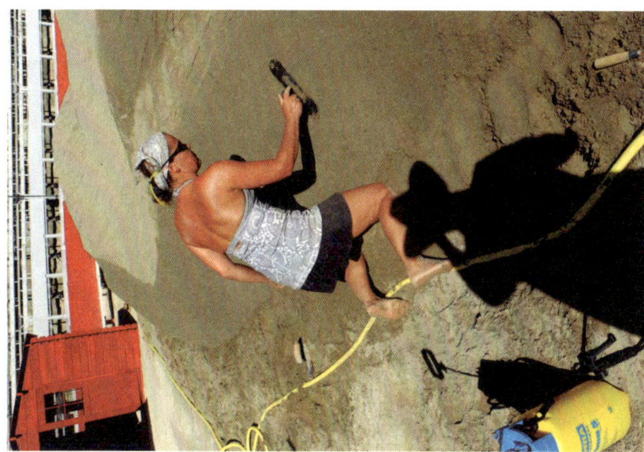

7/6/12—5:26:21 PM

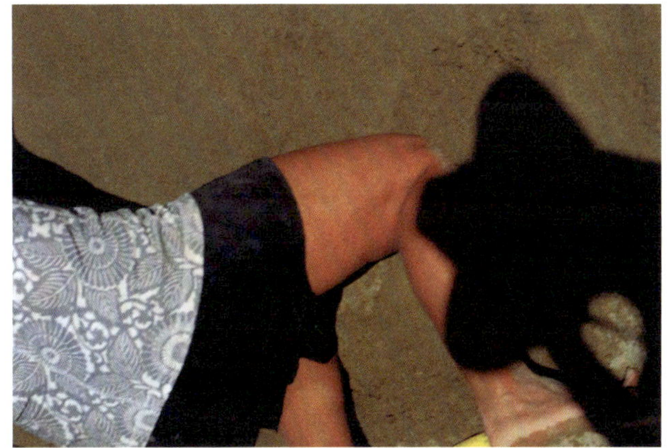

7/6/12—5:26:25 PM

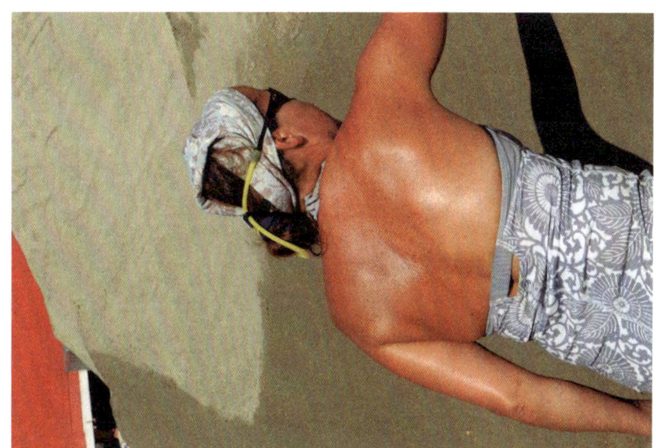

7/6/12—5:26:28 PM

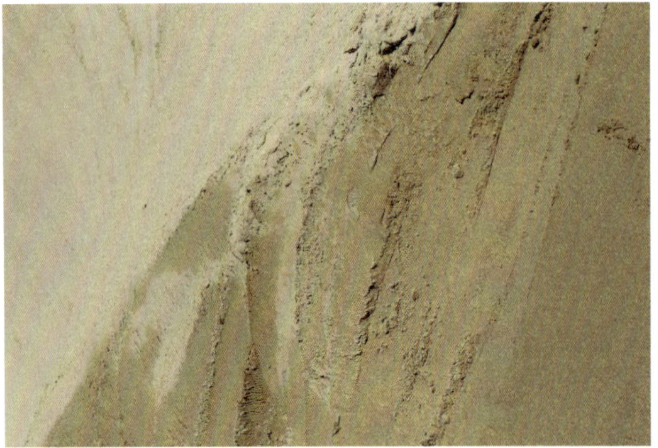
7/6/12—5:26:31 PM

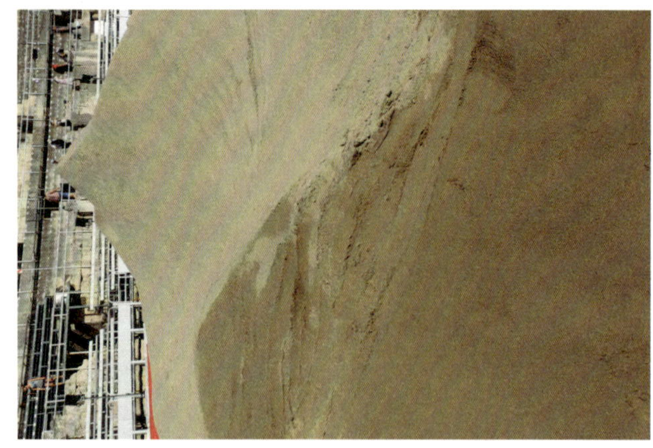
7/6/12—5:26:33 PM

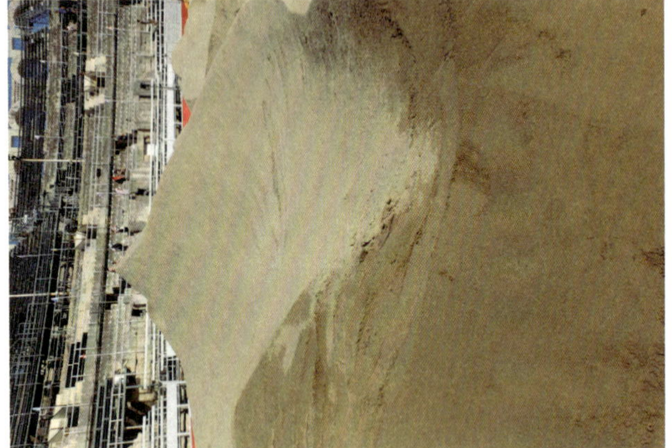
7/6/12—5:26:35 PM

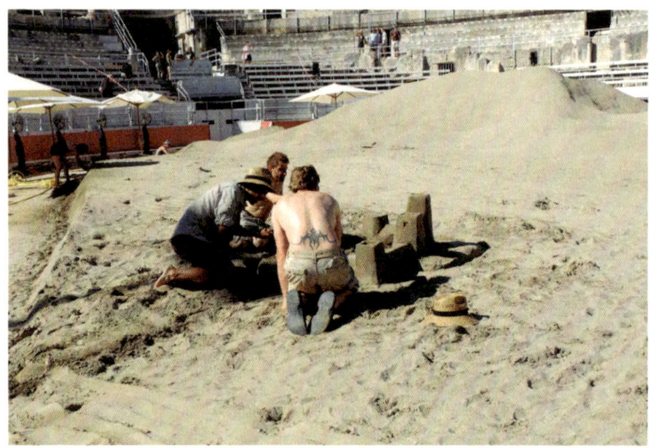
7/6/12—5:30:20 PM

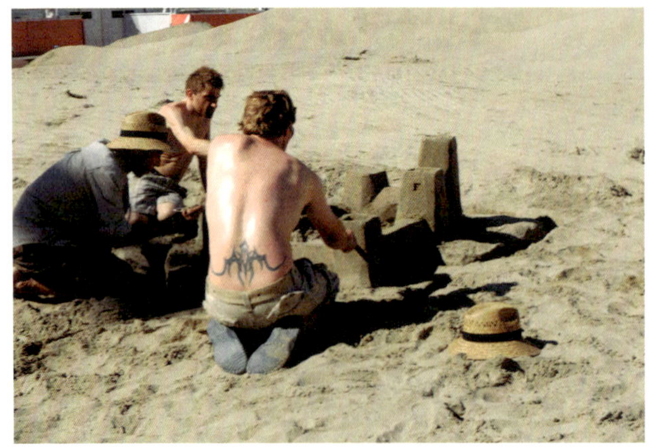
7/6/12—5:30:24 PM

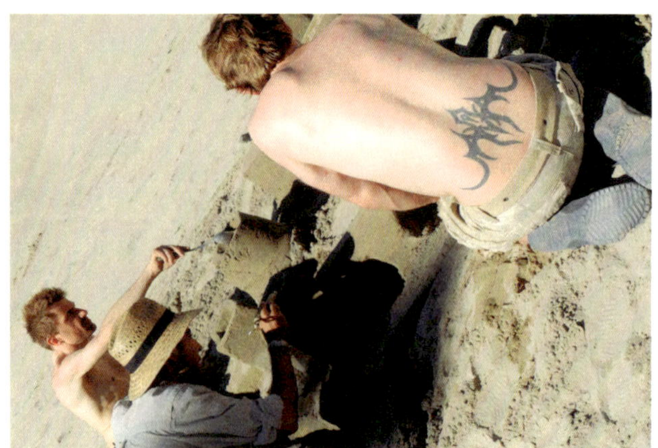
7/6/12—5:30:30 PM

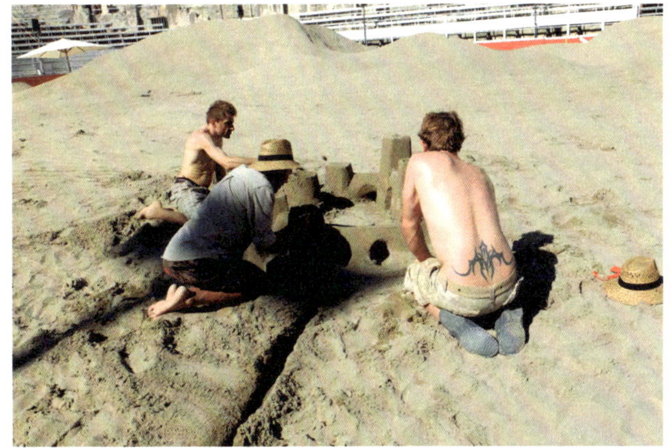

7/6/12—5:30:36 PM

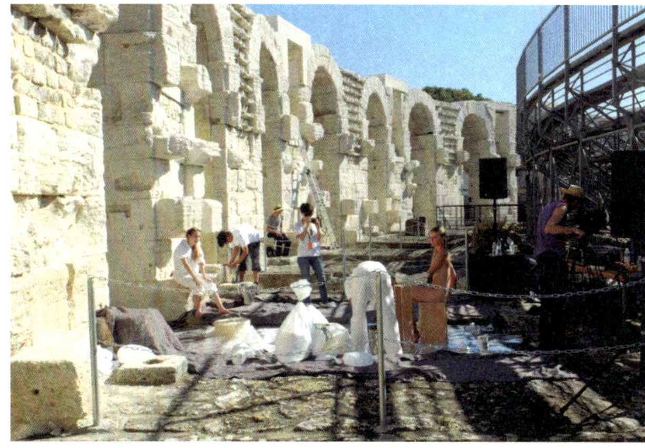

7/6/12—5:35:57 PM

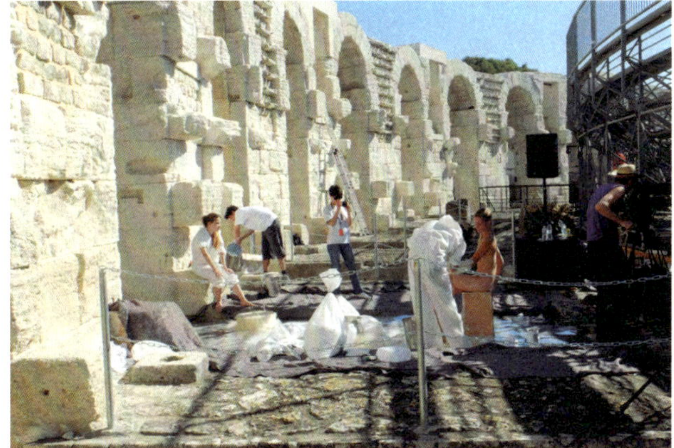

7/6/12—5:36:08 PM

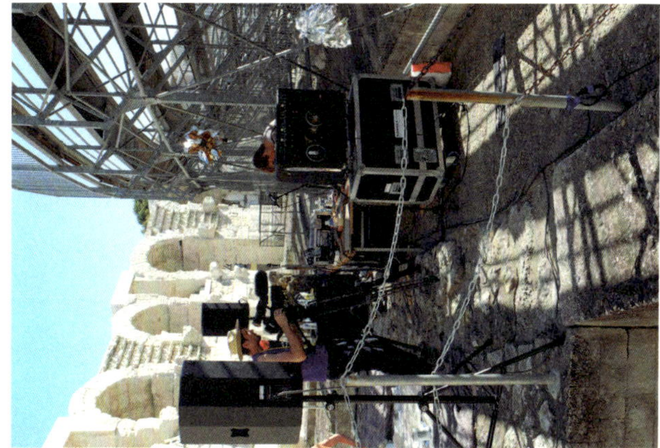

7/6/12—5:36:16 PM

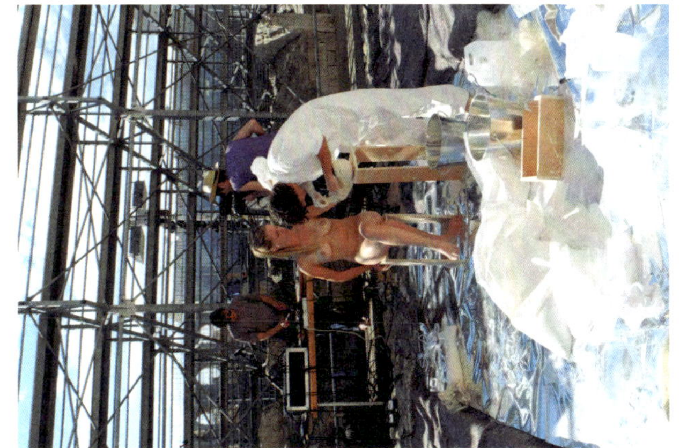

7/6/12—5:36:49 PM

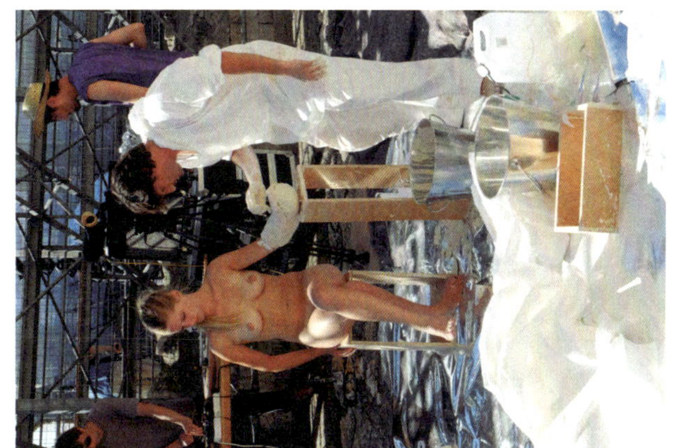

7/6/12—5:37:11 PM

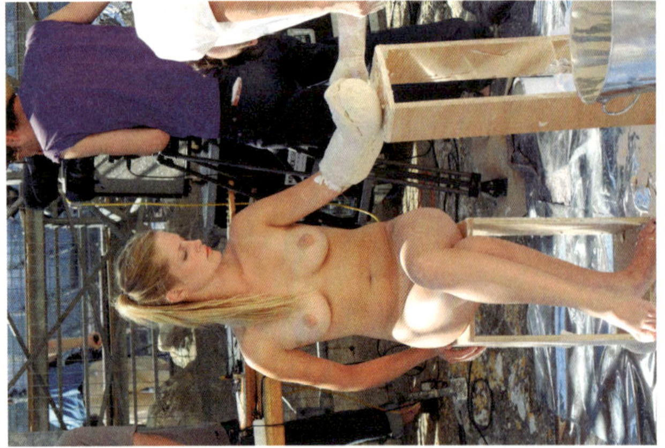

7/6/12—5:37:21 PM

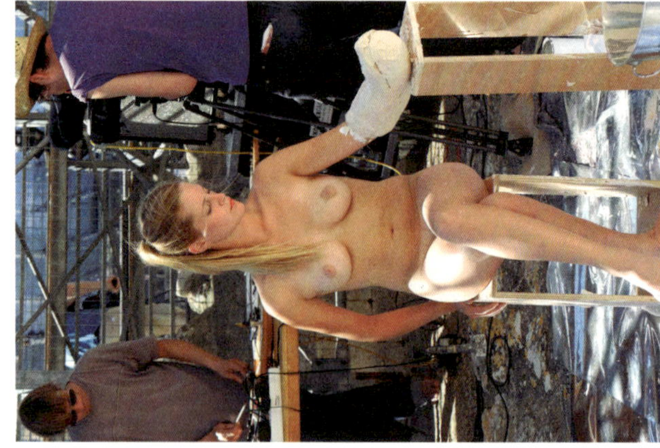

7/6/12—5:37:25 PM

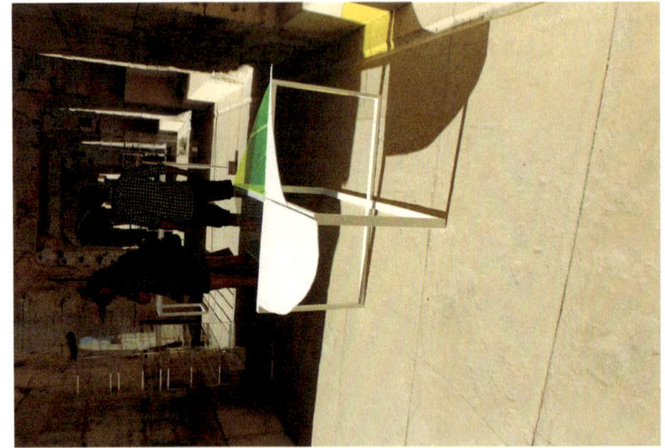

7/6/12—5:41:00 PM

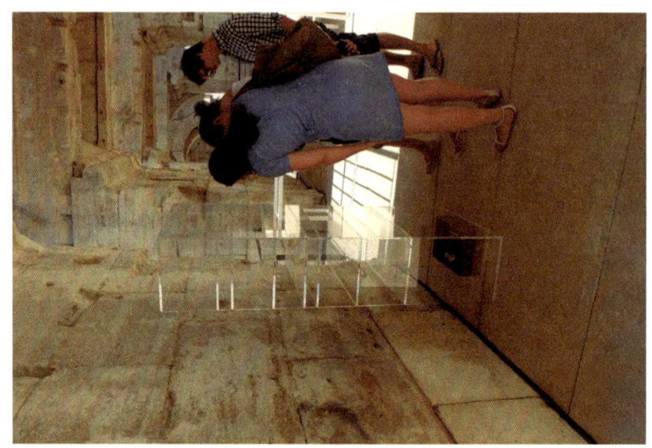

7/6/12—5:41:09 PM

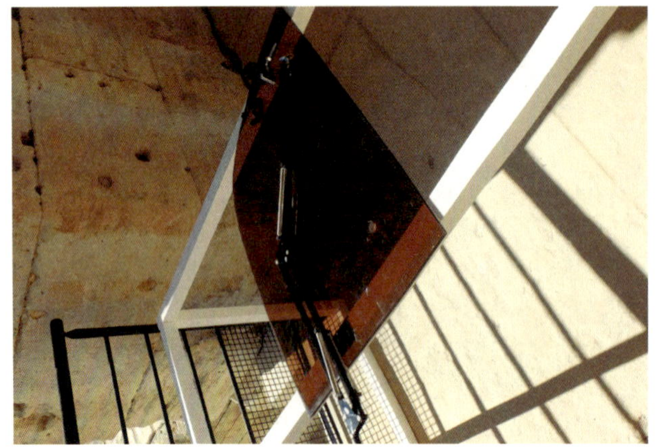

7/6/12—5:41:20 PM

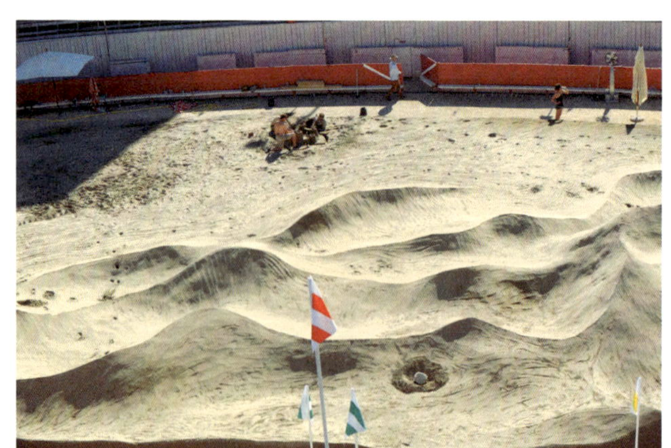

7/6/12—5:43:14 PM

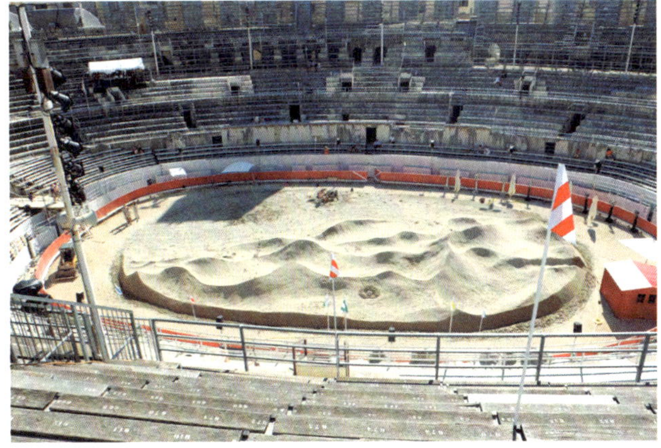
7/6/12—5:43:20 PM

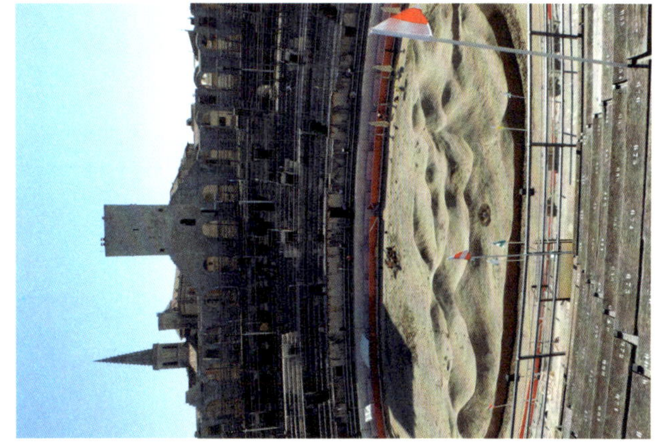
7/6/12—5:43:28 PM

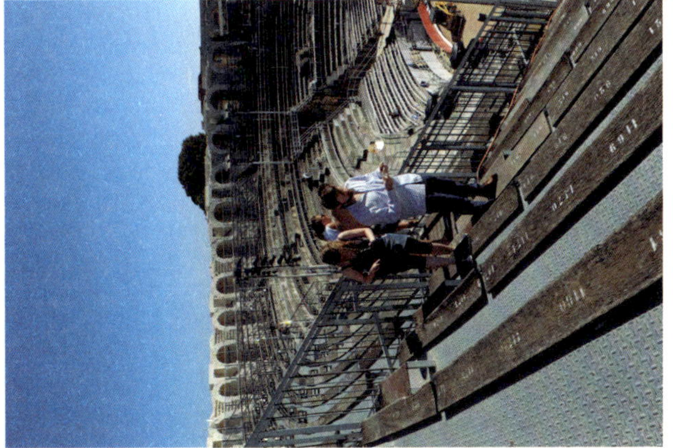
7/6/12—5:43:39 PM

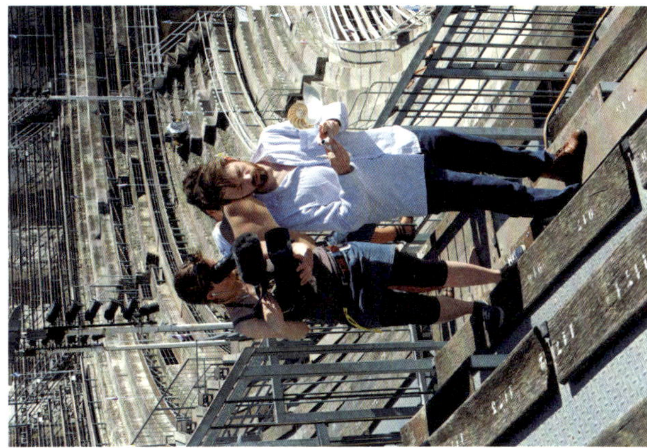
7/6/12—5:43:47 PM

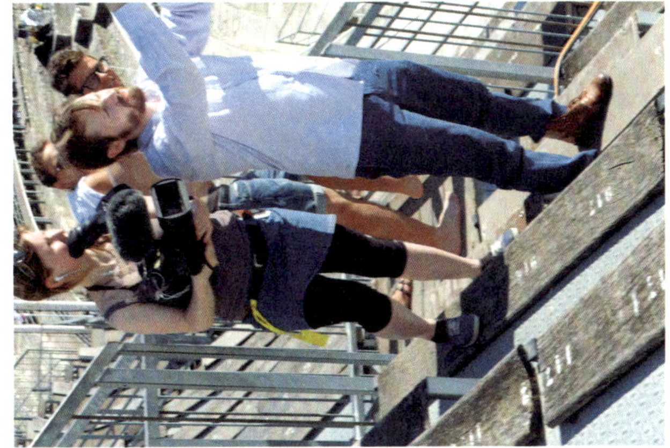
7/6/12—5:43:50 PM

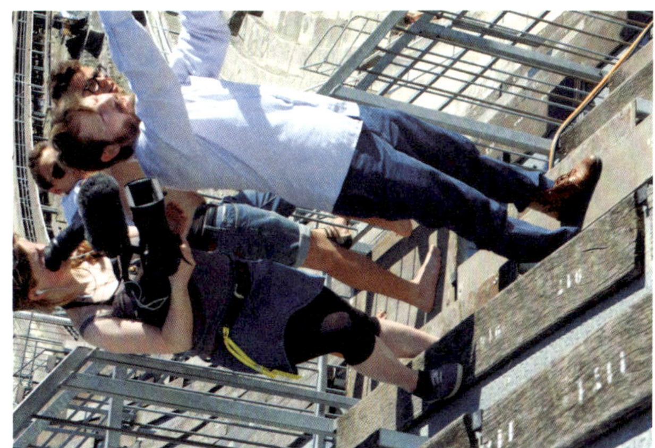
7/6/12—5:43:54 PM

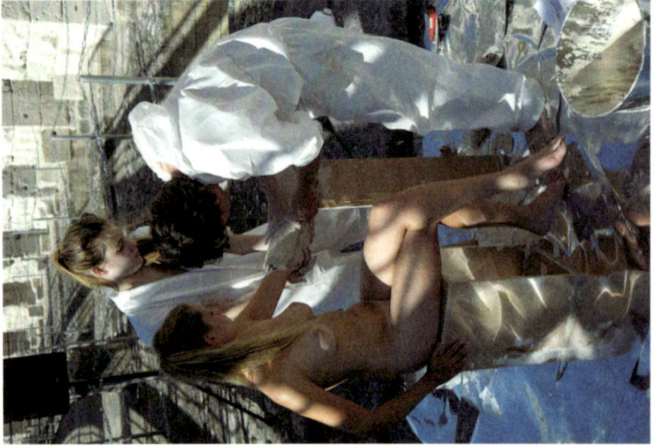

7/6/12—5:44:03 PM

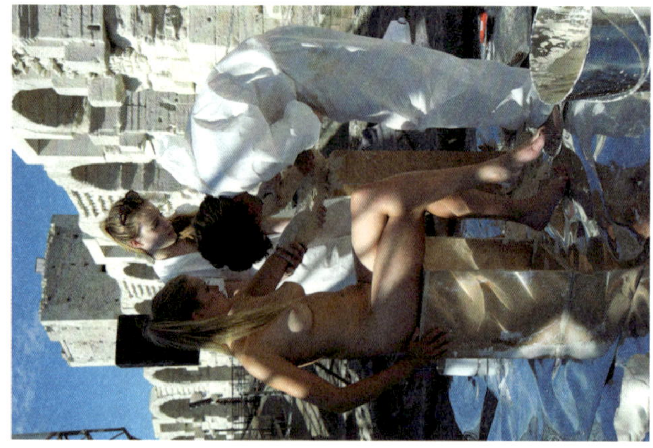

7/6/12—5:44:08 PM

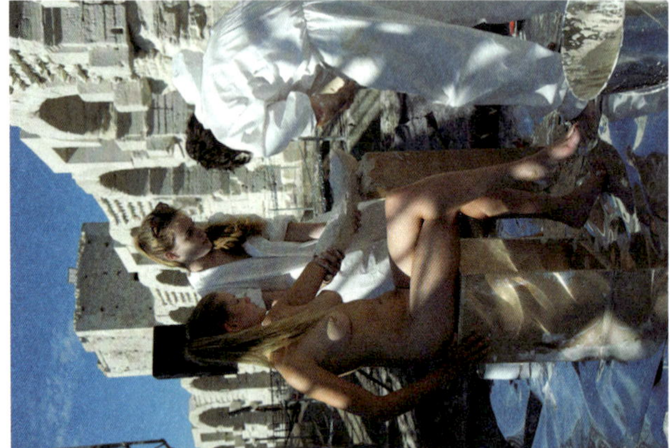

7/6/12—5:44:11 PM

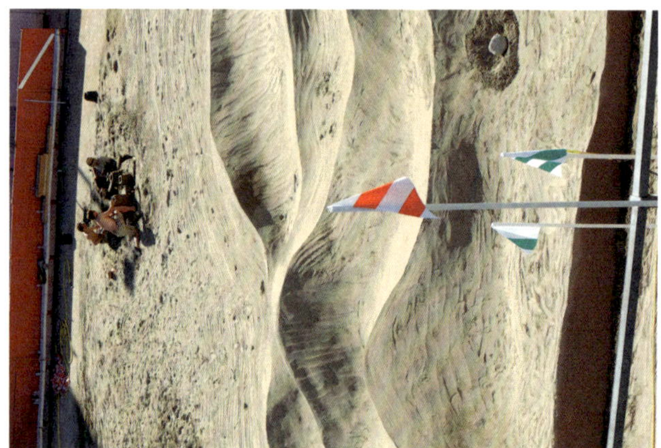

7/6/12—5:44:24 PM

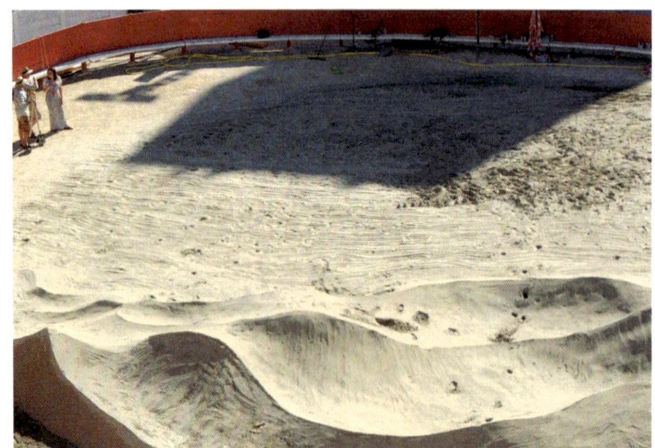

7/6/12—5:44:29 PM

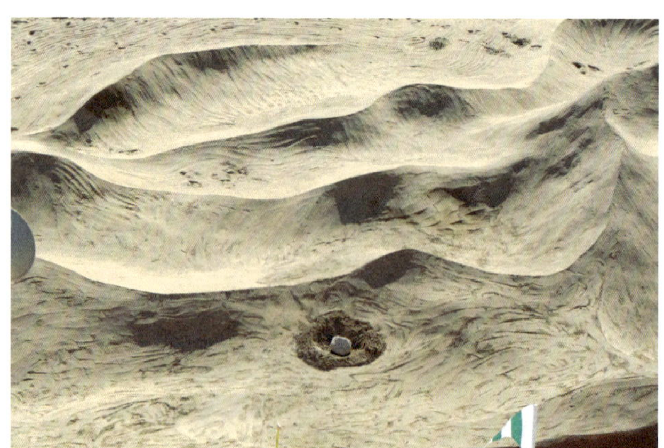

7/6/12—5:44:49 PM

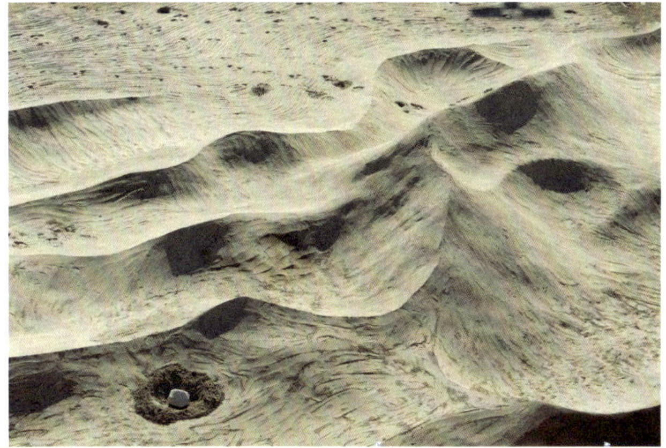

7/6/12—5:44:57 PM

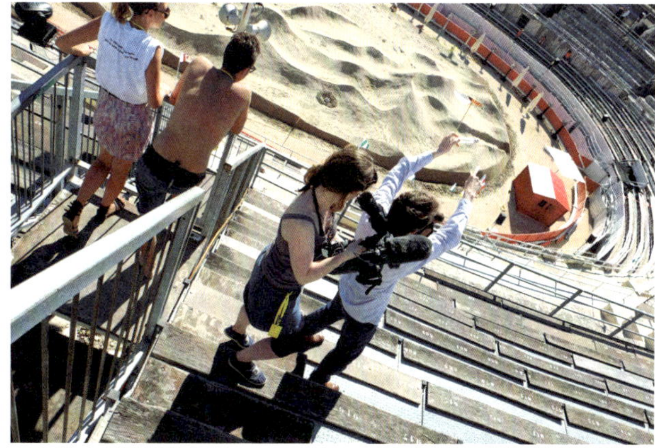

7/6/12—5:45:05 PM

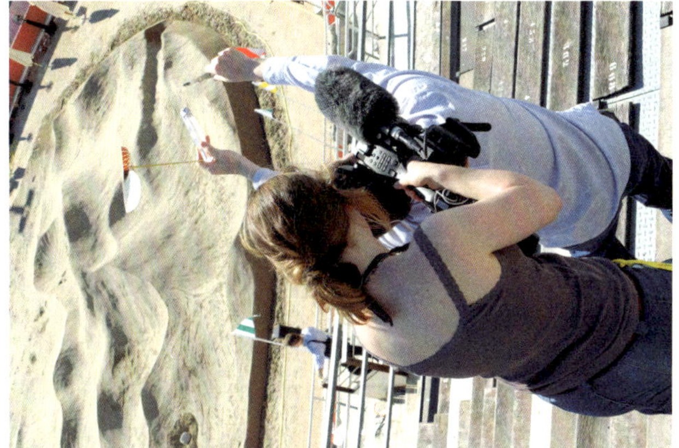

7/6/12—5:45:15 PM

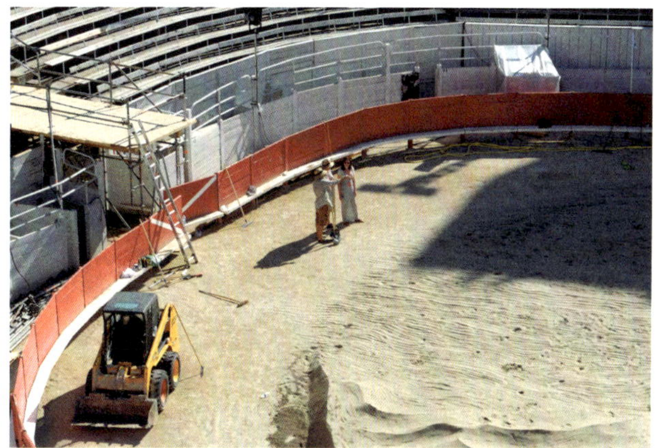

7/6/12—5:45:29 PM

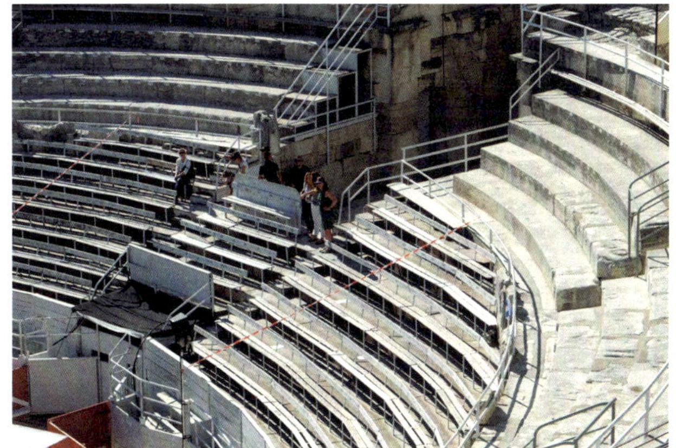

7/6/12—5:45:34 PM

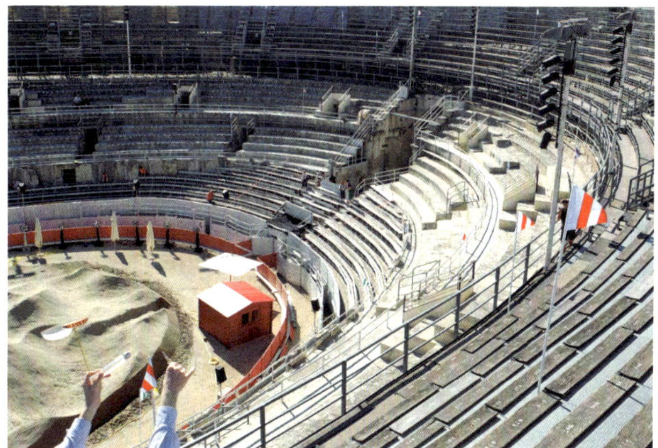

7/6/12—5:45:38 PM

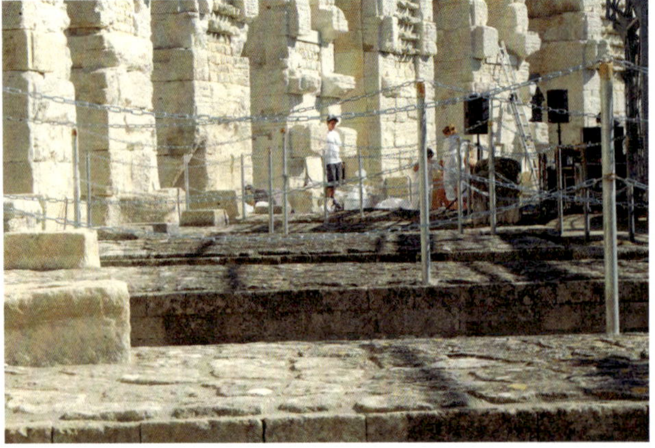

7/6/12—5:46:45 PM

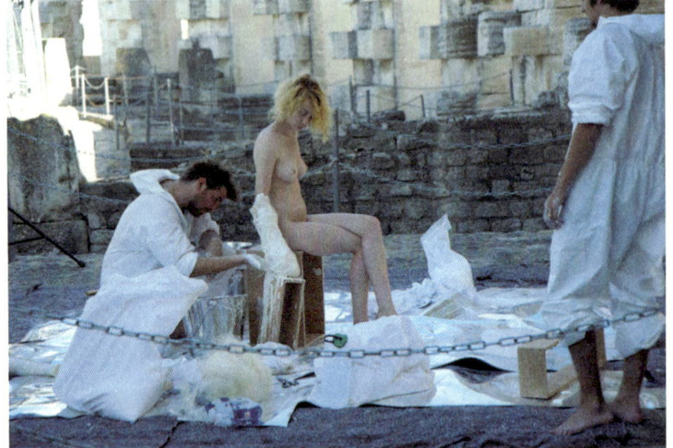

7/6/12—5:49:53 PM

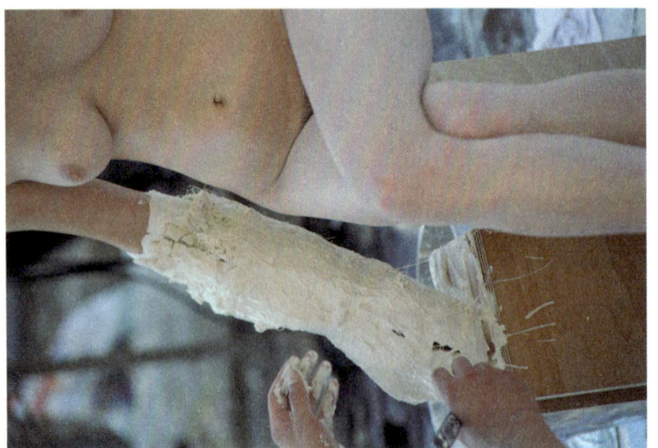

7/6/12—5:51:51 PM

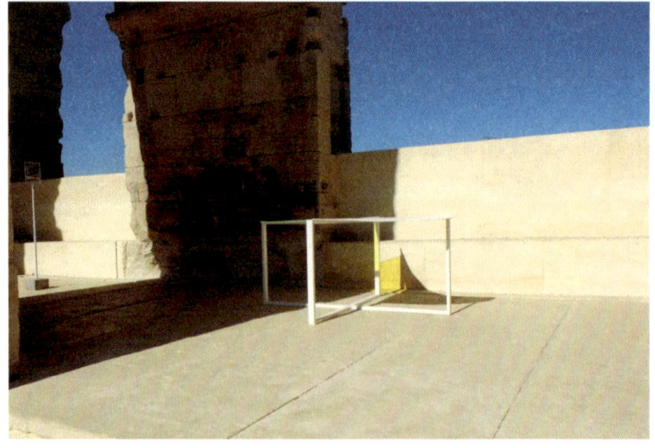

7/6/12—5:46:53 PM

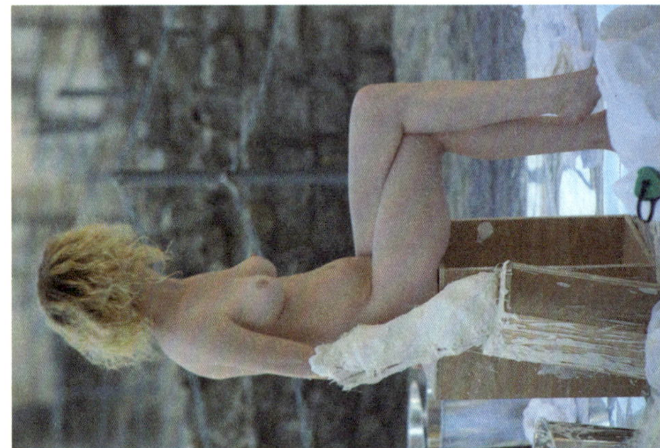

7/6/12—5:51:21 PM

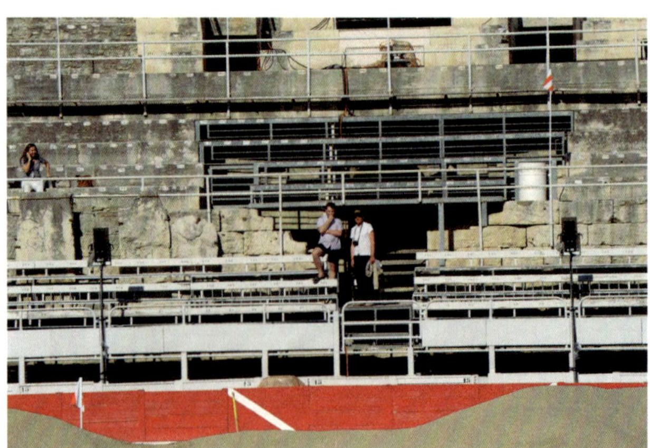

7/6/12—5:56:03 PM

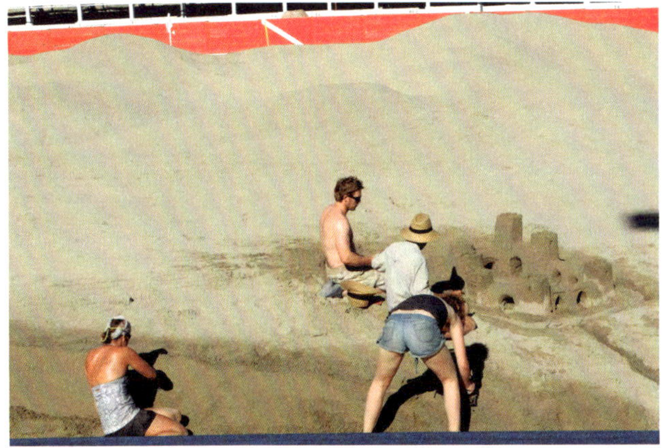
7/6/12—5:56:08 PM

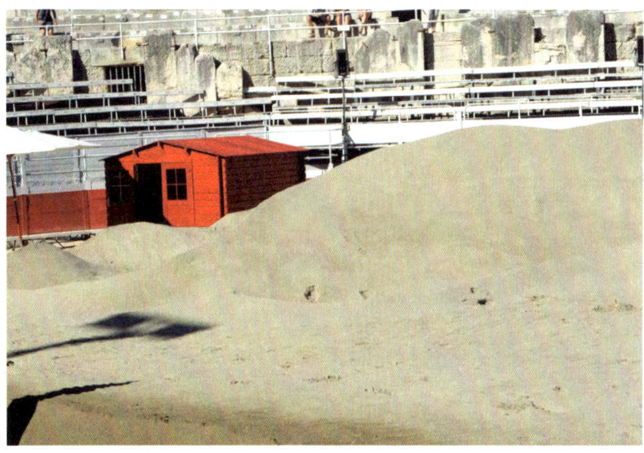
7/6/12—5:56:15 PM

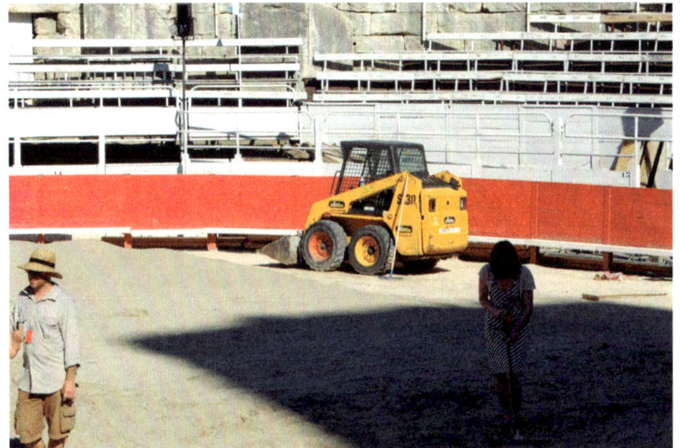
7/6/12—5:56:22 PM

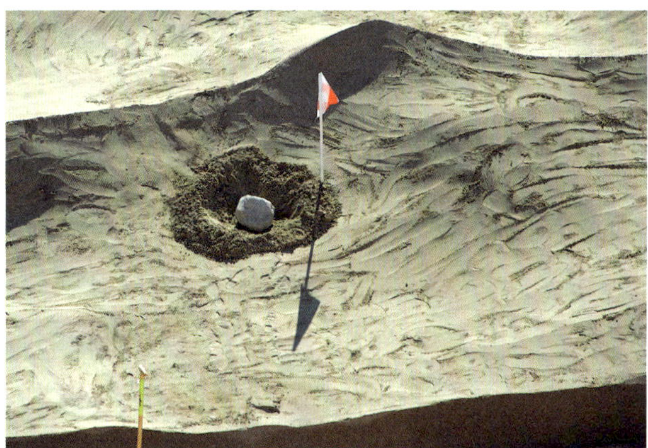
7/6/12—5:58:15 PM

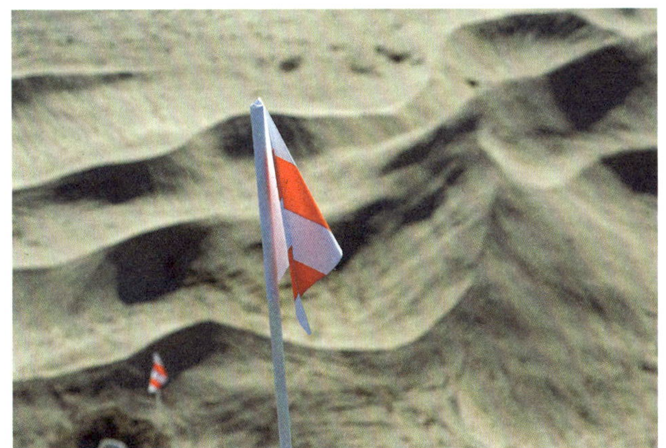
7/6/12—5:58:31 PM

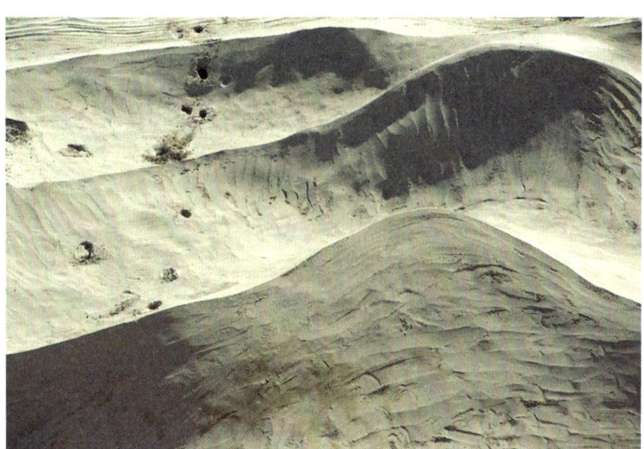
7/6/12—5:58:53 PM

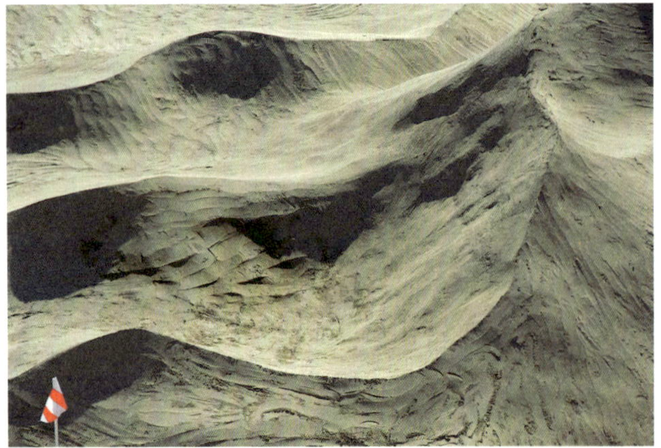

7/6/12—5:58:56 PM

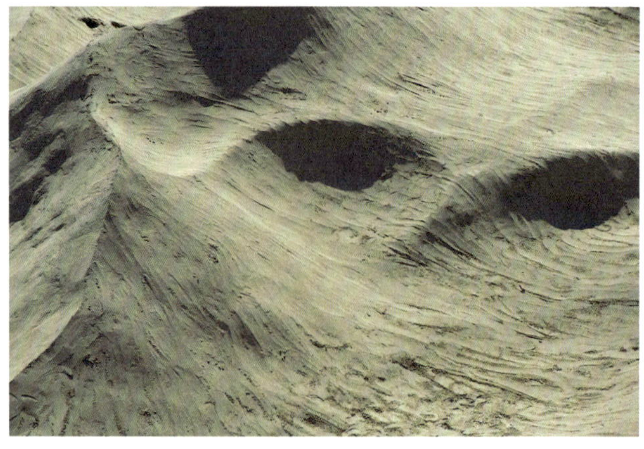

7/6/12—5:58:57 PM

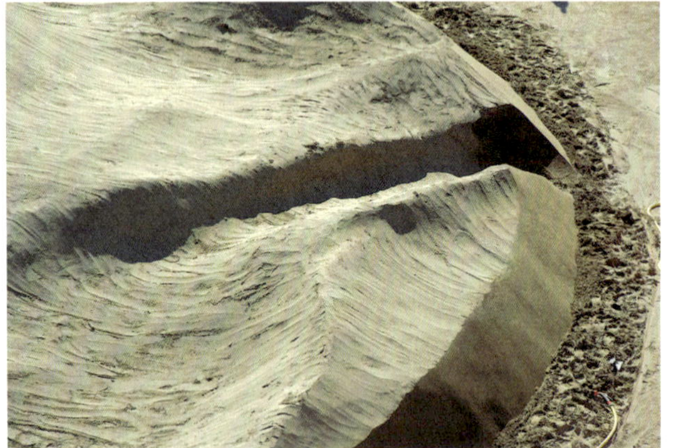

7/6/12—5:59:00 PM

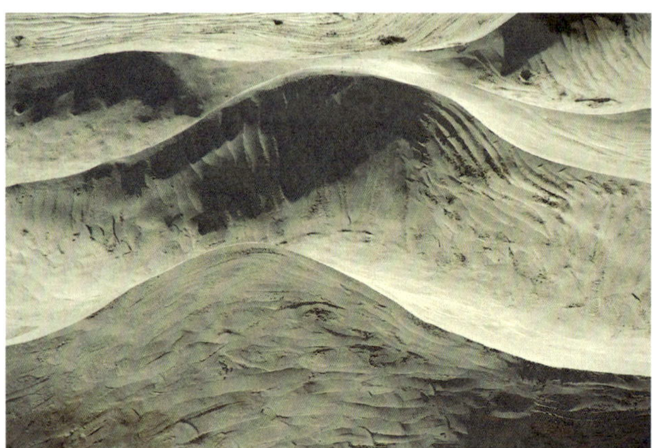

7/6/12—5:59:06 PM

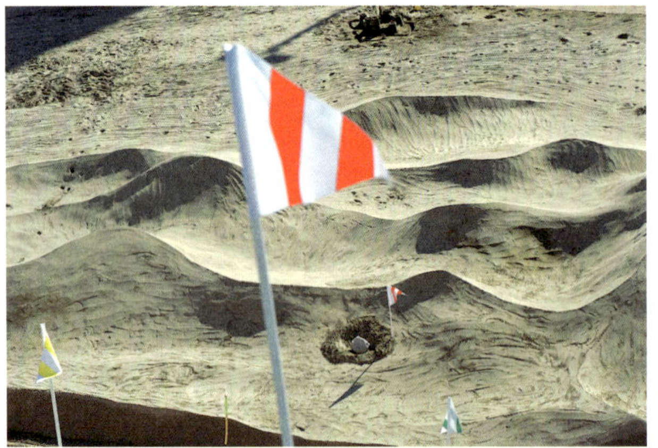

7/6/12—5:59:37 PM

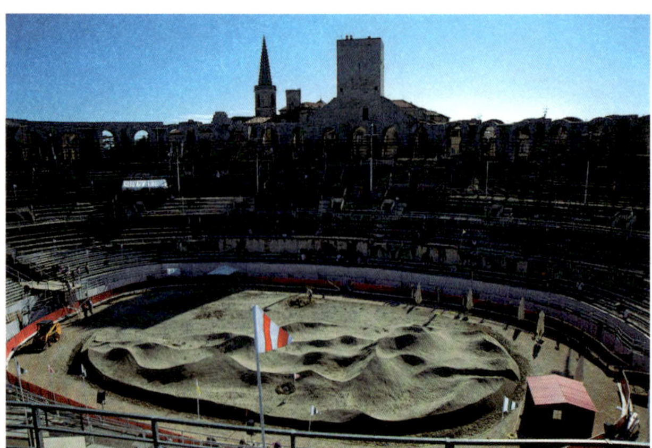

7/6/12—6:00:21 PM

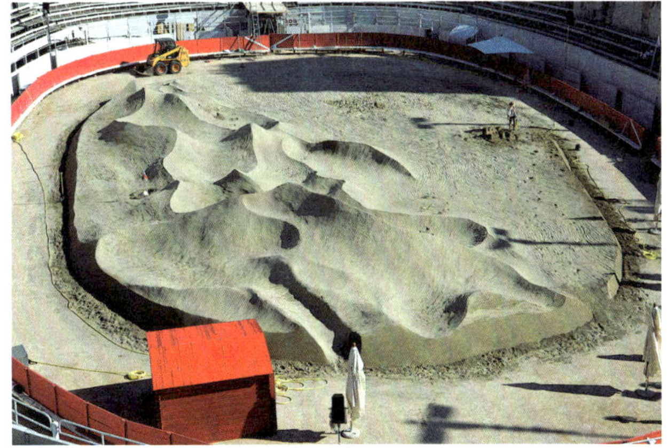
7/6/12—6:01:22 PM

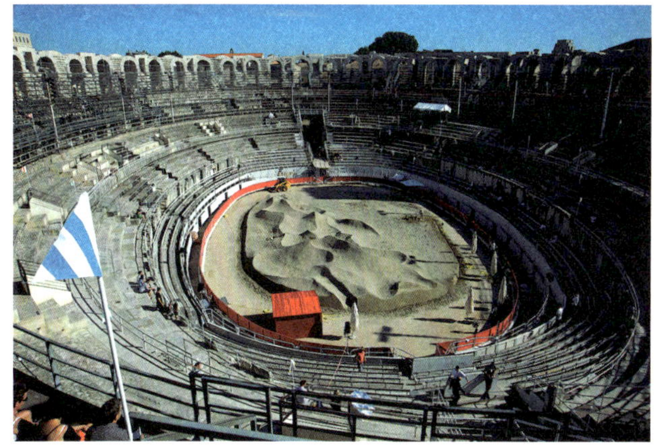
7/6/12—6:01:28 PM

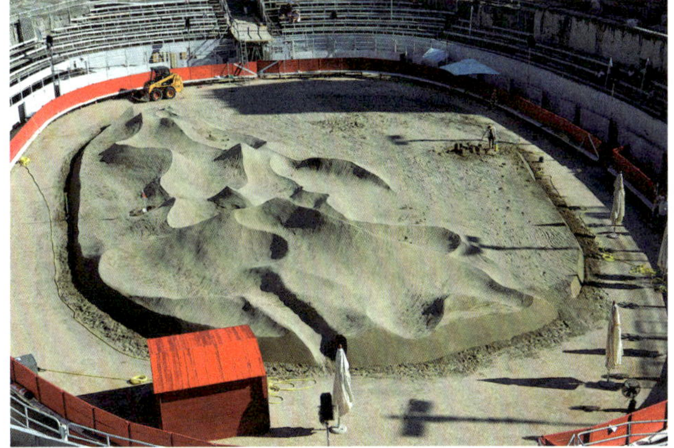
7/6/12—6:01:32 PM

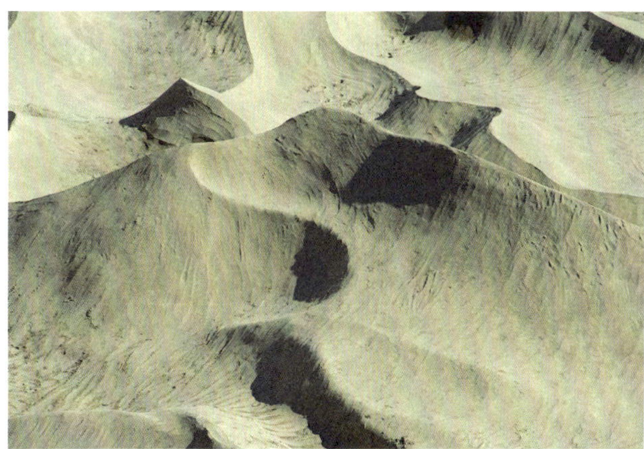
7/6/12—6:02:35 PM

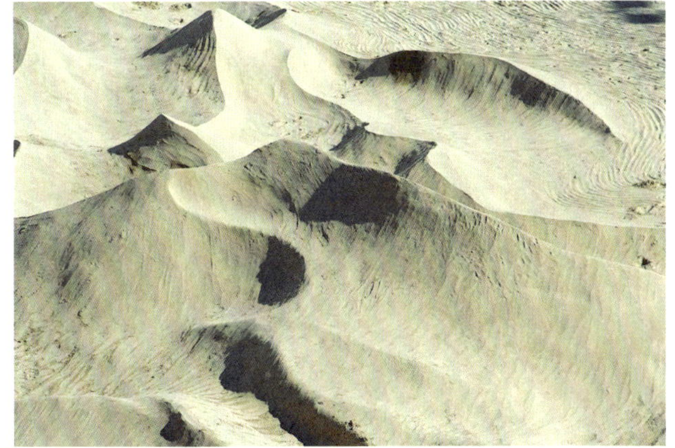
7/6/12—6:02:42 PM

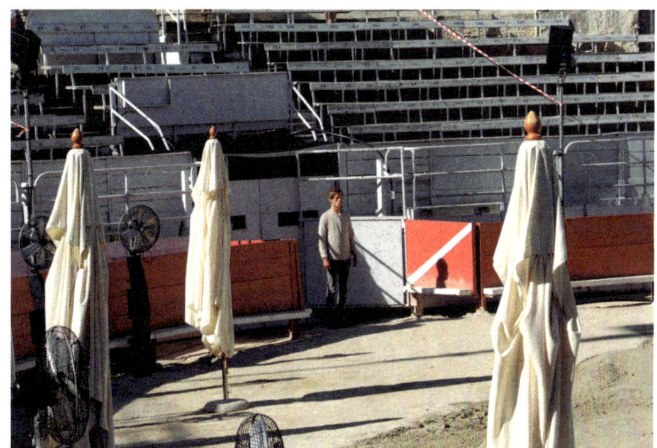
7/6/12—6:04:17 PM

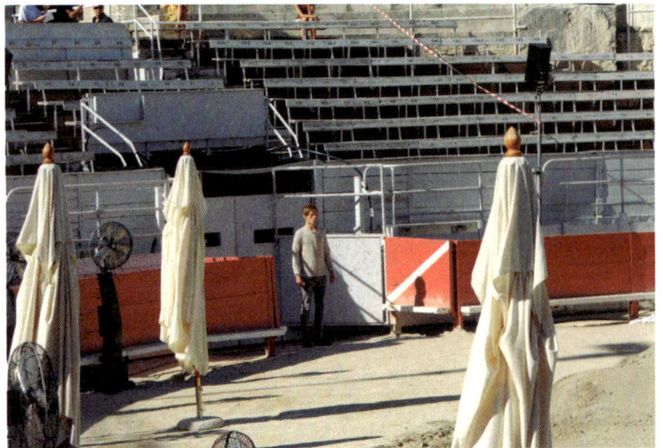

7/6/12—6:04:22 PM

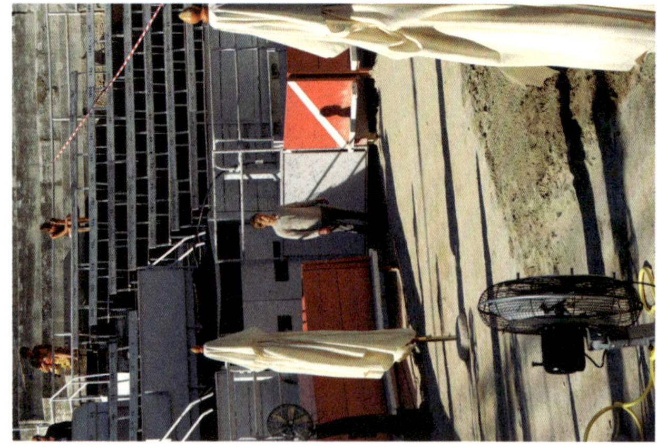

7/6/12—6:04:29 PM

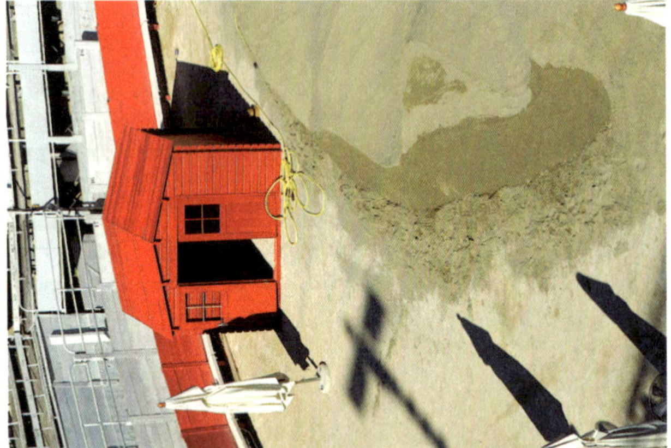

7/6/12—6:07:07 PM

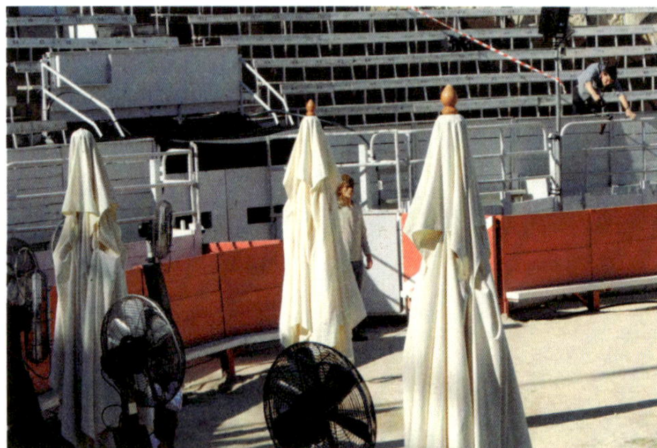

7/6/12—6:12:32 PM

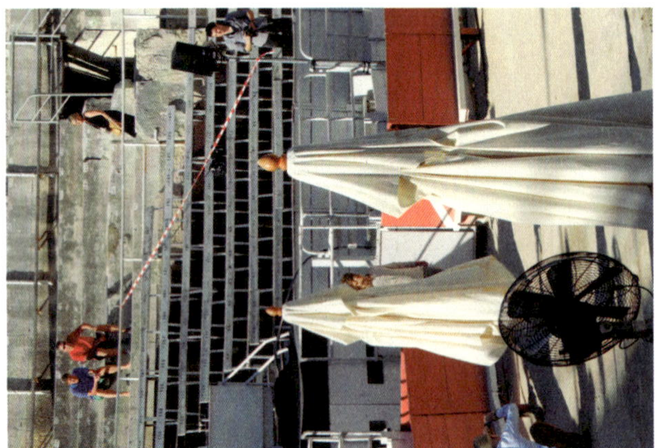

7/6/12—6:12:43 PM

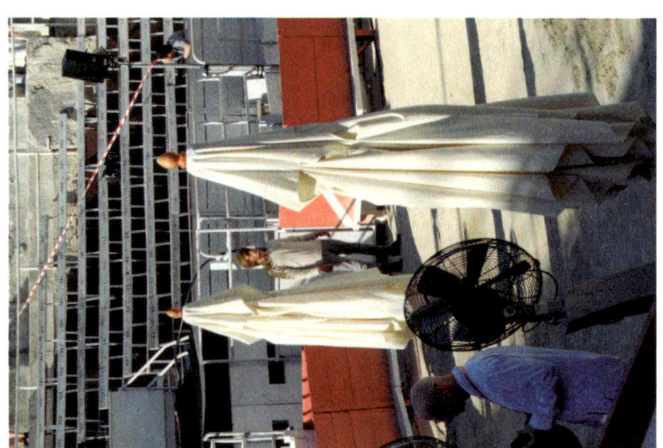

7/6/12—6:13:13 PM

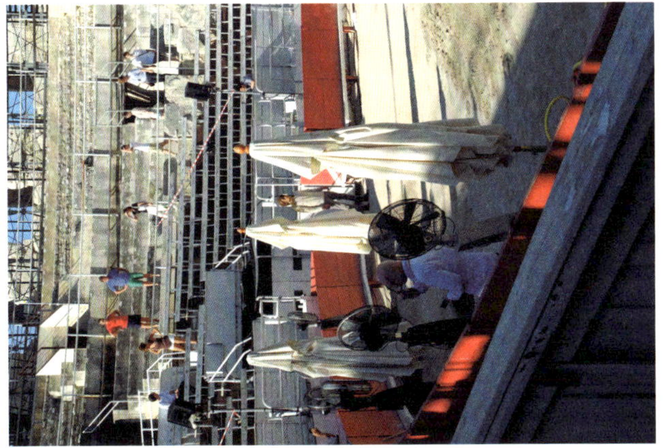

7/6/12—6:13:20 PM

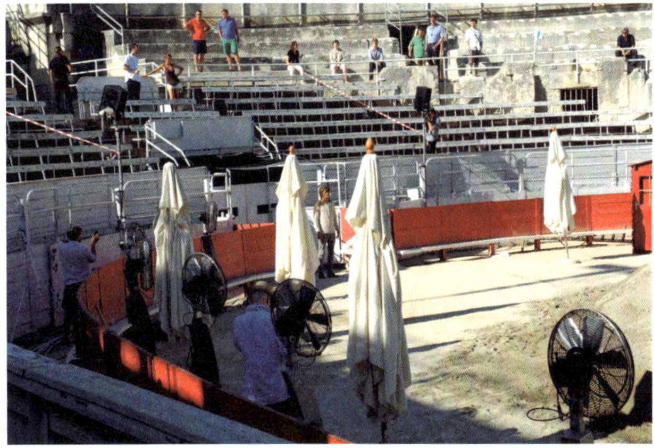

7/6/12—6:13:30 PM

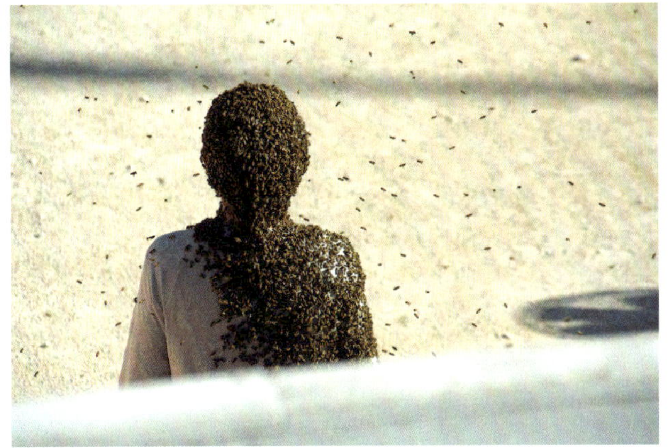

7/6/12—6:15:02 PM

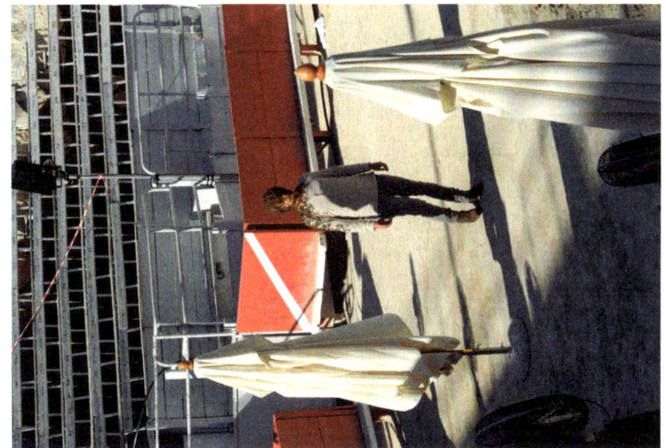

7/6/12—6:16:23 PM

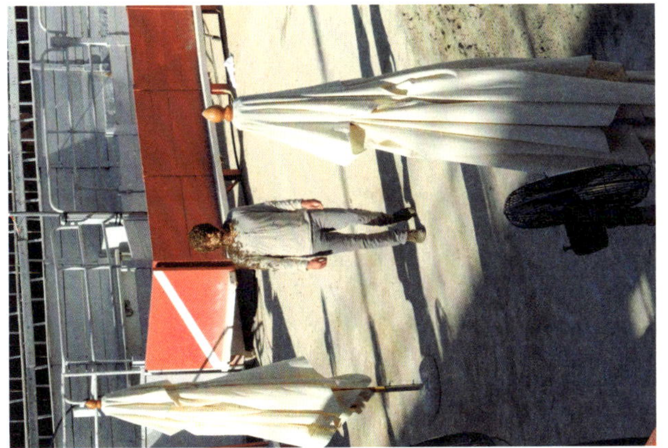

7/6/12—6:16:27 PM

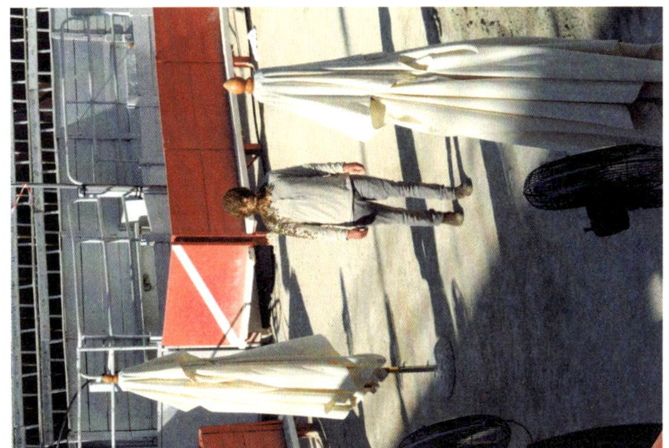

7/6/12—6:16:30 PM

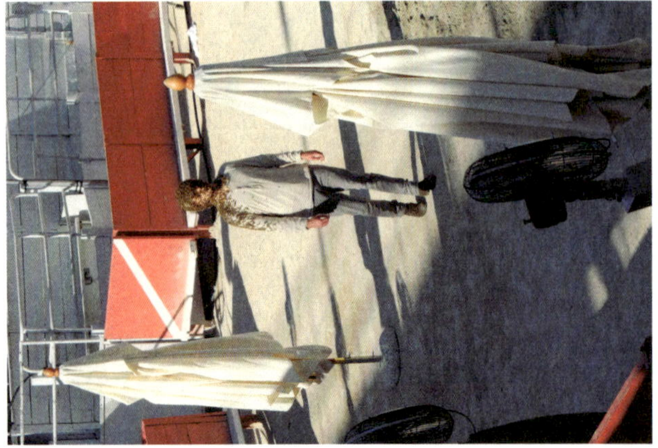
7/6/12—6:16:33 PM

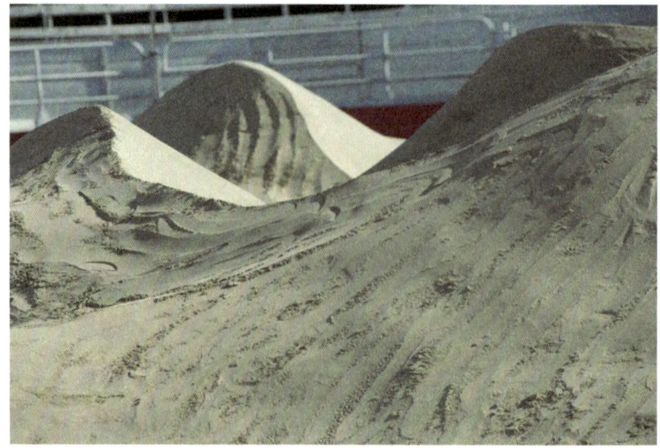
7/6/12—6:16:37 PM

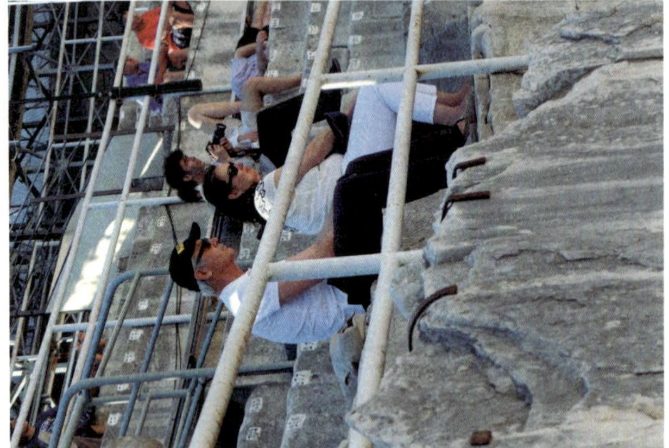
7/6/12—6:16:41 PM

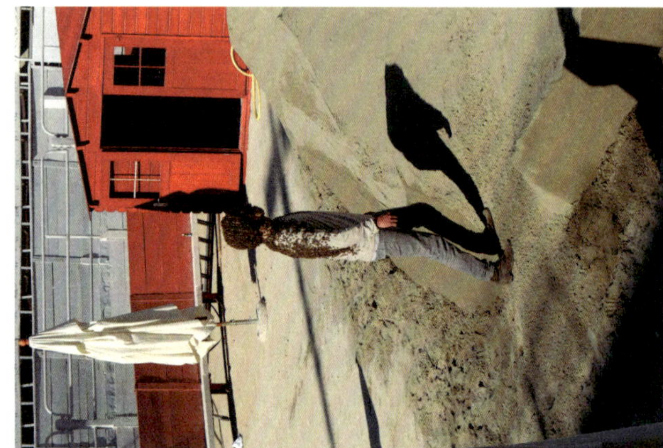
7/6/12—6:16:47 PM

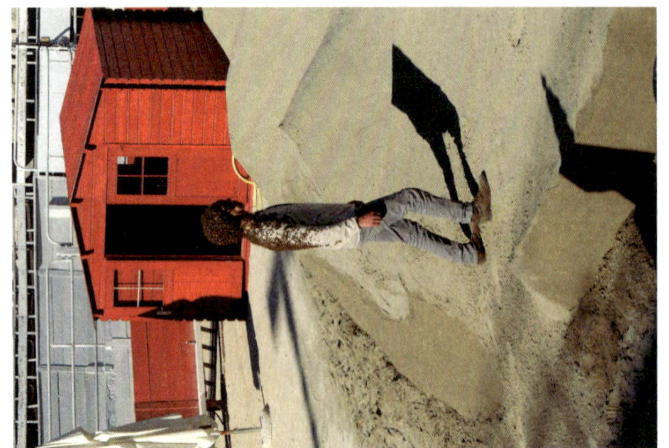
7/6/12—6:16:50 PM

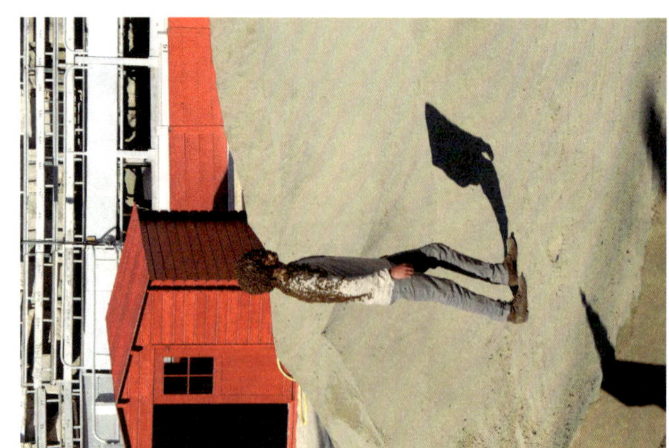
7/6/12—6:16:57 PM

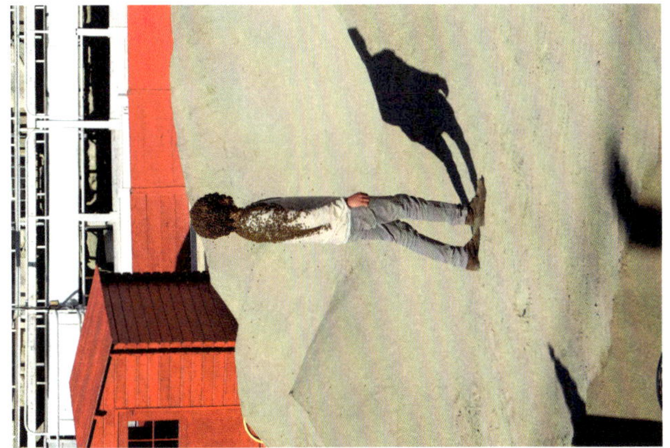
7/6/12—6:17:01 PM

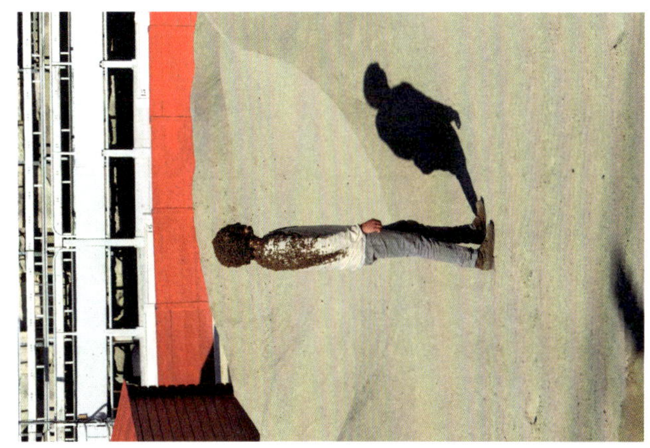
7/6/12—6:17:05 PM

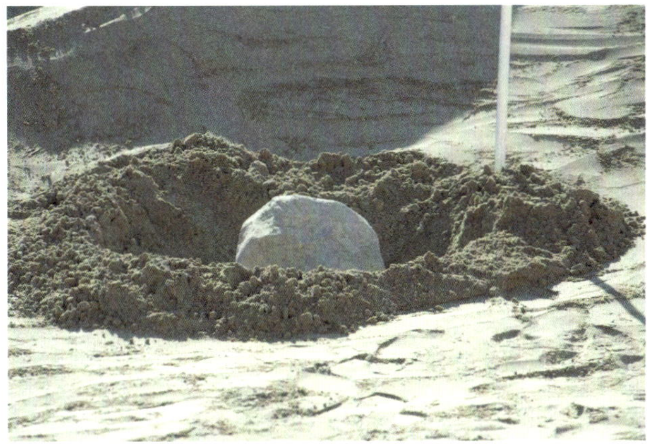
7/6/12—6:17:15 PM

7/6/12—6:17:26 PM

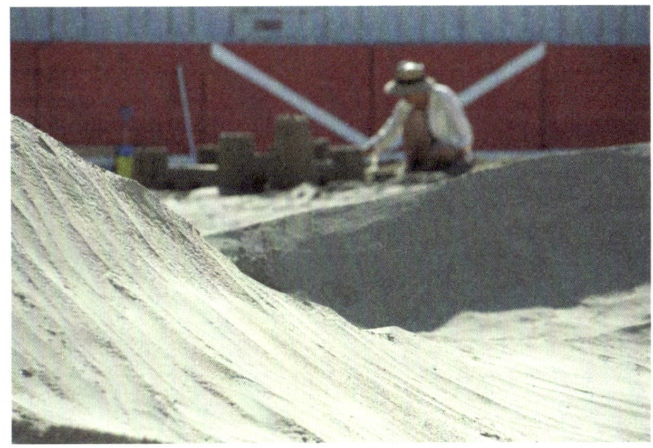
7/6/12—6:17:40 PM

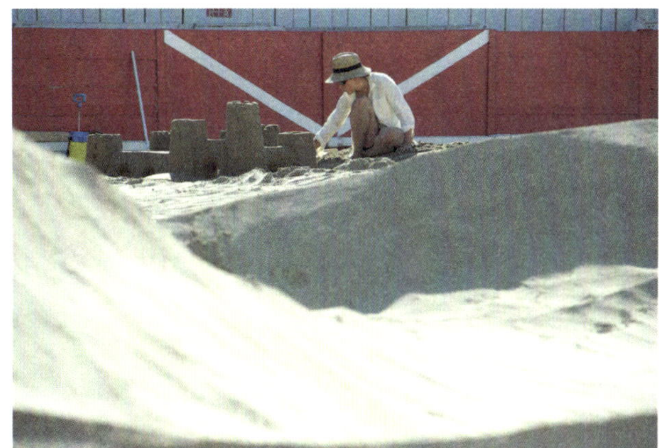
7/6/12—6:17:45 PM

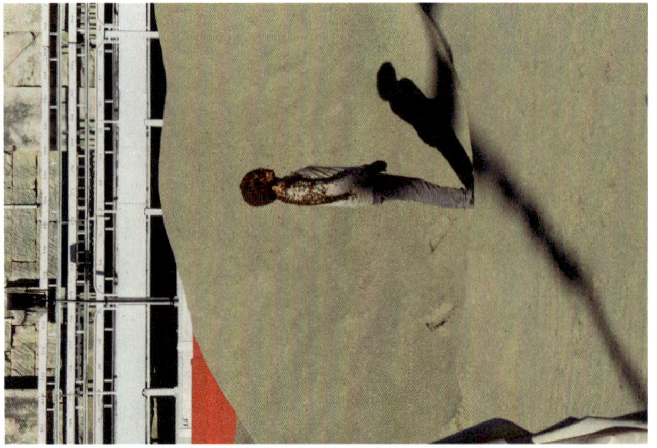
7/6/12—6:17:51 PM

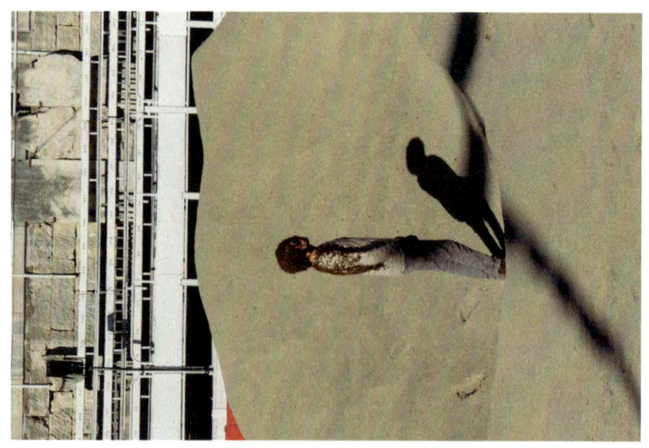
7/6/12—6:18:00 PM

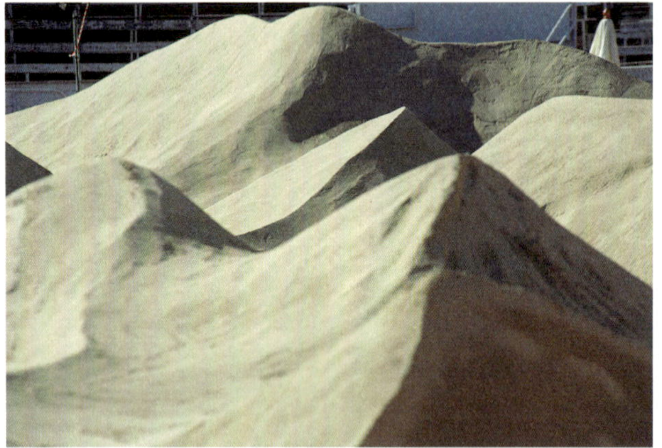
7/6/12—6:18:03 PM

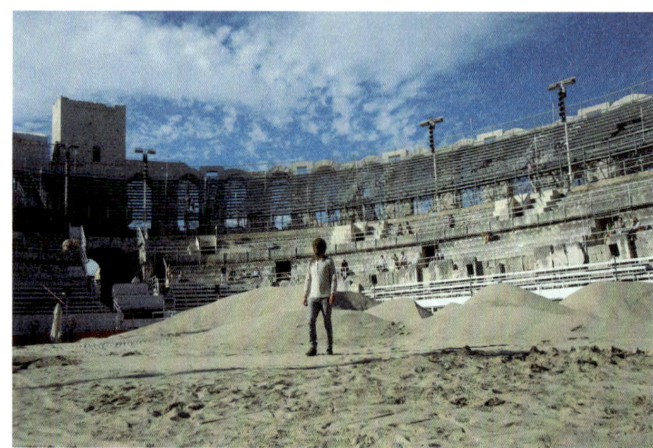
7/6/12—6:22:04 PM

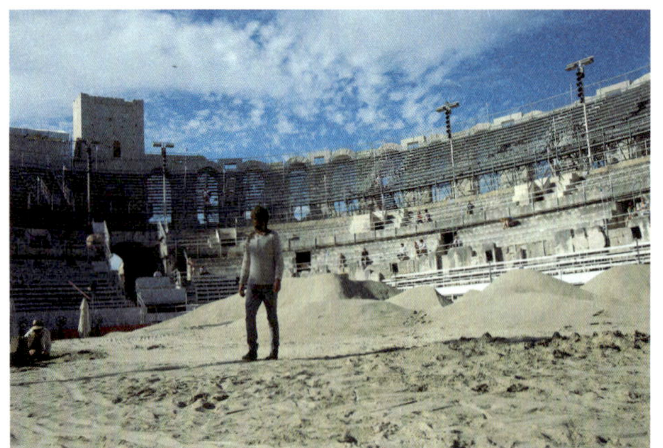
7/6/12—6:22:19 PM

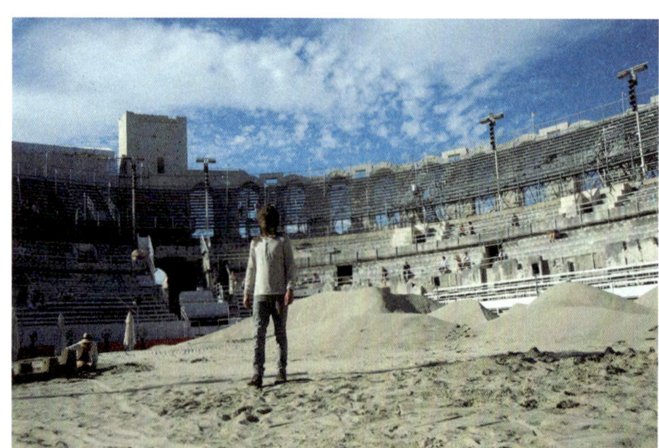
7/6/12—6:22:25 PM

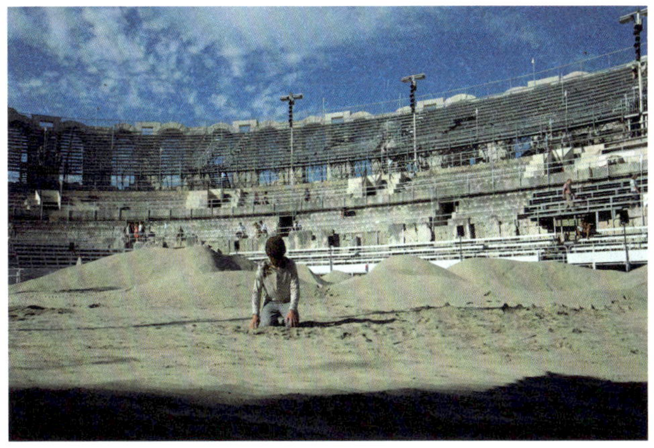
7/6/12—6:23:37 PM

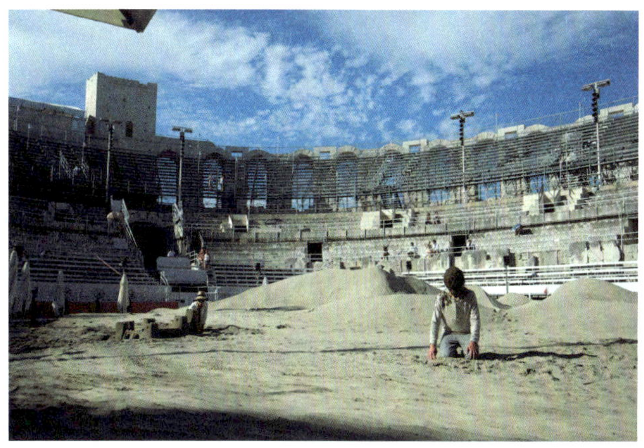
7/6/12—6:24:15 PM

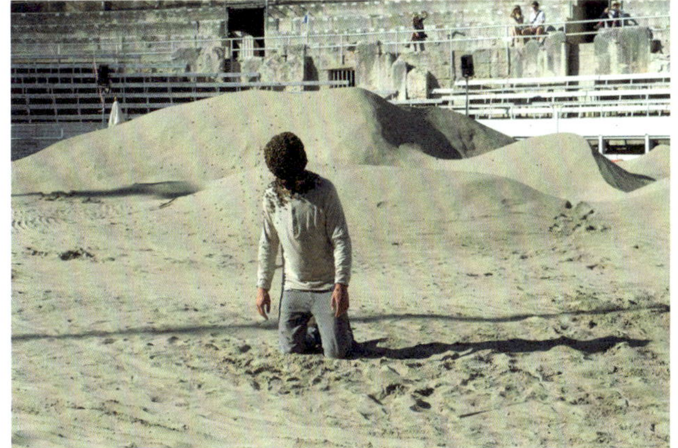
7/6/12—6:26:02 PM

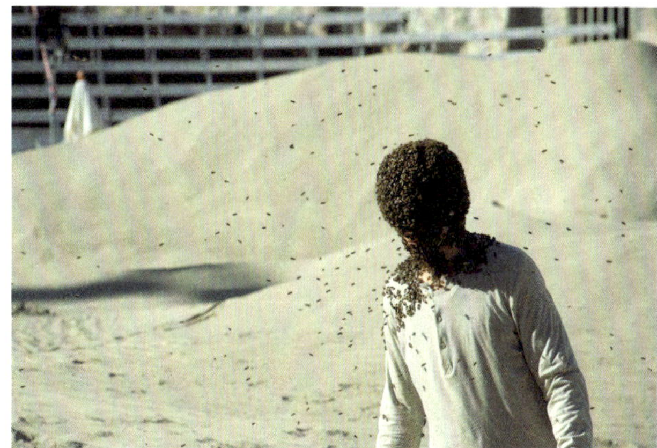
7/6/12—6:26:06 PM

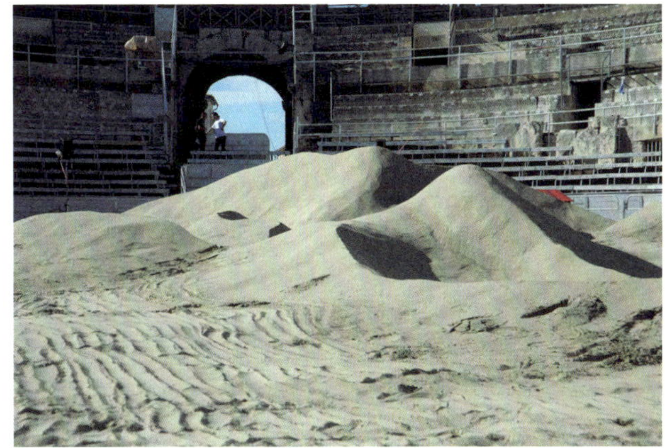
7/6/12—6:27:34 PM

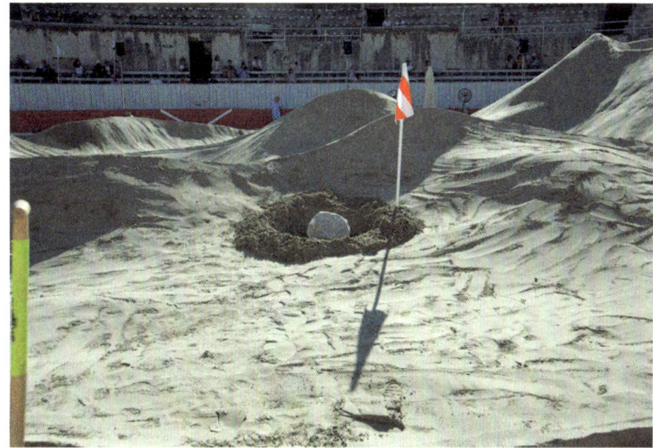
7/6/12—6:28:49 PM

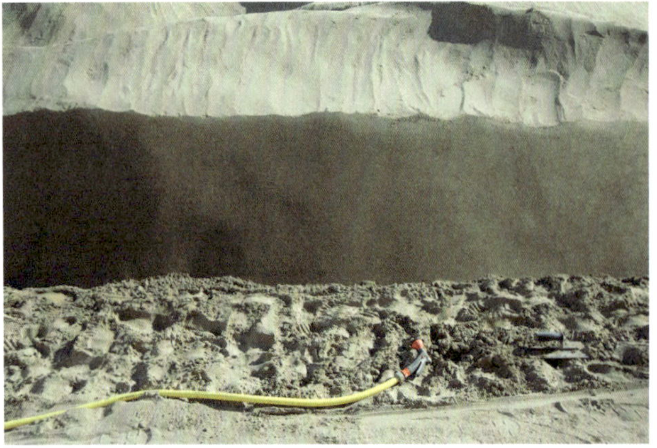
7/6/12—6:29:28 PM

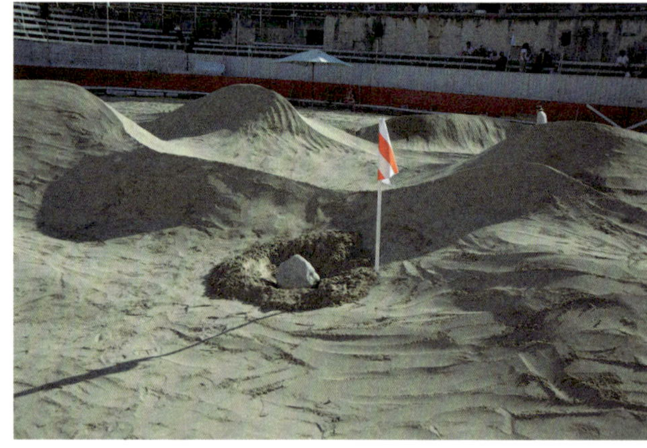
7/6/12—6:29:54 PM

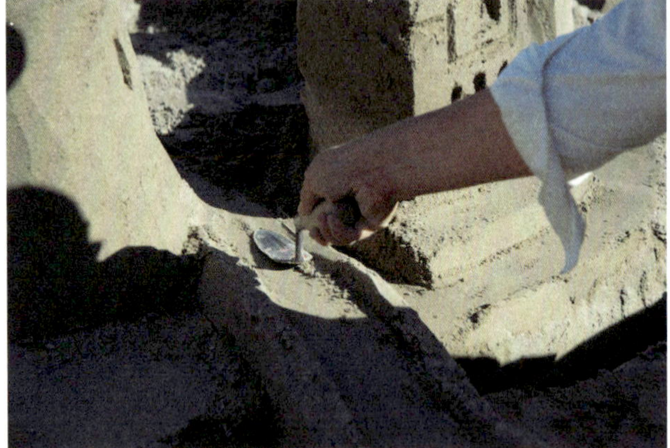
7/6/12—6:31:14 PM

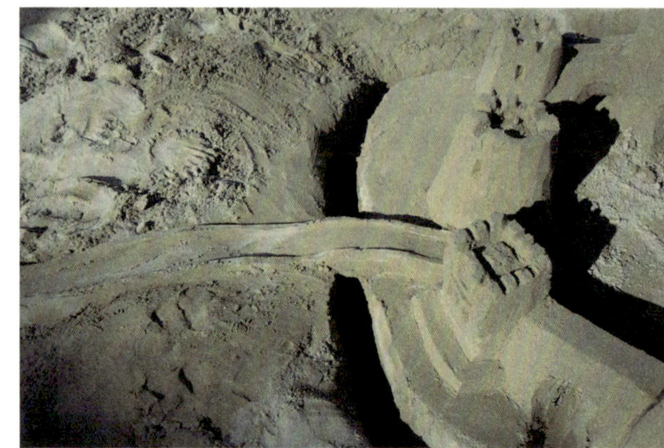
7/6/12—6:33:02 PM

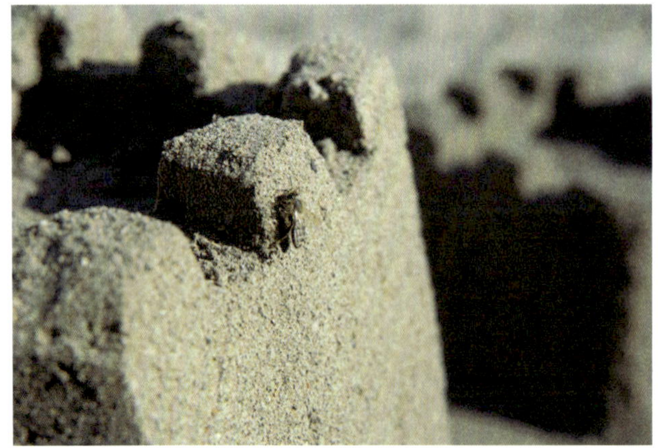
7/6/12—6:33:22 PM

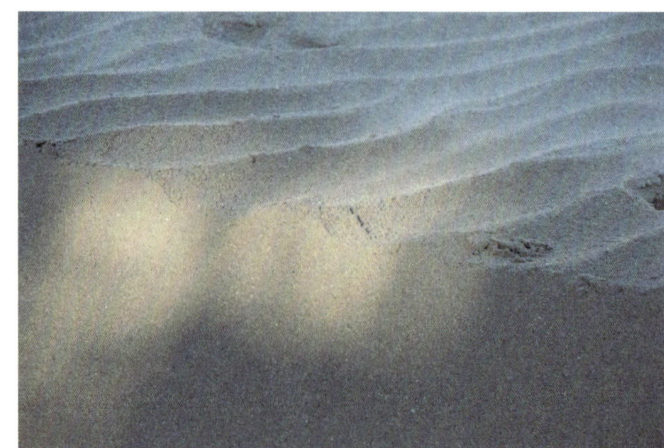
7/6/12—6:34:07 PM

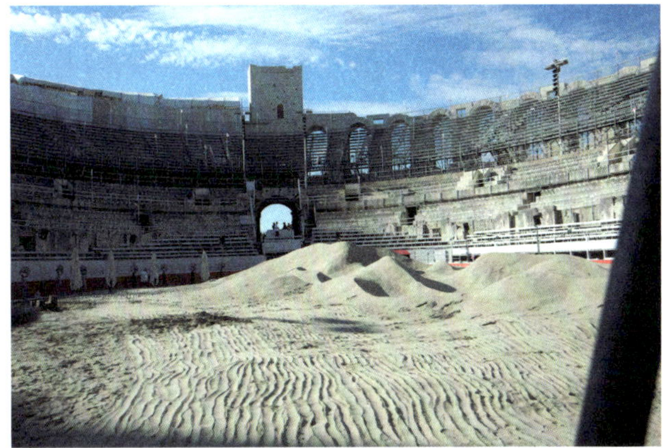

7/6/12—6:37:13 PM

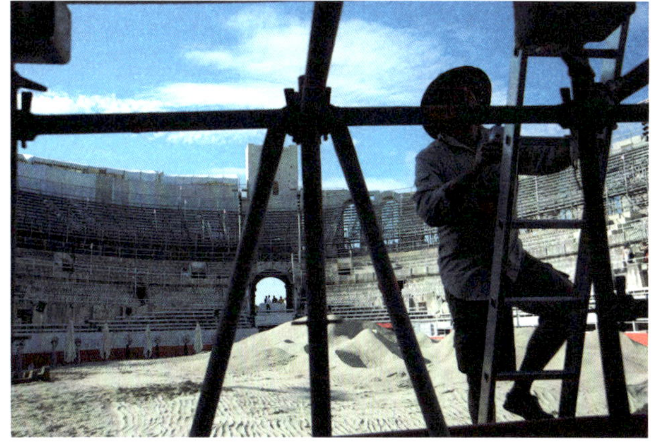

7/6/12—6:37:19 PM

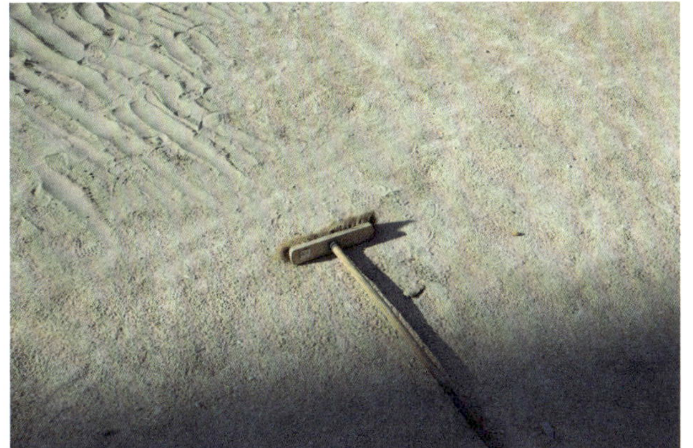

7/6/12—6:46:36 PM

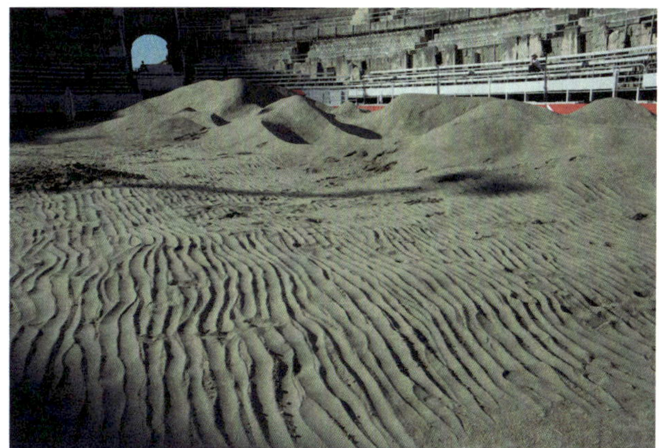

7/6/12—6:50:52 PM

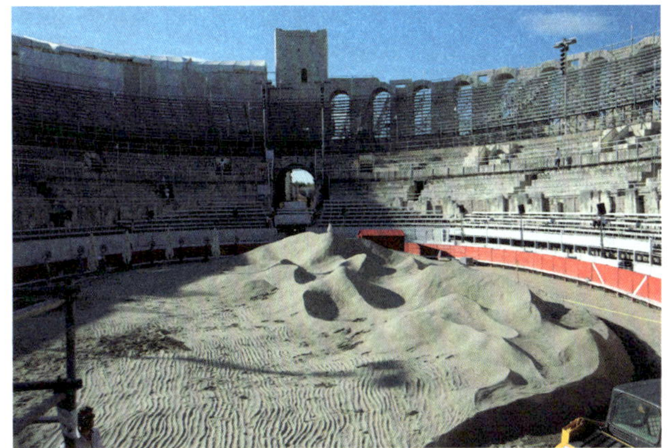

7/6/12—6:52:33 PM

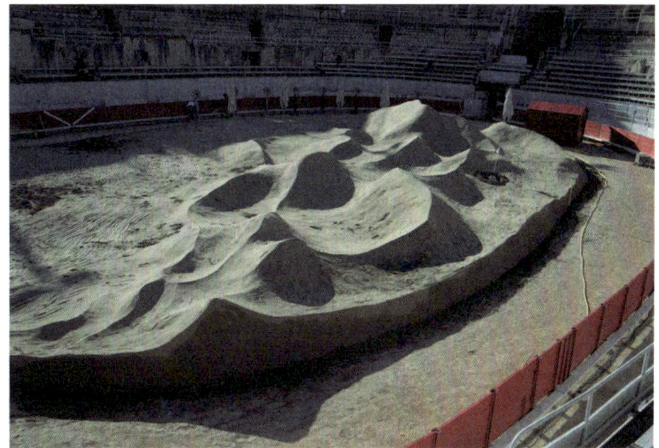

7/6/12—6:53:18 PM

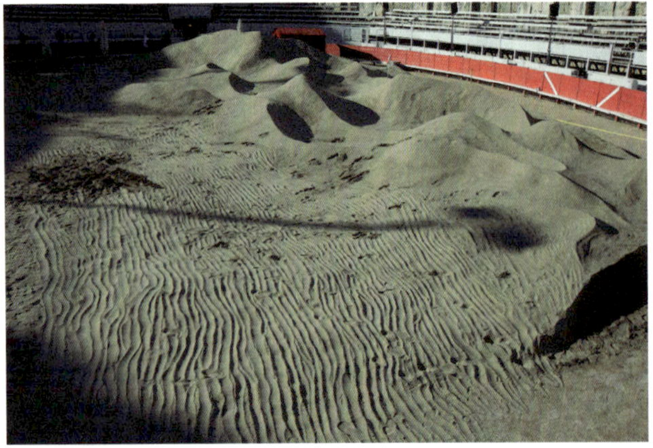

7/6/12—6:56:29 PM

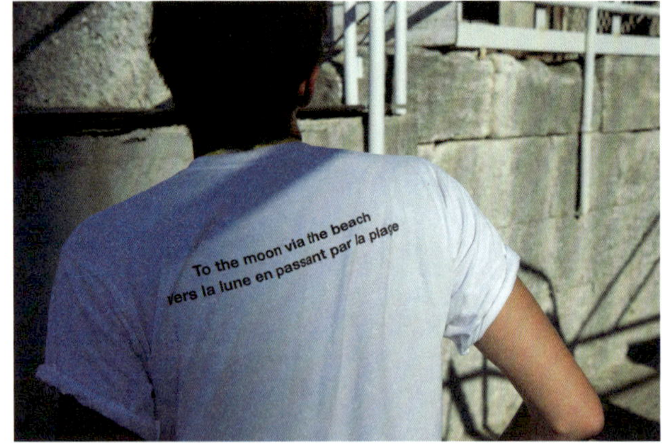

7/6/12—6:57:09 PM

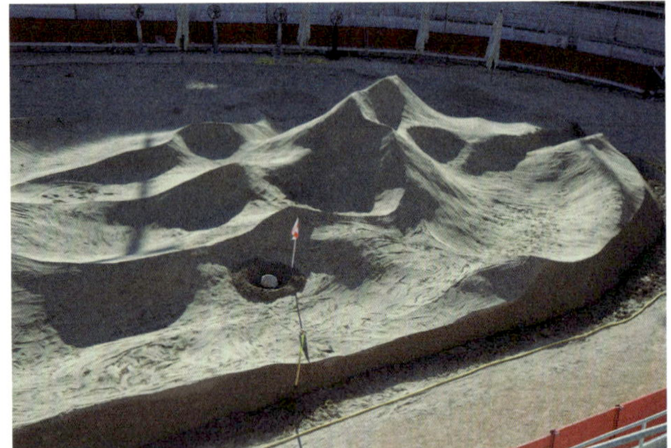

7/6/12—7:01:29 PM

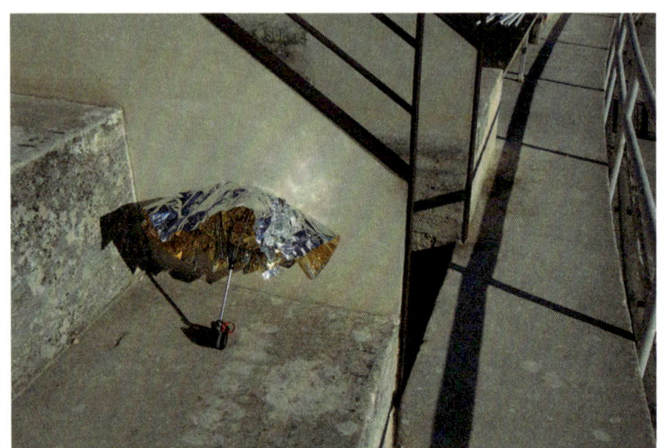

7/6/12—7:02:37 PM

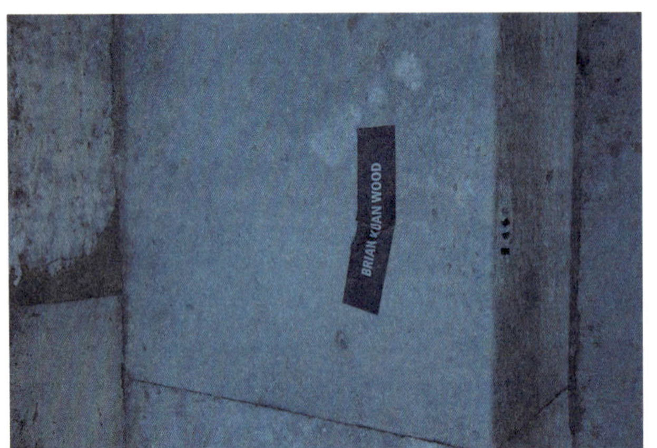

7/6/12—7:06:04 PM

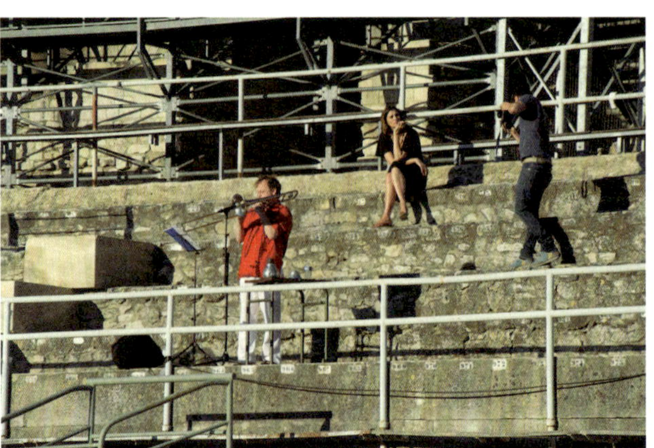

7/6/12—7:56:26 PM

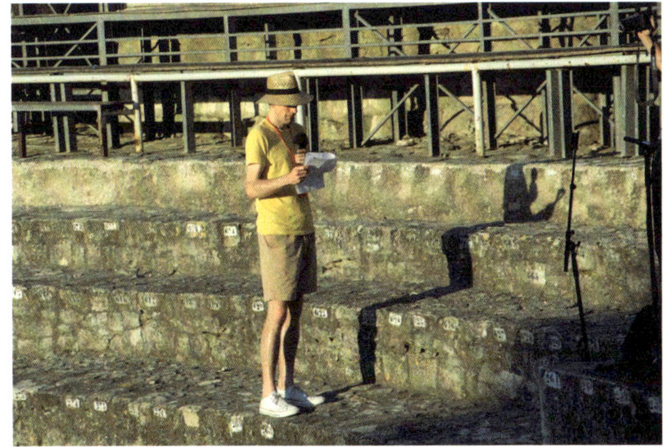

7/6/12—8:21:26 PM

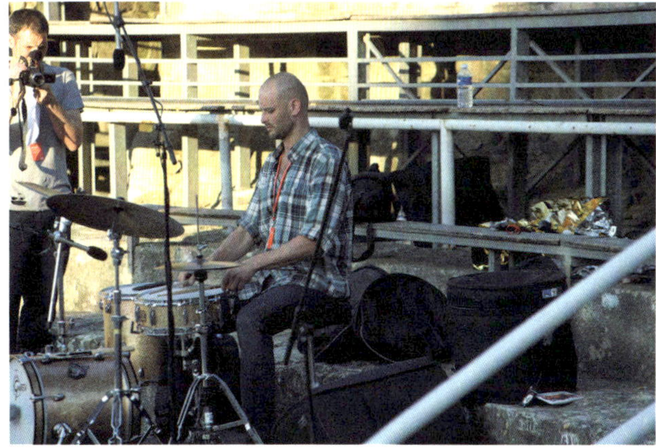

7/6/12—8:22:07 PM

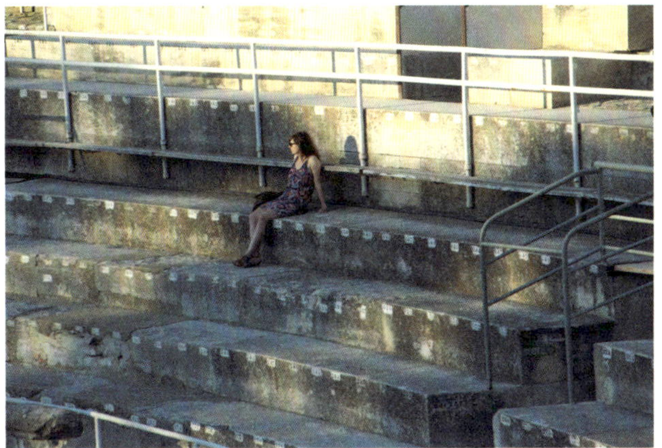

7/6/12—8:22:14 PM

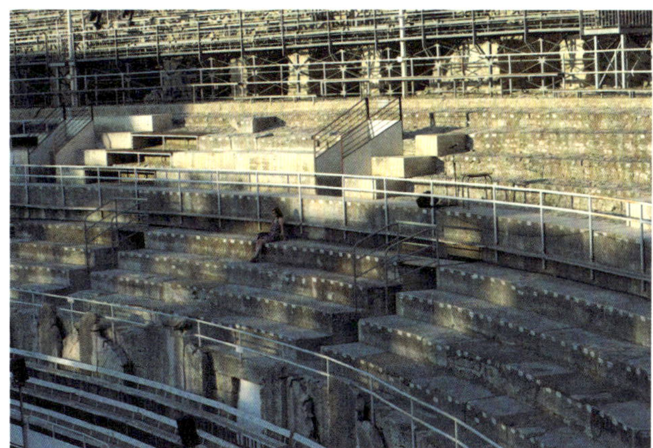

7/6/12—8:23:04 PM

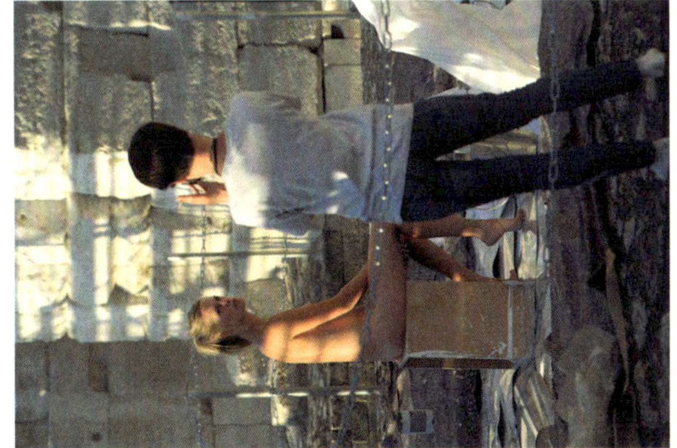

7/6/12—8:25:23 PM

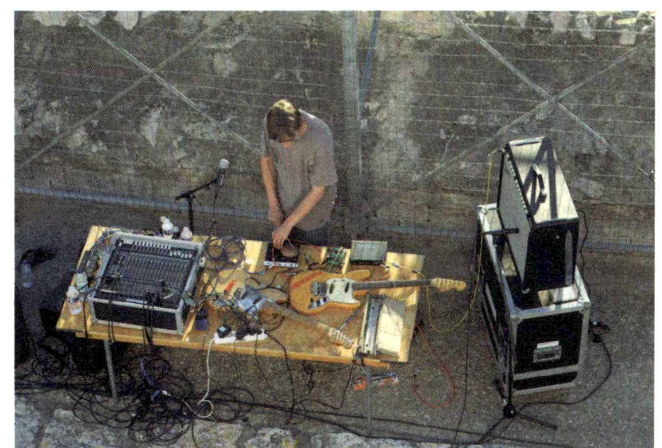

7/6/12—8:26:30 PM

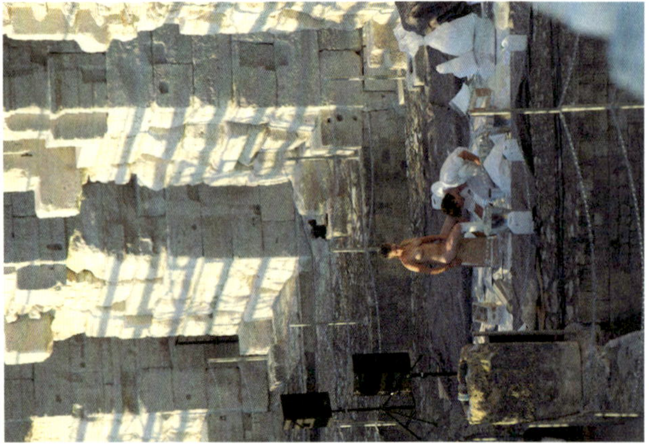
7/6/12—8:37:19 PM

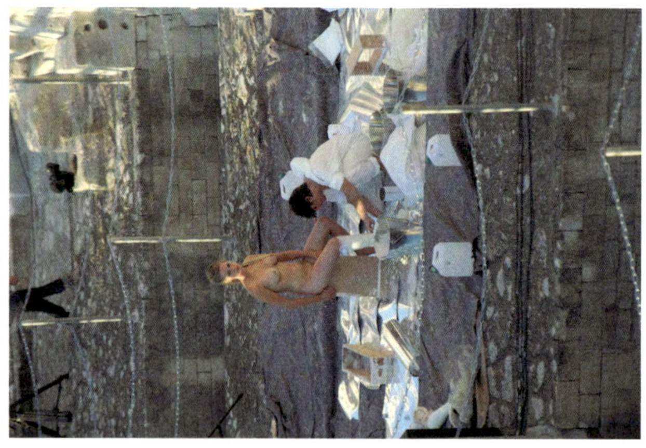
7/6/12—8:37:34 PM

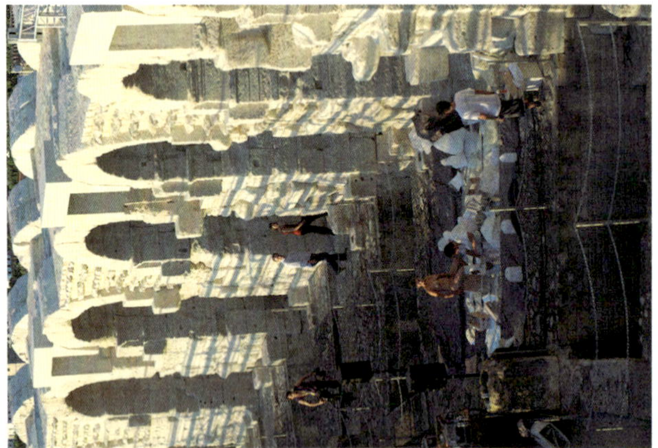
7/6/12—8:37:40 PM

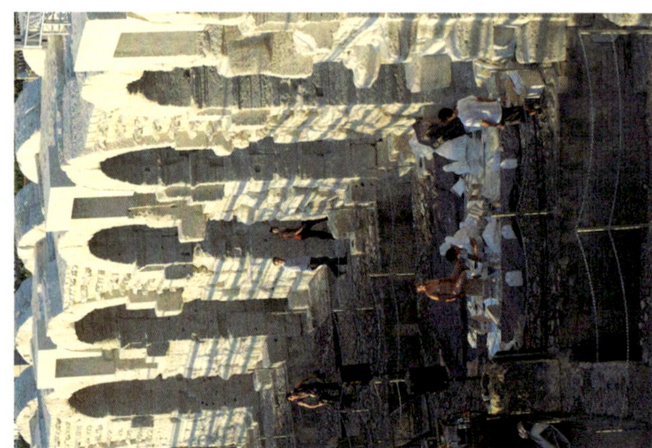
7/6/12—8:37:41 PM

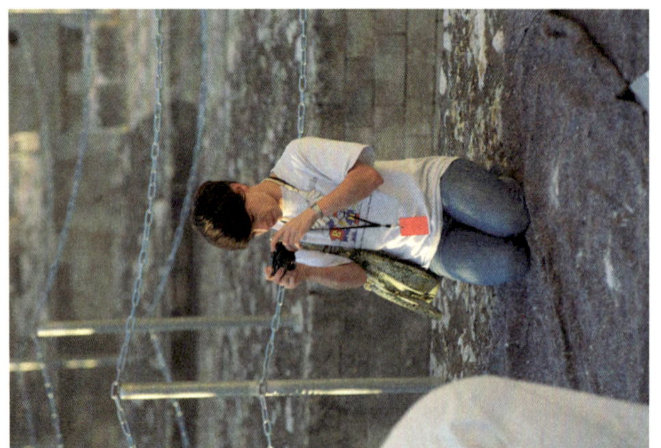
7/6/12—8:43:18 PM

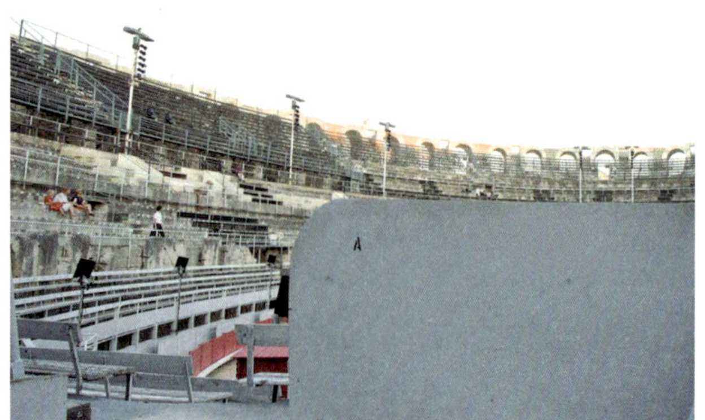
7/6/12—8:43:19 PM

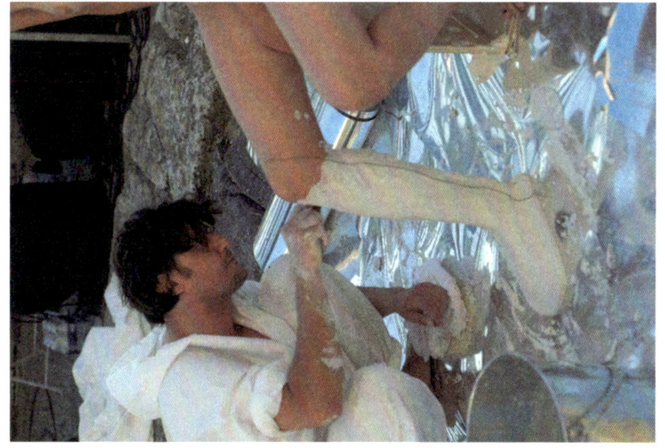
7/6/12—8:45:12 PM

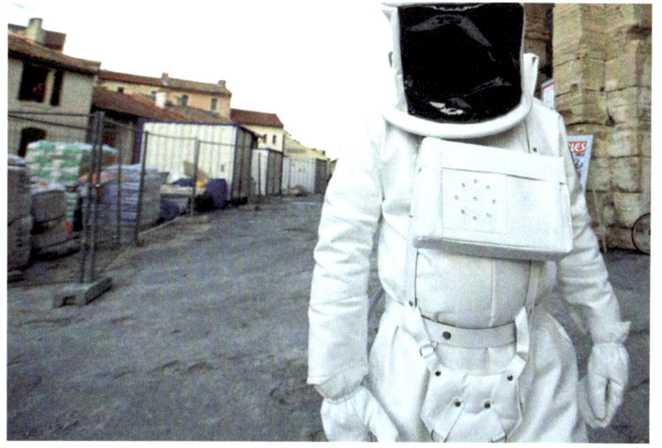
7/6/12—8:45:14 PM

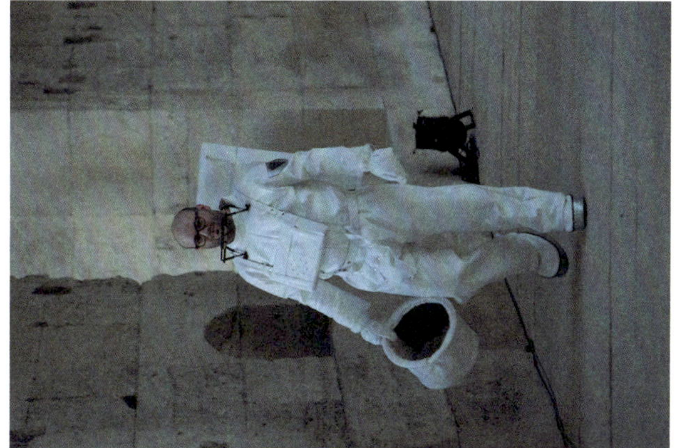
7/6/12—8:46:36 PM

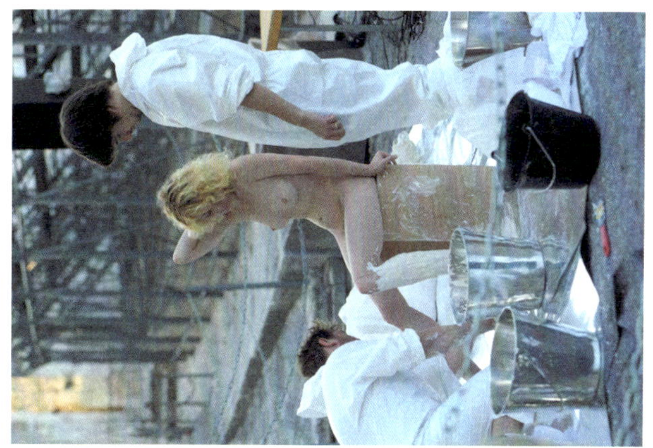
7/6/12—8:47:27 PM

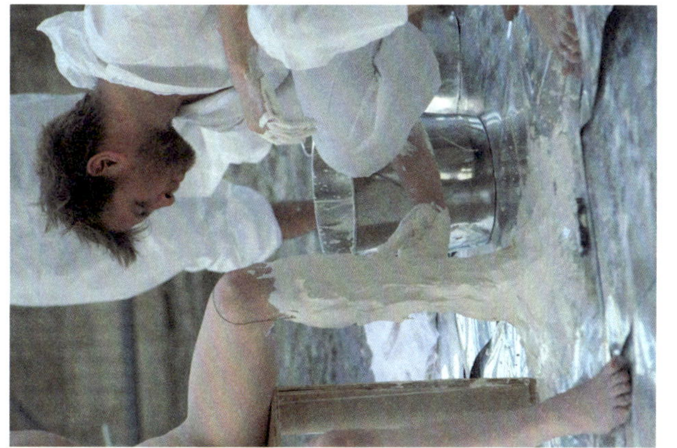
7/6/12—8:51:05 PM

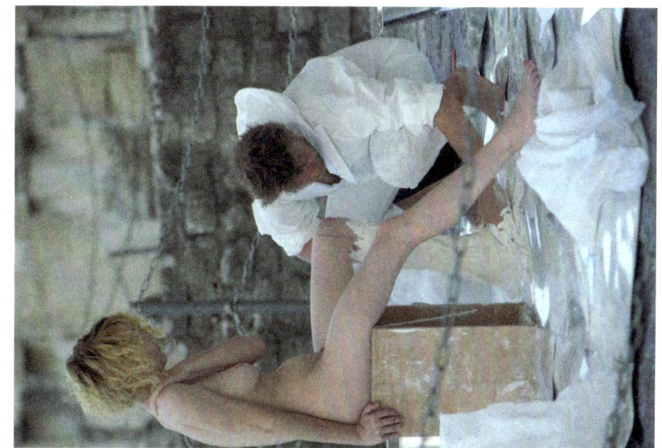
7/6/12—8:51:28 PM

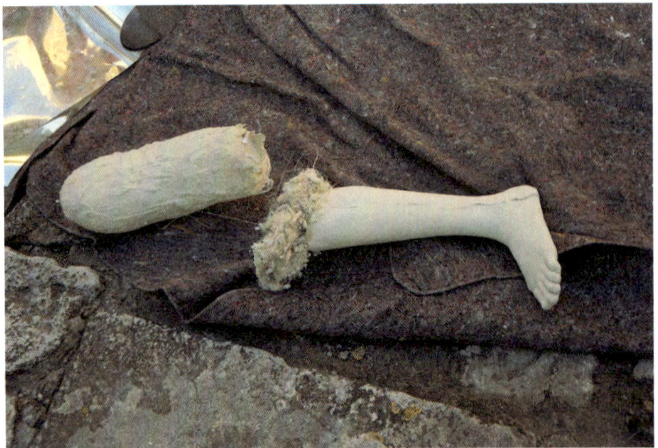

7/6/12—8:54:34 PM

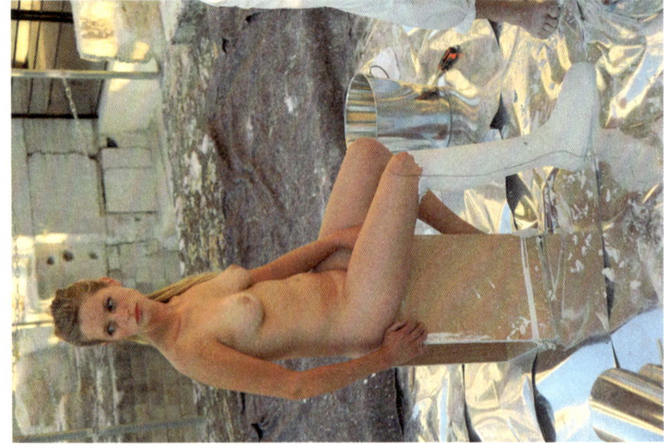

7/6/12—8:54:45 PM

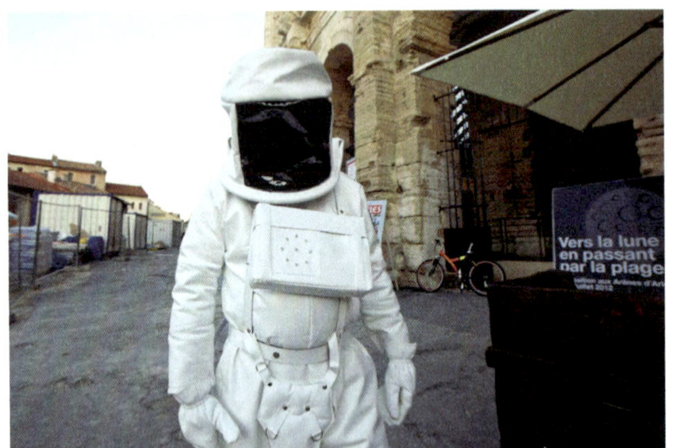

7/6/12—9:13:53 PM

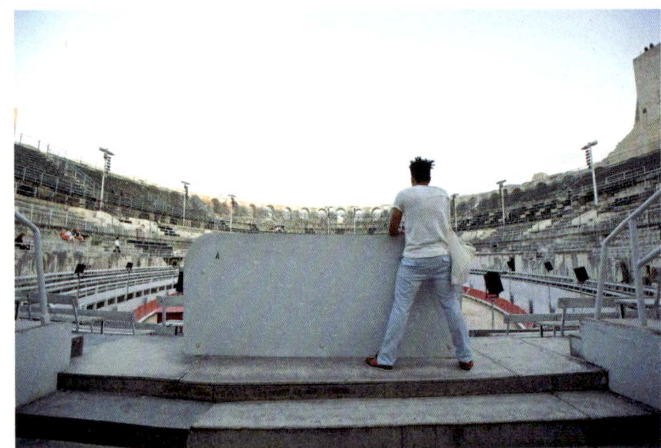

7/6/12—9:17:33 PM

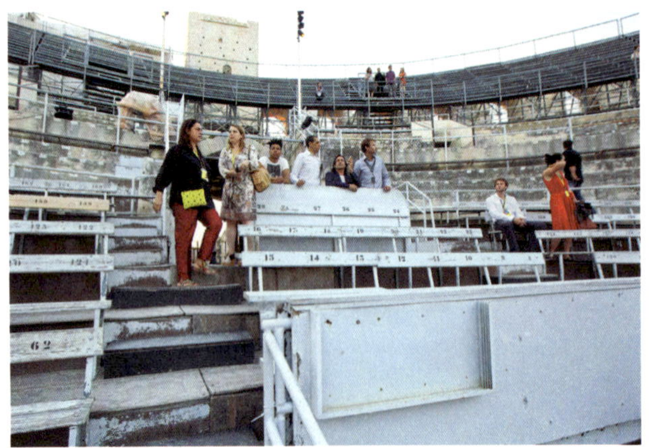

7/6/12—9:21:42 PM

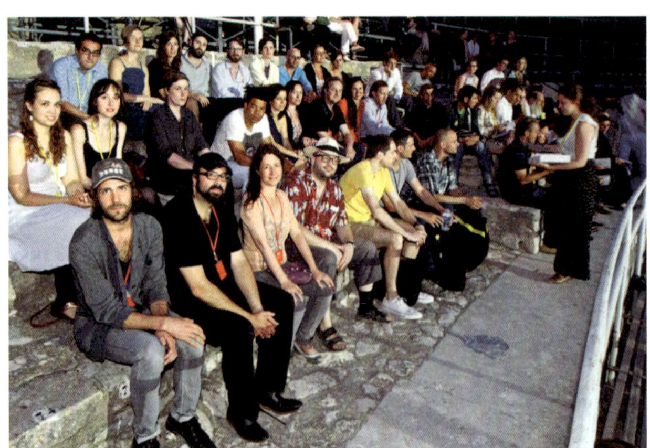

7/6/12—9:53:46 PM

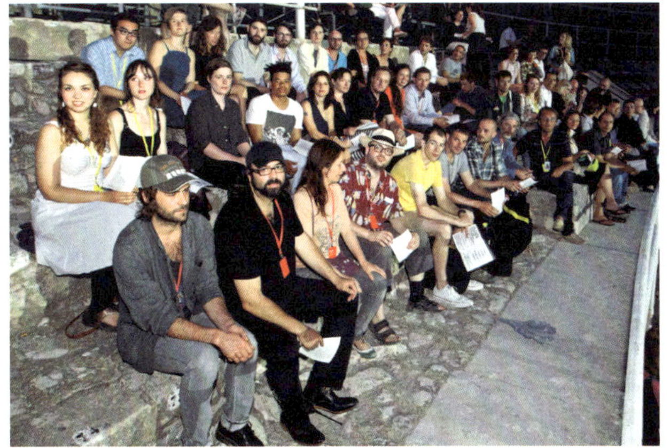

7/6/12—9:54:45 PM

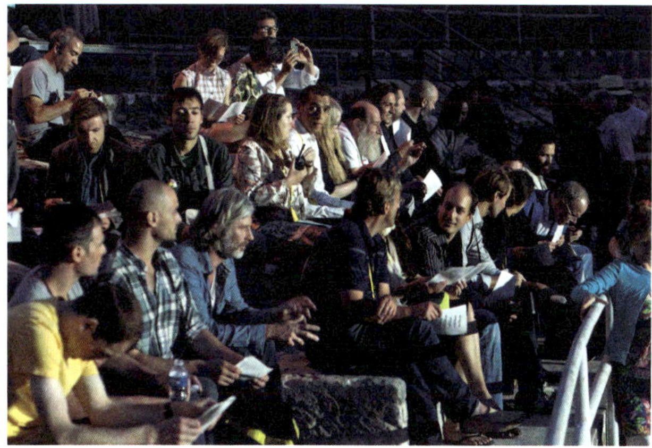

7/6/12—9:55:59 PM

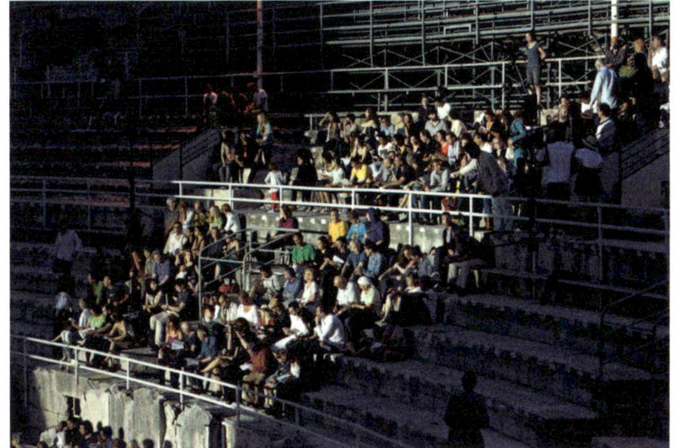

7/6/12—9:57:32 PM

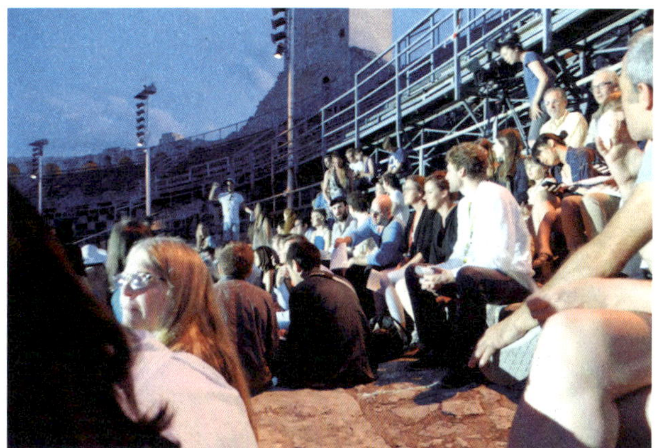

7/6/12—9:57:38 PM

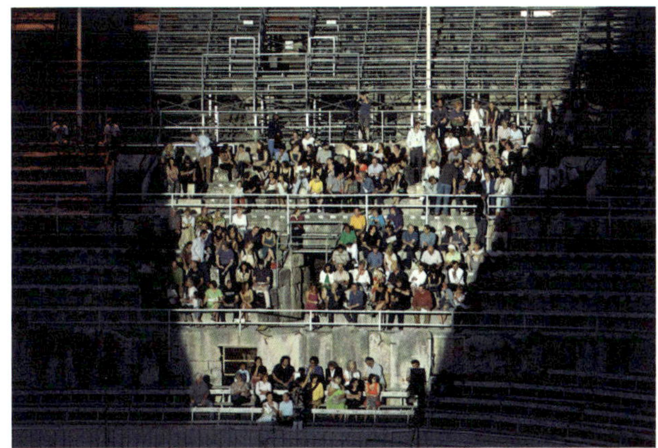

7/6/12—9:58:03 PM

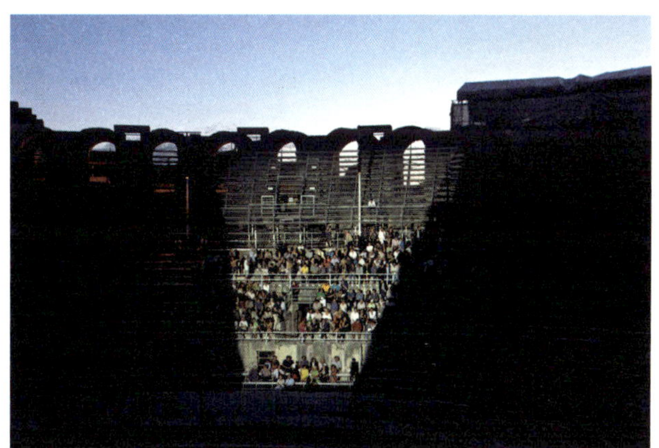

7/6/12—9:59:00 PM

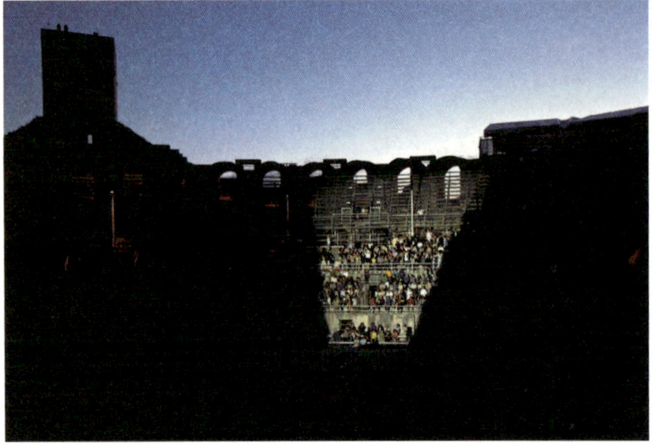

7/6/12—9:59:24 PM

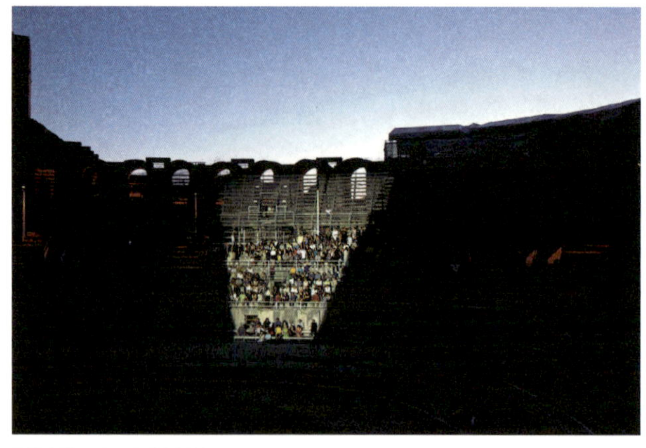

7/6/12—9:59:39 PM

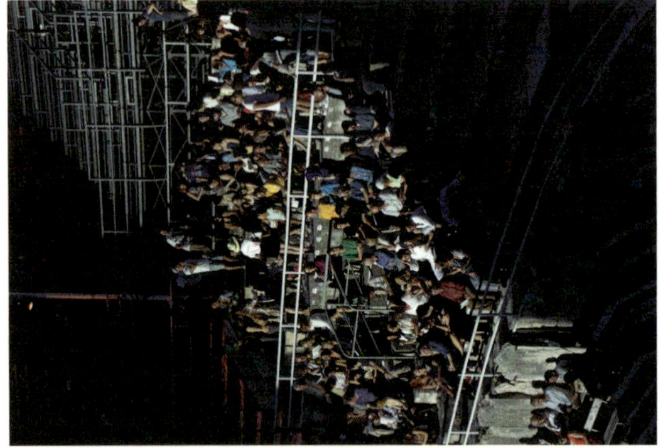

7/6/12—10:00:05 PM

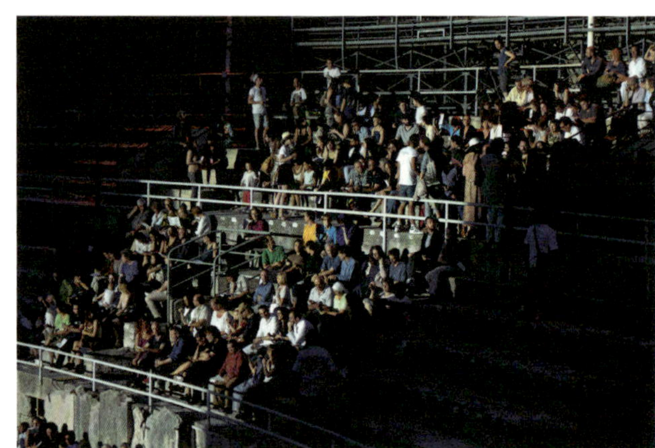

7/6/12—10:00:11 PM

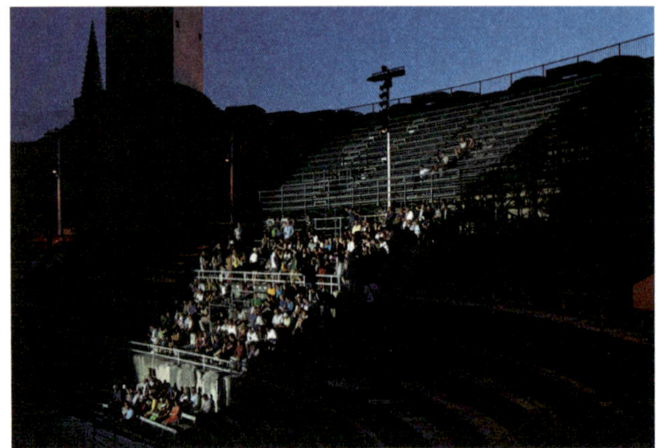

7/6/12—10:00:52 PM

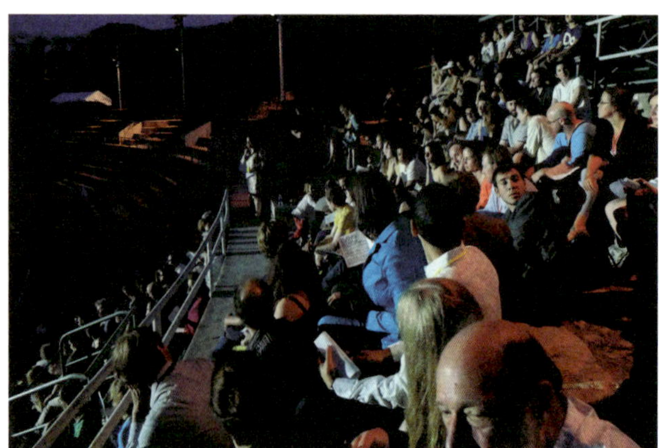

7/6/12—10:01:19 PM

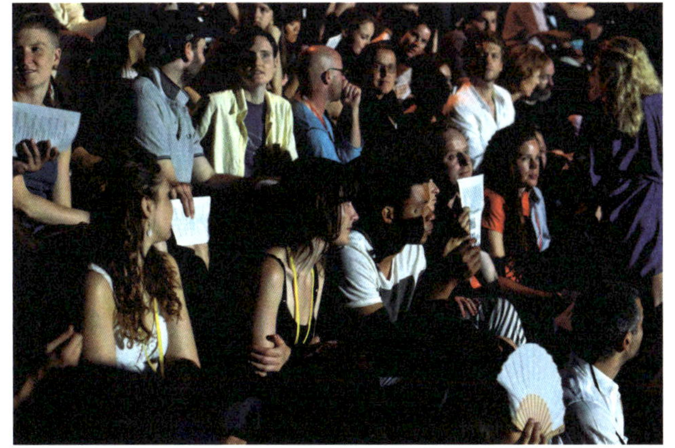
7/6/12—10:09:54 PM

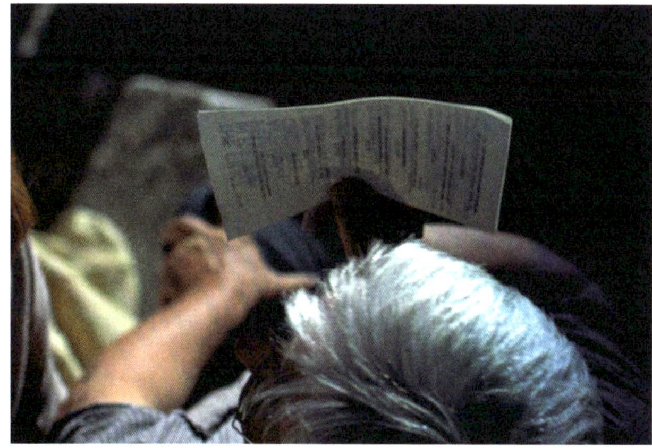
7/6/12—10:10:54 PM

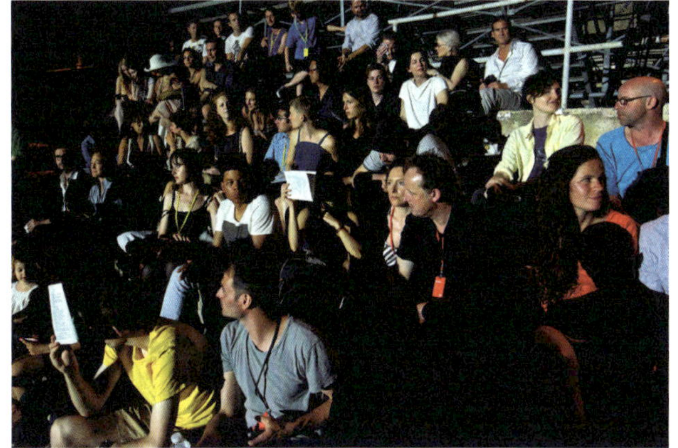
7/6/12—10:12:04 PM

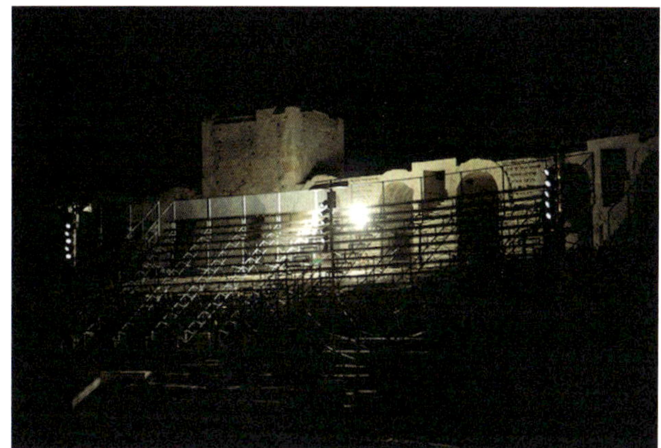
7/6/12—10:22:50 PM

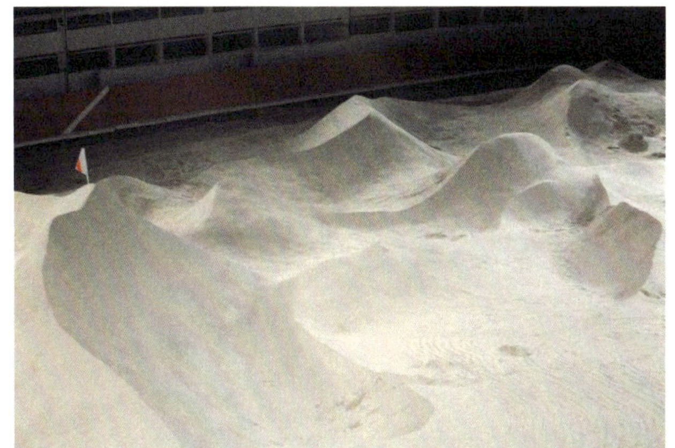
7/6/12—10:22:53 PM

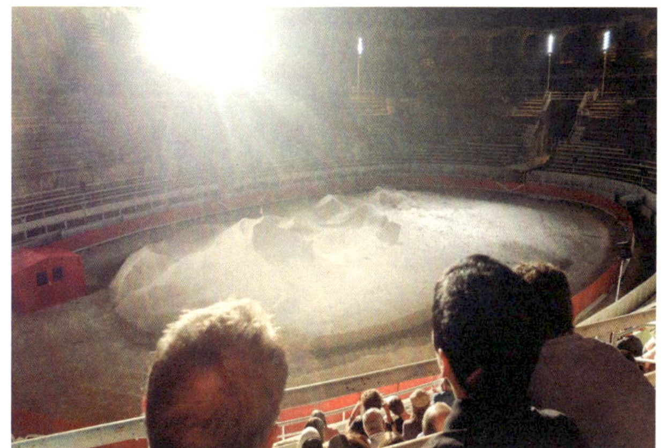
7/6/12—10:22:58 PM

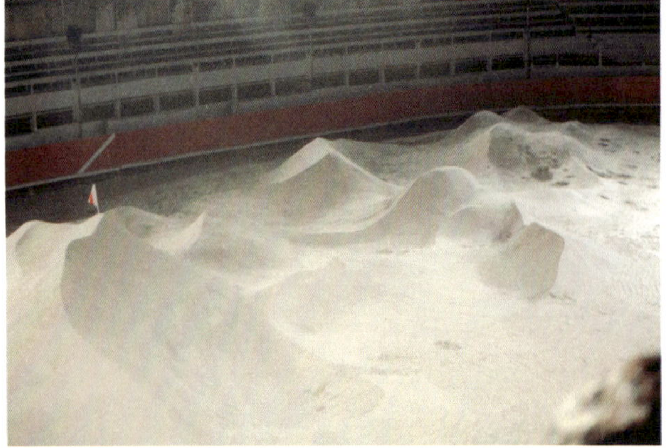

7/6/12—10:23:04 PM

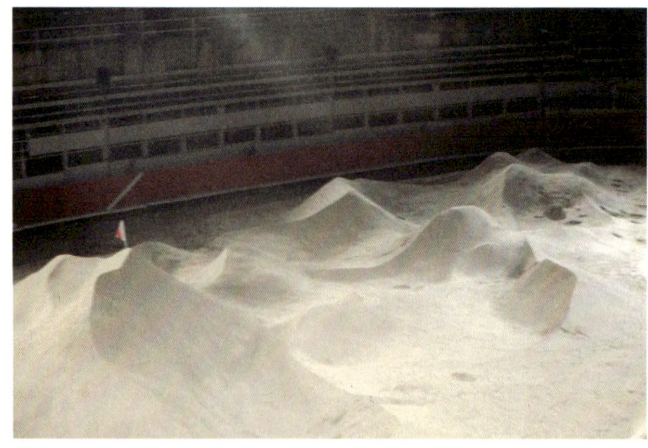

7/6/12—10:23:11 PM

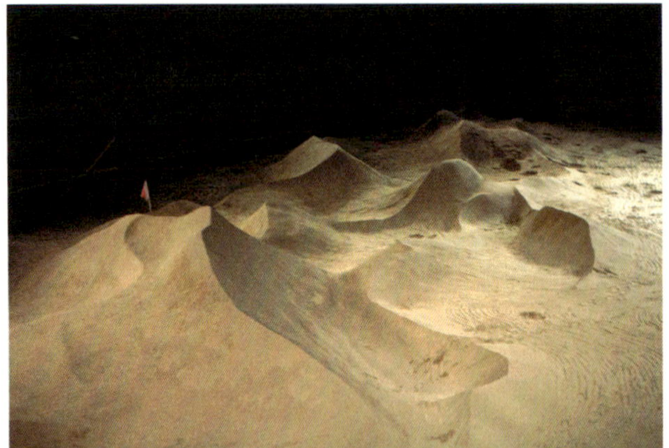

7/6/12—10:25:28 PM

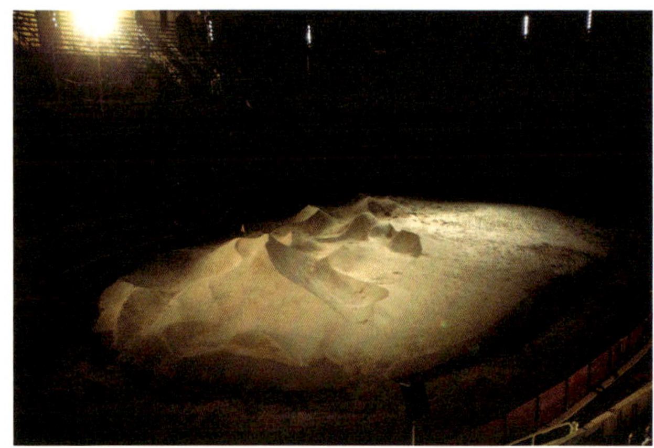

7/6/12—10:25:44 PM

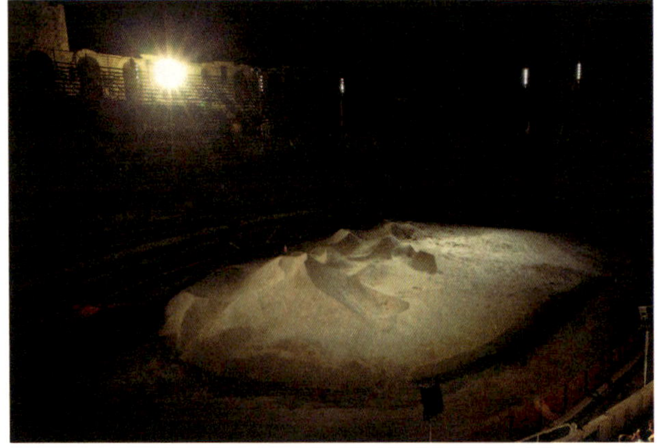

7/6/12—10:25:48 PM

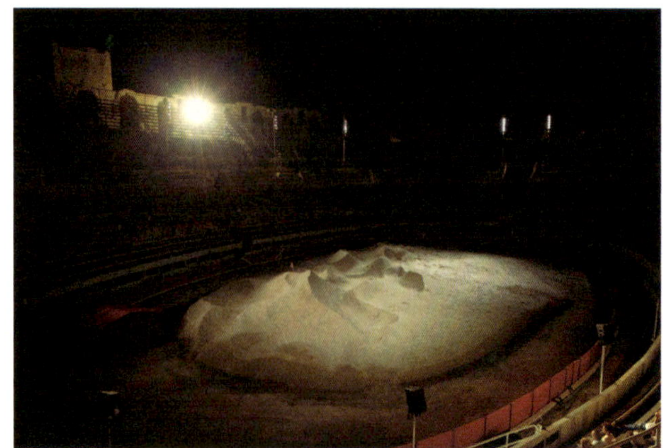

7/6/12—10:25:54 PM

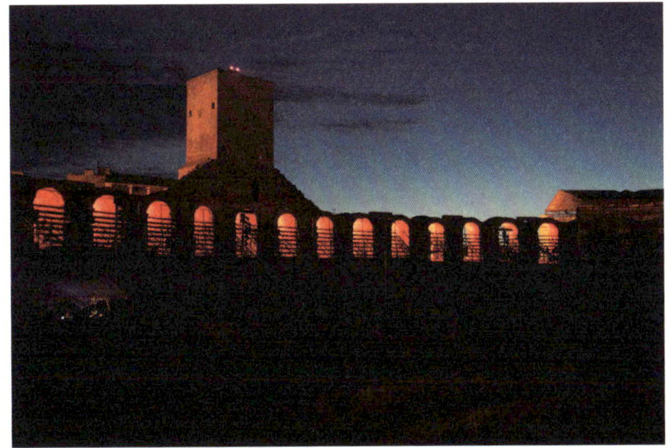

7/6/12—10:27:14 PM

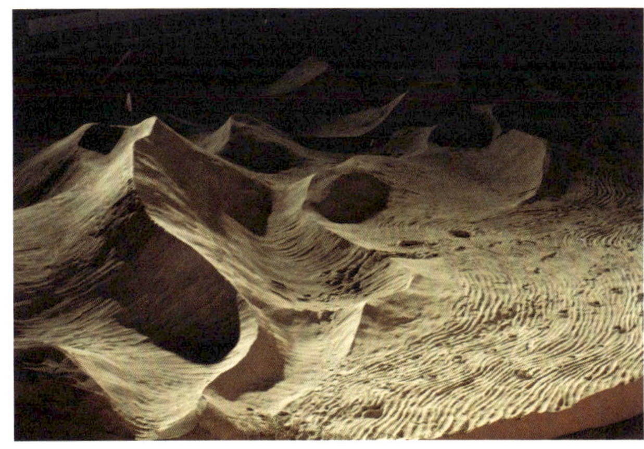

7/6/12—10:27:23 PM

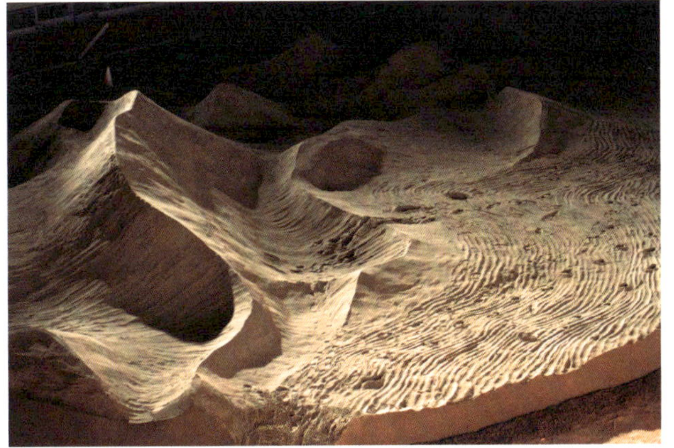

7/6/12—10:27:30 PM

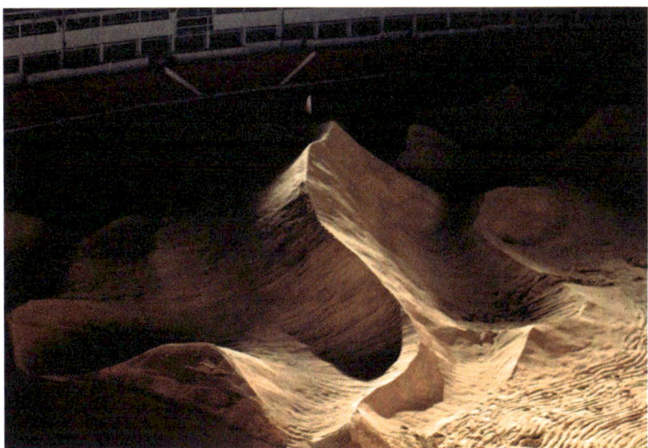

7/6/12—10:27:37 PM

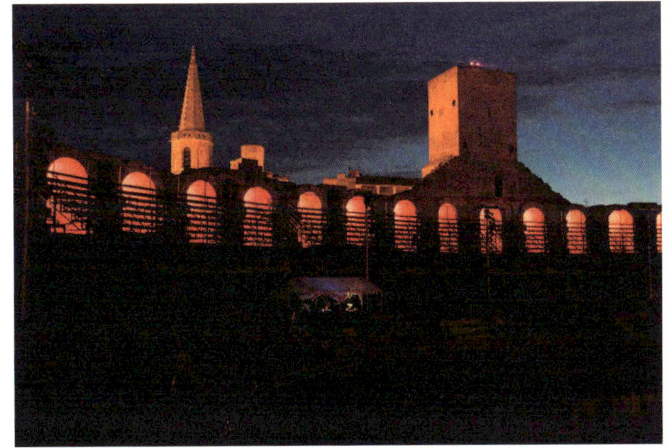

7/6/12—10:28:07 PM

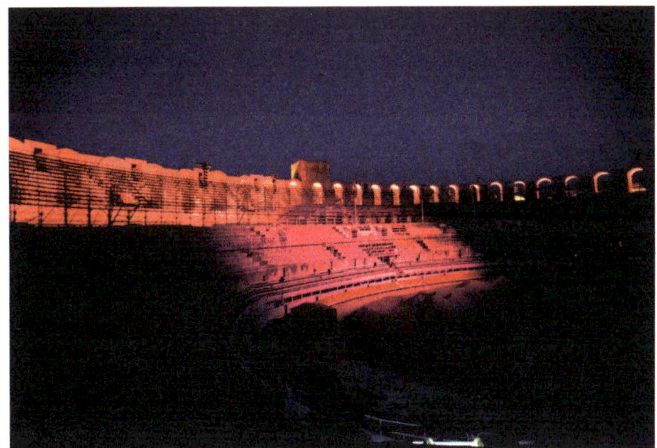

7/6/12—10:29:05 PM

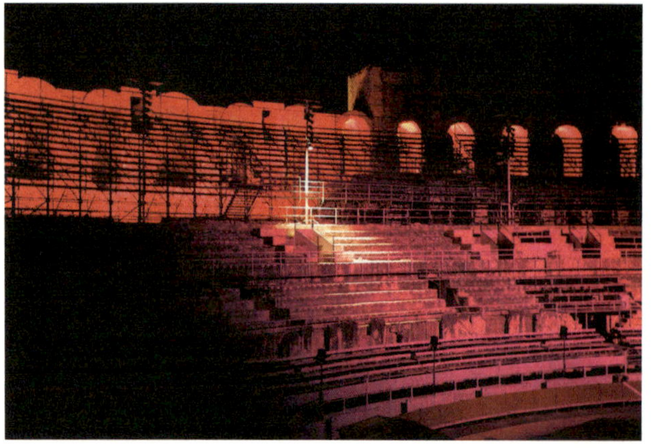
7/6/12—10:30:41 PM

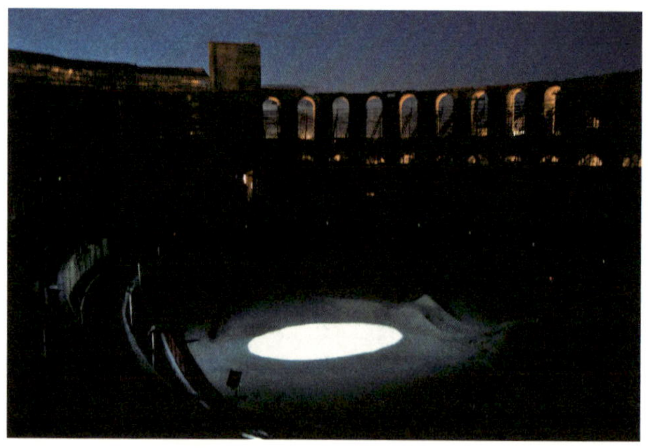
7/6/12—10:32:50 PM

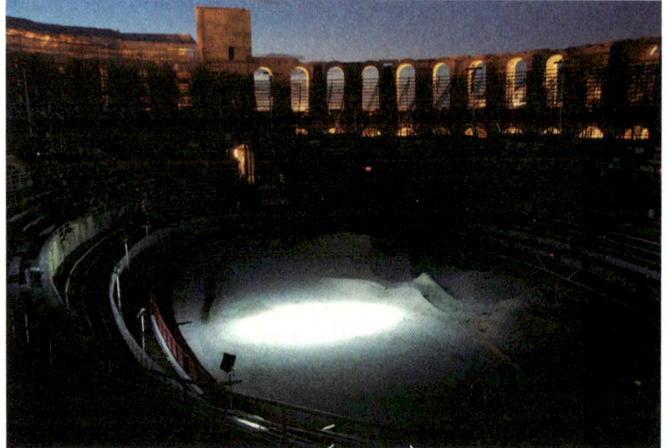
7/6/12—10:33:45 PM

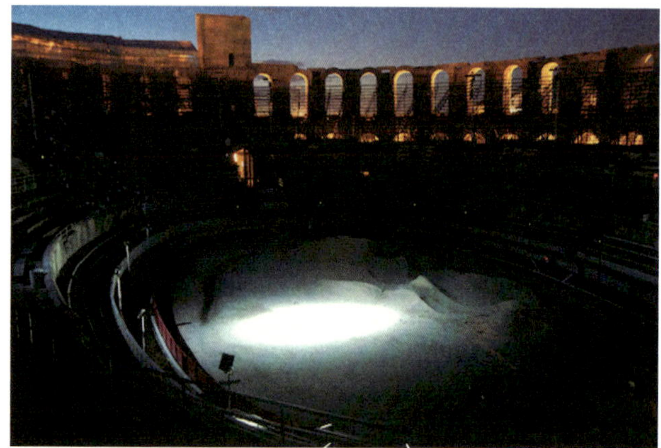
7/6/12—10:33:45 PM

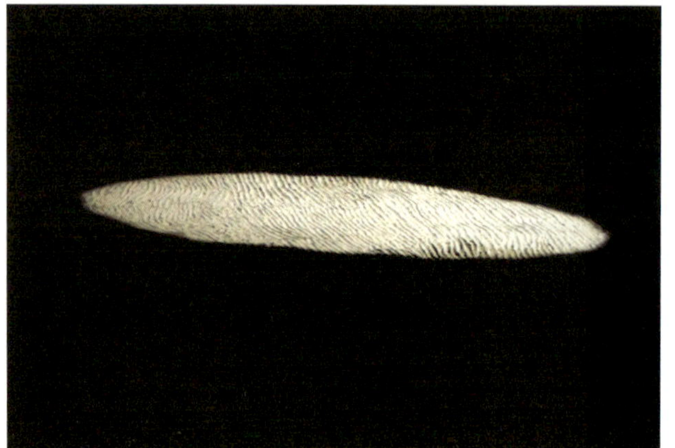
7/6/12—10:35:31 PM

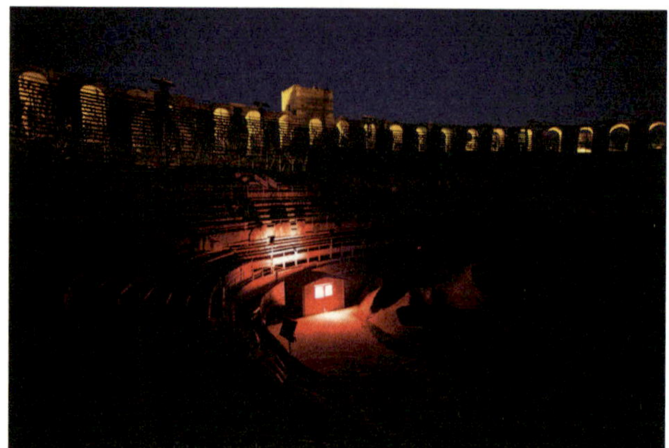
7/6/12—10:42:42 PM

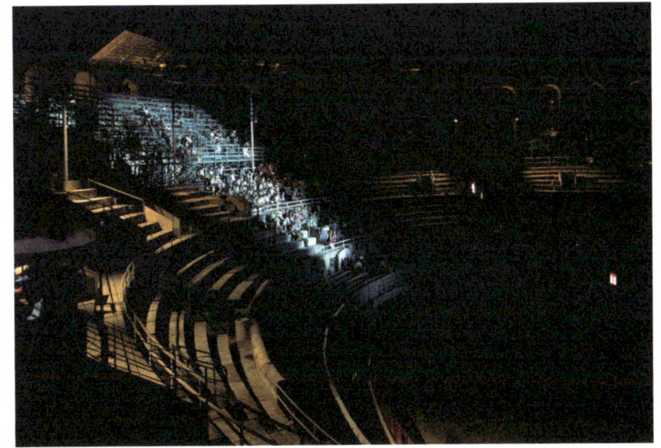

7/6/12—10:42:56 PM

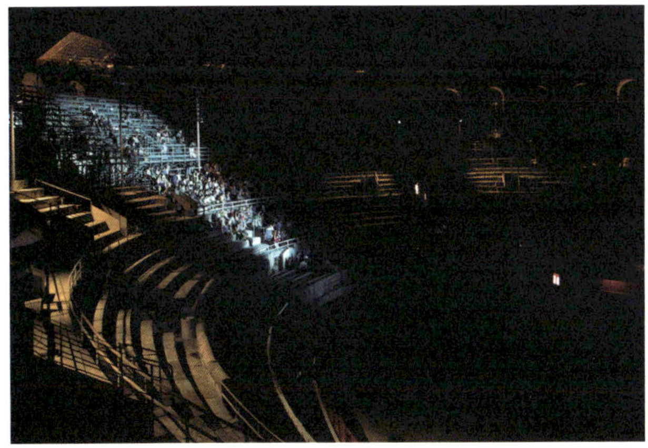

7/6/12—10:42:58 PM

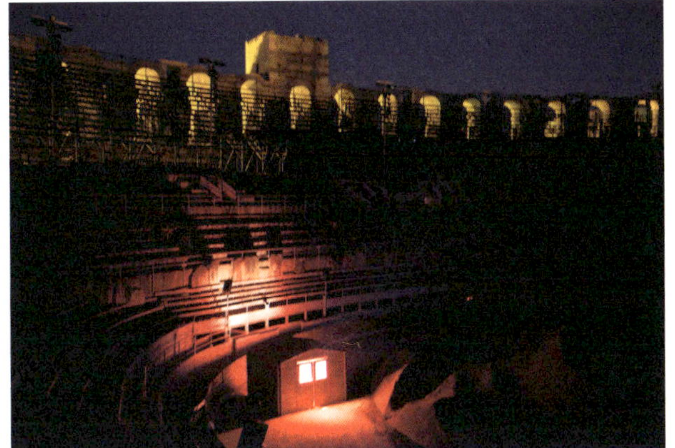

7/6/12—10:43:14 PM

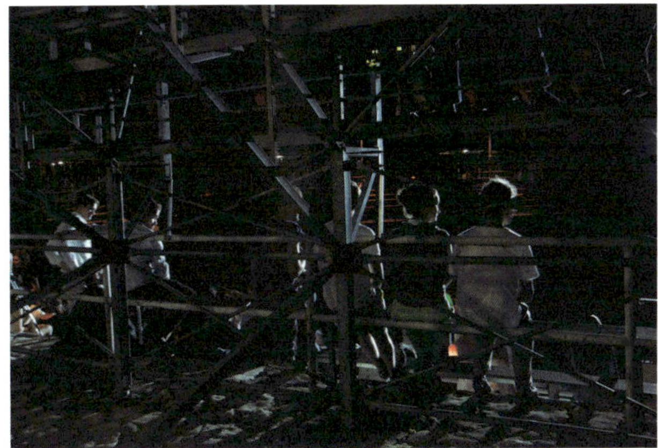

7/6/12—10:44:41 PM

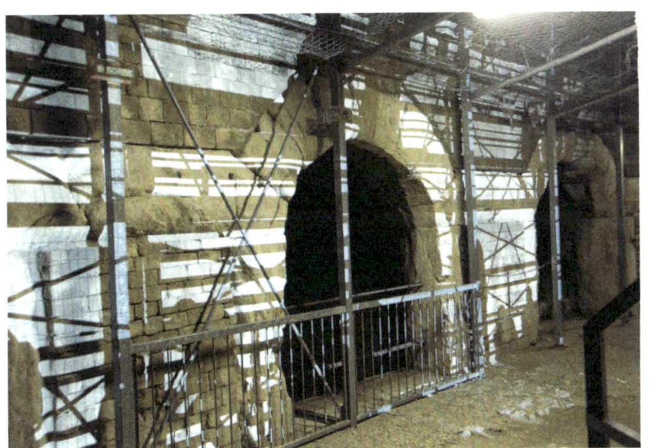

7/6/12—10:44:49 PM

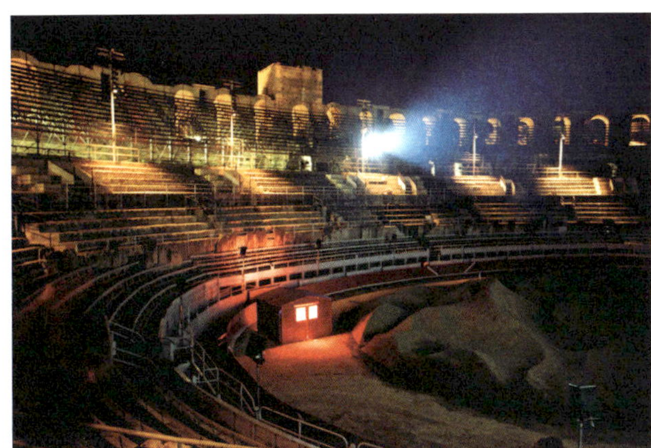

7/6/12—10:46:03 PM

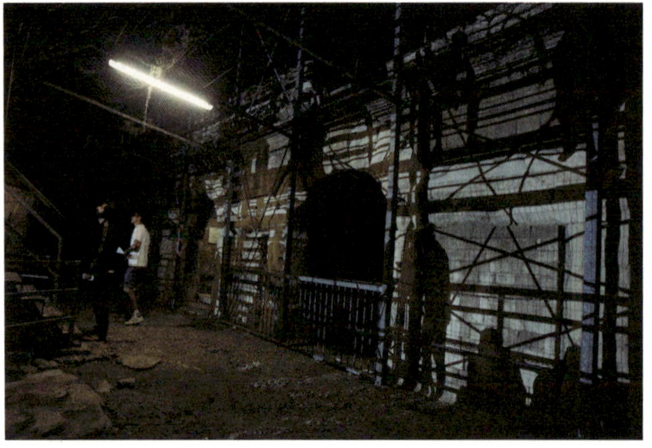
7/6/12—10:47:18 PM

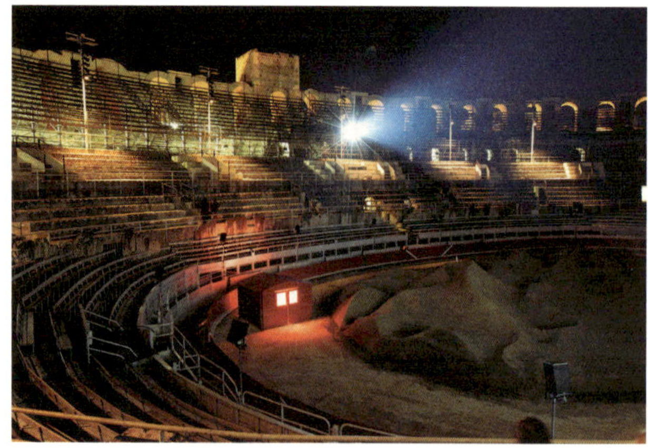
7/6/12—10:47:19 PM

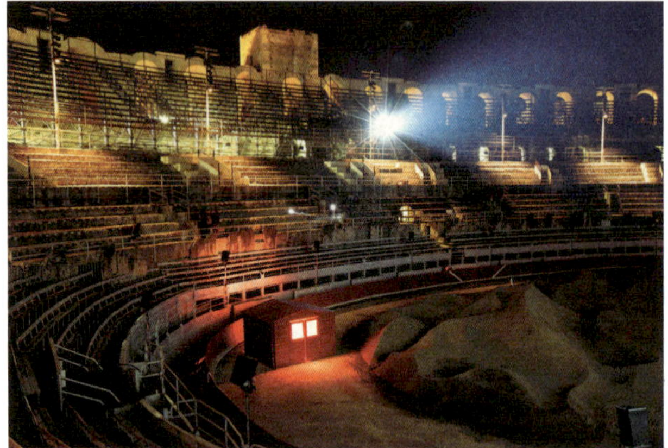
7/6/12—10:48:26 PM

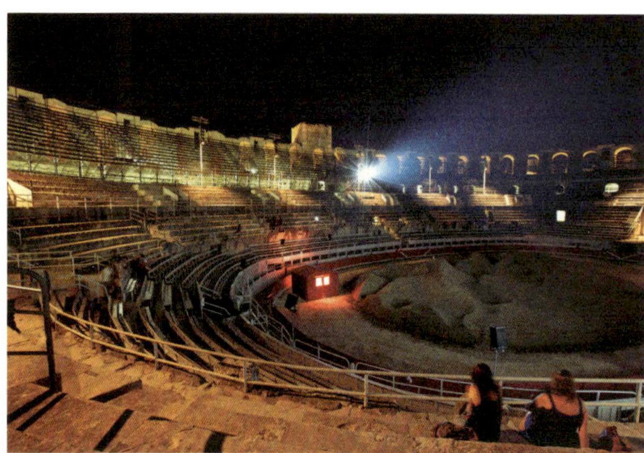
7/6/12—10:48:56 PM

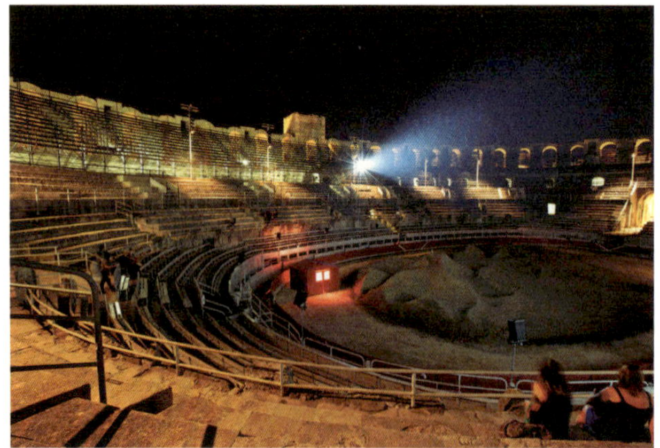
7/6/12—10:49:45 PM

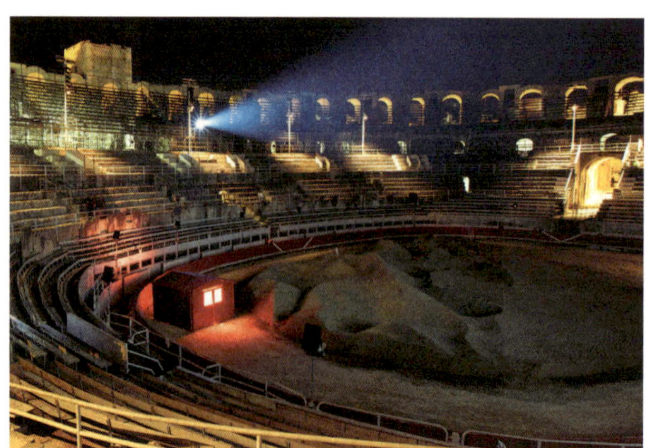
7/6/12—10:50:48 PM

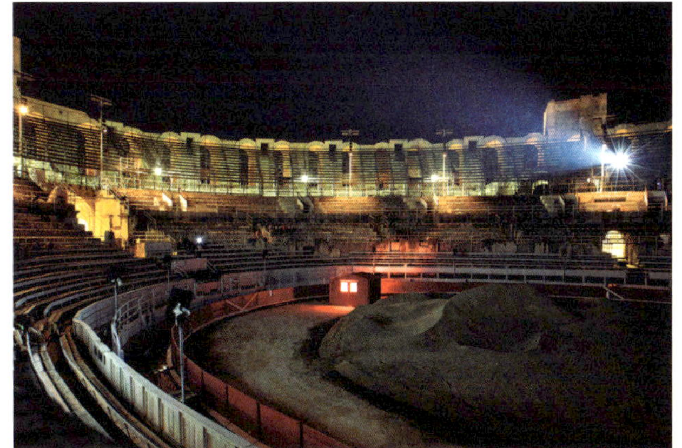

7/6/12—10:52:23 PM

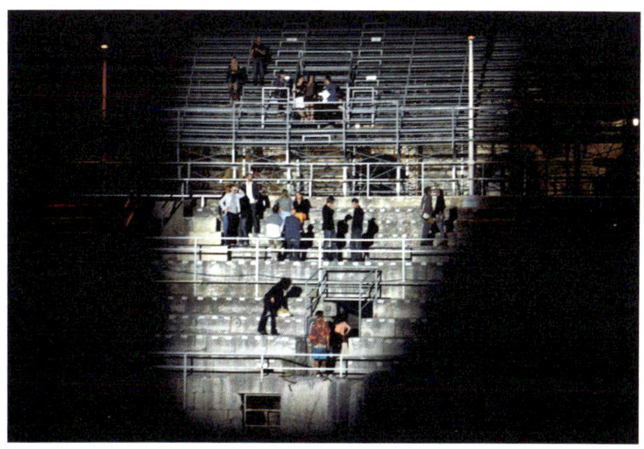

7/6/12—11:09:33 PM

7/6/12—11:10:54 PM

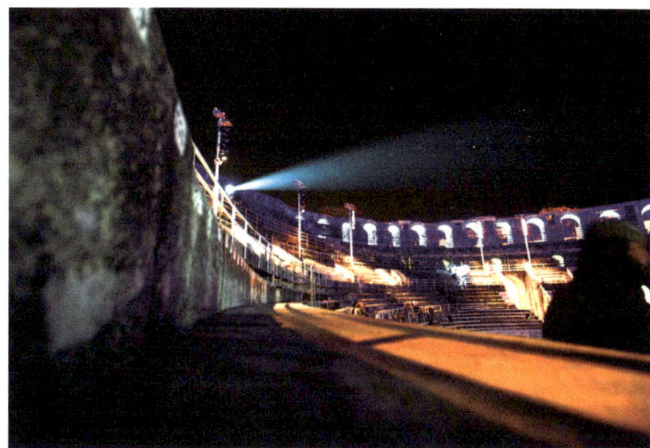

7/6/12—11:13:31 PM

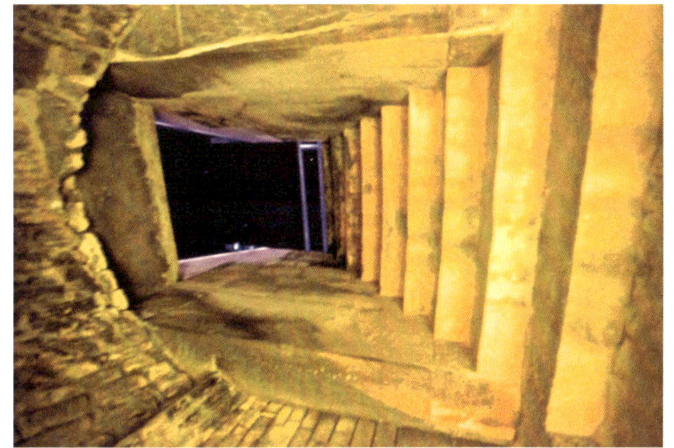

7/6/12—11:15:32 PM

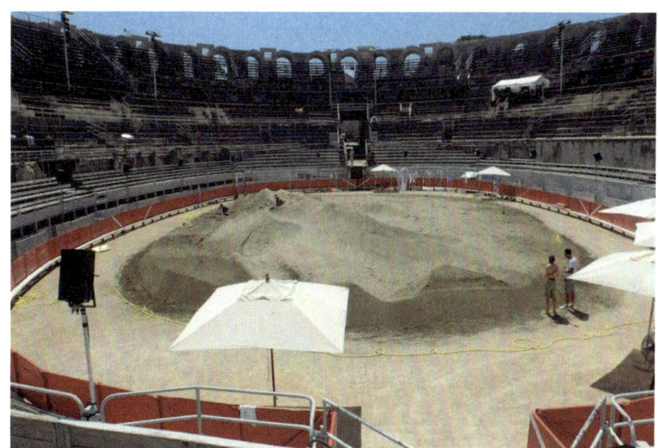

7/7/12—6:57:19 AM

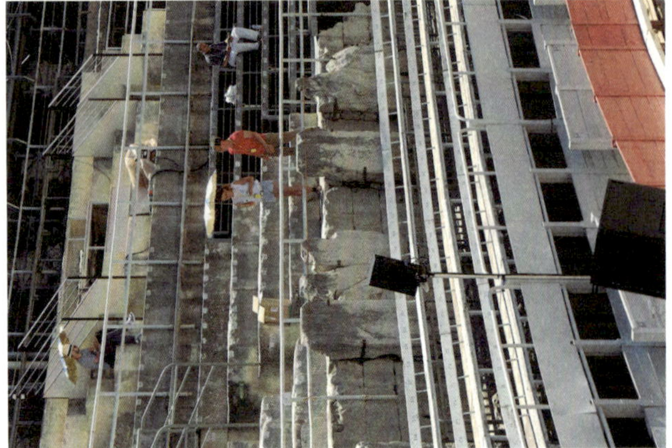
7/7/12—6:57:48 AM

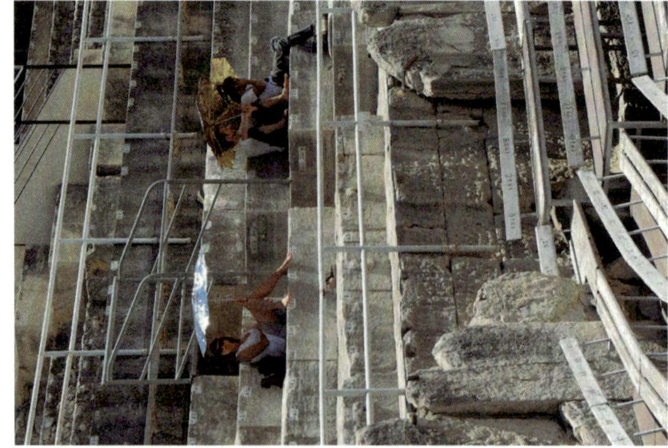
7/7/12—6:57:53 AM

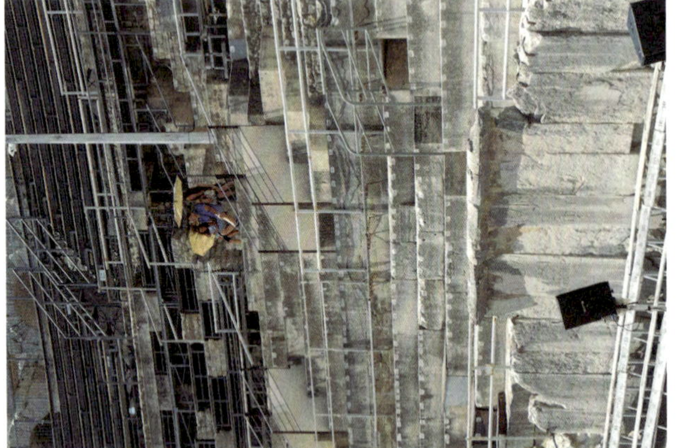
7/7/12—6:58:03 AM

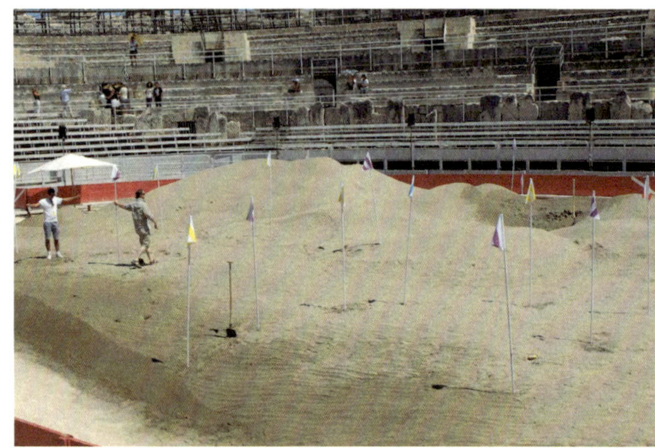
7/7/12—6:59:52 AM

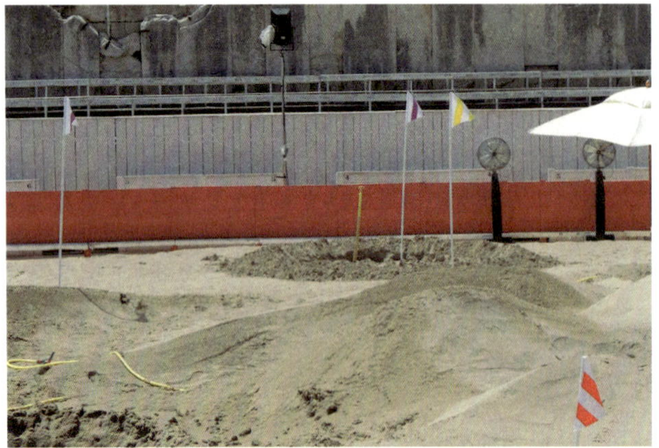
7/7/12—8:44:15 AM

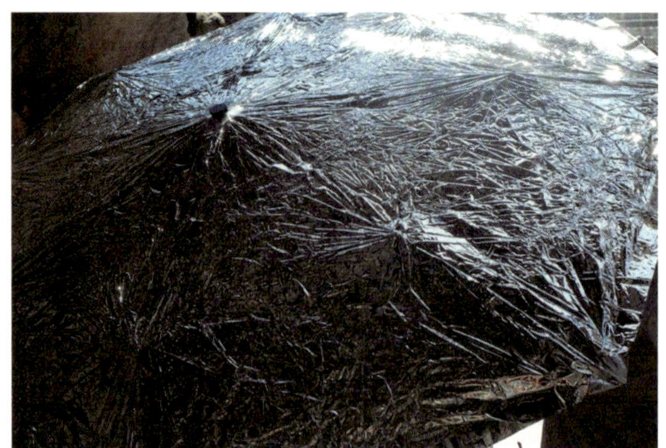
7/7/12—8:57:11 AM

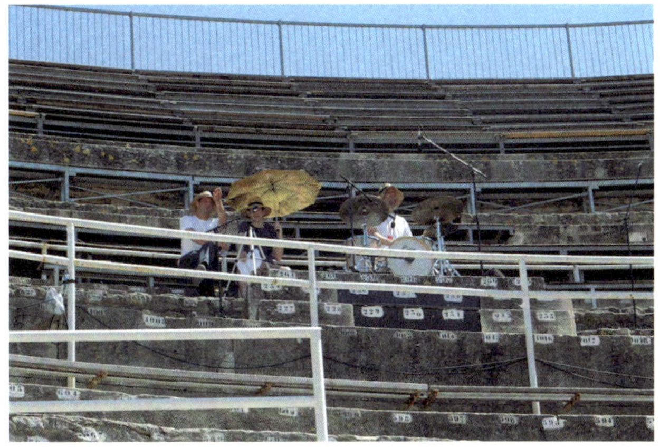
7/7/12—9:15:28 AM

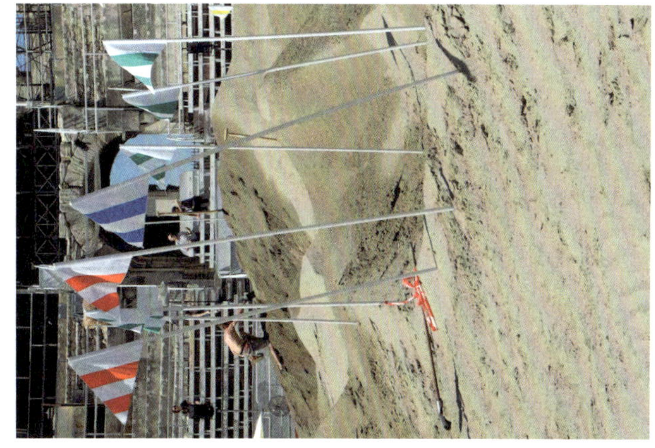
7/7/12—9:16:59 AM

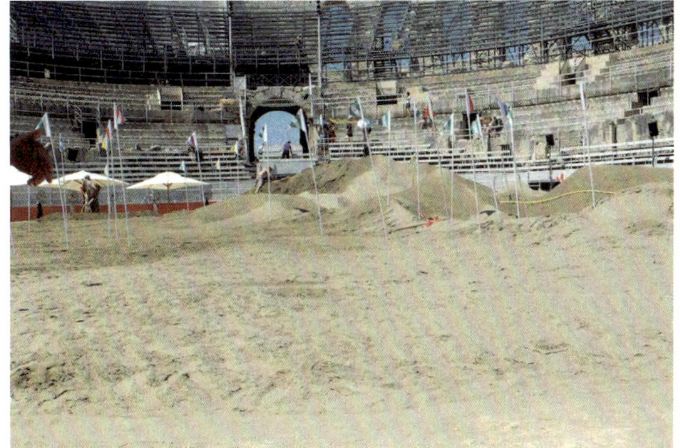
7/7/12—9:17:50 AM

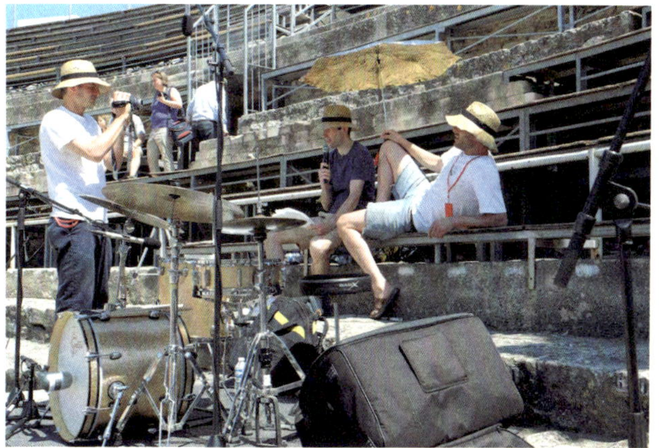
7/7/12—9:21:08 AM

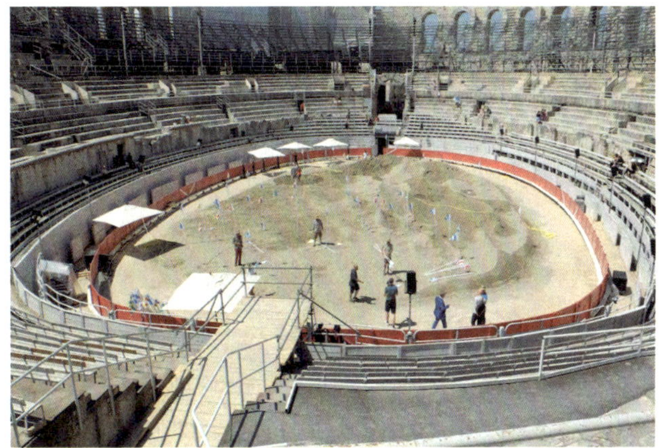
7/7/12—9:21:17 AM

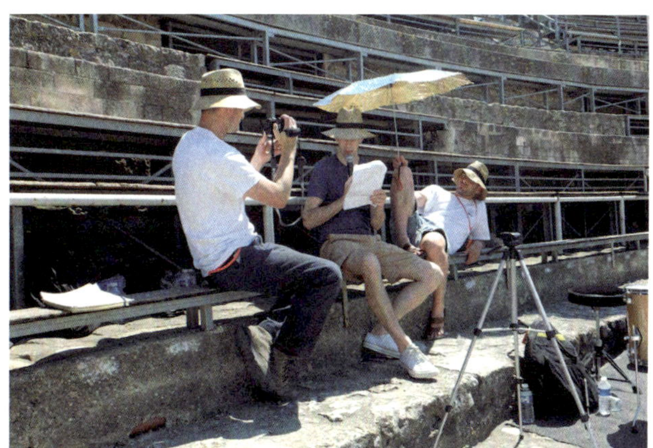
7/7/12—9:22:05 AM

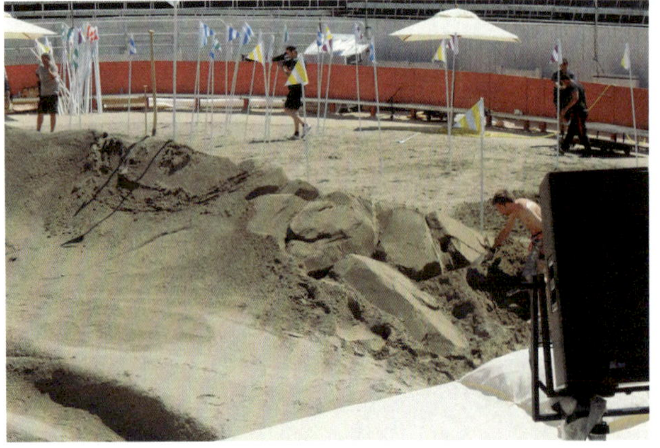

7/7/12—9:28:26 AM

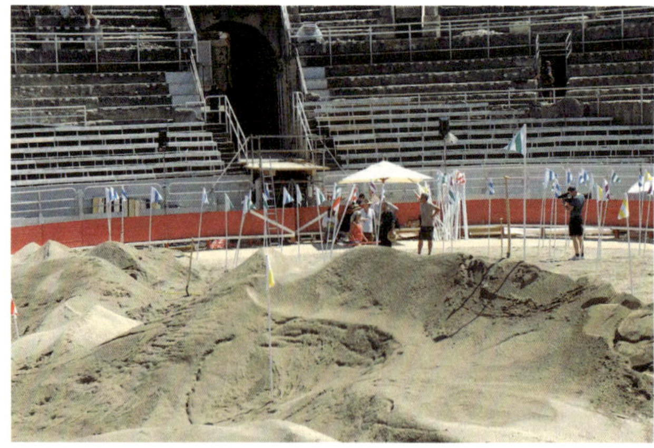

7/7/12—9:28:31 AM

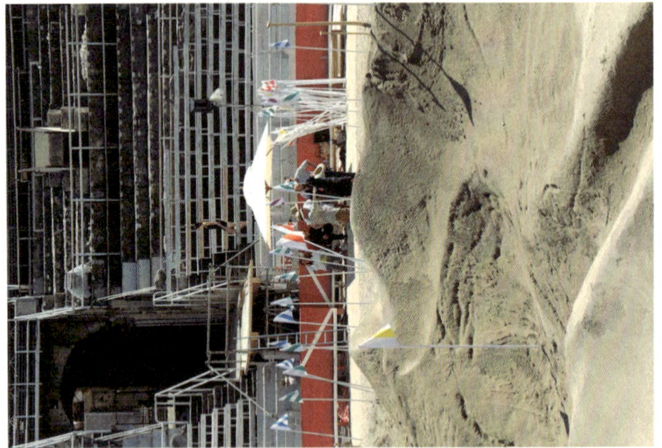

7/7/12—9:29:04 AM

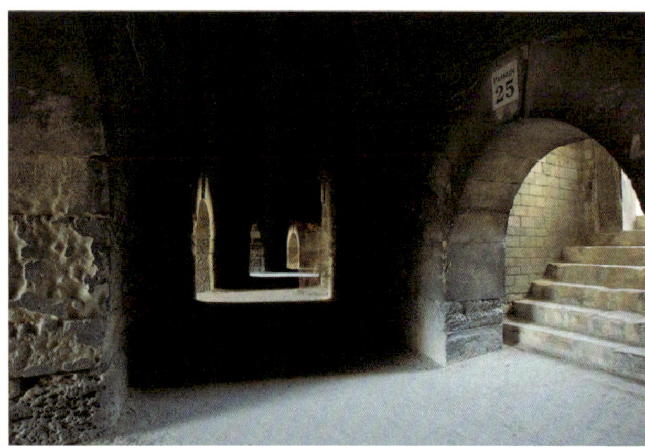

7/7/12—9:31:02 AM

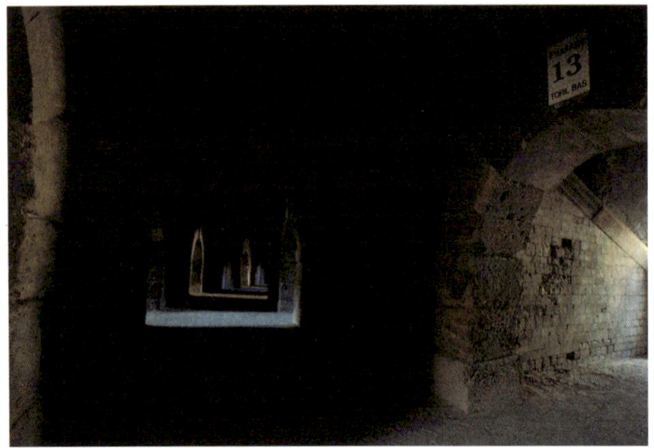

7/7/12—9:34:29 AM

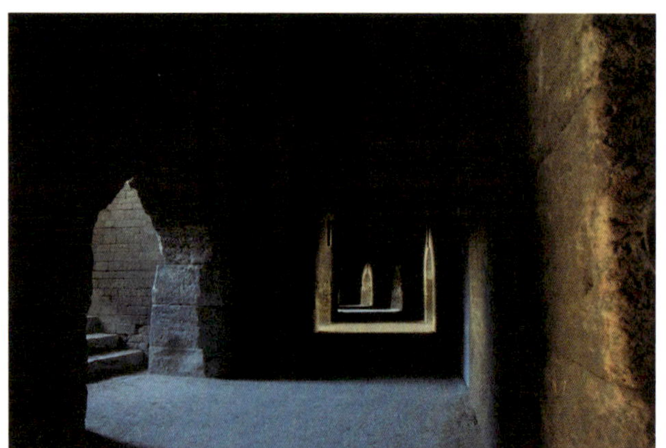

7/7/12—9:35:41 AM

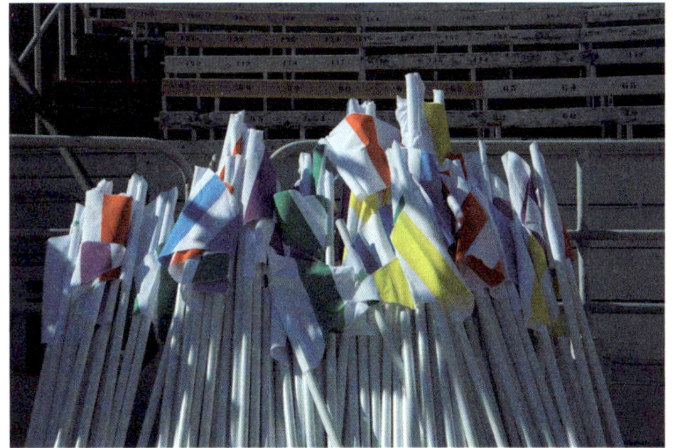

7/7/12—9:53:34 AM

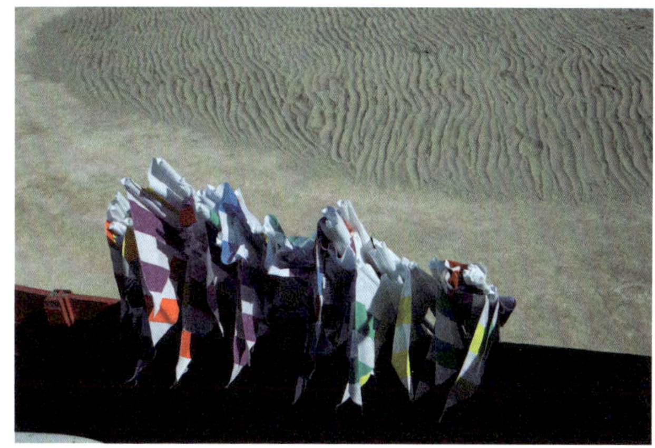

7/7/12—9:59:21 AM

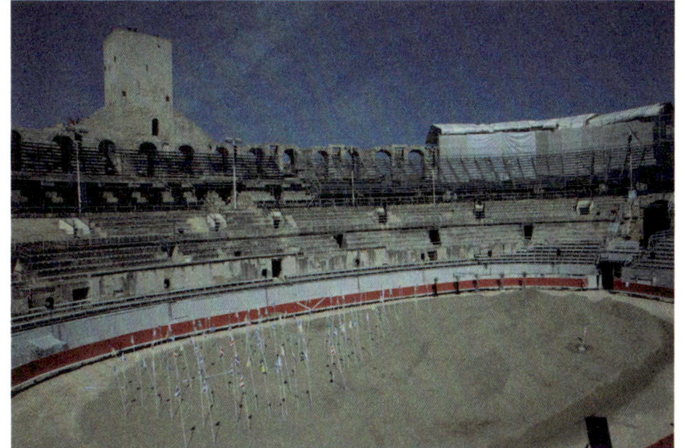

7/7/12—10:52:26 AM

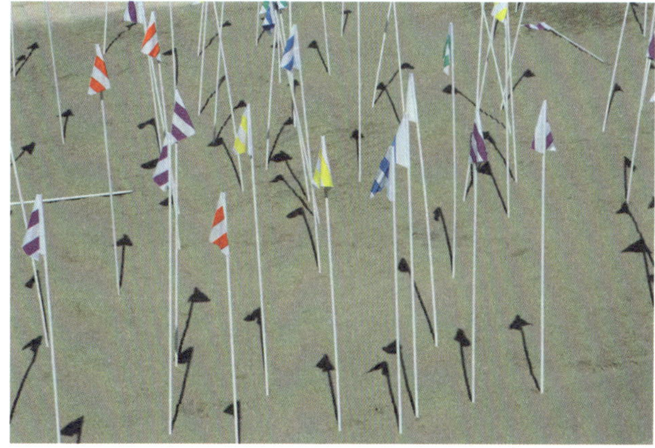

7/7/12—10:53:08 AM

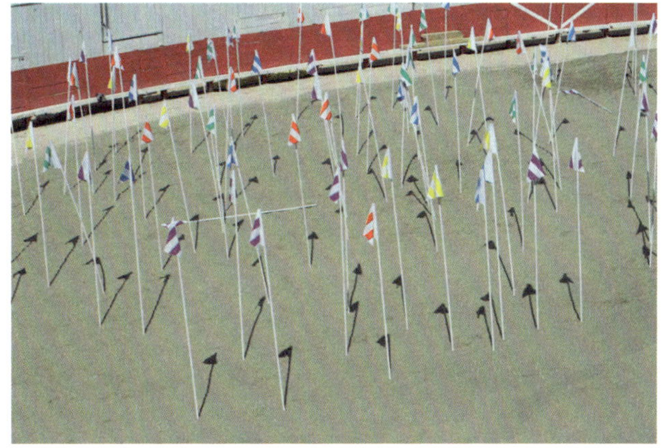

7/7/12—10:53:22 AM

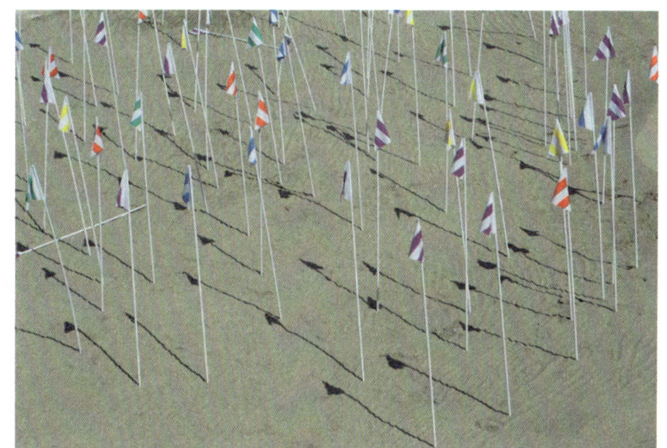

7/7/12—10:53:48 AM

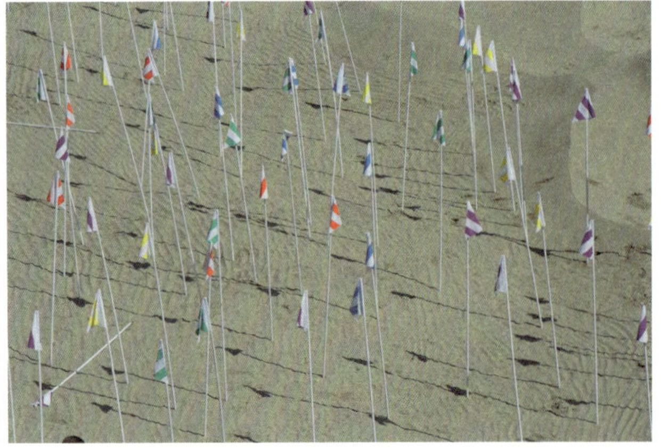
7/7/12—10:54:14 AM

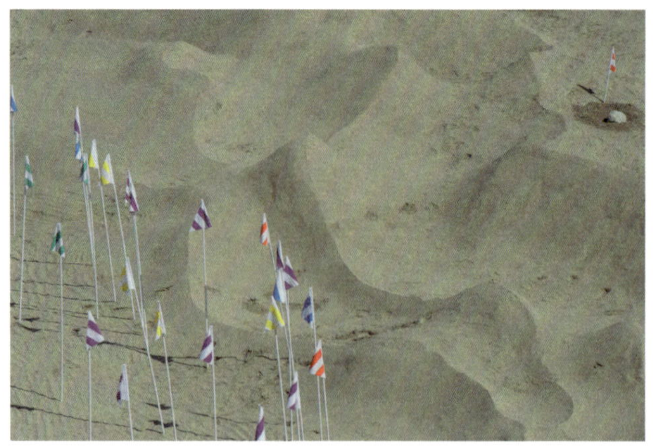
7/7/12—10:54:16 AM

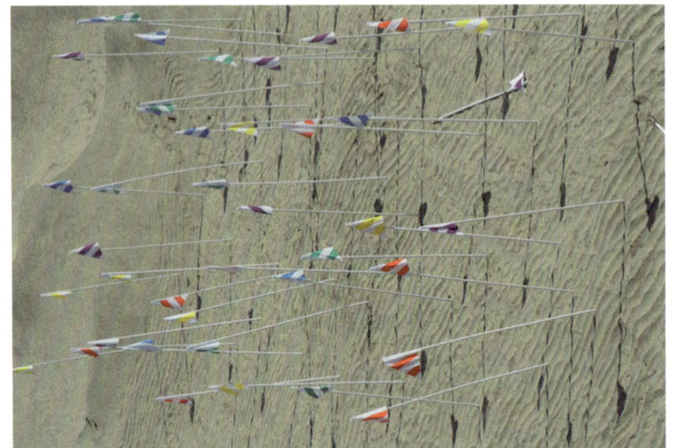
7/7/12—10:54:49 AM

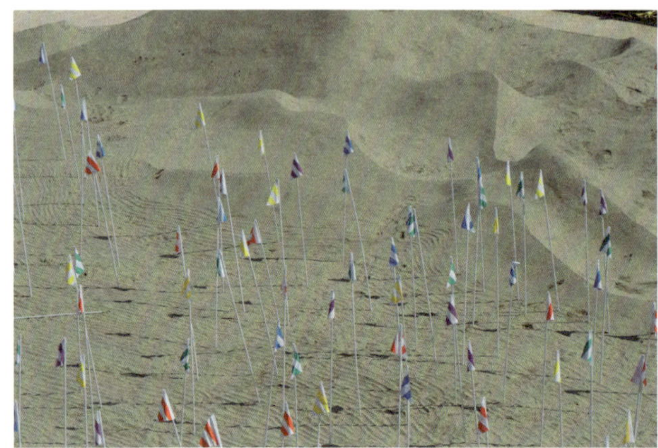
7/7/12—10:54:52 AM

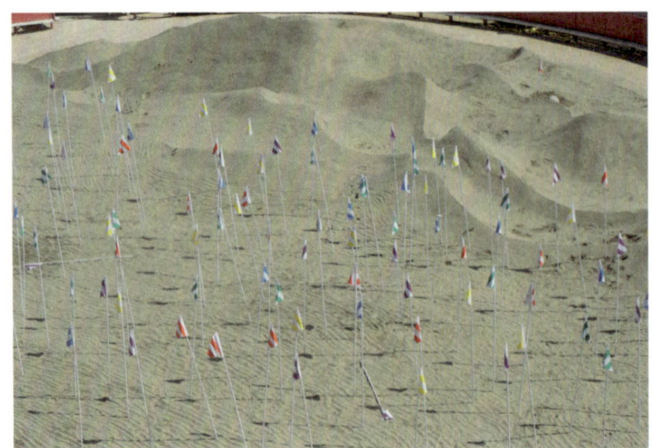
7/7/12—10:54:54 AM

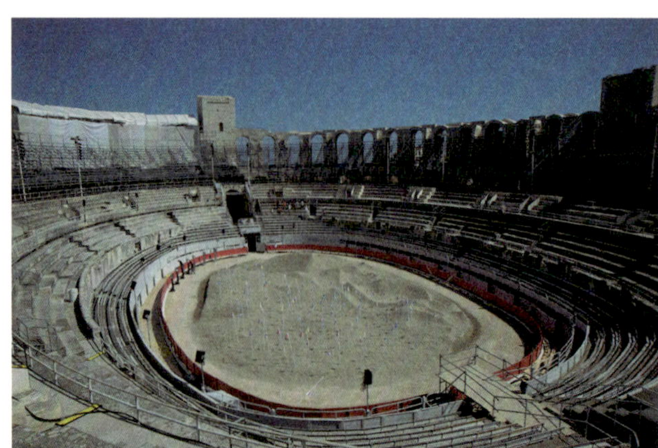
7/7/12—10:55:17 AM

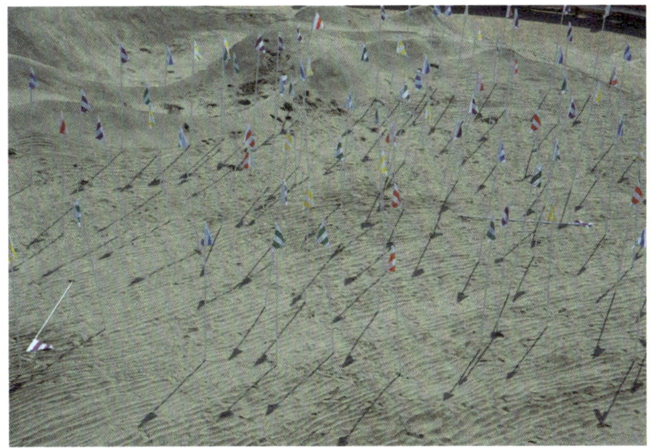

7/7/12—10:56:24 AM

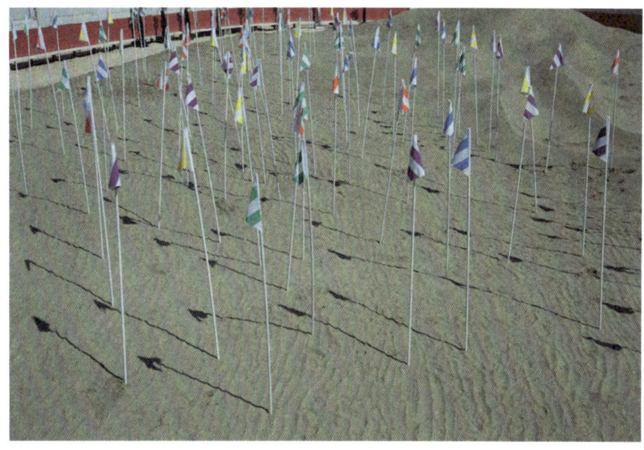

7/7/12—11:06:35 AM

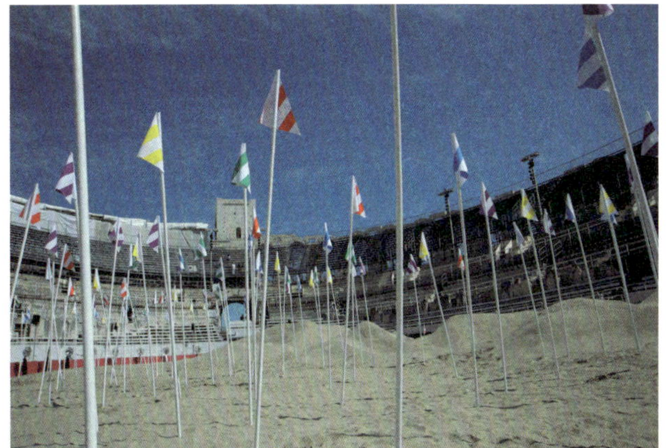

7/7/12—11:08:31 AM

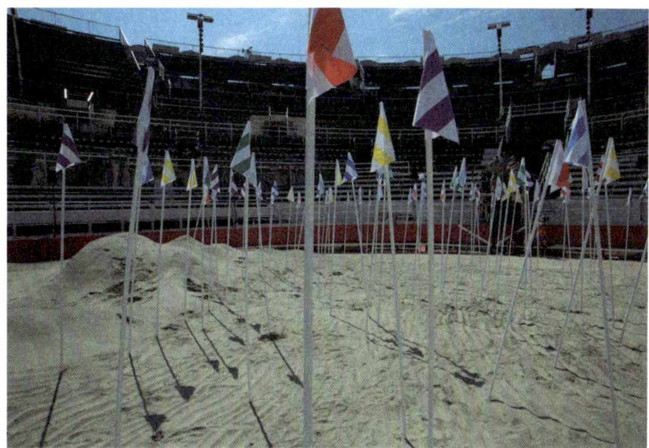

7/7/12—11:10:00 AM

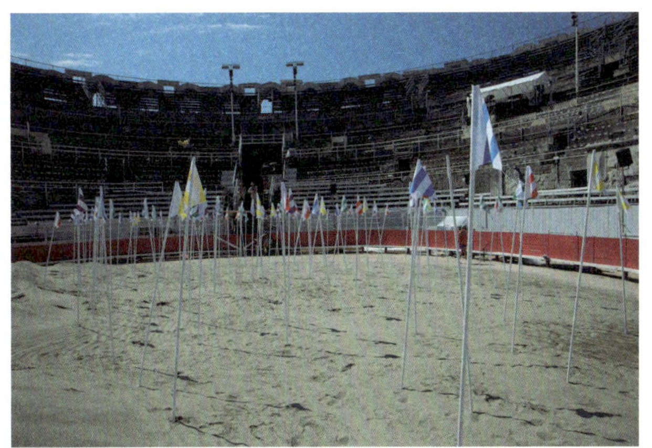

7/7/12—11:10:15 AM

7/7/12—11:10:28 AM

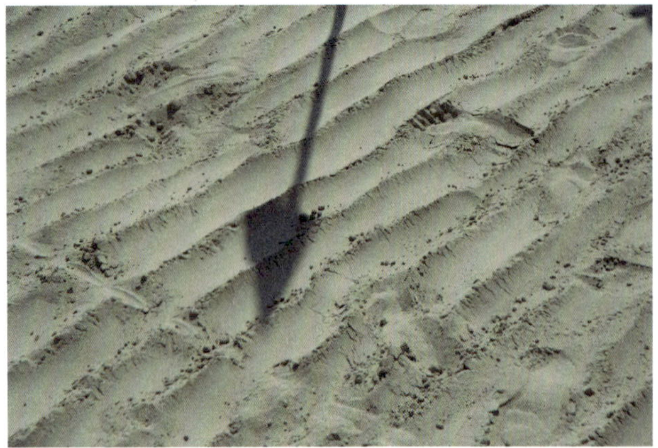
7/7/12—11:10:41 AM

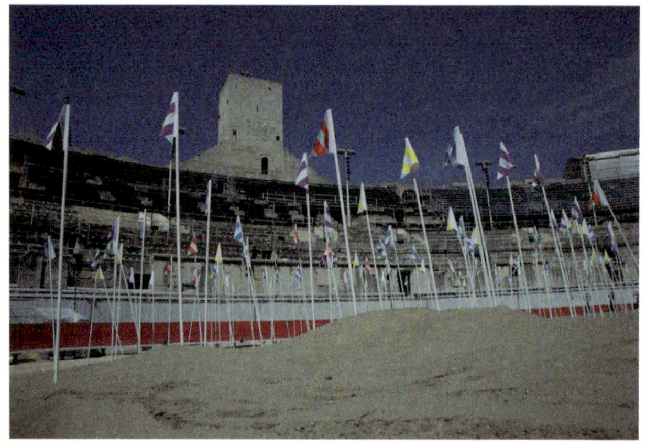
7/7/12—11:12:22 AM

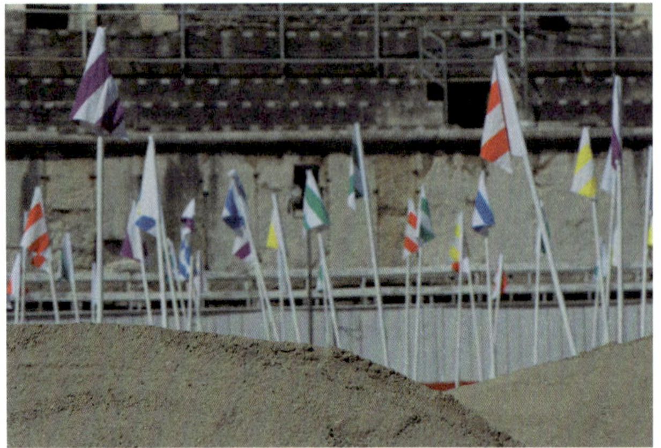
7/7/12—11:15:06 AM

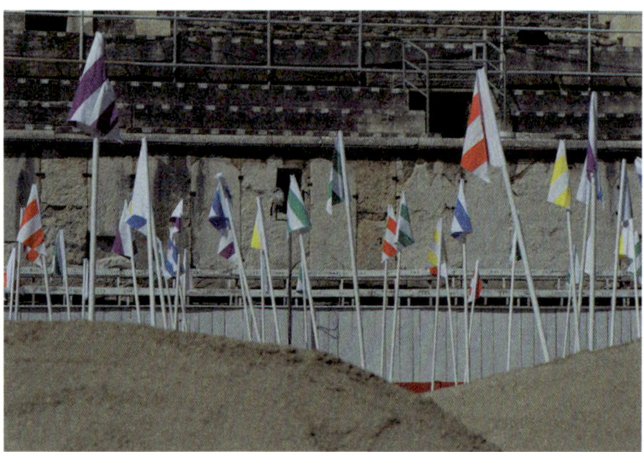
7/7/12—11:15:07 AM

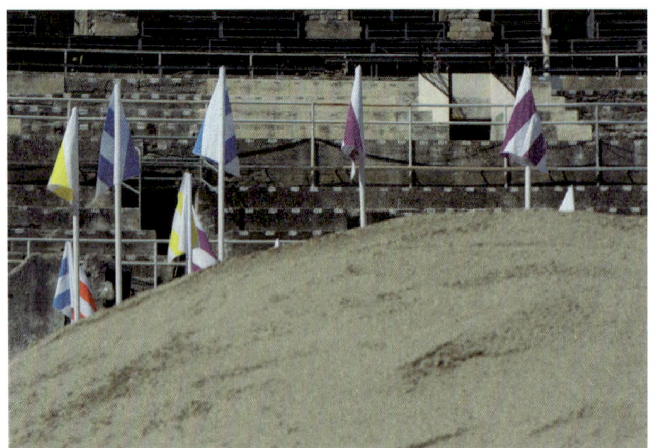
7/7/12—11:15:17 AM

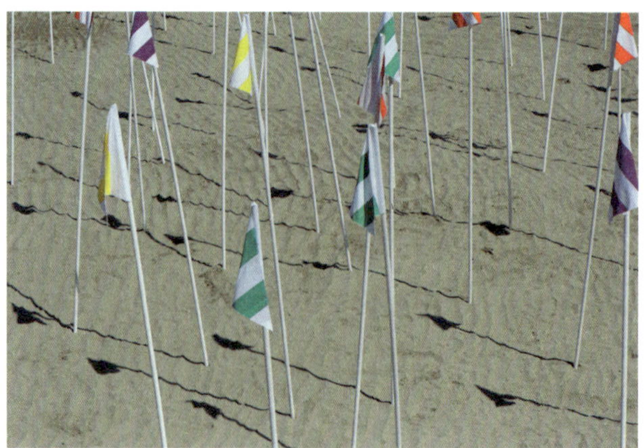
7/7/12—11:16:59 AM

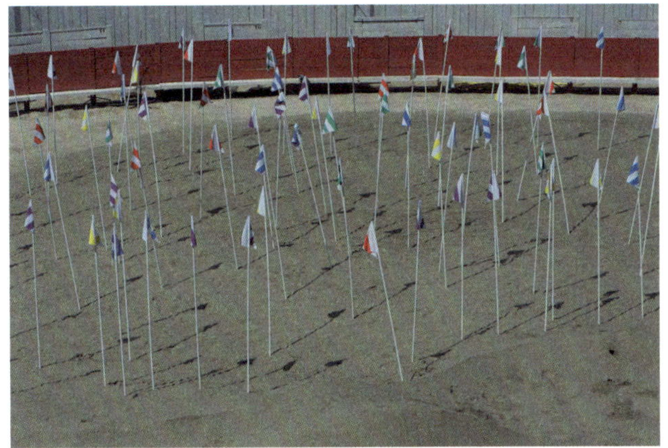

7/7/12—11:20:56 AM

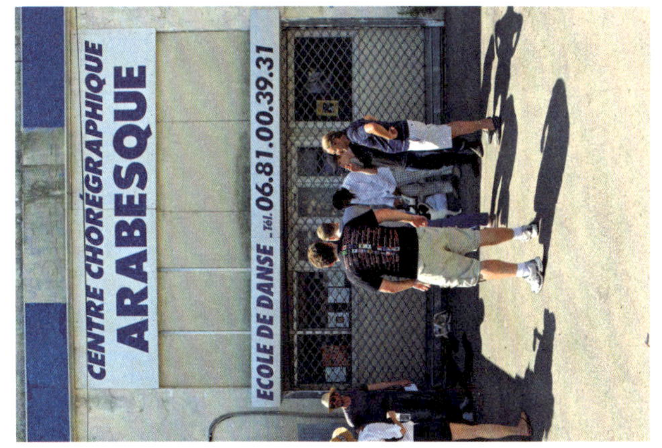

7/7/12—11:29:28 AM

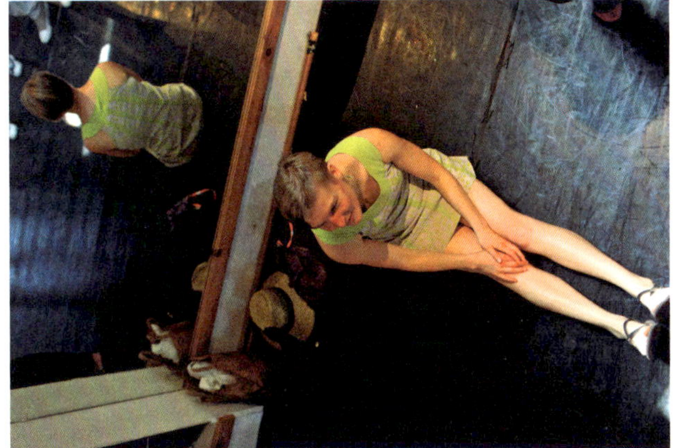

7/7/12—11:32:38 AM

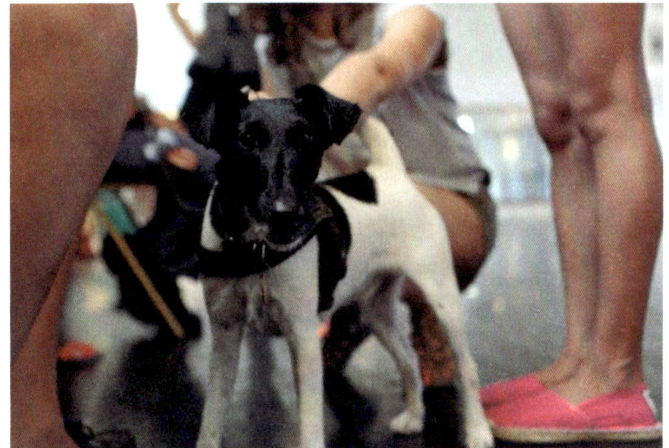

7/7/12—11:34:07 AM

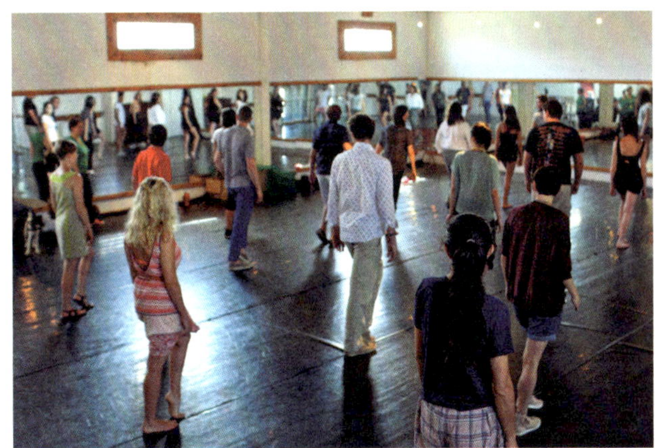

7/7/12—11:37:16 AM

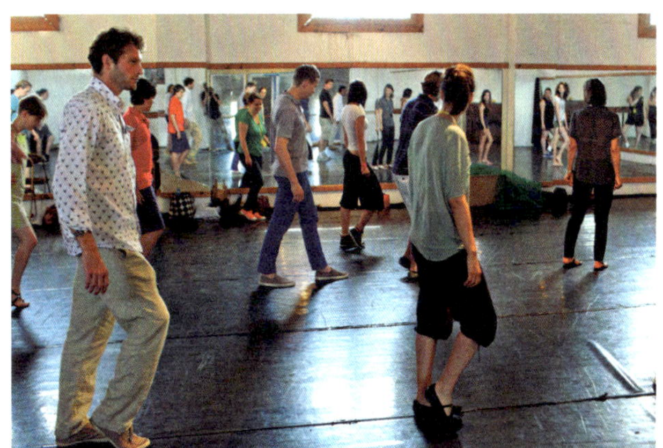

7/7/12—11:37:39 AM

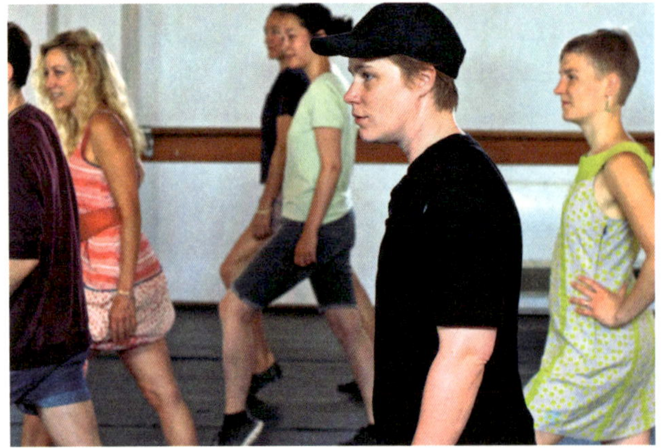
7/7/12—11:42:19 AM

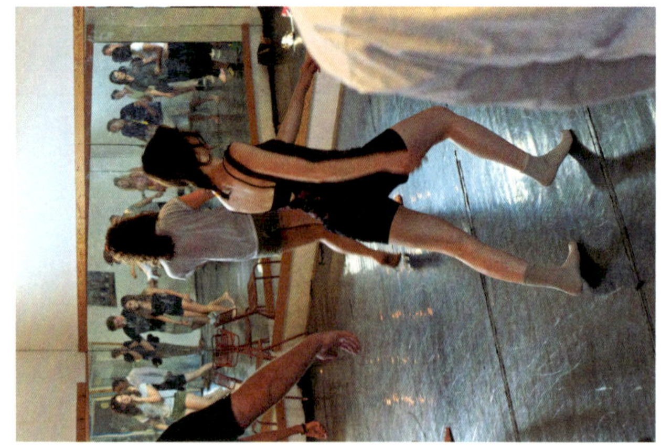
7/7/12—11:43:24 AM

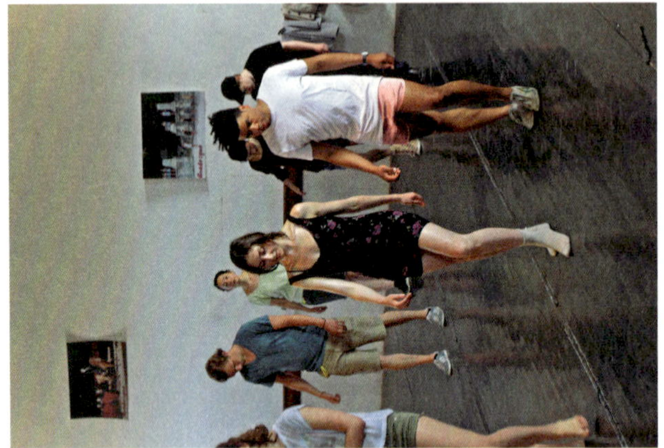
7/7/12—11:48:45 AM

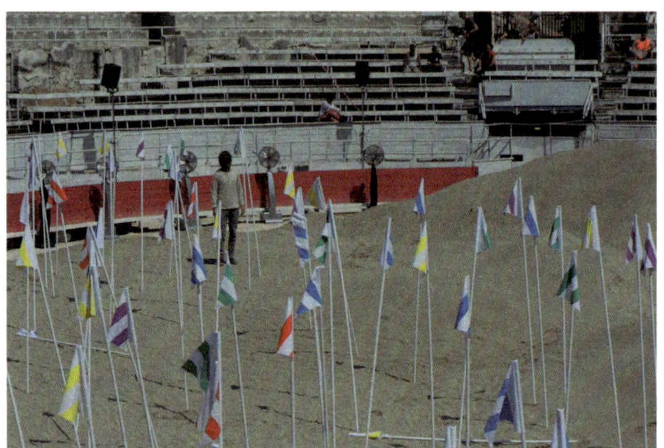
7/7/12—11:51:34 AM

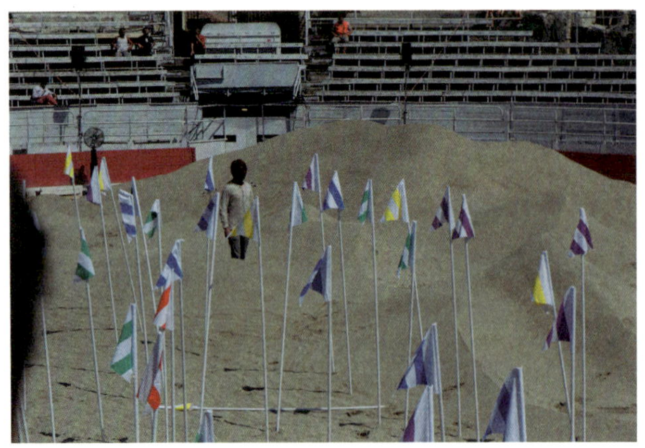
7/7/12—11:52:50 AM

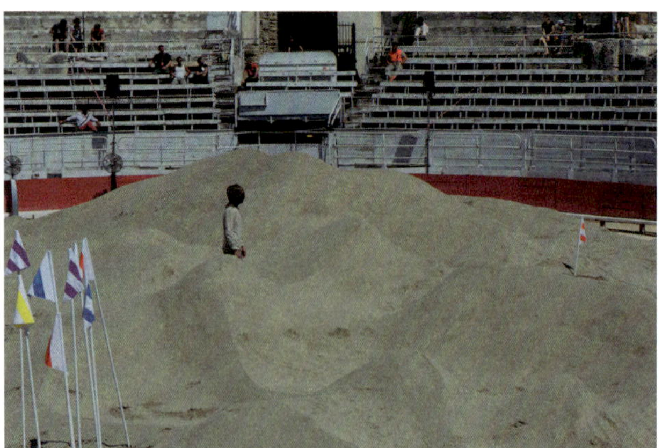
7/7/12—11:53:50 AM

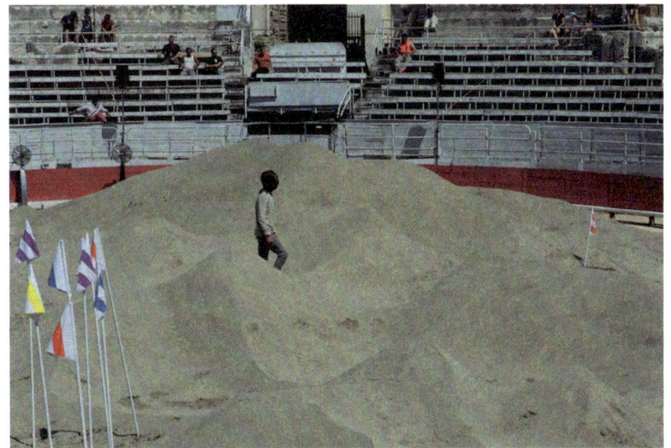
7/7/12—11:53:53 AM

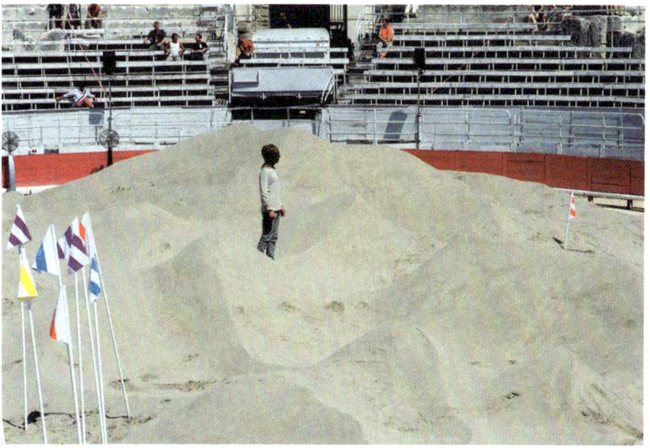
7/7/12—11:54:01 AM

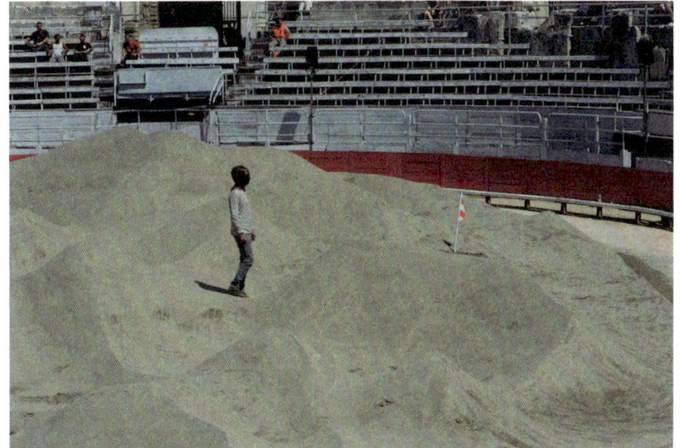
7/7/12—11:54:21 AM

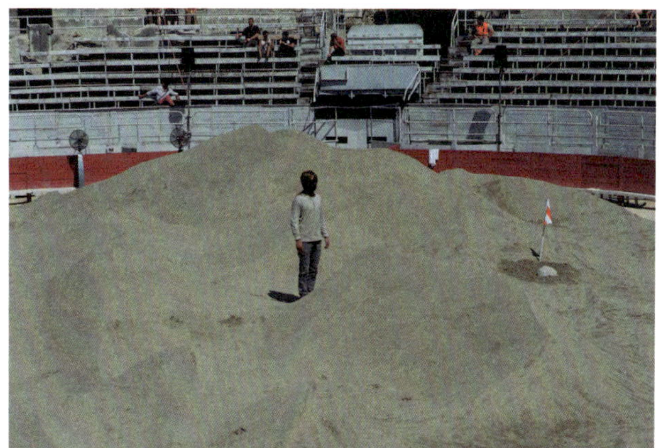
7/7/12—11:54:46 AM

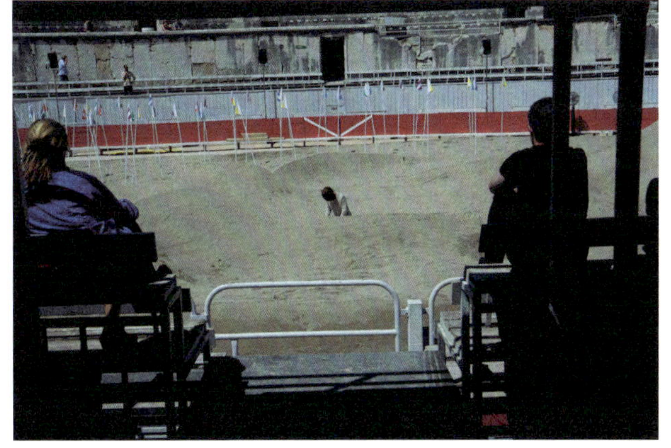
7/7/12—11:56:46 AM

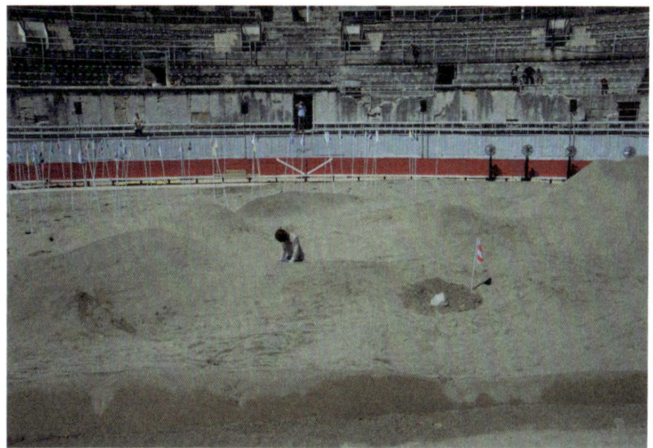
7/7/12—11:57:07 AM

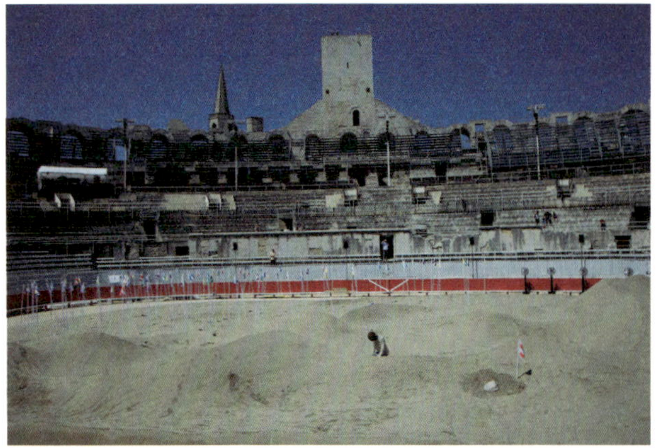
7/7/12—11:57:09 AM

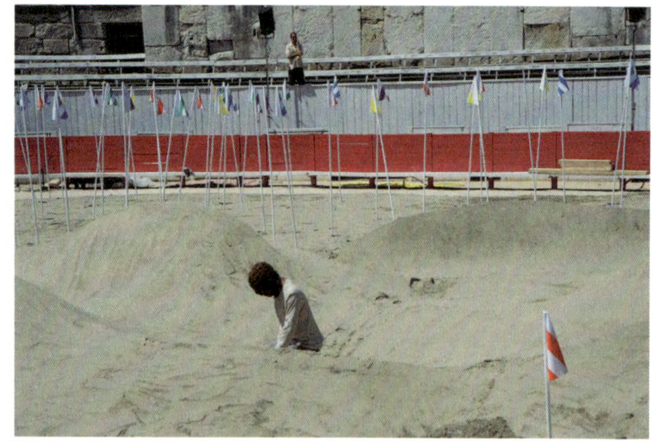
7/7/12—11:57:40 AM

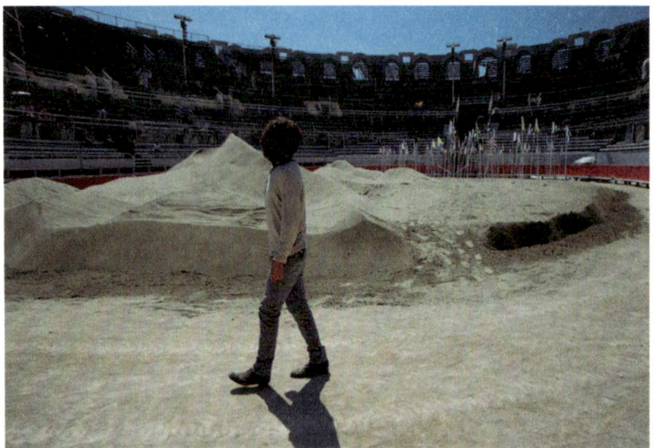
7/7/12—12:00:26 PM

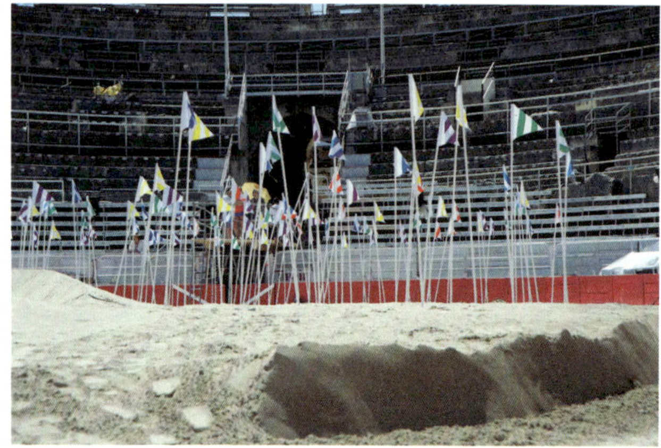
7/7/12—12:00:54 PM

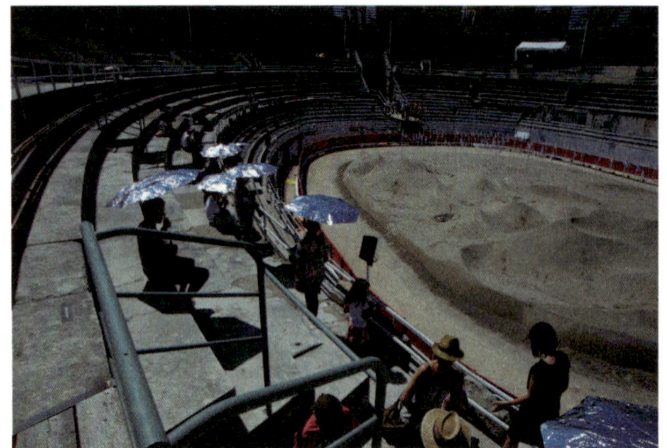
7/7/12—12:03:19 PM

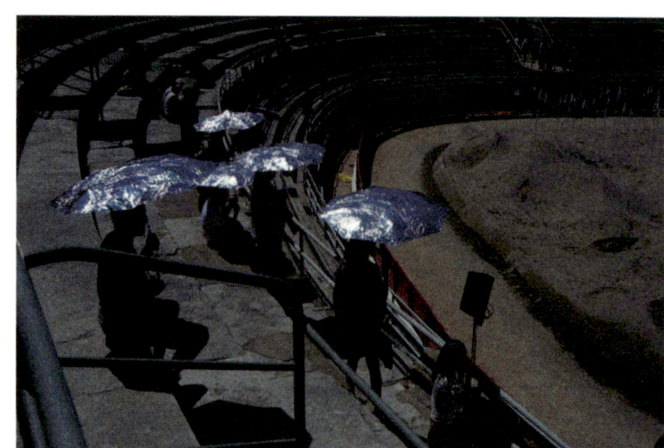
7/7/12—12:03:20 PM

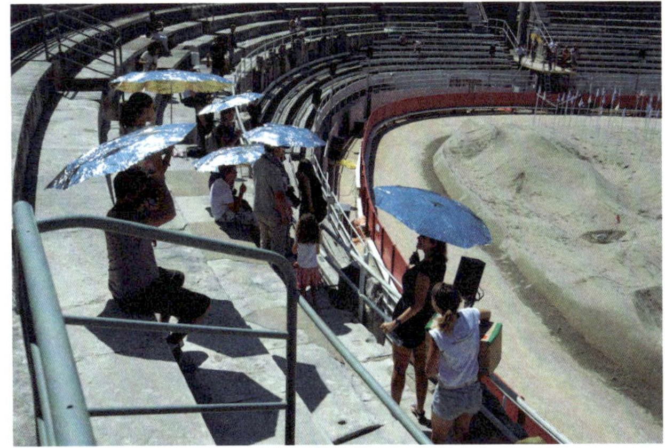
7/7/12—12:03:31 PM

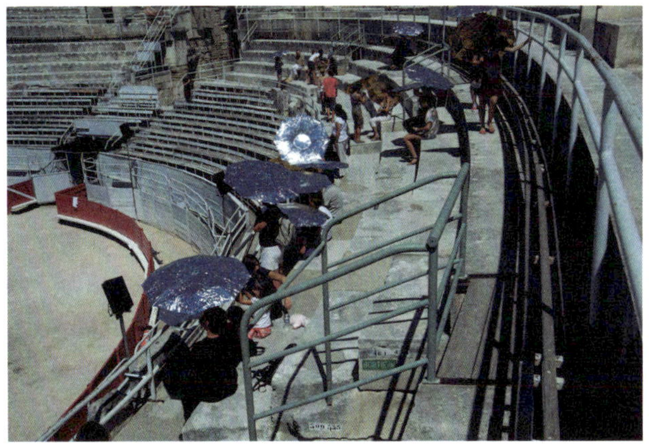
7/7/12—12:03:57 PM

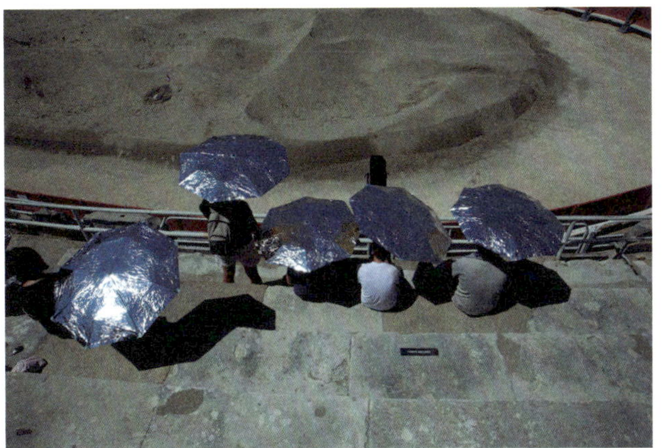
7/7/12—12:04:24 PM

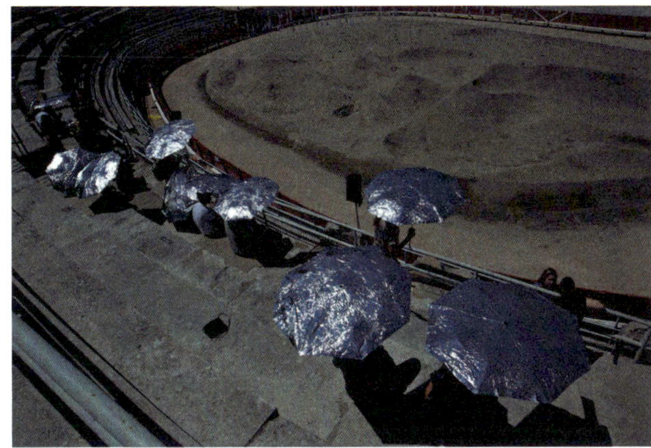
7/7/12—12:04:55 PM

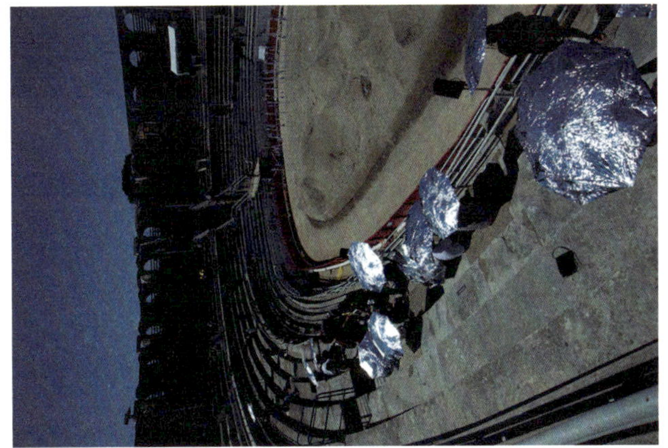
7/7/12—12:04:58 PM

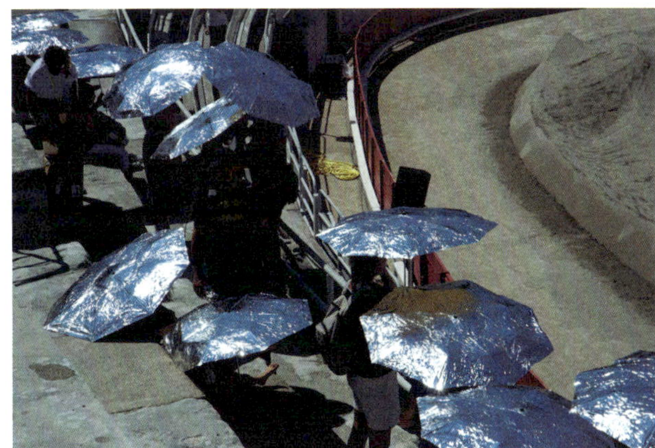
7/7/12—12:06:03 PM

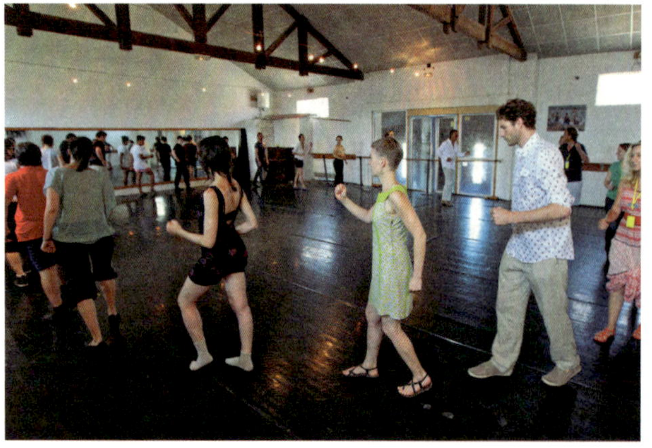

7/7/12—12:06:24 PM

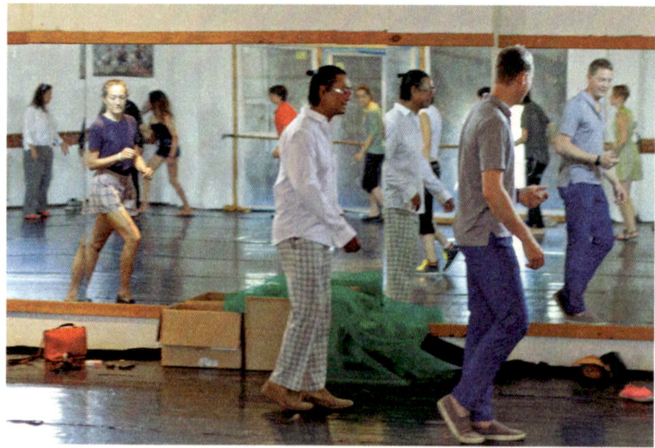

7/7/12—12:07:47 PM

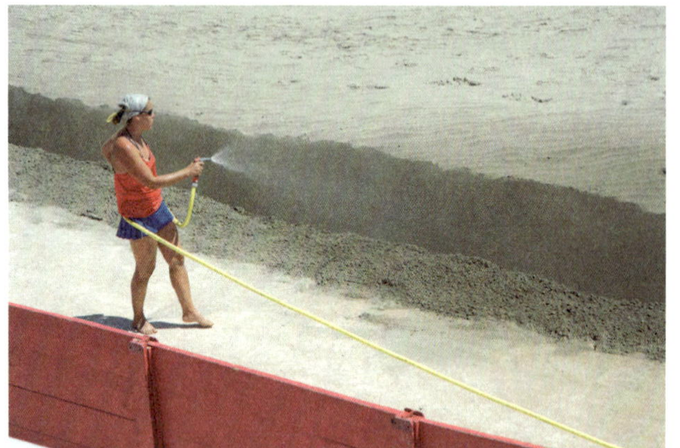

7/7/12—12:24:12 PM

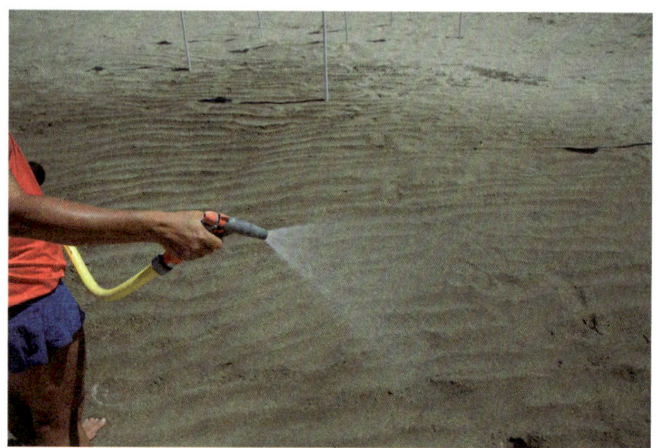

7/7/12—12:25:22 PM

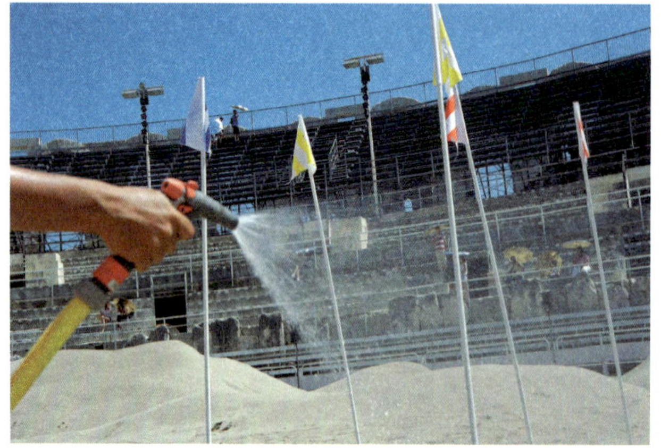

7/7/12—12:25:26 PM

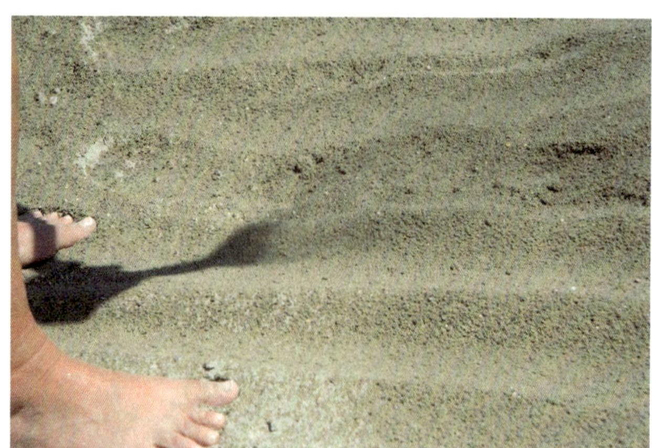

7/7/12—12:25:34 PM

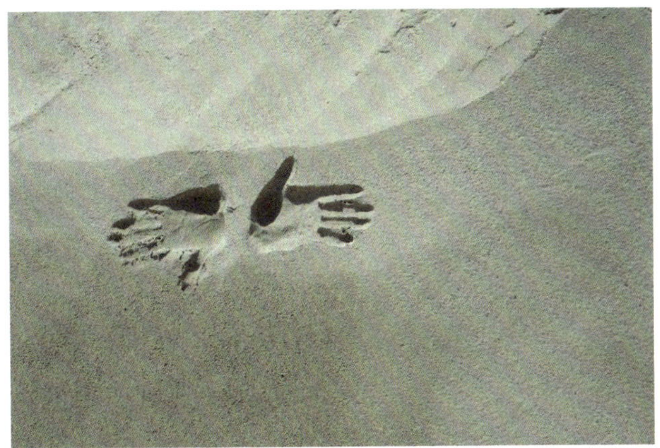

7/7/12—12:28:43 PM

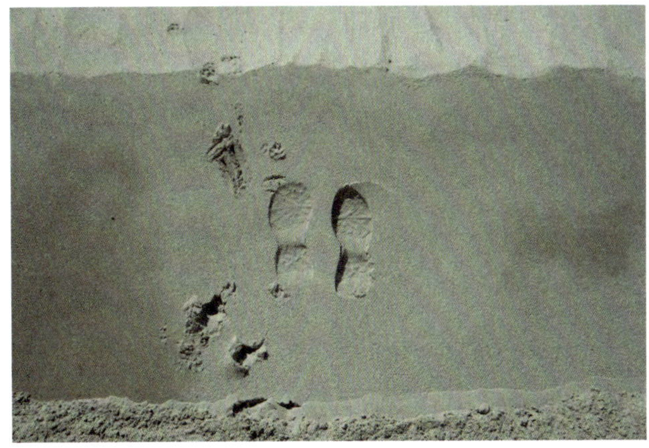

7/7/12—12:29:00 PM

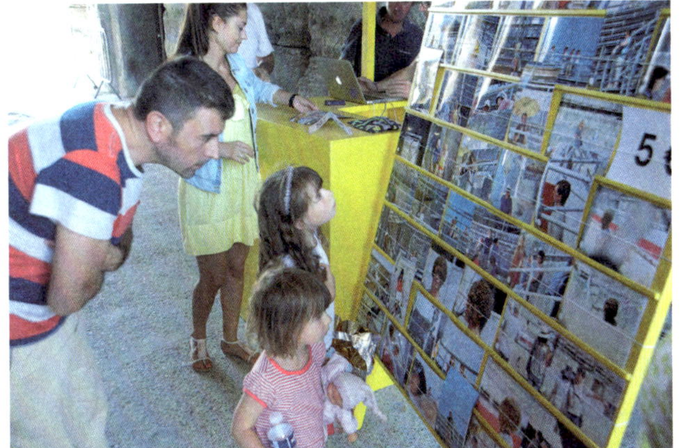

7/7/12—12:33:08 PM

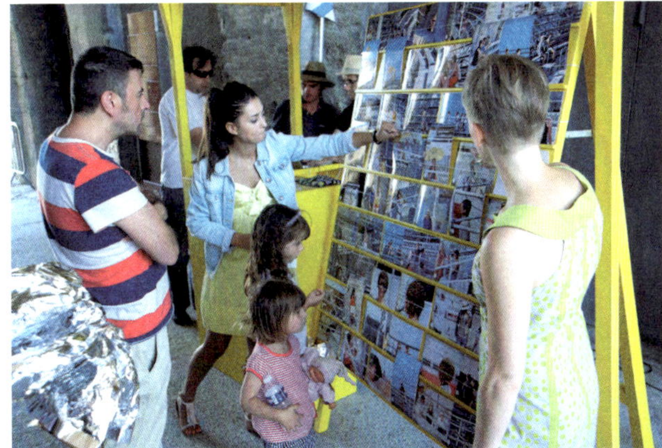

7/7/12—12:33:14 PM

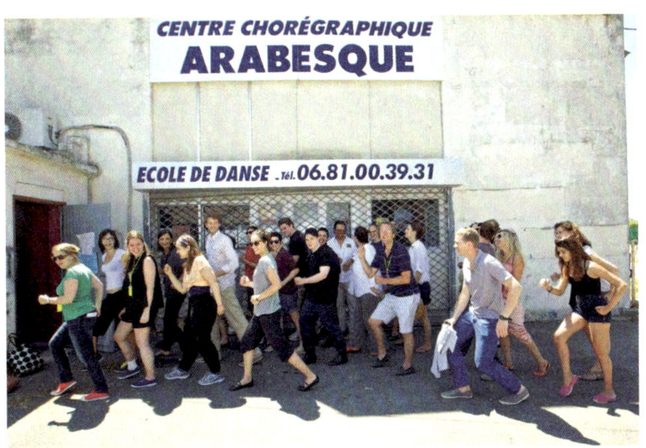

7/7/12—12:39:28 PM

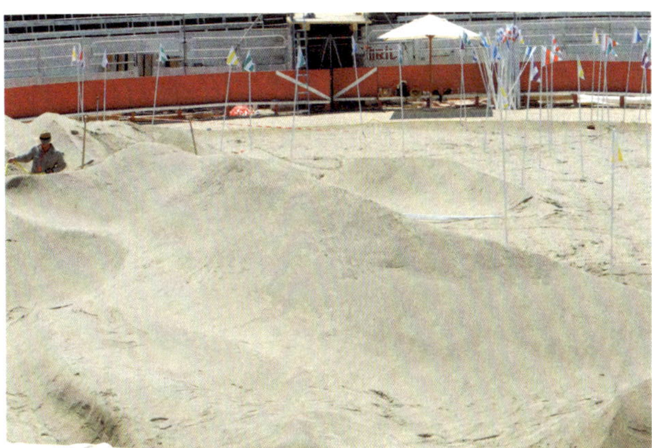

7/7/12—12:57:15 PM

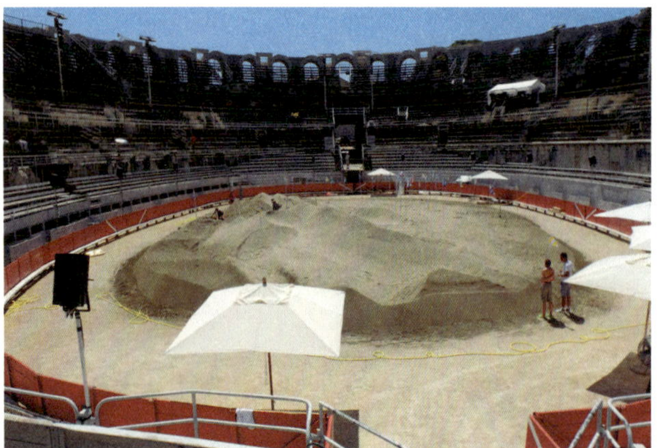

7/7/12—12:57:21 PM

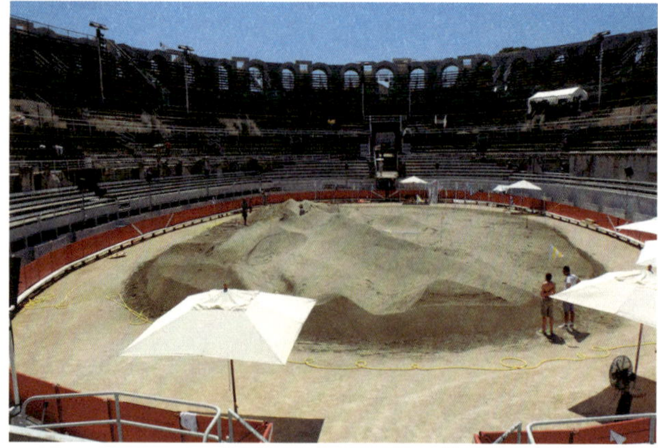

7/7/12—12:57:28 PM

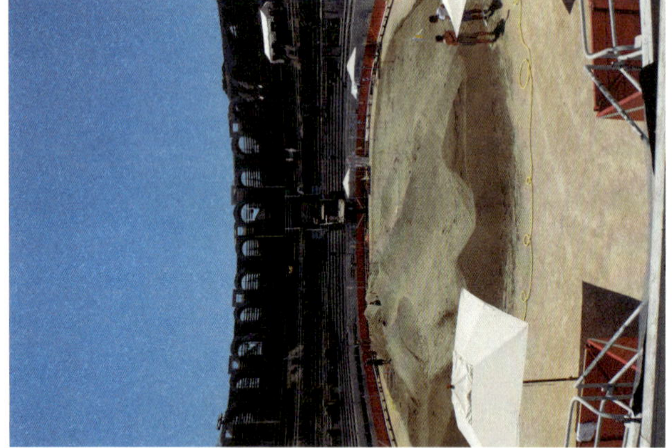

7/7/12—12:57:33 PM

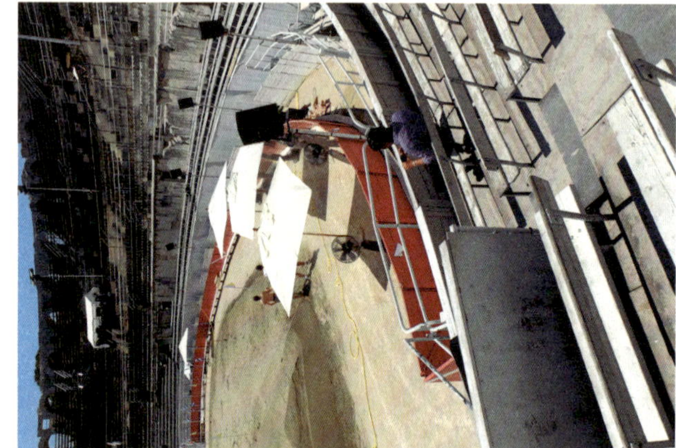

7/7/12—12:57:37 PM

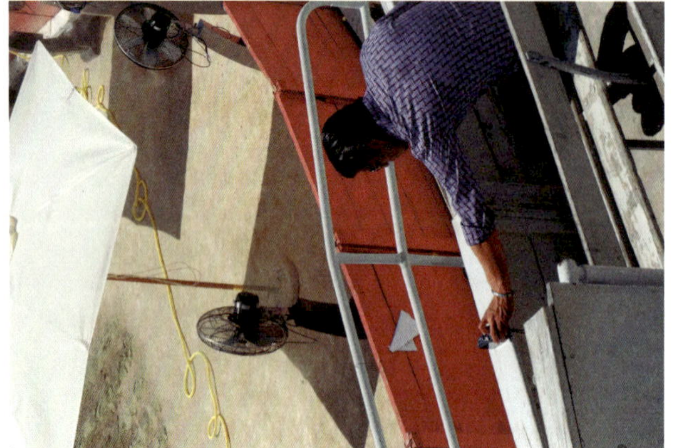

7/7/12—12:57:43 PM

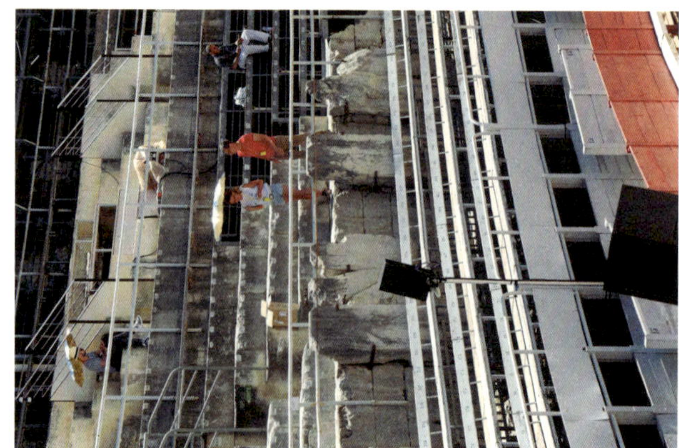

7/7/12—12:57:48 PM

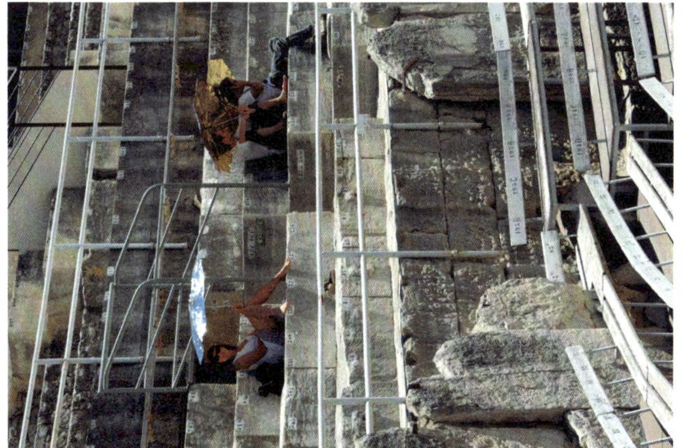

7/7/12—12:57:53 PM

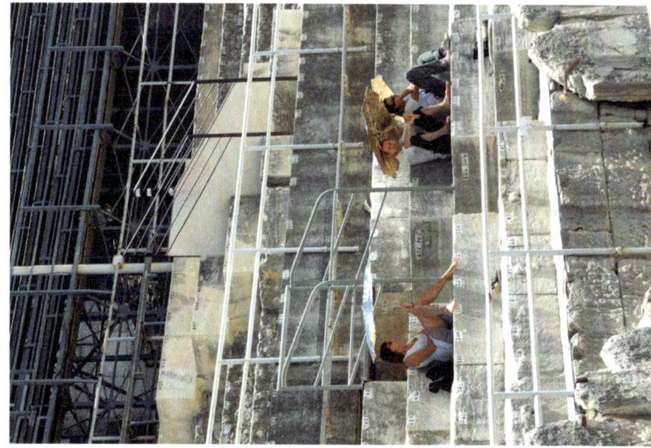

7/7/12—12:57:59 PM

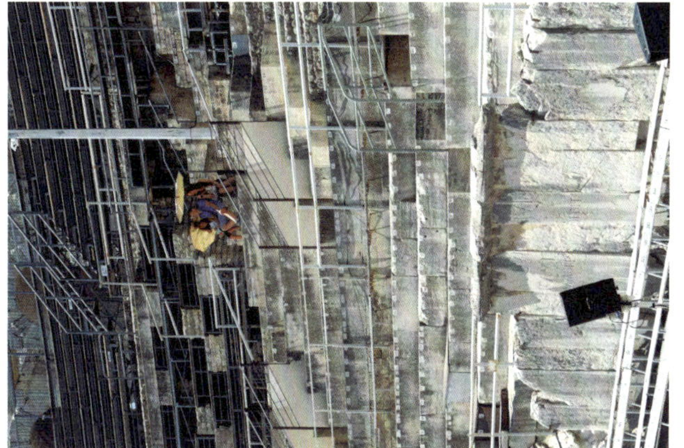

7/7/12—12:58:03 PM

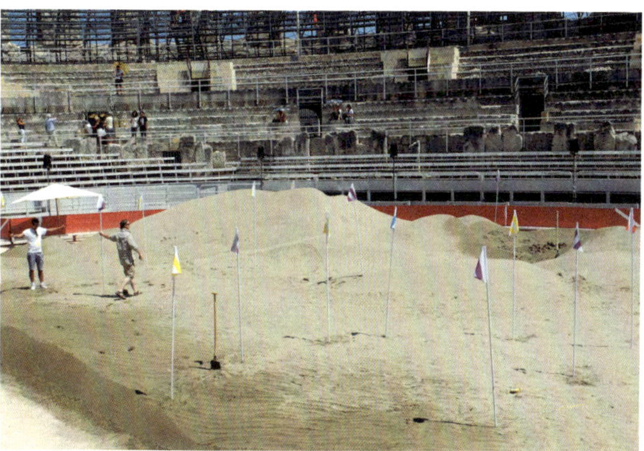

7/7/12—12:59:52 PM

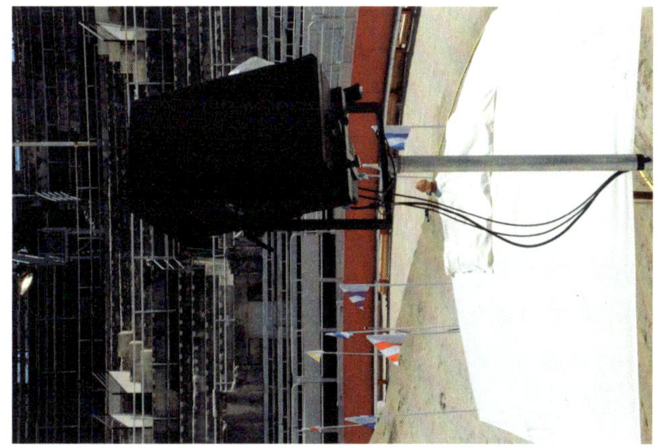

7/7/12—12:59:57 PM

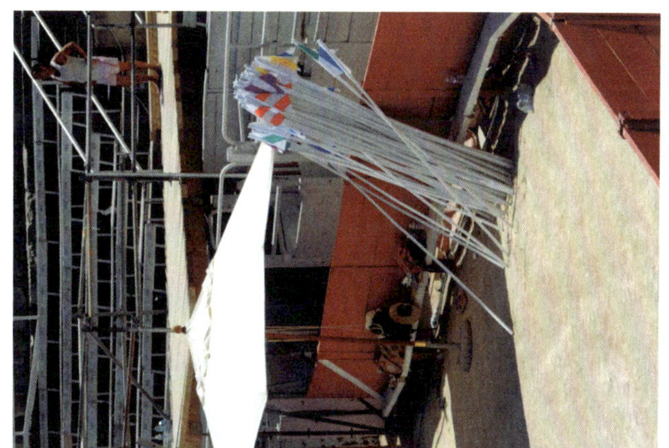

7/7/12—1:00:01 PM

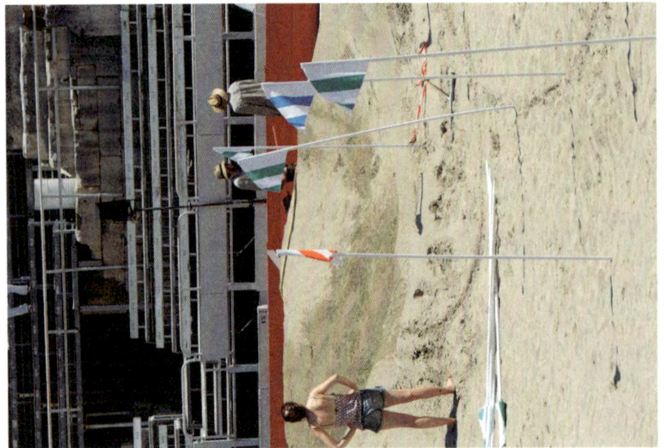
7/7/12—1:00:07 PM

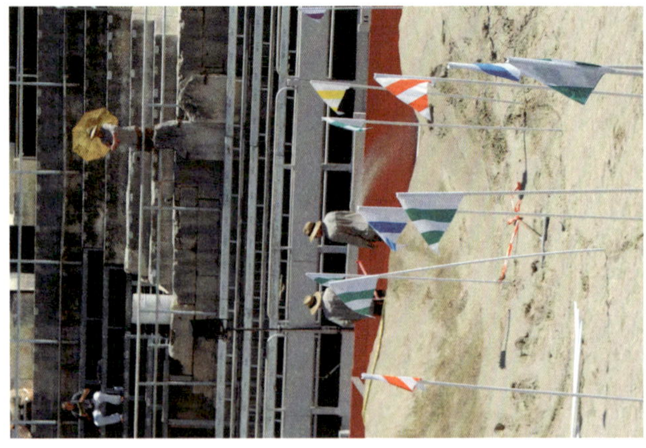
7/7/12—1:00:09 PM

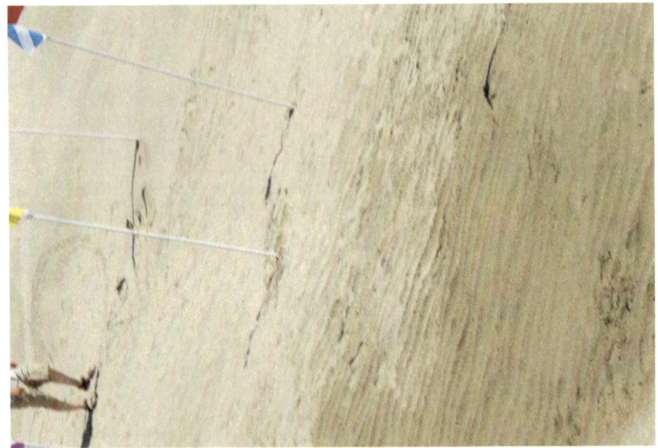
7/7/12—1:00:11 PM

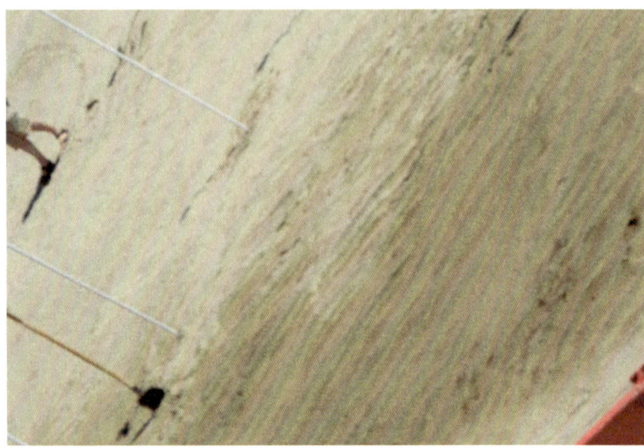
7/7/12—1:00:13 PM

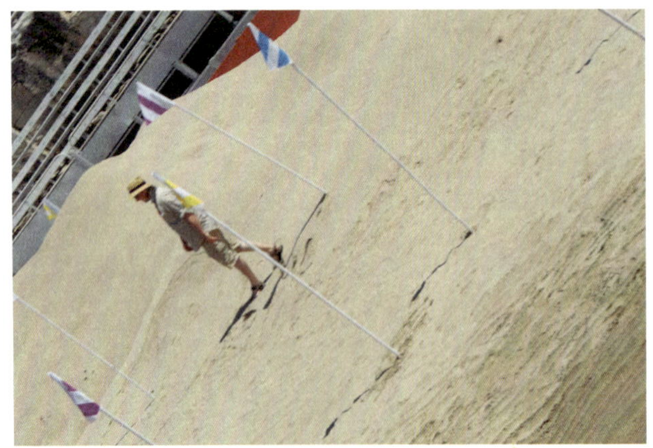
7/7/12—1:00:15 PM

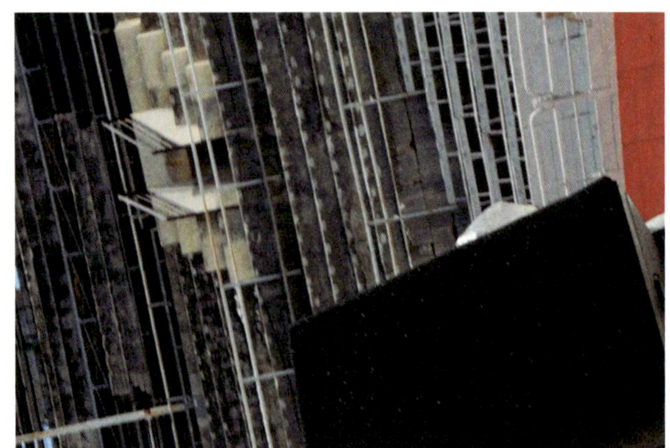
7/7/12—1:00:17 PM

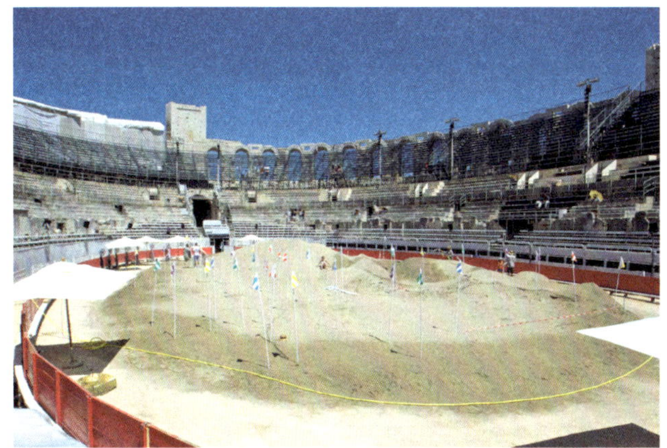

7/7/12—1:02:27 PM

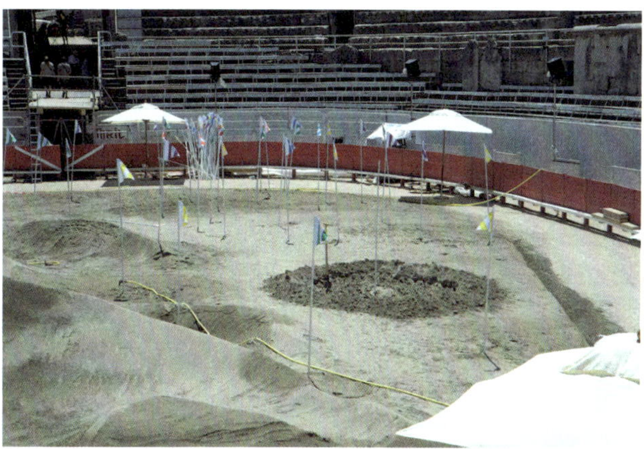

7/7/12—1:38:53 PM

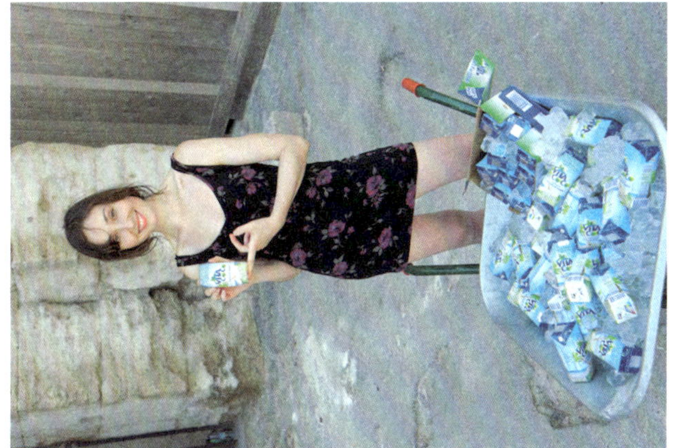

7/7/12—2:38:33 PM

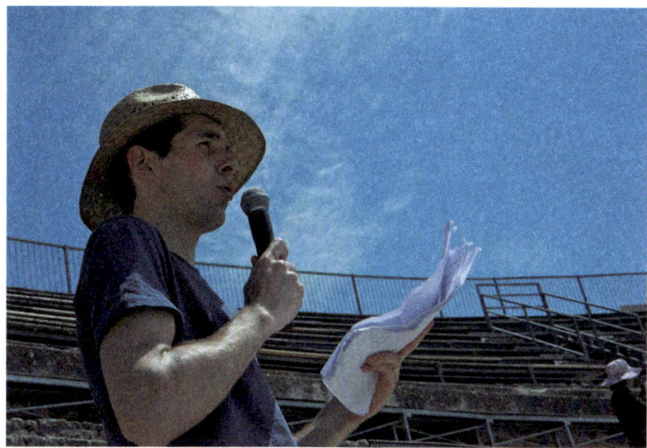

7/7/12—2:43:00 PM

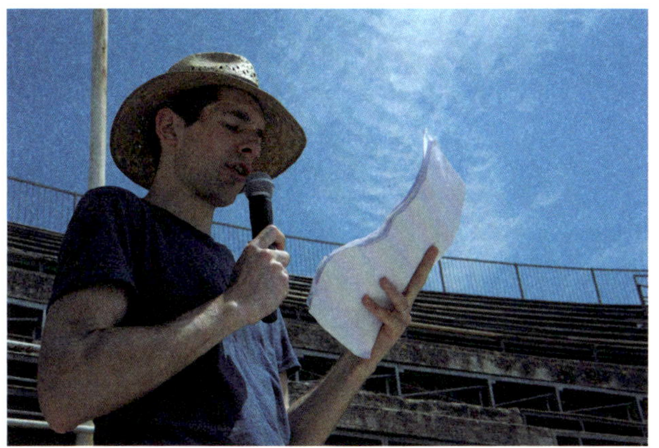

7/7/12—2:43:15 PM

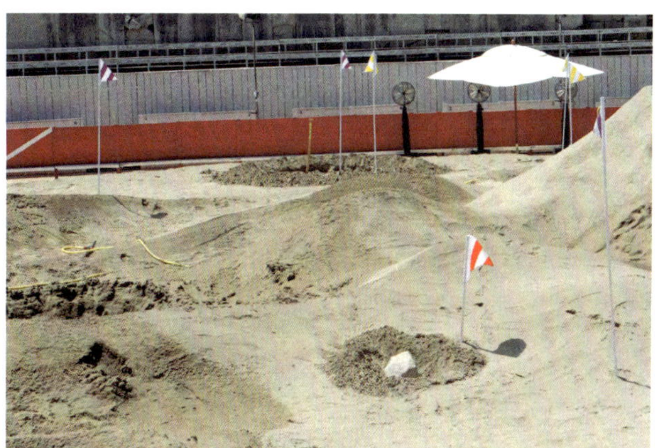

7/7/12—2:43:56 PM

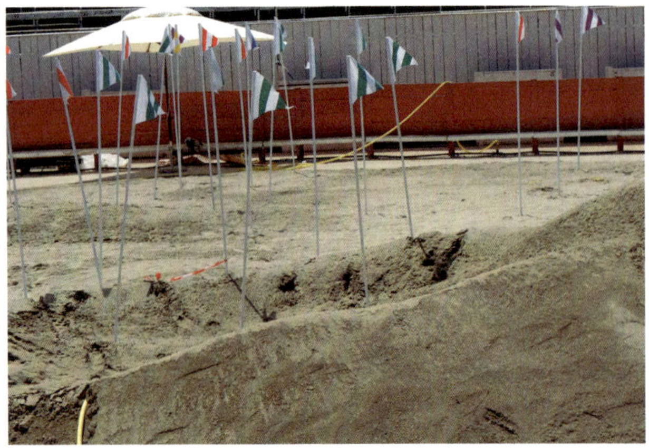

7/7/12—2:44:07 PM

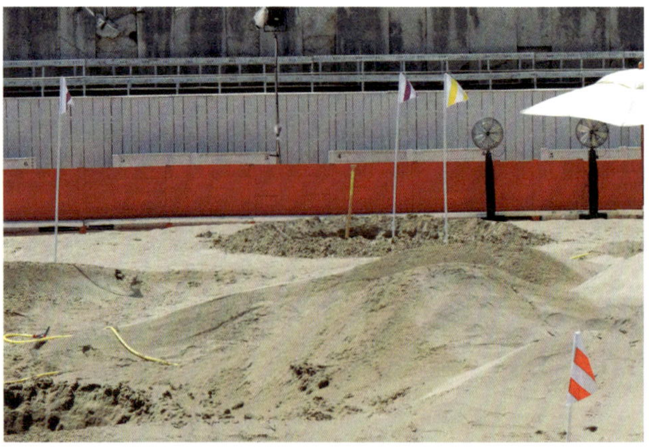

7/7/12—2:44:15 PM

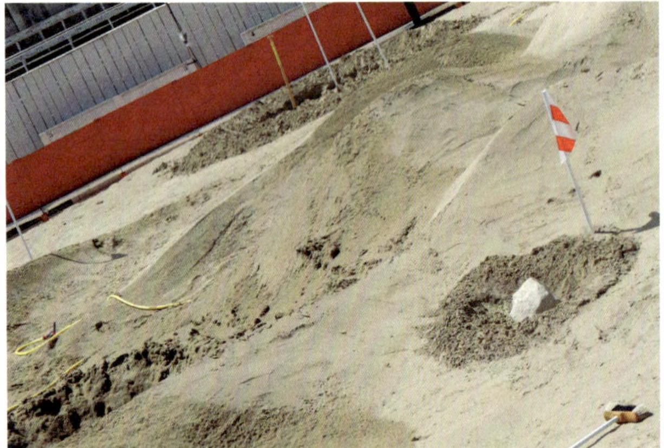

7/7/12—2:44:19 PM

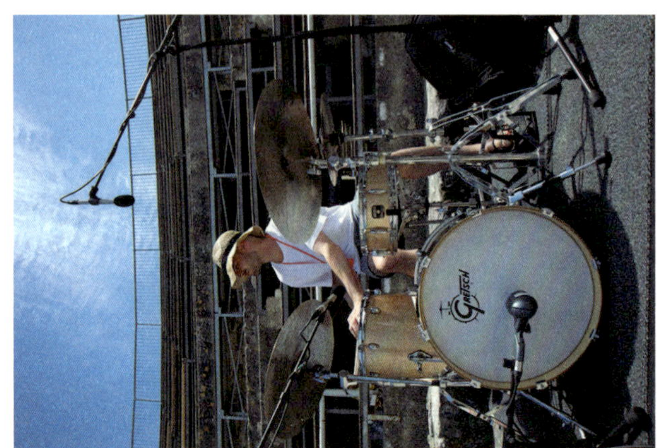

7/7/12—2:44:24 PM

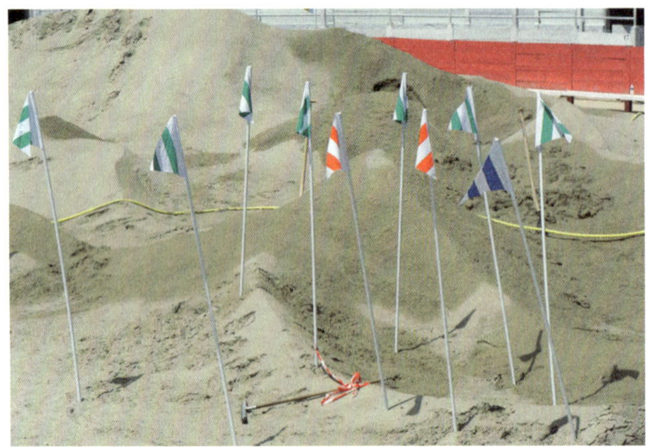

7/7/12—2:47:22 PM

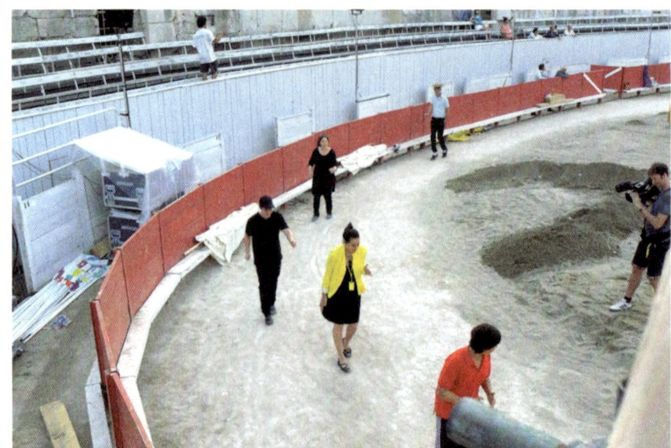

7/7/12—2:50:20 PM

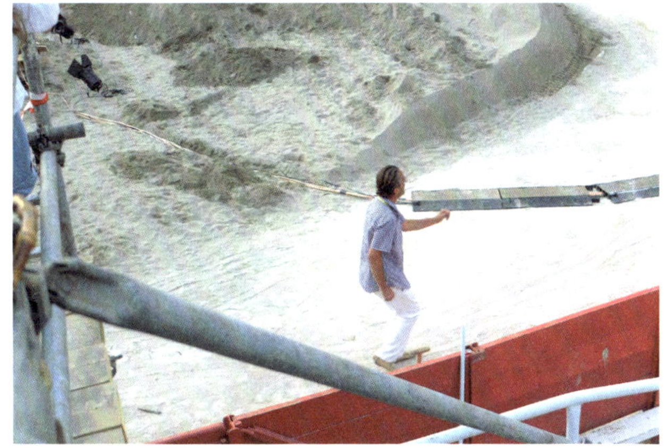
7/7/12—2:50:45 PM

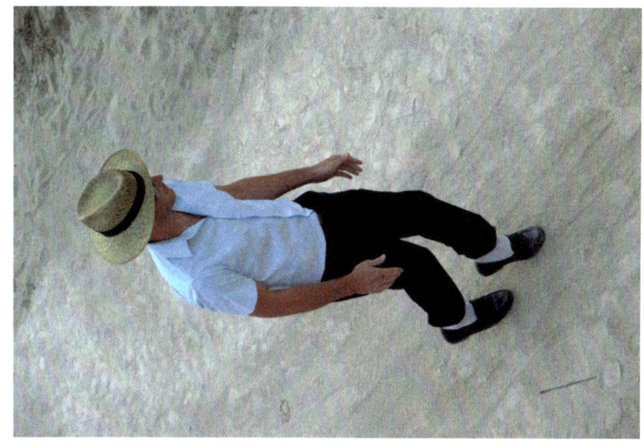
7/7/12—3:01:57 PM

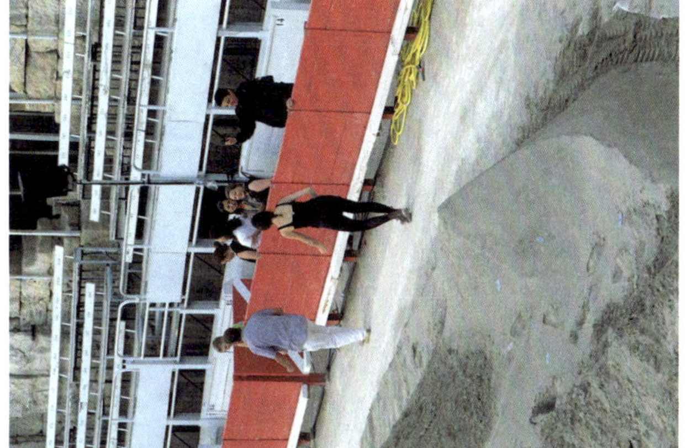
7/7/12—3:02:09 PM

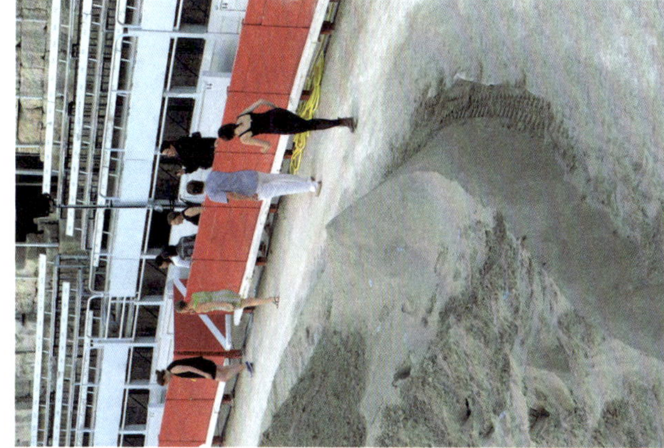
7/7/12—3:02:21 PM

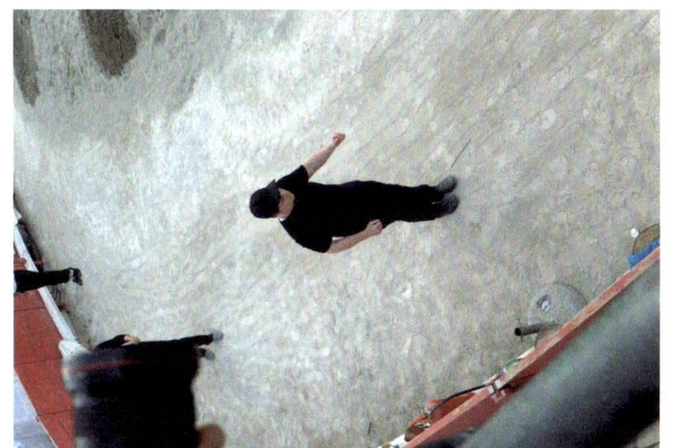
7/7/12—3:02:31 PM

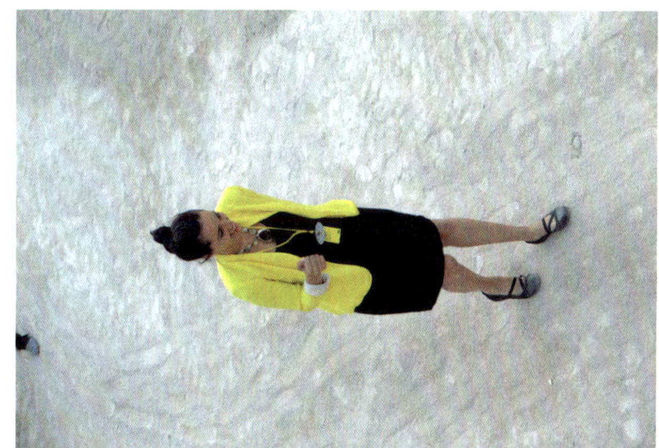
7/7/12—3:02:54 PM

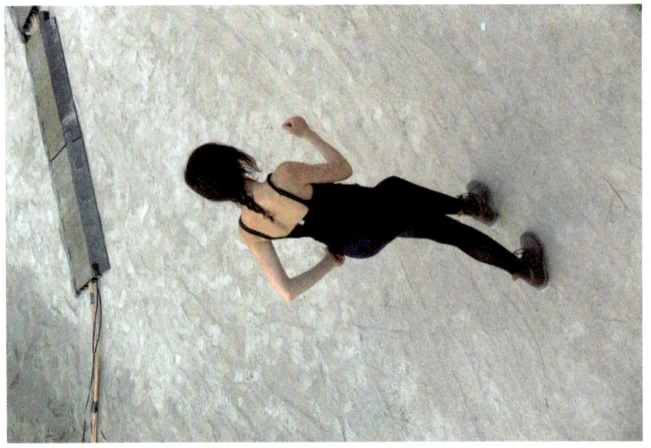
7/7/12—3:03:26 PM

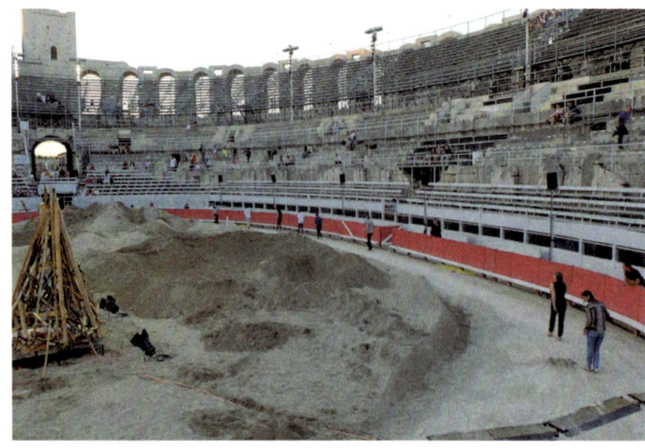
7/7/12—3:03:54 PM

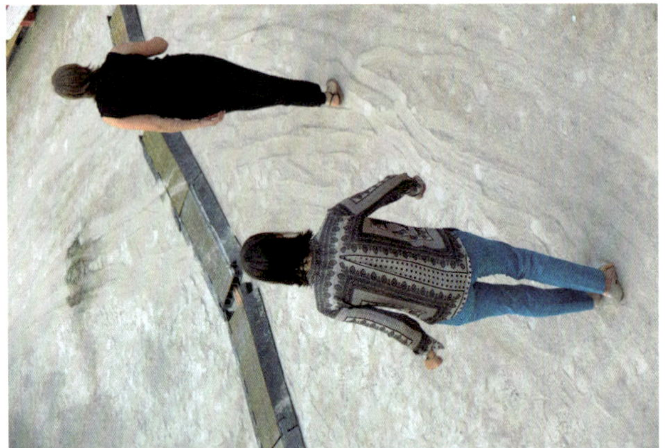
7/7/12—3:04:21 PM

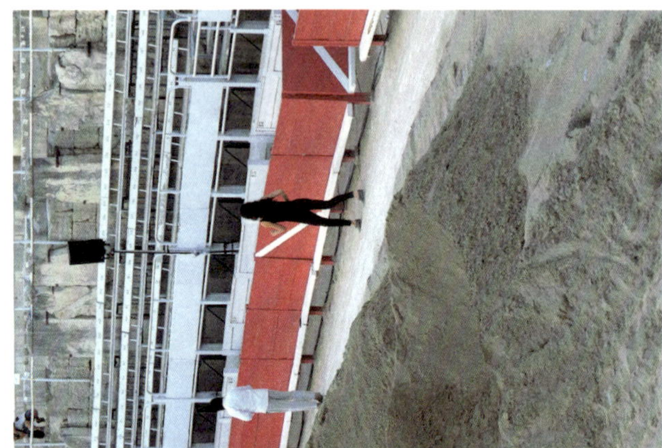
7/7/12—3:04:27 PM

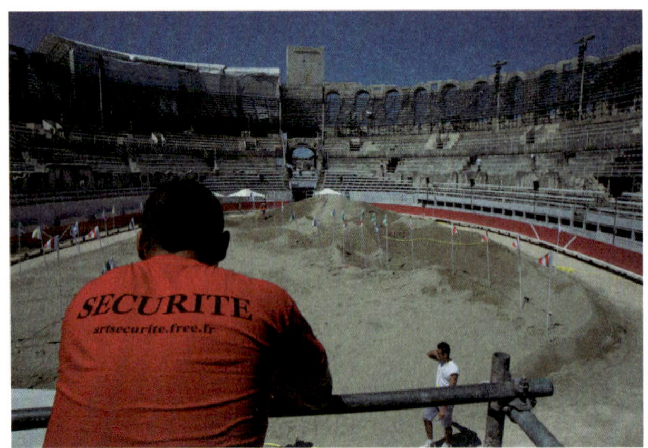

7/7/12—3:05:12 PM

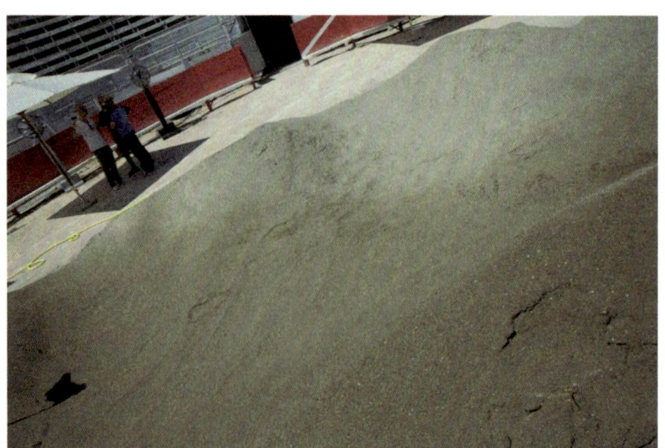
7/7/12—3:11:13 PM

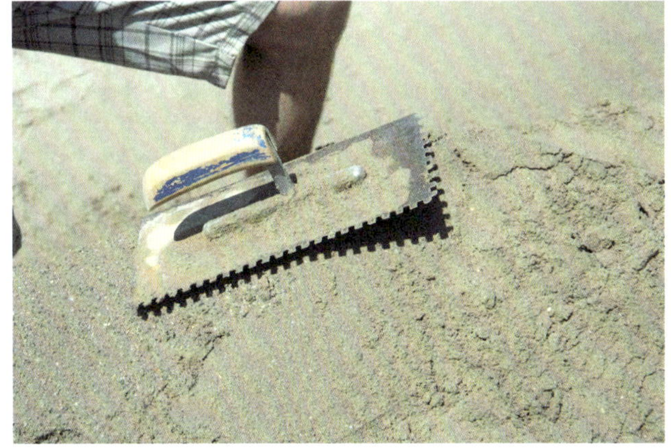
7/7/12—3:12:13 PM

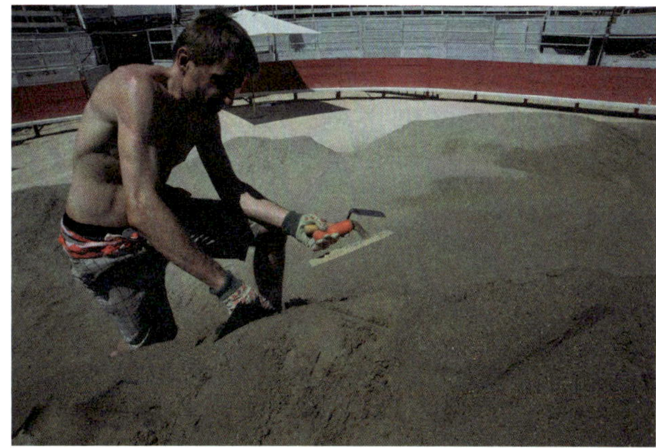
7/7/12—3:12:39 PM

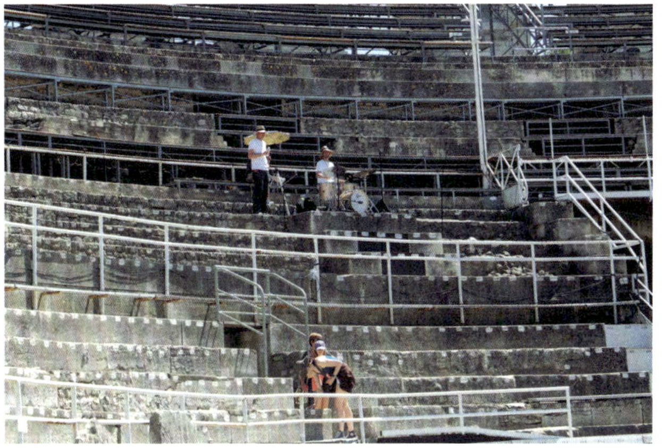
7/7/12—3:14:00 PM

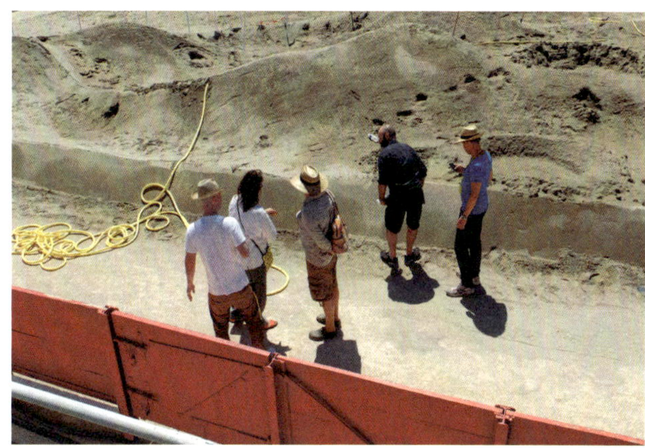
7/7/12—3:14:06 PM

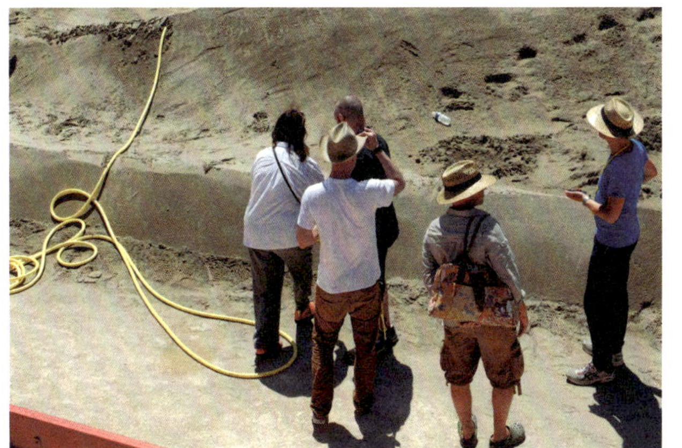
7/7/12—3:14:11 PM

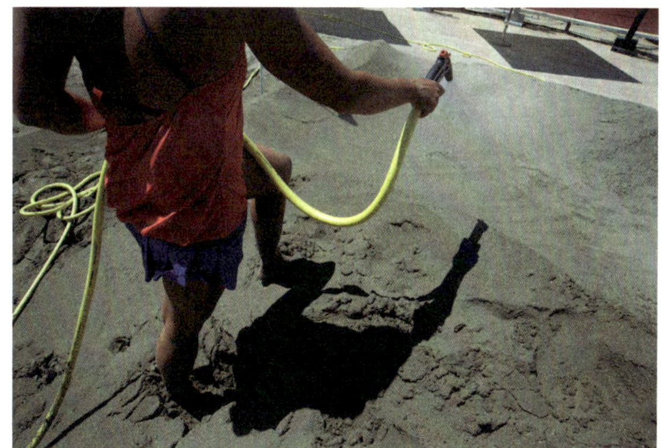
7/7/12—3:14:14 PM

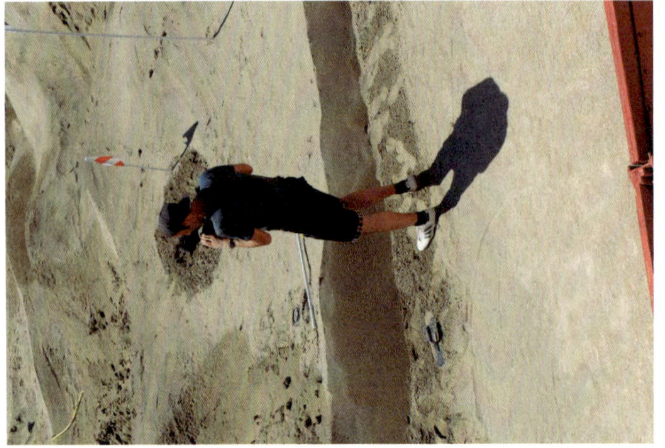
7/7/12—3:14:16 PM

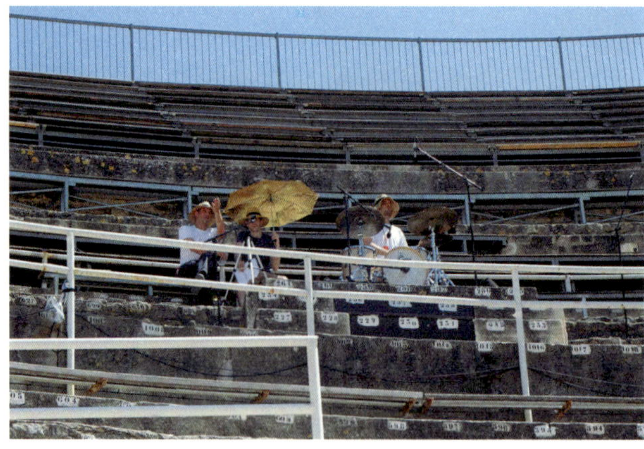
7/7/12—3:15:28 PM

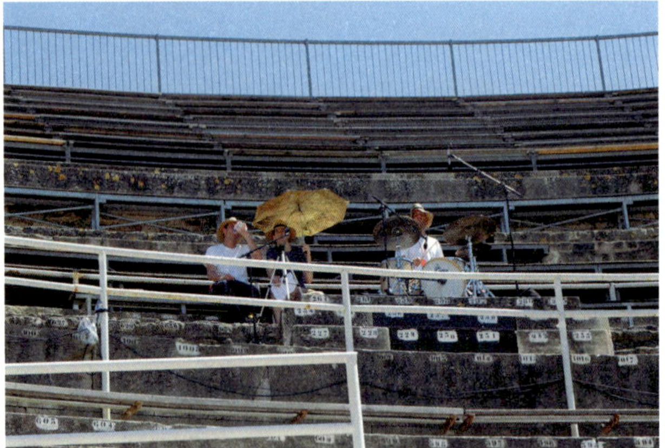
7/7/12—3:15:34 PM

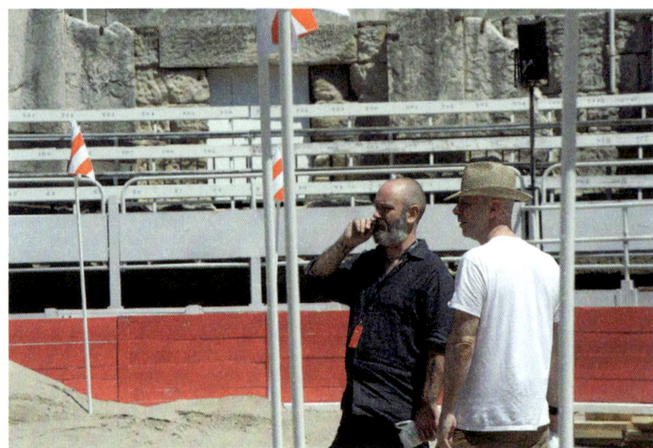
7/7/12—3:15:56 PM

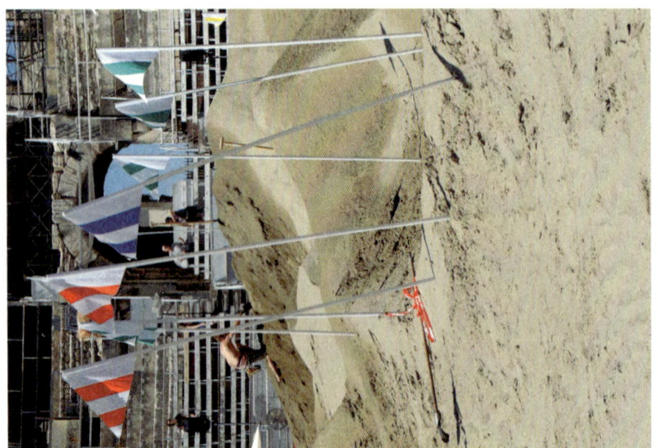
7/7/12—3:16:59 PM

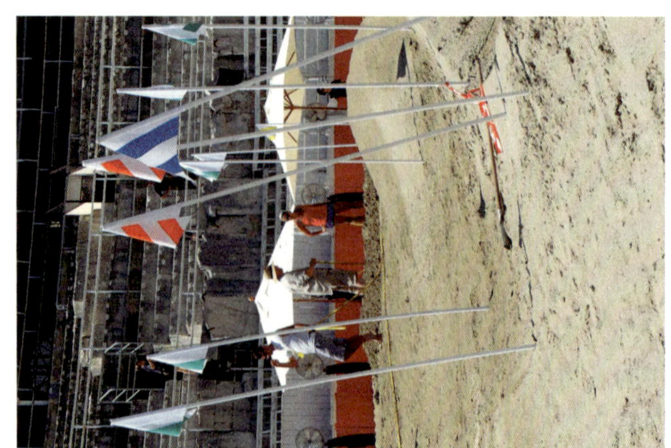
7/7/12—3:17:10 PM

7/7/12—3:17:19 PM

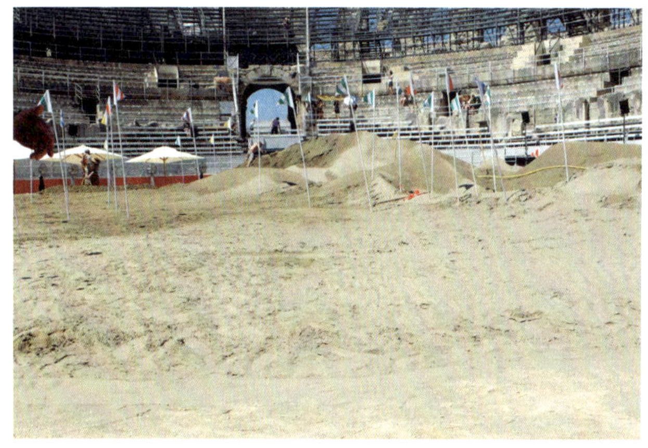
7/7/12—3:17:50 PM

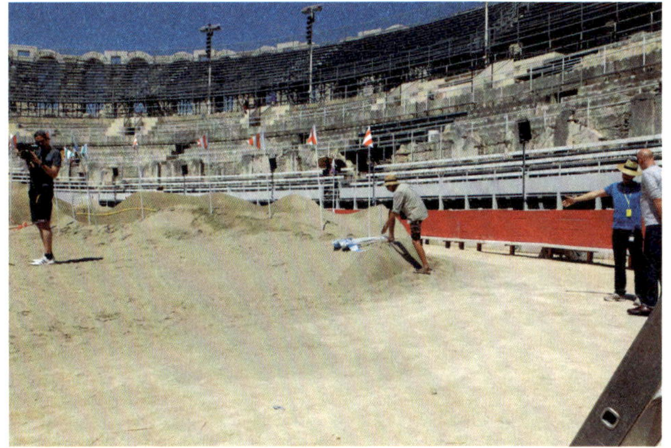
7/7/12—3:19:33 PM

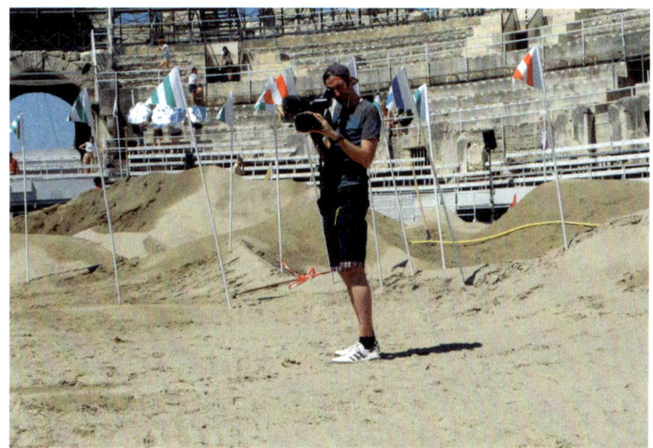
7/7/12—3:19:40 PM

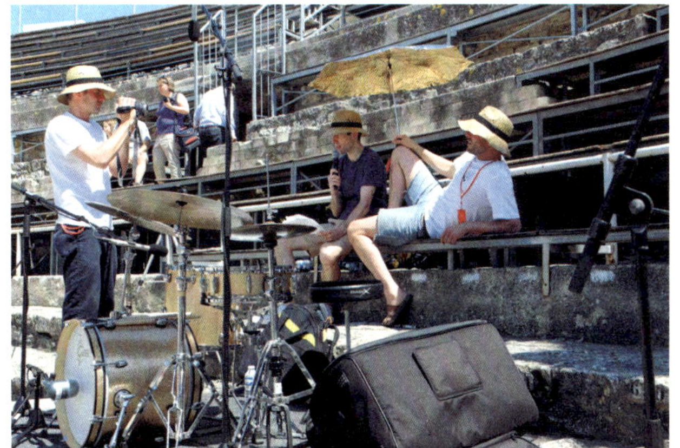
7/7/12—3:21:08 PM

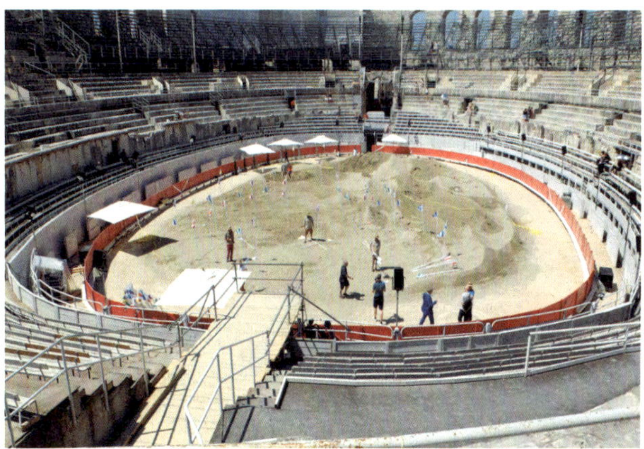
7/7/12—3:21:17 PM

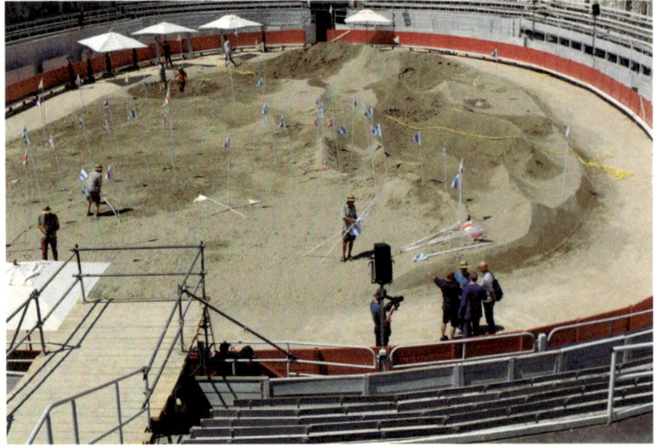
7/7/12—3:21:24 PM

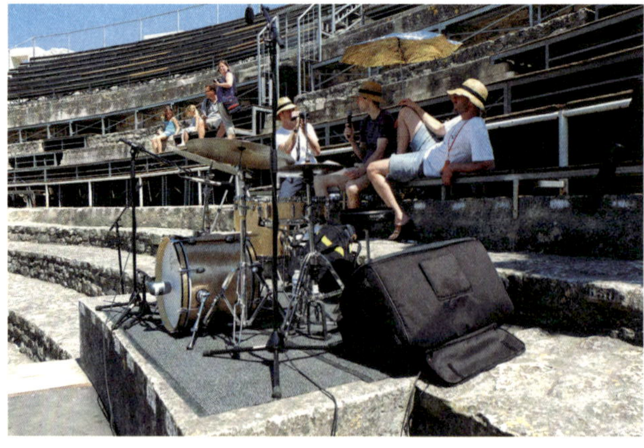
7/7/12—3:21:30 PM

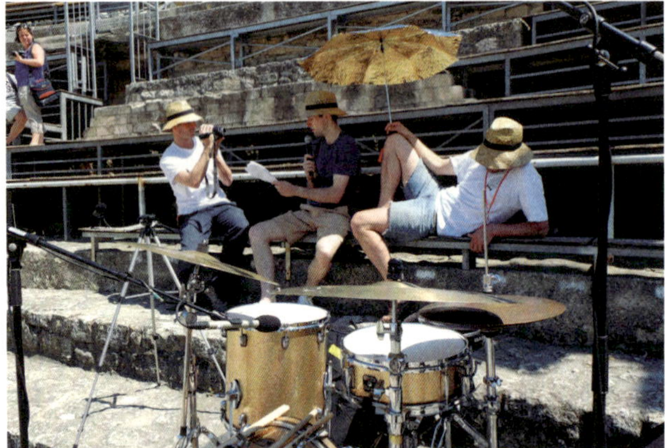
7/7/12—3:21:38 PM

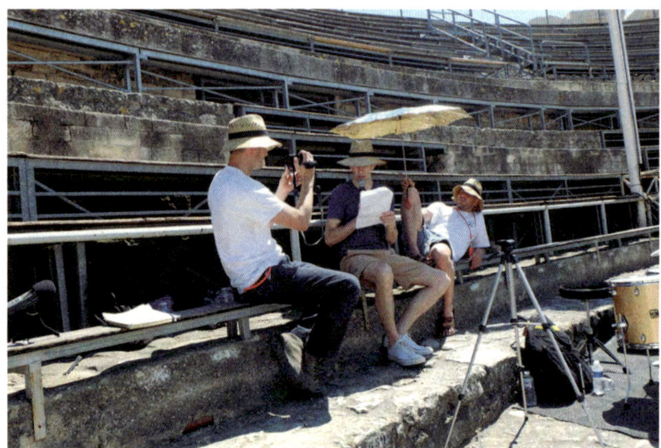
7/7/12—3:22:01 PM

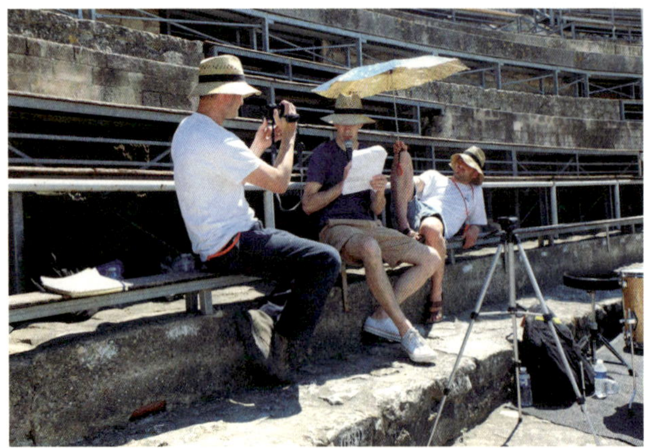
7/7/12—3:22:05 PM

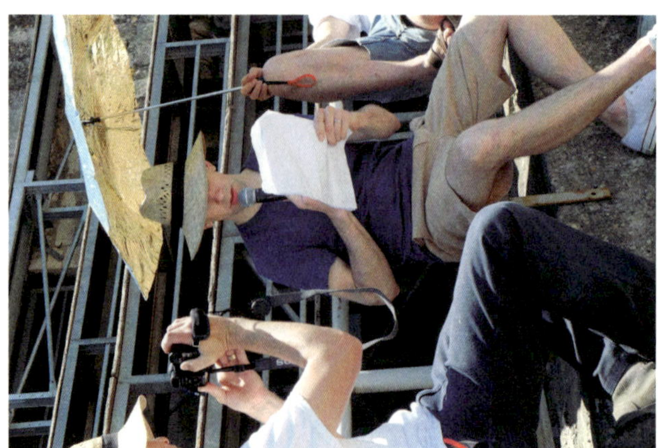
7/7/12—3:22:14 PM

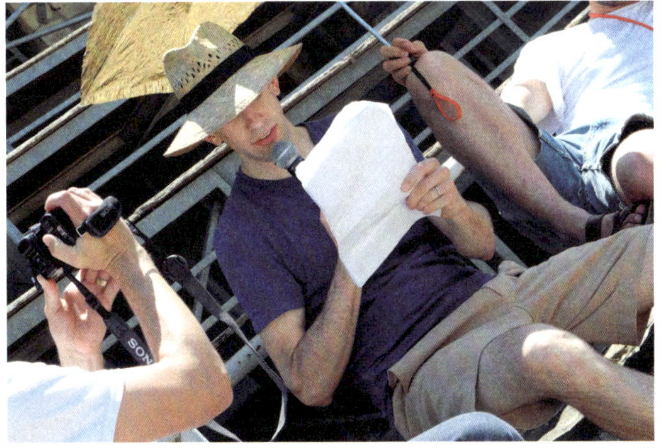

7/7/12—3:22:20 PM

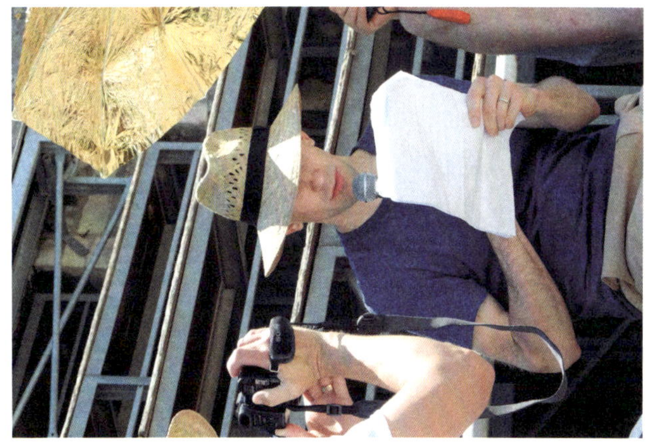

7/7/12—3:22:24 PM

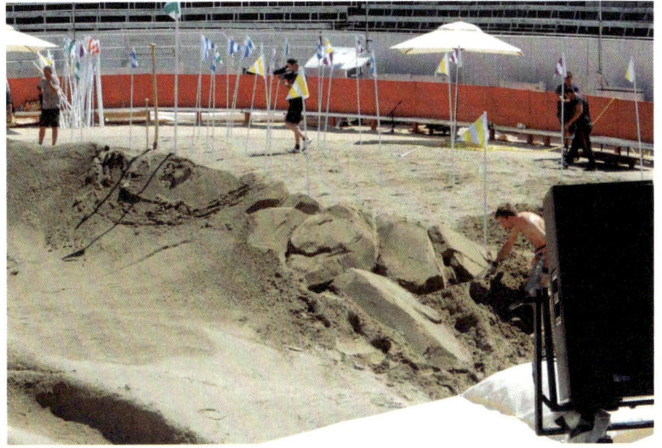

7/7/12—3:28:26 PM

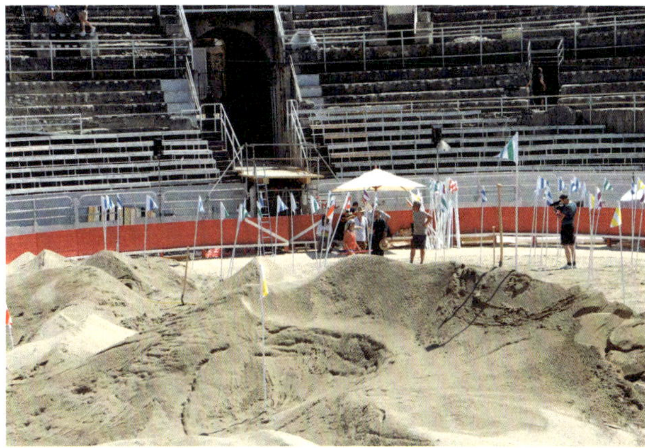

7/7/12—3:28:31 PM

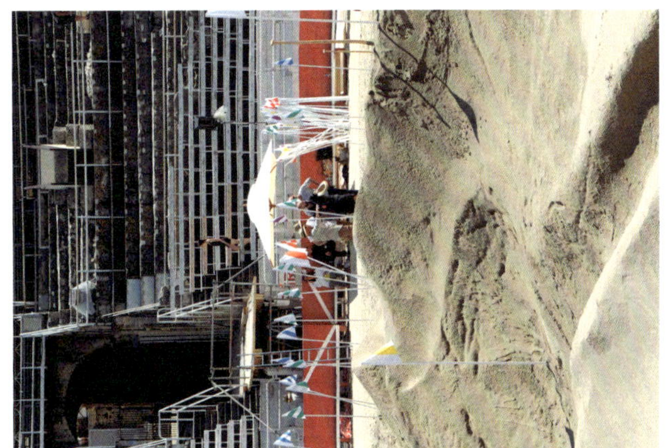

7/7/12—3:29:04 PM

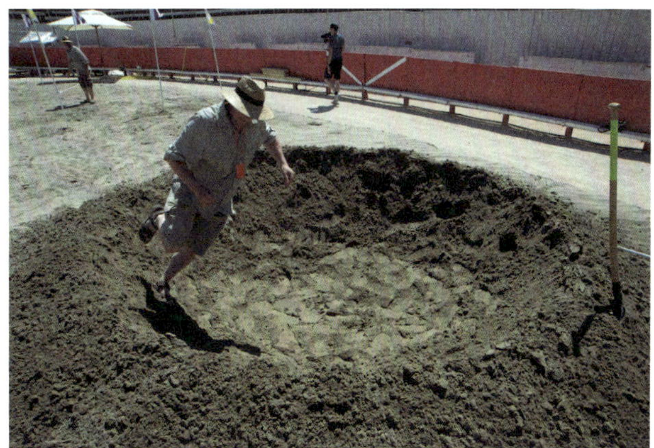

7/7/12—3:36:57 PM

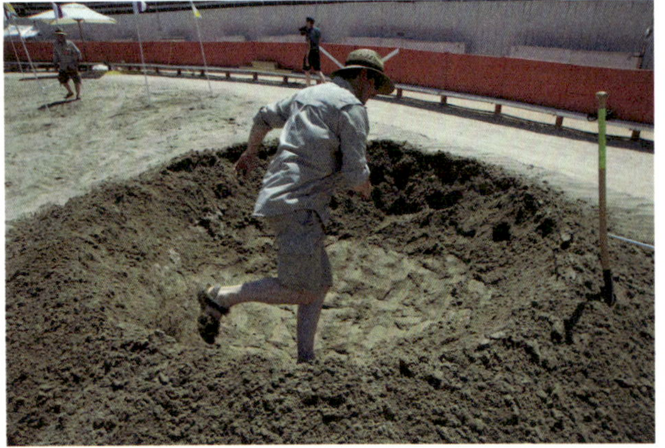
7/7/12—3:36:58 PM

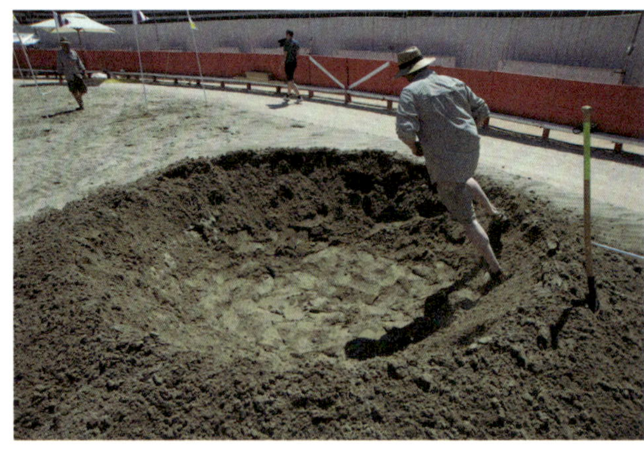
7/7/12—3:36:58 PM

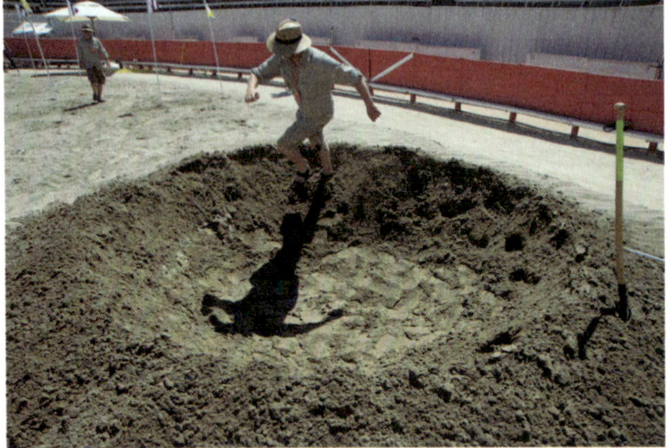
7/7/12—3:36:59 PM

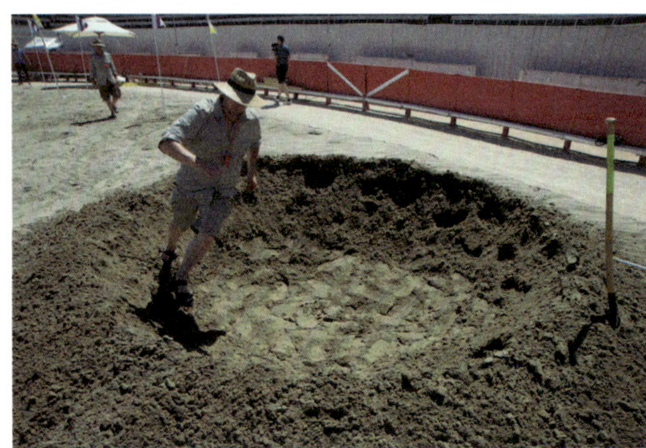
7/7/12—3:37:00 PM

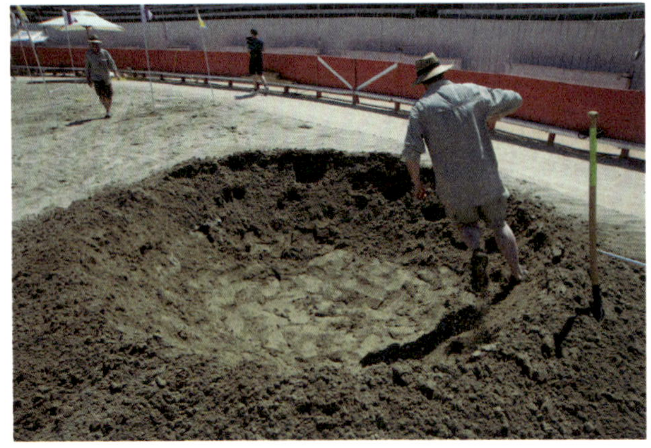
7/7/12—3:37:01 PM

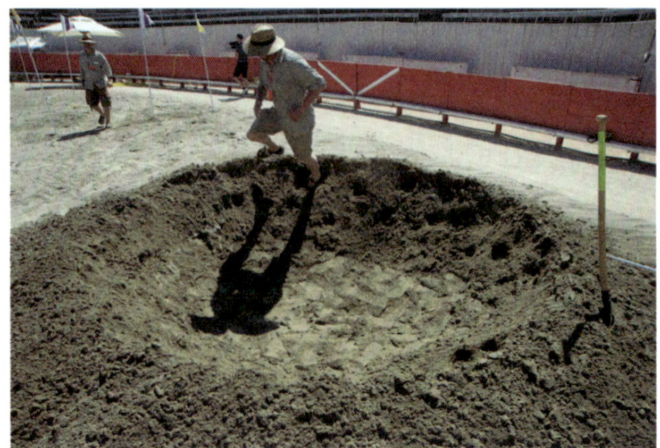
7/7/12—3:37:02 PM

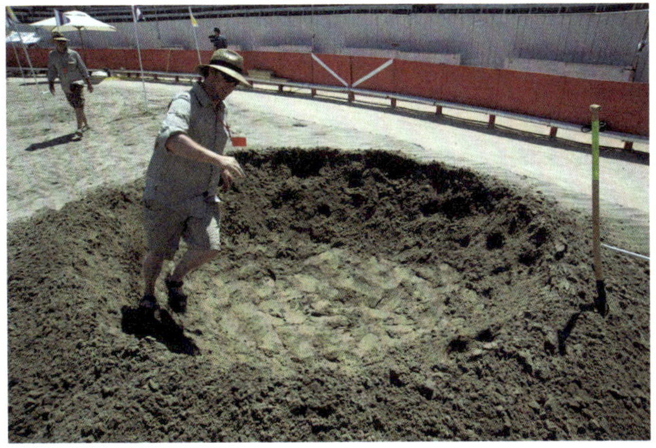
7/7/12—3:37:03 PM

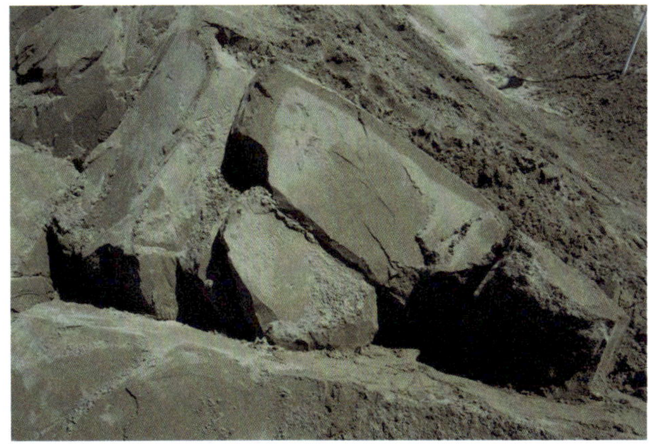
7/7/12—3:37:54 PM

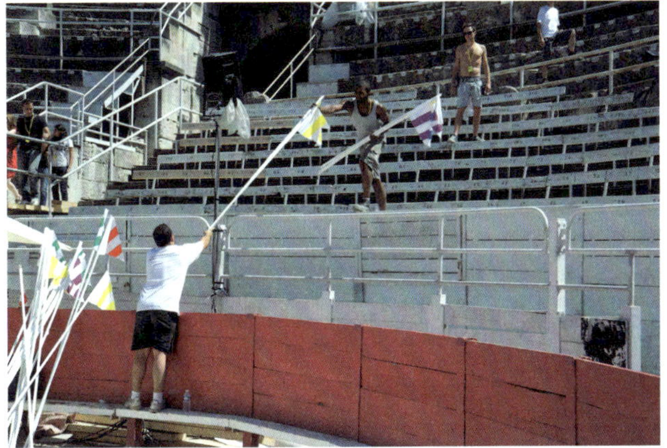
7/7/12—3:39:05 PM

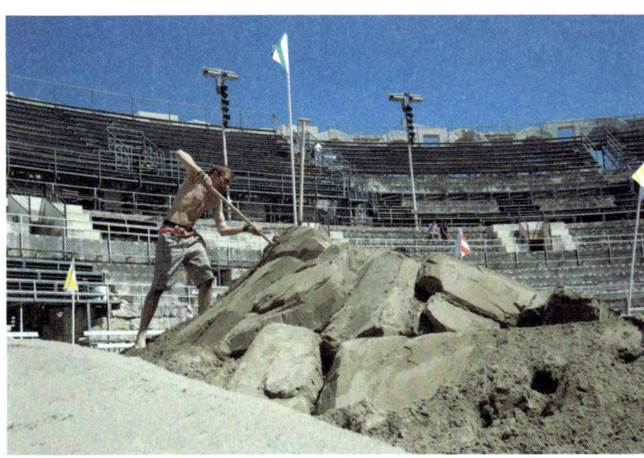
7/7/12—3:42:05 PM

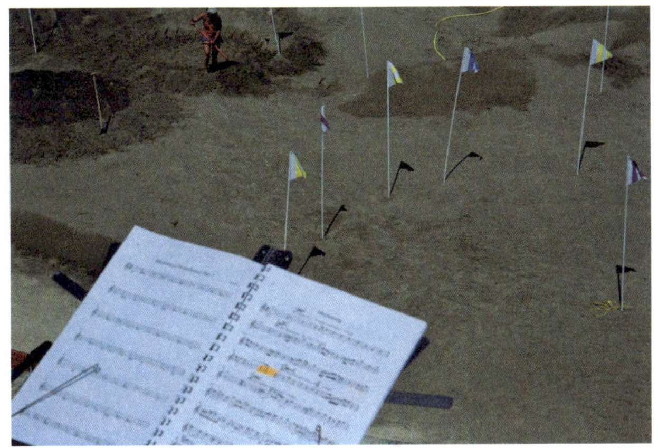
7/7/12—3:48:12 PM

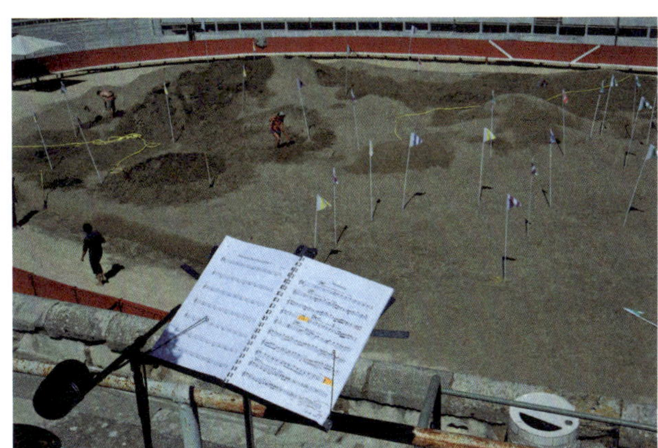
7/7/12—3:48:18 PM

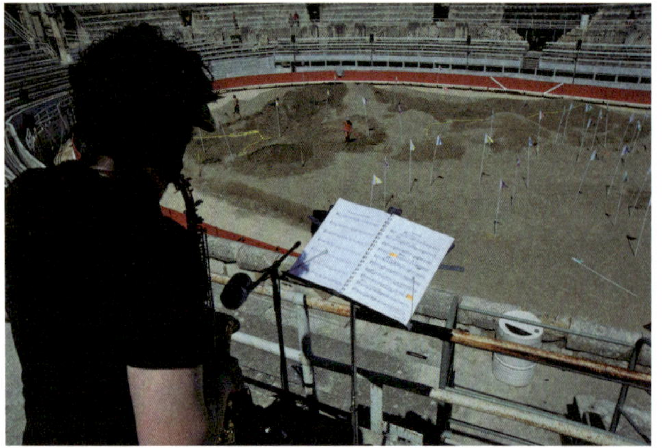
7/7/12—3:48:21 PM

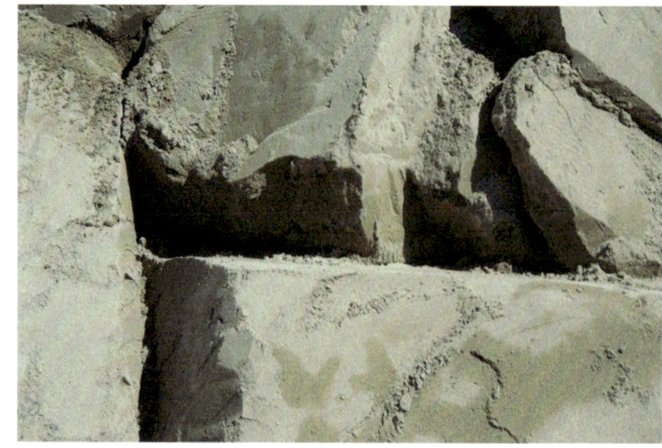
7/7/12—3:55:02 PM

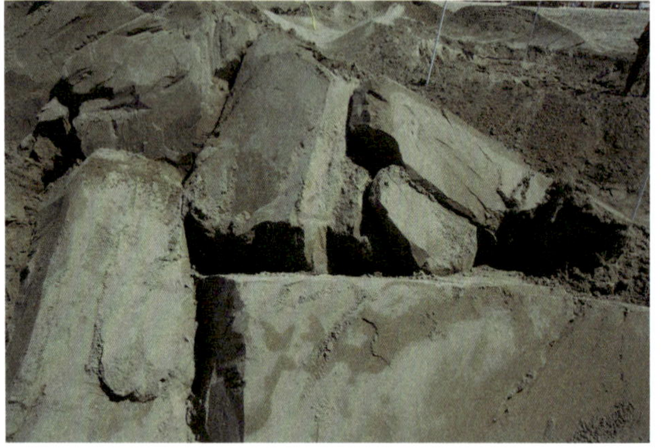
7/7/12—3:55:04 PM

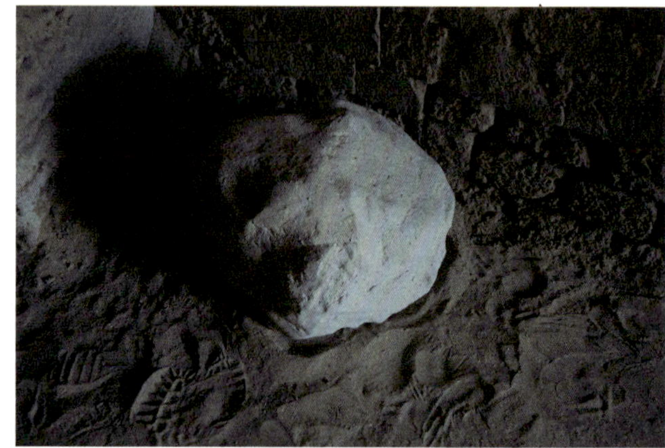
7/7/12—4:06:10 PM

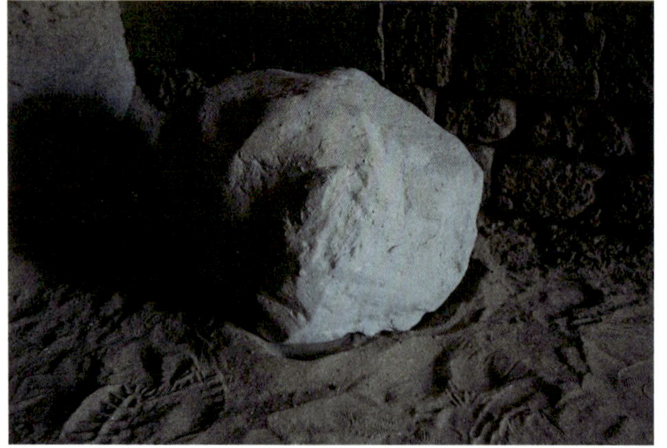
7/7/12—4:06:18 PM

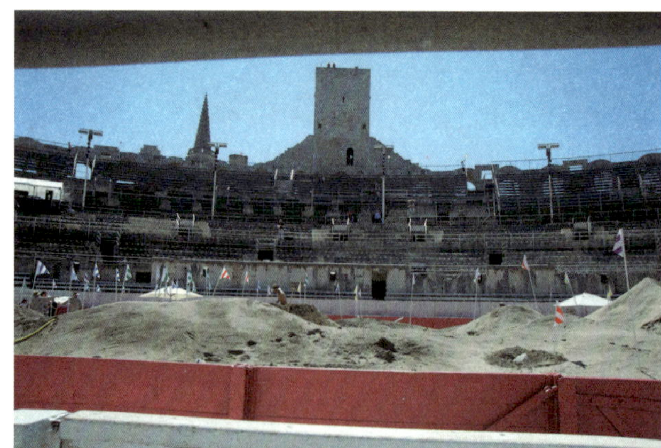
7/7/12—4:10:55 PM

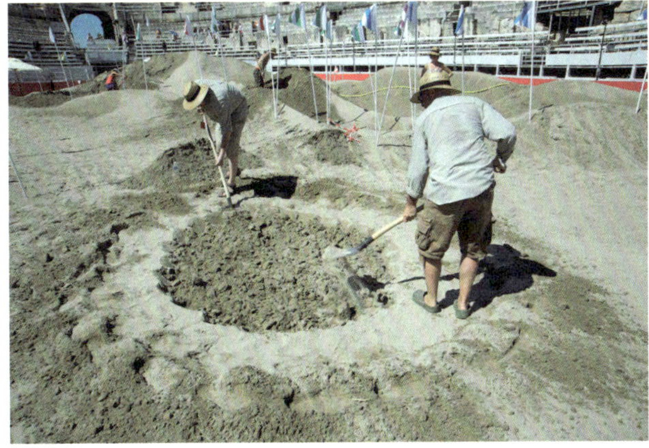

7/7/12—4:14:58 PM

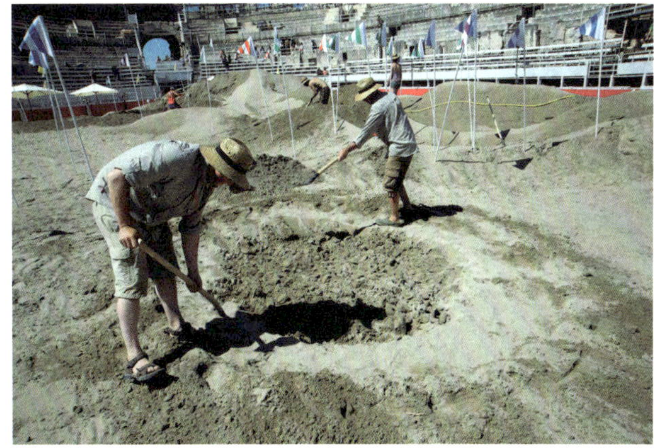

7/7/12—4:15:20 PM

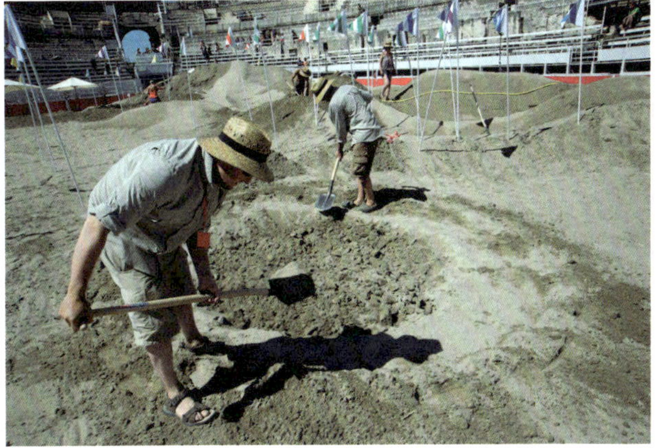

7/7/12—4:15:23 PM

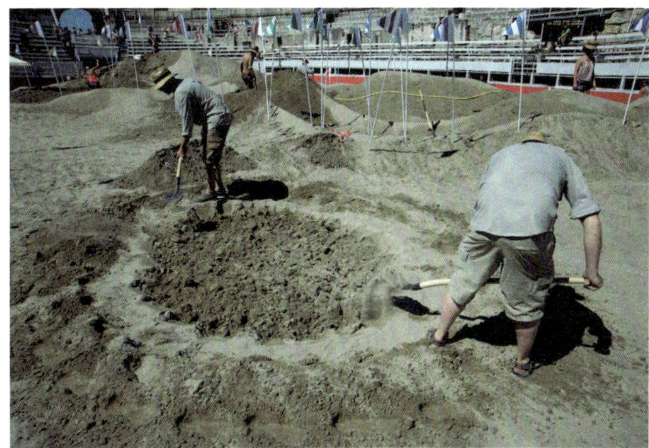

7/7/12—4:15:34 PM

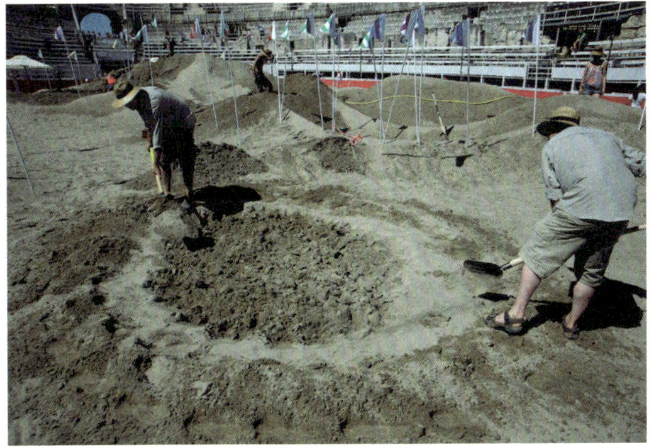

7/7/12—4:15:36 PM

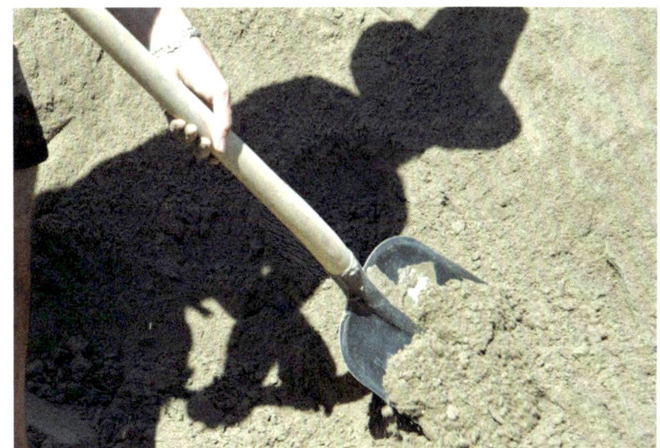

7/7/12—4:16:48 PM

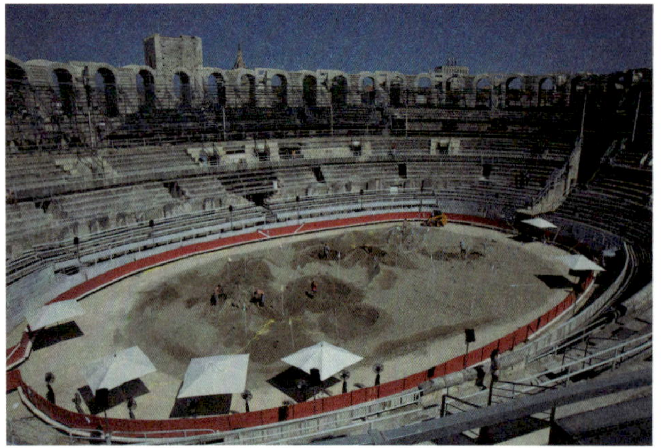

7/7/12—4:21:19 PM

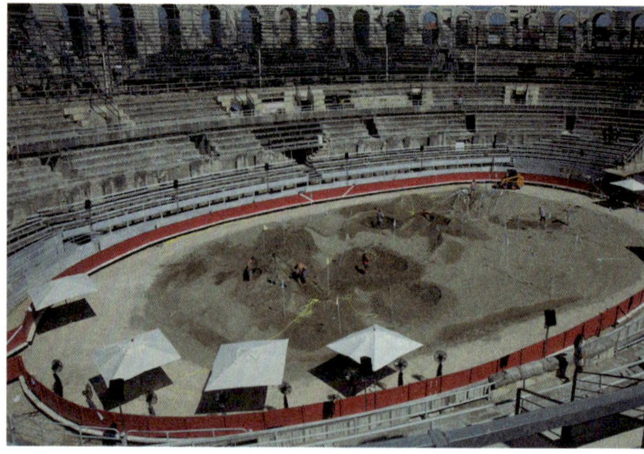

7/7/12—4:21:21 PM

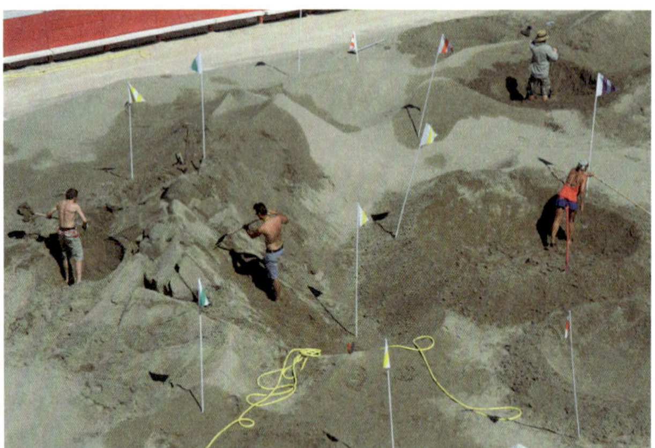

7/7/12—4:21:26 PM

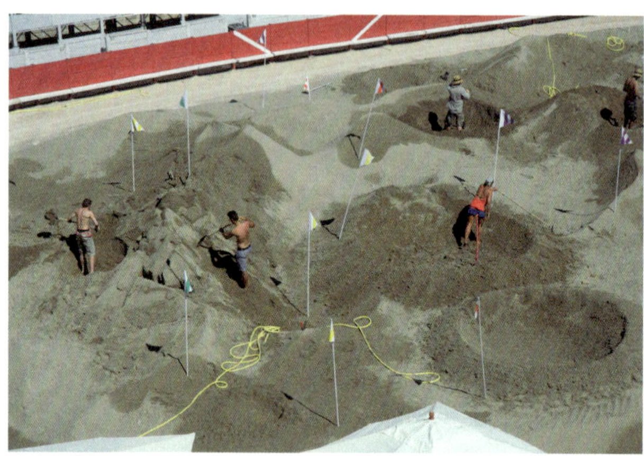

7/7/12—4:21:27 PM

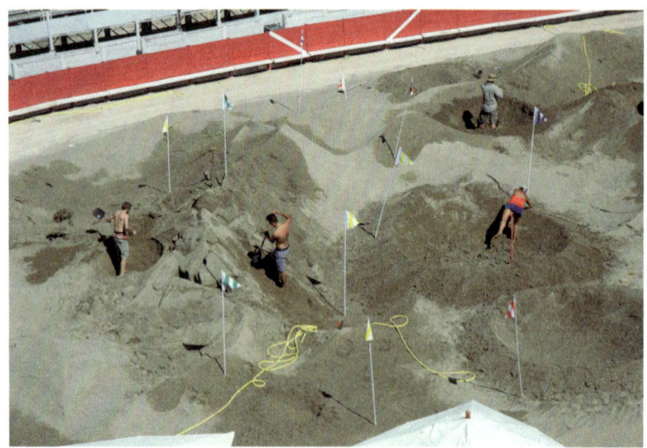

7/7/12—4:21:28 PM

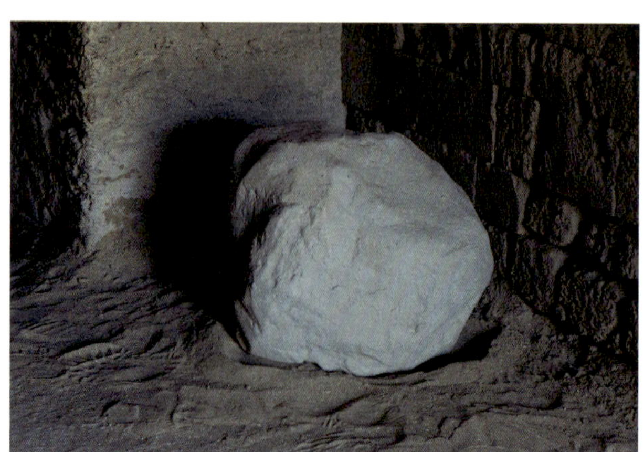

7/7/12—4:30:28 PM

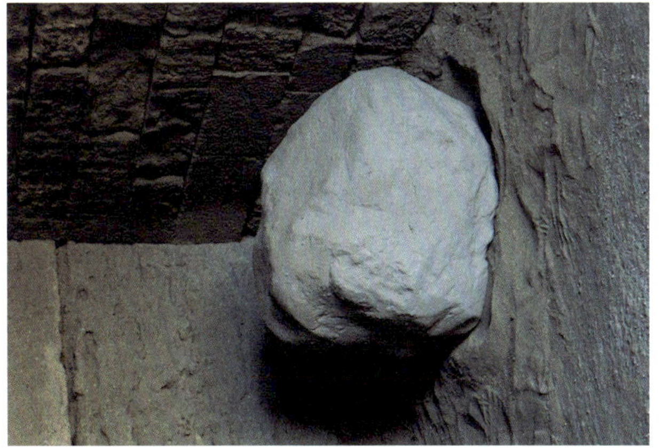
7/7/12—4:30:34 PM

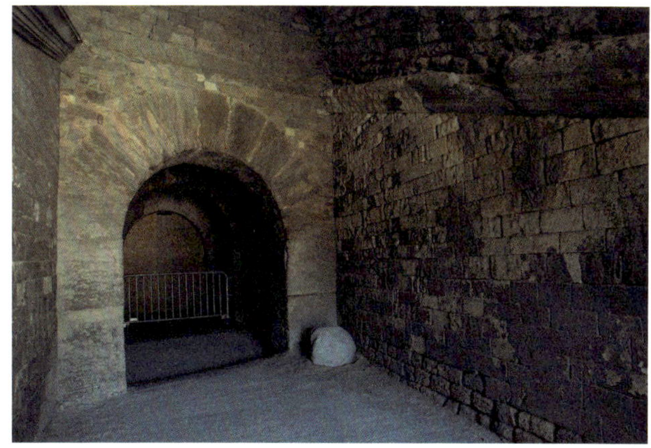
7/7/12—4:32:00 PM

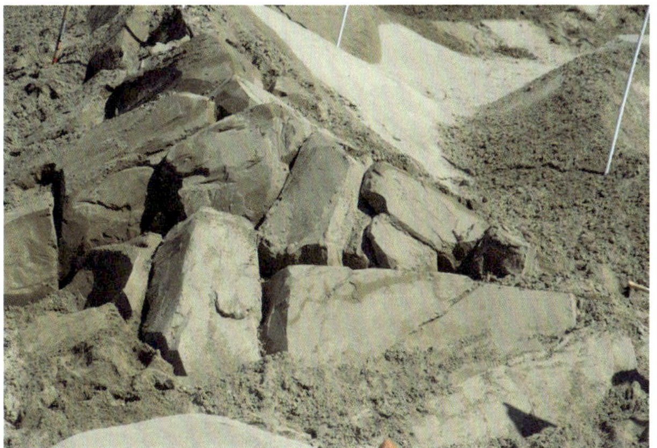
7/7/12—4:33:48 PM

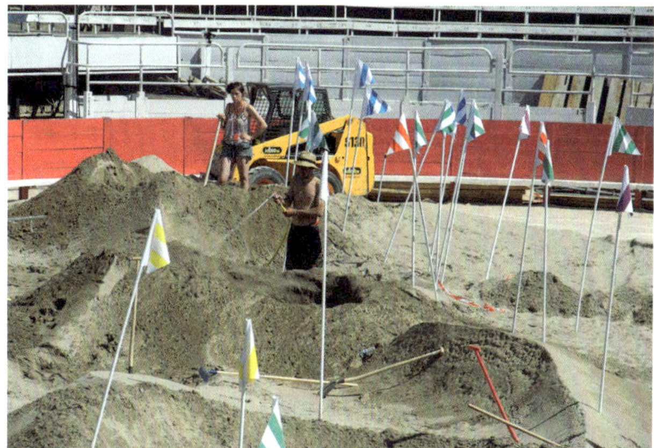
7/7/12—4:34:27 PM

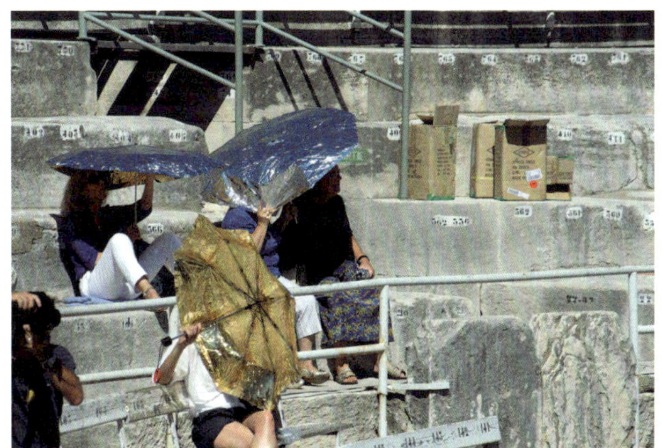
7/7/12—4:35:00 PM

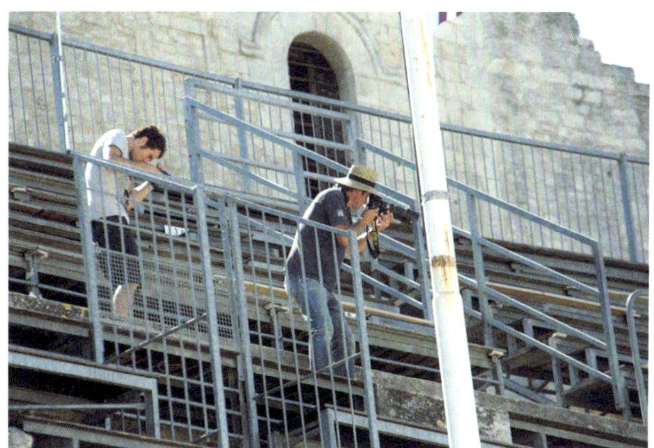
7/7/12—4:42:38 PM

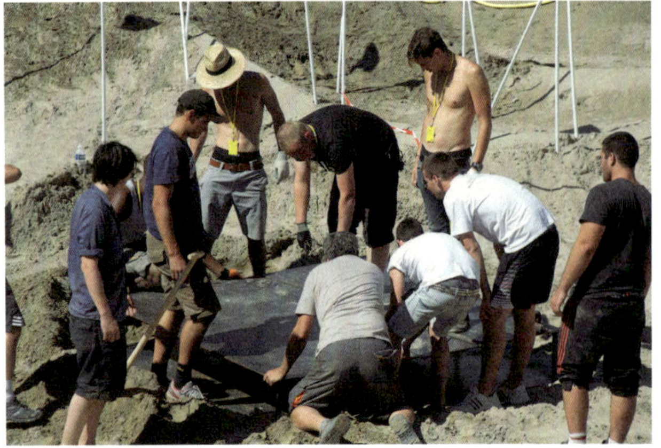
7/7/12—4:43:10 PM

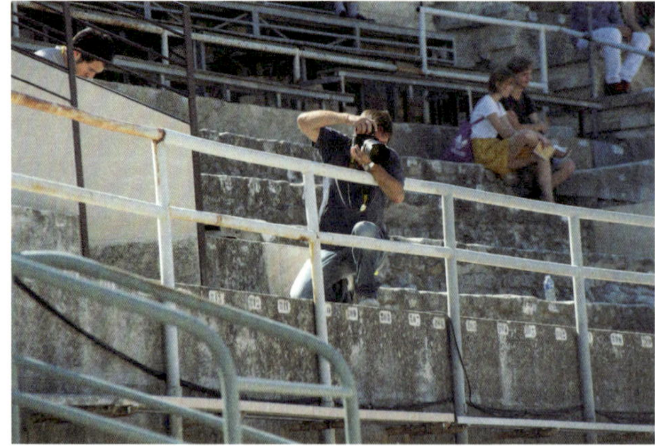
7/7/12—4:43:24 PM

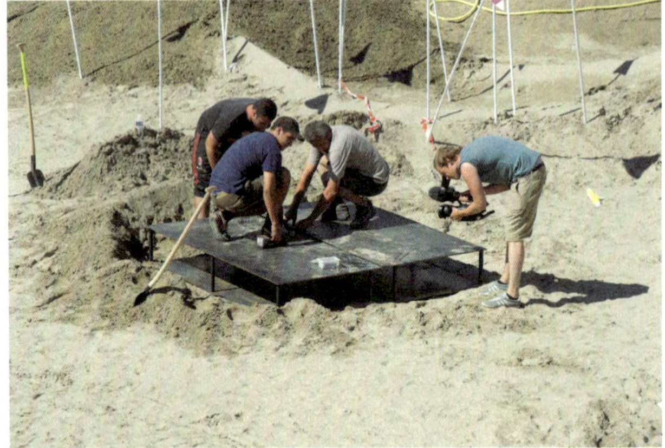
7/7/12—4:45:43 PM

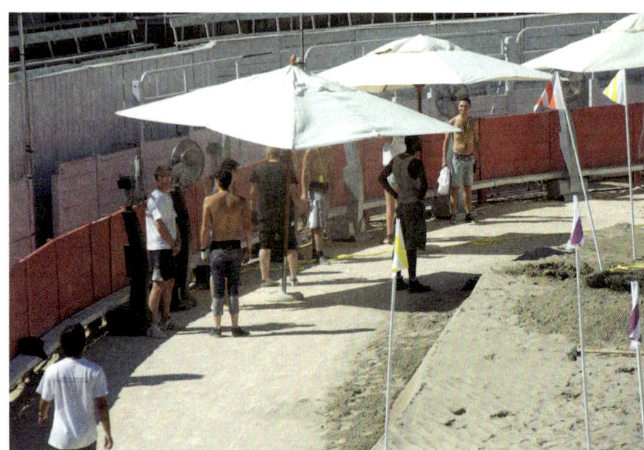
7/7/12—4:45:53 PM

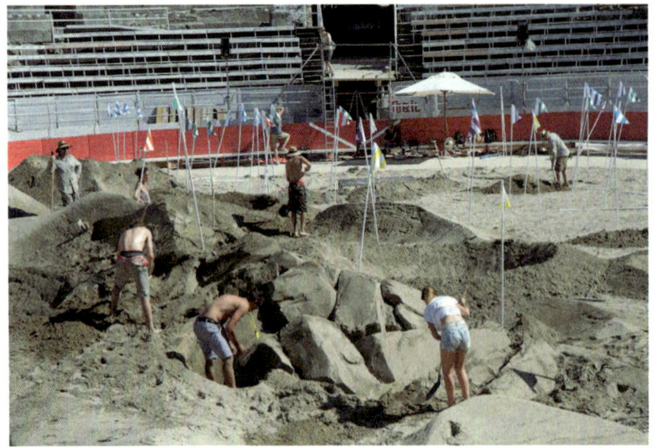
7/7/12—4:55:35 PM

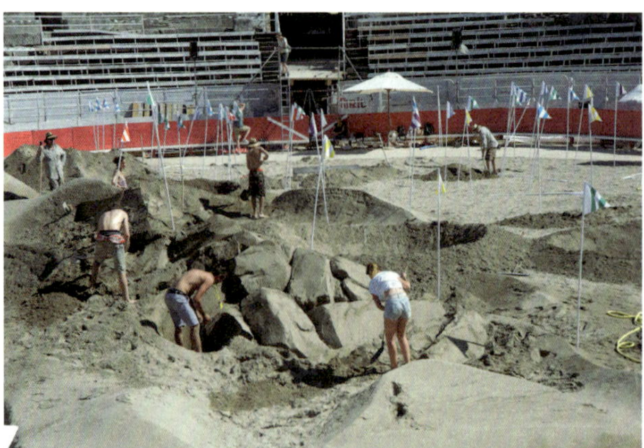
7/7/12—4:55:36 PM

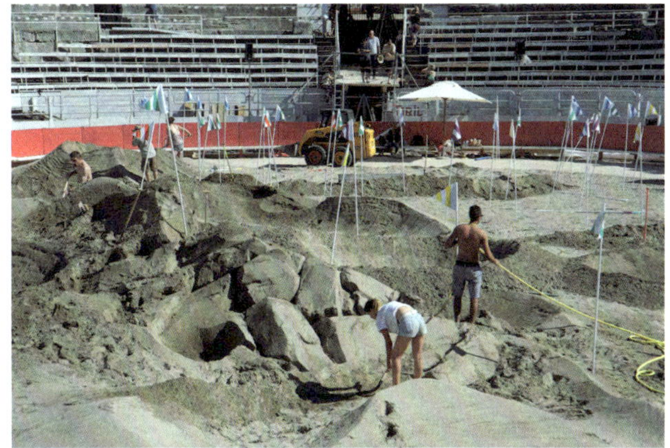
7/7/12—5:13:26 PM

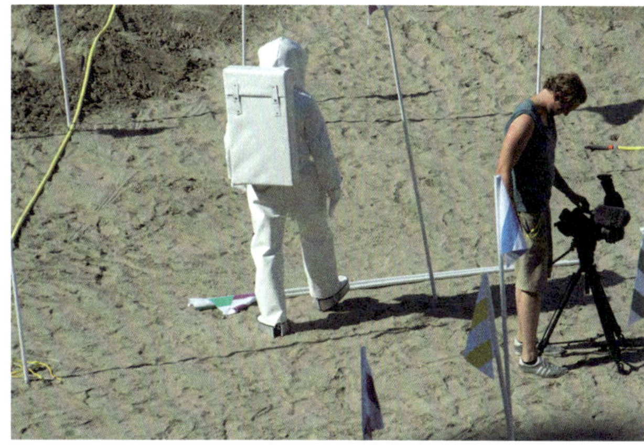
7/7/12—5:31:12 PM

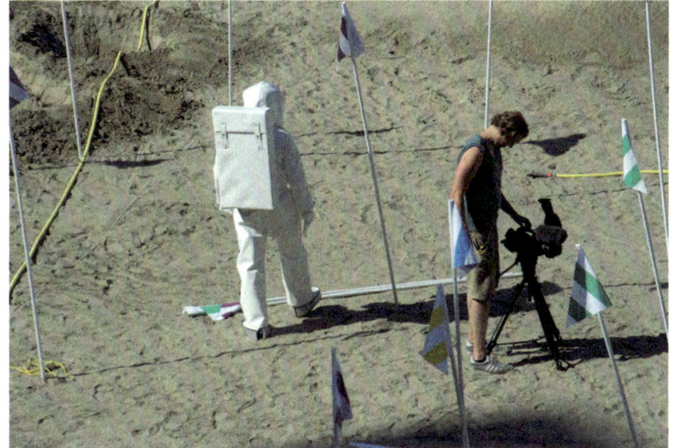
7/7/12—5:31:13 PM

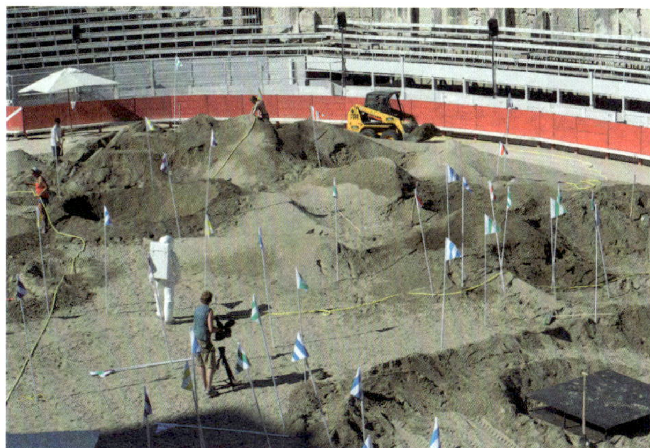
7/7/12—5:31:19 PM

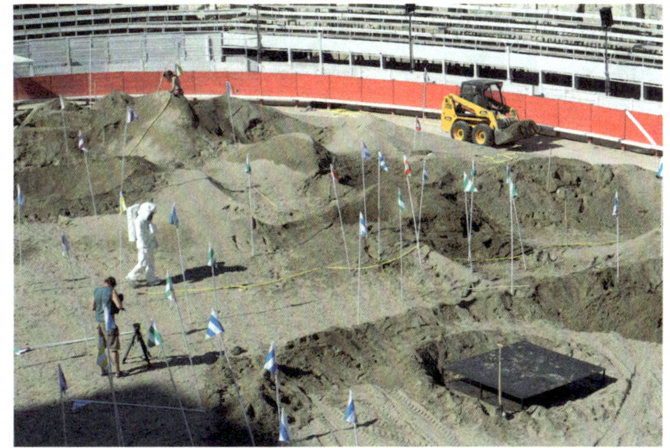
7/7/12—5:31:27 PM

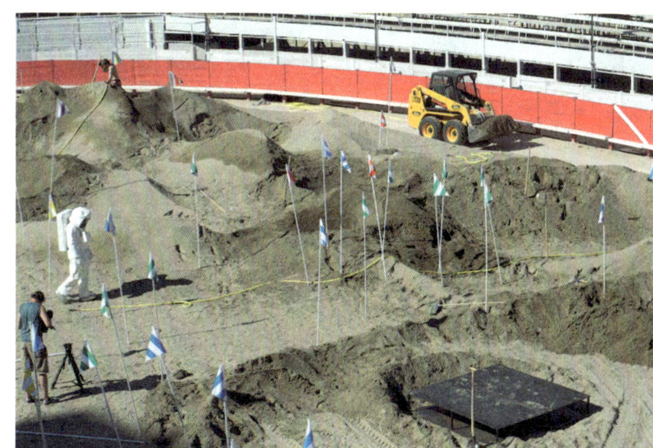
7/7/12—5:31:30 PM

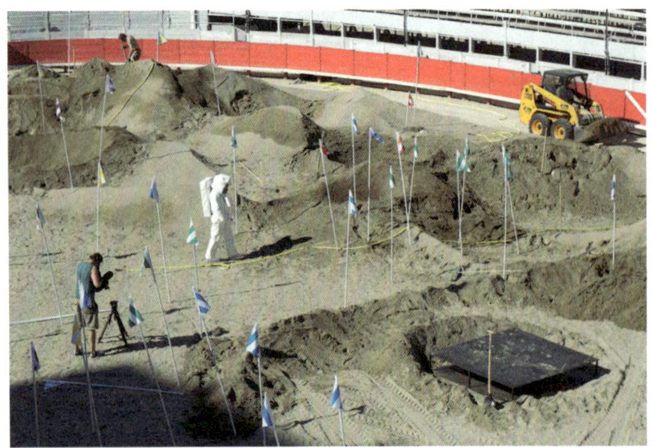

7/7/12—5:31:31 PM

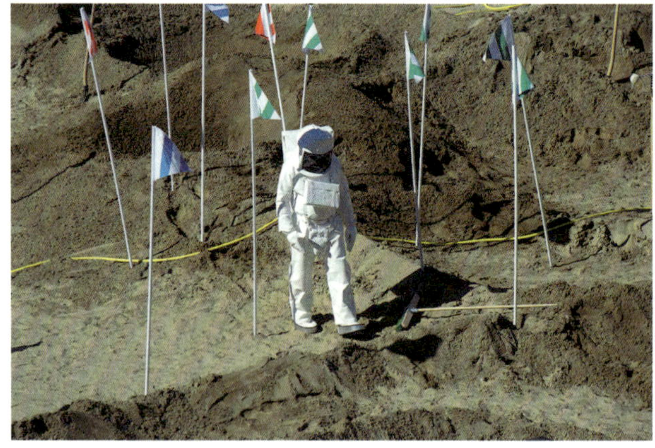

7/7/12—5:31:46 PM

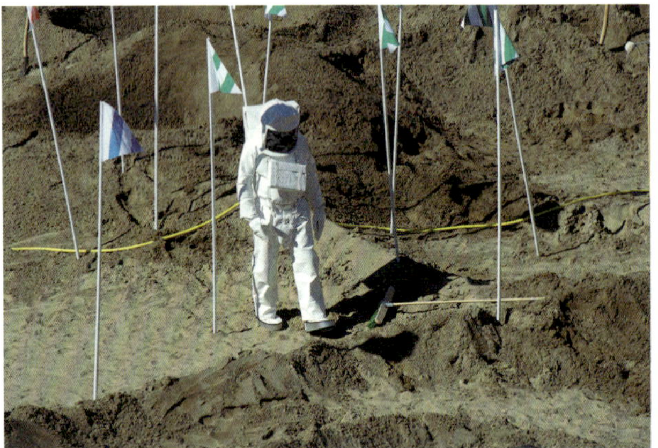

7/7/12—5:31:47 PM

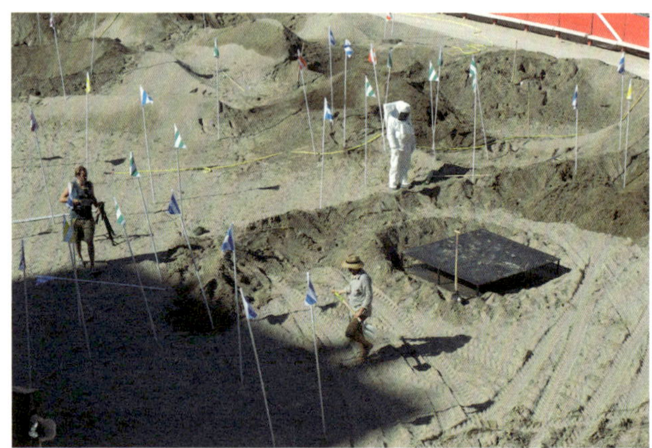

7/7/12—5:31:52 PM

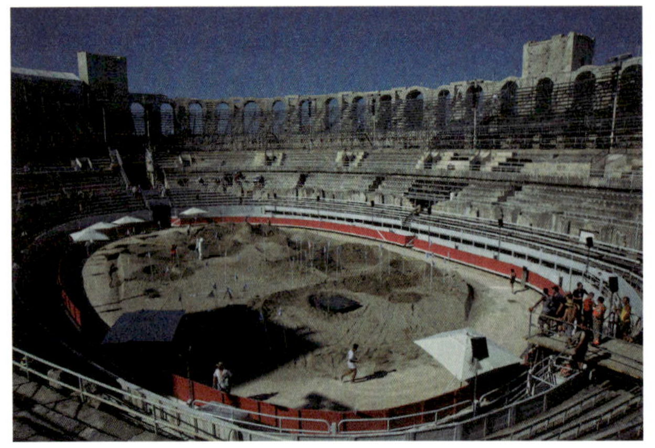

7/7/12—5:32:42 PM

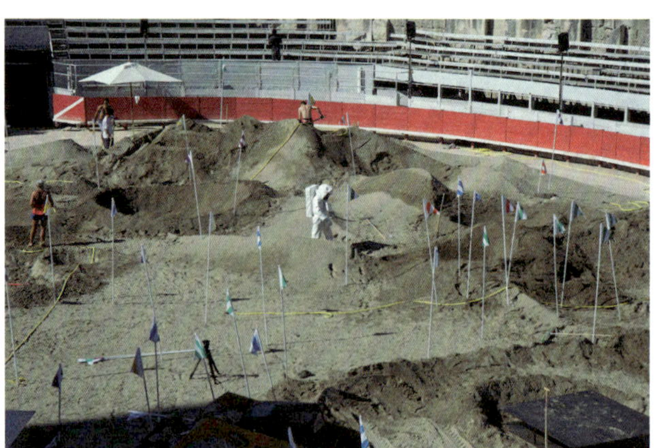

7/7/12—5:32:51 PM

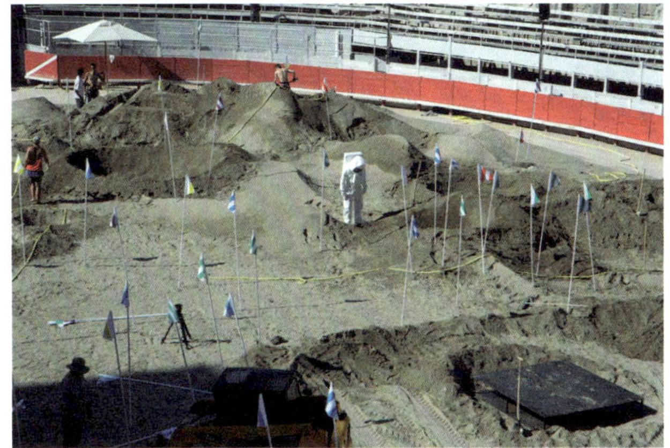

7/7/12—5:32:56 PM

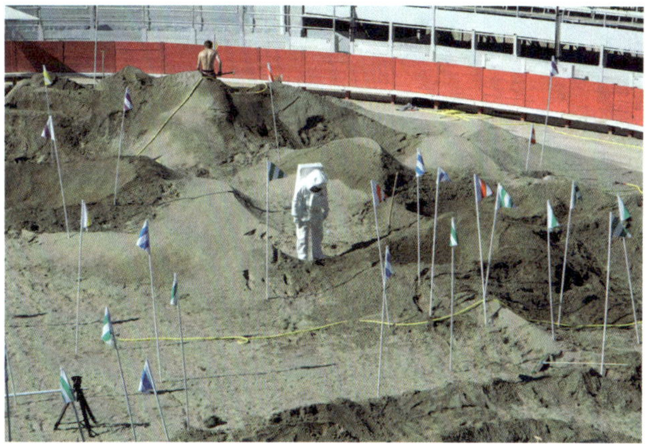

7/7/12—5:32:57 PM

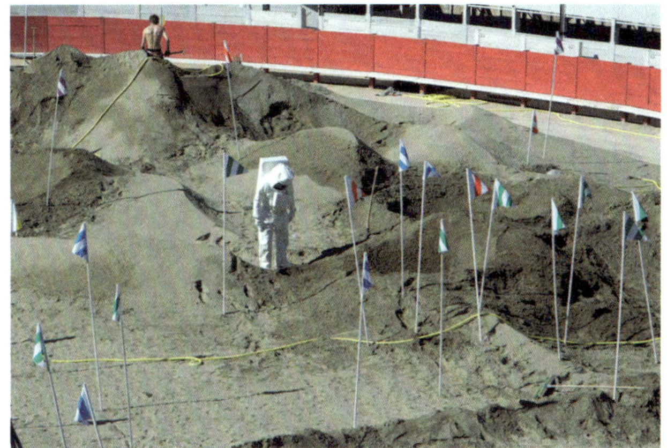

7/7/12—5:32:58 PM

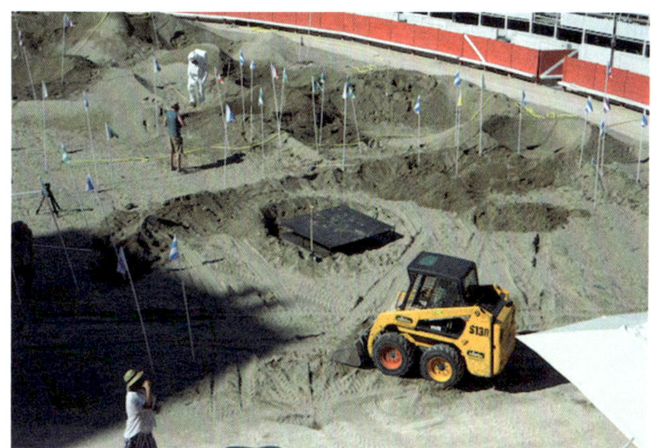

7/7/12—5:33:20 PM

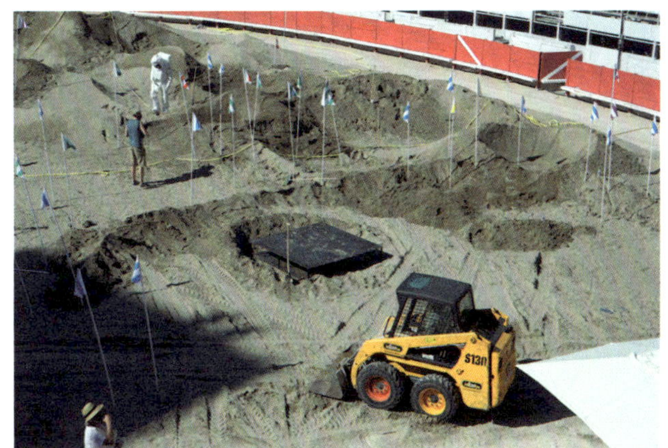

7/7/12—5:33:20 PM

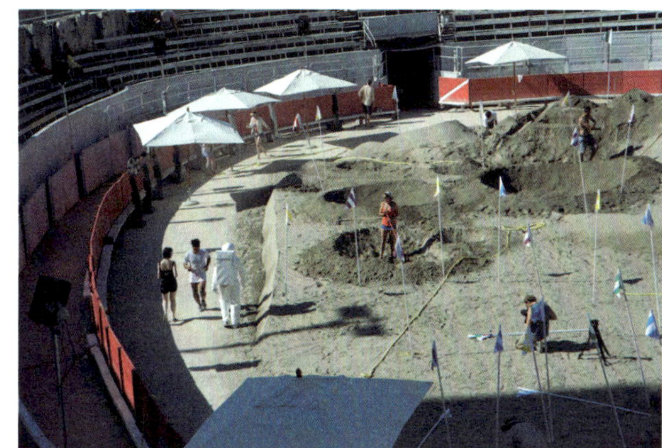

7/7/12—5:33:56 PM

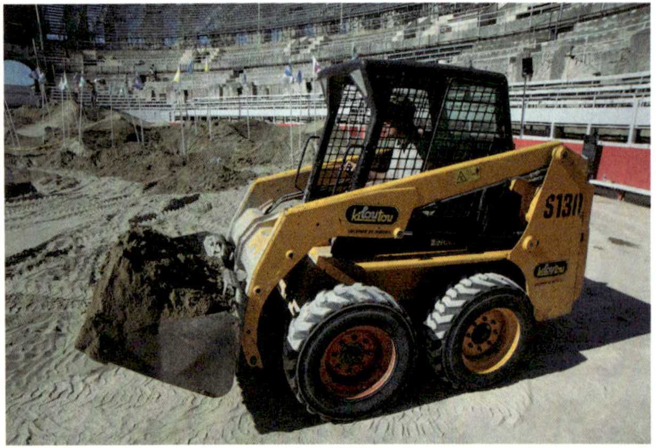

7/7/12—5:35:57 PM

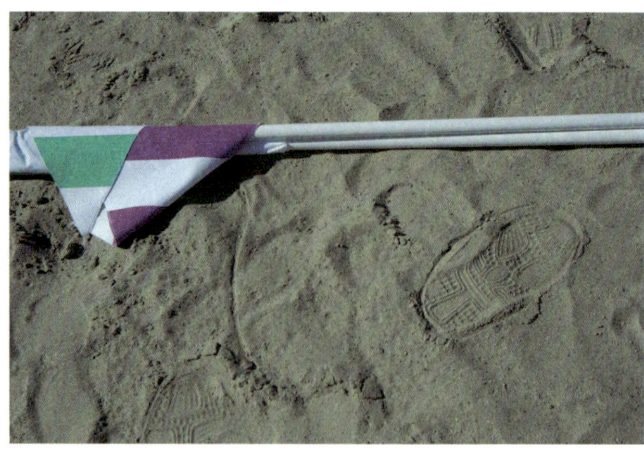
7/7/12—5:36:32 PM

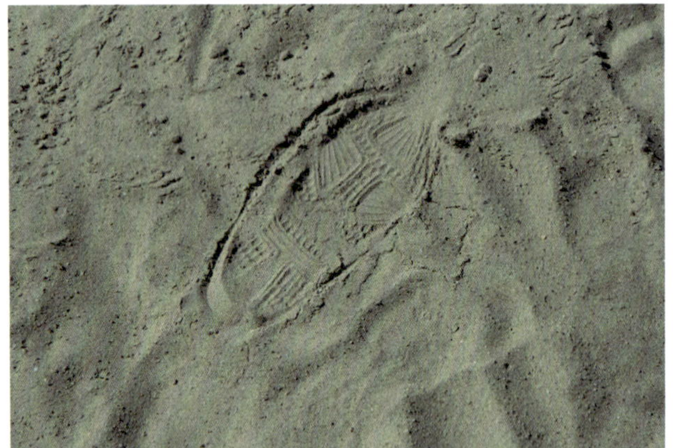
7/7/12—5:36:39 PM

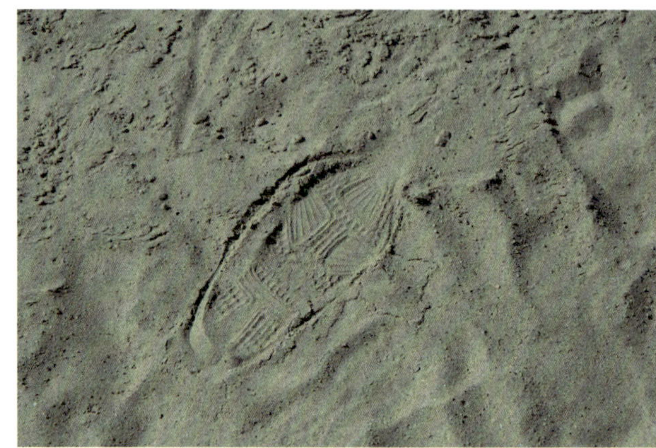
7/7/12—5:36:41 PM

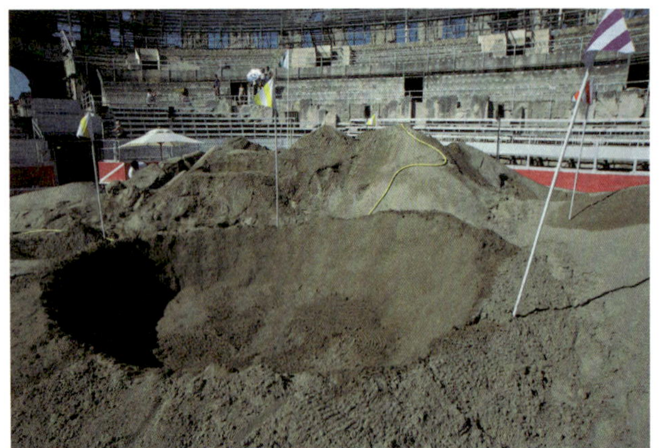
7/7/12—5:36:55 PM

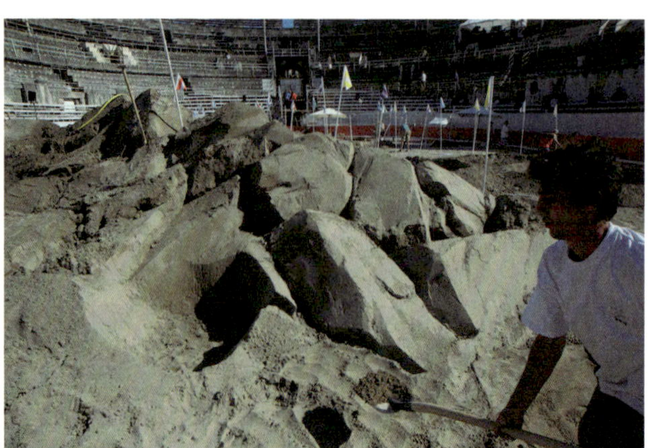
7/7/12—5:37:59 PM

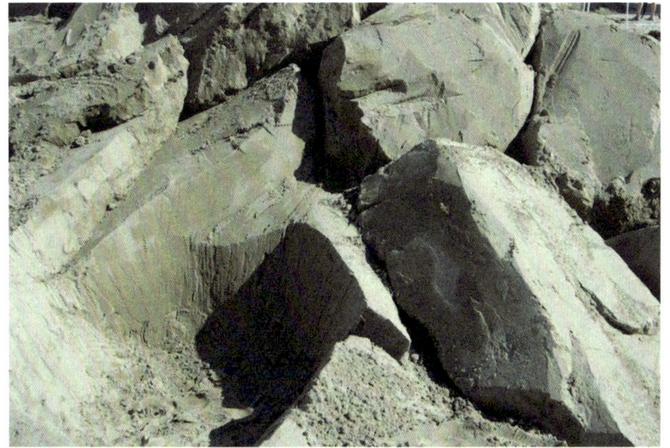

7/7/12—5:38:00 PM

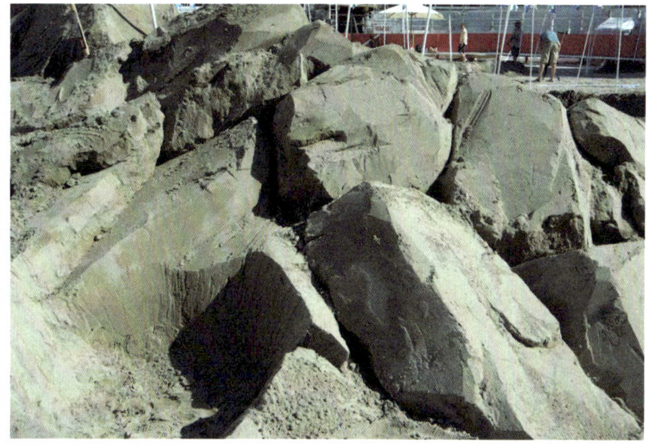

7/7/12—5:38:01 PM

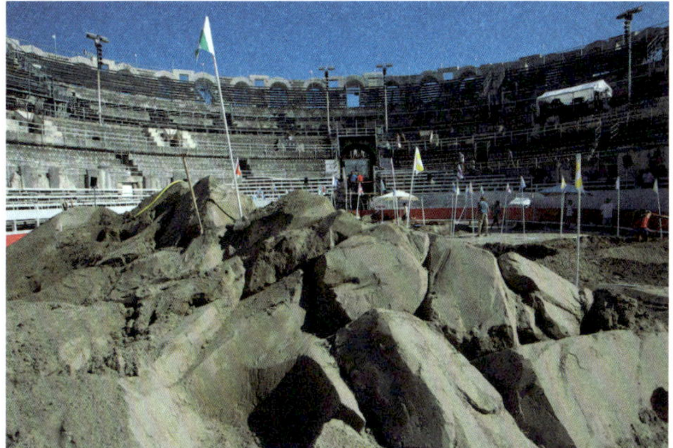

7/7/12—5:38:02 PM

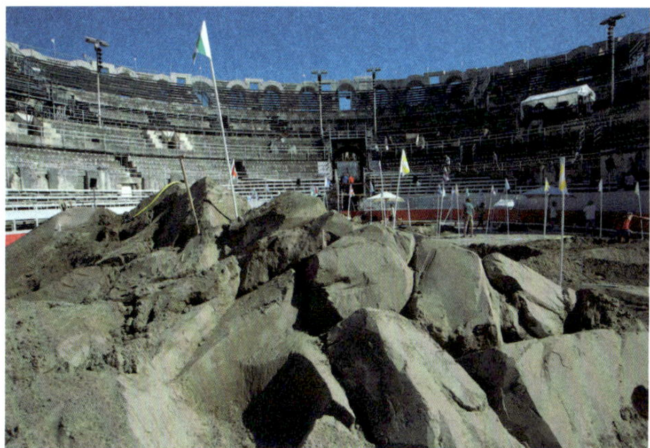

7/7/12—5:38:04 PM

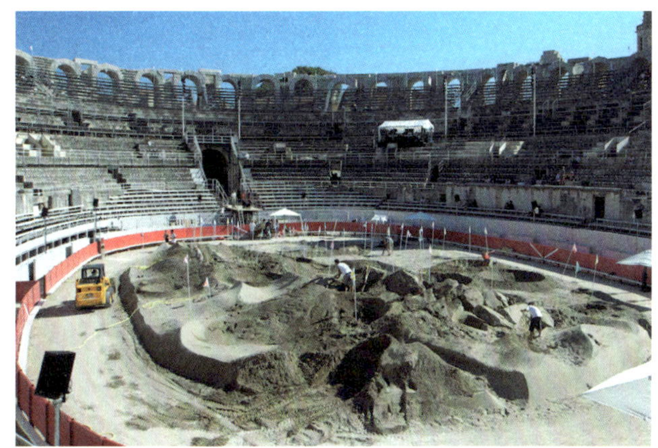

7/7/12—5:40:41 PM

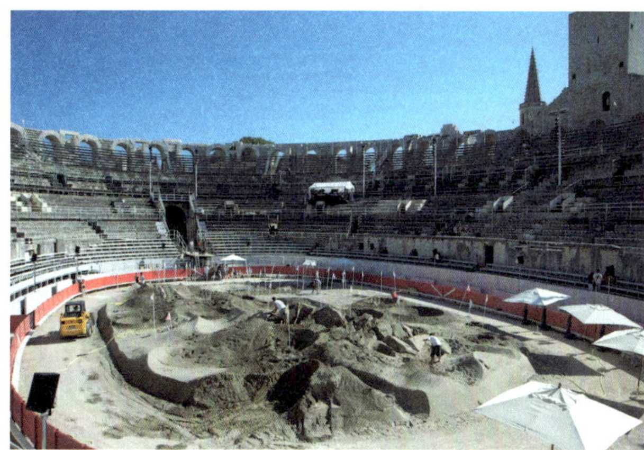

7/7/12—5:40:44 PM

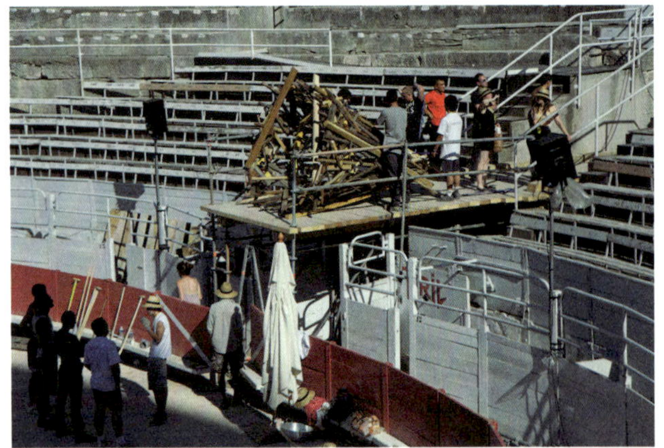
7/7/12—6:02:45 PM

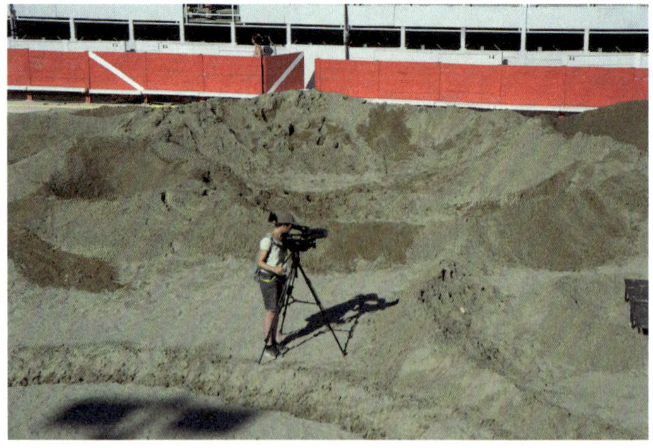
7/7/12—6:03:31 PM

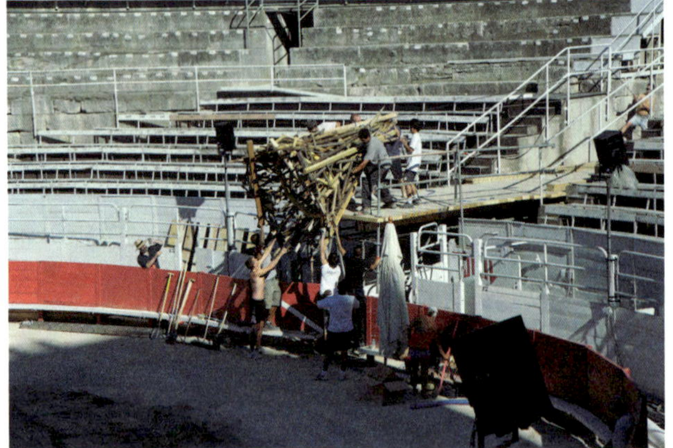
7/7/12—6:05:34 PM

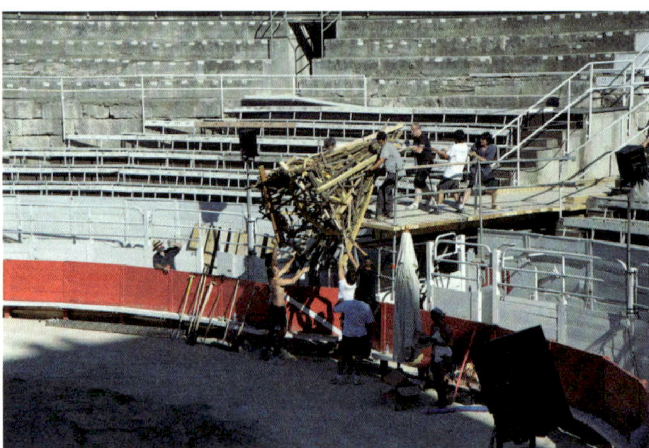
7/7/12—6:05:41 PM

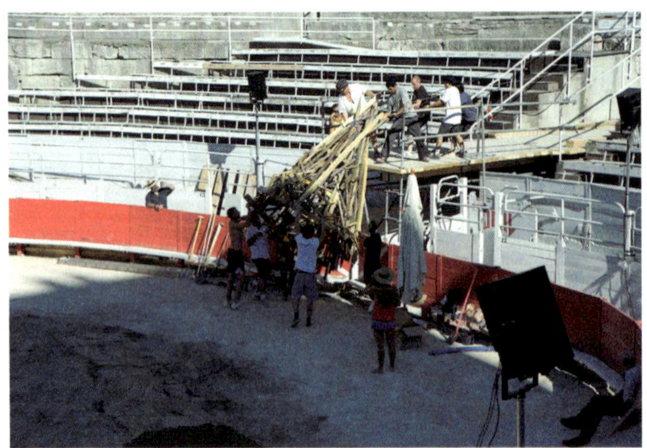
7/7/12—6:05:58 PM

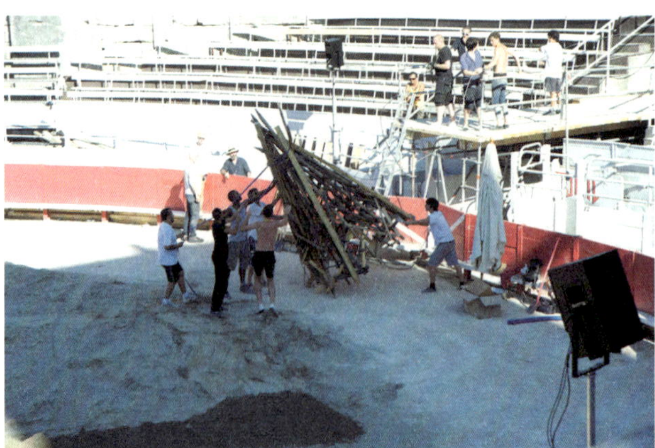
7/7/12—6:06:54 PM

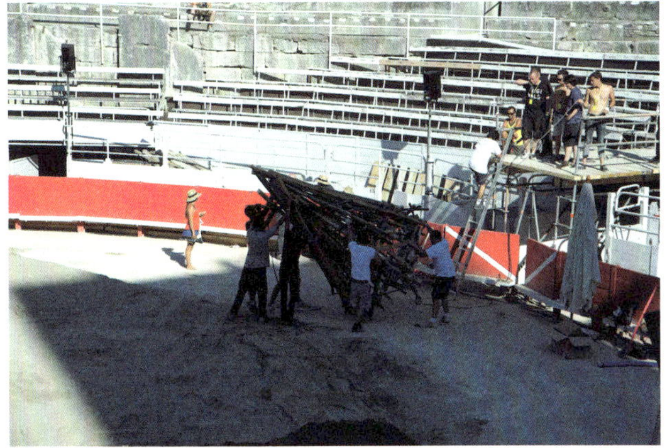

7/7/12—6:07:44 PM

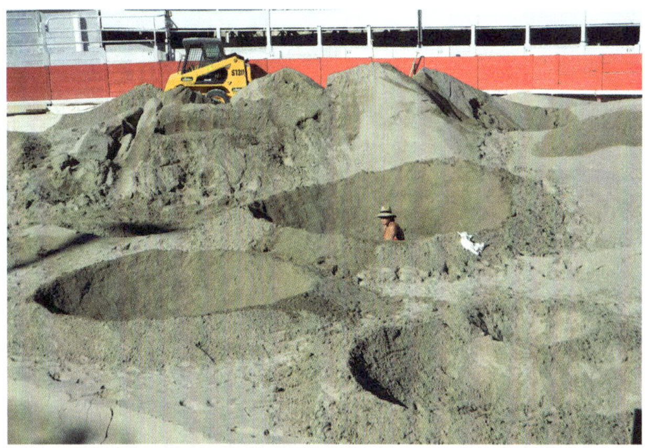

7/7/12—6:11:33 PM

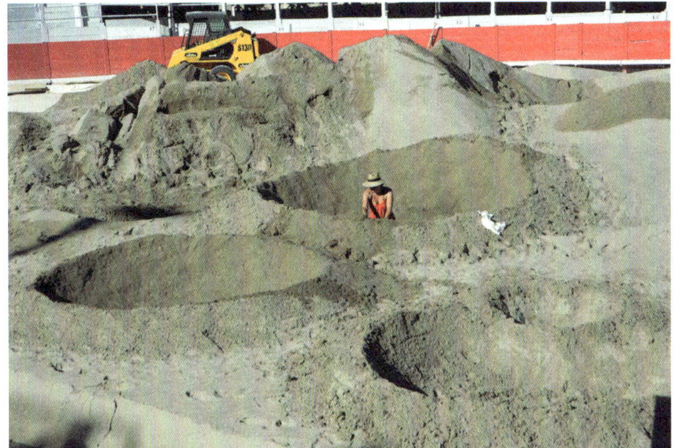

7/7/12—6:11:39 PM

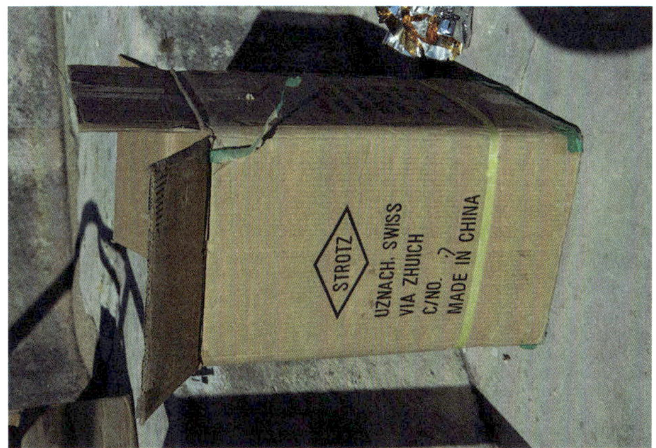

7/7/12—6:14:11 PM

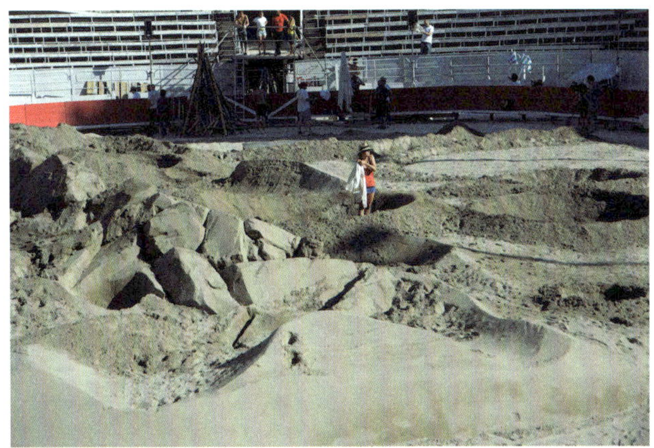

7/7/12—6:14:40 PM

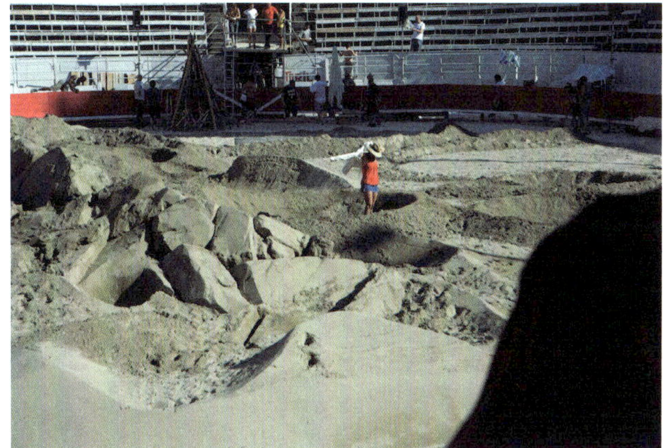

7/7/12—6:14:44 PM

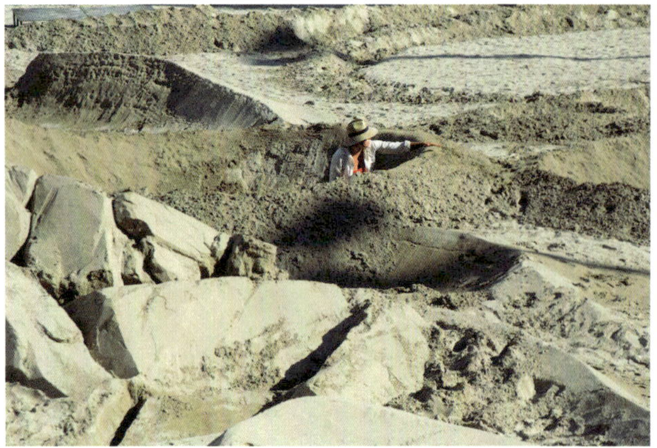
7/7/12—6:15:33 PM

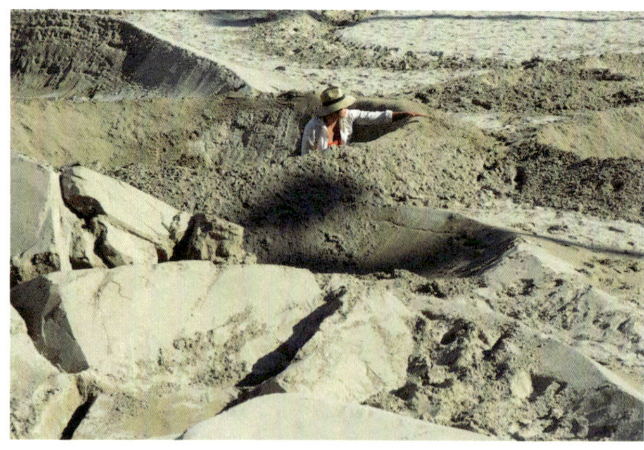
7/7/12—6:15:34 PM

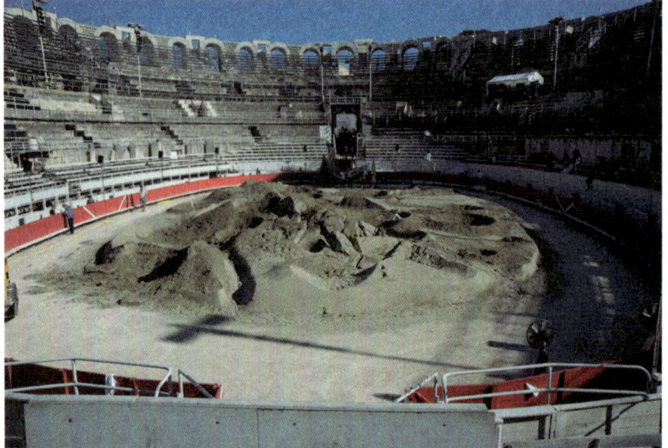
7/7/12—6:18:24 PM

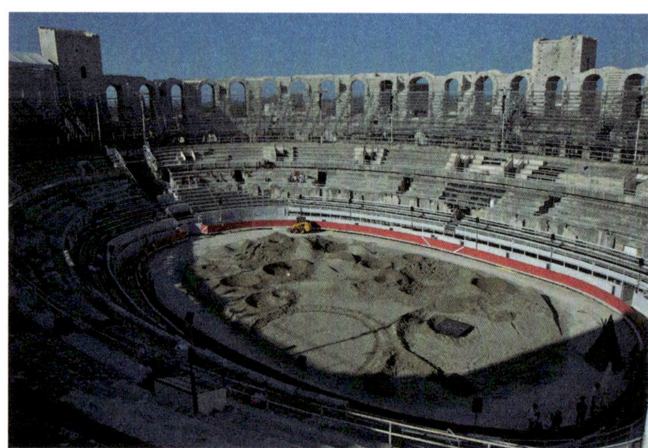
7/7/12—6:26:03 PM

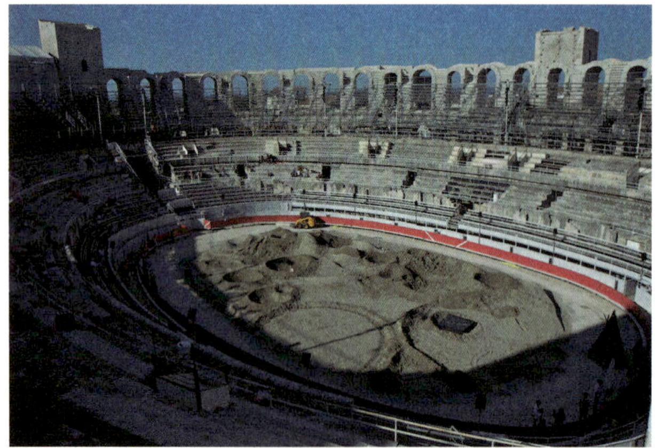
7/7/12—6:26:04 PM

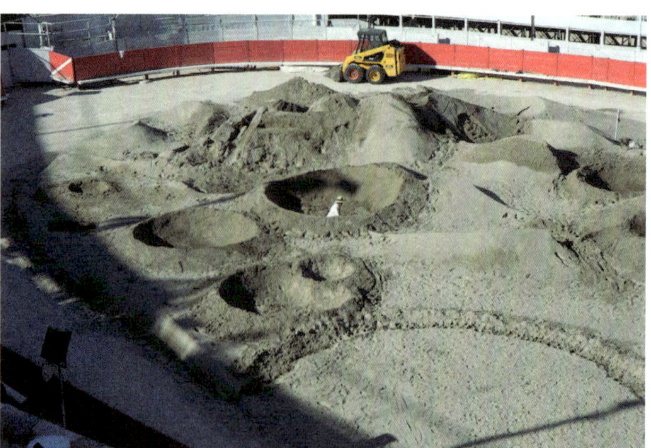
7/7/12—6:27:30 PM

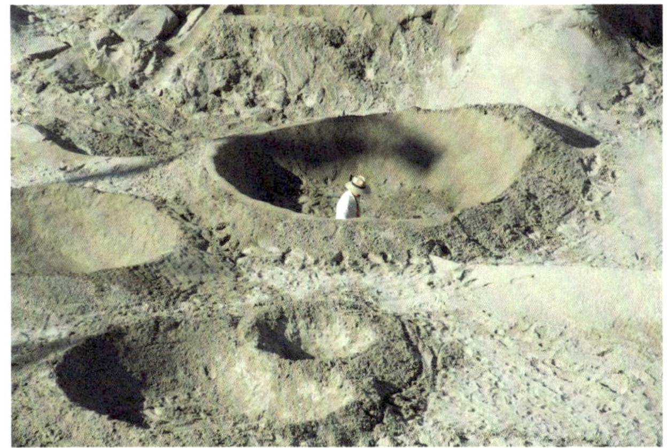
7/7/12—6:28:03 PM

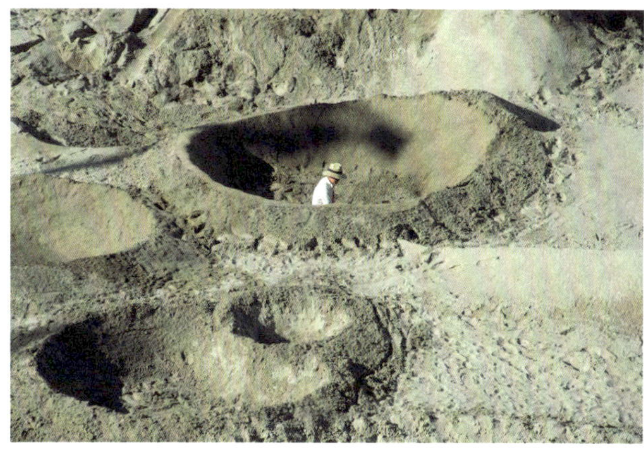
7/7/12—6:28:10 PM

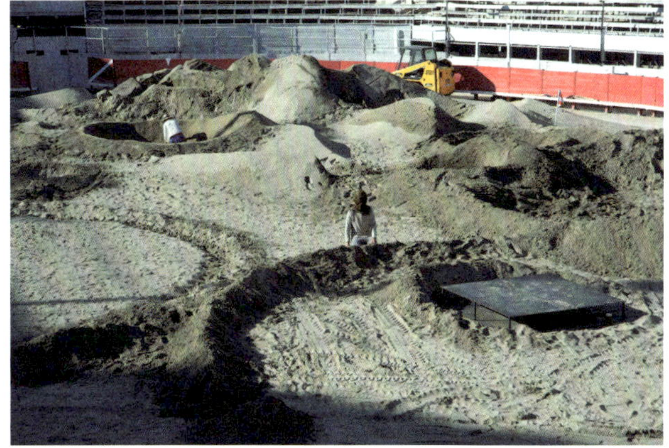
7/7/12—6:41:18 PM

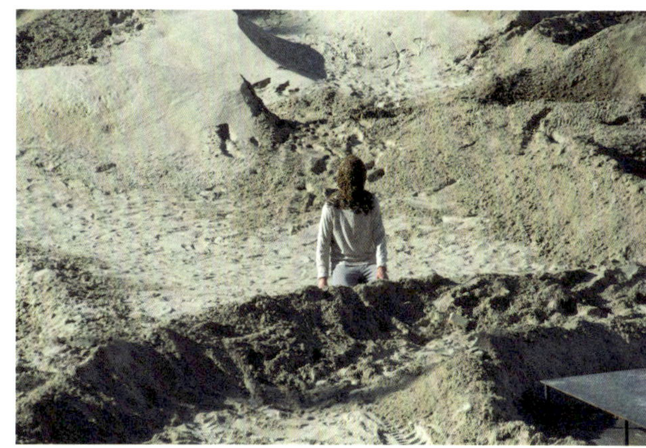
7/7/12—6:41:39 PM

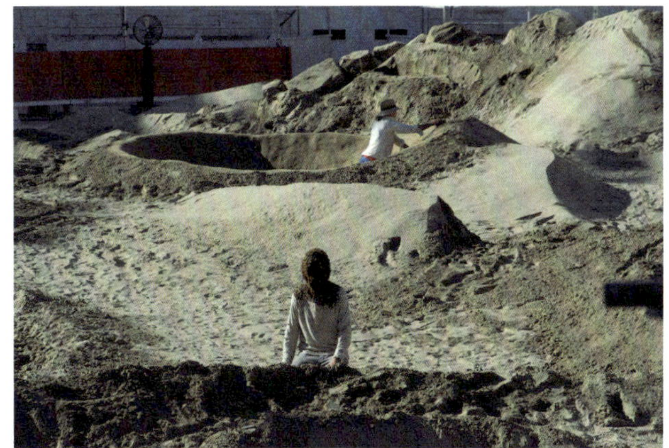
7/7/12—6:42:15 PM

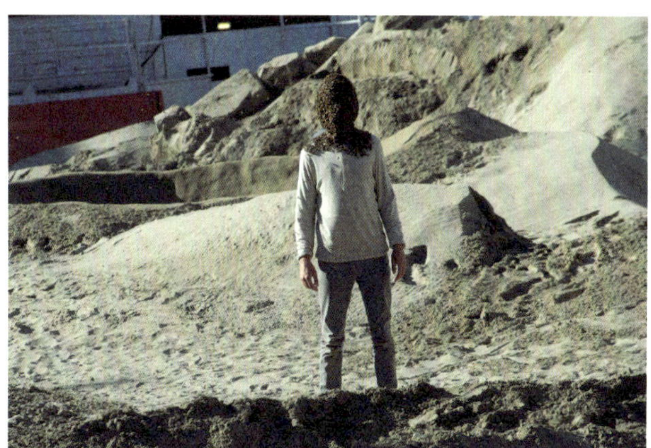
7/7/12—6:42:48 PM

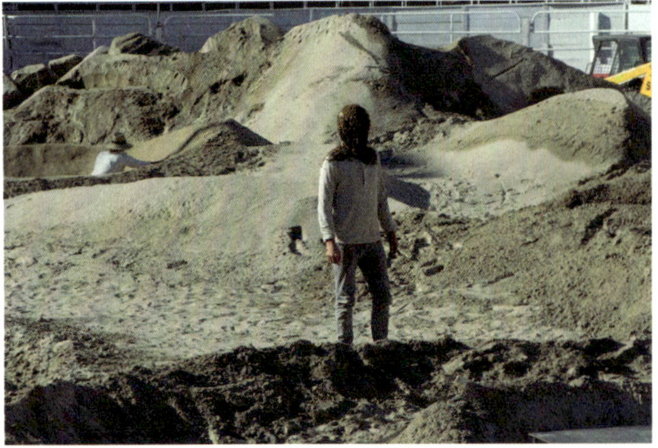

7/7/12—6:43:06 PM

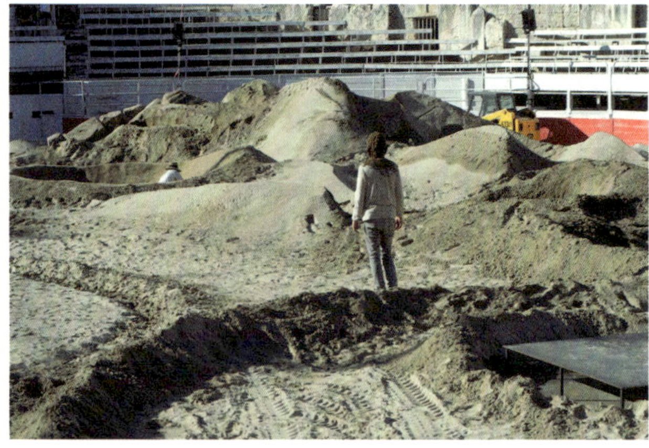

7/7/12—6:43:17 PM

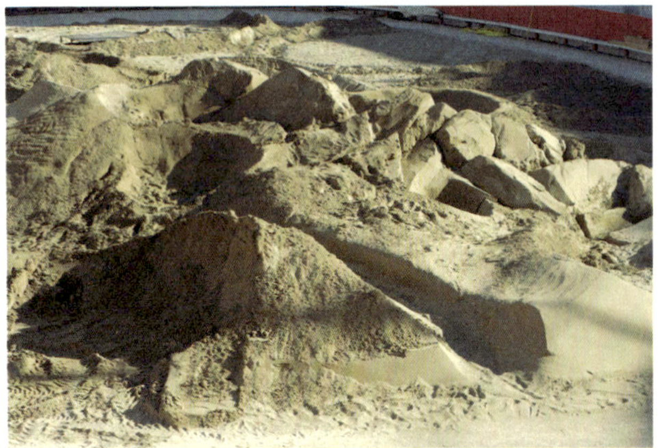

7/7/12—6:46:17 PM

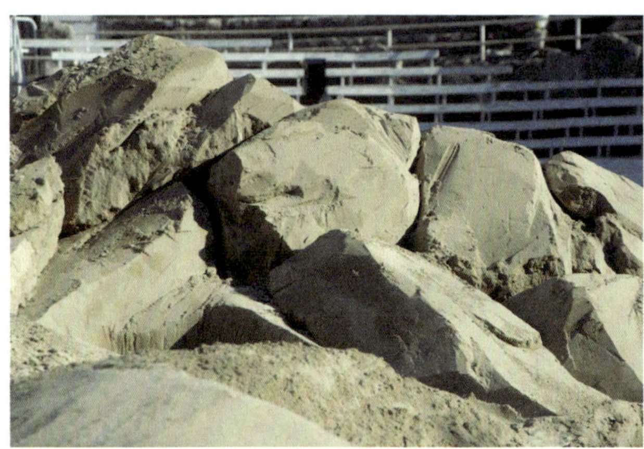

7/7/12—6:49:08 PM

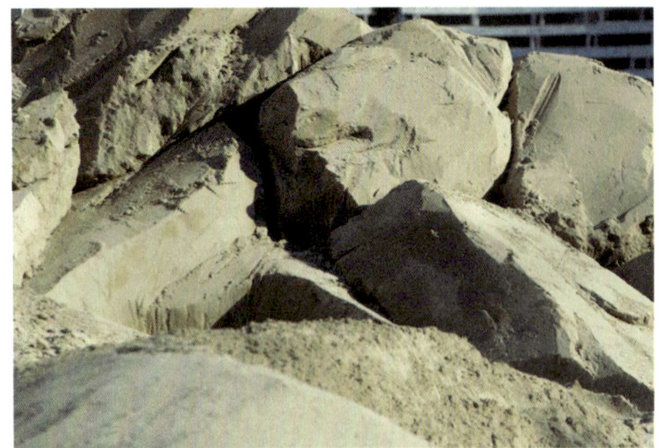

7/7/12—6:49:09 PM

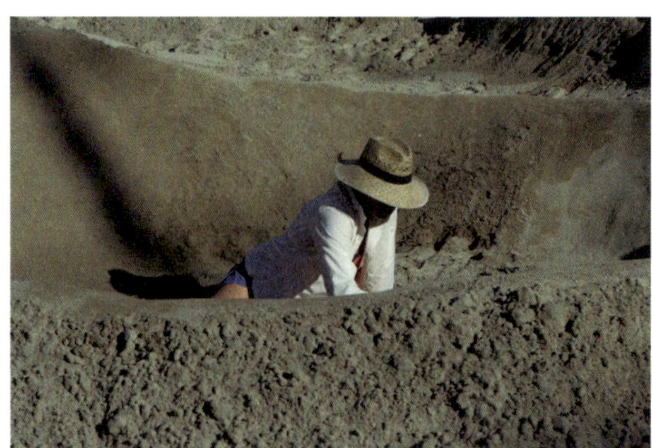

7/7/12—6:50:10 PM

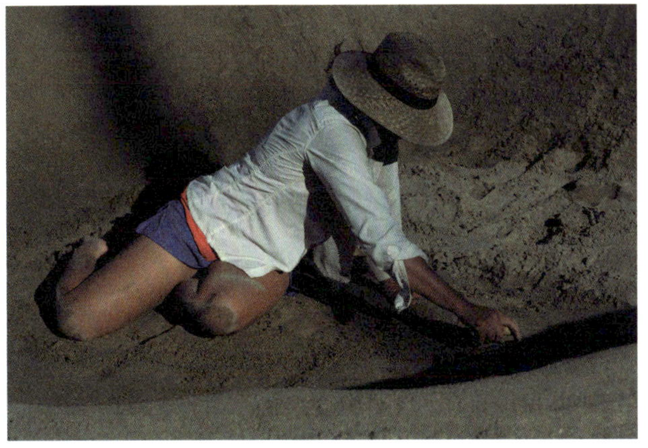

7/7/12—6:50:21 PM

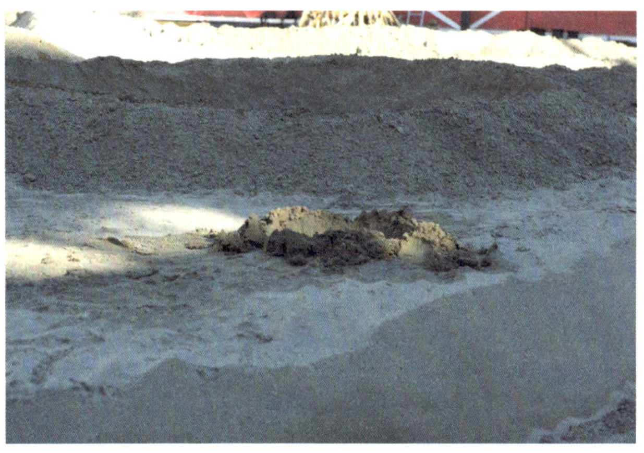

7/7/12—6:50:59 PM

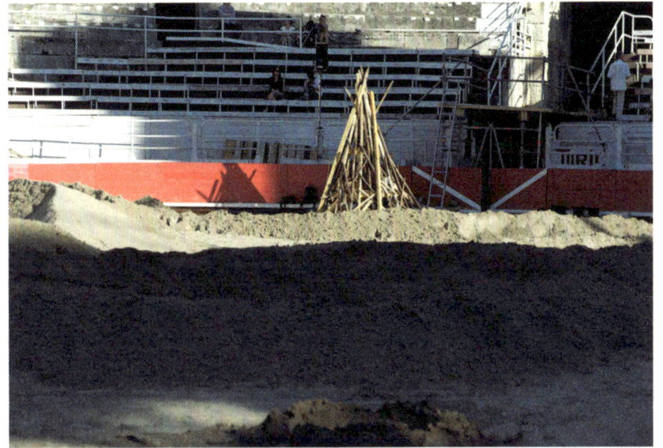

7/7/12—6:51:01 PM

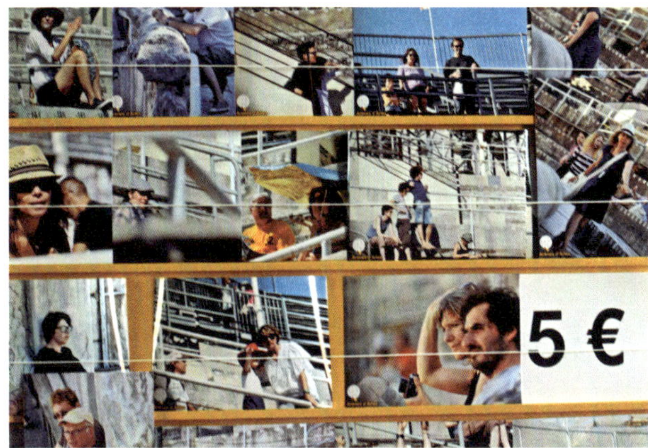

7/7/12—6:51:37 PM

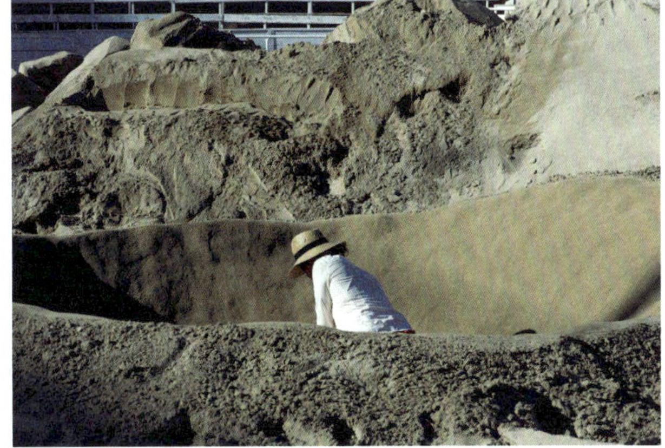

7/7/12—6:51:44 PM

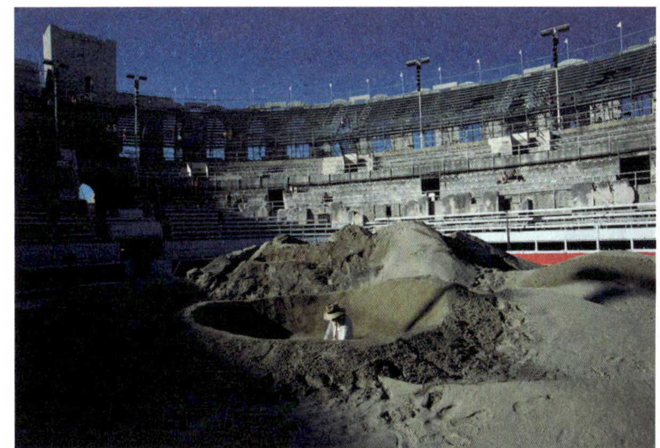

7/7/12—6:52:07 PM

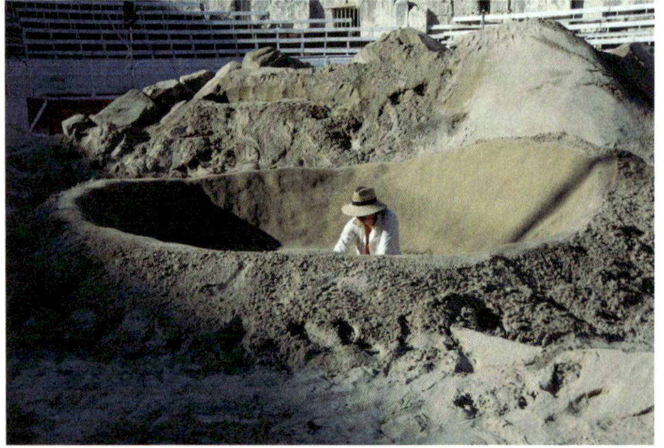
7/7/12—6:52:10 PM

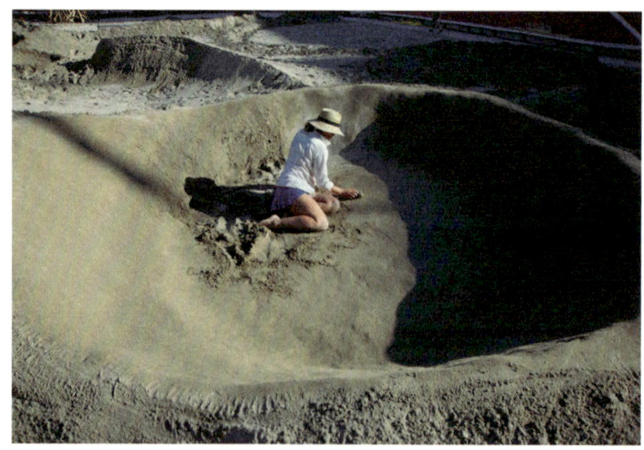
7/7/12—6:52:37 PM

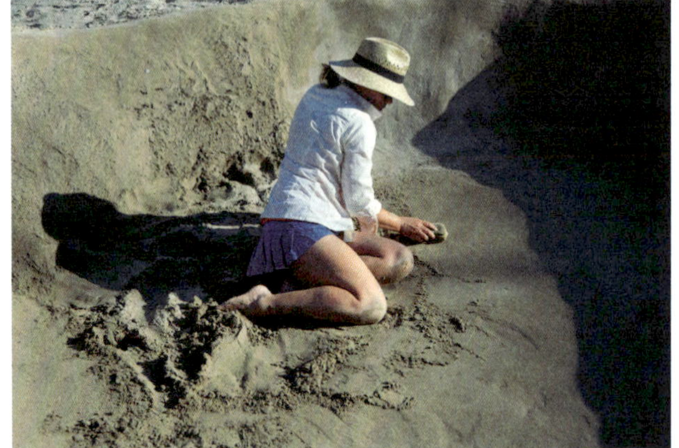
7/7/12—6:52:40 PM

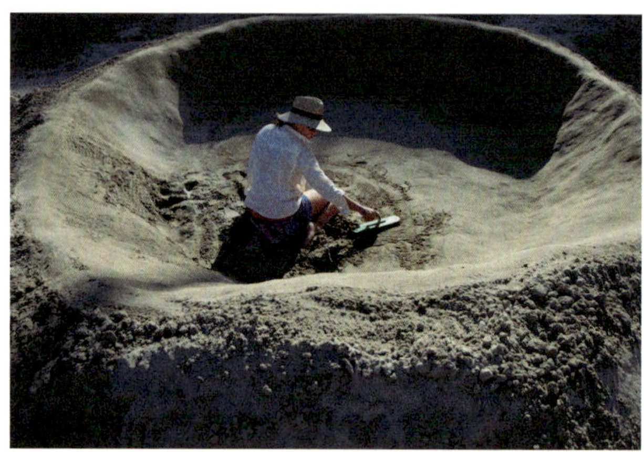
7/7/12—6:52:56 PM

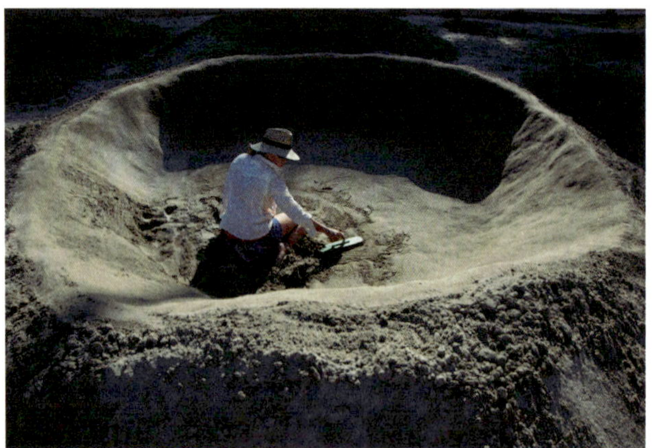
7/7/12—6:52:57 PM

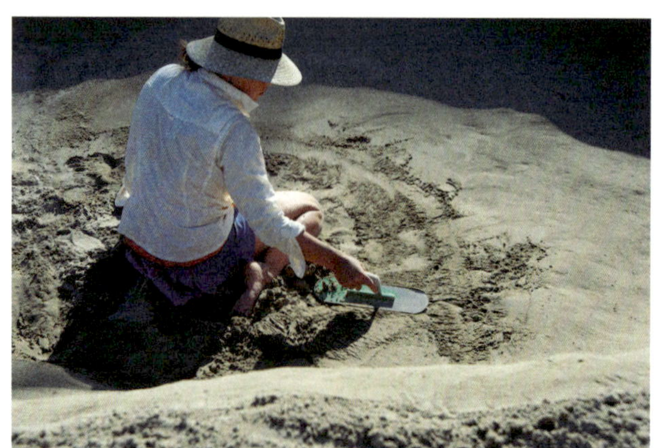
7/7/12—6:52:58 PM

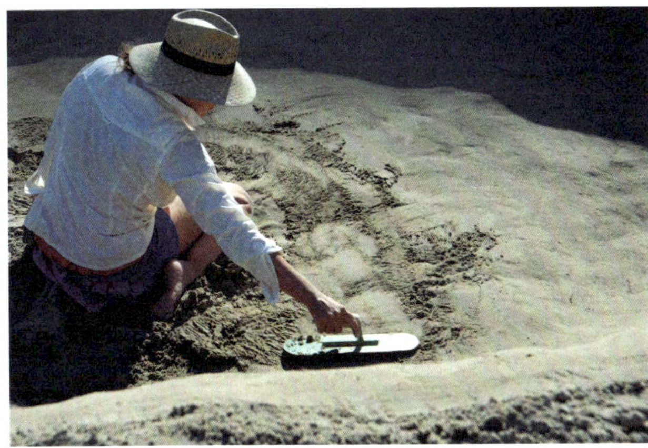

7/7/12—6:52:59 PM

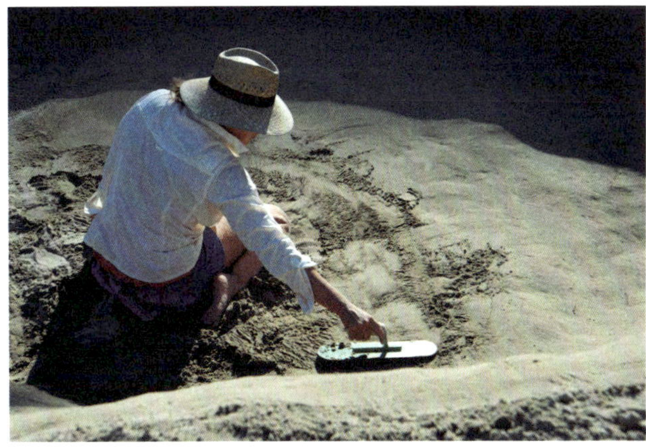

7/7/12—6:53:01 PM

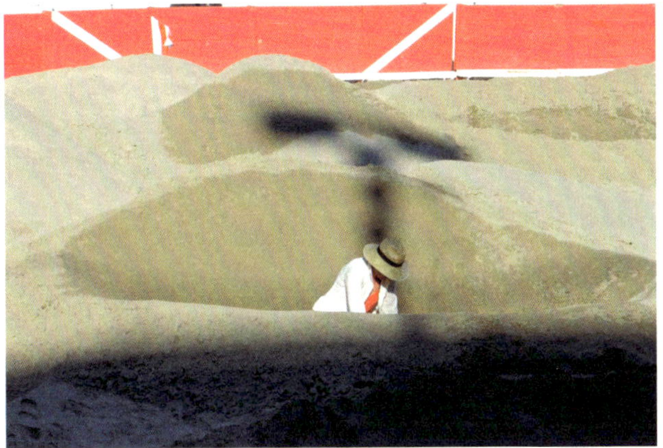

7/7/12—6:53:59 PM

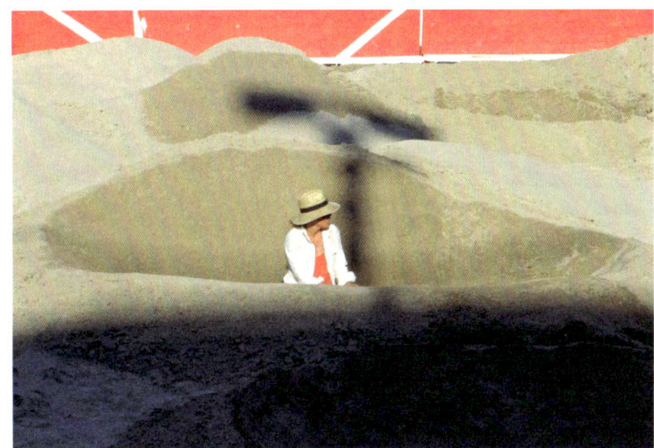

7/7/12—6:54:04 PM

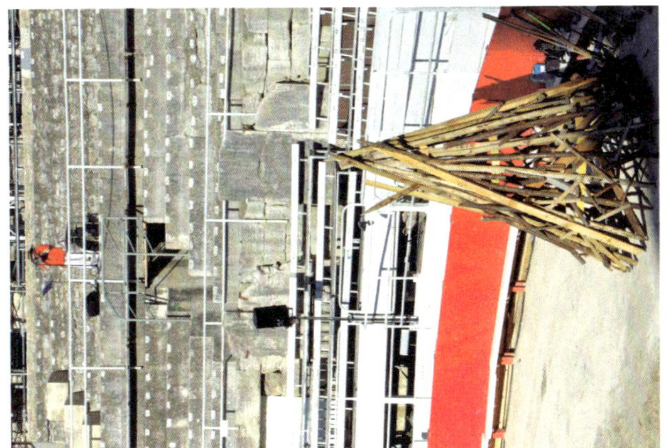

7/7/12—6:56:52 PM

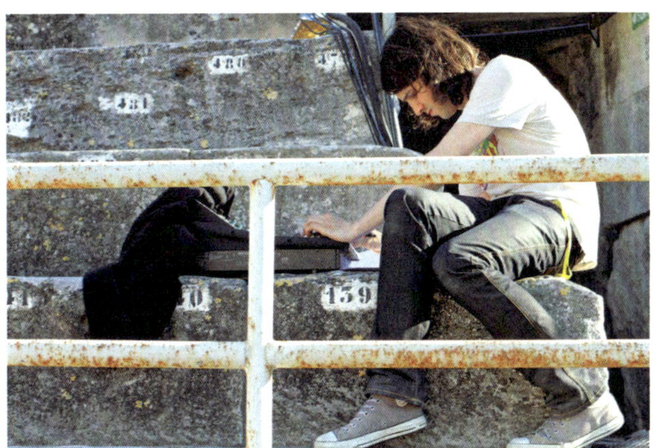

7/7/12—6:57:41 PM

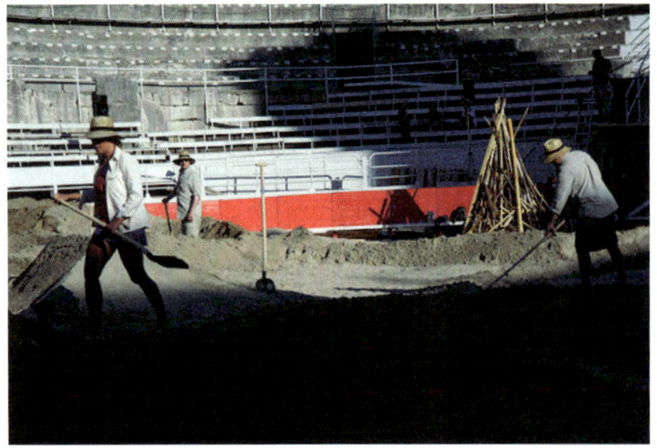

7/7/12—6:57:43 PM

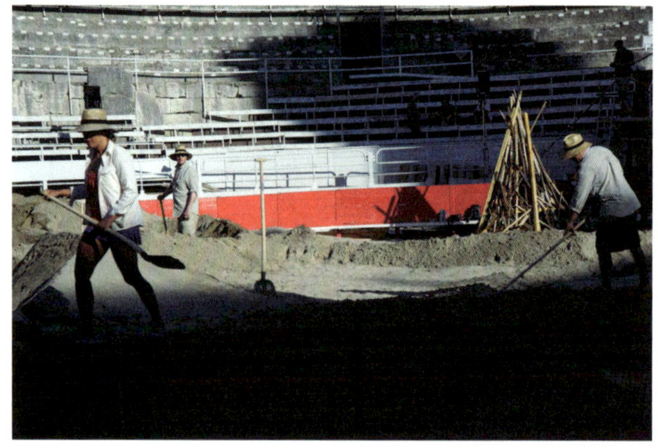

7/7/12—6:57:44 PM

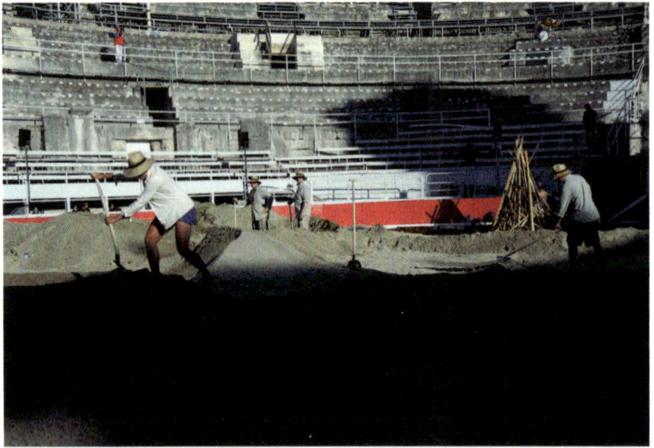

7/7/12—6:57:45 PM

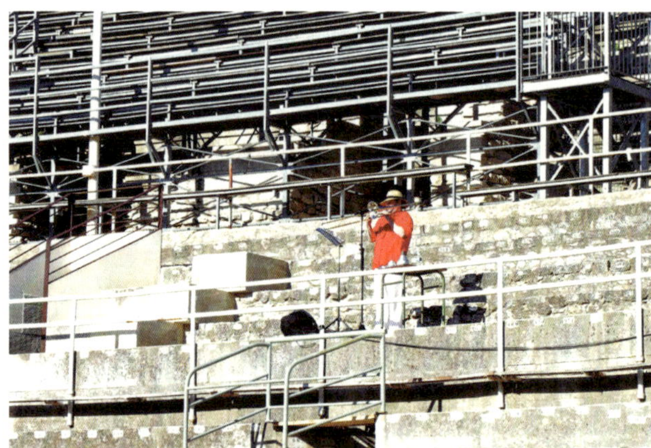

7/7/12—6:58:09 PM

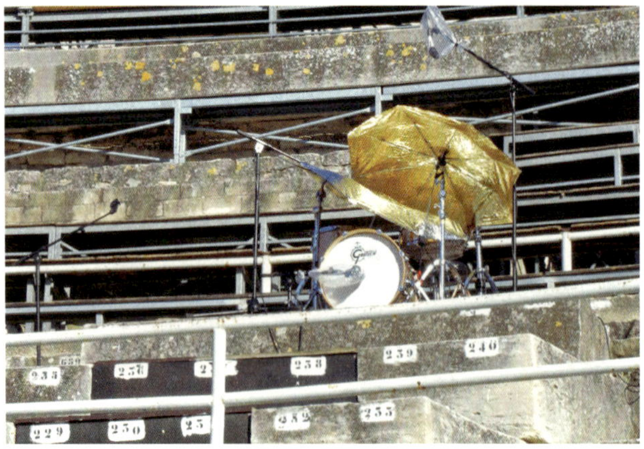

7/7/12—6:59:16 PM

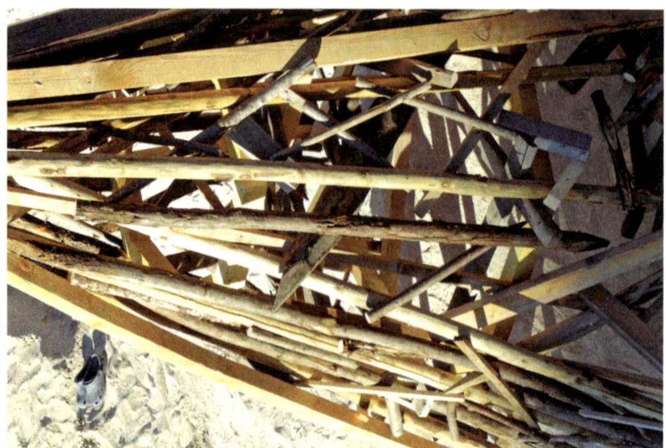

7/7/12—6:59:44 PM

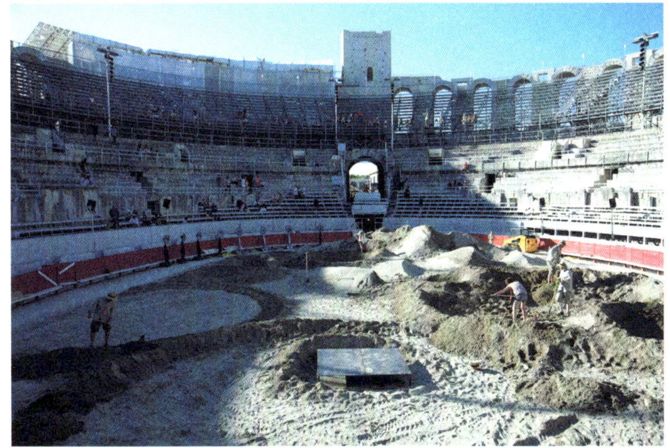

7/7/12—7:00:57 PM

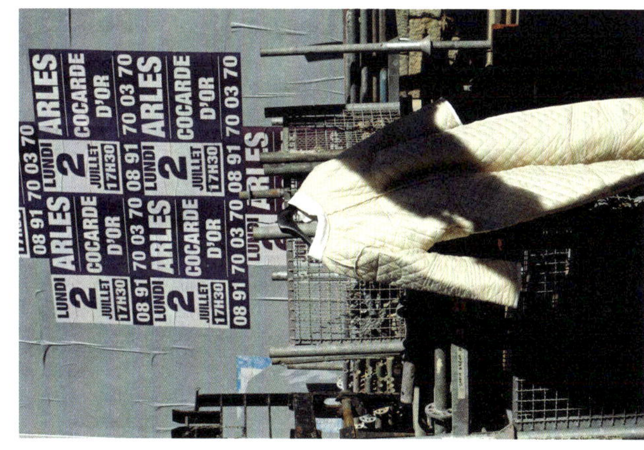

7/7/12—7:08:01 PM

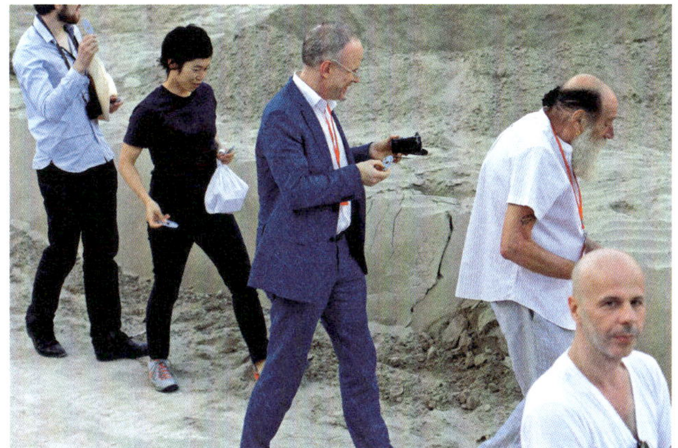

7/7/12—8:28:27 PM

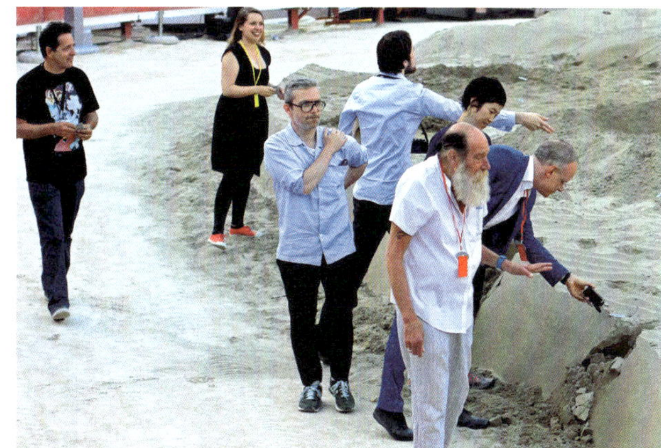

7/7/12—8:28:41 PM

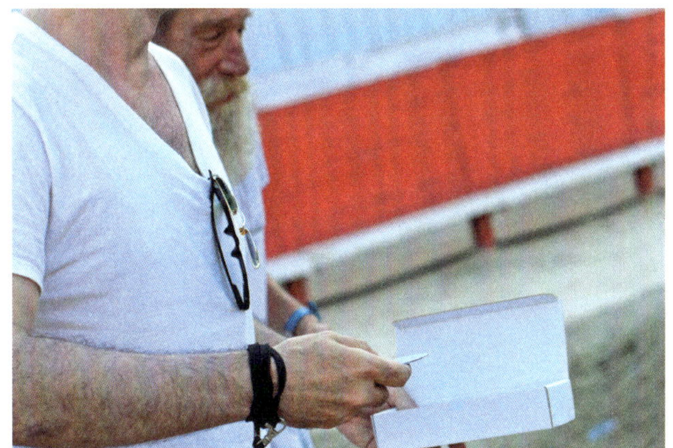

7/7/12—8:29:56 PM

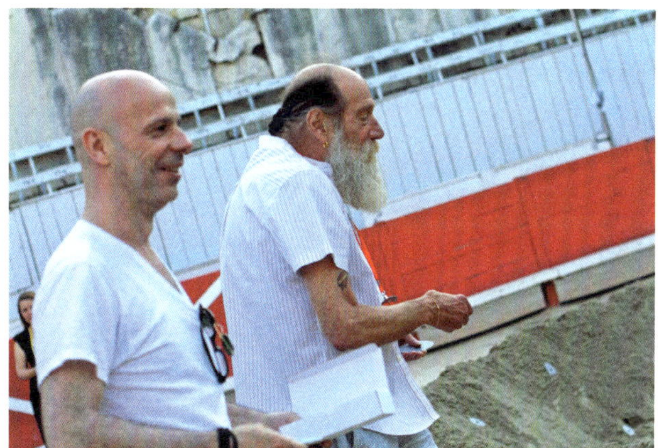

7/7/12—8:30:01 PM

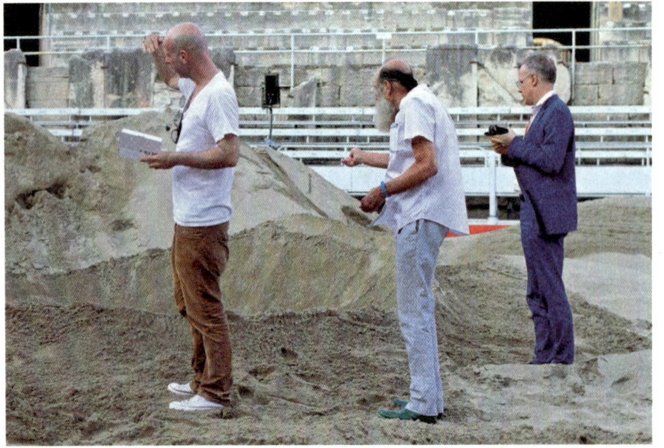

7/7/12—8:30:41 PM

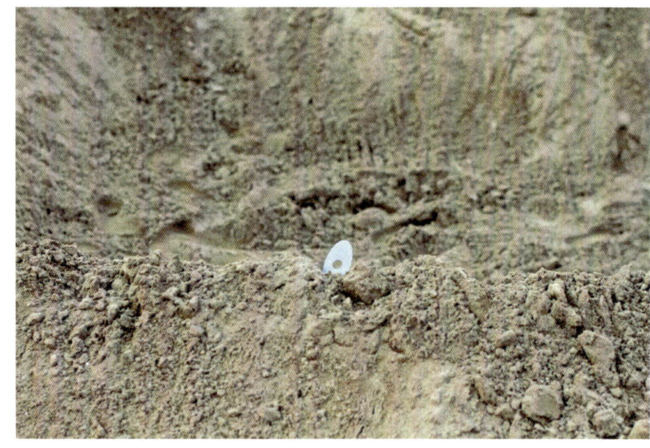

7/7/12—8:30:45 PM

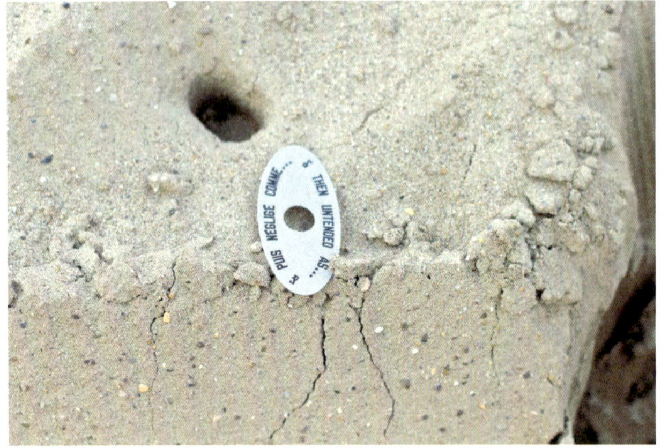

7/7/12—8:31:31 PM

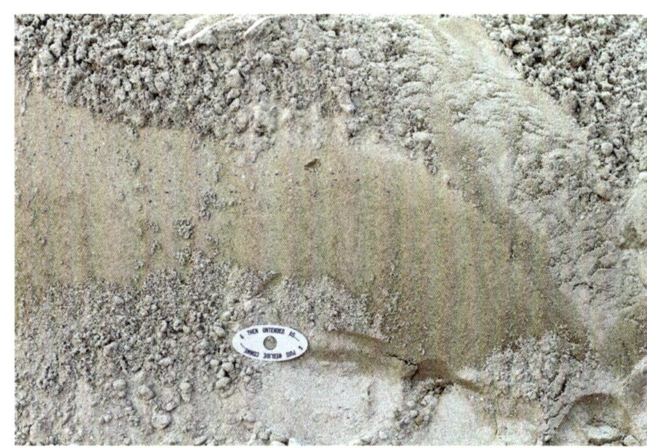

7/7/12—8:31:49 PM

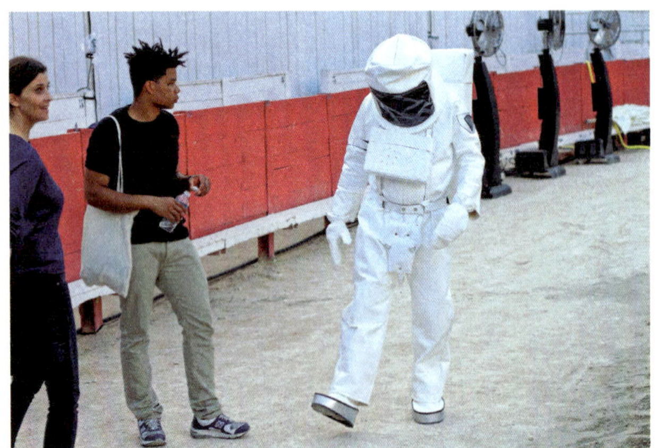

7/7/12—8:33:12 PM

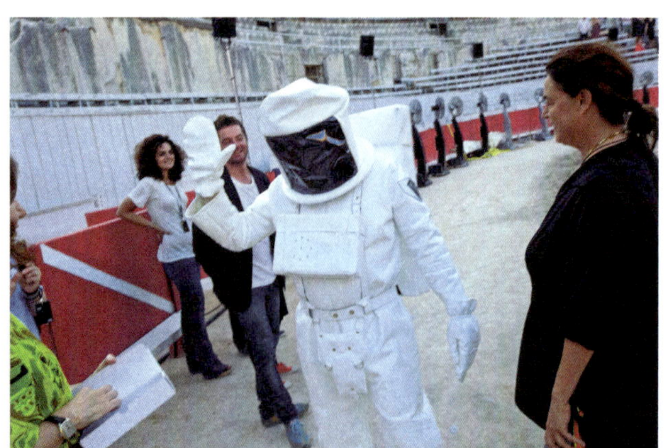

7/7/12—8:33:25 PM

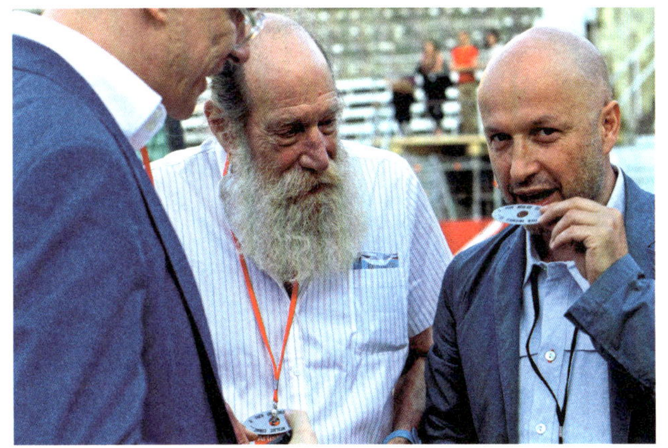
7/7/12—8:33:37 PM

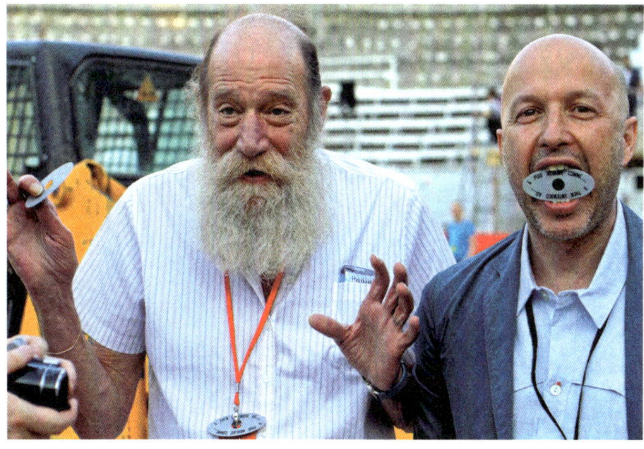
7/7/12—8:33:41 PM

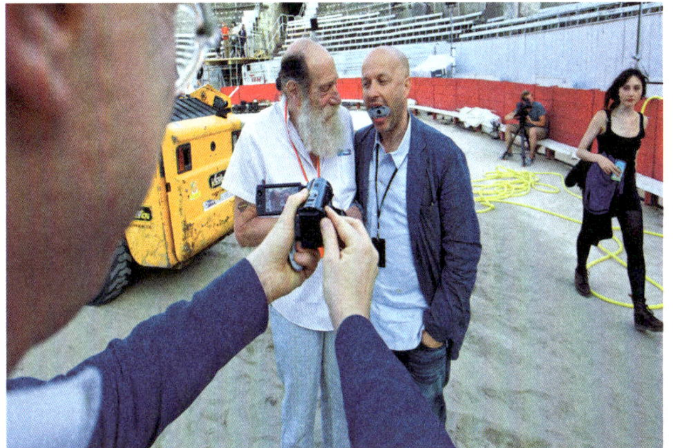
7/7/12—8:33:55 PM

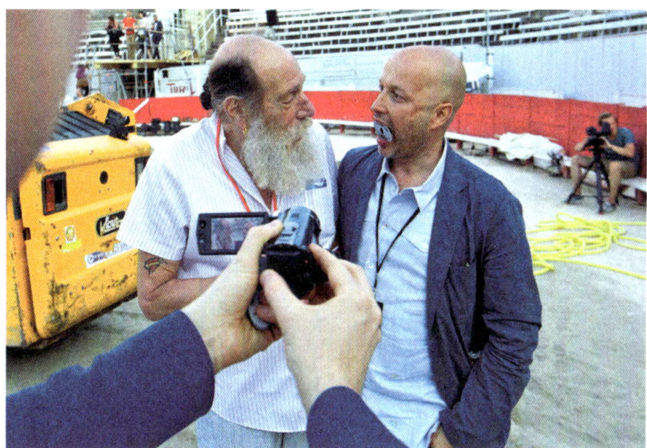
7/7/12—8:33:58 PM

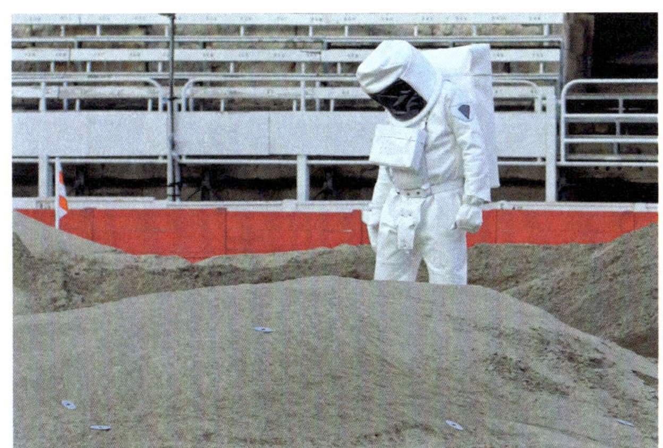
7/7/12—8:34:18 PM

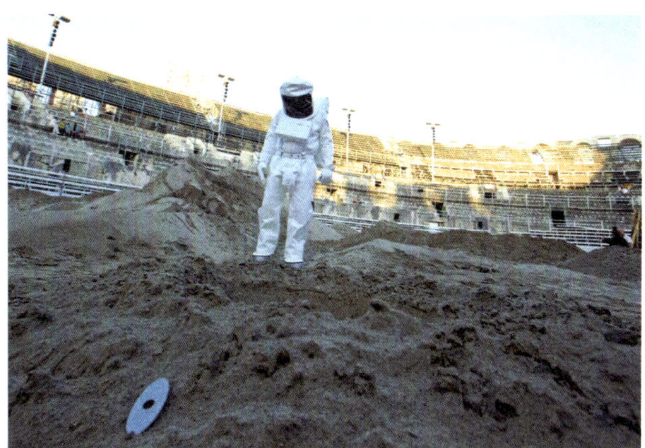
7/7/12—8:35:38 PM

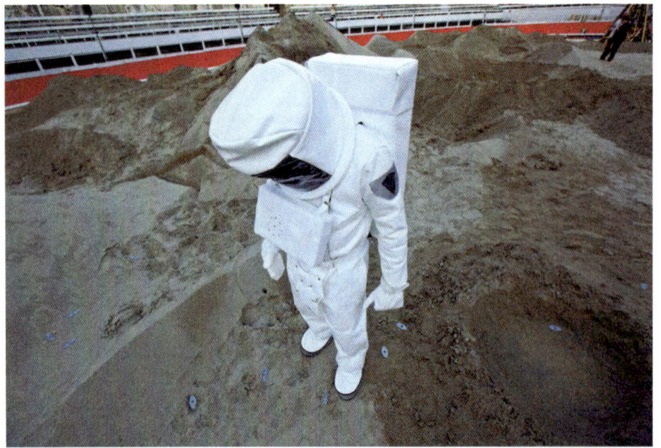

7/7/12—8:35:47 PM

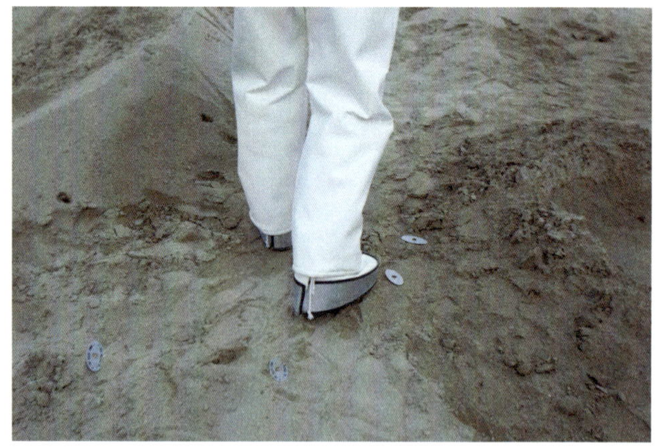

7/7/12—8:35:53 PM

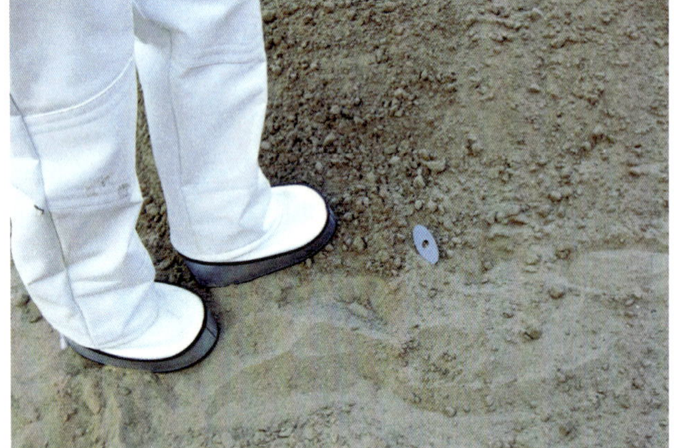

7/7/12—8:36:19 PM

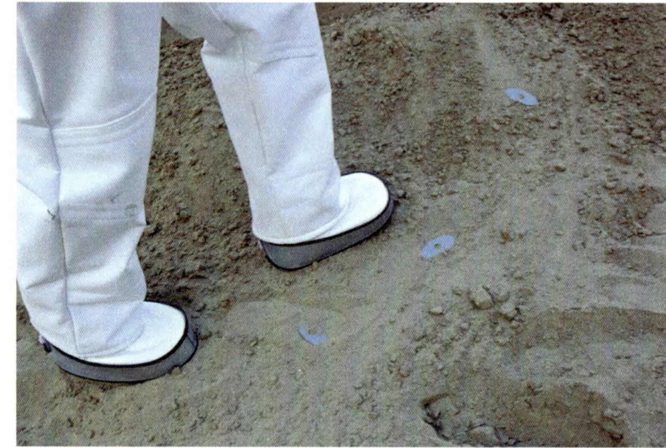

7/7/12—8:36:20 PM

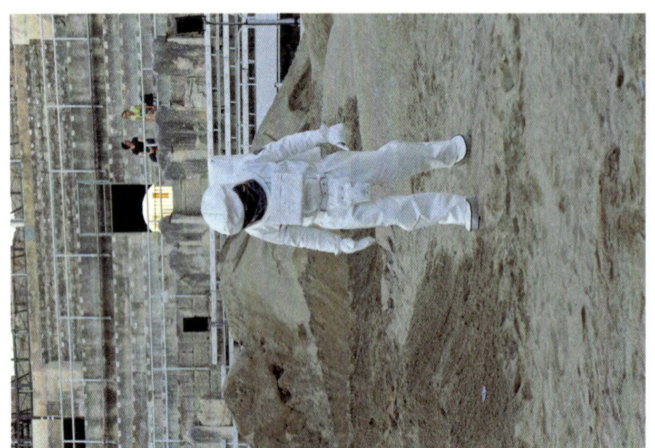

7/7/12—8:36:41 PM

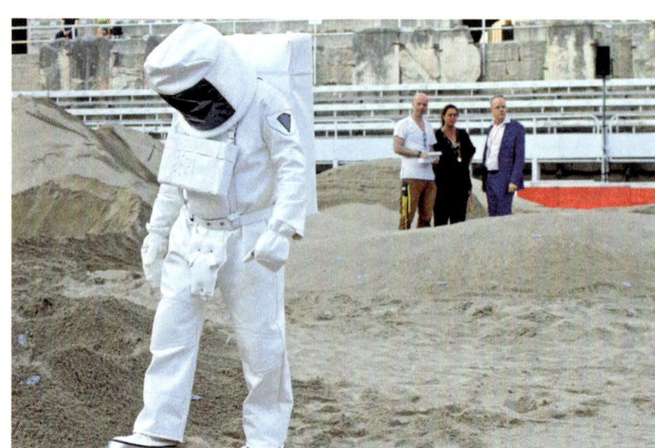

7/7/12—8:36:46 PM

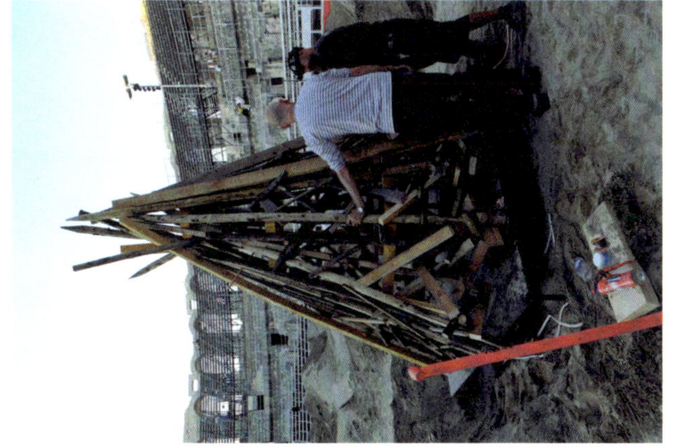

7/7/12—8:38:05 PM

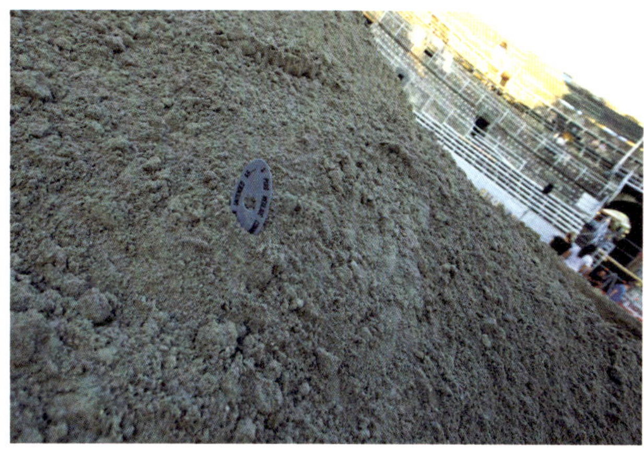

7/7/12—8:38:15 PM

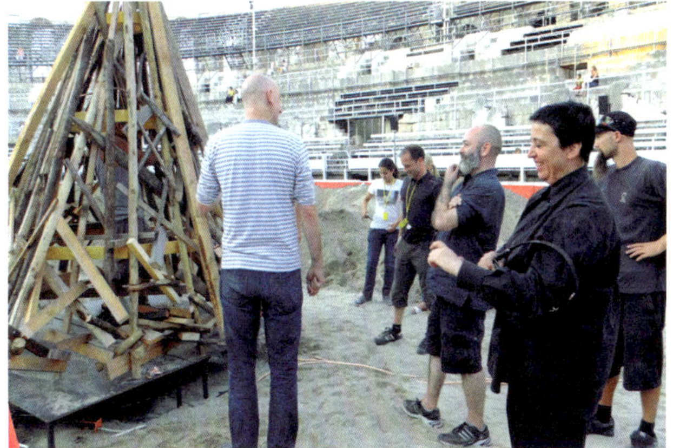

7/7/12—8:38:17 PM

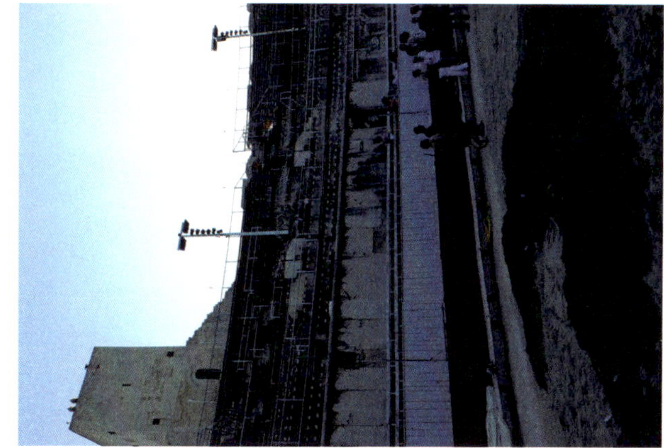

7/7/12—8:38:26 PM

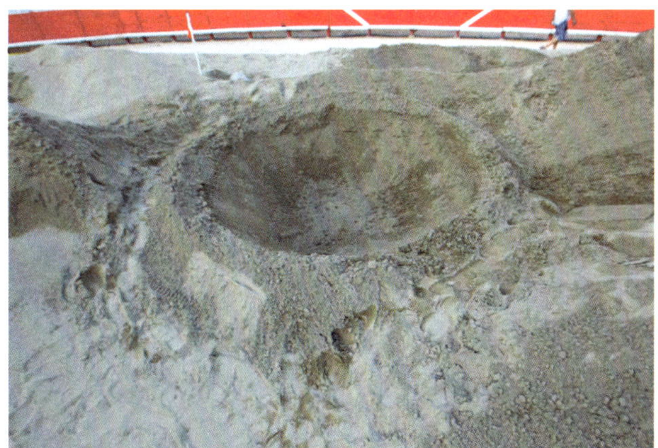

7/7/12—8:38:30 PM

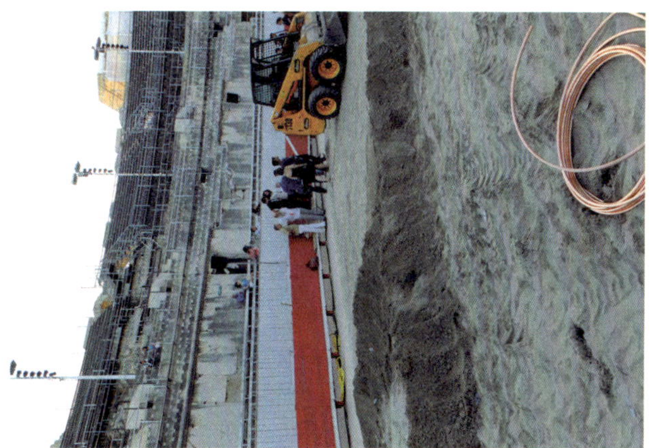

7/7/12—8:38:31 PM

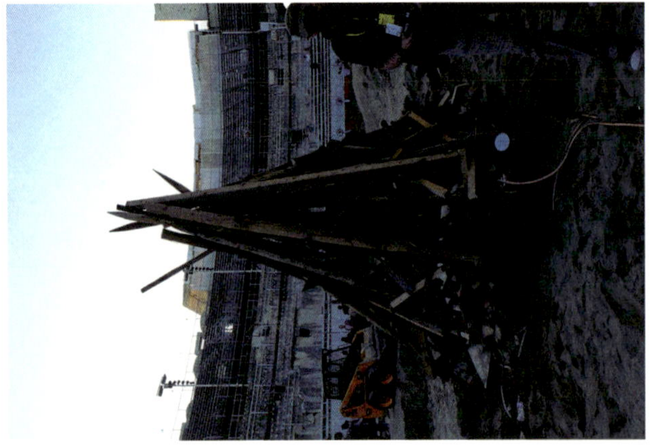

7/7/12—8:38:42 PM

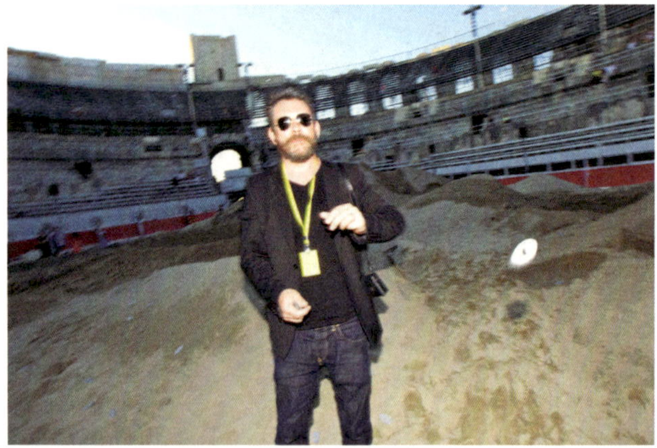

7/7/12—8:39:58 PM

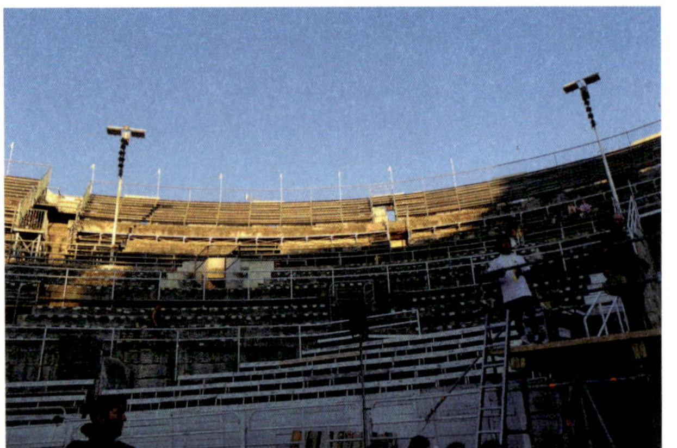

7/7/12—8:40:09 PM

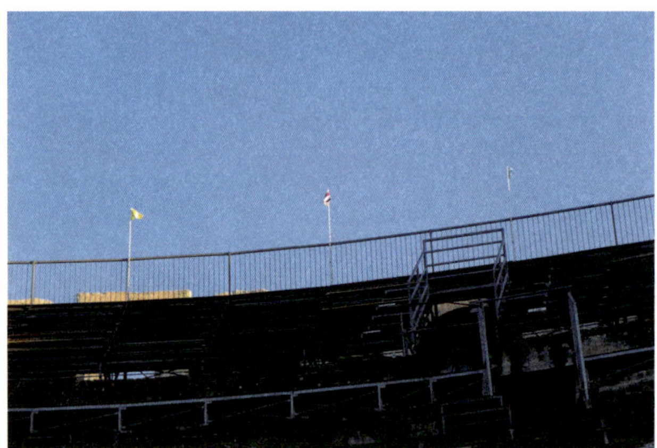

7/7/12—8:40:18 PM

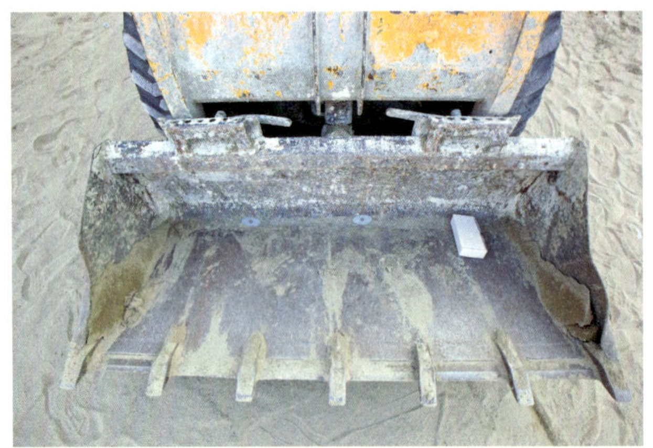

7/7/12—8:40:35 PM

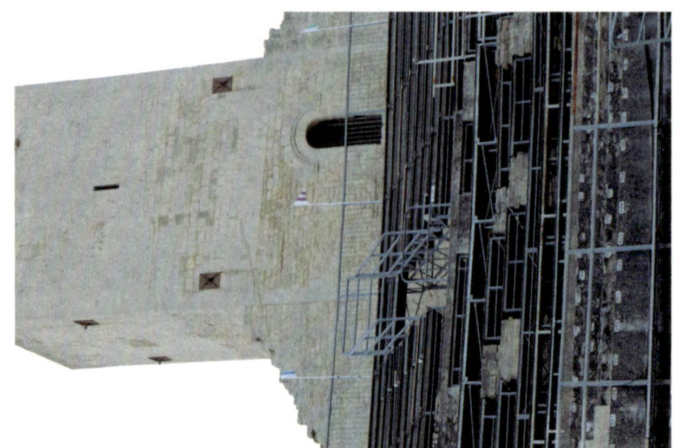

7/7/12—8:41:01 PM

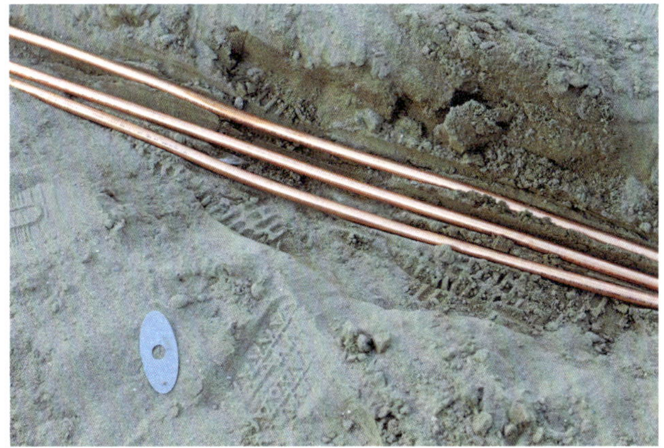

7/7/12—8:41:52 PM

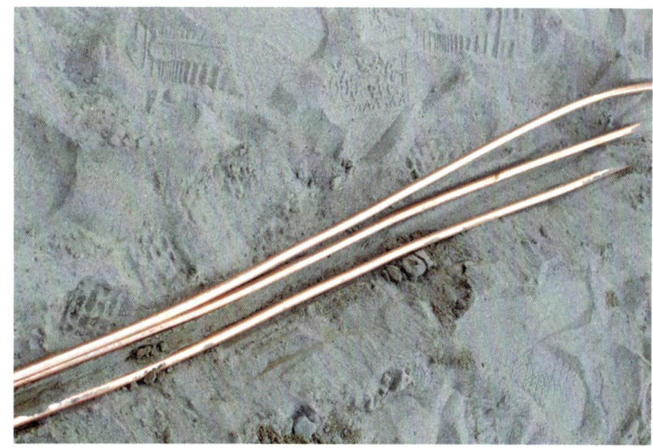

7/7/12—8:42:05 PM

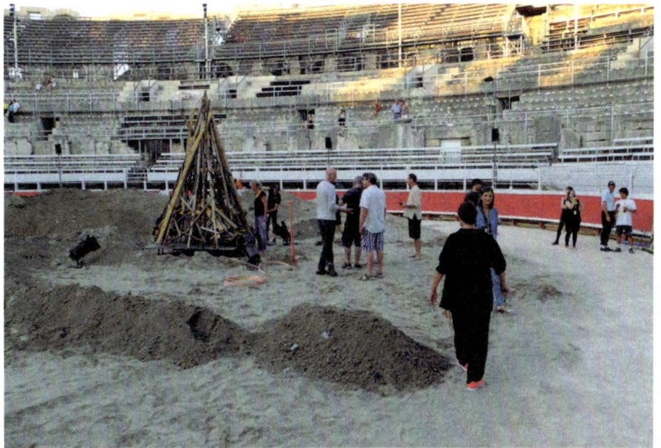

7/7/12—8:43:22 PM

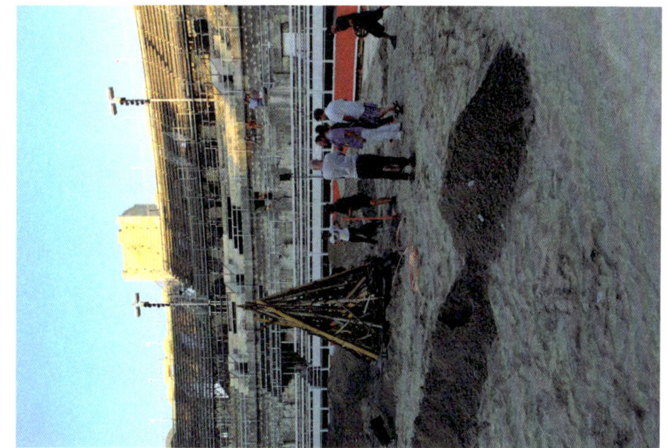

7/7/12—8:43:35 PM

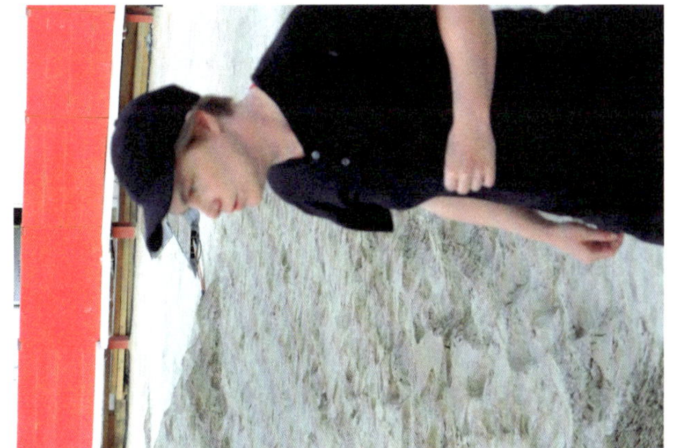

7/7/12—8:43:44 PM

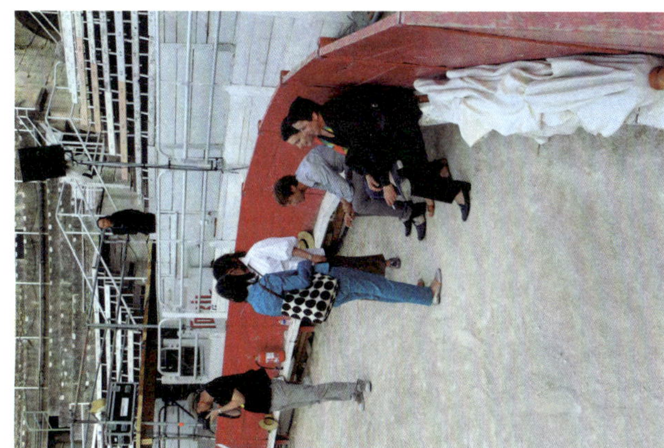

7/7/12—8:43:50 PM

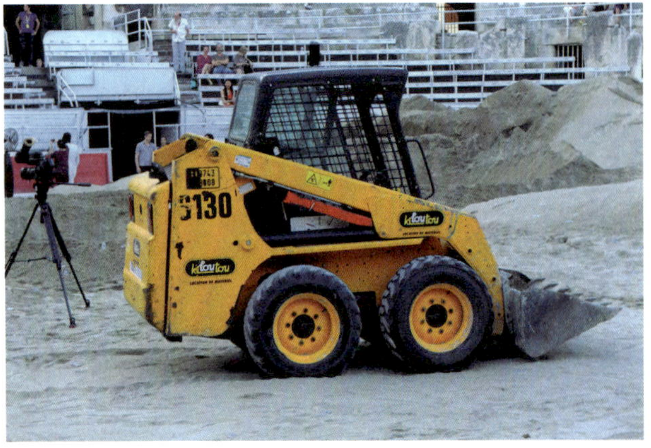

7/7/12—8:44:29 PM

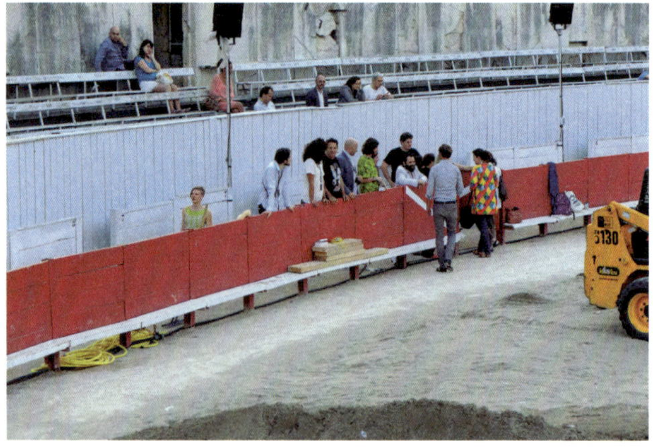

7/7/12—8:46:28 PM

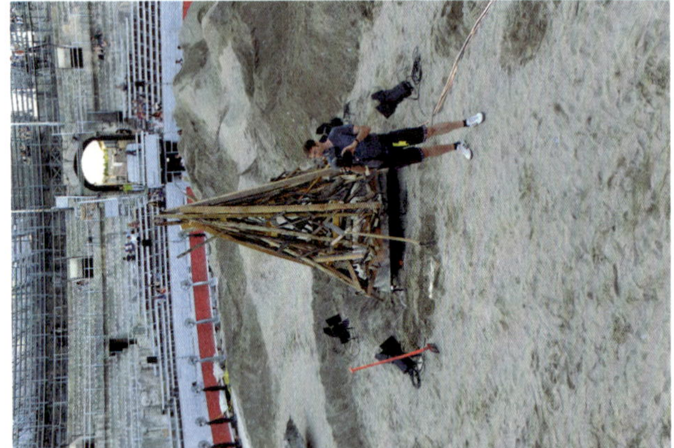

7/7/12—8:47:27 PM

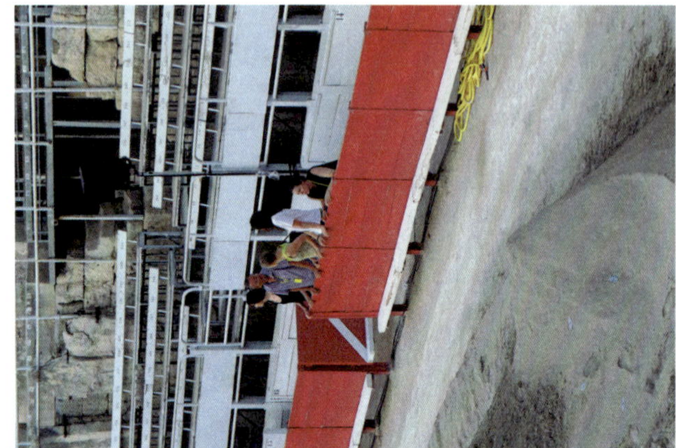

7/7/12—8:47:45 PM

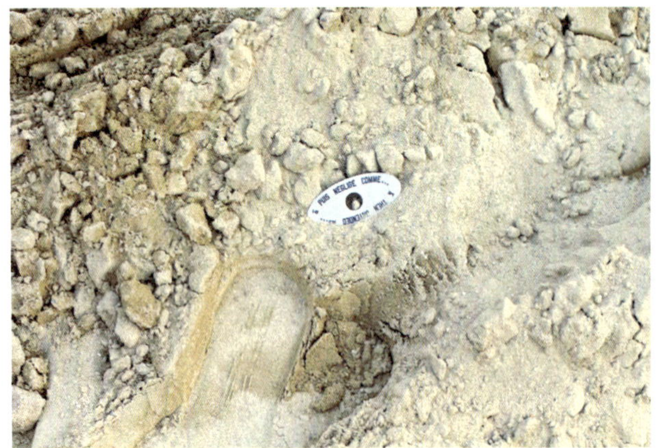

7/7/12—8:48:00 PM

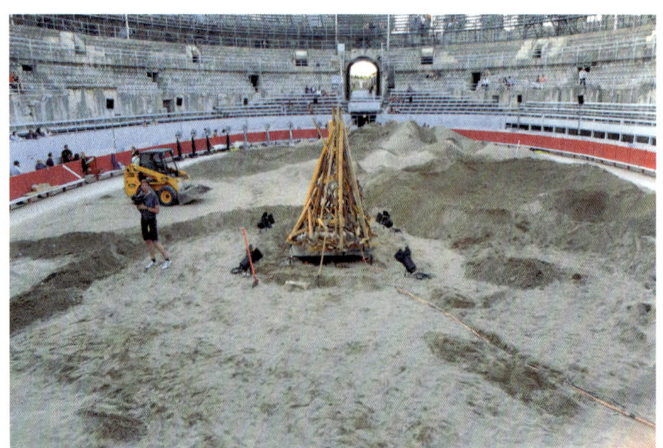

7/7/12—8:48:21 PM

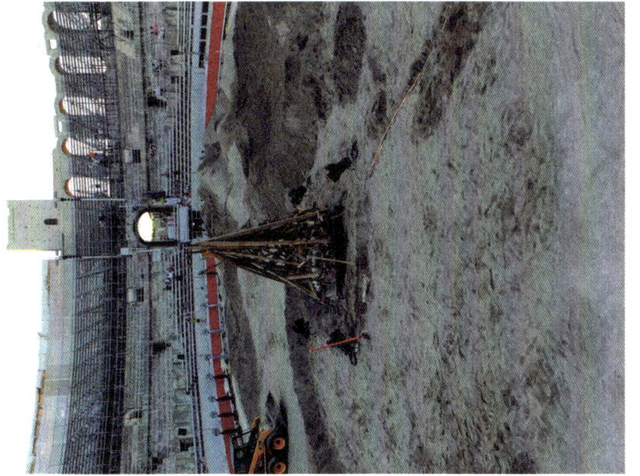
7/7/12—8:48:43 PM

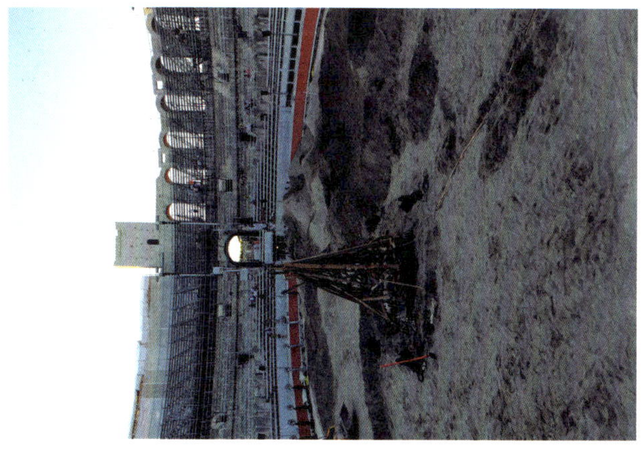
7/7/12—8:48:48 PM

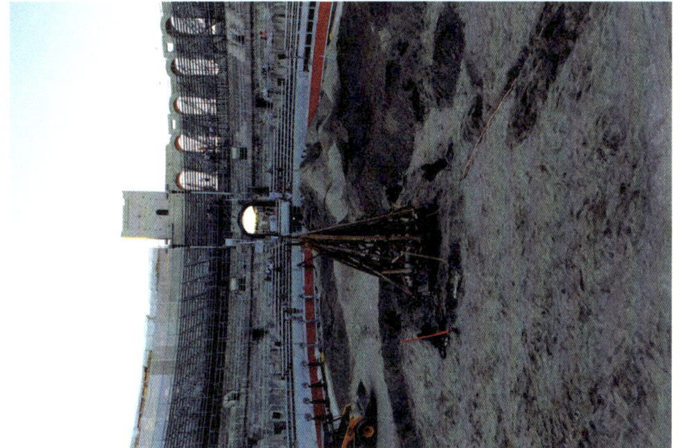
7/7/12—8:48:52 PM

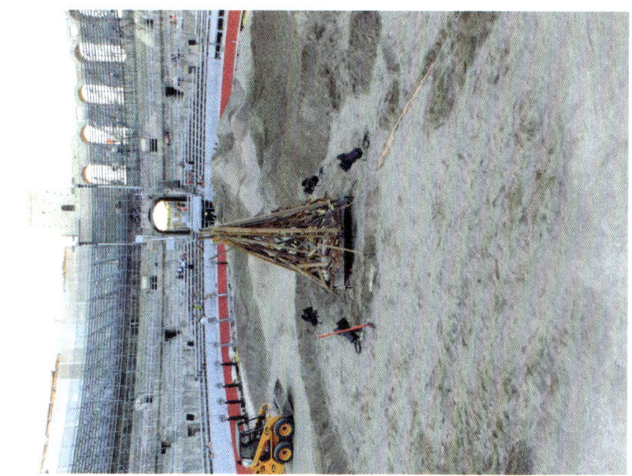
7/7/12—8:49:10 PM

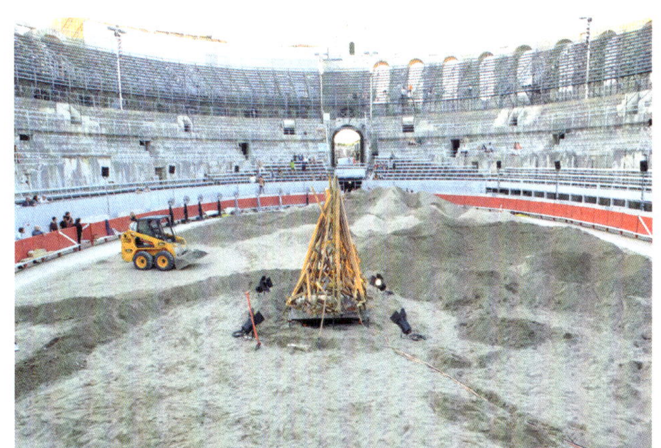
7/7/12—8:49:26 PM

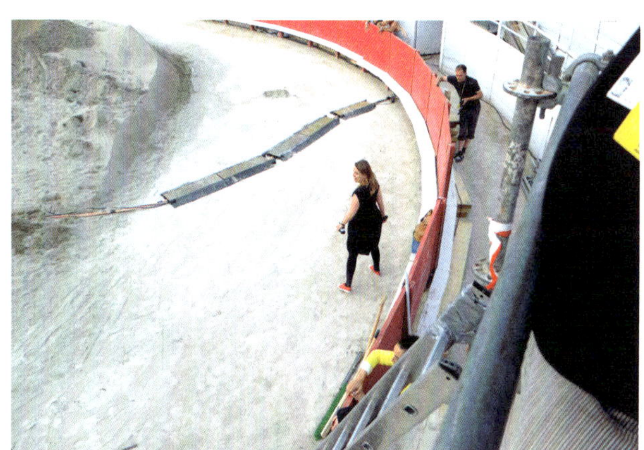
7/7/12—8:49:31 PM

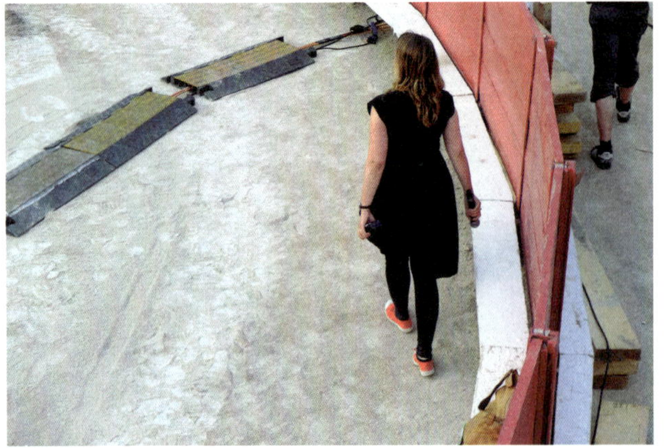

7/7/12—8:49:37 PM

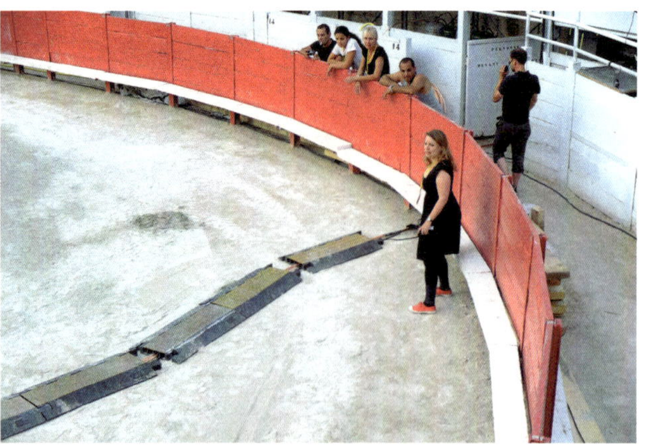

7/7/12—8:49:40 PM

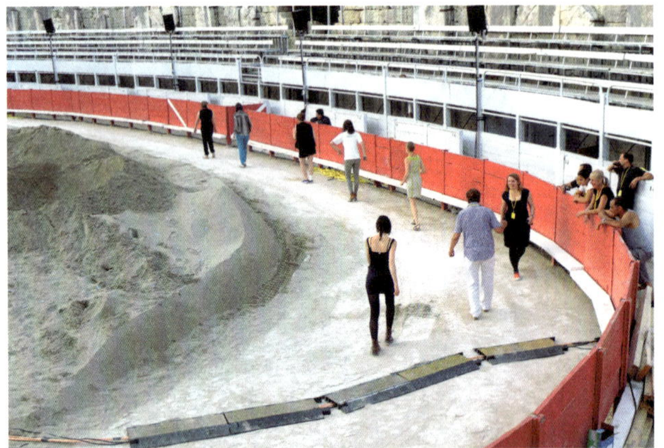

7/7/12—8:50:09 PM

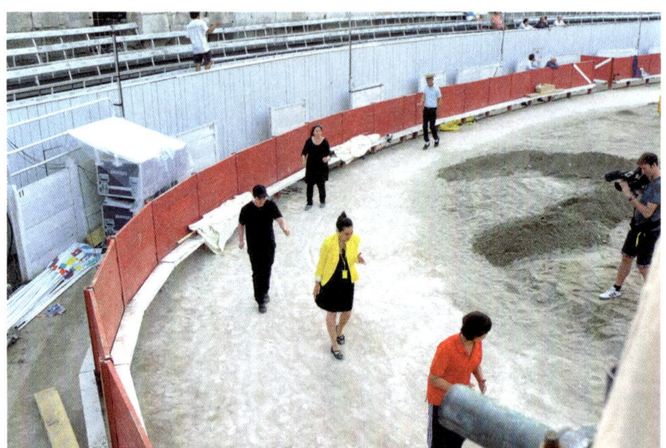

7/7/12—8:50:20 PM

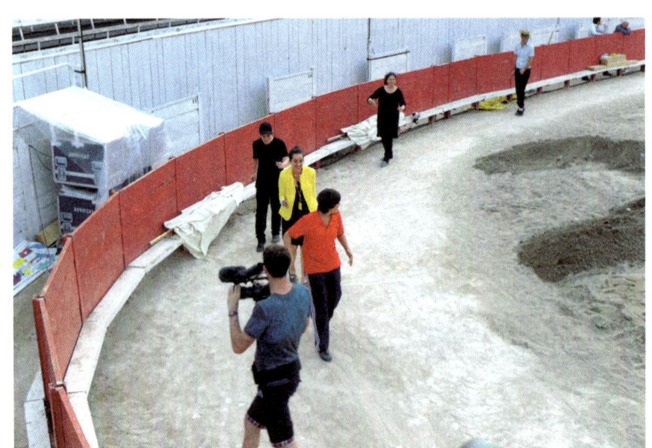

7/7/12—8:50:25 PM

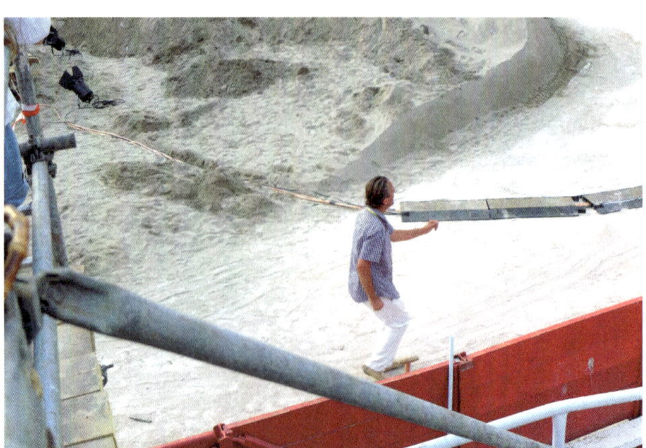

7/7/12—8:50:45 PM

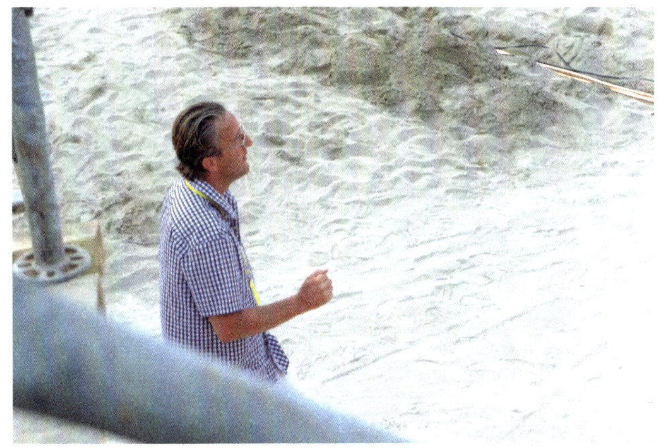
7/7/12—8:50:49 PM

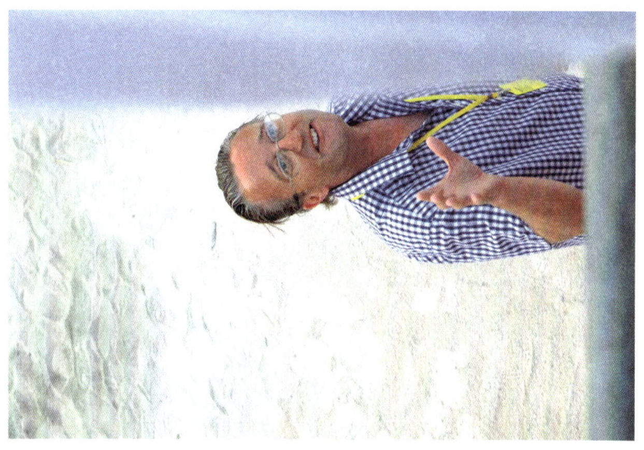
7/7/12—8:50:58 PM

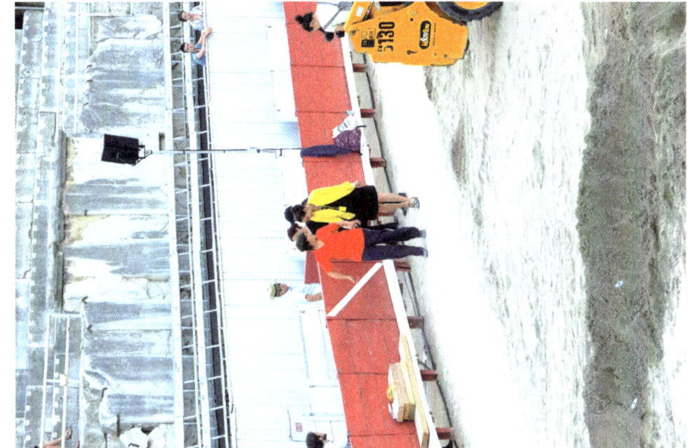
7/7/12—8:51:09 PM

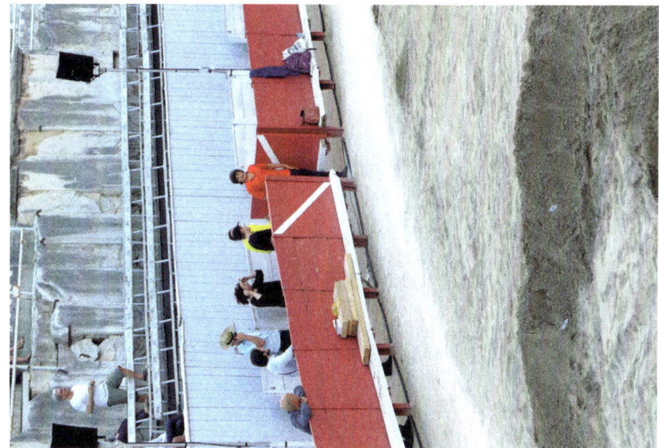
7/7/12—8:51:14 PM

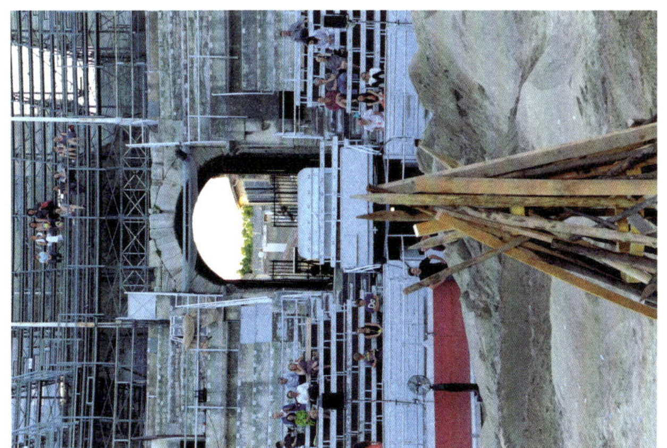
7/7/12—8:51:45 PM

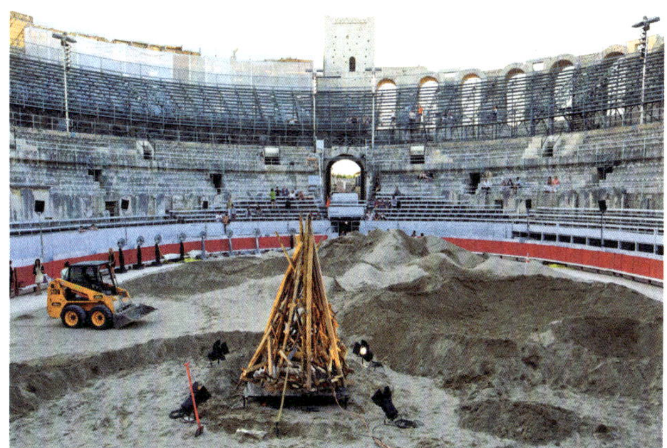
7/7/12—8:52:34 PM

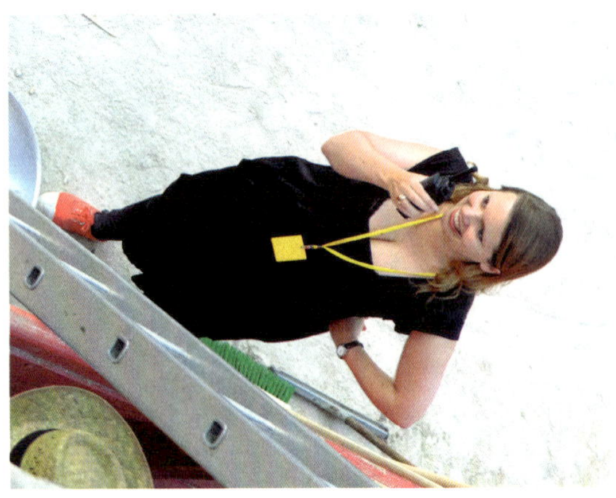
7/7/12—8:52:44 PM

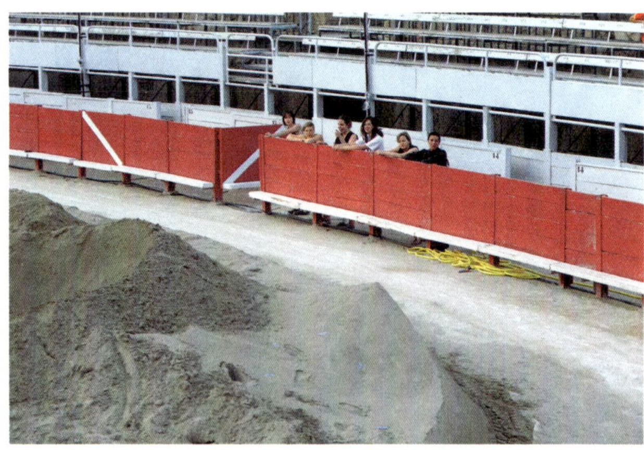
7/7/12—8:52:51 PM

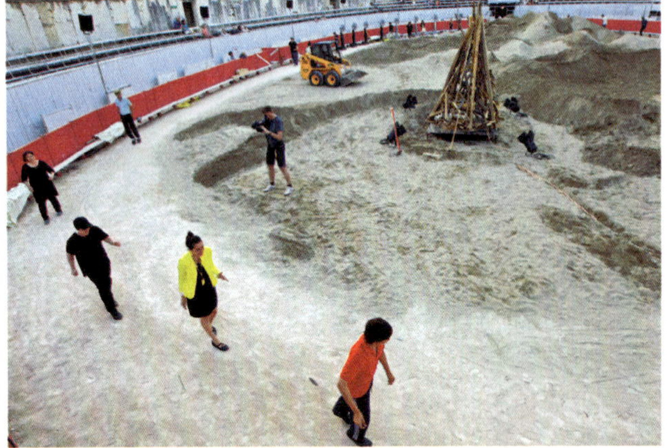
7/7/12—8:53:16 PM

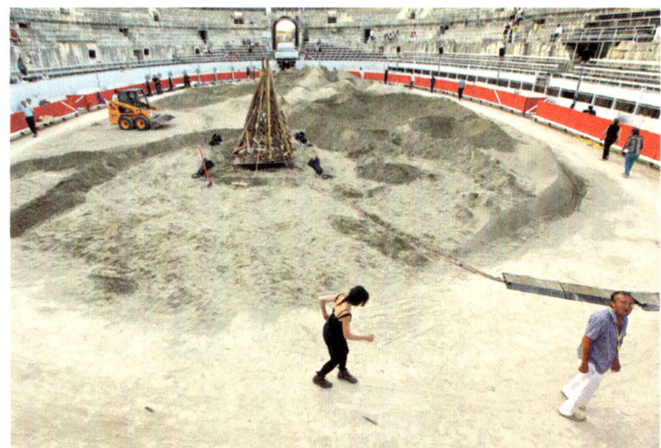
7/7/12—8:53:40 PM

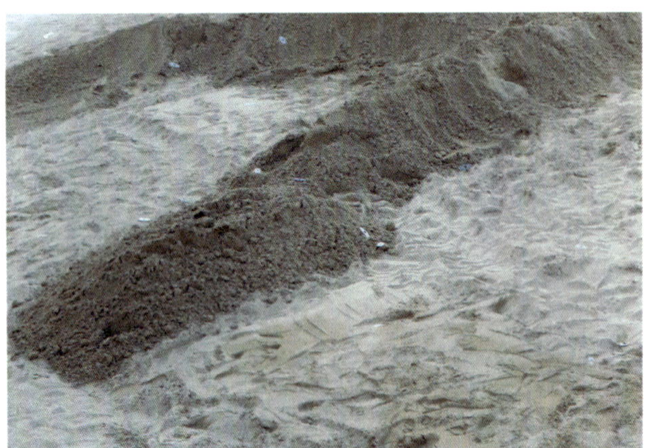
7/7/12—8:53:56 PM

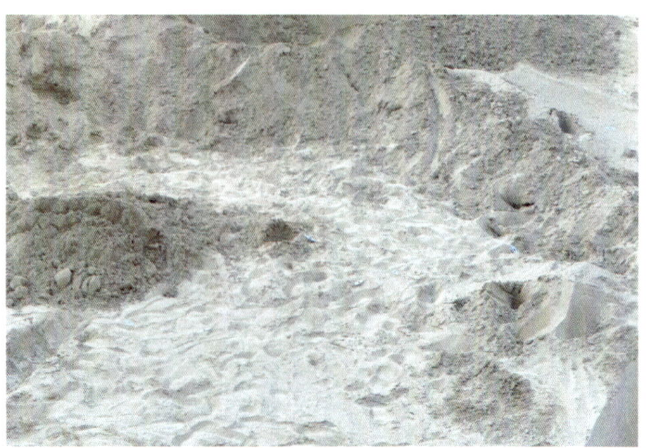
7/7/12—8:54:09 PM

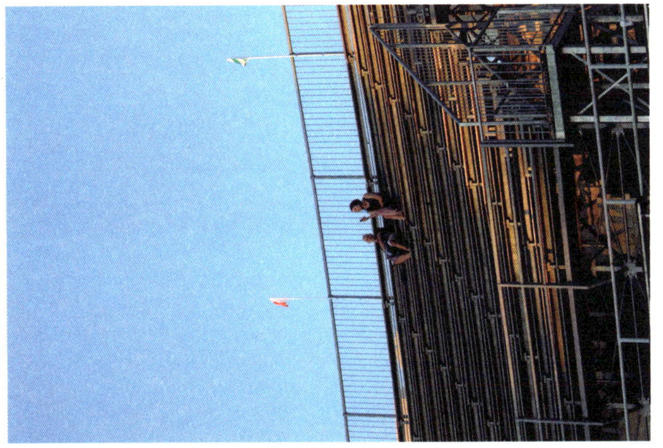

7/7/12—8:58:58 PM

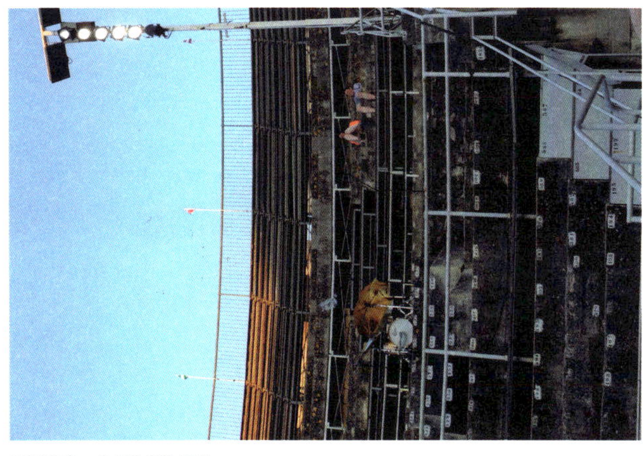

7/7/12—8:59:08 PM

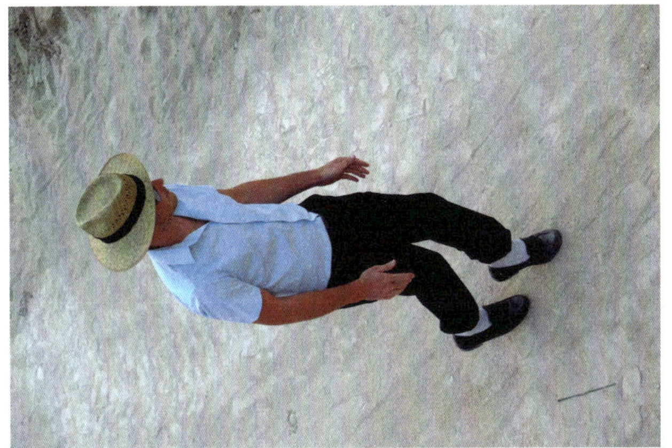

7/7/12—9:01:57 PM

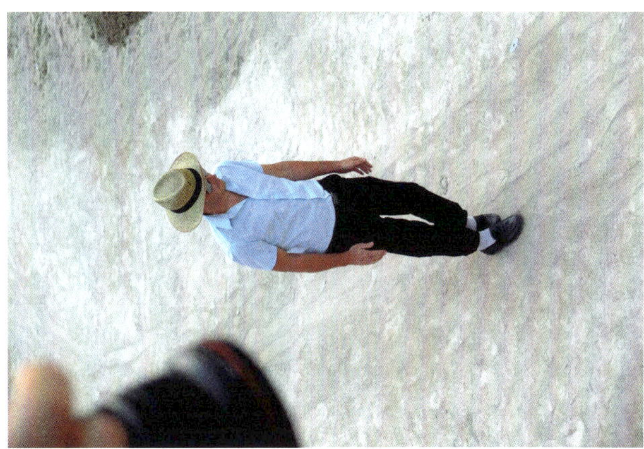

7/7/12—9:02:00 PM

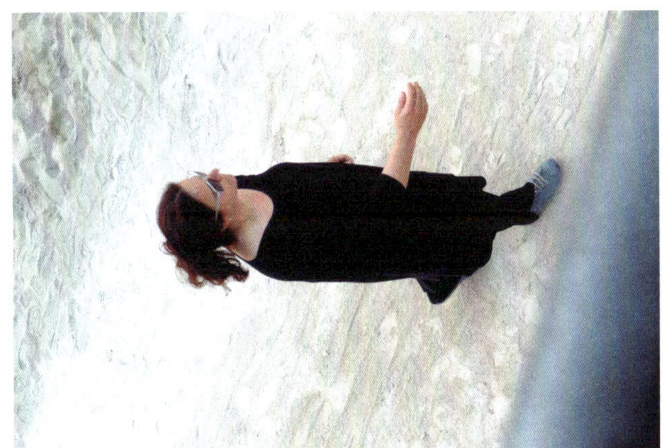

7/7/12—9:02:03 PM

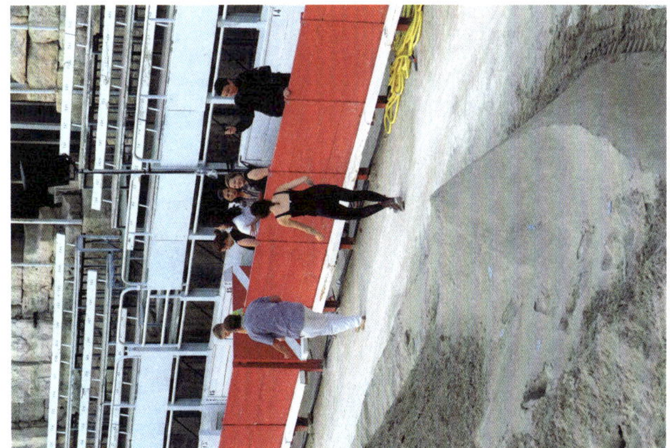

7/7/12—9:02:09 PM

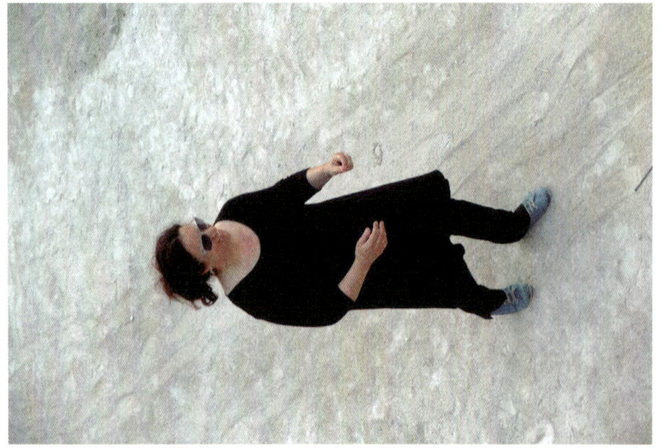

7/7/12—9:02:14 PM

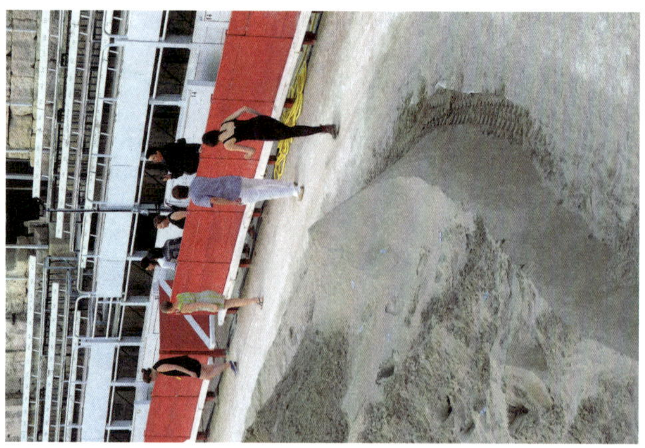

7/7/12—9:02:21 PM

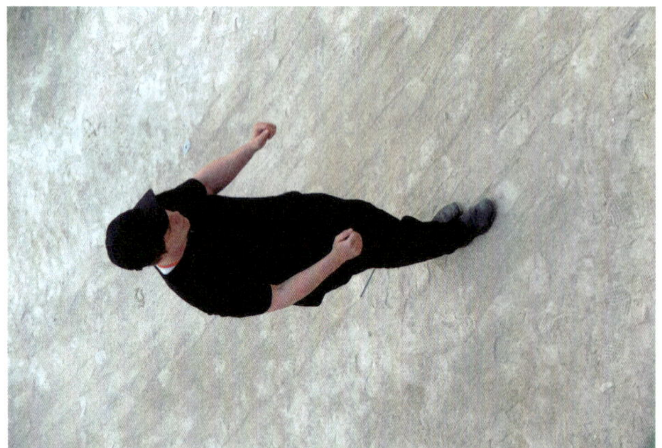

7/7/12—9:02:28 PM

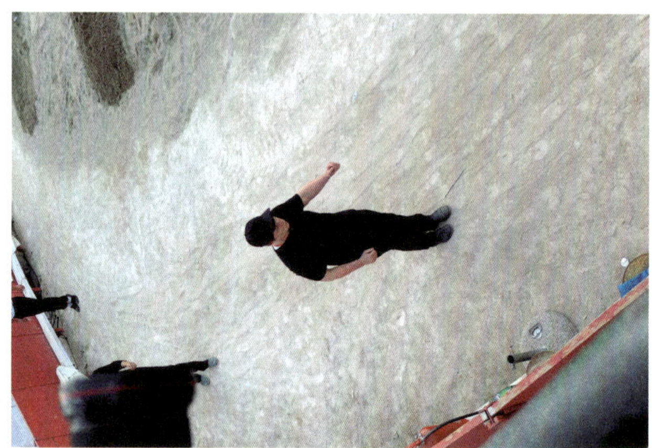

7/7/12—9:02:31 PM

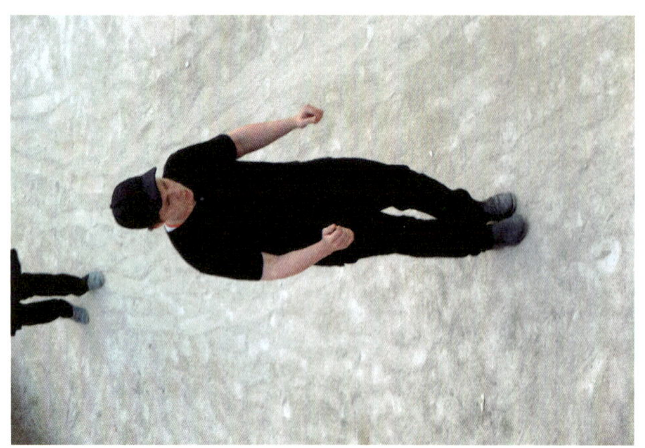

7/7/12—9:02:36 PM

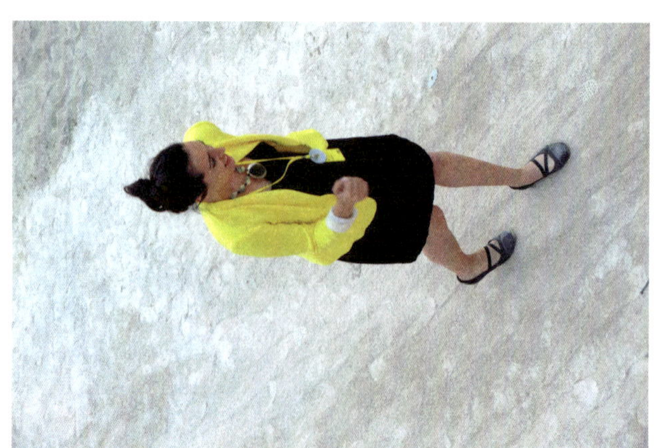

7/7/12—9:02:50 PM

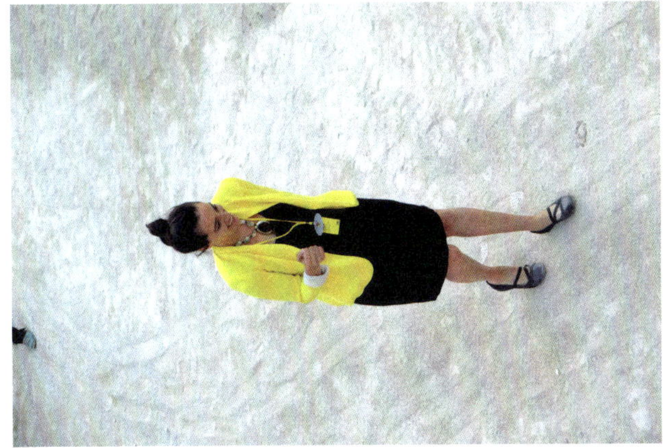
7/7/12—9:02:54 PM

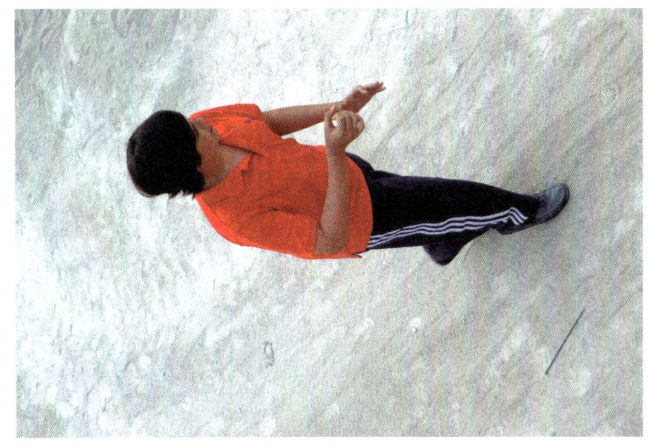
7/7/12—9:02:59 PM

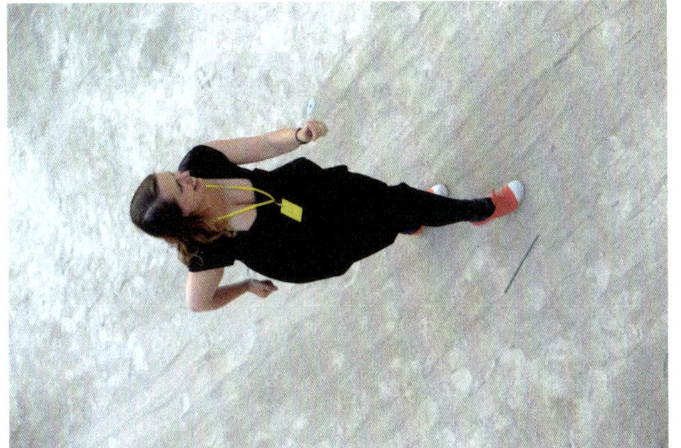
7/7/12—9:03:11 PM

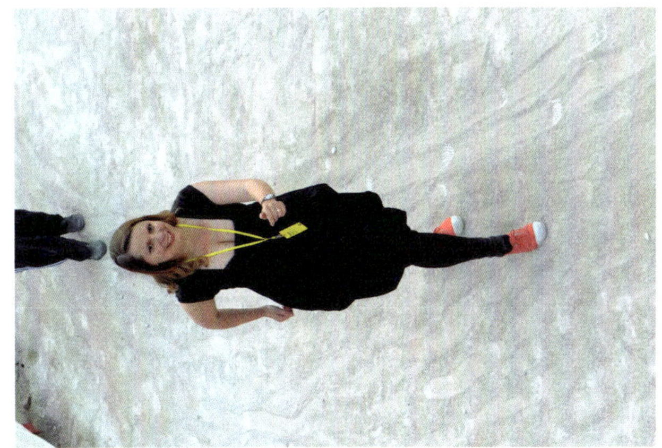
7/7/12—9:03:21 PM

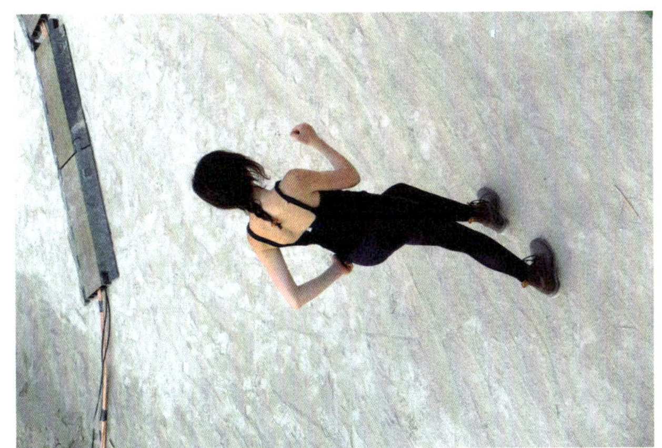
7/7/12—9:03:26 PM

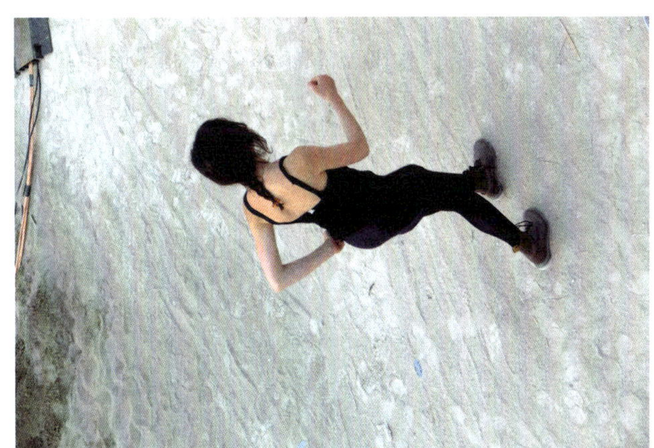
7/7/12—9:03:30 PM

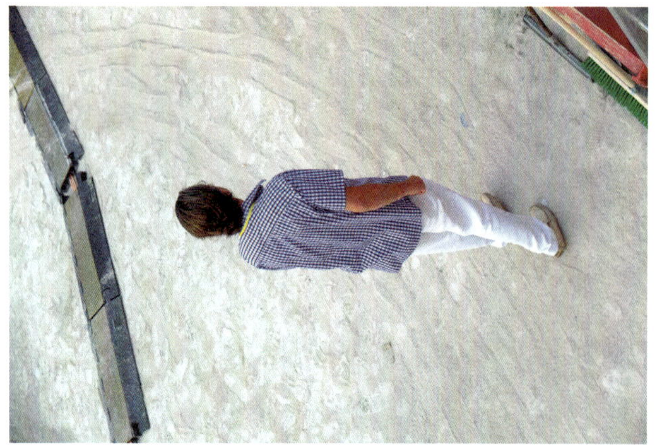
7/7/12—9:03:33 PM

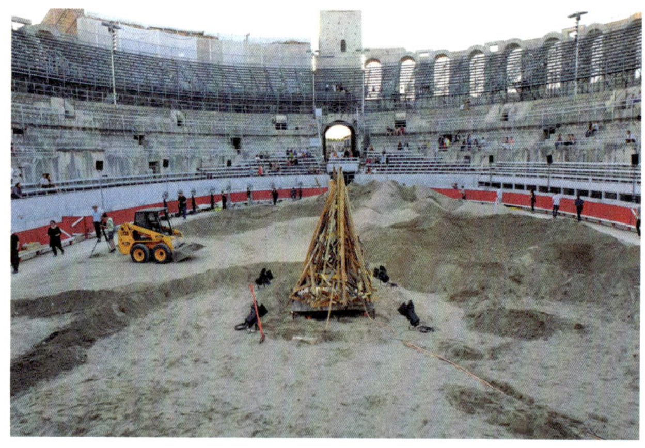
7/7/12—9:03:46 PM

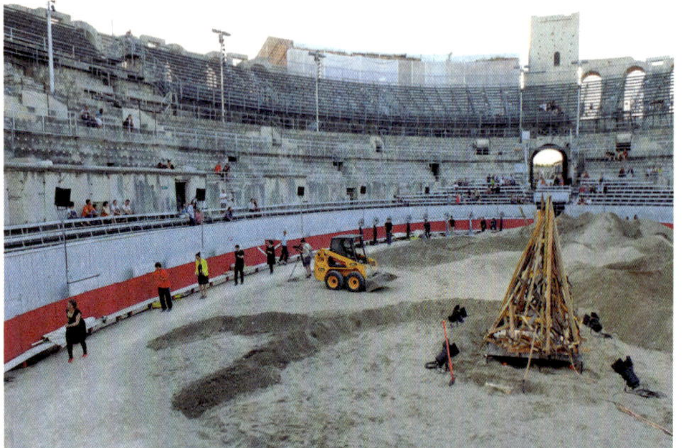
7/7/12—9:03:51 PM

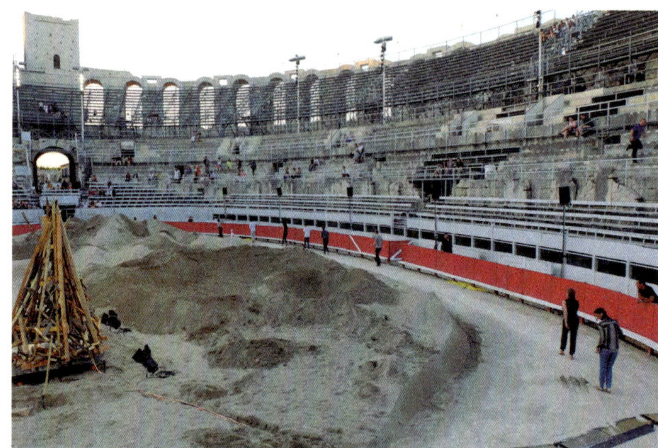
7/7/12—9:03:54 PM

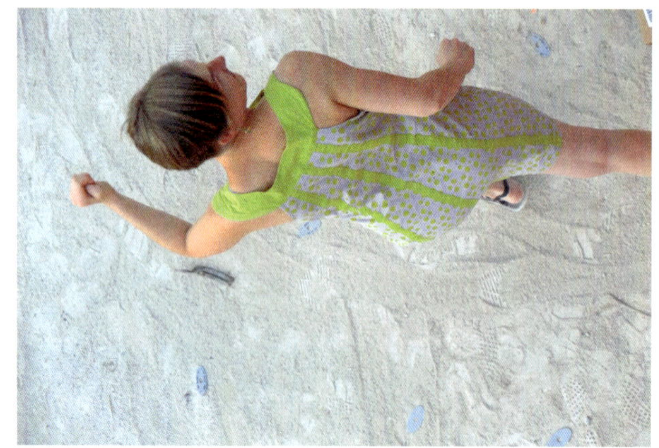
7/7/12—9:04:01 PM

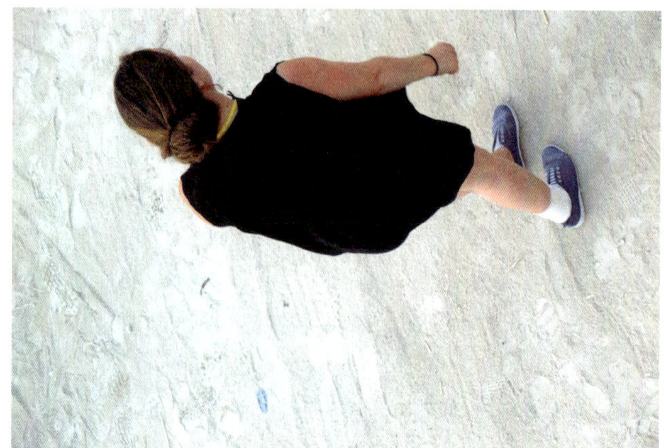
7/7/12—9:04:04 PM

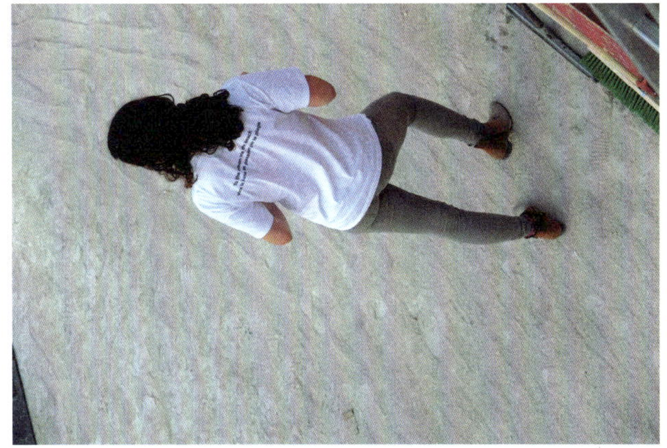
7/7/12—9:04:07 PM

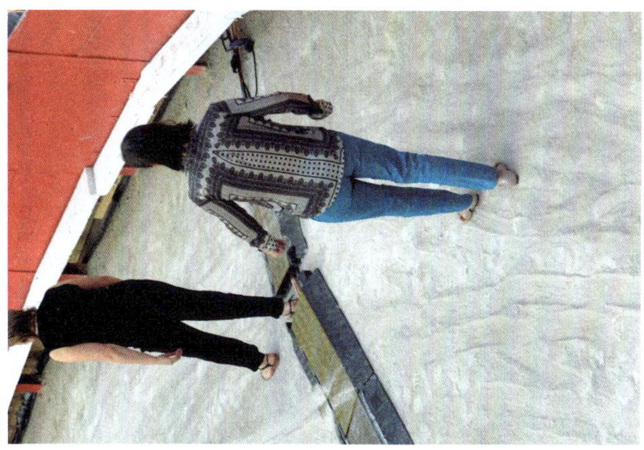
7/7/12—9:04:10 PM

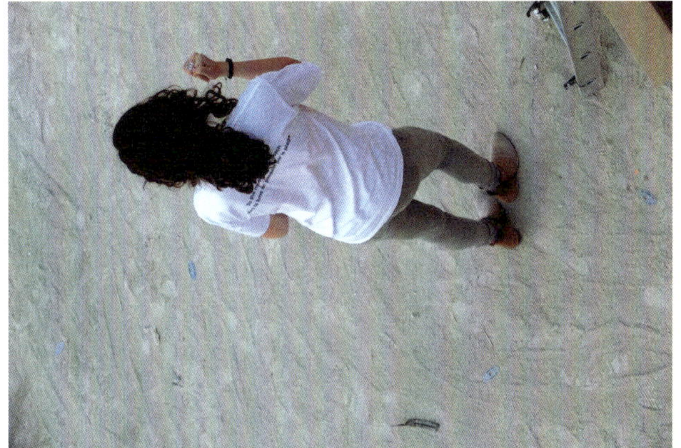
7/7/12—9:04:16 PM

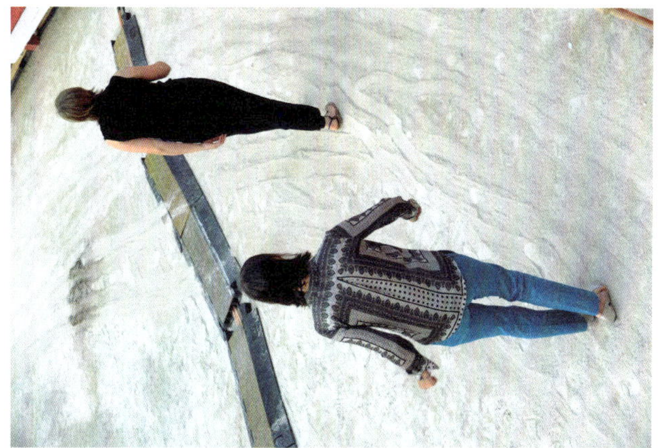
7/7/12—9:04:21 PM

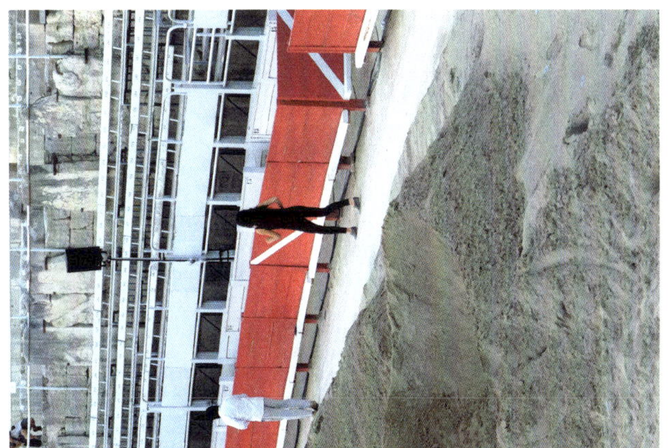
7/7/12—9:04:27 PM

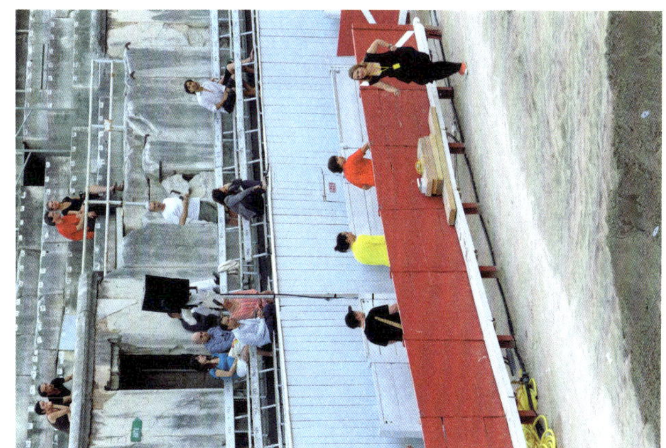
7/7/12—9:04:32 PM

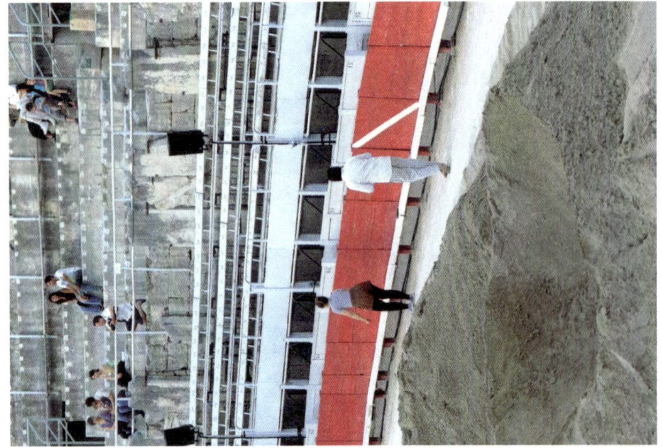
7/7/12—9:04:41 PM

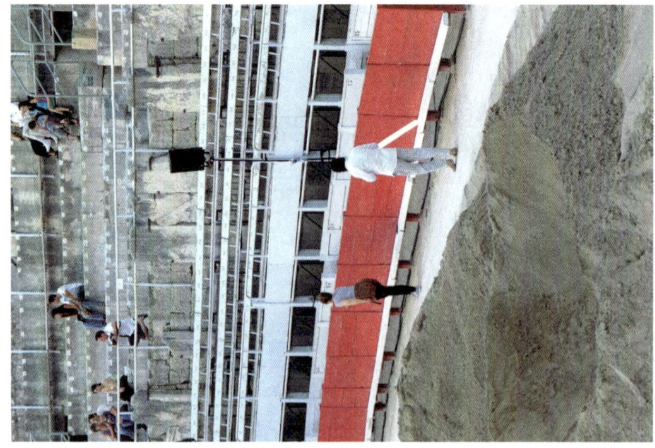
7/7/12—9:04:45 PM

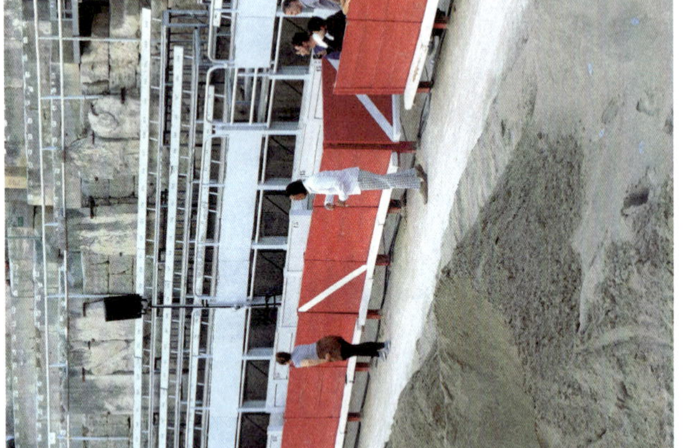
7/7/12—9:04:53 PM

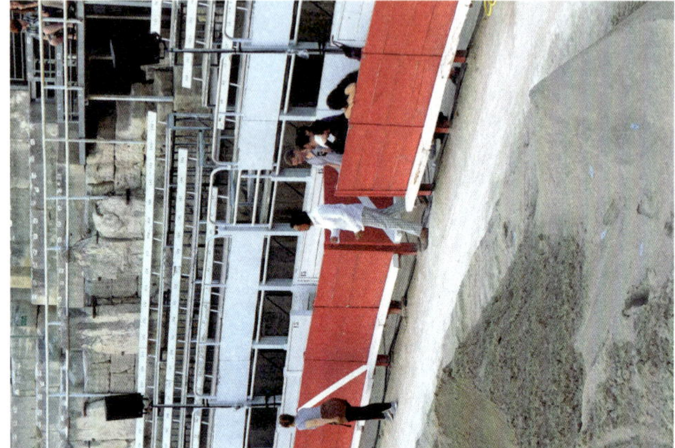
7/7/12—9:04:56 PM

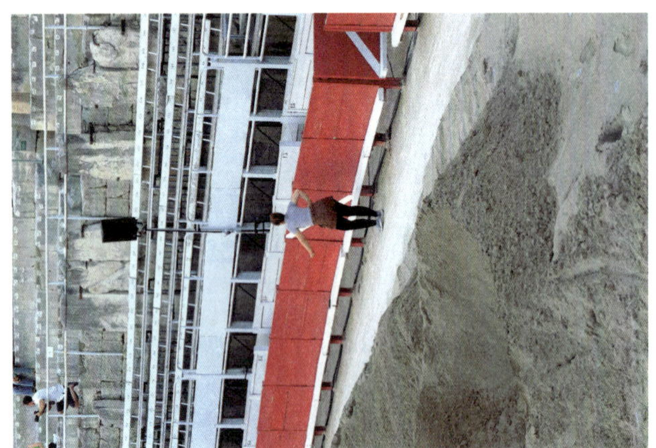
7/7/12—9:04:58 PM

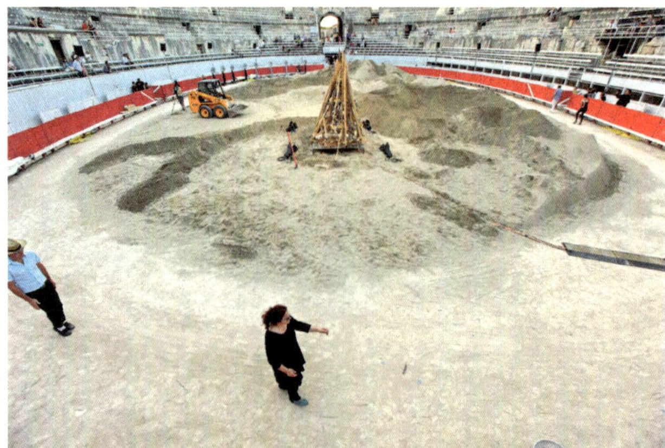
7/7/12—9:05:07 PM

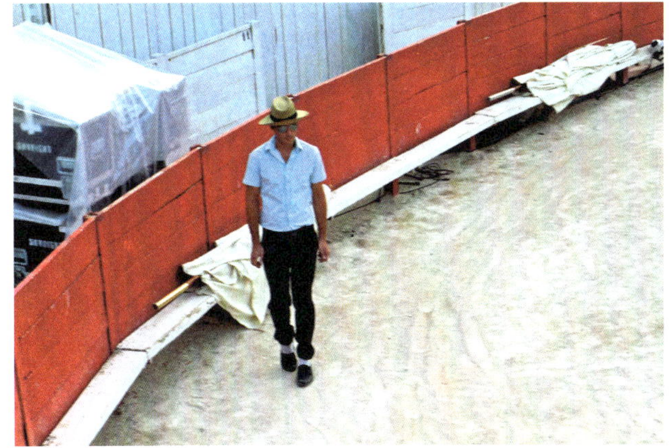

7/7/12—9:05:17 PM

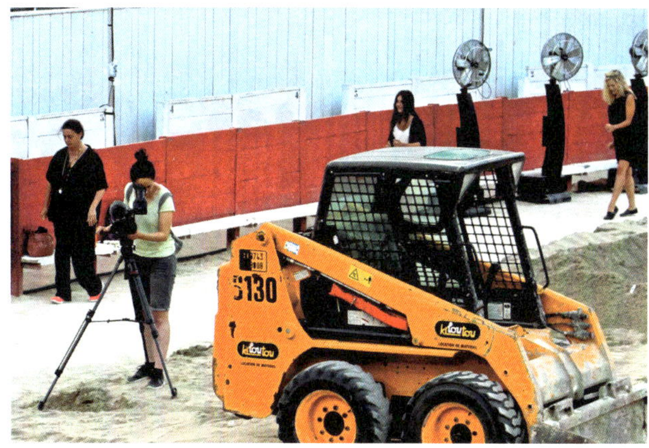

7/7/12—9:05:18 PM

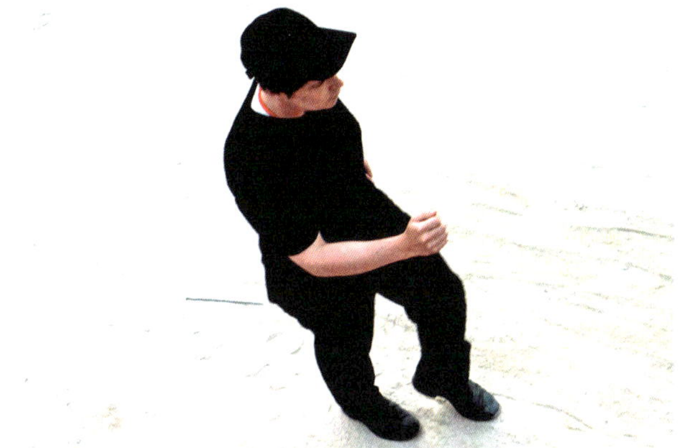

7/7/12—9:05:25 PM

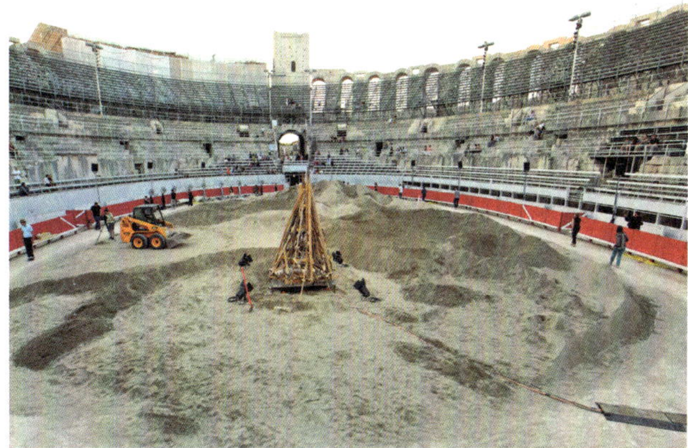

7/7/12—9:06:14 PM

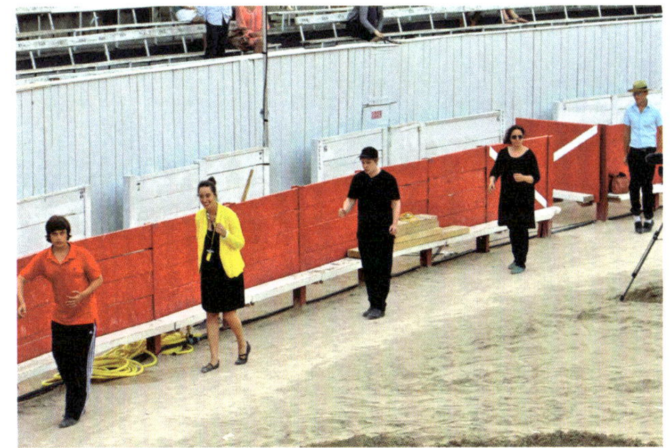

7/7/12—9:06:46 PM

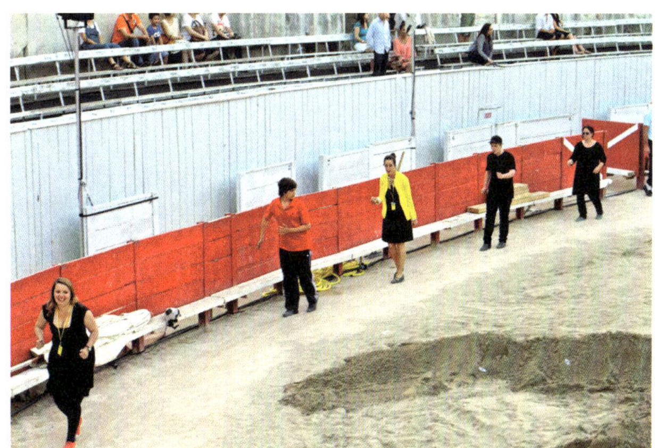

7/7/12—9:06:47 PM

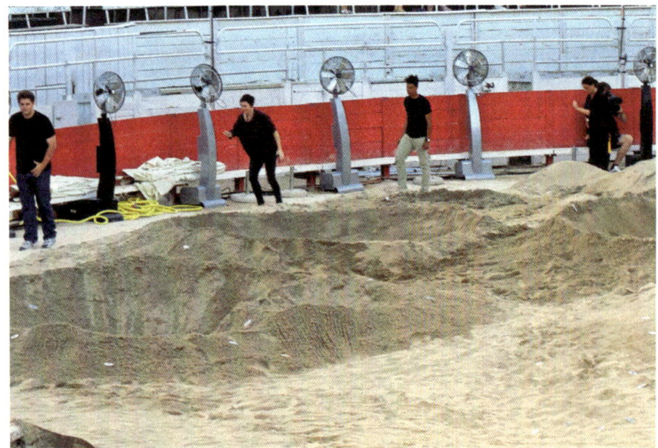
7/7/12—9:06:52 PM

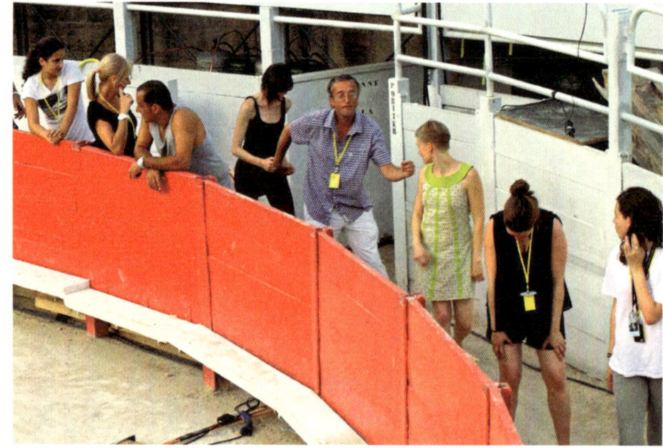
7/7/12—9:07:52 PM

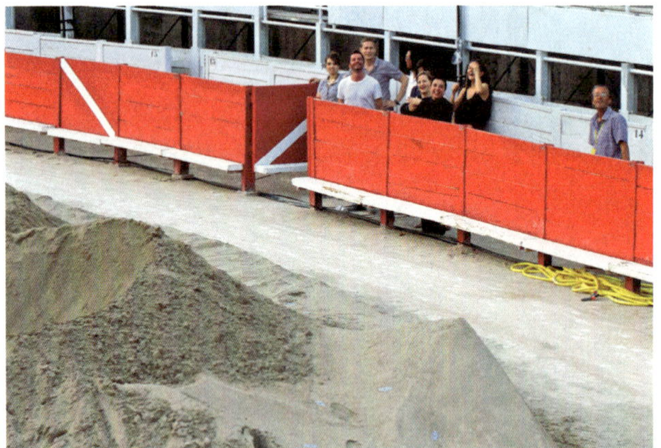
7/7/12—9:08:50 PM

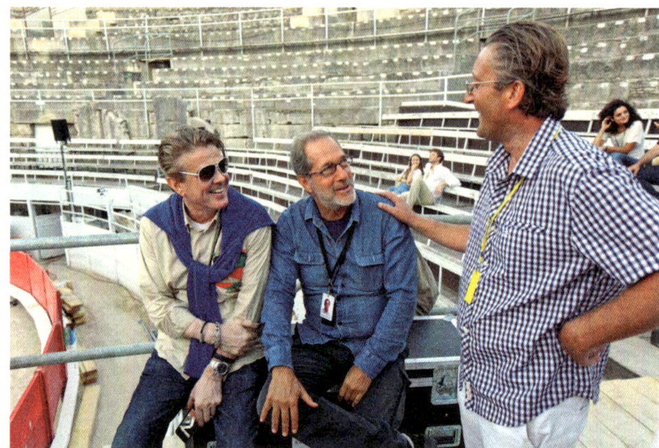
7/7/12—9:12:46 PM

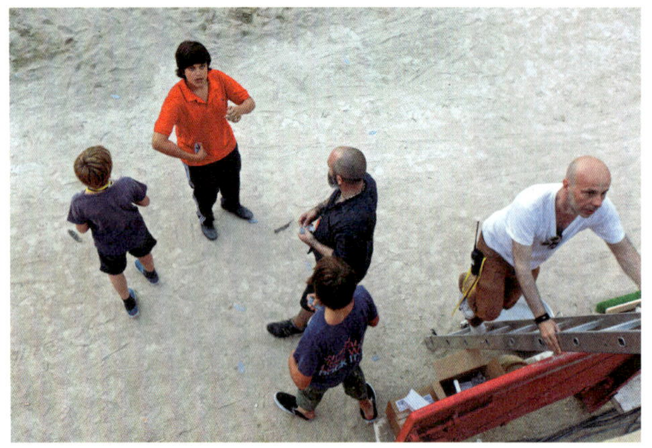
7/7/12—9:15:48 PM

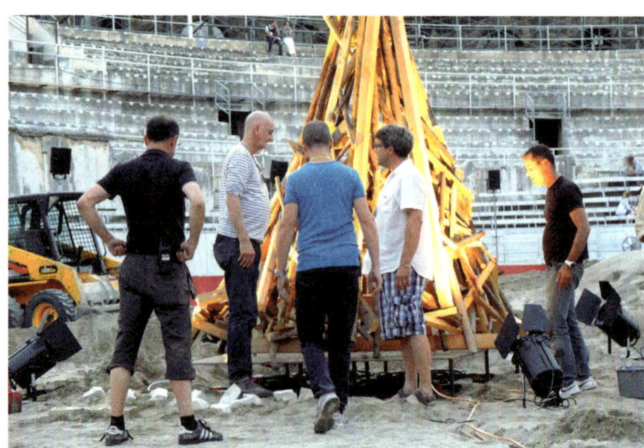
7/7/12—9:17:47 PM

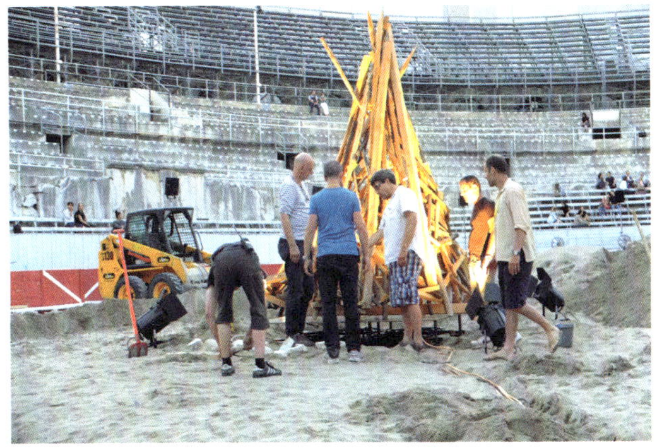
7/7/12—9:17:51 PM

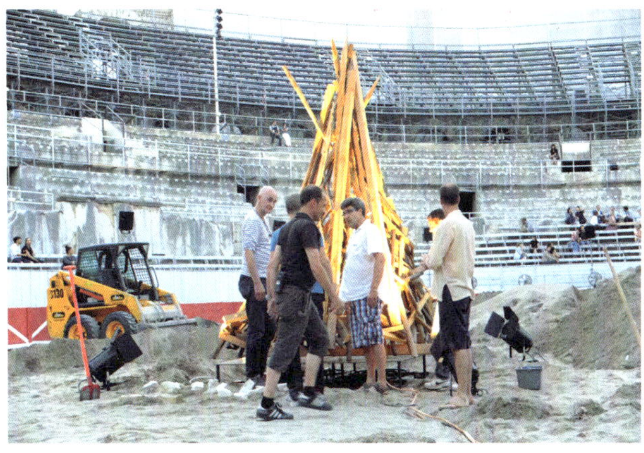
7/7/12—9:17:55 PM

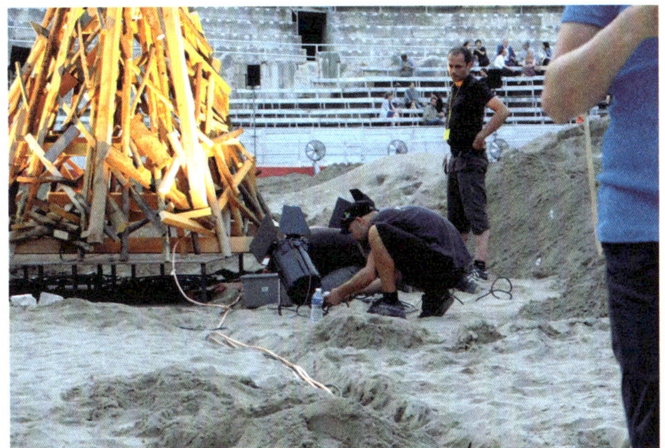
7/7/12—9:20:50 PM

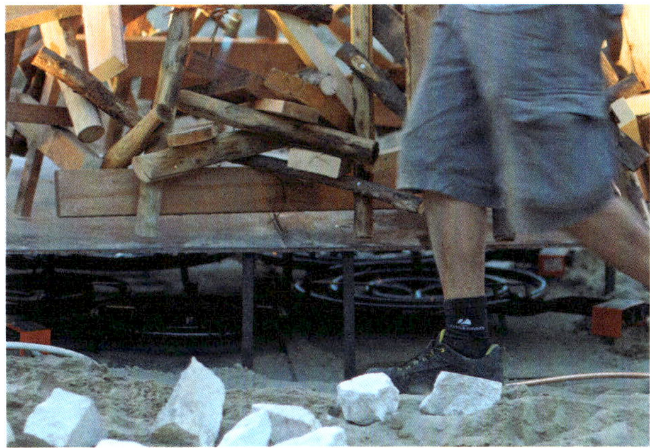
7/7/12—9:24:26 PM

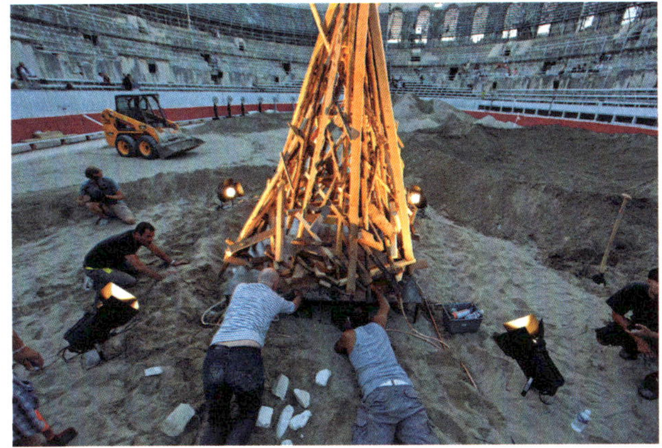
7/7/12—9:26:40 PM

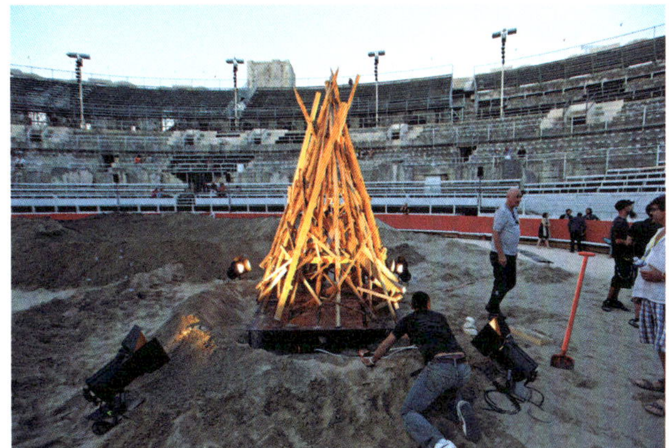
7/7/12—9:27:31 PM

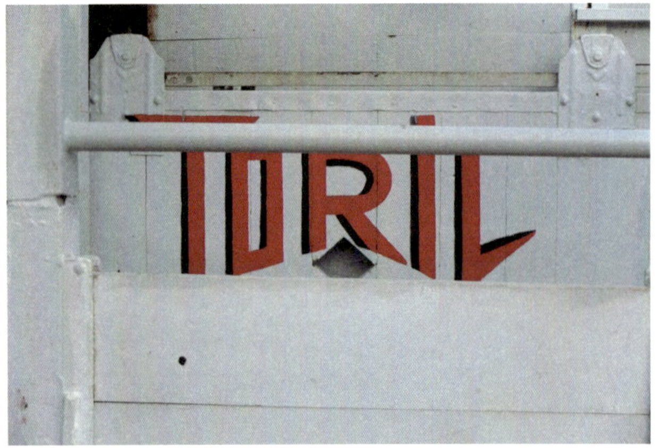

7/7/12—9:28:54 PM

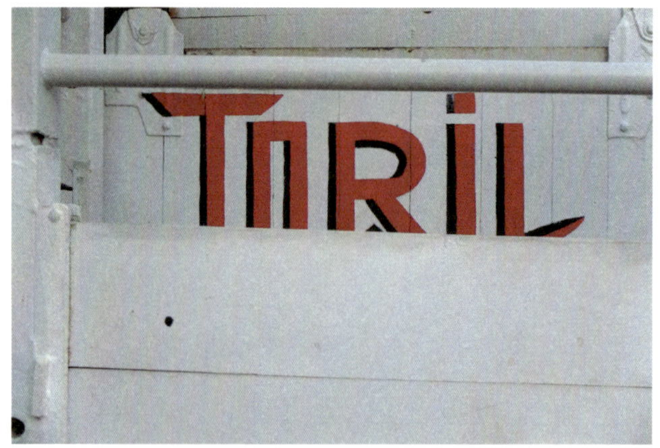

7/7/12—9:28:59 PM

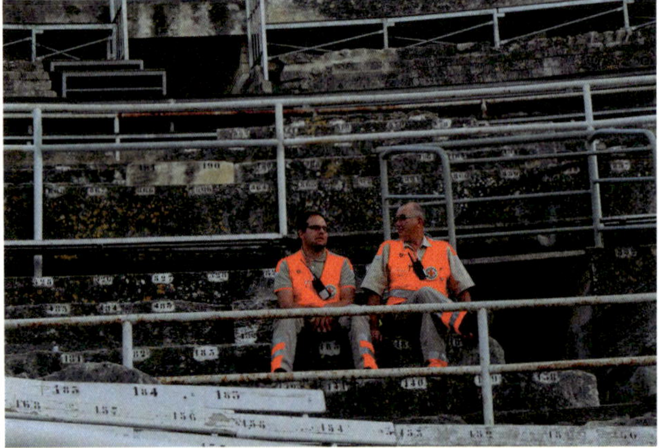

7/7/12—9:29:05 PM

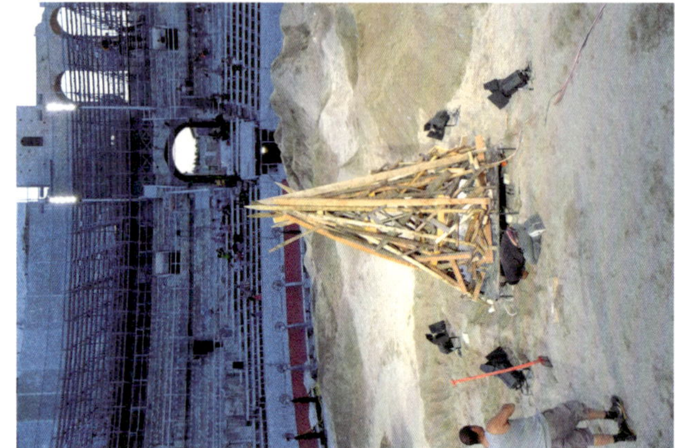

7/7/12—9:32:47 PM

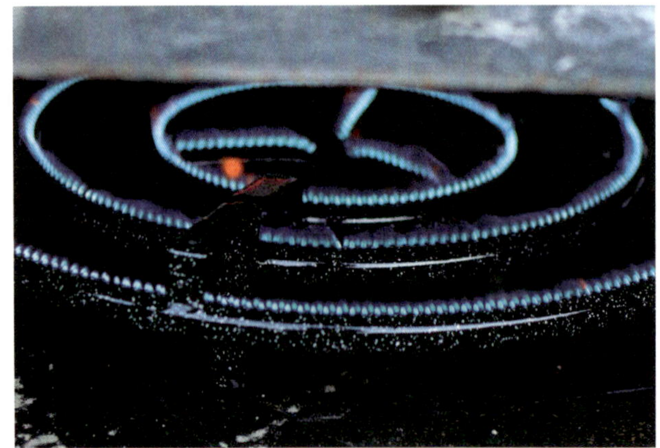

7/7/12—9:32:50 PM

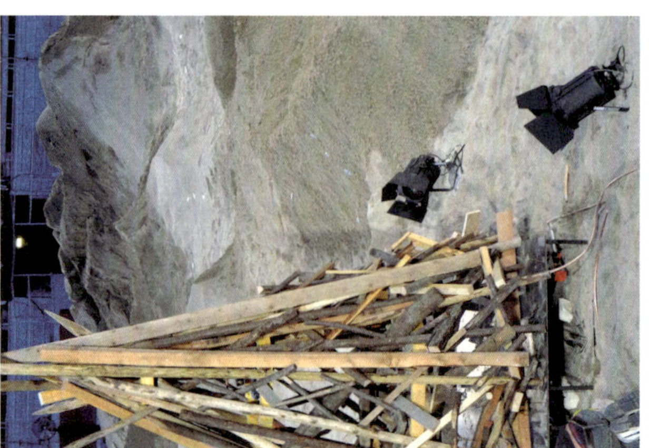

7/7/12—9:32:52 PM

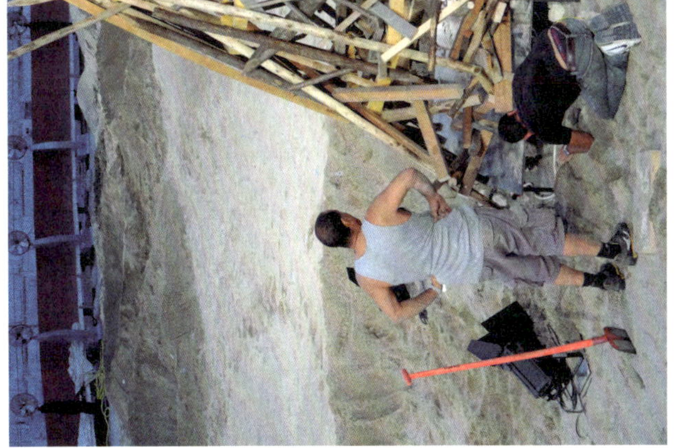

7/7/12—9:32:55 PM

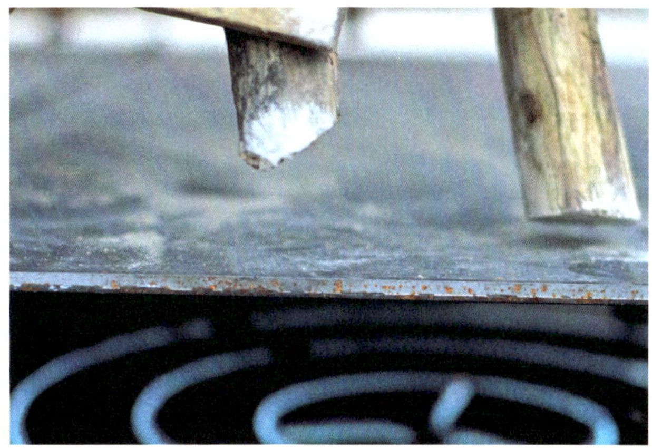

7/7/12—9:32:56 PM

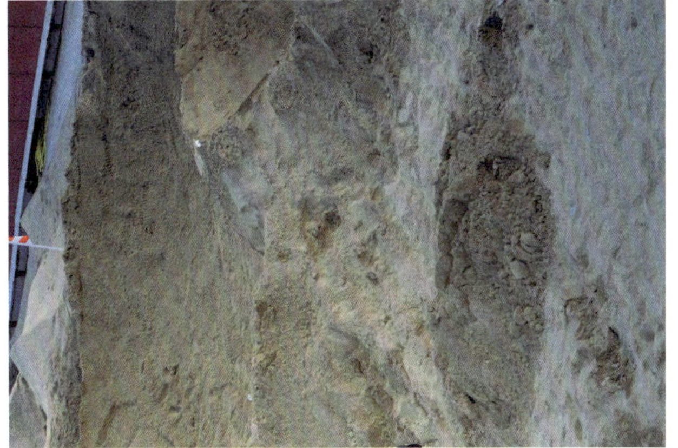

7/7/12—9:32:57 PM

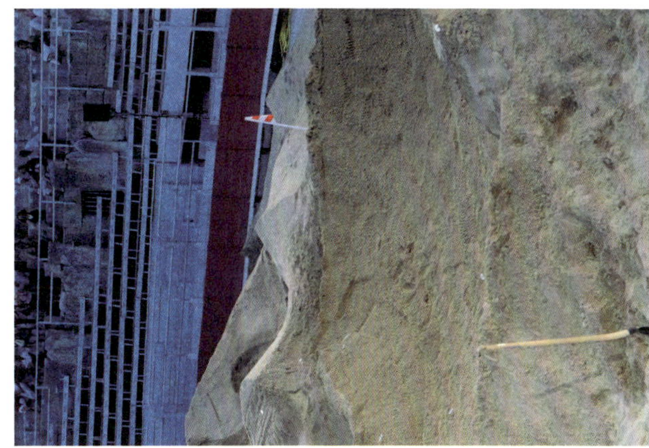

7/7/12—9:33:01 PM

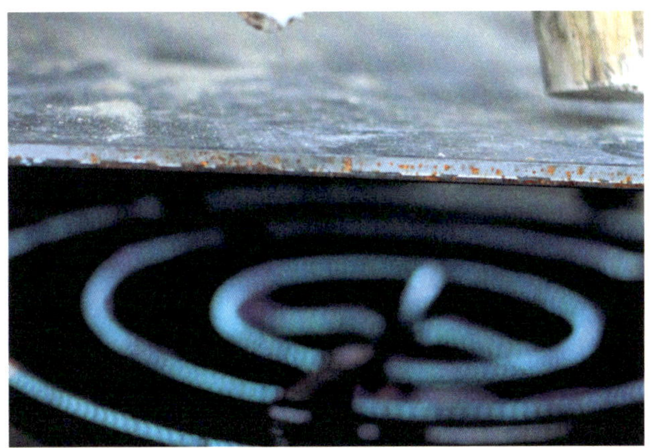

7/7/12—9:33:13 PM

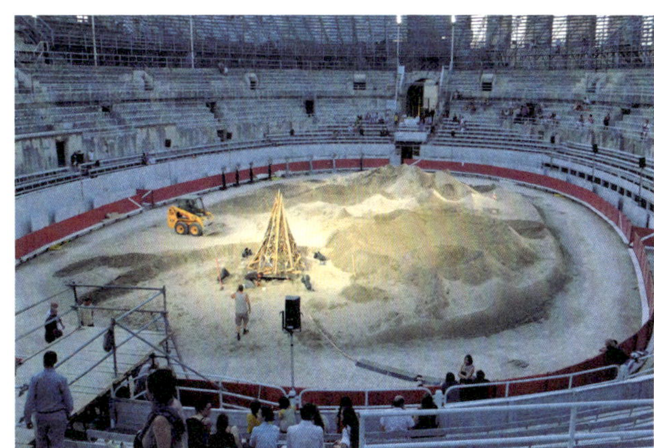

7/7/12—9:33:49 PM

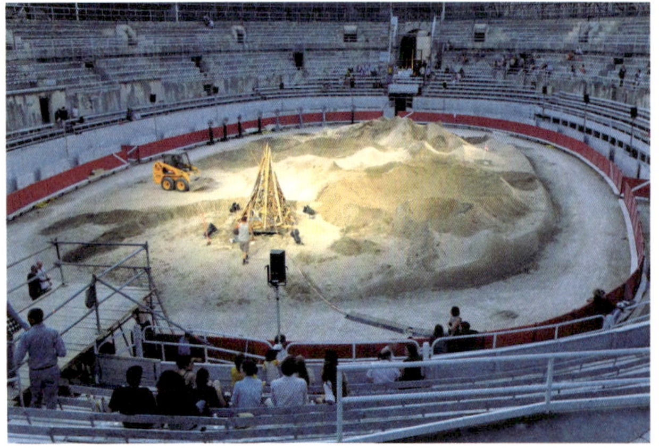
7/7/12—9:33:54 PM

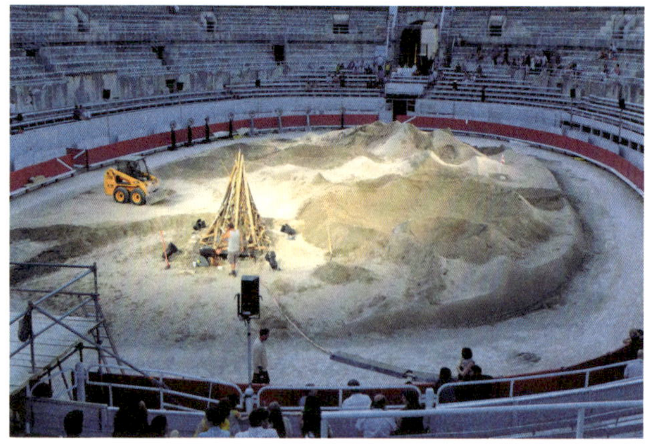
7/7/12—9:33:57 PM

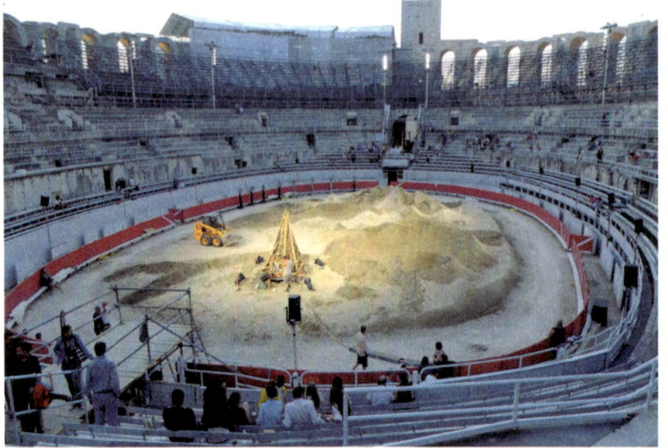
7/7/12—9:34:00 PM

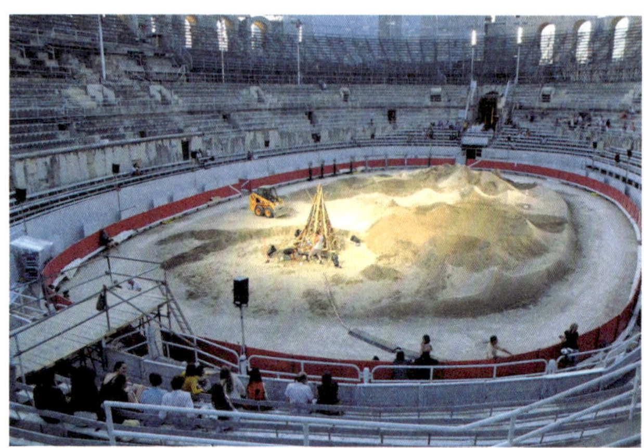
7/7/12—9:34:07 PM

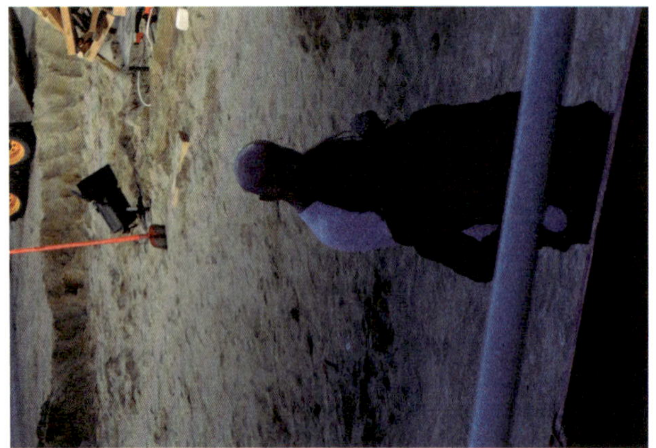
7/7/12—9:38:08 PM

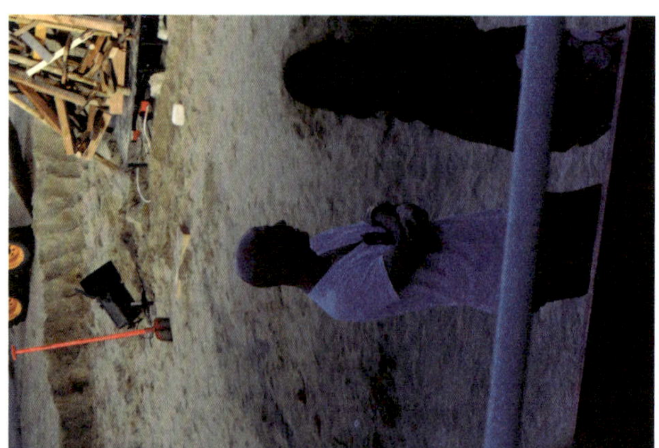
7/7/12—9:38:19 PM

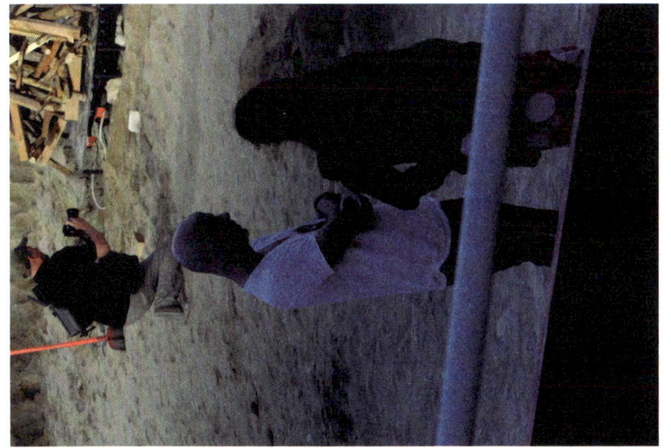

7/7/12—9:38:35 PM

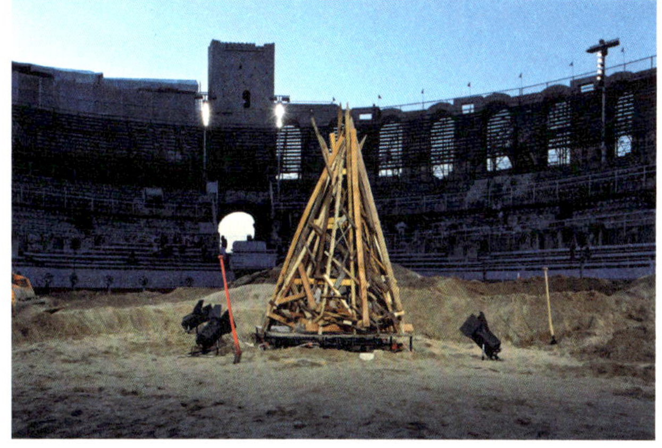

7/7/12—9:39:58 PM

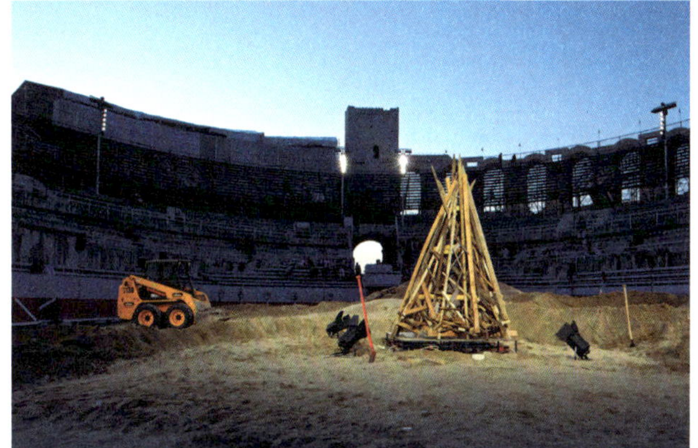

7/7/12—9:40:11 PM

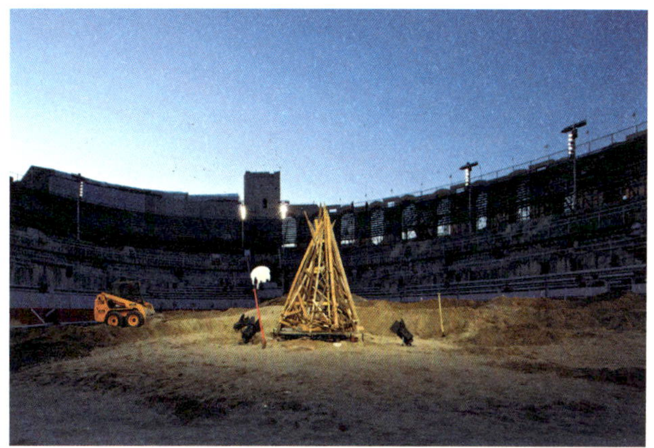

7/7/12—9:40:33 PM

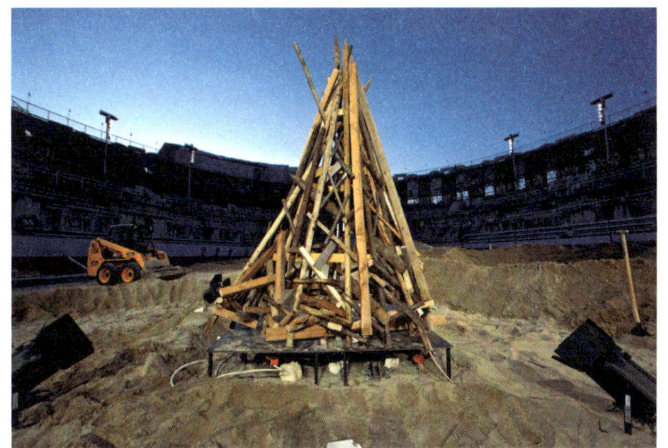

7/7/12—9:41:35 PM

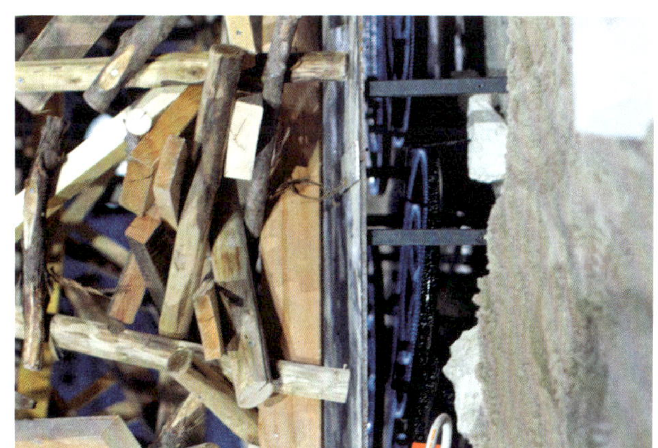

7/7/12—9:41:50 PM

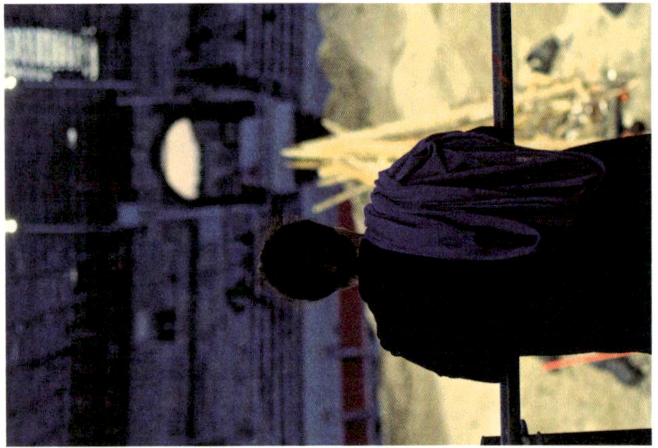

7/7/12—9:45:05 PM

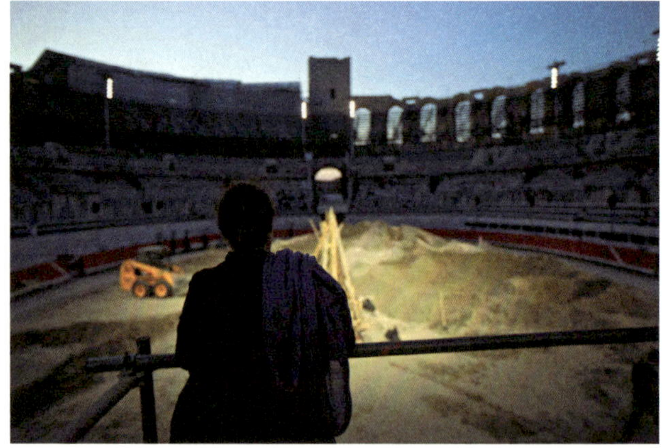

7/7/12—9:45:30 PM

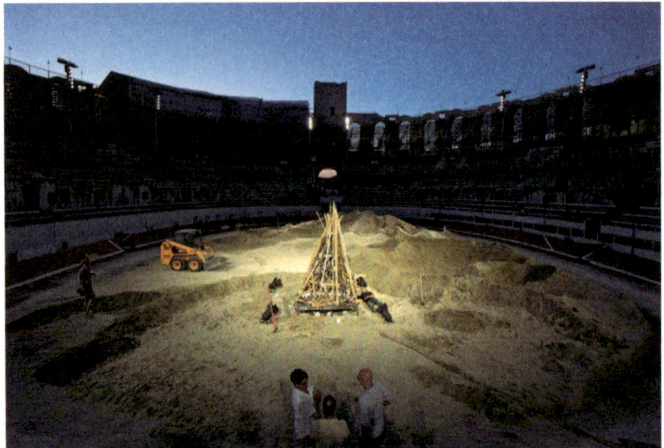

7/7/12—9:49:36 PM

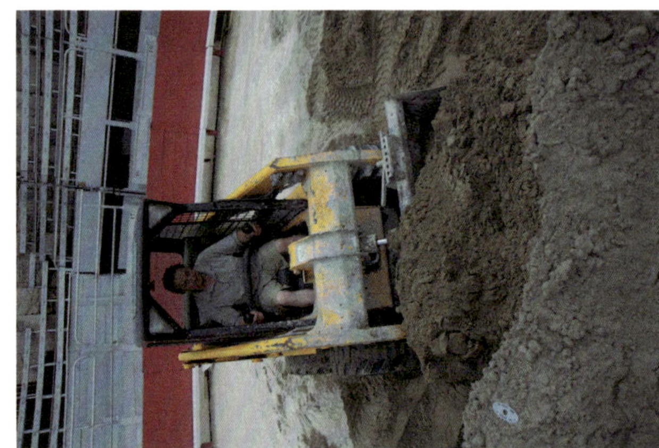

7/8/12—9:32:03 AM

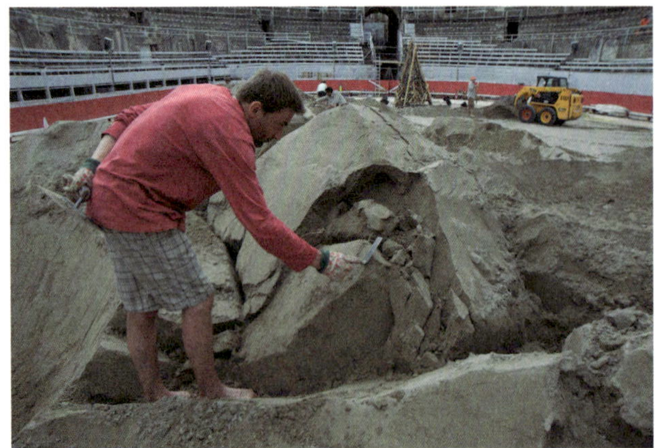

7/8/12—9:33:10 AM

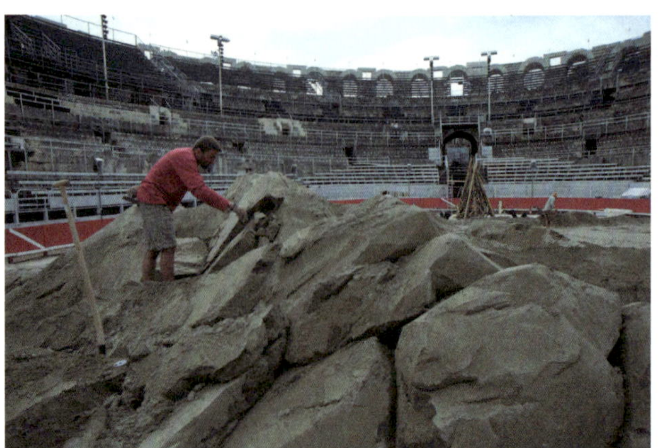

7/8/12—9:33:26 AM

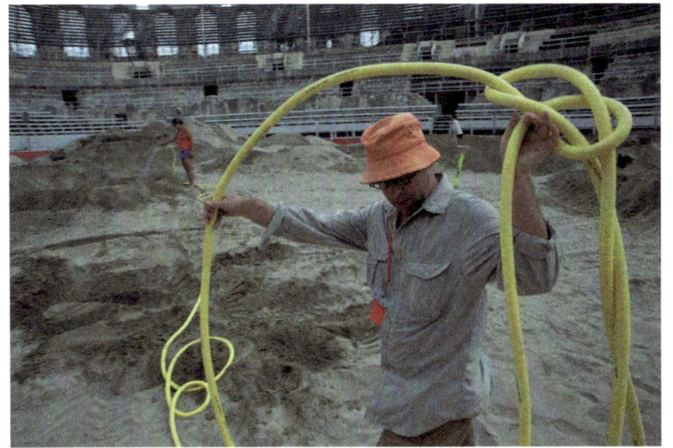

7/8/12—9:35:10 AM

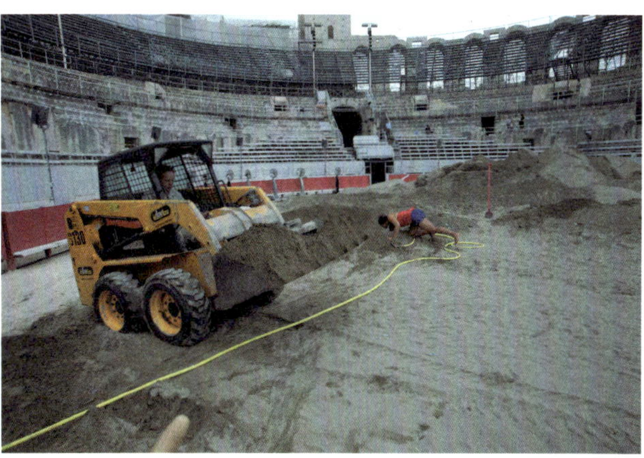

7/8/12—9:35:32 AM

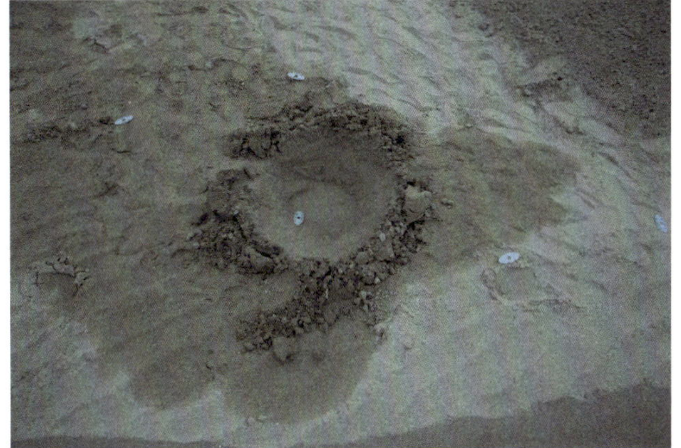

7/8/12—9:38:56 AM

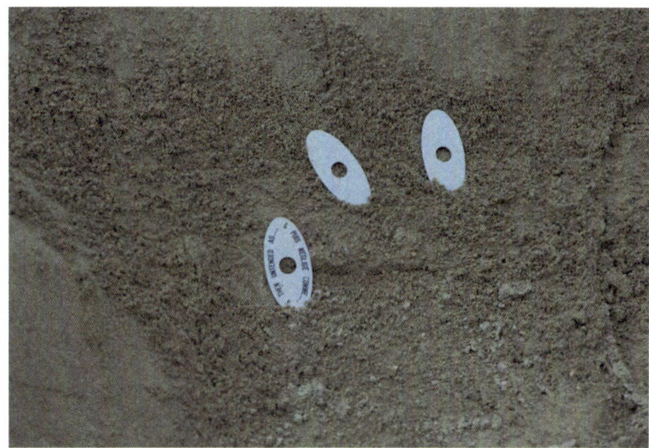

7/8/12—9:40:25 AM

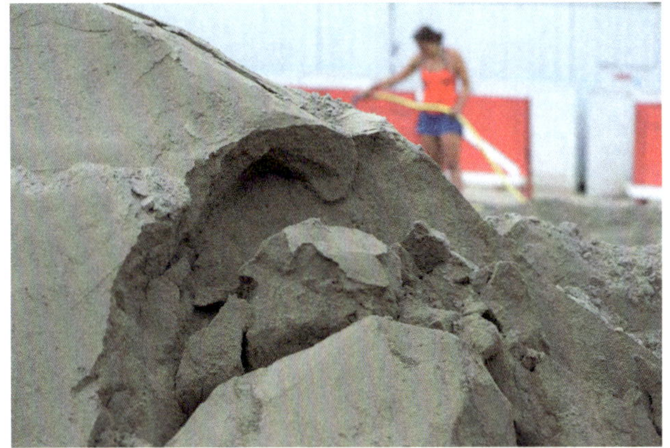

7/8/12—9:40:36 AM

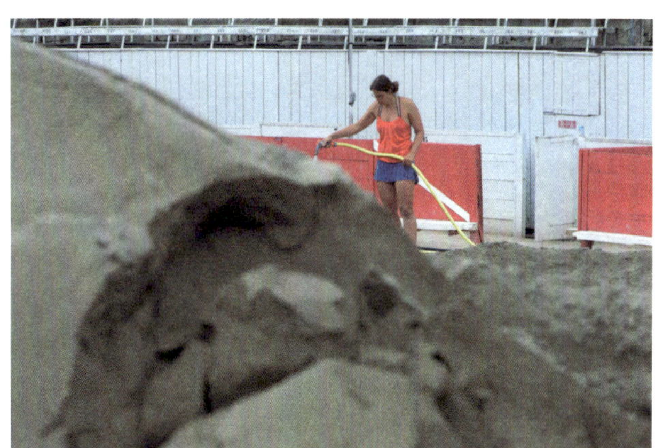

7/8/12—9:40:37 AM

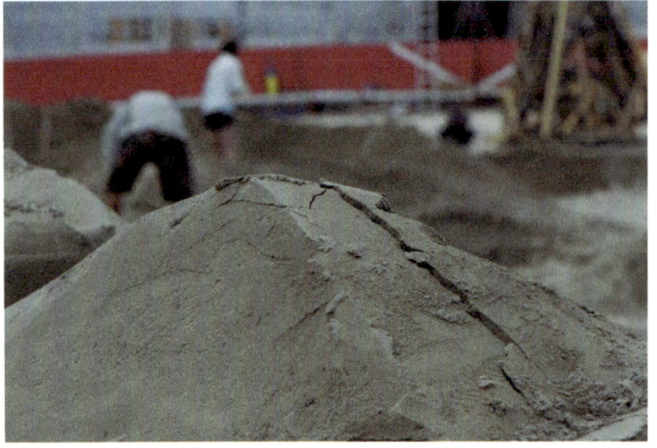
7/8/12—9:41:28 AM

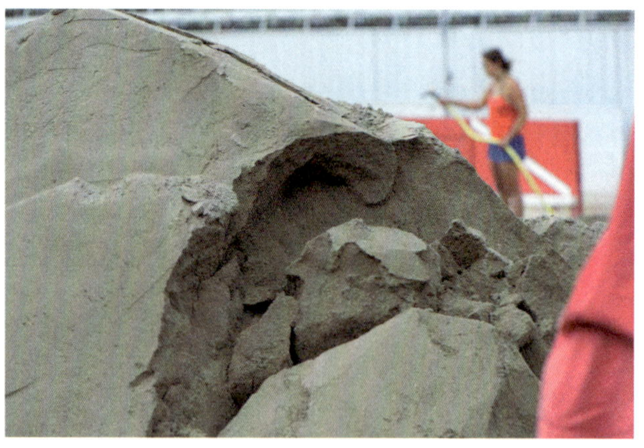
7/8/12—9:42:16 AM

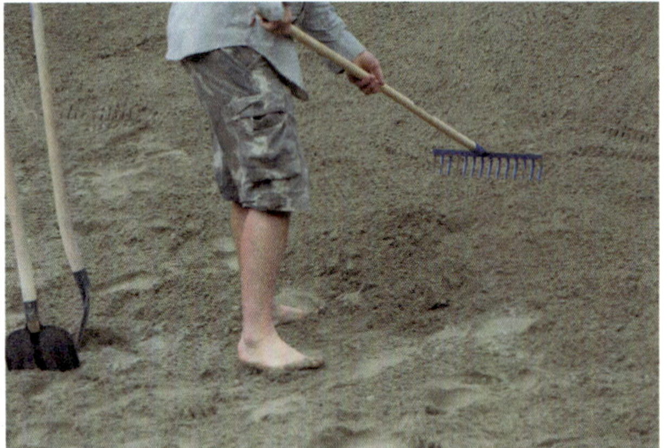
7/8/12—9:43:10 AM

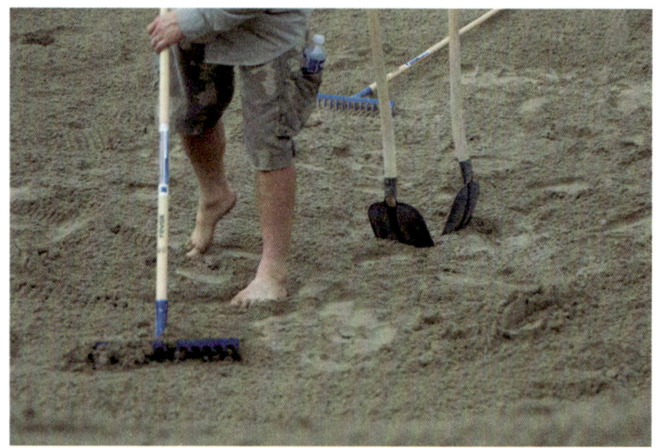
7/8/12—9:43:35 AM

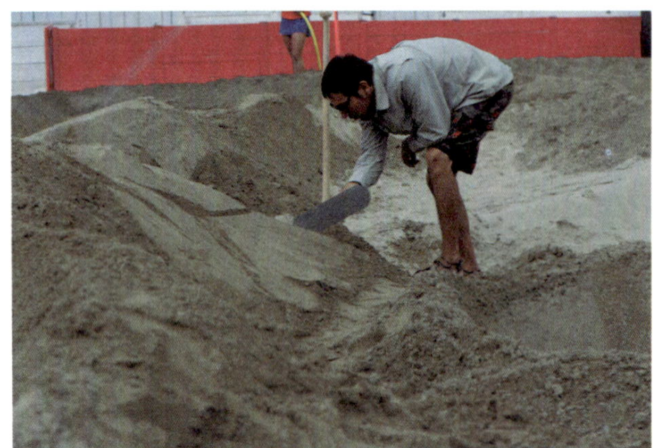
7/8/12—9:43:52 AM

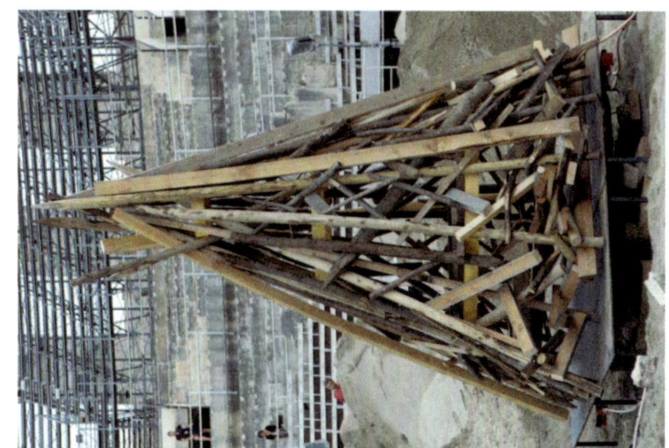
7/8/12—9:45:11 AM

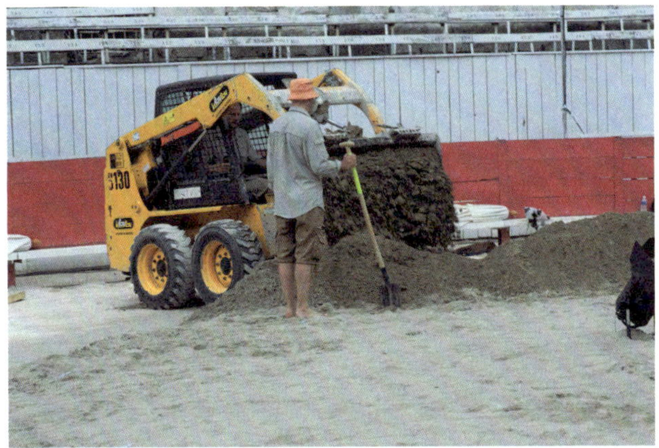

7/8/12—9:46:01 AM

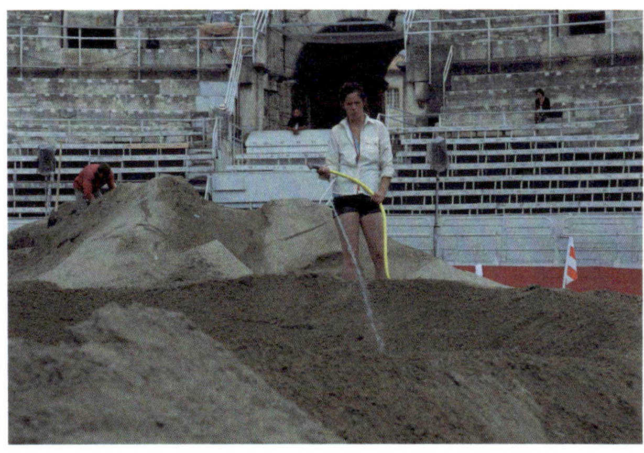

7/8/12—9:46:10 AM

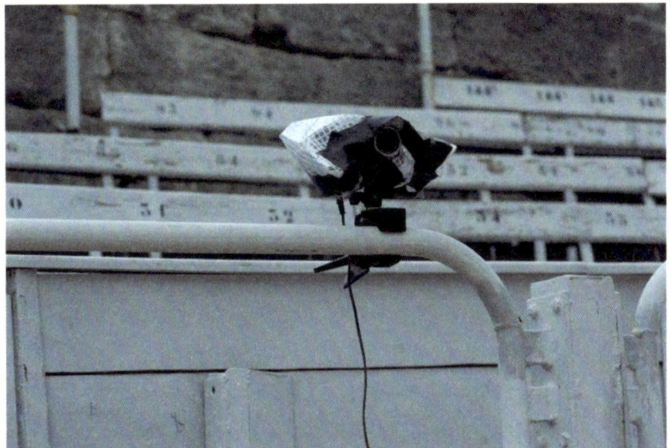

7/8/12—9:46:25 AM

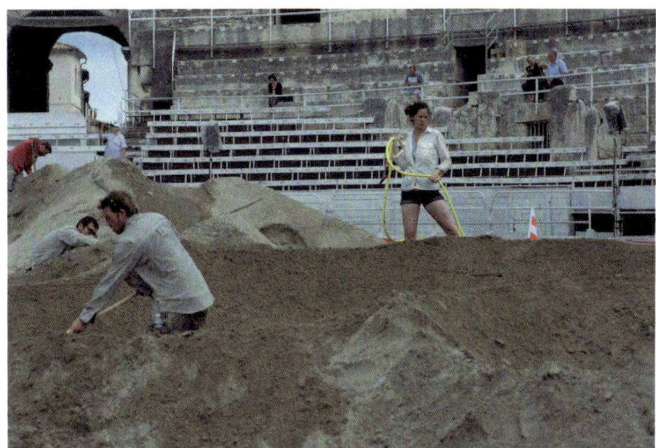

7/8/12—9:46:36 AM

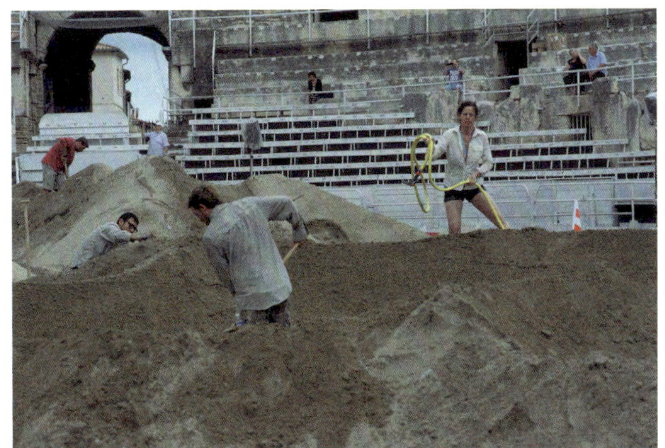

7/8/12—9:46:38 AM

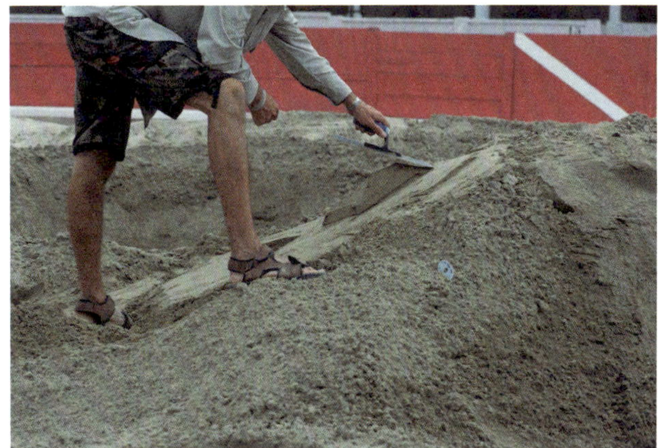

7/8/12—9:47:14 AM

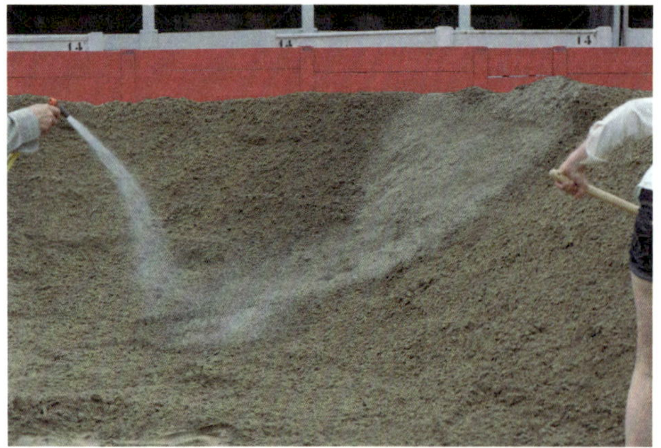

7/8/12—9:47:26 AM

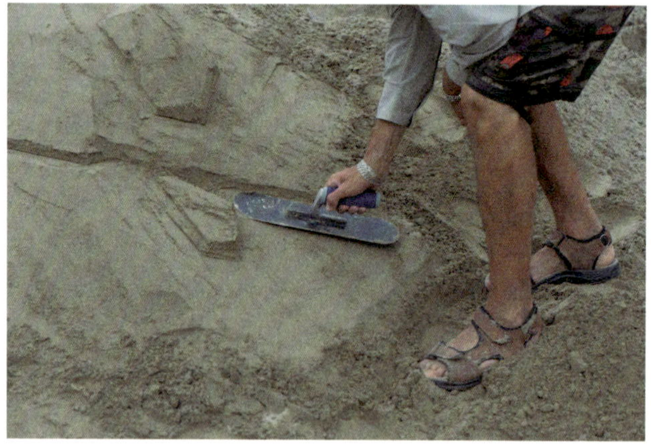

7/8/12—9:47:53 AM

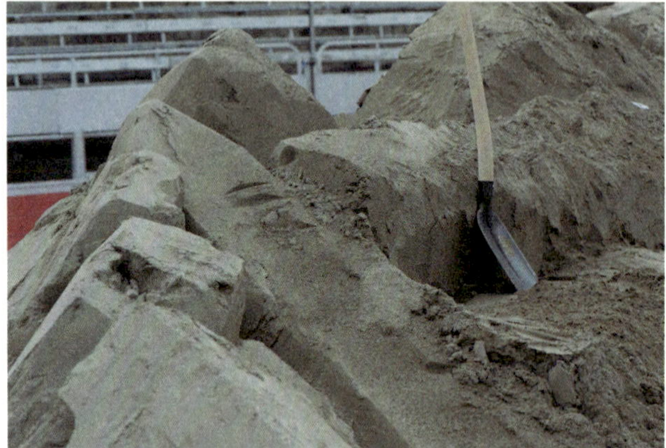

7/8/12—9:48:38 AM

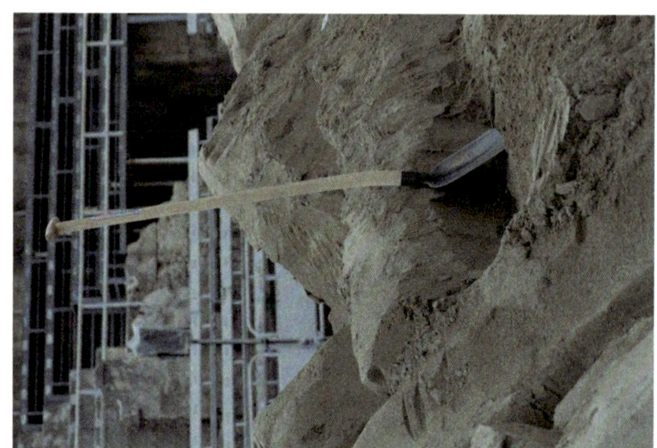

7/8/12—9:48:47 AM

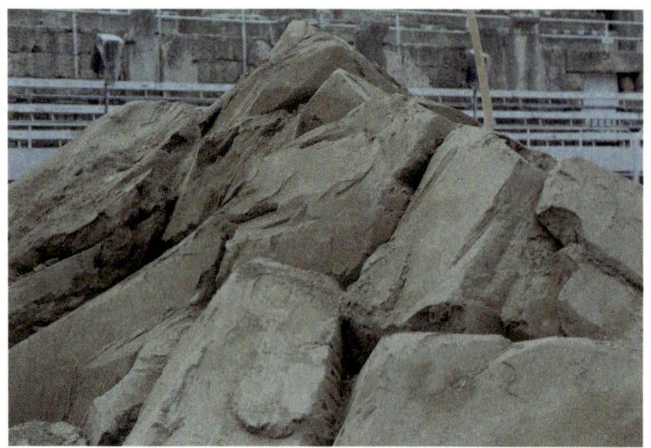

7/8/12—9:49:12 AM

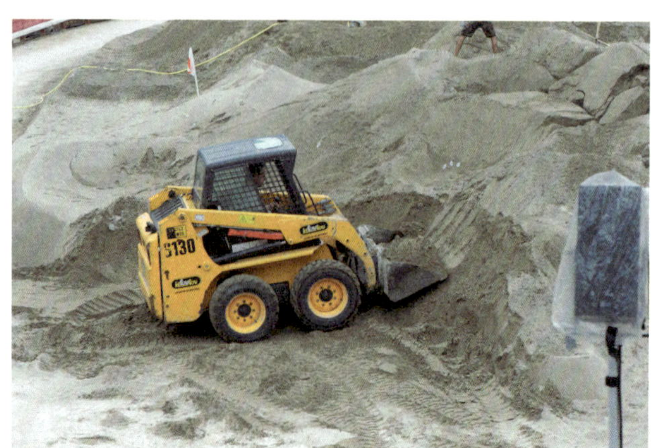

7/8/12—9:50:39 AM

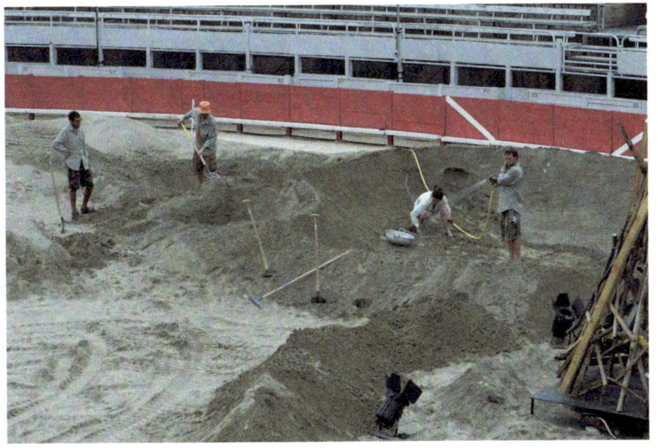

7/8/12—9:53:45 AM

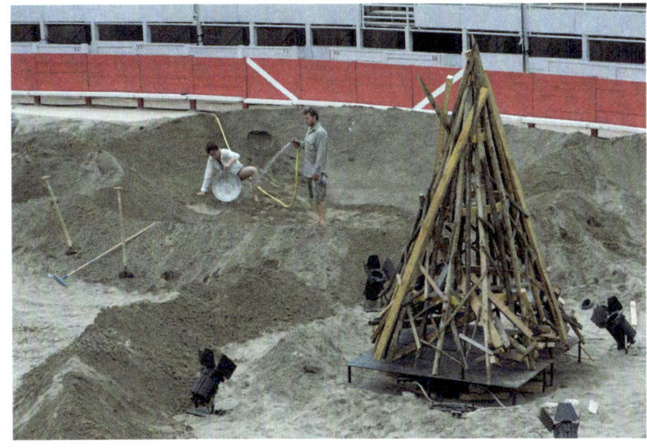

7/8/12—9:53:52 AM

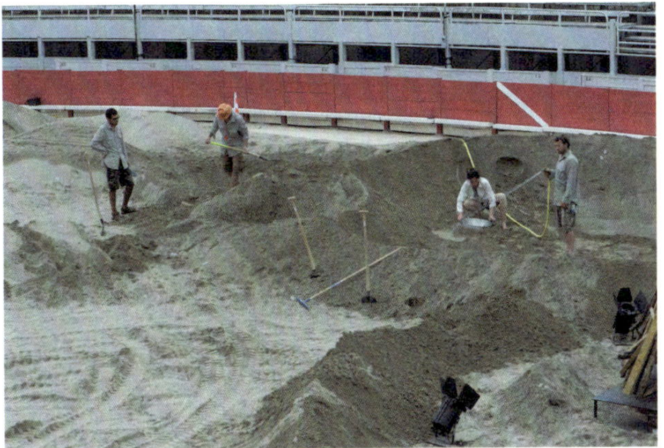

7/8/12—9:53:54 AM

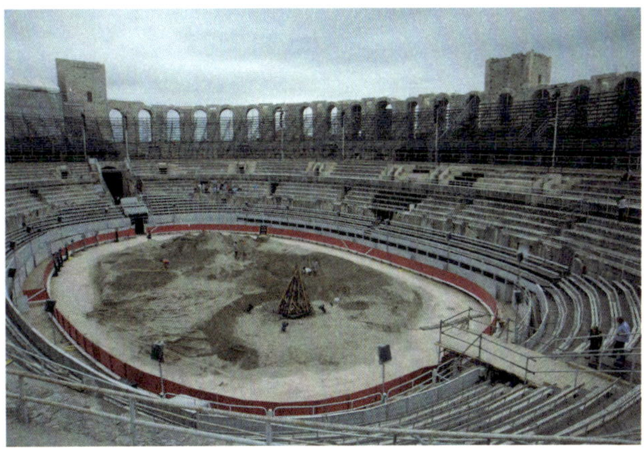

7/8/12—9:59:31 AM

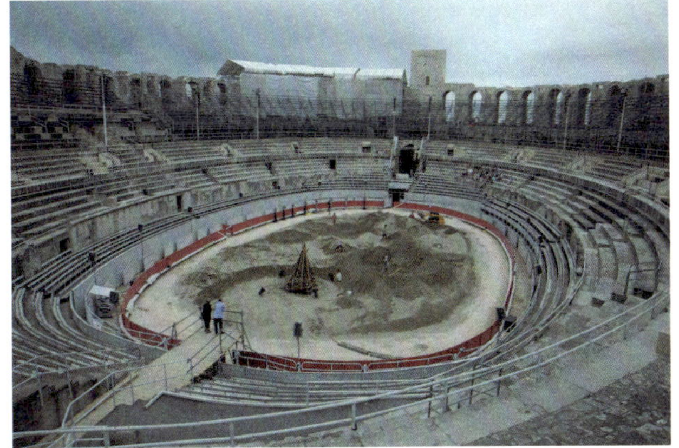

7/8/12—10:00:26 AM

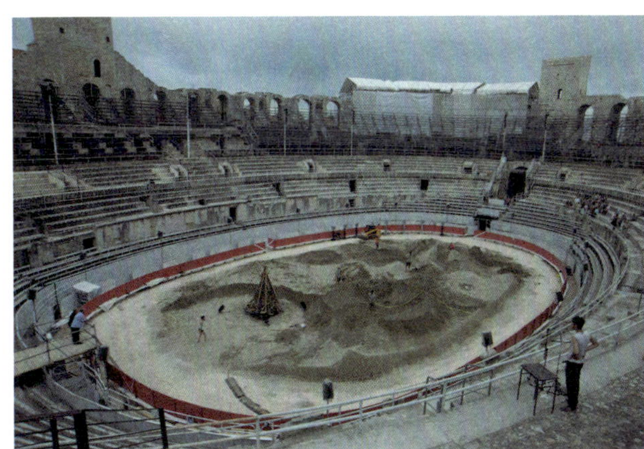

7/8/12—10:00:46 AM

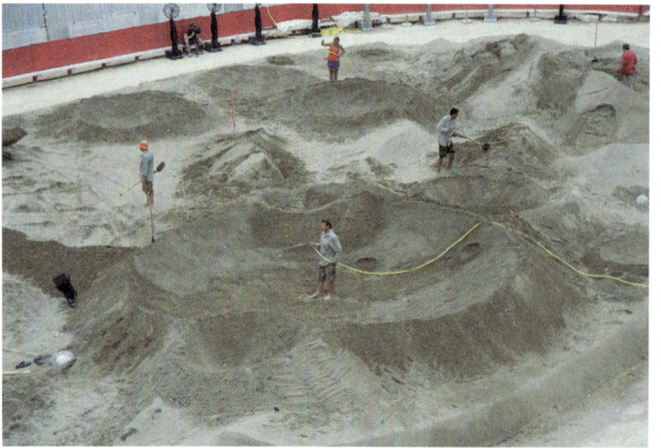

7/8/12—10:01:00 AM

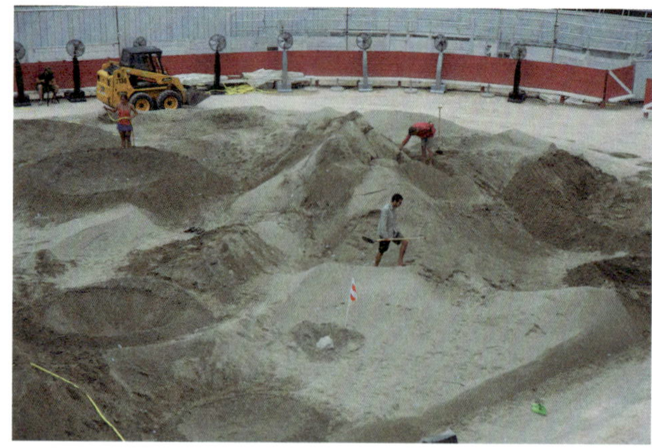

7/8/12—10:01:48 AM

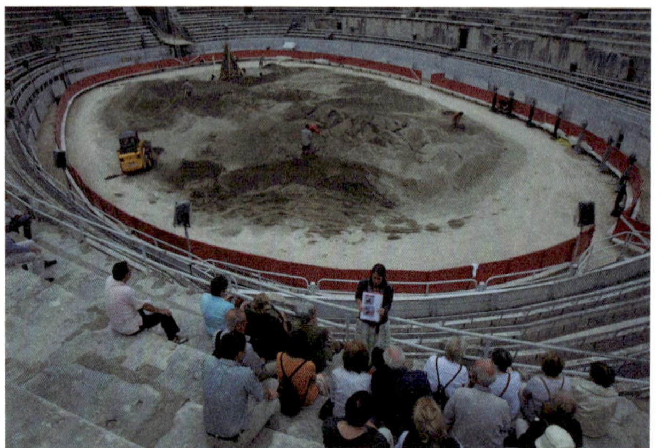

7/8/12—10:03:35 AM

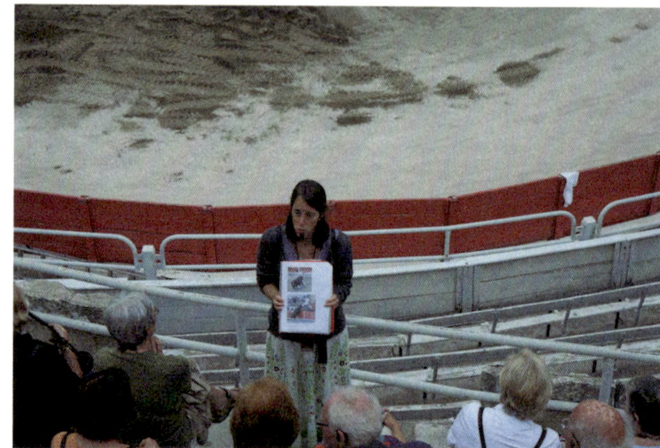

7/8/12—10:03:37 AM

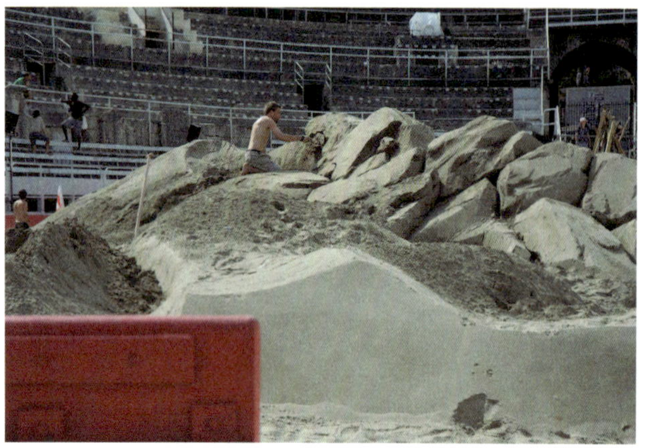

7/8/12—10:48:07 AM

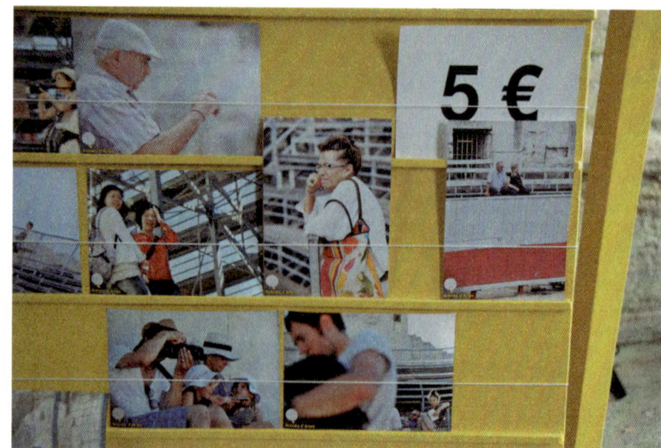

7/8/12—10:58:56 AM

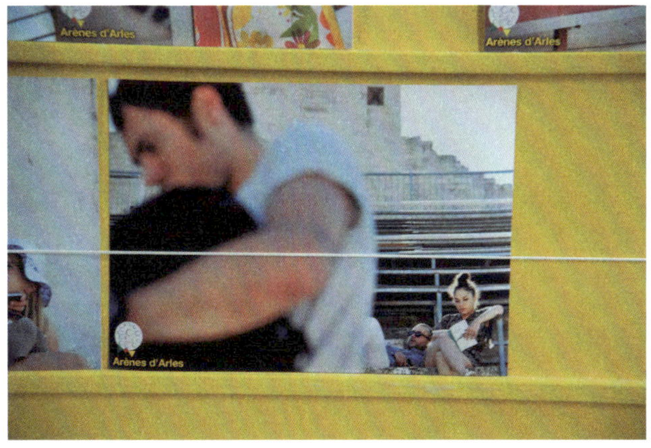

7/8/12—10:59:01 AM

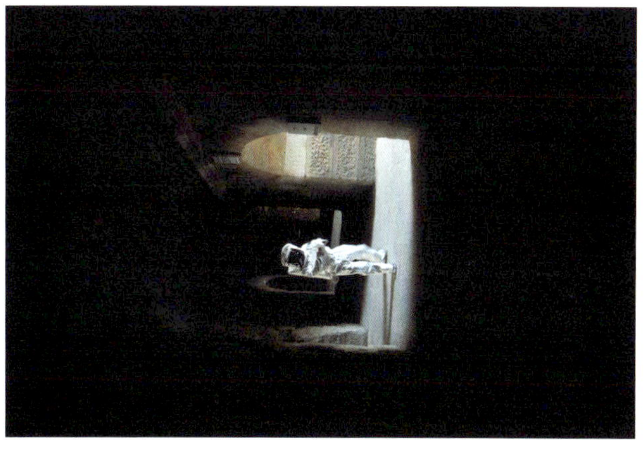

7/8/12—11:09:13 AM

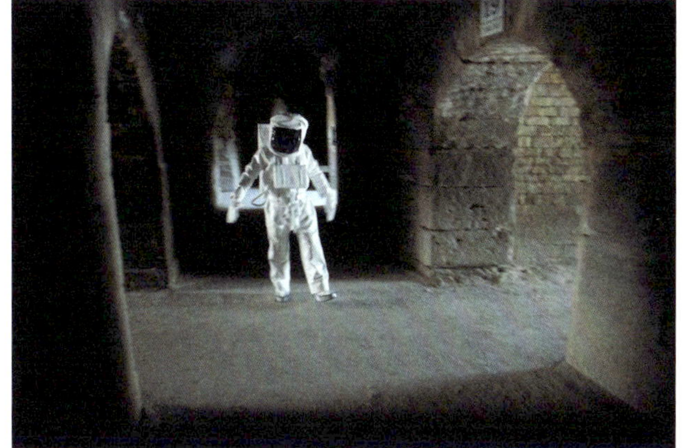

7/8/12—11:09:22 AM

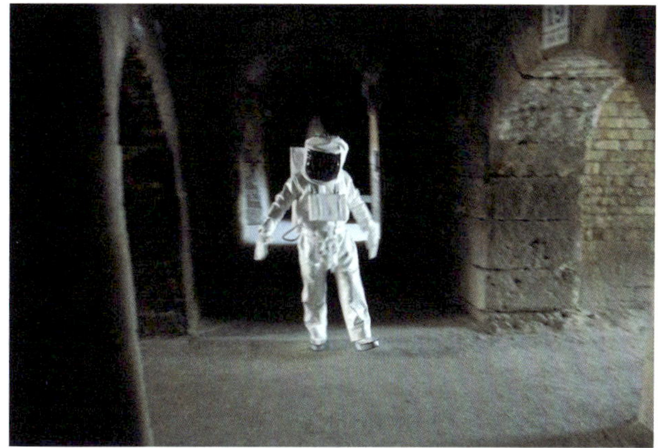

7/8/12—11:09:23 AM

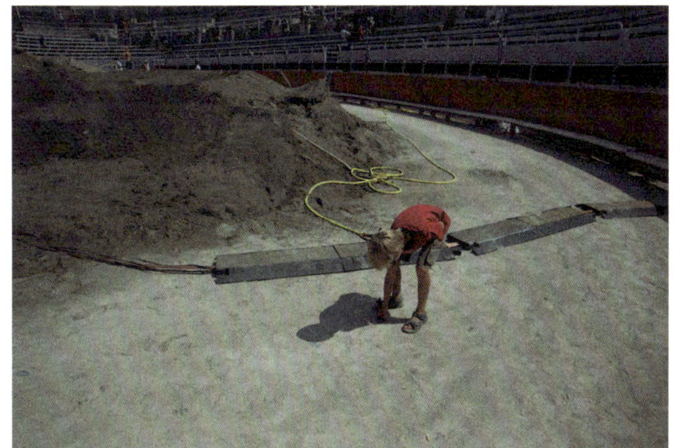

7/8/12—11:34:33 AM

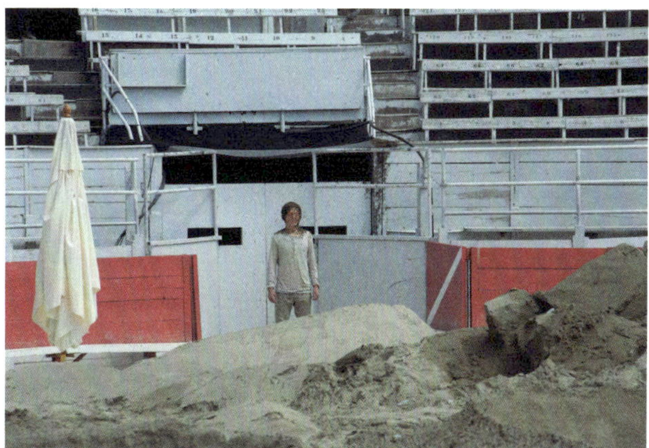

7/8/12—11:40:09 AM

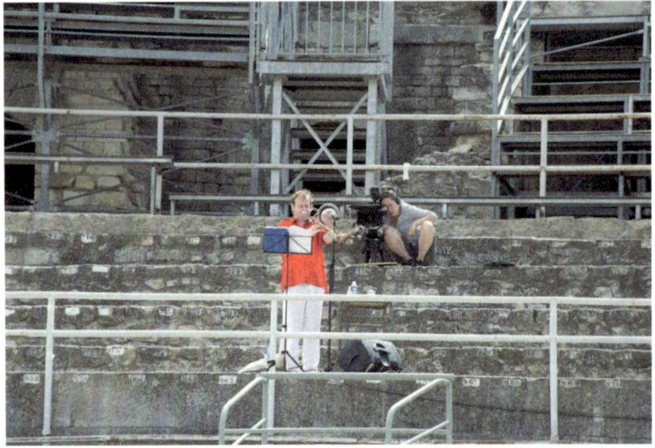
7/8/12—11:40:29 AM

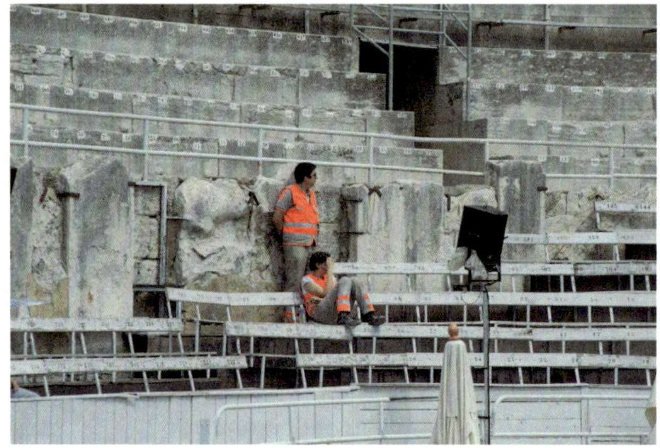
7/8/12—11:40:45 AM

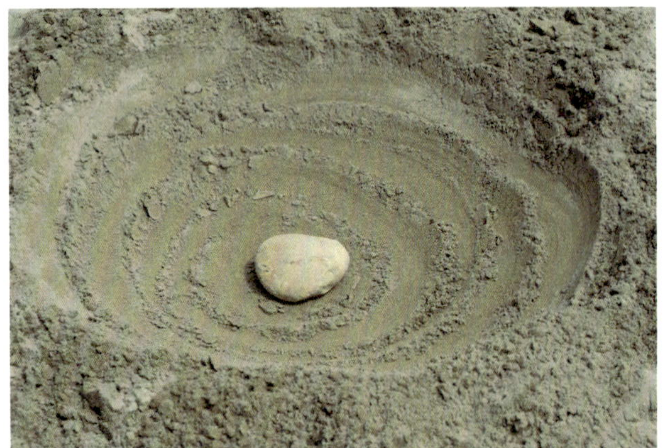
7/8/12—11:41:17 AM

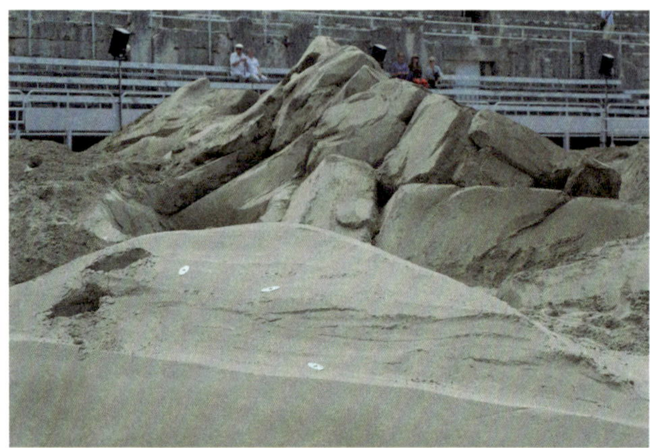
7/8/12—11:44:08 AM

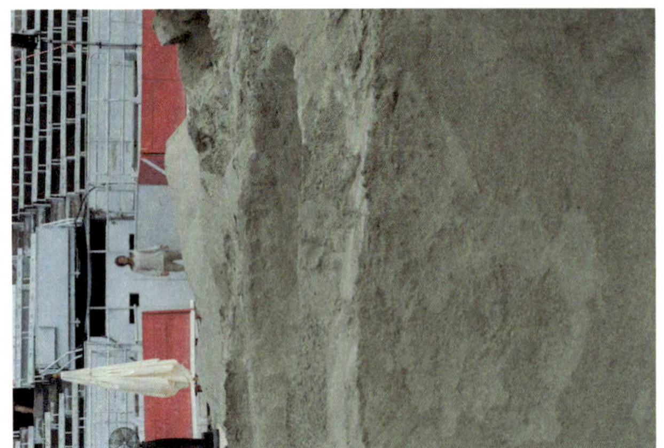
7/8/12—11:46:56 AM

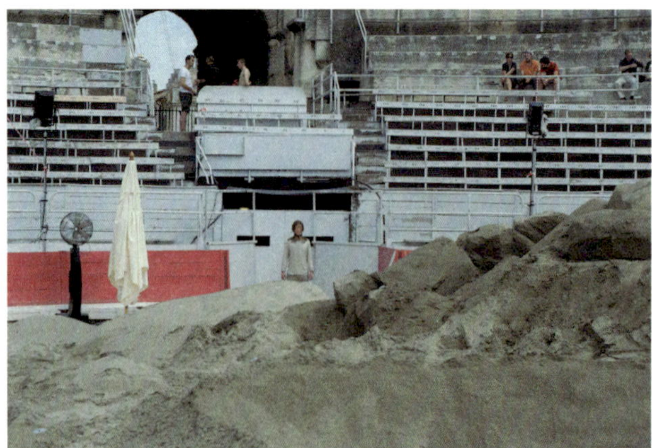
7/8/12—11:47:09 AM

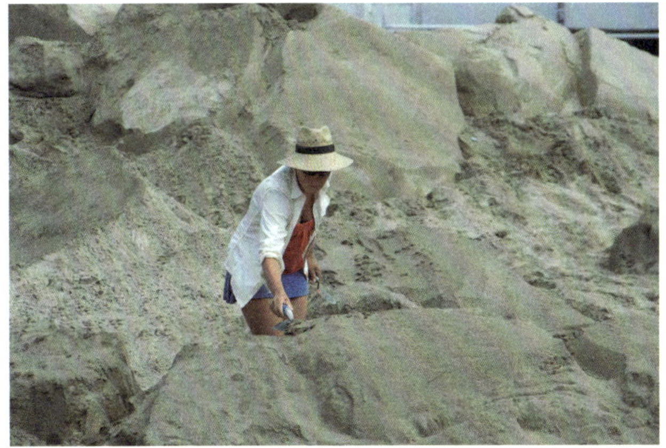

7/8/12—11:47:46 AM

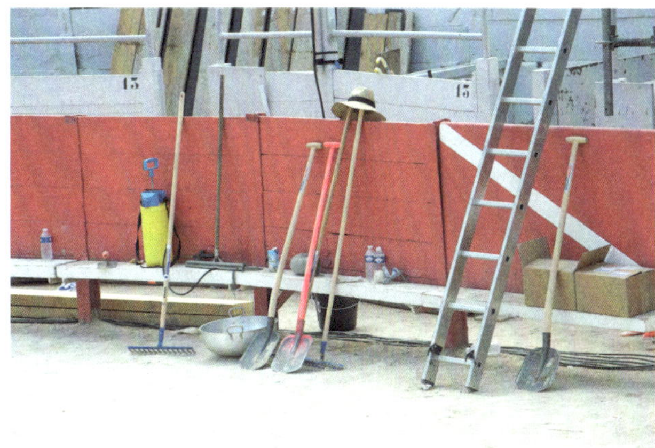

7/8/12—11:51:16 AM

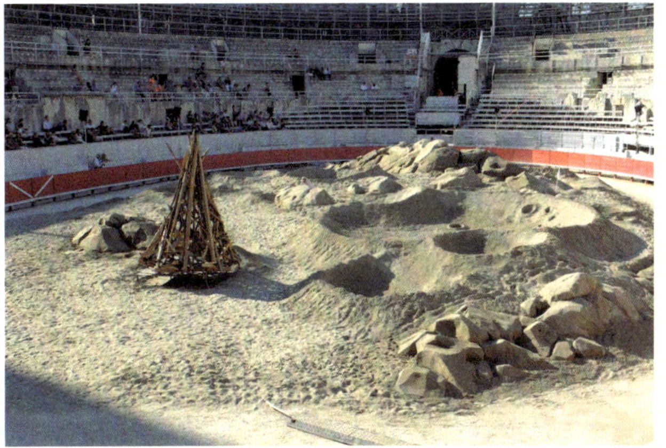

7/8/12—12:35:18 PM

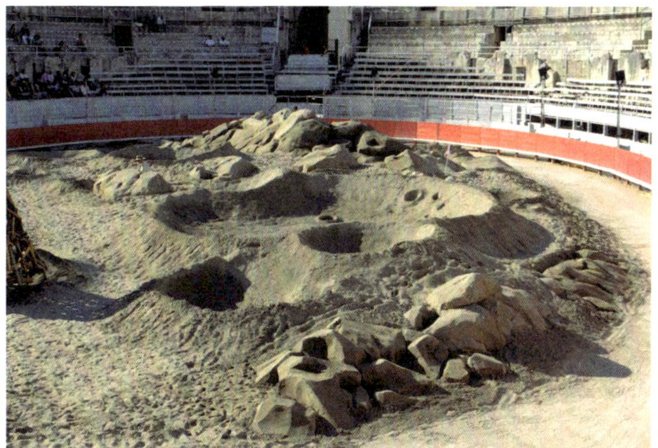

7/8/12—12:35:23 PM

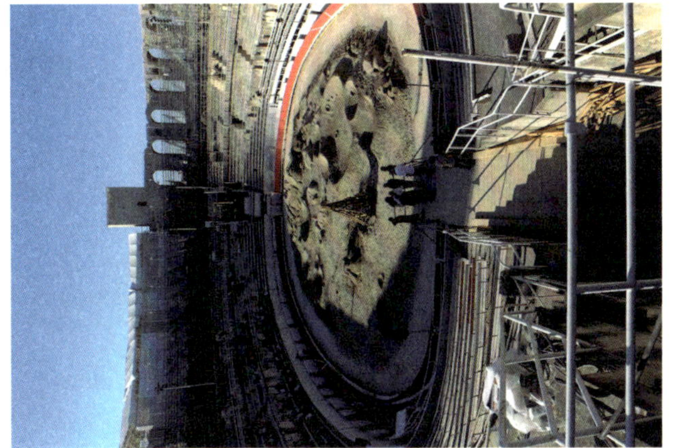

7/8/12—12:36:39 PM

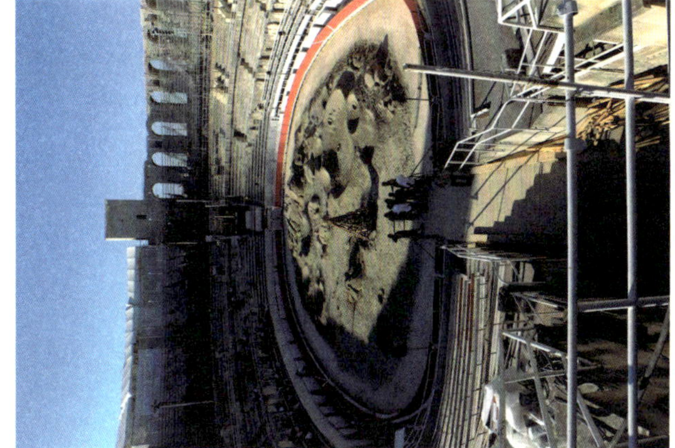

7/8/12—12:36:45 PM

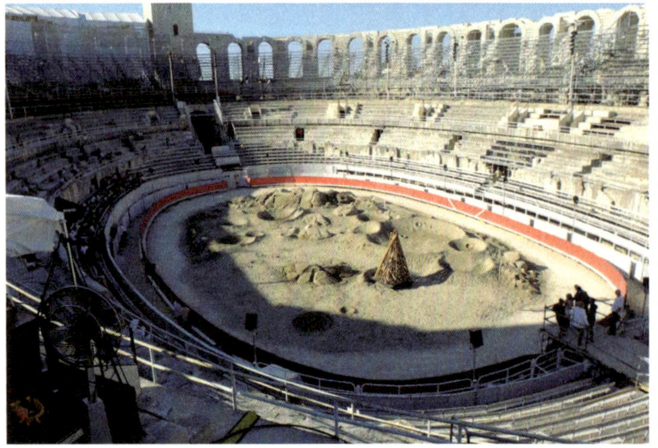

7/8/12—12:37:15 PM

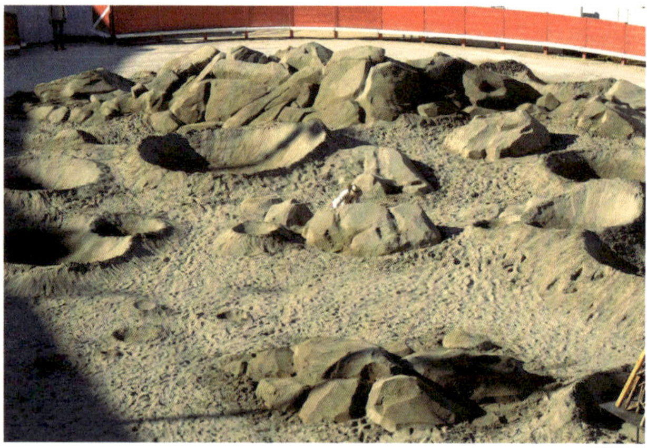

7/8/12—12:37:25 PM

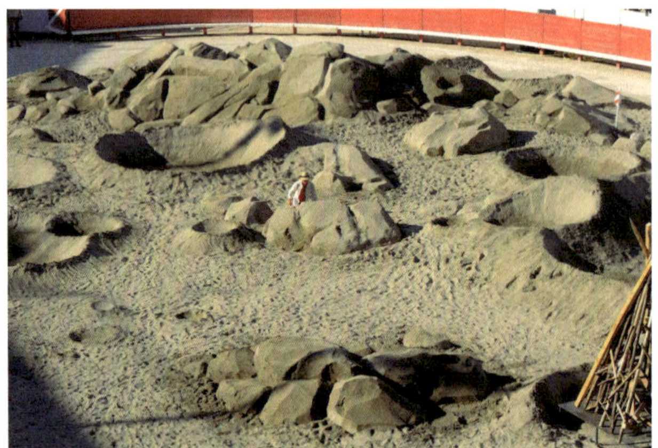

7/8/12—12:37:29 PM

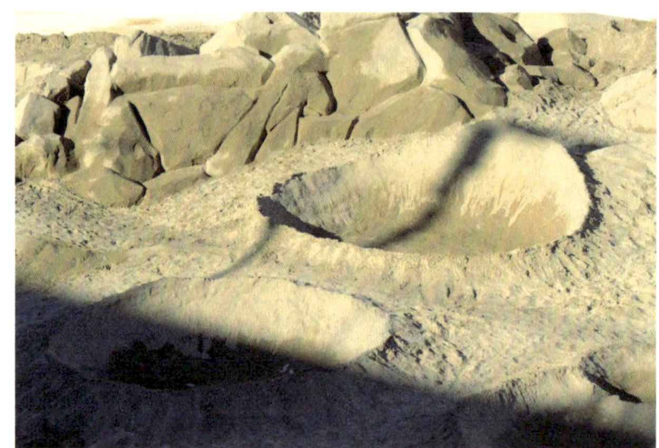

7/8/12—12:39:55 PM

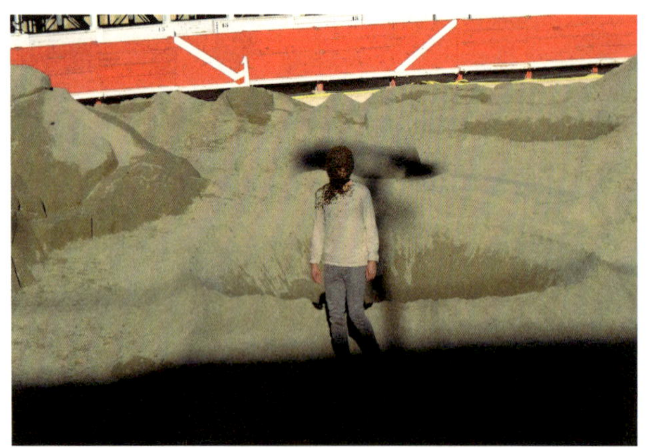

7/8/12—12:48:29 PM

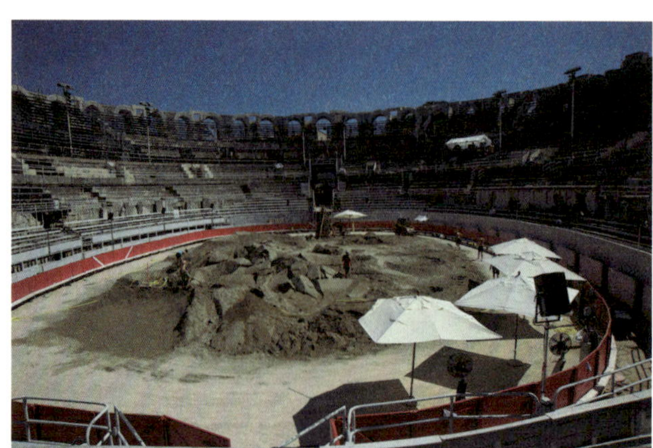

7/8/12—4:09:33 PM

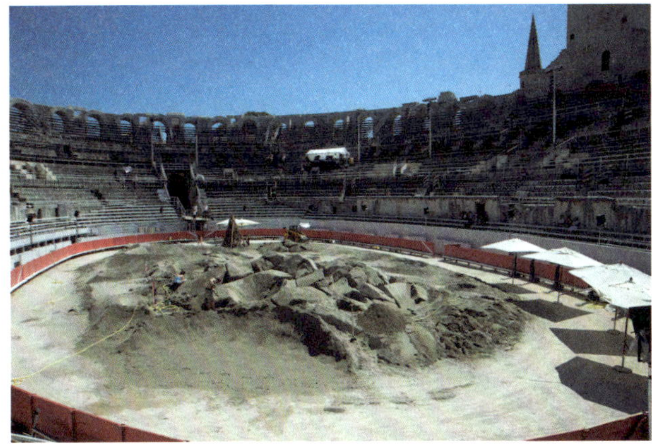
7/8/12—4:11:04 PM

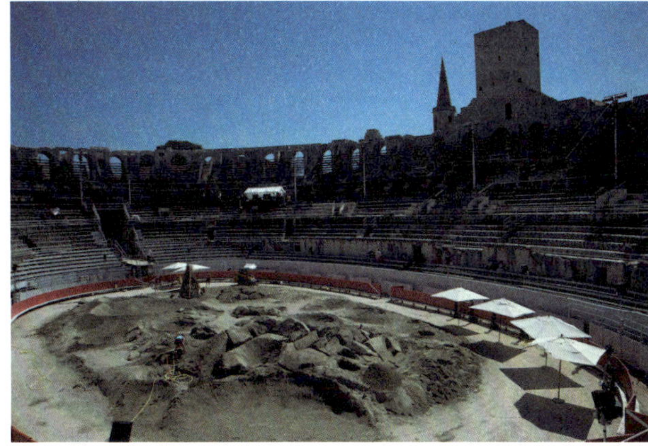
7/8/12—4:11:26 PM

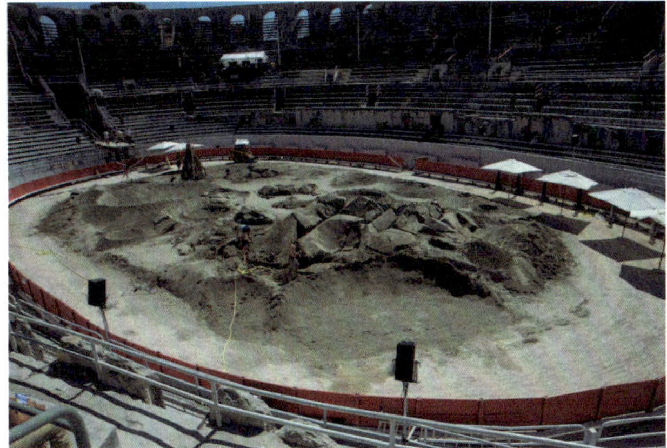
7/8/12—4:11:57 PM

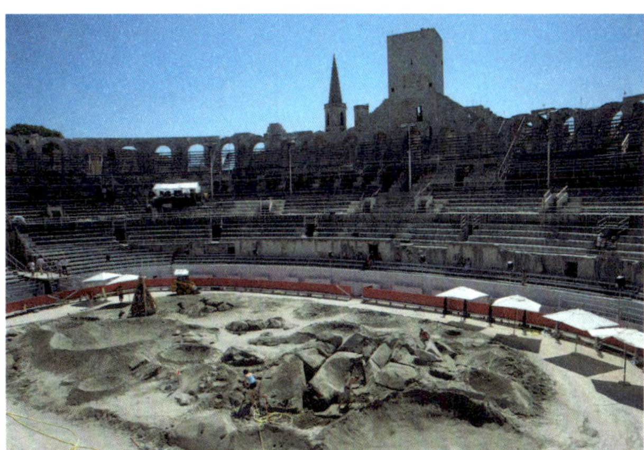
7/8/12—4:12:16 PM

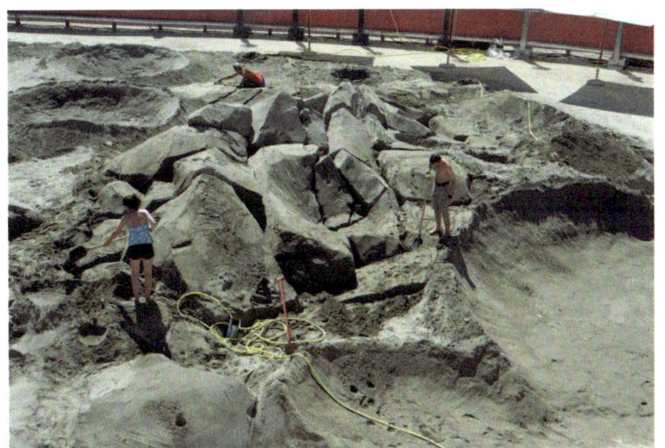
7/8/12—4:14:41 PM

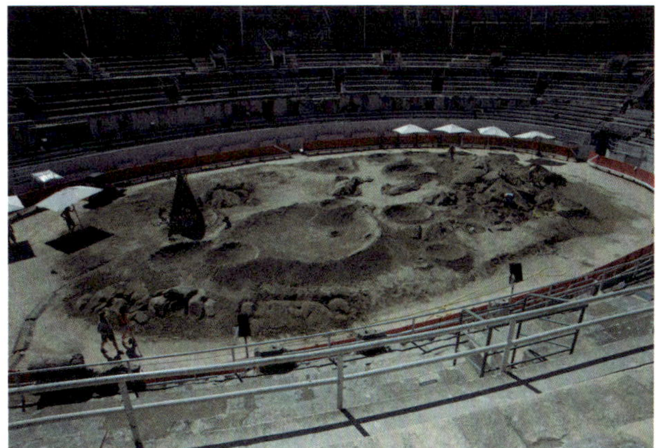
7/8/12—4:15:31 PM

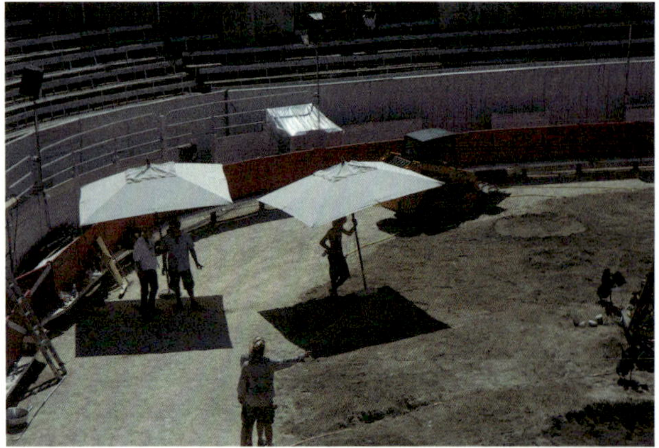
7/8/12—4:15:44 PM

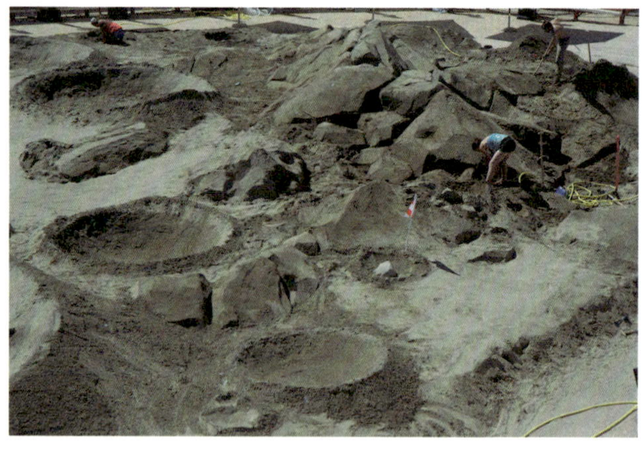
7/8/12—4:16:03 PM

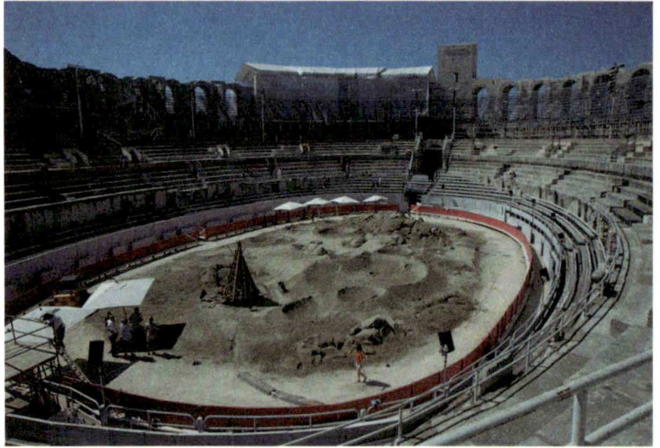
7/8/12—4:16:53 PM

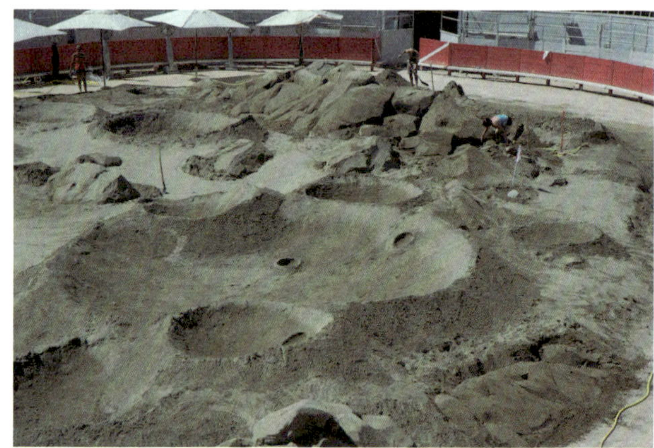
7/8/12—4:16:55 PM

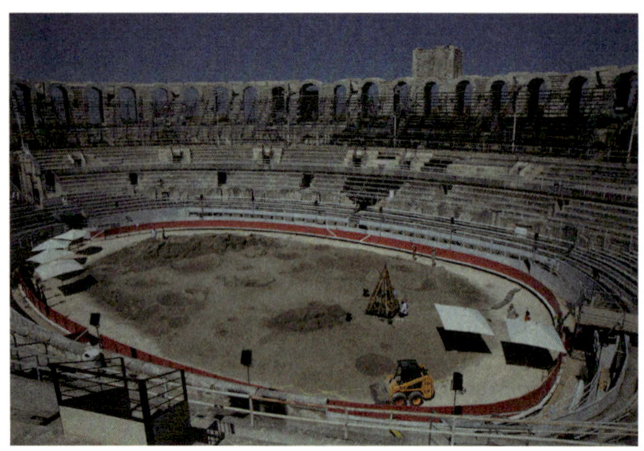
7/8/12—4:18:05 PM

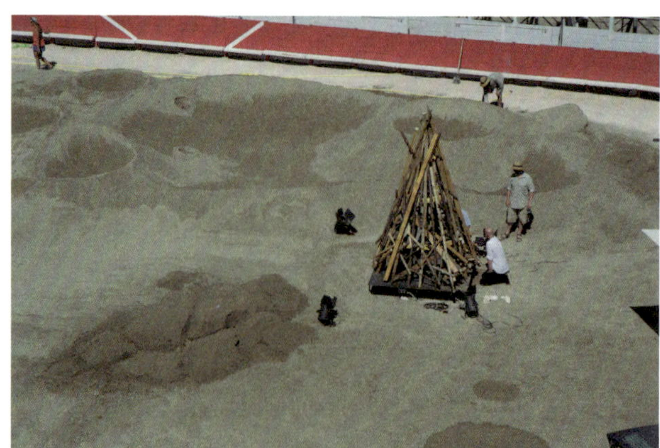
7/8/12—4:18:31 PM

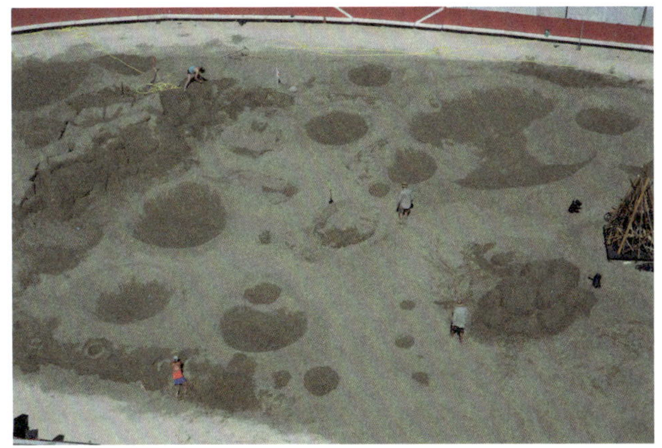
7/8/12—4:23:59 PM

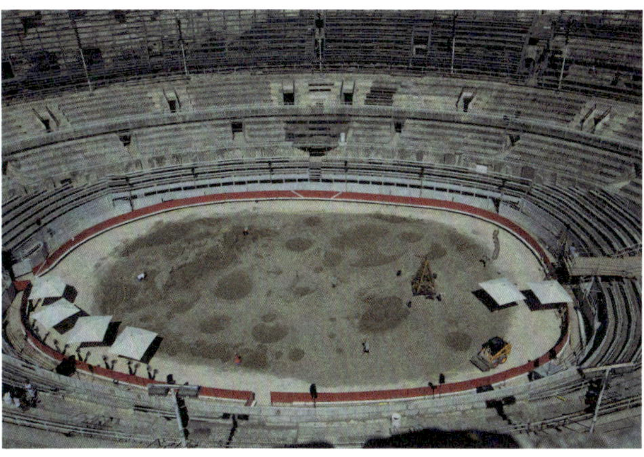
7/8/12—4:24:26 PM

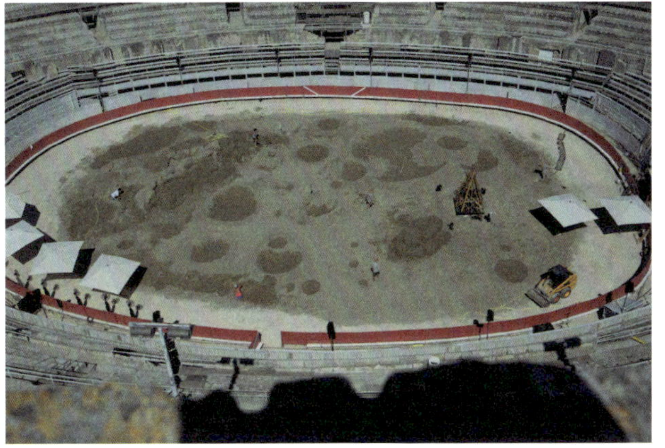
7/8/12—4:24:29 PM

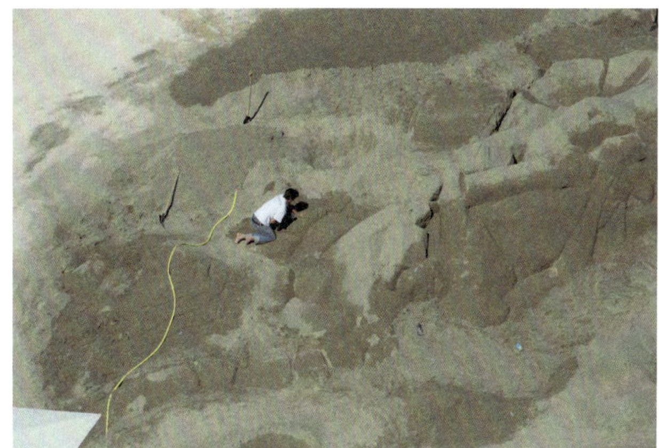
7/8/12—4:25:12 PM

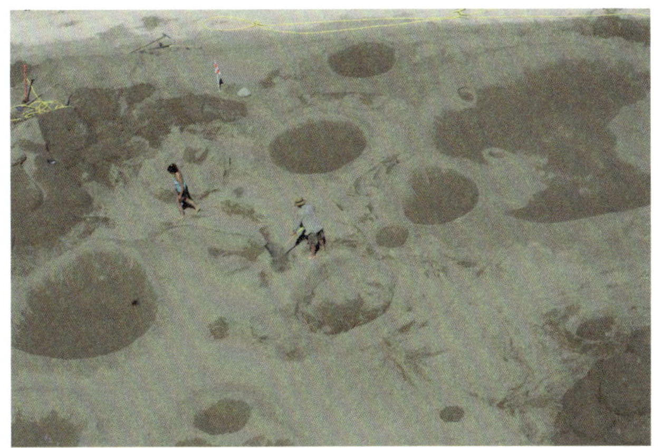
7/8/12—4:25:27 PM

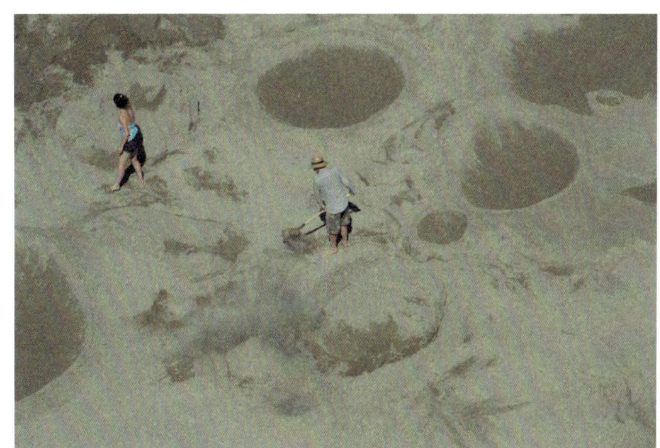
7/8/12—4:25:38 PM

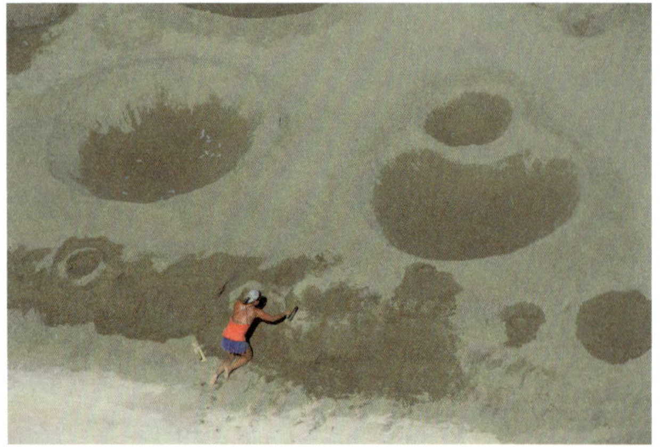
7/8/12—4:25:45 PM

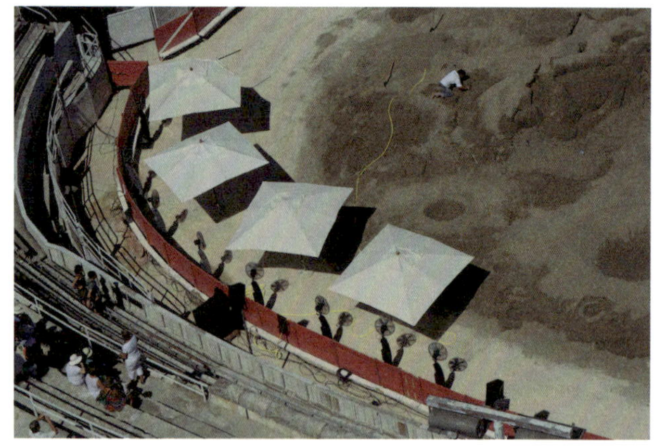
7/8/12—4:26:26 PM

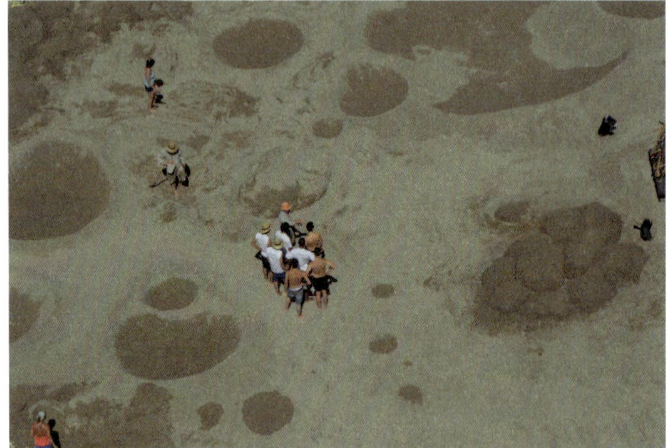
7/8/12—4:26:57 PM

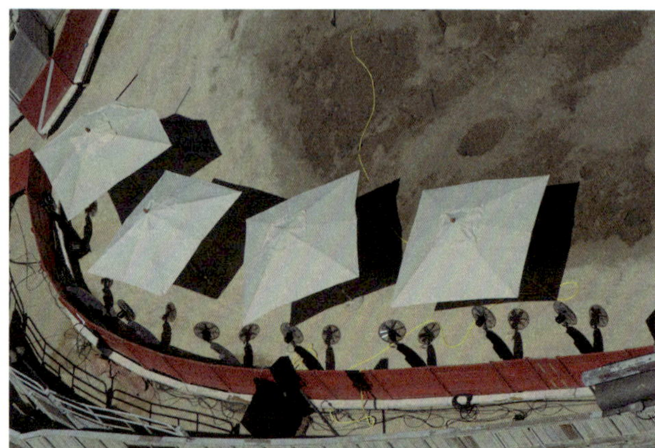
7/8/12—4:27:29 PM

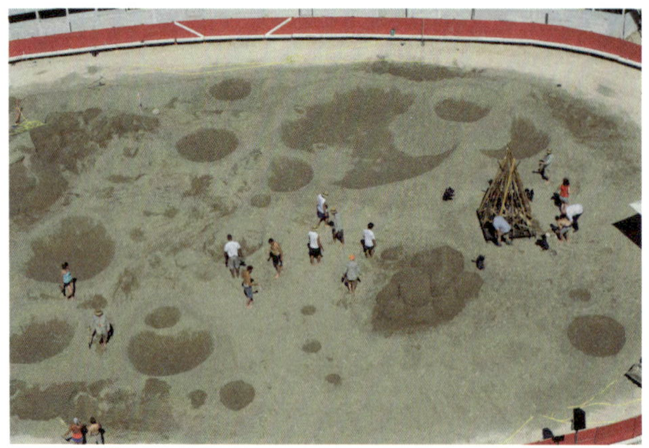
7/8/12—4:28:36 PM

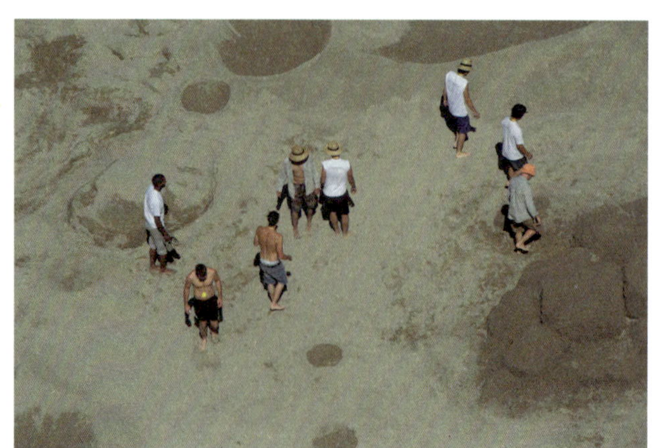
7/8/12—4:28:40 PM

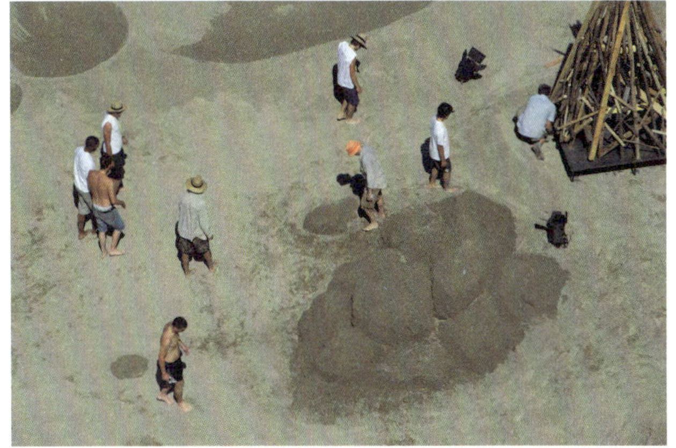

7/8/12—4:28:44 PM

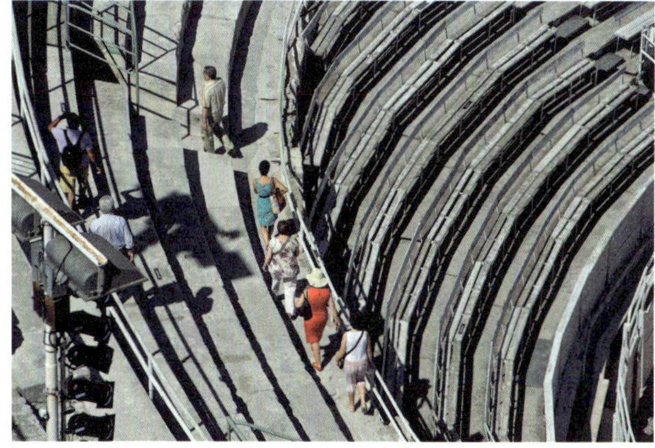

7/8/12—4:29:05 PM

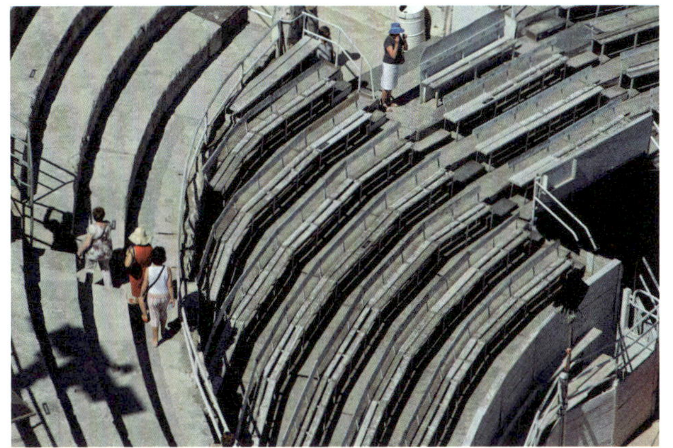

7/8/12—4:29:12 PM

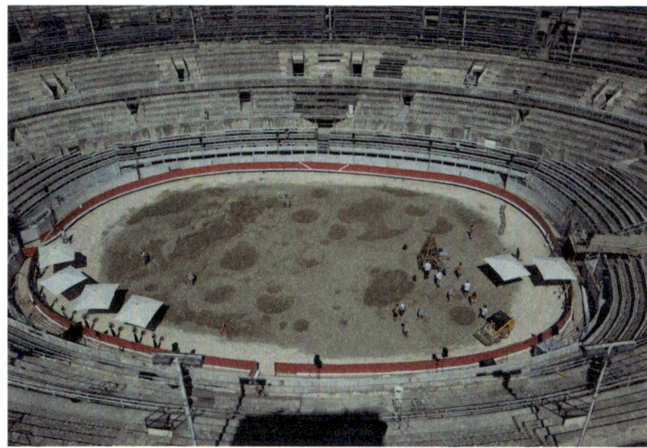

7/8/12—4:31:27 PM

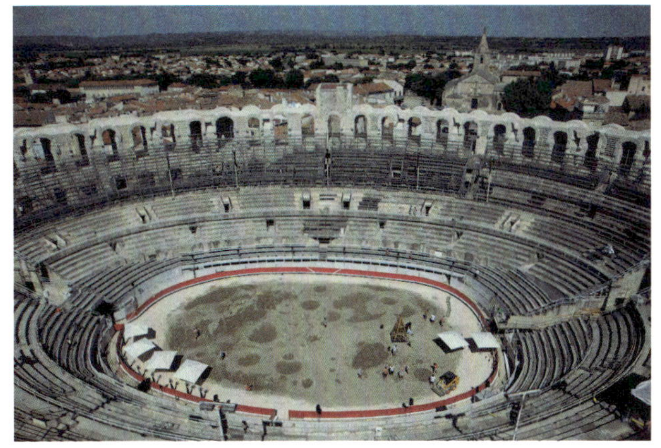

7/8/12—4:31:38 PM

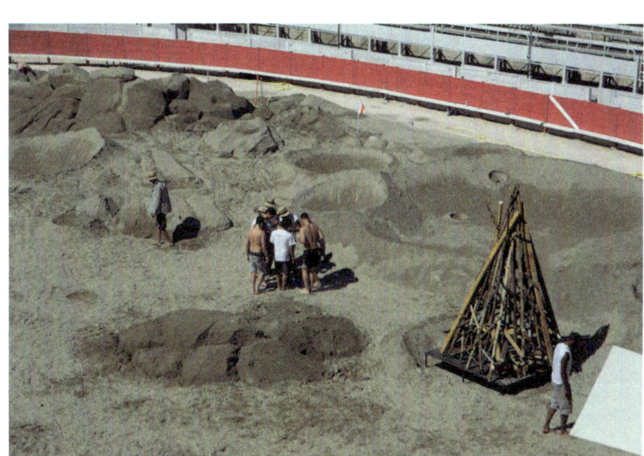

7/8/12—4:37:04 PM

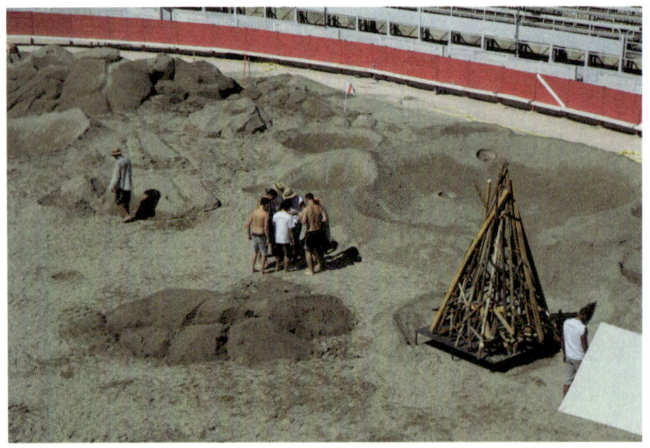

7/8/12—4:37:05 PM

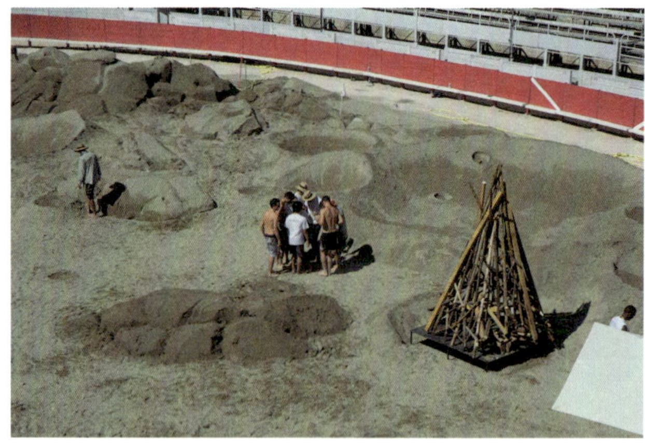

7/8/12—4:37:07 PM

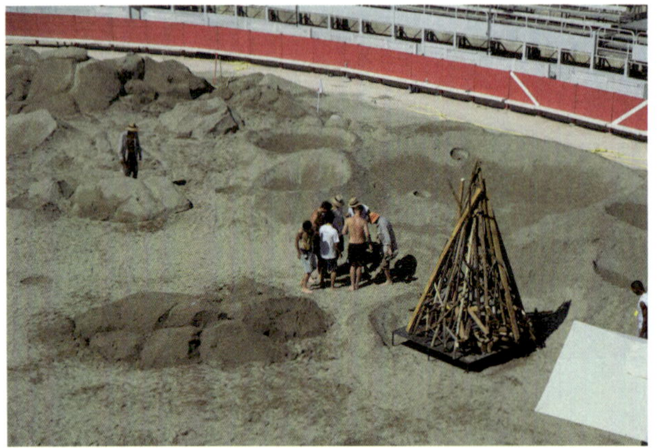

7/8/12—4:37:13 PM

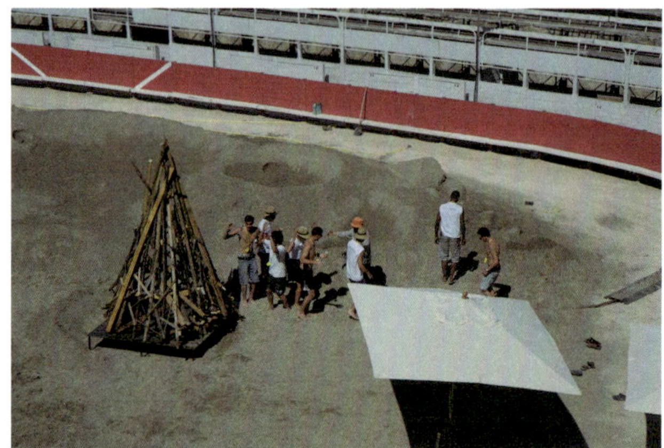

7/8/12—4:37:43 PM

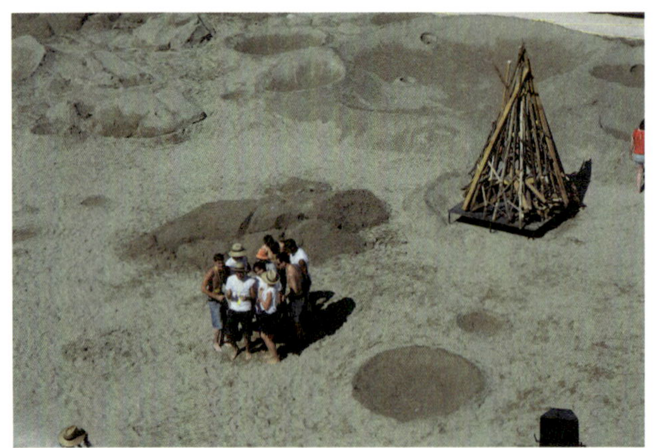

7/8/12—4:39:35 PM

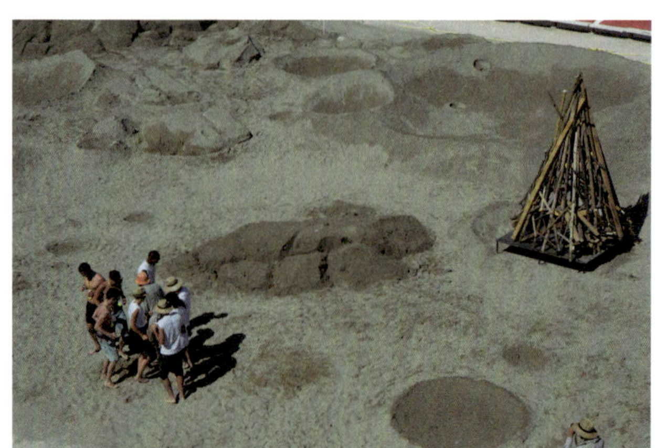

7/8/12—4:39:53 PM

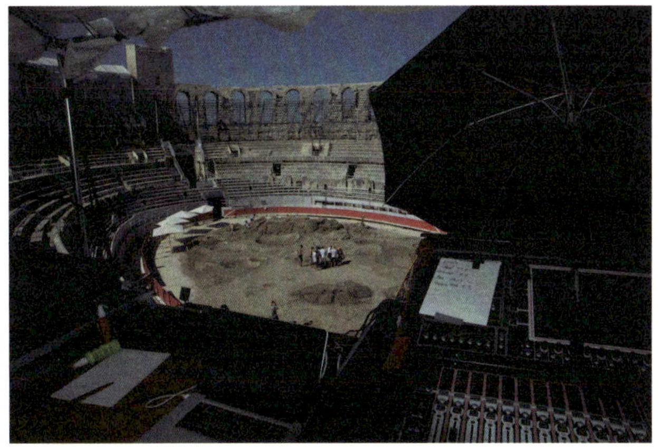

7/8/12—4:40:55 PM

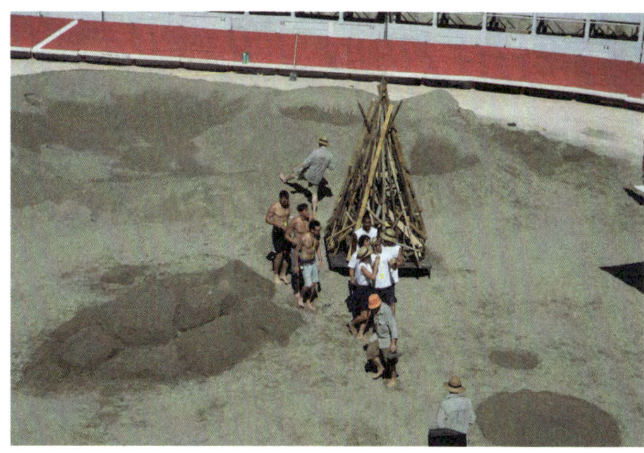

7/8/12—4:41:30 PM

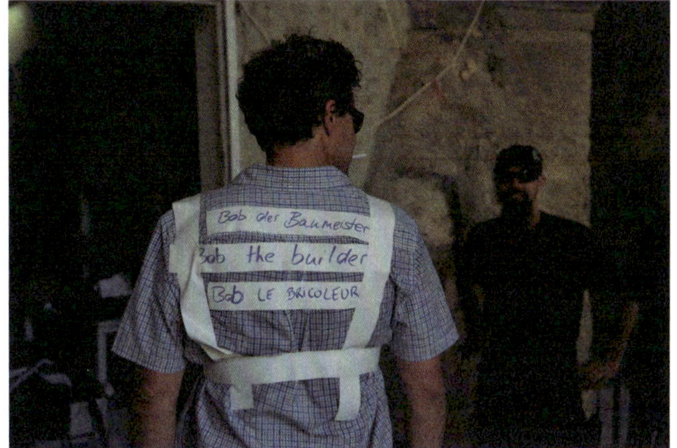

7/8/12—4:43:26 PM

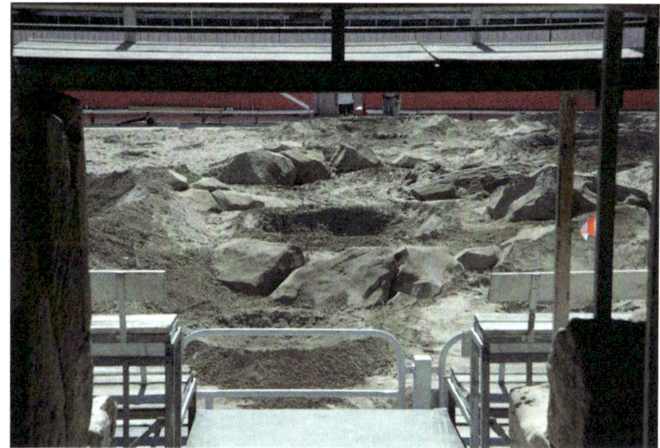

7/8/12—4:47:36 PM

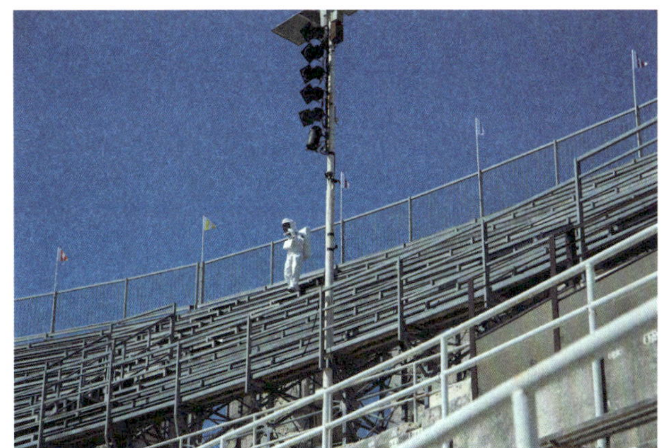

7/8/12—4:48:10 PM

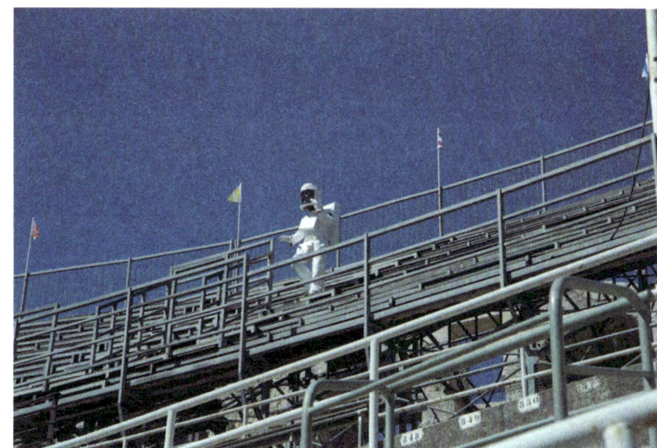

7/8/12—4:48:23 PM

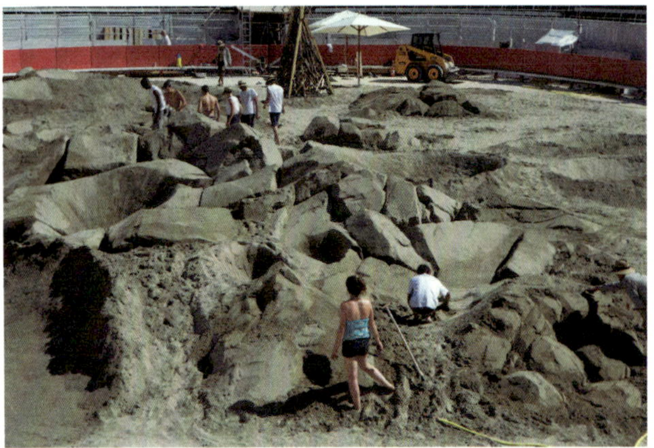
7/8/12—4:49:14 PM

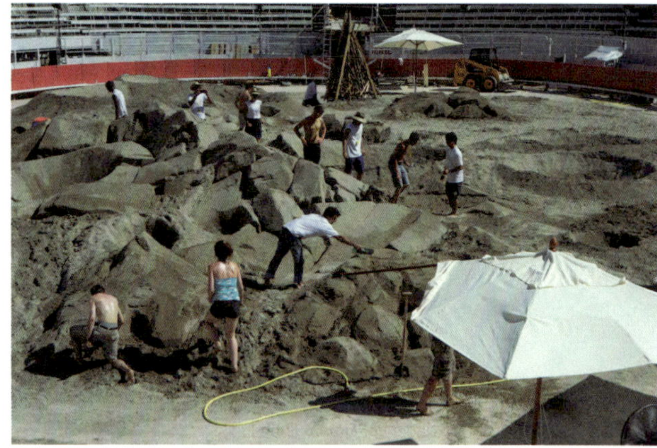
7/8/12—4:50:44 PM

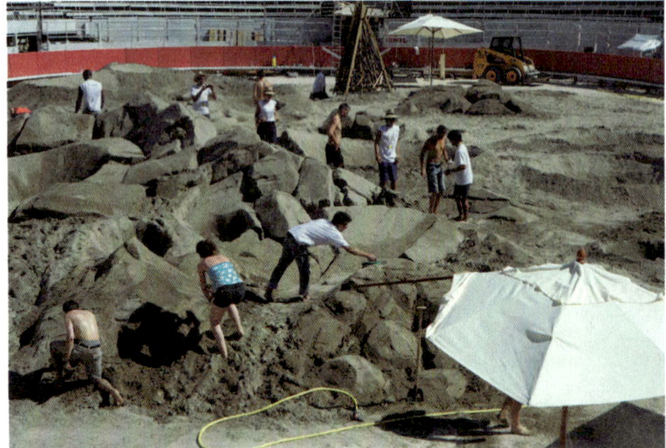
7/8/12—4:50:45 PM

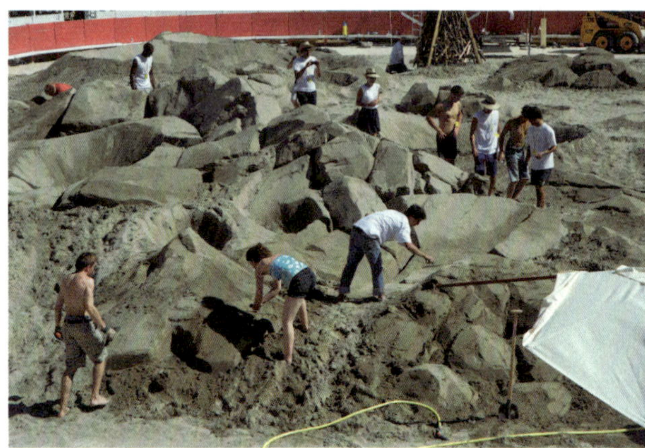
7/8/12—4:50:47 PM

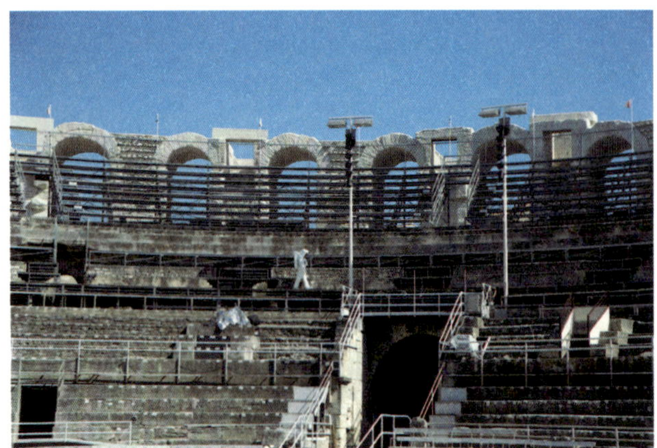
7/8/12—4:52:58 PM

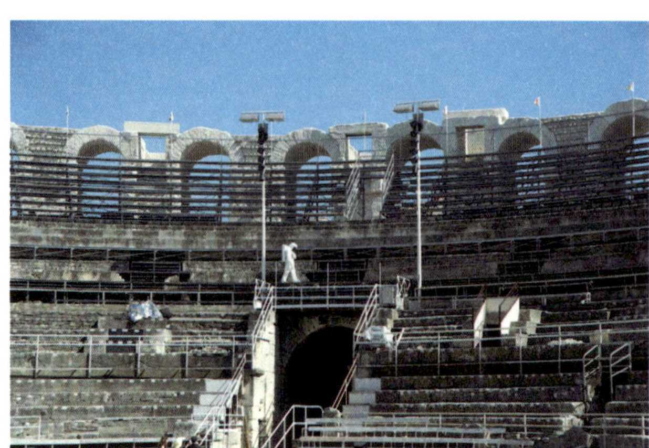
7/8/12—4:53:02 PM

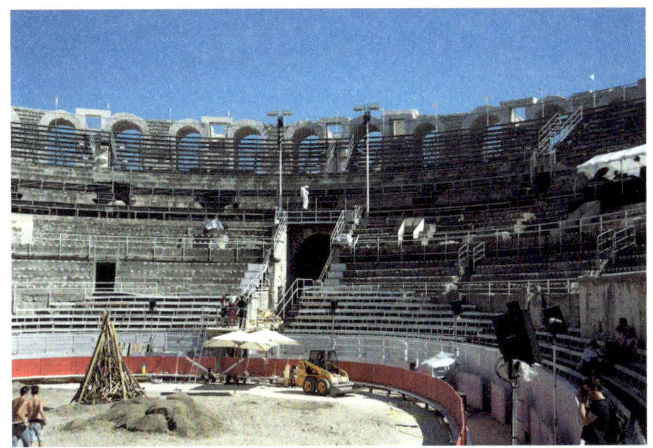
7/8/12—4:53:04 PM

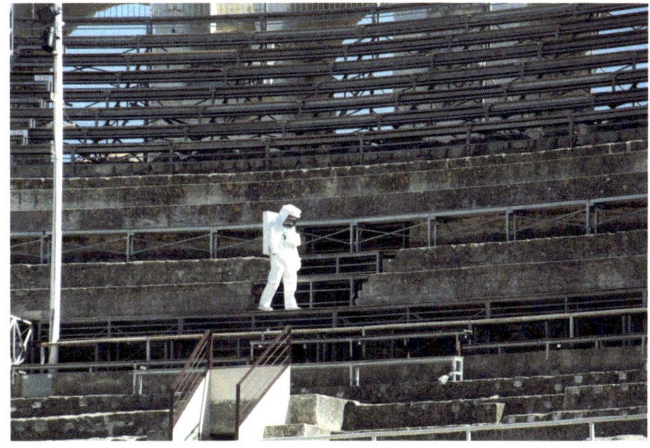
7/8/12—4:53:43 PM

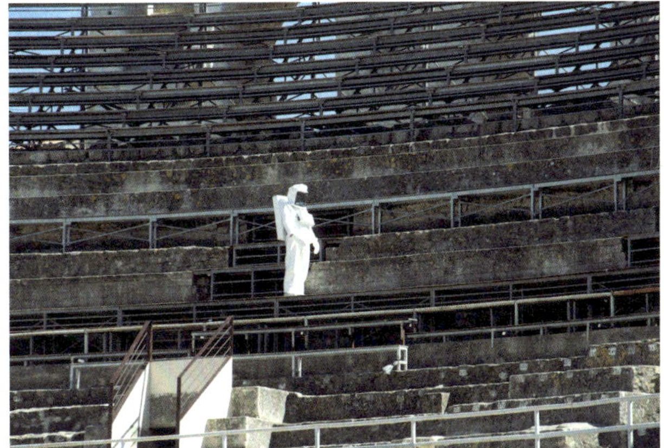
7/8/12—4:53:46 PM

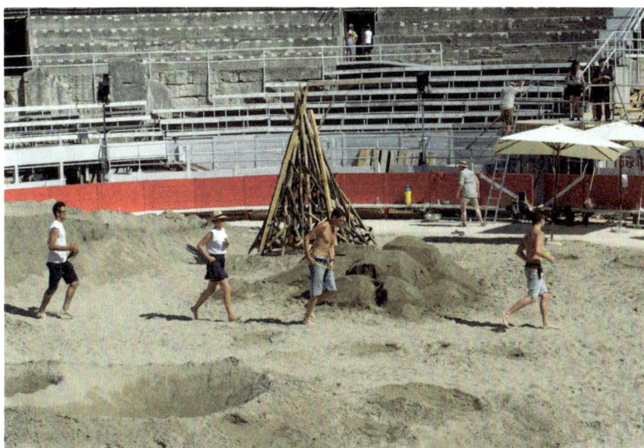
7/8/12—4:53:50 PM

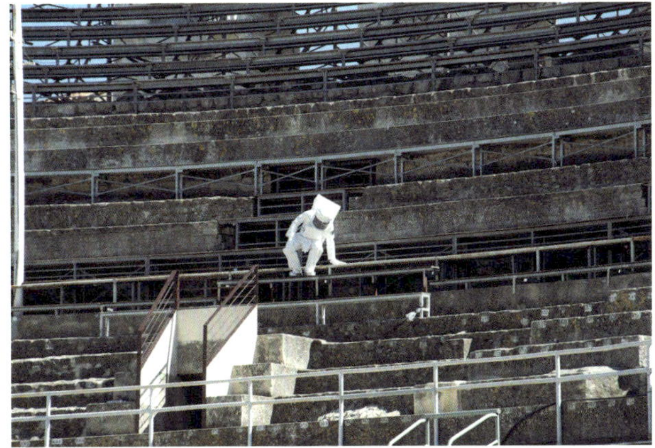
7/8/12—4:54:06 PM

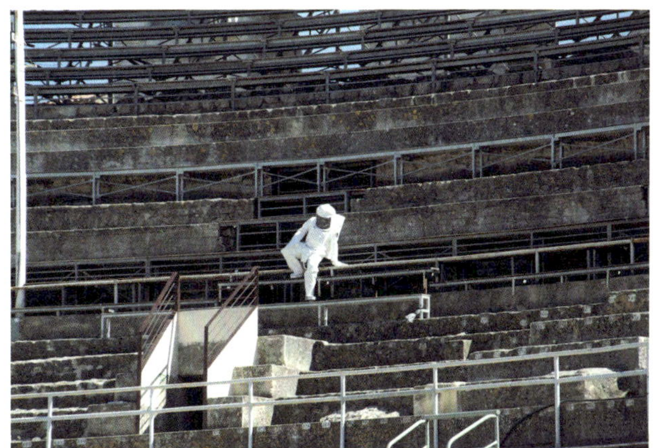
7/8/12—4:54:08 PM

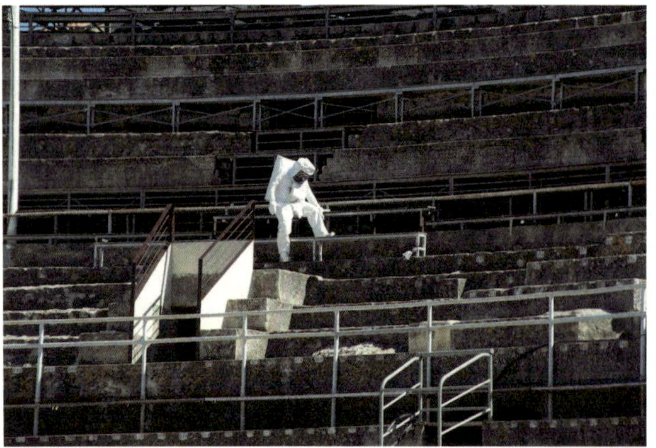
7/8/12—4:54:17 PM

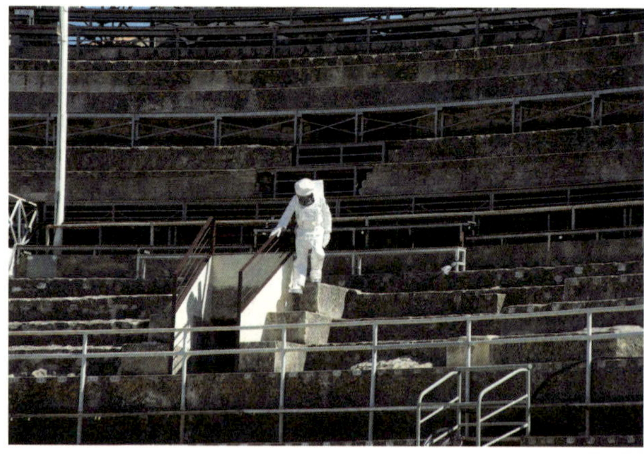
7/8/12—4:54:25 PM

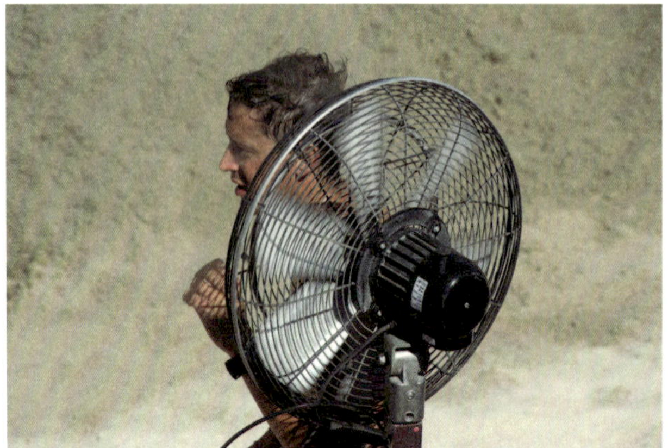
7/8/12—4:54:49 PM

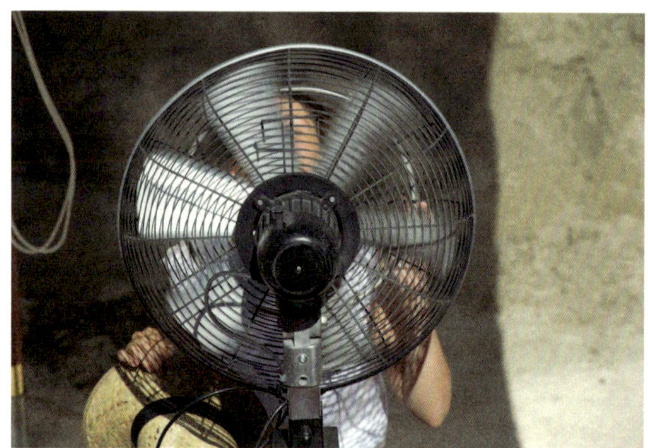
7/8/12—4:54:51 PM

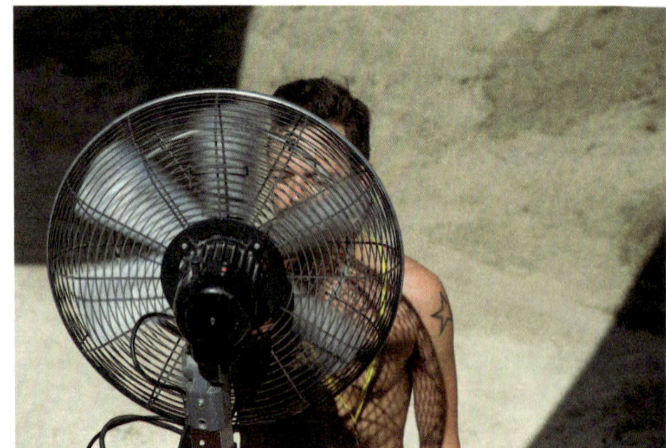
7/8/12—4:55:07 PM

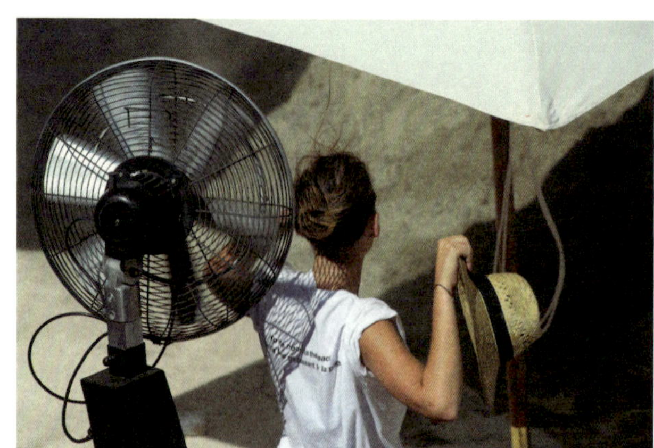
7/8/12—4:55:23 PM

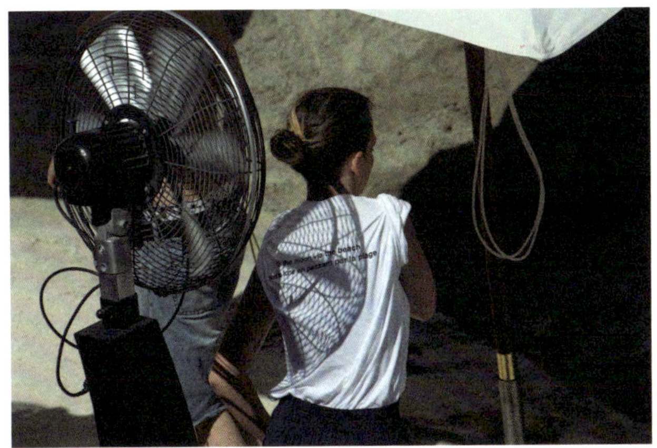

7/8/12—4:55:31 PM

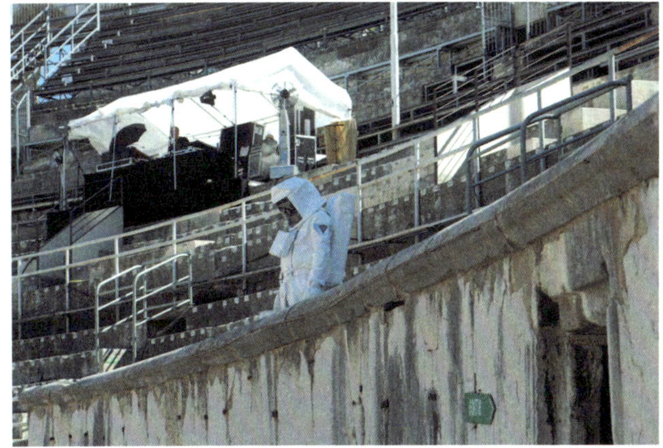

7/8/12—4:55:57 PM

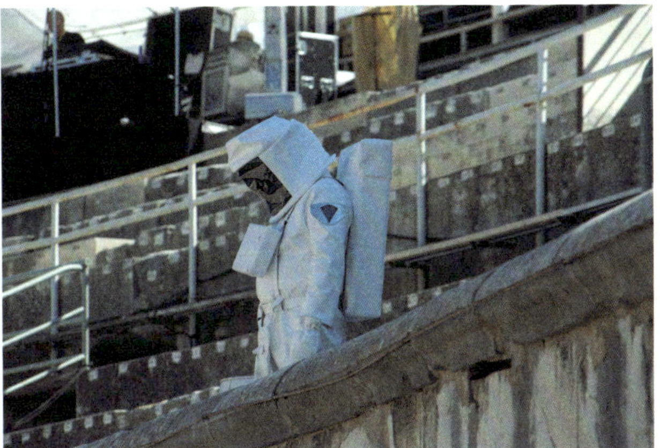

7/8/12—4:56:00 PM

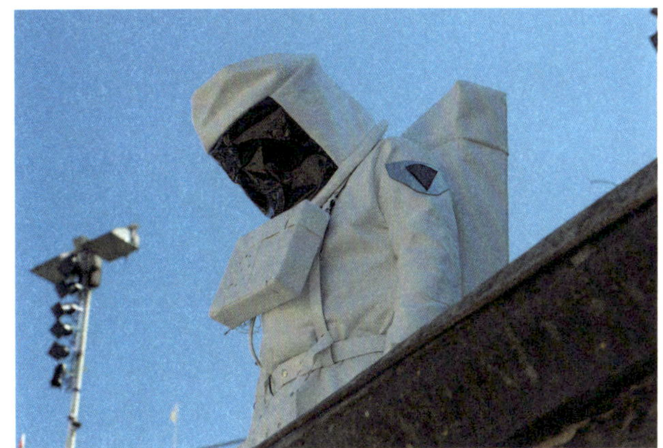

7/8/12—4:56:22 PM

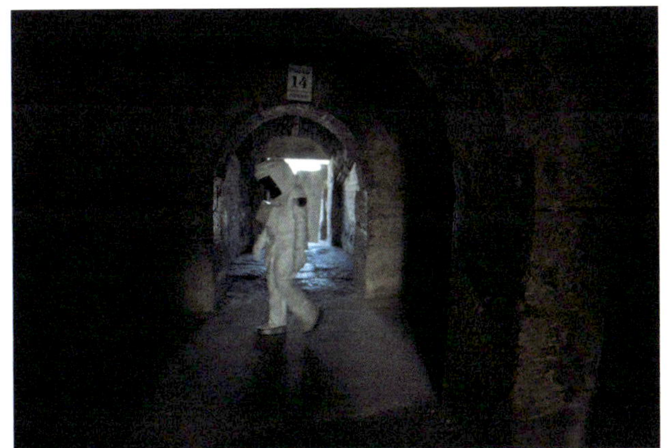

7/8/12—4:57:37 PM

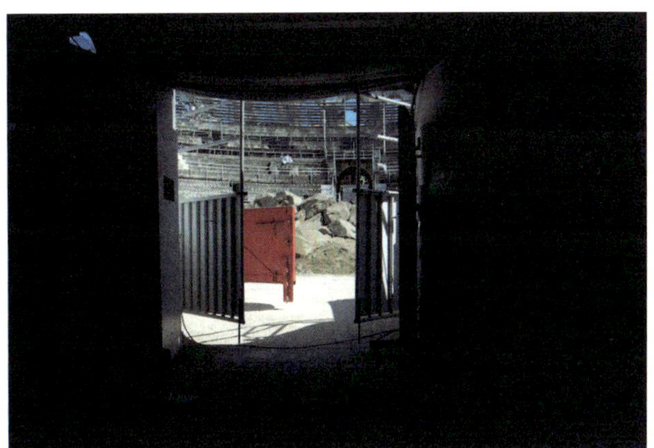

7/8/12—4:59:43 PM

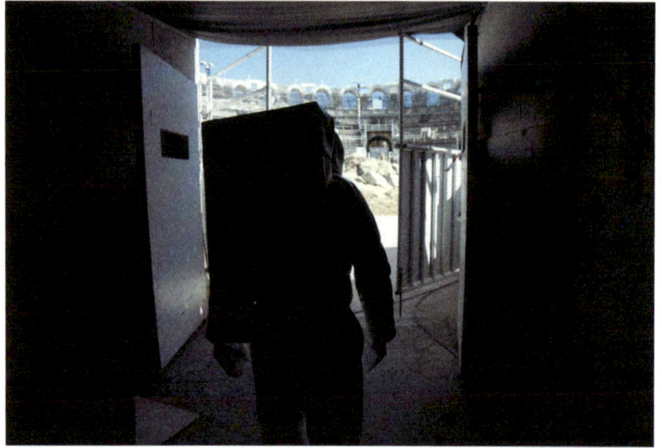

7/8/12—4:59:53 PM

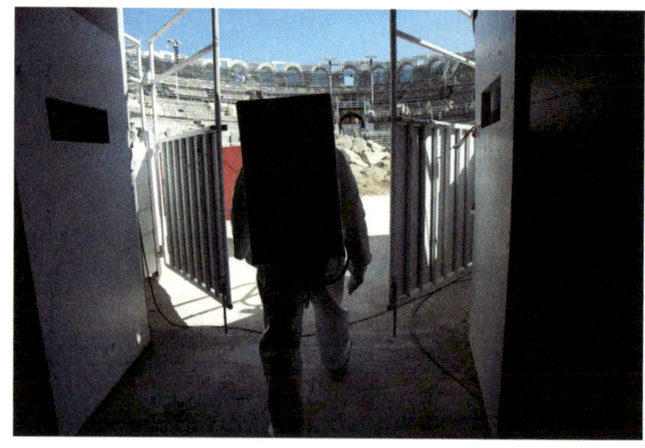

7/8/12—4:59:55 PM

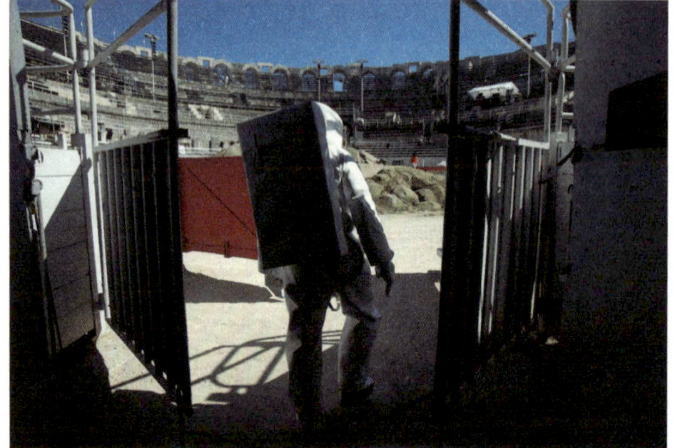

7/8/12—4:59:57 PM

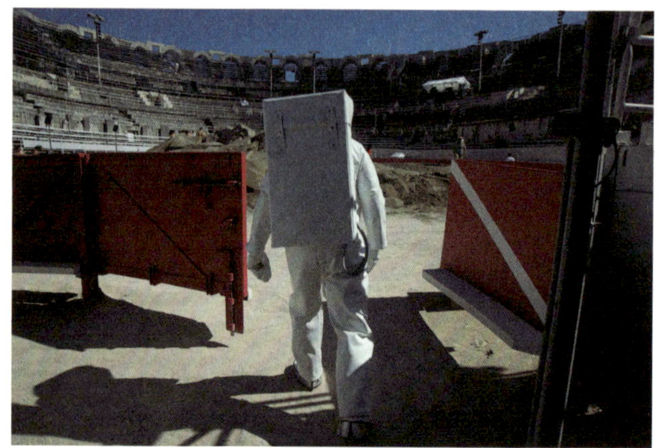

7/8/12—4:59:58 PM

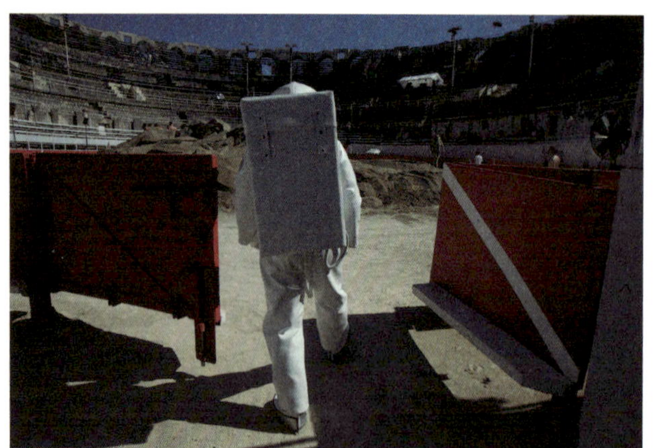

7/8/12—4:59:59 PM

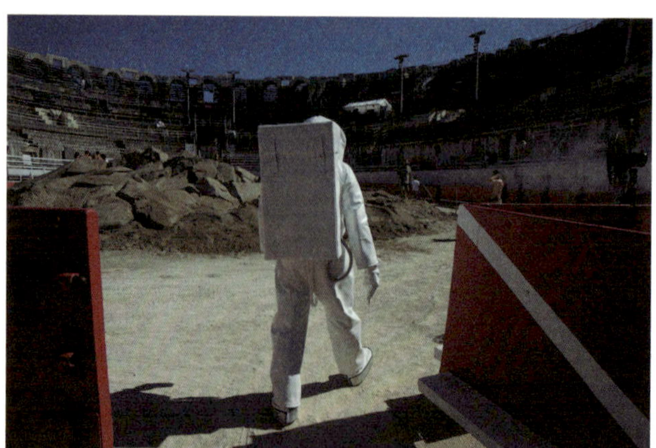

7/8/12—5:00:02 PM

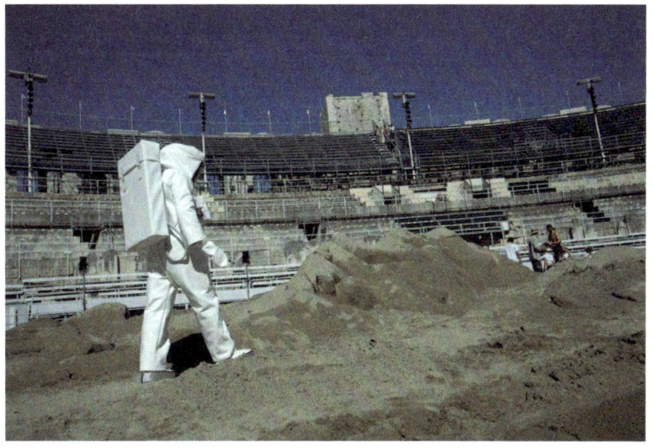
7/8/12—5:00:26 PM

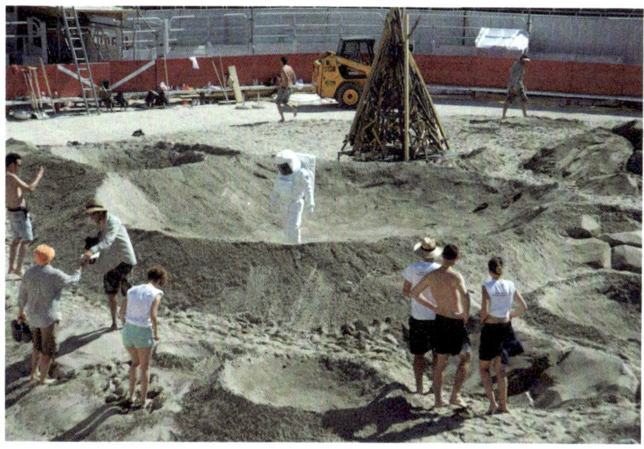
7/8/12—5:01:54 PM

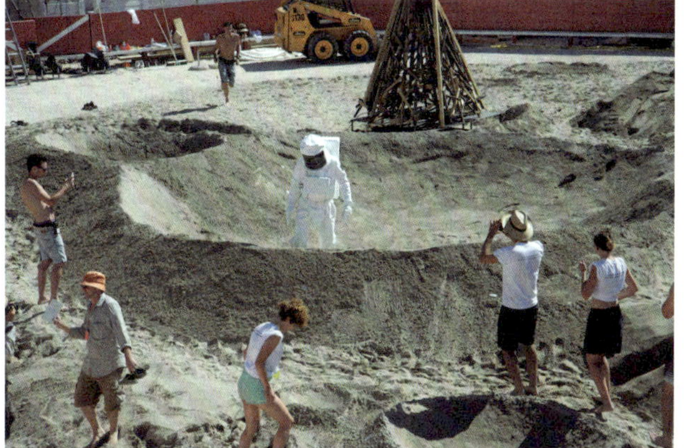
7/8/12—5:02:00 PM

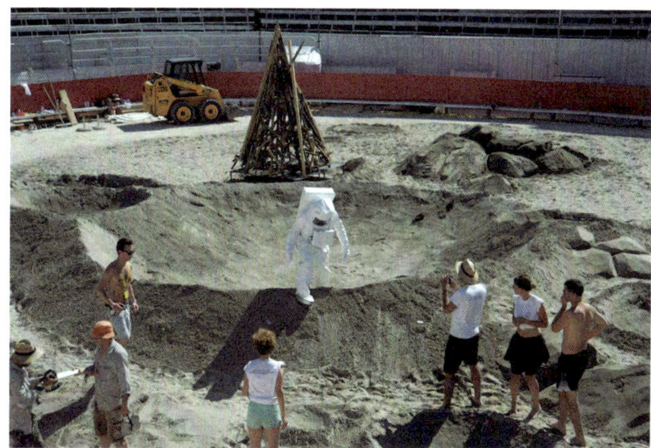
7/8/12—5:02:06 PM

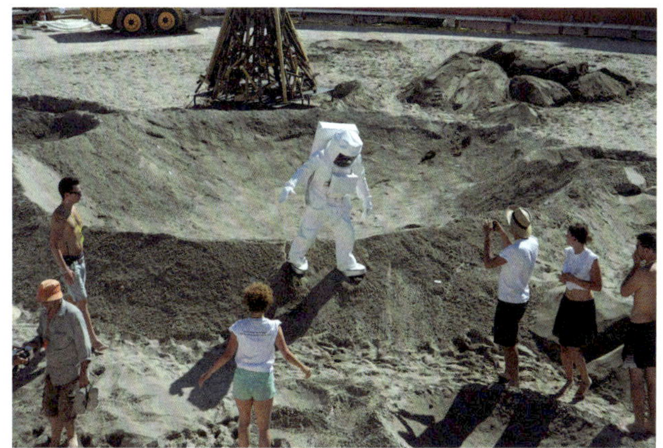
7/8/12—5:02:07 PM

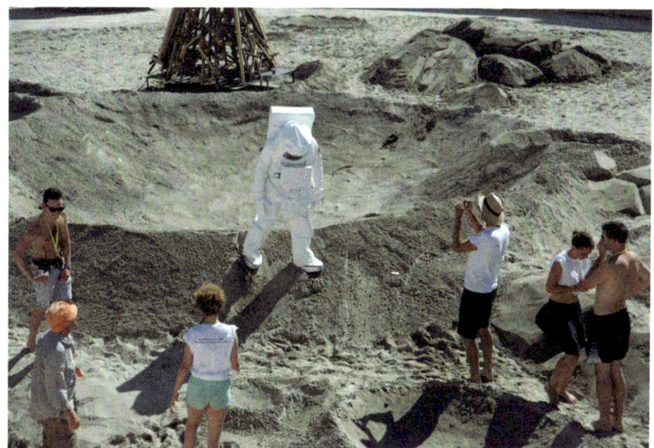
7/8/12—5:02:10 PM

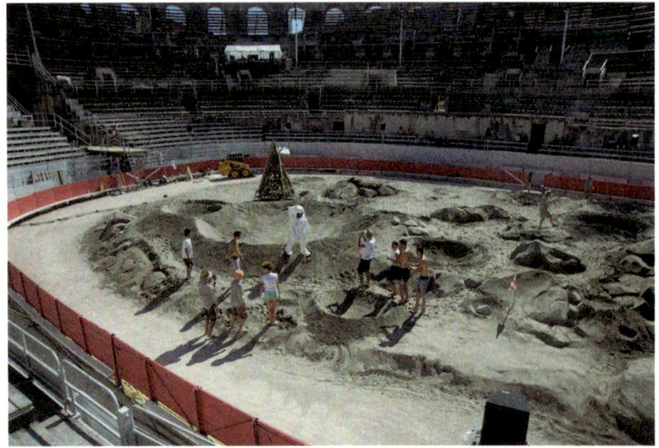
7/8/12—5:02:11 PM

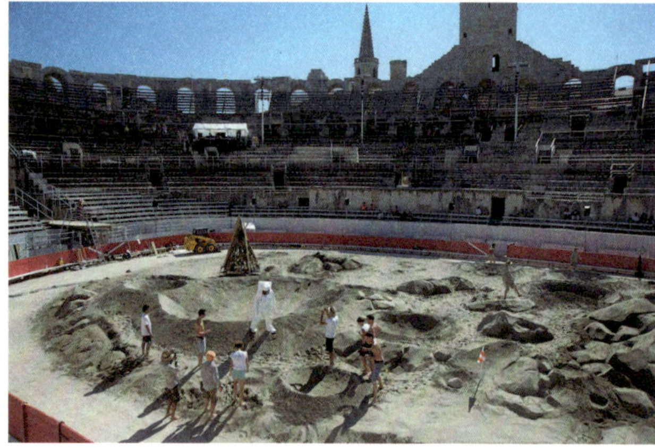
7/8/12—5:02:13 PM

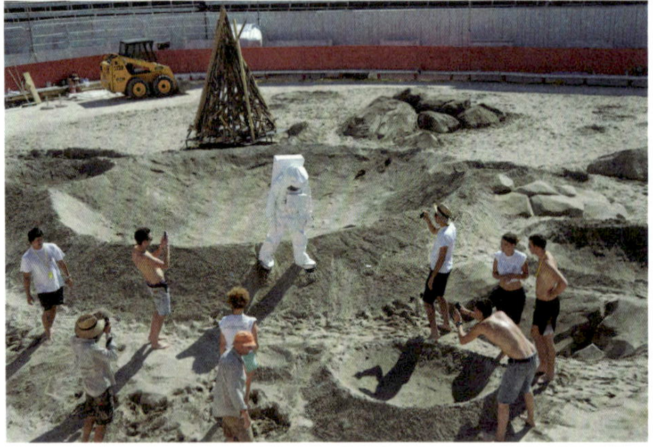
7/8/12—5:02:15 PM

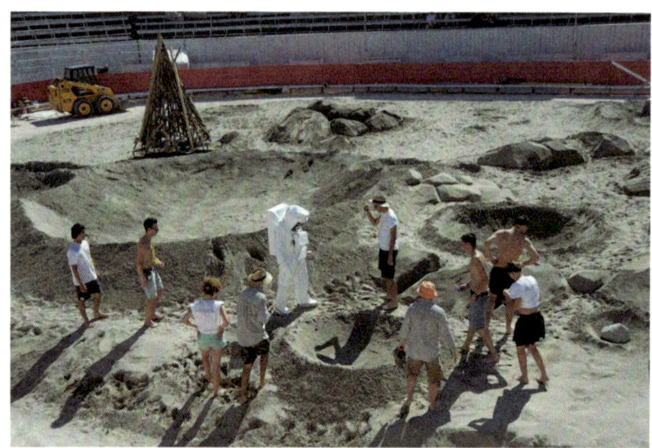
7/8/12—5:02:21 PM

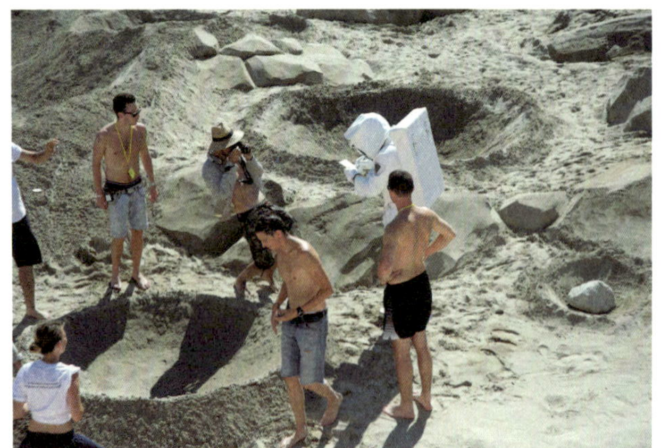
7/8/12—5:02:44 PM

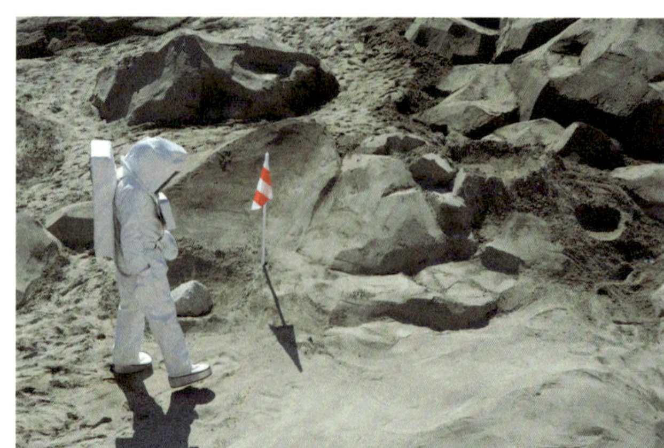
7/8/12—5:02:57 PM

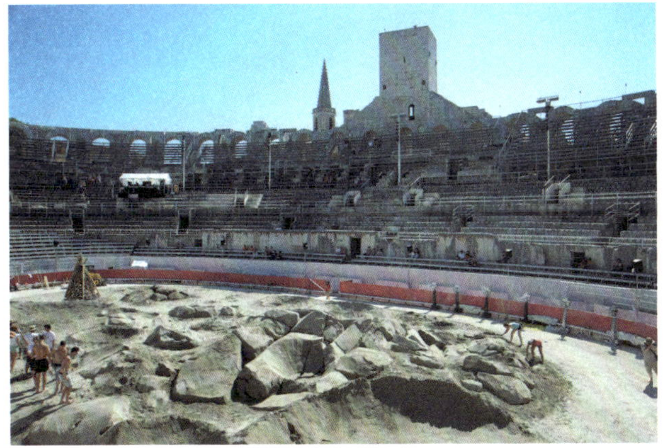

7/8/12—5:04:07 PM

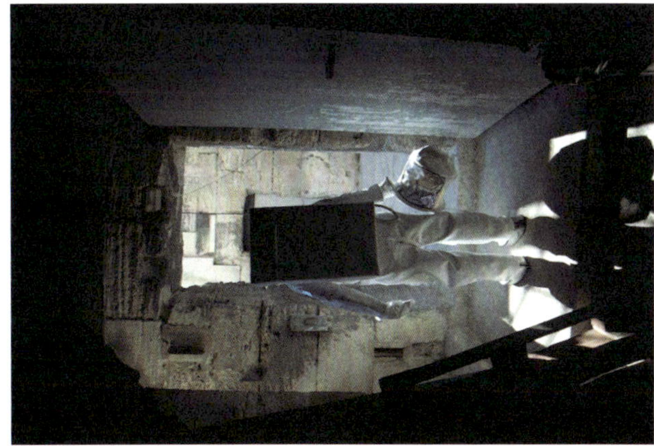

7/8/12—5:05:19 PM

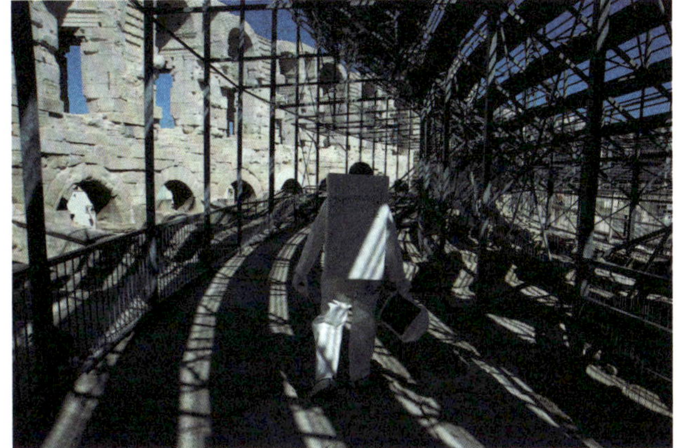

7/8/12—5:07:47 PM

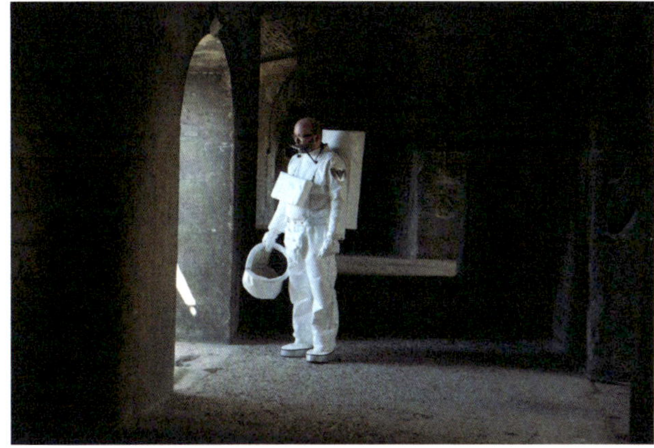

7/8/12—5:10:25 PM

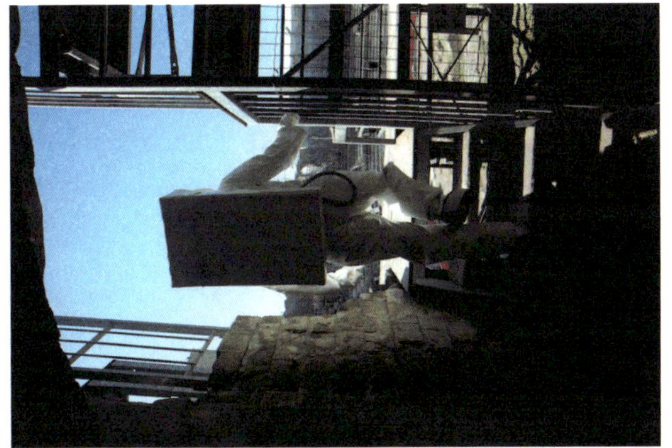

7/8/12—5:10:42 PM

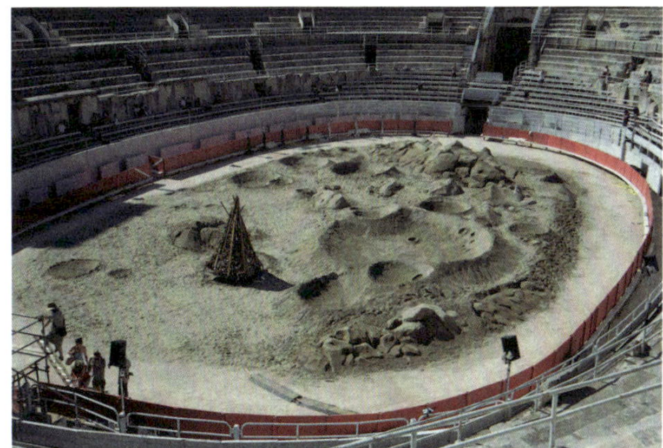

7/8/12—5:11:07 PM

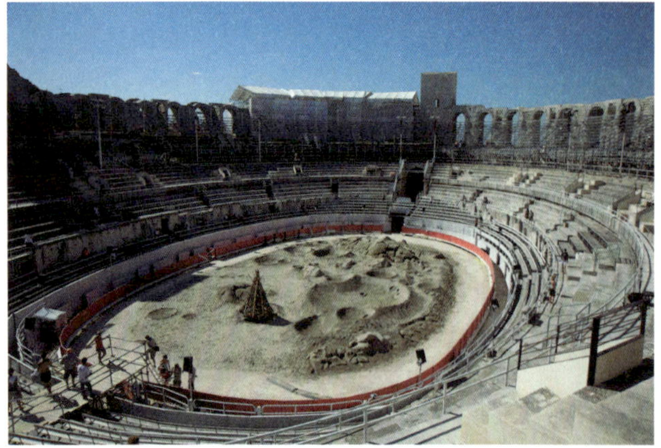

7/8/12—5:11:08 PM

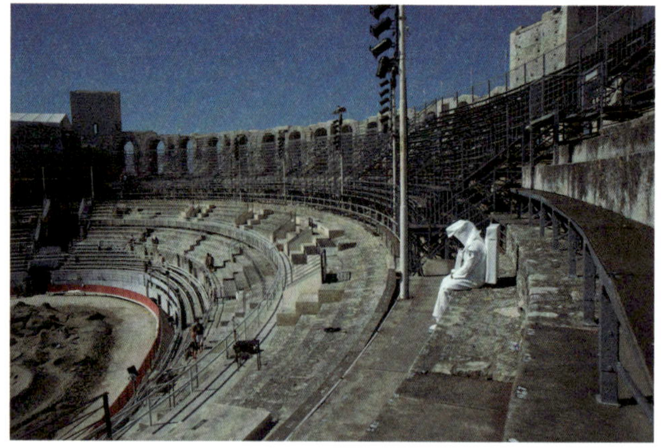

7/8/12—5:11:15 PM

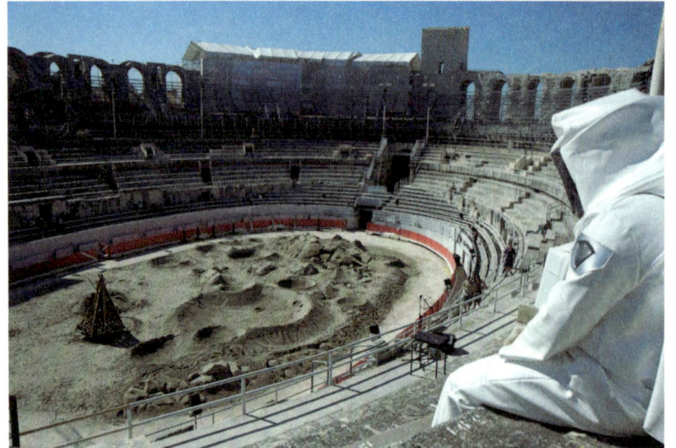

7/8/12—5:12:03 PM

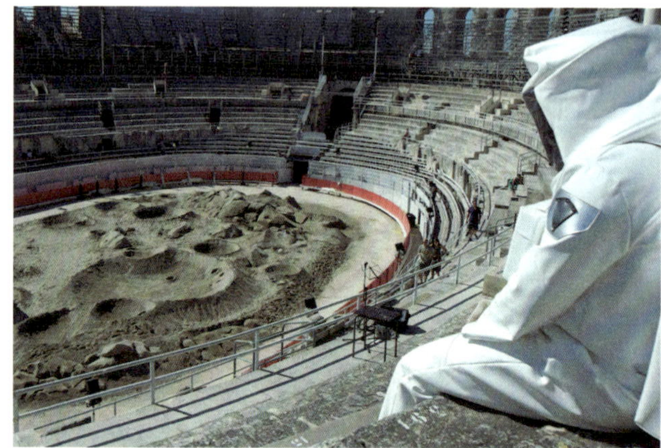

7/8/12—5:12:04 PM

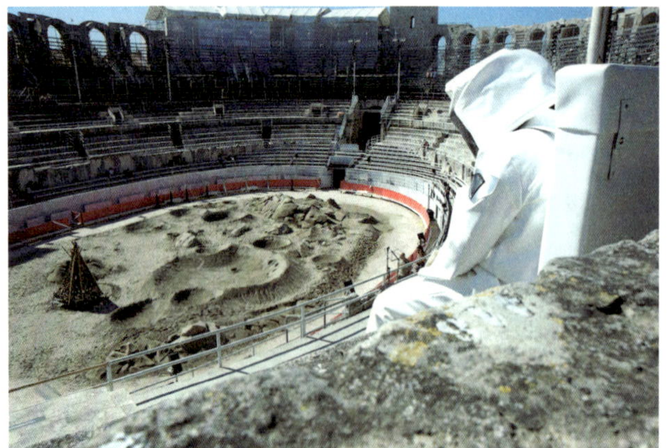

7/8/12—5:12:08 PM

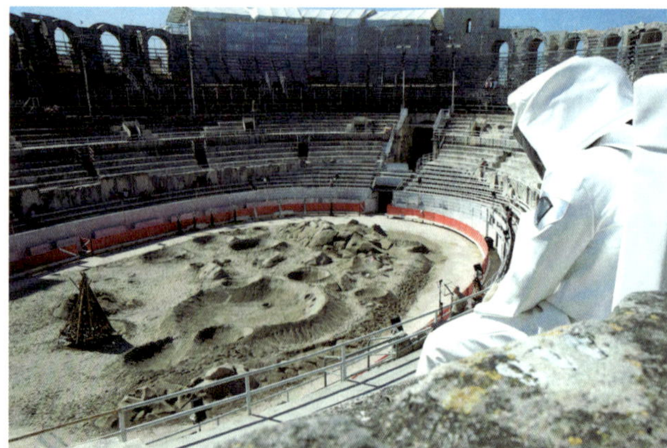

7/8/12—5:12:09 PM

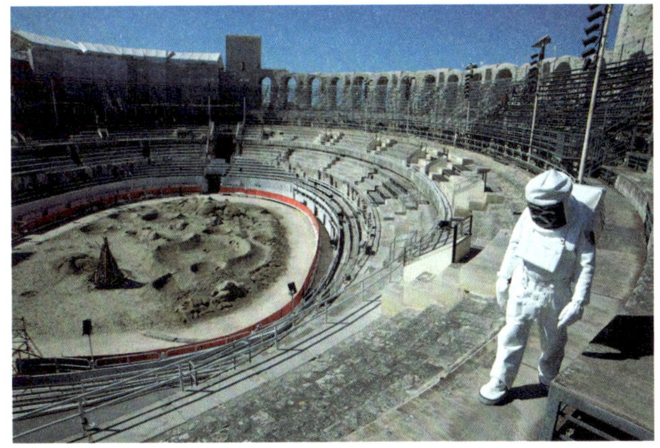
7/8/12—5:13:04 PM

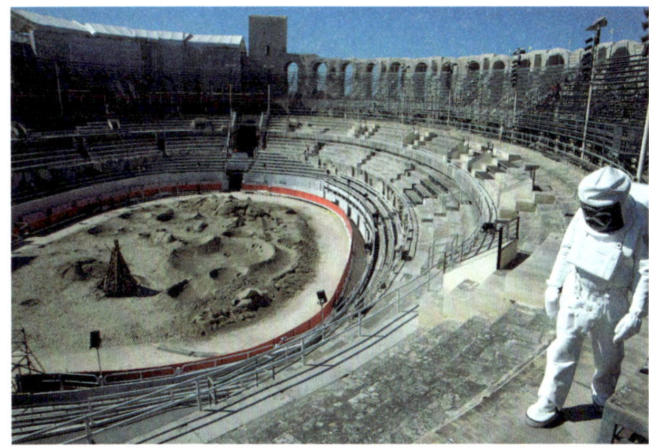
7/8/12—5:13:05 PM

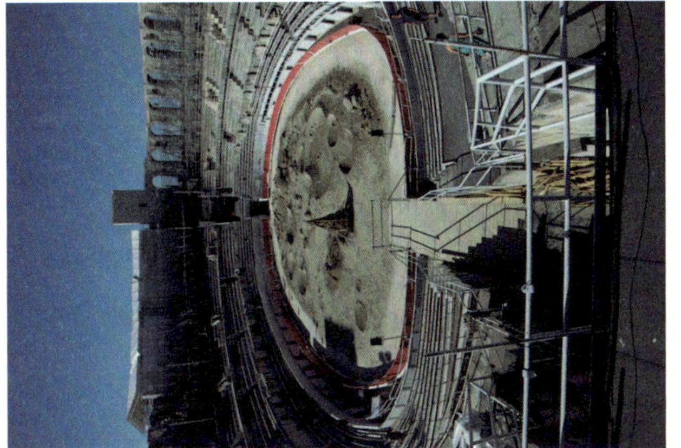
7/8/12—5:13:35 PM

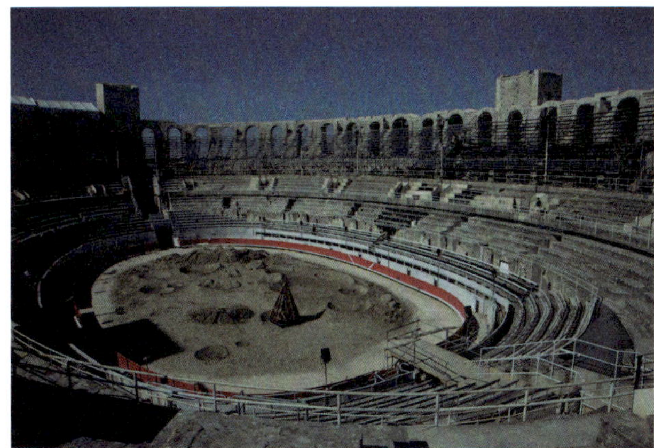
7/8/12—5:14:28 PM

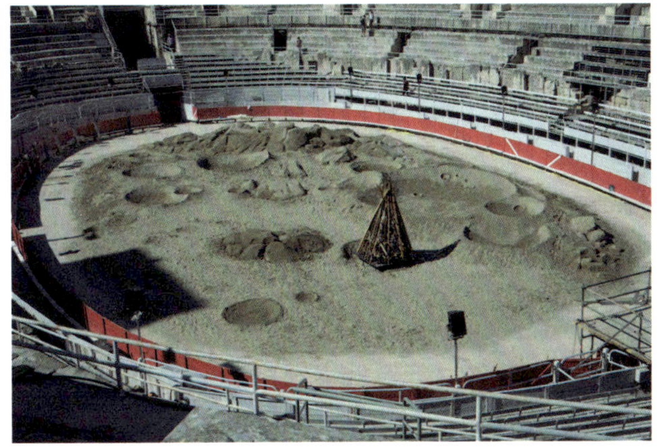
7/8/12—5:14:32 PM

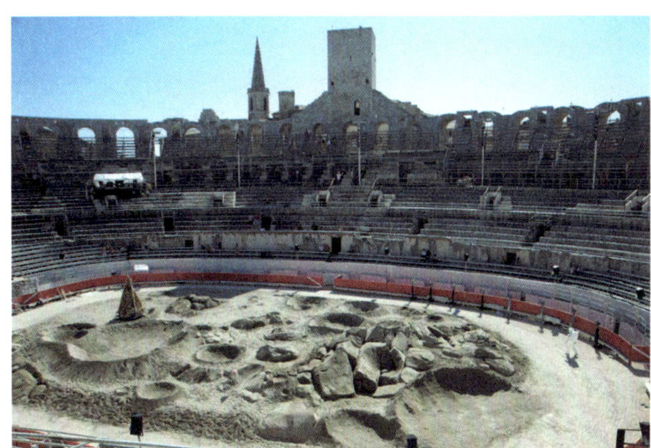
7/8/12—5:23:37 PM

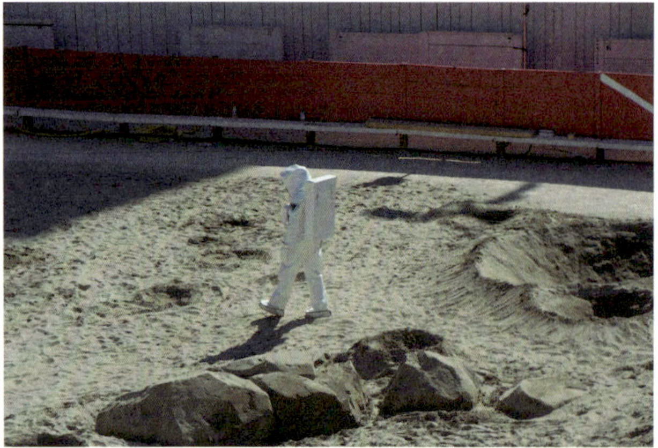
7/8/12—5:24:25 PM

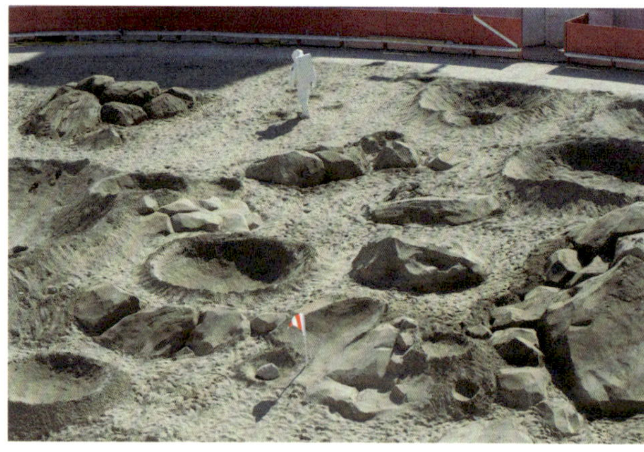
7/8/12—5:24:28 PM

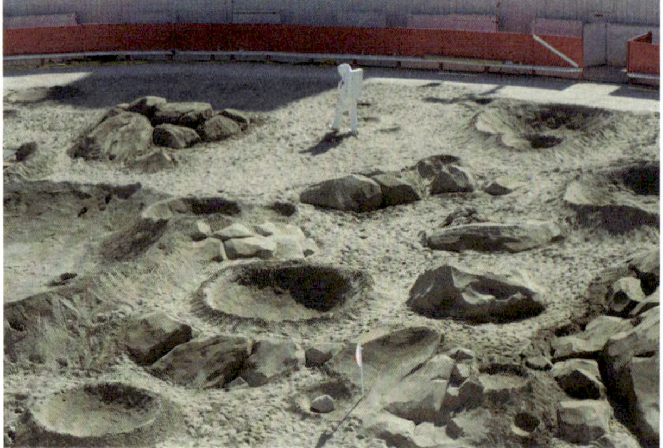
7/8/12—5:24:30 PM

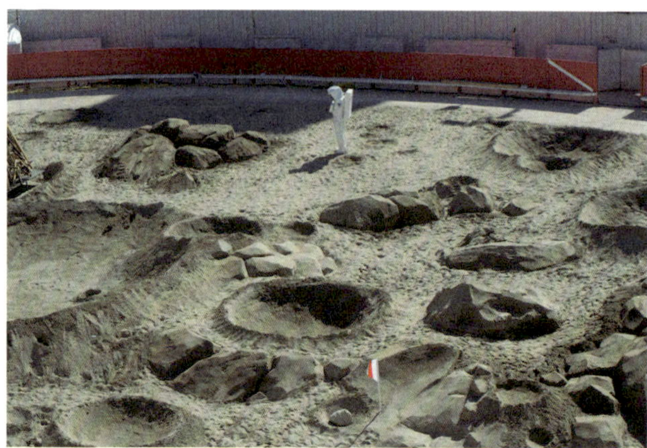
7/8/12—5:24:32 PM

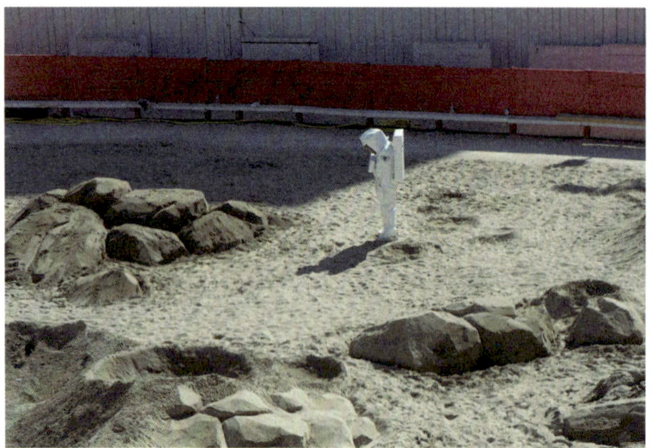
7/8/12—5:24:35 PM

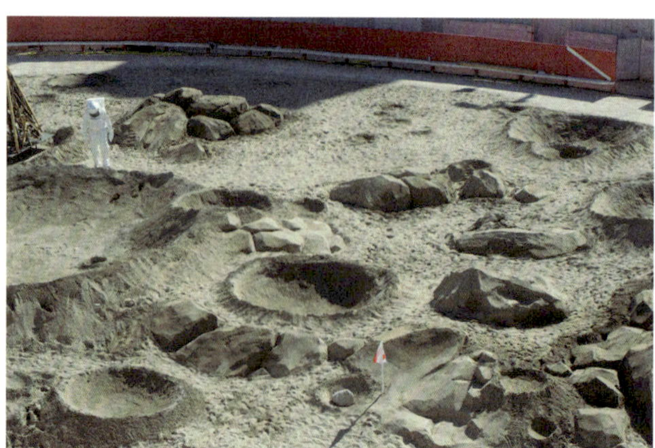
7/8/12—5:25:12 PM

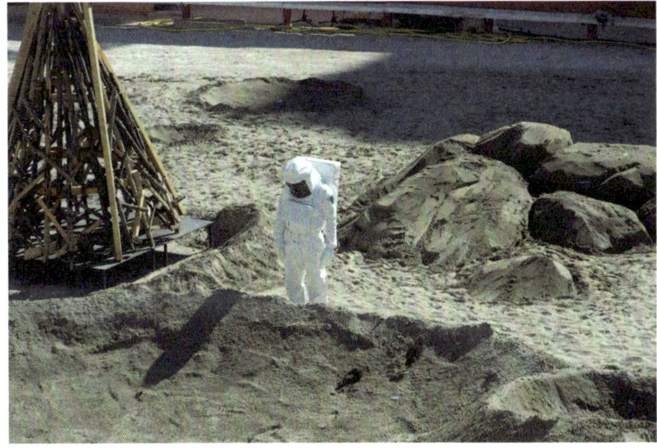

7/8/12—5:25:17 PM

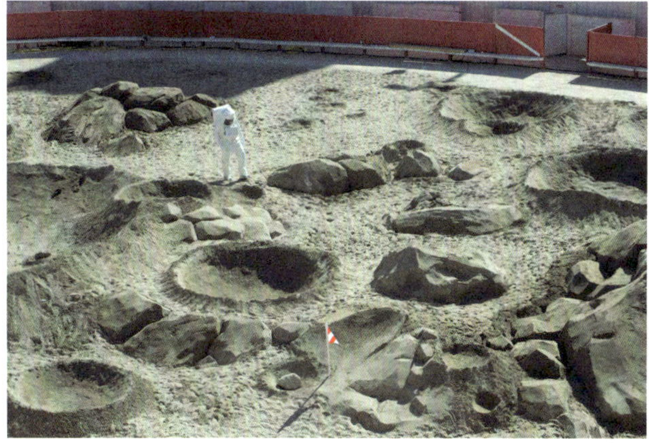

7/8/12—5:25:36 PM

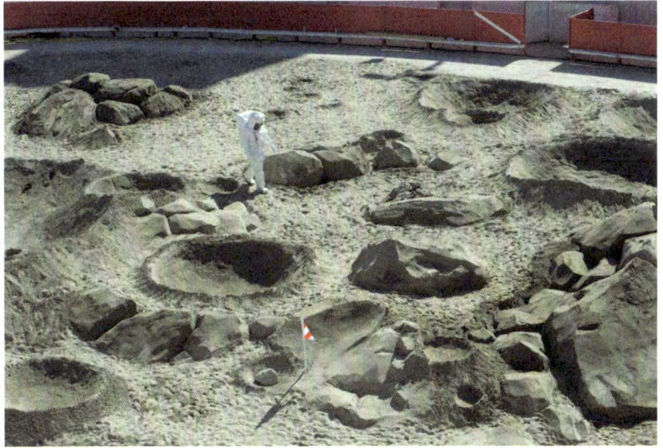

7/8/12—5:25:40 PM

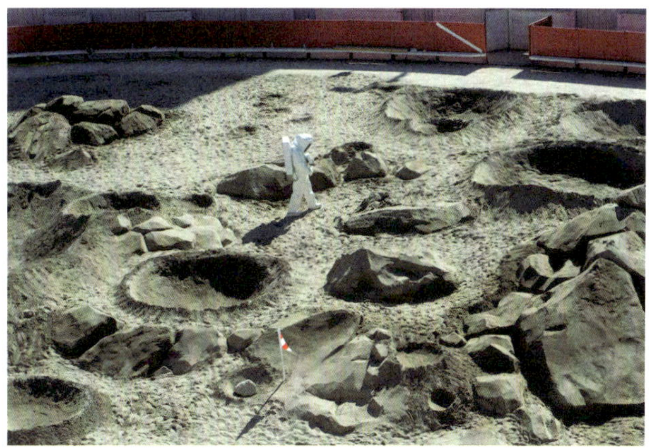

7/8/12—5:25:47 PM

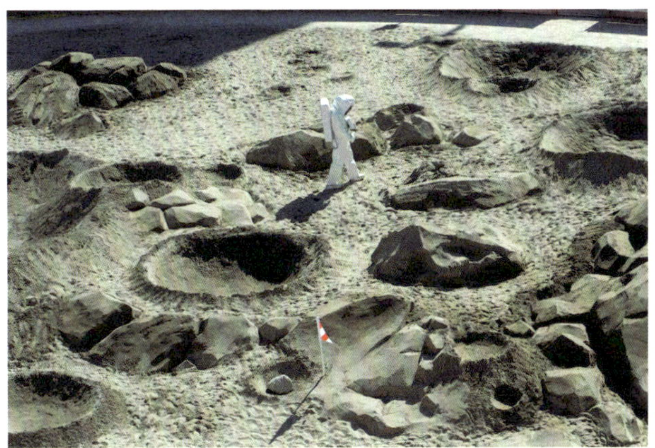

7/8/12—5:25:48 PM

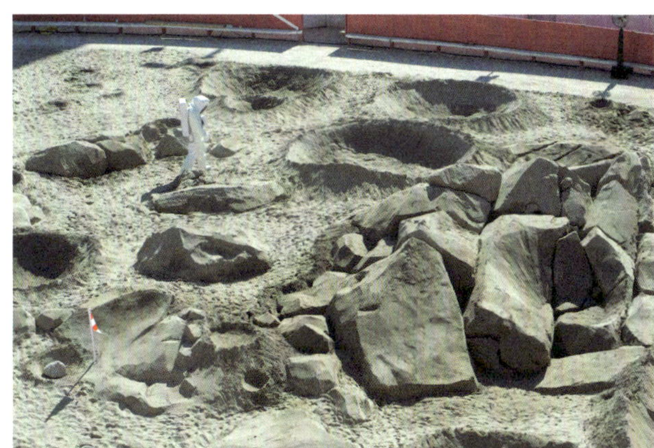

7/8/12—5:25:51 PM

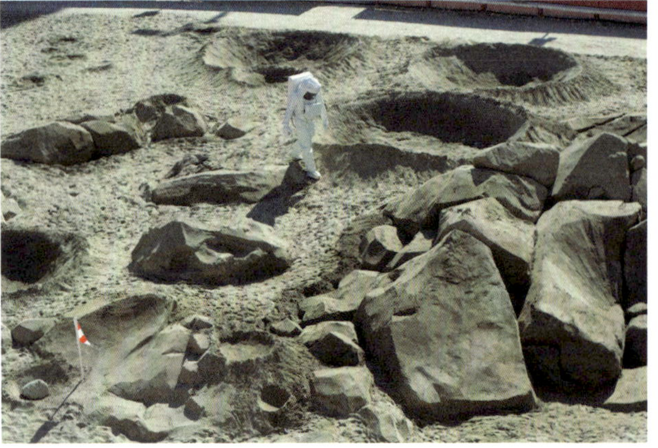

7/8/12—5:26:07 PM

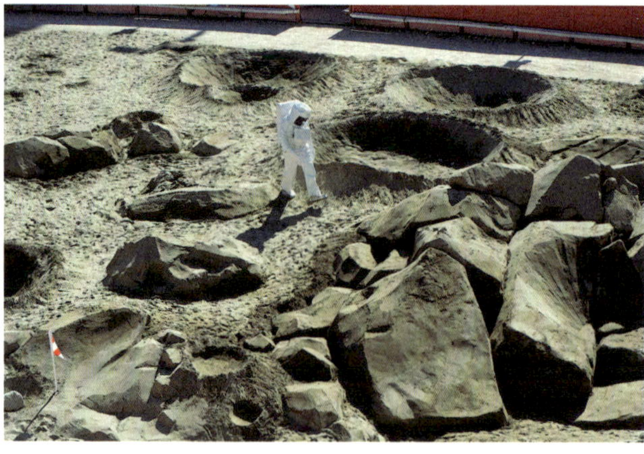

7/8/12—5:26:08 PM

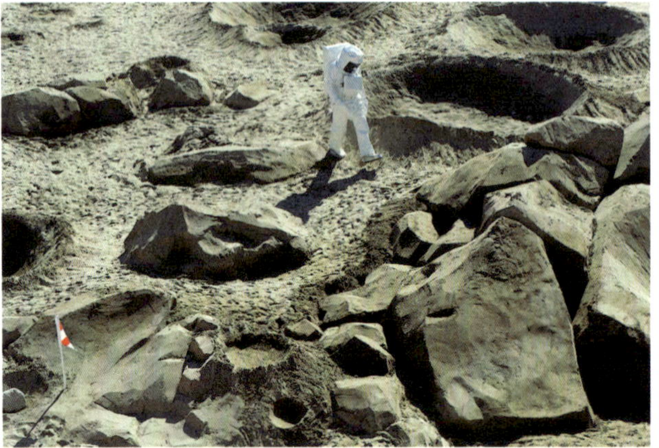

7/8/12—5:26:09 PM

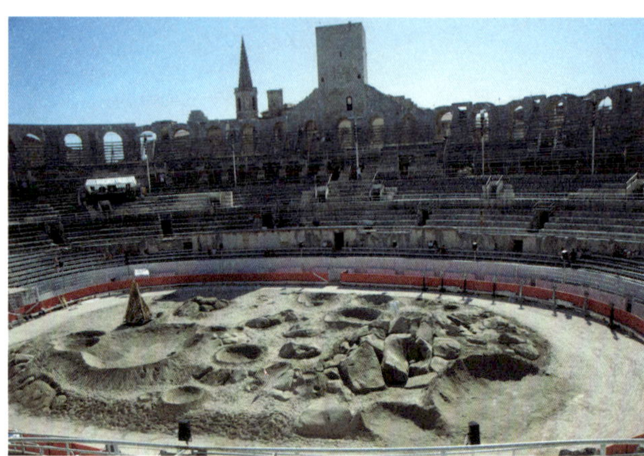

7/8/12—5:26:17 PM

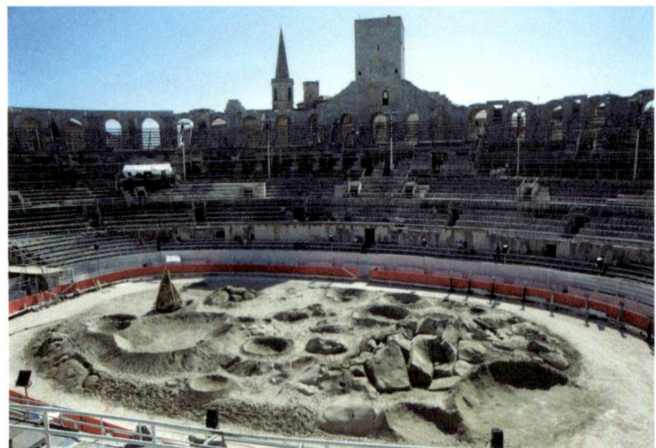

7/8/12—5:27:00 PM

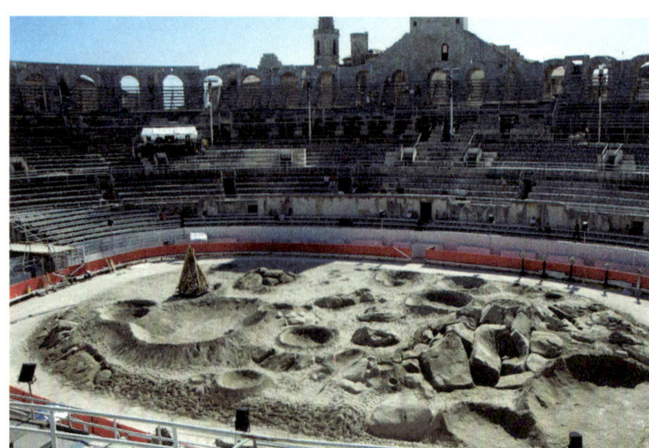

7/8/12—5:27:01 PM

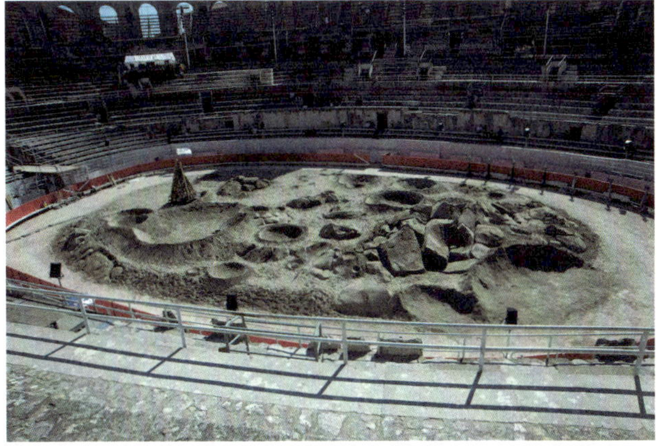

7/8/12—5:27:02 PM

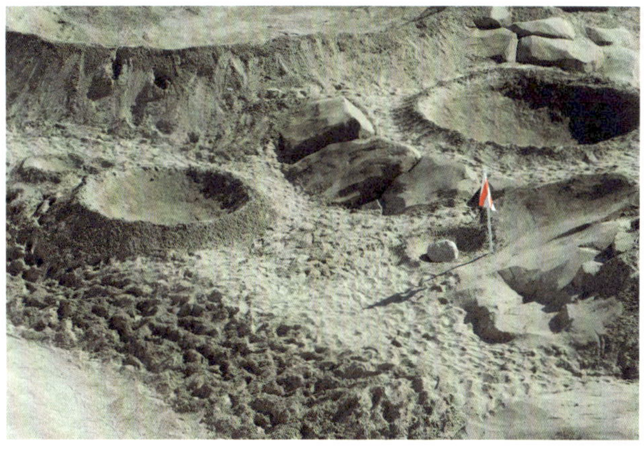

7/8/12—5:28:42 PM

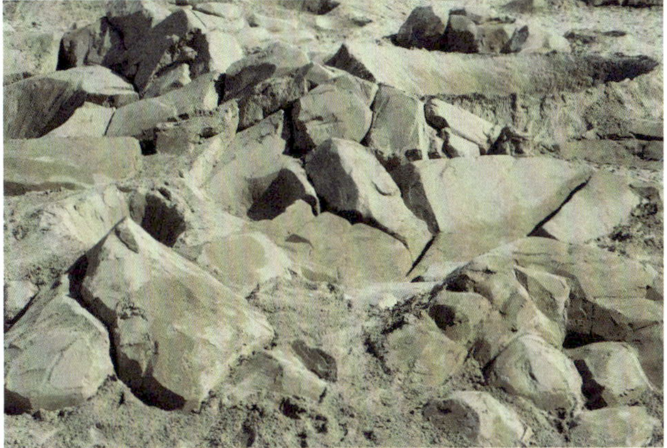

7/8/12—5:30:06 PM

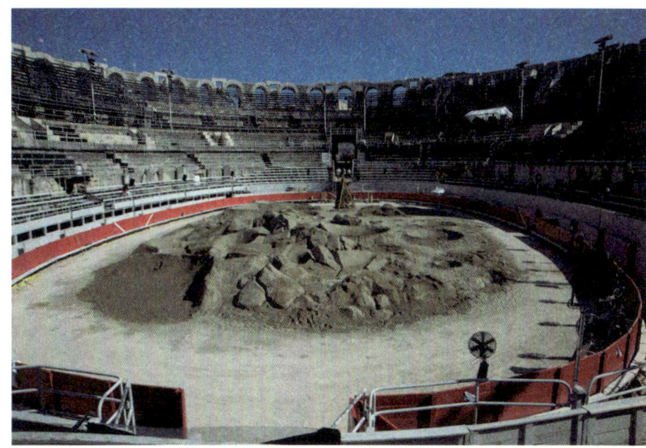

7/8/12—5:30:32 PM

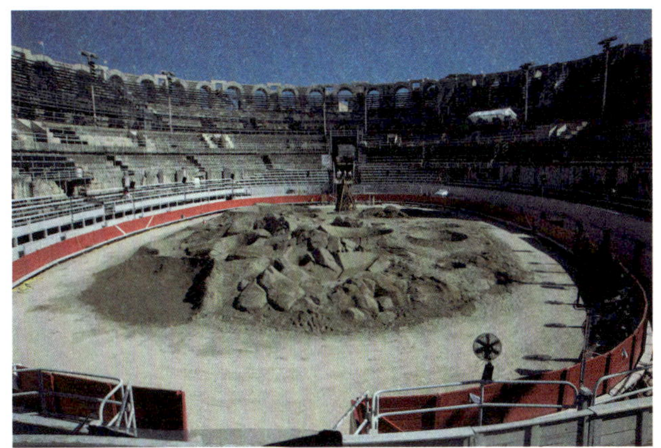

7/8/12—5:30:33 PM

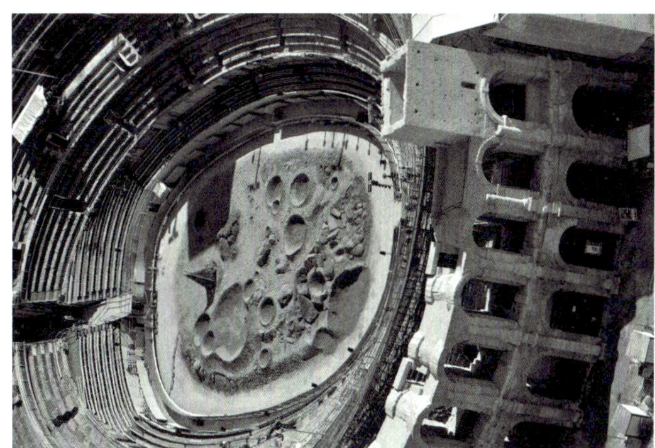

7/8/12—5:35:21 PM

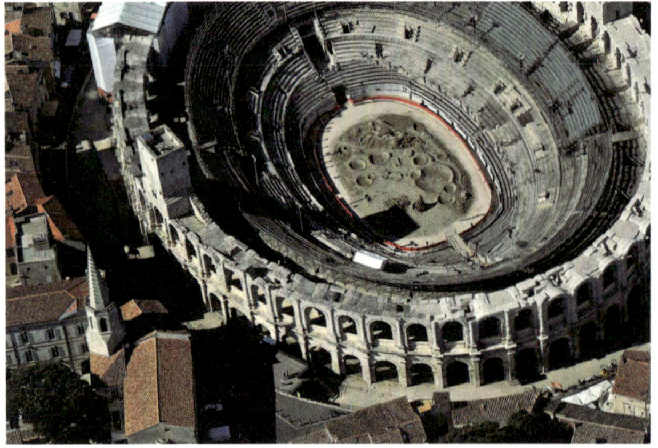

7/8/12—5:35:52 PM

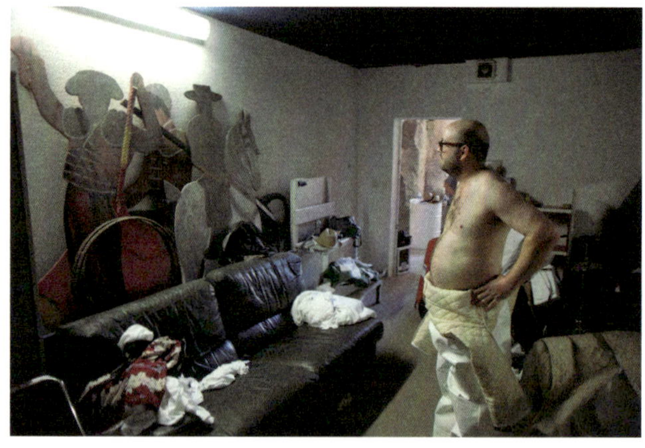

7/8/12—5:36:17 PM

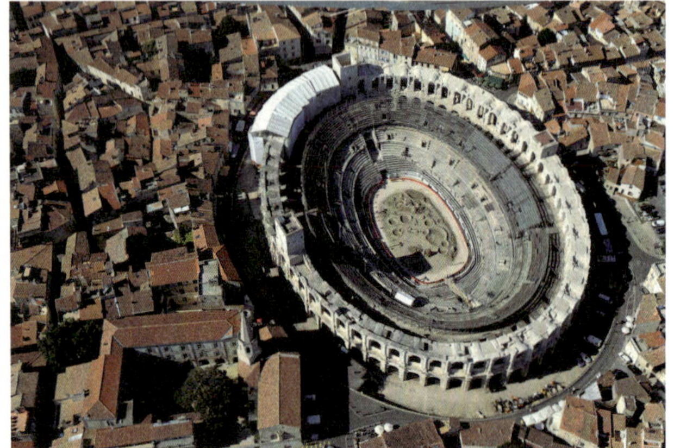

7/8/12—5:45:53 PM

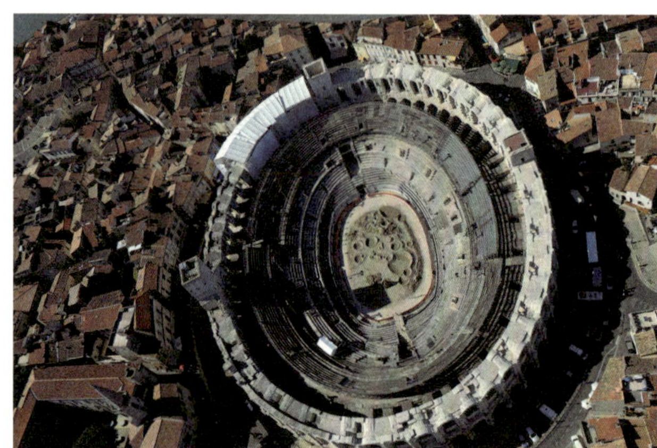

7/8/12—5:49:22 PM

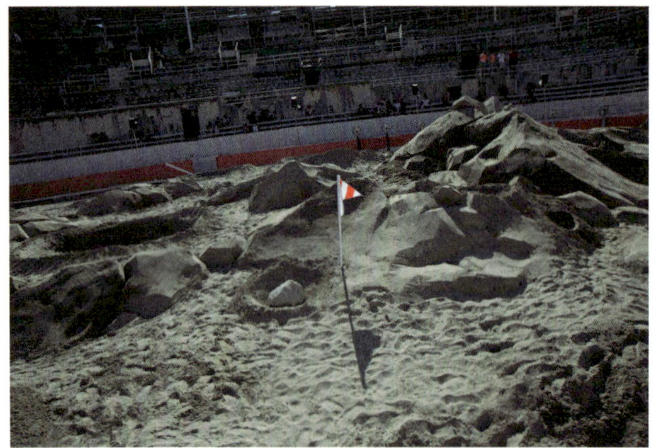

7/8/12—5:52:22 PM

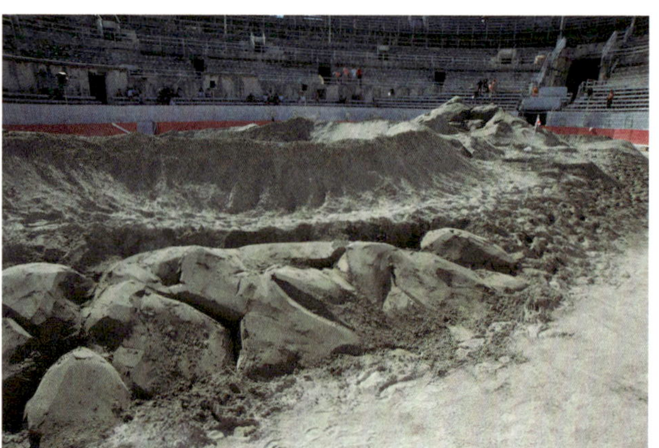

7/8/12—5:52:42 PM

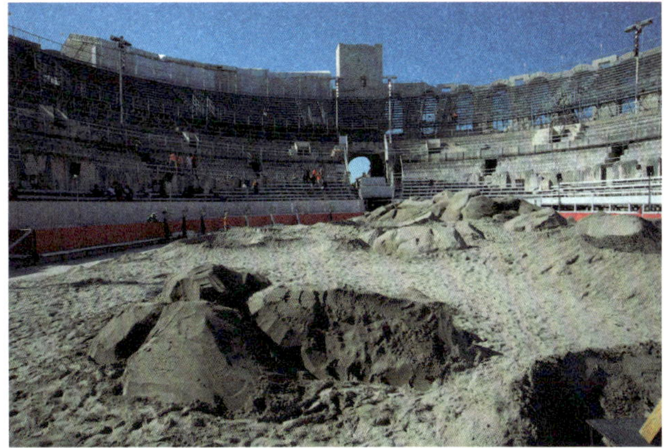

7/8/12—5:53:27 PM

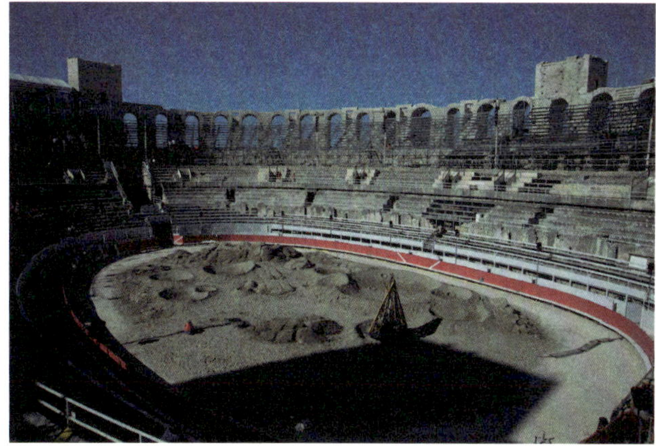

7/8/12—5:55:08 PM

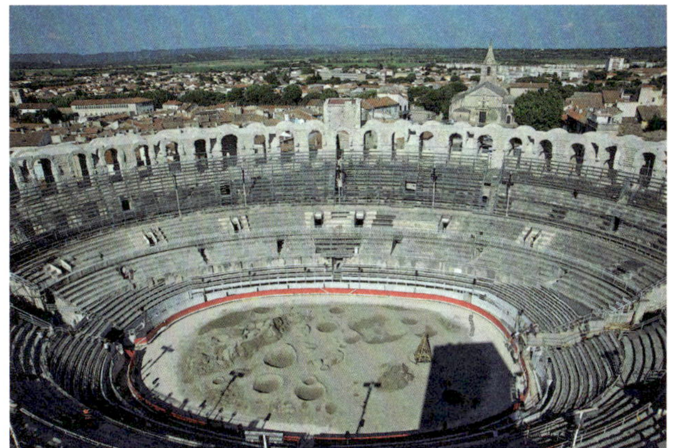

7/8/12—5:59:43 PM

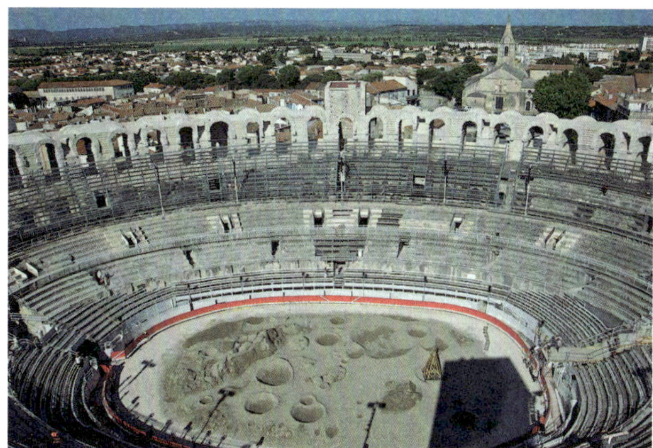

7/8/12—5:59:44 PM

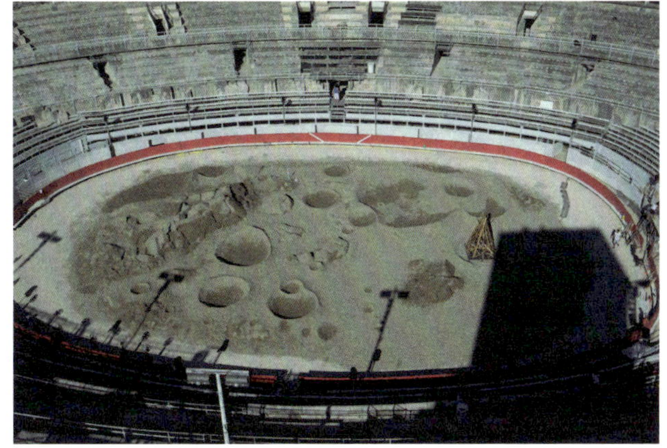

7/8/12—5:59:47 PM

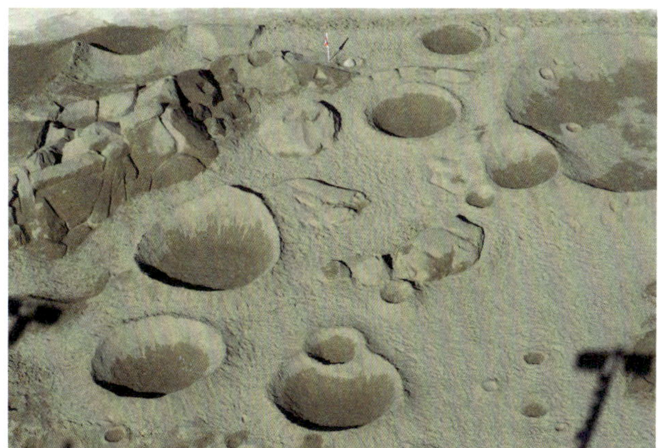

7/8/12—6:01:54 PM

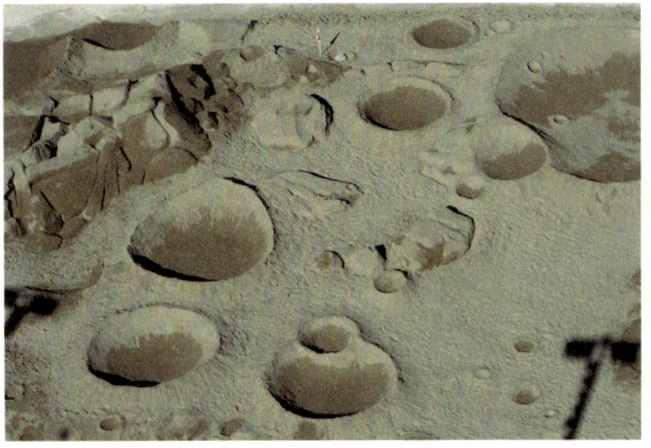
7/8/12—6:01:55 PM

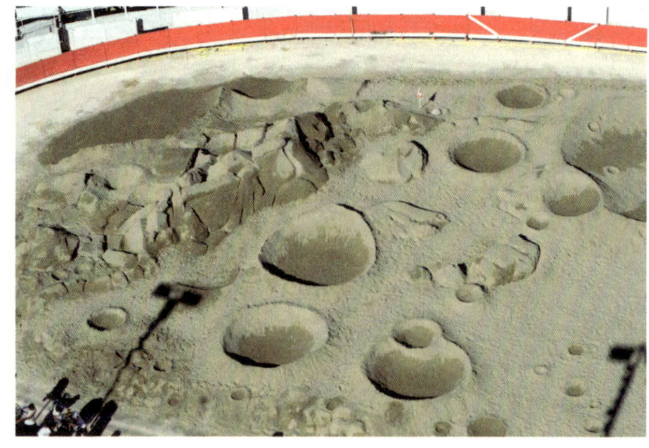
7/8/12—6:02:01 PM

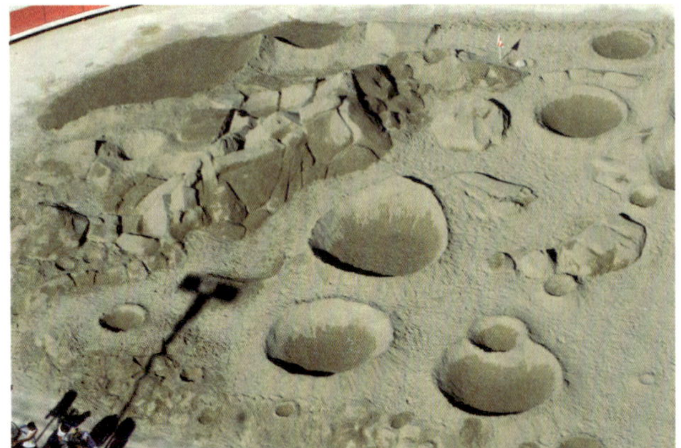
7/8/12—6:02:02 PM

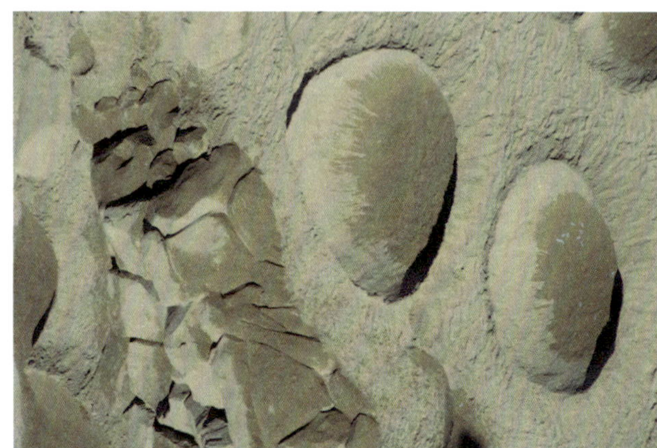
7/8/12—6:02:15 PM

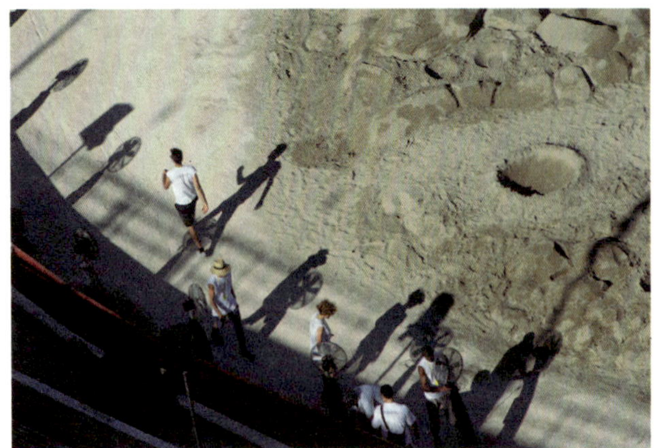
7/8/12—6:04:08 PM

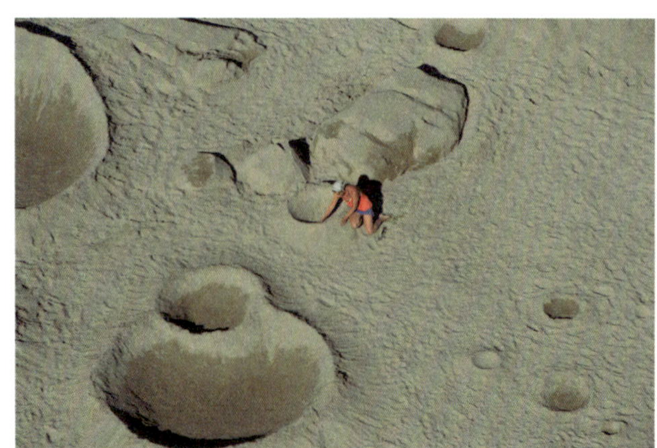
7/8/12—6:06:11 PM

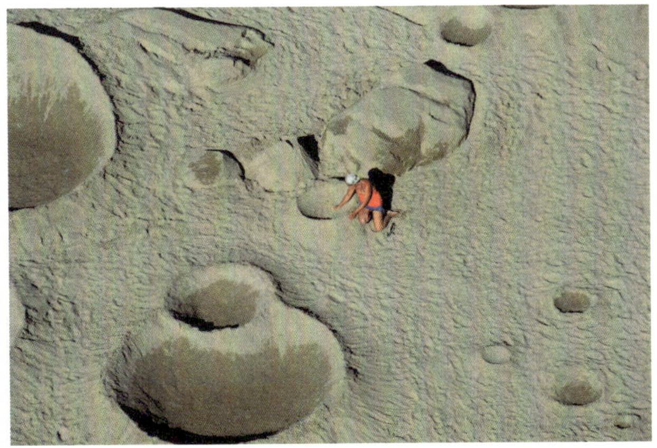
7/8/12—6:06:12 PM

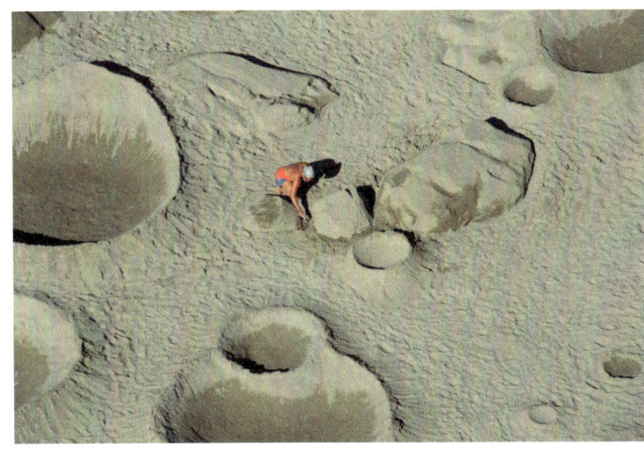
7/8/12—6:08:08 PM

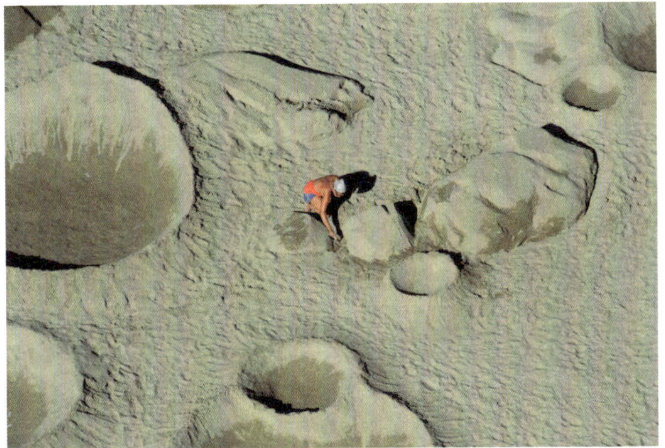
7/8/12—6:08:09 PM

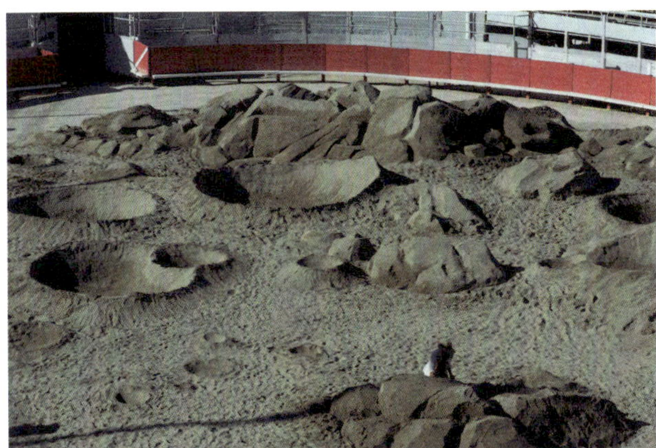
7/8/12—6:16:17 PM

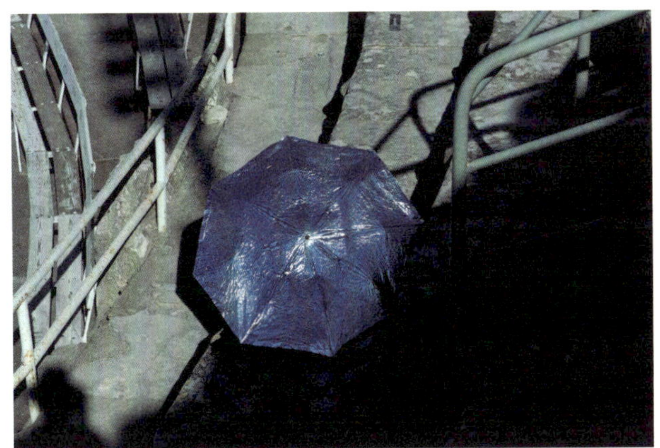
7/8/12—6:16:46 PM

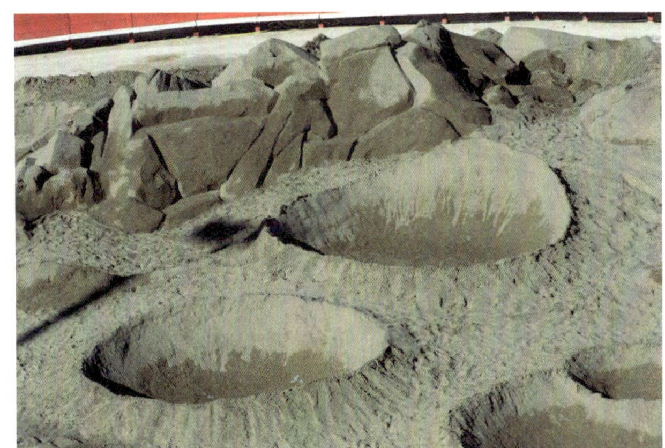
7/8/12—6:17:27 PM

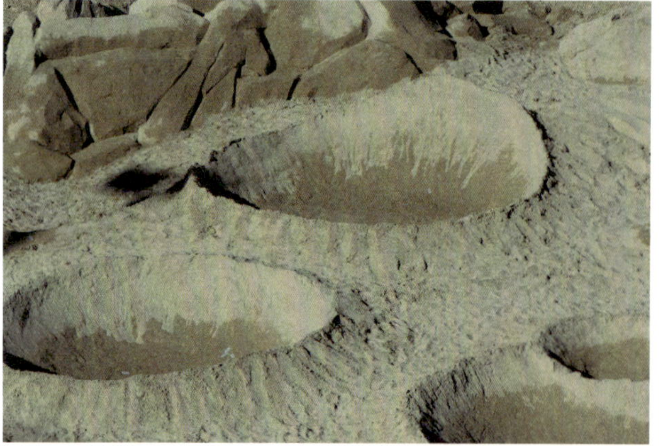
7/8/12—6:17:28 PM

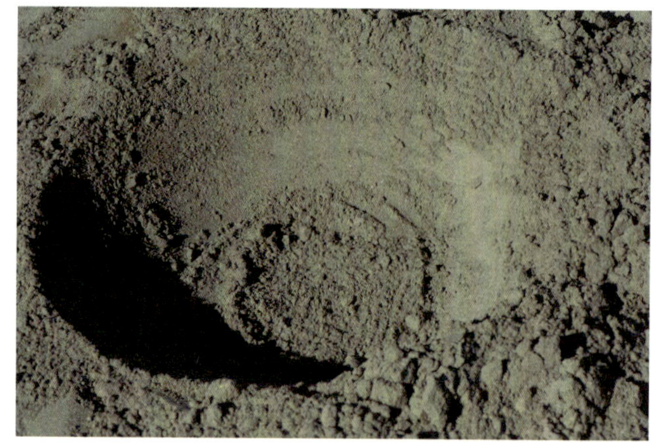
7/8/12—6:22:07 PM

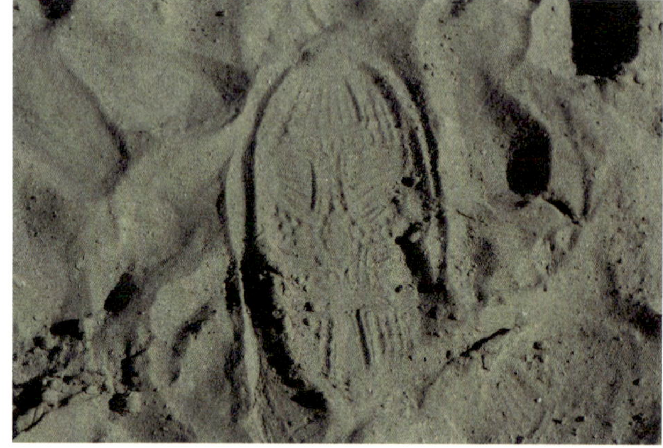
7/8/12—6:22:14 PM

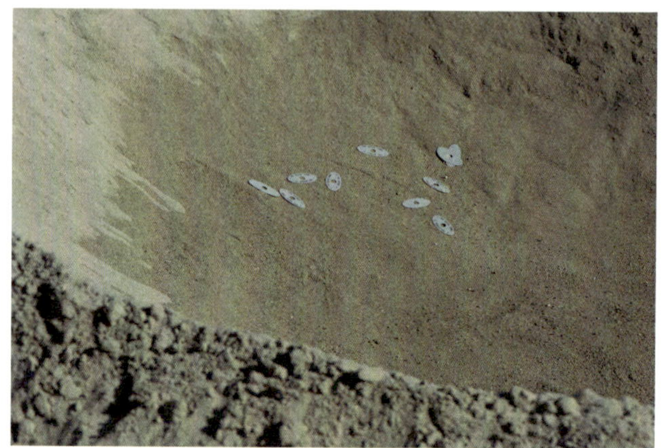
7/8/12—6:22:21 PM

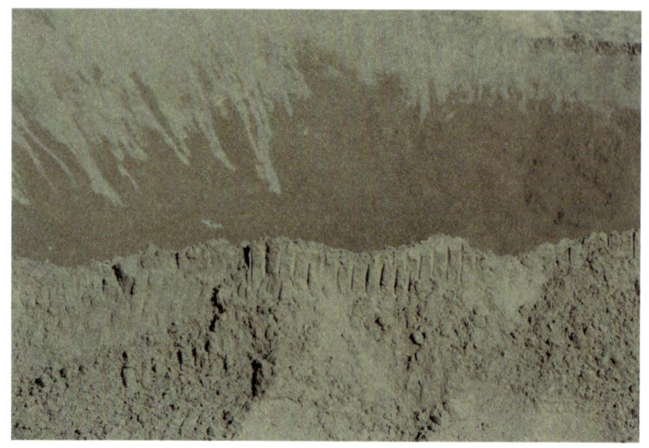
7/8/12—6:22:27 PM

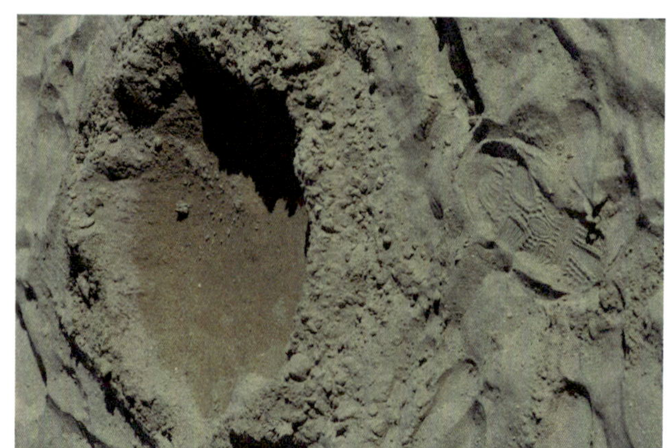
7/8/12—6:22:55 PM

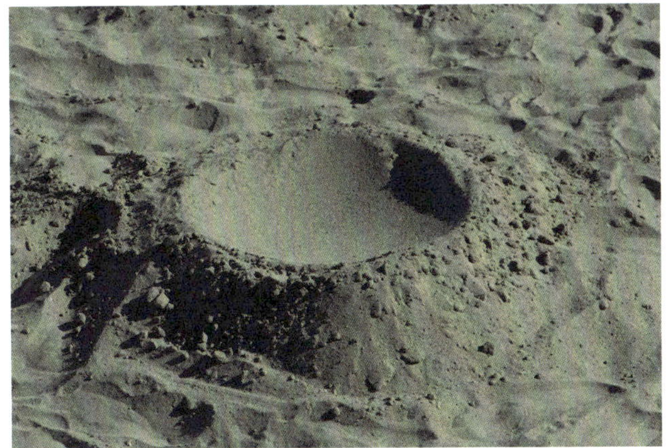

7/8/12—6:23:02 PM

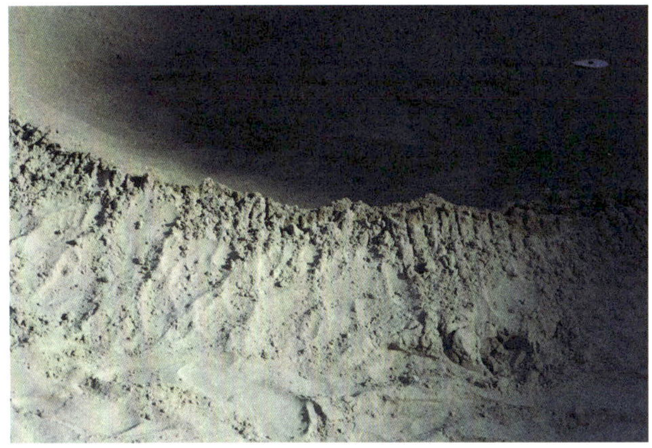

7/8/12—6:23:23 PM

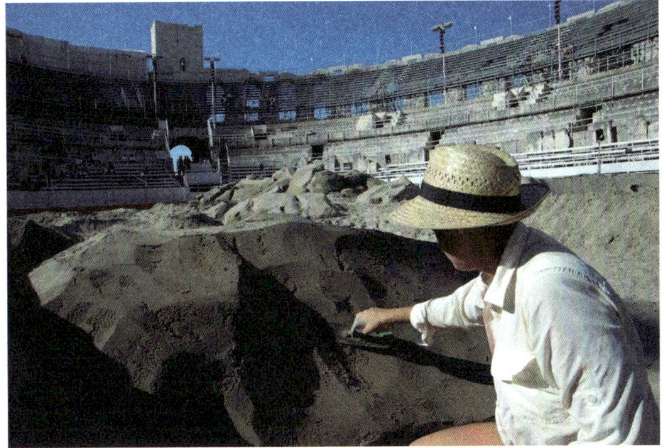

7/8/12—6:24:28 PM

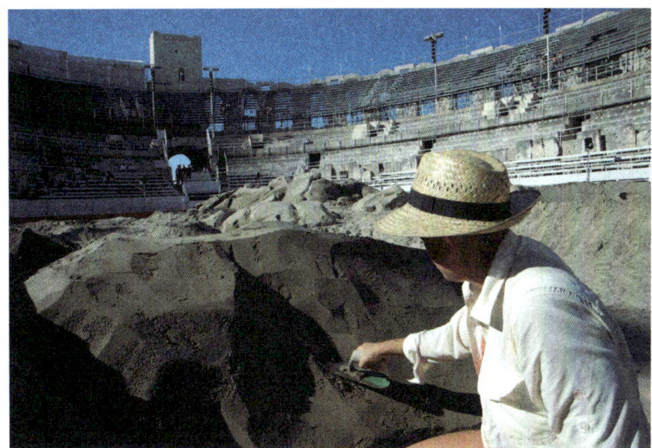

7/8/12—6:24:29 PM

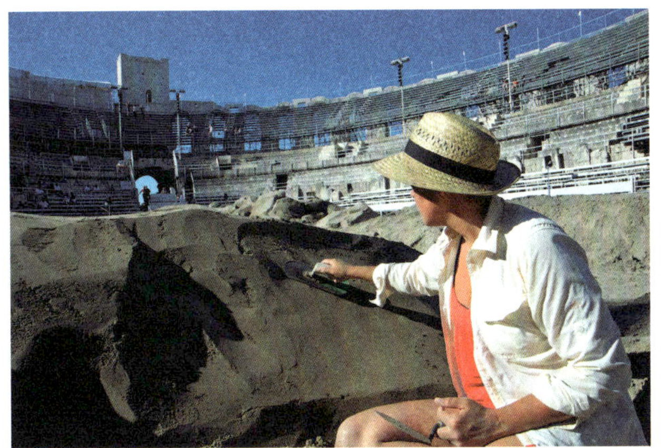

7/8/12—6:25:50 PM

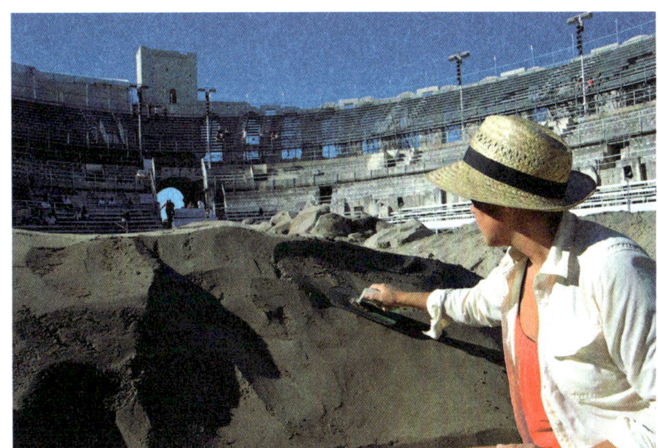

7/8/12—6:25:51 PM

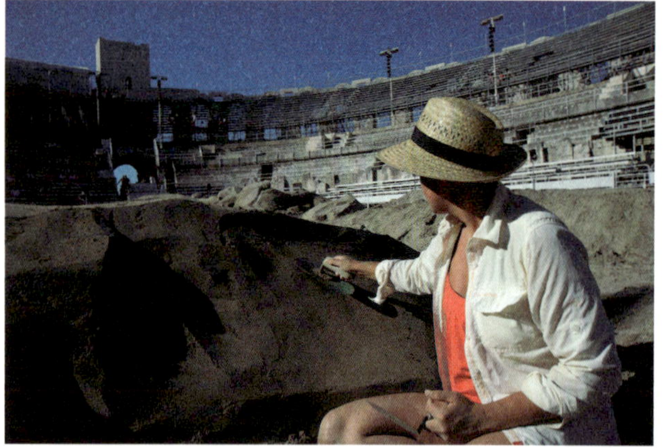

7/8/12—6:25:51 PM

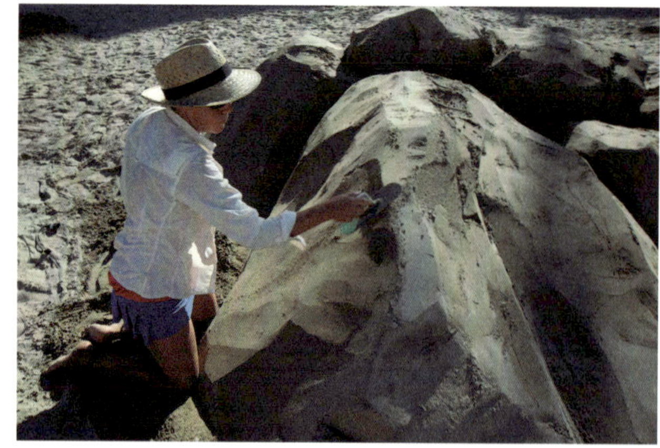

7/8/12—6:26:11 PM

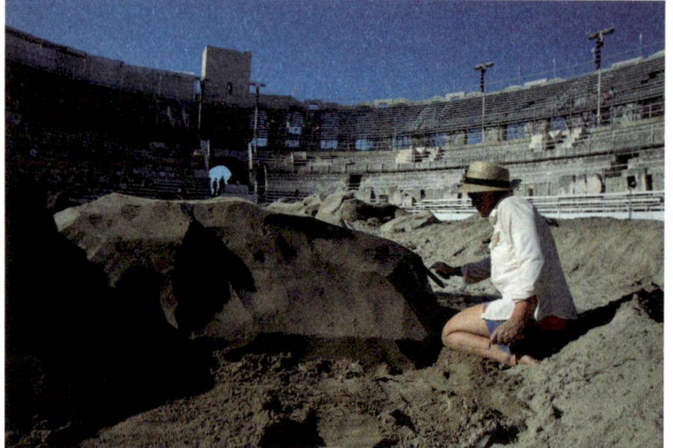

7/8/12—6:26:26 PM

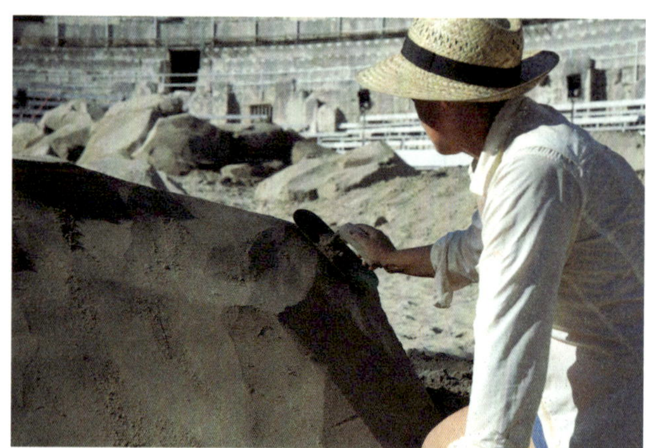

7/8/12—6:26:37 PM

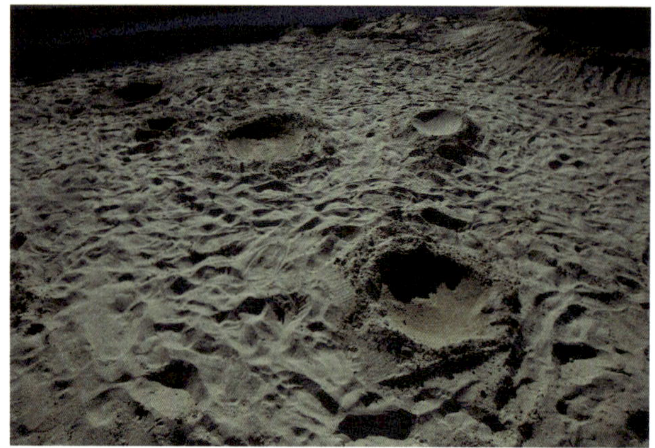

7/8/12—6:27:00 PM

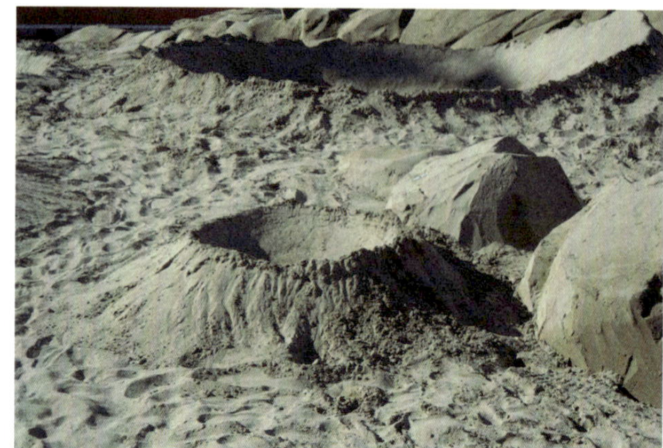

7/8/12—6:27:04 PM

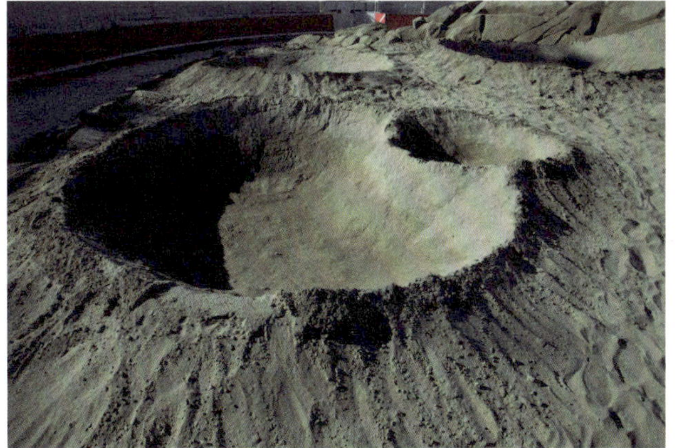

7/8/12—6:27:43 PM

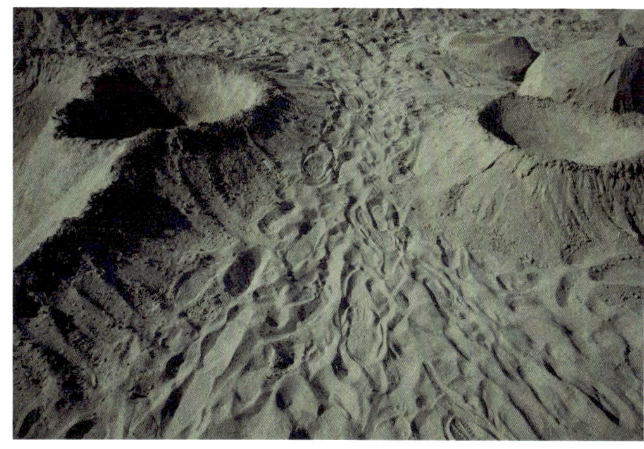

7/8/12—6:27:53 PM

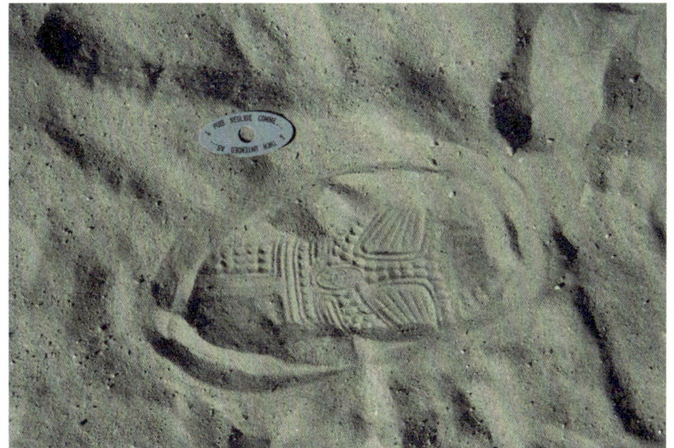

7/8/12—6:28:08 PM

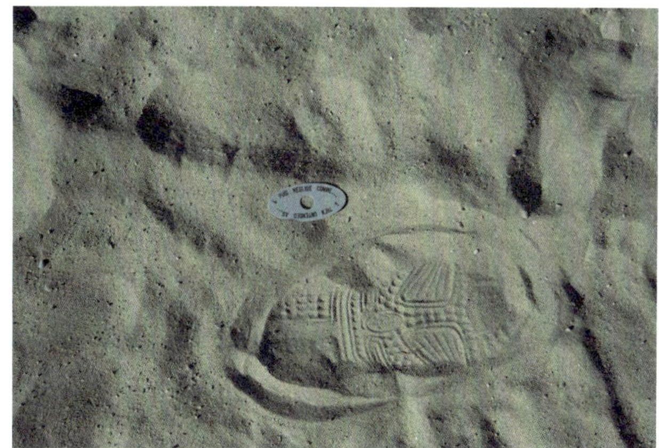

7/8/12—6:28:11 PM

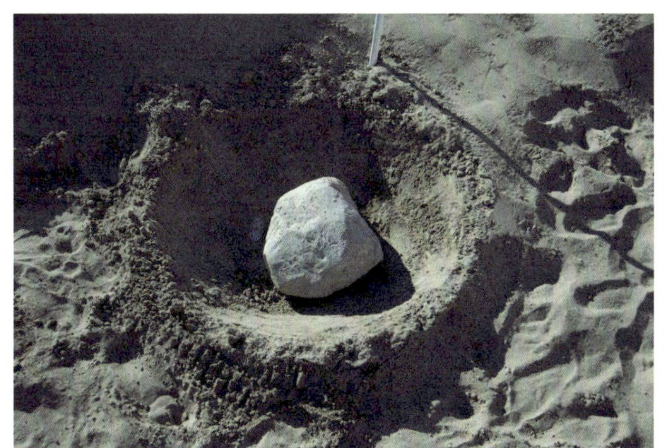

7/8/12—6:28:52 PM

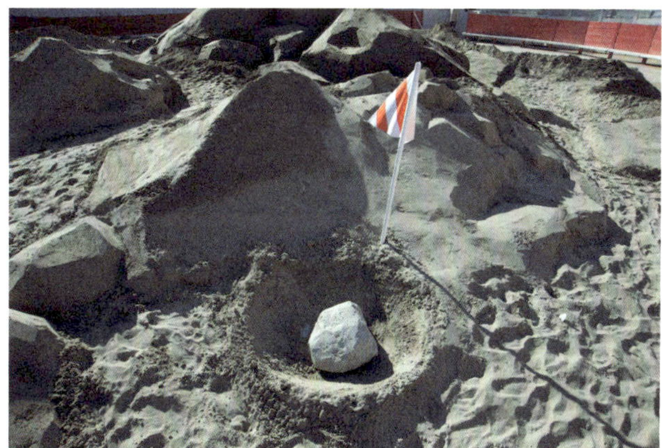

7/8/12—6:28:59 PM

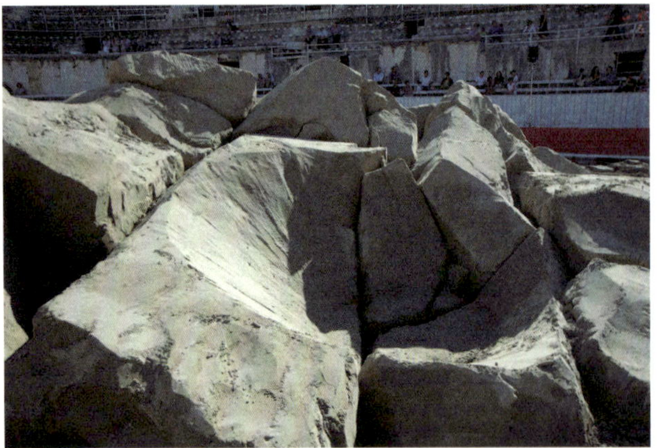

7/8/12—6:29:32 PM

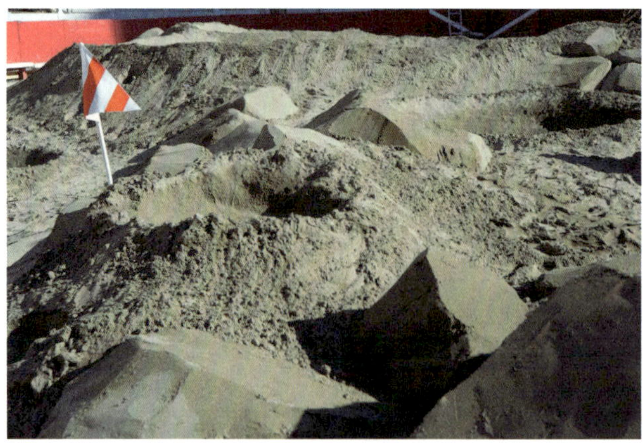

7/8/12—6:29:36 PM

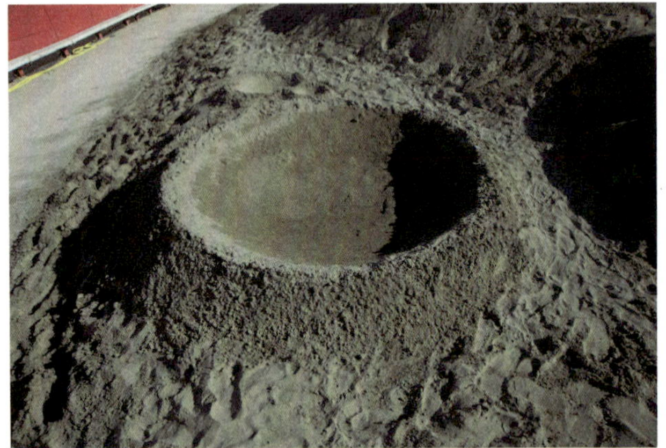

7/8/12—6:29:50 PM

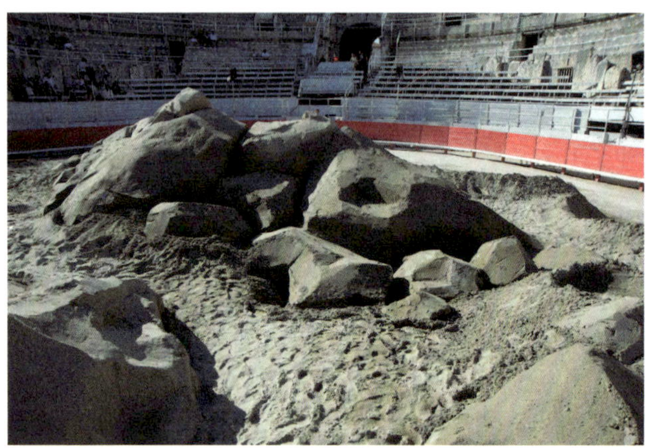

7/8/12—6:30:00 PM

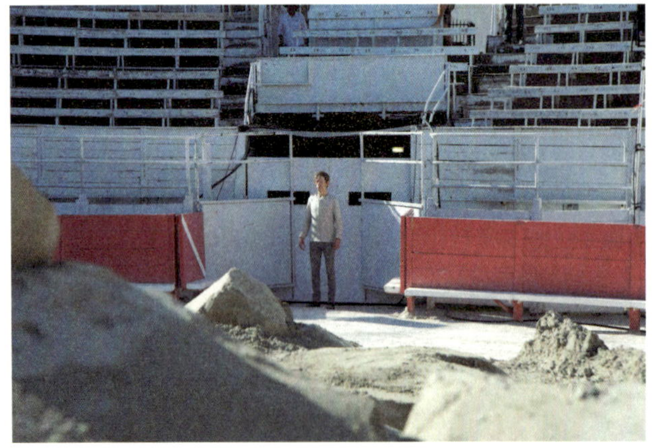

7/8/12—6:30:12 PM

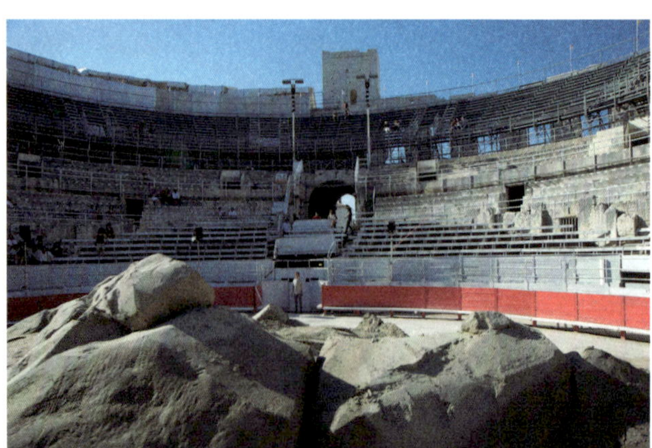

7/8/12—6:30:15 PM

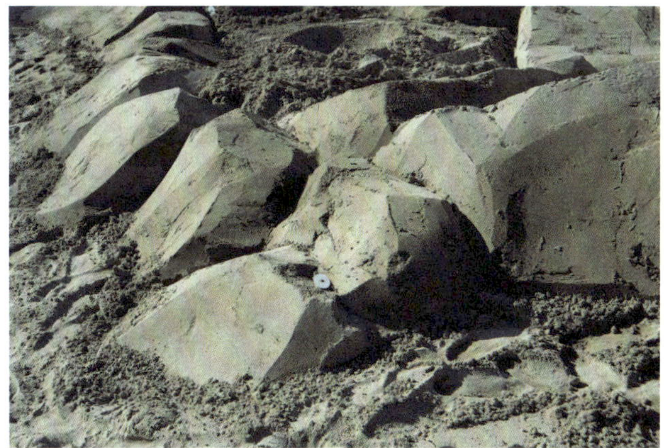

7/8/12—6:30:35 PM

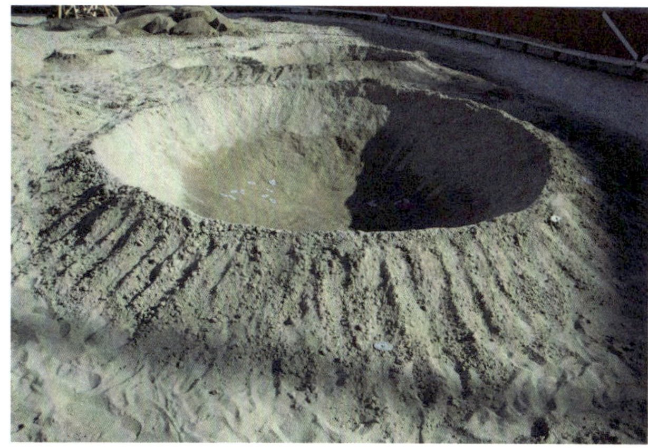

7/8/12—6:30:48 PM

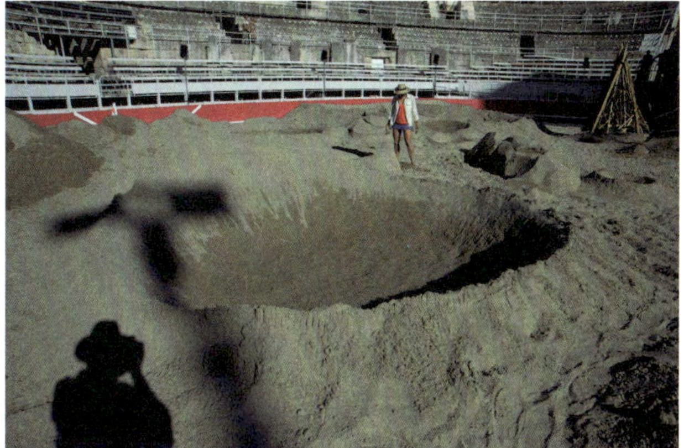

7/8/12—6:30:58 PM

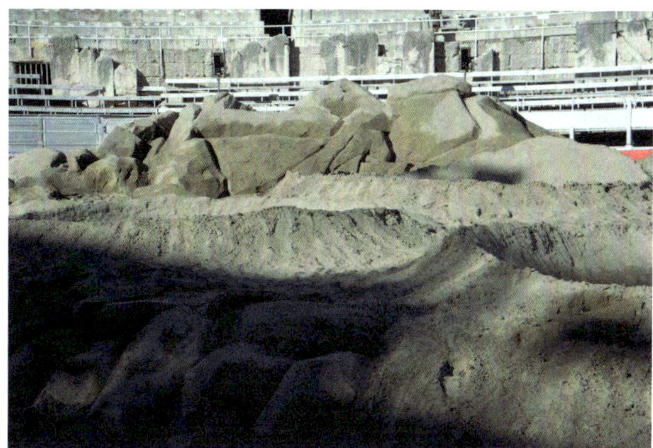

7/8/12—6:31:26 PM

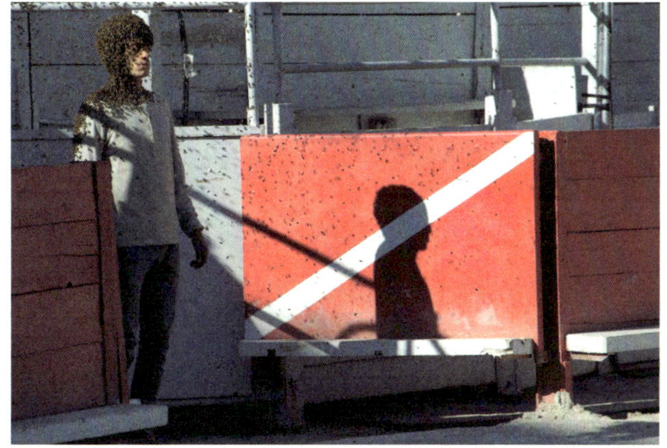

7/8/12—6:33:02 PM

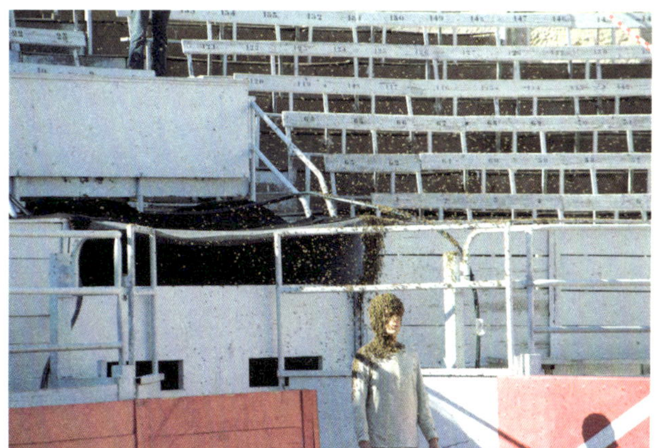

7/8/12—6:34:10 PM

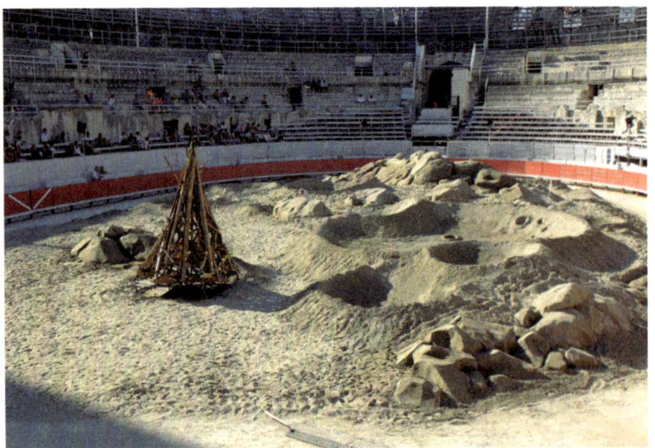

7/8/12—6:35:18 PM

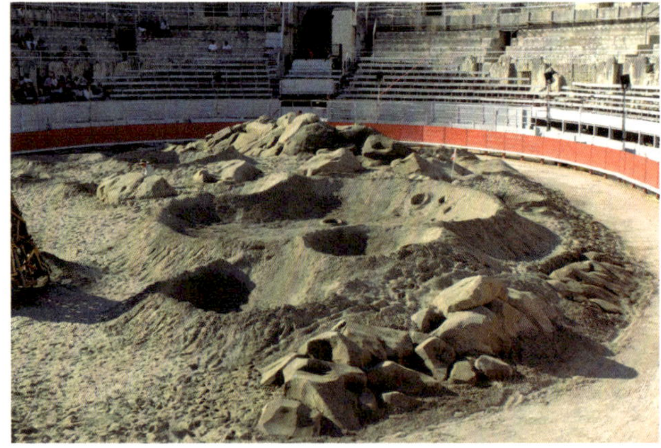

7/8/12—6:35:23 PM

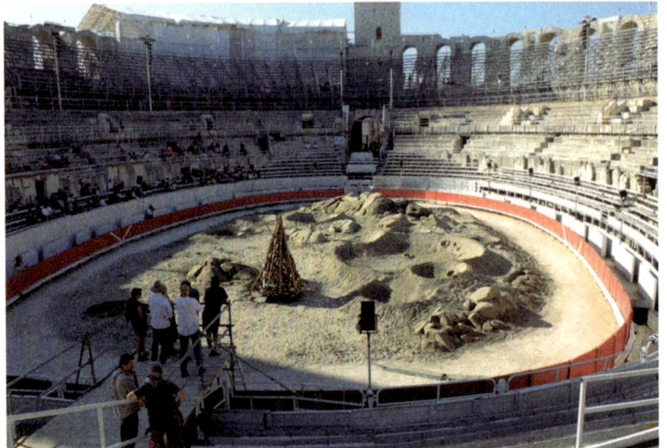

7/8/12—6:35:43 PM

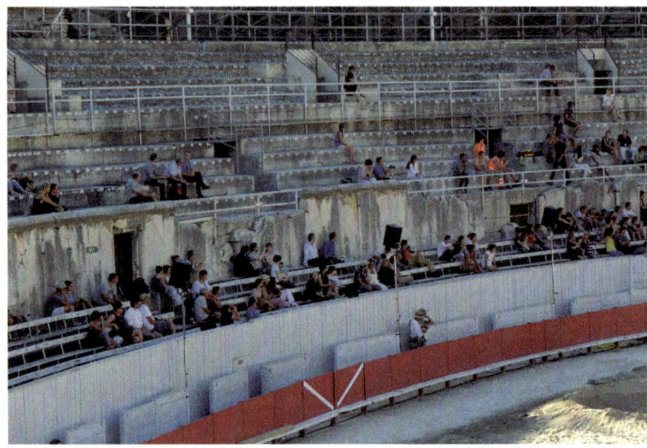

7/8/12—6:35:49 PM

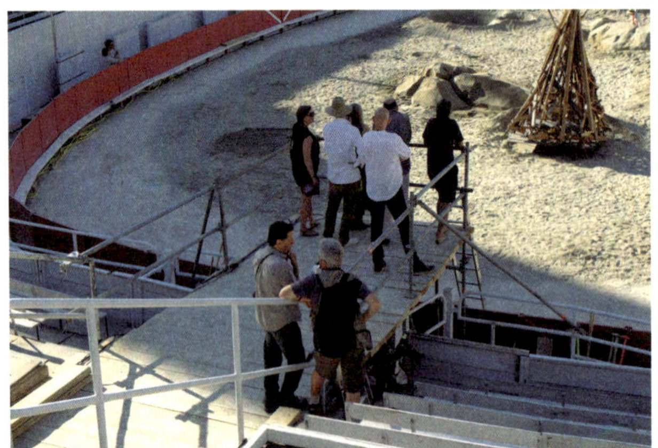

7/8/12—6:35:53 PM

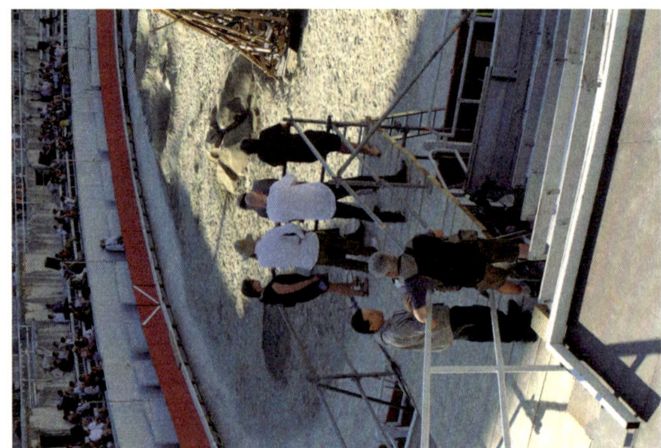

7/8/12—6:35:56 PM

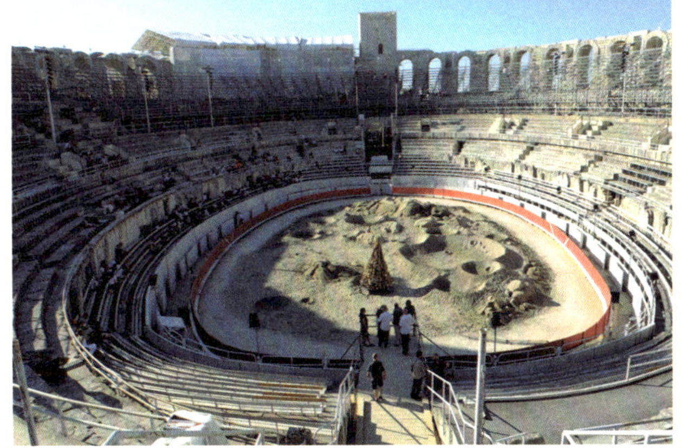
7/8/12—6:36:35 PM

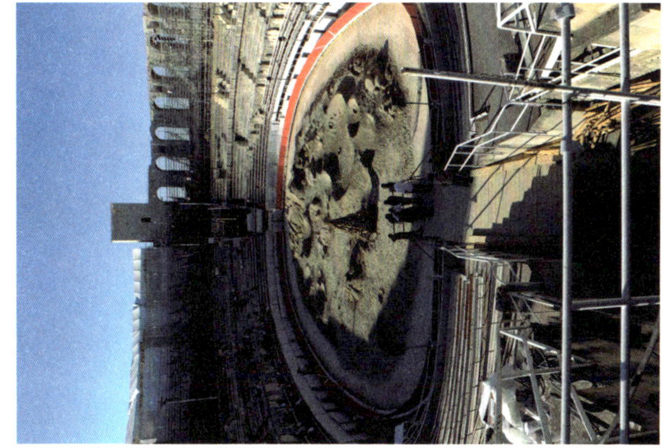
7/8/12—6:36:39 PM

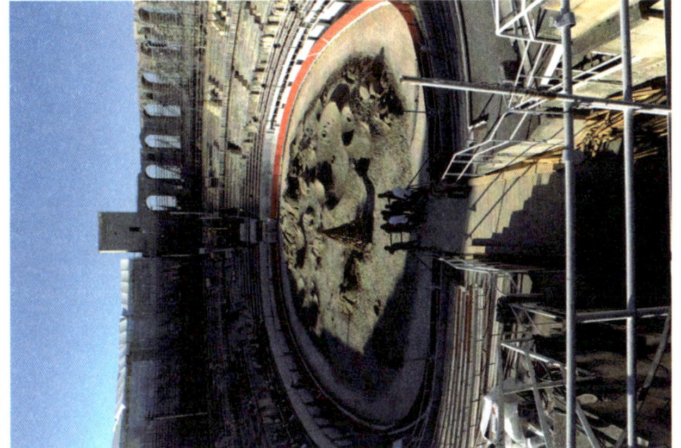
7/8/12—6:36:45 PM

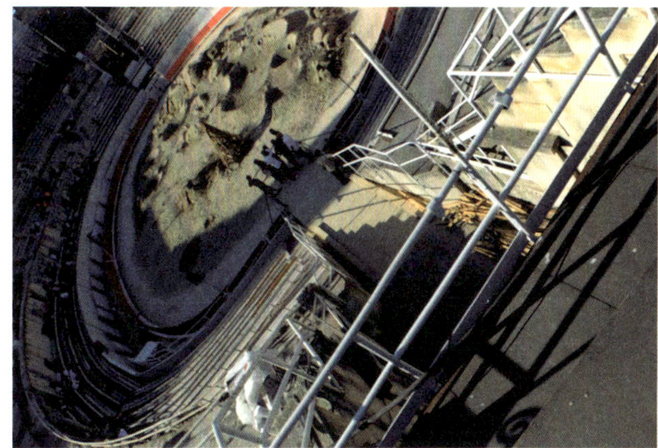
7/8/12—6:36:47 PM

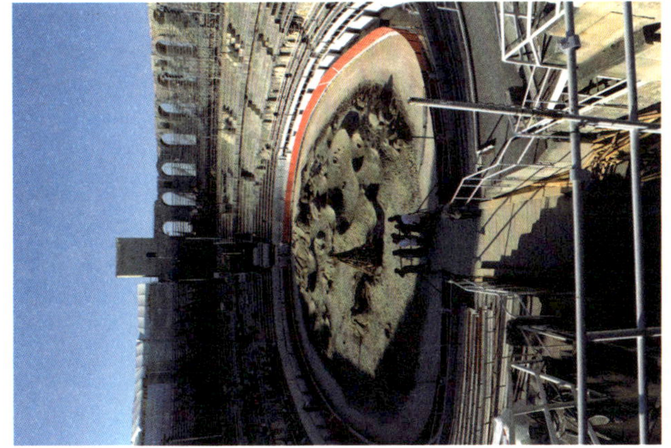
7/8/12—6:36:51 PM

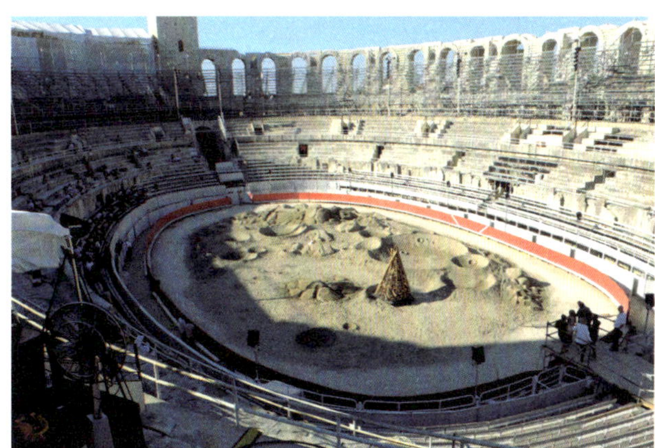
7/8/12—6:37:15 PM

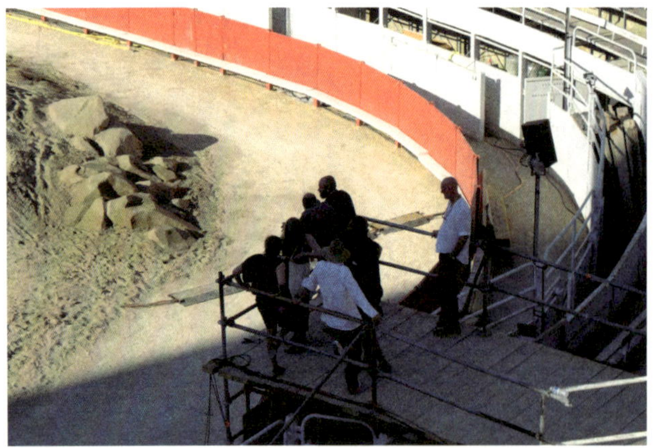
7/8/12—6:37:19 PM

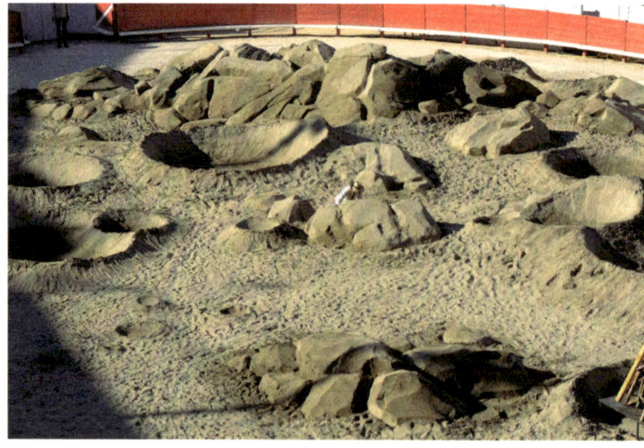
7/8/12—6:37:25 PM

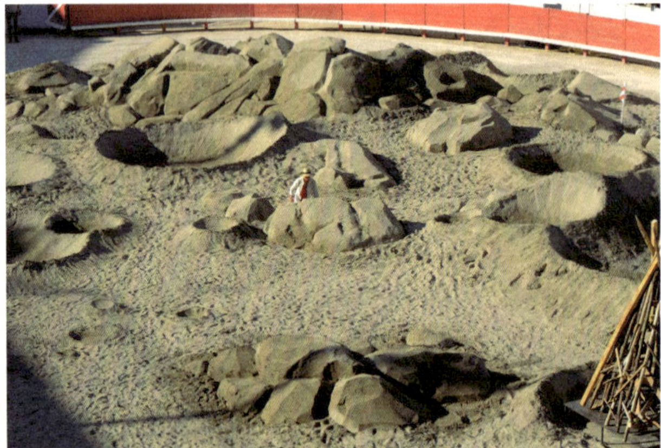
7/8/12—6:37:29 PM

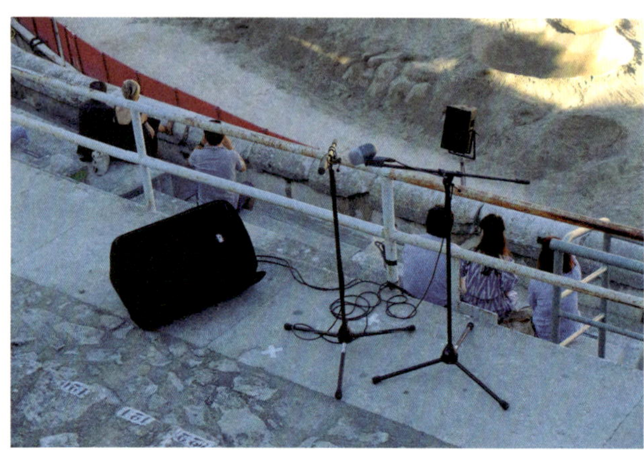
7/8/12—6:39:17 PM

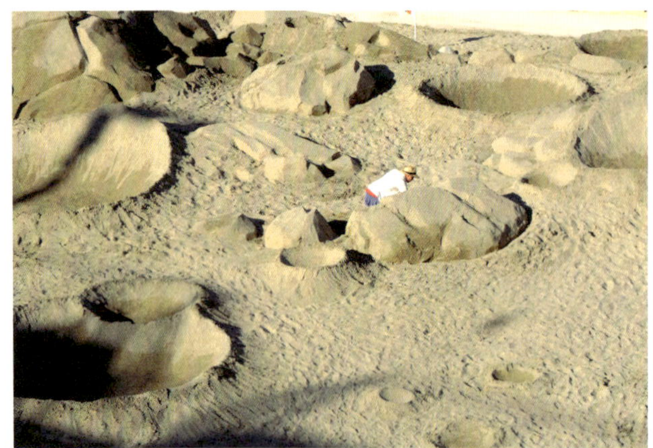
7/8/12—6:39:22 PM

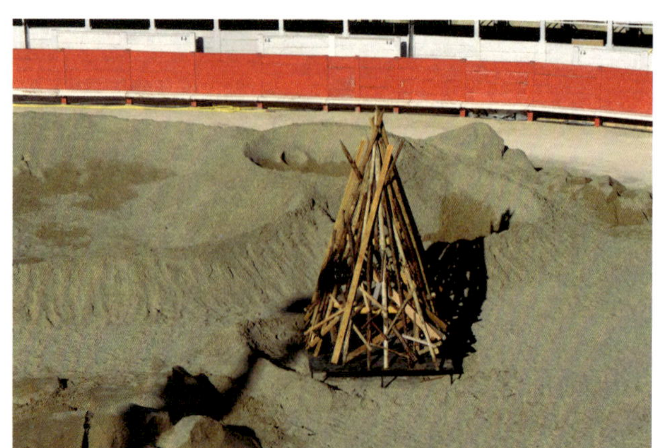
7/8/12—6:39:26 PM

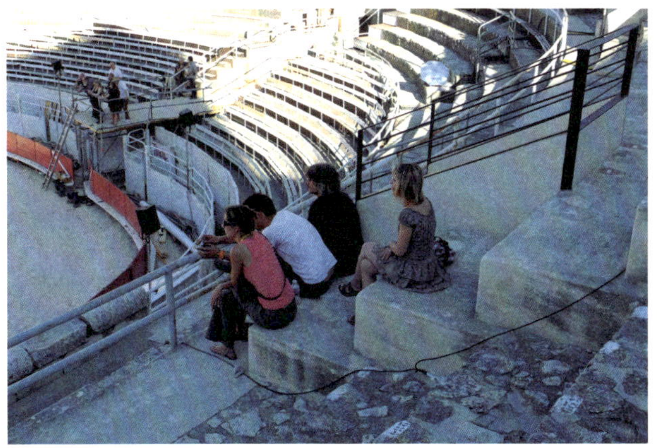

7/8/12—6:39:33 PM

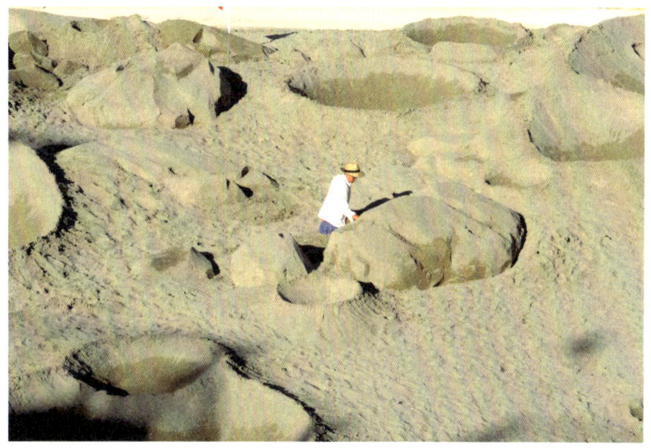

7/8/12—6:39:52 PM

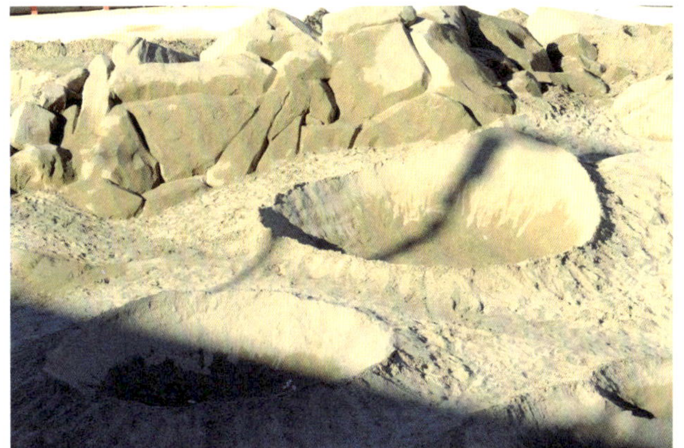

7/8/12—6:39:55 PM

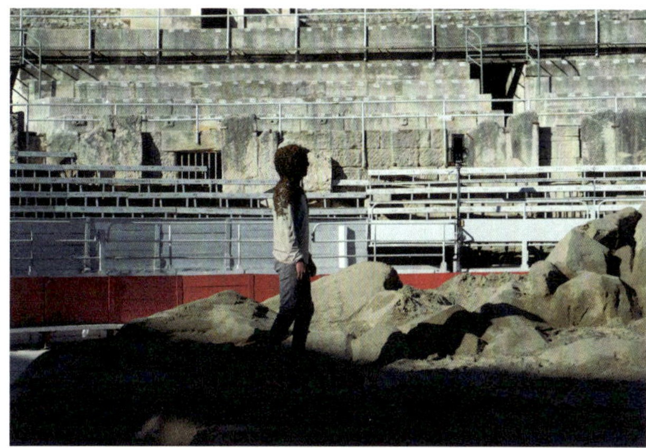

7/8/12—6:39:55 PM

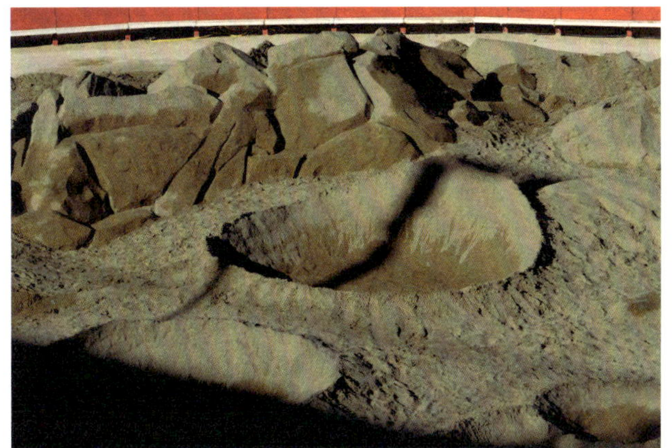

7/8/12—6:40:00 PM

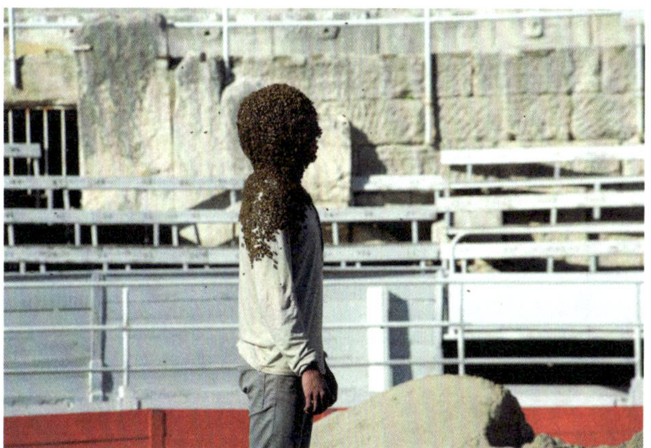

7/8/12—6:40:02 PM

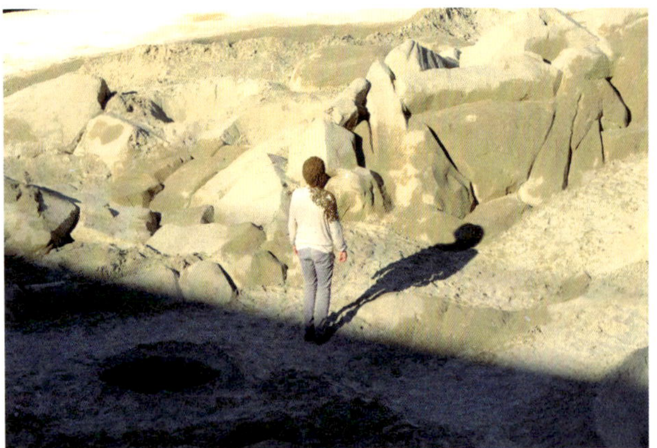

7/8/12—6:40:22 PM

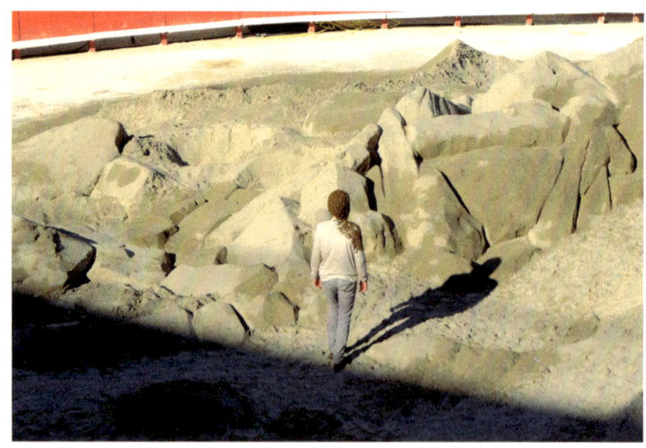

7/8/12—6:40:25 PM

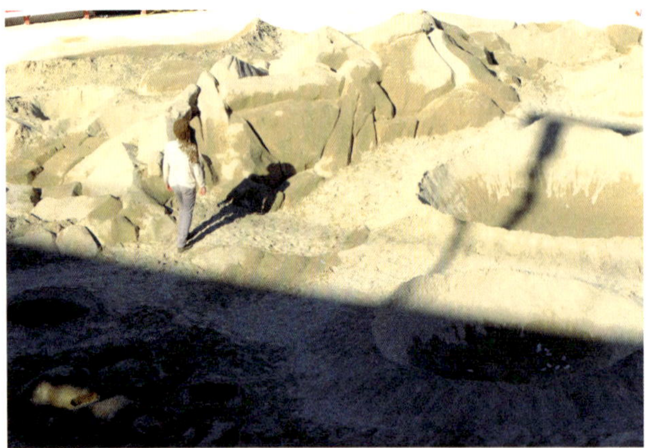

7/8/12—6:40:31 PM

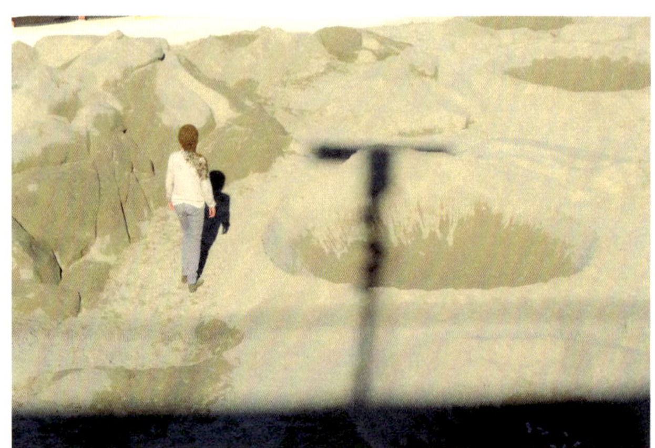

7/8/12—6:40:50 PM

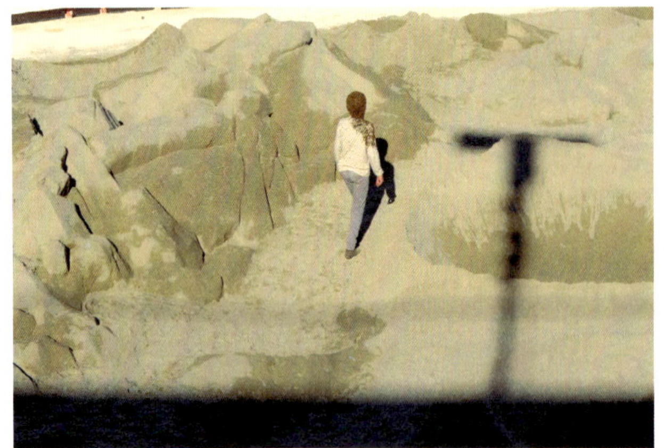

7/8/12—6:40:53 PM

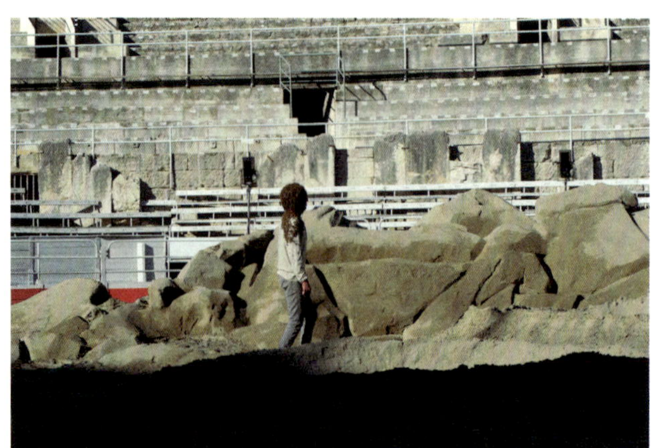

7/8/12—6:40:56 PM

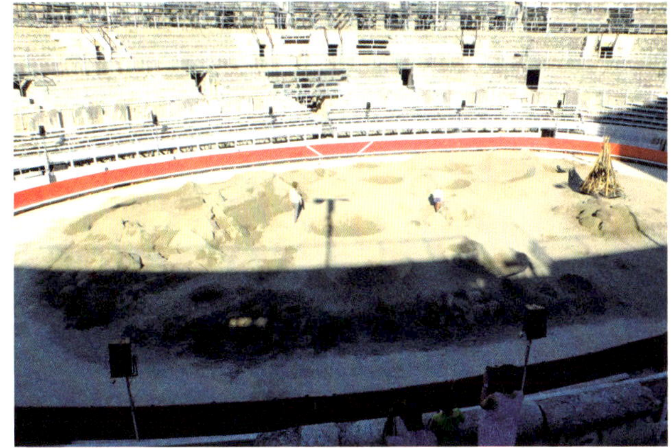
7/8/12—6:40:58 PM

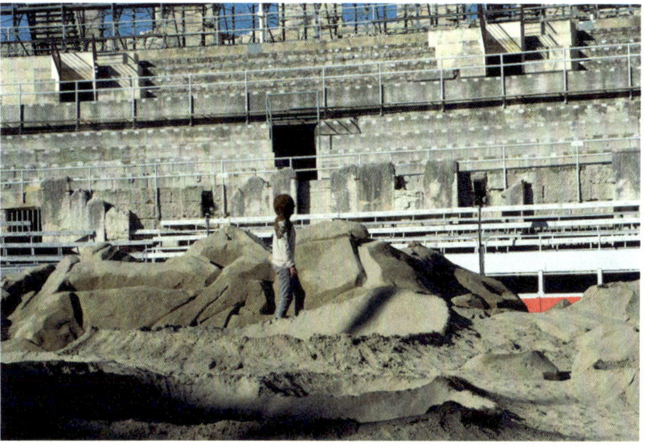
7/8/12—6:41:16 PM

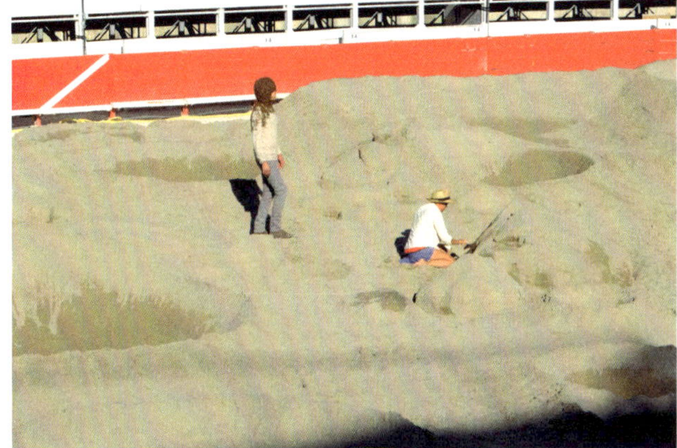
7/8/12—6:41:43 PM

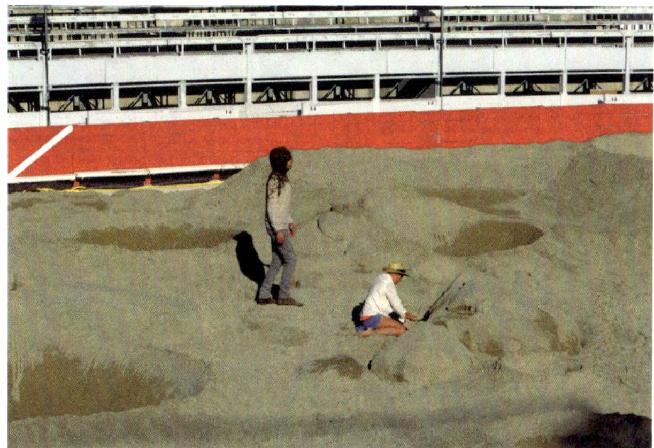
7/8/12—6:41:47 PM

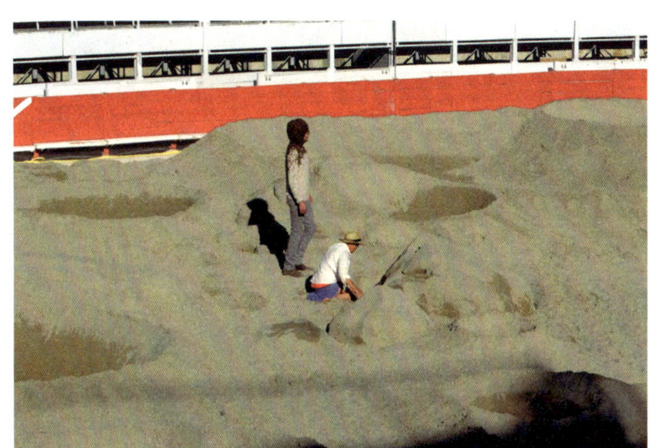
7/8/12—6:41:51 PM

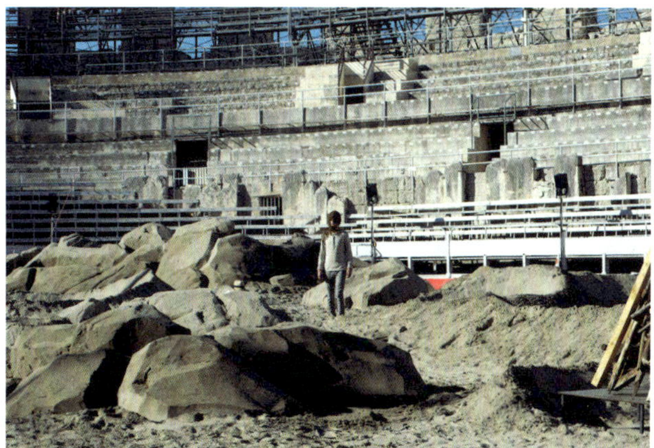
7/8/12—6:41:57 PM

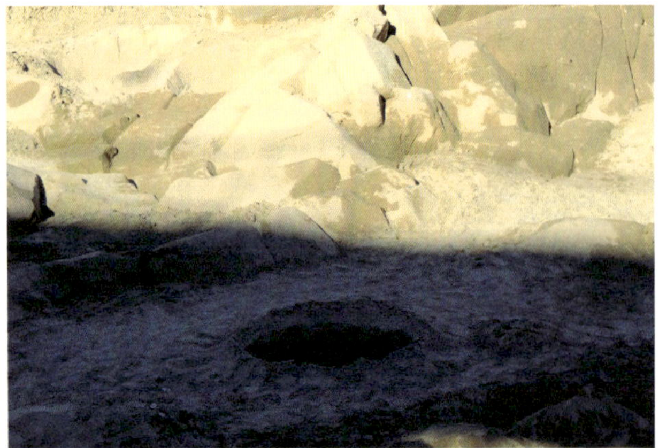
7/8/12—6:42:07 PM

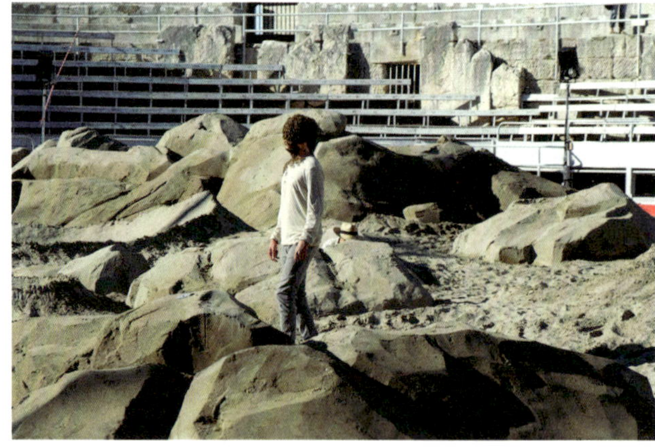
7/8/12—6:43:08 PM

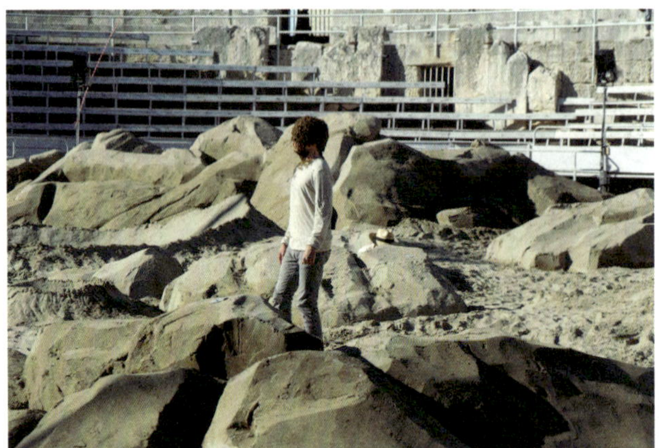
7/8/12—6:43:09 PM

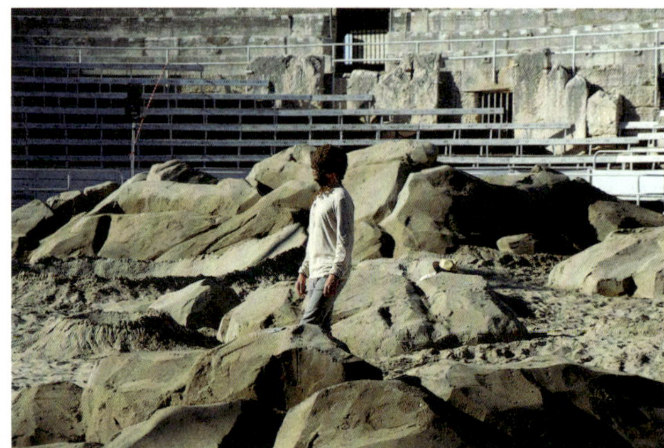
7/8/12—6:43:11 PM

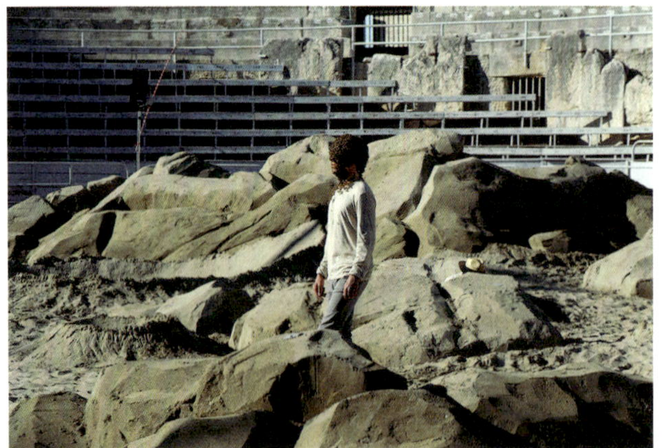
7/8/12—6:43:13 PM

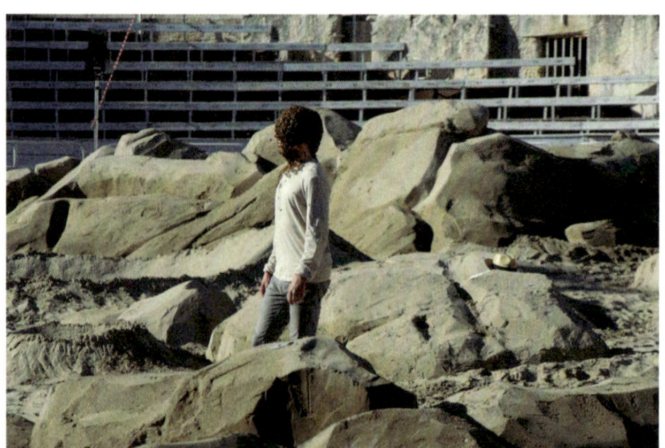
7/8/12—6:43:13 PM

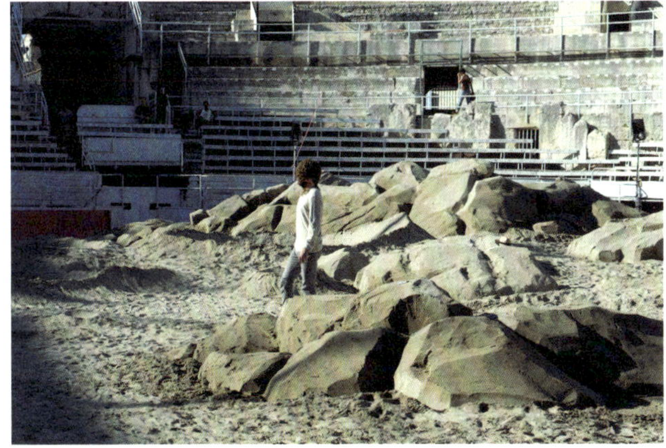

7/8/12—6:43:20 PM

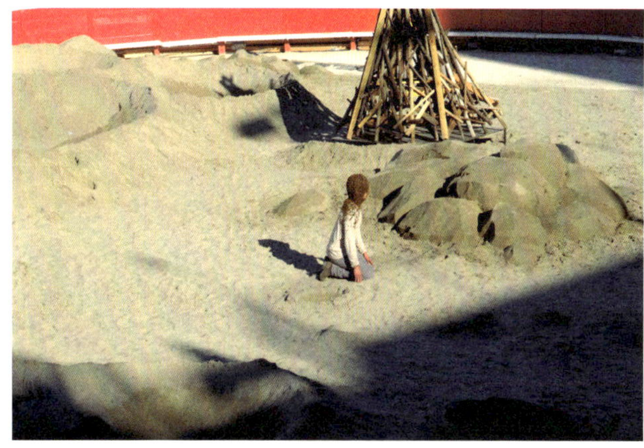

7/8/12—6:44:24 PM

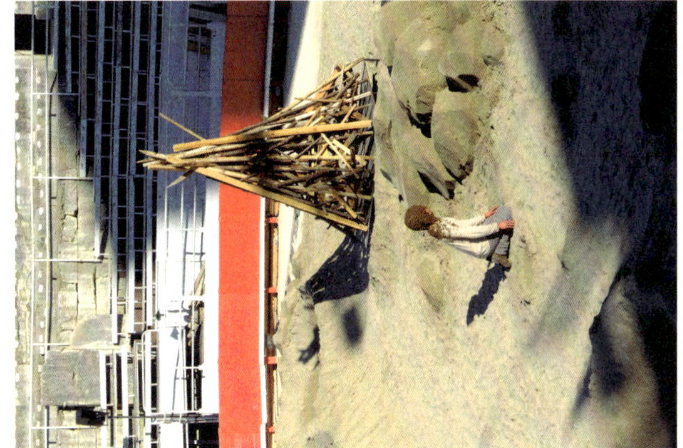

7/8/12—6:44:29 PM

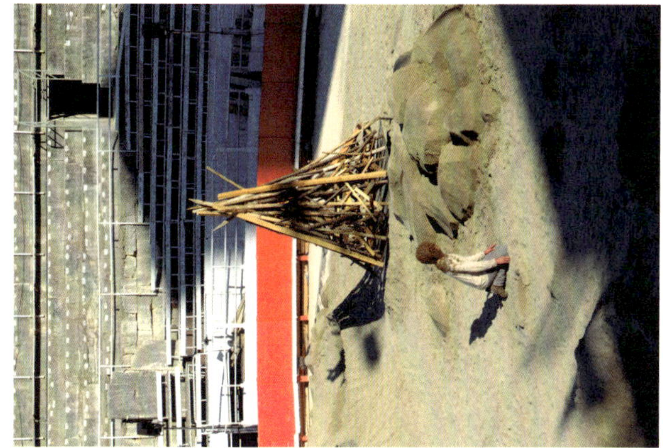

7/8/12—6:44:32 PM

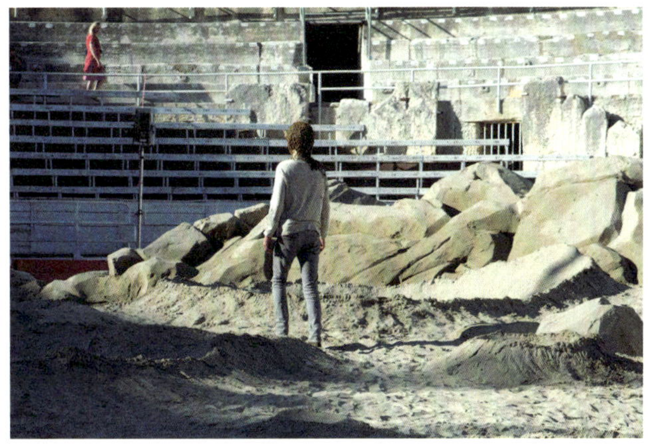

7/8/12—6:47:53 PM

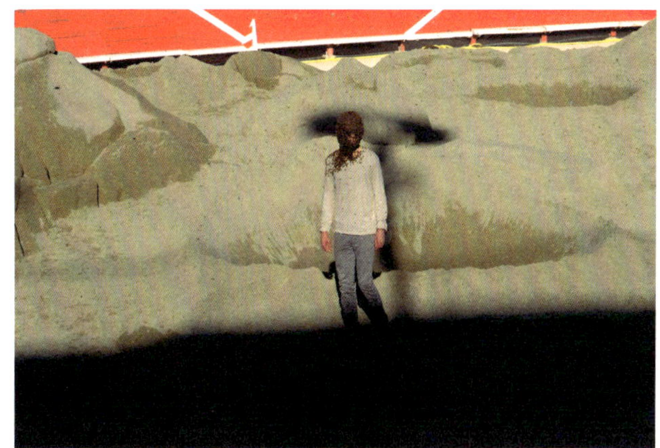

7/8/12—6:48:29 PM

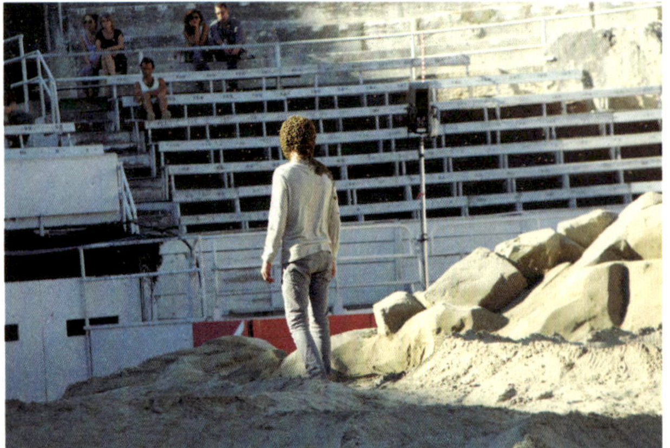
7/8/12—6:48:30 PM

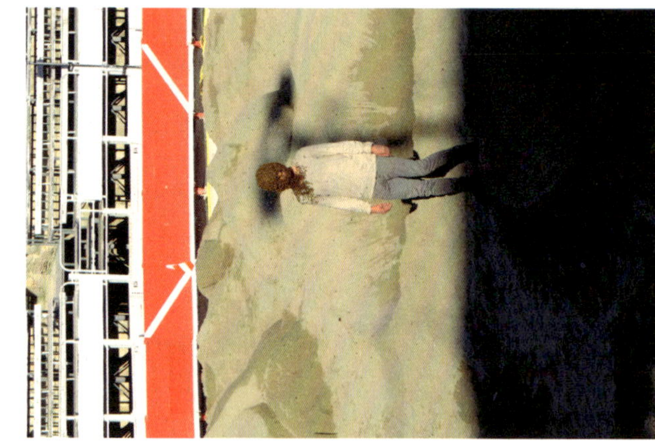
7/8/12—6:48:35 PM

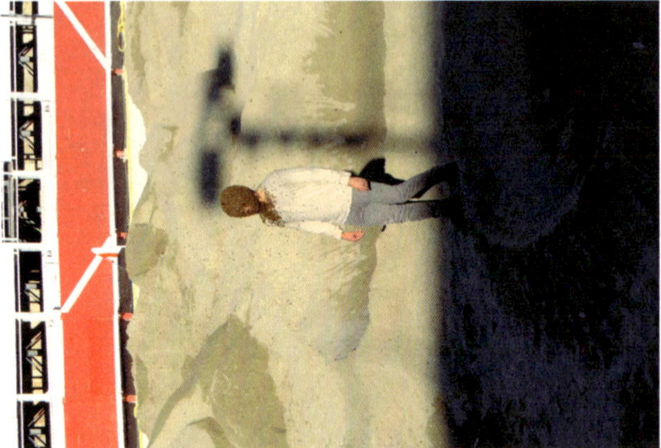
7/8/12—6:48:41 PM

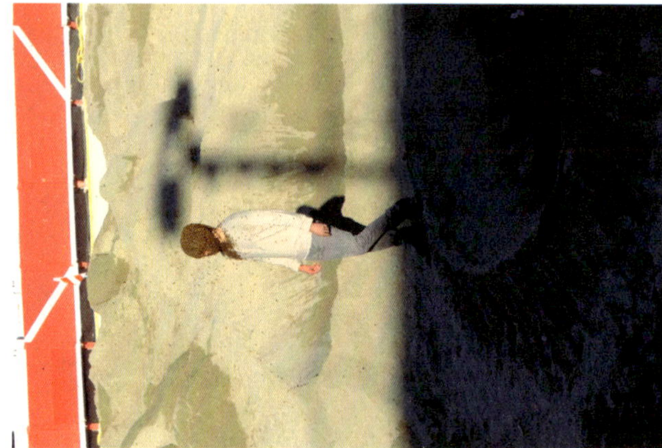
7/8/12—6:48:43 PM

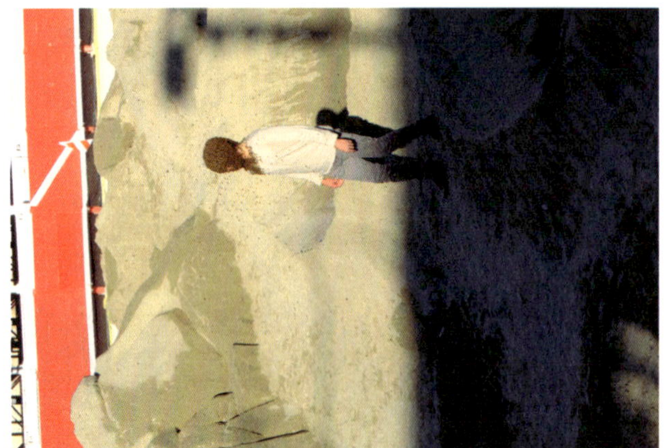
7/8/12—6:48:46 PM

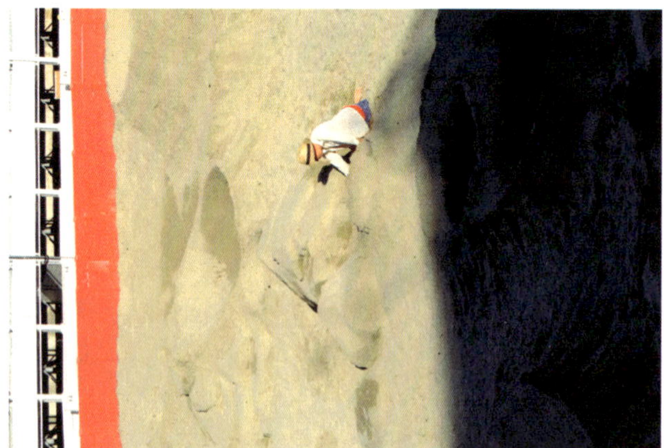
7/8/12—6:48:49 PM

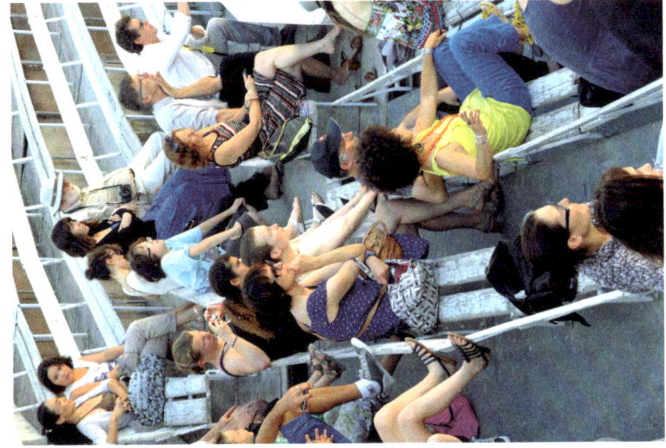

7/8/12—6:49:13 PM

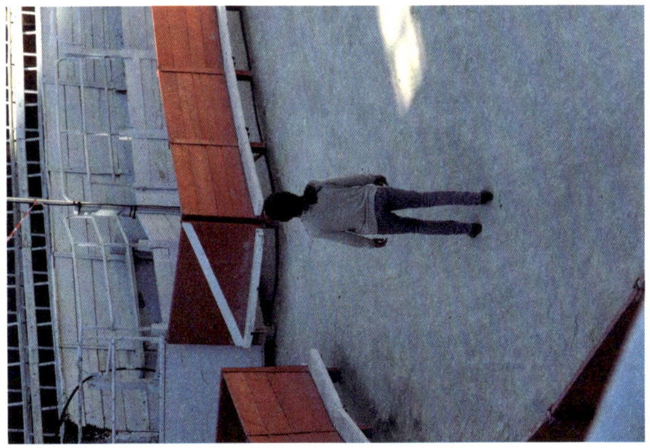

7/8/12—6:50:02 PM

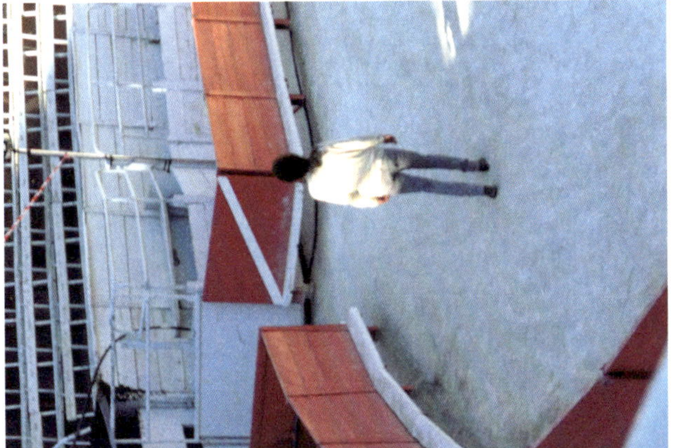

7/8/12—6:50:06 PM

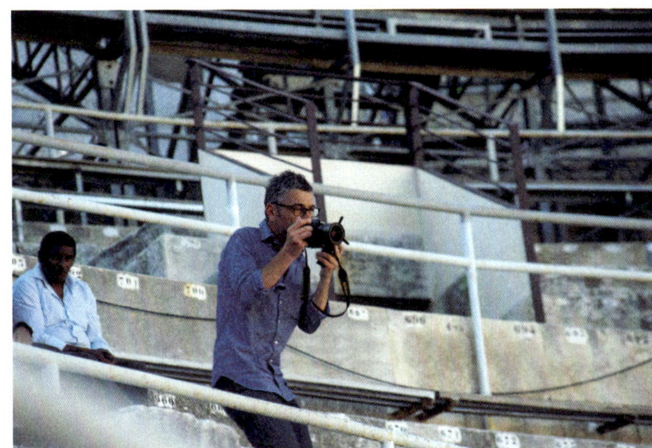

7/8/12—6:50:15 PM

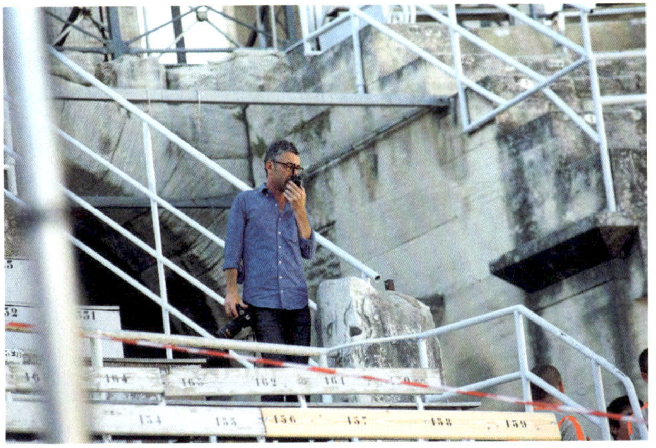

7/8/12—6:50:33 PM

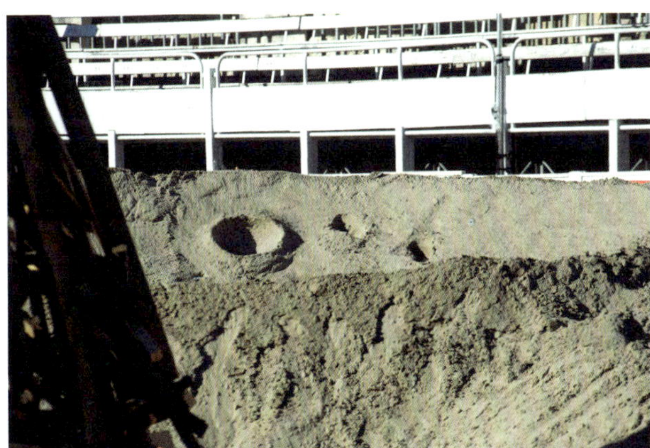

7/8/12—6:55:45 PM

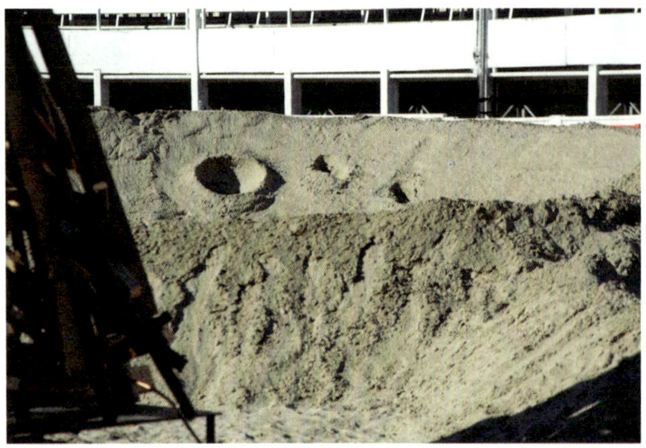

7/8/12—6:55:48 PM

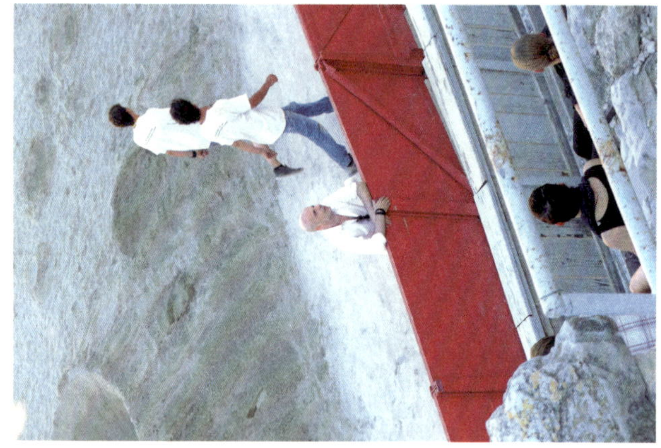

7/8/12—6:56:38 PM

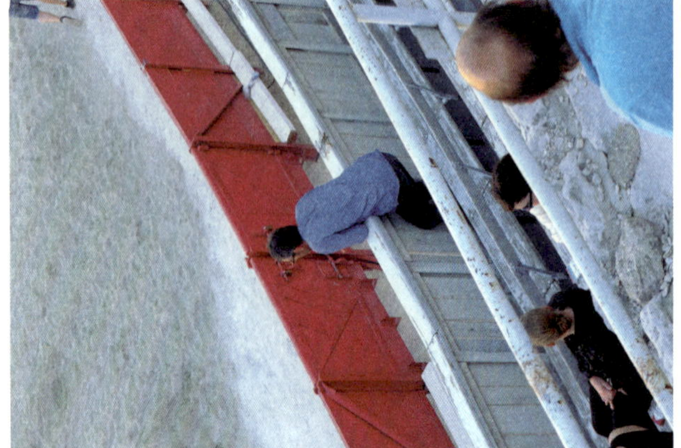

7/8/12—6:56:43 PM

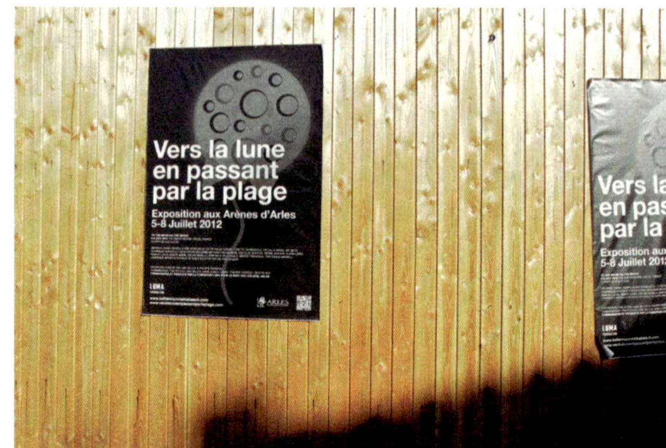

7/8/12—6:58:42 PM

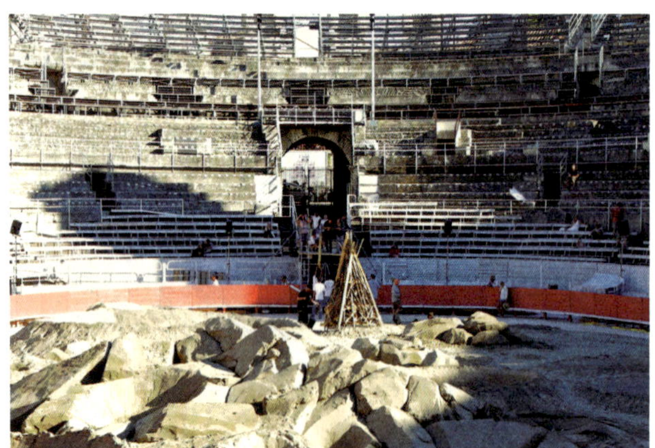

7/8/12—7:00:06 PM

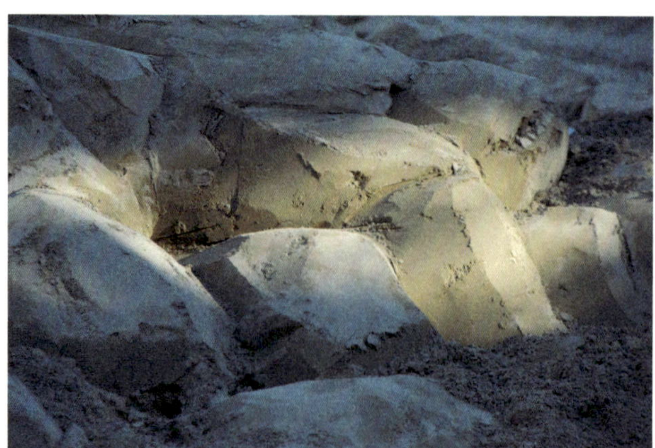

7/8/12—7:04:19 PM

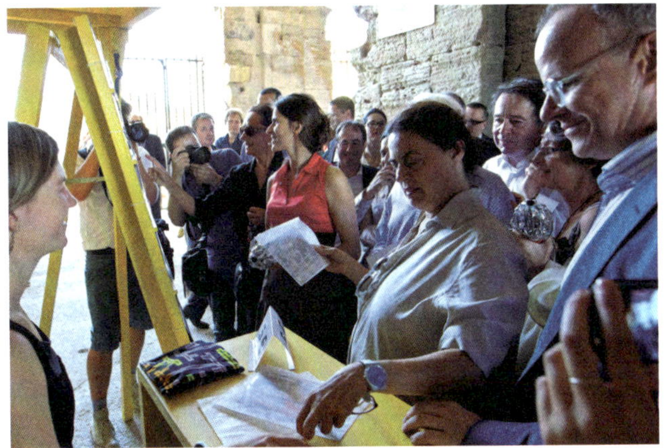
7/8/12—7:22:06 PM

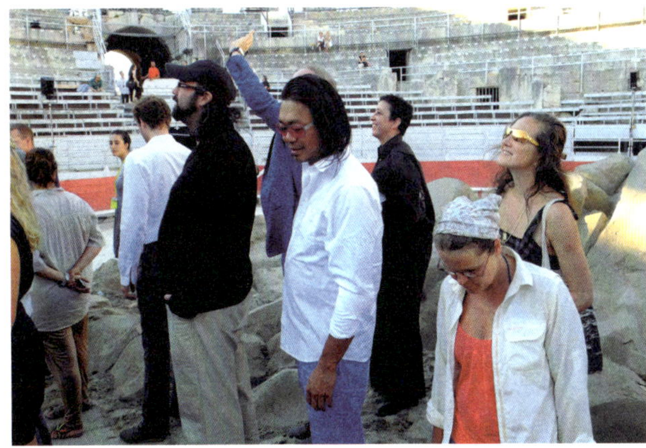
7/8/12—7:28:00 PM

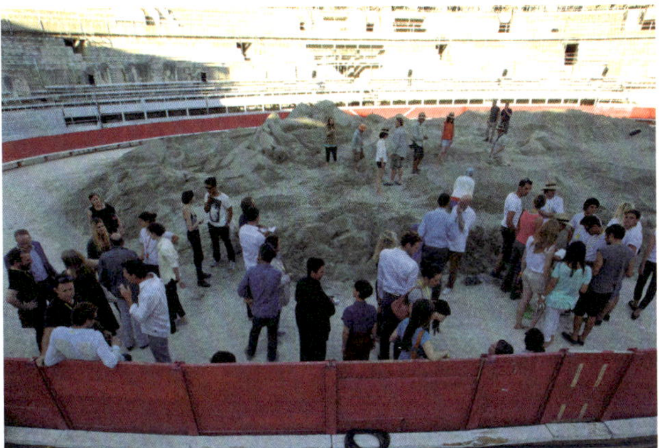
7/8/12—7:39:18 PM

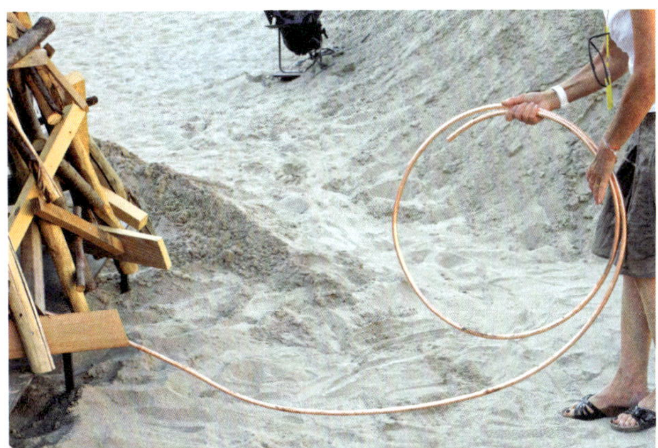
7/8/12—7:52:48 PM

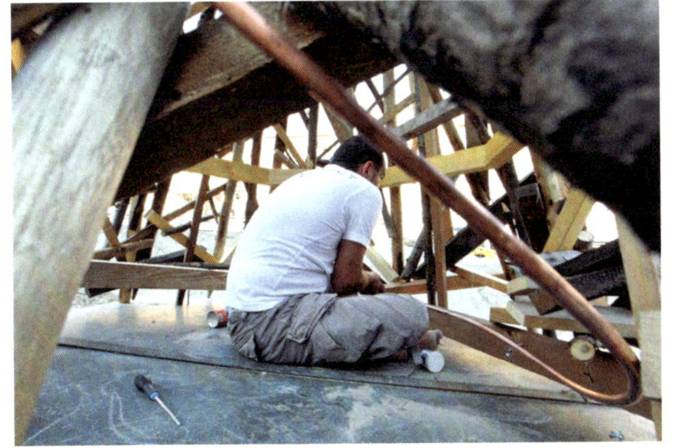
7/8/12—7:53:20 PM

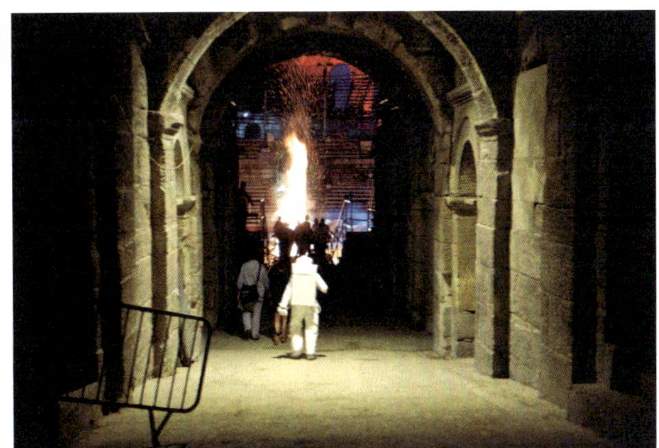
7/8/12—10:31:56 PM

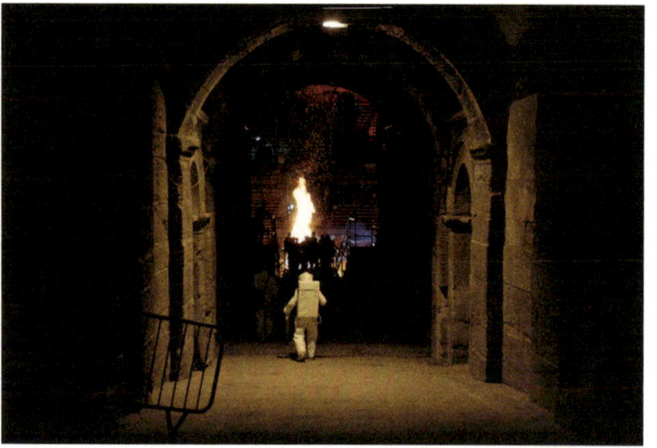

7/8/12—10:31:57 PM

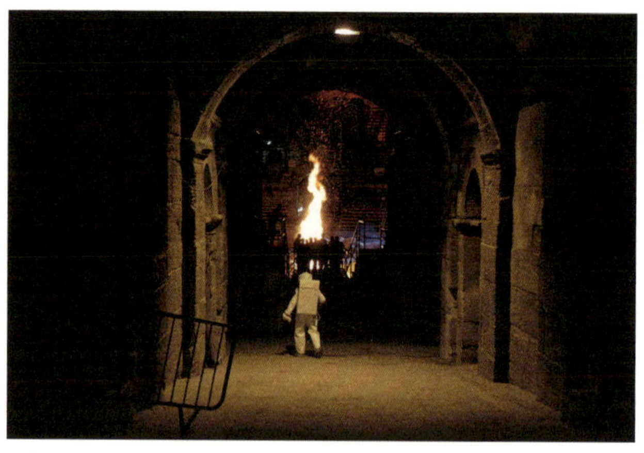

7/8/12—10:31:58 PM

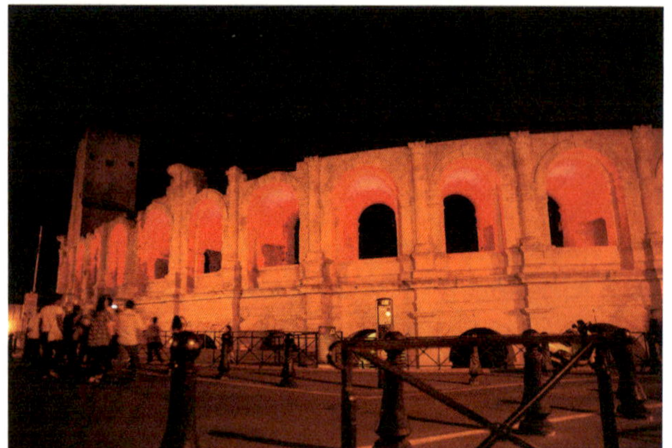

7/8/12—10:32:42 PM

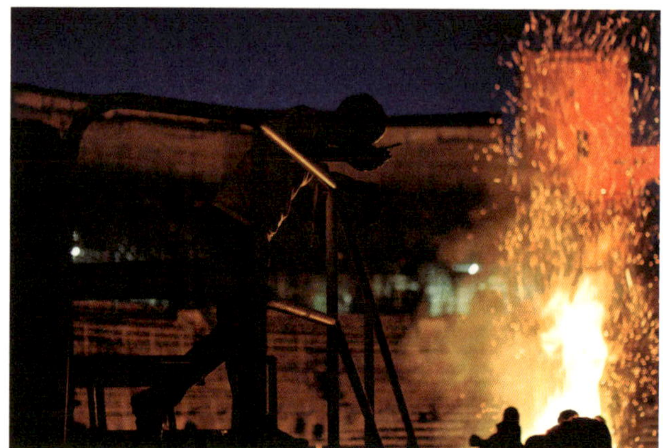

7/8/12—10:33:37 PM

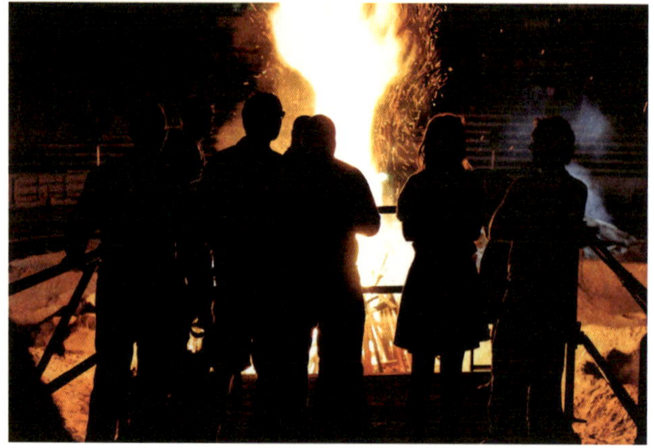

7/8/12—10:33:48 PM

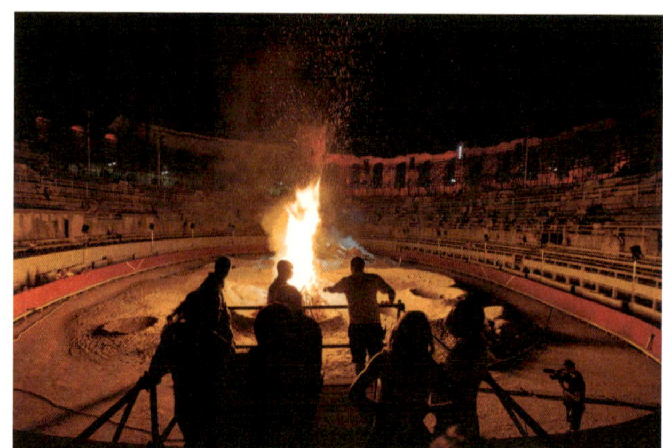

7/8/12—10:34:07 PM

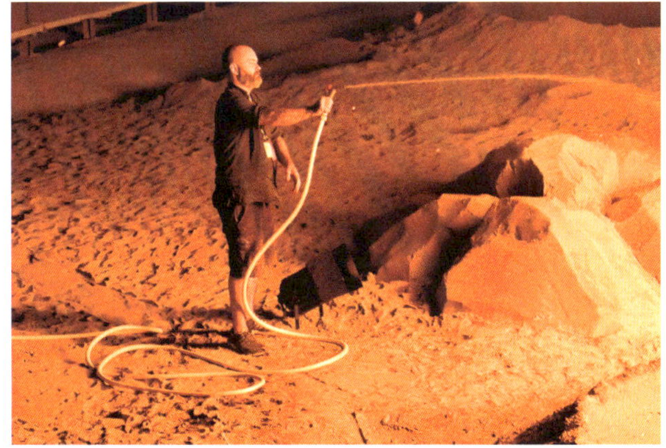
7/8/12—10:34:34 PM

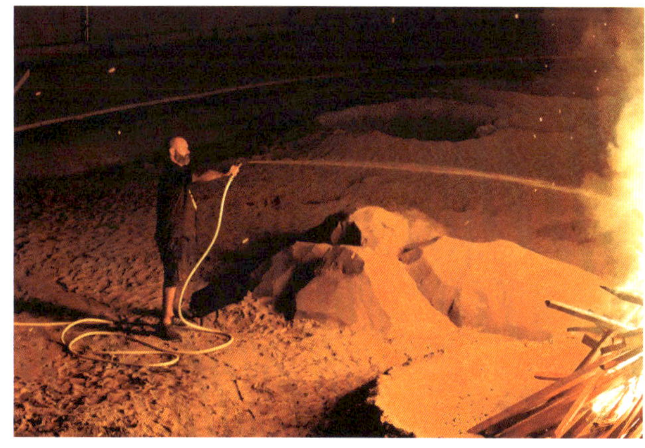
7/8/12—10:34:38 PM

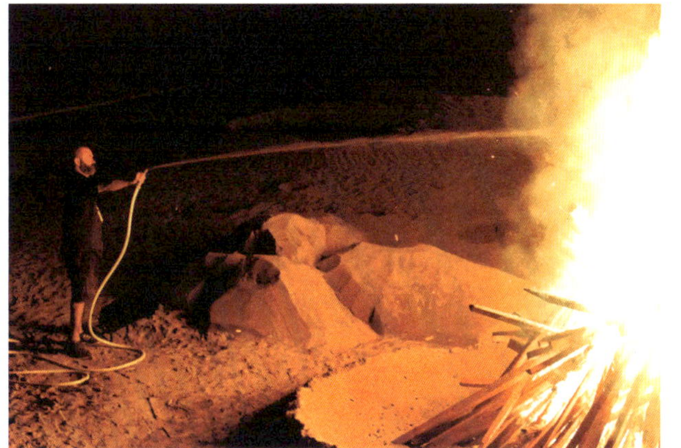
7/8/12—10:34:39 PM

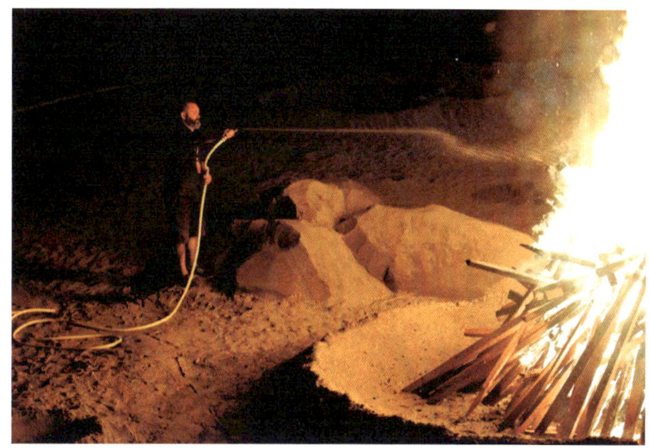
7/8/12—10:34:58 PM

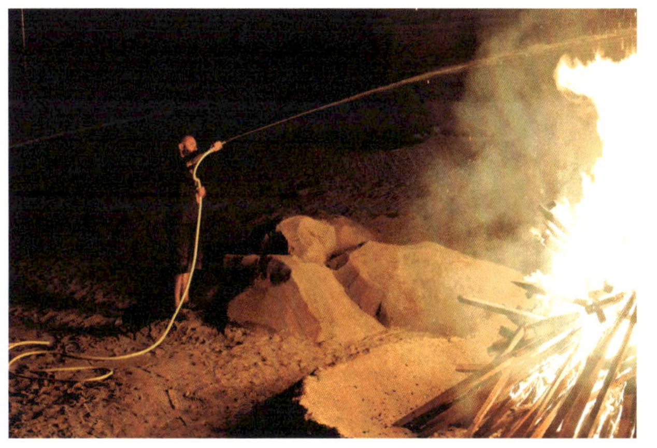
7/8/12—10:35:02 PM

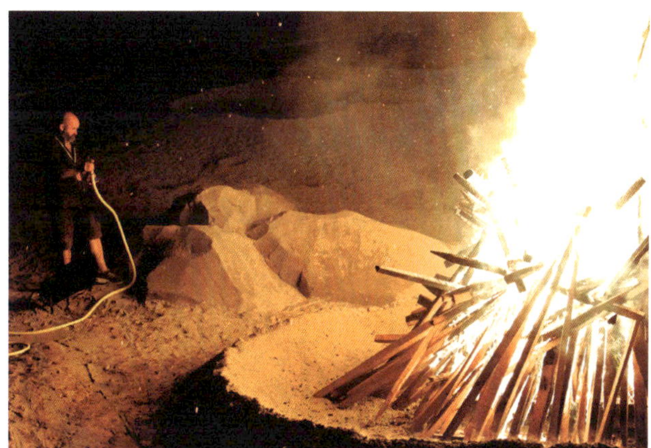
7/8/12—10:35:19 PM

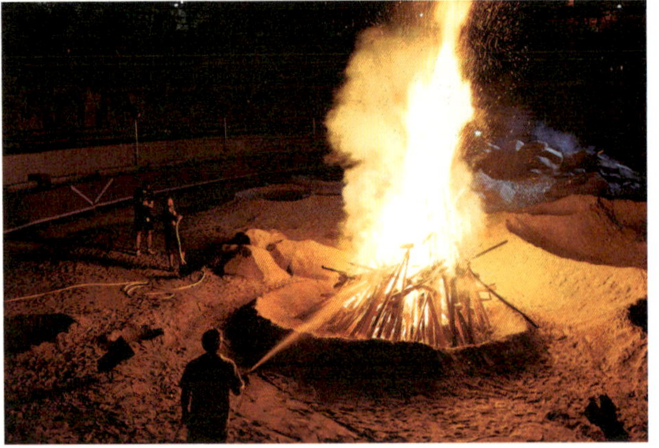

7/8/12—10:36:10 PM

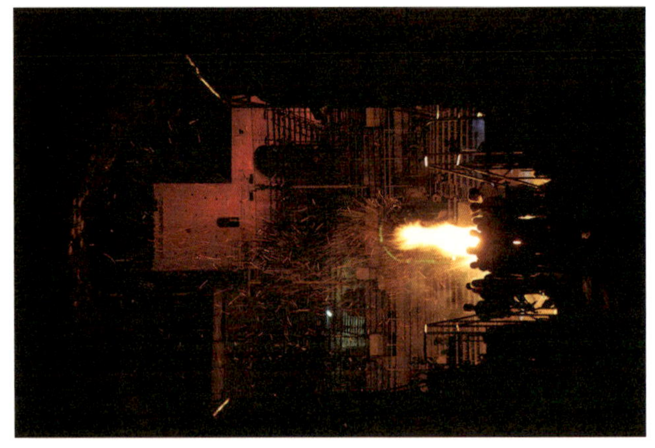

7/8/12—10:37:06 PM

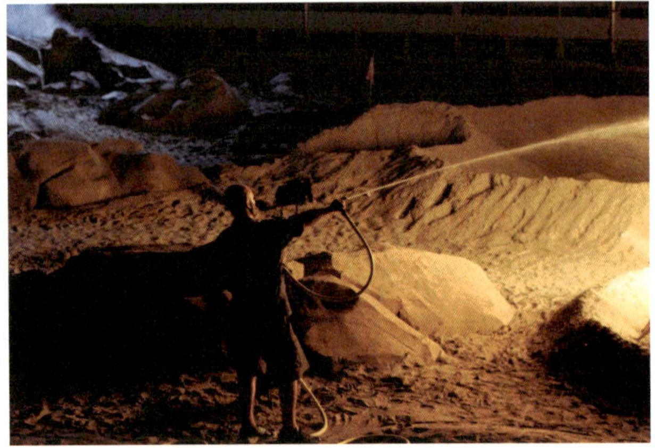

7/8/12—10:37:25 PM

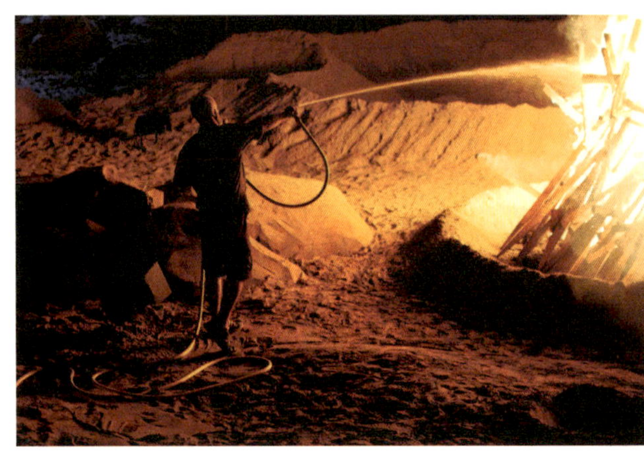

7/8/12—10:37:33 PM

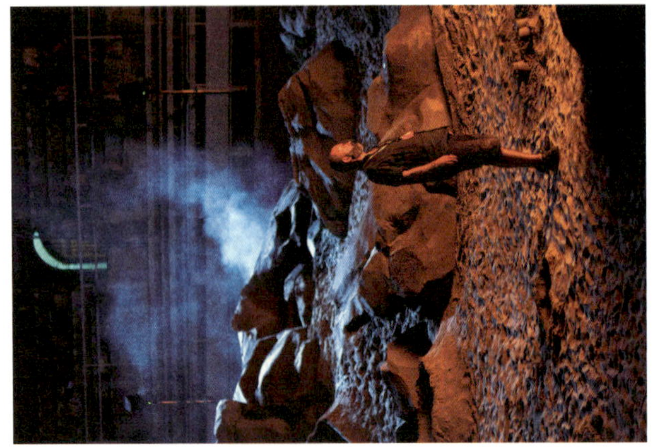

7/8/12—10:37:58 PM

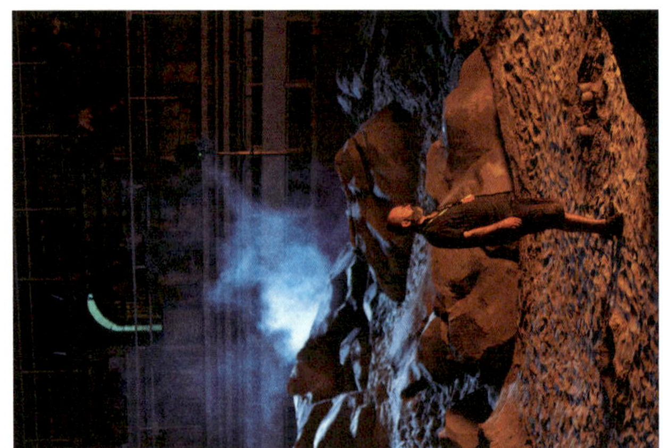

7/8/12—10:38:02 PM

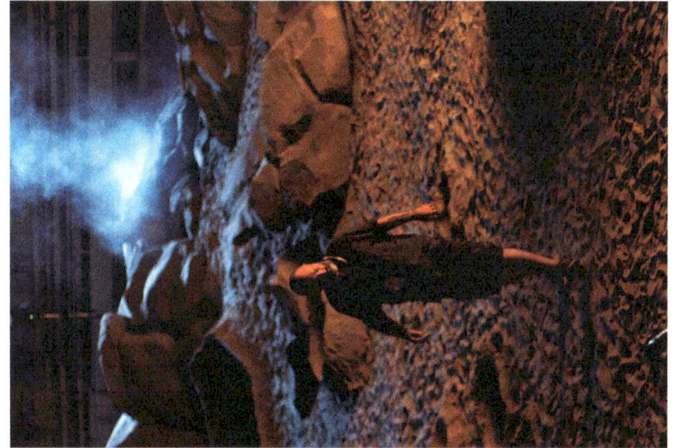
7/8/12—10:38:07 PM

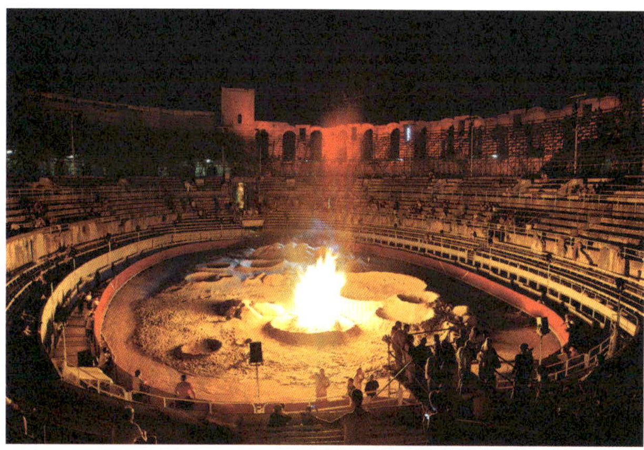
7/8/12—10:38:31 PM

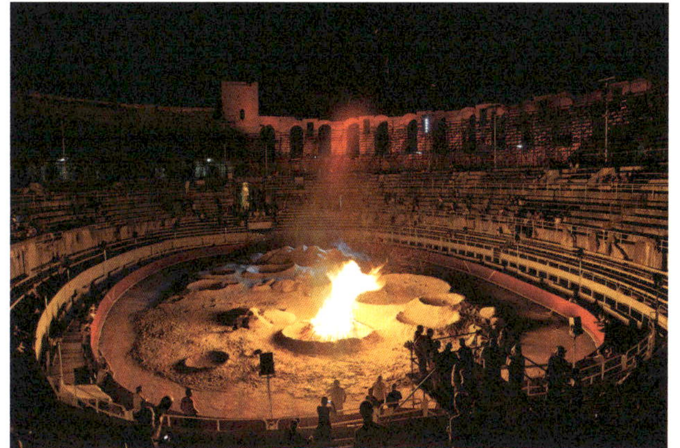
7/8/12—10:38:36 PM

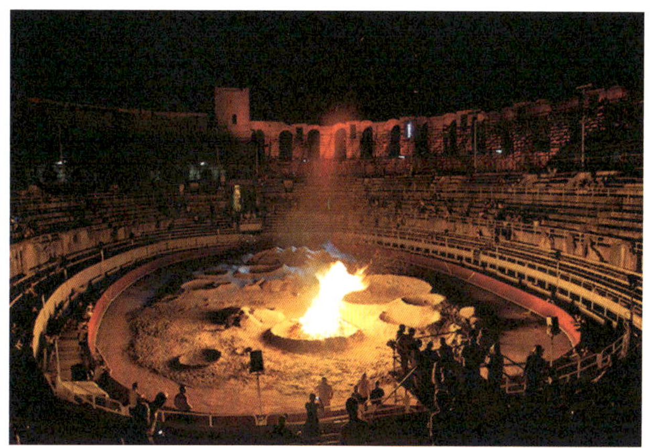
7/8/12—10:38:36 PM

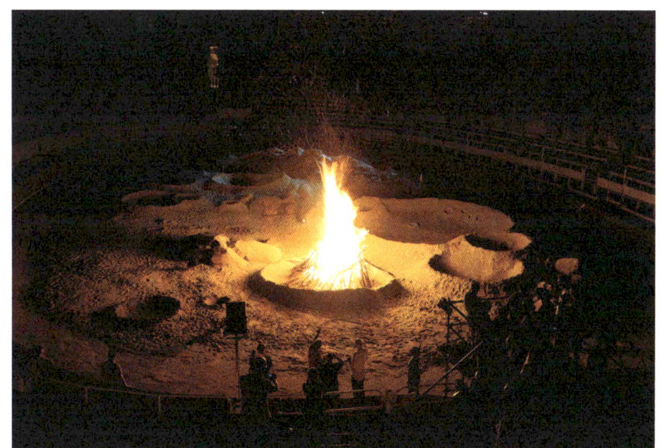
7/8/12—10:39:28 PM

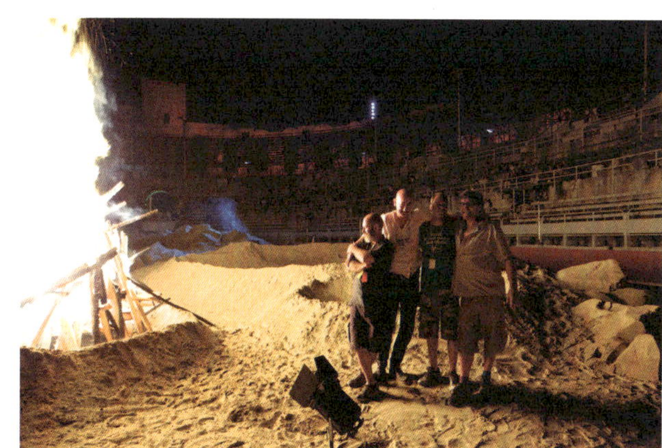
7/8/12—10:40:32 PM

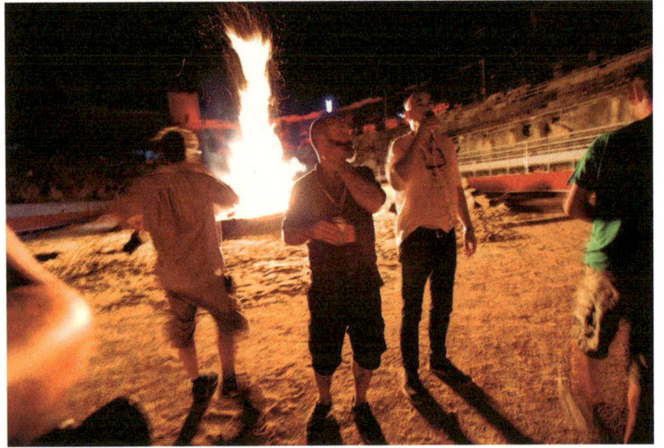

7/8/12—10:42:06 PM

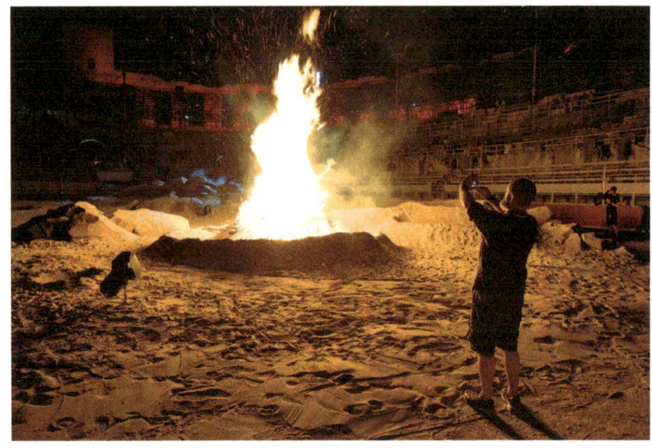

7/8/12—10:42:56 PM

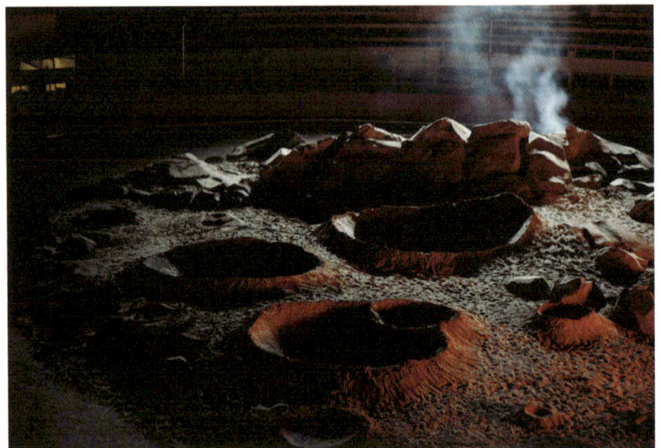

7/8/12—10:43:09 PM

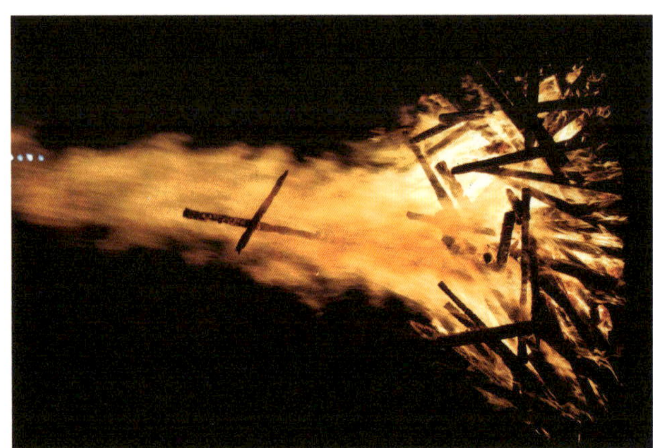

7/8/12—10:43:17 PM

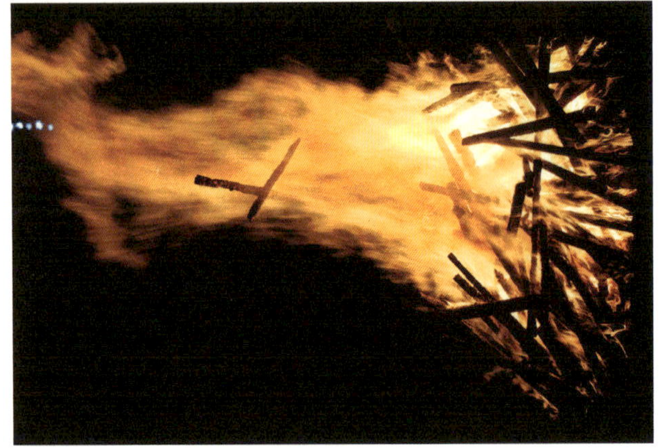

7/8/12—10:43:20 PM

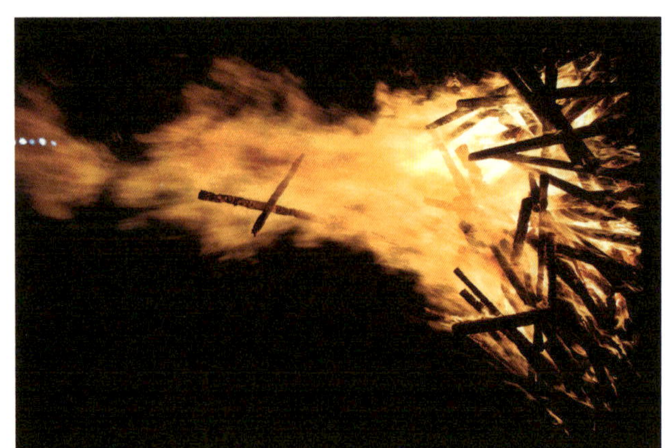

7/8/12—10:43:21 PM

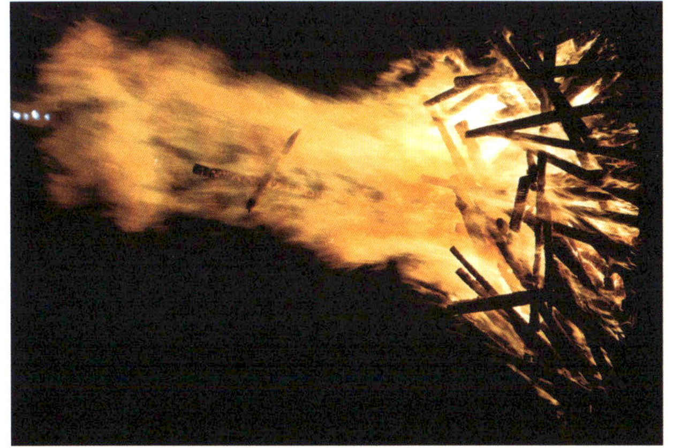

7/8/12—10:43:22 PM

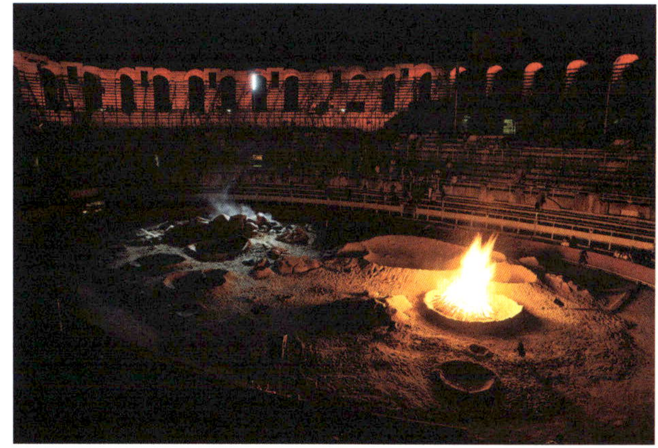

7/8/12—10:44:37 PM

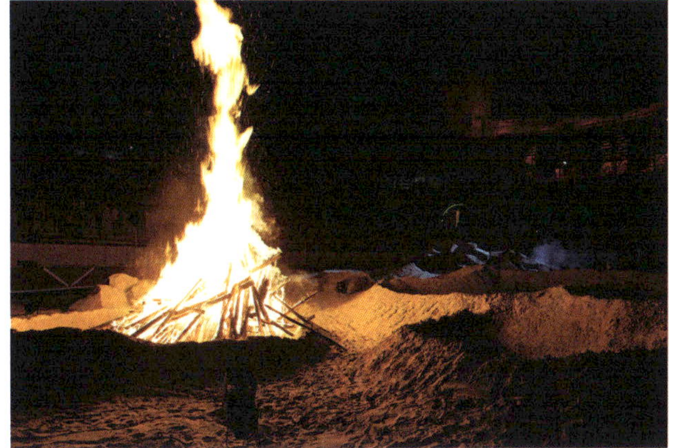

7/8/12—10:44:44 PM

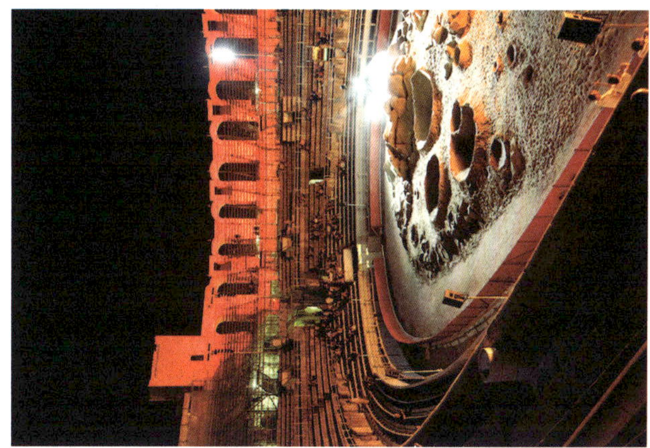

7/8/12—10:46:02 PM

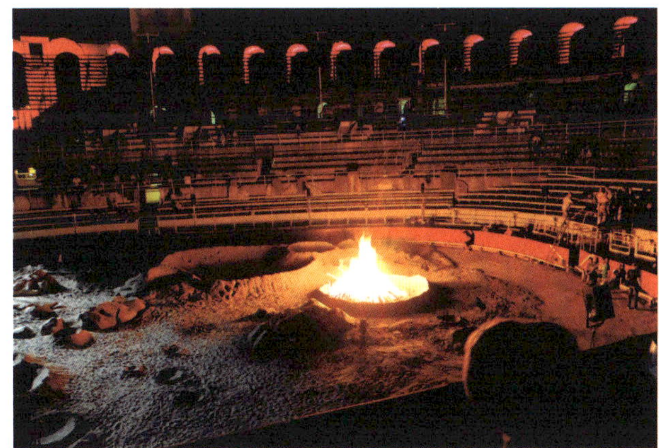

7/8/12—10:46:57 PM

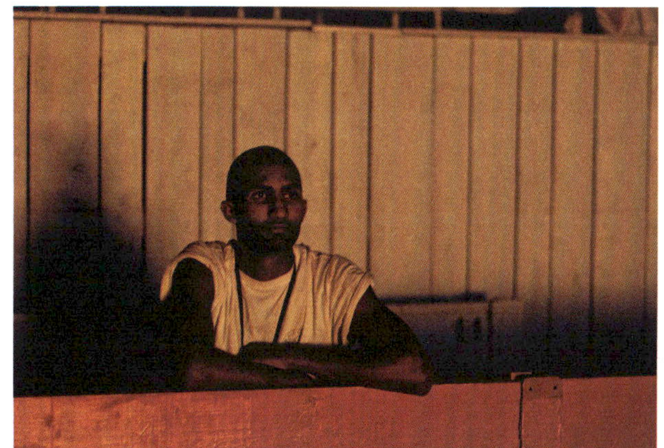

7/8/12—10:47:01 PM

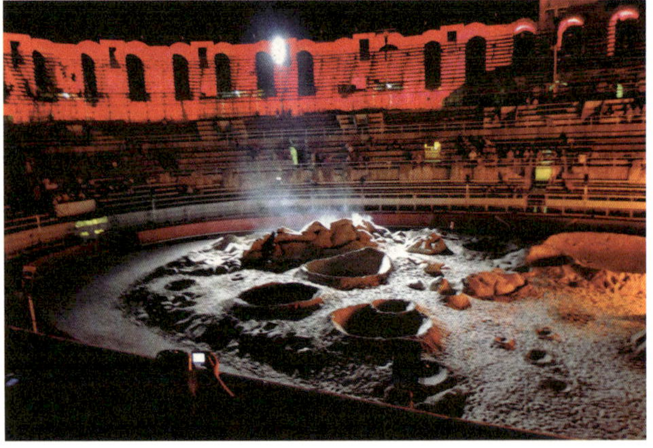
7/8/12—10:47:02 PM

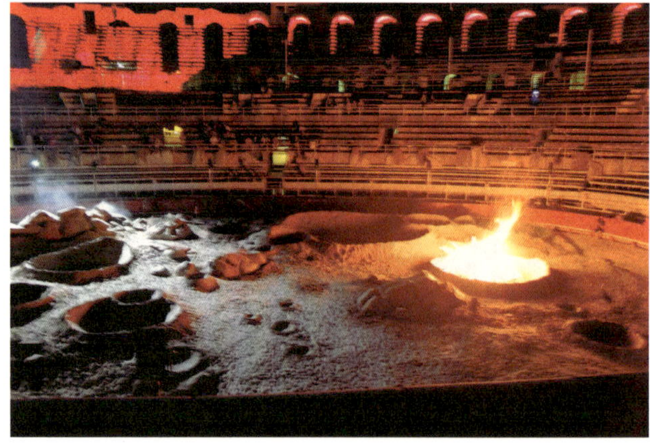
7/8/12—10:47:06 PM

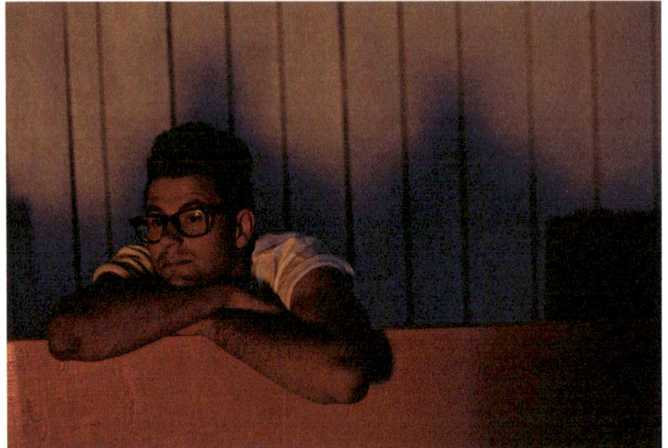
7/8/12—10:47:20 PM

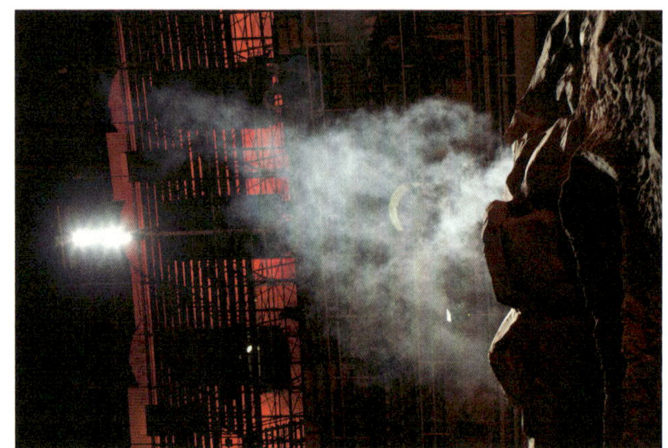
7/8/12—10:47:30 PM

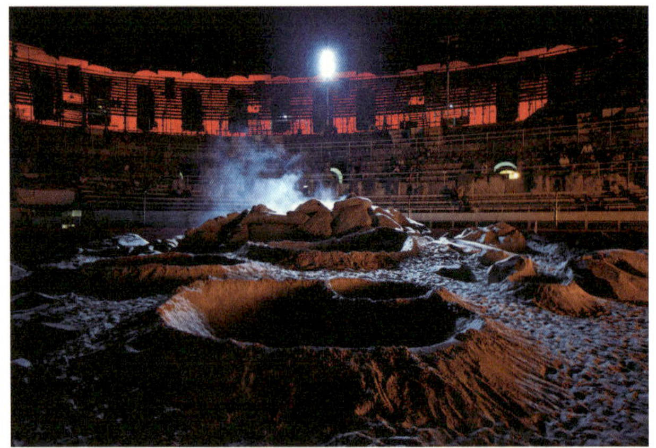
7/8/12—10:47:55 PM

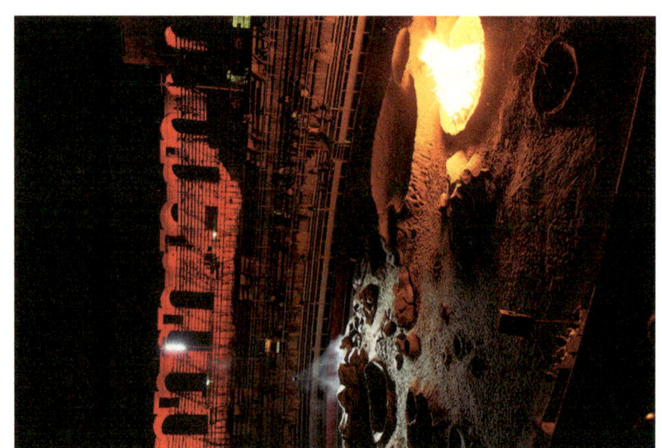
7/8/12—10:48:04 PM

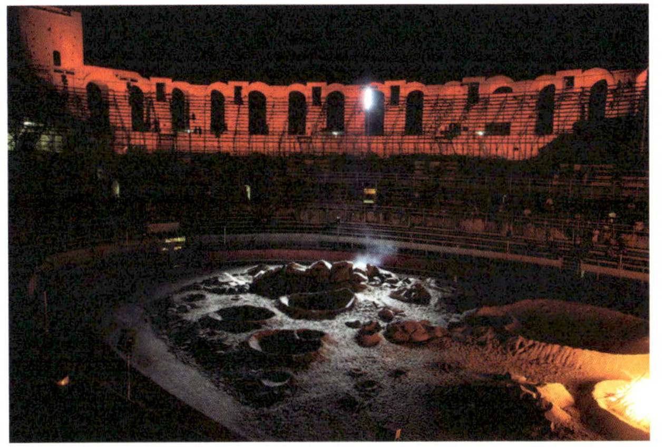

7/8/12—10:48:34 PM

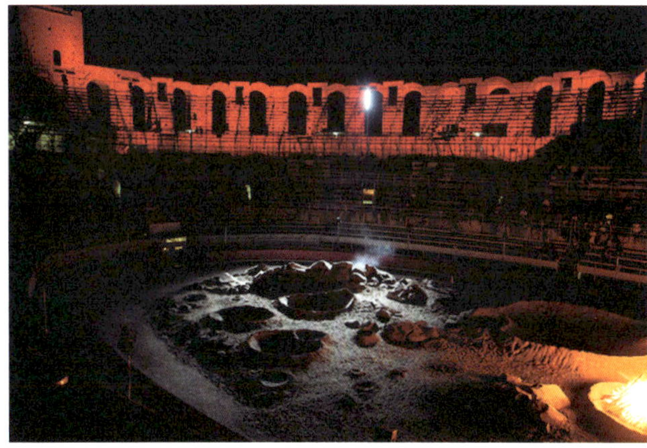

7/8/12—10:48:34 PM

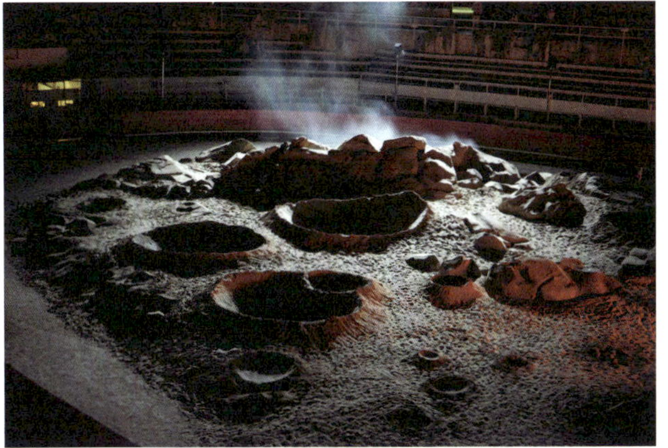

7/8/12—10:48:43 PM

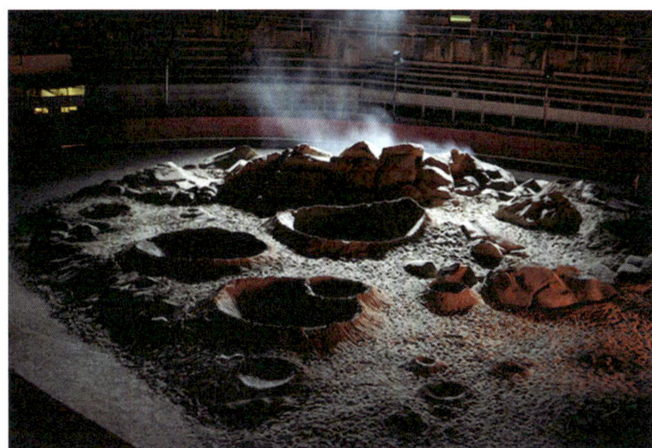

7/8/12—10:48:43 PM

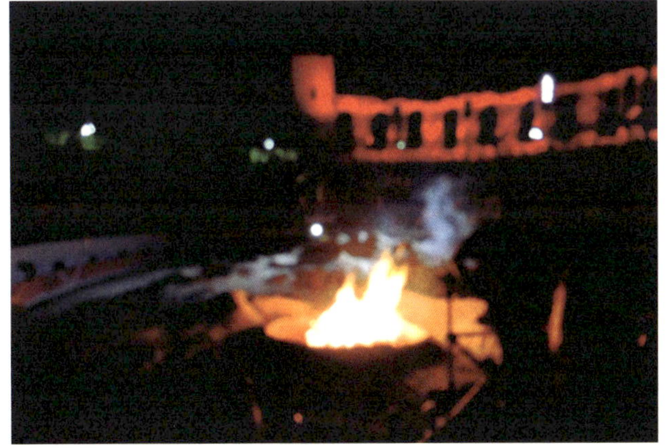

7/8/12—10:49:22 PM

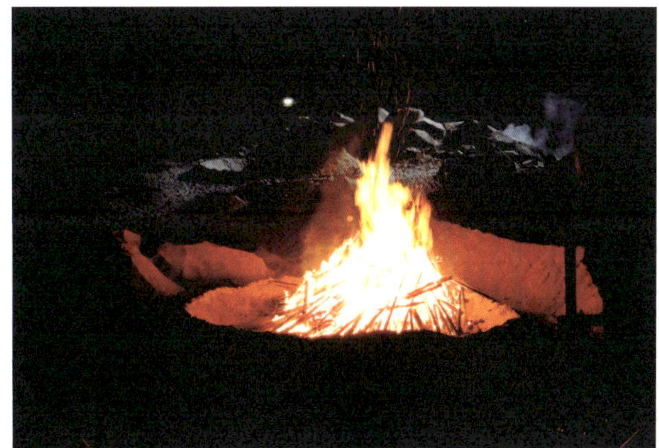

7/8/12—10:49:35 PM

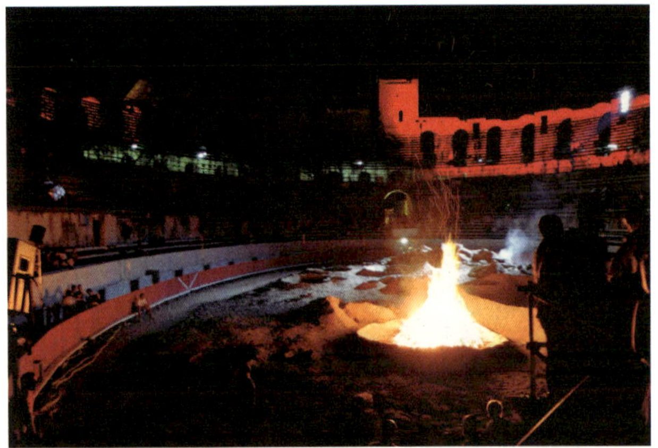
7/8/12—10:49:42 PM

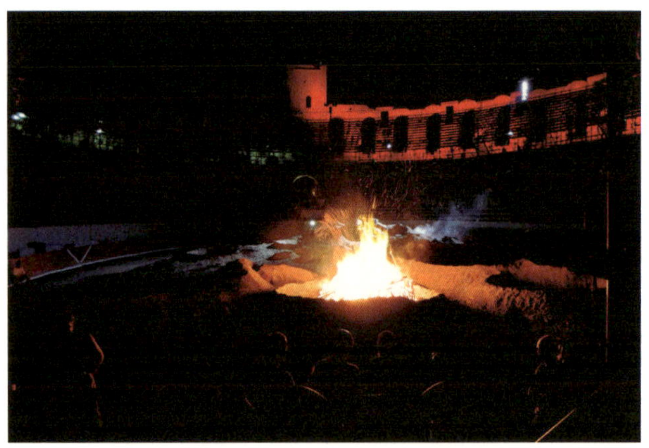
7/8/12—10:50:09 PM

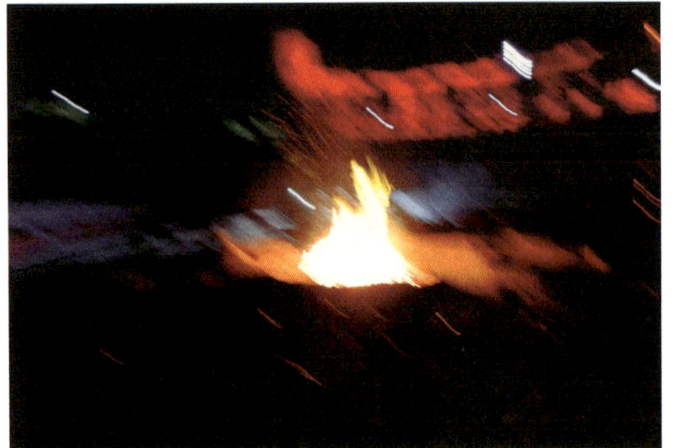
7/8/12—10:50:10 PM

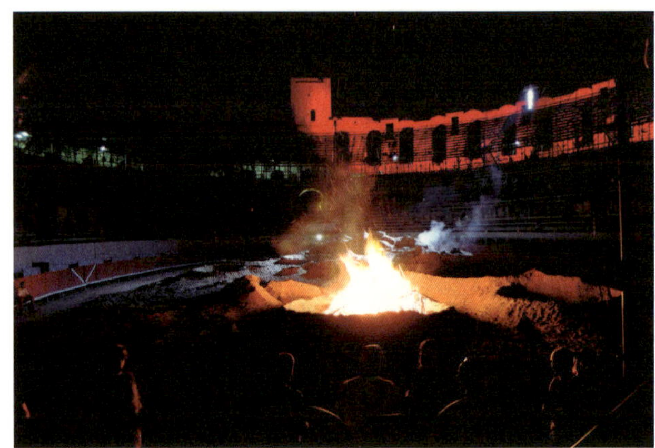
7/8/12—10:50:13 PM

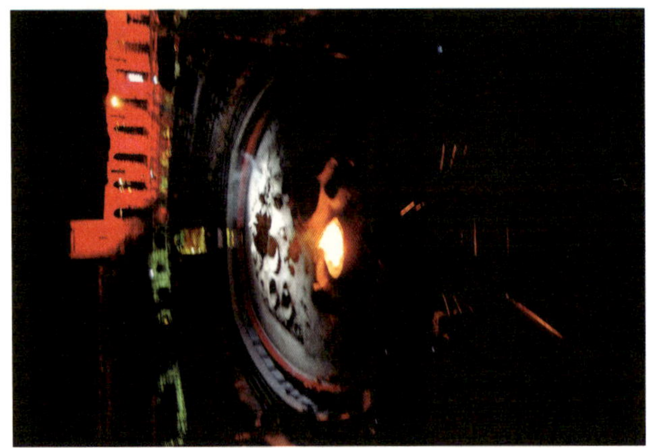
7/8/12—10:53:44 PM

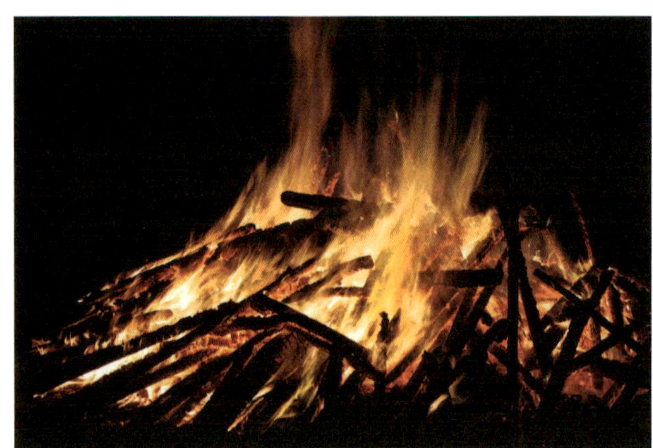
7/8/12—10:53:46 PM

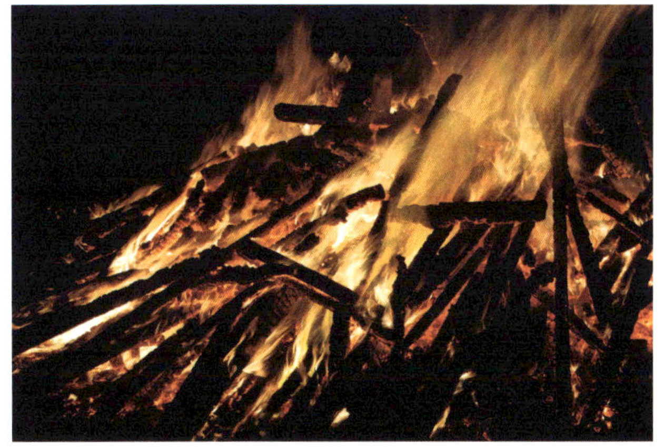

7/8/12—10:54:01 PM

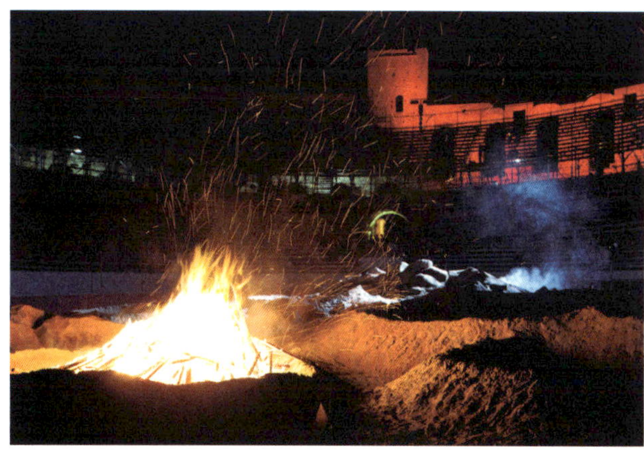

7/8/12—10:54:53 PM

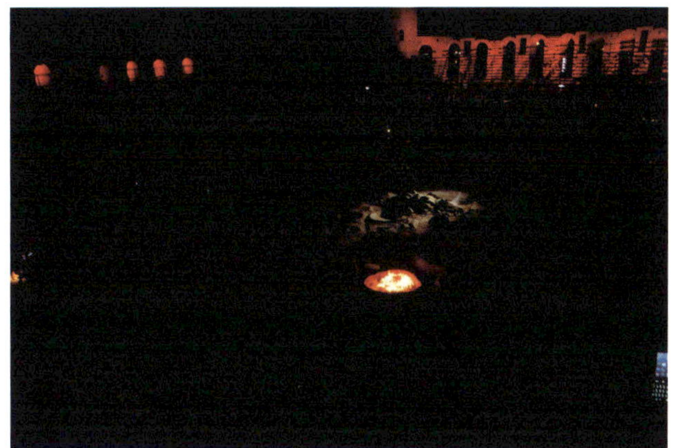

7/8/12—10:55:24 PM

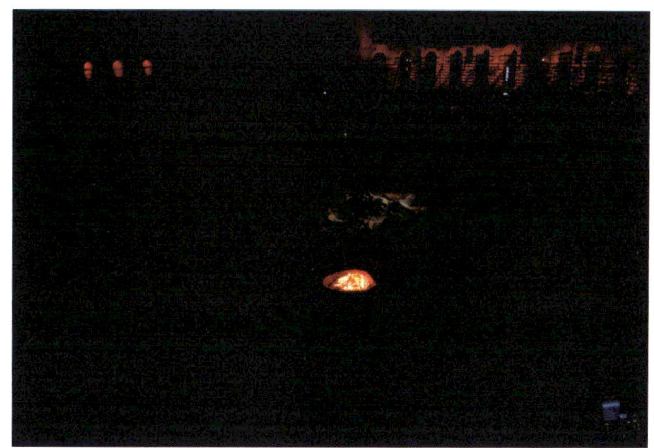

7/8/12—10:55:32 PM

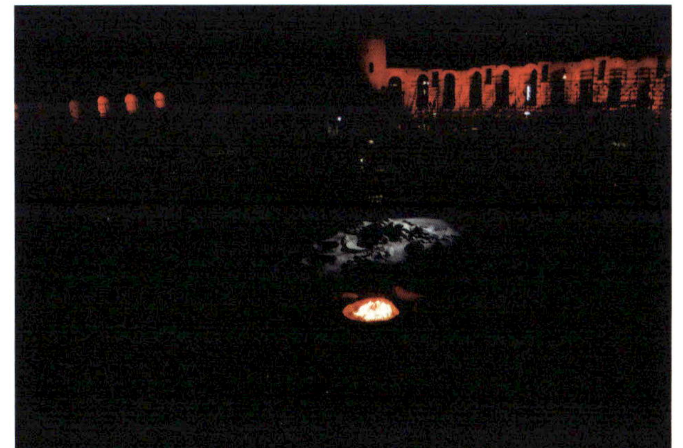

7/8/12—10:55:39 PM

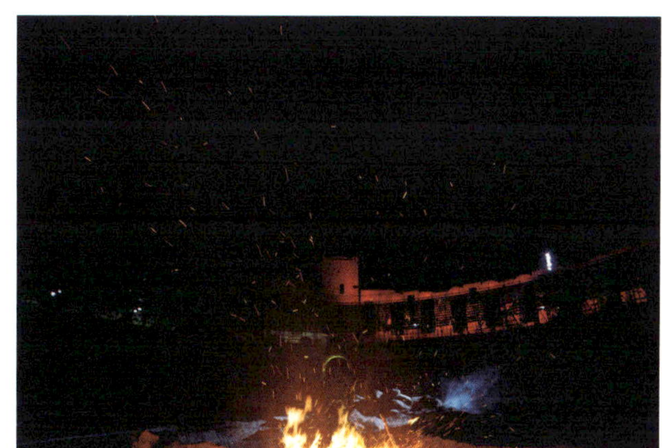

7/8/12—10:55:42 PM

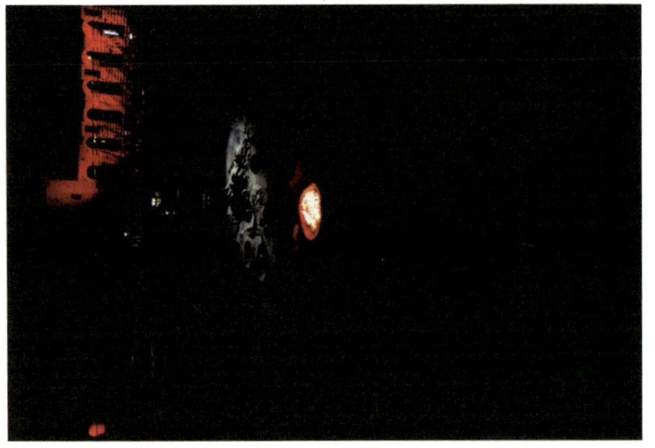
7/8/12—10:55:51 PM

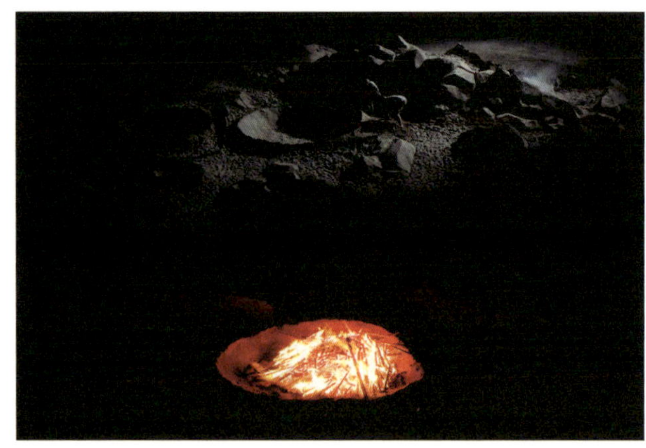
7/8/12—10:55:58 PM

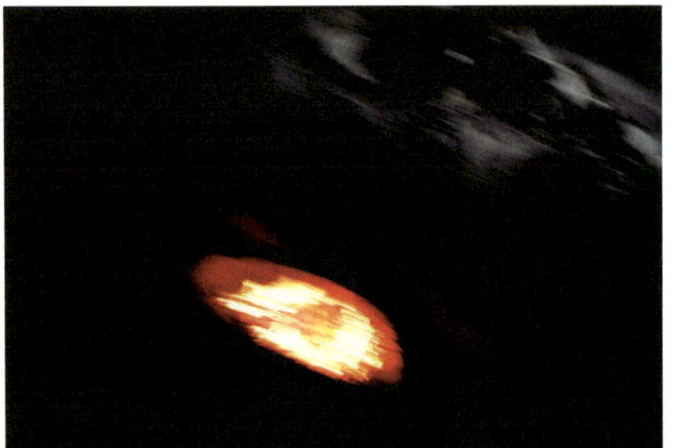
7/8/12—10:56:19 PM

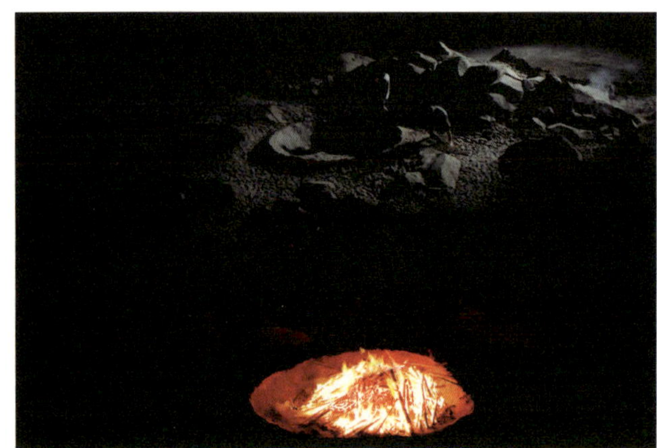
7/8/12—10:56:23 PM

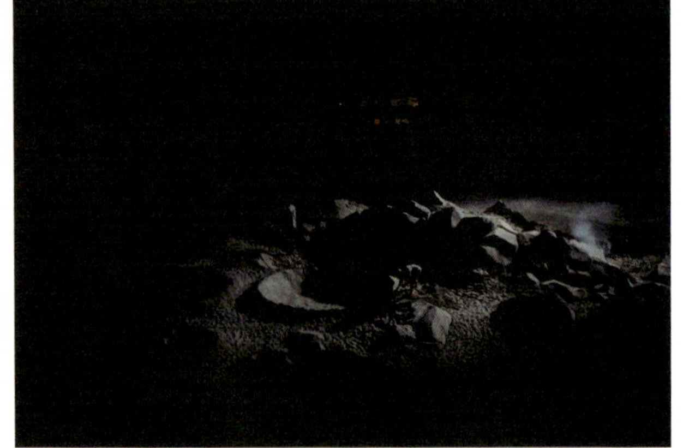
7/8/12—10:56:28 PM

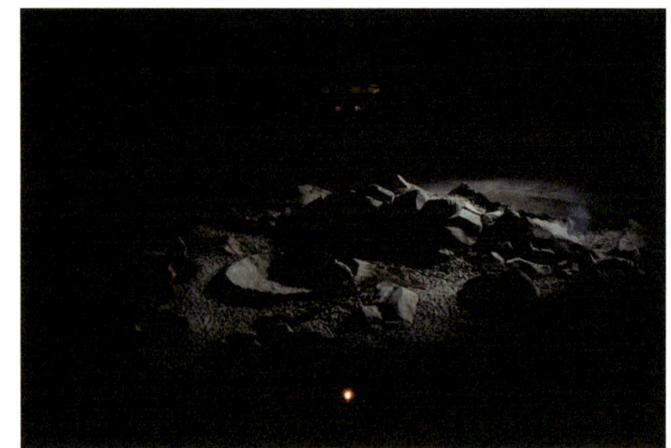
7/8/12—10:56:40 PM

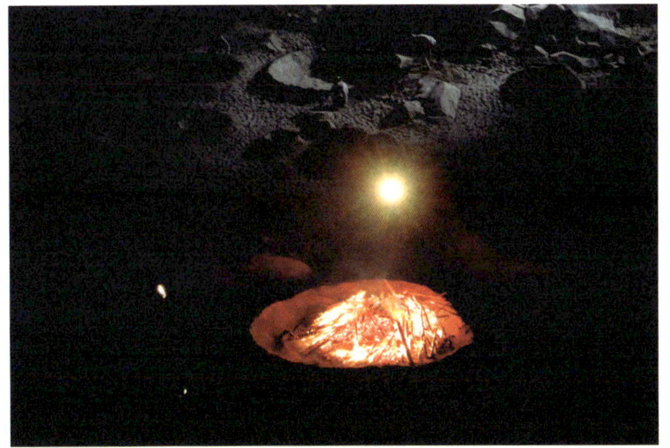

7/8/12—10:56:47 PM

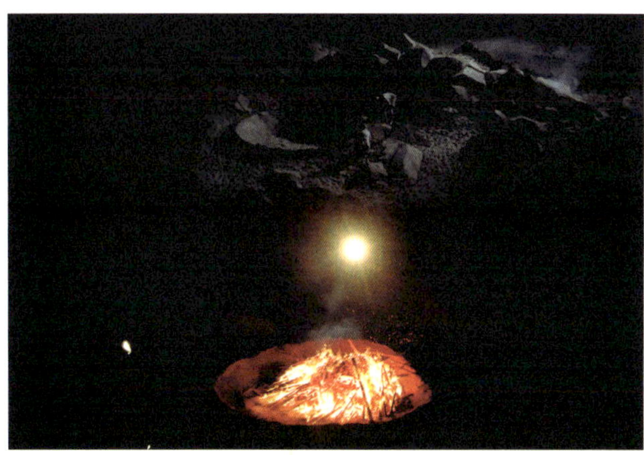

7/8/12—10:56:54 PM

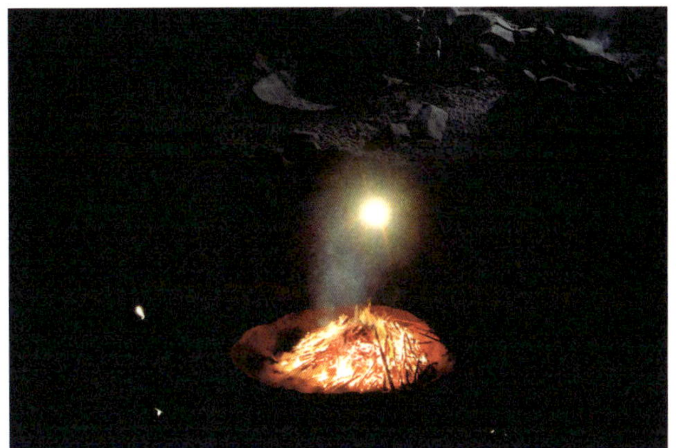

7/8/12—10:57:04 PM

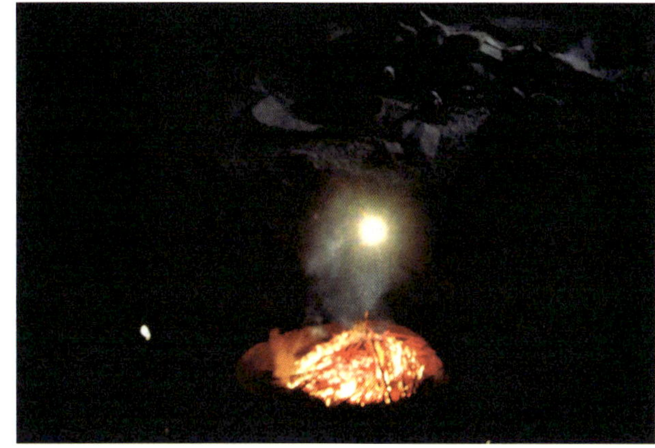

7/8/12—10:57:16 PM

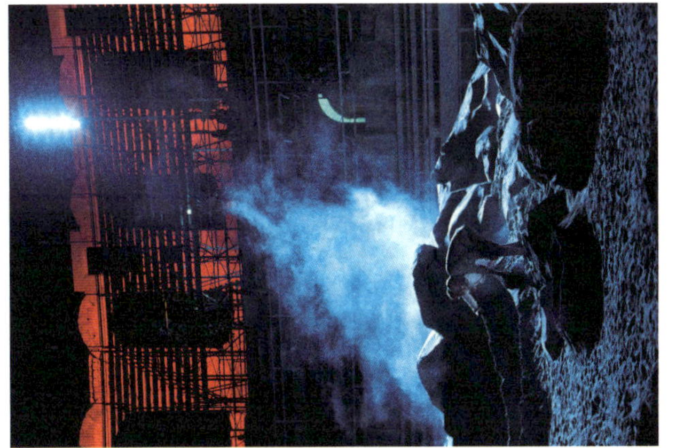

7/8/12—10:57:19 PM

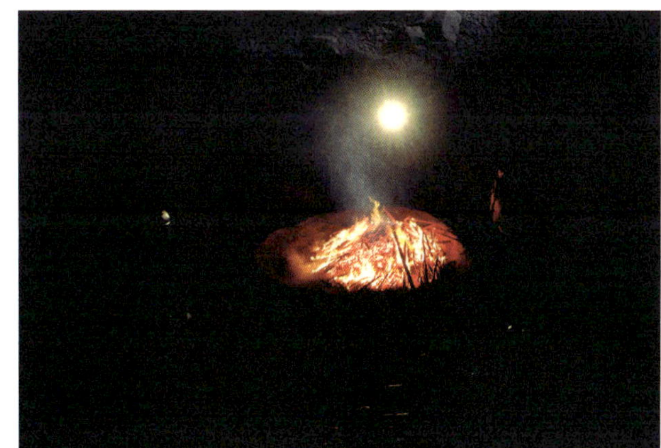

7/8/12—10:57:20 PM

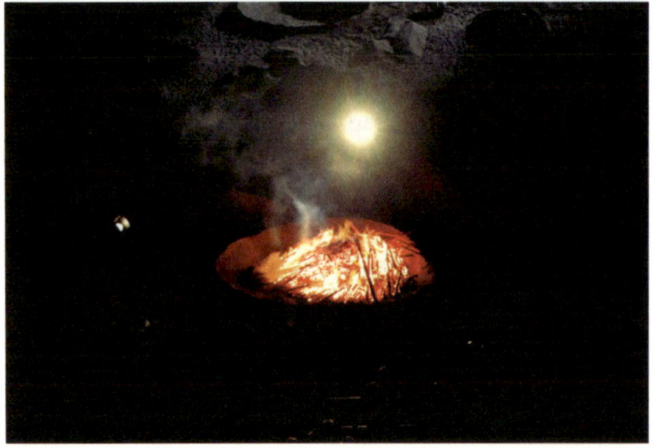

7/8/12—10:57:27 PM

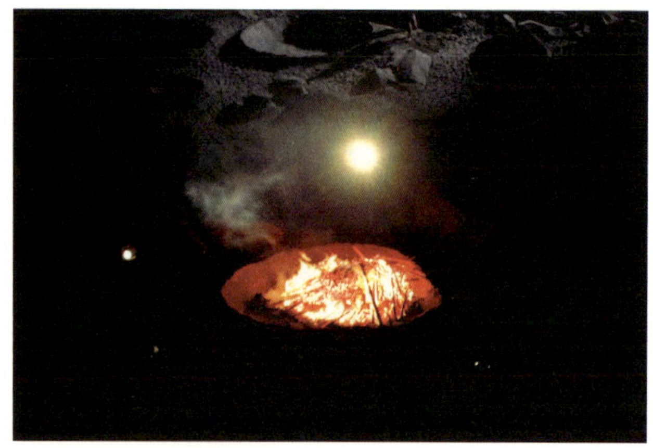

7/8/12—10:57:34 PM

7/8/12—10:57:59 PM

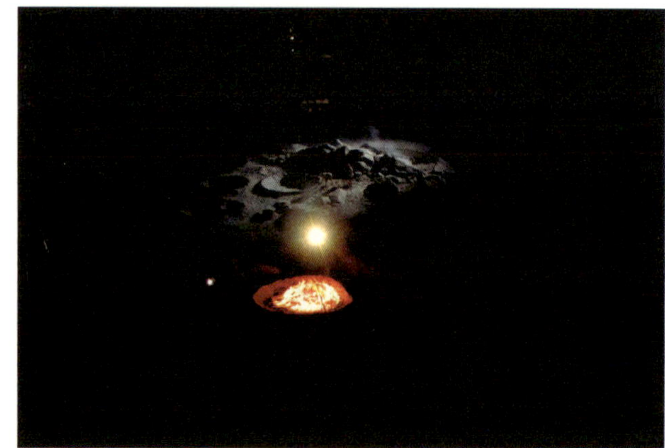

7/8/12—10:58:08 PM

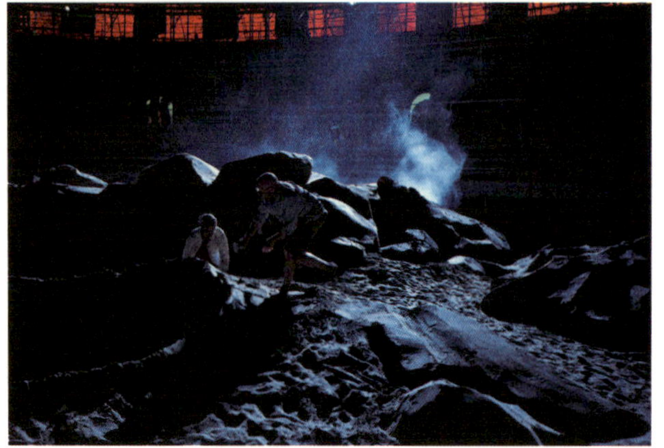

7/8/12—10:58:14 PM

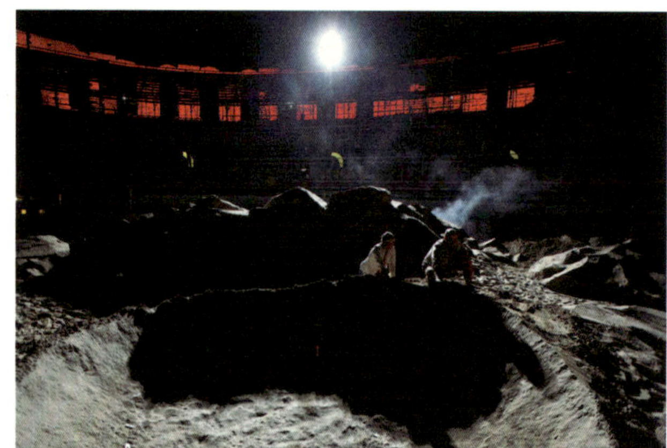

7/8/12—10:58:39 PM

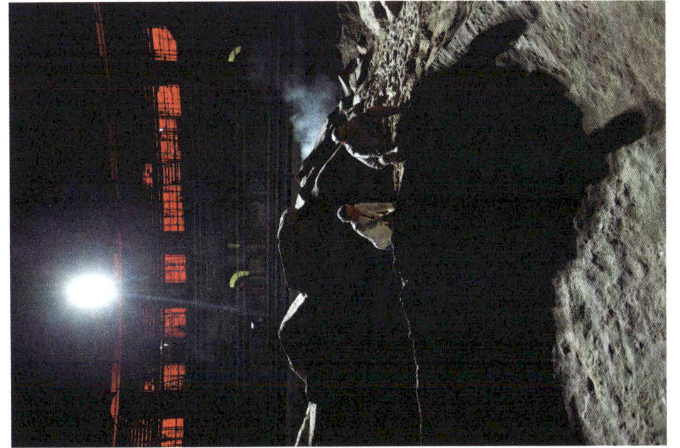

7/8/12—10:58:44 PM

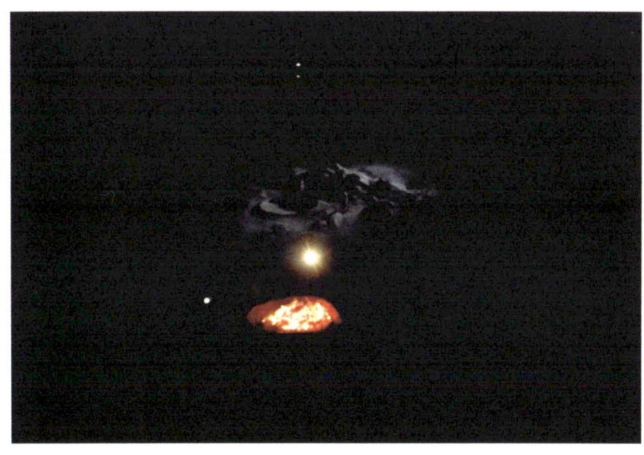

7/8/12—10:59:00 PM

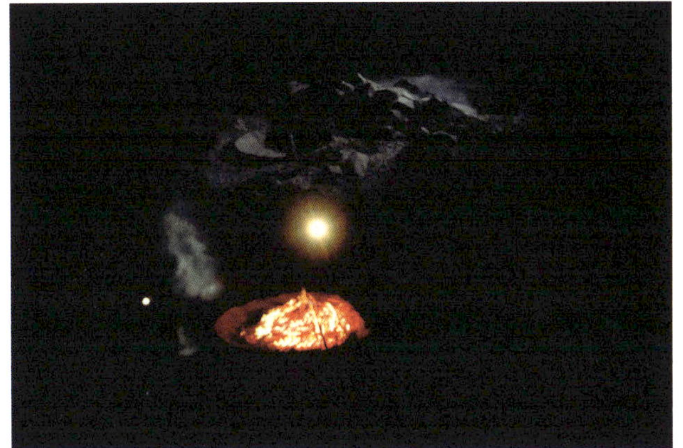

7/8/12—10:59:06 PM

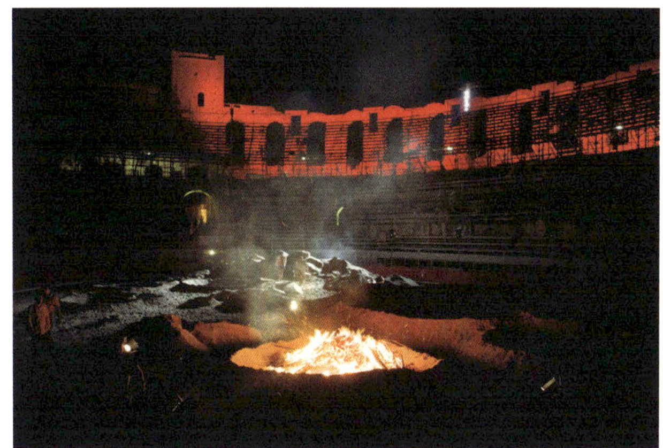

7/8/12—11:00:48 PM

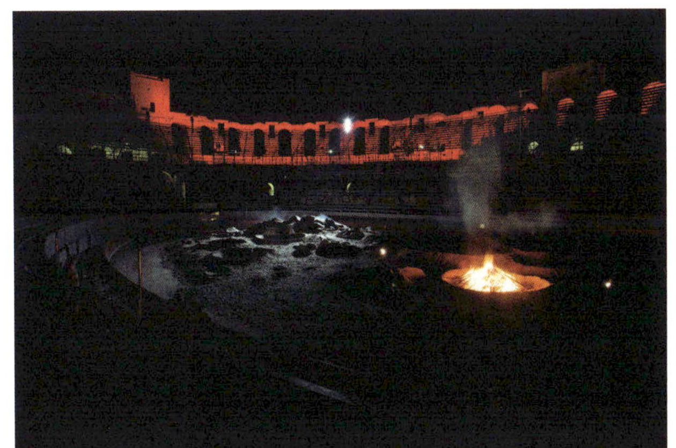

7/8/12—11:01:30 PM

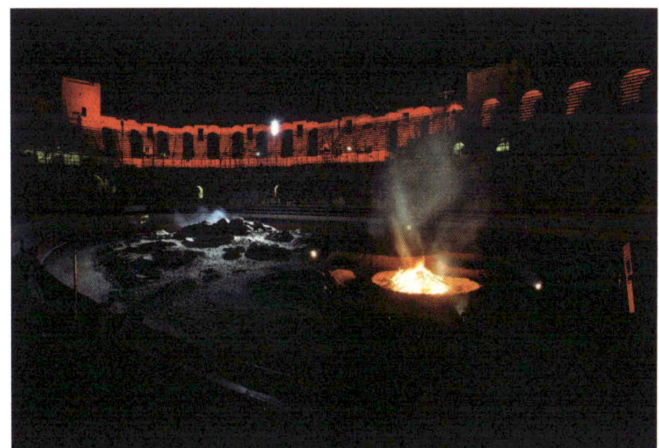

7/8/12—11:02:18 PM

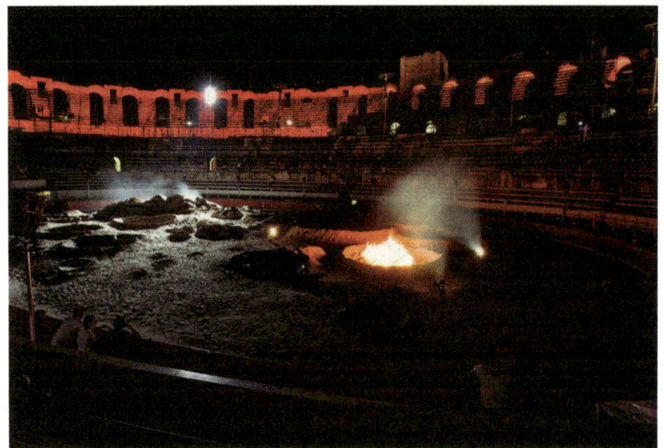
7/8/12—11:02:50 PM

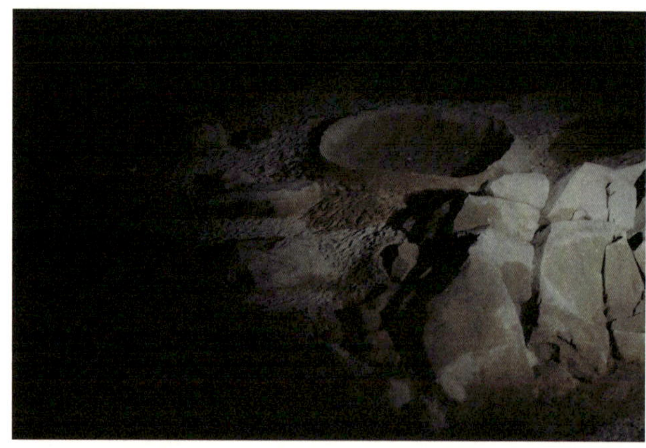
7/8/12—11:03:03 PM

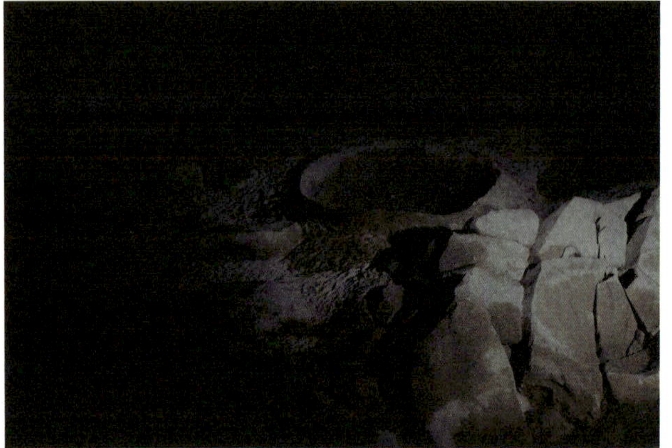
7/8/12—11:03:09 PM

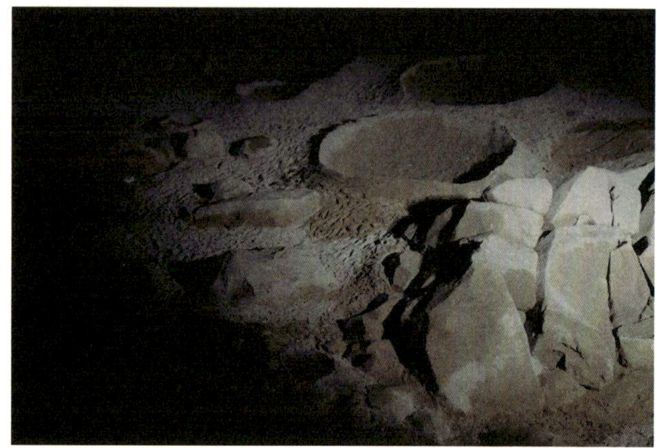
7/8/12—11:03:16 PM

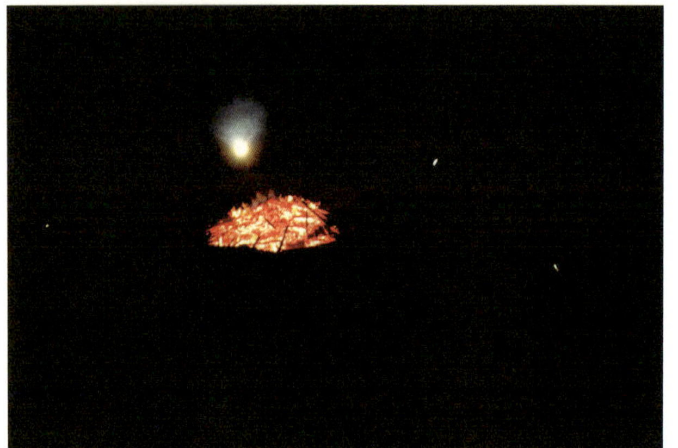
7/8/12—11:03:22 PM

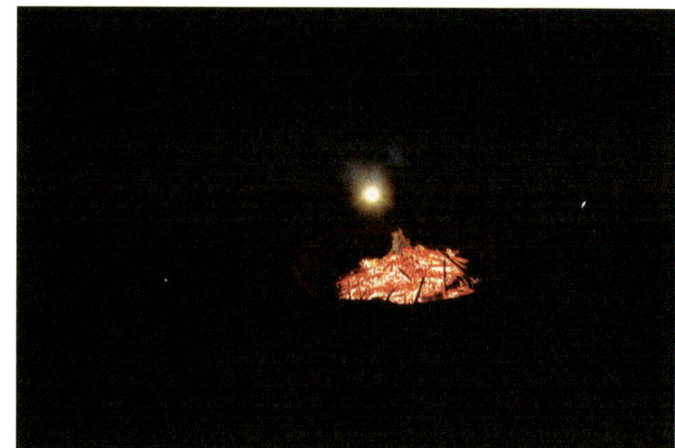
7/8/12—11:03:26 PM

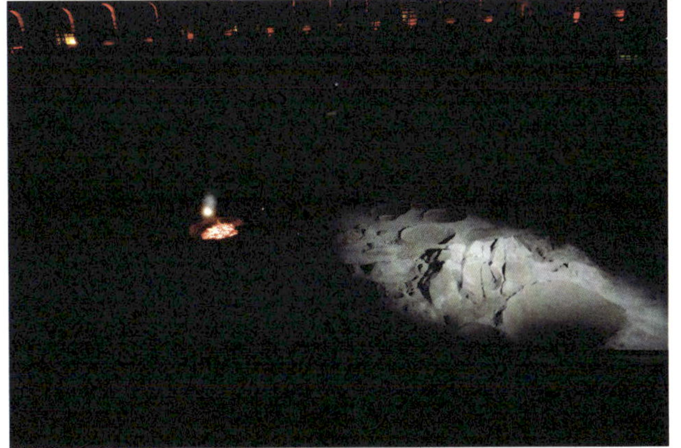

7/8/12—11:03:33 PM

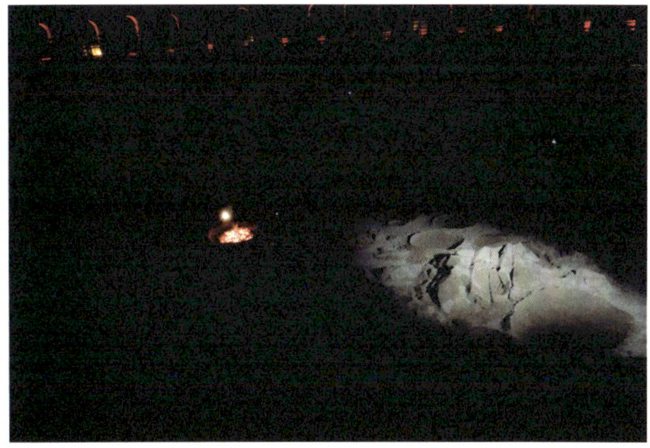

7/8/12—11:03:39 PM

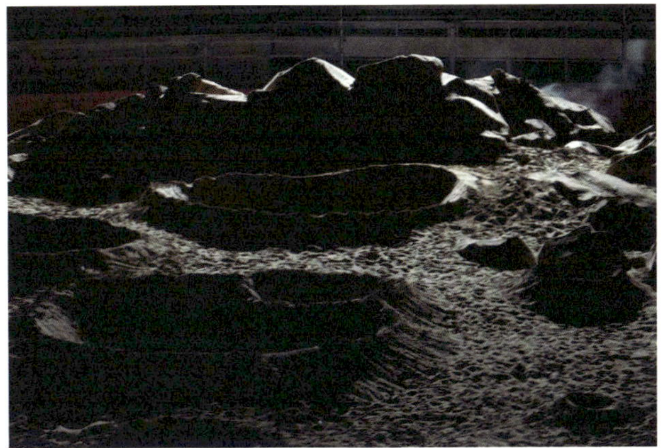

7/8/12—11:03:45 PM

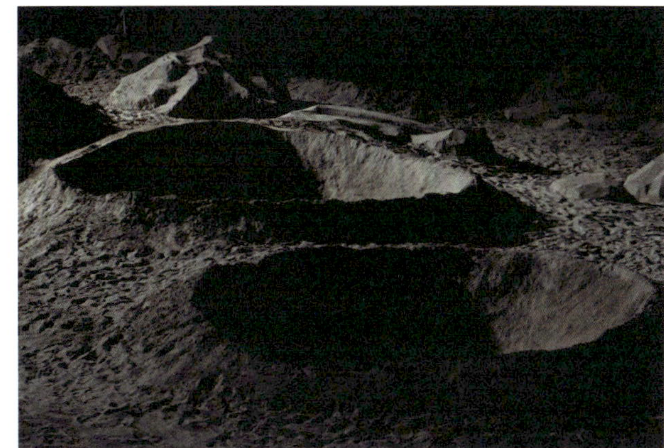

7/8/12—11:04:25 PM

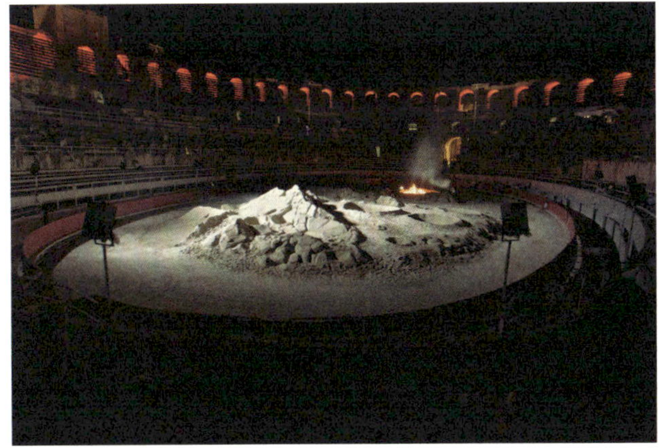

7/8/12—11:05:14 PM

7/8/12—11:05:33 PM

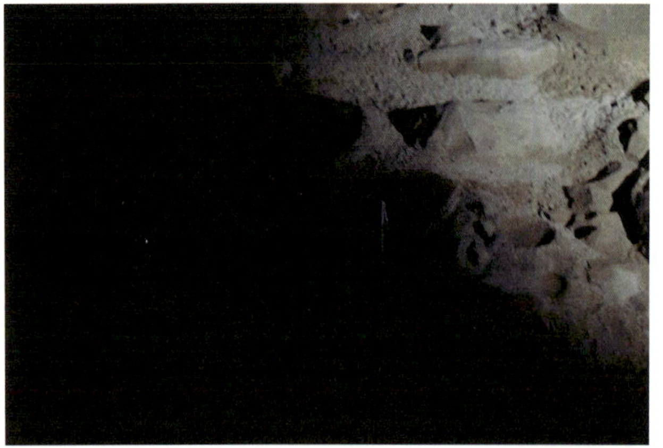

7/8/12—11:05:40 PM

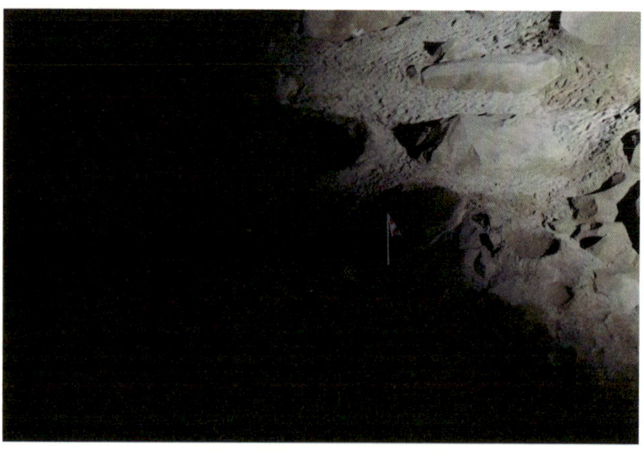

7/8/12—11:05:47 PM

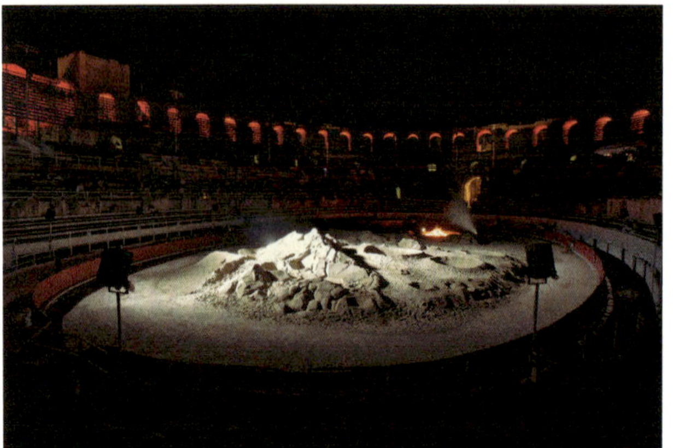

7/8/12—11:06:26 PM

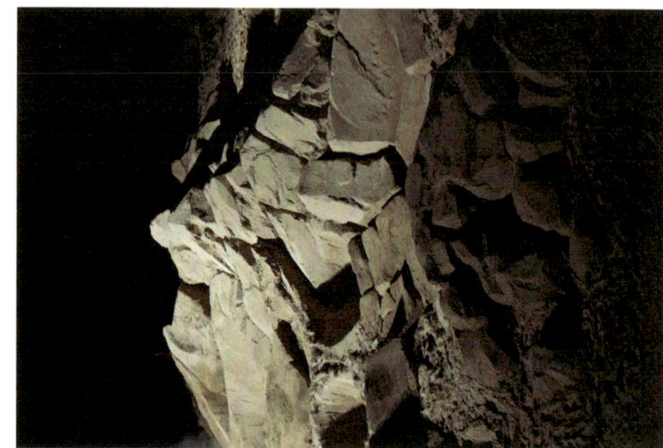

7/8/12—11:06:47 PM

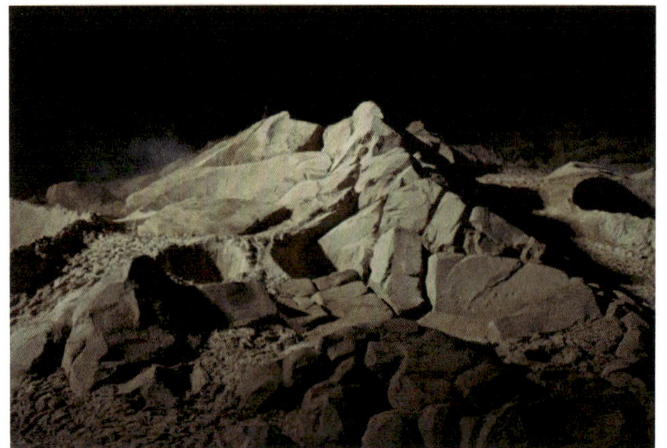

7/8/12—11:06:51 PM

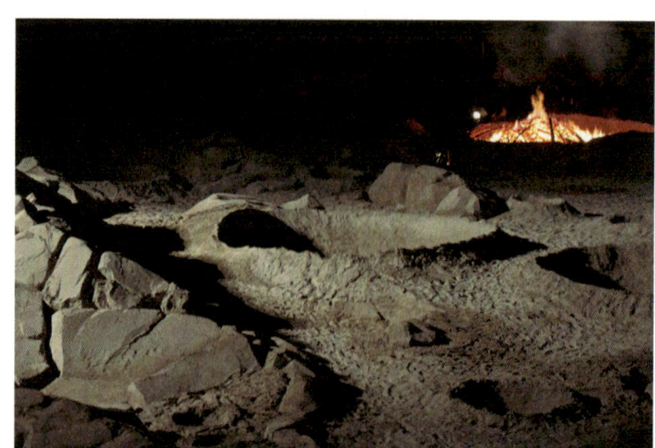

7/8/12—11:06:55 PM

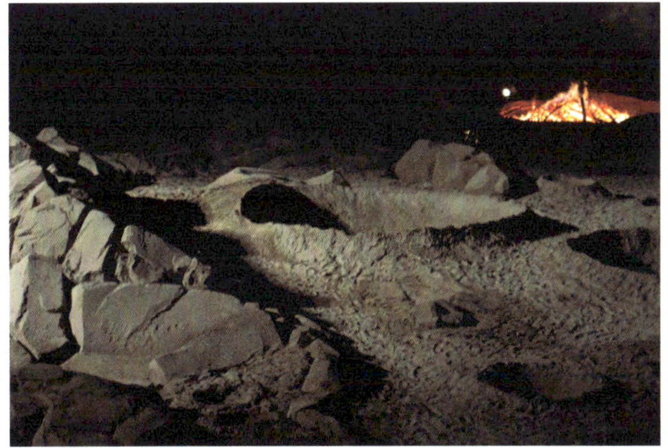

7/8/12—11:07:01 PM

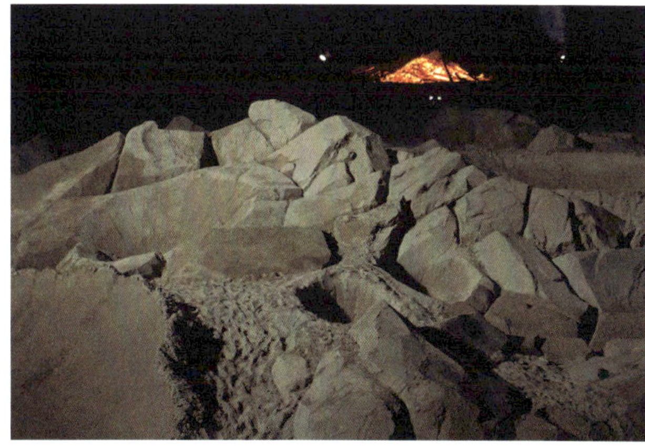

7/8/12—11:12:46 PM

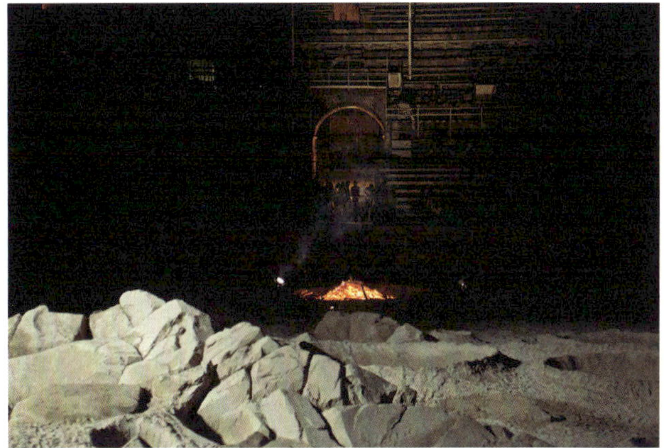

7/8/12—11:16:52 PM

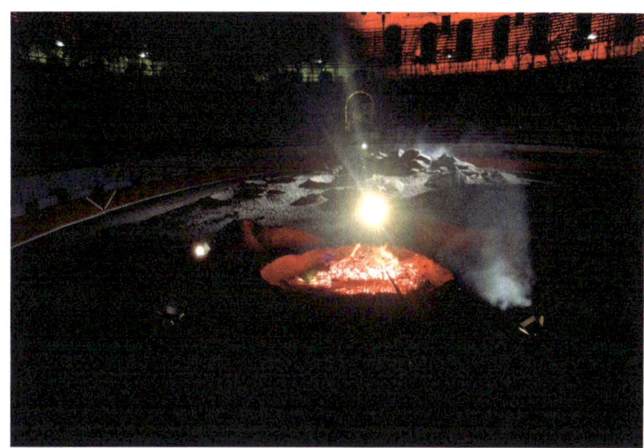

7/8/12—11:17:08 PM

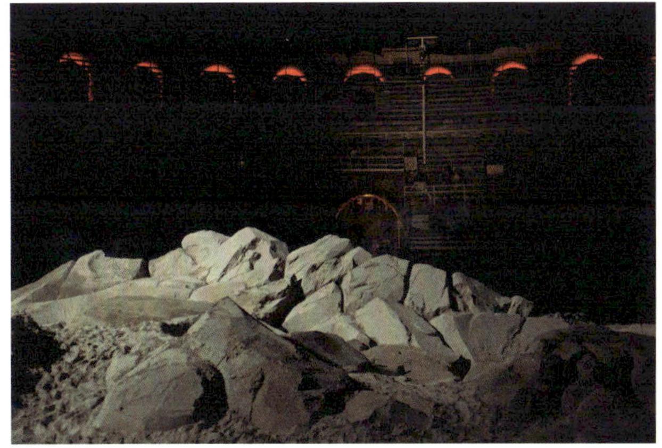

7/8/12—11:21:24 PM

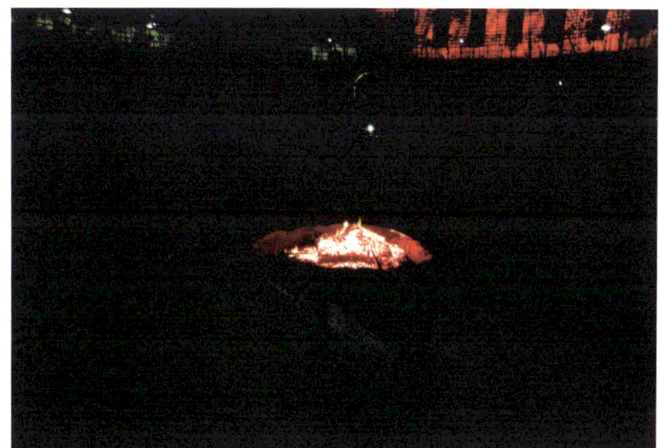

7/8/12—11:21:29 PM

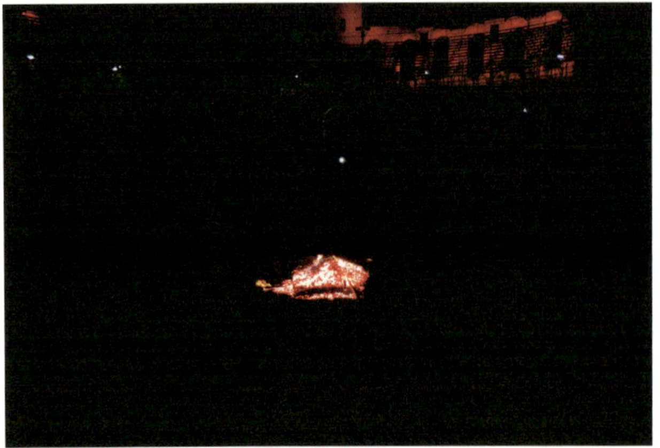
7/8/12—11:21:36 PM

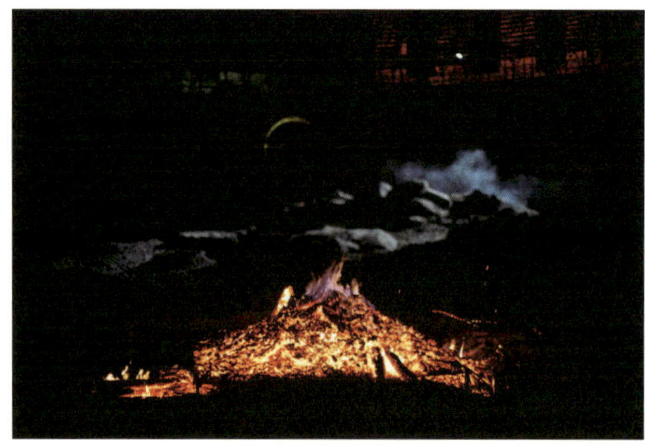
7/8/12—11:23:26 PM

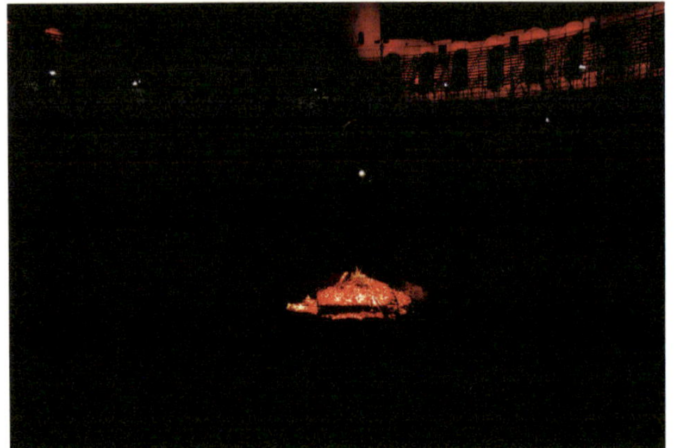
7/8/12—11:23:28 PM

7/8/12—11:23:29 PM

7/8/12—11:23:40 PM

Liam Gillick and Philippe Parreno in Conversation with Hans Ulrich Obrist (Arles, January 2013)

The context for this conversation is the new art center being created by art collector, producer, and patron Maja Hoffmann, and her LUMA Foundation. Hoffmann invited the artists Liam Gillick and Philippe Parreno, and the curators Tom Eccles, Beatrix Ruf, and myself to form a group with her to plan an experimental art center far from any major city, and which will be designed by Frank Gehry. The site chosen is in Arles, in the marshland of France's Camargue, where she grew up. One of Hoffmann's goals is to connect the center to ecology. So, in 2012, we took a step in that direction by creating an exhibition called _To the Moon via the Beach_, which took place in the Roman Amphitheater in Arles, an historical site popular with tourists and often used for bullfighting and festivals. Following an idea by Parreno and Gillick, the Amphitheater was redefined for the duration of the exhibition. At the beginning, visitors encountered an arena covered in tons of sand. This terrain was transformed from a beach to a moonscape by a team of sand sculptors, and also acted as the backdrop for a series of interventions by 20 artists who guided visitors, reacted to the shifting landscape, and produced works in and around the arena. In the end all the sand was moved to Arles' Parc des Ateliers, a former railway engineering yard, where it will be accessible to the public as part of a temporary playground. It will then be once again recycled in the foundations of the forthcoming LUMA center—a new creation, production, and exhibition center, specializing in contemporary art. As the philosopher Michel Serres says, perhaps part of today's fundamental evolution of art could be to open oneself up to living species, to open up to life and to nature.

—Hans Ulrich Obrist

HUO

My first question is to ask you if you remember when you met.

PP

We met in Nice. I was working with Philippe Perrin and Pierre Joseph on an exhibition at the Air de Paris gallery—_Les Ateliers du Paradise_ (1990). We sent out an invitation card in the form of a credit card (called the "carte des figurants"). Liam received it because he was writing for _Artscribe_ at the time. He came to Nice intrigued by this card.

LG

I had the naïveté to believe that a magazine like _Artscribe_ that said "international" on the cover would send people to places. But they weren't in a position to do that financially. So I went with a girlfriend by car from London.

HUO

Did you know about each other at the time?

LG

I knew about him. I don't think he knew about me. Everyone thinks _Les Ateliers du Paradise_ was—and in a way it _was_—the original model of a new type of exhibition that later became a paradigm, but it also included _art_. People think it was just a place of activities and conviviality, but it was as much about the art as anything else.

PP

It was an attempt to experiment with a different model of being in a gallery, trying to produce ideas or just playing video games; it was all about spending time rather than just displaying objects.

LG

Do you remember the sign (_Twin Peaks_, 1991) outside the _No Man's Time_ exhibition (Villa Arson, Nice, 1991)? Philippe did things like that, which were a manifestation of what I was thinking. There had been an earlier moment in France. I was already aware of people like Ange Leccia, IFP (Information Fiction Publicité), and Philippe Thomas, but here was a new feeling … already at art school I felt that there _had_ to be a French art that was as interesting or even _more_ interesting than the theoretical writing of people like Lyotard. It's hard to remember how radical this was and how, for the next few years, people's reaction when I mentioned a French scene would be almost splenetic. There was a refusal to accept it. What I was really fascinated by with Philippe was this relation to cinema, the accommodation of cinema as a structural idea, but without making films at that point. It was a complete revelation to me and it changed everything. It confirmed some of my desires and ideas too.

PP

At the time you were living in London and discussing such ideas with Jack Wendler.

LG

Yes, but for people like Jack something had already happened in the 1980s that had made them think, "We can't deal with this stuff anymore." He was melancholic, and felt the difficulty, the failure of art in the 1980s. What I saw in France was that you don't deal with the failed forms by trying to reproduce them. You actually find new structures.

HUO

This conversation takes place within the context of To the Moon via the Beach, an experimental exhibition and an exhibition as an experiment (Arles Amphitheater, July 2012). You started to do these experiments directly, as a form of collaboration, as in The Trial of Pol Pot at the Magasin in Grenoble (1998).

PP

The first project of this kind was at Le Consortium in Dijon. It all started with Snow Dancing (1995), a project I did there with Xavier Douroux. At the time Xavier was not really keen to work with our generation. He had certain reservations. He sent me a long letter after Snow Dancing saying that he had been wrong to mistrust what we were trying to do, that he was willing to engage with us. He said: "You should take over the space and produce something." At that time I was spending a lot of time with Liam in London, in his apartment in Rotherhithe, and we decided to work on these ideas together.

LG

We had both been in No Man's Time at the Villa Arson in 1991. I had started exhibiting in France and showing with Air de Paris. Snow Dancing first found its form as a book that Philippe proposed that Jack and I publish (G-W Press Ltd., London 1994). I wrote down Philippe's ideas—I was the secretary and Jack asked questions.

PP

At the time Liam was also working with Henry Bond and I was working with Pierre Joseph. It was a kind of "studio practice" in a way. It was quite natural to share ideas, to formulate exhibition ideas.

LG

It was very clear to me that curating was in a dynamic phase, and not art. The idea to work as a group, in itself, was not particularly radical. The idea to work at all was not a question. But it was fascinating to me that Esther Schipper, Dominique Gonzalez-Foerster, Florence Bonnefous, and Edouard Mérino had followed this same curatorial course in Grenoble.

PP

There were also Collins & Milazzo in New York.

HUO

But they were very postmodern.

LG

But not uninteresting. In my head I might also be combining certain artworks, like a photograph by Walker Evans next to an Allan McCollum jar. This seemed all right, but it wasn't quite enough. I was more interested in earlier things such as Six Years (1973), the Lucy Lippard book, and the documenta 5 catalogue (1972).

HUO

And Brian O'Doherty's Inside the White Cube (1981)?

LG

Not so much. Too pure and too much about the spaces of art. What interested me had to do with questions of work, life, and labor—and the division between these things.

HUO

How did this germinate or crystallize in the first instance?

PP

It came really from Liam, because he was working, together with Henry Bond, as a journalist, going to a UN press conference or something, so when he was talking about art it was approached in the same way as any major political event. In many ways, Moral Maze, the project we realized at the Consortium in Dijon in 1995, was a direct extension of Liam's practice and his engagement with Henry. There was an English radio program, popular at the time, called Moral Maze. It always started with the same line— "We are not here to judge you, but to get information from you."

LG

Basically the radio program would address a certain topic, moral or ethical, and, like an investigation, interrogate people who would be asked really tough questions about the subject by a small panel of experts. It had a lot of problems because it took such a typically British form, but there was something within that structure that seemed interesting.

PP

The rules that we came up with for the exhibition were inspired by that. We said to the artists, "You will to come to an exhibition space in Dijon, and while we are thinking about doing a group show we are going to invite a series of specialists." It became a bit like Les Ateliers du Paradise, where different kinds of people met and talked to us in a semi-closed context. It was not a public event.

HUO

It was not a conference?

PP

No, it was only addressed to the artists who were present.

LG

It had a lot to do with Philippe's sense of constantly questioning the exhibition as a form, or as a gesture, and asking where the significance of what you present is ... It was a radical exhibition in its own right. It was closed, but open at the same time, which was indicated by having white paint swirled onto the glass doors, suggesting that the space was in a process of renovation, half-open, half-closed. There was no advertising. No opening.

HUO

Just like To the Moon via the Beach!

LG

It was the occupation of space for a period of time.

PP

Every day different people would come, a lot of them from England. I remember Dunne & Raby for instance.

LG

They said mobile phones would become the paradigm in developing countries, because there is not enough copper in the world to make phone lines in Africa. They were right. They said people would be exchanging money through phones. They were absolutely correct. They said there would be clouds of information—they meant a real cloud, that you could basically sit somewhere and you would be within this electronic cloud. You could receive and send information. There was also someone who was working on educational economics in developing countries, there was a political strategist who was an adviser to Tony Blair's main strategist, etc.

PP

The rule was that every day somebody would come to Dijon and Liam hosted them—taking them for a good lunch. They would then come to the exhibition space and prepare a short presentation, addressed to seven slightly neurotic artists. Some of us would sit and listen, while some, like Maurizio Cattelan, would be bored and walk around. The show opened when all these people left. There were no clear boundaries between the moment of producing art and exhibiting it.

LG

Anxieties such as "Who it is for? How it will be understood? Where is the rhetoric or where is the evidence?" were put in constant tension. It was the same in The Trial of Pol Pot.

PP

I remember that at the time we were talking about Serge Daney not being translated into English, and that there were some cinema critics whose texts were as important as the films that they were describing. At the time, in the early 1990s, that was quite crucial, this blurriness between the analysis and the event itself.

HUO

How did The Trial of Pol Pot came into existence?

LG

To a certain extent it started with Yves Aupetitallot (director of Le Magasin, Grenoble). He brought up the issue of how budgets affect exhibitions; we told him, "You could do an exhibition called The Trial of Pol Pot and in fact not enough money to do it will make it even better." In the summer before we did the project I had been listening to reports that Pol Pot was still alive in the Cambodian jungle near the Thai border. It seemed interesting that these BBC reporters were incapable of understanding who this person was: they were incapable of describing one of the major architects of genocide in the 20th century. We wanted to use this idea, not in a didactic way, but to examine the question of character, to create a search for a character. In a way we were trying to picture a character that couldn't be described and remained elusive. How can you try someone who cannot be described and cannot be seen? It is also somewhat metaphorical.

HUO

What were the rules of the game?

PP

I think we were physically doing all the art. We had a list of people who were ...

LG

... advisers.

PP

We were "controlled" by these people. They were like super-curators, an overwhelming presence during the process.

LG

Some, like Lawrence Weiner, said, "Keep going" and others, like Merlin Carpenter, wrote us long polemical texts about how everything we were trying to do was a posture. Others were just confused.

PP

Liam made some of his first wall texts there. He was working on his computer and said, "I can print out the text sequences from my computer"; it wasn't expensive at all. I began to play with lights and Liam put stickers on walls. It quickly became a designed exhibition where we dealt with complexity by not trying to clarify everything.

LG

I made a poster which had all the comments from the advisors overlapped on top of each other, so you just had this mass of writing.

HUO

Like a palimpsest?

LG

Yes. If you came to the exhibition you could either take one and leave, or pay and come in.

PP

We didn't involve the other artists in the process of making the show—nobody made a "work." We were basically the ones designing the exhibition. In addition to the wall texts there was a big banner in the middle of the space called "La Rue," an open space within the industrial complex. The banner was printed with a moon seen through abstract trees. Then inside there was a broken script, and moving colored lights. It became like a set for an unlikely 1970s TV show.

LG

Then we had—as with To the Moon via the Beach—this apparent crisis of mediation, which of course for me isn't a crisis, but the attempt to find a better way of doing it. Originally I wanted Robert De Niro to come every week to explain the exhibition; I had a contact to reach him, but it eventually fell through. So every Wednesday we did a puppet show for school children that explained why Robert De Niro hadn't come. [Laughter]

HUO

It's interesting to talk about these shows because it's quite difficult to find any information about them.

LG

Yes, the exhibitions made people nervous, they didn't think it was worth putting resources into cataloguing them at the time. They couldn't imagine what to do with these exhibitions—and maybe neither could we.

PP

We knew already that everything—even the title—would be misunderstood. The project was all about that anyway, about misunderstanding and trying to find a position, defining your point of view toward an event. So we were stuck into a set of complex structures.

LG

And the fact that a character evades representation.

PP

Pol Pot was a proto-character, like Annlee.

LG

What connects all these exhibitions is an ambiguous relation to the notions of audience and public. The exhibitions relied on the intelligence and intentionality of any public who would come to such a place, and they played with institutional codes. They had nothing to do with new models of participation. These were absolutely non-participatory exhibitions in fact.

PP

The same is true of No Man's Time, where we basically took over the curatorial agenda—and it is something that Liam did repeatedly in group show situations. He would sit down with the curator, talk about some ideas, and start to write a press release himself. So it was kind of taking the creative director of an institution hostage, dealing with everything ourselves in a way, communication included. Definitely—as in To the Moon via the Beach—the question of the public was very present from the beginning.

HUO

It's also interesting that the notion of time already appears in these early shows. There was a moment when Diaghilev, then a curator of paintings in Russia, said, "I want to curate time": he founded the Ballets Russes and started curating time instead of space.

LG

Yes, but Philippe always had a much more sophisticated understanding of how to play with time in an institution than I did; I'm more of a materialist in a way, which includes writing, because that's also a material fact—you're materializing an idea or a set of projections. It was Philippe who made all the innovations about how to play with time in exhibitions. It has become more and more dominant in his work.

HUO

So, in terms of your collaboration, you think there is a dimension that you were less involved in …

LG

I just think I hadn't thought about it as much as he had. When he was starting to use this dimension it was an incredibly radical thing to do, because most manipulations of time in art were related to performance or happenings. Somehow Philippe played with these codes and temporal games. Suddenly it was not about cinema, but about the creation of a mise-en-scène.

PP

It's about the negotiation of the presence or the appearance of an art object. When you believe that a display in a space can produce knowledge or awareness, then you deal with reading, in a non-authoritarian kind of way, or a non-spectacular way.

HUO

What happened after The Trial of Pol Pot?

PP

There was What if, which Liam co-curated with Maria Lind in Stockholm (Moderna Museet, 2000).

LG

That wasn't a work we did together, but it had some of the qualities we're talking about.

HUO

You didn't want to be called co-curator: you called yourself the "filter."

LG

I didn't want to take responsibility for the artists that Maria selected, because as a good, worthy, new-generation curator, she put artists in that she felt helped tell the story she wanted to tell. I wouldn't have chosen the same people. So I wasn't interested in that side of it. I was interested in the designation of space and how you were supposed to read the exhibition. Most exhibitions are organized traditionally: people are allocated space because the work demands it or things are more or less democratic. I decided to make a plan that was radically neither of these things. So, for example, to Dominique Gonzalez-Foerster, who just needed a small space for a video monitor and a neon work, I gave one fifth of the entire exhibition. It's not what the work itself demands, it's not necessary, but it seemed interesting. So you had these clear areas, then all the films and videos behind grey curtains—you had to find your way through these different rooms.

HUO

What about Bryannnnnn and Ferryyyyyy at the Konstall Lund (2004)?

PP

Bryannnnnn and Ferryyyyyy was a film we did in response to a symposium.

LG

The conference was about law and creativity, and the work was about the idea of art changing the rules of the game, in ten episodes. It was here that I started to see the arrival of a different type of curator, who had heard about projects like Pol Pot, but hadn't seen them, and assumed they had a quality that they did not—as if Pol Pot had presented information about Cambodia, for instance. It's a misunderstanding of Philippe's and my politics probably, and they assumed that we could create some kind of exhibition about this topic of law and creation. We thought we'd make a cartoon series that I wrote and he started to work on visually; then we got a third person involved to do a lot of the technical work.

PP

It's one of the things that was done without discussion really, because it happened really fast.

HUO

But you must have had a discussion about the work.

PP

Not really. It was easy, we had been invited to do something like what we had done together in the past. So we made a cartoon just to show them we were not the artists they thought we were! The basic cartoon, a chase—a cat running after a mouse—took 10 seconds. I sent drawings to Liam and he said, "I'll get somebody to animate them," and that was it.

LG

I always liked the film Philippe made, Ou (Or, 1996), which was mainly credits. I thought it was one of the best films ever made when I saw it, which is ridiculous in a way. There were loads of spelling mistakes, but I thought structurally it was really amazing. For the cartoon series, the credits of each episode were longer than the action. We used the idea of advisors again, but it now reflected a change in the context, so some of those advisors were people who were writers and curators. The question this time was what should we think about, what should we include, what shouldn't we miss out of this process? Those things became part of the credits.

HUO

How did the characters start to develop?

LG

It was a cat and mouse thing. Philippe said something like, "The mouse dies in the first few minutes," and then we did the rest of the series without the classic cat and mouse games. So of course the whole story about conflict and retribution and the infinite resurrection of a character that you find in cartoons doesn't happen. Basically the cat is quite lonely and does things like looking at the Internet, watching New Order videos, thinking about boxing, etc. I decided to write the final draft of the script when I was drunk, so it has a quality of nothing else I've done before. It's melancholic, aggressive.

PP

But that again was quite different from the Moral Maze, don't you think? We haven't really collaborated again until this show in Arles: the sequel to Moral Maze is To the Moon via the Beach.

HUO

In-between there was also Il Tempo del Postino (2007) we co-curated and which somehow …

PP

… which is slightly different.

HUO

But it kind of connects: Il Tempo del Postino was about a prescriptive rule, every artist got 15 minutes, but there is a link, there is an arena of some sort.

LG

I've always felt that for Philippe this project was a way to try to come to terms with theater. It's a difficult thing to do, because in an exhibition space you can play with the whole scene, with time, with everything. When you deal with the formal reality of a theater, it's much more complicated.

PP

It was also a show that came after the Zidane project, which was a proper feature film (with Douglas Gordon, 2006). So again it was the idea of trying to do something with people locked in a room, where the lights are off and we invite them to spend some time. Theoretically it was based on a text I wrote in 1992 in Documents sur l'art, so it was a question we had discussed together for years …

LG

I was just a participant and I when I arrived I thought, "This is going to be fun in some way," meaning discursive, convivial … and all these things that were never necessarily at the center of the exhibitions, but were part of doing them. But I found myself plunged into preparations for a theatrical presentation, which was really stressful. It also introduced new characters, new people arrived who weren't involved before, like Anri Sala, people who became pivotal to the project.

HUO

There was a different generation involved.

LG

Philippe is very generous to other artists, in a way that can make me a little bit … nervous. It made me nervous.

PP

Well it was extreme for me too; I knew that I had to challenge something, but it completely killed me. It went into a paroxysm: how much can one give in order to articulate designs for things to come? It was a kind of extreme experience for me.

LG

It felt like that.

HUO

There was also a big difference: we invited people to Il Tempo del Postino with the idea was that there would be two or three thousand people looking at the stage. Whereas I think shows like Pol Pot or To the Moon via the Beach have more do with what you described when you told me that someone had said about Cities on the Move that they didn't know where to look. When you came into the arena in Arles or at Le Magasin in Grenoble, it wasn't clear where you had to look; that sort of confusion wasn't present in Il Tempo del Postino.

PP

If you put these projects into perspective, you can see that there's something still alive or still operating in To the Moon via the Beach. With Il Tempo del Postino, we used the phrases "the rules of the game" and "the score is the score." There is some kind of automatic principle that we seem to be trying to define, like a machine célibataire. Principles that can be written down in order for something to operate in an automatic way. There is a spirit of automation, which I still find fascinating. For a project like Bryannnnnn and Ferryyyyyy, I think we even addressed how easy it was through the process of making it.

LG

We put into action a set of conditions that started to build something, started to spawn something. "Spawning" for me is the right word because spawning is what frogs and newts do, they spawn and morph …

PP

It's as if you implement something, it starts to work, and then suddenly you start working for it, whatever that is.

HUO

The shows don't have a curatorial master plan.

LG

They're not spontaneous either and they're quite responsible. To the Moon via the Beach had the clearest crediting of any exhibition I've been involved in.

HUO

We have been to Arles together on many occasions. There have been other kinds of projects, such as How Soon Is Now (Arles, 2010). But I remember that you said we should actually make something more spectacular, something not in the context of the festival and not in the context of the art world, but go into what Arles really is, using this famous arena. Do you remember?

PP

I think we had to do something, rather than talk about doing something. It's really impressive when you start to develop ideas about a possible institution. When the work starts to exist, things collapse or have to be redefined, but the prefiguration moment is really exciting, because structures can be invented. While we wait for the architect to come we can work and do things so that a program is already in place. And when the architecture comes to fruition, it will host what has already been engaged. That was an obvious reason to start doing something.

LG

Another way of putting that is to say that when you get people together who are fairly intelligent and reasonably responsible, they can start to self-institutionalize or self-police themselves. That's a problem. I'm very interested in these questions and a lot of my work has been around that recently. We're all very conscious in this group about this problem of self-institutionalizing. To the Moon via the Beach was a way of trying to release that feeling and not institutionalize. Even to the extent where someone might just come to do some sunbathing in the arena and end up watching a guy walk around with bees on his face. It was also important that this person was never given a piece of paper explaining what the artist was doing or that he was Pierre Huyghe, who represented France at the last Venice Biennale, etc.

HUO

You said it's a prefiguration: that's what Johannes Cladders said about Mönchengladbach, where he did the first institutional exhibitions of Joseph Beuys, Daniel Buren, Carl Andre, etc., in a little house in the city's suburbs, while waiting for a museum to be built.

LG

So many exhibitions now are about something; To the Moon was something. It seems to be a fairly simple yet philosophical difference. The same is true of the difference between audience and public. I can create an audience for people watching goats fucking monkeys. I mean it's easy, there's an audience there somewhere that's really into that, but that's not the same as a public. A public is an existing mass of people that is defined by various demographics, differences, and desires, but it's not an audience for anything in particular, it's many audiences that manifest into a public.

PP

When people come to Arles, they have time because they don't have an agenda. They start to hang around and things appear; and the more they look and the more time they spend,the more things appear. So it's really the public that produces what they want to see, in a way. They decide, they edit for themselves what's interesting and what's not. They can decide what's art or what's not art, or what's going to be art and what's not art. It was also interesting for me to see young artists operating in that kind of framework.

LG

Yes, it's the first thing I've done where there are artists in an exhibition who are 20 years older and 20 years younger. It's a little bit melancholic—in a way we're stuck in the middle between these two sets of people. The one thing that characterizes To the Moon via the Beach, The Trial of Pol Pot, and Moral Maze is the attempt to use a rhetorical device, like a title or a set of ideas, in order to make a point, to prove a point. In the case of To the Moon, it was the idea that we can trust artists from different generations, that we can create a backdrop to an activity that is continuous, and that we can make use of this historical monument.

PP

What you have redefined as being the rules of the game. I remember that at some point Liam said we should try to create a formula, a mathematic formula.

LG

Discover a formula—it was about the decision to have a formula in the first place.

HUO

Richard Hamilton said that we only remember exhibitions that have invented a display feature. We remember the Duchamp Surrealist exhibitions, even if they might not have been the best group shows of their time, because of the ropes in New York, the coal bags in Paris. A similar thing is true for many other shows, Yves Klein and Arman, Le Vide and Le Plein. I was wondering if you see the sand in the arena as a display feature in this sense.

PP

Yes, it created context, and more than that it also implied a certain set of actions that might be possible, without being dictatorial. It's also quite relaxing because there's something going on all the time. You don't have to do much or you can even do nothing—and in a way that type of invitation was really clear from the beginning.

LG

But Hans Ulrich has done this in many exhibitions as well, where the structure basically takes the pressure away from the artwork to carry all the significance. Of course, by doing that, it brings new things to the fore.

PP

It allows things to happen. It's like doing chemistry.

LG

I don't want to have a comparative understanding of art that's weighing the mute value of objects against each other—that's pseudo-critical. I want things to be more complicated, and for an exhibition to reflect a more complex understanding of what we ascribe value to and where we are looking and who speaks.

HUO

You came up with the idea to invite sand artists who, according to your instructions, would transform the arena. Then you came up with theses rules for the transformed terrain.

PP

The rules came a day before the doors opened. It wasn't really planned.

HUO

But that doesn't make it less important.

PP

No, that's true. As soon as you start to have principles, they operate. The rules of the game were just corrected a bit sometimes, because people were asking questions that we didn't ask ourselves. So we come up with some ideas to solve some anxieties.

LG

I think that's also true of Il Tempo del Postino. Such a project puts a lot of pressure on the artists, a different kind of pressure than the one in traditional exhibition formats where, basically, the artist is somewhat protected by the architecture. Here, you're only protected in terms of time. You can stop or you can hide, you can withdraw or you can choose a routine. On the other hand, it's harder to have an assertive presence that can protect you. You might notice that some artists we respect, where there's more or less a consensus that they're good for whatever reason, in these situations tend to get louder. Because their response to this problem, as it were, is to get louder. Pierre Huyghe, for example, does something that is going to be memorable and that's a higher volume. It's as if he cranks up the bass or something. You noticed that in Il Tempo del Postino too. Matthew Barney responded by throwing everything at it. It means that the people who have a much clearer vision of how to be visible in the world tend to have an anxiety about how to retain their autonomy and save it in a situation such as To the Moon via the Beach. Dominique Gonzalez-Foerster did this too. Then other people tend toward disappearance or dissipation. Lawrence Weiner's work was incredibly subtle; it was literally dispersed. It was detritus. The exhibitions are not process-driven …

PP

… but they reveal attitudes.

LG

And power structures.

PP

Which is an interesting thing. In a subconscious way it reveals the deep nature of the practice of the different protagonists. Yet, it's also a way to define oneself within a collective. So the structure we came up with was the reflection of this new collectivity, which is also defined while people come together.

HUO

I was really intrigued yesterday when you told me that story about Cities on the Move—that some people asked you how they should look around. I think this exhibition in the arena in Arles has pushed that further. In an arena, vision is usually focused on the bull. It's very panoptical. Not only did this project undermine the panoptical effect, it also created a polyphonic situation where nothing could occupy the center, where protagonists might go on a break or might continue to work on the sand, while Lili Reynaud-Dewar was doing her performance up there or Uri Aran's piece started to play.

LG

I think it was quite a melancholic exhibition in a way. I found it quite moving.

PP

It was a bit like extreme socialism.

LG

It was also set in a strange architecture, which is like a ship.

PP

Exactly.

LG

A very strange venue for playing out political rhetoric.

PP

Today we looked at the footage of the video documenting the project. It reminded me of the trailer of Godard's Film socialisme (2010)—set on a ship—and basically the entire film fast-forwarded. You don't see much, but you see everything and things move fast. There are some things here that are similar, in terms of grammar.

HUO

Your initial idea was to actually have a lot of cameras.

PP

Cameras with a time lapse.

HUO

And the two of you could do a real film out of it.

LG

Well, I'm thinking more and more that this could be a movie, because there's enough material to actually make a movie. It could have a completely different title.

PP

I think we need to see all these elements, put them together, and fast-forward the whole thing. The footage is nice, but it has an institutional quality.

HUO

I would like to bring into this conversation the different inputs the two of you made. Liam, you were very involved before the project opened and really very early on. But the moment it actually opened, you took a back seat. I thought it was an interesting paradox.

LG

You've got to remember that a big part of my work is to make abstract art—and I don't know why I feel I need to do this. But I'm interested in this problem of abstract art, for some reason. Philippe is much more resistant to that—or much more capable of viewing lots of different arcane forms and finding them useful. I'm limited. And there are certain moments where I want to withdraw. I think you need a combination of the two. I said it quite openly to a lot of the artists: "I'm not going to get involved. You do what you need to do." Philippe was more engaged in the realization.

PP

I found it fascinating to see that attitude in operation. I just wanted to be close to it. It's not that I did much.

LG

You didn't stop. You did loads of things!

PP

It's also that, in a way, just by being around, people have discussions with me and that also creates a dynamic.

LG

What happens is that Philippe becomes extremely precise in these situations. The whole thing starts to activate and then he's at the center of it.

PP

In a way I was, although I hate the terminology of choreography, an abstract choreographer.

HUO

Just before the project opened, something very intense happened. Key decisions were made: Should there be a checklist? A program? You also made these radical decisions, which I think became a very important part of the project: to have a musical introduction, to use loudspeakers in the arena to announce and introduce the project, etc.

LG

The thing is, these are all strategies. If you wanted to be a good art historian, you'd look at some of these things and say, "there's an echo here of cinema in the 1950s when the city became the subject or the frame." There are some connections to early Soviet structures, such as the propaganda trains that moved around the countryside. There are some connections to failed forms of architecture that assumed you could come across cultural events in an art-center type of environment. There are ways to analyze and decode these strategies. What's interesting about them is that they are quite fragile. If you think about it in terms of the history of failed revolutions, I think that our principles are quite strong, they're real, and they mean something. They have historical precedents and they have real political meaning. But they are vulnerable.

HUO

I think it's good to mention, for the sake of the interview, to have it recorded somewhere, that the project proceeds from a very unusual situation. In the 25 years I've been in the world of exhibitions, I've never been in this sort of situation. There's often a promiscuity of collaboration. But here there is a very specific situation set up by Maja Hoffmann, with a group of artists and curators, not gathered to think about a show or a biennale, but instead to work over the long term. It took three years of this process with Tom Eccles, and Beatrix Ruf, and the three of us, and Maja of course at the center, to let this institution grow organically, with doubts and questions, until it all started to fall into place.

LG

For me it also has a little bit to do with The Prisoner, the famous TV series, which also takes place in a controlled terrain, a village. There's a Number 1. You know who Number 1 is and you are Number 6. You don't know who the other people in the village are and you can't leave. Sometimes you fight and sometimes you just go along with things, sometimes you collaborate and try to persuade the others that they are also part of this ridiculous inescapable situation. Sometimes you realize you've been instrumentalized, taken along for a ride, or that you've been tricked. After doing this project I watched several episodes of The Prisoners. The last ones, not the first ones.

HUO

After To the Moon via the Beach?

LG

Yes. A lot of it happens on the beach, with Number 6 being chased by big bubbles. In the last episodes, after they'd run out of ideas, it becomes really interesting because they are no longer trying to explain the structure. There is just a sequence of events. With the structure of LUMA I think we're all aware that as soon as you get to the point where the doors of the Foundation open, something will change. It's like what I always say about the failure of modern architecture: it did not have to do with failed forms or a failed utopia of public housing; the failure was enacted on the day the building opened—when someone put a sign on the door saying, "Please use the other door." [Laughter]

PP

It's the classic problem of Beaubourg.

LG

It's exactly that.

PP

It started with walls moving around, and when they became fixed that was the end of things.

HUO

Then segregation started to happen between the departments.

PP

Exactly.

HUO

We've mentioned LUMA and the core group; I think it's important to go back to the context of your collaboration. What about All Hawaii Entries LunaReggae (IMMA, Dublin, 2006)

LG

It was Philippe's exhibition. But it was my title. It's an anagram of "contemporary art gallery" in Irish Gaelic. [Laughter]

PP

We wanted to make a clock. We wanted to have words spinning around as if they were marking time. So each time you went, you might have a different title for the show. Of course we didn't have the technology or the time to do such a thing. We should do it now. It was a good idea.

LG

You see all these things transform into other things, fragments of moments reappearing or borrowed. We're not a collective, and we're not collaborating either. Collectives and collaborations are problematic structures historically.

PP

When I was working with Pierre Joseph, Bernard Joisten, and Dominique Gonzalez-Foerster, we'd come up with a name for a project and that would become the name of the group, so to speak. The next project would carry another name, so people got confused. They'd ask, "Are you the group Ozone or the group Hyper Hyper?" In a way, we were insisting that we were not a group, these were just titles of shows curated by us. Within the shows you had singular works from each artist. I think that is still true. It's not like we're all responsible for the work we do—and yet we put things in common.

Liam's right. There are things that are floating around and that we'll use later, somehow or other. Sometimes I do things that I thought Liam could have done. Still today. It's a way to renegotiate your practice.

LG

If you could say that the discourse around conceptual art was excessively concerned about who did what first, you could say that around our projects the question is who stops first. Who quits the table, quits the game.

HUO

We're talking about an extraordinary project that happened in Arles. It didn't happen in Paris. We're talking about other extraordinary projects in Grenoble and Dijon, outside the capital. That's true for many, many other things our generation has been doing. Il Tempo del Postino happened in Manchester, not in London. Maybe it has to do with the possibility of playing, and the fact that it is difficult to play in New York or London.

LG

I was listening to this lecture the other day about how, when Flaubert checked his texts, he'd read them out loud, virtually shouting. It was a way of checking if the language was okay. It's hard to do that in the city.

PP

So you go to Dijon or Arles.

LG

I think he was probably in Paris, but it feels like it might be easier to shout Madame Bovary when you're not in Paris. [Laughter] I think it's just an illusion. I don't think there's any broader truth you can get from this topic of center and periphery.

PP

It's also partly because, with the works we produce, each time we have to install them we have to renegotiate them. The objects we produce are "quasi," they are not completed. In a way they have to be reinvented. Which is partly why most of the recent monographic exhibitions or retrospectives or semi-retrospectives we've had were a reinvention of some sort. It's there, it stands, it can be in a collection, but as soon as it is brought back into a perspective of a narration, things have to be re-played. They're made for that in a way.

French Translations

Depuis 2010, à Arles, la Fondation LUMA produit des projets artistiques polymorphes comme autant de préfigurations et de tests du projet du Parc des Ateliers d'Arles dont elle conçoit et construit le campus avec les artistes Liam Gillick et Philippe Parreno, les commissaires Tom Eccles, Hans Ulrich Obrist et Beatrix Ruf, les architectes Frank Gehry et Annabelle Selldorf et le paysagiste Bas Smets.

À côté d'expositions centrées sur l'image comme How Soon is Now?[1] et Neue Welt[2], toutes deux présentées au sein du festival des Rencontres Internationales de la Photographie, ou du symposium The Human Snapshot[3] organisé en collaboration avec le Bard College, Vers la lune en passant par la plage, produite en 2012 aux Arènes d'Arles, est une tentative audacieuse et inédite d'affirmer le caractère expérimental de notre action.

À l'invitation de la Fondation LUMA Eccles, Gillick, Obrist, Parreno et Ruf ont choisi vingt artistes de différentes générations, venus du monde entier pour vivre et travailler ensemble dans les Arènes d'Arles. Ce lieu historique majeur et populaire, fréquemment utilisé pour des corridas et des manifestations traditionnelles, a accueilli cette exposition en constante évolution et dont le titre sonnait à la fois comme une expédition, une quête et une recherche. Vers la lune en passant par la plage représentait une réunion de possibles, dilatait l'espace et le temps, laissait les choses advenir.

Nous voulions permettre au public arlésien ou en visite dans la région, de vivre une expérience, de côtoyer des artistes et d’expérimenter une forme différente d’interaction avec l’art, tout en découvrant qu’une exposition peut prendre des formes inattendues.

J’ai convié les deux artistes membres du Core Group de la Fondation LUMA pour Arles (Liam Gillick et Philippe Parreno, à l’origine de cette idée) à en tenter la mise en forme. Ils présentaient le projet très simplement: «Trois sonneries de corne de brume annoncent le commencement du travail – attirant le public aux Arènes. Il s’agit d’une exposition sur le travail, la production et la transformation – des idées en mouvement perpétuel. Un paysage lunaire se composera progressivement, autour duquel les artistes développeront des idées nouvelles. Tout sera visible, sans distinction entre production, présentation et échange.»

Cette exposition est pour moi l'un des actes fondateurs du centre de création, de production et d'exposition d'art et d'idées que la Fondation LUMA a entrepris d'ériger sur le site des Ateliers à Arles. Il a donné forme et vie à la communauté d'artistes que nous souhaitons développer à Arles et qui trouvera dans ce site un outil pour penser, concevoir, formuler, produire les œuvres et les idées marquantes du XXIe siècle.

Ce principe fondateur se retrouve également matérialisé dans le réemploi du sable utilisé pour la création de ce paysage artistique en mouvement : comme un ferment, il sera réutilisé sur le chantier de construction pour stabiliser les fondations du bâtiment conçu par Frank Gehry.

–Maja Hoffmann, mai 2014

1 Exposition collective organisée par Eccles, Gillick, Obrist, Parreno et Ruf en 2010 qui a permis de révéler un autre visage de la photographie.

2 Exposition monographique de Wolfgang Tillmans présentée par Beatrix Ruf en 2013 à la Kunsthalle de Zurich et à Arles.

3 Symposium traitant de la question de l'universalité de l'image et des droits de l'Homme à partir de The Family of Man – l'exposition emblématique organisée par le MoMA de New York en 1953. Le savoir généré par ce colloque est un exemple de ce que sera notre programme post-doc sur le campus LUMA Arles.

Une conversation entre Hans Ulrich Obrist, Liam Gillick et Philippe Parreno Arles, janvier 2013

Le contexte de cet entretien est la création d'un nouveau centre d'art par la Fondation LUMA que préside la collectionneuse, productrice et mécène Maja Hoffmann. Elle a invité les artistes Liam Gillick et Philippe Parreno, ainsi que les curateurs Tom Eccles, Beatrix Ruf et moi-même, à former avec elle un groupe pour penser et mettre en place un centre d'art expérimental éloigné de tout centre urbain et construit par Frank Gehry. C'est Arles, en Camargue, où Maja Hoffmann a grandi, qu'il se construit.

L'un des objectifs de Maja Hoffmann est de connecter ce centre à l'écologie. Un pas dans cette direction a été fait en 2012 avec l'exposition To the Moon via the Beach, qui prit place dans l'Amphithéâtre romain d'Arles, un site historique populaire auprès des touristes et souvent utilisé pour des corridas et des festivals. À l'initiative de Gillick et Parreno, l'amphithéâtre devenait le lieu d'une transformation continue pendant l'exposition. Au début, les visiteurs découvraient l'arène remplie de tonnes de sable. Ce terrain se transformait progressivement d'une plage à un paysage lunaire par le travail d'une équipe de sculpteurs de sable et devenait également le décor d'une série d'interventions de vingt artistes qui tantôt guidaient les visiteurs, tantôt réagissaient au paysage en construction et produisaient des œuvres dans ou autour de l'arène. À la fin du processus, tout le sable fut transporté au Parc des Ateliers d'Arles, un ancien site de construction ferroviaire, pour former une aire de jeu temporaire accessible au public. Le sable sera par la suite réutilisé à nouveau pour stabiliser les fondations du futur bâtiment de la Fondation LUMA, un nouveau centre de création, de production et d'exposition pour la création artistique contemporaine. Comme le disait le philosophe Michel Serres, peut-être que l'une des évolutions fondamentales de l'art d'aujourd'hui est de s'ouvrir à d'autres espèces vivantes, à la vie et à la nature.

–Hans Ulrich Obrist

HUO

Pour commencer, j'aimerais vous demander si vous vous souvenez de votre rencontre.

PP

C'était à Nice en 1990. Je travaillais avec Philippe Perrin et Pierre Joseph sur une exposition à la galerie Air de Paris intitulée Les Ateliers du Paradise. Nous avions envoyé une invitation sous la forme d'une carte de crédit – que nous avions appelée «carte des figurants». Liam l'a reçue parce qu'à l'époque il écrivait pour Artscribe. Intrigué par cette carte, il est venu à Nice.

LG

J'avais eu la naiveté de croire qu'un magazine comme Artscribe, dont la couverture proclamait qu'il était international, envoyait ses journalistes voir sur place les expositions. Mais financièrement, ils n'en avaient pas les moyens. Je suis donc venu de Londres en voiture avec une amie.

HUO

Vous connaissiez-vous à l'époque ?

LG

Je connaissais Philippe mais je crois qu'il n'avait pas entendu parler de moi. Tout le monde pense aujourd'hui que Les Ateliers du Paradise représentent – et c'était vrai, dans une certaine mesure – un nouveau type d'exposition dont la forme originale est par la suite devenue une référence, mais il s'agissait aussi d'art. Les Ateliers sont généralement considérés comme un lieu d'activités et de convivialité, mais il était tout autant question d'art.

PP

Nous tentions d'expérimenter une autre manière d'être dans une galerie : produire des idées ou jouer à des jeux vidéo par exemple ; l'idée, c'était de passer du temps plutôt que de simplement montrer des objets.

LG

Vous rappelez-vous du panneau Twin Peaks (1991) placé à l'extérieur de l'exposition No Man's Time (Villa Arson, Nice, 1991) ? Philippe faisait des objets comme celui-ci et c'était en quelque sorte une manifestation de ce à quoi je pensais. Il s'était bien sûr déjà passé certaines choses en France. J'étais au courant du travail d'artistes comme Ange Leccia, IFP (Information Fiction Publicité) et Philippe Thomas, mais là, un nouveau sentiment émergeait… Aux beaux-arts déjà, mon intuition était qu'il devait exister un art français aussi, voire plus, intéressant que les écrits théoriques d'auteurs comme Jean-François Lyotard. Il est difficile de se rappeler combien c'était radical, combien aussi, au cours des années suivantes, les réactions étaient souvent de l'ordre de l'irritation dès que je parlais d'une scène artistique française. Il y avait un refus d'accepter son existence. Ce qui me fascinait vraiment chez Philippe, c'était sa relation au cinéma, son appropriation du cinéma comme d'une idée structurelle, mais sans réaliser de film à ce stade. Pour moi, ce fut une révélation qui a tout bouleversé – et confirmé certaines de mes envies et de mes idées.

PP

À l'époque, tu vivais à Londres et tu discutais de ces idées avec Jack Wendler.

LG

Oui, mais pour des personnes telles que Jack, il s'était produit dans les années 1980 quelque chose qui les conduisait à penser: «On ne peut plus continuer de cette façon». Il était mélancolique et ressentait la difficulté, voire l'échec de l'art dans les années 1980. Ce que j'ai alors vu en France, c'est que des artistes ne cherchaient pas à sortir de cet échec en reproduisant des formes qui y ont participé: ils cherchaient, en fait, de nouvelles structures.

HUO

Cet entretien prend place dans le cadre de To the Moon via the Beach, à la fois une exposition expérimentale et une exposition en tant qu'expérience, organisée dans l'Amphithéâtre d'Arles en juillet 2012. Vous vous êtes lancés dans ce type d'expériences, sous une forme collaborative, il y a déjà plus d'une décennie, avec Le Procès de Pol Pot au Magasin de Grenoble (1998).

PP

En fait, le premier projet de ce type a eu lieu au Consortium de Dijon. Tout a commencé avec Snow Dancing (1995), un projet que j'ai réalisé avec Xavier Douroux, l'un des directeurs du centre d'art. À l'époque, Xavier n'avait pas vraiment envie de travailler avec notre génération; il avait des réserves. Après Snow Dancing, il m'a envoyé une longue lettre disant qu'il avait eu tort de manquer de confiance envers ce que nous faisions, qu'il désirait collaborer avec nous. Il affirmait: «Vous devriez prendre le contrôle de l'espace pour produire quelque chose». Je passais alors beaucoup de temps avec Liam, dans son appartement de Rotherhithe, à Londres, et nous avons décidé de travailler ensemble sur ces idées.

LG

Nous avions tous deux participé à No Man's Time. J'avais commencé à exposer en France, notamment chez Air de Paris. Snow Dancing a d'abord pris la forme d'un livre que Philippe nous a proposés, à Jack et moi, de publier (G-W Press [pour Gillick-Wendler], Londres, 1994). J'ai mis par écrit les idées de Philippe. J'étais le secrétaire, tandis que Jack posait les questions.

PP

À l'époque, chacun d'entre nous collaborait régulièrement avec un autre artiste: Henry Bond pour Liam, Pierre Joseph dans mon cas. En un sens, c'était une sorte de «pratique d'atelier». C'était assez naturel de partager des réflexions, de mettre en forme des idées d'exposition.

LG

Il était clair pour moi que c'était l'acte d'exposer et non pas l'art, qui se trouvait dans une phase dynamique. En soi, l'idée de travailler en tant que groupe n'avait rien de radical. L'idée même de travailler n'était pas une question intéressante. J'étais fasciné par le fait qu'Esther Schipper, Dominique Gonzalez-Foerster, Florence Bonnefous et Édouard Mérino avaient suivi le même programme curatorial à Grenoble.

PP

Il y avait aussi Collins & Milazzo à New York.

HUO

Mais ils étaient très post-modernes.

LG

Mais pas inintéressants. Dans mon esprit, j'étais capable d'associer certaines œuvres d'art, comme une photographie de Walker Evans et une jarre d'Allan McCollum. Cela paraissait juste, mais pas suffisant. J'étais davantage intéressé par des expériences plus anciennes, comme Six Years (1973), l'ouvrage de Lucy Lippard, ou le catalogue de la documenta 5 d'Harald Szeemann (1972).

HUO

Et peut-être aussi par Inside the White Cube (1981) de Brian O'Doherty?

LG

Pas vraiment. Trop pur, trop centré sur les espaces artistiques. Ce qui m'attirait, c'était ce qui traitait de l'œuvre, de la vie, du travail – et de la division entre ces différents aspects.

HUO

Comment a germé ou s'est cristallisée cette première expérience?

PP

C'est vraiment venu de Liam parce qu'il travaillait, avec Henry Bond, comme journaliste, et qu'il se rendait, par exemple, à une conférence de presse de l'ONU, et donc, quand il parlait d'art, son approche était identique à celle qu'il pouvait adopter pour traiter n'importe quel événement politique majeur. À maints égards, Moral Maze, cet autre projet que nous avons réalisé au Consortium en 1995, était une extension directe de la pratique de Liam et de sa collaboration avec Henry. Il y avait, à l'époque, un programme radiophonique anglais populaire intitulé Moral Maze qui débutait toujours avec cette même phrase: «We are not here to judge you, but to get information from you», soit «Nous ne sommes pas là pour vous juger mais pour obtenir de vous des informations».

LG

Généralement, le programme se concentrait sur un sujet donné, moral ou éthique, et comme dans une enquête, les gens subissaient un interrogatoire très serré sur ce thème, mené par un petit panel d'experts. Cette forme typiquement britannique posait pas mal de problèmes, mais il y avait quelque chose dans la structure qui semblait intéressant.

PP

Les règles établies pour l'exposition s'inspiraient de ce programme. Nous avons ainsi annoncé aux artistes: «Vous viendrez dans un lieu d'exposition à Dijon et, alors que nous avons l'intention d'organiser une exposition collective, nous allons inviter une série de spécialistes». C'était finalement un peu comme Les Ateliers du Paradise, où différentes personnalités se rencontraient et s'adressaient à nous dans un contexte semi-privé. Ce n'était pas un événement public.

HUO

Il ne s'agissait pas d'un format conférence?

PP

Non. Cela concernait seulement les artistes présents.

LG

Moral Maze avait beaucoup à voir avec le questionnement constant de Philippe sur l'exposition comme forme ou comme geste, sur le fait de savoir où réside la signification de ce que tu présentes… En tant que telle, ce fut une exposition radicale. Fermée et ouverte en même temps, ce qu'indiquait la peinture blanche étalée sur les portes vitrées comme pour suggérer que l'espace était dans un processus de rénovation, moitié ouvert, moitié fermé. Il n'y avait pas de publicité. Pas d'inauguration.

HUO

Exactement comme pour To the Moon via the Beach!

LG

C'était une occupation de l'espace sur un temps donné.

PP

Différentes personnes arrivaient chaque jour. Beaucoup d'entre elles venaient d'Angleterre. Je me souviens par exemple des designers britanniques Dunne & Raby.

LG

Ils disaient que les téléphones mobiles deviendraient une référence dans les pays en voie de développement parce qu'il n'existait pas assez de cuivre dans le monde pour établir des lignes téléphoniques en Afrique. Ils avaient raison. Ils affirmaient que les gens échangeraient de l'argent par téléphone. Ils avaient vu juste. Ils disaient qu'il y aurait des nuages d'information – et ils entendaient par là de vrais nuages, c'est-à-dire la possibilité de s'asseoir quelque part et de se retrouver dans un nuage électronique. Et aussi, d'envoyer et de recevoir des informations. Sont également venus un spécialiste de l'économie de l'éducation dans les pays en voie de développement, un conseiller politique qui travaillait auprès du principal stratège de Tony Blair, etc.

PP

La règle, c'était que, chaque jour, un invité était accueilli à Dijon par Liam – qui l'emmenait d'abord faire un bon déjeuner. Puis, il se rendait à l'espace d'exposition pour y donner une courte présentation devant sept artistes légèrement névrosés. Certains d'entre nous restaient assis à écouter, tandis que d'autres, comme Maurizio Cattelan, affichaient leur impatience et marchaient de long en large. L'exposition commençait au moment où toutes ces personnes étaient parties. Il n'y avait pas de limite claire entre l'instant de la production de l'art et celui de sa présentation.

LG

Les attentes du type «Pour qui est-ce? Comment cela sera-t-il compris? Où est la rhétorique, où est la preuve?» étaient soumises à une tension constante. Comme lors du Procès de Pol Pot.

PP

Je me souviens que nous parlions alors du fait que Serge Daney n'était pas traduit en anglais, et qu'il existait des critiques de cinéma dont les textes étaient aussi importants que les films qu'ils décrivaient. Au début des années 1990, ce flou entre l'analyse et l'événement lui-même était assez crucial.

HUO

Comment est né Le Procès de Pol Pot?

LG

Yves Aupetitallot, le directeur du Magasin de Grenoble, en est à l'origine, d'une certaine façon. Il nous parlait des problèmes budgétaires qui affectaient les expositions; nous lui avons répondu qu'il pourrait monter une exposition intitulée Le Procès de Pol Pot dont la qualité serait même améliorée par le fait qu'il n'y avait pas assez d'argent... L'été précédant notre projet, j'avais entendu des reportages sur Pol Pot disant qu'il vivait dans la jungle cambodgienne, près de la frontière thaïlandaise. Ce qui était intéressant, c'est que les journalistes de la BBC étaient incapables de comprendre qui était cette personne: ils étaient incapables de décrire l'un des plus grands génocidaires du XXe siècle. Nous voulions utiliser cette idée, non de façon didactique, mais pour aborder la question du personnage, pour susciter une quête de personnage. Il s'agissait, en un sens, de représenter quelqu'un qui ne pouvait être décrit et restait insaisissable. Comment juger quelqu'un qui ne peut être ni décrit ni vu? C'était également métaphorique, en quelque sorte.

HUO

Quelles étaient les règles du jeu?

PP

Nous prenions en charge, je crois, tout ce qui relevait physiquement de l'art. Nous avions une liste de personnes qui étaient des…

LG

… conseillers.

PP

Nous étions «contrôlés» par ces personnes qui agissaient comme des super-commissaires. Leur présence dominait tout le processus.

LG

Certains, comme Lawrence Weiner, disaient «continuez!». D'autres, je pense notamment à Merlin Carpenter, ont écrit de longs textes polémiques expliquant que notre tentative relevait d'une imposture totale. D'autres, enfin, étaient simplement désorientés.

PP

Liam a réalisé là-bas quelques-uns de ses premiers textes muraux. Il travaillait sur son ordinateur et disait qu'il pouvait imprimer des séquences de texte, ce qui ne coûtait pas grand-chose. J'ai commencé à jouer avec les lumières et Liam a collé des adhésifs sur les murs. C'est rapidement devenu un plan d'exposition où nous abordions une certaine complexité en nous efforçant de ne pas tout clarifier.

LG

J'ai réalisé une affiche qui reprenait tous les commentaires des conseillers, superposés les uns aux autres, si bien qu'on ne voyait qu'une masse d'écrits.

HUO

Comme un palimpseste?

LG

Exactement. En arrivant dans l'exposition, on pouvait prendre une affiche et partir, ou bien payer et entrer.

PP

Nous n'avons pas impliqué les autres artistes dans le processus de réalisation – nul n'a produit d'«œuvre». Nous étions fondamentalement ceux qui concevaient cette exposition. En plus des textes muraux, il y avait une grande bannière au milieu de l'espace nommé La Rue – un lieu ouvert à l'intérieur du bâtiment industriel. Sur la bannière était imprimé le dessin d'une lune se détachant derrière des arbres scématiques. Puis, à l'intérieur des galeries, se trouvaient des extraits de texte, comme une écriture discontinue, avec des lumières colorées et mouvantes. Comme un improbable décor d'un show télévisé des années 1970.

LG

Ensuite, nous avons eu – comme avec <u>To the Moon via the Beach</u> – cette apparente crise de médiation, qui, bien sûr, n'était pas une crise pour moi, mais une volonté d'améliorer le projet. À l'origine, je voulais que Robert de Niro vienne chaque semaine expliquer l'exposition; j'avais un contact pour le joindre, mais c'est tombé à l'eau. Alors, chaque mercredi, nous faisions un spectacle de marionnettes pour écoliers qui expliquait pourquoi Robert de Niro n'était pas venu. [Rires]

HUO

C'est intéressant d'évoquer ces expositions parce qu'il est assez difficile d'obtenir des informations précises à leur sujet.

LG

C'est vrai. Elles rendaient les gens nerveux; ils pensaient que cela ne valait pas la peine de financer un catalogue. Ils n'arrivaient pas à imaginer ce qu'on pouvait faire avec ces expositions – et peut-être bien que nous ne le pouvions pas non plus.

PP

On savait déjà que tout – y compris le titre – serait mal compris. Le projet parlait de ça, de toute façon, de l'incompréhension, de la tentative de trouver une position, de définir son propre point de vue sur un événement. Donc, nous étions pris dans un ensemble de structures complexes.

LG

Sans compter le fait qu'un personnage se dérobait à la représentation.

PP

Pol Pot était un proto-personnage, comme l'est Ann Lee.

LG

Ce qui unit toutes ces expositions, c'est leur relation ambiguë à la notion de public et de spectateur. Elles reposaient sur l'intelligence et l'intentionnalité des différents publics qui se déplaceraient vers ce type de lieu, et elles jouaient avec les codes institutionnels. Rien à voir avec les nouveaux modèles de participation. Il s'agit en fait ici d'expositions totalement non-participatives.

PP

C'est également vrai de No Man's Time, où nous nous étions emparés du programme curatorial – ce que faisait régulièrement Liam dans le contexte d'expositions collectives. Il s'asseyait avec le commissaire, discutait de certaines idées et commençait lui-même à écrire un communiqué de presse. C'était ainsi une façon de prendre en otage le directeur artistique d'une institution, de s'occuper de tout nous-mêmes, y compris de la communication. Dès le début, comme avec To the Moon via the Beach, la question du public était vraiment très présente.

HUO

C'est intéressant que la notion de temps apparaisse dès ces premières expositions. À l'époque où Diaghilev organisait des expositions en Russie, il avait déclaré « Je veux être le conservateur du temps ». Il a ensuite fondé les Ballets Russes et commencé à exposer le temps plutôt que l'espace.

LG

Philippe a toujours eu une compréhension plus raffinée que la mienne de la façon dont il est possible de jouer avec le temps dans une institution ; en un sens, je suis beaucoup plus matérialiste, ce qui inclut l'écriture parce que c'est aussi un fait concret – on matérialise une idée ou une série de propositions. C'est à Philippe que reviennent toutes les innovations sur le jeu avec le temps dans les expositions. Cet aspect a pris une importance croissante dans son travail.

HUO

Du point de vue de votre collaboration, tu penses qu'il y a un aspect sur lequel tu étais moins engagé…

LG

Je pense simplement que je n'avais pas poussé ma réflexion aussi loin que lui. Lorsqu'il a commencé à exploiter cette dimension, la mise en œuvre était assez radicale parce que la plupart des manipulations du temps dans l'art étaient liées aux performances ou aux happenings. D'une certaine façon, Philippe jouait avec ces codes et artifices temporels. Tout à coup, il n'était plus question de cinéma mais de la création d'une mise en scène.

PP

Il s'agit de négocier la présence ou l'apparition d'un objet d'art. Lorsque l'on a cette croyance que la présentation dans un espace produit de la connaissance ou une forme de conscience, on met en alors jeu la lecture, d'une façon non-autoritaire ou non-spectaculaire.

HUO

Qu'y a-t-il eu après Le Procès de Pol Pot?

PP

Il y a eu What if dont Liam fut le co-commissaire avec Maria Lind (Moderna Museet, Stockholm, 2000).

LG

Nous n'avons pas travaillé ensemble sur ce projet, mais il possédait certaines des qualités que nous évoquons.

HUO

Tu ne voulais pas qu'on te nomme co-commissaire ; tu disais être un « filtre ».

LG

Je ne voulais pas avoir la responsabilité des artistes choisis par Maria. En excellente commissaire issue d'une nouvelle génération, elle a sélectionné des artistes dont elle pensait qu'ils soutiendraient l'histoire qu'elle voulait raconter. Je n'aurais pas choisi les mêmes artistes. Donc, cet aspect-là ne m'intéressait pas. Ce qui m'attirait, c'était la conception de l'espace et la façon dont on était censé comprendre l'exposition. La plupart des expositions sont organisées traditionnellement : les artistes obtiennent de l'espace parce que leur œuvre le requiert ou bien tout se passe de façon plus ou moins démocratique. J'ai opté pour un plan qui s'écartait radicalement de cette situation. Dans mon cas, j'ai par exemple alloué à Dominique Gonzalez-Foerster un cinquième de toute l'exposition alors que son écran vidéo et son installation au néon ne nécessitaient pas tant de place. Ce n'était pas que l'œuvre elle-même l'exigeait, ce n'était pas nécessaire, mais cela semblait intéressant. Il y avait donc ces zones dégagées, puis tous les films et vidéos placés derrière des rideaux gris. Il fallait se frayer un chemin à travers ces différentes salles.

HUO

Qu'en est-il de Bryannnnnn and Ferryyyyyy (Konstall, Lund, 2004) ?

PP

Bryannnnnn and Ferryyyyyy est un film tourné en réponse à un symposium.

LG

La conférence portait sur la loi et la créativité, et notre travail sur l'idée que l'art change les règles du jeu, le tout en dix épisodes. C'est à ce moment que j'ai vu arriver des commissaires d'un genre différent, qui avaient entendu parler de projets comme Le Procès de Pol Pot, mais ne les avaient pas vus et leur prêtaient une qualité qu'ils ne possédaient pas – comme le fait, par exemple, que l'exposition contiendrait des informations sur le Cambodge. C'était un malentendu sur ma façon de faire et sur celle de Philippe, et ils ont pensé qu'on pouvait créer une sorte d'exposition autour de ce sujet de la loi et de la créativité. Nous avons réfléchi à une bande dessinée que j'ai rédigée, et Philippe a commencé à la travailler visuellement ; puis, une troisième personne a collaboré pour réaliser une grande partie du travail technique.

PP

Cela s'est fait sans qu'on en parle vraiment, tout est allé tellement vite.

HUO

Mais vous avez sûrement dû discuter de l'œuvre.

PP

Pas réellement. C'était facile, nous étions invités à produire quelque chose que nous avions déjà réalisé par le passé. Alors, nous avons fabriqué un dessin animé, juste pour montrer que nous n'étions pas les artistes qu'ils pensaient que nous étions ! Le dessin animé, une chasse – un chat courant après une souris –, durait 10 secondes. J'ai envoyé les dessins à Liam qui m'a répondu « Je vais trouver quelqu'un pour les animer », et voilà.

LG

J'ai toujours aimé le film Ou (1996) de Philippe. Il se compose essentiellement d'un générique. Quand je l'ai vu, je me suis dit que c'était l'un des meilleurs films jamais tournés – ce qui est ridicule en un sens. Il y avait beaucoup de fautes d'orthographe mais je pense que, structurellement, c'était vraiment étonnant. Pour le dessin animé, le générique de chaque épisode était plus long que l'action. Nous avons repris l'idée des conseillers mais, en accord avec le changement de contexte, certains de ces conseillers étaient écrivains ou commissaires. La question était alors : que devons-nous penser, inclure ou ne pas manquer de ce processus ? Ces aspects ont fini par faire partie des génériques.

HUO

Comment les personnages se sont-ils mis en place ?

LG

C'était un truc de chat et de souris. Philippe a dit quelque chose comme « La souris meurt au cours des premières secondes », et nous avons réalisé le reste de la série sans le jeu classique du chat et de la souris. Donc, bien sûr, toute l'histoire à propos du conflit et du châtiment, et de l'infinie résurrection d'un personnage que nous retrouvons dans les dessins animés, n'est pas présente. En fait, le chat est assez solitaire, fait des choses telles que surfer sur Internet, regarder des vidéos de New Order, penser à faire de la boxe, etc. J'ai décidé d'écrire la version finale en état d'ivresse, ce qui lui donne du coup une qualité qui ne ressemble à rien de ce que j'ai réalisé jusque-là. C'est mélancolique, agressif.

PP

Mais c'était cette fois encore assez différent de Moral Maze, non ? Nous n'avons plus vraiment collaboré jusqu'à cette exposition aux Arènes d'Arles. La suite de Moral Maze, c'est To the Moon via the Beach.

HUO

Entre-temps, il y a eu Il Tempo del Postino (2007), que nous avons co-organisée et qui, d'une certaine façon…

PP

… est légèrement différent…

HUO

… tout en étant malgré tout très lié. Il Tempo del Postino reposait sur une règle normative : tout artiste disposait de quinze minutes. Mais il y a un lien, il y a en quelque sorte une arène.

LG

J'ai toujours eu le sentiment que pour Philippe, ce projet était une façon de trouver un accord avec le théâtre. C'est quelque chose de difficile à accomplir parce que dans une exposition, on peut jouer avec la totalité de l'espace, avec le temps, avec tout. Quand on est confronté à la réalité formelle d'un théâtre, c'est bien plus compliqué.

PP

C'est aussi une exposition venant après le projet du Zidane, un vrai film de cinéma réalisé avec Douglas Gordon (2006). Une nouvelle fois, l'idée était de tenter quelque chose avec des personnes enfermées dans une pièce, lumières éteintes, où elles étaient conviées à passer un certain temps. Du point de vue théorique, c'était fondé sur un texte que j'avais publié en 1992 dans Documents sur l'art ; c'était donc une question dont nous avions discuté ensemble plusieurs années auparavant…

LG

Pour Il Tempo del Postino, je n'étais qu'un participant et lorsque je suis arrivé, je me suis dit « Je crois qu'on va s'amuser », parler à bâtons rompus, de manière conviviale… et toutes ces choses qui ne sont pas nécessairement au cœur des expositions, mais qui en font partie. En fait, je me suis retrouvé plongé dans la préparation d'une représentation théâtrale, ce qui est vraiment stressant. De nouvelles personnes sont également apparues, de nouvelles personnalités qui n'étaient pas impliquées jusque-là, comme Anri Sala ; elles sont devenues essentielles au projet.

HUO

Une génération différente était impliquée.

LG

Philippe est très généreux avec les autres artistes, ce qui peut me rendre un peu… nerveux. Cela me rendait nerveux.

PP

C'était intense pour moi aussi ! Je savais qu'il y avait un défi mais cela m'a épuisé. Cela s'est révélé d'une manière paroxystique : combien pouvons-nous donner pour mettre en place un projet ? C'était une expérience extrême pour moi.

LG

Nous l'avons ressenti.

HUO

La différence d'échelle était énorme. Nous avons lancé des invitations pour Il Tempo del Postino dans l'idée que deux à trois mille spectateurs verraient la pièce. Alors que des expositions comme Le Procès de Pol Pot et To the Moon via the Beach ont, je crois, davantage à voir avec ce que tu décris quand tu me disais qu'un spectateur ne savait pas où regarder dans Cities on the Move (1999). Quand on descend dans l'arène, à Arles ou au Magasin à Grenoble, nous ne savons pas où nous devons regarder ; cette sorte de confusion n'était pas présente dans Il Tempo del Postino.

PP

Si tu mets ces projets en perspective, tu peux constater qu'il y a toujours quelque chose de vivant ou d'actif dans To the Moon via the Beach. Avec Il Tempo del Postino, nous nous sommes servis des expressions « la règle du jeu » ou « une partition est une partition ». Il y a une sorte de principe automatique que nous essayons, je crois, de définir, comme une machine célibataire. Des principes qui peuvent être couchés sur le papier pour que quelque chose fonctionne de manière mécanique. Il existe un esprit d'automatisation que je trouve toujours fascinant. Pour un projet comme Bryannnnnn and Ferryyyyyy, nous avons même évoqué combien c'était facile d'être dans le processus de mise en œuvre.

LG

Nous avons activé un ensemble de conditions qui ont commencé à construire quelque chose, à pondre quelque chose. Pondre, pour moi, est le terme juste parce que c'est ce que font les grenouilles et les tritons, ils fraient et se transforment…

PP

C'est comme mettre quelque chose en œuvre ; ça commence à fonctionner et tout à coup, toi, tu te retrouves à travailler pour cette chose, quelle qu'elle soit.

HUO

Sur le plan curatorial, ces expositions n'avaient pas de schéma directeur.

LG

Elles ne sont pas non plus spontanées ; elles sont plutôt responsables. De toutes les expositions auxquelles j'ai participé, c'est To the Moon via the Beach qui avait le générique le plus clair.

HUO

Nous nous sommes rendus ensemble à Arles à plusieurs occasions. Il y a eu d'autres types de projet, comme How Soon Is Now? (Arles, 2010). Mais tu affirmais, Philippe, je m'en souviens, que nous devions réaliser quelque chose de plus spectaculaire, qui ne se situe pas dans le cadre d'un festival, ni dans celui du monde de l'art, mais qui aurait à voir avec ce qu'Arles est vraiment, en exploitant cette fameuse arène. Tu t'en rappelles ?

PP

Mon idée, c'était que nous devions – plutôt que dire que « nous allions » – faire quelque chose. C'est vraiment impressionnant ce moment où l'on entreprend de réfléchir sur une institution possible. Lorsqu'elle commence à exister, les choses s'effondrent ou doivent être redéfinies, mais l'instant de préfiguration est réellement passionnant parce que nous pouvons inventer des structures. Avant que n'arrive l'architecte, nous pouvons travailler et concrétiser des choses, de sorte à mettre en place un programme. Et quand l'architecture prend forme, elle accueille ce qui a été élaboré. C'était une indéniable raison pour initier le projet.

LG

Pour le dire autrement, quand on rassemble des personnes plutôt intelligentes et assez responsables, il y a des chances pour qu'elles commencent à s'auto-institutionnaliser, s'autoréguler. Ce qui pose problème. Ces questions me passionnent, et une grande partie de mon travail récent y est consacré. Dans notre groupe – ce que nous appelons le « core group » de la Fondation Luma –, nous sommes tous très conscients de ce risque d'auto-institutionnalisation. To the Moon via the Beach était une façon de se libérer de ce sentiment et de ne pas s'institutionnaliser. Jusqu'à imaginer qu'une personne venant simplement prendre le soleil dans l'arène se retrouve à regarder un type déambulant avec des abeilles sur le visage. C'était important que cette personne ne reçoive pas un bout de papier expliquant ce que l'artiste était en train de faire, ou bien qu'il s'agissait de Pierre Huyghe, qui a représenté la France à la dernière Biennale de Venise, etc.

HUO

Tu parles de préfiguration. C'est ce que Johannes Cladders disait à propos de Mönchengladbach lorsqu'il a monté les premières expositions muséales de Joseph Beuys, Daniel Buren, Carl Andre et d'autres dans une petite maison située en banlieue, en attendant que le musée soit construit.

LG

Tant d'expositions aujourd'hui portent sur quelque chose : To the Moon via the Beach était quelque chose. Il s'agit, je crois, d'une différence aussi simple que philosophique. On peut en dire autant de la distinction entre spectateurs et public. Je peux créer des spectateurs en présentant des chèvres qui copulent avec des ânes. Je veux dire, c'est facile, il y a quelque part des spectateurs pour ça, mais qui ne s'identifient pas au public. Le public, c'est une masse de personnes existantes, définies par des données démographiques, des différences et des désirs variés, mais qui ne se confond pas avec les spectateurs d'une chose donnée. Ce sont ces nombreux ensembles de spectateurs qui se manifestent sous la forme d'un public.

PP

Ceux qui viennent à Arles ont du temps, parce qu'ils n'ont pas un agenda trop rempli. Ils vont ici et là, et les choses apparaissent. Et plus ils regardent, plus ils passent du temps, plus des choses apparaissent. C'est donc vraiment le public qui produit ce qu'il veut voir, en un sens. Ils décident, ils choisissent pour eux-mêmes ce qui vaut la peine ou pas. Ils peuvent décider de ce qui relève de l'art ou pas, de ce qui deviendra de l'art ou pas. C'était également passionnant pour moi de voir de jeunes artistes intervenir dans ce type de cadre.

LG

C'est la première fois que j'organise une exposition qui réunit des artistes qui ont vingt ans de plus et vingt ans de moins que moi. C'est un peu mélancolique – nous sommes en quelque sorte coincés entre ces deux générations. Ce qui caractérise To the Moon via the Beach, Le Procès de Pol Pot et Moral Maze, c'est le procédé rhétorique que nous essayons d'utiliser, comme un titre ou une série d'idées, pour marquer ou prouver quelque chose. Dans le cas de To the Moon via the Beach, c'était l'idée que nous pouvions faire confiance à des artistes de générations différentes, que nous pouvions créer la toile de fond d'une activité continue, et que nous pouvions exploiter ce monument historique.

PP

Ce que tu as redéfini comme étant les règles du jeu. Je me souviens qu'à un moment donné, Liam a dit que nous devions créer une formule, de type mathématique.

LG

Découvrir une formule – l'idée était de partir d'une formule.

HUO

Richard Hamilton affirmait que nous nous souvenons seulement des expositions qui ont inventé un mode de présentation. Nous nous rappelons des expositions surréalistes de Marcel Duchamp, même si ce n'était peut-être pas les meilleures expositions collectives de leur temps, à cause des cordes à New York et des sacs de charbon à Paris. C'est vrai de nombreuses autres expositions, par exemple du Vide d'Yves Klein et du Plein d'Arman. Voyez-vous le sable dans l'arène comme un mode de présentation compris dans ce sens ?

PP

Oui. Cela crée du contexte et, plus encore, cela implique une série d'actions rendues possibles, sans être dictatoriales. C'est également assez reposant parce qu'il se passe toujours quelque chose. Pas besoin, ou presque, de faire quelque chose – en un sens, ce type d'invitation était très clair dès le départ.

LG

Mais, c'est ce que tu avais fait, Hans Ulrich, dans plusieurs expositions où la structure détournait la pression exercée sur les œuvres d'art pour porter l'intégralité de la signification. Ce type d'interventions génère bien sûr de nouvelles significations.

PP

Cela permet que des choses se produisent. C'est comme de pratiquer la chimie.

LG

Je ne souhaite pas avoir une approche comparative de l'art et évaluer la valeur silencieuse des objets les uns par rapport aux autres – c'est de la pseudo-critique. Je veux que ce soit bien plus compliqué et que l'exposition témoigne d'une compréhension plus complexe de ce à quoi nous accordons de la valeur, vers où nous portons notre regard et de ce qui s'exprime.

HUO

Vous avez eu l'idée d'inviter des «artistes de sable» qui, conformément à vos instructions, ont transformé l'arène. Puis, il y a eu cette règle du jeu une fois le terrain modifié.

PP

Les règles se sont mises en place la veille de l'inauguration. Ce n'était pas vraiment programmé.

HUO

Ce qui ne les rend pas moins importantes.

PP

Exact. Dès que des principes sont posés, ils agissent. On a simplement modifié les règles du jeu à quelques reprises, parce qu'on nous posait des questions auxquelles nous n'avions pas songé. Donc, on a eu des idées pour répondre à certaines anxiétés.

LG

Je pense que c'est également vrai pour Il Tempo del Postino. Ce genre de projet exerce une grande pression sur les artistes, différente de celle générée par les formats traditionnels de l'exposition où l'artiste est en quelque sorte fondamentalement protégé par l'architecture. Ici, nous ne sommes protégés que par le temps. On peut arrêter, se cacher, se retirer ou encore opter pour une routine. D'un autre côté, c'est plus difficile d'avoir une force de présence qui vous protège. Tu noteras que certains des artistes que nous respectons, pour lesquels il existe un consensus quant à la qualité de leur travail, quelle qu'en soit la raison, tendent à s'affirmer plus fortement dans un tel contexte. Parce que s'affirmer plus fortement est leur réponse, en quelque sorte, à ce problème. Ce que réalise Pierre Huyghe, par exemple, est destiné à être mémorable, c'est plus «bruyant». Comme s'il augmentait le volume de la basse. C'est aussi le cas dans Il Tempo del Postino. La réponse de Matthew Barney a été d'y jeter toutes ses forces. Ce qui veut dire que ceux qui savent très clairement comment se rendre visible dans le monde ont tendance à s'inquiéter pour leur autonomie et à la préserver dans une situation comme celle de To the Moon via the Beach. Dominique Gonzalez-Foerster a réagi de la même façon. D'autres, au contraire, tendent à disparaitre ou à se disperser. L'œuvre de Lawrence Weiner était incroyablement subtile; elle était littéralement disséminée. C'était un débris. Les expositions ne sont pas mûes par un processus …

PP

… mais elles révèlent des attitudes.

LG

Et les structures de pouvoir.

PP

Ce qui est intéressant. De manière inconsciente, cela dévoile la nature profonde de la pratique des différents protagonistes. Pourtant, c'est aussi un moyen de se définir à l'intérieur d'un collectif. La structure que nous avons élaborée était donc le reflet de cette nouvelle collectivité qui se détermine aussi au moment où les protagonistes se rencontrent.

HUO

J'étais très intrigué lorsque vous m'avez raconté cette histoire à propos de Cities on the Move – ces personnes qui vous ont demandé comment elles devaient regarder. J'ai le sentiment que cette exposition aux Arènes d'Arles va encore plus loin de ce point de vue. Dans une arène, le regard se concentre habituellement sur le taureau. C'est très panoptique. Ce projet sape non seulement l'effet panoptique mais crée également une situation polyphonique dans laquelle rien ne peut occuper le centre, dans laquelle les protagonistes peuvent marquer une pause ou continuer à travailler sur le sable, cependant que Lili Reynaud-Dewar exécute sa performance ou que la pièce d'Uri Aran commence à être jouée.

LG

C'est une exposition assez mélancolique, je pense. Je l'ai trouvée assez émouvante.

PP

C'est un peu comme un «socialisme extrême».

LG

Et le décor offrait une architecture étrange, celle d'un navire.

PP

Exactement.

LG

Un lieu très singulier pour y mettre en scène une rhétorique politique.

PP

Aujourd'hui, nous avons regardé les rushs de la vidéo tournée sur le projet. Cela m'a rappelé la bande-annonce de Film socialisme (2010) de Jean-Luc Godard – dont l'action se situe sur un navire –, laquelle fait défiler la totalité du film en accéléré. On ne discerne pas grand-chose, mais on voit tout avancer très vite. Du point de vue de la grammaire, il y a des choses similaires ici.

HUO

Votre idée initiale était de recourir à de nombreuses caméras.

PP

Oui, à des caméras qui filment en accéléré (time lapse).

HUO

Et vous pourriez en tirer un vrai film.

LG

Je suis de plus en plus convaincu que ce pourrait être un film parce qu'il existe assez de matière pour cela. Il pourrait avoir un titre complètement différent.

PP

Je pense que nous devons visionner tous les éléments, les assembler et accélérer l'intégralité du film. Les rushs sont bien mais encore un peu institutionnels.

HUO

Je voudrais maintenant aborder vos propres contributions. Liam, tu étais impliqué très tôt avant l'inauguration du projet. Mais, dès l'ouverture, tu t'es mis en retrait. C'est un paradoxe intéressant, je trouve.

LG

Tu ne dois pas oublier qu'une grande partie de mon travail c'est de faire de l'art abstrait – et je ne sais pas pourquoi je ressens ce besoin. Mais cette question de l'art abstrait m'intéresse pour une raison ou une autre. Philippe y est bien plus réfractaire – ou plus à même de considérer simultanément différentes formes et de les juger utiles. Je suis plus limité. Et il y a certains moments où j'ai envie de me retirer. Je pense qu'il faut une combinaison des deux. Je l'ai affirmé assez ouvertement devant un grand nombre d'artistes : « Je ne vais pas m'impliquer. Vous faites ce que vous avez à faire ». Philippe était plus engagé dans la réalisation.

PP

J'ai trouvé fascinant de voir cette attitude à l'œuvre. J'avais simplement envie d'en être proche. Je n'en ai pas fait tant que ça.

LG

Tu n'as pas arrêté. Tu as fait des tonnes de choses !

PP

C'est aussi que, d'une certaine façon, les gens discutent avec moi et cela crée alors une dynamique.

LG

Ce qui se passe, c'est que Philippe devient extrêmement précis dans ces situations. Le projet commence à se mettre en place et il se retrouve alors au centre.

PP

J'étais en quelque sorte, même si je n'aime pas la terminologie de la chorégraphie, un chorégraphe abstrait.

HUO

Juste avant l'inauguration, il s'est produit quelque chose de très intense. Il fallait prendre des décisions fondamentales : doit-il y avoir une check-list ? Un programme ? Vous avez également décidé d'avoir une introduction musicale, d'utiliser des haut-parleurs dans l'arène pour annoncer et introduire le projet, etc.

LG

Le fait est que tout cela, ce sont simplement des stratégies. En regardant certaines de ces choses, un bon historien d'art pourrait dire : « On retrouve ici un écho du cinéma des années 1950, lorsque la ville est devenu le sujet ou le cadre ». Il existe un lien avec les premières structures soviétiques, tels ces trains de propagande qui se déplaçaient à travers le pays. Également avec des formes d'architecture avortées qui postulaient qu'il était possible de découvrir des événements culturels dans un environnement de type centre d'art. Il y a plusieurs façons d'analyser et de décoder ces stratégies. Ce qui les rend intéressantes, c'est leur relative fragilité. Si on les considère du point de vue de l'histoire des révolutions échouées, nos principes sont, je crois, assez puissants ; ils sont réels et ont un sens. Ils se fondent sur des précédents historiques et possèdent une vraie signification politique. Mais ils sont vulnérables.

HUO

Je pense que c'est bien de mentionner ici, pour que nous en gardions la trace, que ce projet est né d'une situation très inhabituelle. Depuis vingt-cinq ans que je fréquente l'univers des expositions, je ne me suis jamais retrouvé dans ce type de situation. Il y a souvent une collaboration dûe à une promiscuité temporelle. Alors qu'ici Maja Hoffmann a instauré une situation très particulière, avec un groupe d'artistes et de commissaires rassemblés non pour réfléchir à une exposition ou une biennale mais pour travailler sur le long terme. Ce processus avec Tom Eccles et Beatrix Ruf, nous trois, et Maja au centre, bien sûr, dure depuis trois ans – trois ans durant lesquels l'institution s'est développée de manière organique, avec des doutes et des questions, jusqu'à ce que tout commence à se mettre en place.

LG

Pour moi, cela a un peu à voir avec la célèbre série télévisée Le Prisonnier, qui se déroule aussi sur un terrain contrôlé, un village. Il y a Numéro 1. Vous savez qui est Numéro 1 et vous êtes Numéro 6. Vous ignorez qui sont les autres habitants du village et vous ne pouvez pas partir. Parfois, vous vous battez; parfois, vous vous accommodez de la situation; parfois vous collaborez et vous vous efforcez de convaincre les autres qu'ils font également partie de cette situation inéluctable et ridicule. À d'autres moments encore, vous prenez conscience que vous avez été instrumentalisé et embarqué pour un long voyage, ou qu'on vous a piégé. Après avoir réalisé ce projet, j'ai regardé plusieurs épisodes du Prisonnier. Les derniers épisodes, pas les premiers.

HUO

Après To the Moon via the Beach?

LG

Oui. Une bonne partie des scènes se déroule sur la plage où Numéro 6 est poursuivi par de grosses bulles. Une fois que les scénaristes ont été à court d'idées, les derniers épisodes sont devenus vraiment intéressant parce qu'ils n'essayaient plus d'expliquer la construction. Il y avait simplement une suite d'événements. Avec la structure de LUMA, nous avons tous conscience, je crois, que dès que les portes de la Fondation s'ouvriront, un changement se produira. C'est comme ce que je dis toujours à propos de l'échec de l'architecture moderne: cela n'a rien à voir avec une utopie ou des formes ratées de logement public. Le fiasco a lieu le jour où le bâtiment est inauguré – le jour où quelqu'un accroche sur la porte une pancarte indiquant «Merci d'utiliser l'autre porte». [Rires]

PP

Le problème classique de Beaubourg.

LG

Précisément.

PP

À l'origine, l'on pouvait déplacer les murs librement. Puis, le jour où ils ont été fixés, ce fut le début de la fin.

HUO

Et la ségrégation entre les services et les disciplines s'est mise en place.

PP

Exactement.

HUO

Nous avons évoqué LUMA et le groupe fondateur. Je pense que c'est important de revenir au contexte de votre collaboration. Qu'en est-il d'All Hawaii Entries Luna Reggae (IMMA, Dublin, 2006)?

LG

C'était l'exposition de Philippe. Mais c'était mon titre, créé d'après l'anagramme de «contemporary art gallery» [galerie d'art contemporain] en gaëlique d'Irlande. [Rires]

PP

Nous voulions faire une horloge. Nous voulions que des mots tournent comme s'ils marquaient le temps. Donc, chaque fois que vous veniez, vous pouviez découvrir un titre différent pour l'exposition. Bien sûr, nous n'avions ni la technologie ni le temps pour réaliser ce projet. Nous devrions le réaliser maintenant. C'était une bonne idée.

LG

Tu vois, toutes ces choses se transforment en d'autres choses, des fragments de moments qui réapparaissent ou sont empruntés. Nous ne sommes pas un collectif, et nous ne collaborons pas non plus. Les collectifs et les collaborations sont historiquement des structures problématiques.

PP

Quand je travaillais avec Pierre Joseph, Bernard Joisten et Dominique Gonzalez-Foerster, nous trouvions un nom pour chaque projet qui devenait, pour ainsi dire, le nom du groupe. Le projet suivant apportait un autre nom, alors les gens étaient perdus. Ils demandaient: «Êtes-vous le groupe Ozone ou le groupe Hyper Hyper?» Nous insistions en quelque sorte sur le fait que nous n'étions pas un groupe, qu'il s'agissait juste de titres d'expositions dont nous étions les commissaires. À l'intérieur de ces expositions, chacun présentait des œuvres singulières. Je pense que c'est toujours vrai. Ce n'est pas comme si nous étions tous responsables du travail que nous faisions – et pourtant, nous mettions des choses en commun. Liam a raison. Ce sont des choses qui flottent dans l'air et que nous utiliserons plus tard, d'une façon ou d'une autre. Parfois, ce que je réalise, Liam aurait pu le faire, je crois. Aujourd'hui encore. C'est une façon de renégocier notre pratique.

LG

Si l'on considère que le discours sur l'art conceptuel se préoccupait excessivement de qui avait fait quoi en premier, alors, on peut affirmer que, dans nos projets, la question est de savoir qui arrête le premier. Celui qui quitte la table, quitte le jeu.

HUO

Nous parlons d'un projet extraordinaire qui s'est passé à Arles. Pas à Paris. Nous évoquons d'autres projets extraordinaires à Grenoble et Dijon, en région. C'est vrai pour de très nombreuses autres productions de notre génération. Il Tempo del Postino a eu lieu à Manchester, pas à Londres. Cela a peut-être à voir avec la possibilité de jouer, et le fait qu'il est difficile de jouer à New York ou Londres.

LG

J'écoutais cette conférence, l'autre jour, sur la façon dont Gustave Flaubert vérifiait ses textes en les lisant à voix haute, en gueulant littéralement. C'était une manière de vérifier si la langue lui convenait. Difficile de faire ça dans une ville.

PP

Donc, il faut aller à Dijon ou Arles.

LG

Je pense qu'il était probablement à Paris, mais j'avais le sentiment que c'était plus facile de crier Madame Bovary lorsque l'on n'était pas à Paris. [Rires] Je pense que c'est juste une illusion. Je ne crois pas qu'il existe de vérité plus riche sur ce sujet du centre et de la périphérie.

PP

C'est également en partie parce qu'avec les œuvres que nous produisons, chaque fois que nous les installons, nous devons renégocier avec elles. Les objets que nous réalisons sont «quasi»; ils ne sont pas complets. En un sens, ils doivent être réinventés. Ce qui est en partie la raison pour laquelle la plupart des expositions monographiques, rétrospectives, semi-rétrospectives que nous avons eues, constituent une sorte de réinvention. Elles sont là, elles sont visibles, ou bien, dans une collection, mais dès qu'elles sont de nouveau placées dans la perspective d'une narration, tout se rejoue. Elles sont faites pour cela en un sens.

To the Moon via the Beach/
Vers la lune en passant par la plage (July 2012)

Presented by
Maja Hoffmann
Tom Eccles
Liam Gillick
Hans Ulrich Obrist
Philippe Parreno
Beatrix Ruf

With
Uri Aran
Daniel Buren
Elvire Bonduelle
Lili Reynaud-Dewar
Loretta Fahrenholz
Fischli & Weiss
Jef Geys
Dominique Gonzalez-Foerster/
Ari Benjamin Meyers/Tristan Bera
Douglas Gordon
Pierre Huyghe
Klara Lidén
Renata Lucas
Benoît Maire
Oscar Murillo
Anri Sala
Pilvi Takala
Rirkrit Tiravanija
Tris Vonna-Michell
Lawrence Weiner

Coordinated by
Marc Baettig
Zoë Gray

Thanks to
Harry Ackland, Nina Alexandersen, Julien André, Dan Aran, Martina Aschbacher, Valentina Atamirano, Fabrice Auffret, Julie Autin, Erica Bartrum, Louise Basilien, Diana Becker, Charles Bellagambi, Mustapha Bouhayati, Friedrich Brühl, Geoffrey Buscail, Christophe Cachera, Josephine Dupuy-Chavanat, Mark Church, Jean-Baptiste Couronne, Guillaume Crouvezier, Enguerrand David, Dazin Azur Montage (Arles), Tatiana Defraine, Idrissa Diagne, Daniel Fintan Doyle, Martin Ehrencrona (Kobra Studio, Stockholm), Cendrine Fons, Fanette Gauzargues, Inge Godelaine, Zoë Gray, Orestes Grediaga, Christopher Green, Anna Mayrhofer-Grünbühel, Tony Guerrero, Giuliani Hanspeter, Hendrik Hegray, Hervé Hôte, Jörg Hurschler, Darren Jackson, Eldar Jakubov, Hilary Jeffery, Danny Jöckel (Kassel), Florence Kahn, Diana Kaur, Etienne Kitenge, Daniel Kreis, Gabriel Kreis, Nicolas Legrand, Robert Leslie, Simon Lichtenberger, Jean-Baptiste Marcant, Jung Martina, Francis Mary, the Mayor of Arles and la Mairie d'Arles, Paul McGuinness (London), Antonia Meile, Margaux Metais, Eric Métais, Marlon Middek, Erik Minkinnen, Sami Moor, Joel Muggleton, Tony Pastor, Eric Pérez, Andreas Pfeiffer, Victor Picon, Hugo Pouliquen, the President of the Région Provence Alpes Côte d'Azur, Greg Hausmann-Prior, Stephanie Quayle, Christian Camacho Reynoso, Pierre Rivalin, Sandra Roemermann, Lionel Roux, Olivier Roux, Thomas Royez, Hildegard Spielhofer, Sebastian Stebler, Brunner Stephan, Willem Stijger, Dominik Suppiger, Christine Taris, Laure-Anne Tillieux, Berganger Tourneboeuf, Marion TP (Arles), Zaza Tralala, Todd Uzel, Anais Vandevyver, Andrea Vasile, Andre Vida, Simon Weber, Edith Van de Wetering

Publication

LUMA Foundation President/
Fondation LUMA Présidente
Maja Hoffmann

Core Group
Tom Eccles
Liam Gillick
Hans Ulrich Obrist
Philippe Parreno
Beatrix Ruf

Edited by
Maja Hoffmann
Liam Gillick
Hans Ulrich Obrist
Philippe Parreno

Editorial Coordination
Lionel Bovier

Editing and Proofreading
Clément Dirié
Clare Manchester

Translations
Alice Boucher (Conversation),
Suzanne Pickford (Preface)

Design
Nicolas Eigenheer/Vera Kaspar,
JRP|Ringier

Assistance
Nicolas Leuba

Typeface
Antique

Photographs
Lionel Roux, Hervé Hôte, Robert Leslie

Color Separation & Print
Musumeci S.p.A., Quart (Aosta)

Printed in Europe

Published by

JRP|Ringier
Limmatstrasse 270
CH-8005 Zurich
T +41 (0) 43 311 27 50
F +41 (0) 43 311 27 51
E info@jrp-ringier.com
www.jrp-ringier.com

ISBN 978-3-03764-371-6

JRP|Ringier books are available internationally at selected bookstores and from the following distribution partners:

Switzerland
AVA Verlagsauslieferung AG, Centralweg 16, CH-8910 Affoltern a.A., verlagsservice@ava.ch, www.ava.ch

France
Les presses du réel, 35 rue Colson, F-21000 Dijon, info@lespressesdureel.com, www.lespressesdureel.com

Germany and Austria
Vice Versa Distribution GmbH, Immanuelkirchstrasse 12, D–10405 Berlin, info@vice-versa-distribution.com, www.vice-versa-distribution.com

UK and other European countries
Cornerhouse Publications, 70 Oxford Street, UK-Manchester M1 5NH, publications@cornerhouse.org, www.cornerhouse.org/books

USA, Canada, Asia, and Australia
ARTBOOK|D.A.P., 155 Sixth Avenue, 2nd Floor, USA-New York, NY 10013, orders@dapinc.com, www.artbook.com

For a list of our partner bookshops or for any general questions, please contact JRP|Ringier directly at info@jrp-ringier.com, or visit our homepage www.jrp-ringier.com for further information about our program.